GUIDE TO

REFERENCE MATERIAL

Second edition

edited by

A. J. WALFORD
M.A., Ph.D., F.R.Hist.S., F.L.A.

Volume 2

PHILOSOPHY & PSYCHOLOGY, RELIGION
SOCIAL SCIENCES, GEOGRAPHY
BIOGRAPHY & HISTORY

Assistant editors

A. L. SMYTH, F.L.A., and C. A. TOASE, A.L.A.

THE LIBRARY ASSOCIATION
1968

PUBLISHED BY
THE LIBRARY ASSOCIATION
7 RIDGMOUNT STREET, STORE STREET, LONDON, W.C.1

SBN 85365 081 0

Reprinted 1971

Made and printed in England by
STAPLES PRINTERS LIMITED
at their Rochester, Kent, establishment

Set in Intertype 8 pt. Times with 8 pt. Bodoni Bold

CONTENTS

INTRODUCTION

Aim. The object of the *Guide to reference material* is to provide a signpost to reference books and bibliographies published mainly in recent years. It is international in scope, with some emphasis on items published in Britain. It is intended for librarians, in the building up and revision of reference library stock; for use in general and special library enquiry work; as an aid to students taking examinations in librarianship and subject bibliography; and for the research worker, in the initial stages of research.

Coverage of the three volumes. The second edition of the *Guide* is planned in three volumes, to be published roughly one per alternate year:

> v. 1: *Science and technology.* 1966.
> v. 2: *Philosophy, psychology and religion; social & historical sciences.*
> v. 3: *Generalia; language & literature; the arts.*

Some subjects, as classified by U.D.C., have a divided allegiance, and the policy in these three volumes is to concentrate at a given place, or at two places, with rare exceptions, rather than to scatter according to viewpoint. This does not mean that in some cases the user must refer to more than one volume. Thus, military, naval and air force matters are to be found at both 355 and 623; economics and business affairs, at both 33 and 65; transport, at 385/388, 629 and 656; geography, at 91 and 551.4. Duplicate entries, updated where possible, have sometimes been made.

Volume 2. This volume, covering U.D.C. classes 1, 2, 3 and 9, has main entries for about 3,300 items, plus subsumed entries for a further 1,500, at least. (C. M. Winchell's *Guide to reference books* (8th ed., 1967) has about 3,770 entries covering the same classes.) This represents an increase of about 50% over the corresponding total in the original *Guide* (1959) and its *Supplement* (1963). The avowed British slant is less evident in this volume, except in such subjects as law, social services and local history, where the national element is bound to have prominence. Less-developed countries in Africa, Asia and Latin America receive more attention. The U.D.C. number 908 now accommodates area studies, although the index must be consulted for further references to countries. There is also an appreciable increase in the number of entries for the following: individual philosophers; non-Christian religions; statistics; economics; trade; atlases and maps; archaeology. The amount of older material included has increased, especially if these items are now available as reprints. "Hidden" bibliographies, appearing in periodicals or as parts of books, also figure more prominently. Entries are given for leading reviewing journals (*e.g., American economic review; English historical review*), and reviews have been increasingly drawn upon to provide more critical annotations. When two prices are given for a work, the cheaper is usually for the paperback edition.

The index, again compiled by C. A. Toase, gives detailed coverage of countries as well as of subjects and forms.

Date line. In general this volume includes entries for items published up to the end of 1967. Some 1968 material has been noted at galley-proof stage and announcements of forthcoming books also find a place. The editor is grateful for the expedition—and patience—with which the printers and Mr. F. J. Cornell (the Library Association Publications Officer) have handled copy, much of it in longhand.

Acknowledgements. The editor is indebted to the following, in particular, for advice on items to be included and sometimes for annotations, although the great majority of the annotations are his own.

22/28	Christianity	Miss I. R. Elliott, A.L.A., Deputy Librarian, Dr. Williams's Library.
29	Non-Christian religions	A. Lodge, B.A., The Library, School of Oriental and African Studies, University of London.
325	Colonial administration	C. D. Overton, F.L.A., formerly Deputy Librarian, Commonwealth Office Library.
327	International affairs	Miss D. M. Hamerton, M.A., A.L.A., Librarian, Royal Institute of International Affairs.
328	Parliament	D. J. T. Englefield, M.A., House of Commons Library.
33	Economics	A. L. Smyth, F.L.A., Librarian, Commercial Library, Manchester Public Libraries.
332	Banking	G. O. Randle, Librarian, Bank of England.
34	Law	W. A. F. P. Steiner, LL.M., Librarian, Institute of Advanced Legal Studies, Univ. of London.
355	Military science	D. W. King, O.B.E. F.L.A., Chief Librarian, Central and Army Library, Ministry of Defence.
36	Social relief & welfare	C. A. Toase, A.L.A., Senior Reference Librarian, Merton Public Libraries.
37	Education	D. J. Foskett, M.A., F.L.A., Librarian, Institute of Education, Univ. of London.
38	Commerce, Trade	A. L. Smyth, F.L.A.
39	Costume, Folklore, etc.	C. A. Toase, A.L.A.
908(5)	Area studies: Asia	A. Lodge, B.A.
92	Biography	Harold Smith, F.L.A., Deputy Librarian, Wandsworth Public Libraries.
929	Heraldry	F. R. Pryce, F.L.A., Reference Librarian, Holborn Central Library, Camden Public Libraries.
93, 94	History	A. T. Milne, M.A., F.R.Hist.S., Secretary, Institute of Historical Research, Univ. of London.
941	British local history	F. R. Pryce, F.L.A.
941.1	Scotland	C. S. Minto, F.L.A., Librarian, Edinburgh Public Libraries.
941.2	London	D. A. Dawe, A.L.A., F.R.Hist.S., Guildhall Library, London.

The assistant editors, A. L. Smyth and C. A. Toase, gave valuable counsel and contributed a number of annotated entries.

Libraries visited. Most of the items recorded in this volume have been examined by the editor. The stocks—and staffs—of the following libraries in the London area proved particularly helpful:

(a) *General.* London Library; University of London Library; Westminster Central Reference Library; St. Marylebone Reference Library; Holborn Reference Library; Kensington Central Reference Library.

(b) *Special libraries.* Library Association; Aslib; Institute of Archaeology, Institute of Education, Institute of Historical Research, Institute of Advanced Legal Studies, Institute of Hispanic Studies, and School of Oriental and African Studies, University of London; Institute of Psychology; British Library of Political and Economic Science; Royal Institute of International Affairs; Central and Army Library, Ministry of Defence; Board of Trade Central Library and Statistics Library; Royal Commonwealth Society; Royal Geographical Society; British Institute of Management.

A. J. WALFORD

September 1968

ABBREVIATIONS

Listed below are the chief bibliographical abbreviations used in this *Guide*. They do not include such generally accepted abbreviations as *c.*, c / o, Co., Corpn., *d.*, *e.g.*, *i.e.*, Inc., Ltd., p.a., *q.v.* and *s.*

A.G. (German): Aktiengesellschaft: *Co.*
A.L.A.: *American Library Association*
Abt. (German): Abteilung: *part*
ampl. (Italian): ampliata: *enlarged*
Aufll. (German): Auflage: *edition*
augm. (French): augmenté: *enlarged*
Ausg. (German): Ausgabe: *printing, edition*
B.S.: *British Standard*
Bd. (German): Band: *volume*
bearb. (German): bearbeitet: *compiled, edited*
Belg.: *Belgian*
chron.: *chronology, chronological*
Cmnd., etc.: *Command Paper*
col.: *colour, coloured*
cols.: *columns*
comp.: *compiler*
corr.: *corrected*
D.fl.: *Dutch florins*
Dan.: *Danish*
diagrs.: *diagrams*
DM. (German): *Deutsche Mark*
druk (Dutch): *edition*
ea.: *each*
ed.: *edition, editor(s)*
ed. (Italian): edizione; (Spanish) edición: *edition*
éd. (French) édition: *edition*
enl.: *enlarged*
erw.; erweit. (German): erweiterte: *enlarged*
F.: *francs*
F.I.D.: *Fédération Internationale de Documentation*
facsim(s).: *facsimile(s)*
fasc(s).: *fascicule(s)*
fig.: *figures*
fldg.: *folding*
F.: *new francs*
fr.: *francs*
front.: *frontispiece*
gänz. (German): gänzlich: *complete*
glav. red. (Russian): glavnyĭ redaktor: *editor-in-chief*
gldrs. (Dutch): *guilders*
GmbH. (German): Gesellschaft mit beschränkter Haftung: *Ltd.*
Gosud. (Russian): Gosudarstvo: *State*
H.M.S.O.: *Her (His) Majesty's Stationery Office*
Hft. (German): Heft: *part, number*
hrsg. (German): herausgegeben: *edited, published*
illus.: *illustrations, illustrated*
imp. (French): imprimé, imprimerie: *printed, printing firm*
izd. (Russian): izdanie: *edition*
Izdat. (Russian): izdatel': *publisher*
Jahrg. (German): Jahrgang: *annual publication*

kr. (Danish, Norwegian): *kroner*
L. (Italian): *lire*
l.: *leaves*
Lfg. (German): Lieferung: *number, part*
m.fl. (Danish): med flere: *and others*
n.d.: *no date*
NF. (French) (also F.): *new francs*
neubearb. (German): neubearbeitet: *revised*
no.: *number*
Nor.: *Norwegian*
nouv. (French): nouvelle: *new (edition)*
n.p.: *no place of publication*
Nr. (Danish; German): Nummer: *number*
n.s.: *new series*
N.V. (Dutch): naamloze vennootschap: *Limited Company*
o.p.: *out of print*
O.T.S.: *Office of Technical Services*
omarb. (Swedish): omarbetad: *revised*
opl. (Danish) oplag: *edition*
p.: *pages*
pl.: *plate(s)*
port.: *portrait(s)*
pt(s).: *part(s)*
pub.: *publication*
réd. (French): rédigé: *edited, compiled*
rev.: *revised; revision*
riv. (Italian): riveduto: *revised*
R. (South African): *rand; rubles*
Rs.: *rupees*
Sch.: *Schillings*
ser, sér.: *series*
suppt.: *supplementary; supplement(s)*
Sw.: *Swiss*
Swe.: *Swedish*
t. (French): tome(s): *volume(s)*
T. (German): Teil(e): *part(s)*
u. (German): und: *and*
udg. (Danish): udgave: *edition*
uit. (Dutch): uitgaaf: *publication*
uitg. (Dutch): uitgegeven: *published*
umgearb. (German): umgearbeitete: *revised*
Univ.: *University*
uppl. (Swedish): upplaga: *edition*
utg. (Norwegian): utgave: *edition*
v.: *volume(s)*
v.p.: *various pagings*
VEB (German): Volkseigener Betrieb: *People's Concern*
veränd. (German): verändert: *revised*
verb. (German): verbesserte: *improved*
verm. (German): vermehrte: *enlarged*

1. PHILOSOPHY & PSYCHOLOGY

Bibliographies

1:016

ALBERT, E. M., and **KLUCKHORN, C.,** *with others.* **A selected bibliography on values, ethics and esthetics** in the behavioral sciences and philosophy, 1920-1958. Illinois, Free Press of Glencoe, 1959. xviii, 342p. $9.95.

2,006 annotated entries, systematically arranged: 1. Anthropology—2. Psychology, social and educational psychology, psychiatry and psycho - analysis — 3. Sociology — 4. Political science, public administration and government — 5. Economics — 6. Philosophy — 7. Related sciences. Author index.

1:016

BERG, J. Selektiv bibliografi i teoretisk filosofi. Stockholm, 1960. 81p. Supplement. 1961. 7p. Mimeographed. (Filosofiska studier utg. av Filosofiska Institutionen vid Stockholms Universitet. H.5). Swe.kr. 5.

A systematically arranged selected list of books and periodical articles, intended for university students. No index.

1:016

Bibliographie de la philosophie. 1937-. Paris, Vrin, 1937-. 1-. Quarterly (1954-; 2 p.a., 1937-49; annual for 1950 and 1951; 1 v. for 1952/53). NF.35-40 p.a.; ea. NF.12.50.

At head of title-page: Institut International de Philosophie. Published for the International Federation of Philosophical Societies, under the auspices of the International Council of Philosophy and Human Studies, with the aid of UNESCO, etc.

Aims at completeness of coverage; confined to books (v. 10 (1963): 1,551 entries). Entries for new books are annotated, the length of annotation depending on the importance of the book. Reprints, new editions, paperbacks and translations are merely listed at the end of each section. Sections: Philosophy in general.—Logic.—Philosophical psychology.—Philosophy of art.—Philosophy of value.—Social philosophy.—Philosophy of history.—Philosophy of religion.—History of philosophy (general; special).—Reference books. Dictionaries. Bibliographies. Annuals.

Annotations in English, French, German, Italian and Spanish, according to language of original. Annotations in English or French for books in other languages (*e.g.,* Japanese; Polish). Annual indexes only: general index (authors, anonymous titles, catchword title entries); indexes of publishers, writers of prefaces, translators and authors cited; geographical index of publishers (by country, A-Z).

1:016

BOCHENSKI, I. M., *ed.* **Bibliographische Einführungen in das Studium der Philosophie.** Berne, Francke, 1948-53. 23v.

1. *Allgemeine philosophische Bibliographie,* by I. M. Bochenski and F. Monteleone. 1948. 42p. (*See at 1:016.*)
2. *Amerikanische Philosophie,* by R. B. Winn. 1948. 32p. (*See at 1 (73):016.*)
3. *Symbolische Logik,* by E. W. Beth. 1948. 28p. (*See at 164:016.*)
4. *Kierkegaard,* by R. Jolivet. 1948. 32p. (*See at I/KIE.*)
5. *Antike Philosophie,* by O. Gigon. 1948. 52p. (*See at 1 (091) "—":016.*)
6. *Arabische Philosophie,* by P. J. de Menasce. 1948. 48p. (*See at 297:016.*)
7. *Italienische Philosophie der Gegenwart,* by M. F. Sciacca. 1948. 36p. (*See at 1 (45):016.*)
8. *Aristoteles,* by M.-D. Philippe. 1948. 48p. (*See at I/ARI.*)
9. *Französische Existenzphilosophie,* by R. Jolivet. 1948. 34p. (*See at 141.3 (44).*)
10. *Augustinus,* by M. F. Sciacca. 1948. 32p. (*See at I/AUG.*)
11. *Der logische Positivismus,* by K. Dürr. 1948. 24p. (*See at 165:73.*)
12. *Platon,* by O. Gigon. 1950. 30p. (*See at I/PLA.*)
13/14. *Thomas von Aquin,* by P. Wyser. 1950. 78p. (*See at I/AQU.*)
15/16. *Der Thomismus,* by P. Wyser. 1951. 120p. (*See at I/AQU.*)
17. *Philosophie des Mittelälters,* by F.v. Steenberghen. 1950. 52p. (*See at 1 (091) "04/14":016.*)
18. *Patristische Philosophie,* by O. Perler. 1950. 44p. (*See at 276:016.*)
19. *Judische Philosophie,* by G. Vajda. 1950. 40p. (*See at 296:016.*)
20/21. *Buddhistische Philosophie,* by C. Regamey. 1950. 86p. (*See at 294.3:016.*)
22. *Johannes Duns Scotus,* by O. Schäfer. 1953. 34p. (*See at I/DUN.*)
23. *Deutsche Existenzphilosophie,* by O. F. Bollnow. 1953. 40p. (*See at 141.3 (43).*)

Each volume includes an introduction and is systematically arranged (aids; biography and work; philosophy), with numbered entries and a name index. A valuable bibliographical series.

1:016

BOCHENSKI, I. M., and **MONTELEONE, F. Allgemeine philosophische Bibliographie.** Berne, Francke, 1948. 42p. (Bibliographische Einführungen in das Studium der Philosophie).

A valuable small-scale guide to *c.* 400 items, with annotated entries for more important works. Two main sections, one on more inclusive bibliographies (p. 12-25) and the other on philosophy and related fields (p. 26-40) in 7 sections: Ueberwegs *Grundriss;* retrospective bibliographies; current bibliographies; dictionaries and handbooks; biographies; periodicals; and bibliographies on related fields. Name index.

W. Totok's *Bibliographischer Wegweiser der philosophischen Literatur* (Frankfurt am Main, Klostermann, 1959. 36p. DM.3) is an outline guide to the literature of philosophy. Eight sections: guides; current bibliographies; abstracts and indexes; reviews; non-current bibliographies; encyclopaedias and dictionaries; national bibliographies; bibliographies of special fields (science; symbolic logic; Thomism; etc.). Only about 50 items are dealt with, but each is briefly analyzed and evaluated. Index of authors and anonymous titles.

Philosophy: an introductory book-list, compiled by P. N. Johnson-Laird (London, Hendon [now Barnet] Public Libraries, 1964. 24p.) is chiefly concerned with books by and on the great philosophers, from the Greeks to the Existentialists, with notes on individual philosophers and schools.

Reader's guide to books on philosophy (London, Library Association, County Libraries Section, 1957. 32p.) is a systematically arranged list of *c.* 500 briefly annotated items in English. With some few exceptions, works of the classic philosophers (to *c.* 1900) have not been included. Final sections cover Ethics (p. 27-30) and Logic (p. 31-32). Books considered of value to beginners are asterisked.

H. J. Koren's *Research in philosophy: a bibliographical introduction to philosophy* . . . (Pittsburgh, Duquesne Univ. Press, [1966]. 203p. $3.95) includes a competently done section of 40p. on bibliographical tools, according to *College and research libraries,* v. 28, no. 4, July 1967, p. 293.

Also noted: *The bibliography of philosophy: a descriptive account,* by C. L. Higgins (Ann Arbor, Michigan, Department of Library Science, Univ. of Michigan, 1965. 29p.).

1:016
Bulletin signalétique. 19-24: Sciences humaines. Philosophie . . . Paris, Centre National de la Recherche Scientifique, 1961-. Quarterly. NF.80 (foreign, NF.85) p.a.

Formerly *Bulletin analytique. Philosophie* (v. 1-9. 1947-55); then *Bulletin signalétique.* 19: *Philosophie. Sciences humaines* (1956-60). The Philosophy section in the new form (1961-) carries *c.* 3,000 indicative abstracts on aspects of philosophy. Coverage: Histoire de la philosophie. —Métaphysique et philosophie générale.— Théorie des valeurs.—Morale.—Esthétique.— Philosophie de l'histoire.—Logique et philosophie de la connaissance. Annual index of authors and concepts. Not published separately, unlike the other sections of *Bulletin signalétique,* 19-24.

Preceding *Bulletin analytique. Philosophie* is *Philosophic abstracts* (New York, Russell F. Moore Co., 1939-54. V. 1-16. Quarterly). The index to v. 1-12 (*Decennial index to philosophical literature, 1939-1950.* 1952) comprises author, title and subject indexes.

1:016
DE BRIE, G. A., *ed.* **Bibliographia philosophica, 1934-1945.** Utrecht & Brussels, Spectrum, 1950-54. 2v.

v. 1: *Bibliographia historiae philosophiae.*
v. 2: *Bibliographia philosophiae.*
Aims at listing every book, article and book review published during the period. 48,178 numbered items, covering philosophical literature published in Danish, Dutch, English, French, German, Italian, Latin, Norwegian, Portuguese, Spanish and Catalan, Swedish. Chronological order of philosophers in v. 1; systematic order with name index in v. 2.
Further issues are planned to cover five-year periods.

1:016
Philosophical books. January, 1960-. Leicester Univ. Press, 1960-. v. 1, no. 1-. Quarterly, then 3 p.a. 14s. p.a.; ea. 3s.

Now (1965-) edited by Professor J. Kemp.
Signed reviews, each of *c.* 1,000 words, of about 20 books (in English only) per issue. Miscellaneous collections and source books are not reviewed but a summary of their contents is given.

Philosophischer Literaturanzeiger (Munich, Reinhardt, 1949/50-. 8 p.a.) is a reviewing journal on an international scale. It reviews *c.* 100 items p.a. and lists others. Author index, cumulated for v. 1-10 in v. 10 (1957).

1:016
RAEYMAEKER, L. de. Introduction à la philosophie. 4. éd., revue et corrigée. Louvain, Publications Universitaires de Louvain, 1956. 291p.

At head of title-page: Cours publiés par l'Institut Supérieur de Philosophie.
3rd ed. (in German), 1948.
A survey of Western philosophy and its history occupies p. 8-168; this is documented and includes footnote biographical data. A guide to the literature (p. 188-276) covers: organizations (academic and other) and congresses; introductions; biographical dictionaries, encyclopaedias and dictionaries; histories of philosophy (general; by period; by country; by type); editions of texts; commentaries and manuals; periodicals; recent and current bibliographies. Parts of series are set out and entries for the major bibliographies are annotated. Name index only. A basic guide to the literature.

D. Huisman's *Guide de l'étudiant en philosophie* (Paris, Presses Universitaires de France, 1956. xii, 109p.) is much less a guide to the literature than outlines of study for French college and Sorbonne courses in philosophy (*Bulletin des bibliothèques de France,* v. 1, no. 3, March 1956, p. 239-41).

An older bibliography, J. Hoffmans. *La philosophie et les philosophes: ouvrages généraux* (*répertoire des ouvrages à consulter*) (Brussels, Van Oest, 1920 [ii], xvii, 395p.), has 2,716 entries.

1:016
RAND, B. Bibliography of philosophy, psychology, and cognate subjects. New York, Macmillan, 1905 (reprinted 1949). 2v.

Forms v. 3 of *Dictionary of philosophy and psychology,* edited by J. M. Baldwin (at 1 (031)= 20).
The most comprehensive bibliography of its kind, for both books and periodical articles. 70,000 items, systematically arranged: *1.* Bibliographical (general bibliographies; dictionaries; periodicals). *2.* Literary (A. Histories of philosophy. Philosophers (A-Z)—B. Systematic philosophy—C. Logic—D. Aesthetics—E. Philosophy of religion—F. Ethics—G. Psychology). Subarrangement is alphabetical. No author index.
Now much dated, particularly in section G. Psychology. Section D, Aesthetics, is supple-

mented by W. A. Hammond's *A bibliography of aesthetics . . . from 1900-1932* (Rev. and enl. ed., 1934).

1:016
Répertoire bibliographique de la philosophie.
Publié sous les auspices de l'Institut International de Philosophie, avec le patronage de l'Unesco. 1949-, Louvain, Editions de l'Institut Supérieur de Philosophie, 1949-. v. 1-. Quarterly (issued as supplement to *Revue philosophique de Louvain*).

At head of title: Société Philosophique de Louvain.

A comprehensive bibliography, covering books and periodical articles in Dutch, English, French, German, Italian, Portuguese, Spanish and Catalan; works in other languages may be included, but without the aim of completeness. The order is systematic, but the November issue of each year contains an alphabetical name index and also a separate index of reviews in alphabetical order of authors of books reviewed.

V. 6, 1964, carried 6,646 items, and included a 'Répertoire des comptes rendus'.

The Philosopher's index: an international index to philosophical periodicals (Bowling Green, Ohio, Bowling Green Univ., 1967-. v. 1, no. 1-. Quarterly. $8.50 p.a.) covers 76 periodicals, but these are largely British, U.S. and French, according to *College and research libraries* (v. 28, no. 4, July 1967, p. 293-4). KWIC index.

1:016
TOTOK, W., with SCHRÖER, H. Handbuch der Geschichte der Philosophie, Frankfurt am Main, Klostermann, 1964-. v. 1-.

v. 1: *Altertum. Indische, Chinesische, Griechisch-romänische Philosophie.* xxiv, 400p. 1964. DM.54.50; 62.50.

Despite its title, a detailed bibliography of philosophy, arranged chronologically by periods. Occasional very brief notes in italics indicate basic works. V. 1 has the following main parts: Allgemeine Geschichte der Philosophie (covering all branches of philosophy, including Aesthetics, Ethics, Logic, Philosophy of history, Philosophy of science, Legal and political philosophy and Philosophy of religion)—Die Philosophie des Orients (India; China; p. 13-67)—Die Philosophie des Abendlandes (Graeco-Roman philosophy, Hellenistic-Roman philosophy, up to Boethius; p. 68-353). Author index (p. 355-94) has about 5,000 entries; over 10,000 references in all, heavily abbreviated and set solid but arranged A-Z by authors after sub-headings in bold. Subject index (p. 395-400); list of journals cited (p. xvii-xxiv). No annotations, but each section has introductory matter.

V. 2, to cover the Middle Ages and v. 3, Modern times, are in preparation. When completed this will be a major bibliography of philosophy.

1:016
VARET, G. Manuel de bibliographie philosophique. Paris, Presses Universitaires de France, 1956. 2v.

v. 1: *Les philosophies classiques.* Fr. fr. 1,800.
v. 2: *Les sciences philosophiques.* Fr. fr. 1,960.

Forms v. 9 of *Logos: introduction aux études philosophiques* (see at 1 (021)). Lists both books and periodical articles, arrangement being systematic. Coverage of v. 1 is ancient (Eastern as well as Western) and Christian philosophy (up to Kant), and the influence of these on modern philosophers. Chapter 1 notes encyclopaedic works of reference. V. 2 covers modern philosophical schools and includes a detailed index (p. 923-1045).

Manuals

1 (021)
Logos. Introduction aux études philosophiques.
Fondée par L. Lavelle et continuée par René Le Senne et Gaston Berger. Paris, Presses Universitaires de France, 1939-. v. 1-.

A full-scale treatise, v. 9 being devoted to the bibliography of philosophy. Volumes carry chapter bibliographies.

1. *Introduction à la philosophie,* by R. Le Senne. 4th ed. 1958.
2. *Traité de morale générale,* by R. Le Senne. 3rd ed. 1949.
3. *Traité de psychologie générale,* by M. Pradines. 2nd ed. 1946. 3v.
4. *Traité de caractérologie,* by R. Le Senne. 3rd ed. 1949.
5. *Traité de pédagogie générale,* by R. Hubert. 2nd ed. 1948.
6. *Histoire de la philosophie,* by A. Rivaud. 1948-63. 4v. (*see at* 1 (091)).
7. *Traité des valeurs,* by L. Lavelle. 1951-55. 2v.
8. *Traité de psychologie animale,* by F. J. J. Buytendijk. 1952.
9. *Manuel de bibliographie philosophique,* by G. Varet. 1956. 2v. (*see at* 1:016).
10. *Traité de l'argumentation,* by Ch. Perelman and L. Olbrechts-Tyteca. 2v.
11. *Traité de l'action morale,* by G. Bastide. 1961-62.
12. *Traité de psychologie sociale,* by R. Daval. 1963-.

Encyclopaedias

1 (031)=20
BALDWIN, J. M., *ed.* **Dictionary of philosophy and psychology,** including many of the principal conceptions of ethics, logic, aesthetics, philosophy of religion, mental pathology, anthropology, biology, neurology, physiology, economics, political and social philosophy, philology, physical science and education, and giving a terminology in English, French, German and Italian. New York, Macmillan, 1901-05. 3v. in 4. New ed., with corrections, 1925. Reprinted New York, Peter Smith, 1960.

Mainly concerned with philosophical subjects; articles on psychology are hopelessly dated and biography is treated very summarily. Signed articles by experts, chiefly American and British. Thus the 3-column article on 'Scepticism' by Professor John Dewey, states etymology and discusses philosophical, ethical and religious aspects, with ten references. But the article on 'Plato' is 20 lines only, with cross-references.

Appended to v. 2 are indexes of Greek, Latin, German, French and Italian terms. The editor was assisted by 17 consulting editors from various countries and 50 contributing subject-specialists. Now termed 'antiquated' in *Times literary supplement*, no. 3,420, 14th September 1967, p. 809.

For v. 3, *Bibliography of philosophy*, by B. Rand (1905), *see entry at* 1:016.

1 (031)=20
The Encyclopedia of philosophy. Paul Edwards, editor-in-chief. New York, Macmillan Co. and The Free Press; London, Collier-Macmillan, 1967. 8v. $219.50; £117.

The only major English-language dictionary of philosophy since Baldwin, and commendably up-to-date. 1,450 comprehensive signed articles (including more than 900 on individual thinkers); 500 contributors from 24 countries; international editorial board of 153. Systematic bibliographical coverage is a feature. Thus, the contribution on 'Alienation' (10½ cols.; 5 sections) has a bibliography of 1¾ cols. in 6 sections, including one for periodical articles up to 1963; that on 'Hinduism' (8½ cols.) has a bibliography of 1¼ cols. in 8 sections that on 'A. N. Whitehead' (6 pages; 5 main sections) has a bibliography of works by Whitehead (nearly 1 col.) and material on him (¾ col.), with some comments. The lengthy article, 'Logic, history of', runs to 58p., including 7 cols. of bibliography. Also rewarding bibliographically are the 3 articles. 'Philosophical bibliographies' (v. 6, p. 166-9), 'Philosophical dictionaries and encyclopedias' (v. 6, p. 170-99) and 'Philosophical journals' (p. 199-216). Copious cross-references. V. 8 has a detailed subject index (p. 387-544), with c. 40,000 entries.

Articles are scholarly but readable. Physically the volumes are also pleasing, with large, attractive print and stout paper. Given a full-length review in *Times literary supplement*, no. 3,420, 14th September 1967, p. 809-10. Recommended in *Library journal* (v. 92, no. 8, 15th April 1967, p. 1603-4) for all but the smallest public libraries.

1 (031)=30
EISLER, R. Wörterbuch der philosophischen Begriffe, historischquellenmässig bearbeitet. 4. völlig neubearb. Aufl. weitergeführt und vollendet durch K. Roretz. 4. Aufl. Berlin, Mittler, 1927-30. 3v.

Very full definitions (in German) of philosophical terms, with detailed documentation of their use by philosophers. Bibliographical references are given in the articles themselves, and a list of books is given at the end of v. 3 (p. 695-906).

Abridged edition (*Handwörterbuch*. 2nd ed. Berlin, Mittler, 1922) in 1v.

1 (031)=50
Enciclopedia filosofica. Centro di Studi Filosofici di Gallarate. Venice and Rome, Istituto per la Collaborazione Culturale, 1957. 4v. illus.

Similar in layout to the *Enciclopedia italiana*. Articles (*c*. 12,000 in all) are signed and bibliographies provided. Comprehensive and fairly well balanced. Descartes receives 12¼ pages, including ½ col. of bibliography; Bertrand Russell, 4½ cols.,

including ½ col. of bibliography; Wittgenstein, 2½ cols., including 18½ lines of bibliography. But whereas Oscar Wilde is given 2½ cols. (with 11½ lines of bibliography), Jung has a mere ¾ col. (with 8½ lines of bibliography). Entries tend to be under philosophers rather than under individual philosophies, *e.g.*, under Sartre, not under Existentialism; under Smuts, not under Holism. V. 4 includes indexes of theories and of historical aspects, of terms which are not given entries, and of illustrations.

1 (031)=82
Filosofskaya entsiklopediya. Glav redaktor F. V. Konstantinov. Moscow, 'Sovetskaya Entsiklopediya', 1960-. v. 1-. ea. *c*. 25s.

V. 1-3 (1960-64). To be completed in 4v.
A general encyclopaedia of philosophy, written from a Marxist-Leninist viewpoint. Thus, the article on 'Dialectical materialism' runs to more than 19 double-column pages, while Karl Barth is dismissed in a few lines. The major articles carry lengthy bibliographies. "Especially valuable for its detailed coverage of the theoretical bases of Communist doctrine" (Neiswender, R. *Guide to Russian reference and language aids* (1962), p. 38-39). Includes sociological topics, *e.g.*, marriage.

1 (032)=20
URMSON, J. O., *ed.* **The concise encyclopædia of Western philosophy and philosophers.** London, Hutchinson, 1960. 431p. illus. (incl. 8 col. pl.). (Rev. ed. 1968. 432p. 63s.).

Although the *Introduction* states that priority is given to the needs of more specialist readers, this compilation is not particularly scholarly; it assumes, for instance, that the reader is not an expert linguist; it has no index. It claims "a fairly narrow interpretation of what constitutes philosophy", but the inclusion of an entry for Freud and the lack of one for Jung seem arbitrary. A preponderance of biographical articles. 48 contributors, but no indication of who has written what. The style is clear and simple, and references in the text to other topics are in bold. 112 illustrations, of good quality. 'For further reading' (p. 421-31), A-Z by topics, but Existentialism, on which there is a 2-page article, is not among them.

1 (032)=30
HOFFMEISTER, J. Wörterbuch der philosophischen Begriffe. 2. Aufl. Hamburg, Meiner, 1955. viii, 687p.

Previously published 1944.
Concisely written articles, some with references. Includes psychological terms; omits biographies. Gives etymology

1 (032)=30
NEUHÄUSLER, A. Grundbegriffe der philosophischen Sprache. Begriffe viersprachig. Munich, Ehrenwirth Verlag, 1963. 276p. DM.22.80.

About 500 entry-words, with English, French and Italian equivalents and German explanation, plus bibliography (*e.g.*, 'Metaphysik': 1½p., with 26 lines of bibliography) and U.D.C. number). Appended is a U.D.C. classified list of topics treated.

1 (032)=30
SCHMIDT, H. Philosophisches Wörterbuch. 16.
Aufl. durchgesehen, ergänzt und hrsg. von Georgi
Schischkoff. Stuttgart, Kröner, 1961. vii, 656p.
DM.15.

First published 1935.
Entries range from brief definitions to lengthy
articles (*e.g.,* 'Geist': 4 columns), including biographies (*e.g.,* 'Leibniz': 4 columns). About 2,000
entries, most of them with bibliographies appended (*e.g.,* 'Geist': 12 items; 'Leibniz': 26
items). Chronological table, p. 647-56 (up to
1960).
The approach is non-Christian, in contrast with
the Roman Catholic approach of Walter Brug-
ger's *Philosophisches Wörterbuch* (8. neubearb.
Aufl. Freiburg, Herder, 1961. xxxix, 511p.
DM.19.80), while G. Klaus and M. Buhr's
Philosophisches Wörterbuch (Leipzig, VEB
Bibliographisches Institut, 1965. xv, 635p.) takes
a Marxist-Leninist viewpoint. It has about a
thousand entries; no bibliographies, but text
references; many cross-references.

1 (032)=40
FOULQUIÉ, P., and **SAINT-JEAN, P. Diction-
naire de la langue philosophique.** Paris, Presses
Universitaires de France, 1962. xvi, 776p. NF.50.

About 1,500 entry-words, with different applications lettered and supporting quotations numbered. Under 'Imagination' (p. 342-5) are grouped
related terms, with 76 numbered quotations in all
(*e.g.,* 'Image' (applications, A-D; 28 numbered
quotations, with sources cited); 'Imaginer',
'Imaginaire', 'Imaginatif', 'Imagination'). 'Indications bibliographiques', p. 773-6 (reviews, dictionaries and encyclopaedias, textbooks).

1 (032)=40
LALANDE, A., *ed.* **Vocabulaire technique et
critique de la philosophie.** 9. éd., rev. et augm.
Paris, Presses Universitaires de France, 1963.
xxiv, 1324p. NF.60.

At head of title: Société Française de Philosophie.
First published in *Bulletin de la Société Française de Philosophie,* 1902-23.
Definitions of philosophical concepts and
terms, with reference to their use by philosophers
and the evolution of their present meaning. German, English and Italian equivalents of terms are
given; also etymology. Numerous citations and
footnotes. The 8th ed. (1960. xxiv, 1323p.) showed
revision and amendments on some points of
detail and its supplement contains further articles
and notes. The 9th ed. adds very little.

D. Julia's *Dictionnaire de la philosophie* (Paris,
(Larousse, 1964. 320p. illus., tables. NF.14),
unlike the dictionaries by Foulquié and Lalande,
is addressed to the layman. It gives clear and
precise definitions and explanations, and includes
potted biographies, with numerous illustrations.

A. Cuvillier's *Nouveau vocabulaire philosophique*, first published in 1956 (Paris, Colin.
204p.) had its 7th edition in 1961.

1 (032)=50
ABBAGNANO, N. Dizionario di filosofia. Turin,
Unione Tipografico—Editrice Torinese, 1961.
xii, 905p. L 10,000.

About 2,000 unsigned entries; no biographies.
Different applications of terms are explained;
French, English and German equivalents, and
Greek or Latin origins are given. Some articles
are fairly lengthy (*e.g.,* 'Identità', Filosofia della:
3 columns). References are given to primary
sources, these being listed on p. ix-xii.

1 (032)=60
FERRATER MORA, J. Diccionario de filosofía.
4. ed. Buenos Aires, Editorial Sudamericana,
1958. 1481p.

First published 1941.
About 2,000 entries, including biographies.
Particularly strong on bibliographies. Thus the
article on Kant (5½ p.) has 6 columns of bibliography (works by; material on); that on Logic
(p. 810-27) has 7 columns of bibliography.
Supplementary general bibliography, p. 1449-57;
chronological table, p. 1459-81.

Periodicals

1 (05):016
UNITED STATES. LIBRARY OF CONGRESS.
Reference Department. **Philosophical periodi-
cals:** an annotated world list, by D. Baumgardt.
Washington, Government Printing Office, 1952.
vi, 89p.

489 numbered entries are listed, covering some
71 countries. Arrangement is alphabetical by
titles under countries A-Z, with title index. The
brief annotations indicate subject coverage. More
general periodicals have been included where
they have philosophical references or contributions, the frequency of these being noted in the
annotation. Particulars given for each periodical
include: frequency; editor; imprint; date of commencement. Locations in the Library of Congress
are indicated.

Directories

1 (058.7)
VARET, G., and **KURTZ, P.,** *ed.* **International
directory of philosophy and philosophers.**
New York, Humanities Press, Inc., 1965. 295p.
$12.50.

Prepared under the auspices of the International Institute of Philosophy, with the aid of
UNESCO.
Lists more than 15,000 names and addresses,
of philosophers, college and university departments of philosophy, philosophical journals,
organisations, research centres and publishers
in the field. A section on international bodies is
followed by sections (in English, French, Spanish
and German) on 63 countries. The country directories are often preceded by short surveys reviewing the state of philosophical research and teaching in the country concerned.

V. 1 of the biennial *Directory of American
philosophers,* edited by A. J. Bahm (Department
of Philosophy, Univ. of New Mexico. Albu-
querque, New Mexico, the Editor, 1962. $6)
ostensibly covers the period 1962-63; v. 2: 1964-
65 ($11.25) appeared in 1964.

History

1 (091)
BRÉHIER, É. Histoire de la philosophie. 4.-6. éd. Paris, Presses Universitaires de France, 1950-51. 2v.; 2 supplementary v. 1948, 1949.

> v. 1: *L'antiquité et le moyen âge.* 7. éd. 1960.
> v. 2: *La philosophie moderne.* 6. éd. 1962.
> fasc. supplémentaire: *La philosophie en Orient,* by P. Masson-Oursel (1948).
> *La philosophie byzantine,* by B. Takatis (1949).
> English translation (Chicago & London, Chicago Univ. Press, 1963-): v. 1: *The Hellenic Age* (1963. 50s.); v. 2: *The Hellenistic and Roman Age* (1965. 56s.); v. 3: *The Middle Ages and the Renaissance* (New ed. 1966. 14s.); v. 4: *The seventeenth century* (1966. 50s.); v. 5: *The eighteenth century* (1967. 63s.).

A clear and comprehensive study of the development of philosophical thought, with chapter-bibliographies. The author is Professor of Philosophy at the Sorbonne.

1 (091)
COPLESTON, F. C. A history of philosophy. London, Burns, Oates & Washbourne [now Burns & Oates], 1947-66. 8v.

> v. 1: *Greece and Rome.* 1947. 42s.
> v. 2: *Augustine to Scotus.* 1950. 42s.
> v. 3: *Ockham to Suárez.* 1953. 42s.
> v. 4: *Descartes to Leibniz.* 1958. 42s.
> v. 5: *Hobbes to Hume.* 1959. 42s.
> v. 6: *Wolff to Kant.* 1960. 42s.
> v. 7: *Fichte to Nietzsche.* 1963. 42s.
> v. 8: *Bentham to Russell.* 1966. 50s.

A lucid and scholarly work, written from "the standpoint of the scholastic philosopher". The only recent extensive history of philosophy in English. Each volume has a substantial bibliography and an analytical index (*e.g.,* v. 7: bibliography, p. 443-63 index, p. 464-96). Father Copleston, S.J. is Professor of the History of Philosophy at Heythrop College, Oxford (1939-) and at Gregorian University, Rome (1952-).

1 (091)
RADHAKRISHNAN, *Sir* E., *and others, ed.* **History of philosophy, Eastern and Western.** London, Allen & Unwin, 1952-53. 2v.

A history of philosophy, prepared under the auspices of the Ministry of Education, Government of India. Comprises some 60 contributions by different scholars, mainly Indian. Each chapter contains a brief bibliography.

1 (091)
RIVAUD, A. Histoire de la philosophie. Paris, Presses Universitaires de France, 1948-63. 4v. (Logos. Introduction aux études philosophiques, v. 6).

> v. 1: *Des origines à la scolastique.* 1948. 2. éd., mise à jour par Gilbert Varet. 1960.
> v. 2: *De la scolastique à l'époque classique.* 1950.
> v. 3: *L'époque classique.* 1950.
> v. 4: *Philosophie française et philosophie anglaise, de 1700 à 1830.* 1963. NF.22.

The author (1876-1956) died before v. 4 was completed. The 2nd ed. of v. 1 has 38 chapters, each with a bibliography general bibliography, p. xvii-xxiii; name index only. Roman Catholic viewpoint.

1 (091)
UEBERWEG, F. Grundriss der Geschichte der Philosophie. 11.-12. Aufl. Berlin, Mittler, 1923-28 (and reprints). 5v.

> v. 1: *Die Philosophie des Altertums,* by K. Praechter. 12th ed., 1926.
> v. 2: *Die patristische und scholastische Philosophie,* by B. Geyer. 11th ed., 1928.
> v. 3: *Die Philosophie der Neuzeit bis zum Ende des 18. Jahrhunderts,* by M. Frischeisen-Köhler and W. Moog. 12th ed., 1924.
> v. 4: *Die deutsche Philosophie des 19. Jahrhunderts und der Gegenwart,* by T. K. Oesterreich. 12th ed., 1923.
> v. 5: *Die Philosophie des Auslandes vom Beginn des 19. Jahrhunderts bis auf die Gegenwart,* by T. K. Oesterreich. 12th ed., 1928.

Indispensable to the student of the history of philosophy by reason of its very full bibliographies. The several volumes are also valuable as expositions of the period by acknowledged experts.

A new ed. in 8v., edited by Paul Wilpert, began publication in 1965 (Basle, Schwabe).

W. Windelband's *History of philosophy* (New York, Harper, Row, 1958. 2v. $4.70) is a reprint of a translation by J. H. Tuft of the rev. ed. of *Geschichte der Philosophie* (1901). It has been described (*The Observer. Suppt.* 27 Nov. 1966, p. 46) as "the best medium-sized, one-man history of philosophy, for all its late-Victorian upholstery".

Ancient Philosophy

(*See also* 1 (38).)
1 (091) "—":016
GIGON, O. Antike Philosophie. Berne, Francke, 1948. 52p. (Bibliographische Einführungen in das Studium der Philosophie, 5).

Includes sections on Socrates, Plato, Aristotle, Cicero, Epicurus and philosophical systems. Some annotations; name index.

Mediæval Philosophy

1 (091) "04/14"
GILSON, É. History of Christian philosophy in the Middle Ages. London, Sheed & Ward, 1955. xvii, 829p. 42s.

Based on the French original, *La philosophie au moyen âge, des origines patristiques à la fin du XIVᵉ siècle* (Paris, Payot, 1922; 2nd ed., 1944), being not a translation but a "reworking of the material". Roman Catholic viewpoint.

The work of a leading expert, with bibliographical notes on each of the leading philosophers. Bibliographical and other notes, p. 549-804.

J. R. Weinberg's *A short history of medieval philosophy* (Princeton, N.J., Princeton Univ. Press, 1964. ix, 304p. $6) is considered by *Philosophical review* (v. 75, no. 3, July 1966, p. 407-9) to be a work of first-rate scholarship and something of a classic. Selective bibliography, p. 295-300.

1 (091) "04/14"

STEENBERGHEN, F. van. Histoire de la philosophie. Période chrétienne. Louvain, Publications Universitaires, 1964. 196p. Belg. fr. 80.

At head of title-page: 'Cours publiés par l'Institut Supérieur de Philosophie'.
The author is Professor of Mediæval Philosophy at Louvain University, in succession to M. de Wulf. Period covered is end of 5th century to end of 12th century, and pt. 3 deals with philosophy in the Arab world. The bibliography (p. 181-6) notes both sources for research work and items for further reading.

1 (091) "04/14"

WULF, M. de. Histoire de la philosophie mediévale. 6. éd. Louvain, Institut Supérieur de Philosophie; Paris, Vrin, 1934-47. 4v.

First published 1900. The 3rd English ed., based on the 6th French ed., *History of mediæval philosophy,* translated by E. C. Messenger, appeared in 1935-38 (London, Nelson. 2v.).
A scholarly, well documented work by the then Professor of Mediæval Philosophy at Louvain University. General bibliography in v. 1; footnote references and chapter bibliographies. Bibliographies are intended to update and supplement F. Ueberweg's *Grundriss der Geschichte der Philosophie* (11-12th ed. Berlin, Mittler, 1923-28. 5v.). Accordingly only the principal editions of texts and the most important works are mentioned up to 1928, with a more complete recording thereafter.

1 (091) "04/14":016

STEENBERGHEN, F. von. Philosophie des Mittelälters. Berne, Francke, 1950. 52p. (Bibliographische Einführungen in das Studium der Philosophie, 17).

A bibliography in four sections: general bibliographies; Scholasticism (three periods, ending with Nicolaus Cusanus). Very occasional annotations. Name index.

Modern Philosophy

1 (091) "18/19"

PASSMORE, J. A hundred years of philosophy. 2nd ed. London, Duckworth, 1966. 574p. 50s.

First published 1957.
Author is Professor of Philosophy at the Australian National University. An excellent survey of 19th century and contemporary philosophers (starting with J. S. Mill and ending with Nagel and Feyerabend). The 2nd ed. adds considerably to accounts of Ayer, Popper, Wittgenstein and Sartre, completely rewritten and much enlarged sections on Austin, Jaspers and Heidegger, and a new section on Merleau-Ponty, etc. Extensive footnote references and notes; 'Further reading', p. 147-9. Index of names; index (non-analytical) of subjects.

1 (091) "19"

INSTITUT INTERNATIONAL DE PHILOSOPHIE. Philosophy in the mid-century: a survey; edited by Raymond Klibansky. Florence, 'La Nuova Italia'; etc. 1958-59. 4v.

Published under the auspices of UNESCO.
Surveys the period 1949-55; in all those cases in which the subject matter demanded it, the time limits have been extended in either direction. About eighty contributions, under main headings: v. 1, Logic and philosophy of science; v. 2, Metaphysics and analysis; v. 3, Philosophy of value, of history and of religion; v. 4, History of philosophy; Contemporary philosophy in Eastern Europe and Asia. Each contribution normally includes a "selective" bibliography. Contributions are in English or French. Critically reviewed in a leading article in the *Times literary supplement,* no. 3,030, 25th March 1960, p. 193.

Dictionnaire des idées contemporaines, edited by M. Mourre (Paris, Éditions Universitaires, 1964. 718p. illus. NF.35) consists of a prefatory series of survey articles on aspects of 20th-century philosophy (*c.* 200p.) and then the dictionary proper, with short articles on some 200 contemporary thinkers, plus portraits and bibliographies. Index of names. *Bulletin critique du livre français* (v. 20, no. 3, March 1965, no. 63,203) notes omission of de Saussure and N. Wiener.

Also noted: *Les grands courants de la pensée mondiale contemporaine:* ouvrage publié sous la direction de M. F. Sciacca (Milan, Marzorati, [*c.* 1958]-).

Individual Philosophers

1/AQU

WYSER, P. Thomas von Aquin. Berne, Francke, 1950. 78p. (Bibliographische Einführungen in das Studium der Philosophie, 13/14).

——— **Der Thomismus.** Berne, Francke, 1951. 120p. (Bibliographische Einführungen in das Studium der Philosophie, 15/16).

Thomas von Aquin is a bibliography in 3 main sections: 1. Aids and collected works—2. Life and work—3. Philosophy (p. 33-78). *Der Thomismus* continues the earlier bibliography in 2 main sections: 1. History of Thomism—2. Systematics of Thomism. Combined name index to the 2v., p. 103-19.

"Thomistic bibliography, 1920-1940", by V. J. Bourke, appeared as supplement to v. 21 (1945) of *The modern schoolman* (viii, 312p.). It lists 4,764 titles. *Bibliographie thomiste,* by P. Mandonnet and J. Destrez (2. éd. Paris, Vrin, 1960. xxii, 121p.) is continued in the *Bulletin thomiste.*

A lexicon of St. Thomas Aquinas on the 'Summa theologica' and selected pages of his other works, by R. F. Deferrari and M. I. Barry, with I. McGuiness (Washington, Catholic Univ. of American Press, 1949-54. x, 1185p.) is an excellently produced concordance. The Latin entry-word is followed by its genitive form, part of speech, meanings and references, with citations.

1/ARI

ARISTOTELIAN SOCIETY. A synoptic index to the 'Proceedings' of the Aristotelian Society, 1900-1949. Edited by J. W. Scott. Oxford, Blackwell, 1954. v.p.

Pt. 1 consists of entries, arranged by authors of papers, A-Z. Synopses of arguments are given for all the papers listed. Synopses are asterisked if the contributor has not collaborated in making them. Pt. 2 is an index of subjects, with cross-references to pt. 1. An appendix gives contents lists of the separate volumes of the 'Proceedings' for the period preceding 1900 (*i.e.*, 1887-96), for 1900-49, and for 1950-53.

Covers a wide range of aspects of philosophy. Considered "a major new tool for the subject, an indexing and abstracting service" (Staveley, R. *Notes on subject bibliography* (1959), p. 34).

A detailed bibliography of works by and studies on Aristotle appears in W. Totok's *Handbuch der Geschichte der Philosophie* (Frankfurt on Main, Klostermann, 1964-. v. 1, p. 214-64). *Aristoteles*, by M. D. Philippe (Berne, Francke, 1948. 48p. Bibliographische Einführungen in das Studium der Philosophie series, 8) has a similar scope. 17 sections; name index.

Index Aristotelicus, by H. Bonitz, is part of v. 5 (1870) of the K. Preuss. Akademie der Wissenschaften's edition of Aristotle's works (Berlin, Reimer; reprinted Graz, Akademische Druck- und Verlagsanstalt, 1955. vi, 878p.). There is also *An index to Aristotle in English translation,* by T. W. Organ (Princeton, N.J., Princeton Univ. Press, 1949. 181p.).

1/AUG
SCIACCA, M. F. Augustinus. Berne, Francke, 1948. 32p. (Bibliographisches Einführungen in das Studium der Philosophie, 10).

A bibliography in 14 sections, including 1. General, including bibliographies (*e.g.*, Nebreda, E. *Bibliographia augustiniana.* Rome, 1928), indexes, and a chronology of St. Augustine's works).—2. Writings.—3. Editions and translations.—4. Biographies. Name index.

Based on the bibliographies appearing in the quarterly *Augustiniana*, T. J. van Bavei's *Répertoire bibliographique de Saint Augustin, 1950-1960* (Steenbergen, Abbatia Sancti Petri, 1963. 991p.) has author, subject and name indexes.

1/DES
SEBBA, G. Bibliographia Cartesiana: a critical guide to the Descartes literature. 1800-1960. The Hague, Nijhoff, 1964. xv, 510p. D.fl.54.

In 3 pts.: (*1*) bibliographical and biographical studies of Descartes (11 subheadings); (*2*) an exhaustive bibliography of Descartes' writings; (*3*) a bibliography of all works devoted to Descartes (excluding items in (*1*)), published 1800-1960. Classified and A-Z subject indexes. Reviewed in *Bulletin des bibliothèques de France,* v. 11, no. 1, 1966, p. 62.

1/DUN
SCHÄFER, O. Johannes Duns Scotus. Berne, Francke, 1953. 34p. (Bibliographische Einführungen in das Studium der Philosophie).

A bibliography in three main sections: 1. Aids —2. Life and work—3. Philosophy. Name index (analytical).

Also noted: O. Schäfer's *Bibliographia de vita, operibus et doctrina Duns Scoti . . . saec. XIX-XX* (Rome, Orbis Catholicus Herder, 1955. xxv, 223p.): 4,506 entries.

1/ERA
BIBLIOTHÈQUE NATIONALE, Paris. Catalogue des ouvrages d'Érasme, conservés au Département des Imprimés. Paris, Imprimerie Nationale, 1912. iip., 136 col.

Reprint from v. 47 of the *Catalogue général des livres imprimés de la Bibliothèque Nationale.* 958 items.

1/HEG
GLOCKNER, H. Hegel-Lexikon. Stuttgart, Frommann, 1935-39. 4v. (xxxii, 2777p.).

A concordance-dictionary, forming v. 23-26 of the Jubilee edition of Hegel's collected works. Entries under key-words consist of quotations and sources, with commentary (*e.g.*, 'Kant', p. 1194-1222). Ingenious system of cross-references.

1/HUM
JESSOP, T. E. A bibliography of David Hume, and of Scottish philosophy, from Francis Hutcheson to Lord Balfour. London, Brown, 1938. xiv, 201p.

See entry at 1 (411):016.

1/KAN
EISLER, R. Kant-Lexikon. Nachschlagewerk zu Kants sämtlichen Schriften, Briefen und Handschriftlichen Nachlass. Berlin, Mittler, 1930 (reprinted 1964). viii, 642p.

Compiled with the co-operation of the Kantgesellschaft. A dictionary-index to key-words in Kant's writings, with numerous cross-references. Some lengthy entries (*e.g.*, 'Freiheit des Willens', p. 160-9; 'Imperativ'. p. 267-72). List of Kant's works, p. 640-2.

1/KIE
JOLIVET, R. Kierkegaard. Translated by O. Gigon. Berne, Francke, 1948. 32p. (Bibliographische Einführungen in das Studium der Philosophie, 4).

Three main sections: 1. Introduction (appreciation; bio-bibliographical chronology, p. 3-13).—2. Editions and translations of works.—3. Critical works on Kierkegaard (by subjects). Name index.

Also noted: *Søren Kierkegaard: international bibliografi,* by J. Himmelstrup, with K. Birket-Smith (Copenhagen, Nyt Nordisk Forlag, 1962. 216p.).

1/LEI
MÜLLER, K. Leibniz-Bibliographie: die Literatur über Leibniz. Frankfurt am Main, Klostermann, 1967 [*i.e.* 1966]. xx, 478p.

3,392 items on Leibniz. 7 main sections: 1. General—2. Leibniz' life—3. General characteristics—4. Special characteristics—5. Leibniz' work (p. 83-208)—6. Philosophy—7. Connections, activities.

A complementary bibliography is: *Biblio-*

graphie des œuvres de Leibniz, by E. Ravier (Paris, Alcan, 1937. v, 703p.).

1/LOC
CHRISTOPHERSEN, H. O. A bibliographical introduction to the study of John Locke. Oslo, I Kommisjon Hos Jacob Dybwad, 1930. 134p.

Chapter 1 is a chronologically arranged account of Locke's works, 1686-1704, with footnote references. Chapter 2 lists posthumous works, letters, lives and collected works; chapter 3, separate editions of Locke's works after 1704. Author index.

1/PLA
GIGON, O. Platon. Berne, Francke, 1950. 30p. (Bibliographische Einführungen in das Studium der Philosophie. 12).

A bibliography in 10 sections, beginning with bibliography and indexes, and followed by a list of Plato's works, biographies, complete editions and translations, individual works, and commentaries.

A more recent bibliography is available in W. Totok's *Handbuch der Geschichte der Philosophie* (Frankfurt on Main, Klostermann, 1964. v. 1, p. 146-212).

Key-word indexes. (Greek): *Lexicon Platonicum...,* by F. Ast (Leipzig, Weidmann, 1835-38. 3v. (reprinted Bonn, 1956); supplemented by J. Zurcher's *Lexicon Academicum* (Paderborn, Schöningh, 1954. 36p.); (English): *Index to Plato, compiled from the second edition of Professor Jowett's translation of the Dialogues,* by E. Abbott (Oxford, Clarendon Press, 1875. 64p.).

1/SCHE
SCHNEEBERGER, G. Friedrich Wilhelm Joseph von Schelling: eine Bibliographie. Berne, Francke, 1954. 190p.

1,012 items.

1/SCHO
WAGNER, G. F. Schopenhauer-Register. Neu hrsg. von Arthur Hübscher. Stuttgart, Frommann, [1960]. viii, 530p.

First published 1909.
An index to keywords in Schopenhauer's works. In addition to references, quotations are frequently given. Numerous cross-references. List of keywords, p. 484-99.

1/SPI
OKO, A. S., *comp.* **The Spinoza bibliography.** Published under the auspices of the Columbia University Libraries. Boston, Mass., G. K. Hall, 1964. xxiii, 700p. $40.

A photolithographed reproduction of about 7,000 cards (10 per page). Classified arrangement: A. Bibliographies—B. Works—C. Life, Contemporaries—D. Works on Spinoza's philosophy —E. Philosophical works with references to Spinoza—F. Non-philosophical literature and Spinoza—G. History and Spinoza—H. Influence in different countries—1. Special topics—J.

Reviews—K. Notes about authors—L. Fiction, poetry, drama—M. Miscellaneous (Spinoza's library; 'Spinozahouses'). 2 appendices; no indexes. The cards reproduced are either Library of Congress printed cards or else typed,—in both cases very legible.

Biographies

1 (092)
ZIEGENFUSS, W., and **JUNG, G. Philosophen-Lexikon:** Handwörterbuch der Philosophie nach Personen. Berlin, de Gruyter, 1949-50. 2v.

Biographical articles on philosophers, with emphasis on the second half of the 19th century and on the 20th century, especially in Germany. Living philosophers are included. Entries include a list of works, contributions to encyclopaedias, etc., as well as material on the philosopher concerned (*e.g.,* Bertrand Russell: 2½ pages, including 1 page of bibliography).

The *Dictionnaire illustré des philosophes* (Paris, Seghers, 1962. 376p. illus.) consists of biographical notes on philosophers, both deceased and living (296p.), and a glossary of terms (79p.). The *Bulletin des bibliothèques de France* (v. 8, no. 3, March 1963, p. 197-8) finds it particularly good on modern philosophers.

Only v. 1 (*Anglo-American philosophers*) of *Who's who in philosophy,* edited by D. D. Runes (New York, Philosophical Library, 1942. 293p. $5) was published. Stronger on the American than on the British side, it has biographical data and a bibliography of the published works and major periodical contributions of then living philosophers.

1 (092) "13/16"
RIEDL, J. O., *ed.* **A catalogue of Renaissance philosophers (1300-1650).** Milwaukee, Marquette Univ. Press, 1940. 179p.

In 102 sections, compiled by 17 undergraduate students under the direction of John O. Riedl. Includes "many scientists, theologians and rhetoricians ... partly because some of their writings either were philosophical or had an influence on philosophy". Arrangement is by schools, each entry consisting of biographical data followed by a tabulated list of writings by the philosopher. A bibliography (p. 167-72) is followed by an author index.

Greek Philosophy

1 (38)
ARMSTRONG, A. H., *ed.* **The Cambridge history of later Greek and early medieval philosophy.** Cambridge, Univ. Press, 1967. xiv, 710, [1]p. 95s.

"Originally planned in connexion with W. K. C. Guthrie's *History of Greek philosophy,* but has developed on rather different lines. . . . It is an independent survey designed to show how Greek philosophy took the form which it was known to and influenced the Jews, the Christians of East and West and the Moslems, and what these inheritors of Greek thought did with their heritage during, especially, the first millennium A.D." (*Preface*). Coverage: from the Old Academy 4th century B.C.) to St. Anselm (beginning of 12th century A.D.). Final chapter 8: 'Early Islamic philosophy'. Select bibliography, by chapters, p. 670-91. Index of ancient and medieval books referred to in the text general, analytical index; index of Greek terms.

1 (38)
GUTHRIE, W. K. C. A history of Greek philosophy. Cambridge, University Press, 1962-. v. 1-.

> v. 1. *The earlier Presocratics and the Pythagoreans.* 1962. 63s.
> v. 2. *The Presocratic tradition, from Parmenides to Democritus.* 1965. 75s.
> A scholarly survey, to be completed in five volumes, by the Professor of Ancient Philosophy in Cambridge University. The study of Anaxageras in v. 2 (p. 266-344) provides a detailed analysis of his writings, with citations and footnote references. Each volume carries an index of passages quoted or referred to, and a general, analytical index (with main page-references in bold), plus a bibliography (unhelpfully arranged A-Z by authors). One reviewer (*Philosophy* v. 39, no. 148, April 1964, p. 184-5) notes the paucity of Greek quotations, confined to footnotes and appendices.

British Philosophy

1 (410) (08)
MUIRHEAD, J. H., *ed.* **Contemporary British philosophy:** personal statements. London, Allen & Unwin, 1924-56. 3v. (Library of philosophy).

> 28 philosophers give brief accounts of their thought and development. "Principal publications" are appended to each contribution. The third series includes biographical notes.
> *First series:* J. B. Baillie; B. Bosanquet; C. D. Broad; H. W. Carr; Viscount Haldane; L. T. Hobhouse; Dean Inge; J. Laird; J. S. Mackenzie; J. E. McTaggart; C. Lloyd Morgan; J. H. Muirhead; C. Read; B. Russell; F. C. S. Schiller; W. Temple.
> *Second series:* Jas. Ward; E. B. Bax; D. Fawcett; G. D. Hicks; R. F. A. Hoernlé; C. E. M. Joad; G. E. Moore; J. A. Smith; W. R. Sorley; A. E. Taylor; J. Arthur Thomson; C. C. J. Webb.
> *Third series,* edited by H. D. Lewis: R. I. Aaron; H. B. Acton; A. J. Ayer; W. H. F. Barnes; C. A. Campbell; F. C. Copleston; A. C. Ewing; J. N. Findlay; S. Hampshire; H. A. Hodges; W. C. Kneale; H. D. Lewis; J. D. Mabbott; D. M. Mackinnon; H. J. Paton; K. R. Popper; H. H. Price; L. J. Russell; G. Ryle; F. Waismann.

1 (410) (091)
METZ, R. A hundred years of British philosophy; translated [from the German] by J. W. Harvey, T. E. Jessop and H. Sturt. London, Allen & Unwin, 1938. 828p.

> The period covered is "from about the middle of the 19th century to the present day" (1934). Useful brief accounts of the thought of the leading philosophers, with a note on their chief written contributions. The German original was published in 1935, but was largely revised—and the bibliographies brought up to date—for the translation.

1 (41) (091)
SORLEY, W. R. A history of British philosophy, to 1900. Cambridge, Univ. Press, 1965. xx, 386p. 15s.; 30s.

> First published 1920.
> The text is based upon a series of chapters contributed to *The Cambridge history of English literature* and is ably written. The lengthy chapter bibliographies in the 1st ed. (p. 323-73) have been revised and brought up to date.

Scottish Philosophy

1 (411):016
JESSOP, T. E. A bibliography of David Hume, and of Scottish philosophy from Francis Hutcheson to Lord Balfour. London, Brown, 1938. xiv, 201p.

> Hume (p. 3-71): Collected works—Works published by Hume and translations of these—Posthumously published works—Spuria—Works on Hume.
> Scottish philosophy: chronological list of authors; general; philosophers, A-Z. An appendix on the Gifford Lectures gives a complete list of the lecturers and of the lectures published. Index of names.

Italian Philosophy

1 (45):016
Bibliografia filosofica italiana dal 1900 al 1950. A cura dell' Istituto di Studi Filosofici e del Centro Nazionale di Informazioni Bibliografiche, con la collaborazione del Centro di Studi Filosofici Cristiani di Gallarate. Rome, Edizioni Delfino, 1950-56. 4v.

> A bibliography of editions of works by Italian philosophers and of studies on them published 1900-50. Arranged under names of philosophers, A-Z. 'Vico' has 28 columns, 4½ of them devoted to editions of his works. V. 4 (U-Z. Aggiunte) consists largely of a supplementary sequence and an annotated list of Italian philosophical journals, 1900-55, with locations in Italian libraries.
>
> Supplemented by the annual *Bibliografia filosofica italiana.* Anno 1949-. (Milan, Marzorati, 1951-), also edited by the Centro di Studi Filosofici Cristiani di Gallarate.

1 (45):016
SCIACCA, M. F. Italienische Philosophie der Gegenwart. 1948. 36p. (Bibliographische Einführungen in das Studium der Philosophie, 7).

> Includes bibliographical aids and periodicals as well as works on individual philosophical systems, concluding Existentialism and Marxism. Some annotations. Name index.

Spanish Philosophy

1 (46):016
MARTÍNEZ GÓMEZ, L. Bibliografía filosófica española e hispanoamericana (1940-1958). Barcelona, Flors, 1961. iii-xxv, 500p.

PHILOSOPHY AND PSYCHOLOGY

A bibliography (10,166 items) of writings on philosophy by Spanish and Hispanic American authors and of others writing on Spanish philosophical theories, states *College and research libraries* (v. 24, no. 1, January 1963, p. 33). Author index. Based chiefly on bibliographies in the quarterly *Pensamiento* (Madrid, 1945-).

Library trends (v. 15, no. 3, January 1967, p. 464-5) cites two serial bibliographical media for the Spanish-speaking world: *Enciclopedia de orientación bibliográfica,* edited by T. Zamarriego (Barcelona), of which v. 3-4 (Ciencias humanas) includes philosophy and religion; and *Documentación crítica iberoamericana* (October 1964-).

Russian Philosophy

1 (47):016
Bibliographie der sowjetischen Philosophie. Dordrecht, Reidel, [1959-64]. 5v. (Sovietica. Veröffentlichungen des Osteuropa-Instituts, Universität Freiburg, Schweiz).

1. *Die 'Voprosy filosofii', 1947-1956.* [1959]. D.fl. 12.25.
2. *Bücher, 1947-1956. Bücher und Aufsätze, 1957-1958. Namenverzeichnis, 1946-1958.* [1959]. D.fl. 15.75.
3. *Bücher und Aufsätze, 1959-1960.* [1962]. D.fl. 18.50.
4. *Ergänzungen, 1947-1960.* [1963]. D.fl. 28.75.
5. *Register, 1947-1960.* [1964]. D.fl. 20.50.
The first volume lists articles that appeared in the Academy of Sciences' official journal, *Voprosy filosofii,* during 1947-56 the second includes a list of books published 1947-56. 7,217 items in all.

Studies in Soviet thought (Univ. of Fribourg, Switzerland, Institute of East-European Studies, 1961-. Quarterly) lists books and periodical articles and also features specialised bibliographical surveys.

1 (47) (038)
BALLESTREM, K. G. Russian philosophical terminology . . . Dordrecht, Reidel, [1965]. viii, 116p. D.fl.20.

A Russian-English-German-French dictionary. About 1,000 Russian philosophical terms, with equivalents and indexes in the other languages. Emphasises terms that have a special use in Soviet philosophy. A publication of the Institute of East European Studies, University of Fribourg, Switzerland.

1 (47) (091)
ZENKOVSKY, V. V. A history of Russian philosophy. Authorized translation from the Russian by George L. Kline. London, Routledge & Kegan Paul, 1953. 2v.

Author was Professor of Philosophy and Psychology, Russian Orthodox Seminary, Paris. "Written primarily for Russian readers; it thus presupposes a certain acquaintance with Russian creative work and Russian culture generally" (*Author's preface to the English edition*). A survey from the Middle Ages to the 20th century

(Lenin, v. 2, p. 434-53), in 4 main parts. Footnote references. Analytical index, v. 2, p. 927-47.

Chinese Philosophy

1 (51) (091)
BRIÈRE, O. Fifty years of Chinese philosophy, 1898-1950; translated from the French by L. G. Thompson. London, Allen & Unwin, 1956. 159p.

Originally published as *Les courants philosophiques en Chine depuis 50 ans* (Shanghai, 1949). Two main aspects are examined,—the impact of Western thought, as represented by Marx, Kropotkin, Dewey and Russell; and the traditional Chinese line of thought. Valuable bibliographies are included.

Also noted: *An outline and an annotated bibliography of Chinese philosophy,* by Wing-Tsit Chan (New Haven, Conn., Yale Univ. Press, 1961. vi, 127p. 22s. 6d.), and *Chinese philosophy, 1949-1963: an annotated bibliography of Chinese Mainland publications,* by the same author (Honolulu, East-West Center Press, 1967. xiv, 290p. 60s.).

1 (51) (091)
FUNG, YU-LAN. A history of Chinese philosophy; translated by D. Bodde. London, Allen & Unwin, 1937-53 (reprinted 1966). 2v. £10.

v. 1: *The period of the philosophers* (from the beginnings to *c.* 100 B.C.).
v. 2: *The period of classical learning* (from the 2nd century B.C. to the 20th century A.D.).
A thorough and scholarly presentation of a subject hardly covered (especially as regards the period of v. 2) in Western writings. Well translated. Detailed chronological tables, bibliographies (v. 1: p. xxiii-xxvi, 410-22; v. 2: p. 726-54) and indexes at the end of each volume.
Library of Congress catalogue enters author under 'Fêng, Yu-Lan'.

The *Times literary supplement* review (no. 1903, 6th August 1938, p. 516) notes that there is nothing in English to compare with A. Forke's monumental trilogy: *Geschicht der alten chinesischen Philosophie* (Hamburg, Friederichsen, 1927); *Geschicht der mittelalterlichen chinesischen Philosophie* (1934); and *Geschicht der neueren chinesischen Philosophie* (1938).

Indian Philosophy

1 (54) (091)
DASGUPTA, S. A history of Indian philosophy. Cambridge, Univ. Press, 1922-55. 5v. £19 8s.

See entry at 294.

American Philosophy

1 (73):016
WINN, R. B. Amerikanische Philosophie. Berne, Francke, 1948. 32p. (Bibliographische Einführungen in das Studium der Philosophie, 2).

The author was editor of *Philosophic abstracts*. Lengthy annotations of 38 works (including histories); list of 24 periodicals, with brief notes on coverage. Name index.

"Bibliography of current philosophical works published in North America" has appeared as a regular supplement to the November and May issues of *The modern schoolman: a quarterly journal of philosophy* (St. Louis Univ., St. Louis, Mo.) since November 1955.

Latin American Philosophy

1 (8):016

See 1 (46):016.

Occultism

133:016

BESTERMAN, T., *comp.* **Library catalogue of the Society for Psychical Research.** Glasgow, Maclehose, 1927. viii, 368p.; **Supplements,** 1927-1928; 1928-1929; 1929-30; 1931-1933.

An author catalogue, giving full sub-titles and, occasionally, annotations or bibliographical notes. 9,350 items in all.

The Society's brief list, *Psychical research: a selected guide to publications in English* (1949. 11p.) takes the form of a running commentary.

The 'Author and title catalogues of the collection of the Society for Psychical Research', announced by G. K. Hall of Boston, Mass. for 1964, will not now be published.

133:016

CAILLET, A. L. Manuel bibliographique des sciences psychiques ou occultes . . . Paris, Dorbon, 1912-13 (reprinted Nieuwkoop, de Graaf, 1964). 3v. NF.360.

Sub-title: "Sciences des Mages—Hermétique—Astrologie — Kabbale — Franc-Maçonnerie—Médicine ancienne—Mesmerisme—Sorcellerie — Singularités — Abérrations de tout ordre — Curiosités—Sources bibliographiques et documentaires sur ces objets, etc."
A detailed, annotated bibliography of the ccoult sciences; 11,648 items. The fullest of its kind. Bibliothèque Nationale press-marks are given. The reprint is a limited edition of 300 copies.

133 (032)

FODOR. N., *comp. and ed.* **Encyclopædia of phychic science.** London, Arthurs Press, 1933. Iv, 415 [1]p. illus.

The compiler, who was assisted by an editorial committee, states: "Of occultism, theosophy and mysticism I steered clear." Articles give evidence pro and con, citing a variety of opinions. Biographical articles are occasionally lengthy, as also are entries on certain topics (*e.g.*, Table-training The entry under the Proceedings of the old A.S.P.R. (American Society for Psychical research) gives a detailed list of contributions.

Occasional bibliographical references; illustrations (plates). p. xix-lv.

Also noted: Fodor, N. *Encyclopædia of psychic science* (New Hyde Park, New York, University Books, [1966]. xxix, 415p. $17.50).

Magic. Witchcraft

133.4 (032)

ROBBINS, R. H. The encyclopedia of witchcraft and demonology. New York, Crown; London, Nevill, 1959. 571p. illus., facsim. $7.50.

The articles, some of which are lengthy, include biographies. A source book of curiosa rather than an encyclopædia proper, being stocked with numerous quotations from contemporaneous writings and fully illustrated with facsimiles of title pages and reproductions of prints (gruesome in some cases, *e.g.*, in the article on the Inquisition). The select bibliography of 1,140 items is an author list, and is preceded by a subject index.

133.4 (091)

THORNDIKE, L. History of magic and experimental science. New York, Columbia Univ. Press, 1923-58. 8v. ea. $12.

See main entry in v. 1 of Guide, at 5/6 (091).

Alchemy

133.5:54

READ, J. Prelude to chemistry: an outline of alchemy, its literature and relationships. 2nd ed. London, Bell, 1939. xxiv, 328p. illus. (pl.).

First published 1936.
Glossary (p. 291-4); chapter bibliographies and notes (p. 295-318). Chapter 2: "The literature of alchemy."

The Science Museum. *Book Exhibitions. Catalogues.* No. 1 is entitled *A hundred alchemical books* (1952. 32p.).

Existentialism

141.3 (43)

BOLLNOW, O. F. Deutsche Existenzphilosophie. Berne, Francke, 1953. 40p. (Bibliographische Einführungen in das Studium der Philosophie, 23).

Pt. 1, Introduction; pt. 2, Bibliography, including items by and on individual existentialists,—Jaspers, Heidegger and Lipps. Name index.

141.3 (44)

JOLIVET, R. Französische Existenzphilosophie. Berne, Francke, 1948. 34p. (Bibliographische Einführungen in das Studium der Philosophie, 9).

5 sections, the first 2 (definition; guidance on studies) being in narrative form. Texts and critical studies are then listed, often with annotations. Name index.

159.9 PSYCHOLOGY

Bibliographies

159.9:016

L'Année psychologique. 1894-. v. 1-. Paris, Presses Universitaires de France, 1895-.

Since the 52nd issue, for 1952 (1953), published in 2 fasc. p.a.
Sub-title: "Publiée avec le concours du Centre National de la Recherche Scientifique".
Fasc. 2 of the 1964v. has two main sections, the first (p. 353-502) consisting of four original contributions and three critical review-articles, and the second consisting of "Analyses bibliographiques" (p. 503-699),—signed abstracts of *c*. 150 periodical articles (classes 1-17) and *c*. 50 signed book reviews (6 classes). International coverage. Annual indexes of authors (of items reviewed) and subjects.

159.9:016

BAYNE, H., and **BRY, I. "Problems and projects in the bibliography of psychiatry and psychology".** In *Libri*, v. 3, 1954. p. 363-87.

The bibliography has three sections (p. 373-87): A. Bibliographies in psychiatry, neurology, psychology and psycho-analysis.—B. Bibliographic aids in psychiatry and related fields.—C. Publications of reference use. Items are not annotated.

159.9:016

Bulletin signalétique. 20: Psychologie. Pédagogie. Paris, Centre National de la Recherche Scientifique, 1961-. Quarterly. 30F. (foreign, 35F.) p.a.

Formerly part of Pt. 3 of the *Bulletin signalétique.—Philosophie. Sciences humaines.* As from 1961, issued as a separate service, carrying about 8,000 abstracts p.a. Coverage: Social psychology — Applied psychology — Pathological psychology — Child psychology — Educational methods—Organisation of school life—Social psychology. About 60% of the abstracts concern aspects of psychology. Quarterly subject index ('Liste des concepts') for 'Psychologie'.

159.9:016

Contemporary psychology: a journal of reviews. Washington, D.C. and subsequently Lancaster, Pa., American Psychological Association, 1956-. v. 1, no. 1-. Monthly. ea. $1; $10 (foreign, $10.50) p.a.

Each issue is largely devoted to *c*. 25 thousand-word reviews of books and films; short notices; and a list of *c*. 50 books received. Apparently confined to English-language material. Qualifications of reviewers and authors of books are stated in detail. Coverage extends to psychiatry, public opinion and animal behaviour.

159.9:016

DANIEL, R. S., and **LOUTTIT, C. M. Professional problems in psychology.** New York, Prentice-Hall, 1953. 416p. $5.50.

Functions in part as a guide to the literature of psychology, superseding C. M. Louttit's *Handbook of psychological literature* (Bloomington,

Indiana, Principia Press, 1932. viii, 273p.).
Includes an annotated bibliography of some 300 reference books in psychology and a list of 300 psychological journals.

R. S. Daniel's article "Psychology" in *Library trends* (v. 15, no. 4, April 1967, p. 670-84. 38 references) has notes on the chief serial bibliographical aids, and on bibliographical control, and analyses the provision of literature in various psychological journals.

Guide de l'étudiant en psychologie, by R. Carron and R. Lombès (Paris, Presses Universitaires de France, 1953. xii, 239p.) deals with the development of psychology. It is weakest in this last field (p. 65-118), according to *Bulletin critique du livre français* (v. 19, no. 3, March 1964, entry no. 24126).

159.9:016

The Harvard list of books in psychology; compiled and annotated by the psychologists in Harvard University. 3rd ed. Cambridge, Mass., Harvard Univ. Press; London, Oxford Univ. Press, 1965. viii, [1], 111p. $2.50; 20s.

First published 1938; 2nd ed. 1949; suppt. 1958.
21 collaborators; 704 numbered items (304 new, 283 as in the previous ed. and suppt., and 117 updated), with brief critical annotations. 31 sections, including 1. Reference works and basic handbooks (nos. 1-11)—2. General handbooks and textbooks (nos. 13-25) . . . 28. Industrial psychology and organizational behavior—29. Psychology of religion—30. Psychic research and parapsychology—31. Non-technical books (nos. 683-704). According to *Contemporary psychology* v. 20, no. 9, September 1965, p. 388-9) its five strongest areas are: history of psychology; psychological statistics and measurement; comparative animal psychology; physiological psychology; and theories and systems of psychology. Author index. An invaluable selective list for students, librarians and the ordinary public, although confined to English-language publications.

The British Psychological Society's *Psychology: a selected list of books* (Cambridge, Univ. Press, for the National Book League, 1951. 32p. o.p. N.B.L. Book lists. Second series) has *c*. 400 annotated entries in 19 sections, but badly needs updating.

Readers' guide to books on psychology (Library Association, County Libraries Group, 1962. 40p. 2s. 6d. (New series, no. 69) is a selection of *c*. 500 books under 32 headings, A-Z. For the serious student of psychology; omits unscientific or popular books, as also advanced medical textbooks and works. Very few annotations; no pagination or index; prices given. Critically reviewed in *The assistant librarian*, v. 56, no. 7, July 1963, p. 146, 148.

159.9:016

Psychological abstracts. Lancaster, Pa., American Psychological Association, 1927-. v. 1-. Originally monthly, then bi-monthly, now (1966-) monthly. ea. $2; $20 ($20.50 foreign) per v.

The leading abstracting journal in the field. V. 39 (1965): 16,619 indicative and informative, evaluative and signed abstracts of books, official documents and dissertations as well as periodical articles. 11 main sections, with sub-divisions: General (including obituaries; history; philosophy; general books & reference works; bibliographies & reviews)—Methodology and research technology—Experimental psychology—Physiological psychology—Animal psychology—Developmental psychology—Social psychology—Personality—Clinical psychology—Educational psychology—Military and personnel psychology. Each issue carries an author index; annual cumulated author and permuted subject indexes. The retrospective value of this abstracting service is enhanced by the following indexes:

Cumulative author index to 'Psychological index', *1894-1935 and* 'Psychological abstracts', *1927-58;* compiled by Columbia University (Boston, Mass., G. K. Hall, 1960. 4v. $295) consists of 320,000 mounted entries, photolithographically reproduced.
Cumulative author index to Psychological abstracts. *First supplement, 1959-1963* (Boston, Mass., G. K. Hall, 1965. $90) consists of 43,100 mounted entries, similarly reproduced. A *Second supplement, 1964-1968* is to follow.
Cumulated subject index to Psychological abstracts, *1927-1960* (Boston, Mass., 1966. 2v. $650) comprises *c.* 350,000 entries, with some regrouping of headings to provide consistency.

Psychological abstracts: abstract references (Columbus, Ohio, American Psychological Association, 1940-41. 2v.) covers the period 1894-1928, and usefully precedes *Psychological abstracts.*

Psychological index: an annual bibliography of the literature of psychology and cognate subjects, 1894-1935, v. 1-42 (Princeton, N.J., Psychological Review Co., 1895-1936) continues section G of v. 3 (*Bibliography of philosophy*, by B. Rand (1905)) of J. M. Baldwin's *Dictionary of philosophy and psychology.*

"Index of literature reviews and summaries in the Psychological bulletin, *1940-1966"*, by T. G. Andrews and F. E. Kerr (*Psychological bulletin,* v. 68, no. 3, September 1967, p. 178-212) is an author index. Each review article has 20 or more references.

159.9:016
STEIN, M. I., and **HEINZE, S. J. Creativity and the individual**: summaries of selected literature in psychology and psychiatry. Glencoe, Ill., Free Press of Glencoe, 1960. [xi], 428p. $10.95.

A publication of the Graduate School of Business, University of Chicago.
An annotated bibliography of *c.* 500 books, periodical articles and papers. 500-word annotations. 13 sections, including 10. 'Psychopathology and other illnesses', and 13. 'Symposia and surveys of the literature'. Index of authors and subjects (analytical).

159.9:016
VOUTSINAS, D. Documentation sur la psychologie française. Paris, Groupe d'Études de Psychologie de l'Université de Paris, 1957-. fasc. 1-.

1. *Dix années de psychologie française (1947-1956). Recueil des articles de psychologie parus dans le revues françaises.* 1957.
2. *Recueil des articles parus en 1957. Liste des ouvrages publiés depuis 1947. Index des auteurs signalés dans les dix années.* 1958.
3. *Recueil des articles publiés de 1843 à 1946. Ouvrages et articles parus en 1958.* 1959.
4. *Ouvrages et articles (1947-1959).* 1960.
5. *Ouvrages et articles publiés en 1960.* 1961.
6. *Éléments de bibliographie, 1746-1946.* 1963.

An important retrospective bibliography. *Bulletin des bibliothèques de France* (v. 3, no. 5, May 1958, p. 406) describes fasc. 1 as a valuable tool for students.

A comparable German bibliography is *Gesamtverzeichnis der deutschsprachigen psychologischen Literatur der Jahre 1942 bis 1960,* edited by A. Wellek (Göttingen, Verlag für Psychologie, 1965. 876p.).

For Eastern Europe there is the *Bibliographie der psychologischen Literatur der sozialistischen Länder* (Berlin, Volk und Wissen, 1959-. Annual. (v. 4. 1964. 2v. ea. MDN.14), arranged by country of origin.

159.9:016
WATSON, R. I., and *others.* **"Psychology".** In *Sources of information in the social sciences,* by C. M. White and others (Totowa, N.J., Bedminster Press, 1964), p. 273-309.

This chapter comprises a survey of aspects and branches of psychology (but not psychiatry), with references to 249 numbered items, and a 'Guide to the literature' (nos. 250-302). This last feature is well annotated and particularly valuable; sections: Reviews of the literature—Abstracts and digests—Bibliographies, current—Bibliographies, retrospective—Dictionaries—Encyclopedias and encyclopedic sets—Directories and biographical information—Handbooks, manuals, compendia—Sources of scholarly contributions—Sources of current information.

159.9:016:016
LOUTTIT, C. M., *comp.* **Bibliography of bibliographies on psychology, 1900-1927.** Washington, National Research Council, 1928. 108p. (*Bulletin of the National Research Council,* no. 65, November 1928).

2,129 numbered entries (2,134 less 5 blank). Pt. 1. Periodicals and general works searched—Pt. 2. Further bibliographical sources (with occasional notes)—Pt. 3. List of bibliographies, under author, A-Z—Pt. 4. Subject index (p. 87-108; analytical). A valuable early list that badly needs supplementing.

Manuals

159.9 (021)
GOTTSCHALDT, K., LERSCH, P., *and others, ed.* **Handbuch der Psychologie.** Göttingen, Verlag für Psychologie, 1959-.

1 (2 pts.). *Allgemeine Psychologie.* 1964-66.
2. *Motivation.* 1965.
3. *Entwicklungspsychologie.* 1959.
4. *Persönlichkeitsforschung.* 1960.

5. *Ausdruckspsychologie.* 1965.
6. *Psychologie Diagnostik.* 1964.
9. *Betriebspsychologie.* 1961.
10. *Pädagogische Psychologie.* 1959.

A systematic survey of the whole field of modern psychology, each volume by specialists. V. 1, pt. 1 (*Der Aufbau des Erkennens.* xxiv, 1179p.), chapter 26, *Der Traum* (p. 1097-1134), has bibliography, p. 1129-34 and extensive name and subject indexes (p. 1135-79). To be completed in 12v.

159.9 (021)
KOCH, S., *ed.* **Psychology: a study of a science.** New York, London, McGraw-Hill, 1959-. v. 1-. diagrs.

Study 1. Conceptual and systematic.
  v. 1. *Sensory, perceptual and systematic formulations.* 1959.
  v. 2. *General systematic formulations, learning and general processes.* 1959.
  v. 3. *Formulations of the person and the social context.* 1959.
Study 2. Empirical substructure and relations with other subjects.
  v. 4. *Biologically oriented fields.* 1962.
  v. 5. *The process areas, the person and some allied fields.* 1963.
  v. 6. *Investigations of man as socius.* 1963.
Postscript to the Study.
  v. 7. *Psychology and the human agent.*
Prompted by the American Psychological Association's decision in 1952 on the need for a thorough and critical examination of the status and development of psychology. V. 1 (x, 710p.), has contributions by *c.* 80 authors. 'Color theory', by C. H. Graham (p. 145-287) has 209 references. Name and subject indexes.

159.9 (021)
Logos. Introduction aux études philosophiques. Fondée par L. Lavelle et continueé par René Le Senne et Gaston Berger. Paris, Presses Universitaires de France, 1959-. v. 1-.

  3. *Traité de psychologie générale,* by M. Pradines. 2nd ed. 1946. 3v.
  8. *Traité de psychologie animale,* by F. J. J. Buytendijk. 1952.
  12. *Traité de psychologie sociale,* by R. Daval. 1963-.
Volumes carry chapter bibliographies.

Dictionaries

159.9 (031)
The Encyclopedia of philosophy. Paul Edwards, editor-in-chief. New York, Macmillan Co. and The Free Press; London, Collier-Macmillan, 1967. 8v. $219.50; £117.

Includes a basic article on Psychology (v. 7, p. 1-27), with short bibliography and references to 36 other headings in the *Encyclopedia.*

159.9 (032)
HARRIMAN, P. L., *ed.* **Encyclopedia of psychology.** New York, Philosophical Library, 1946 (reprinted 1951). vii, 897p. o.p.

Included as being the only English-language

encyclopædia of psychology. Signed articles by many contributors, with brief bibliographies. Index of topics. "Unfortunately, quality of articles varies widely and the length of the articles frequently has little relation to the importance of the topics" (White, C. M., and others. *Sources of information in the social sciences* (1964), item F.284).

See also the article on psychology (v. 7, p. 1-27) and various aspects of it (listed at 'Psychology, Articles on') in *The Encyclopedia of philosophy,* at 1 (031)=20.

159.9 (038)=20
DREVER, J. A dictionary of psychology. Rev. ed., revised by Harvey Wallenstein. Harmondsworth, Middlesex, Penguin Books, 1964. 320p. 5s.

First published 1952.
Concise definitions (5-100 words) of *c.* 4,000 terms, with adequate cross-references. Includes terms in German and certain other languages, as well as medical terms and abbreviations. Omits biographical notes but has entries for schools. The author was Emeritus Professor of Philosophy in the University of Edinburgh. The revised ed. updates and corrects some errors.

159.9 (038)=20
ENGLISH, H. B., and **ENGLISH, A. C. A comprehensive dictionary of psychological and psychoanalytical terms:** a guide to usage. New York, Longmans, Green, 1958 (reprinted New York, McKay, 1964). xiv, 594p. diagrs. $10.75; 60s.

More than 13,000 terms and abbreviations are explained. The aim (*Preface*) is to include all terms frequently used in a special or technical sense by psychologists, with one set of definitions for the comparative layman and another set for the person working in the field of psychology. Pronunciation is given for unusual or difficult words. Extended treatment is given to certain generic and other terms (see *Science reference notes,* v. 1, no. 6, January 1959, p. 26). The inclusion of compound-word terms is a feature (*e.g.,* 'Reinforcement' and its compounds occupy five pages). Extensive cross-references. "The best dictionary of psychological terms" (*Harvard list of books in psychology* (3rd ed., 1964), p. 1).

159.9 (038)=20
VERPLANCK, W. S. "A glossary of some terms used in the objective science of behavior". In *Psychological review,* v. 64, no. 6, 1957, p. i-viii, 1-42.

Extended definitions of *c.* 200-300 terms (*e.g.,* 'Conditioning' and its 11 applications: 5 cols. (*c.* 2,000 words). Includes "laboratory slang". Categorises terms (*e.g.,* [*eth*]=usage of ethnologists). Many cross-references. 36 references to the literature.

D. C. Fraser's *Basic concepts in modern psychology* (Cambridge, Heffer, 1963. vi, 64p. 8s. 6d.) is a rev. ed. of his *A psychological glossary* (1954), intended primarily for the adult extramural student. It defines and discusses *c.* 30 terms, with references to the literature.

159.9 (038)=20
WARREN, H. C. Dictionary of psychology. London, Allen & Unwin, 1935. x, 371p.

A comprehensive dictionary, with about 7,500 entries. The dictionary proper (p. 1-299) is followed by useful appendices, including a list of technical dictionaries and vocabularies, a glossary of French terms (p. 343-58) and of German terms (p. 359-71). A valuable work of reference, though dated.

159.9 (038)=30
DORSCH, F., with TRAXEL, W. Psychologisches Wörterbuch. 7. umgearb. und erw. Auflag. Testverzeichnis und Testerklärungen mit einem Anhang . . . Hamburg. Meiner; Berne, Huber, 1963. viii, 552p. DM.38.

The psychological dictionary proper, with its many cross-references, has an appendix of authors, a special appendix by Wilhelm Witte ('Einführung in die mathematische Behandlung psychologischen Probleme'), and a bibliography (p. 502-52) that includes periodical articles. The basic German-German dictionary.

W. Hehlmann's *Wörterbuch der Psychologie* (3. Aufl. Stuttgart, Kröner, 1965. viii, 684p. illus.) includes biographical notes, a chronology and a short bibliography.

159.9 (038)=40
PIÉRON, H. Vocabulaire de la psychologie, publié avec la collaboration de l'Association des Travailleurs Scientifiques. 3. éd., entièrement rev. et augm. Paris, Presses Universitaires de France, 1963. xiii, [1], 524, [1]p. NF.40.

First published 1951; 2nd ed. 1957.
Signed definitions of *c.* 6,000 terms, stating sources (author; date). Index of names cited (p. 435-55); appendices of abbreviations, formulae, etc., and of Greek roots. No formal bibliographies. Designed for the advanced student or professional in the field of experimental and field psychology and psychiatry rather than for the layman who wishes to look up an unfamiliar word (*Science reference notes,* v. 1, no. 6, January 1959, p. 27, on the 2nd ed.). The author is Director of the Institut de Psychologie de l'Université de Paris.

Reports of Progress

159.9 (047.1)
The Annual review of psychology. Palo Alto, Cal., Annual Reviews, Inc., 1950-. v. 1-. ea. $8.50 (U.S.A.), $9 (elsewhere).

A systematic review of developments in various fields of psychology, so arranged that the fields are surveyed at regular intervals (1, 2 or 3 years). "For example, by appropriate selection and scheduling of two chapters annually, the entire field of Learning and Motivation would be covered every three years" (*Preface,* v. 11 (1960)). V. 17 (1966) comprises 17 papers, including for the first time one on Japanese psychology. Date of coverage of the literature survey is stated. The paper "Perceptional learning", by J. F. Wohlwill (p. 201-32), has 162 references. Author and subject indexes; cumulative index of contributing

authors, v. 13-17 and of chapter titles, v. 13-17. Cumulative 5-yrly. and 10-yrly indexes.

Periodicals

159.9 (05):016
Psykologiske tidsskrifter. Liste over ikke-nordiske tidsskrifter av psykologisk interesse på nordiske biblioteker. 2. utg. Oslo, Munksgaard; Copenhagen, A/S Bokhjørnet, 1955. 44p.

A union list of about 350 non-Scandinavian psychological periodicals in 56 libraries in Norway and Denmark. This substantially supplements the Scott and Smith union list (1950) (q.v.).

159.9 (05):016
SCOTT, J. W., and SMITH, F. V. A handlist of psychology periodicals in the learned libraries of Great Britain. London, Aslib, 1950. 15p. (offprint).

Originally published in *Journal of documentation,* v. 6, no. 3, September 1950, p. 152-66.
Lists 179 periodicals holdings in 62 libraries. Imperfections in runs are indicated. Holdings of the National Institute of Industrial Psychology are omitted. A handy list which needs updating.

"List of periodicals and serial publications contained in the British Psychological Society's Library (1962)" (in *British Psychological Society bulletin,* no. 49, October 1962, p. 55-60) comprises *c.* 250 titles, including those of ceased periodicals.

The mimeographed *List of periodicals* issued by the Tavistock Institute of Human Relations and Tavistock Clinic Joint Library (September 1965. 15p.) records *c.* 230 titles.

Directories

159.9:058.7
International directory of psychologists, exclusive of the U.S.A. Prepared by the Committee on Publication and Communication of the International Union of Psychological Science. 2nd ed., edited by H. C. J. Duijker and E. H. Jackson. Assen (Netherlands), Van Gorcum, 1966. xxiv, 577p. fl.15.75.

First published 1958.
About 10,000 entries, arranged under 80 countries A-Z. Entries average *c.* 60 words and state specialisation but do not mention works written by the biographee. For quick reference sexes are indicated ('M' or 'F'). Index of names, under headings.

Complementary to the American Psychological Association's *Directory of psychologists in the U.S.* (Washington, the Association, 1916-. Annual), which gives details of careers, professional positions and addresses of *c.* 20,000 American psychologists.

History

159.9 (091)
BRETT, G. S. A history of psychology. London, Allen & Unwin, 1912-21. 3v. (Muirhead library of philosophy).

v. 1: *Ancient and Patristic.* 1912. xx, 388p.
v. 2: *Medieval and early modern period.* 1912. 394p.
v. 3: *Modern psychology.* 1921. 322p.
A basic general history. Each volume includes bibliographical notes and references; v. 3 carries a list of general works consulted.

A shortened and modernised version, *Brett's History of psychology,* edited and abridged by R. S. Peters (London, Allen & Unwin, 1962. 778p. 60s.) bears the mark of its dual authorship. It includes a final chapter, 'Twentieth-century themes', a list of major omitted sections, a bibliography (p. 769-72), and an index of proper names, but no subject index.

159.9 (091)
FLUGEL, J. C. A hundred years of psychology. [3rd ed.], revised by D. J. West. London, Methuen, 1964. viii, 394p. 21s.

First published 1933. 2nd ed. 1951.
The 3rd ed. consists of the text of the 1st ed. plus a 52-page section ("Developments, 1933-63"), by D. J. West. The original text dealt with the period 1833-1933. The bibliography (by authors, A-Z, p. 359-74) has been updated and so has the chronology (to 1962). Index of subjects (non-analytical) and names. According to *The British journal of psychology* (v. 56, pt. 243, August 1965, p. 341-2), the editing of the added section has been very poor indeed (thus, some names mentioned in the text are not indexed, and some books mentioned by author and date are not in the bibliography); but this is "an attractive and stimulating work covering the chosen areas with remarkable accuracy".

159.9 (091)
WORDSWORTH, R. S., with SHEEHAN, M. R. Contemporary schools of psychology. 9th ed. London, Methuen, 1965. viii, [1], 457p.

First published 1931.
Deals with schools established in the 20th century, up to *c.* 1960 (*e.g.,* chapter 4. 'Soviet psychology as a "school" '; 8. 'Gestalt psychology'; 9. 'Psychoanalysis and related theories'). Succinct explanations of theories, with many cross-references. References and author index, arranged under authors, A-Z, then chronologically (p. 405-40; *c.* 500 references in all), preceded by 'Robert S. Wordsworth: a bibliography', 1897-1959. Analytical subject index.

British Psychology

159.9 (410)
HEARNSHAW, L. S. A short history of British psychology, 1840-1940. London, Methuen, 1964. vii, 331p. 35s.

"Likely to be a standard work on its subject for many years to come. It will encourage students to attain what is necessary in a human science—a sense of historical and social process . . . " (*The British journal of psychology,* v. 56, pts. 2 & 3, August 1965, p. 321-2). 'Select bibliography', p. 298-316 (arranged by chapters).

Research

159.9.001.5
GREAT BRITAIN. WARREN SPRING LABORATORIES. Register of research in the human sciences. . . . London, H.M. Stationery Office, 1962-. Annual.

See entry at 3.001.5.

Experimental Psychology

159.9.07
BORING, E. G. A history of experimental psychology. 2nd ed. New York, Appleton-Century-Crofts, 1950 (reprinted 1957). xxi, 771p. $7.50.

First published 1929.
Author was Professor of Psychology at Harvard University. Ranges from the time of Copernicus up to 1950. Particularly valuable for its bio-bibliographical data (*e.g.,* Wundt, p. 316-27). 26 chapters, each with notes and references appended chapter 27: 'Retrospect'. Index of names and analytical index of subjects.

Child Psychology

159.922.7:016
AXFORD, W. A., *comp.* **Handicapped children in Britain:** their problems and education. Books and articles published in Great Britain, from the 1944 Education Act to 1958. London, Library Association, 1959. 53p. (Special subject list no. 30).

About 900 entries, arranged A-Z by subject. Covers all types of physical and mental handicap, but not psychological or social handicaps such as maladjustment or deprivation. Autobiographies and biographies, Bibliographies, Directories and other special aspects of subjects appear as sub-headings. "Theses have not been included as they are already listed by subject in Mrs. Blackwell's *Lists of educational researches*" (*Introduction*).

159.922.7:016
BALINT, E. Child psychology. Cambridge, Univ. Press, for the National Book League, 1956. 24p. (National Book League. Reader's guides. Second series, 4).

An annotated reading list of 106 items in four sections: *1.* Some basic text-books and researches. *2.* The child in the family. *3.* Child psychology applied to education. *4.* Psychological treatment of the disturbed child. Prices are given. Aims to provide information to readers who are not themselves working in the field of child psychology but who may be interested in its history, theory and practical applications.

159.922.7:016
BRACKBILL, Y., *ed.* **Research in infant behavior:** a cross-indexed bibliography. Baltimore, Md., Williams & Wilkins, 1964. xi, 281p. $6.25.

1,733 entries, chiefly for periodical articles (the first article referred to is dated 1876), drawing on *c.* 290 serial publications and *c.* 150 books. Material intentionally omitted: "Theoretical papers, retrospective studies and papers available only at high duplication costs. The number of missed entries must be minimal" (*Contemporary psychology*, v. 11, no. 8, August 1966, p. 384-5). A form of co-ordinate indexing is used.

159.922.7:016
Child development abstracts and bibliography. Chicago, Ill., Society for Research in Child Development, Inc., 1927-. Bi-monthly (3 p.a., 2 nos. per issue). ea. $3; $8 p.a. (domestic), $8.50 (Western hemisphere), $9 (other countries).

Originally published by the National Research Council's Committee on Child Development.
Main sections: Biology—Clinical medicine and public health—Developmental and comparative psychology—Experimental psychology—Personality—Sociology and psychology—Education and educational psychology—Psychiatry and clinical psychology—Book notices. Also a list of 'Books received' and author per issue. 1965 (v. 39): 797 signed and numbered informative abstracts (*c.* 120-150 words apiece) p.a., stating location of author (or first author, if several). Annual cumulative author index and subject index.

159.922.7:016
CHOYNOWSKI, M. "La psychologie de l'adolescence". In *Revue analytique de l'éducation,* v. 14, no. 4, 1962. 54p.

80 entries, each with lengthy annotation. 5 pts.: 1. Textbooks and general works on adolescence (17 items)—Various problems of adolescence—Instruments and methods of research—Bibliographic sources (including the Studienbüro für Jugendfragen's *Handbuch zur Jugendforschung* (Munich, Juventa Verlag, 1961. 349p.), which lists more than 4,000 titles of publications, 1945-60).

159.922.7:016
STATENS PÆDAGOGISKE STUDIESAMLING. Katalog over litteratur om börne- og ungdomspsykologi, psykologi i almindelighed, personligheds- og karaktertests, pædagogisk psykologi med standpunktspröver, psykologiskpædagogiske studiesamling. 4. udg. Copenhagen, the Association, 1954. 107p. **Supplement, 1954-59.** 1960. 56p. (Statens pædagogiske studiesamling).

Bibliography of child and adolescent psychology, psychology and general, personal and character tests, and educational psychology.

159.922.7 (032)
GRUENBERG, S. M., *ed.* **The encyclopedia of child care and guidance.** Rev. ed. New York, Doubleday, 1963. 1008p. illus. $7.50.

Concerned with all aspects of child development: physical, psychological, educational, emotional, cultural, spiritual, as well as juvenile delinquency and adoption. Non-technical treatment.
In two parts: (1) an encyclopedia (p. 38-604) with medium length articles under fairly specific headings; extensive cross-references; agencies and organisations; for further reading (annotated; p. 629-72). (2) a 30-chapter survey of the background to child development. Both parts are linked by cross references.

Encyclopedia of child guidance, edited by R. B. Winn (New York, Philosophical Library, 1943. 456p. o.p.) contains nearly 230 signed contributions, usually with short bibliographies. Fairly extensive cross-references. Deals only with work in U.S.A.

159.922.7 (038)=40
LAFON, R., *and others.* **Vocabulaire de psychopédagogie et de psychiatrie de l'enfant.** Paris, Presses Universitaires de France, 1964. xx, 604p. 48F.

The work of 21 specialists, apart from the author. Gives *c.* 2,000 signed definitions and, according to *Bulletin critique du livre français* (v. 19, no. 6, June 1964, entry no. 60131), is more serviceable than any treatise or handbook on the subject. Numerous cross-references. German, English, Spanish and Italian equivalents of entrywords; etymology. Occasional short bibliographies appended (*e.g.,* 'Psycho-somatique' (Médecine): 3 cols.; bibliography of 4 items, plus quotations in text).

159.922.7 (058.7)
NATIONAL ASSOCIATION FOR MENTAL HEALTH. Directory of child guidance and school psychological services. Rev. ed. London, the Association, 1966. 139p. 25s.

1962 ed. has title: *Directory of child guidance services in England, Wales and Scotland and Northern Ireland, the Channel Islands and Eire, and school psychological services in England and Wales.*

Aptitude

159.928
MEDICAL RESEARCH COUNCIL. Applied Psychology Research Unit. **Human performance reports.** London, the Unit, 1956-. no. 1-. Unpriced.

List no. 12 (Autumn 1966) contains 36 one-page abstracts (*c.* 120 words each) under 7 headings: 1. Perception and division of attention—2. Decision—3. Memory—4. Control mechanisms and response—5. Stress—6. Methodology—7. Reviews. 'Work completed' is noted under the same 7 headings.

Special Mental Conditions

159.961:016
ZORAB, G., *comp.* **Bibliography of parapsychology.** New York, Parapsychology Foundation, Inc., 1957. 127p. $3.75.

A selected bibliography of *c.* 1,200 books, periodical articles, etc. 10 sections, including 'Reference books' and 'Bibliographies'. No annotations. Entries give author, title, place and date of publication only. Author and subject indexes.

Psychoanalysis

159.964.2:016
GRINSTEIN, A. The index of psychoanalytic writings. New York, International Universities Press, Inc., 1956-. v. 1-.

v. 1-5 (1956-60).

v. 6-9 (1964-66).

A revision and updating of J. Rickman's *Index psychoanalyticus* (covering 1893-1926). V. 1-4 list 37,121 numbered items under authors, A-Z, followed by anonymous items and reports, and cover the period 1900-52. All of Freud's that are known or currently available, including the non-psychological writings, are listed at nos. 10,350-10,714. V. 5, the subject index to v. 1-4, includes additions and corrections. V. 6-8 list supplementary items, with v. 9 as subject index.

159.964.2 (038)

STRACHEY, A. A new German-English psycho-analytical vocabulary. Published for the Institute of Psycho-Analysis, by London, Ballière, Tindall & Co., 1943. viii, 84p.

Enlarged and revised ed. of "Glossary for the use of translation of psycho-analytical works", suppt. 1 to the *International journal of psychoanalysis*, 1924, plus additions and emendations. About 2,000 German terms, with English equivalents.

Noted: *The encyclopedia of psychoanalysis,* by L. Eidelberg (New York, Collier-Macmillan, 1967. £10); 6,000 references.

159.964.2 (047.1)

The Annual survey of psychoanalysis: a comprehensive survey of current psychoanalytic theory and practice, 1950-. New York, International Universities Press; London, Hogarth Press, 1952-. v. 1-. (v. 9: 1958. 1967. $12; 100s.).

V. 8 (1964, covering publications of 1957) has 9 chapters, by 8 different authors: 1. History—2. Critique—3. Theoretical studies—4. Clinical studies—5. Dream studies—6. Psychoanalytic child psychiatry—7. Psychoanalytic therapy—8. Psychoanalytic education—9. Applied psychoanalysis (I. Religion, mythology and folklore. II. Sociological studies and anthropology. III. Literature, arts and aesthetics). Bibliography, p. 349-60 (281 text references); analytical index. Considerable time-lag.

Abnormal Psychology

159.97:016

"Bibliography and epitome." In *The Journal of mental science* (subsequently (1963-) *British journal of psychiatry*), 1854-.

Appears very sporadically in the January and July issues of the *Journal,* a quarterly published by authority of the Royal Medico-Psychological Association. A contents-listing of a half-year's issues of some 44 journals, plus abstracts (usually the author's) of one or more important articles in those journals. Coverage: all aspects of psychology and psychiatry. About 2,000 items are listed and some 200 are abstracted p.a. Annual index of 'Authors referred to in epitome'; annual general index covers reviews (about 12 per issue) and epitomes, the latter being indexed by catch-word in title. Considerable time-lag.

159.97:016

DRIVER, E. D. The sociology and anthropology of mental sickness: a reference guide. Amherst, Univ. of Massachusetts Press, 1965. xiv, 146p. $3.50.

A bibliography, drawing on articles from *c.* 300 periodicals. 9 main sections: 1. General studies in social psychiatry—2. Attitudes toward mental illness—3. Frequency and distribution of mental illness—4. Characteristics of the mentally ill—5. Etiology of mental illness—6. The mental hospital and clinic—7. The former patient in the community.—8. Impact of mental illness on the patient's family—9. Mental illness, crime and suicide. Detailed, analytical, author and subject index (p. 117-46). Items are not annotated and the absence of commentary belies the sub-title, "a reference guide".

159.97:016

MENNINGER, K. A. A guide to psychiatric books, with some suggested reading lists. 2nd rev. ed. New York & London, Grune & Stratton, 1956. xv, 157p. $5.

First published 1950.

A checklist of *c.* 3,500 items; no annotations. 7 main sections: 1. Basic and related disciplines —2. General psychiatry—3. Specialized psychiatry—4. Psychiatric therapies—5. Preventive psychiatry and mental hygiene—6. Psychiatric book lists and bibliographies—7. Reading lists. Index. Heavy U.S. slant.

159.97:016

Mental health book review index. Flushing, N.Y., the Index, 1956-. no. 1-. 2 p.a., then annually. $5 p.a.

Sponsored by the World Federation for Mental Health, the International Council of Psychologists, and the Research Center for Mental Health, New York University.

Lists references to signed book-reviews of *c.* 300 new books p.a. in three or more of *c.* 130 journals in English. Indexing began with volumes current in January 1955. Covers not only psychology and psychiatry, and sociological aspects, but also a good many books of general cultural interest, states *Nature,* v. 197, no. 4867, 9th February 1963, p. 542.

Also noted: Schermerhorn, R. A. *Psychiatric index for interdisciplinary research: guide to the literature, 1950-1961* (U.S. Vocational Rehabilitation Administration. Washington, U.S. Government Printing Office, 1964. 1249p. $6.50).

159.97:016

NATIONAL ASSOCIATION FOR MENTAL HEALTH, New York. **Recommended books for a mental health library.** 2nd rev. ed. New York, the Association, [1966]. [i], 16p. 25c.

About 200 items in three main sections: Background readings and general references—Books on special mental health subjects—Books for professional groups (teachers; physicians; nurses; clergymen). Some items are annotated.

159.97 (02)

ARIETI, S., *ed.* **American handbook of psychiatry.** New York, Basic Books, Inc., 1959-66. 3v. v. 1-2. $25; v. 3 (1966). $20.

A comprehensive survey, by more than a hundred contributors; primarily for professionals. Each contribution has a short bibliography (*e.g.,* 'Personality theory', v. 1, p. 88-113; bibliography of 37 items). V. 2 includes a name index, and an excellent analytical subject index (p. 2009-98).

V. 3 aims to include new material and update v. 1-2 principally in three areas: biochemical psychiatry, community psychiatry and conceptual psychiatry. Reviewed in *Contemporary psychology,* v. 12, no. 6, June 1967, p. 330.

Noted: Gruhle, H. W. *Psychiatrie der Gegenwart: Forschung und Praxis* (Berlin, Springer Verlag, [1966?]-.), to be completed in 3v. and numerous parts; articles in German, French and English.

159.97 (02)

EYSENCK, H. J., *ed.* **Handbook of abnormal psychology:** an experimental approach. London, Pitman Medical Publishing Co., 1960. xvi, 816p. illus., diagrs., tables.

Editor is Professor of Psychology, University of London. 20 chapters (19 contributors), in 3 pts.: 1. Description and measurement of abnormal behaviour—2. Causes and determinants of abnormal behaviour—3. Experimental study and modification of abnormal behaviour. Each contribution has summary or conclusion, and references. Index of authors cited in text; index of subjects (detailed, but not analytical; *e.g.,* 'Neuroticism': 72 unspecified references to the text).

159.97 (031)

DEUTSCH, A. Encyclopedia of mental health. New York, Watts, 1963. 6v. $49.50.

141 contributors; 172 major-subject chapters of interest both to mental health professionals and the layman (*e.g.,* aging, brain damage, creativity, learning and reading, mental hospitals, nervous breakdown, sleep). Includes a directory of agencies, a glossary of *c.* 1,000 psychiatric and psychological terms and a name index. The unclassified bibliography of 8 pages at the end of v. 6 is inadequate. Expensive.

159.97 (032)

HINSIE, L. E., and **CAMPBELL, R. J.,** *ed.* **Psychiatric dictionary.** 3rd ed. New York, Oxford Univ. Press, 1960. ix, 788p. $17.50; £7.

First published 1940.

The 2nd ed. contained more than 8,000 entries, "Approximately thirteen hundred of these have been eliminated, and nearly two thousand listings added" (*Preface to the third edition*). Encyclopædic treatment of terms, giving pronunciation, etymology and citations, plus references to sources of information. The planning of the very brief biographical entries has been criticised as lacking in balance (*Library journal,* v. 85, no. 8, 15th April 1960, p. 1605-6).

Stone, C. P., *comp. Abnormal psychology glossary: technical terms for beginning students in abnormal psychology, mental hygiene and medical social service* (Stanford, Cal., Stanford Univ. Press; London, Oxford Univ. Press, 1954. 24p.), first published in 1944, has *c.* 600-700 very brief definitions and biographies (*e.g.,* of J. M. Charcot).

159.97 (038)=00

MOOR, L. Lexique français-anglais-allemand des termes usuels en psychiatrie, neuropsychiatrie infantile, et psychologie pathologique. Paris, L'Expansion Scientifique Française, 1965. 198p. chart. *c.* 26s.

A concise dictionary of *c.* 2,000 terms in 3 parts: French-English-German (p. 11-71); German-French-English (p. 75-133); English-French-German (p. 138-98). Bibliography, p. 7-8.

159.97 (038)=20

AMERICAN PSYCHIATRIC ASSOCIATION. A psychiatric glossary: the meaning of words most frequently used in psychiatry. 2nd ed. Washington, the Association, 1964. 79p. $1.

First published 1957.

Nearly 700 terms are defined in simple, good English. Of these *c.* 150 are new terms "derived primarily from psycho-pharmacology, neurophysiology, biochemistry, mental retardation and community psychiatry. . . . Fewer than 100 definitions in the first edition survived in their original form. . . ." (*Introduction*). Includes 1-5 line biographical notes. Full cross-references. Neatly produced.

159.97 (038)=82

TELBERG, I., and **DMITRIEFF, A. Russian-English glossary of psychiatric terms.** New York, Telberg Book Corpn., 1964. iv, 86 l. Mimeographed. $9.80.

Posthumously published; completed by A. Dmitrieff.

The first part (l. 1-60) consists of *c.* 1,000 Russian terms with English equivalents. Names of some leading psychiatrists are included. The second part is 'Materials for a Russian-English index of proper names and titles in psychiatry'. List of sources (7 items). Expensive.

Mental Retardation

159.973:016

HEBER. R., *and others.* **Bibliography of world literature on mental retardation,** January 1940–March 1963. Washington, Public Health Service, [1963]. vii, 564p. $40. **Supplement** . . . , March 1963–December 31, 1964. 1965. $1.75.

The original *Bibliography* lists *c.* 16,000 classified citations, with an author-subject index. The Supplement adds 2,372 citations. Covers both behavioural and biological aspects, states *Contemporary psychology* (v. 11, no. 10, October 1966, p. 511).

Psychological Tests

159.98 (083)

BUROS, O. K., *ed.* **Tests in print:** a comprehensive bibliography of tests for use in education, psychology and industry. Highland Park, N.Y., Gryphon Press, 1961. xxix, 479p. $7.

Lists 2,104 (plus interpolations) different tests in print in 1961, with concise descriptions and references to reviews. Closely classified. Appended list of out-of-print tests. Publishers directory and index; distributors directory and index; title and name indexes.

159.98 (083)

BUROS, O. K., *ed.* **The sixth mental measurements yearbook.** Highland Park, N.J., Gryphon Press, 1965. xxxvi, 1714p. $32.50.

V. 1, 1938; v. 5 (1959), covering 1952-58.

An encyclopædic account of all types of

psychological test and assessment. It enables test users to locate and evaluate tests through book and journal references and original reviews. The 6th *Yearbook*, nearly one-third as large again as the 5th, includes for the first time the status of all tests formerly listed in *Tests in print* (q.v.). Indexes of titles and names, plus classified index of tests. Author is now Visiting Professor of Education, University College, University of East Africa, Nairobi, Kenya.

159.98 (083)

BURT, Sir C. Mental and scholastic tests. 4th ed. London, Staples Press, 1962. xxx, [1], 551p. tables. 65s.

Memoranda: 1. The Binet-Simon scale: practical use of the method—2. The Binet-Simon scale: theoretical validity of the results—3. Tests of educational attainments. Indexes of subjects and of names. 65 tables.

16 LOGIC

16:016

RISSE, W. Bibliographia logica. Verzeichnis der Druckschriften zur Logik mit Angabe ihrer Fundorte. Hildesheim, G. Olms Verlagsbuchhandlung, 1965-. v. 1-.

v. 1: *1472-1800.* 1965.
v. 2: *1800 bis zu Gegenwart.*
v. 3: *Zeitschriftenartikel.*

V. 1 contains *c.* 6,000 entries, arranged chronologically by year; locations in 65 libraries. Four indexes, of authors, anonymous works and commentators, and a systematic index.

The *Notre Dame journal of formal logic: devoted to symbolic logic* . . . (Notre Dame, Indiana, Univ. of Notre Dame Press, 1960-. Quarterly. $6 p.a.) includes a survey of the current literature.

16 (031)

The Encyclopedia of philosophy . . . New York, Macmillan Co. and the Free Press, London, Collier-Macmillan, 1967. 8v. $219.50; £117.

Includes articles on various aspects of logic, v. 4, p. 504-71 and v. 5, p. 1-83 (including 'Logical terms, Glossary of', v. 5, p. 57-77), as well as elsewhere.

16 (091)

BOCHENSKI, I. M. A history of formal logic. Translated and edited by Ivor Thomas. Notre Dame, Indiana, Notre Dame Univ. Press, 1961. xxii, 567p. $20.

Parts: 2. Ancient logic—3. Scholastic logic—4. Classical logic—5. Mathematical logic—6.

Indian logic. The extensive bibliography runs to several thousand entries.

164:016

CHURCH, A. "A bibliography of symbolic logic, 1660-1935." In *The journal of symbolic logic,* v. 1, no. 4, December 1936, p. 121-218; v. 3, no. 4, December 1938, p. 178-212.

A chronologically arranged bibliography for the period 1666-1935, with an author index of the 547 items cited. Items obelisked are works recommended for their expository value for topics covered by the bibliography. The second article consists of additions and corrections, and author and subject indexes to the whole.

A more recent bibliography is included in C. I. Lewis's *A survey of symbolic logic* (New York, Dover Publications; London, Dover, [1960]. 327p. illus. $2.20; 16s.). *Symbolische Logik und Grundlegung der exakten Wissenschaften,* by E. W. Beth (Berne, Francke, 1948. 28p. (Bibliographische Einführungen in das Studium der Philosophie, 3)) has three main sections: *A.* General: Logic and general methodology—*B.* Special: Laying the foundation of the sciences—*C.* Supplement ('Geschichtsschreibung der Logik und Grundlagenforschung'). Author index.

165.73:016

DÜRR, K. Der logische Positivismus. Berne, Francke, 1948. 24p. (Bibliographische Einführungen in das Studium der Philosophie, 11).

14 sections. Periodicals are listed in section 6. Annotated entries name index.

17 ETHICS

17 (031)

HASTINGS, J., *ed.* **Encyclopaedia of religion and ethics.** Edinburgh, Clark, 1908-26. 12v. and index. illus. 80s. per v.

Includes extensive articles by leading experts on philosophers and ethical and philosophical subjects with bibliographical references. Thus, the article 'Ethics and morality' (p. 436-522) has 18 sections ('American', 'Australian', 'Babylonian' . . .), each by a specialist; 'Drunkenness': 6 sections (11 columns), with 54½ lines of bibliography. Extensive quotations, in very small type. The final volume consists almost entirely of an analytical subject index.

(For main entry, see at 2 (031).)

See also articles on various aspects of ethics in *The Encyclopedia of philosophy* (at 1 (031)= 20), v. 3, p. 87-134.

17 (091)

DITTRICH, O. Geschichte der Ethik. Die Systeme der Morale vom Altertum bis zur Gegenwart. Leipzig, Meiner, 1926-32. v. 1-4 (pt. 1).

The basic history. Author was Professor of Philosophy at the University of Leipzig. V.3 (*Mittelalter bis zum Kirchenreformation.* 1926. viii, 510p.) has profuse footnote references, a bibliography (p. 433-440) and an excellent subject index (p. 441-510). Only pt. 1 of v. 4 was completed: *Kirchenreformation bis zum Ausgang. 1. Die Reformation* . . . (1932).

2. RELIGION

Bibliographies

2:016

ADAMS, C. J., *ed.* **A reader's guide to the great religions.** New York, The Free Press; London, Collier-Macmillan, 1965. xv, [1], 304p. $6.95; 75s.

See entry at 29:016.

2:016

Bulletin signalétique. 19. Sciences religieuses. Paris, Centre National de la Recherche Scientifique, 1961-. Quarterly. 25F. (foreign, 30F.) p.a.

Part of sections 19-24. *Sciences humaines. Philosophie,* published separately. Formerly part of *Bulletin analytique. Philosophie* (v. 1-9. 1947-55), then of *Bulletin signalétique. 19. Philosophie. Sciences humaines* (1956-60).
About 4,000 indicative abstracts p.a. Four main sections: 1. Philosophie de la religion—2. Histoire des religions—3. Exégèse et critiques bibliques—4. Theologie.

2:016

DARLING, J. Cyclopaedia bibliographica: a library manual of theological and general literature, and guide to books for authors, preachers, students, and literary men: analytical, bibliographical and biographical. London, J. Darling, 1854-59. 2v.

A bibliography of theology and all kindred subjects, with enumerations of lengthy collections, brief biographical details of authors, and some annotations. V. 1 is arranged by authors; v. 2 is devoted chiefly to the Holy Scriptures and works on them, with a selective subject index. A further volume was planned but never published.

2:016

DIEHL, K. S. Religions, mythologies, folklores: an annotated bibliography. 2nd ed. New York, Scarecrow Press, 1962. 573p. $12.50.

See entry at 29:016.

2:016

DR. WILLIAMS'S LIBRARY, London. **Catalogue of the Library.** London, 1841. 2v. (v. 2: Tracts and pamphlet material).

—— **Catalogue of the Library.** v. 3 [1842-1885]. London, 1885. 3 pts.

—— **Author catalogue of additions, 1900-1932** [with supplement of publications of learned societies, connected series, etc.]. London, 1933. 3 pts.

—— **Catalogue of accessions, 1900-1950;** being a catalogue of books published and added to the Library during that period [with supplement of titles of periodicals, publications of learned societies, connected series, etc.]. London, 1955. viii, 776, cxlv p.

—— **Catalogue of accessions,** v. 2; being a catalogue of books published in the twentieth century and added to the Library, 1951-1960. London, 1961. xi, 181, xxxv p.

A catalogue, by authors, of a library founded in 1715 and now possessing some 100,000 volumes covering all aspects of religion, philosophy and kindred subjects; especially strong in early Nonconformist material. No printed catalogue exists for the years 1886-99, and the latest two catalogues do not list books published before 1900 and added since then.

2:016

HOULDEN, J. L., *comp.* **6s. and under:** an annotated and classified list of 368 important religious and theological books for all readers. London, S.P.C.K., 1960. 30p.

20 sections, including 'Bible translations', 'Religious autobiography and experience', 'Modern issues and problems', 'Psychology and healing', 'Non-Christian religions'. About one item in ten is very briefly annotated. Books asterisked are specially suitable for church stalls; those obelisked are more specialised. Mostly paper backs. For clergy and laity, listing works by authors of various confessions. Gives prices.

2:016

Index to religious periodical literature: an author and subject index to periodical literature, including an author index of book reviews. . . . American Theological Library Association (distributed by the American Library Association, Chicago, Illinois), 1953-.

v. 1: 1949-1952. 1953.
v. 2: 1953-1954. 1956.
v. 3: 1955-1956. 1964.
v. 4: 1957-1959. 1960.
v. 5: 1960-1962. 1963.
v. 6: 1963-1964. 1965.

Published in 3-year cumulated v., the first two years being issued separately, paperbacked. V. 6 contains *c.* 14,000 entries for *c.* 3,500 articles from 104 scholarly journals, plus *c.* 4,000 book reviews, entered under authors of books in a separate sequence. The 1965 annual (1966) shows a marked increase in size. None of the journals scanned is indexed in the *Reader's guide* or *International index* (now *Social sciences and humanities index*). International in scope; basically Protestant, but with some Roman Catholic and Jewish items. "An excellent instrument" (*Library trends,* v. 15, no. 3, June 1967, p. 470).

An alphabetical subject index and index encyclopaedia to periodical articles on religion, 1890-99, by E. C. Richardson (New York, Scribner, 1907-11. 2v.) covers American and foreign material. V. 1 is arranged by subjects A-Z, each subject being clearly and briefly defined; v. 2, which can be used independently, is arranged by authors (titles, in the case of anonymous works).

2:016

MORRIS, R. P. A theological book list. Naperville, Ill., Allenson's; Oxford, Blackwell, 1960. xiv, 242p. $6.

Prepared [by the librarian of the Yale University Divinity School] on behalf of the

Theological Education Fund of the International Missionary Council "to assist in the efforts to strengthen and improve the theological colleges and seminaries training for the Christian ministry in the churches of Africa, Asia and Latin America" (*Preface*).

A list of 5,472 works, primarily in English, but other Western languages are used when there were no satisfactory substitutes; basic books, even if o.p., have been included. Printed in double columns; basic arrangement: Bible, Church history, doctrine and practical theology; elaborately divided and subdivided, with 6 double-column pages of 'Table of contents', and 14 four-column pages of index, authors' names only. Some entries have brief indications of their nature and/or value. Approximately one-third of the list are Biblical materials, but the whole is a very convenient tool for anyone interested in theology generally.

1st supplement: Theological Book Fund. *A theological book list of works in English, French, German, Portuguese, Spanish* (Oxford Blackwell, 1963 [*i.e.* 1964]. 221p. 50s.). A different compiler for each language; English book list compiled by A. Marcus Ward.

2:016

Répertoire général de sciences religieuses. Bibliographie hors commerce publiée avec le concours de la Direction des Relations Culturelles au Ministère des Affaires Étrangères pour le Service Bibliographique du Centre d'Études, Saint - Louis - de - France. Rome, "L'Airone" (later, Paris, Éditions Alsatia Colmar), [*c.* 1952]-. Année 1950-.

The volume for 1957 (1966) has 20,528 numbered, unannotated items—books and periodical articles. About 1,500 periodicals are indexed. Eleven divisions: Histoire des religions—Bible et théologie biblique—Théologie catholique—Histoire de la théologie et de la littérature chrétienne. Théologie historique protestante—Théologie protestante. Théologie systematique. Théologie pratique. Les églises diverses—Unité de l'église. Oecuménisme—Philosophie. Sociologie religieuse. Education religieuse. Education chrétienne—Droit canonique et ecclésiastique. Histoire de l'église. Art et archéologie, etc.—Missions catholiques. Missions protestantes—Littératures. Author index is included with each volume.

2:016

Scripta recenter edita. New publications. Nijmegen, Bestel Centrale V.S.K.B., 1959-. v. 1. 10 nos. $5 p.a.

An international bibliographical bulletin that "aims to give information immediately about all books that may be of interest to theological and philosophical libraries". Edited by the Dutch Vereniging voor Seminarie- en Kloosterbibliothecarissen (V.S.K.B.). Sections: Philosophica—Philosophica historica—Psychologica et paedagogica — Sociologica — Theologica generalia et dogmatica—Theologica moralia et pastoralia—Scripturistica — Liturgica — Canonica—Historica et patrologica—Historica religionum et missologica — Theologica spiritualia — Varia. About

4,000 items p.a. Prices of books given, but no annotations. Each issue has author index.

2:016

UNION THEOLOGICAL SEMINARY LIBRARY, New York City. **Shelf list . . .** Boston, Mass., G. K. Hall, 1960. 10v. $715.

—— **Alphabetical arrangement of main entries from the 'Shelf list'** . . . Boston, Mass., G. K. Hall, 1960. 10v. $975.

The Union Theological Seminary Library has *c.* 350,000 items and is particularly strong in the historical field. Its *Shelf list* is classified and comprises *c.* 203,000 cards, photolithographically reproduced in these 10 volumes. The *Alphabetical arrangement* . . . comprises *c.* 191,000 cards and is basically an author catalogue.

2:016:016

BARROW, J. G. A bibliography of bibliographies in religion. Ann Arbor, Michigan, Edwards, 1955. xi, 489p. $15.

An important research tool that attempts to list, fairly completely up to 1950, all separately published bibliographies in Christian and non-Christian religions. Arrangement is chronological in order of publication date, under subjects, with full bibliographical description, evaluations, and, generally, locations. Author, title and subject index.

Encyclopaedias

2(031)=20

Encyclopaedia of religion and ethics; edited by J. Hastings, with the assistance of J. A. Selbie and other scholars. Edinburgh, Clark; New York, Scribner, 1908-26. 12v. and index. illus. ea. 80s.

The fullest work of its kind, the words "religion" and "ethics" being used in their most comprehensive sense. The aim is to include articles on every religious belief or custom, every ethical movement, every philosophical idea, and every moral practice. Persons and places famous in the history of religion and morals are included. Particularly valuable for the comparative approach (*e.g.*, the series of articles: Faith, Buddhist; Faith, Christian; Faith, Greek; Faith, Hindu; Faith, Muslim; etc.).

Articles are signed and well documented; systematic treatment of major subjects (*e.g.*, "Architecture" ((v.1, p. 677-773) has 24 sections, from 'Ægean' to 'Shinto'. The index volume comprises a general, analytical index (p. 1-660), an index to foreign words, an index to scripture passages, and an index to authors of articles. Diacritical markings are given.

2(031)=20

SCHAFF, P. New Schaff-Herzog encyclopedia of religious knowledge, embracing Biblical, historical, doctrinal and practical theology and Biblical, theology and ecclesiastical biography, from the earliest time. S. M. Jackson, editor-in-chief. New York, Funk, 1908-12. 12v. and index (reprinted, Grand Rapids, Michigan, Baker Book House, 1949-50. 13v.).

Based on the 3rd ed. of the *Realencyklopädie für protestantische Theologie und Kirche,* founded by J. J. Herzog and edited by A. Hauck (3rd. ed. Leipzig, Hinrichs, 1896-1913. 24v.), and therefore Protestant in tone. Valuable for its biographies and particularly for its bibliographies, appended to articles and also prefatory to each volume. Supplemented by:

Twentieth - century encyclopedia of religious knowledge: an extension of the "New Schaff-Herzog encyclopedia of religious knowledge". Editor-in-chief, L. A. Loetscher. Michigan. Grand Rapids, Baker Book House, 1953-55. 2v.

Nearly 500 contributors, all American. Corrects and supplements data, to 1954, in the *New Schaff - Herzog encyclopedia.* Signed articles; bibliographies.

2(031)=30
Evangelisches Kirchen Lexikon. Kirchlich-theologisches Handwörterbuch. Hrsg. von Heinz Brunotte und Otto Weber. Göttingen, Vanderhoeck & Ruprecht, 1956-61. 4v. DM.310.

V. 13: A-Z; v. 4: *Register.*
The work of nearly 800 contributors. Signed, often lengthy and sectionalised articles with bibliographies (*e.g.,* 'Mission': cols. 1336-71; 5 sections, each with bibliography; statistical table). V. 2 includes a valuable tabular approach to church history as a whole (*Kirchengeschichte,* p. 663-730). V. 4. consists largely of a subject index (col. 41-272); 'Ökumenische Bewegung': 17 lines), and an extensive name index—'Biographischer Anhang' (cols. 273-924)—to v. 1-3, with *c.* 20,000 entries (some note chief works, in small type). German Protestant standpoint.

2(031)=30
Lexikon für Theologie und Kirche. Begründet von Michael Buchberger. Hrsg. von J. Höfer und K. Rahner. 2. völlig neu bearb. Aufl. Freiburg, Herder, 1957-65. 10v. DM.888. Suppty. v. 1966-.

First published 1930-38.
Signed short articles, each with brief bibliography, are a feature. Has 119 entries, plus cross-references, under 'GU', whereas *Evangelisches Kirchenlexikon,* with its lengthy, sectionalised contributions, has only 3 entries. Biographical and place entries included. Many cross-references (*e.g.,* more than thirty under 'Calvinism'), but no general index. V. 1-10 cover the main A-Z sequence. Supplementary v. 1-2: *Das zweite Vatikanische Konzil. Dokumente und Kommentare* (1966-67). Roman Catholic standpoint.

2(031)=30
Die Religion in Geschichte und Gegenwart. Handwörterbuch für Theologie und Religionswissenschaft. 3. völlig. neu bearb. Aufl. in Gemeinschaft mit Hans Freiherr v. Campenhausen [u.a.]; hrsg. von Kurt Galling. Tübingen, Mohr, 1957-65. 7v. illus., maps.

First published 1909-13. 5v.; 2nd ed. 1927-32. 5v.
A scholarly work, all articles being signed, with bibliographies. A feature is the lengthy, systematic treatment of subjects. The article 'Kirchenbau' (v. 3) covers columns 1347-1411, including 58 plans, 16 pages of plates, and treats the subject in terms of its major periods. 10p. on Buddhism; 18p. on Islam. Valuable, too, for its articles on marginal topics and appropriate men of letters (*e.g.,* articles on the ikon, existentialism, the film, and Franz Kafka).
V. 7, the index, comprises biographical notes on the *c.* 3,000 contributors, a subject index (p. 272-1102); 'Zwingli': 2/3 col.), and errata. German Protestant standpoint.

2 (031)=40
Encyclopédie des sciences ecclésiastiques, redigée par les savants catholiques les plus éminents de France et de l'étranger. Paris, Letouzey, 1907-.

The parts of this monumental undertaking are as follows:
1. Vigouroux, F. G., and Pirot, L. *Dictionnaire de la Bible.* 1907-12. 5v.; Supplément, v. 1-. 1928-. (In progress). *See entry at 22 (031).*
2. Vacant, A., *and others. Dictionnaire de théologie catholique.* 1909-50. 15v.; Tables générales. 1951-. (In progress). *See entry at 282 (03).*
3. Cabrol, F., and Leclercq, H. *Dictionnaire d'archéologie chrétienne et de liturgie.* 1928-53. 15v. in 30. *See entry at 27(03).*
4. Baudrillart, A. *Dictionnaire d'histoire et de géographie ecclésiastiques.* 1929-. v. 1-. *See entry at 27 (03).*
5. *Dictionnaire de droit canonique.* 1935-. v. 1-. *See entry at 348 (031).*

2 (032)=20
PIKE, E. R. Encyclopaedia of religion and religions. London, Allen & Unwin, 1951. [ii], 406p. 35s.

The author claims to have "no propagandist aim to serve" (*Foreword*). The entries include many very brief definitions (*e.g.,* of Greek, Hebrew, etc. words) and biographies. Taoism receives $2\frac{3}{4}$ columns; Jehovah's Witnesses, $1\frac{1}{2}$ columns; Quakers, $4\frac{1}{2}$ columns; Vedanta, 1 column. Mythology is included. No bibliographies. Pronunciation list, p. 405-6. Useful for the occasions when a short, simple and unbiased statement on a minor religion is required.

An encyclopedia of religion, edited by V. Ferm (London, Owen, 1956. xix, 844p. o.p.), first published *c.* 1945 (New York, Philosophical Library) has a wide range of articles, with bibliographies; profuse cross-references. Entries for variant spellings of terms. Protestant standpoint.

2 (032)=30
KÖNIG, F. Religionswissenschaftliches Wörterbuch. Die Grundbegriffe. Freiburg, Herder, 1956. 954 cols. maps.

Signed articles, with brief bibliographies. Covers a wide range of religions and doctrines, and thus handy for quick reference. 4 maps. Roman Catholic standpoint.

Religious Quotations

2 (082.2)
MEAD, F. S., *ed. and comp.* **Encyclopedia of religious quotations.** London, Peter Davies, 1965. [vii], 534p. 126s.

More than 10,000 quotations, arranged A-Z by topic, from 'Advertising' (19 entries, authors A-Z, anonymous preceding) to 'Zeal' (16 entries). 170 subject headings. Covers verse and prose and draws on non-Christian as well as Christian (including Biblical) sources. Quotations are sometimes lengthy, but there are obvious omissions. Index of authors does not include Biblical authors; index of topics. Critically reviewed in *Times literary supplement,* no. 3333, 13 January 1966, p. 29.

2 (082.2)

WOODS, R. L., *comp. and ed.* **The world treasury of religious quotations.** New York, Hawthorn, 1966. 1106p. $15.

10,000 quotations, chronologically arranged under 1,500 subject headings. Universal coverage; no poetry and only two verses from the Bible. Author, title and date of publication for each quotation. Author index; no keyword index.—a definite drawback. Reviewed in *Library journal,* v. 92, no. 6, 15th March 1967, p. 1145.

History of Religions

2 (091)

Histoire générale des religions. [2. éd.]. Paris, Quillet, 1960. 2v. illus.

> v. 1. *Les primitifs. L'ancien orient. Les indo-européens. L'antiquité classique.*
> v. 2. *Indo-iraniens. Judaïsme. Christianisme. Islam. Extrême Orient. Folklore et religion.*

First published 1944-51 (by M. Gorce and R. Mortier). 5v.

The 2nd ed. show some overhaul: contributions have been dropped and other features added. V. 1 has 20 chapters, and v. 2, 10 chapters, by various hands. Chapter notes and bibliographies are appended (v. 1, p. 671-719; v. 2, p. 581-619). V. 2 has a lengthy chronological table (p. 510-577), showing contemporaneous political and religious events up to 1960. Name index, v. 2, p. 623-95. One or more photogravure illustrations on nearly every page are a feature. The review in *Bulletin des bibliothèques de France,* v. 6, 1961, p.*251, notes omissions in the bibliographies.

2 (091):016

International bibliography of the history of religions. Bibliographie internationale de l'histoire des religions . . . 1952-. Leiden, Brill. 1954-. Annual & cumulated. D.fl.16 p.a.; D.fl.14 to subscribers to *Numen*).

Published by the International Association for the History of Religions.

"This bibliography", states the compiler, "attempts to give as complete a list as possible of the books and articles relating to the history of religion which were published during the year under review". It also notes book reviews. No annotations. Main sections: 1. General works—2. Prehistoric and primitive religions—3. Religions of antiquity—4. Judaism and ancient Israel—5. Christianity—6. Islam—7. Hinduism—8. East Asian religions. About 2,000 entries p.a. Cumulated v. for 1957-61 published 1963; 1963 v. published 1966.

2(091):016

PUECH, H.-Ch. "Bibliographie générale de l'histoire des religions". In Vandier, J. *La religion égyptienne* (2. éd. Paris, Presses Universitaires de France, 1949. Mana. Introduction à l'histoire des religions, v. 1), p. xvii-lxiii.

First published 1944.

A bibliography, with occasional notes, of *c.* 500 items. 6 main sections: 1. Instruments généraux de travail (introductions; manuals and general histories; bibliographies; dictionaries & encyclopaedias; sources, selected documents, texts; collections of illustrations, maps, statistics; periodicals; series)—2. Enseignement, sociétés, musées, congrès—3. Histoire de la discipline—4. Questions connexes: mythologie, magie—5. Méthodes et divisions de la science religieuse—6. Monographies concernant un thème général (*e.g.,* symbols, symbolism; sacrifice; death, immortality of the soul).

Rationalism

211(032)

KAHANE, E., *and others, ed.* **Dictionnaire rationaliste.** Paris, Éditions de l'Union Rationaliste 1964. 503p. 38F.

Published two centuries after Voltaire's *Dictionnaire philosophique,* to which tribute is paid. 82 contributors (index of contributors and articles, p. 499-503); articles sometimes fairly lengthy (*e.g.,* 'Mythe (religion)': 5½ columns, with 14 quotations. Includes biographies, listing main works (*e.g.,* Luther (5 columns), Heine, Helvétius, Newton, Réaumur).

211(032)

McCABE, J. A rationalist encyclopædia: a book of reference on religion, philosophy, ethics and science. 2nd. ed. London, Watts, 1950. vi, 633p.

First published 1948.

An attempt to refute the prevailing belief that Christianity is the mainspring of social progress and individual morality (cf. *Foreword* to 1st ed.). Includes a number of brief biographies; references in the text to literature.

J. McCabe's *A biographical dictionary of modern rationalists* (London, Watts, 1920. xxxii p., 934 cols.) has *c.* 2,000 entries covering those still living at the time. Some unexpected inclusions (*e.g.,* William Pitt, Prince Jerome Bonaparte, Turgenev, Pestalozzi). Acknowledgements are made to *Who's who* and the *D.N.B.*

Religion and Science

215:016

MALTBY, A. Religion and science. London, Library Association, 1965. 36p. (Special subject list no. 46). 10*s.* (7*s.* 6*d.* to members).

238 numbered items, some with brief annotations, in 3 sections: A. The history of the conflict between religion and science. Controversy prior to the 19th century—B. The great 19th century struggle. Man—ape or angel?—C. The relationship between religion and science in the 20th century. 23 periodicals (all in English) are cited. Name index. Author is Lecturer in Librarianship, Liverpool College of Commerce.

22/28 CHRISTIANITY

(See also 29:016.)

22/28:016

Christian periodical index: a subject index to selected periodical literature. Buffalo, N.Y., Christian Librarians Fellowship, 1959-. Annual. ea. $3. Cumulated 5-yrly.

"Index to selected Christian periodicals of interest to Bible institutes, seminars and Christian liberal arts colleges" (*The Standard periodical directory, 1964-65*, p. 411).

22/28:016

NATIONAL BOOK LEAGUE. Christianity in books: a guide to current Christian literature. London, National Book League, 1964. 141p. 5s.

1,004 numbered and briefly annotated entries in 8 main sections: The Bible and commentaries—Christian doctrine—Christian history and biography—Worship and devotion—The Church and the world today—Christian education and religious instruction—Children's books—Christianity and the arts—Postscript. Mainly for the general reader and representative of Anglican, Free Church, Roman Catholic and other traditions. Author and editor index.

W. M. Smith's *A list of bibliographies of theological and Biblical literature published in Great Britain and America, 1595-1931; with critical, biographical, and bibliographical notes* (Coatesville, Pa., 1931) excludes church history, Christian missions, religious education and non-Christian religions, all of which are covered in Barrow (*see at 2:016:016*).

22/28:016

WALSH, H. H. "Christianity". In *A reader's guide to the great religions,* edited by C. J. Adams (New York, The Free Press; London, Collier-Macmillan, 1965), p. 229-86.

A running commentary on the literature, by the Professor of Church History, Faculty of Divinity, McGill University. Sections: The Christian view of history—The Holy Scriptures—Text and canon of the New Testament—New Testament interpretation—Patristics and patrology—Christian doctrines—Christian philosophy—Christian sociology—Christian worship—Christianity and civilization—The Ecumenical movement—Tradition and traditions—Crusades [and Reformation]—Christianity and other religions.

22 THE BIBLE

Bibliographies

22:016

BRITISH MUSEUM. General catalogue of printed books. Photographic ed. to 1955. v. 17-19. **Bible.** London, 1965.

These 3 volumes provide an excellent bibliography of the Bible. V. 1-2 list editions of the Bible in all languages, the Old Testament, Apocrypha, and New Testament; v. 3 forms an appendix, covering works about the Bible. Arrangement is by languages alphabetically, sub-arranged chronologically. New Testament Apocryphal works are not included.

22:016

"Elenchus bibliographicus biblicus". In *Biblica.* Rome, Pontificio Istituto Biblico, 1920-. Quarterly.

A quarterly selected bibliography of writings on the Bible. About 5,500 items p.a. in 16 sections (*e.g.,* XI. Vita Christi, with 11 sub-divisions). Separate, continuous pagination. Annual list of journals indexed. Annual subject index. Roman Catholic standpoint.

Internationale Zeitschriftenschau für Bibelwissenschaft und Grenzgebiete. International review of Biblical studies . . . , 1951/52 (Stuttgart (then Düsseldorf), Verlag Katholisches Bibelwerk, 1952-. Heft 1-. 2 p.a.) notes articles in *c.* 400 periodicals as well as Festschriften and reports, and lists series. Helpful coverage of such allied subjects as archaeology, and Egyptology.

22:016

GLANZMAN, G. S., and FITZMYER, J. A. An introductory bibliography for the study of Scripture. Westminster, Md., The Newman Press, 1962. xix, 135p. $1.50.

First published 1960; 2nd printing, slightly corrected, 1962.

342 numbered entries, with evaluative annotations in 21 sections. These latter embrace periodicals, series, texts and versions of the Bible, lexica, grammars, concordances, commentaries in series, dictionaries, subject aspects, New Testament apocrypha, Rabbinical literature (on the New Testament) and bibliography. Index of modern authors. Asterisk denotes a Roman Catholic author or editor. Aims "to present a list of titles of reasonable length with which the student who is beginning theology or the study of Scripture in a serious way might do well to familiarize himself" (*Preface*). Also valuable as a library check-list. The authors are both Jesuits.

Encyclopaedias

22 (031)=20

HASTINGS, J., ed. A dictionary of the Bible, dealing with its language, literature, and contents, including Biblical theology. Edinburgh, Clark, 1898-1904 (and reprints). 5v.

The standard dictionary, containing articles, some of considerable length and sectionalised, by Biblical scholars, on persons, places, antiquities, archaeology, ethnology, geology, natural history, Biblical theology and ethics. Etymology given. The article 'Jerusalem' (34½ large columns; 1 plan) has 8 sections, the last, 'Literature' (34 lines), being an evaluative survey. The fifth, "extra" volume contains supplementary articles, with maps and indexes. Protestant standpoint.

The one-volume *Dictionary of the Bible,* edited by J. Hastings, with the co-operation of J. A. Selbie (Edinburgh, Clark, 1909. 992p.) is an independent work. A 2nd ed., revised by F. C. Grant and H. H. Rowley (1963. xvi, 1059, 16p. 100s.) is a thorough overhaul, based on the Revised Standard Version, with cross-references from both A.V. and R.V. forms 148 contributors; sectionalised longer articles. No appended bibliographies, but abbreviated references in text. The 16 coloured maps are identical with those on *Peake's Commentary on the Bible.* Accurate and up-to-date. For clergy. Protestant standpoint.

Encyclopædia Biblica: a critical dictionary of literary, political and religious history, the archæology, geography and natural history of the Bible (London, Black, 1899-1903. 4v.; reprinted, with minor corrections, 1914) was edited by T. K. Cheyne and J. S. Black. Cheyne had quite exceptional gifts of exegesis, but "his textual criticism had grown reckless to the point of mental aberration", particularly in v. 3-4 (*Adam & Charles Black, 1807-1957* (1957), p. 76).

22 (031)=20
The Interpreter's dictionary of the Bible: an illustrated encyclopedia, identifying and explaining all proper names and significant terms and subjects in the Holy Scriptures, including the Apocrypha; with attention to archaeological discussions and researches into the life and faith of ancient times. New York, Nashville, Abingdon Press, 1962. 4v. $45.

George Arthur Buttrick, directing editor; 4 associate editors; about 250 contributors, mostly American. Signed longer articles with brief bibliographies (*e.g.,* 'Daniel'. I. The man. II. The book. Nearly 8 pages. Bibliography of 26 lines: 'Jerusalem': p. 843-66; 4 illus., 5 maps; bibliography of 6 items). V. 1 has 24 pages of coloured maps. About 1,000 black-and-white illustrations and 32 col. pl. (apart from the maps). Scholarly; gives etymology. Intended as companion to the 12-v. *Interpreter's Bible* (q.v.).

22 (031)=30
REICKE, B., and **ROST, L.,** *ed.* **Biblisch-historisches Handwörterbuch.** Landeskunde. Geschichte. Religion. Kultur. Literatur. Göttingen, Vandenhoeck & Ruprecht, 1962-66. 3v. illus., tables, maps. (v. 2. DM.106).

v. 1: A-G; v. 2: H-O; v. 3: P-Z.
A scholarly Bible dictionary. Nearly 200 contributors to v. 1. Signed articles; short bibliographies. (*e.g.,* 'Joshuabuch': 1¾ columns; 21 lines of bibliography; 'Jerusalem': 28½ pages; 3 plans (1 with overlay), 2 illus.; bibl. of ⅔ col.)

22 (031)=40
VIGOUROUX, F. G. Dictionnaire de la Bible, contenant tous les noms de personnes, de lieux, de plantes, d'animaux mentionnés dans les Saintes Écritures, les questions théologiques, archéologiques, scientifiques, critiques relatives à l'Ancien et au Nouveau Testament et des notices sur les commentateurs anciens et modernes, avec de nombreuses renseignements bibliographiques. Paris, Letouzey, 1907-. illus.

5v. 1895-1912; Supplément (commenced under the editorship of L. Pirot and A. Robert; continued under H. Cazelles and A. Feuillet). 1928-. v. 1- (fasc. 40-41: Pharisiens-Pirot. 1965. ea. 30F.) Part of the *Encyclopédie des sciences ecclésiastiques.* A full-scale encyclopaedia of the Bible, from the French Catholic viewpoint. Each volume contains some 2000p. Lengthy, signed articles, well-documented and illustrated. The supplementary volumes (fasc. 40 of v. 7 (1965): Pharisiens-Philistins) deal in particular with theological questions.

22 (032)
Catholic Biblical encyclopedia; by J. E. Steinmuller and K. Sullivan. **Old Testament.** New York City, Wagner, 1956. xviii, 1166p. **New Testament.** New York City, Wagner, 1950. xvi, 679, xiiip. 2v. in 1. illus., maps. o.p.

Claims to be "the first Catholic Biblical encyclopedia in the English language" (*Introduction, Old Testament*). Gives pronunciations and defines Hebrew and Greek words. In the New Testament section a list of cross-references precedes the text. Illustrations and maps are fairly adequate, without being of high quality. Appended to the volume is a contribution on Mariology.

22 (032)
CORSWANT, W. A dictionary of life in Bible times. Completed and illustrated by Édouard Urech. Translated from the French by Arthur Heathcote. London, Hodder & Stoughton, 1960. illus. 308, [1]p. 25s.

Originally published as *Dictionnaire d'archéologie biblique* (Neuchâtel & Paris, Delachaux & Niestlé, 1956). Professor Willy Corswant, Professor of the History of Religions and of Biblical Archaeology in the Faculty of Theology at Neuchâtel, died in 1954.
About 1,200 entries, ranging from 2-3 lines to as many columns; copious Biblical references appended; many line-drawings. The article on 'Shoe' runs to 1½ pages, has 20 illustrations of types of shoe and some 60 Biblical references, giving the dictionary value as a Bible concordance. No biographies. Simple language is used. Systematic classification of principal articles, p. ix-xii sources of illustrations appended.

22 (032)
DOUGLAS, J. D., *ed.* **The new Bible dictionary,** London, The Inter-Varsity Fellowship, 1962. xvi, 1375p. illus. (16 pl.), maps. 45s.

"The major product of the Tyndale Fellowship for Biblical Research" (*Preface*). 2,300 signed articles, with short bibliographies, by more than 130 contributors. Longer articles (*e.g.,* 'Messiah': 7 columns; bibliography of 26 items) are sectionalised. Each book of the Bible is analysed; Biblical references. Strong on archaeology (*e.g.,* 'Palestine': p. 918-25; 5 maps; 3 diagrams; bibliography of 11 items). Better layout than McKenzie (*q.v.*). Reliable and reasonably up to date. The *Times literary supplement* (no. 3148, 29th June 1962, p. 482-3) finds the article on 'Inspiration' bewildering and doubts whether the 200-odd line-drawings are worth the space. Protestant viewpoint.

22 (032)
HARTMAN, L. F. Encyclopedic dictionary of the Bible. A translation and adaptation of A. van den Born's *Bijbels woordenboek* (2nd rev. ed. 1954-57). New York, London, etc., McGraw-Hill, 1963. xvp., 2,634 cols. illus. (32 pl.), tables. $27.50.

A more or less free adaptation rather than a strict translation of the original. 32 authors of articles in the original 2nd ed.; 15 collaborators in the English translation. Signed articles, with etymology; short bibliographies for longer articles (*e.g.*, 'Palestine': 10 columns; no illustrations; 27 lines of bibliography; 'Dead Sea Scrolls': 14 columns; ¾ col. bibliography). Profuse references to Bible text. Sparing of illustrations. Author is Executive Secretary of the Catholic Biblical Association of America.

The Zondervan pictorial Bible dictionary (general editor, M. C. Tenney. Grand Rapids, Mich., Zondervan; London, Marshall, Morgan & Scott, 1963. 927, xxiip. illus., maps. $9.75; 70*s*.) is unreservedly recommended in *Library journal*, v. 88, no. 12, 15th June 1963, p. 2500) as a 1-v. Bible dictionary. It has more than 5,000 entries, the work of 65 co-operating Bible scholars ("almost without exception theological conservatives or fundamentalists"). 700 small but well-chosen illustrations; 40 maps.

22 (032)
McKENZIE, J. L. Dictionary of the Bible. Milwaukee, Wis., Bruce; London & Dublin, G. Chapman, 1965. xviii, [1], 954p. illus., maps. $17.95; 90*s*.

About 2,000 scholarly yet readable articles; etymology given. Each book of the Bible is analysed, but not the Apocrypha, which is dealt with as a whole. 'Acts of the Apostles': 7 columns; 'Messiah': 6½ columns; 'Palestine': 5 columns; 'Qumran' (Dead Sea) Scrolls: 13 columns. Many cross-references; Biblical references in text but no appended bibliographies. Bibliography, p. xi-xiv (U.S. imprints, usually). Roman Catholic standpoint.

22 (032)
MILLER, M. S., and **MILLER, J. L.,** *comp.* **Black's Bible dictionary.** 2nd ed., rev. London, Black, 1960. x, 850, [4]p. illus., tables, maps. 55*s*.

1st British ed. 1954.
Originally published as *Harper's Bible dictionary* (New York, Harper, 1952).
A one-volume dictionary intended to embody recent discoveries in archaeology, geography, chronology, textual criticism and other fields of contemporary Biblical investigation. Illustrations (photographs, drawings) are interesting, if not always relevant; coloured maps, charts and diagrams.
The 2nd ed. shows some slight revision and bringing up to date (*e.g.*, the article on Dead Sea

scrolls). "Besides the two British editions there have been five in the U.S.A. since the first of 1952, with constant revision" (*Heythrop journal*, v. 1, no. 3, October 1960, p. 358)

22 (032)
MILLER, M. S., and **MILLER, J. L. Encyclopedia of Bible life.** London, Black, 1957. xvii, 493p. illus., maps. 45*s*. (2nd British ed., 1960).

First published 1944 (New York, Harper); rev. ed. 1955. 1957 is the date of the first British ed.
22 sections, from 'Agriculture' to 'Water supply' and 'Worship', each with its own Bible references and bibliography of modern works. The map section of 14 coloured maps is preceded by a 16-page gazetteer and followed by a chronology, index of Biblical quotations and a general, analytical index. A compact source book, the 245 illustrations being mainly the author's own photographs. Deliberately complementary to *Black's Bible dictionary*, by the same compilers.

Dictionaries

22 (038)
ALLMEN, J.-J. von, *ed.* **Vocabulary of the Bible**; translated by P. J. Allcock [and others]. English translation edited by H. A. Wilson. London, Lutterworth Press, 1958. 479p. 35*s*.

A well-known continental work (*Vocabulaire biblique* (Neuchâtel & Paris, Delachaux & Niestlé, 1954), translated wholly into English (*i.e.*, without Greek or Hebrew transliterations). 36 scholars, apart from the general editor, have contributed articles on 350 important Biblical words. Longer articles are signed. The whole belongs to the field of theology rather than of dictionaries; the linguistic information is slight, but the work is comprehensive and authoritative. It bridges the gap between the very scholarly Kittel's *Theologisches Wörterbuch* (*q.v.*) and the ordinary Bible reader. Comparable to Alan Richardson's *Theological word book of the Bible* (*q.v.*). Adequate cross-references. The Scriptural quotations are from the Revised Standard Version of the Bible (1952).

22 (038)
BRIDGES, R., and **WEIGLE, L. A. The Bible word book:** concerning obsolete or archaic words in the King James Version of the Bible. London, Nelson, 1960. x, 422p. 36*s*.

Intended for general reading as well as for reference, this contains 827 articles on words in the King James Version that have been affected by changing English use, explains what the King James translators meant by these words, and shows what words replace them in the Revised Standard Version. Index of over 2,600 entries, including over 1,800 words which modern translations have substituted for the archaic terms. Supersedes L. A. Weigle's *Bible words in living language* (1957).

22 (038)
RICHARDSON, A., *ed.* **A theological word book of the Bible.** London, S.C.M. Press, 1950 (reprinted 1963). 290p. 18*s*.

A work on the lines of Kittel's *Theologisches Wörterbuch* (*q.v.*), by a team of English-speaking scholars, elucidating the theological meanings of the main Bible keywords, and based on the Revised Version. All Hebrew and Greek words are transliterated and historical details are included where necessary for theological understanding.

Atlases

22 (084.4)

GROLLENBERG, L. H. Atlas of the Bible; translated and edited by J. M. H. Reid and H. H. Rowley. London, Nelson, 1956. 166p. illus., maps. 90*s*.

First published as *Atlas van den Bibjel* (Amsterdam, 1954).

Contains 37 excellent maps in colour and 408 photogravure illustrations. The three media—maps, illustrations and text—are interdependent. The illustrations, which include aerial views, cover ancient monuments and sites, landscapes and localities in the Holy Land.

The 26-page index of places and persons aims "to catalogue and describe all the *geographical indications* provided by the Bible . . . Non-Biblical place-names and personal names are included when their mention on the maps or in the text appear to require further elucidation". Index entries give etymology, map reference and Biblical reference. "Absolutely essential to any intelligent study of the Bible, whether privately or in schools and universities" (*Times literary supplement,* no. 2859, 14th December 1956, p. 753). Page size: $14'' \times 10\frac{1}{4}''$.

——— **The shorter atlas of the Bible;** translated by Mary F. Hedlund. London, Nelson, 1959. 184p. illus., maps. 12*s*. 6*d*.; 25*s*.

A popular edition of the larger *Atlas*. The text has been rewritten and the maps specially redrawn, with less detail. 200 gravure illustrations; 10p. of maps. Smaller format than the parent work. This edition should be in all small libraries that do not possess the earlier work.

22 (084.4)

KRAELING, E. G. H. The Rand McNally Bible atlas. Chicago, Rand McNally, [1956]; London, Collins, 1957. 487p. illus., maps. $9.95.

Comprehensive; well illustrated with drawings, photographs, and 51 maps, plans and tables. There are also 22 coloured maps, geographical and political, showing different periods of Bible history. Introductory section deals with the finding of the Dead Sea Scrolls, and then goes back into Patriarchal times. The survey of geographical and geological features of Palestine on both sides of the Jordan has value.

E. G. H. Kraeling's *Rand McNally historical atlas of the Holy Land* (Chicago, Rand McNally, 1959; London, Vane, 1960. 88p. 25*s*.) is an abridgement. It contains 22 coloured maps, with an index-gazetteer, apart from black-and-white maps in the text.

22 (084.4)

MAY, H. G., *and others, ed.* **Oxford Bible atlas.** London, Oxford Univ. Press, 1962. 144p. illus., maps. 21*s*.

Consists of a well-illustrated introduction (p. 9-45) and notes on the maps, followed by the atlas proper (physical, historical and archæological maps, p. 48-97), a further well-illustrated article, 'Archæology and the Bible', a gazetteer with notes (p. 116-42) and a list of sources of illustrations. The 48-page map section was prepared at the Cartographic Department of the Clarendon Press. The 73 illustrations are well chosen, but unattractively displayed, comments *Heythrop journal* (v. 4, no. 2, April 1963, p. 215-6). Remarkably cheap, by modern standards. Page size: $10'' \times 7\frac{1}{2}''$. Editor is Professor of Old Testament Language and Literature, Graduate School of Theology, Oberlin College, Ohio.

22 (084.4)

WRIGHT, G. E., and **FILSON, F. V.,** *ed.* **The Westminster historical atlas to the Bible.** 5th ed., rev. London, S.C.M. Press, 1957. 130p. illus., maps. 50*s*.

First published 1945 (Philadelphia, Westminster Press). 1st British ed., 1946.

Text, maps and illustrations have been revised. 33 coloured maps and one inset, on 18 plates. Special articles accompanying each map; information on modern excavations. 88 illustrations. Table of dates. Index to text and a gazetteer-index—"a topographical concordance of all places mentioned in the Bible", with "modern names of places where ancient sites are located". The 5th ed. adds an 'Index of Arabic names' (p. 129-30). Page size: $14'' \times 9\frac{1}{2}''$.

Biography

22 (092)

LOCKYER, H. All the men of the Bible: a portrait gallery and reference library of more than 3,000 Biblical characters. London, Pickering & Inglis, 1958. 381p. 30*s*.

Most entries are short, and the longer ones appear to be somewhat imaginatively extended. Occasionally supplements Hastings' *Dictionary of the Bible*.

Edith Deen's *All the women of the Bible* (London, Independent Press, 1959. xxii, 410p. 15*s*.) is a complementary work.

Geography

22:551.4

BALY, D. Geographical companion to the Bible. London, Lutterworth Press, 1963. 196p. illus., diagrs., maps. 35*s*.

Introduction—Land of the Bible (p. 13-137; 58 references)—Cartography of the Bible (p. 139-44, with 16 pages of coloured maps)—Camera and the Bible (16 pages of plates)—Place names of the Bible (p. 163-181; contains all the places mentioned in the Bible, with modern equivalents) —Index of Biblical references—Index to the text. Author is Associate Professor of Religion, Kenyon College, Gambier, Ohio.

Noted: *Land of the Bible: a historical geography,* by Y. Aharoni; translated from Hebrew by A. F. Rainev (London, Burns & Oates, 1967. 409p. 34 maps. 63*s*.).

Natural History

22:59

MOLLER-CHRISTENSEN, V., and **JORGENSEN, K. E. J. Encyclopedia of Bible creatures.** Edited by M. T. Heinecken. Philadelphia, Pa., Fortress Press, 1965. 302p. illus. $6.75.

Translated from Danish by Carol Wilde. The editor has added footnotes based on the Revised Standard Version and current Biblical research. Gives scientific and popular names, dictionary definition, Greek and Hebrew names, and habitat of every known creature in the Bible; explanation of Bible references. Three indexes: Latin and common names; Biblical names and places; Scriptural index. "Will be appreciated by Church workers and animal naturalists" (*The booklist,* v. 62, no. 18, 15th May 1966, p. 890).

Chronology

22:930.24

FINEGAN, J. Handbook of Biblical chronology: principles of time reckoning in the ancient world and problems of chronology in the Bible. Princeton, N.J., Princeton Univ. Press; London, Oxford Univ. Press, 1964. xxvi, 338p. tables. 60s.

Pt. 1 includes an account of Egyptian, Babylonian, Israelite and other calendars, of official and regnal years, of different eras and of the early Christian chronographers. Pt. 2 discusses some of the more interesting problems in Old and New Testaments (*Heythrop journal,* v. 6, no. 2, April 1965, p. 256). Full indication of sources; further reading.

Archaeology

22:930.26

WRIGHT, G. E. Biblical archaeology. New and rev. ed. Philadelphia, Pa., The Westminster Press; London, Duckworth, 1962. 291p. illus., maps. 50s.

First published 1957.
Aims "to summarize the archaeological discoveries which illumine biblical history" (*Foreword*). 14 chapters, each with "Further reading" appendix. 8 black-and-white maps and plans; 220 illustrations. Indexes: modern names, Biblical names, Biblical places, subjects and Biblical references. Quarto size. G. E. Wright has been Packman Professor of Divinity at Harvard since 1958.

Noted: *The Biblical world: a dictionary of Biblical archaeology;* edited by C. F. Pfeiffer (Grand Rapids, Baker Book House, 1966. 912p. $8.95), with numerous black-and-white illustrations.

Introductions

22.01

Helps to the study of the Bible. 2nd ed., with many corrections, alterations and additions, by the Bishop of Bradford [A. W. T. Perowne], G. H. Box, C. H. Dodd, etc. London, Oxford Univ. Press, 1931. xx, 289, 247, 56p. illus. (104 pl.); maps. 12s. 6d.

Originally edited by J. Ridgway, 1880, and revised and enlarged by G. F. Maclear, 1893.
Summarises the books of the Bible, plus dictionary of proper names, Biblical index and concordance. In this edition the historical, critical and archaeological sections were re-written in view of later discoveries, forming a handy book of reference which covers Bible study in all its aspects.

22.01

MANSON, T. W. A companion to the Bible. New ed., edited by H. H. Rowley. Edinburgh, Clark, 1963. xii, 628p. maps. 35s.

First published 1959. Prof. Manson died 1958; H. H. Rowley, Emeritus Professor of Hebrew, Manchester University, in revising, recruited American and continental scholars.
Main parts: 1. The book (chapters 1-7)—2. The land and the people (8-11)—3. The religion of the Bible (12-18). Each chapter has an appended bibliography. Six folding maps and plans. Four indexes: Scripture references; authors; general; Latin, Greek and Oriental words. Retains the original high level of scholarship. "Invaluable for systematic accounts of the revelation against the historical and geographical background" (*British book news,* no. 283, March 1964, p. 176).

22.01

NEIL, W., *ed.* **The Bible companion:** a complete pictorial and reference guide to the people, places, events, background and faith of the Bible. London, Skeffington, 1959. xii, 468p. illus. (inc. col. pl.), maps. 50s.

"For the ordinary reader who is unfamiliar with the jargon of the theologian" (*Introduction*). Edited by a well-known New Testament scholar, with a team of distinguished collaborators. Includes a section on archaeology, alphabetical glossaries of people, places, plants, animals, etc. and articles on the arts and sciences, social life, books and writers of the Bible. Keyed to the A.V. Well illustrated; 16 good maps (p. 453-68). Bibliography (p. 433-6) corresponds in arrangement with that of the book. Protestant standpoint.

Catholic companion to the Bible, edited by R. L. Woods (Philadelphia, Pa., Lippincott, 1956. $3.95) is an anthology of inspirational and critical writings from St. Jerome to Jacques Maritain.

Concordances

22.03

CRUDEN, A. A complete concordance to the Old and New Testaments . . . , with . . . a concordance to the Apocrypha. 3rd ed. London, Warne, 1769 (frequently reprinted, *e.g.,* Religious Tract Society, [1920] xvi, 719p.).

First published 1737, and forms the basis of modern concordances. Some reprints (*e.g.,* Lutterworth Press. 37s. 6d.) omit the Apocrypha, although it is the inclusion of the latter which makes Cruden's *Concordance* particularly valuable. About 250,000 entries in all. Arranged A-Z by English word, with appendices of proper names and the concordance to the Apocrypha. "Cruden's work is accurate and full, and late:

concordances only supersede his by combining an English with a Greek and Hebrew concordance" (*Encyclopædia Britannica* (11th ed.), v. 6, p. 832).

22.03

ELLISON, J. W., *comp.* **Nelson's Complete concordance of the Revised Standard Version Bible.** Edinburgh, etc., Nelson, 1957. [vi] [1], 2157p. 105s.

All words in the Revised Standard Version are listed, except a few of very frequent occurrence, with their text location. Original Hebrew or Greek words are not given. The double column allows for a larger and more legible type. Computer-compiled and produced only 5 years after the R.S.V.
Useful in conjunction with the R.S.V., but not essential in every library.

The Oxford concise concordance to the Revised Standard Version of the Holy Bible, compiled by Bruce M. Metzger and Isobel M. Metzger (London, Oxford Univ. Press, 1962. 158p. 10s. 6d.) is a selective concordance for the general reader.

22.03

JOY, C. R., *comp.* **Lutterworth topical concordance.** 2nd ed. London, Lutterworth, 1961. xii, [i], 628p. 30s.

First published as *Harper's Topical concordance* (1940); reprinted as *A concordance of subjects* (London, Black, 1952. ix, 478p.).
A new type of Biblical concordance, enabling texts and quotations to be easily found. Verses are arranged under 2,775 topics (1st ed.: 2,150 topics), and a fairly complete list of texts specifically connected with these topics is given. Appended list of cross-references. The 625 new topics include Integration, Segregation, Morale, Reverence for life, Well-being and Unemployment.

The home book of Bible quotations, compiled by B. E. Stevenson (New York, Harper, 1949. xxiv, 654p. $10) is a selection arranged A-Z by subjects, with a concordance-type index. It is based on the Authorised Version.

22.03

THOMPSON, N. W., and **STOCK, R. Complete concordance to the Bible (Douay version).** 4th rev. and enl. ed. St. Louis, Mo., Herder, 1945. 2, (1), 1914p.

First published 1942.
Uses the text of the Roman Catholic Bible, which differs in several ways from the A.V., in being translated from the Latin Vulgate. The Old Testament in this version has 46 books, as opposed to 39 in the A.V., although the additional books appear in the Protestant Apocrypha.

22.03

YOUNG, R. Analytical concordance to the Bible. 8th ed. London, Lutterworth Press, 1939 (and reprints). viii, 1090, 146 p. 63s.

First published 1879. The rev. ed., revised by W. B. Stevenson (1902), provides the text for all later editions.

Sub-title: "about 311,000 references, subdivided under the Hebrew and Greek originals, with the literal meaning and pronunciation of each." Includes names of persons and places. Supplemented by index lexicons to the Old and New Testaments, and a complete list of Scripture proper names.

The exhaustive concordance of the Bible, by J. Strong, first published in 1894 (reprinted 1948. London, Hodder, 1800p. 147s.), is even fuller. The main concordance (p. 5-1218) has *c.* 400,000 entries. An appendix lists occurrence of 47 common words such as 'and' and 'their'. Appended: a comparative concordance of A.V. and R.V. (with the American variations); Hebrew and Chaldee dictionary; and Greek dictionary of the New Testament.

Versions

22.04/.05 (091)

GREENSLADE, S. L., *ed.* **The Cambridge history of the Bible.** Cambridge, Univ. Press, 1963-.

1st v.: *The West from the Reformation to the present day.* 1963. x, 590p. pl. 45s.
"The two volumes originally planned will deal with the history of the Bible in the West, that is, in Western Europe and America" (*Preface*), *i.e.,* "accounts of the texts and versions of the Bible used in the West, of its multiplication, in manuscript and print, and its circulation; of attitudes towards its authority and exegesis; and of its place in the life of the Western Church". An extensive history of the Bible in English is envisaged, "and further volumes may take up other aspects of the story or cover other areas".
The 1963 v. has 13 chapters, with sub-divisions, each by a specialist. It does not discuss the composition of individual books. Appendices: 1. 'Aids to the study of the Bible: a selective historical account of the major grammars, lexicons, concordances, dictionaries and encyclopædias, and atlases'. 2. 'Commentaries: a historical note'. Bibliography, p. 536-49 (by chapters, sub-divided by types of material). General index; index to Bible references.

22.04/.05 (091)

ROBINSON, H. W. The Bible in its ancient and English versions. Oxford, Clarendon Press, 1940 (lithographic reprint, with appendix, 1954). vii, 337p.

A symposium, each contributor having complete freedom, presenting the history of the Bible from its origins. Supplements Sir F. G. Kenyon's *Our Bible and the ancient manuscripts* (1939; 5th ed. London, Eyre & Spottiswoode, 1958) by emphasizing the English versions, ending with the Revised Version. Bibliographies; indexes.

22.05

The Interlinear Bible: The Authorized Version and the Revised Version; together with the marginal notes of both versions and central references. Cambridge, Univ. Press, 1906 (and reprints).

The quickest and most convenient reference book for showing at a glance the alternative renderings of the A.V. and R.V.

The Holy Bible, containing the Old and New Testaments: Revised Standard Version (London, Nelson, 1957. 15s.) first appeared in two pts. (*New Testament*. 1946; *Old Testament*. 1952).

The New English Bible. New Testament (Oxford Univ. Press, Cambridge Univ. Press, 1961. 21s.) is the first part of a translation of the original Greek, undertaken by the major Christian bodies (other than the Roman Catholic) of Britain. Translation of the Old Testament and Apocrypha has been completed, and world-wide simultaneous publication of the complete *New English Bible* is expected not later than 1970 (*The bookseller*, no 3,184, 31st December 1966, p. 2688).

Of the Roman Catholic versions of the Bible, the Rheims or Douay version, like that by Mgr. Ronald Knox (*New Testament*. Burns & Oates. 1945. 6s.; *Holy Bible*, Burns & Oates, 1958. 35s.) is based on the Latin Vulgate, and so, too, is *The Holy Bible. Revised Standard Version* (*Catholic*) (1965). *The Jerusalem Bible* (London, Darton, Longman & Todd, 1966. 84s.), on the other hand, is a translation into contemporary English from the original Greek and Hebrew, with introductions (*e.g.*, to the *Pentateuch*, the Historical Books) and footnotes. Reviewed in *Times literary supplement*, no. 3382, 22nd December 1966, p. 1191.

For a detailed survey of editions, versions, commentaries and studies of the Bible, see *The reader's adviser and bookman's manual*, by H. R. Hoffman (10th ed. New York, Bowker, 1964), p. 100-39.

22.05:016
BRITISH AND FOREIGN BIBLE SOCIETY. Historical catalogue of the printed editions of Holy Scripture in the Library of the ... Society. Compiled by T. H. Darlow and H. F. Moule. London, Bible House, 1903-11. 2v. in 4 (New York, Kraus Reprint, 1964. $97.50).

The most important bibliography of the Bible. V. 1 covers English Bibles, arranged chronologically, with appendices of additional items and a list of the Books translated into provincial dialects. The other volumes, arranged alphabetically by language and then chronologically, describe polyglot Bibles and those in foreign languages. Nearly 10,000 entries. Annotations; full indexes.

A bibliography of Scriptures in African languages, compiled by G. E. Coldham (London, British and Foreign Bible Society, 1966. 2v. Mimeographed. Private circulation) is "a revision of the African sections of the Darlow and Moule ..., with additions to 1964" (title-page note). V. 1: Polyglot. Acholi—Mousgoum; v. 2: Mpama —Zulu. 3,580 numbered items. 5 indexes: languages and dialects; translators, revisers, editors, etc.; printers and publishers; places of printing and publication; miscellaneous.

Commentaries

22.07
The Abingdon Bible commentary, edited by F. C. Eiselen, and others. London, Epworth Press, 1932. xvi, 1452p. maps.

First published 1929 (New York, Abingdon Press).

Probably the best of the single-volume Bible commentaries, by 66 scholars. Chapter-by-chapter commentary on the various books, plus more general treatment. Includes bibliographies.

Other well-known single-volume commentaries:

GORE, C., *and others, ed.* **A new commentary on Holy Scripture,** including the Apocrypha. London, S.P.C.K., 1928 (reprinted 1951). xvi, 697, 158, 743p. 31s. 6d.

A commentary by 56 Anglican scholars; intended to combine modern research and criticism with the spirtual use of the Bible. Helpfully includes the Apocrypha. List of reference books; select subject index.

Peake's Commentary on the Bible. New ed., edited by Matthew Black and H. H. Rowley. London, Nelson, 1962. xv, 1126p., 4 p. illus., maps. 70s.

First published 1919.
Based on the R.S.V. 62 contributors have revised text of this new ed. Not only updated on archæological discoveries but also slanted to present trend in Biblical theology. Bibliographies. 12 pages of maps.

CLARKE, W. K. L. Concise Bible commentary. London, S.P.C.K., 1952. xiii, 996p. 30s.

The work of a single author and therefore more consistent in its views than Gore or Peake. 28 essays precede commentaries on individual books. A deficiency, compared with Gore and Peake, is the absence of bibliographies.

22.07
CATHOLIC BIBLICAL ASSOCIATION. A Catholic commentary on Holy Scripture, edited by B. Orchard, [and others]. London, Nelson, 1953. xvi, 1312p. maps. 84s.

The work of 43 contributors, the commentary being based on the Douai Version. Three main sections; General; Old Testament; New Testament, articles in each section being followed by commentaries. A selective bibliography (including books by Protestant writers) (precedes each commentary. Detailed index (p. 1209-89); maps (p. 1297-1312) and index of names in the maps.

22.07
International critical commentary on the Holy Scriptures; under the editorship of S. R. Driver, A. Plummer and C. A. Briggs. 2nd ed. Edinburgh, Clark, 1930 (1963 reprint). 43v. in 46.

A scholarly series of commentaries on individual books of the Bible, contributed by specialists and bringing modern research and criticism to bear on questions of authorship, etc. Each volume, which is complete in itself, carries a bibliography.

22.07
The Interpreter's Bible: The Holy Scriptures in the King James and Revised Standard versions, with general articles and introduction, exegesis, exposition for each book of the Bible. [Edited

by N. B. Harmon]. New York, Abingdon-Cokesbury Press, 1952-57. 12v.

1. General articles on the Bible; general articles on the Old Testament; Genesis; Exodus.
2. Leviticus [to Samuel].
3. Kings [to Job].
4. Psalms [to Proverbs].
5. Ecclesiastes [to Jeremiah].
6. Lamentations [to Malachi].
7. General articles on New Testament; Matthew; Mark.
8. Luke; John.
9. Acts; Romans.
10. Corinthians; Galatians; Ephesians.
11. Philippians [to Hebrews].
12. James [to Revelation]. General articles (including one on Dead Sea Scrolls). Indexes (*e.g.*, index of subjects, p. 706-817).

Aimed at the general reader, teacher and preacher of the Bible. Contributors represent almost every branch of the Christian Church; consulting editors, from larger Protestant groups. Bibliographies throughout the work. Each page has text of A.V. and R.S.V.; below that, exegesis followed by exposition. Contributors include a number of eminent British theologians and Biblical scholars.

22.07
Nelson's Bible commentary. Based on the Revised Standard Version. General editor, Frederick C. Grant. London, Nelson, 1963-. ea. 42s.

v. 6: *Matthew to Acts.* 1963.
v. 7: *Romans to Revelations.* 1963.

Old Testament

221:016
SOCIETY FOR OLD TESTAMENT STUDY. Booklist. [London], [1496?]-. Printed for private circulation. 7s. 6d. p.a.

Each volume carries critical and lengthy reviews (ea. *c.* 150 words). The 1966 volume reviewed *c.* 300 books. Reviews are signed; 38 contributors. Sections: General—Educational—Archaeology and epigraphy—History and geography—Text and versions—Exegesis and modern translations—Literary criticism and introduction—Law, religion and theology—The life and thought of the neighbouring people—The Dead Sea scrolls—Apocrypha and post Biblical Judaism—Philology and grammar—Books received too late for notice. Author index. Items recommended for inclusion in school libraries are asterisked.

———**Eleven years of Bible bibliography:** the book lists of the Society for Old Testament Study, 1946-56; ed. by H. H. Rowley. Indian Hills, Colorado, Falcon's Wing Press, [c. 1957]. vii, 804p. $7.50.

A photographic reproduction of the original annuals plus an author index covering 11 years, and a brief composite subject index, pointing out pages on which the several topical groupings will be found. Handier for use than the separate lists, but it is regrettable that the lists were not merged into one sequence.

———**A decade of Bible bibliography:** The book lists of the Society for Old Testament Study, 1957-1966; edited by G. W. Anderson. Oxford, Blackwell, 1967. ix, 706p. 84s.

A further cumulation,—*c.* 1,500 entries, well annotated. 12 sections. Author index.

Zeitschrift für die alttestamentliche Wissenschaft (Berlin, Töpelmann, 1881-. 3 p.a.) has comprehensive coverage of periodical articles ('Zeitschriftenschau', under titles of periodicals, A-Z) and books ('Bücherschau',—short reviews of *c.* 100 items per issues, under authors, A-Z) on the Old Testament.

221:91
SIMONS, J. The geographical and topographical texts of the Old Testament: a concise commentary in XXXII chapters. Leiden, Brill, 1959. xiv, [1], 613p. maps.

Intended as a vademecum for schools and students. Four parts: 1. The geographical background of the Old Testament—2. The division of the Promised Land—3. From Abraham to Simon the Maccabee—4. Supplementary chapters (*e.g.*, 'The world of the Prophets'). 10 maps. Index: list of texts; list of Biblical (p. 544-613) and extra-Biblical names, and gazetteer of maps.

221.03
HATCH, E., and REDPATH, H. A. A concordance to the Septuagint and the other Greek versions of the Old Testament, including the Apocryphal books. Supplement by H. A. Redpath. Oxford, Clarendon Press, 1892-7, 1906. 2v. in 1 and suppt. (Facsimile reprint in 4v. 1955).

Designed to be a complete concordance to the Septuagint version of the Old Testament, to the Greek text of the Apocryphal books, and to the remains of other versions forming part of Origen's Hexapla, using Field's edition of this work. Supplement contains Greek proper names, etc., and index to Hebrew words.

New Testament

225:016
LYONS, W. N., and PARVIS, M. M., *ed.* **New Testament literature:** an annotated bibliography. Chicago, Univ. of Chicago Press, 1948-. (v. 1. 1948. 392p.).

Continues series of *New Testament literature* in 1940, 1941, and 1942, published annually by the New Testament Club of Chicago University.

Designed to present an exhaustive bibliography of books, articles and book reviews in New Testament and related fields covering 1943-45. Author and Scripture index. Further volumes were promised.

Zeitschrift für die neutestamentliche Wissenschaft (Berlin, Töpelmann, 1900-. Quarterly) has a sytematically arranged bibliography of periodical articles ('Zeitschriften—Bibliographie'), citing *c.* 42 journals, in each issue.

225:016
New Testament abstracts: a record of current periodical literature. Weston, Mass., Theological

Faculty of Weston College. May 1956-. v. 1, no. 1-. 3 p.a. ea. $1.75; $4.50 p.a.

Each issue has *c*. 300 concise and readable signed, 150-word abstracts of articles in more than 200 periodicals in ten languages. Sections: Introduction—Gospels—Acts—Epistles—Apocalypse—Biblical theology—Early church—Dead Sea scrolls. Other features: 'Books and opinions', devoted to some half-a-dozen books, with possibly several opinions of different critics; 'Biographical notes'; Book notices' is a list of recent publications with short descriptions of contents. Annual indexes only, to principal Scriptural texts; authors; 'Books and opinions'; 'Book notices'. Annual list of journals abstracted.

225 (03)

KITTEL, G., *ed.* **Theologisches Wörterbuch zum Neuen Testament;** hrsg. von G. Kittel. Stuttgart, Kohlhammer, 1932-. v. 1-.

v. 1-7 (1932-64): A-E.
An important work, planned by a distinguished Rabbinist with specialist collaborators, on a scale comparable with the new Liddell and Scott. It defines specific meanings which Greek terms have come to possess within Christian thought as a whole, and many articles amount to complete monographs, some of which have been translated in J. R. Coates's *Bible key-words* (London, Black, 1949-52. 6v.).

A full, authorised English translation, edited by G. W. Bromiley, with the title *Theological dictionary of the New Testament* (Grand Rapids, Mich., Eerdmans; Exeter (Devon), Paternoster Press, 1964-) is to appear in 7 or 8v. V. 1-3 (1964-66): A-K.

225 (092)

GUY, H. A. Who's who in the Gospels. London, Macmillan, 1966. 152p. 12s. 6d.

Articles on people, places and subjects mentioned in the Gospels, arranged A-Z, with appended citations and cross-references. Accurate and in the form of 'model answers' (*Times literary supplement,* no. 3,357) 30th June 1966, p. 581). For the general reader.

225.01

McNEILE, A. H. An introduction to the study of the New Testament. 2nd ed., revised by C. S. C. Williams. Oxford, Clarendon Press, 1953. viii, 486p.

First published 1927.
A conspectus for the general reader of historical and literary New Testament material, with special emphasis on canon and textual criticism. This edition incorporates findings in recent studies, and has a new chapter on form criticism. Bibliographies; indexes.

W. G. Kümmel's *Introduction to the New Testament,* founded by Paul Feine and Johannes Behm; translated [for the 14th rev. German ed.] by A. J. Mattill, in collaboration with the author (London, S.C.M. Press, 1966. 444p. 50s.) provides a guide to each book of the N.T. and discusses the origin of the canon and history of the text, with a bibliography of 'Important modern tools

for study' (*Heythrop journal,* v. 7, no. 4, October 1966, p. 481).

A. Robert and A. Feuillet's *Introduction to the New Testament* (Translated from the French. New York & Tournai, Desclee Co., 1965. xviii, [5], 912p. maps) is an updated and adapted translation of *Introduction à la Bible.* V. 2. *Nouveau Testament* (1959). The work of 13 contributors, it is heavily footnoted and has section bibliographies. Indexes of authors, subjects and Biblical references.

225.03

BULLINGER, E. W. A critical lexicon and concordance to the English and Greek New Testament, together with an index of Greek words, and several appendices. 8th ed. London, Lamp Press, 1957. 999, xiip.

First published 1877.
Gives every English word in alphabetical order, and under each the Greek word or words so translated, with variants; thus a Greek word with its literal and derivative meanings may be found for every word in the English N.T. The index is of Greek words in alphabetical order, with the English translation following. A helpful and handy work.

A comparable work with wider scope is the translation and adaptation of Walter Bauer's *Griechisch-deutsches Wörterbuch zu den Schriften des Neuen Testaments . . . ,* by W. F. Arndt and F. W. Gingrich,—*A Greek-English lexikon of the New Testament and other early Christian literature* (London, Oxford Univ. Press, 1964. xxxviii, 910p. 110s.). A condensed version is F. W. Gingrich's *Shorter lexicon of the Greek New Testament* (Chicago, Univ. of Chicago Press, 1965. 304p. $5; 33s. 6d.).

A German lexicon, to appear in 10 pts., is: *Theologisches Begriffslexikon zum Neuen Testament,* edited by L. Coenen and others (Wuppertal, Brockhaus, 1905-. Lfg. 1-. ea. DM.16.80), the work of *c*. 100 contributors.

Standard Version (1946).

225.03

MOULTON, W. F., and **GEDEN, A. S.,** *ed.* **A concordance to the Greek Testament.** 2nd ed. Edinburgh, Clark, 1899 (and reprints). xi, 1033p.

First published 1897.
The standard and complete concordance, following the text of Westcott and Hort, but equally available for Tischendorf and the "revisers' text". Marginal readings are included in all cases, and Hebrew text is given beneath the Greek in all direct quotations from the Old Testament.

225.05

The New Testament octapla: eight versions of the New Testament in the Tyndale-King James tradition. Edited by Luther A. Weigle. Edinburgh, Nelson, 1962. xviii, 1489p. facsim. 168s.

The full text of 8 major English versions: Tyndale (1525), Great Bible (1539), Geneva Bible (1560), Bishops' Bible (1568), Rheims (1582), King James (1611), Revised Version (1881), Revised Standard Version (1946).

Gospels

226:016
METZGER, B. M., *comp.* **Index to periodical literature on Christ and the Gospels.** Leiden, Brill, 1966. xxiii, 602p. (New Testament tools and studies, v. 6). 98s. 6d.

10,090 numbered items from *c.* 160 journals in 16 languages. 6 main sections: 1. Bibliographical articles—2. Historical studies of the life of Jesus —3. Critical studies of the Gospels—4. Early non-canonical literature related to Christ and the Gospels—5. Theological studies concerning Jesus Christ and the Gospels—6. The influence and interpretation of Jesus Christ and the Gospels in worship, the fine arts and culture in general. No annotations. Author index only. The compiler is Professor of New Testament Language and Literature, Princeton Theological Seminary.

Professor Metzger has also produced an *Annotated bibliography of the textual criticism of the New Testament, 1914-1939* (Copenhagen, Munksgaard, 1955. xviii, 133p.), listing nearly 1,200 items, and an *Index of articles on the New Testament and the Early Christian Church published in 'Festschriften'* (Philadelphia, Society of Biblical Literature, 1951. xv, 182p.), which lists 2,150 items.

226.03
HASTINGS, J., *ed.* **A dictionary of Christ and the Gospels;** edited with the assistance of J. A. Selbie and J. C. Lambert. Edinburgh, Clark, 1906-08. 2v.

Complementary to Hastings's *Dictionary of the Bible,* but articles are written by new authors from a new angle, and with greater range. Designed to give an account of everything relating to Christ in the Bible and world literature, with detailed investigation of the Gospels. Signed articles with bibliographies; indexes of subjects and Greek terms. Protestant standpoint.

H. A. Guy's *Who's who in the Gospels* (London, Macmillan, 1966. 152p. $2.95) is a dictionary with entries for places, institutions, practices, etc. as well as persons mentioned in the four Gospels.

Acts of the Apostles

227:016
MATTILL, A. J., and **MATTILL, M. B. A classified bibliography of literature on the Acts of the Apostles.** Leiden, Brill, 1966. xviii, 513 p. (New Testament tools and studies, v. 7). $13.20.

6,646 numbered items, drawn from *c.* 200 journals. 9 main sections: 1. Bibliographical studies—2. General studies—3. Textual studies —4. Philological studies—5. Literary studies—6. Form-critical studies—7. Historical studies (p. 181-265)—8. Theological studies—9. Exegetical studies of individual passages. Entries date from the period of the Church Fathers up to 1961. Index of authors ('Anonymous', at end) only. A. J. Mattill is Professor of New Testament Language and Literature, Winebrenner Theological Seminary.

227 (03)
METZGER, B. M., *comp.* **Index to periodical Church.** Edinburgh, Clark, 1915-18. 2v. ea. 50s.

This work is complementary to the same editor's *Dictionary of Christ and the Gospels* and, together with it, forms a complete dictionary of the New Testament, in which the history of the early Church to the end of the first century is covered.

Apocrypha

229
CHARLES, R. H. The Apocrypha and Pseudepigrapha of the Old Testament in English. . . . Edited, in conjunction with many scholars, by R. H. Charles. Oxford, Clarendon Press, 1913 (reprinted 1963). 2v. £10.

The most important collection in English of all the non-canonical Jewish literature from 200 B.C.-A.D. 100. Each book is translated from the best critical text, with an introduction giving detailed textual and bibliographical information, with critical and explanatory notes; general index in v. 2.

An introduction to the books of the Apocrypha, by W. O. E. Osterley (London, S.P.C.K., 1935 (reprinted 1953)) is in two parts, Prolegomena, and Books; each book is treated separately, with its own bibliography; well indexed.

Dogmatic Theology

23 (032)
HARVEY, Van A. A handbook of theological terms. New York, Macmillan; London, Allen & Unwin, 1966. 217p. 30s.

Explains *c.* 300 Christian theological terms (Abba—Works) in precise terms, with history and background (*e.g.,* 'Resurrection of Christ': 2¼p.; 'Natural theology': 3p.). Gives both Catholic and Protestant views on the Eucharist, etc. For laymen. "Particularly useful in a student's library as a guide to modern radical theology" *Times literary supplement,* no. 3395, 23rd March 1965, p. 253).

W. M. Mosse's *A theological German dictionary* (New York, Macmillan, 1955. 148p. o.p.) gives English equivalents of *c.* 3,000 German theological terms, plus quotations from the Bible in both languages.

Miracles

231.73
BREWER, E. C. A dictionary of miracles, imitative, realistic and dogmatic. London, Chatto & Windus, 1884. 582p.

The only reference book of its kind, intended to reproduce in a handy form impartial information about a mode of religious thought. Divided into three parts: miracles of saints, relating to Scripture miracles or secular stories; realistic miracles, founded on literal interpretation of Scripture; and dogmatic miracles, to prove ecclesiastical dogmas. Full index.

Virgin Mary

232.931

ATTWATER, D., *comp.* **A dictionary of Mary.**
London, Longmans, Green, 1957. vii, 312p.

Originally published 1956 (New York, Kennedy).

The aim is "to provide the reader, whether a member of the Catholic Church or not, with a quick reference to matters connected with the many aspects of the life, significance and veneration of the Blessed Virgin Mary in ordinary, non-technical language" (*Preface*).

According to the reviewer in *Library journal*, v. 85, no. 15, 1st October 1960, p. 2920, the richly illustrated *Lexikon der Marienkunde* (Ratisbon, Pustet, 1960-. fasc. 1-), to be completed in 3v., "will be the definitive reference book on all aspects of Mariology".

Saints

235.3:016

"Bulletin des publications hagiographiques".
In *Analecta Bollandiana*, 1882-. Brussels, Société des Bollandistes. Quarterly.

235.3 (092)

BUTLER, A. The lives of the saints. New ed., rev. and copiously supplemented by H. Thurston, [N. Leeson and D. Attwater]. London, Burns, Oates, 1926-38). 12v. (Rev. ed., 1942-49. 12v. and suppt.).

A greatly expanded edition of a work published 1756-59, intended for the general reader, 1v. for each month, biographies being arranged according to the saint's day. Short biographies are appended.

A general index to the rev. ed. (giving date for each saint) is published as *A dictionary of saints* . . ., compiled by D. Attwater. (New ed. London, Burns & Oates, 1958. vii, 280p. 30s.).

——. **Butler's Lives of the saints;** edited, revised and supplemented by H. Thurston and D. Attwater. 2nd ed. London, Burns, Oates, 1956. 4v.

In this edition certain abbreviations have been made to the 1926-38 text (*e.g.,* Butler's daily exhortations have been discarded). Each volume has an index, v. 4 including a cumulated index.

The Book of saints: a dictionary of persons canonized or beatified by the Catholic Church; compiled by the Benedictine Monks of St. Augustine's Abbey, Ramsgate (5th rev. ed. London, Black, 1966. xiv, 740p. 48s.) gives concise biographical data. It adds to the 4th ed. (1947) entries on person beatified or canonised during the last 25 years. The calendar of saints has been dropped.

235.3 (092)

COULSON, J., *ed.* **The saints: a concise biographical dictionary.** London, Burns & Oates, 1958. 496p. illus. (incl. 16 col. pl.).

About 2,500 entries arranged A-Z by anglicised form of Christian name. Entries vary in length from 3-4 lines to 3 columns (*e.g.,* St. Thomas Aquinas: 2¼ columns; St. Teresa of Avila: 2¼ columns, plus an illustration). Many cross-references. 'Calendar of feast days', p. 473-85; 'For further reading', p. 489-91. Articles are unsigned;

the impressive list of some 65 contributors does not indicate the specific contributions.

D. Attwater's *The Penguin dictionary of saints* (Harmondsworth, Middlesex, Penguin Books, 1965. 362p. 6s.) identifies more than 500 saints, especially those of Great Britain and Ireland. Many other individuals are mentioned in the biographical sketches, with cross-references.

235.3 (092)

Vie des saints et des bienheureux selon l'ordre du calendrier avec l'historique des fêtes, par les RR.PP. Bénédictins de Paris. Paris, Letouzey, 1935-39. 13v. (v. 13: Supplément et table générale).

235.3 (4)

SHARP, M. A traveller's guide to saints in Europe. London, Evelyn, 1964. xv, 251p. 21s.

Identifies more than 400 European saints, arranged A-Z, with chronological list of saints (by century and then date of death). Entries give name, dates, attributes in art, and patron. Bibliography (p. vii); glossary of terms (p. viii); index of churches containing relics (by countries, p. 241-51). The *Times literary supplement* notes some omissions and misspelling (no. 3241, 9th April 1964, p. 297).

235.3 (410)

BARING-GOULD, S., and **FISHER, J. The lives of the British saints,** the saints of Wales and Cornwall and such Irish saints as have dedications in Britain. London, published for the Honourable Society of Cymmrodorion, by C. J. Clark, 1907-13. 4v. illus., maps.

A useful introduction (v. 1, p. 1-99) is followed by a series of saints' lives, arranged alphabetically. (A chronological arrangement, by saints' days, is provided in S. Baring-Gould's *Lives of the Saints* (New and rev. ed. Edinburgh, Grant, 1914. 16v. illus.).) Sources are quoted; index.

The main source for Irish saints is: O'Hanlon, J. *Lives of the Irish saints . . . with the commemorations and festivals of holy persons, noted in calendars, martyrologies . . . relating to the ancient church history of Ireland* (Dublin, Duffy, 1875-1903. 9v. & 7 pts. of v. 10). This covers January to 21st October. No more published.

G. H. Doble's *Saints of Cornwall* (Truro, Cathedral Chapter, 1960-. v. 1-.), to be completed in 6v., deals with saints by locality. V. 1-4, 1961-65.

235.3:929.6

DRAKE, M., and **DRAKE, W. Saints and their emblems.** London, Laurie, 1916. xiii, 235p.

A dictionary of some 4-5,000 names alphabetically listed, of saints, with dates, where ascertainable, indications of further printed information, and an alphabetical cross-index of emblems, with appendices. In spite of some inaccuracies, the work remains of use to ecclesiastical craftsmen and students.

Not so full as Drake, but a modern and available substitute is: Roeder, H. *Saints and their attributes; with a guide to localities and patronage* (London, Longmans, Green, 1955. xxviii, 391p.). Arrangement is by subjects A-Z, sub-arranged under saints' names (giving date of death; religious order). Indexes of saints, patronage and localities; short bibliography (p. xiv).

For the general reader there is: Milburn, R. L. P. *Saints and their emblems in English churches* (Rev. ed. Oxford, Blackwell, 1957. xxxviii, 283p. illus. 15s.). This provides short biographies and emblems, but excludes Celtic and continental saints. Locations of portraits of saints and the emblems associated with them are often given.

St. Paul

235.3/P:016
METZGER, B. M., *comp.* **Index to periodical literature on the Apostle Paul.** Leiden, Brill, 1960. xi, 183p. (New Testament tools and studies, v. 1).

2,987 numbered entries in 6 sections: 1. Bibliographical articles on Paul—2. Historical studies on the life of Paul—3. Critical studies of the Pauline literature—4. Pauline apocrypha—5. Theological studies—6. The history of the interpretation of Paul and his work. Includes articles from some 135 journals in 14 languages, and goes up to the end of 1957. Author index.

Creeds

238 (091)
CURTIS, W. A. **A history of creeds** and confessions of faith in Christendom and beyond. Edinburgh, Clark, 1911. xx, 502p.

An admirable survey of religious creeds throughout the ages, with extensive and representative quotations from the authoritative documents, bibliographies, and appendices of historical tables. Index.

Moral Theology

241 (03)
ROBERTI, F., *cardinal.* **A dictionary of moral theology . . . ;** translated under the direction of Henry J. Yannone. London, Burns & Oates, 1962. xli, 1353p. 189s.

Translated from the 2nd ed. of *Dizionario di teologia morale.*
"A standard work which includes new problems of psychology, medicine, sociology and international law" (*Heythrop journal,* v. 4, no. 2, April 1963, p. 220). Includes entries on leading moral theologians of the past. Bibliography, p. 1313-52.

A dictionary of Christian ethics, edited by J. MacQuarrie (London, S.C.M. Press, 1967. 366p. 63s.) is the work of contributors who represent Protestant, Anglican, Roman Catholic, Orthodox and Jewish faiths.

Hymns

245
See entries at 264-068.

Personal Religious Life

248 (03)
VILLER, M., *and others, ed.* **Dictionnaire de spiritualité, ascétique et mystique, doctrine et histoire.** Paris, Beauchesne, 1937-. v. 1-.

First published in fascicules.
v. 1-5 (1937-64): A-FYOT.

A scholarly work, with long signed articles, rich in biographies. Bibliographies appended to articles include references to sources. The article on St. Bernard of Clairvaux, for instance, occupies p. 1454-99 of v. 1 and is in 5 sections (life; spiritual works; source of teaching; doctrine (20 pages); influence on spirituality) and has 1½ columns of bibliography; that on Jakob Boehme runs to 6 columns (life and work; doctrine) and has a ½ column of bibliography (works; literature on).

CHRISTIAN CHURCH
Dictionaries

26 (032)
The Oxford dictionary of the Christian Church; edited by F. L. Cross. London, Oxford Univ. Press, 1957. xix, 1492p. 90s.

"It is addressed to the needs not merely of those whose primary vocation lies in the Christian ministry or in the professional study of theology or church history, or even only to the general body of professing Christians who seek information about their faith and its growth, but to the educated public as a whole" (*Preface*).
Over 6,000 entries, particularly strong on biographies, definitions, theologies and heresies; bibliographies are usually of generous length (*e.g.,* 24½ lines on "St. Paul's Cathedral"). 94 contributors are listed, but the entries themselves are unsigned. Asterisks indicate cross-references. Treatment is fairly well balanced, although the entry for Church of England (5½ cols.) is equal in length to those for the Methodist Churches (3½ cols.) and for Roman Catholicism (2 cols.) combined.

26 (038)
BUMPUS, J. S. **A dictionary of ecclesiastical terms;** being a history and explanation of certain terms in architecture, ecclesiology, liturgiology, music, ritual, cathedral constitution, etc. London, Laurie, 1914. 324p.

Fairly substantial definitions of terms are given (*e.g.,* 4½p. on "Minor canons") and adequate references appear in the text. Etymology and equivalent terms in other languages are given where considered necessary.

26 (038)
DUBOULAY, F. R. H., *comp.* **A handlist of medieval ecclesiastical terms.** London, National Council of Social Service, for the Standing Conference for Local History, 1952. 31p. (Local history series, no. 9).

"This handlist is intended principally for beginners and amateurs who wish to search . . . into the records of their parish or diocese" (*Foreword*). Some 500 terms are defined, a feature being the frequent inclusion of references to monographs and other works which provide further information and, often, bibliographies. 'Some works of general reference', p. 4.

26 (038)
PURVIS, J. S. **Dictionary of ecclesiastical terms.** London, Nelson, 1962. vii, 204p. 30s.

Concise explanations of more than 1,000 liturgical, legal and hierarchical terms. Terms exclusively Greek in form and origin and related only to the Eastern Church have been omitted. Not a dictionary in the strict sense, but contains chiefly historical notes (*Heythrop journal*, v. 4, no. 1, January 1963). Bibliography.

Also noted: *A practical church dictionary*, compiled by J. M. Malloch. Edited by K. Smallzried (New York, Morehouse-Barlow, 1964. 576p. $13.95). with 4,500 very brief articles. Episcopal Church slant (*Library journal*, v. 90, no. 8, 15th April 1965, p. 1816).

Ecumenical Movement

261.8:016
BRANDRETH, H. R. T. Union and reunion. 2nd ed. London, Black, 1948. lxiv, 160p.

A survey, within defined limits, of the literature of Christian reunion since the beginning of the 19th century, listing English translations where they exist; annotations, and separate indexes of authors and subjects.

261.8:016
CROW, P. A. The Ecumenical movement in bibliographical outline. New York, Department of Faith and Order, National Council of the Churches of Christ in the U.S.A., 1966. 80p. $2.

A comprehensive but not exhaustive bibliography of books published up to 1964. Supplements are due at intervals (*Library journal*, v. 91, no. 8, 15th April 1966, p. 1993).

The more extensive *Christian unity: a bibliography [of] selected titles concerning international relations between the churches and international Christian movements*, by A. Senaud (Geneva, World's Committee of Y.M.C.A.'s, 1937. xvi,[1], 173p.) lists more than 2,000 items; author index.

H. Delfs' *Ökumenische Literaturkunde*, hrsg. von D. F. Siegmund-Schultze (Soest, Westfälische Verlagsbuchhandlung Mocker & Jahn, 1966. xii, 580p.) has 3 main parts: 1. Die ökumenische Bewegung (sections 1-27)—2. Kirchen und Gemeinschaften (28-72)—3. Länder und Kontinente (73-100). Confined to books; no annotations, but introduction on each section or country. Author index.

Also noted: Lescrauwaet, J. F. *Critical bibliography of Ecumenical literature* (Nijmegen, Bestel Centrale V.S.K.B., 1965. 104p. D.fl. 14.50), in the Bibliographia ad usum seminariorum series, v. 7.

261.8 (091)
ROUSE, R., and NEILL, S. C., *ed.* A history of the Ecumenical movement, 1517-1948. London, S.P.C.K., 1954. xxiv, 822p. (2nd rev. ed. 1967. 55s.).

A symposium, sponsored by the Ecumenical Institute at Bossey, Geneva, by sixteen authors; intended to present a straightforward history of the efforts made for Christian unity since the Reformation, stressing the influence of evangelical revivals. List of contributors; full bibliography; glossary and notes; index.

Papacy

262.13
JOHN, E., *ed.* The Popes: a concise biographical history. London, Burns & Oates, 1964. 496p. illus. (16 col. pl.). 84s.

Gives precise information on each papal reign, from St. Peter to Paul VI. Historical surveys by Douglas Woodruff; biographical articles by J. M. W. Beau and others. 9 contributors. 130 good black-and-white illustrations, apart from col. plates. Annotated list of books for further reading, p. 481-2; index, p. 483-96.

262.13
PASTOR, L., *Freiherr von.* The history of the Popes, from the close of the Middle Ages. Drawn from the secret archives of the Vatican and other original sources. From the German. Translated and edited by F. I. Autrobus [and others]. London, Hodges; Kegan Paul; Routledge and Kegan Paul, 1891-1953. 40v.

"Unlikely ever to be superseded" (John, E. *The Popes* (1964), p. 482). V. 1 commences with Clement V (1305-14); v. 40 deals with Pius VI (1775-99). 2v. are devoted to some Popes (*e.g.*, Leo X, Paul III, Clement VIII, Pius VI). Each volume carries a list of most cited works; each is heavily footnoted and has an index of names.

Church Councils

262.5 (031)
PALAZZINI, P., and MORELLI, G., *ed.* Dizionario dei Concili. Tivoli, [?], 1963-. v. 1-. (v. 4. 1966).

v. 1: AACHEN-CZESTOCHOWA.
A dictionary of Church Councils, arranged A-Z by place of assembly. According to *Stechert-Hafner book news* (v. 18, no. 9, May 1964, p. 123), the final volume will contain indexes, including a chronological index.

Liturgy

264:016
"Liturgies". In British Museum. Department of Printed Books. *General catalogue of printed books*, v. 138 (243 cols.), 139 (whole v., 1,238 cols.). Photo-offset ed. London, Trustees of the British Museum, 1962. 130s. per v.

Pt. 1: Greek rite; Lesser Eastern rites; Latin rite. Pt. 2: Church of England, [etc.]. Pt. 3: Lutheran churches Calvinistic and Zwinglian churches; Evangelical Union churches; Lesser reformed bodies. Index (v. 139, cols. 1175-1238).

The *Yearbook of liturgical studies* (Collegeville, Minn., Liturgical Press, 1960-) gives a comprehensive and concise survey, well-indexed, of the literature of worship and church music, according to *Library trends* (v. 15, no. 1, January 1967, p. 473). The *Jahrbuch für Liturgik und Hymnologie* (Kassel, J. Stauda, 1955-) is its German counterpart.

264 (031)
CABROL, F. Dictionnaire d'archéologie chrétienne et de liturgie. Paris, Letouzey, 1907-53. 15v. (176 fasc.). illus.

See entry at 27 (031).

264 (038)
LERCARO, G. A small liturgical dictionary. Edited by J. B. O'Connell. London, Burns & Oates, 1959. 248p.

A translation from the 2nd Italian ed. of *Piccolo dizionario liturgico* (1950).

The author is the archbishop of Bologna. The dictionary (p. 33-248) consists of brief and simple entries explaining terms in the Roman Catholic liturgy, in the light of the present liturgical movement. Fills a gap in the literature on the subject.

The *New dictionary of the liturgy*, by G. Podhradsky (English ed., edited by L. Sheppard. Translated by R. Wells and M. Baring. London, G. Chapman, 1967 [*i.e.*, 1966]. 208p. 50*s*.) was originally *Lexikon der Liturgie* (Innsbruck, Tyrolia, 1962). Reviewed in *Times literary supplement*, no. 3395, 23rd March 1967, p. 250.

J. G. Davies' *A select liturgical lexicon* (London, Lutterworth Press, 1965. 146p. 20*s*.) is written from the Anglican standpoint.

Vestments

264-03
NORRIS, H. Church vestments: their origin & development. London, Dent, 1949. xv, 190p. illus. 45*s*.

A work which grew out of the author's *Costume and fashion,* dealing with classical garments that were the ancestors of church vestments. Attention given to accurate dating; coloured, and black-and-white illustrations, brief historical data; index.

Hymns

264-068·016
CHEVALIER, C. U. J. Repertorium hymnologicum: catalogue des chants, hymnes, proses, séquences, tropes en usage dans l'église latine depuis les origines jusqu'à nos jours. Louvain, Société des Bollandistes, 1892-1920. 6v. (v. 1-5 reprinted 1959. ea. Belg. fr. 350). Belg. fr. 1900.

Reprinted from *Analecta Bollandia,* v. 1-3, 5.

The standard bibliography of Latin-rhymed poetic texts for liturgical use, with details of *incipit,* sources, etc. V. 6: *Préface et tables.*

V. Duckles (*Music reference and research materials: an annotated bibliography* (1964), entry no. 676) mentions a volume of additions and emendations by Clemens Blume,—*Repertorium repertorii* (Leipzig, 1901).

264-068 (03)
JULIAN, J. A dictionary of hymnology, setting forth the origin and history of Christian hymns of all ages and nations . . . Rev. 2nd ed., with new supplement. London, Murray, 1907 (reprinted 1915). xviii, 1768p. (Reprinted New York, Dover, 1956. 2v. $17.50.)

First published 1892.

Still the standard work on hymnology, with biographical and critical notices of authors and translators, historical articles on national and denominational hymnody, breviaries, etc., the English language being the keynote of the work. There are lists of contributors, MSS., abbreviations, and indexes of first lines and names.

Being revised by the Rev. L. H. Bunn for the Hymn Society (Davies, J. H. *Musicalia* (1966), p. 31).

The *Judson concordance to hymns,* by T. B. McDormand and F. S. Crossman (Valley Forge, Pa., Judson Press, 1965. 375p. $7.50) indexes nearly 2,400 hymns from 27 hymnals of major U.S. and Canadian denominations. The user is referred from the keyword in any line to the 'Line index' and thence to the first line of the hymn.

K. S. Diehl's *Hymns and tunes—an index* (Metuchen, N.J., Scarecrow Press, 1966. 1242p. $30) is advertised as an index to songs found in 78 hymnals, chiefly in English and representing British and North American Jewish-Christian institutions.

264-068 (091)
FROST, M., ed. Historical companion to 'Hymns ancient and modern'. London, Clowes. 1962. xvi, 761p. illus., ports., facs., mus. examples. 63*s*.

First published 1909, as W. H. Frere's *Historical edition of 'Hymns ancient and modern'.*

Gives notes on the words and tunes of 636 hymns in the revised ed. of *Hymns ancient and modern,* with biographical sketches of hymn writers, translators and composers, indexes of first lines and tunes, a metrical index, list of sources, and other aids.

R. W. Thomson's *Who's who of hymn writers* (London, Epworth Press, 1967. 104p. 15*s*.) contains concise biographical sketches of 277 British and American as well as European hymn-writers.

Breviaries

264-13
BOHATTA, H. Bibliographie der Breviere, 1501-1850. 2. unveränderte Aufl. Stuttgart, Hiersemann, 1963. vii, 349p. 94*s*.

First published 1937.

2,891 numbered items. Main sections: 1. Breviarium Romanorum—2. Orden (Canonici Regulares. Ordines Monastici. Ordines Mendicantium—Ordines Militares)—3. Diözesen. Title index; chronology; list of sources quoted (p. 275-8); country (sub-divided by town) index.

Also noted: *Bibliographie analytique de la liturgie,* by Th. A. Vismans and L. Brinkhoff. Édition française. Traduit de l'allemand. (Nijmegen, Association des Bibliothèques de Séminaires et de Couvents, 1960. 79p. D.fl. 6.65).

Prayer Book

264-19
HARFORD, G., and STEVENSON, M., ed. The Prayer Book dictionary. London, Pitman, 1912. xx, 832p. (1925 reprint. xxiii, 832p.).

An attempt to provide for the Anglican Book of Common Prayer a dictionary comparable to existing Bible dictionaries. Aims at covering origins, history, use and teaching of the Prayer Book, with full, accurate data, and fairness in controversial questions. Signed articles; list of contributors; appendix of contents in Prayer Book order.

Christian Missions

266:016
"Bibliography on world mission and evangelism." In *International review of missions.* London, International Missionary Council (now Geneva. World Council of Churches), 1911-. Quarterly. ea. 6s.; 20s. p.a.

About 1,000 items (some briefly annotated), p.a. 8 main sections: 1. The Christian world mission in Bible and Church: its nature, principles and methods—2. The Christian mission at home and overseas—3. Christian institutions and the Church's mission—4. Anthropological, sociological and political factors in relation to the Church's mission.—5. The living faiths of men —6. Regional, national and local studies of Church and society—7. Works of reference—8. Miscellaneous.

266:016
STREIT, P. Bibliotheca missionum. Begonnen von R. Streit, fortgeführt von P. J. Dindinger; hrsg. von P. J. Rommerskrichen and P. N. Kowalsky. Freiburg, Herder, 1916-. v. 1-.

1. *Grundlegender und allgemeiner Teil.*
2-3. *Amerikanische Missionsliteratur, 1493-1699; 1700-1909. 2. Aufl. 1963.*
4-5. *Asiatische Missionsliteratur, 1245-1599; 1600-1699.*
6. *Missionsliteratur Indiens, der Philippinen, Japans und Indochinas, 1700-1799.*
7. *Chinesische Missionsliteratur, 1700-1799.*
8. *Missionsliteratur Indiens und Indochinas, 1800-1909.*
9. *Missionsliteratur der Philippinen, 1800-1909.*
10. *Missionsliteratur Japans und Koreas, 1800-1909.* (In preparation)
11. *Missionsliteratur Indochinas, 1800-1909.* (In preparation)
12-14. *Chinesische Missionsliteratur, 1800-1884; 1885-1909; 1910-1950 (3 pts).*
15-20. *Afrikanische Missionsliteratur, 1053-1599; 1600-1699; 1700-1879; 1880-1909; 1910-1940 (2v.)*
21. *Missionsliteratur von Australien und Ozeanien, 1525-1950.*
22. *Grundlegender und allgemeiner Teil, 1910-1935 und Nachtrag zu Bd.1.*
23. *Afrikanische Literatur. Grundlegender und allgemeiner Teil.*
24. *Amerikanische Missionsliteratur, 1910-1924. 1967.*

Each volume has c. 2000 entries, chronologically arranged. Roman Catholic viewpoint.

266:016
VRIENS. Le P. L., *and others.* **Critical bibliography of missiology.** English ed., translated from the Dutch MS. by Deodatus Tummers. Nijmegen, Édition Bestel Centrale V.S.K.B.,

1960. 127p. (Bibliographie ad usum seminariorum, v. 2). D.fl.12.35.

206 items. Does not include Protestant missions or Protestant work in the mission field.

The *Dictionary catalog of the Missionary Research Library, New York* is to be published by G. K. Hall (Boston, Mass.) in 1968. (17v. $1125 (U.S.); $1237.50 (outside U.S.)). It will contain 298,000 photolithographed author, title and subject entries covering more than 100,000 catalogued items.

266 (091)
LATOURETTE, K. S. A history of the expansion of Christianity. London, Eyre & Spottiswoode, 1938-47. 7v. maps.

A work of encyclopaedic range, by a well-known authority on Christian missions, likely to remain the standard history for many years to come, on the missionary enterprise of Christianity from its earliest times up to the present day. Each volume has its own index, full bibliography, and maps. "Latourette handles temperately, charitably and with immense erudition every part of Christian expansion—Roman Catholic, Protestant, and Orthodox" (Neill, S. *A history of Christian missions* (1965), p. 579).

266 (6)
GROVES, C. P. The planting of Christianity in Africa. London, Lutterworth Press, 1948-60 (reprinted 1965). 4v. maps. 168s.

Published under the auspices of the Department of Missions, Selly Oak Colleges, Birmingham.

Chronological treatment. V. 1 covers the period from the 1st century A.D. to 1840; v. 2: 1840-1878; v. 3: 1878-1914; v. 4: 1914-1954. Numerous footnote references. The author was formerly Professor of Missions in the Selly Oak Colleges. Protestant standpoint.

Salvation Army

267.12 (058)
The Salvation Army year book, 1906-. London, Salvationist Publishing & Supplies, Ltd., 1906-. illus. Annual. (1967, published 1966. 6s. 6d.; 10s. 6d.).

The 1965 year book contains a record of events and articles, followed by book reviews and directory information, international and by territories (p. 97-214). A list of retirements and obituaries precede a who's who (p. 232-70).

The History of the Salvation Army (v. 1-3, by R. Sandall (1947-55), v. 4, by A. S. Wiggins (1964). London, Nelson) is a detailed official account of the organisation. V. 1-2, 4 carry the narrative from 1865 to 1904; v. 3 is subtitled *1883-1953: Social work and reform.* V. 5 (1968. 35s.) covers the years 1904-14. Each vol. has illustrations, a bibliography and an analytical index.

HISTORY OF CHRISTIAN CHURCH

27:016
CASE, S. J., *ed.* **A bibliographical guide to the history of Christianity,** compiled by S. J. Case, J. T. McNeill, W. W. Sweet, W. Pauck, M.

Spinka. Chicago, Univ. of Chicago Press, 1931. xi, 265p. Reprinted Magnolia, Mass., Peter Smith, 1952. $4.50.

A select list, covering the history of Christianity in the Western hemisphere, its career in Eastern Europe and Western Asia, and its growth in Africa, Asia and the Pacific Islands. Contents, which include periodical articles, are classified by subject, with an author and subject index.

27:016
CHADWICK, O. The history of the Church: a select bibliography. [New ed.] London, Historical Association, 1962. 52p. (Helps for students of history, no. 66). 6s.

Previous ed., 1923.
About 700 entries, most of them annotated, in 5 sections: 1. General works on Church history —2. The Early Church—3. The medieval Church —4. The Reformation and Counter-Reformation —5. The modern Church. A valuable bibliography, with further references included in annotations. Handicapped by lack of author and subject indexes.

27 (021)
JEDIN, H., and DOLAN, J., *ed.* **Handbook of Church history.** Translated from the 3rd rev. German ed. Freiburg, Herder; London, Burns & Oates, 1965-. v. 1-.

Original German: *Handbuch der Kirchengeschichte* (1962-). To be in 6v. V. 1. *From the Apostolic community to Constantine.* 1965. xxiii, 523p. 90s. Provisional titles of later v.: 2. Christianity as the state religion after Constantine—3. The Western Church and the struggle for power in the Middle Ages—4. Schism and reform—5. The Church and the secularization of the West— 6. The Church from 1918 to the present. A large-scale, scholarly history, written from the Roman Catholic standpoint. Heavily documented. V. 1 has a lengthy bibliography (by chapters) with evaluative commentary (p. 435-503).

Even more extensive is M. J. H. S. A. Fliche and V. Martin's *Histoire de l'Église depuis les origines jusqu'à nos jours* (Paris, Bloud & Gay, 1938-). Pt. 2 of v. 14, on the period of the Great Schism and the conciliary crises (1378-1449), appeared in 1964.

27 (021)
LATOURETTE, K. S. Christianity in a revolutionary age: a history of Christianity in the nineteenth and twentieth centuries. London, Eyre & Spottiswoode, 1959-63. 5v. ea. 63s.

v. 1: *The nineteenth century in Europe: background and the Roman Catholic phase.* 1959. xiv, 498p.
v. 2: *The nineteenth century in Europe: the Protestant and Eastern churches.* 1960. vii, [1], [1], 532p.
v. 3: *The nineteenth century outside Europe: the Americas, the Pacific, Asia and Africa.* 1961. viii, [1], 527p.
v. 4: *The twentieth century in Europe: the Roman Catholic, Protestant, and Eastern Churches.* 1962. viii, 568p.
v. 5: *The twentieth century outside Europe: the Americas, the Pacific, Asia and Africa; the*

emerging world Christian community. 1963. viii, 568p.

Discusses all aspects of Christianity throughout the world since 1815,—theology, organisation, devotional life and influence on the social, political and educational scene (*Christianity in books* (1964), p. 63). Well documented (*e.g.,* the chapter on Latin America in v. 3 has 187 footnotes; each v. carries an annotated bibliography of *c.* 17 pages of works cited more than once. Analytical index. Author is Stirling Professor of Missions and Oriental History, Emeritus and Associate Fellow of Berkeley College, Yale University.

27 (021)
LATOURETTE, K. S. A history of Christianity. London, Eyre & Spottiswoode, [1954]. xxviii, 1516p. maps. 63s.

An attempt to summarize the entire history of Christianity in all its phases, from the immediate background of Christ's life up to the present day. Not a condensation, then, of the same author's *History of the expansion of Christianity (266 (091))*, but a tracing of the development of Christianity in the setting of human history. Select chapter bibliographies; full index; 20 maps.

27 (031)
BAUDRILLART, A. Dictionnaire d'histoire et de géographie ecclésiastiques. Paris, Letouzey, 1912-. v. 1-. maps.

v. 1-15 (1912-63): A-EUSÉBIE.
Part of the *Encyclopédie des sciences ecclésiastiques.* Later volumes edited under the direction of R. Aubert and É. van Couwenbergh, both professors at the University of Louvain.
The scope is, broadly, that of the history of the Roman Catholic Church, and events, persons, countries and localities are included and treated accordingly (*e.g.,* article in v. 12 on China, p. 694-730 deals with religious history, Roman Catholic missions, ecclesiastical divisions, churches, etc.). Very useful for biographies and ecclesiastical data on localities. Signed articles; adequate bibliographies (*e.g.,* article in v. 15 on St. Eusebius, p. 1478-83, has ¾ col. of bibliography). Volumes carry a list of major sources used.

27 (031)
CABROL, F. Dictionnaire d'archéologie chrétienne et de liturgie. Paris, Letouzey, 1907-53. 15v. (176 fasc.). illus.

Part of the *Encyclopédie des sciences ecclésiastiques.*
Authorship of v. 15 (2 pts. 1950-53) is given as "R. R. dom F. Cabrol et dom H. Leclerq, publié sous la direction de Henri Marrou".
A scholarly work, covering all aspects of early Christian art, institutions, customs, etc. Articles are lengthy, signed, systematically arranged and well documented (*e.g.,* the article "Salonique", cols. 623-713, has 29 sections, each with a short bibliography, with a final general bibliography of 1½ cols.). Numerous footnote references.
Illustrations take the form of line drawings and plans in the text.

27 (031)
SMITH, *Sir* **W.,** and **CHEETHAM, S. A dic-**
tionary of Christian antiquities. London,
Murray, 1875-80. 2v. illus.

Intended to provide, with the *Dictionary of
Christian biography,* a complete account of the
leading persons, institutions, art, social life, etc.,
of the early Christian Church, up to the age of
Charlemagne, treating the same class of subjects
as Smith's *Dictionary of Greek and Roman
antiquities,* but in relation to Christianity.

27 (031)
SMITH, *Sir* **W.,** and **WACE, H. A dictionary of**
Christian biography, literature, sects and doc-
trines during the first eight centuries. London,
Murray, 1877-87. 4v.

A continuation of Smith's *Dictionary of the
Bible* (1860-5); designed to furnish a complete
collection of materials for the history of the
Church to the age of Charlemagne, excluding
Christian antiquities, which is treated separately.
An excellent one-volume abridgement has been
compiled by H. Wace and W. C. Piercy (1911)
(*see at* 27 (*092*)).

A reprint, costing £66, is in preparation.

27 (084.4)
MEER, F. van der, and **MOHRMANN, C. Atlas**
of the early Christian world; translated and
edited by Mary F. Hedland and H. H. Rowley.
London. Nelson, 1958. 216p. illus. (incl. pl.),
maps. 105s.

Complementary to the Nelson *Atlas of the
Bible.* Together they form an indispensable guide
to the origins of the Christian Church and its
development down to the 7th century. 42 six-
colour maps (page size: $14\frac{1}{2}'' \times 10\frac{1}{4}''$) and a commentary divided into three parts, of which part 2
is a valuable description of Church life A.D. 303-
600. Quotations from patristic writings and inscriptions are a notable feature. Geographical
index to the maps and plates; index of authors
and inscriptions. 613 gravure illustrations.

*The 'Universe' atlas of the Christian world:
the expansion of Christianity through the ages,*
by A. Freitag and others (London, published for
Associate Catholic Newspapers by Burns &
Oates, [1964]. xii, 200p. illus., maps, facsim. 63s.),
was originally published as *Atlas du monde
chrétien* (Paris, Meddens, 1959). It has 29 col-
oured plates of maps ($13\frac{3}{4}'' \times 10''$), many illustrations and text, and covers missions of Churches
not in communion with Rome.

27 (092)
WACE, H., and **PIERCY, W. C.,** *ed.* **A dictionary**
of Christian biography and literature to the
end of the sixth century A.D., with an account of
the principal sects and heresies. London, Murray,
1911. xi, 1028p.

An abidged edition of Smith and Wace's four-
volume work, published 1877-87 (*see at* 27 (*031*)),
which cuts off two centuries, and improves upon
the larger work by excluding many insignificant
names.

27 (093)
STEVENSON, E., *ed.* **A new Eusebius:** docu-
ments illustrative of the history of the Church to
A.D. 337. London, S.P.C.K., 1957. 448p. 21s.; 30s.

—— **Creeds, Councils and controversies:** documents illustrative of the history of the Church.
London, S P.C.K., 1966. 408p. 45s.

Planned to replace B. J. Kidd's *Documents
illustrative of the history of the Church* (London,
S.P.C.K., 1920-41. 3v. o.p.) and better arranged;
whereas Kidd arranged his material according to
the date of the writing cited, thus separating
comments from originals, Stevenson adopts the
order of events (*Times literary supplement,* no.
3,384, 5th January, 1967, p. 12).

27 (093.3)
BARDENHEWER, O. Geschichte der altkirch-
lichen Literatur. Darmstadt, Wissenschaftliche
Buchgesellschaft, 1962. 5v.

V. 1 covers the period from the end of the
Apostolic era to the close of the 2nd century
(xii, 633p.). V. 5 (ix, 423p.) includes a section on
the oldest Armenian document. Arrangement is
by authors, with biographical data and quotations. Thus 'Boethius' (p. 250-64) is dealt with
under five headings, each with a bibliography;
De consolatione philosophiae has $\frac{3}{4}$p. listing
editions, translations, commentaries and studies
on it. Semi-analytical name index to each volume.

Religious Orders

271 (410)
ANSON, P. F. The religious orders and congre-
gations of Great Britain and Ireland. Worcester, Stanbrook Abbey Press, 1949. 423p.

Pt. 1: Orders and congregations of men (arranged alphabetically by orders); pt. 2: Orders
and congregations of women (similarly arranged).
Details are given of background history, activities, habit and location of communities. Index to
each part.

271 (410)
Directory of religious orders, congregations and
societies of Great Britain and Ireland. Glasgow,
Burns. Annual. (1967. 5s.)

An alphabetical list of Roman Catholic orders
and congregations. 'Outline of history and activities' (priests; brothers; nuns: addresses and telephone numbers of provincial and regional
superiors). Alphabetical index (priests; brothers;
nuns).

271 (411)
EASSON, D. E. Medieval religious houses:
Scotland; with an appendix on the houses in the
Isle of Man. London, Longmans, Green, 1957.
xiii, 204p. maps. 45s.

A companion volume to Knowles and Hadcock's *Medieval religious houses: England and
Wales* (q.v.).
Arranged by orders (*e.g.,* monks, regular
canons, mendicant orders, nuns, military orders),
with sub-divisions, and then A-Z by name of
house. Appendix 1: The religious houses of the
Isle of Man; 2: The income of the Scottish
religious houses; the sources. Preliminary essay
(p. 1-39) on 'The development of monasticism in
Scotland'. List of sources (p. 40-48); footnotes
and references; index of religious houses.

271 (42)

KNOWLES, D., and HADCOCK, R. N. Medieval religious houses: England and Wales. London, Longmans, Green, 1953. xxiii, 387p. maps.

A much expanded and revised version of D. Knowles' *Religious houses of medieval England* (1940).

Basic list of religious and secular communities. Arranged by order (Benedictine, etc.), then A-Z by name of house. Details for each house; county; rank (*e.g.*, abbey, priory, etc.); income in 1535; dates of foundation and dissolution; parent house. Index of religious houses.

271 (420)

KNOWLES, D. The monastic order in England: a history of its development from the times of St. Dunstan to the Fourth Lateran Council, 940-1216. 2nd ed. Cambridge, Univ. Press, 1963. xxii, 780p. 30s.

First published 1940.

An account, historical rather than antiquarian, of English monastic life during an important period of religious history; based on contemporary sources, quoted in full where space allows. Detailed bibliography and notes. Continued by:

271 (420)

——**The religious orders in England.** Cambridge, Univ. Press, 1948-59. 3v. 155s.

v. 1: 1948. xvi, 348p. 50s.
v. 2: *The end of the Middle Ages.* 1955. xii, 408p. 50s.
v. 3: *The Tudor age.* 1959. xiv, 522p. 55s.

The standard work, making use of many published records of episcopal visitations. Includes the history of the Friars in England. V. 3 has an extensive bibliography (p. 497-506) and a detailed index, as well as valuable appendices (*e.g.*, 2. 'Religious houses suppressed by Wolsey'; 10. 'Regulars as Bishops' (a list)).

Sir William Dugdale's *Monasticon Anglicanum* (London, Bested, 1817-30. 8v.; first published in 1693) is assessed by J. L. Hobbs (*Local history and the library*, p. 200) as an essential source book; it "details the charters of foundation and other deeds of monasteries and religious houses, with a historical summary of each".

271:282 (02)

HEIMBUCHER, M. Die Orden und Kongregationen der katholischen Kircher. 3. Aufl. Paderborn, Schöningh, 1933-34. 2v.

First published 1896-97; 2nd ed. 1907.

An updated condensation of the chief repertory for historical information,—Helyot's *Histoire des ordres religieux* (1714. 8v.; 2nd ed. 1792, with its many coloured plates showing habits and dress). V. 1 deals with beginnings and the Benedictine, Dominican and Franciscan orders. V. 2 concludes the Franciscans and also covers the Carmelites, the Jesuits and other orders, such as the Sulpicians. "This most useful handbook is equipped throughout with an excellent and well-chosen bibliography" (*Encyclopædia Britannica.* 11th ed. 1910-11. v. 18, p. 691, on the 2nd ed.).

For reference works on individual orders, see Totok, W., and others. *Handbuch der bibliographischen Nachschlagewerke* (3rd ed., 1966), p. 177.

271:282 (03)

KAPSNER, O. L. Catholic religious orders, listing conventional and full names in English, foreign languages and Latin; also, abbreviations, date and country of origin, and founders. 2nd ed., enl. Collegeville, Minn., St. John's Abbey Press, 1957. xxxviii, 594p.

First published 1948.

Sponsored by the Catholic Library Association and "primarily . . . intended for the use of library cataloguers" (*Preface*). 1,777 main entries; abbreviations are cross-referred to full names. Glossary, p. xiii-xxvi; list of authorities consulted, p. xxvii-xxxvii.

271:283

ANSON, P. F. The call of the cloister: religious communities and kindred bodies in the Anglican communion. London, S.P.C.K., 1955. xvi, 641p. illus.

Provides a complete list of all Anglican communities throughout the world, with a brief history of each. An excellent bibliography (p. 598-609); appendix of communities in order of foundation; indexes. Likely to prove the standard work of reference on this subject. By a former member of the Benedictine community at Caldey.

271:283

CHURCH OF ENGLAND. Advisory Council on Religious Communities. **Guide to the religious communities of the Anglican Communion.** New ed. London, Mowbray, 1955. xi, 140p.

First published 1951.

Contents: Men's communities (England, Ireland, U.S.A.); Women's communities (England, Wales, etc.). Index of communities; index of places.

The Church Fathers

276:016

ALTANER, B. Patrology. Translated by Hilda C. Graef. Freiberg, Herder; Edinburgh & London, Nelson, 1960. xxiv, 660p. 60s.

A translation based on the 5th German edition of *Patrologie* (1958), revised and augmented.

Not a "mere bibliography of patrology", but rather a literary history, with brief biographies and extensive bibliographical references. The section on St. Jerome, for example, covers p. 462-77. Index. "This indispensable manual for patristic studies is notable for the completeness of coverage and for its separate bibliographies for individual writers and subjects" (*Heythrop journal*, v. 1, no. 3, October 1960, p. 359).

276:016

PERLER, O. Patristische Philosophie. Berne, Francke, 1950. 44p. (Bibliographische Einführungen in das Studium der Philosophie, 18).

Lists, with occasional annotations, the chief texts, histories of Patristics and studies of the Apostolic, Greek and Latin Fathers. Name index.

276:016

QUASTEN, J. Patrology. Westminster, Maryland, Newman Press; Utrecht, Spectrum, 1950-. v. 1-.

v. 1: *The beginnings of Patristic literature.* 1950. $7.50.

v. 2: *The ante-Nicene literature after Irenaeus.* 1953. $9.

v. 3: *The golden age of Greek Patristic literature, from the Council of Nicaea to the Council of Chalcedon.* 1960. $12.50.

An important bibliography, designed to inform both specialist and student on the literature of the subject; the latter comprises (1) critical editions, (2) translations, especially into English, and (3) articles and monographs.

The fullest collection of Patristic texts is that produced by J.-P. Migne,—*Patrologiae cursus completus* (Latin series. Paris, 1844-64. 221v.; Greek series (Greek text with Latin translation). Paris, 1857-66. 166v.; Latin texts of Greek authors. Paris, 1856-67. 81v. "Its vast scope leaves it still unique and valuable, where other editions of special works do not exist" (*Encyclopædia Britannica* (11th *ed.*), v. 18, p. 426).

Corpus Christianorum. Series Latina (Turnhout, Brépols, 1954-), to be published in 175v., is to cover all Patristic texts in Latin.

E. Dekkers' *Clavis patrum latinorum* (Steenbergen, Abbatia Sancti Petri, 1961. xxviii, 640p.) provides a valuable key to Patristic texts in Latin that have appeared in collections, etc.

276:016
SCHNEEMELCHER, W., *ed.* **Bibliographia patristica:** internationale patristische Bibliographie. Berlin, de Gruyter, 1959-. v.1-.

V. 1 lists 1067 publications (including reviews) for 1956; v. 8 (1966) covers 1963. 9 sections, with sub-divisions: 1. Generalia—2. Novum Testamentum atque Apocrypha—3. Auctores—4. Liturgica—5. Iuridica, symbola—6. Doctrina auctorum et historia dogmatum—7. Gnostica—8. Patrum exegesis Veteris et Novi Testamenti—9. Recensiones. Author indexes to pts. 1-8 and 8.

276 (038)=75
LAMPE, G. W. H., *ed.* **A Patristic Greek lexicon.** London, Methuen, 1961-67. 5 fasc. ea. 84s.

A summary history of the use of all theologically important words by the Greek Christian writers of the period from the Apostolic Fathers to A.D. 800. Each fascicle has *c.* 300 pages. The editor is Ely Professor of Divinity in the University of Cambridge.

276 (091)
LABRIOLLE, P. de. History and literature of Christianity, from Tertullian to Boethius. London, Kegan Paul, 1924. xiii, 555p.

Translated from the French; one of the "History of civilization" series, this is an authoritative work by a former Professor of Classic Latin Literature at Fribourg-en-Suisse. Has an excellent introductory chapter, and tables surveying the field of Latin Christian literature; authors are discussed individually. Footnotes; no bibliography.

The original work, *Histoire de la littérature latine chrétienne* had a 3rd rev. and enl. ed. in 1947 (Paris, Belles-Lettres. 2v.) which carries bibliographies.

CHRISTIAN CHURCHES

28 (02)
MOLLAND, E. Christendom: the Christian churches, their doctrines, constitutional forms and ways of worship. London, Mowbray, 1959. xiv, 418p. 35s.

First published in Norwegian in 1953. The author is Professor of Ecclesiastical History in the University of Oslo.

Pt. 1: 'The churches of Christendom' (p. 11-328), consisting of 20 chapters, ranging from 1, 'The Orthodox Church' to 20, 'The Society of Friends (Quakers)'. Pt. 2: 'Religious systems containing elements derived from Christianity' (Unitarians; Christian Science; Jehovah's Witnesses; Mormonism'). Bibliography, p. 387-402 (first a general section and then arranged in text sequence), annotations on more important items. Indexes of persons, places and subjects. An important work.

28 (032)
GRÜNDLER, J. Lexikon der Christlichen Kirche und Sekten, unter Berücksichtigung der Missionsgesellschaften und Zwischenkirchlichen Organisationen. Freiburg, Herder, 1961. 2v.

V. 1, pt. 1: Die Katholische Kirche; pt. 2: Die Nichtkatholischen Kirchen, Sekten . . . (continued into v. 2, which carries an index of places and bodies). 2,659 entries (a number of them with no details), A-Z, stating name, address, historical background, type of church or sect, and religious connections.

28 (083.4)
World Christian handbook, 1968. Editors, H. W. Coxill and Sir K. Grubb. London, Lutterworth Press, for the Survey Application Trust, 1967. xvii, 378p. tables. 42s.

First published 1949. 5th ed., 1968 (1967).

Part 1: Articles (p. 1-55). Part 2: Statistical section, by continents and countries (Protestant and Anglican churches and missions, p. 59-219; Roman Catholic statistics; African independent churches; Jewish statistics; Non-Christian religions)—Part 3: Directory section (Ecumenical and international Christian organisations—Protestant and Anglican churches, missions and Christian organisations, by continents and countries—African independent churches). Indexes: Contents of statistical and directory sections—General index (p. 357-78).

Also noted: Littel, F. H. and Walz, H. H., *ed. Weltkirchenlexikon. Handbuch der Ökumene* (Stuttgart, Kreuz-Verlag, 1961. 1792 cols. illus. (pl.). This has a comprehensive keyword and subject index.

Great Britain

28 (410):016
UNION THEOLOGICAL SEMINARY, New York. **Catalogue of the McAlpin Collection of British history and theology;** compiled and edited by C. R. Gillett. New York, the Seminary, 1927-30. 5v.

Important for older material, especially for publications between 1641 and 1700, which are covered by v. 2-4. Over 15,000 entries are listed chronologically, with author arrangement under each year; full bibliographical details and references to similar copies in British catalogues. V. 5 consists of a detailed index of authors, anonymous titles, etc.

Scotland

28 (411):016
MACGREGOR, M. B. The sources and literature of Scottish church history. Glasgow, McCallum, 1934. 4, [11], 260p.

A classified and annotated bibliography; includes biographical sketches of leading personalities.

28 (411):026/027
LAMB, J. A. "Theological and philosophical libraries in Scotland." In Library Association record, v. 61, no. 12, December 1959, p. 327-333.

Notes on the history and collections of theological and philosophical libraries connected with the Church of Scotland, the Scottish universities, and denominations other than the Church of Scotland.
This article, entitled "The Scottish scene", appeared in the Bulletin of the Association of British Theological and Philosophical Libraries, no. 5, March 1958, p. 5-8; no. 6, June 1958, p. 3-7; no. 7, November 1958, p. 7-10.

28 (411)(091)
BURLEIGH, J. H. S. A church history of Scotland. London, Oxford Univ. Press, 1960. x, 456p. maps. 42s.

A survey from the coming of Christianity down to 1957. Addressed to the general reader and not to the specialist (Preface). The selective bibliography (p. 423-4) is a guide to the more important literature available for consultation. Includes a very useful diagram showing the Church's divisions and reunions, 1690-1929. Detailed index (p. 427-56). The author is Professor of Ecclesiastical History at Edinburgh University.

Ireland

28 (415):091
KENNEY, J. F. The sources for the early history of Ireland: an introduction and guide. V. 1. Ecclesiastical. New York, Columbia Univ. Press, 1929. xvi, 807p. maps. Reprinted New York, Octagon, 1966. $12.50.

659 numbered and annotated items in 8 chapters, arranged chronologically up to the 12th century. Many footnote references. References to manuscripts and to printed editions and commentaries, plus notes. General bibliography, p. 91-109. Analytical index.

U.S.A.

28 (73):016
MODE, P. G. Source book and bibliographical guide for American church history. Boston,

Mass., Canner, 1964. xxiv, 735p. $17.50.

First published 1921.
29 chapters, each with a bibliography and documents. Regional as well as period coverage. Chapter 29: 'Since the Civil War' (to c. 1917). Index, p. 723-35. The author is Assistant Professor of Church History in the Divinity School of the University of Chicago.

A critical bibliography of religion in America, by N. R. Burr (Princeton, N.J., Princeton Univ. Press, 1961. 2v. $17.50) is a valuable and comprehensive narrative bibliography in 5 main parts, of which pt. 1 is 'Bibliographical guides; general surveys and histories'.

28 (73)(083)
MEAD, F. S. Handbook of denominations in the United States. 4th ed. Nashville, Tenn., Abingdon Press, 1965. 271p. $2.95.

First published 1951.
Basic data on the history, organisation and doctrines of more than 250 religious denominations. Bibliographies.

E. S. Gaustad's Historical atlas of religion in America (New York, Harper & Row, 1962. $8.95) covers the period from 1620 to the 1960's. It contains 78 maps and 57 charts, tables and graphs.

Eastern Church

281.9:016
BRANDRETH, H. R. T. An outline guide to the study of Eastern Christendom. London, S.P.C.K., 1951. 34p.

An annotated book list for English readers. The eleven sections include: 10, Iconography and art; 11, Periodicals. No index.

281.9:264
KING, A. A. Rites of Eastern Christendom. London, Burns, Oates, 1950. 2v. illus.

Intended to provide a manual for those, other than the expert liturgical scholar, who want information about the rites of the Eastern Church, including the separated Churches. Historical, ritual and ceremonial detail is given, with liturgical texts. Illustrations; bibliography and index to each volume.

Roman Catholic Church

282:016
Catholic periodical index: a cumulative author and subject index to a selected list of Catholic periodicals. 1930-. Haverford, Pa., Catholic Library Association, 1939-. Quarterly, with 2- and 5-yr. cumulations. Service basis.

Indexes articles and book reviews in more than 200 Catholic periodicals and newspapers.

The "Elenchus" in Ephemerides theologicae Lovanienses (Univ. of Louvain. Gembloux, Duclot, 1924-. Quarterly) covers books and periodical articles, grouped under theological subject headings, in Latin (*e.g.,* 'Theologia moralis'). Praised in *Library trends* (v. 15, no. 3, June 1967, p. 471) for its coverage and its author index.

282 (031)
DAVIS, H. F., *and others, ed.* **A Catholic dictionary of theology.** London, Nelson, 1962-. v. 1-.

v. 1-2: A-HEAVEN. 1962-67. (v. 1. 42*s.*; v. 2. 105*s.*).
To be in 4v. Aims to provide a connected account of Roman Catholic theology in article form. Scholarly, signed contributions; appended bibliographies include readings as well as source material. The articles on Atonement, Apologetics and Anglicanism merit special attention, states the reviewer in *Heythrop journal*, v. 4, no. 3, July 1963, p. 315-6. Well produced. Two of the editors attended the Vatican Council, yet, according to the *Times literary supplement* (no. 3, 412, 20th July 1967, p. 643), the *Dictionary* gives "little hint of any serious assessment of recent theological development"; it is not comprehensive enough for the serious scholar, yet "too elaborate for the day-to-day use of the general reader".

K. Rahner and H. Vorgrimler's *Concise theological dictionary*, edited by Cornelius Ernst and translated by Richard Strachan (Freiburg, Herder; London, Burns & Oates, 1965. 493p. 45*s.*) was first published in 1961. Is intended to explain briefly "the most important concepts of modern Catholic dogmatic theology for readers who are prepared to make a certain intellectual effort" (*Author's Preface*).

282 (031)
Enciclopedia cattolica. Vatican City, Ente per l'Enciclopedia Cattolica e per il Libro Cattolico, 1948-54. 12v. illus.

Deals with all matters pertaining to the Roman Catholic Church, historical and contemporary. Well-produced; of major importance. Articles, which are signed, are mainly by Italian scholars, and the adequate bibliographies include periodical articles. Each volume contains some 2,000 pages, and there are photogravure plates as well as illustrations in the text. The work is self-indexing, but v. 12 includes an "Indice sistematico" that classifies the articles under 42 main headings, with sub-divisions.

282 (031)
Enciclopedia ecclesiastica, pubblicata sotto la direzione dell'Eccellenza Mons. Adriano Bernareggi. Milan, Villardi; Turin, Marietti, 1942-. v. 1-. illus.

v. 1-7: A-PAM. 1942-63.
An encyclopaedia of religion, with a decided Roman Catholic slant. Particularly rich in biographies of Italian clerics. Articles are not signed, although 96 contributors are listed in v. 4. The article on Gregory VII has 4 columns of text and 1¼ cols. of bibliography; that on the Virgin Mary (v. 5, p. 333-401) is divided in to 12 sections, each with bibliographies. Plates, including some in colour. Poorly produced,—binding, paper, typography and illustrations. Delayed appearance of v. 7 (v. 6. 1955).

282 (031)
New Catholic encyclopedia: an international work of reference on the teachings, history, organization and activities of the Catholic Church, and on all institutions, religions, philosophies, and scientific and cultural developments affecting the Catholic Church from its beginning to the present. Prepared by the editorial staff at the Catholic University of America. New York, McGraw-Hill, 1967. 15v. illus., maps. $450; £220.

"Not a revision of *The Catholic encyclopedia* (1907-14), but a completely new work, abreast of the present state of knowledge and reflecting the outlook and interests of the second half of the 20th century" (*Preface*). 15,350 pages; *c.* 17,000 articles by some 4,800 contributors; 7,400 illustrations (32 col. pl.) and 300 maps. V. 15, the index, has *c.* 300,000 entries (including entries for maps and illustrations). All articles are signed and carry select bibliographies, some briefly annotated. The article on St. Anselm of Canterbury (5¼ cols.) has 2 illustrations and 15 lines of bibliography; that on the Bible runs to 140p. Wide coverage (*e.g.,* 'Psychiatry': 13 cols.; 'Zionism': 3 cols.; 'Hungarian art': 30p.). Some unusual articles (*e.g.,* 'Translation literature, Greek and Arabic'). No biographies of living persons, although the text goes up to the close of Vatican Council II (article, v. 14, p. 563-72, with bibliography of ¾ col.). Especially valuable on scholastic philosophy and theological writers. Excellently produced and illustrated. A major special encyclopaedia. Praised in *Times literary supplement* (no. 3, 422, 28th September 1967, p. 899) for its open attitude, and for the importance given to Biblical and patristic evidence.

The Catholic encyclopedia (New York, Encyclopedia Press, [1907-22]; Gilmary Society, 1950-59. 18v.), to which *New Catholic encyclopedia* is the successor, is still of value to the student of the Middle Ages as well as Catholic doctrine and history.

282 (031)
VACANT, A., and **MANGENOT, E. Dictionnaire de théologie catholique,** contenant l'exposé des doctrines de la théologie catholique, leurs preuves et leur histoire. Commencé sous la direction de A. Vacant et E. Mangenot; continué sous celle de É. Amann. Paris, Letouzey, 1909-.

v. 1-15. 1909-50; *Tables générales,* par B. Loth et A. Michel, 1951-.
Part of the *Encyclopédie des sciences ecclésiastiques.* Lengthy, signed articles, with good bibliographies; fuller treatment than in the *Catholic encyclopedia.*
The *Tables générales* (fasc. 1-12 (1951-65): A-MAGIE) function as commentary, supplement and analytical index to the main work.

Another major contribution in this field is: *Catholicisme: hier, aujourd'hui, demain. Encyclopédie.* Dirigée par G. Jacquemet (Paris, Letouzey, 1948-), to be completed in 7v. (fasc. 1-24 (1948-64): A-JÉSUS). Treatment is briefer than in the *Catholic encyclopedia* and the *Dictionnaire de théologie catholique,* but the bibliographies are up-to-date.

282 (032)

ADDIS, W. E., and **ARNOLD, T. A Catholic dictionary**: containing some account of the doctrine, discipline, rites, ceremonies, councils and religious orders of the Catholic Church. Revised by T. B. Scannell; further revised, with additions, by P. E. Hallett. 15th ed. London, Routledge & Kegan Paul, 1951. viii, 843p. (17th ed. 1960. viii, 860p. 50s.).

First published 1886.

A standard work, valuable for its articles on doctrine, history and orders. Articles are unsigned and biographies are excluded, but there are detailed references to material and many cross-references. A list of works frequently cited, etc., appears on p. vii-viii.

The *"Catholic encyclopedia" dictionary* (New York, Gilmary Society, 1941, 1095p. illus.) includes biography. Sub-title: "containing 8,500 articles on the beliefs, devotions, rites, symbolism, tradition and history of the church; her laws, organizations, dioceses, missions, institutions, religious orders, saints; her part in promoting art, science, education and social welfare".

282 (058)

Annuaire pontifical catholique. 1898-. Paris, Maison de la Bonne Presse, 1897-. v. 1-.

Contains a list of popes in alphabetical and chronological order, with data on the present pope, and a list of pontifical documents, discourses and allocutions, etc.

Orbis catholicus; edited by Donald Attwater (London, Burns, Oates, 1938-) is described as a first draft of an equivalent in English of the *Annuario pontifico* and the *Annuaire pontifical catholique*.

Chronological lists of dignitaries (popes, archbishops and cardinals) of the Roman Catholic Church appear in P. B. Gams' *Series episcoporum Ecclesiae Catholicae, quotquot innotuerunt a beato Petro Apostolo* (Ratisbon, Manz, 1873. xxiv, 963p.) and its supplement, covering 1870-85 (Ratisbon, Manz, 1886. iv, 148p.). Part of the ground (1198-1799) is re-covered by Conrad Eubel's *Hierarchia catholica medii et recentioris ævi* (2nd ed. Monasterii, Regensberg, 1913-58. 6v.), based on Vatican archives.

282 (082.2)

CHAPIN, J., ed. **The book of Catholic quotations**; compiled from approved sources, ancient, medieval and modern. London, Calder, 1957. xi, 1073, [1]p. 50s.

More than 10,400 quotations, arranged alphabetically by subject. Quotations, p. 1-932; detailed analytical index of subjects, p. 933-1056; index of sources, p. 1057-73; corrigenda appended.

282 (092)

The Catholic who's who, 1908-. London, Burns, Oates, 1908-. Irregular. (latest v.: 1952).

Until 1935, the title was *The Catholic who's who and year book*. The 1952 v., edited by Sir H. J. Hood, was the first to be issued since 1941.

About 5,000 biographies, listing writers' works. List of abbreviations, p. xiii-xxv; cross-reference list of archbishops, bishops, abbots and priors (under sees and A-Z); necrology.

Who is who in the Catholic world. v. 1. *Europe: a biographical dictionary, containing about 5,500 biographies of prominent personalities in the Catholic world*; edited by S. S. Taylor and L. Melsheimer (Düsseldorf, 1967) has an appended account of the hierarchial organisation of the Catholic Church outside the Vatican and in European countries, with data on religious orders and the like.

282 (092)

DELANEY, J. J., and **TOBIN, J. E. Dictionary of Catholic biography.** Garden City, N.Y., Doubleday, 1961; London, Hale, 1962. xi, 1245p. $18.50; 105s.

Biographies of c. 13,000 leading Roman Catholics (churchmen and laymen), from the founding of the Church to the present day. Bibliographies appended; numerous cross-references. Appendices: the saints as patrons of vocations; the saints as patrons of places; symbols of the saints in art; 12-page chart correlating papal and secular reigns.

282 (410)(058.7)

The Catholic directory, . . . 1838-. London, Burns, Oates, 1838-. illus., maps. Annual. (1967. 12s. 6d.).

Directory information on the Roman Catholic hierarchy in Great Britain and Ireland and on the dioceses of England, Scotland and Wales. Lists the church dignitaries (cardinals, archbishops, bishops) of the British Commonwealth and U.S.A.; the priests of Great Britain; religious orders in England and Wales. Also, hospitals, societies, religious orders. Index of places.

Supplemented, for the rest of the British Isles, by: *The Irish Catholic directory and almanac* (Dublin, Duffy. Annual), which includes census, parliamentary and postal information relating to both Eire and Northern Ireland; and *The Catholic directory for the clergy and laity in Scotland* (Glasgow, Burns. Annual).

282 (420)(092)

GILLOW, J. A literary and biographical history, or bibliographical dictionary, of the English Catholics, from the breach with Rome, in 1534, to the present time. London, Burns, Oates, [1885-1902]. Reprinted in New York, Franklin, 1961. 5v. $125.

"The object . . . is to present . . . a concise record of the literary efforts, educational struggles and the sufferings for religion's sake of the Catholics in England down to the present time." (*Preface*, v. 1). A good example of bio-bibliography. Following the biographical sketch are given brief references to biographical dictionaries, histories, etc. for further material and then a full, numbered list of works (c. 15,000 items).

Protestantism

283/284:016

COMMISSION INTERNATIONALE D'HIS-TOIRE ECCLÉSIASTIQUE COMPARÉE. Bibliographie de la Réforme, 1450-1648: ouvrages parus de 1940 à 1955. Leiden, Brill, 1958-. fasc. 1-.

fasc. 1: *Allemagne. Pays-Bas.* 1958. 2nd ed. 1961.
2: *Belgique. Suède. Norvège. Danemark. Ireland. États-Unis.* 1960.
3: *Italie. Espagne. Portugal.* 1961.
4: *France. Angleterre. Suisse.* 1963.
5: *Pologne. Hongrie. Tchécoslovaquie. Finlande.* 1965.

Sponsored by the International Commission of Ecclesiastical History, part of the International Committee of Historical Sciences. The section on Germany, by G. Franz, in fasc. 1, comprises 1,745 unannotated entries plus 4 indexes (1. Begriffe und Institutionen—2. Deutsche Länder und Städte—3. Ausland—4. Biographien); 38 journals are cited. The section on England, by Basil Hall and W. H. C. Frend, in fasc. 4 comprises 176 entries and no indexes.

283/284 (032)
WRIGHT, C. H. H., and NEIL, C., *ed.* **A Protestant dictionary,** containing articles on the history, doctrines, and practices of the Christian Church. New ed., edited by C. S. Carter and G. E. A. Weeks. London, Harrison Trust, 1933. xv, [1], 832p. illus.

First published 1904 (xvi, 832p.).

A controversial work, not professing to be complete as a historical or theological lexicon, but intended to provide a handy work of reference for Protestants on the divisions between the Roman and Reformed Churches, comparable to the *Catholic Dictionary* of Addis and Arnold (*see at 282 (032)*). Signed articles.

283/284 (091)
LÉONARD, É.-G. A history of Protestantism. Edited by H. H. Rowley. London, Nelson, 1966-.

v. 1: *The Reformation.* Translated by J. M H. Reid. 1966.
v. 2: *The Establishment.* Translated by R. M. Bethell. 1967. 126s.

To be published in 3v. The original, *Histoire générale du protestantisme* (Paris, Presses Universitaires de France, 1961-64) has as v. 3, *Déclin et renouveau* (xviiiə-xxə siècle). The author died in 1966.

V. 1 of the English translation covers the period from the origins of Protestantism up to 1564 (when Calvin died); v. 2, from the establishment of Protestantism to the end of the 17th century. Prof. Rowley has greatly improved the work in its translated form. Even so, the critical review of v. 1 in *The listener* (v. 76, no. 1950, 11th August 1966, p. 212-3) points out Léonard's marked dislike of Calvin and the sketchy coverage of the medieval background of the Reformation and of English institutions and thought. The impressive bibliography (not always up-to-date) occupies one-third of the volume.

V. 2 is adversely criticised in the *Times literary supplement* (v. 3,423, 5th October 1967, p. 943).

Church of Scotland

283 (411)(092)
SCOTT, H. Fasti Ecclesiae Scoticanae: the succession of ministers in the Church of Scotland

from the Reformation. New ed., rev. and continued to the present time under the superintendence of a committee appointed by the General Assembly. Edinburgh, Oliver & Boyd, 1915-. v. 1-.

First published 1866.
v. 1. *Synod of Lothian and Tweeddale.* 1915.
2. *Synods of Merse and Teviotdale.* 1917.
3. *Synod of Glasgow and Ayr.* 1920.
4. *Synods of Argyll, and of Perth and Stirling.* 1923.
5. *Synods of Fife, and of Angus and Mearns.* 1925.
6. *Synods of Aberdeen and of Moray.* 1926.
7. *Synods of Ross, Sutherland and Caithness, Glenelg, Orkney and Shetland, the Church in England, Ireland and overseas.* 1928.
8. *Ministers of the Church from . . . 1914-28 to . . . 1929, and addenda and corrigenda, 1560-1949.* 1950.
9. *Ministers of the Church from 1929-54.* 1961. 90s.

Records briefly lives, writings and families of ministers; volumes are arranged in Synods and Presbyteries according to the Roll of the General Assembly, with parishes alphabetically under Presbyteries. V. 1-7 each have a lengthy bibliography of local literature; index of parishes and ministers, but no cumulative index.

Church of Ireland

283 (415):026/027
TALLON, M. Church of Ireland diocesan libraries. Dublin, Library Association of Ireland, 1959. 30p. map. 3s.

A short account, with lists of the most important holdings. Also published in *Leabharlann,* v. 17, no. 1, March 1959, p. 17-27. Bibliography.

283 (415)(058.7)
The Irish Church directory and year-book. Dublin, Church of Ireland Printing and Publishing Co., 1862-. Annual. (1965. 17s. 6d.).

Chief contents: list of clergy; provinces and dioceses; alphabetical index of parishes; succession of bishops of the Church of Ireland.

283 (415)(091)
PHILLIPS, W. A., *ed.* **History of the Church of Ireland,** from the earliest times to the present day. London, Oxford Univ. Press, 1933-34. 3v. o.p.

v. 1: *The Celtic Church.*
v. 2: *The movement towards Rome, the medieval church and the Reformation.*
v. 3: *The modern Church.*

The standard history. Each volume carries about a dozen pages of bibliography. V. 3 has a list (p. 433-58) of the succession of bishops of the Church of Ireland.

283 (415)(092)
COTTON, H. Fasti ecclesiae Hibernicae: the succession of the prelates and members of the cathedral bodies of Ireland. Dublin, Parker, 1848-78. 5v. and Supplement.

v. 1 : *Munster.* 2nd ed., 1848.
v. 2 : *Leinster.* 1848.
v. 3 : *Ulster.* 1849.
v. 4 : *Connaught, and consecrations.* 1850.
v. 5 : *Illustrations, corrections and additions, with general indexes.* 1860.
Supplement, continuing the work until the end of 1870 (Disestablishment), 1878.

Although this work gives the succession only of bishops and cathedral dignitaries and has in part been superseded by J. B. Leslie's lists (see below), it remains a valuable and useful work.

The following are by, or edited by, J. B. Leslie: *Armagh clergy and parishes* (Dundalk, Tempest, 1911; *Supplement.* 1948); *Clogher clergy and parishes* (Enniskillen, Fermanagh Times, 1929); *Ossery clergy and parishes* (Enniskillen, Fermanagh Times, 1933); *Ferns clergy and parishes* (Dublin, Church of Ireland Printing & Publishing Co., 1936); *Derry clergy and parishes* (Enniskillen, Fermanagh Times, 1937); *Ardfert and Aghadoe clergy and parishes* (Enniskillen, Fermanagh Times, 1940); *Raphoe clergy and parishes* (Enniskillen, Fermanagh Times, 1940); Swanzy, H. B. *Succession lists of the diocese of Dromore;* edited by J. B. Leslie (Belfast, Caswell, 1933); Leslie, J. B., and Swanzy, H. B. *Biographical succession lists of the clergy of the diocese of Down* (Enniskillen, Fermanagh Times, 1936).

Church of England

283 (420):026/027
CHURCH OF ENGLAND. Central Council for the Care of Churches. **The parochial libraries of the Church of England:** report of a committee appointed to investigate the number and condition of parochial libraries belonging to the Church of England; ... with an historical introduction, notes on early printed books and their care, and an alphabetical list of parochial libraries, past and present. Edited by Neil Ker. London, Faith Press, in conjunction with the College of the Faith, 1959. 125p. illus. 42s.

Each entry in the list of libraries contains a brief description of contents with dates, etc. There is a list of medieval MSS. now belonging to parish churches, or now or formerly in the libraries included in the alphabetical list.

283 (420)(03)
OLLARD, S. L., *and others, ed.* **A dictionary of English Church history.** 3rd rev. ed. London & Oxford, Mowbrays, 1948. xx, 698p. o.p.

First published 1912.
A standard work of reference intended for the churchman and general reader; also useful for historians seeking succinct information outside their own special field. The scope is confined to the Provinces of Canterbury and York; certain articles have been brought up-to-date according to the results of recent research, and new articles and biographies have been added to this edition. Bibliographical references appended to most articles.

283 (420)(058.7)
The Church of England year book . . . : the official year book of the National Assembly of the Church of England, 1883-. London, Church Information Office & S.P.C.K., 1883-. Annual (1967. 45s.).

Diocesan lists; directory information on other Churches in the British Isles; Churches and Provinces overseas; list of organizations; statistics; who's who in the Church Assembly and some of its Boards, Councils, etc.; legal information; etc. Index.

283 (420)(058.7)
Crockford's Clerical directory . . . 1858-. London, Oxford Univ. Press, 1858-. illus. Annual (now biennial). (1967. £11 10s.).

First published 1858.
Sub-title of 1967 ed.: "a reference book of the clergy of the Provinces of Canterbury and York, and of other Anglican provinces and dioceses." An essential source of information on all matters relating to Anglican clergy; primarily concerned with those ordained in the British Isles. The who's who of bishops and clergy of the Church of England, Scottish, Episcopal, Irish and overseas churches contains about 25,000 brief biographies. Also includes obituaries, indexes of parishes, rural deaneries, cathedral establishments, etc., and a Church overseas section. Map section.
The preface provides a lively survey of events concerning the Church since the previous issue.

283 (420)(083)
CHURCH OF ENGLAND. Central Board of Finance. Statistical Unit. **Facts and figures about the Church of England.** Number 3. London, Church Information Office, 1965. 96p. tables, diagrs. 30s.

Attractively produced data. 89 tables and 27 diagrams, giving figures back to 1844 and up to 1962. Covers such matters as arrangement of parish, churches, livings, etc., statistics on clergy and membership, and parochial finance. Explanatory notes appended; analytical index.

283 (420)(091)
STEPHENS, W. R. W., and HUNT, W., *ed.* **A history of the English Church.** London, Macmillan. 1899-1910 (and reprints). 8v. in 9. maps.

The standard history, based on a careful study of original authorities, and the best ancient and modern writers, in moderate-sized volumes. Goes beyond purely ecclesiastical history (*e.g.,* v. 2, chapter 16: 'Popular religion, learning and art'). Each volume is by a specialist in the period covered, with its own analytical index, chronological tables and maps. A list of sources is appended to each chapter.

2 volumes have so far been published of *An ecclesiastical history of England* (London, Black, 1961-): v. 1. *The pre-Conquest Church,* by M. Deanesly (38s.) and v. 5. *The Victorian Church,* by O. Chadwick. pt. 1 (1966- 63s.). This latter volume has numerous footnote references, an extensive bibliography (p. 575-83) and an analytical index.

283 (420)(092)
LE NEVE, J. Fasti Ecclesiae Anglicanæ, 1300-1541. New and expanded ed. London, Univ. of London, Institute of Historical Research, Athlone Press, 1962-67. 12v.

CHRISTIAN CHURCH

1. *Lincoln diocese.* 1962. 25s.
2. *Hereford diocese.* 1962. 17s 6d.
3. *Salisbury diocese.* 1962. 25s.
4. *Monastic cathedrals (Southern Province).* 1963. 17s. 6d.
5. *St. Paul's, London.* 1963. 25s.
6. *Monastic cathedrals (Northern Province):* York, Carlisle, Durham. 1963. 35s.
7. *Chichester diocese.* 1964. 25s.
8. *Bath and Wells diocese.* 1964. 30s.
9. *Exeter diocese.* 1964. 30s.
10. *Coventry and Lichfield diocese.* 1964. 30s.
11. *The Welsh dioceses.* 1965. 35s.
12. *Introduction, errata and index.* 1967. 55s.

First published 1716; rev. ed. by T. D. Hardy (covering the period from the earliest times to *c.* 1850), 1854 (3v.).

Sub-title of 1st ed. begins: "a calendar of the principal ecclesiastical dignitaries of England and Wales". V. 3, *Salisbury diocese,* compiled by Joyce M. Horn (1962. x, 117p.) has a list of references (works in print; manuscript) preceding the calendar (bishops, deans, subdeans, archdeacons, precentors, chancellors, treasurers, prebendaries, with dates of collation, election and death, and sometimes fuller notes, *e.g.,* Prebendary Thomas Butiller: 21 lines); detailed indexes of persons and places.

This series is to be followed in due course by volumes on the period before 1300. Thus the 1854 ed. is unlikely to be completely superseded for some years.

Noted: W. Stubbs's *Registrum sacrum Anglicanum: an attempt to exhibit the course of episcopal succession in England from the records and chronicles of the Church.* 2nd ed., with an appendix of Indian, colonial and missionary consecrations, collected and arranged by E. E. Holmes (Oxford, Clarendon Press, 1897. xvi, 248p.).

283 (420)(093)
POWICKE, Sir F. M., and CHENEY, C. R., *ed.* Councils and Synods with other documents relating to the English Church. Oxford, Univ. Press, 1964-.

v. 2: *A.D. 1205-1313.* 2 pts. £15 15s.
Planned under the general editorship of F. W. Powicke, in continuation of A. W. Haddan and W. Stubbs' *Councils and ecclesiastical documents of Great Britain and Ireland* (Oxford, Clarendon Press, 1969-78. 3v.).
Pt. 1, covering A.D. 1205-1265, includes a list of printed books and articles cited p. xliii-li. Documents are reprinted in Latin, without translation but in each case with an introduction and profuse footnotes. Pt. 2 has an index of manuscripts and general analytical index (p. 1403-50).

Canon J. S. Purvis's *An introduction to ecclesiastical records* (London, St. Anthony's Press, [1953]. 96p.) deals fully with the records to be found in diocesan record offices,—archbishops' and bishops' registers; visitations; records of ecclesiastical courts, etc.

Church of Wales

283 (429)
WILLIAMS, G. The Welsh Church, from Con-

quest to Reformation. Cardiff, Univ. of Wales Press, 1962. xiv, 602p. 63s.

A scholarly survey, the author being Professor of History at the University College of Swansea. Fully documented in footnotes. Bibliography, p. 567-82.

Lutheran Church

284 (031)
BODENSIECK, J. H., *ed.* The encyclopedia of the Lutheran Church. Minneapolis, Minn., Augsburg Publishing House, 1965. 3v. illus. $37.50.

Published under the auspices of the Lutheran World Federation.
About 3,000 entries, contributed by 723 Lutheran scholars and specialists from 34 countries. Includes 1,000 biographical sketches and articles on places, etc., pertinent to Lutheranism. Bibliographies.

Free Churches

285/287 (410) (058.7)
Free Church directory. 1965-67 ed., edited by John McNicol. Modern, Surrey, Crown House, 1965. 35s.

Lists more than 20,000 ministers, with addresses and telephone numbers. Sections: Methodist Church—Baptist—Congregational—Presbyterian —Church of England—United Free Church of Scotland—Others (including Christian Brethren, Church of Christ and Salvation Army)—Free Church statistics — Book reviews (p. 317-23). Valuable on recently developed Evangelical sects, as well as the older established faiths, but has no biographical data as in *Who's who in the Free Churches.* It excludes Society of Friends and Unitarians.

285/287 (410) (092)
Who's who in the Free Churches (and other denominations). Editor, L. G. Pine. London, Shaw 1951. xxxv. 500p.

Section two gives a series of biographical entries under each of 22 Nonconformist denominations, beginning with the Baptist Union and ending with the Salvation Army. Other sections give directory information on organizations, societies, missions, schools and colleges. The general index is to sections only.
Dated; for more recent information the yearbooks, etc. of the respective denominations should be referred to.

285/287 (420) (093)
POWELL, W. R. "The sources for the history of Protestant Nonconformist churches in England". In *Bulletin of the Institute of Historical Research,* v. 25, no. 92. 1925.

Locations of the principal surviving records of this kind are given in the British Records Association's *Archives of religious and ecclesiastical bodies and organisations other than the Church of England* (London, the Association, 1936. Reprints from Committees, no. 3).

Presbyterian Churches

285.1 / .6 (411) (058.7)
The Church of Scotland year-book, 1884-. Edinburgh, Clark (now, Edinburgh, etc., Church of Scotland, Department of Publicity and Publication), 1884-. Annual. (1967: 82nd year of issue). 10s.

Directory information on synods, presbyteries and parishes; alphabetical list of ministers, probationers and lay missionaries; index of places.

285.1 / .6 (411) (092)
LAMB, J. A., ed. **The Fasti of the United Free Church of Scotland, 1900-1929.** Edinburgh & London, Oliver & Boyd, 1956. xi, 639p. 84s.

Biographical data, with index of congregations and index of ministers.

Preceded by: (a) Small, R. History of the congregations of the United Presbyterian Church, 1733-1900 (Edinburgh, Small, 1904. 2v.), which includes biographical notices of ministers, and (b) Ewing, W., ed. Annals of the Free Church of Scotland, 1843-1900 (Edinburgh, Clark, 1914. 2v.), v. 1 of which includes bibliographies.

The Handbook of the United Free Church of Scotland, 1964-65 (Glasgow, Offices of the Church. [1965]. 66p. 3s.) gives details of Presbyteries and more than a hundred individual churches.

285.1 / .6 (415) (092)
McCONNELL, J., and McCONNELL, S. G. Fasti of the Irish Presbyterian Church, 1613-1840. Belfast, Presbyterian Historical Society, 1936-59.

Issued in 16 fascicles, the Fasti are divided into seven periods (1613-41, 1642-61, 1661-90, 1690-1720, 1721-77, 1778-1820, 1820-40), each with its own alphabetical arrangement of names. No consolidated index has so far been issued.
Of considerable value for genealogical research.

The formal history is covered by: Reid, J. S. History of the Presbyterian Church in Ireland (new ed., with additional notes by W. D. Killen. Belfast, Mullan, 867. 3v.), first published in 1833.

Of special value for Irish-American genealogical research is: Stewart, D., ed. Fasti of the American Presbyterian Church; treating of ministers of Irish origin who laboured in America during the eighteenth century (Belfast, Bell & Logan, 1943. 26p. and suppt. (4p.)).

285.1 / .6 (420) (058.7)
The Official handbook of the Presbyterian Church of England, 1887/88-. London, Publishing Office of the Presbyterian Church, 1887-. (1966/67. 10s.).

Directory information on the offices and officers of the Presbyterian Church of England, the General Assembly, the Presbytery of England, the Presbyterian Church of Wales, the World Presbyterian Alliance, Presbyterian Churches overseas and the presbyteries in England (Berwick to Yorkshire). List of ministers; index to churches.

Congregationalism

285.8:016
DEXTER, H. M. The Congregationalism of the last 300 years, as seen in its literature. New York, Harper, 1880. xl, 716, 326p.

Consists of twelve lectures, with a bibliographical appendix (326p.): "Collections toward a bibliography of Congregationalism".

285.8 (42)(058.7)
The Congregational year-book, 1846-. London, Congregational Union of England and Wales (now Independent Press). (1966/67. 1967. 45s.).

Directory information on the Congregational Union of England and Wales, its Council, committees, boards, societies; alphabetical list of ministers and others obituary notices. Includes the proceedings of the Congregational Union.

For Scotland,—Congregational Union of Scotland year book (Glasgow, the Union. 1966-67 ed., published 1966. 3s.).

Baptists

286:016
STARR, E. C. A Baptist bibliography; being a register of printed material by and about Baptists; including works written against the Baptists. Philadelphia, Judson Press; subsequently Rochester, N.Y., American Baptist Historical Society, 1947-. v. 1-. ea. $2.50-$7.

v. 1-12 (1947-67): A-J.
Arranged A-Z by authors; gives library locations in U.S.A. Nearly 4,000 entries per volume. Index of Baptist publishers, distinctive titles and subjects appended to each volume.

286:016
WHITLEY, W. T. Baptist bibliography; being a register of the chief materials for Baptist history, whether in manuscript or in print, preserved in Great Britain, Ireland and the Colonies . . .; compiled for the Baptist Union of Great Britain and Ireland. London, Kingsgate Press, 1916-22. 2v. o.p.

v. 1 (1916): 1526-1776; v. 2 (1922): 1777-1837, and addenda for 1613-53. Chronological arrangement, with indexes of anonymous pamphlets, authors, places and subjects. Locations are given in 30 libraries in England and Wales, and one library in U.S.A.

286 (058.7)
The Baptist handbook, 1860-. London, Baptist Union (now Baptist Church House). 1860-. illus. Annual. (1967. 17s. 6d.).

Imprint varies.
Directory information on the Baptist Union of Great Britain and Ireland, with a list of associations and churches, theological colleges, etc.; statistical information for the British Isles and for the rest of the world; list of accredited Baptist ministers; obituaries.

There are also: The Scottish Baptist year-book (Glasgow, Baptist Union Office. Annual since 1903. 1967: 7s. 6d.); and Handbook of the

National Federation of Strict and Peculiar Baptist Churches (1949; Supplement, 1953).

Methodists

287 (058.7)

The Minutes of the Annual Conference of the Methodist Church held in . . . London, Methodist Publishing House. Annual. (1966. 20s.).

First issued 1744; title varies.
The official year-book, with membership statistics, names and addresses of ministers, probationers and lay members of committees, obituaries, a list of circuits and a report on the overseas missions of the Methodist Church in Britain.

There is also: *Ministers and probationers of the Methodist Church . . . , with their appointments in chronological and alphabetical order; . . . together with an alphabetical list of deceased ministers.* (London, Methodist Publishing House, 1847-. 1964 ed. 25s.)

287 (091)

DAVIES, R., and RUPP, G., *ed.* **A history of the Methodist Church in Great Britain.** London, Epworth Press, 1965-. v. 1-. (v. 1. 63s.).

To be in 3v., plus a volume of documents and primary sources.
V. 1, dealing with the 18th century, is the work of 9 contributors (*e.g.*, "England in the eighteenth century", by Herbert Butterfield). Bibliography of primary and secondary sources (p. 317-9).

Indexes of subjects (non-analytical), names and places.

Unitarianism

288 (058.7)

The Unitarian and Free Christian Churches. Year-book of the General Assembly, 1890-. London, Lindsey Press, 1890-. (1966. 6s.).

10 sections. 1. The General Assembly . . . 3. List of congregations and ministers . . . 8. Ministerial and other societies and activities.

Society of Friends

289.6:016

SMITH, J. A descriptive catalogue of Friends' books, or books written by members of the Society of Friends. . . . London, J. Smith, 1867. 2v. and Supplement (London, Hicks, 1893).

An author catalogue, covering broadsheets as well as books. The heading "Periodical publications" is followed by a list of contents of issues of various periodicals. Editions and reprints are recorded. Analytical notes are provided as necessary, as well as very brief biographical data (place of birth or residence; time and place of death).

A Guide to Quaker literature, prepared by the Friends Literature Committee (London, Bannisdale Press, [1952]. 24p. 9d.) is an annotated list, systematically arranged. Essential titles that are out of print are asterisked.

29 NON-CHRISTIAN RELIGIONS

Bibliographies

29:016

ADAMS, C. J., *ed.* **A reader's guide to the great religions.** New York, The Free Press; London, Collier-Macmillan, 1965. xx, [1], 364p. $6.95; 75s.

Eight bibliographical essays by specialists of professorial rank in U.S. or Canadian universities. 1. Primitive religion—2. The religions of China (excepting Buddhism)—3. Hinduism—4. Buddhism—5. The religions of Japan—6. Judaism—7. Christianity—8. Islam. Each essay provides a sectionalised survey of the literature with running commentary, often evaluative; some have appendices listing reference works (with comments) and relevant periodicals. Works in English predominate, although many European languages are included. Index of authors, editors, translators and compilers; index of subjects. Well produced and scholarly. Reviewed in *The booklist,* v. 62, no. 5, 1st November 1965, p. 238.

29:016

DIEHL, K. S. Religions, mythologies, folklores: an annotated bibliography. 2nd ed. New York, The Scarecrow Press, Inc., 1962. 573p. $12.50.

First published 1956 (315p.).
"It includes books of general and specific reference, literatures, literary and historical

guides, various scriptures and their commentaries, records of institutional accomplishment, and biographies of men and women . . . " (*Preface,* 2nd ed.).
2,388 numbered items (as against 1,240 in the 1956 ed.), with concise annotations, in 6 chapters: 1, Universal religious knowledge (items 1-247)—2. Fine arts (248-493)—3. Folklore (494-721)—4. Religions exclusive of Judaism and Christianity (722-1168)—5. The Judaeo-Christian tradition (1169-2259)—6. Periodicals (2260-2388). Annotations state if items carry bibliographies, footnotes or indexes; sometimes introduction or preface is quoted, and sometimes there is contents-listing. Index of authors and titles (p. 467-573). Very wide-ranging coverage, including magic, crystal gazing and church music. A valuable bibliography, despite some surprising omissions. The absence of a subject index, in view of the many topics covered, is a serious one. As a piece of book production does not compare with Adams.

29:016

Religious and theological abstracts. Youngstown, Ohio, Religious and Theological Abstracts, Inc., 1958-. v. 1-. Quarterly. $7 p.a.

Abstracts articles in *c.* 60 Christian, Jewish and Muslim journals, giving "fairly complete coverage to the periodical literature in all theological disciplines, though not done as extensively as we could wish" (*Library trends,* v. 15, no. 3, June

1967, p. 470). One year's time-lag. Annual author, subject and Biblical indexes.

29 (02)
ZAEHNER, R. C., *ed*. The concise encyclopædia of living faiths. London, Hutchinson, 1959 (reprinted 1964). 431p. illus. (pl.). (New horizon books). 63*s*.

"Attempts to describe in a brief compass those faiths which have withstood the test of time and which must, therefore, correspond to some fundamental need in man" (*Introduction*). Chapters on Judaism, Christianity in its diverse forms (5 chapters), Islam, Zoroastrianism, Hinduism, Jainism, Buddhism (3 chapters), Shintó, Confucianism and Taoism, each by an appropriate authority. A final chapter entitled 'A new Buddha and a new Tao' deals with Jungian Psychology and Marxism. A list of items 'for further reading', followed by acknowledgements, p. 418-23. Non-analytical index. Suitable for the general reader and the public library.

B. Y. Landis's *World religions: a brief guide to the principal beliefs and teachings of the religions of the world and to the statistics of organized religion* (New rev. ed. New York, Dutton, 1965. 127p. 95*cs.*; $2.95), first published 1957, is arranged A-Z. The statistics need to be used with caution since some have not been updated since the 1st ed.

Comparative Religion

291 (021)
FRAZER, *Sir* J. G. The golden bough: a study in magic and religion. 3rd ed., rev. and enl. London, Macmillan, 1911-15. 12v. ea. 50*s*; £30.

1st ed. 1890; 2nd ed. 1900.
v. 1: *The magic art and the evolution of kings.* 1911. 2v.
v. 2: *Taboo and the perils of the soul.* 1911.
v. 3: *The dying God.* 1911.
v. 4: *Adonis, Attis, Osiris.* 1914. 2v.
v. 5: *Spirits of the corn and of the wild.* 1912. 2v.
v. 6: *The scapegoat.* 1913.
v. 7: *Balder the beautiful. The fire-festivals of Europe and the doctrine of the external soul.* 1913. 2v.
v. 8: *Bibliography and general index.* 1915.

——. **Aftermath:** a supplement to the "Golden Bough". London, Macmillan, 1936. xx, 494p.

A monumental contribution on primitive beliefs and customs, and their place in the comparative history of religion. The general index provides an adequate key to the many examples and analogies. Much of what is called "primitive religion" is classified as magic by Frazer, and his views have accordingly been attacked as unscientific.

An abridged edition of the *Golden Bough* was published in 1957 (London, Macmillan. 2v.).

291 (031)
KLAUSER, T., *ed*. Reallexikon für Antike und Christentum. Sachwörterbuch zur Auseinandersetzung des Christentums mit der antiken Welt. Leipzig (subsequently Stuttgart), Hiersemann, 1950-. v. 1-. illus.

v. 1-6 (fasc. 1-48; 1950-66): A—EXITUS. £110.
An encyclopaedia of the classical world and its relationship to early Christianity. Scholarly, signed articles, sometimes lengthy, with bibliographies (*e.g.*, Constantine the Great is the subject of a monograph (v. 3, p. 306-79), sectionalised A-G, with sub-divisions nearly two columns of bibliography, apart from references in the text). Occasional line-drawings.

291.37 (03)
CIRLOT, J. C. A dictionary of symbols. Translated from the Spanish by Jack Sage. London, Routledge & Kegan Paul, 1962. liv, 400p. illus. (32 pl.). 50*s*.

An A-Z sequence of descriptive entries, sometimes fairly lengthy (*e.g.*, 'Zodiac': 3½p.). References from text to the black-and-white plates; author references only to the two appended bibliographies ('Bibliography of principal items', p. 367-8; 'Additional sources', p. 369-77). Non-analytical index.

The lost language of symbolism, by H. Bayley (London, Williams & Norgate, 1912 (reprinted 1951). 2v. illus.) is particularly helpful for its 1,418 line-drawings in the text.

291.8
FINEGAN, J. The archeology of world religions: the background of primitivism, Zoroastrianism, Hinduism, Jainism, Buddhism, Confucianism, Taoism, Shinto, Islam and Sikhism. Princeton, N.J., Princeton Univ. Press, 1952 (reprinted Princeton Univ. Press; Oxford Univ. Press, 1966. 3v. 60*s*.). xi, 599p. illus., maps.

The study being primarily archaeological, attention is focused upon the ancient monuments and documents of the various religions. Thus chiefly concerned with the early history of the religions rather than with their recent and contemporary aspects. Bibliographical footnotes; 260 plates; 9 maps.

Mythology

292/293 (021)
GRAY, L. H., *ed*. Mythology of all races. Boston, Archaeological Institute of America, Marshall Jones Co., 1916-32. 13v. illus. (Reprinted New York, Cooper Square Publishers, 1964. $150).

v. 1: *Greek and Roman*, by W. S. Fox, 1916.
v. 2: *Eddic*, by J. A. MacCulloch. 1930.
v. 3: *Celtic*, by J. A. MacCulloch; *Slavic*, by J. Machal. 1918.
v. 4: *Finno-Ugric. Siberian*, by U. Holmberg. 1927.
v. 5: *Semitic*, by S. H. Langdon. 1931.
v. 6: *Indian*, by A. B. Keith; *Iranian*, by A. J. Carnoy. 1917.
v. 7: *Armenian*, by M. H. Ananikian; *African*, by A. Werner. 1925.
v. 8: *Chinese*, by J. C. Ferguson; *Japanese*, by M. Anesaki. 1928.
v. 9: *Oceanic*, by R. B. Dixon. 1916.
v. 10: *North American*, by H. B. Alexander. 1916.
v. 11: *Latin American*, by H. B. Alexander. 1920.

v. 12: *Egyptian,* by W. M. Müller; *Indo-Chinese,* by J. G. Scott. 1918.

v. 13: Complete index to v. 1-12. 1932.

"Much of the material here given appears for the first time in the English language on Slavic and Finno-Ugric, Oceanic, Armenian and African [mythology]. No survey of American mythology as a whole has hitherto been written. Even where—as in Indian, Teutonic and Semitic —English monographs exist, new points of view are represented" (*Editor's Preface,* v. 1).

Each volume of this comprehensive work carries some 20 to 50 plates, in addition to figures in the text; also, some 20 pages of bibliography. The detailed index (v. 13; under subjects (*e.g.* floods, eclipses) and mythological personages) runs to 477 pages.

292/293 (021)

GRIMAL, P., *ed.* **Larousse world mythology.** Translated by Patricia Beardsworth. New York, Putnam, 1965; London, Hamlyn, 1966. 560p. illus., col. pl. $25; 100s.

Originally as *Mythologies* (Paris, Larousse, 1963).

23 specialist contributions (Prehistory—Egypt — Sumer — Babylon — The Hittites — Greece — Rome—Persia—India. The Celts—Germans—Slavs — Ugric - Finns — China — Japan — North America—Central America—South America—Oceania—Africa—Siberia), ranging from prehistoric times to the present day. Profusely illustrated (40 pages of colour plates; 600 black-and-white illus.). Bibliography of suggested readings (p. 546-7); index. Lacks maps.

292/293 (021)

GUIRAND, F., *ed.* **Larousse encyclopedia of mythology.** Translated by Richard Aldington and Delano Ames, and revised by a panel of editorial advisors. London, Batchworth Press, 1959. xii, 500p. illus. (incl. 8 col. pl.). maps. (Reprinted Hamlyn, 1963. 25s.; 84s.).

First published as *Larousse mythologie générale* (1935).

17 long articles or essays by specialists, covering prehistoric, Egyptian, Assyro-Babylonian, Phoenician, Greek, Roman, Celtic, Teutonic, Slavonic, Finno-Ugric, Ancient Persian, Indian, Chinese, Japanese, American, Oceanian and Black African mythology. In his introduction, Robert Graves declares that the work is not an encyclopaedia, but a story book. Reviewers (e.g., *Library journal,* 1st April 1960, p. 1477-8) have found it lacking in scholarship, while admitting the excellence of the illustrations. Appended is 'A selected list for further reading' (p. 493-4). Index of names, covering both text and illustrations. 1,000 illustrations, whose excellence compensates a little for other faults.

292/293 (031)

HAUSSIG, H. W., *ed.* **Wörterbuch der Mythologie.** Stuttgart, Klett, 1961-. Lfg. 1-. tables, maps.

Section 1: Die alten Kulturvölker, v. 1: *Götter und Mythen im Vorderen Orient.* 1965. x, 601p. Other volumes in Section 1 (not sold separately) to follow: 2. Das alte Europa—3. Die Iranischen Völker—4. Zentral-und Ostasien—5. Altamerika.

V. 1, the work of 6 contributors, is divided by countries or areas, each with an introduction and short bibliography preceding an A-Z sequence of entries. Entries have references to the literature. Profuse cross-references; semi-analytical index, p. 569-601. Sections: Mesopotamie—Kleinasien—Syrien—Ägypten—Die Stammesgruppen Nord- und Zentralarabiens in vorislamischer Zeit.

292/293 (032)

CUROTTO, E. Dizionario della mitologia universale, con tavole fuori testo, fonti e bibliografia. Turin, Società Editrice Internazionale, 1958. vii, 488, [3]p. illus.

Ten sections: Mondo classico—Asia orientale and centrale—Asia occidentale—Islam—Egitto e Africa—Etruschi—Celti, Germani, Slavi e Scandinavi—America precolombiana—Primitivi. About 18,000 very brief entries, averaging some 12 words. Sources are cited as footnotes. The bibliography (p. 474-88) is international in scope. Good illustrations.

Classical Mythology
(See also 937/938.)

292 (031)

ROSCHER, W. H. Ausführliches Lexikon der griechischen und römischen Mythologie. Leipzig & Berlin, Teubner, 1884-1937. 6v.; 4 suppt. v. illus.

v. 1-6: A-Z; Nachträge.

Supplementary v.: *Epitheta deorum.* 1893, 1902. 2v.; *Mythische Kosmographie der Griechen.* 1904. *Geschichte der klassischen Mythologie und Religionsgeschichte.* 1921.

A scholarly work, for the large library. Signed articles, with extensive references to sources as well as to secondary material. Many illustrations.

292 (032)

GRIMAL, P. Dictionnaire de la mythologie grecque et romaine. Paris, Presses Universitaires de France, 1951 (reprinted 1958). xxxi, 579p.

Greek or Latin names are given within brackets following the French entry-word. Footnotes give the references to sources. 40 genealogical tables; index of proper names and index of subjects in mythology (*e.g.,* "Enfants, dévorés"; "Colombes, transfiguration en").

A. R. A. van Aken's *The encyclopedia of classical mythology,* translated from the Dutch [*Elseviers Mythologische encyclopedie.* 1961], by D. R. Welsh (Englewood Cliffs, N.J., Prentice-Hall, 1965. 155p. illus. $2.45; $5) is a compact factual guide, with entry under Latin form of name. Line drawings. Considered (*Library journal,* v. 90, no. 7, 1st January 1965, p. 1107) particularly useful to art students.

292 (032)

HUNGER, H. Lexikon der griechischen und römischen Mythologie, mit Hinweisen auf das Fortwirken antiker Stoffe und Motive in der bildenden Kunst, Literatur und Musik des Abendlandes bis zur Gegenwart. 5. Aufl. Vienna, Hollinek, 1959. xii, 387p. illus. (3 pl.).

4th ed. 1953 (xii, 387p.).

An A-Z sequence, with profuse cross-references. Entries carry references to sources. Particularly valuable for detailing use of myths and mythical personages as motifs in plastic and graphic arts, drama, poetry, novels, music, operas, as well as for bibliographies of material on the subject (*e.g.*, in the 4th ed. the article on Hercules extends to 6 pages of text and 3½ pages of 'documentation', including 2 pages of literature on Hercules). General bibliographies, p. 381-7.

292.1 (022)

ROSE, H. J. A handbook of Greek mythology, including its extension to Rome. 6th ed. London, Methuen, 1958 (and reprints). ix, 363p. 18*s.*; 36*s.*

First published 1928 (ix, 363p.).
A standard, scholarly manual by the then Professor of Greek in the United College of St. Salvator and St. Leonard, St. Andrews. Chapter footnotes and bibliographical references (*e.g.*, chapter 9, 'The legends of Greek lands', has 82 references); bibliography, p. 335-9. Index of mythological names; index of real names. Alterations to the text since 1928 appear to be minor.

Teutonic, etc. Mythology

293/299

SYKES, E., *comp.* **Everyman's Dictionary of non-classical mythology.** New [3rd] ed. London, Dent, 1961. 288p. illus. (Everyman's Reference library). 20*s.*

Previous ed., 1952.
Comprises *c.* 2,000 short articles, with cross-references and a brief general bibliography. Covers Chinese, Japanese and American mythology, as well as Scandinavian, Teutonic and Near Eastern, but omits *One thousand and one nights* as a source. The 1961 ed. adds 30 articles as an appendix. 16 pages of illustrations.

293 (=3)

GRIMM, J. Teutonic mythology. English translation from the 4th ed. [of *Deutsche Mythologie*] by J. S. Stallybrass. London, Bell, 1882-3. 4v.

A storehouse of facts relating to Teutonic mythology, from Iceland to the Danube. Very considerable attention is paid to philological detail, and comparisons are drawn with classical myths and the cycle of Slavic, Lettic and other traditions.

293 (51)

WERNER, E. T. C. Dictionary of Chinese mythology. Shanghai, Kelly, 1932. xvii, [i], 627p. (Reprinted New York, Julian Press, 1961. $12.50).

"A who's who of the Chinese other world, compiled from the Chinese and foreign works named in the Bibliography (p. 625-27) from personal observations in Chinese temples, houses and streets, and conversations with Chinese scholars, priests and peasants" (*Preface*). Gives Chinese equivalents (accordingly to Diehl, K. S. *Religions, mythologies, folklores* (2nd ed., 1962), entry no. 998).

Eastern Religions

294/299:016

JAMES, E. O. The comparative study of religions of the East (excluding Christianity and Judaism). Cambridge, Univ. Press, for the National Book League, 1959. 32p. (Reader's guides. Third series, 5). 3*s.*

A selective, annotated bibliography of about 150 priced items; compiled for the educated intelligent reader rather than the specialist. Indications of further reading on more technical lines are given when necessary. Has an introduction on the history of the study of religions. Appended sections 'For reference' and 'Forthcoming titles'; index of authors and editors. The author is Emeritus Professor of the History of Religion in London University.

294/299.8

The Sacred books of the East. Translated by various Oriental books of the East and edited by F. Max Müller. Oxford, Clarendon Press. 1879-1910 (reprinted 1962-66). 50v. £100.

A major collection of translated Eastern religious literature, including the Upanishads, Sacred Laws of the Aryas, Texts of Confucianism, Zend-Avesta, Pahlavi Texts, Qur'an and Institutes of Vishnu. V. 50 is the General index to the series, by M. Winternitz (*q.v.*).

Another important collection is the *Harvard Oriental series,* edited by C. R. Lanman, and others (Cambridge, Harvard Univ. Press, 1891-1950. 44v.).

294/299.8

WINTERNITZ, M., *comp.* **A concise dictionary of Eastern religion;** being the index volume to "The sacred books of the East". Oxford, Clarendon Press, 1910 (reprinted 1925). xvi, 683p.

Forms v. 50 of *The sacred books of the East.* A remarkably detailed analytical index (*e.g.*, 'Prayers': 15 columns, set solid). Many cross-references. It is designed on the basis of a "scientific classification of religious phenomena".

Indian Religions

294:016

TOTOK, W., and **SCHRÖER, H.** "Die Philosophie der Inder". In their *Handbuch der Geschichte der Philosophie.* v. 1 (1964), p. 13-50.

About 1,000 references in 7 sections (Die Veden—Die Brähmanatexte—Die älteren Upanishaden—Die Systeme der Brahmanen—Jaina—Der Materialismus der Cārvākas—Der Buddhismus).

294 (038)

A Glossary of philosophical terms. Madras, Tirumalai-Tirupati Devasthanams Press, 1941. 88p. (Sri Venkatesvara Oriental Series, no. 3).

A Sanskrit-English glossary, embracing all systems of Indian philosophy.

294 (093.3)

FARQUHAR, J. N. An outline of the religious literature of India. London, Oxford Univ. Press, 1920. xxviii, 451, [1]p.

A survey of the religious history of India as an individual whole, a long process of development. Attention is restricted to the literature as the chief source of knowledge of the religions. The extensive bibliography covers the important religious works, their translations into European languages, and pertinent modern critical works published in book form and as articles in journals. Old, but "remains an indispensable guide to authors and documents and can be used still as a provisional encyclopedia of Hinduism" (*A reader's guide to living faiths*, p. 47).

294.1
DASGUPTA, S. A history of Indian philosophy. Cambridge, Univ. Press, 1922-55. 5v. £19 8s.

Mainly intended as an exposition of Indian thought, strictly on the basis of the original texts and commentaries. Often the ground covered has been wholly new and the materials have been obtained by a direct and first-hand study of all available texts and manuscripts. No attempt has been made to draw any comparison or contrasts with Western philosophy (*Preface* to v. 2). Each volume has footnotes and an analytical index.

294.11:016
RENOU, L. Bibliographie védique. Paris, Adrien-Maisonneuve, 1931. v, 339p.

6,750 items. Has as its sequel *Vedic bibliography*, by R. N. Dandekar (v. 1. Bombay, xxiii, 760p. Rs. 30; 60s.). The three volumes provide excellent bibliographical aid for the earlier periods; excludes modern Hinduism. V. 2 of Dandekar gives comprehensive and critical coverage of publications between 1946 and 1960.

294.2 (03)
DOWSON, J. Classical dictionary of Hindu mythology and religion, geography, history, and literature. London, Trubner, 1879 (and reprints). xix, 411p.

GARRETT, J. A classical dictionary of India. . . . Madras, Higginbotham, 1871. xii, 793, [iv], 160p.

See entries at 934 (03).

294.28
The Sacred books of the Hindus. Allahabad, The Panini Office, 1909-37. 32v.

In this valuable collection, as in Müller's *Sacred books of the East* (at 294/299.8), the most notable Hindu scriptures appear as complete documents. Some 30 extensive works have been translated and published in the two collections (*A reader's guide to great religions*, ed. C. J. Adams (1965), p. 47).

Buddhism

294.3:016
Bibliographie bouddhique. Paris, Librairie d'Amérique et d'Orient, 1930-. v. 1-. Irregular (each v. covers 1 yr.). (v. 28-31. 1961. vii, 363p. 189s.).

Founded in 1928. A current bibliography, systematically arranged, of books and periodical articles relevant to Buddhist studies. V. 23 *bis* (fascicule annexe) includes a general index to v. 7-23, and v. 6 has a general index to v. 1-. Publisher is latterly given as 'Adrien Maisonneuve (Librairie d'Amérique et d'Orient)'.

Bibliography on Buddhism, by Shinshō Hanayama, Professor Emeritus of the University of Tokyo (Tokyo, Hokaseido Press, 1961. xiii, 869p.). Arranged by authors A-Z, with catchword index.

A Buddhist bibliography, compiled by A. C. March (London, Buddhist Lodge, 1935. xi, 257p.), with *Annual supplement, 1-5* (1936-40), is an author list of books (mostly in English) and periodical articles. The 1935 v. has 2,110 entries. Analytical subject indexes.

294.3:016
REGAMEY, C. Buddhistische Philosophie. Berne, Francke, 1950. 86p. (Bibliographische Einführungen in das Studium der Philosophie, 20/21).

Six main sections: 1. Allgemeinen Teil—2. Vorkanonische Philosophie—3. Das 'Kleine Fahrzeug' (Hīnayāna)—4. Das 'Grosse Fahrzeug' (Mahāyāna)—5. Ausserindische Schulen [Tibet, China, Japan]—6. Einzelprobleme [Ontology, Psychology, Soteriology, Ethics, etc.]. Introductory notes to Sections; some items are annotated.

294.3 (02)
HUMPHREYS, C., *ed.* **A Buddhist students' manual.** London, The Buddhist Society, 1956. 279p. illus.

Edited by the founder-President of the Buddhist Society. Includes A brief glossary of Buddhist terms', by A. C. March, amended and enlarged by C. Humphreys (p. 119-89) and 'An analysed bibliography of books on Buddhism in English' (p. 263-72; no annotations).

The same author's *A popular dictionary of Buddhism* (New York, Citadel, 1963. 223p. $1.75; $4) gives definitions and brief explanations of c. 1,000 terms.

Also noted: Nyanatiloka. *Buddhist dictionary: manual of Buddhist terms and doctrines* (2nd rev. ed. Colombo, Frewin 1956), first published in 1950.

294.3 (031)
MALALASEKERA, G. P., *ed.* **Encyclopaedia of Buddhism.** Colombo, Government of Ceylon; London, Luzac, 1961-. v. 1, fasc. 1-.

v. 1 (fasc. 1-4): A—AOKI. xv, 786p.; v. 2, fasc. 1 (1966), to ASITA DEVALA.

Published under the auspices of the International Association for the History of Religions. The *Encyclopaedia*, which covers religion, culture and all aspects of history, is to run to c. 15,000 pages and be completed in about ten years. Signed, scholarly articles, with bibliographies. The 50-page article on Amida-Buddhism is considered (*Assistant librarian*, v. 60, no. 7, July 1967, p. 142, 144) to be "what is perhaps the most succinct and informative article on the subject to appear in English". Physical production is fairly good.

294.3 (51)

SOOTHILL, W. E., and HODOUS, L. A dictionary of Chinese Buddhist terms, with Sanskrit and English equivalents and Sanskrit-Pali index. London, Kegan Paul, 1937. 510p.

"Indexed by the number of strokes in the Chinese symbol, with definitions in clear and concise English" (Diehl, K. S. *Religions, mythologies, folklores* (2nd ed. 1962), item no. 931).

294.3 (52)

BANDO, S., *and others, ed.* **A bibliography on Japanese Buddhism.** Tokyo, Cultural Interchange Institute for Buddhists Press, 1958. xiii, 180p. front. 40s.

1,660 items, chiefly in European languages. Lists (p. 1-7) other bibliographies that contain references to Japanese Buddhism.

294.38

A Buddhist Bible; edited by D. Goddard. 2nd ed., rev. and enl. Thetford, Vermont, D. Goddard. 1938 (reprinted London, Harrap, 1956). viii, 677p.

First published 1932.
The work represents a collection of translations of texts from Pali, Sanskrit, Chinese and Tibetan sources and from Japanese modern collections. The appendix contains bibliographical and other notes. Additional material in the 2nd ed. is the work of Bhikshu Wai-tao and other Buddhist scholars.

294.38

NANJIO, B. A catalogue of the Chinese translation of the Buddhist Tripitaka: the sacred canon of the Buddhists in China and Japan. Oxford, Clarendon Press, 1883. xxxvi, 240p. (Reprinted, with additions, Tokyo, 1929).

Lists 1,662 different works, arranged and classified as in the original Chinese catalogue. Based on a copy of the Japanese edition in the India Office Library, London. Three appendices systematically lists authors' and famous translators' works; indexes of the original Sanskrit titles (where identified), and of Indian and Chinese authors and translators.

Hôbôgirin: dictionnaire encyclopédique du Bouddhisme d'après les sources chinoises et japonaises. Redacteur en chef, P. Demiéville (Tokyo, Maison Franco-Japonaise) is an incomplete source. Only 4 fasc. (A—CHI and a fasc. annexe) has been published (1929-37. £15), but further parts are in preparation.

Yoga

294.527

SIVANANDA, S. S. Yoga Vedanta philosophy. Rishikesh. Yoga Vedanta Forest Univ., 1950. viii, 144p. Rs.5.

A dictionary of Yoga terms, with definitions and terms in Sanskrit.

E. Wood's *Yoga dictionary* (New York, Philosophical Library, 1956. xi, 177p.) includes both definitions and longer notes. All technical terminology is taken from Sanskrit works. No diacritical markings.

E. Wood's *Zen dictionary* (London, Owen, 1957. [vii], 165p. 25s.) includes brief biographies and some quotations, with a select bibliography (authors and titles only). Diacriticals shown. His *Vedanta dictionary* (London, Owen, 1964. vii, 225p. 25s.), a companion work, is on similar lines.

Judaism

296:016

JEWISH INSTITUTE OF RELIGION. Hebrew Union College, Cincinnati Library. **Dictionary catalogue of the Cincinnati Library.** Boston, Mass., G. K. Hall, 1963. 32v. $1,750 ($1,925 outside U.S.).

Photolithographic reproduction of 483,000 cards, including analytical entries for periodical articles. The Cincinnati, or Klan Library has a stock of more than 175,000 v. and takes more than 1,000 current serials. Specialisations: Spinoza; Jewish music; 15th and 16th century Judaica and Hebraica, as well as Jewish bibliography, history, philosophy, Hebrew and Yiddish literature, Bible studies and the ancient Near East (G. K. Hall prospectus, p. 2).
V. 28-32, comprising titles using Hebraic characters, are available separately at $325.

296:016

NEW YORK. PUBLIC LIBRARY. Dictionary catalog of the Jewish Collection of the New York Public Library, Reference Department. Boston, Mass., G. K. Hall, [n.d.]. 14v. $590.

270,000 entries, the catalogue (not seen) being a photo-litho copy of the card catalogue. 12,600p.; 21 cards to a page. "In addition to works in Hebrew and Yiddish, this catalogue lists publications in all European languages on the history and traditions of the Jewish people throughout the ages and in all lands. It covers archaeological and Biblical studies as well as belles-lettres, rabbinic and philosophical texts. It is particularly strong in entries for Jewish periodical publications in various languages and in analytical entries" (W. Heffer's Catalogue. *The Oriental and travel supplement.* No. 128 (1961), p. 7).

296:016

ROTH, C. Magna bibliotheca anglo-judaica: a bibliographical guide to Anglo-Jewish history. New ed., rev. and enl. London, Jewish Historical Society of England, 1937. xiii, 464p.

First published as *Bibliotheca anglo-judaica,* by J. Jacobs and L. Wulf (1888).
About 3,000 items. 2 main pts.: 1. Histories (sections A1-14, including biography and periodicals)—2. Historical material (B1-22). Items in the Mocatta Library and allied collections in University College, London, are asterisked. Author index. The sequel is:

LEHMANN, R. P. Nova bibliotheca anglo-judaica: a bibliographical guide to Anglo-Jewish history, 1937-1960. London, Jewish Historical Society of England, 1961. 30s.

About 1,800 items. Similarly arranged to the parent work. Author index. The compiler is Librarian, Jews' College, London.

296:016

VAJDA, G. Jüdische Philosophie. Berne, Francke, 1950. 40p. (Bibliographische Einführungen in das Studium der Philosophie, 19).

Five sections, the first dealing with general aids and the others with broad periods (Rabbinical thought; Middle Ages; Jewish mysticism; Jewish philosophy in modern times). Name index.

296:016:016

SHUNAMI, S. Bibliography of Jewish bibliographies. 2nd ed., enl. Jerusalem, The Magnes Press, The Hebrew University (distributed in Great Britain, the British Commonwealth and Europe by Oxford Univ. Press), 1965. xxiv, 992, xxiiip. £1 50 (180s.).

First published 1936.
4,727 numbered items, with very brief annotations, in 27 sections (including 1. Encyclopaedias—2. Bibliography of bibliography—3. General bibliographies—4-5. Catalogues of public and private collections—6. Booksellers' and publishers' catalogues (a selection)—7. Bibliographical periodicals—8. Lists of periodicals—9-25. Subject sections—26. Manuscripts—27. Personal bibliographies). Index of names and subject; index of Hebrew titles. The 2nd ed. has entries on the Dead Sea Scrolls and the holocaust of the Nazi régime.

296 (031)

Encyclopaedia Judaica: das Judentum in Geschicht und Gegenwart. Berlin, Verlag Eschkol, [c. 1928-34]. v. 1-10. illus.

v. 1-10: A-LYRA. (No more issued, publication being interrupted by the Nazi persecution of the Jews.)
A scholarly work, well produced. The signed articles are almost invariably accompanied by bibliographies. A feature is the number of short biographies, each of some 15 lines in length. The Hebrew form of a word is frequently given within brackets. Well illustrated; the article "Krakau" in v. 10 is 6p. in length, and includes 6 illustrations, 1 facsimile, and half a page of bibliography.

296 (031)

The Jewish encyclopedia: a descriptive record of the history, religion, literature and customs of the Jewish people from the earliest times to the present day. . . . I. Singer, managing editor. New York & London, Funk & Wagnalls, 1901-06. 12v. illus. (Reprinted New York, Ktav Publishing House, 1964. $69.50).

Contents include Assyriology, Egyptology, archaeological investigation in Palestine in the 19th century, the relation of the Hellenistic literature to the Jewish and Greek thought of the period, and the literature of the New Testament. Signed articles extensive bibliographies; 2,000 plates.
Less scholarly than the *Encyclopaedia Judaica* for the topics covered by the latter, it is also somewhat dated. Biographical and historical data are still invaluable, nevertheless.

296 (031)

The Universal Jewish encyclopedia . . .: an authoritative and popular presentation of Jews and Judaism since the earliest times; edited by I. Landman. New York, Universal Jewish Encyclopedia, Inc., 1939-44. 10v. and reading guide and index. illus.

Admirably supplements the *Jewish encyclopedia*, having the same broad scope, if less scholarly treatment. Articles are often signed and well illustrated; numerous short bibliographies. Very useful for biographical sketches, living persons being included.
The supplementary reading guide, *The seven-branched light: a reading guide or index to "The Universal Jewish encyclopedia"*, consists of 100 systematically arranged subject sections, with an alphabetical index.

296 (032)

The Junior Jewish encyclopedia. 3rd rev. ed., edited by Naomi Ben-Asher, Hagim Leaf [and others]. New York City, Shengold Publishers, 1959. 350, [2]p. illus., ports. (4th ed. 1961. 75s.).

First published 1957; 2nd ed. 1958.
The work of 30 contributors, articles being signed. Very well illustrated; many cross-references. The appended two pages of bibliography have entries arranged A-Z by subject. This encyclopaedia "seeks to provide a dependable and accurate guide for the young Jew to the past and present of his people" (*Preface*).

296 (032)

ROTH, C., *ed*. The standard Jewish encyclopedia. London, W. H. Allen, 1959. 1,978 cols. [2]p. illus. (incl. 12 col. pl.). maps. 90s.

A handy reference book which "throws special stress on . . . recent historic developments, although at the same time covering every phase of Jewish life, literature and thought from their beginning" (*Preface*). More than 8,000 articles; the list of some 250 contributors indicates the articles written by each. Handy for biographies of people (many of them living) who, though Jews, have no religious significance, *e.g.*, musicians, authors. 600 illustrations, portraits accompanying a number of the biographies. No bibliographies. Suitable for most types of libraries as a very convenient compendium.
The *Encyclopedia* has been accused (*Times literary supplement*, no. 3,067, 9th December 1960, p. 799) of attempting to cover too much, so that "every tinge of colour or emotion has been squeezed out. . . . The article on Hebrew Literature, for example, sounds like a catalogue of names". It is suggested that fewer titles should have been included and fuller treatment given to more important subjects.
A "New, revised and updated edition" (New York, Doubleday, 1963) has the same pagination.

296 (032)

WERBLOWSKY, R. J. Z., and WIGODER, G., *ed*. The encyclopedia of the Jewish religion. Jerusalem & Tel Aviv, Masada - P.E.C. Press, Ltd., 1966; London, Phoenix House, 1967. [vii], 415p. pl. 70s.

Aims to provide the interested layman "with concise, accurate and non-technical information on Jewish beliefs and practices, religious movements and doctrines, as well as the names and concepts that have played a rôle in Jewish religious history" (*Preface*). Short, unsigned articles (*e.g.* 'Moses': 2 cols.; 'Cantorial music': ¾ col.; 'Song of Songs': ¾ col.), A-Z. Numerous cross-references; etymology. No bibliographies.

H. A. Cohen's *A basic Jewish encyclopaedia* (Hartford, Conn., Hartford House; London, Wyndham & Stacey, 1967. 205p. 37s. 6d.) is a concise encyclopaedia of Judaism. 150 Hebrew terms are transliterated and translated. Appended Hebrew index and references to the Talmud. Reviewed in *Times literary supplement,* no. 3,425, 19th October 1967, p. 997.

296 (058.7)
The Jewish year book, 5657- (1896-). London, "Jewish Chronicle" Publications, 1896-. (1967. 30s.).

Includes details of Anglo-Jewish institutions, a directory of synagogues (London; provinces; Commonwealth), chief institutions in other countries, statistics, 'A Jewish book list', a who's who of British Jews (1967 ed.: p. 213-317) and obituaries. Index; 2 maps.

The Zionist year book, 5712- (1951/1952-). London. Zionist Federation of Great Britain and Ireland, 1951-. Annual. (5727. 1966/67. 21s.) includes a directory of Zionism, a list of selected books, a directory of Jewish organisations in Britain, obituaries, a who's who (1967 ed.: p. 371-472). Index.

296 (082.2)
BARON, J. L., *ed.* **A treasury of Jewish quotations.** New York, A. S. Barnes; London, Yoseloff, 1966. 623p. 45s.

First published 1956 (New York, Crown. 623p.).
A dictionary of quotations about Judaism and Jewish history, from the Bible to the present. Arranged under topics A-Z. Precise references to sources. It is estimated that 10,000 of the quotations have never been published in English. One criticism made in the *Times literary supplement* (no. 3348, 28th April 1966, p. 373) is that the selection is too generous; "the half might have been better than the whole".

296 (091)
BARON, S. W. A social and religious history of the Jews. 2nd ed. New York, Columbia Univ. Press, 1952-. v. 1-. (v. 11-12. 1967. ea. 72s.).

First published 1937.
A comprehensive work that provides a fresh approach for students, in that it deals with major patterns of development rather than events. Thus v. 12 (announced) has the title *Economic catalyst.* According to *A reader's guide to the great religions,* edited by C. T. Adams (1965) (p. 198), it provides one of the most comprehensive bibliographies on Jews and Judaism.

World history of the Jewish people, edited by Cecil Roth (London, W. H. Allen, 1964-) reached its eleventh volume in 1966, with second series:

Medieval period. v. 2: The Dark Ages. *Jewish in Christian Europe, 711-1096.* This contains 15 chapters by different hands, supported by chapter notes and bibliographies, illustrations and end-paper maps.

296 (092)
Who's who in world Jewry: a biographical dictionary of outstanding Jews. Rev. ed., edited by H. Schneiderman and I. J. C. Karpman. New York, Who's Who in World Jewry, Inc. (London, "Jewish Chronicle") 1965. xxxii, 1087p. $37.50; £12.

First published 1955 (xliv, 898p.).
Biographical data (p. 3-1087) on more than 11,000 Jews from many parts of the world, particularly the U.S.A. (*e.g.,* S. W. Baron: 32 lines). Yugoslavia and Hungary appear, but not the U.S.S.R. and other Communist countries. Works of writers are listed, with dates. Large page; well bound. Appended directory of Jewish organisations and institutions, and list of Jewish periodicals of the world are omitted from the 1965 ed.

296 (093)=016
BURCHARD, C. Bibliographie zu den Handschriften vom Toten Meer. Berlin, Töpelmann, 1957. xv, 118p.

A bibliography of 1,538 numbered items (mainly periodical articles) on the Dead Sea Scrolls, for the period 1948-55. Arranged in Latin, Greek and Hebrew sections. Appended list of *c.* 180 journals cited.
Kept up to date by entries in the *Revue de Qumran.*

296 (4/9)
FEDERBUSH, S., *ed.* **World Jewry today.** London, W. H. Allen, 1959. [iii], 748 cols. 75s.

A new reference book, sponsored by the World Jewish Congress. In addition to articles on world Jewry, it gives statistics and other information on the religious, cultural and social life in the Jewish communities of over a hundred countries. Jewish press, by countries, p. 37-70. Reviewed in *International affairs,* v. 36, no. 1, January 1960, p. 150.

296.18
The Babylonian Talmud; translated, with notes, glossary and indices, under the editorship of I. Epstein. London, Soncino Press, 1935-52. 35v. (including index v.). Rev. ed. (to be in 18v.), 1961-.

The only complete English translation of the Talmud. The index is comprehensive; it covers all cited Scriptural passages, lists foreign-language glossaries and abbreviations, and gives a complete list of Rabbis mentioned in the Talmud, with their sayings (*Stechert-Hofner book news,* April 1959, p. 100).

The Soncino Press has also published the *Soncino books of the Bible,* edited by A. Cohen (1945-52. 14v.), consisting of Hebrew text and English translation plus expositions based on the classical Jewish commentaries, in association with the Jewish Publication Society of America; and *The Midrash* (the classical Jewish commentaries).

translated into English, with notes, glossary and indexes; and edited by H. Freedman and M. Simon (1951. 10v.).

Mohammedanism

297:016

Index islamicus, 1906-1955: a catalogue of articles on Islamic subjects in periodicals and other collective publications; compiled by J. D. Pearson and J. F. Ashton. Cambridge, Heffer, 1958 (reprinted 1961, with minor corrections). xxxvi, 895p. 126s. **Supplement,** 1956-60. 1962. 70s.; **Second supplement,** 1961-1965. 1968. 105s.

See entry at 908 (5/6=927).

297:016

NEW YORK. PUBLIC LIBRARY. Dictionary catalog of the Oriental Collection of the New York Public Library, Reference Department. Boston, Mass., G. K. Hall, 1960. 16v. $960.

See entry at 908/5/6=927).

297 (031)

The Encyclopædia of Islam. New ed., prepared by a number of leading Orientalists under the patronage of the International Union of Academies. Leyden, Brill; London, Luzac, 1954-. v. 1, fasc. 1-. illus., plans, maps. ea. fasc., 28s.

v. 1 (fasc. 1-22): A-B. 1960. xx, 1360p. £25.
v. 2 (fasc. 23-40): C-GYPSUM. 1965. xxi, 1146p. £28 10s.
v. 3 (fasc. 41-50): HA—al-HUSRI. 1965-67.

Originally as *The Encyclopaedia of Islam: a dictionary of the geography, ethnography and biography of the Muhammadam peoples* (1913). 4v.; *Supplement.* 1933.

The new ed. will be in 5v. It resembles the 1st ed. in size and presentation but gives more emphasis to economic and social topics and to artistic production. A general index and an atlas of the Islamic world are also planned.

Signed articles, with bibliographies. Many biographies and entries under localities (*e.g.,* Afghānistān: v. 1, p. 221-33; 5 pts.,—geography; ethnography; languages; religion; history—each with a bibliography; folding black-and-white map). The article on 'Crusades' (v. 2, p. 63-66) has a bibliography of 1¼ columns, with running commentary. A minor difficulty is the entry of articles under the appropriate Arabic word instead of the English (*e.g.,* mosques are dealt with under the Arabic term 'Masdjid'). Diacritical markings. A definitive, scholarly work.

The *Encyclopaedica arabica,* edited by F. E. Boustany (Beirut, 1956-. v. 1-) has Arabic text only.

297 (032)

RONART, S., and RONART, N. Concise encyclopaedia of Arabic civilization. Amsterdam, Djambatan, 1959-66. 2v. maps.

See entry at 908 (5/6=927) (032).

[*The Cambridge history of Islam,* edited by P. M. Holt, A. K. S. Lambton and B. Lewis, is to be published in 1968-69 (2 v.).]

297 (032)

The Shorter encyclopaedia of Islam; edited on behalf of the Royal Netherlands Academy by H. A. R. Gibb and J. H. Kramers. Leyden, Brill; London, Luzac, 1953. viii, 677p. illus. 90s.

Comprises all the articles in the 1st ed. and supplement of the *Encyclopaedia of Islam* (1913-33) relating particularly to the religion and law of Islam. Most of these articles have been reproduced without material alteration; some have been shortened or revised; a few new entries have been added. Bibliographies have been brought up-to-date. Included is a "Register of subjects", which gives the English translation of Arabic words used as headings. A-Z index of articles, stating authors. Invaluable.

297 (058)

Annuaire du monde mussulman.

See entry at 908 (5/6=927).

297.1:016

MENASCE, P. J. de. Arabische Philosophie. Berne, Francke, 1948. 48p. (Bibliographische Einführungen in das Studium der Philosophie, 6).

14 sections, including sections on individual Arab philosophers (*e.g.,* Avicenna; Averroes). Occasional annotations. Name index.

297.1 (091)

SHARIF, M., ed. A history of Muslim philosophy, with short accounts of other disciplines and the modern Renaissance in Muslim lands. Wiesbaden, Harrassowitz; London, Luzac, 1963-66. 2v. (viii, 1792p.). ea. £11 11s.

The work of 56 specialists. V. 1 covers the earlier centuries of Islam and the fundamental teachings of the Qur'ān in 83 chapters (each with a bibliography). V. 2 covers the period 1258 A.D. onwards, also discussing other disciplines and the influence of Muslim thought; general index, p. 1663-1792. The *History* deals with literature, architecture, the arts and other branches of learning, as well as history proper. Heavily footnoted.

297.18

PICKTHALL, M. The meaning of the glorious Koran: an explanatory translation of the Koran. 3rd ed. London, Allen & Unwin, 1953 (reprinted London, Muller, 1956). xix, 464p. 35s.

First published 1930.
This is the first English translation of the Koran, by an English convert to Islam.

A. J. Arberry's *The Koran interpreted: a new version of the Koran* (London, Allen & Unwin, 1955 (reprinted 1963). 2v. 45s.) has a valuable prefatory note on previous English translations, and an index of subjects and names in v. 2. Arberry has been Professor of Arabic at Cambridge University since 1947.

Ancient Egyptian Religion

299.3 (03)

BONNET, H. Reallexikon der ägyptischen Religionsgeschichte. Berlin, de Gruyter, 1952. xv, 883p. illus. DM.92.

An encyclopaedic dictionary of ancient Egyptian religious history. Articles are unsigned and the appended bibliographies are brief, but there are numerous references in the text. 199 line-drawings.

Chinese Religion

(See also 1 (51).)

299.5:016

Index sinicus: a catalogue of articles relating to China in periodicals and other collective publications, 1920-1955. Compiled by John Lust, with the assistance of Werner Eichhorn. Cambridge, Heffer, 1964. xxx, 663p. 168s.

See entry at 908 (51):016.

299.5:016

TOTOK, W., and SCHRÖER, H. "Die Philosophie der Chinesen". In their *Handbuch der Geschichte der Philosophie.* v. 1 (1964), p. 50-67.

About 500 references. Sections: Lao-tse—Konfuzius—Mo Ti—Yang Chu—Chuang-tse—Die Sophisten—Die Yin-Yang—Theorie—Mencius—Hsün-tse—Han Fei-tse—Der chinesische Buddhismus—Tung Chung-shu—Wang Ch'ung—Der Neu—Konfuzianismus—Chu Hsi—Wang Shou—Jen.

299.5 (021)

DE GROOT, J. J. M. The religious system of China: its ancient forms, evolution, history and present aspect, manners, customs and social institutions connected therewith. Leyden, Brill, 1892-1910. 6v. illus.

Book 1 (v. 1-3): Disposal of the dead; Bk 2 (v. 4-6): On the soul and ancestral worship. An extensive survey, with many illustrations; bibliographical footnotes; short index.

Japanese Religion

299.52:016

HOLZMAN, D., and others. Japanese religion and philosophy: a guide to Japanese reference and research material. Ann Arbor, Michigan Univ. Press (London, Mayflower Publishing Co.), 1959. vii, 142p. (Michigan Univ. Center for Japanese Studies. Bibliographic series no. 7).

992 numbered items, giving author and title in Japanese, with English translation. Limited to Japanese books dealing with the doctrines and histories of the religions and philosophies of Japan published since the Meiji era. In nearly all cases entries are annotated briefly. Sections: 1. General—2. Shintó—3. Buddhism—4. Confucianism—5. Bushidó, Kokugaku and Yogaku—6. Christianity—7. Meiji and after. Appendices: List of publishers; List of authors and editors; Subject index.

Shuntō shoseki mokuroku [A bibliography of Shintoism] (2nd ed. Tokyo, Meiji Seitoku Kinenkai, 1943. 646p.) and its continuation, *Meiji taishô shôwa Shintô shoseki mokuroku* [A bibliography of Shintoism of the Meiji, Taishô and Showâ eras] (Tokyo, Meiji Jingû Shamusho, 1953. 707p.), both edited by Genchi Katô, list *c.* 15,000 and *c.* 16,000 items respectively, up to 1940.

299.52:016

KOKUSAI BUNKA SHINKOKAI. K.B.S. bibliography of standard reference books for Japanese studies, with descriptive notes. Vol. 4. **Religion.** Tokyo, Univ. of Tokyo Press, 1966. [vii], 181p. 20s.

327 numbered and annotated entries (plus numerous sub-entries) in 7 sections: 1. General—2. Shinto—3. Buddhism—4. Confucianism—5. Christianity—6. Popular beliefs—7. Periodicals. Confined to books and periodicals published in Japan and in Japanese. Entries consist of romanised form of title, author and publisher, followed by the vernacular form and English translation of title. Evaluative English annotations which indicate level and often sketch in background. Index of authors and editors. "Primarily intended to give the first orientation to beginners though it may be doubtlessly useful for specialists" (*Introduction*).

3 SOCIAL SCIENCES

3:002.6

UNITED NATIONS EDUCATIONAL, SCIEN-TIFIC AND CULTURAL ORGANIZATION. International repertory of social science documentation centres. Paris, Unesco, 1952. 42p. (Documentation in the social sciences).

Details (director; organization; subjects covered; services; publications) are given of 59 social science documentation centres in some 16 countries, together with international organizations. Arrangement is by countries A-Z, with A-Z order of organization under each country. No subject index. Now considerably dated.

Bibliographies

3:016

The ABS guide to recent publications in the social and behavioral sciences. New York, the American Behavioral Scientist, Metron Inc.; Oxford, Pergamon Press, 1965. xxi, 781p. $19.95; 147*s*. **1966 supplement.** 1966. 220p. $12.50; 95*s*. **1967 supplement.** 1967. 212p. 95*s*.

6,664 numbered and annotated entries for books, and periodical articles, some government reports and a few pamphlets compiled from *The American behavioral scientist*, 1957-64. Unhelpfully arranged under authors, A-Z; an outline classification scheme precedes and there is a 'topical and methodological' index, based on the classification. Book-title index; proper name (*e.g.,* locality) index. A significant proportion of the items are not in English; French predominates, followed by Italian, German and Spanish. *Bulletin of the P.A.I.S.* (q.v.) is far more current and comprehensive, carrying *c.* 25,000 entries for 1957/64, emphasising factual and statistical information and citing a higher percentage of popular material (see review in *The booklist,* v. 62, no. 16, 15th April 1966, p. 781-8). The four Unesco 'International bibliographies of the social sciences' together list 15,-20,000 items p.a., but they suffer from a marked time-lag and are not annotated. Entries in the *ABS guide* not infrequently omit price and pagination, and show inconsistency in author entry.

3:016

ADLER, C. E. M., *comp.* **Social studies: an annotated list of recent books** on politics, sociology, economics, international relations and world affairs, for the use of librarians, teachers, adult students, students in universities and technical colleges and sixth forms in schools. London, School Library Association, 1965. iv, 36p. 9*s*. 6*d*. (6*s*. to members). **Supplement.** 1966.

244 numbered and annotated items, mainly books published 1950-55 that "will provoke thinking and discussion both on their own subject and on allied subjects". Prices are very rarely in excess of 63*s*. Presence of bibliographies, tables and maps is indicated. 20-word annotations. 13 sections. Indexes of authors and subjects.

3:016

Bibliographie der Sozialwissenschaften. Internationale Dokumentation der Buch- und Zeitschriftenliteratur des Gesamtgebietes der Sozialwissenschaften. Göttingen, Vandenhoeck & Ruprecht, 1905-43, 1950-.

1937-42, as *Bibliographie der Staats- und Wirtschaftswissenschaften.* Since 1950, as suppt. to *Jahrbuch für Sozialwissenschaft.*
About 7,500 items p.a., systematically arranged in 15 sections (15: Bibliographien. Biographien. Festschriften. Handbücher.). Covers books and periodical articles in economics and social sciences. Annual author and subject indexes. Complements the *Bulletin of the P.A.I.S.* (q.v.).

3:016

BRITISH LIBRARY OF POLITICAL AND ECONOMIC SCIENCE. London School of Economics and Political Science, University of London. **Guide to the collections.** London, the Library, 1948. 136p.

A revised edition of the second part of "A Reader's guide", of which three editions were published from 1934 to 1945. (*Foreword*). The library is probably the largest of its kind in the world, having some 300,000 bound volumes at the time this *Guide* was produced.
16 of the 18 chapters deal with types of material (*e.g.,* general reference books; government publications) and subject material (*e.g.,* statistics; law). Ch. 16 deals with Russian publications. Major and typical items are cited, with annotations and the library's classification number, for the benefit of undergraduate users. Index of subjects and collections. A new edition is much needed.

3:016

Bulletin analytique et documentation politique, économique et sociale contemporaine. Fondation Nationale des Sciences Politiques. Paris, Presses Universitaires de France, 1946-. 10 p.a. ea. NF.2; 20 F. p.a. (foreign, 24 F.).

Preceded by *Bulletin bibliographique de documentation internationale contemporaine.* 1965: 4,376 indicative (*c.* 40-word) abstracts. Coverage is of periodicals in all European languages and also official documents. An abstract sometimes has appended to it the titles of other articles on the same topic. Systematic arrangement: 1. Problèmes nationaux (arranged under countries, A-Z, then by subjects, as necessary)—2. Relations internationales et études comparatives (Études politiques. Études économiques. Développement et assistance internationale. Problèmes régionaux (by regions, A-Z)). Cross-references. Annual subject index and list of periodicals scanned.

The Fondation's *Index to post-1944 periodical articles on political economic and social problems* is to be published by G. K. Hall, Boston, Mass., early in 1968, in 17v. The 304,000 cards, photolithographically reproduced, are arranged initially by countries or areas and then by a decimal classification. $1190 in U.S.A. and France.

SOCIAL SCIENCES

3:016

Bulletin of the Public Affairs Information Service: a selective subject list of the latest books, pamphlets, government publications, reports of public and private agencies, and periodical articles, relating to economic and social conditions, public administration and international relations, published in English throughout the world. New York, the Service, 1915-. v. 1, no. 1-. Weekly. $100 p.a. (extra copy, $50 p.a.); annual cumulation, $25.

Cumulated 5 times p.a., the fifth cumulation being the bound annual volume.

About 30,000 entries p.a. Not primarily an index to periodicals, although more than a thousand periodicals are scanned each year (*Preface*). Emphasis on factual and statistical information. Entries for subjects and countries (*e.g.,* 'Russia' in the issue of v. 53, no. 12, 17th December 1966 has sub-headings: 'Bibliography'; 'Economic assistance program—Syria'; 'Economic planning'; 'Foreign relations—Japan'). Author entries, but only for the most important authors (v. 42, 1956-). Adequate cross-references. The annual volume has a key to periodical references, a directory of publishers and organisations, and a list of publications analysed (including some 40 year-books). The entry 'Directories' (sub-divided by subject or country) in the 1965v. occupies p. 242-71. Because of its frequent appearance and comprehensive coverage of English-language material, the *P.A.I.S. bulletin* (as it is called) is the major indexing service in its field in English.

V. 1-31 (1915-45), v. 38 (1952) were reprinted in 1962; v. 1-31, ea. $22, $594 the set; with v. 38, $693.

Current contents: your twice monthly survey of the social sciences, including management sciences (Philadelphia, Pa., Institute for Scientific Information) ran only for the period 1956-62 (v. 1-7).

3:016

Current issues: a selected bibliography on subjects of concern to the United Nations. New York, United Nations, Dag Hammarskjold Library, December 1965-. no. 1-. Irregular. (ST/LIB/SER.G/2). nos. 1-2, ea. $1; no. 3, 75c.; no. 4 (June 1967). $1.50.

Succeeds the United Nations Library (New York) *List of selected articles* (1949-. Monthly), last published September 1963. About 1,200-1,500 entries per issue. The No. 3 issue (September 1966) has 8 main sections (International organization — League of Nations — United Nations—International agencies related to the U.N.—Non-governmental organizations—Legal questions—Scientific and technological questions —Social and humanitarian questions), Nos. 2 and 4 deal with aspects of economic development. No. 1 includes references to periodical articles and books received by the library between August 1963 and September 1965. 111 periodicals were scanned for no. 2 (June 1966).

3:016

GRANDIN, A. Bibliographie générale des sciences juridiques, politiques, économiques et sociales de 1800 à 1925/26. Paris, Recueil Sirey, 1926. 3v.; Supplements 1-19, 1926-50. 1928-51.

Systematic arrangement, with 16 subject groups. The bibliography is of books and only those in the French language, published in France or elsewhere. Supplement 19 carries about 5,000 items. Theses and government publications are included. No annotations, but frequent cross-references. Subject and author indexes. Aspects of law preponderate.

3:016

HOSELITZ, B. F., ed. A reader's guide to the social sciences. Glencoe, Ill. (then New York), The Free Press, 1959 (reprinted 1965). 256p.

Chapters: 1. The social sciences in the last two hundred years—2. History—3. Geography—4. Political science—5. Economics—6. Sociology —7. Anthropology—8. Psychology. In each chapter the ramifications and development of the subject are explained and a running commentary follows on the literature (*e.g.,* on economics: 'classics'; works of specialised sub-disciplines; popular works; items of special interest). Rather wordy and occasionally uneven (*e.g.,* no periodicals are listed in the chapter on Political science). Only author, title and date are given for books cited. Index of authors cited, but no subject index.

L. R. Wynar's *Social science general reference: a selective list* (Boulder, Univ. of California Libraries, 1962-. no. 1-. Mimeographed. Gratis on exchange) is annotated and due to appear in 8 parts. So far: 1. Social sciences in general (6p.) —2. Sociology (25p.)—3. Political science (66p.) —History (1963. 348p.). Criticised in *Library quarterly* (v. 33, no. 3, July 1963, p. 288-9) for failing to record the latest edition of a title.

Research materials in the social sciences, compiled by J. A. Clarke (Madison, Wis., Univ. of Wisconsin Press, 1959. 42p. 75c.) is an annotated list of 193 items for graduate students preparing to do research in the social sciences. 6 sections, with emphasis on more inclusive encyclopaedias, bibliographies and abstracting journals.

3:016

International bibliography of the social sciences. Paris, Unesco, 1951-.

Consists of 4 series:
International bibliography of economics. v. 1-8. 1955-61. *See at 33:016.*
International bibliography of political science. v. 1-8. 1954-61. *See at 32:016.*
International bibliography of social and cultural anthropology. v. 1-5. 1958-61. *See at 572:016.*
International bibliography of sociology. v. 1-9. 1951-59. *See at 301:016.*
As from 1962 all 4 series are published by Stevens and subsequently (1963-) Tavistock Publications (London) and Aldine Publishing Co. (Chicago), each v. at 63s. or $10; £10 10s., the set.

3:016

International information service. Chicago, Ill., Library of International Relations, 1963-. v. 1, no. 1-. Quarterly. ea. $3; $10 p.a.

As *The world in focus* (1963).

About 2,500 annotated entries p.a. Systematic arrangement, with numerous cross-references: General — Geography — History — Political factors—Economic factors—Social and cultural factors—International political and military factors—International economic and social factors—International organization and law—Atlases; yearbooks (including statistical yearbooks); bibliographies; directories. Each issue has a geographical index.

3:016

LEWIS, P. R. The literature of the social sciences: an introductory survey and guide. London, Library Association, 1960 (reprinted 1967). xx, 222p. 48s. (36s. to members).

Nine chapters: 1. Social sciences in general—2. Economics—3. Economic history and conditions—4. Economic history: Great Britain.—5. Statistics—6. Commerce and industry—7. Political science and public administration—8. Law—9. International affairs—10. Sociology. In each case the appropriate general and special bibliographies, guides, reference books, text-books, histories, source material, libraries and library problems are noted. The survey (which, the author admits, is bound to be superficial) usually takes the form of a brief running commentary. The period of coverage is "from about 1800 onwards, and concentrated particularly on the twentieth century". Intended for those "whose work brings them into contact with the social sciences" (*Preface*), as well as for students preparing for the Library Association List C examination papers. Education, Anthropology and Criminology are subjects omitted. The 'Index of publications' is a most useful addition to a survey which was badly needed in this degree of detail.

3:016

A London bibliography of the social sciences, being the subject catalogue of the British Library of Political and Economic Science at the London School of Economics, the Goldsmiths' Library of Economic Literature at the University of London, the libraries of the Royal Statistical Society and the Royal Anthropological Institute, and certain special collections at University College, London, and elsewhere. Compiled by B. M. Headicar and C. Fuller. London, London School of Economics, 1931-32. 4v.; Supplements: 1st and 2nd, v. 5-6 (covering 1929-31), 1934-37; 3rd, v. 7-9 (covering 1936-50), 1952-55; 4th, v. 10-11 (covering 1950-55), 1958-60. ea. 100s.; 6th, v. 12: A-F (1956-62), 1966 (v. 12. £15).

V. 1-5 record works in the nine libraries specified up to 31st May 1931. In v. 6 (1937), only the holdings of the British Library of Political and Economic Science and the Edward Fry Library of International Law at the London School of Economics are recorded, plus some 5,000 additional items in the Goldsmiths' and University of London libraries. The holdings in v. 7 onwards are confined to the British Library of Political and Economic Science and the Edward Fry Library, less non-governmental periodicals and material in Slavonic languages for the period concerned.

The largest subject (A-Z) bibliography of its kind; arrangement is chronological under subjects or their country/topic sub-divisions. References from countries or areas to subjects (*e.g.*, 'Finland' in v. 12 has 53 lines of references to subject headings with items on Finland. The form "Government publications" is a separate sub-division under each heading or sub-heading. Extensive entries under country, with many sub-divisions; bibliographical details are brief, but the presence of a bibliography is indicated. References in v. 7 onwards are fuller than those in v. 1-6.

Supplemented by the Library's *Monthly list of additions* (ea. 3s.; 35s. p.a.), each with *c.* 1,200 items arranged in some 22 subject classes plus lists of new (and ceased) official and non-official serials. Quarterly *Russian supplement,* similarly priced.

3:016

MUKHERJEE, A. K. Annotated guide to reference materials in the human sciences. London, Asia Publishing House, 1962. xv, 267p. 35s.

1,164 annotated entries. Pt. 1: Anthropology; pt. 2: Sociology, social psychology and allied topics. Each subject field has sub-divisions for reference material proper, journals and serials, and source materials and standard treatises. The brief annotations, sometimes gratuitous, average *c.* 20 words. Prices not given. Author and subject indexes. Asiatic slant provides a valuable corrective. (Duplicate of entry at 572:016 in v. 1 of the *Guide to reference material.*)

3:016

UNITED NATIONS. Dag Hammarskjold Library, New York. **New publications in the Dag Hammarskjold Library.** New York, 1950-. Monthly. ea. 50c.; $5 p.a.

Succeeds the United Nations Library (New York) *New publications in the United Nations Headquarters Library* as "a monthly list of recent books, periodicals and newspapers added to the . . . Library. It is planned as a practical finding list rather than as a bibliography or a list of suggested readings" (*Foreword*). Excludes U.N. and Specialized Agency publications.

About 400 items per issue. 13 sections (1-10, on political, economic, governmental and social subjects, etc., using U.D.C. numbers. 11. Reference books (general; bibliography and bibliographies; biographies and biographical dictionaries; cartography and maps; dictionaries and encyclopaedias. 12. Miscellaneous. 13. Periodicals and newspapers). Titles of items in Arabic. Chinese and Russian are in native characters.

3:016

UNITED NATIONS Library. Geneva. **Monthly list of books** catalogued in the library of the United Nations. Geneva, League of Nations. 1928-45; United Nations, 1946-. Monthly. 36s.; $5 p.a.

"A selected list of works relating to questions of every kind studied by the organs of the United Nations" (*Explanatory note*).

Carries about 350 items monthly: systematic arrangement in seven groups, as in the *Monthly list of selected articles* (*q.v.*), except that section 7 is devoted to reference works and library science. U.D.C. classification numbers are given; no annotations.

3:016

UNITED NATIONS. Library. Geneva. **Monthly list of selected articles.** Geneva, 1929-. v. 1-. 6 double nos. p.a. $7.50 p.a.

"The object of this publication is to provide a list of selected articles on political, legal, economic, financial and other questions of the day." (*Explanatory note*). About 1,500 periodicals are regularly examined for this purpose; purely informative articles, in the nature of news and periodical statistical notices, are not included. Carries about 7,000 entries yearly; titles of articles in languages other than English are not translated, but there are occasional very brief indications of subject content. Wide international coverage; annual list of periodicals (in November/December issue). No annual indexes. Sections: 1. United Nations; international tions—4. Social, humanitarian and educational questions — 5. Economics and population — 6. Finance—7. Communications and transport.

3:016

UTZ, A. Grundsatzfragen des öffentlichen Lebens. Bibliographie (Darstellung und Kritik). Recht, Gesellschaft, Wirtschaft, Staat. . . . Bases for social living. A critical bibliography embracing law, society, economics and politics. Freiburg, Herder, 1960-. v. 1-.

v. 1 (1956-1959). 1960.
v. 2 (1959-1961). 1962.
v. 3 (1961-1963). 1964.
v. 4 (1963-1965). 1966.
Unusual arrangement: pt. A consists of a classified list of items; pt. B, of reviews ('Besprechungen') or abstracts of the items (*c.* 600 in v. 4). In German, French, English and Spanish. Draws on *c.* 370 journals.

3:016

WHITE, C. M., *and others.* **Sources of information in the social sciences:** a guide to the literature. Totowa, N.J., Bedminster Press, 1964. xiii, 498p. $10.50.

Preliminary ed. 1959.
10 contributors; 8 chapters: 1. The literature of social science—2. History—3. Economics and business administration — 4. Sociology — 5. Anthropology—6. Psychology—7. Education—8. Political science (including international law). For each chapter a specialist presents "a bibliographical review of basic monographic works for a collection of substantive material. This review is followed by a list of reference works [compiled by librarians]" (*Preface*). Items are numbered in each chapter; they total 2,741 and can easily be traced via the full author and title index. Subject coverage is wider than in P. S. Lewis's *The literature of the social sciences* (q.v.); although law is omitted, history, anthropology and psychology are included. Lewis himself admits that treatment of some sectors in White is superior to his own (*Library Association record,* v. 66, no. 10, October 1964, p. 443-6). In this review-article, however, Lewis finds two serious weaknesses in White: the complete absence of either a subject index or a detailed contents list, and the lack of co-ordination between the specialists' contributions on mono-

graphs and the librarians' annotated lists of reference works. These last do not single out the most relevant items, or those to be tackled first. after the monographs, but simply deal with each in turn.

3:016=82

SORBONNE. École Pratique des Hautes Études. **Ouvrages cyrilliques concernant les sciences sociales:** liste des reproductions disponibles. Cyrillic publications concerning the social sciences. Current list of reproductions. Paris & The Hague, Mouton, 1964-65. 2v.

Forms suppts. 1-2 to *Cahiers du monde russe et soviétique.* A systematically arranged list of more than 4,000 Russian works and periodicals on the social sciences available in offset or microform reproduction. 'Periodicals', nos. 113-782. Symbols denote state (*e.g.,* offset, xerox, microcard, microfiche). 20 publishing concerns are involved.

3:016:016

FRYKHOLM, L. Översikt över samhällsvetens-kapliga bibliografiska hjälpmedel. A survey of the bibliographical aids in the social sciences. Stockholm, Beckman, 1960. 160p. Sw. kr. 10.

A select list of 2,088 bibliographies in the social sciences. Three main sections: general; subject; regions. Author and anonymous-title index. Of value for its inclusion of marginal fields (*e.g.,* religion, philosophy, history) and its international coverage. Occasional brief annotations.

3:016:016

Index bibliographicus. 4th ed. v. 2: **Social sciences.** The Hague, Fédération Internationale de documentation, 1964. [iv], 34p. 10*s.*

"A complete revision" of the 3rd ed. of v. 2 (1952).
Designed as a classified (U.D.C.) directory of the more important current abstracting and bibliographic services. About 390 items in the social sciences, including 'Regional studies' and 'Psychology', but excluding philosophy, history and the humanities. Details for each item include: title (with previous titles and dates), subtitle; issuing body; publisher; date of start; frequency and availability (by subscription or free); number of bibliographical references, annotated entries, abstracts and critical reviews; arrangement; language of abstracts, etc., if not apparent from title; frequency and nature of indexes; subject coverage. Subject index (in English and French); index of titles. Some important omissions (e.g., *P.A.I.S. bulletin, Excerpta criminologica*).

3:016:016

UNITED NATIONS EDUCATIONAL, SCIENTIFIC AND CULTURAL ORGANIZATION. A selected inventory of periodical publications. Paris, Unesco, 1951. 129p. facsim.; Supplement 1. [1953]. 12p. (Bibliographies in the social sciences).

Pt. 1 deals with the problem of documentation services in the social sciences; pt. 2 provides an inventory of 59 leading abstracting, indexing and allied services in that field. Details of publication, subject coverage, special features, time lag, etc. are systematically stated in each case. Facsimiles of pages of 14 of these journals form a valuable appendix. Indexes of titles, countries of publication, languages of publication, kinds of services, disciplines, and geographical areas follow. The supplement covers a further 15 services and includes corrigenda. Badly needs updating.

Encyclopaedias

3 (031)=20

Encyclopaedia of the social sciences. Editor-in-chief, E. R. A. Seligman; associate editor, A. Johnson. New York & London, Macmillan, 1930-35. 15v. (Reprinted 1951. 15v. in 8.).

A comprehensive work, projected under the auspices of ten learned societies; signed articles by specialists. Some subject articles are lengthy and are provided with lists of contents (*e.g.,* "Agriculture"; 9 sections; 8 contributors); treatment is usually systematic (*e.g.,* a subject will be introduced by giving historical background surveyed in various countries, and then discussed in terms of its problems). Although about one-half of the articles are biographies, these are usually comparatively brief, being chiefly concerned with the person's achievements in the social sciences. Bibliographies, generally excellent, even if dated, are appended to articles. V. 15 includes the index and a classification of the articles in subject and biography groups.

A new edition, entitled *The international encyclopedia of the social sciences* is being published in 1968 by the Collier-Macmillan Co., New York in 17v. at £230.

3 (031)=30

Handwörterbuch der Sozialwissenschaften. Tübingen, Mohr; Stuttgart, Fischer, 1951-. Lfg. 1-. DM.14 per Lfg.

v. 1-11 (1951-65): A-WERT.
To be completed in 12v., plus an index volume. The Lieferungen started from three points in the alphabet,—A, H and R.
This encyclopedia is the successor to the *Handwörterbuch der Staatswissenschaften,* hrsg. von L. Elster, A. Weber, Fr. Wieser (4. gänz. ungearb. Aufl. Jena, Fischer, 1923-29. 8v. and suppt. (*see at 32 (031)*). It has the same international scope, lengthy signed articles and extensive bibliographies (*e.g.,* the article "Banken", v. 1, p. 539-60, covers first the history, with subdivision by periods and a bibliography (books and articles) of *c.* 125 items; then, banking theory, with a bibliography of *c.* 56 items). Intended to cover all branches of the social sciences, whereas its predecessor was primarily concerned with political science.

3 (031)=30

Staatslexikon: Recht, Wirtschaft, Gesellschaft. Hrsg. von der Görres-Gesellschaft zur Plege der Wissenschaft im Katholischen Deutschland. 6. völlig neu bearb. und erw. Aufl. Freiburg, Herder, 1959-63. 8v. DM. 76 per v.

First published 1887; 5th ed. 1926-32 (5v.}.
About 4,000 signed articles, arranged A-Z. Systematic and lengthy treatment of subjects from the Roman Catholic viewpoint; bibliographies appended to articles. Of particular interest are the articles on the Federal Republic of Germany, Ghana and Communism. Biographies are included (*e.g.,* of Gandhi, Hitler); that of Karl Marx (1. Life; 2. Appreciation) has 3 columns of text and nearly one column of bibliography. The 6-column article on Laos has a bibliography of items up to 1958. See reviews in *International affairs,* v. 35, no. 1, January 1959, p. 136, and v. 36, no. 2, April 1960, p. 281.

3 (031)=50

Enciclopedia di scienze politiche, economiche e sociali. [Capo della redazione, Rodolfo Sommaruga]. Bologna, Zuffi, 1956-. v. 1-.

v. 1: A-BEN (1956). No further volumes have so far been published. International in scope, but with an Italian slant (*e.g.,* the article 'Agricoltura', p. 139-53, in 15 sections). Some 400 contributors. Signed articles, usually carrying bibliographies (*e.g.,* 'Behaviorismo'—2 columns; 10 lines of bibliography; but 'Atlantico Patto'—4 columns; no bibliography). Bibliographies may include periodical articles. Biographical and country entries included.

3 (032)=20

GOULD, J., and **KOLB, W. K.,** *ed.* **A dictionary of the social sciences.** London, Tavistock Publications, 1964. xvi, 761p. 126*s.* 6*d.*

Compiled under the auspices of Unesco, and "the first of a series of unilingual dictionaries in the social sciences" (*Foreword*).
About 270 British and U.S. social scientists survey 1,022 terms and concepts, especially in political science and sociology. Signed articles, sectionalised for different meanings; references to the literature in text; cross-references (*e.g.,* 'Gold standard': nearly 4 columns; sections A-D; 3 references in text; 2 cross-references). The aim is to provide extended discussion of each concept, determine its role in the social sciences, and its historical development. Intended for the student or practitioner in the social sciences and also for specialists in other disciplines (*Foreword*). Includes no articles on closed shop, conscientious objection, disarmament, inferiority complex, materialism, pragmatism, social science, points out *The philosophical quarterly* (v. 16, no. 65, October 1966, p. 403-4), which also criticises the entries as being explanations rather than definitions, and of uneven quality. Very well produced (print; paper; binding). "Undoubtedly the best one-volume dictionary of the language of the social scientist available today" (*Library journal,* v. 90, no. 2, 15th January 1965, p. 231).

Dictionaries

3 (038)=00

PAENSON, I., *comp.* **Systematic glossary, English-French-Spanish-Russian, of selected economic and social terms.** Oxford, Pergamon Press, 1963. xxxv, 414p. diagrs. Loose-leaf. £10.

English-French-Russian text compiled by I. Paenson; Spanish translation prepared by Luis de la Plaza and others. Prepared in co-operation with the N.I.E.S.R. (for the English text), Institut National de Statistique et d'Études Economiques (for the French text), U.N.E.C.L.A. (for the Spanish text) and the Institute of World Economy and International Relations, Moscow (for the Russian text).

About 7,000 terms are defined and explained (sometimes at length) in all 4 languages. 8 chapters, with detailed sub-division: 1. Demand —2. Production—3. Business economics—4. Labour and social security questions—5/6. Financial questions—7. Economic theories—8. International trade and other forms of international economic relations. Alphabetical index for each language.

3 (038)=20
ZADROZNY, J. T. Dictionary of social science. Washington, Public Affairs Press, 1958. 367p.

Some 4,000 terms are clearly and concisely defined. Concentrates on current usage of the more important terms, especially in sociology, political science and economics. Terminology of population statistics, psychology, physical anthropology, psychiatry, jurisprudence and statistics is also covered.

3 (038)=30
ERDSIEK, G., and DIETL, C. E. Wörterbuch für Recht, Wirtschaft und Politik, mit erläuternden und rechtsvergleichenden Kommentaren. . . . Schloss Bleckede bei Hamburg, Meissner, 1964-. v. 1-.

v. 1. *Englisch-deutsch,* pt. 1: A-K. 1964. xii, 300p. DM.58.50.

Incorporates American usage. About 5,000 entries, with numerous sub-entries in bold (*e.g.,* 'Bank': ¾ col.). Many examples of usage, with some comment. *Babel* (1965, no. 4) notes inconsistency in entry of nouns—under qualifying adjective plus noun, or under noun plus qualifying adjective? Lengthy appended list of abbreviations, A-K (p. 273-300). Promises to be a valuable addition to dictionaries in this field.

3 (038)=40
SUAVET, T. Dictionnaire économique et sociale. 3. éd. revue. Paris, Éditions Ouvrières, 1965. 479p. maps, graphs. 19.95F.

First published 1961.
A few hundred entries,—definition plus comment and usually a brief bibliography (*e.g.,* 'Cooperative': 7 columns, including a 2-column bibliography; 'Malthusianisme': 2 columns; bibliography has anti-Malthusian items). Appended chronology, 1830-1964; indexes of names and subjects. Numerous cross-references. No biographies.

A. Birou's *Vocabulaire pratique des sciences sociales,* from the same press (1966. 315p.) is on a slightly smaller scale. Articles (*e.g.,* 'Entreprise': 2½ columns; 'National-socialisme': 1 column) have no bibliographies, but there is a general bibliography (p. 297-9) of 61 items. Includes a list of names cited and an index of terms that have no main entries but are defined in the text.

3 (038)=82
SMITH, R. E. F. A Russian-English dictionary of social science terms. London, Butterworths, 1962. xii, 495p. 95s.

The compiler is Research Fellow, Department of Economics and Institutions of the U.S.S.R., University of Birmingham. About 10,000 entrywords, including entries for abbreviations; *c.* 35,000 definitions, some with explanations (*e.g.,* 'Produktsiya' has 3¾ columns of definitions and explanations; different meanings are numbered and idioms included). Indicates stress and gives different forms of the infinitives of Russian verbs. An important contribution to an area in which terminology is often equivocal or difficult to render into English (*Babel,* v. 9, no. 4, 1963, p. 197). Clear layout.

Theses

3 (043)
UNITED NATIONS EDUCATIONAL, SCIENTIFIC AND CULTURAL ORGANIZATION. Thèses de sciences sociales. . . . Theses in the social sciences: an international analytical catalogue of unpublished doctorate theses, 1940-1950. Paris, Unesco, 1952. 236p.

3,215 items, arranged under broad subjects and then by countries (French form of name) A-Z 31 countries are included. U.D.C. index and also subject, author and geographical indexes.

See also 3.001.5.

Opinions

3 (049.3)
ROBINSON, A. Pros and cons: a newspaper-reader's and debater's guide to the leading controversies of the day. 15th ed. London, Routledge and Kegan Paul, 1965. vii, 192p. 10s.

First published 1896.
Pros and cons of controversial points of current interest, religious, political, social and educational, in parallel columns. Brief notes introduce each topic (*e.g.,* closed shop, pacificism, vegetarianism). Index.

Periodicals

3 (05):016
GREAT BRITAIN. NATIONAL LENDING LIBRARY FOR SCIENCE AND TECHNOLOGY. Select list of social science serials in the N.L.L. Boston Spa, Yorkshire, N.L.L., 1966. 25p.

"The list relates only to the serials listed in (a) *International bibliography of the social sciences,* 1963, or (b) *Index bibliographicus.* 4th edition. Vol. II. *Social sciences.* 1964. . . ." About 350 titles, arranged by titles A-Z, with N.L.L. shelfmarks.

3 (05):016
UNITED STATES. BUREAU OF THE CENSUS. Foreign Manpower Research Office. **Bibliography of social science periodicals and monograph series.** Washington, U.S.G.P.O., 1961-65.

A series on 22 Communist *bloc* and other countries using so-called "difficult" languages, in general for the period 1950-60:

1. *Rumania, 1947-1960*. 1961. 25c.
2. *Bulgaria, 1944-1960*. 1961. 30c.
3. *Mainland China, 1949-1960*. 1961. 25c.
4. *Republic of China, 1949-1961*. 1961. 25c.
5. *Greece, 1950-1961*. 1962. 20c.
6. *Albania, 1944-1961*. 1962. 15c.
7. *Hong Kong, 1950-1961*. 1962. 20c.
8. *North Korea, 1945-1961*. 1962. 15c.
9. *Republic of Korea, 1945-1961*. 1962. 15c.
10. *Iceland, 1950-1962*. 1962. 15c.
11. *Denmark, 1945-1961*. 1963. 60c.
12. *Finland, 1950-1962*. 1963. 50c.
13. *Hungary, 1947-1962*. 1964. 70c.
14. *Turkey, 1950-1962*. 1964. 50c.
15. *Norway, 1945-1962*. 1964. 40c.
16. *Poland, 1945-1962*. 1964. $1.50.
17. *U.S.S.R., 1950-1963*. [1965]. $2.25.
18. *Yugoslavia, 1945-1963*. [1965]. 75c.
19. *Czechoslovakia, 1948-1963*. [1965]. 65c.
20. *Japan, 1950-1963*. [1965]. $1.75.
21. *Soviet Zone of Germany, 1948-1963*. [1965]. $1.
22. *Sweden, 1950-1963*. [1965]. 50c.

The short list covering Mainland China (no. 3. iv, 32p.) records 142 publications, 107 of them periodicals and 35, serial monographs. Entries consist of transliterated title, translated title, title in Chinese characters, place of publication, date of start, frequency, detailed statement of coverage, language. Indexes of subjects, titles and issuing organisations.

3 (05):016

World list of social sciences periodicals. 3rd ed., rev. and enl. Paris, Unesco, 1966. 448p. (Documentation in the social sciences). 60s.

First published 1952; 2nd ed. 1956.

About 1,300 entries under 'International organisations' and 92 countries, arranged A-Z. Entries under each country are numbered. Details: Title (including abbreviated form, if any, and previous titles)—Publisher—Frequency; date of start—Number of pages; number of articles and average length of each; subjects covered (with allotment of pages); number of reviews (with allotment of pages); other contents (number of pages). Title, institution and subject indexes, in French and English. Excludes periodicals that contain only statistics or regular features about economic conditions, and purely bibliographical periodicals (for which see *Index bibliographicus*, v. 2. 4th ed. (1964), at 3:016:016.

Almanacks

3 (058)=20

'Daily mail' year book. London, Associated Newspapers, Ltd., 1901-. Annual. (1967. 5s.).

The 1966 issue, the 66th year, published 1965, has 14 sections: Almanac—Current affairs—The Royal family—Religion—People—International—Education — General — Household — Holiday guide—Entertainment—Science, commerce, industry—Sport—Parliamentary. Index, p. 377-84. A popular version of *Whitaker's Almanack,* for home use.

3 (058)=20

Information please almanac. . . . New York, Macmillan, Simon & Schuster, 1947-. maps. Annual. (1966 (1965). $1.60; $2.95).

Much information not usually found in a year-book, and varying from year to year (*e.g.,* crossword-puzzle guide, cookery). Who's who and who was who, with single-line entries. Occasional descriptive articles on the year's achievements in certain fields. Useful supplementary material, but no substitute for the *World almanac.*

3 (058)=20

WHITAKER, J. An almanack for the year of Our Lord . . . London, Whitaker, 1868-. illus. Annual. (1968. 100th ed. (1967). Complete ed. 27s. 6d.; shorter ed. 15s.).

Divided into main sections: calendar (includes astronomy, time, weather), the world, Great Britain, British Commonwealth. The following are omitted from shorter ed.: Commonwealth countries, foreign countries, reviews of the year in science, literature, drama, films, and sport. Other contents in the complete ed. include government and public offices (Ministers and senior civil servants, with their salaries), lists of peers, baronets, knights, M.P.s, judges, sheriffs, county and borough councils, holders of the V.C. and George Cross, societies. Information on the churches, forces, education (lists of public schools, professional education), insurance companies and their rates, postal regulations, tide tables, income tax, national insurance, and legal notes. The index has 25,000 entries (but lacks cross-references) and excludes most personal names. Since 1954 has included illustrations of events of the previous year. The 1967 ed. has, for the first time, a list of official overseas information bureaux in London.

Invaluable in any library, and particularly useful for the variety of miscellaneous information which does not come into any of the sections listed above and must be found through the index.

3 (058)=20

The World almanac and book of facts. New York, World-Telegram, 1868-. maps. Annual. (1967. $2.75).

Similar content to *Whitaker's almanack* and equally dependent on a detailed index (with cross-references). The nearest approach to a general U.S. year-book. Includes a detailed annual chronology, memorable dates, U.S. associations and institutions, U.S. population statistics for places of 2,500 or more, and has sections on noted personalities (not all U.S.), foreign countries (A-Z; 1967: p. 593-671) and sporting events. Quotes sources of statistics.

3 (058)=40

Almanache Hachette . . . : 1001 réponses à tout. Paris, Hachette, illus. Annual. (70th year, 1965).

A mine of information on a wide range of subjects, from literary prize-winners and sports records to classification charts for zoology, botany and minerals, a chronology, a calendar and a list of leading banks in France. Subject index.

Organisations

3:06.058

UNITED STATES. NATIONAL REFERRAL CENTER FOR SCIENCE AND TECHNO-

LOGY. A directory of information resources in the United States: social sciences. Washington, Library of Congress, 1965. vi, 218p. $1.50.

Supported, like the first directory (on the physical and biological sciences, and engineering), by the National Science Foundation.

About 700 entries, arranged A-Z under names of major organisations. Indexes of subjects and organisations.

3:061 (100)
INSTITUT INTERNATIONAL DES CIVILISATIONS DIFFÉRENTES. Répertoire international des centres d'étude des civilisations et de leurs publications. International guide to study centres on civilizations and their publications. Brussels, the Institute, 1955. 156p. Belg. fr. 75; 11s.

A directory of 275 research centres concerned with anthropological, historical and socio-economic study of civilizations; classified in 23 civilization-groups or areas. Details: address; date of constitution; status; person in charge; aims; publications (periodical and other) issued since 1945 or due shortly or in preparation. Name and locality (i.e., of research centre HQs) indexes. In French and English.

3:061 (100)
UNITED NATIONS EDUCATIONAL, SCIENTIFIC AND CULTURAL ORGANIZATION. International organizations in the social sciences: a summary description of the structure and activities of non-governmental organizations specialized in the social sciences and in consultative relationship with Unesco (categories A and B). [3rd] ed. Paris, Unesco, [1965?]. 147p.

2nd ed. 1961.
In English and French. The 14 organizations dealt with (2nd ed.: 18) all belong to categories A ('consultative and associate') and B ('information and consultative') as of 1 April 1964. Details on each: organization and aims; activities (meetings; research and studies; activities in progress from 1963; recent publications); annex (officers; council members; statutes (articles in full)).

Social History

3 (091):016
International review of social history. Assen, Netherlands, Royal Van Gorcum Ltd., 1956-. v. 1-. 3 p.a. D.fl. 25 or 49s. 6d. p.a.

Previously (1937-40, 1950-55) as Bulletin of the International Institute of Social History. Edited by the Internationaal Instituut van Sociale Geschiedenis.

Each issue contains about 65 pages of annotated bibliography, c. 250 items, systematically arranged (A. General issues: 1. Religions and philosophy—2. Social and political science—3. History—4. Contemporary issues. B. Continents and countries: 1. Africa—2. America—3. Asia—4. Australia and Oceania—5. Europe). Annotations or abstracts average c. 100 words. Annual author and geographical indexes.

Biographies

3 (092) (73)
American men of science: a biographical directory. The social and behavioral sciences. 10th ed. Tempe, Arizona, Arizona State Univ., Jacques Cattell Press, 1962. ix, 1220p. $25.

Forms v. 5 of 10th ed. of American men of science (1960-62).

The 9th ed., the first in which social and behavioral sciences were treated separately, listed c. 18,000 such specialists. The 10th ed., v. 5 adds a further 4,000. Follows the same criteria for inclusion as in v. 1-4: (1) achievement plus continued activity in the field (2) research activity of high quality, as evidenced by contributions to journals of standing; (3) attainment of a position of responsibility. About 12 lines per entry. Fields covered include psychology, geography, anthropology, economics, sociology, political science and statistics.

3 (092):(6)
UNITED NATIONS EDUCATIONAL, SCIENTIFIC AND CULTURAL ORGANIZATION. Social scientists specializing in African studies. Paris & The Hague, Mouton, 1963. 375p. 57s. 6d.

Data on 2,072 social scientists, with subject index (p. 355-75). The biographical sketches average c. 30 lines and cover career, particular fields of interest, past and present activity, membership of learned societies, latest publications and postal address. "Social science" is interpreted fairly generously. Text in English and French.

3 (092):(8=6)
UNITED STATES. LIBRARY OF CONGRESS. HISPANIC FOUNDATION. National directory of Latin Americanists. Washington, D.C., the Foundation, 1966. 351p. (Hispanic Foundation. Bibliographical series, no. 10). $2.

Bio-bibliographical data on 1,884 specialists in social sciences and humanities in the Latin American field. Confined to specialists in the U.S.A.

Race Relations

(See also Guide, v. 1, at 572.9 (=96):016.)

3-054:016
VIET, J., comp. Selected documentation for the study of race relations. Paris, Unesco, 1958. 81p. (Reports and papers in the social sciences, no. 9).

Three parts: 1. Bibliography of books and articles on race relations, 1953-1956 (5 sections; 952 items)—2. Periodicals dealing, either generally or occasionally, with race relations—3. Research institutions and relevant research in the field of race relations (subdivided geographically; publications of institutions are mentioned).

3-054 (680)
SOUTH AFRICAN INSTITUTE OF RACE RELATIONS. Survey of race relations in South Africa. Johannesburg, the Institute, 1951/52-. Annual.

"A valuable summary review of developments and trends in legislation, government action and opposition" (Musiker, R. *Guide to South African reference books.* 4th ed., 1965, entry no. 72).

3-054 (73)

MILLER, E. W., *comp.* **The negro in America: a bibliography.** [Published] for the American Academy of Arts and Sciences [by] Harvard Univ. Press, Cambridge, Mass., 1966 xvii, [1], 190p.

About 4,000 items, mainly 1954-65 publications, some with very brief annotations. 14 sections: 1. Background (general; history; demography; biography)—2. Definition and description (race; social institutions and conditions; individual characteristics; health; literature and folklore)—3. Intergroup relations—4. Racial problems—5. Urban problems—6. Economic status and problems—7. Employment—8. Housing and urban renewal—9. Education—10. Public accommodations—11. Political rights and suffrage—12. The freedom revolution—13. Black nationalism—14. Tools for further research (p. 169-70). Index of authors.

3-054 (73)

WELSCH, E. K. The negro in the United States: a research guide. Bloomington & London, Indiana Univ. Press, 1965. 142p. 13s. 6d.

A narrative bibliography of *c.* 450 items, with pithy annotations and admirably arranged in four chapters: 1. Science, philosophy and race—2. Historical and sociological background (p. 8-41)—3. The major issues today (p. 42-74)—4. The negro and the arts (p. 75-93). Each chapter has an introduction; period, subject or form divisions follow, as required. Appendixes: A. Bibliographies—B. Periodicals—C. National and state organizations. Bibliography of works cited and author index; subject index. Reviewed in *Race,* v. 8, no. 1, July 1966, p. 97-98.

The American negro reference book, edited by J. P. Davis (Englewood Cliffs, N.J., Prentice-Hall, [1966]. xxii, 969p. diagrs., tables, charts. $19.95) has 22 chapters, covering all major aspects of negro life in America,—social, economic, religious, political, legal, professional, military, sports, literary and artistic. Intended for consecutive reading. Reviewed in *The booklist,* v. 62, no. 1, 1st July 1966, p. 1005-8.

3-054.001.5

Research on race relations: articles reprinted from the *International social science journal.* Paris, Unesco, 1966. 265p. tables. 25s.

Contributions, mostly by sociologists and anthropologists, mainly drawn from the *International social science journal* and *Bulletin,* 1958-61. Includes trend reports on current research. Supplemented by a specially commissioned study on the Pacific area; selected, up-to-date bibliography. Reviewed in *Race,* v. 8, no. 2, October 1966, p. 210.

Research

3.001:016

GREAT BRITAIN. DEPARTMENT OF EDUCATION AND SCIENCE, and **BRITISH**

COUNCIL. Scientific research in British universities and colleges, 1966-67. v. 3. **Social sciences** (including Government Departments and other institutions). London, H.M. Stationery Office, 1967. xxvii, 272p. 32s. 6d.

This volume replaces the *Register of research in the human sciences,* hitherto produced by the Warren Spring Laboratory, Ministry of Technology (see below). Compiled at the request of, and in co-operation with, the Social Science Research Council.
14 sections: 1. Economics—2. Politics and public administration—3. Law—4. Sociology—5. Social administration—6. Industrial administration—7. Social anthropology—8. Psychology—9. Mental health—10. Social medicine—11. Human geography—12. Human biology—13. History and philosophy of science—14. Information science. "Includes research in Government Departments and other non-academic institutions and indicates starting and finishing dates and names of sponsors where supplied" (*Introduction*). 235 institutions; name index; analytical subject index (p. 234-72).

3.001.5:016

GREAT BRITAIN. WARREN SPRING LABORATORY. Register of research in the human sciences . . . London, H.M. Stationery Office, 1962-65. Irregular. (3rd ed.: 1962-65. 1965. 37s. 6d.).

1st ed. (1962) covered 1959-61; 2nd ed. (1963), 1960-63.
Information on research in progress on the science of human relations in industry. The 3rd ed. carried 1,291 numbered entries in 19 sections, including for the first time information from Northern Ireland. Index of institutions and their entries; subject index.
Now replaced by *Scientific research in British universities and colleges.* v. 3. *Social sciences* (q.v.).

3.001.5:016

NATIONAL INSTITUTE OF ECONOMIC AND SOCIAL RESEARCH. Register of research in the social sciences in progress and in plan, nos. 5-13. 1947/48-1956/57. London, Cambridge Univ. Press; London, Aslib, 1948-57.

Nos. 1-4: 1943-46/47, were not for sale.
Projects and developments in the U.K. and Eire, arranged under broad headings (anthropology; demography; economics; economic and social history, education, geography; industrial relations and management; international relations; political sciences; public administration; social psychology; social medicine; social surveys; sociology), with sub-division by sponsoring body. The 1955 volume covered 1,811 such projects. Ph.D. theses in progress or recently accepted are also listed.
A valuable feature is the appended Directory of research institutions and university research sections (name, address, telephone number; foundation and policy; organization; research arrangements; publications). Index of institutions and their entries; subject index; author index.

3.001.5:016

UNITED STATES. BUREAU OF INTELLI-GENCE AND RESEARCH. External research: a list of current social science research by private scholars and academic centers. Washington, 1952-. 7 pts. Irregular.

An annual series of 7 booklets, one for each of six geographical areas (1. U.S.S.R. and Eastern Europe—2. Asia—3. Western Europe, Great Britain and Canada—4. Middle East—5. Africa —6. American republics—7. International affairs). As from 1965 includes studies both in progress and completed. Entries cover dissertations, contributions to be included in collective works, periodical articles and the like. Estimated date of completion (EDC) is stated, where appropriate. Based on information submitted by scholars and research centres in the U.S.A., and therefore largely U.S.-slanted. The 1966 v. on *Asia* ([vii], 124p.) is arranged by countries A-Z and includes the Pacific area. The section on India has subdivisions: economics, education, foreign relations, geography, government and politics, history, language and literature, law, philosophy and religion, social conditions. The 1966 v. on *International affairs* ([v], 111p.) has *c.* 1,300 entries in 19 subject sections.

3.001.5 (6)

LYSTAD, R. A., *ed.* **The African world:** a summary of social research. Published for the African Studies Association by Pall Mall Press, London, 1965. xv, 575p. tables, map. 126s.

Aims "to summarise and show relationships among current, recent and pertinent earlier research 'within' a particular discipline or area of knowledge. . . . The greatest attention . . . is given to sub-Saharan material published in the English language" (*Editor's Preface*). 18 chapters in 3 main parts: 1. Historical and socio-cultural studies—2. Physico-biological studies—3. Psycho-cultural studies. Chapter notes and bibliographies, p. 493-560. A valuable and well-produced survey. Very favourably reviewed in *Geographical journal,* v. 132, pt. 1, March 1966, p. 103; also *Africa,* v. 36, no. 3, July 1966, p. 331-2. The author is Professor of African Studies at the School of Advanced International Studies, Johns Hopkins Univ.

B. Rupp's *Inventaire des registres de la recherche en cours dans le domaine des sciences sociales et humaines en Afrique noire* (Paris, École Pratique des Hautes Études. Centre d'Analyse et de Recherche Documentaires pour l'Afrique Noire, 1966. 32 l. Mimeographed) is a draft, annotated bibliography of 66 numbered items.

3.001.5 (94):016

SOCIAL SCIENCE RESEARCH COUNCIL OF AUSTRALIA. Bibliography of research in the social sciences in Australia, 1960-1963. Canberra, Australian National Univ. Press, 1966. xx, 278p. $A.50.

An author index. Previous issues were confined to research projects at universities and resulting publications. The 1960-1963 list has been extended to cover research projects and resulting publications in the social sciences carried out by Government departments and other non-university agencies. 3,117 authors are listed under 21 subjects. Includes research in progress as well as completed. List of *c.* 500 journals cited. Index of names.

SOCIOLOGY

301:016

BOTTOMORE, T. B. Sociology: a guide to problems and literature. London, Allen & Unwin, 1962 [*i.e.,* 1963]. 330p. 21s., 30s.

The aim is to "present sociological concepts, theories and methods in relation to the culture and institutions of Indian society" (*Preface*). 6 parts (each with 'Notes on reading' appended): 1. The scope and methods of sociology—2. Population and social groupings—3. Social institutions—4. Social control—5. Social change—6. Applied psychology. Numerous footnote references. Non-analytical index of subjects and names.

301:016

Bulletin signalétique. 21. Sociologie. Ethnologie. Paris, Centre National de la Recherche Scientifique, 1961-. Quarterly. 20F. (foreign, 25F.) p.a.

Part of sections 19-24. *Sciences humaines. Philosophie,* published separately. Formerly part of *Bulletin analytique. Philosophie* (v. 1-9. 1947-55), then of Bulletin signalétique. 19. *Philosophie. Sciences humaines* (1956-60).

About 4,000 indicative abstracts p.a. Sociologie: 19 sections; Ethnologie: 14 sections. Subject index to each issue.

301:016

Current sociology . . . Paris, Unesco, 1952-57; Oxford, Blackwell, 1958-. Quarterly. 25s. p.a.

Prepared for the International Sociological Association under the auspices of the International Committee for Social Sciences Documentation.

An international bibliography of sociology. Certain issues of v. 1-4 form annual volumes of *International bibliography of sociology* (q.v.) for 1951-54. Each v. now comprises a trend report (with résumé in French), plus supporting bibliography. V. 14, no. 3, 1966: 'Learning and behavior: a trend report and bibliography', by F. J. Stendenbach (trend report, p. 7-51; classified and annotated bibliography, of 858 numbered items, p. 62-132; list of periodicals with abbreviations; author index); v. 14, no. 2, 1966: 'Comparative sociology, 1950-1963: a trend report and bibliography', by R. M. Marsh (trend report, p. 5-34; classified and annotated bibliography of 976 items, p. 41-138; etc.).

301:016

International bibliography of sociology . . . Paris, Unesco, 1952-61; London, Stevens (subsequently Tavistock Publications), 1962-. v. 1-9, 10-.

Prepared by the International Committee for Social Sciences Documentation. Earliest volumes (1951-54) formed part of *Current sociology* (q.v.).

V. 15: 1965 (1966) contains 5,251 items. 6 main sections: A. History and organization of social studies—B. Theories and methods of sociology —C. Social structure—D. Social control and communication—E. Social change—F. Social problems and social policy. Author and subject (only partly analytical) indexes. V. 15 was received in December 1966—virtually an 18-months' time-lag.

301:016

Sociological abstracts. New York, Sociological Abstracts, Inc., 1952-. v. 1, no. 1-. 8 p.a., including cumulative index issue. ea. $15; $100 p.a.

About 5,000 informative and indicative signed abstracts p.a. of books and periodical articles from a wide range of journals. 21 sections, with sub-divisions: Methodology and research technology—Sociology: history, theory and the sociology of knowledge—Social psychology—Culture and social structure—Complex organizations (management)—Social change and economic development—Mass phenomena—Political interactions—Social differentiation—Community development and rural sociology —Urban structure and ecology—Sociology of the arts—Sociology of education—Sociology of religion—Social control—Sociology of science—Demography and human biology—The family and socialization—Sociology of health and medicine—Social problems and social welfare. Appended to sections are listed journals from which abstracts are taken. Cross-references. Each issue carries an author index. A major source in the field, updating *International bibliography of sociology*.

301 (02)

OGBURN, W. F., and **NIMKOFF, M. F.** A **handbook of sociology.** 5th ed., rev. London, Routledge & Kegan Paul, 1964. xii, 644p. tables, graphs, charts. (International library of sociology and social reconstruction). 40s.

First published 1947 in U.S.A.; 3rd U.S. ed. (1958) as *Sociology*.
26 chapters, each with summary, questions for study and selected readings, as well as numerous footnote references. 7 parts: 1. Introduction—2. Society—3. Group behaviour—4. Personality—5. Human ecology and population—6. Social organization—7. Socio-cultural change. The U.S. material "is purely illustrative and not integral to the argument" (*Preface to the first English edition*). Analytical index, p. 618-64. A basic textbook.

Traité de sociologie, edited by G. Gurvitch, (Paris, Presses Universitaires de France, 1958-60. 2v. ea. 30 F.) is a collection of essays that between them cover many of the social sciences. Like Ogburn and Nimkoff, has chapter bibliographies, but no index.

301 (03)

FAIRCHILD, H. P., ed. **Dictionary of sociology.** New York. Philosophical Library, 1944. [iv], 342p. (New ed. London, Transatlantic Book Service, 1962. 341p. 16s.).

Signed entries, varying from brief definitions to lengthier comments. Some 500 entries in all;

many cross-references. Biographies are excluded. The author was first President of the Population Association of America.

Dictionary of sociology, edited by G. D. Mitchell is due for publication by Routledge & Kegan Paul in 1968 (viii, 224p. 25s.). It covers nearly 300 entries. The editor is Professor of Sociology, Univ. of Exeter, and the book is designed for students of the social sciences in universities and colleges.

A. Cuvillier's *Manuel de sociologie, avec notices bibliographiques* (4. éd. Paris, Presses Universitaires de France, 1960-62. 2v.) is equipped with lengthy general and chapter bibliographies. Each volume has an index of names and concepts.

301 (038)=30

BERNSDORF, W., and **BÜLOW, F. Wörterbuch der Soziologie.** Stuttgart, Enke, 1955. vii, 640p.

Signed articles on topics and terms in the field of sociology by 84 leading social scientists, chiefly German. Biographies are omitted. Brief bibliographies are appended to lengthier articles. No index, but abundant cross-references.
A successor, in some sense, to the *Handwörterbuch der Soziologie;* hrsg. von A. Verkandt (Stuttgart, Enke, 1931. 690p.).

301 (047.1)

L'Année sociologique. Paris, Alcan, 1896-1925; Paris, Presses Universitaires de France, 1948-. Annual.

More than half of each annual consists of a selective survey of the significant literature of sociology in 9 or 10 sections (general sociology; collective psychology; social morphology; social systems and civilisation; sociology of religion, etc.). About 200-300 reviews of varying length p.a. Author index.

301 (092)

BERNSDORF, W., and **KNOSPE, H.,** ed. **Internationales Soziologen-Lexikon,** unter Mitarbeit zahlreicher Fachleute des In- und Auslandes. Stuttgart, Enke, 1959. viii, 662p. DM.49.

Complementary to *Wörterbuch der Soziologie*, by W. Bernsdorf and F. Bülow (q.v.).
A biographical dictionary, including living sociologists. About 1,000 entries; 55 contributors, none of them British. Signed articles; the chief works of writers are listed; if they are deemed important, material on them is also given (*e.g.,* Mao Tse-tung: 1½p.; 12 items by him; 11 items on him). Some German slant (*e.g.,* Sidney Webb —1¼p.; Max Weber—10p.).

Supplemented by biographical entries in E. Willems' *Dictionnaire de sociologie. Adaptation française*, par Armand Cuvillier (Paris, Rivière, 1961. 272p.).

301 (-202):016

"Rural sociology". In *World agricultural economics and rural sociology*, April 1959-. Amsterdam, North-Holland Publishing Co., 1959-64; Farnham Royal, Bucks., Commonwealth Agricultural Bureaux, 1965-. Quarterly. 60s. p.a. to subscribers in C.A.B. contributing countries; 100s. to subscribers in other countries.

As from 1965 prepared by the Commonwealth Bureau of Agricultural Economics, Oxford.

About 300 informative abstracts p.a. on rural sociology. Sub-divisions: O. General—1. Demography—2. Rural communities—3. Migrations—4. Rural/urban contrasts and relations—5. Living standards and conditions—6. Leadership—7. Adoption of innovations.

"WAERSA" has a quarterly author index; annual author, and subject and geographical indexes.

French bibliographical digest. Rural sociology, by H. Mendras (New York, French Embassy, 1964. 156p. (no. 39, series 2), "intended primarily to make the contributions of French scholars and scientists better known in the United States", consists of 506 annotated entries in 8 sections. Appendix: Bibliographies — Periodicals — Archives and documentation centers—Maps and atlases.

301.001.5:061.6
UNITED NATIONS EDUCATIONAL, SCIENTIFIC AND CULTURAL ORGANIZATION. International repertory of sociological research centres outside the United States of America. Prepared by the International Committee for Social Sciences Documentation, Paris, December 1961. Paris, Unesco, 1965. 125p. (Reports and papers in the social sciences, no. 20). 6s.

Includes only fully-fledged institutions or centres with a permanent staff and some remunerated research workers. Entries state full name and address, date of foundation, status, management, scientific and administrative staff, finances, information on recent and current research, equipment and publications. Reviewed in *Board of Trade journal,* v. 188, no. 3561, 18th June 1965, p. 1345.

Public Opinion

301.153:016
SMITH, B. L., and SMITH, C. M. International communication and public opinion: a guide to the literature. Prepared for the Rand Corporation by the Bureau of Social Science Research, Washington, D.C. Princeton, N.J., Princeton Univ. Press, 1956. xi, 325p.

2,563 numbered, annotated entries (annotations average *c.* 100 words). 7 sections: 1. Theoretical and general writings relevant to international communication and censorship—2. Political persuasion and propaganda activities (by country of origin)—3. Specialists in political persuasion—4. Channels ('Media') of international communication (to, from and in particular areas)—5. Audience characteristics—6. Methods of research and intelligence—7. Bibliographies. Appendix A is a note on current sources, and B, a list of journals. Author and subject index.

Communities

301.18:016
LONDON. UNIVERSITY. INSTITUTE OF EDUCATION. Community Development Library.

Bulletin of acquisitions: a selective list of articles, reprints and publications received by the Library. August 1960-. Irregular. Mimeographed.

The Community Development Library was the Community Development Clearing House until v. 4, no. 1, March 1966.
The December 1966 issue (v. 4, no. 4) contains *c.* 100 annotated entries, systematically arranged.

Community development abstracts (Washington, Department of State, Rural & Community Development Service, Office of Technical Cooperation & Research, [1964], [iv], [i], 282p.) comprises *c.* 1,108 abstracts, covering the literature from the early 1950s. Pt. 1, periodical literature (19 sections); pt. 2, monographs, books, reports, etc. Four indexes: author, periodical title, subject and nation-tribe-society.

Social Geography

308 (4/9):016
Geographical abstracts. D. Social geography. Edited by Christopher Board; published by K. M. Clayton. London, Geo Abstracts, Dept. of Geography, London School of Economics, 1966-. 6 p.a. 54s. p.a.

1966: 1,103 signed informative abstracts. Covers periodical articles, books, reports, British government publications and mimeographed material. 16 sections: General human—Social—Population distribution—Population movement and change—Man and environment—Regional studies—Cultural (including agrarian studies)—Political—Planning problems—Urban: general and theoretical—Urban: regional and descriptive —Rural settlement—Methodology—Techniques —Bibliography and source material—Miscellaneous. Annual author and regional indexes included in last issue of each year. A comprehensive annual subject index to all 4 parts of *Geographical abstracts* for 1966 appeared in 1967 (180s. p.a.).

308 (4/9) (02)
UNITED NATIONS. Progress of the non-self-governing territories under the Charter. New York, United Nations, 1960-61. 5v.

v. 1: *General review.* 1961.
v. 2: *Economic conditions.* 1961.
v. 3: *Social conditions.* 1961.
v. 4: *Educational conditions.* 1961.
v. 5: *Territorial surveys.* 1960.
A report on progress achieved by the non-self-governing territories in pursuance of Chapter XI of the Charter. V. 5 provides an economic survey, territory by territory, with numerous tables (statistics up to 1956 or 1957) and maps.

308 (4/9) (058)
UNITED NATIONS. Department of Economic and Social Affairs. 1963 report on the world social situation. New York, United Nations, 1963. x, 191p. tables. (E/CN.5/375/Rev. 1). $2.50.

To be issued biennially, covering, in alternate editions, social conditions and social programmes, on one hand, and urgent comprehensive social problems on the other. Later reports are for 1965 (E/CN.5/402) and 1967 (E.CN.5/417).

The 1963 v. "has as its main task the summing-up of trends in social conditions and social programmes since 1950" (*Preface*). 14 chapters, including chapters on social development in Latin America, the Middle East, Asia and Africa. Many tables numerous footnote references.

308 (4/9) (083.4)
UNITED NATIONS. Statistical Office. Compendium of social statistics, 1963 (data available as of 1 November 1962). New York, United Nations, 1963. xii, 586p. tables. (Statistical papers, series K, no. 2). $7.

104 tables, with statistics up to 1960 and retrospective: population and vital statistics (11)—Health conditions (12-17)—Food consumption and nutrition (18-53)—Housing (54-57)—Education and cultural activities (58-65)—Labour force and conditions of employment (66-93, with some sub-divided)—Social security (94-99)—Income and expenditure (100-104). Many footnote definitions; explanatory notes. In English and French.

308 (410)
GREAT BRITAIN. THE GOVERNMENT SOCIAL SURVEY. List of published Social Survey reports. [London, the Survey, 1966.] 40p. Unpriced.

About 300 annotated items, stating date of fieldwork and price (if any) of reports. Items asterisked are o.p. 3 parts: 1. Reports on surveys carried out by the Social Survey (a) individual studies; (b) based on a number of studies; (c) consumer expenditure surveys—2. Papers by staff of Social Survey—3. Reports by other bodies, based on or including the results of, Social Survey work.

308 (47):016
Soviet periodical abstracts. Soviet society. New York, Slavic Languages Research Institute, 1961-. Quarterly.

1961, as *Selective Soviet annotated bibliographies. Soviet society.*
Nearly 1,000 abstracts and references p.a., systematically arranged. Covers new Soviet books and periodical articles in the field of education, sociology, philosophy, public administration and non-governmental institutions.

308 (5-013):016
Southern Asia social science bibliography (with annotations and abstracts). Delhi, [Unesco] Research Centre on Social and Economic Development in Southern Asia, 1959-. Annual.

Resulted from the merging of *South Asia social science abstracts* (1952-58) and *South Asia social science bibliography.*
No. 12: 1963 (1965): 1,519 items. Countries covered: India, Pakistan, Ceylon, Burma, Indonesia, Malaya and Singapore, Philippines, Thailand and Vietnam. 6 main sections: 1. Social sciences—2. Sociology—3. Social anthropology—4. Social psychology—5. Political science—6. Economics. Draws on 162 periodicals. Author and subject indexes.

308 (56):016
UNITED NATIONS EDUCATIONAL, SCIENTIFIC AND CULTURAL ORGANIZATION. Middle East Science Co-operation Office. Retrospective bibliography of social science works published in the Middle East, 1945-1955. Cairo, the Office, 1959. vi, 299p.

A bibliography of works published in Iraq, Jordan, Lebanon and the United Arab Republic. It lists books, periodical articles and mimeographed reports, but not unpublished theses and articles in the daily press. See also Unesco *Bibliographical news*, v. 9, no. 3, May 1960, p. 11.

308(6):016
"Bibliographie africaniste". In *Journal de la Société des Africanistes.* Paris, Société des Africanistes, 1931-. v. 1-. Annual.

About 1,000 items p.a., systematically arranged, listing books and periodical articles on the social sciences in Africa. Author index.

308 (8=6):016
Handbook of Latin American studies. Prepared by a number of scholars for the Hispanic Foundation of the Library of Congress. Earl J. Pariseau, editor. no. 27: **Social sciences,** Gainesville, Univ. of Florida Press, 1965. xvi, 515p. $20.

As from no. 26, the *Handbook* covers *Humanities* and *Social sciences* in alternate years. No. 27 contains 4,264 numbered, annotated entries (with numerous intercalations). Some entries are signed. 8 main sections: Bibliography and general works—Anthropology—Economics—Education—Geography—Government and international relations—Law—Sociology. Sub-divided by area and country. 66 contributing editors (all U.S.); 5 foreign corresponding editors. Nearly 600 journals are cited. Subject and author indexes. Special article: 'Latin American studies in Japan'.

308 (8=6) (047)
INTER-AMERICAN DEVELOPMENT BANK. Social Progress Trust Fund. . . . Annual report, 1961-. Washington, the Bank, 1962-. tables, maps.

"The principal source of the Trust Fund is to contribute to the social development and the institutional progress of Latin America through long-term, low-interest loans and technical assistance" (*Preface*). The annual reports are, in effect, social, economic and institutional surveys of progress in 19 Latin American republics, both regionally and individually. Thus, in the *Fifth annual report, 1965* (xi, [1], 626p. 1966), the section on Chile (p. 199-228) has headings: 1. Population and level of living—2. Recent economic trends—3. Progress achieved in implementing the Act of Bogotá and the Charter of Punta del Este—Sources of basic data. 6 tables.

308 (910):016
PAMUNTJAK, R., *comp.* **A regional bibliography of social science publications: Indonesia.** [Djakarta?]. National Bibliographic Center, [1955?]. ii, 65p.

Sponsored by Unesco.
594 numbered items in 4 sections: 1. Anthropology—2. Sociology—3. Political science—4.

Economics. Author and subject indexes. List of periodicals, with abbreviations. Includes books, periodical articles and texts of political speeches. Covers works by Indonesian writers or non-Indonesian affairs, as well as contributions by foreign writers.

A second bibliography is to cover the post-1954 period.

308 (94):016

Australian public affairs information service: a subject index to current literature. Canberra, National Library of Australia, 1945-. Monthly (except December), cumulated annually (since 1955). Mimeographed. ea. $0.50; $2.50, annual cumulation; $8 for complete service.

'APAIS' is a current guide to material on Australian political, economic, social and cultural affairs. The November 1966 issue had *c*. 375 items, arranged under subjects A-Z, with subdivisions. 134 periodicals, published both in Australia and overseas, indexed; 34 of them comprehensively indexed (e.g., *Current notes on international affairs; Local government administration*). Some annual reports of government agencies and other important organisations are also indexed.

Australian social science abstracts (Melbourne, Australian National Research Council, nos. 1-18. March 1946-November 1954. 2 p.a.) was systematically arranged, with *c*. 300-350 abstracts p.a. and annual index.

31 STATISTICS

(for Economic statistics, see under 33.)

Dictionaries

31 (032)

MULHALL, M. G. The dictionary of statistics. 4th ed., rev. to November 1898. London, Routledge, 1899. [vi], 853p. tables.

Arrangement is by subjects, alphabetically; numerous tables. Period covered is from *c*. A.D. 300 to 1898. List of books of reference, p. 822-25. Index of places and topics. Sources are sometimes quoted for the statistics cited.

Supplemented by:

31 (032)

WEBB, A. D. The new dictionary of statistics: a complement to the fourth edition of Mulhall's "Dictionary of Statistics". London, Routledge, 1911. xii, 682p. tables.

Covers the period 1899-1909. Similar in pattern to Mulhall, but it does give sources for all figures cited. On the other hand, Webb only cites data for which he can quote chapter and verse, thereby excluding a certain amount of useful information. The 325 sources cited are listed on p. 648-54.

31 (038)=00

KENDALL, M. G., and BUCKLAND, W. R. A dictionary of statistical terms. 2nd ed., with a combined glossary in English, French, German, Italian and Spanish. Edinburgh, Oliver & Boyd, 1960. xi, 575p. 32*s*.; Supplement only, 10*s*. 6*d*.

First published 1957.

Prepared for the International Statistical Institute with the assistance of Unesco.

The English dictionary (1,500 terms and definitions), an unchanged reprint, occupies p. 1-320. Supplementary glossaries of French, German, Italian and Spanish terms, with English equivalents and page references, p. 321-575. A reverse key (*e.g.*, English-French, etc.) would have been helpful.

A 2nd ed. of the Inter-American Statistical Institute's *Statistical vocabulary* (Washington, Pan American Union, 1960. xi, 83p. $3; 1st ed. 1950) lists *c*. 1,500 terms in English. with Spanish, Portuguese and French equivalents and indexes.

The Hungarian Statistical Office's *Statisztikai szótár* (Budapest; London, Collet's, 1961. viii, [1], 142, [1]p. 40*s*. is a statistical dictionary of 1,700 terms in seven languages,—Russian, Hungarian, Bulgarian, Czech, Polish, German, English).

31 (038)=40

NIXON, J. W. Glossary of terms in official statistics, English-French, French-English. Published for the International Statistical Institute by Oliver & Boyd, Edinburgh & London, 1964. xiv, 106p. 42*s*.

Pt. 1, English-French (p. 3-43); pt. 2, French-English (p. 47-104); *c*. 3,500 and 4,500 specialised entry-words respectively, with equivalents. Appendix 1: 'List of principal sources consulted'; 2: 'Existing glossaries or dictionaries giving terms in English and French used in official statistics'. Clear layout; good use of bold type. Compiler was formerly Chief Statistician, International Labour Office.

World statistics

31 (4/9):016

BALL, J., *ed.* **Foreign statistical documents:** a bibliography of general, international trade and agricultural statistics, including holdings of the Stanford University Libraries. Stanford Univ., Stanford, Cal., Hoover Institution on War, Revolution and Peace, 1967. vii, 173p.

About 1,700 entries, under countries A-Z. Arrangement under each country: general statistics (annuals; bulletins)—trade statistics (annuals; bulletins)—agricultural statistics (annuals; bulletins)—annual reports of departments of agriculture. Entries double-asterisked are for items not held in the Stanford, Hoover or Food Research Institute libraries but recorded in Gregory's *List of the serial publications of foreign governments, 1815-1931*. Call numbers given; gaps in holdings stated in detail.

31 (4/9):016

"Bibliography". In *1963 supplement to the 'Monthly bulletin of statistics'*: definitions and explanatory notes (fifth issue) (New York, United Nations, 1964), p. 238-54.

A valuable current list of "the most important government and central bank publications, a part of which is used as sources from the statistical data contained in the *Monthly bulletin of statistics*". Arrangement is by countries A-Z. Continents and larger regions (*e.g.,* Latin America) are not covered as such. Under each country the official source of statistical data (central statistical office or equivalent institution) is given first, then all the other publishing authorities, including private and/or semi-official institutions. Includes official statistical annuals and bulletins as well as bank reports.

31 (4/9):016

UNITED NATIONS. Statistical Office. Department of Economic and Social Affairs. **List of statistical series collected by international organizations.** New York, February 1955. viii, 78p. (Statistical papers. Series M, no. 11. Rev. 1).

First published 1951.
"The list is confined to statistics appearing in periodical international or regional tables; compilations appearing only once, or referring to a single country are not listed. . . . For the most part the information refers to 1954" (*Introduction*). 53 publications (year-books, monthlies, quarterlies; semi-annual and *ad hoc* publications) of 25 agencies are analysed. Of these agencies, 5 are U.N. Commissions, 10 are U.N. Special Agencies, and 10 are other agencies (*e.g.,* International Rubber Study Group; Commonwealth Economic Committee; Lloyd's *Register of shipping*).
Arranged by subject. Columns show subject, frequency, name of organization, and name of publication.

31 (4/9):016

VERWEY, G., and RENOOIJ, D. C. The economist's handbook: a manual of statistical sources. Amsterdam, Economist's Handbook, 1934. viii, 1460p.; **Supplement.** 1937. iii, 79p.

The main section consists (p. 39-200) of subjects, arranged alphabetically, with country subdivision. Column form is used to facilitate reference, sources of information being given in the right-hand column. An equally extensive section follows (p. 203-415), listing the sources quoted (general; then by countries A-Z; then by frequency of publication—annual, quarterly, monthly, etc.), with notes on their scope. Finally, there is an alphabetical index of sources. Countries drawn upon are: Belgium, France, Germany, Netherlands, Switzerland, the U.K., and U.S.A. The Supplement lists additional source material and gives corrigenda. Now largely of historical value only.

31 (4/9) (051):016

ORGANISATION FOR EUROPEAN ECONOMIC CO-OPERATION. Bibliographie des périodiques statistiques cataloguées à la Bibliothèque. 7. éd. Paris, O.E.E.C., 1957. 159p. Mimeographed.

4th ed. 1954.
The 7th ed. lists 1,062 statistical periodicals of 81 countries and territories, and 122 statistical periodicals published by 23 international, govern-

mental and non-governmental organisations. Excludes economic or technical periodicals that publish statistics or that sometimes contain articles illustrated with statistical data. Entry consists of full present title, issuing body, frequency, and the O.E.E.C. Library's holdings.

31 (4/9) (051):016

UNITED STATES. LIBRARY OF CONGRESS. Census Library Project. **Statistical bulletins:** an annotated bibliography of the general statistical bulletins of major political sub-divisions of the world; prepared by P. G. Carter. Washington, Library of Congress, 1954. 93p. 75c.

Arranged by continent and then by country or area. Concerned with official periodical bulletins recording current statistics on a variety of subjects. Annotations state the type of current statistical data that appear regularly and also indicate presence of bibliographies, plus background information. Locations in Washington are given.

31 (4/9) (051/)

UNITED NATIONS. Statistical Office. **Monthly bulletin of statistics.** New York, United Nations, 1947-. no. 1, August 1946-. Monthly. ea. $1; $10 p.a.

The January 1967 issue has 70 subject tables from more than 180 countries and territories. Annual figures for five or six recent years, as well as monthly figures for up to two years. Special features: A. World trade: index numbers by regions—B. World railway traffic—C. International sea-borne shipping: world total. 'List of new series and revisions', p. 213-4. Provides current economic and social data for many of the tables published in the United Nations *Statistical yearbook* (see at 31 (4/9) (058)).
A *Supplement* of definitions and explanatory notes to the *Monthly bulletin* is issued every few years (*e.g.,* 1954, 1956, 1959, 1963) (see at 31(4/9):016).

31 (4/9) (058):016

UNITED STATES. LIBRARY OF CONGRESS. Census Library Project. **Statistical year books:** an annotated bibliography of the general statistical year-books of major political sub-divisions of the world; prepared by P. G. Carter. Washington, Library of Congress, 1953. 123p. 90c.

Arranged by continent and then by country or area (some 200 countries and areas in all). Annotated entries with information on historical background, contents of the most recent issue, and the location in Washington, of the last five issues.

31 (4/9) (058/)

UNITED NATIONS. Statistical Office. **Statistical yearbook . . .** New York, United Nations, 1949-. v. 1-. Annual. (18th issue, 1966. 1967. 112s. 6d.).

Continues the *Statistical year-book of the League of Nations,* 1926-1942/44 (Geneva, 1927-45).
The 17th issue (1966) has sections: World survey—Population—Manpower—Agriculture—Forestry — Fishery — Industrial production—Mining, quarrying—Manufacturing (tables 82-

138)—Construction — Energy — Internal trade — External trade—Transport—Communications—Consumption—Balance of payments—Wages and prices — National accounts — Finance — Public finance—Social statistics—Housing—Education, culture. 204 tables. Appendix: Conversion coefficients and factors. Over 150 countries and areas covered. Country index is non-analytical (*e.g.,* Zambia: 5½ lines of blind references). In English and French. Sources are cited.

Current data on many of the tables appear regularly in the *Monthly bulletin of statistics* (see at 31 (4/9) (051/)).

31 (4/9-77)
EUROPEAN COMMUNITIES. Statistical Office. **Associés d'outre-mer: annuaire de statistiques générales.** Brussels, the Office, 1966-. Annual.

Population, social, economic, financial and trade statistics of overseas countries, territories and departments associated with the European Communities. These are: Burundi, Cameroun, Central African Republic, Chad, Congo (Brazzaville), Congo (Kinshasa), Dahomey, Gabon, Ivory Coast, Malagasy, Mali, Mauretania, Niger, Rwanda, Senegal, Somalia, Togo, Upper Volta, Surinam, Netherlands Antilles, St. Pierre & Miquelon, Comoro Archipelago, French Somaliland, New Caledonia, French Polynesia, Guadeloupe, French Guiana, Martinique and Réunion.

Europe
(See also 31 (7).)

31 (4)
EUROPEAN COMMUNITIES. Statistical Office. **Basic statistics of the community;** comparison with some European countries, Canada, the United States of America, Japan and with the Union of Socialist Soviet Republics. 7th ed. Brussels, the Office, 1966. 204p. tables, bar diagrs. Belg.fr. 50.

A handy pocket-sized paperback, comprising 130 tables in 12 sections, with statistics up to 1965, and retrospective to 1955 in some cases. Footnotes to tables.

The European Communities are the European Coal and Steel Community, the European Economic Community and the European Atomic Energy Authority.

Supplemented by the Statistical Office's *General statistical bulletin* (1959-. 11 p.a.) and *Statistical information* (1960-. Quarterly). Both are in Dutch, English, French, German and Italian editions.

The Council of Europe's *Données statistiques. Statistical data . . . : population, employment, agriculture, industry, trade, transport, external trade, finance* (Strasbourg, the Council of Europe), first published in 1955, has not appeared since the 1959 v. (1960, cviii, 605p.), with its 438 tables.

31 (4)
HARVEY, J. Statistics—Europe: sources for market research. Beckenham, Kent, CBD Research, Ltd., 1968. xi, [170]p. 60s.

Aims "to provide market researchers with up-to-date information on published statistics and to

indicate the availability of unpublished statistics . . ." (*Introduction*). Covers the 38 countries of Europe, A-Z ('Europe' (20p.) precedes). For each country, data on central statistical office, statistics libraries, bibliographies of statistics, and statistical publications (general; production; external trade; internal distribution; population; standard of living), stating coverage and time factor. Cross-references; indexes of titles and of organisations. Well produced and arranged.

31 (4)
ROSS, I. "Statistical and other information sources". In *Aslib proceedings,* v. 14, no. 6, June 1962, p. 152-75.

A survey of sources in the European Economic Community, with a valuable appendix: 'Guide to sources of statistics in Common Market countries' (International statistics—Country statistics—Publications of official and non-official organizations—European market surveys—Publications relating to Common Market activities—Advertising—Bank reviews—Tariff and tax information—Important directories—Leading financial newspapers).

Commonwealth

31 (41-5)
GREAT BRITAIN. COMMONWEALTH OFFICE. Dependent Territories Division. **Digest of statistics.** London, H.M. Stationery Office, 1965-. no. 57-. Annual. (no. 58. August 1966).

Originally as Colonial Office. *Digest of colonial statistics,* 1950-59 (6 p.a.), then as Colonial Office. *Quarterly digest of colonial statistics,* 1959-62, and then Colonial Office. *Digest of statistics,* 1963-65. Designed as a companion to the *Monthly digest of statistics.*

Covers some 30 territories (trade; industrial production; prices; finance). Retrospective figures; explanatory footnotes.

Great Britain

31 (410)
GREAT BRITAIN. CENTRAL STATISTICAL OFFICE. Statistical digest of the War. London, H.M. Stationery Office and Longmans, Green, 1951. xii, 1248p. tables. (History of the Second World War. United Kingdom civil series).

192 tables in 12 sections: 1. Population and vital statistics—2. Manpower—3. Social conditions—4. Agriculture and food—5. Fuel and power—6. Raw materials—7. Production—8. External trade—9. Transport—10. Public finance—11. National income—12. Wages and prices. Definitions and explanatory notes. Analytical index. Covers the years 1939 (or 1940)-1945.

31 (410):016
GREAT BRITAIN. H.M. TREASURY. Government statistical services. 2nd ed. London, H.M.S.O., 1962. 34p. 3s.

Outlines the work of the British Government's statistical services (collection of data; methods of tabulation and analysis; provision of statistical information; statutory provisions re collection and publication of official statistics; organisation; staff). Valuable appendices: *A.* Statistics collected by Government Departments (p. 19-23: Department or office; Subjects covered)—*B.* Principal statistical publications (general; then A-Z by subject, from Agriculture to War Pensions; headings: subject—title of publication—frequency—department or other organisation responsible). (For latest year of issue of publications under *B,* see index of sources in *Annual abstract of statistics.*)

The Central Statistical Office's *List of principal statistical services available* (London, H.M. Stationery Office, 1965. 36p. 4s. 6d.) is in three sections: 1. Economic statistics—2. Financial statistics—3. Regional statistics (arranged by Ministries or Departments). Notes on frequency and coverage of each series.

The Permanent Consultative Committee on Official Statistics' *Guide to current official statistics* (v. 1-17, 1922-38. London, H.M.S.O., 1924-38), published annually, consists of (1) a list of publications, containing statistics, grouped under the Department responsible; (2) a very detailed subject index to the statistics included in each item listed in (1). V. 2 (1923) contained a 48p. appendix on publications of permanent statistical interest, selected from Government publications issued between 1900 and 1923.

31 (410):016
GREAT BRITAIN. INTERDEPARTMENTAL COMMITTEE ON SOCIAL AND ECONOMIC RESEARCH. Guides to official sources. London, H.M. Stationery Office, 1948-. no. 1-.

1. *Labour statistics.* Rev. ed. 1958. 5s. (*See at 331 (410):31.*)
2. *Census reports of Great Britain, 1801-1931.* 1951. 3s. 6d. (*See at 312 (410):016.*)
3. *Local government statistics.* 1953. 1s. 6d. (*See at 352 (410):31.*)
4. *Agricultural and food statistics.* 1961. 8s. (*See Guide, v. 1, p. 302.*)
5. *Census of production reports.* 1961. 5s. (*See at 338.45 (410):016.*)

"Intended to assist research workers, students and others who have occasion to use the extensive range of information on economic and social matters made available by Government Departments [in official reports and papers]".

31 (410):016
KENDALL, M. G., *ed.* **The sources and nature of the statistics of the United Kingdom.** London & Edinburgh, Oliver & Boyd, for the Royal Statistical Society, 1952-57. v. 1-2.

Two cumulations of a series of articles giving guidance on statistics in various fields and written by experts in those fields; arranged and classified under the headings: General surveys.—Statistics of particular commodities.—Statistics of transport.—Miscellaneous. Bibliographies are appended. The articles originally appeared in the *Journal of the Royal Statistical Society.* Series A.

A very brief and now dated survey is provided by: *Statistical sources for market research* (Market Research Society (Inc.), in association with the Oakwood Press, 1957. ii, 32p.). This gives short notes on the official, semi-official and private statistical sources under ten heads, with a final section on advertising and readership. Subject index.

31 (410) (051)
GREAT BRITAIN. CENTRAL STATISTICAL OFFICE. Monthly digest of statistics, 1946-. London, H.M. Stationery Office, 1946-. Monthly. ea. 8s 6d.

Source of the current official statistics of the United Kingdom. A summary of the principal series, in the form of annual totals, appears in each February issue. The December 1966 has 168 tables under 19 heads, from 1. National income and expenditure—2. Population and vital statistics to 18. Entertainment—19. Weather. Annual figures for five or six recent years and monthly figures for up to two years. In many respects supplements the *Annual abstract of statistics* (*q.v.*).

Annual supplement of *Definitions and explanatory notes,* in January (*e.g.,* 1967. 81p. 3s.).

Economic trends (monthly) is a companion publication, showing by charts and key statistics the main trends of the U.K. economy.

31 (410) (058)
GREAT BRITAIN. CENTRAL STATISTICAL OFFICE. Abstract of regional statistics. London, H.M. Stationery Office, 1965-. Annual. (no. 2: 1966. 1966. 9s.).

Brings together the main economic and social statistics available for 11 standard regions of the U.K. (Scotland, Wales and Northern Ireland are each represented by a region). The 1966 v. has statistics for 1965 under 10 heads (51 tables): 1. Population—2. Employment—3. Fuel and power—4. Production—5. Construction—6. Distribution—7. Transport—8. Income and expenditure—9. National health service—[10]. Education. Appended map of standard regions and index of sources (p. 63-64).

Handelshögskolan, Stockholm. *England and Wales: statistical data for standard regions and administrative counties.* Compiled at the Department of Geography, the Stockholm School of Economics, under the direction of William William-Olsson (Stockholm, Almqvist & Wiksell, 1963. xx, 124p. Sw.kr.54) is arranged by counties and has maps and plans.

31 (410) (058)
GREAT BRITAIN. CENTRAL STATISTICAL OFFICE. Annual abstract of statistics. 1935/46-. London, H.M. Stationery Office, 1948-. v. 84. Annual. (v. 103. 1966. 26s. 6d.).

v. 1-83: Board of Trade. *Statistical abstract for the United Kingdom.*

Gives a wide selection of U.K. statistics for 10-year periods. The 1966 v. has 14 chapters and 384 tables. Source for each table is stated; footnotes. Index of sources, by chapters, p. 333-41. Appendix 1: Standard regions and conurbations for statistical purposes—2: Standard Industrial Classification. Index, p. 346-64. Clear sanserif type on stout paper.

Supplemented in many respects by *Monthly*

digest of statistics, although the *Annual abstract* generally gives greater detail for comparable series and includes many other series that, by their nature (*e.g.,* crime), can only be included in an annual publication.

Scotland

31 (411)
GREAT BRITAIN. SCOTTISH COUNCIL OF SOCIAL SERVICE. The third statistical account of Scotland. Edinburgh, Oliver & Boyd, 1951-53; Glasgow, Collins, 1958-. illus., maps.

See entry at 908 (411).

31 (411)
GREAT BRITAIN. SCOTTISH STATISTICAL OFFICE. Digest of Scottish statistics. Edinburgh, H.M. Stationery Office, 1953-. no. 1, April 1963-. 2 p.a. ea. 7s. 6d.

No. 28, October 1966, has 9 sections: 1. Industrial activity—2. Transport and communication—3. Trade through Scottish ports—4. Labour—5. Population and vital statistics—6. Social services—7. Finance—8. Miscellaneous. 72 tables; graphs. Sources stated; footnotes; index.

Northern Ireland

31 (416)
NORTHERN IRELAND. MINISTRY OF FINANCE. Digest of statistics. Belfast, H.M. Stationery Office, 1954-. no. 1, March 1954-. 2 p.a.

Prepared by the Ministry of Finance in collaboration with other Departments.

Eire

31 (417)
EIRE. CENTRAL STATISTICS OFFICE. Statistical abstract of Ireland. 1931-. Dublin, Stationery Office, 1931-. v. 1-. Annual. (v. 34, 1965. 10s. 6d.).

The 1965 issue (xviii, 377p.) has 13 sections and 371 tables. Introduction to each section; list of sources precedes; subject index. Appendix: The six counties (36 tables). Statistics up to 1964.
Kept up to date by the quarterly *Irish statistical bulletin* (1926-. ea. 2s. 6d.).

London

31 (421)
LONDON COUNTY COUNCIL. London statistics. London, L.C.C., 1890-. tables; maps. (New series, v. 1: 1945-54. 1957).

V. 6, new series, covering 1952-1961 (1965. 40s.) has 12 parts (214 sections; 264 tables): 1. Franchise—2. Population—3. Employment and wages—4. Health—5. Care of deprived children. Education. Housing—6. Ambulance service. Fire service. Police and justice, etc.—7. Baths and washhouses. Libraries. Museums. Town planning, etc.—8. Port of London—9. Air transport. Road and rail transport. Post Office—10. Electricity, Gas, Water—11. Finance—12. Cemeteries and crematoria. Charities. Inquests. Weather. Bibliography of sources for further reference, p. 272; index.

Wales

31 (429)
GREAT BRITAIN. OFFICE OF THE MINISTER FOR WELSH AFFAIRS. Digest of Welsh statistics, 1954-. London, H.M. Stationery Office, 1954-. no. 1-. Annual. (no. 12: 1965. 1966. 11s.).

A statistical review of Welsh affairs (social, economic, financial, legal, etc.) on the pattern of the *Annual abstract of statistics.* Includes Monmouthshire. No. 12: 1965 (79p.) has 10 sections and 100 tables, with statistics up to 1964/65.

German Democratic Republic

31 (43-11)
GERMANY (Democratic Republic). **STAATLICHEN ZENTRALVERWALTUNG FÜR STATISTIK. Statistisches Jahrbuch der Deutschen Demokratischen Republik.** 1955-. Berlin, VEB Deutscher Zentralverlag, 1956-.

On somewhat the same lines as the *Statistisches Jahrbuch für die Bundesrepublik Deutschland.* 27 sections on the Democratic Republic, statistics being broken down by Länder, etc. and covering a five-year period. Supplement on green-tinted paper deals with Comecon and international statistics.
The *Statistical pocket book of the German Democratic Republic* consists of extracts from the *Statistisches Jahrbuch* in English. The 1965 pocket book gives statistics for 1964 under 16 main headings.

German Federal Republic

31 (43-15)
GERMANY (Federal Republic). **STATISTISCHEN BUNDESAMT. Statistisches Jahrbuch für die Bundesrepublik Deutschlands,** 1952-. Stuttgart, Kohlhammer, 1952-. tables, maps. Annual. (1967. DM.42).

23 sections on the Federal Republic and West Berlin, followed by one on East Germany, East Berlin and former German territories now in Poland. Appendix on international statistics, on green-tinted paper. List of German statistical publications; subject index. Tables cover a five-year period, usually. Headings in German only.
The pocket edition, issued every 3 years (*i.e.,* 1961, 1964, 1967), is entitled *Statistisches Taschenbuch für die Bundesrepublik Deutschlands.* The English translation is entitled *Handbook of statistics for the Federal Republic of Germany.*
Supplemented by the monthly *Wirtschaft und Statistik* (April 1949-), the second half of which consists of 'Statistisches Monatszahlen'.

Berlin

31 (431.5)
STATISTISCHES LANDESAMT BERLIN. Statistisches Jahrbuch Berlin. Berlin, Kulturbuch-Verlag. Annual.

The 1964 volume (388, 16p.) gives statistics up to 1963. 23 sections, plus a 16-page supplement of statistics for the Soviet Zone of Germany. Catchword index. Insert lists publications of the Statistisches Landesamt Berlin since 1945.

Luxembourg

31 (435.9)
LUXEMBOURG. SERVICE CENTRAL DE LA STATISTIQUE. Annuaire statistique. Luxembourg, STATEC. graphs, maps. Annual.

The 1964 v. has 203 tables in 20 main sections, plus a section of international statistics. Tables give annual figures for 1938 and 1953-63 and monthly figures for 1962-63. Footnote definitions; subject index. In French only.

Austria

31 (436)
AUSTRIA. STATISTISCHES ZENTRALAMT. Statistisches Jahrbuch für die Republik Österreich. Vienna, 1950-. Annual.

The 1965 v. (with statistics for 1964) has 32 sections, with an internation section on yellow-tinted paper.
Supplemented by the monthly *Statistische Nachrichten*, 1946-.

Hungary

31 (439.1)
HUNGARY. KÖZPONTI STATISZTIKAI HIVATAL. Statisztikai évkönyv. Budapest, 'Kultura', Hungarian Trading Co. for Books & Newspapers. Annual.

The Hungarian Central Statistical Office's Statistical year book. The 1964 ed., published 1965, gives figures for 1963 and 1964. 25 chapters.
The English and Russian edition,—*Statistical yearbook* (1965 ed., published 1966) has 20 sections followed by a lengthy explanation of terms. Figures are often retrospective to 1950.
The *Statistical pocket book for Hungary* (Budapest, Publishing House for Economics and Law) is in English. The 1966 v. gives statistics for 1965 and retrospectively under 17 main headings.
Supplemented by the monthly *Statisztikai havi közlemények*.

Czechoslovakia

31 (437)
CZECHOSLOVAKIA. STATNI URAD STATISTICKY. Statistická ročenka Československé Socialistické Republiky. Prague, SNTL. Annual.

'Statistical yearbook of the Czechoslovak Socialist Republic'. Text in Czech only. The 1966 yearbook has 24 chapters and gives statistics for a ten-year period. Footnotes and explanations; bar diagrams.
A pocket edition (*Cisla do kapsy*) is also available.
Supplemented by the quarterly *Statistické zpravy*.

Poland

31 (438)
POLAND. GLÓWNY URZAD STATYSTYCZNY. Rocznik statystyczny. Warsaw. Annual.

The Polish Central Statistical Office's Statistical yearbook. In Polish only. The 1965 v. (Rok XXV) has 925 tables under headings A-L. An international statistical section is appended; subject index. Statistics are retrospective for about ten years. Clear sanserif type.
A shorter form is the *Maly rocznik statystyczny*, of which there is an English ed.,—*Concise statistical yearbook of the Polish People's Republic*.
Supplemented by the monthly *Biuletyn statystyczny*.

France

31 (44)
FRANCE. INSTITUT NATIONAL DE LA STATISTIQUE ET DES ÉTUDES ÉCONOMIQUES. Annuaire statistique de la France. Paris, Imprimerie Nationale (now Presses Universitaires de France), 1878-. v. 1-. Annual.

Previously issued by the Direction de la Statistique Générale. 'Partie française' is in 7 pts., 58 chapters; 'partie internationale' (including franc-zone countries) forms a 64-page appendix on tinted paper in the 1965 ed. A fair proportion of textual comment accompanies the tables. Maps; index. V. 66 (N.S. no. 8) (1961) is retrospective to 1861, 1870, etc. Kept up to date by the *Bulletin mensuel de statistique*, 1950- (formerly *Bulletin de la statistique générale de France*, 1911-49), and its quarterly supplement.

French overseas territories are covered by the I.N.S.E.E.'s *Données statistiques* (1961-. Quarterly) and *Résumé des statistiques d'Outre-mer*. *Bulletin accéléré* (Monthly).

31 (44):016
FRANCE. INSTITUT NATIONAL DE LA STATISTIQUE ET DES ÉTUDES ÉCONOMIQUES. Répertoire des sources statistiques françaises. Paris, Imprimerie Nationale, 1962. 400p. Loose-leaf.

Classified arrangement. Detailed statement of subject interests of organisations, and frequency and subject coverage of their publications (*e.g.*, I.N.S.E.E., p. 288-309). Detailed subject index precedes (p. 5-74); appended index of publications and contents list.

Italy

31 (45)

ITALY. ISTITUTO CENTRALE DI STATISTI-CA. Annuario statistico italiano, 1878-. Rome, Istituto Poligrafico dello Stato, 1878-. diagrs., maps. Annual.

Sections cover geography and climate; population and social statistics; agricultural, industrial, trade and labour statistics; public administration; retrospective data; international statistics. The 1965 v. has 465 tables in 20 sections and gives statistics for a five-year period. Analytical subject index.

The *Compendio statistico italiano* is a shorter version, with 308 tables, in a smaller format.

Supplemented by the monthly *Bollettino mensile de statistica* (November 1926-).

Malta

31 (458.2)

MALTA. CENTRAL OFFICE OF STATISTICS. Annual abstract of statistics. [Valetta], the Office. Annual. Mimeographed.

The 1964 v. (no. 18) is in 13 sections, with statistics for 1960-63 and longer periods. 1 map. No subject index.

Malta statistical handbook (1965-) is a pocket, abridged version in 17 sections, with graphs and bar diagrams. No subject index.

Supplemented by a monthly *Statistical summary* and a *Quarterly digest of statistics* (1960-).

Spain

31 (46)

SPAIN. INSTITUTO NACIONAL DE ESTAD-ÍSTICA. Anuario estadístico de España, 1912-. Madrid, 1913-. Annual. (Año 40. 1965).

Parte primera: *Totales nationales* (chapters 1-15, including 14: Provincias africanas; 15: Internacional). Parte segunda: *Detalle provincial.* Subject index.

The *Edición manual* (1941-) is a slightly abridged version in a smaller format.

Supplemented by the monthly *Boletín mensual de estadística* (1939-).

Portugal

31 (469)

PORTUGAL. INSTITUTO NACIONAL DE ESTATÍSTICA. Anuário estatístico. Lisbon, 1877-. Annual.

v. 1. *Metrópole.*
v. 2. *Ultramar.*
V. 2 deals with Portuguese territories in Africa and the Far East. Both volumes have maps and a subject index. Headings in Portuguese and French.

Supplemented by the monthly *Boletin mensal do Instituto Nacional de Estatística* (1929-). This includes a list of Portuguese official statistical publications and a 'Bibliografia' (items, national and foreign, received by the Library of the Institute).

U.S.S.R.

31 (47)

U.S.S.R. TSENTRAL'NOE STATISTICHESKOE UPRAVLENIE. Narodnoe khozyaĭstvo SSSR . . . : statisticheskiĭ ezhegodnik. Moscow, Statistika, 1956-. tables. Annual.

A comprehensive annual statistical survey of the Soviet economy. In the 1964 volume (published 1965), the tables (p. 7-796) are grouped under 14 main headings (*e.g.,* population, trade, industry, agriculture, employment, education, public health, investment and national income, construction). Retrospective figures, to 1940. Explanatory notes; index.

A pocket-sized version is *SSSR v tsifrakh . . . : kratkiĭ statisticheskiĭ sbornik.* The 1965 volume (Collet's, 1966. 168p. 2s. 3d.) has retrospective figures, to 1913, 1928, etc.; footnotes; index.

Vestnik statistiki (1949-. Monthly) is not a statistical bulletin in the accepted sense but a review on statistical methodology, with some articles on special statistical data.

31 (47):016

KASER, M. C. "Soviet statistical abstracts, 1956-65". In *Soviet affairs,* number 4 (St. Antony's papers, no. 19), p. 134-55.

A cumulation of the 8 lists (comprising 431 abstracts) that have appeared annually in the January issue of *Soviet studies* (v. 10, no. 3, January 1959, p. 312-9, and thereafter). 8 library holdings are cited (Library of Congress, United Nations Library (Geneva) and 6 in Britain).

The series continues with M. C. Kaser's "Ninth list of Soviet statistical tables", in *Soviet studies,* v. 18, no. 3, January 1967, p. 394-6. This lists 41 abstracts, incorporating entries in *Knizhnaya letopis'* up to no. 33, 1966; all are re-issues, with later material. "Tenth list . . .", Soviet studies, v. 19, no. 3, January 1968, p. 457-9.

Scandinavia

31 (48)

NORDIC COUNCIL. Yearbook of Nordic statistics, 1962-. Stockholm, Nordic Council, 1963-. tables, bar diagrs., map. Annual. (1966, published 1967).

128 tables in 19 sections and 34 charts in the 1966 v., covering all the important economic and social statistics for Denmark, Finland, Iceland, Norway and Sweden. Tables are retrospective for 5-10 years, in some cases, and up to 1965. Explanatory footnotes; sources (p. 132). Introduction and headings in English and Swedish.

Finland

31 (480)

FINLAND. TILASTOLLINEN PÄÄTOIMISTO. Suomen tilastollinen vuosikirja. Helsinki, Tilastollinen Päätoimisto. Annual.

The Finnish Central Statistical Office's Statistical yearbook of Finland. In Finnish, Swedish and English. The 1965 v. has 25 chapters and 424 tables, with statistics retrospective for about a five-year period. List of official statistical publications (p. 469-78); subject index.

Supplemented by the monthly *Tilastokatsauksia-Statistiska Översikter* (1924-).

Norway

31 (481)

NORWAY. STATISTISK SENTRALBYRA. Statistisk årbok. Statistical yearbook of Norway. Oslo, Aschehoug. Annual.

In Norwegian and English. The 1966 yearbook (85th issue) has 21 chapters and 444 tables. Chapter 21, International statistics, has headings in Norwegian only. Footnote references. List of Norwegian statistical publications, p. 365-7.

Supplemented by the monthly *Statistisk månedshefte* (1882-), also in Norwegian and English.

Fortegnelse over Norges offisielle statistikk, 1828-1950 (Oslo, Aschehoug, 1951. 97p.) lists all the Norwegian Central Statistical Office's publications for the period concerned.

Sweden

31 (485)

SWEDEN. STATISTISKA CENTRALBYRAN. Statistisk årsbok. för Sverige. Stockholm, AB Nordiska Bokhandel. Annual. (1965. Arg. 52).

In Swedish and English.

30 sections; 498 tables. 30: 'Comparative international statistics' (headings in Swedish only). Detailed list of Swedish statistical publications and subject index.

Supplemented by the monthly *Allmän manadsstatistisk* (1963-).

For historical statistics,—*Historisk statistisk för Sverige* (1. *Befolkning,* 1720-1950 (1955); 2. *Väderlek* . . . [climate, land surveying, agriculture, forestry, fisheries, to 1955] (1959)).

Denmark

31 (489)

DENMARK. DET STATISTISKE DEPARTEMENT. Statistisk årbog. Copenhagen, Munksgaard. Annual. (1966. Argang 70).

Contents list, table main headings and index in Danish and English. In the 1966 v., tables 1-330 cover Denmark proper; tables 331-354: Faroe Islands; 355-383: Greenland; 384-425: International. List of official statistical publications; subject index.

Supplemented by the *Statistiske Efterretninger* (1909-; *c.* 90 issues p.a.).

Netherlands

31 (492)

NETHERLANDS. CENTRAAL BUREAU VOOR DE STATISTIEK. Jaarcijfers voor Nederland, 1881-. The Hague, the Bureau, [1882]-. maps. Annual.

The 1959-1960 yearbook (Zeist, de Haan, 1962)

has chapters A-X, with 477 tables. Statistics for 1954-60. Headings in Dutch and English. Subject index; list of official statistical publications.

The *Statistisch zakboek, 1962* (Zeist, de Haan, 1962) is a pocket edition, with 293 tables in classes A-X. Maps and graphs. Attractively produced.

Supplemented by the monthly (8-10 p.a.) *Maandschrift* (The Hague, Staatsuitgerverij, 1906-), which includes articles as well as statistical tables.

Belgium

31 (493)

BELGIUM, INSTITUT NATIONAL DE STATISTIQUE. Annuaire statistique de la Belgique, 1870-. Brussels, I.N.S., 1870-. Annual. (v. 86: 1965. [1966?]. Belg. fr. 250. (foreign, Belg. fr. 300.)).

V. 86: 1955 has tables on p. 3-637, with detailed contents-list and analytical subject index. Statistics are usually for a 5- or 10-year period up to 1965. 15 sections, the first being 'Aperçu international', on yellow-tinted paper.

Kept up to date by the monthly *Bulletin de statistique* (1966: 52nd year), which includes regional statistics.

Switzerland

31 (494)

SWITZERLAND. EIDGENÖSSISCHES STATISTISCHES AMT. Statistisches Jahrbuch der Schweiz. Annuaire statistique de la Suisse, 1891-. Basle, Birkhäuser Verlag, 1891-. v. 1-. Annual.

In German and French.

In the 1966 v., statistics on Switzerland (p. 1-546) are followed by international statistics, for comparison (p. 547-600), list of sources and of Swiss official statistical publications. Subject index.

Supplemented by the monthly *Die Volkswirtschaft* (1928-). (The French edition, *La vie économique,* appears a fortnight later.)

Greece

31 (495)

GREECE. ETHNIKE STATISTIKE YPERESIA. Statistical yearbook of Greece, 1930-. Athens, National Printing Office, 1931-. Annual.

Title varies. In Greek and English. The 1964 v. has pt. 1, National tables (25 chapters), and pt. 2, International. Statistics for about ten-year periods. No index.

Supplemented by the Bank of Greece's *Monthly statistical bulletin,* in English and Greek, with tables (6 sections) and graphs.

Albania

31 (496.5)

ALBANIA. DREJTORIA E STATISTIKES. Vjetari statistikor i R.P.SH. Tirana, the Directorate. diagrs., graphs, maps. Annual.

'Statistical yearbook of the People's Republic of Albania'. 15 chapters (15: International data). The 1964 v. gives statistics for 1950, 1955 and 1960/63. No subject index but a detailed contents list.

The *Statistical pocketbook of the P.R.A.*, 1964 (Tirana, 1965) is an English translation of the headings only in the *Vjetari statistikor*.

Yugoslavia

31 (497.1)
YUGOSLAVIA. SAVEZNI ZAVOD ZA STATISTIKU. **Statistički godisnjak FNRJ.**, 1954-. Belgrade, S.Z.S.E., 1954-. graphs. Annual.

The Serbo-Croat only. The 1966 v. (12th year) has 5 main sections: 1. the Yugoslav Socialist Federal Republic (56 sections; p. 63-340)—2. The constituent Socialist republics—3. Communes—4. Cities—5. International. Subject index; list of official statistical publications.

The *Statistical yearbook of the Socialist Federal Republic of Yugoslavia,* 1966 (13th issue). Belgrade, S.Z.S.E., 1966) is a translation of only the headings in the original.

The *Statistical pocket-book of Yugoslavia* (4th year, 1958) consists of extracts from the original, plus much factual information (*e.g.*, on the principal Yugoslav holidays; the railway tariff). Supplemented by the monthly *Indeks.*

Bulgaria

31 (497.2)
BULGARIA. TSENTRALNO STATISTICHESKO UPRAVLYENIE . . . **Statisticheski godishnik na Narodna Republika Bulgariya.** Sofia, 1966. xii, 574, [1]p.

About 800 tables in 3 main sections: the Republic; regions; international statistics. Statistics cover a ten-year period (1955/65) and sometimes give 1938, 1948 and 1952 figures. Some introductory text to sections. Graphs; bar diagrams; map. Subject index, p. 566-74.

Rumania

31 (498)
RUMANIA. DIRECTIA CENTRALA DE STATISTICA. **Anuarul statistic al Republicii Socialiste Românie.** Bucharest, the Directia. diagrs. Annual.

First published in 1942. The 1966 v. has 16 chapters, with 322 tables (15: Municipal services; 16: International statistics). Statistics for 1950/65. List of official statistical publications; subject index.

The *Statistical yearbook of the Socialist Republic of Romania,* 1966 (Bucharest, 1966) is an English translation of the headings of the 322 tables in the original.

The *Statistical pocket book . . . , 1966* is a concise version of the original (chapters 1-14), with bar diagrams.

Supplemented by the quarterly *Buletin statistic trimestrial* (1958-).

South-east Asia

31 (5-012)
INSTITUTE OF ASIAN ECONOMIC AFFAIRS, Tokyo. **Bibliography of the statistical materials on Southeast Asia.** Tokyo, the Institute, 1960. ix, 66p.

A union catalogue of 24 leading libraries in Japan, detailing holdings up to the end of March 1960. Items are primarily post-World War II publications. Countries: British Borneo; Burma; Cambodia, Laos and Vietnam, Ceylon, India, Indonesia, Malaya and Singapore, Pakistan, Philippines and Thailand. Sections: General—By countries—Appendix—Reports and annuals. Country section is sub-divided by types of statistics (*e.g.*, regional, census, economic, banking, financial, industrial, price, trade, electricity). Contents of annuals, etc. are stated.

Communist China

31 (510)
CHINA. STATE STATISTICAL BUREAU. **Economic and cultural statistics of Communist China.** Washington, D.C., 1960. 187p. (U.S. Central Intelligence Agency. Foreign Documents Division. Translation no. 737).

Translation of the series of statistical compilations issued in Peiping, 1959 (*Current geographical publications,* v. 23, no. 4, April 1960, p. 140).

Hong Kong

31 (512.317)
HONG KONG. **Special supplement . . . to the 'Hong Kong Government gazette'.** Hong Kong. Monthly.

The Special supplement no. 4, for 5th January 1968, has 42 tables, giving November 1967 and January-November 1967 figures.

Korea

31 (519)
KOREA. BUREAU OF STATISTICS. **Korea statistical yearbook.** [Seoul], 1952-.

The 1966 v. (13th ed.) has 32 sections, with 444 tables. Section 32, International statistics. Sources; footnotes. Detailed contents-list; no subject index. Modelled on the *Japan statistical yearbook.*

Japan

31 (52)
JAPAN. BUREAU OF STATISTICS. **Japan statistical yearbook.** Tokyo, 1949-.

Aims to present all the basic statistical information on land, population, economy, and the social and cultural aspects of Japan. The 1965 ed. (16th issue) has 383 tables in 30 sections (30: International statistics). In Japanese and English. Detailed contents-list and subject index. 26 charts. Well produced.

Supplemented by *Monthly statistics of Japan* (1947-).

Nationalist China

31 (529)

CHINA (National Republic). **COUNCIL FOR INTERNATIONAL ECONOMIC CO-OPERATION AND DEVELOPMENT. Taiwan statistical data book.** Taipei.

The 1965 v. has tables in 15 sections (15: International statistics), mostly for the period 1952-64. Detailed contents-list; no index. Sources stated. Oblong format.

Saudi Arabia

31 (532)

SAUDI ARABIAN MONETARY AGENCY. Research Department. **Statistical summary.** Jeddah, [1963?]-. v. 1, no. 1-. Quarterly.

As from v. 3, no. 1 (November 1965), includes "a brief review of the domestic economic condition, especially of the monetary, fiscal and oil sectors of the economy". This issue has 13 tables.

Kuwait

31 (536.8)

KUWAIT. CENTRAL STATISTICAL OFFICE. **Statistical abstract.** Kuwait, Government Press, [1964?]-. Annual.

The 1964 v. has 78 tables in 10 sections (section 6. Oil). Statistics for 1963 and 1964. Sources stated. No index.
Supplemented by a monthly *Bulletin of statistics.*

India

31 (540)

INDIA. CENTRAL STATISTICAL ORGANISATION. **Statistical abstract of the Indian Union.** New Delhi, Manager of Publications. Annual.

The 1963 & 1964 v. (1965) has 248 tables in 36 sections, with a subject index. (vi, 763p.). Sources stated; footnotes and explanatory notes.
The *Statistical pocket-book of the Indian Union* (1957-) is a condensed version. The 1965 (9th) issue has 114 tables in 24 sections.
Supplemented by the *Monthly abstract of abstracts* (1947-), which has a *Weekly supplement.*

Ceylon

31 (548.7)

CEYLON. DEPARTMENT OF CENSUS AND STATISTICS. **Statistical abstract of Ceylon.** Colombo, Government Publications Bureau. Annual.

The 1959 v. has 14 sections, with 301 tables. Sources; footnotes. Subject-index. Statistics for ten-year periods. Clear sanserif type.

Pakistan

31 (549)

PAKISTAN. CENTRAL STATISTICAL OFFICE. **Statistical yearbook.** Karachi, Manager of Publications, 1952-. Irregular.

The 7th issue, for 1964 (published 1966), has 14 chapters, with an additional chapter on the Five-year plan; 185 tables. Sources stated; explanatory notes begin each chapter.
The *Statistical pocket book of Pakistan,* 1966 (fifth issue) is a condensed edition. 14 sections; 82 tables, with statistics for 1964/65.
Supplemented by the *Monthly statistical bulletin* (March 1952-), which includes a "one-time" special feature in each issue (*e.g.,* July 1966: average wholesale prices of oilseeds and tobacco in various markets of Pakistan, 1957-1965).

Turkey

31 (560)

TURKEY. ISTATISTIK GENEL DIREKTORLUGÜ. **Türkiye istatistik yilligi. Annuaire statistique de la Turquie.** Ankara, Istatistik. Enstitüsü (Institut National de la Statistique).

First published for 1928.
The 1964/65 volume has 22 sections, with 548 tables. Statistics up to 1965. No index; detailed contents. In Turkish and French.
Supplemented by the monthly *Aylik istatistik bülteni.*

Cyprus

31 (564.3)

CYPRUS. STATISTICS AND RESEARCH DEPARTMENT. **Statistical abstract.** [Nicosia] Republic of Cyprus Printing Office, 1955-. Mimeographed. Annual. (1964 ed. 10s.).

23 sections of tables. Sources stated; some footnotes. Detailed contents list; no index.
Supplemented by the monthly *Statistical summary.*

Iraq

31 (567)

IRAQ. CENTRAL BUREAU OF STATISTICS. **Statistical abstract.** [Baghdad], Government Press. Annual.

In Arabic and English. The 1964 v. (13" × 10") has 42 sections, with 437 titles, and gives 1963 and 1964 statistics. Introductory text to sections. Detailed contents-list; no index. Bar diagrams.
Supplemented by *Quarterly bulletin of statistics* (1952-).

Syria

31 (569.1)

SYRIAN ARAB REPUBLIC. DIRECTORATE OF STATISTICS. **Statistical abstract,** 1948-. Damascus, Government Press, 1949-. Annual (18th year, 1965. 1966).

13 chapters, 223 tables in the 1965 v., covering the various aspects of the economic and social activities of the Republic. Sources stated. Headings in Arabic and English. Maps. No index.

Supplemented by quarterly *General bulletin of current statistics.*

A. A. Sharif's *Sources of statistics in Syria: a reference manual for research work* (Damascus, Bureau des Documentations Syriennes et Arabes, 1964. xv, 711. Mimeographed) gives detailed analysis of publications (including annual reports) in 20 sections, mostly arranged by Ministries.

Lebanon

31 (569.3)

LEBANON. DIRECTION CENTRALE DE LA STATISTIQUE. Recueil de statistiques libanaises. Année 1963. Beirut, [1967?]. 275p.

In Arabic and French. 11 sections. Tables of statistics (p. 14-275) for 1963 and earlier years. Good maps in colour; graphs. No index.

Kept up to date by the *Bulletin statistique mensuel* (1963-). Each issue has statistics for 13 months. 15 sections (15: 'Indicateurs économiques divers'); graphs.

Israel

31 (569.4)

ISRAEL. CENTRAL BUREAU OF STATISTICS. Statistical abstract of Israel. Jerusalem, 1950-. Annual.

In two parts, English and Hebrew. Introduction to tables; 24 sections of tables, with statistics retrospective to 1951/52, 1962/63, and up to 1964 (or 1963/64) in the 1965 v. (16th issue). Very detailed contents list; sources and explanatory notes. Maps; graphs.

Supplemented by monthly *Statistical bulletin of Israel,* in 5 pts. Pt. 5: English summary, in English and Hebrew.

Jordan

31 (569.5)

JORDAN. DEPARTMENT OF STATISTICS. Statistical yearbook. Amman, Department of Statistics Press, [1950?-]. Annual.

In English and Arabic. The 1964 v. (no. 15) gives 1964 figures and retrospectively to 1958. Introduction; 17 sections of tables in 4 parts (demographic, agricultural, economic and miscellaneous statistics). Subject index. List of Department of Statistics publications.

Supplemented by *Quarterly bulletin of current statistics.*

The Jordan Department of Statistics also produces a pocket-sized *Statistical guide to Jordan* (No. 1-: 1962-. 1963-), in English and Arabic.

Afghanistan

31 (581)

AFGHANISTAN. DEPARTMENT OF STATISTICS AND RESEARCH. Survey of progress. Kabul. Annual.

In English. The first half of the 1964/65 v. (published 1965) consists of text. The appended tables are in 7 sections: Public finance—Money and banking—Foreign trade—Industry—Transportation and communications—Education—Health. No index.

Burma

31 (591)

BURMA. CENTRAL STATISTICAL AND ECONOMICS DEPARTMENT. Economic survey of Burma. Rangoon, Central Press. Annual.

The 1964 v. has 112 tables in 3 pts.: 1 (A-G): Economic activity in the Union—2 (1-14). Institutional changes and development progress—3. Government finances, 1963/64 and 1964/65. 14 charts. Includes an appreciable amount of text.

Supplemented by *Quarterly bulletin of statistics* (bilingual, Burmese and English).

Thailand

31 (593)

THAILAND. CENTRAL STATISTICAL OFFICE. Statistical year book. Bangkok.

The 1965 v. (no. 26) has 220 tables in 20 sections. Contents list, titles of tables, and headings are in Siamese and English. Footnotes. Siamese and English subject indexes.

Supplemented by *Quarterly bulletin of statistics.*

Malaysia

31 (595)

MALAYSIA. DEPARTMENT OF STATISTICS. Annual bulletin of statistics. Kuala Lumpur, the Department. Mimeographed. Annual. (1966, published [1967]. $3).

"An attempt to bring together a range of selected statistics for Sabah, Sarawak and West Malaysia and to provide, where possible, data for Malaysia" (*Foreword,* 1966 ed.). The 1964 ed. has 62 tables in 12 sections, and gives figures up to 30th September 1964.

Supplemented by *Monthly statistical bulletin of the States of Malaya.*

Singapore

31 (595.13)

SINGAPORE. CHIEF STATISTICIAN. Monthly digest of statistics. Singapore, 1962-. Monthly.

Replaces the monthly *Digest of economic and social statistics.* 10 sections.

Cambodia

31 (596)

CAMBODIA. DIRECTION DE LA STATISTIQUE . . . Annuaire statistique rétrospectif du Cambodge, 1958-1961. Phnom-Penh, [1962].

86 tables in 15 chapters. Sources are cited. Contents list, but no subject index. The preceding

Annuaire statistique rétrospectif is for 1937-1957 (published [1958]).
Supplemented by *Bulletin mensuel de statistique*.

Vietnam

31 (597.3)
VIETNAM. NATIONAL INSTITUTE OF STATISTICS.... **Statistical yearbook** of Vietnam. Saigon. Annual.

The 8th v., for 1958-1959, appeared in 1960. 259 tables in 14 chapters. In Vietnamese, French and English. Subject index; map. Includes a lengthy chapter on climatology (p. 1-40).
Supplemented by *Monthly bulletin of statistics* (1957-).

Laos

31 (598)
LAOS. DIRECTION DE LA STATISTIQUE. **Annuaire statistique.** Vientiane. Annual (irregular).

The *Annuaire statistique* du Laos, 4th v.: 1953-1957, was published in 1961, and give some statistics up to 1960. 13 sections, plus census figures in Annexe 1. No index.
Supplemented by quarterly *Bulletin de statistique du Laos.*

Africa

31 (6):016
UNITED NATIONS. Economic Commission for Africa. **Bibliography of African statistical publications, 1950-1965** . . . [Addis Ababa], 1966. vii, 256p. Mimeographed. (E/CN.14/LIB. SER. C/2).

Preceded by *Bibliography of African statistical publications* (Addis Ababa, 1962. (E/CN.14/112)).
Arranged by countries and areas, A-Z, from Algeria to Zanzibar (53 countries). The items for Nigeria (p. 141-4) cover: general; development plans; national accounts and economic surveys; population, housing; agriculture; industry; external trade; transport; education; public health; labour; consumption; miscellaneous.

31 (6) (084.4)
AFRICA INSTITUTE, Pretoria. **Africa: maps and statistics.** Pretoria, the Institute, 1962-65. 10v. maps. ea. 75c.; R 9, the set.

See entry at 33 (084.4) (6).

Tunisia

31 (611)
TUNISIA. SERVICES DES STATISTIQUES. **Annuaire statistique de la Tunisie.** Tunis, Présidence du Conseil. Annual.

The 12th v., for 1960 (published [1963?] has 15 chapters and gives statistics for 1959-60. In French. Contents list; subject index. Clear sanserif type.

Supplemented by *Bulletin mensuel de statistique* (1954-).

Libya

31 (612)
LIBYA. CENSUS & STATISTICAL DEPARTMENT. **Statistical abstract.** Tripoli, the Department. 1958/62-. Annual.

The 1964 v. has 17 sections, with 178 main tables. In English and Arabic. Statistics for 1961-64. Contents-list; explanatory notes; graphs and bar diagrams.
Supplemented by quarterly *Statistical summary.*

United Arab Republic

31(621/623)
UNITED ARAB REPUBLIC. CENTRAL AGENCY FOR PUBLIC MOBILISATION & STATISTICS. **Statistical handbook of the United Arab Republic, 1952-1965.** Cairo, 1966. xi, 333p. diagrs., graphs, map.

A pocket-sized handbook; English, Arabic and French editions. The fifth annual *Statistical handbook.* 16 sections, mainly statistical; includes 'The High Dam', 'Political information', 'Diplomatic Missions'. Statistics reflect particularly what has been achieved under the First Five-Year Plan, 1960/65.

Sudan

31 (624)
SUDAN. MINISTRY OF FINANCE & ECONOMICS, Economics Branch. **Economic survey.** Khartoum, the Ministry. Annual. Mimeographed.

The 1963 v. (published 1964) has 8 chapters of text and 35 supporting tables with figures for 1961/62 and 1963 or 1962/63. List of tables; no subject index.

Ethiopia

31 (63)
ETHIOPIA. CENTRAL STATISTICAL OFFICE. **Statistical abstract.** Addis Ababa, 1963-. Annual. Mimeographed.

The 1965 issue is for the first time in Amharic as well as in English. It has 16 sections, each with an introduction, and 96 tables. Detailed contents-list; no subject index. Sources; explanatory notes. Statistics cover a ten-year period up to 1964.
Kept up to date by *Monthly statistical bulletin.*

Morocco

31 (64)
MOROCCO. SERVICE CENTRAL DES STATISTIQUES. **Annuaire statistique du Maroc.** Rabat, the Service. Annual.

The 1959 v., in French and English, has 16 chapters. Statistics cover a 2-3-year period. Subject index.

Supplemented by *Bulletin mensuel de statistique,* and the quarterly *Bulletin économique et social du Maroc* (text, with supporting tables).

Algeria

31 (65)
ALGERIA. SERVICE DE LA STATISTIQUE GÉNÉRALE. Annuaire statistique de l'Algérie. Algiers, the Service, 1949-.

The 1960 v. has 12 headings and 40 tables, with statistics for a five or ten-year period. Some graphs; few footnotes. Subject index.
Supplemented by the monthly *Bulletin mensuelle de statistique générale* (1949-) and the quarterly *Statistiques générales.*

West, Central & East Africa

31 (66/67)
MALI. Direction de la Statistique Générale. *Annuaire statistique.* Bamako-Koulouba, 1963-. Annual. Supplemented by *Bulletin mensuel de statistique.*

UPPER VOLTA. Bureau des Études Économiques et de la Statistique. *Bulletin annuaire statistique statistique et économique.* Ouagadougou. Annual. Supplemented by *Bulletin mensuel de statistique.*

NIGER. Service de la Statistique. *Bulletin de statistique.* Niamey, 1959-. Quarterly. Mimeographed. (No. 29, 1966, 1st quarter, has 7 sections, 28 tables. Source stated; some footnotes.)

SENEGAL. Service de la Statistique. *Bulletin statistique et économique mensuel.* Dakar Monthly.

SIERRA LEONE. Central Statistical Office. *Quarterly statistical bulletin.* Freetown. (September 1964 issue: 11 sections, 55 tables, with statistical for October/December 1962. Sources stated.)

GAMBIA Government. *Statistical summary.* 1965-. Bathurst, Government Printer, 1966-. Annual.

GUINEA. Service de la Statistique Générale. *Bulletin mensuel de statistique.* [Conakry].

LIBERIA. Bureau of Statistics. *Statistical newsletter.* [Monrovia]. Quarterly.

IVORY COAST. Direction de la Statistique. . . . *Bulletin mensuel de statistique.* [Abidjan].

GHANA. Central Bureau of Statistics. *Quarterly digest of statistics.* [Accra].

TOGO. Service de la Statistique Générale. *Bulletin de statistique.* [Lomé].

NIGERIA. Federal Office of Statistics. *Annual abstract of statistics.* Lagos. Supplemented by quarterly *Digest of statistics* (1952-).

NIGERIA (Northern Region). Ministry of Economic Planning. *Statistical yearbook.* Kaduna, 1964-. Annual.

UNION DOUANÌERE ÉQUATORIALE. *Bulletin des statistiques générales* . . . Brazzaville, 1963-. Quarterly. (Succeeds *Bulletin mensuel statistique de l'Afrique Equatoriale Française.*)

CAMEROUN. Service de la Statistique. *Annuaire statistique du Cameroun.* Yaoundé. Annual. (Supplemented by monthly *Bulletin de la statistique générale du Cameroun.*)

GABON. Service National de la Statistique. *Bulletin mensuel de statistique de la République Gabonaise.* Libreville, 1959-. Monthly.

CENTRAL AFRICAN REPUBLIC. Direction de la Statistique. . . . *Annuaire statistique de la République Centrafricaine.* Paris, COGIPA. (Supplemented by monthly *Bulletin mensuel de statistique.*)

CHAD. Service de la Statistique Générale. *Bulletin mensuel de statistique.* [Fort-Lamy]. Monthly.

CONGO. Service de la Statistique. *Bulletin mensuel de statistique.* Léopoldville. Monthly.

EAST AFRICA. East African Statistical Department. *Economic and statistical review.* Entebbe. 1961-. Quarterly. (June 1966 (no. 19) issue has 12 sections, 71 tables, with statistics for 1961-65, plus monthly figures. Graphs; list of current publications.

UGANDA. Statistics Division. . . . *Statistical abstract.* Entebbe, Government Printer. Annual. (22 sections, including 'Land and climate', 'Public health', 'Education' and 'Justice'. List of statistical publications appended. Maps are no longer included; for these see the new *Atlas of Uganda* (at 912/676.1). The *Uganda quarterly digest of statistics* (December 1965-) replaces the *Monthly economic and statistical bulletin.*)

TANZANIA (United Republic). Central Statistical Bureau. *Monthly statistical bulletin.* (Previously *Tanganyika monthly statistical bulletin* (New series, 1951-). V. 16, no. 6 (August 1966) has 13 sections (3. 'National accounts of Tanganyika'). Appended list of statistical publications currently available.)

MOZAMBIQUE. Repartição de Estatística Geral. *Anuário estatístico.* Lourenço Marques. Ano 1: 1926. 1927. 1928. (A detailed statistical survey, in Portuguese only. The 1962 v. (ano 35, published 1963) has 13 chapters; tables, p. 11-626.) Supplemented by the monthly *Boletin mensal de estatística.*

South Africa

31 (680)
SOUTH AFRICA (Republic). **BUREAU OF STATISTICS. Statistical year book.** Statistiese jaarboek, Pretoria, the Bureau, [1964]-. Annual. 1964-.

The first issue (1964) covers 1945 to 1963; future issues will be confined to relatively recent years (*Preface*). 23 sections (A-W), with footnote definitions and explanations. 4 charts. In English and Afrikaans.
Supplemented by *Monthly bulletin of statistics.*

The Union of South Africa. Bureau of Census and Statistics' *Union statistics for fifty years* (Pretoria, [1960]. v.p.) is a jubilee issue covering 1910-60.

31 (680):016

GEERTSEMA, G., with **KIERCK, J. R.,** *comp.* **A guide to statistical sources in the Republic of South Africa.** Pretoria, Bureau of Market Research, Univ. of South Africa, 1962. 2v. R.14.

V. 1 gives an A-Z list of institutions collecting statistics, with notes on their publications and a subject index. V. 2 reproduces "60 different statistical questionnaires currently used by 7 institutional sources" (Musiker, R. *Guide to South African reference books.* 4th rev. ed., 1965. item 60).

31 (686.1)

LESOTHO. BUREAU OF STATISTICS. Annual statistical bulletin. Maseru. Annual. Mimeographed.

Lesotho was, until independence (1966), Basutoland.
The 1965 *Bulletin* (published 1966) omits the report on the year's work included in 1963/64 *Bulletin.* The 38 tables give statistics for 1965 and earlier years, and include data on the 1966 population census. Complete accuracy is not claimed, particularly with trade statistics.

Rhodesia

31 (689.1)

RHODESIA. CENTRAL STATISTICAL OFFICE. Monthly digest of statistics. Salisbury, 1933-.

Originally as *Economic and statistical bulletin of Southern Rhodesia.*
The February 1966 issue (latest available) has 80 tables under 14 main headings. Supplementary notes; list of statistical publications currently on sale.

Zambia

31 (689.4)

ZAMBIA. CENTRAL STATISTICAL OFFICE. Monthly digest of statistics. Lusaka, C.S.O., 1965-.

The October 1966 (v. 2, no. 10) issue has 45 tables in 9 sections. Few explanatory notes or definitions. List of publications obtainable from the C.S.O. precedes.

Malawi

31 (689.7)

MALAWI. Compendium of statistics, 1965. [Zomba, 1966].

Collects into one volume "statistical data that are available within Ministries and Statutory bodies in Malawi. It must not be regarded as a proper Statistical Abstract". 148 tables, with statistics for July 1961 - December 1962 and 1963-65. Sources stated; folding map.
Supplemented by a mimeographed *Quarterly digest of statistics* (April 1964-), issued by the Ministry of Finance, Zomba.

Malagasy

31 (691)

MALAGASY REPUBLIC. Service de Statistique. **Bulletin mensuel de statistique.** Tananarive, Imprimerie Nationale. Monthly.

Americas

31 (7/8)

PAN AMERICAN UNION. Department of Statistics, and **INTER-AMERICAN STATISTICAL INSTITUTE. América en cifras, 1965.** Washington, Secretaría General de la Organización de los Estados Americanos, 1966-.

Situación demográfica. Estado y movimiento de la población.
Situación económica. 1. *Agricultura, ganadería.* 1966.
    2. *Industria.* 1966.
    3. *Comercio, servicios, transportes, communicaciones y turismo.* 1966.
    4. *Balanza de pagos, producto e ingreso nacionales y finanzas.* 1966.
    5. *Precios, salarios, consumo y otros aspectos de la situación económica.*
Situación social. Hozar, habitación, mejoramiento urbano, provisión social, asistencia medica y de salud.
Situación cultural. Educación y ostros aspectos de la situación cultural. 1967.
Previous ed.: 1963 (1963-64. 2v.). *América en cifras* covers 21 countries, including Canada and the U.S.A.

North America

31 (7)

MUELLER, B. A statistical handbook of the North Atlantic area. New York, Twentieth Century Fund, 1965. 239p. tables. $6.

Covers N.A.T.O. countries of America and Europe. Has chapters on population, employment, public and private expenditure, productivity, national product, resources and foreign trade. Text and table headings in French and English.

Canada

31 (71)

CANADA. DOMINION BUREAU OF STATISTICS. Canada year book. . . : official statistical annual of the resources, history, institutions and social and economic conditions of Canada. Ottawa, Queen's Printer. Illus., tables, maps, charts. Annual. (1966 v. $3; $5).

The 1966 v. has 27 chapters and many tables. Chapter 27: 'Official sources of information and miscellaneous data (pt. 1. 'Official sources of information', including 'Books about Canada' (p. 1121-38); pt. 2. 'Special material published in former editions' [of the *Year book*]. Detailed analytical index.
The *Canadian statistical review* (1926-) is monthly, with annual supplement.

STATISTICS

31 (71)
URQUHART, M. C., and BUCKLEY, K. A. H.,
ed. **Historical statistics of Canada.** Toronto,
Macmillan; London, Cambridge Univ. Press,
1965. xvi, 672p. tables. $15; 115s.

Sponsored by Canadian Political Science Association and Social Science Research Council of
Canada.
Patterned after the *Historical Statistics of the
United States.* Covers economic, social and political affairs, 1867-1960. 21 subject areas. Detailed
table of contents; comprehensive subject index.
Reviewed in *College and research libraries,* v. 27,
no. 1, January 1966, p. 47-48.

Mexico

31 (72)
MEXICO. DIRECCIÓN GENERAL DE ESTAD-
ISTICA. **Anuario estadístico compendiado de
los Estados Unidos Mexicanos.** Mexico. Annual.

The 1964v. (published 1965) has 16 sections,
with 336 tables. Statistics for three or six-year
periods. Sources are cited. Detailed contents-list;
no subject index. Small, clear type.
The fuller annual is the *Anuario estadístico de
los Estados Unidos Mexicanos.*
Supplemented by the monthly *Revista de
estadística* (1952-). The February 1967 issue contained 122 tables in 10 sections.

U.S.A.

31 (73)
UNITED STATES. BUREAU OF THE CENSUS.
**Historical statistics of the United States, 1789-
1945:** a supplement to the "Statistical abstract
of the United States". Washington, Government
Printing Office, 1949. viii, 363p.

Arranged systematically, by chapters; in each
chapter a lengthy introduction precedes tables.
Chronological and subject indexes.
A *Continuation to 1952, with revisions of
selected series,* was published in 1954.

—— ——**Historical statistics of the United
States, colonial times to 1957:** a "Statistical
abstract" supplement. Washington, Government
Printing Office, 1960. xi, 789p. $6.

Based on the earlier volumes, but in a number
of cases series have been replaced or supplemented. Text material has been made more uniform in scope and quality, and critical notes and
further bibliography added. The earlier v. still
need to be consulted, since (*Library journal,* 15th
April 1966, p. 1992) explanatory text, source notes
and most of the footnotes are not repeated. The
States of Alaska and Hawaii are now included.
Analytical index.

—— ——**Historical statistics of the United
States, colonial times to 1959;** continuation to
1962 and revisions . . . Washington, Government
Printing Office, 1965. iv, 154p.

Table 1 (p. 1-104): Continuations of series in
"Historical statistics"; table 2 (p. 105-50): Revisions of series in "Historical statistics". Source
notes, p. 151-4.

*The Statistical history of the United States,
from colonial times to the present* (Stamford,
Conn., Fairfield Publications, Inc.; New York,
Horizon Press, 1965. xxiv, 789p. $9.95), issued
under the direction of the U.S. Bureau of the
Census, with the co-operation of the Social
Sciences Research Council, is based on *Historical
abstracts* (1960) and its continuation (above).

31 (73)
UNITED STATES. BUREAU OF THE CENSUS.
Statistical abstract of the United States, 1878-.
Washington, Government Printing Office, 1879-.
v. 1-. Annual. (87th annual ed. 1966. $3.75).

"The standard summary of statistics on the
industrial, social, political and economic organization of the United States" (*Preface*). Particularly valuable for the retrospective nature of
tables, spanning 15-20 years. The 1966 ed. contains more than 1,300 tables and charts in 33
sections (section 33: 'Comparative international
statistics'). Appendix 2. Historical appendix:
Index to tables having *Historical statistics,
colonial times to 1957* series. Appendix 3. Guide
to sources of statistics (p. 941-96), including
'Publications of recent censuses', 'Guide to state
statistical abstracts', and 'Source agencies and
table numbers'. Analytical index, p. 997-1039.
Statistical abstract supplements: *Pocket data
book, U.S.A.; Directory of Federal statistics for
local areas; County and city data book; Congressional district data book* and *Supplements;
Historical statistics of the United States* (q.v.).

The U.S. Bureau of the Budget. Division of
Statistical Standards' *Statistical services of the
United States Government* (Rev. ed. Washington,
1963. 136p.) includes a list of *c.* 100 periodical
statistical publications of federal agencies, and
describes the general organisation of the U.S.
statistical system and types of economic statistics.

*Statistical sources: a subject guide to date on
industrial, business, social, educational, financial
and other topics for the United States and selective foreign countries,* by P. Wasserman and
others (Detroit, Gale Research Co., 1965. 387p.)
is a revised ed. of the compilation published in
1963, which gave sources on more than 9,000
items under 6,152 headings, A-Z.

31 (8=6)
Latin America in maps, charts, tables. Mexico,
the Center of Intercultural Formation, 1963-. no.
1-. tables, bar diagrs., maps. Spiral binding.

1. *Socio-economic data.* 1963.
2. *Socio-religious data (Catholicism).* 1964.
3. *Socio-educational data.* 1965.
4. *Socio-religious data (non-Catholic).*
5. *Socio-cultural data.*
6. *Data on health and medical care.*
Gives detailed statistical data up to 1960.
Includes directory information. Further publication was suspended after v. 3.

31 (8=6)
Statistical abstract of Latin America. Los
Angeles, Cal., Univ. of California, Center of
Latin American Studies, 1956-. Annual (irregular).
(1964 ed., published 1965. xiv, 164p. $10).

"As comprehensive a set of statistics as possible on the general social, economic and financial structure of the Latin American republics and the European and the U.S. dependencies in the Americas" (*International affairs,* v. 42, no. 4, October 1966, p. 777). The 1965 ed. has 102 tables in 5 subject groups: Area and land use (tables 1-2)—Population (3-14)—Social organization (15-36)—Economy (37-82)—Finance (including trade, prices; 83-102). Figures up to 1964. Includes Canada, U.S.A. and the Caribbean. Bibliography of sources, p. 152-78.

31 (8=6)
UNITED NATIONS. Economic Commission for Latin America. **Boletín estadístico de América latina.** Statistical bulletin for Latin America. New York, United Nations, 1964-. v. 1, no. 1-. 2 p.a. ea. 19s.

Previously (October 1958-) as statistical supplement to *Economic bulletin for Latin America.* In Spanish and English.
V. 1, no. 1 has *c.* 100 tables. Sections: General —Population—National accounts—Finance and prices—Production—International trade. Explanatory notes, citing sources.

Brazil
31 (81)
BRAZIL. INSTITUTO BRASILEIRO DE GEOGRAFIA E ESTATISTICA. Anuário estatístico do Brasil. Rio de Janeiro, 1936-. Annual.

V. 27, 1966 has statistics (tables, p. 15-534) for 1963 and 1964. In Portuguese only. Six broad groups: Situação física—Situação demográfica—Situação econômica—Situação social—Situação cultural — Situação administrativa e política. Sources are cited. 24 graphs, bar-diagrams; maps. Subject index.
Supplemented by quarterly *Boletim estatístico.*

Argentina
31 (82)
ARGENTINA. DIRECCIÓN NACIONAL DE ESTADISTICA Y CENSOS. Boletín de estadística. Buenos Aires, 1947-. Quarterly.

The July/September 1966 has 12 sections of tables and two special features. List of publications of the Dirección Nacional.

Chile
31 (83)
CHILE. DIRECCIÓN DE ESTADISTICA Y CENSO. Boletín. Santiago de Chile. Monthly.

The December issue contains annual statistics (*Sinopsis*).
The Banco Central de Chile's *Boletín mensal* (1930?-) includes supporting statistical tables covering a ten-year period, plus recent months.

Peru
31 (85)
PERU. DIRECCIÓN NACIONAL DE ESTADISTICA Y CENSOS. Boletín de estadística peruana. Lima, 1958-. Mimeographed. Annual.

The 1964 v. (año 7) has four main parts: Comercio exterior—Comercio interior—Transportes—Communicaciones. Statistics for ten-year periods and up to June 1964.

Colombia
31 (86)
COLOMBIA. DEPARTAMENTO ADMINISTRATIVO NACIONAL DE ESTADISTICA. Anuario general de estadística. Bogotá, 1905-. Annual.

The 1963 v. (published 1965) is a detailed survey (861p.) in 11 chapters, with 451 tables. Statistics for 8-year periods (1956-63). Detailed contents-list; no index. Introductory notes to chapters.

Venezuela
31 (87)
VENEZUELA. DIRECCIÓN GENERAL DE ESTADISTICA Y CENSOS NACIONALES. Anuario estadístico de Venezuela, 1957-1963. Caracas, 1964. 2v.

A detailed compilation (1801p.) in 11 parts, with 1,191 tables. Statistics are mainly for ten-year periods. Detailed contents-list; no subject index or citation of sources.
Supplemented by *Boletín mensual de estadística* (1941-).

Uruguay
31 (899)
URUGUAY. DIRECCIÓN GENERAL DE ESTADISTICA Y CENSOS. Anuario estadístico, 1955-1960. Montevideo, [1960]. v.p. Mimeographed.

17 sections; more than 300 tables. Detailed contents-list; no subject index. Sources stated.

Uruguay en cifras, by A. E. Solari, and others (Montevideo, Departamento de Publicaciones, Universidad de la República, 1966. 176, [14]p. tables, diagrs.) has text and supporting tables with statistics up to 1965. Six sections: 1. Population—2. Geographical distribution—3. Employment and distribution of occupations—4. Literacy and level of education—5. Urban and rural housing—6. Gross national product.

Indonesia
31 (910)
INDONESIA. BIRO PUSAT STATISTIK [Central Bureau of Statistics]. **Statistical pocketbook of Indonesia.** Djakarta, [the Bureau], [1956?-].

The 1961 issue (the 6th post-war) has *c.* 200 tables in 18 sections, with footnotes. States sources. Appendix 3: List of 97 publications issued by the Central Bureau of Statistics. Detailed contents; no index.

31 (910)

NUGROHO. Indonesia: facts and figures.
Djakarta, Terbitan Pertjobaan, 1967. xxxiv, 608p.
tables, maps. Mimeographed.

Mainly statistical data, in the form of tables,
up to 1965. 9 chapters: 1. The country—2. Population and labour—3. Social statistics (education,
religion, culture, health & law enforcement)—4.
Agriculture—5. Manufacturing, electricity, gas &
steam, mining—6. Trade, transport & communications, co-operatives—7. Money & banking,
wages & prices—8. National income and comparative statistics—9. Appendix (1-6); general
references (p. 607-8). Sources are cited; chapter
references.

New Zealand

31 (931)

**NEW ZEALAND. DEPARTMENT OF STATIS-
TICS. Statistical publications 1840-1960**
(mainly those produced by the Registrar-General,
1853-1910 and the Government Statistician, 1911-
1960). Wellington, Government Printer, 1961.
66p.

Includes a section, 'Select bibliography on
early New Zealand', p. 25-26.
The Department's *Catalogue of New Zealand
statistics* (Rev. ed. 1966. 156p. 10s.), first published in 1962, gives detailed coverage (*e.g.,* 2
pages on the *Monthly abstract of statistics*).

31 (931)

New Zealand official yearbook. Wellington, Department of Statistics, 1892-. illus., tables, maps.
Annual. (71st issue, 1966. 21s.).

See entry at 908 (931).

Supplemented by the *Monthly abstract of
statistics* (1914-).

Australia

31 (94)

**AUSTRALIA. COMMONWEALTH BUREAU OF
CENSUS AND STATISTICS. Official year
book of the Commonwealth of Australia.**
Canberra (originally Melbourne), 1908-. Annual.

The 1965 year book (no. 51) has 31 chapters
of text, with many tables and maps, and an
appended statistical summary (p. 1279-1320), giving statistics up to 1964-65. Analytical index, p.
1327-52.
The Commonwealth Bureau also produces an
annual *Pocket compendium of Australian statistics* (1965 issue. 2s. 5d.).

Statistical Science

311:016

Statistical theory and method abstracts. Published for the International Statistical Institute
by Oliver & Boyd, Edinburgh & London, 1959-.
v. 1-. Quarterly. ea. 45s.; 150s. p.a.

See entry in v. 1 of the Guide (2nd ed.),
at 519.2:016.

311:016

"Bibliographie". In *Revue de l'Institut International de Statistique.* The Hague, Stockum,
1933-. v. 1-. 3 p.a.

The frequency of the *Revue* has varied from
1 to 3 issues p.a.
In 1966 the "Bibliographie" carried 2,285
entries, in four main sections, with detailed
sub-division: General—General theory and
methods—Fields of application—Data collection:
methods & results. No annotations. Covers
periodical articles, books (asterisked items),
annuals and official documents. Not cumulated.

311:016

**BUCKLAND, W. R., and FOX, R. A. Biblio-
graphy of basic texts and monographs on
statistical methods, 1945-1960.** 2nd ed., rev.
and enl. Published for the International Statistical Institute by Oliver & Boyd, Edinburgh &
London, 1963. vii, 297p. 35s.

First published 1951 (The Hague, I.S.I.).
About 200 annotated entries in ten subject
groups (*e.g.,* General introductory texts—Mathematical statistics—Demography). The annotations
consist of contents lists (chapter headings) and
extracts from 22 leading statistical, etc. journals
published in English that include a regular book-
review section. Appended: list of journals; list of
publishers; supplementary list of book titles
(1960-62); author index.
(Also entered in the *Guide* (2nd ed.), v. 1, at
519.2:016.)

311:016

**KENDALL, M. G., and DOIG, A. G. Biblio-
graphy of statistical literature, 1950-1958.**
Edinburgh & London, Oliver & Boyd, 1962. xii,
297p. 63s.

9,802 numbered entries under authors, A-Z. 26
specialists collaborated in providing references to
works published in their respective countries or
languages (19 in all). For 12 journals almost all
the articles are indexed; for 42 others, relevant
articles only.
Two more v. are to follow, making 25-30,000
references in all.

312 POPULATION

Bibliographies

312:016

**ELDRIDGE, H. T. The materials of demo-
graphy:** a selected and annotated bibliography.
New York, International Union for the Scientific
Study of Population, and the Population Association of America, 1959. xi, 222p.

Aims "to identify and describe significant published works in the field of population analysis"
(*Introduction*). Well annotated entries for 411
English-language works, chosen with the teacher
of demography in mind. 10 sections, each with an
introduction. Lists papers read at conferences
and asterisks works of major importance;
includes yearbooks and statistical bulletins.

Narrow two-column page. Has drawn heavily on *Population index.*

A comparable bibliography for French material (850 books and periodical articles) is J.-C. Chasteland's *Demographie: bibliographie et analyse d'ouvrages et d'articles en français* (Paris, I.N.É.D. & U.N.I.E.S.P., 1961. 182p.).

312:016
LEGEARD, C. Guide de recherches documentaires en demographie. Paris, Gauthiers-Villars, 1966. xiv, 322p. 40F.

Part 1: Le domaine de la documentation démographique (with reading lists appended to sections); part 2: Caractéristiques, moyens, fonctions de la documentation demographique. Chapter 5 (p. 189-208): Les bibliographies, les recueils et revues bibliographiques périodiques français, étrangers et internationaux (with brief notes on items). Chapter 6 (p. 208-60): Les revues françaises, étrangères et internationales. No index.

C. Legeard's "Select bibliography" (in *International social science journal*, v. 17, no. 2, 1965, p. 307-31) is a list of books and periodical articles on demography (in all languages) published 1959-64. 20 sections (from bibliographies, dictionaries, journals and the teaching of demography to international migration and internal migrations.

312:016
Population index. Princeton, N.J., School of Public Affairs (latterly, Office of Population Research), Princeton University, and the Population Association of America, 1935-. v. 1-. Quarterly. $10 p.a.

18 sections (A-S): General population studies and theory—Regional population studies—Spatial distributions—Trends in population size—Mortality—Fertility and natural increase—Marriage, divorce and the family—International migration —Internal migration—Characteristics—Demography and economic interrelations—Other interrelations—Politics—Methods of research and analysis—Organization and administration—Professional meetings and conferences—Bibliographies—New periodicals—Official statistical publications.
1966: 4,916 indicative, analytical abstracts. A first-class example of an annotated bibliography in a special field, the material dealt with ranging from periodical articles to books, statistical yearbooks and new journals. Regularly recurring compilations of official statistics such as are listed in the bibliographies of the U.N. *Demographic yearbook* are not normally covered. An article or two on some current demographic subject, supported by a bibliography, usually precedes the abstracts. Quarterly geographical and author indexes, cumulated annually.

312:016
POPULATION REFERENCE BUREAU, Washington. **Bibliography on population.** Washington, the Bureau, 1966. 20p.

A reference supplement to *Population bulletin,* August 1966.
262 items in 10 sections. Standard works of outstanding merit are asterisked. Sections: 1. Population. General studies—2. Population. Special studies—3. Fertility and fertility control —4. Mortality and health—5. Migration—6. Urbanism—7. Food, land, resources and ecology —8. Demographic and economic interrelations— 9. Demographic and social interrelations: marriage, family, ageing, etc.—10. Catholic views on population and fertility—11. Bibliographies—12. U.N. and U.S. Government publications—13. Periodicals (25 titles). No index.

Dictionaries

312 (038)
UNITED NATIONS. Department of Economic and Social Affairs. **Multilingual demographic dictionary.** Prepared by the Demographic Dictionary Committee of the International Union for the Scientific Study of Population. **English section.** New York, United Nations, 1958. viii, 77p. (ST/SOA/Ser. A/29. Population studies, no. 29).

Provisory ed., 1954. Other language "sections": French (1958); Spanish (1959); Italian (1959); German (1960); Swedish (1961); Finnish (1962); Czech (1965). A Russian section is in the press.
The English section consists of 931 passages in subject chapters, showing terms, compounds, etc. in their context, preceded by an A-Z index of terms (nearly 1,500 in all). Terms are given the same number in each language "section".

Other multilingual dictionaries: *Wörterbuch demographischen Grundbegriffe* (Hamburg, Deutsche Akademie für Bevölkerungswissenschaft, 1960. 136p.), covering German, French Italian and English; *Demographic terms in five languages (including Hungarian)* (Budapest, National Statistical Centre, 1959. 156p.).

Organisations

312:061
UNITED NATIONS EDUCATIONAL, SCIENTIFIC AND CULTURAL ORGANIZATION. International repertory of institutions conducting population studies. Paris, Unesco, 1959. 240p. (Reports and papers in the social sciences, no. 11).

Two parts: International organizations (16)— National institutions (393 in 84 countries, A-Z by country; 'United Kingdom' includes British colonies), p. 25-217. For each institution (governmental agencies; universities and university institutes; autonomous bodies) are given: name, address, name of director, names of professional staff, finance, research activities, teaching and training, use of basic demographic data, publications (including films). No index.

International

312 (4/9):016
TEXAS. UNIVERSITY. Population Research Center. **International population census bibliography.** Austin, Texas, Bureau of Business Research, Univ. of Texas, 1965-67. 5v. Suppt. 1968.

1. *Latin America and the Caribbean.* 1965. $3.
2. *Africa.* 1965. $3.
3. *Oceania.* 1966. $2.
4. *North America.* 1966. $3.
5. *Asia.* 1966. $4.   6. *Europe.* 1967. $6.
Foreword to each volume mentions more general sources (*e.g.,* Kuczynski; U.N. *Demographic year book*). No. 5 deals with 47 countries, A-Z, with items in chronological order. Prefatory note on each country; parts of multi-volume works are detailed. Coverage of national, provincial, state and city censuses (India: 102p.). Cites census taken but not published.

312 (4/9):016
UNITED NATIONS. Statistical Office. **Bibliography of recent official demographic statistics.** Bibliographie des publications officielles récentes présentant des statistiques démographiques. New York, 1954. iv, 80p. (Statistical papers. Series M, no. 18).

A reprint of the bibliography included in the *Demographic year-book,* 1953. Prepared for the United Nations by the U.S. Library of Congress, Census Library Project.
Sections: International compilations—Africa—America, North—America, South—Asia—Europe —Oceania. Order within each section is by countries alphabetically. 214 areas or countries in all are dealt with. Usually the latest census in each case is listed. Occasional annotations; index of countries.

312 (4/9):016
ZELINSKY, W. A bibliographic guide to population geography. Chicago, Ill., Chicago Univ. Press, 1962. xxx, 270, [1]p. (Univ. of Chicago, Department of Geography. Research paper no. 80).

Lists 2,588 numbered, unannotated items (1,042 in English; 461, French; 442, German; 154, Italian; 118, Spanish), including many periodical articles. "Intended primarily as a convenience for scholarly investigation" (*Introduction*). Pt. 1, General statistics. Bibliographies and general aids, etc.; pt. 2, Regional statistics (nos. 292-2563; Americas: nos. 297-840; Africa: nos. 2272-2487). Author index.

Periodicals

312 (4/9):05
Population bulletin of the United Nations. New York, United Nations, Department of Economic and Social Affairs, 1951-. no. 1-. Irregular. (no, 7:1963. 1965. $2).

Each issue concentrates on a particular theme; well documented; many tables. Thus, no. 6:1962 is entitled "The situation and recent trends of mortality in the world" (p. 3-145). It includes an annotated list of selected demographic publications of the United Nations (p. 203-10). No. 7:1963 concentrates on conditions and trends of fertility in the world. Chapter 3, "Levels and trends of fertility in Africa" (p. 15-41; 2 maps, 11 tables, 152 footnote references).

Year-books

312 (4/9) (058)
UNITED NATIONS. Statistical Office. **Demographic yearbook . . .** 1948-. New York, 1949-. Annual. (17th issue, 1965. 1966. $11; $15).

Presents population, nationality, mortality, nuptiality, divorce and migration statistics, life-table values, an explanatory chapter entitled "Technical notes on the statistical tables". Detailed contents-list. The 1965 v. has a cumulative subject index to issues 1-17. The 1965 yearbook includes census results covering nearly 250 separate areas of the world. In accordance with a rotation plan, each issue presents special tables on one aspect of the subject (*e.g.,* 17th issue, 1965: the 4th natality volume; 48 tables, with statistics for 1955-64; 14th, 15th and 16th issues, 1962/64: population census statistics). In English and French.

Supplemented by United Nations. *Statistical papers. Series A.—Population and vital statistics reports* (*e.g.,* v. 19, no. 4 (1967. $1), giving data as of 1 October 1967).

Atlases

312 (4/9) (084.4)
Welt-Bevölkerungs-Atlas. Verteilung der Bevölkerung der Erde um das Jahr 1950. World atlas of population: distribution of population on the earth about the year 1950. Hrsg. von F. Burgdörfer. Hamburg, Falk-Verlag, 1955-57. maps.

Based on results of the first world population census, 1950. Ten excellent double-page following maps 1. Europe (1:10M)—2. Central Europe (1:2½M)—3. Mediterranean area (1:5M)—4. Africa (1:20M)—5. U.S.A. and adjoining territories (1:7½M)—6. Australia (1:20M)—7. North America (1:15M)—8. South America (1:15M)—9. Asia (1:22½M)—10. World map (1:45M). The maps are physical and operate on the dot principle, towns being graded in some 13 sizes, with populations of from 1,000 upwards. Map 3 is backed by a map of the Nile delta and tables. Page size: *c.* 16″ × 23″.

An example of a national population atlas: Hilton, T. E. *Ghana population atlas: the distribution and density of population in the Gold Coast and Togoland under United Kingdom Trusteeship* (London, Nelson, 1960. 40p. maps. 50s.), based on the 1948 census.

Europe & Asia

312 (4/5)
UNITED STATES. BUREAU OF THE CENSUS. International population statistics [reports]. Series P-90. Washington, Government Printing Office. 1952-65. 22v.

The object of the series is "the compilation and evaluation of population data and related information which are often available only in scattered sources or in languages other than English". Chiefly on Sino-Soviet bloc countries.

1: *The population of Germany and West Berlin.* 1952.

2: *The population of Israel.* 1952.
3: *The population of Czechoslovakia.* 1953.
4: *The population of Poland.* 1954.
5: *The population of Yugoslavia.* 1954.
6: *The population of Communist China, 1953.* 1955.
7: *The population of Manchuria.* 1958.
8: *The population and manpower of China: an annotated bibliography.* 1958.
9: *The population of Hungary* [with list of sources]. 1958.
10: *The 1959 census of population of the U.S.S.R.: methodology and plans.* 1959.
11: *The labor force of the Soviet Zone of Germany and the Soviet Zone of Berlin.* 1959
12: *The Soviet statistical system. Labor force recordkeeping and reporting.* 1960.
13: *The labor force of Czechoslovakia.* 1960.
14: *The labor force of Rumania.* 1961. (P-60).
15: *The size, composition and growth of the population of Mainland China.* 1961.
16: *Labor force of Bulgaria.* 1962.
17: *Soviet statistical system: labor force recordkeeping and reporting since 1957.* 1962.
18: *Labor force of Hungary.* [1962].
19: *Soviet mineral - fuels industries, 1925 - 58.* [1963].
20: *Labor force of Poland.* [1964].
21: *Non - agricultural employment in Mainland China, 1949-58.* 1965.
22: *Labor force of Yugoslavia.* [1965].

Europe

312 (4):016
UNITED STATES. LIBRARY OF CONGRESS. Census Library Project. **National censuses and vital statistics in Europe, 1918-1939:** an annotated bibliography. Washington, Government Printing Office, 1948. vii, 215p. 40c.

The national censuses cover industry, housing, agriculture and the like, as well as population; statistical year-books are also dealt with. Forty-two countries are covered, arrangement being alphabetically by country.

——————. **1940-1948 supplement:** an annotated bibliography. 1949. v, 48p. 15c.

Similar in pattern, but there is a general British entry under "United Kingdom" and not under "England and Wales", "Scotland" and "Northern Ireland", as in the main volume.

Commonwealth

312 (41-5)
KUCZYNSKI, R. R. Demographic survey of the British colonial empire. London, Oxford Univ. Press, 1948-53. 3v.

v. 1: *West Africa.* 1948. xiii, 821p.
v. 2: *South Africa High Commission territories. East Africa. Mauritius and Seychelles.* 1949. x, 983p.
v. 3: *West Indian and American territories.* 1953. xiii, 497p.
The work was originally planned in 4 volumes; v. 4 was to have included a synopsis of all the birth and death registration laws in force. The author died in 1947, and v. 3 has a brief index only, as opposed to the analytical indexes in

v. 1-2. Sections are included in each volume on census-taking, composition of population, native fertility, etc. There are numerous statistical tables, with extensive quotations from original reports, making the survey an important source book on colonial social and medical development. The bibliographies must be sought in the extensive lists of sources quoted and in footnote references.

A reprint is due for publication, at *c.* £25.

Great Britain

312 (410)
GREAT BRITAIN. GENERAL REGISTER OFFICE, ENGLAND and WALES; SCOTLAND. Census, 1961, Great Britain. Summary tables. London, H.M. Stationery Office, 1966. lii, 158p. 39s.

Statistics on population, birthplace and nationality, housing, household composition, migration, occupation, industry, education and fertility for Great Britain as a whole.

Another joint publication of the two General Register Offices: *Census, 1961, Great Britain. Scientific and technical qualifications.* 1962. 6s. 6d.

312 (410):016
GREAT BRITAIN. INTERDEPARTMENTAL COMMITTEE ON SOCIAL AND ECONOMIC RESEARCH. Guide to official sources. No. 2: **Census reports of Great Britain, 1801-1931.** London, H.M. Stationery Office, 1951. iv, 119p.

"The aim . . . is to give a brief account for research workers and others of the development of the Census and of the wide range of information and analyses published in the long series of official Reports." Chapter 5: Selected subjects of census enquiry. Numerous tables and reproductions.

Scotland

312 (411)
GREAT BRITAIN. GENERAL REGISTER (formerly **REGISTRY) OFFICE, SCOTLAND. Annual estimates of the population of Scotland.** Edinburgh, H.M. Stationery Office, 1958-. Annual. (1966, published 1967. 1s. 4d.).

Estimate of population by regional divisions, conurbations, counties of cities, large burghs, small burghs, and landward areas by district of county.

312 (411)
GREAT BRITAIN. GENERAL REGISTER (formerly **REGISTRY) OFFICE, SCOTLAND. Annual report** of the General Registrar for Scotland, 1855-. Edinburgh, H.M. Stationery Office. (1966, published 1967. 40s.).

Vital statistics of Scotland: population estimates, statistics of births, still-births (since 1939), marriages and deaths (including causes of death and still-births). Also fertility statistics, since 1938.
Supplement to the Annual report, issued for

the decades 1861-70, 1881-90, 1891-1900, 1921-30, including occupational mortality, life tables, etc

Quarterly return: Births, deaths (including causes of death) and marriages; weather report. 4s.; 17s. p.a.

Weekly return: Births, deaths and marriages; infectious diseases; new claims for sickness benefit; weather report. 9d.; 52s. p.a.

312 (411)
GREAT BRITAIN. GENERAL REGISTER (formerly **REGISTRY) OFFICE, SCOTLAND. Census, 1961. Report on the sixteenth census of Scotland.** Edinburgh, H.M. Stationery Office, 1961-67.

Preliminary report. 1961. 5s.
v. 1. County reports.
v. 2. Usual residence. 1965. 7s.
v. 3. Age, marital condition and general tables. 1965. 35s.
v. 4, pt. 1. Housing and households. 1966. 50s.
pt. 2. Household composition tables. 1966. 53s.
v. 5. Birthplace and nationality. 1966. 14s.
v. 6. Occupation, industry and workplace. 3 pts. 1966. 47s. 6d., 43s., 16s.
v. 7. Gaelic. 1966. 10s. 6d.
v. 8. Internal migration. 1966. 33s.
v. 9. Terminal education age. 1966. 95s.
v. 10. Fertility. 1966. 30s.
Place names and population. 1967. 27s. (See at 914.11 (083.86).)
Leaflets no. 1-8, 10-27 (on population, housing, occupation and industry, internal migration; Gaelic supplementary leaflet). 1963-66. Various prices.

312 (411)
GREAT BRITAIN. GENERAL REGISTER (formerly **REGISTRY) OFFICE, SCOTLAND. Sample census, 1966: Scotland. County reports.** Edinburgh, H.M. Stationery Office, 1967-.

Chiefly tables. Reports so far issued: Edinburgh, East Lothian, Midlothian, Stirling and West Lothian (15s. 6d.); Dundee, Angus and Perth (14s.); Dumbarton and Renfrew (14s. 6d.); Ayr and Bute (11s.); Clackmannan, Fife and Kinross (14s. 6d.).

Northern Ireland

312 (416)
NORTHERN IRELAND. GENERAL REGISTER OFFICE. Annual report of the Registrar General, 1922-. Belfast, H.M. Stationery Office. Annual. (44th report. 1965. 18s. 6d.).

Contains general abstracts of births, deaths and marriages, returns of infectious diseases, and a meteorological summary.

Other publications of the Northern Ireland G.R.O.:
The Registrar-General's Quarterly returns, 1922-. Of births, deaths and marriages, notification of infectious diseases, and a meteorological report.
Weekly return, 1922-. Of births and deaths for principal towns, notifications of infectious diseases.

312 (416)
NORTHERN IRELAND. GENERAL REGISTER OFFICE. Census of population of Northern Ireland, 1961. Belfast, H.M. Stationery Office.

1. Preliminary report. 1961. 4s.
2. County Antrim. 1964. 15s.
3. County Armagh. 1964. 15s.
4. Belfast County Borough. 1963. 15s.
5. County Down. 1964. 15s.
6. County of Fermanagh. 1964. 12s. 6d.
7. County and County Borough of Londonderry. 1964 17s. 6d.
8. County Tyrone. 1964. 15s.
9. General report. 1965. 20s.
10. Fertility report. 1965. 8s.
Topographical index. 1962. 25s.

——— —— Census of population, 1966. Preliminary report. 1967. 4s. 6d.

Eire

312 (417)
EIRE. CENTRAL STATISTICS OFFICE. Census of population of Ireland, 1961. Dublin, Stationery Office, 1961-66.

Excludes Northern Ireland.

Preliminary report. 1961. 2s.
1. Population, area and valuation of each district electoral division and of each larger unit of area. 1963. 6s.
2. Ages and conjugal conditions classified by areas only. 1963. 7s. 6d.
3. Occupations of males and females . . . 1963. 6s. 6d.
4. Industries. 1964. 6s.
5. Occupations classified by ages and conjugal conditions. 1964. 7s.
6. Housing and social amenities. 1964. 6s.
7. Pt. 1. Religions. Pt 2. Birthplaces. 1965. 5s.
8. Fertility of marriage. 1965. 7s.
9. Irish language. 1966. 2s. 6d.

312 (417)
——— —— Census of population of Ireland, 1966. Dublin, Stationery Office, 1966-.

Preliminary report. 1966. 2s.
1. Population of district electoral divisions, towns and larger units of area. 1967. 6s.

Other Eire, C.S.O. publications:
Report on vital statistics, 1953-. (Previously, Annual reports of the Registrar General, 1922-52).
Quarterly report, 1922-. Statistics of births, deaths and marriages, and infectious diseases.
Weekly returns, 1922-. Statistics of births and deaths for the principal towns.

England and Wales

312 (42)
GREAT BRITAIN. GENERAL REGISTER OFFICE, ENGLAND and WALES. Annual estimates of the population of England and Wales and of local authority areas. London, H.M. Stationery Office, 1948-. Annual. (1966. 2s. 6d.)

Contains the mid-year estimates of the population (both sexes combined) of each administrative area. For England and Wales as a whole the estimate is divided by sex and by certain age-groupings with each year of age under 21.

312 (42)

GREAT BRITAIN. GENERAL REGISTER OF-FICE, ENGLAND AND WALES. Census, 1961. England and Wales: reports. London, H.M. Stationery Office, 1961-.

Preliminary report. 1961. 7s. 6d.
County reports. 62v. 11s.-77s.
Greater London tables. 1966. 15s. 6d.
Report on Jersey, Guernsey and adjacent islands. 21s.
Report on the Isle of Man. 2 pts. 12s. 6d.
Report on Welsh speaking population. 10s.
Age, marital and general tables. 1964. 22s.
Birthplace and nationality tables. 15s.
Classification of occupations. 1966. 40s. (See at 331.7.)
Commonwealth immigrants in the conurbations. 1965. 21s.
Education tables. 1966. 24s.
Fertility tables. 1966. 58s.
Housing tables. 1964. 2s. 6d.
Housing national summary tables. o.p.
Household composition tables. 1966. 67s.
Household composition national summary tables. 4s.
Index of place names. 1965. 2v. 100s. (See at 914.2 (083.86).)
Industry tables. 2 pts. 81s.
Migration tables. 1966. 67s.
Migration national summary tables. 2 pts. 8s. 6d.
Occupation tables. 55s.
Occupation and industry national summary tables. 3s.
Occupation, industry, socio-economic groups. 58 leaflets. 3s. 6d. - 8s.
Population, dwellings, households. Leaflets 1-19. 1s. 3d. - 2s. 6d.
Socio-economic group tables. 24s.
Usual residence tables. 12s.
Workplace tables. 58s.

———————**Sample census, 1966.** England and Wales. **County reports.** London, H.M. Stationery Office, 1967-.

312 (42)

GREAT BRITAIN. GENERAL REGISTER OF-FICE, ENGLAND and WALES. Matters of life and death. 4th ed. London, H.M. Stationery Office, 1958. 28p.

First published 1948.
"A short account of the growth of the population of England and Wales, with particular reference to the facts about births, deaths, migrations, etc. collected by the General Register Office since 1837" (*Government publications. Sectional list no. 56* (1964), p. 10.

312 (42)

GREAT BRITAIN. GENERAL REGISTER OF-FICE, ENGLAND and WALES. Statistical review of England and Wales, 1921-. London, H.M. Stationery Office, 1923-. Annual. (1964, published 1966-67. 3 pts. 79s.).

Previously as *Annual report,* the number of the report preceding this title; the first report covers 1st July 1837 - 30th June 1838.
The three parts of the 1964 review are: pt. 1. *Tables, medical* (38s.); pt. 2. *Tables, population* (18s.); pt. 3. *Commentary* (25s.). Pt. 3 has detailed analyses of the statistics published in pts. 1-2, with comment on the trend of mortality from different causes of death, notification of infectious diseases, population trends, marriage, birth and fertility rates and the like.

Also supplements (e.g., *Supplement on mental health; Supplement on cancer*).
Quarterly return: Births, deaths and marriages. Infectious diseases. Weather. Population estimates. 2s. 6d.
Weekly return: Births and deaths. Infectious diseases. Weather. 2s.; 117s. p.a.

312 (42):016

GREAT BRITAIN. H.M. STATIONERY OF-FICE. Government publications. Sectional list no. 56, revised to 31st October 1967: **General Register Office, England and Wales.** London, H.M.S.O., 1968. 15p. *Gratis.*

Entries, often annotated; headings: Census 1966—Sample Census 1966—Census 1961—Census 1951—Decennial supplement, England and Wales—Official list—Report on hospital in-patient enquiry—Returns—Statistical review of England and Wales—Studies on medical and population subjects—Miscellaneous publications —A selection of Public General Acts.

Asia

312 (5):016

DEMOGRAPHIC TRAINING AND RESEARCH CENTRE, Bombay, *and others.* **A select annotated bibliography on population & related questions in Asia and the Far East.** New Delhi, U.N. Economic Commission for Asia and the Far East, 1963. 158, 61p. Mimeographed.

Annotated bibliography of 869 items in classified order (classes A-M; M: Bibliographies and yearbooks). Appended list of periodicals. Author and subject-country indexes.
Supplements are promised.

Americas

312 (7/8)

PAN AMERICAN UNION. Department of Statistics. **América en cifras, 1963.** v. 2: **Situación demográfica;** estado y movimiento de la población. Washington, Secretaría General de la Organización de los Estados Americanos, 1964. 155p.

Population statistics, 1963, covering North, Central and South America. The corresponding volume in *América en cifras, 1965,* has not yet been published.

An annotated list of past censuses appears in the U.S. Library of Congress. Census Library Project. *General censuses and vital statistics in the Americas* (Washington, Government Printing Office, 1943. 151p.).

U.S.A.

312 (73)

UNITED STATES. LIBRARY OF CONGRESS. Census Library Project. **Catalog of United States census publications, 1790-1945.** Washington, Government Printing Office, 1950. 320p.

An annotated list of the publications of the U.S. Bureau of the Census and its predecessors. Supplemented by the Bureau's quarterly *Census publications* (1945-), cumulated annually.

Births & Deaths

312.1 / .2 (4/9)
WORLD HEALTH ORGANIZATION. World health statistics annual, 1962. Geneva, W.H.O., 1965-66. 3v.

v. 1. *Vital statistics and causes of death.* 1965. 80c.
v. 2. *Infectious diseases: causes, deaths and vaccinations.* 1966. 26s. 8d.
v. 3. *Health personnel and hospital establishments.* 1966. 26s. 8d.
Previously as *Annual epidemiological and vital statistics . . . ,* 1939/46-1961. V. 1: 1963 (1966)

has 516p. of tables. Many statistics are for 1963 only, but some (*e.g.,* estimated population) are retrospective.

312.2 (410)
HOWE, G. M. National atlas of disease mortality in the United Kingdom. London, Nelson, 1963. [8], 111p. maps. 35s.

Aims "to show through the medium of maps the spatial patterns of variations in disease mortality in the United Kingdom" (*Introduction*). 56 black-and-white maps (all at 1:3,000,000), with 2 overtraces, for location of administrative units. Divided by type and nature of fatal disease (*e.g.,* cancer: circulatory system; respiratory system; digestive system; miscellaneous causes). Includes accidents and suicides as categories. Statistical appendix. Page size: $11\frac{1}{4}'' \times 6\frac{3}{4}''$. Claims to be the first British atlas of its kind.

32 POLITICAL SCIENCE

Bibliographies

32:016
BROCK, C. "Political science". In *Library trends,* v. 15, no. 4, April 1967 ('Bibliography: current state and future trends'. Part 2), p. 628-47.

A valuable survey under two heads: Literature sector—Data sector (*i.e.,* data sources and services). 48 references, of which a list is appended.
Mentions an annual annotated list of German works on political science, *Literatur-Verzeichnis der politischen Wissenschaften* (Munich, 1952-) that has no U.S. counterpart.

32:016
Cumulative index to the 'American political science review', v. 1-57: 1906-1963. Edited by Kenneth Janda. Evanston, Ill., Northwestern Univ. Press, 1964. xxvi, 225p. 35s.

A KWIK index covering 2,614 articles. Sections: 1. Keyword listing—2. Author-alphabetized bibliography—3. Author cross-references.

32:016
HARMON, R. B. Political science: a bibliographic guide to the literature. New York & London, Scarecrow Press, 1965. 388p. $8.75.

About 2,000 items in 10 chapters: 1. The literature of politcal science—2. General research materials—3. Political science and the theory of politics—4. Comparative government—5. State and local government—6. Political parties, public opinion and electoral processes—7. Political theory.—8. Law and jurisprudence—9. Public administration—10. Industrial relations. Appendixes: A. Periodicals—B. Government documents —C. Agencies and institutions engaged in political research. Author-title index; subject index. Brief introductions to sections; items in chapters 1, 2 and 8 are annotated and occasionally items elsewhere. For students; U.S. slanted. Clear type; near-printed.

A comparable survey is *Guide to reference materials in political science: a selective bibliography,* by L. R. Wynar, with L. Fystrom (Denver, Colorado Bibliographic Institute, 1966. 318p.). "Though neither [Wynar nor Harmon] pretends to comprehensiveness, both are valuable additions in a field which has lacked any general guide for thirty years" (*Library trends,* v. 15, no. 4, April 1967, p. 632).

32:016
International bibliography of political science. Bibliographie internationale de science politique, 1953-. Paris, Unesco (now London, Tavistock Publications; Chicago, Aldine Publishing Co.), 1954-. v. 1-. Annual. (v. 13: 1964. 1965.) (International bibliography of the social sciences).

Prepared by the International Committee for Social Sciences Documentation.
V. 13 contains 4,293 items (books; periodicals; documents), in 6 main sections: A. Political science—B. Political thought—C. Government and public administration (items 508-1753; detailed country divisions)—D. Governmental process—E. International relations—F. Area studies (items 3881-4293; country divisions). List of periodicals, p. xv-lvii (*c.* 2,000 titles—the same list as that used for the other parts of the International bibliography of the social sciences series. Author and analytical subject indexes.

32:016
International political science abstracts. Documentation politique internationale. Oxford, Blackwell, 1951-. v. 1-. Quarterly. ea. 16s.; 55s. p.a.

Prepared by the International Political Science Association and the International Studies Conference, with the support of the Co-ordination Committee on Documentation in the Social Services.
V. 15, no. 1, 1965: abstracts of articles published from October to December 1964 (copy received 25th January 1966) has 352 numbered

informative and indicative c. 150 word-abstracts. 6 main sections: 1. Political science—2. Political theory—3. Government and public administration —4. Governmental process—5. International relations—6. Area studies. English abstracts of articles in English; otherwise French abstracts. About 150 periodicals (listed in each issue) are covered. Subject index in each issue; annual author and cumulated subject index.

Complementary to the *International bibliography* in that it is selective, devoted to periodical articles, annotated and more frequent. An identical pattern of arrangement would have helped.

Encyclopaedias & Dictionaries

32 (031)

Handwörterbuch der Staatswissenschaften, hrsg. von L. Elster, A. Weber, Fr. Wieser. 4. gänz. ungearb. Aufl. Jena, Fischer, 1923-29. 8v. and supplement.

The leading encyclopaedia of political science; supplemented to some extent by the *Handwörterbuch der Sozialwissenschaften* (1952-) (*see at* 3 (*03*)). Well known for its lengthy, signed articles and adequate bibliographies (*e.g.,* the article on "Trusts" runs to 24p., including two columns of bibliography). Biographical articles give a full list of works by the writer, with material on him (*e.g.,* "Karl Marx"—6p., about one-third of it being bibliography, including periodical articles).

V. 8 includes a supplement and a subject index to the whole. The supplementary volume carries its own subject index.

32 (032)=00

BACK, H., *and others.* **Polec: dictionary of politics and economics.** Berlin, de Gruyter, 1964. xvi, 961p. DM.35.

14,000 English, French and German terms in one A-Z sequence, with definitions and frequently descriptive data, plus adequate cross-references. The definition and data are in the language of the entry-word, the equivalent of which is then given in the other two languages. Includes entries under names of States and political parties. English entry-words are sometimes suspect (*e.g.,* 'suddentrip'; 'exceptional law') and English definitions can be awkwardly phrased (*e.g.,* 'VVB' is translated as 'Society of people's owned industry').

32 (032)=20

ELLIOTT, F., and **SUMMERSKILL, M. A dictionary of politics.** 5th ed. Harmondsworth, Middlesex, Penguin Books, 1966. 423p. (Penguin reference books). 7s. 6d.

First published 1957; 4th ed. 1964.

Includes political developments up to 1965. Entries comprise definitions and lengthier articles. Biographies of living persons (*e.g.,* Ho Chi-Minh); articles on countries (*e.g.,* Canada: 3½p.) and areas, doctrines, policies, parties and organisations. References from abbreviations to full names.

W. Theimer's *Encyclopaedia of world politics*; edited, rev. and enl. by P. Campbell (London, Faber, 1950. 471p. maps) is now outdated,

although a 6th ed. in German was published in 1962 (*Lexikon der Politik*. Berne, Francke. 763p.).

32 (038)=20

SPAULL, H. The new ABC of civics: a dictionary of terms used in connection with Parliament, local authorities, courts of law, diplomacy. NATO, the Common Market and the United Nations. [4th] new, rev. and enl. ed. London, Barrie & Rockliff, 1967. 142p. 15s.

3rd ed. 1963.

Deals with fairly elementary terms (*e.g.,* "condominium"; "left-wing") and is suitable for the school library.

32 (038)=20 (73)

SPERBER, H., and **TRITTSCHUH, T. American political terms:** an historical dictionary. Detroit, Wayne State Univ., 1962. x, 516p. $12.75 (New York, McGraw-Hill, 1964. $3.95).

On *O.E.D.* lines: definition; different meanings; changes in usage, with quotations (*e.g.,* 'loco foco'; 'egghead'). About 1,000 entries. A few politically unimportant words are included solely because they do not appear in *O.E.D.,* Matthews' *Dictionary of Americanisms* and Craigie and Hulbert's *Dictionary of American English*. Rather narrow columns.

Annuals

32 (058)

Political handbook and atlas of the world: parliaments, parties and press as of January 1 . . . New York & London, Harper & Row, for the Council on Foreign Relations, [*c.* 1927]-. v. 1-. Annual. (1966. 68s.).

Title varies. As from 1963 includes a 32-page map supplement in colour.

Under 130 countries and areas, A-Z, basic information plus notes on form of government and holders of chief offices; recent political events; members of cabinet; party programmes; the press (leading newspapers and periodicals: editors and political slant). Includes International Court of Justice, United Nations and Vatican City. No index. Supplements *Statesman's year book* to some extent, but is no substitute.

World handbook of political and social indicators, by B. M. Russett and others (New Haven & London, Yale Univ. Press, 1964. x, 372p. 72s.) is described in the *Economic journal* (v. 75, no. 299, September 1965, p. 616-7) as a "wonderful quarry of information" with a "terribly inadequate index". Comparisons of growth rates and projections to 1975 for most countries of the world.

Biography

32 (092)

KOSCH, Wilhelm. Biographisches Staatshandbuch. Lexikon der Politik, Presse und Publizistik. Fortgeführt von E. Kuri. Berne, Francke, 1963. 2v. Sw. fr. 148.

Biographical articles (*c.* 5,000) on leading public figures in German-speaking countries during the past 150 years: politicians, statesmen, journalists and political writers, plus articles on political press and periodicals. Bibliographical references (material by and on the biographee).

Great Britain

32 (410)

BUTLER, D., and FREEMAN, J. British political facts, 1900-1960. London, Macmillan, 1963. xvi, 245p. tables. 40s.

Arranged in 21 sections (*e.g.,* 1. Ministries (with biographical notes)—2. Parties—3. Parliament—4. Elections—5. Major social legislation—6. Nationalisation—7. Treaties and international organisations—8. Civil service . . . 15. Trade unions—16. Churches—17. National newspapers —18. Broadcasting authorities—19. Pressure groups—20. Statistics, 1900-1960 (79 tables)—21. Bibliographical note (p. 239-40)). The index omits individual names (except where biographies are supplied) and entries in tables and bibliographies; but 'Index of ministers' (p. 58-88) provides supplementary entries. Sources are stated.

Middle East

32 (5-011)

Middle East record: a comprehensive annual survey of political developments in the Middle East. Jerusalem, The Reuven Shiloah Research Centre, [1962]-. v. 1-. Annual.

v. 1: 1960 ([1962]. 105s.); v. 2: 1961 (1966. 140s.).

The first reference work of its kind in English. V. 1 has 3 main sections: 1. The Middle East in world affairs—2. Relations between the Middle East countries—3. Countries—International political affairs and international relations. Numerous maps and tables. V. 2 has a detailed subject-index to both volumes and fuller statistical information. The term "Middle East" includes Libya, Ethiopia, Somalia and Sudan.

Japan

32 (52):016

WARD, R. E., and WATANABE, H. Japanese political science: a guide to Japanese reference and research materials. Rev. ed. Ann Arbor, Univ. of Michigan Press, for the Center for Japanese Studies, 1961. xi, 210p. 55s.

1,759 annotated items in 27 sections, each with an introduction (1. Bibliographies—2. General reference works—3. Periodicals—4-27. Subject aspects (*e.g.,* Constitutional law; National Diet; Allied occupation of Japan). Author's name in entry is first given in romanised form, then in Japanese characters, and similarly with title. Cross-references. Index of authors and editors.

West & Equatorial Africa

32 (66/67)

BALLARD, J. A. "Politics and government in former French West and Equatorial Africa: a critical bibliography". In *Journal of modern African studies,* v. 3, no. 4, December 1965, p. 589-605.

A running commentary in 4 sections: The colonial period—Post-war politics—The period of independence—Research needs. Covers material up to 1964. Author is Lecturer in Political Science, University of Ibadan, Nigeria.

Canada

32 (71)

CARELTON UNIVERSITY, Ottawa. Library. Sources of information for research in Canadian political science and public administration: a selected and annotated bibliography prepared for the Department of Political Science and the School of Public Administration. Ottawa, Carelton Univ. Library, 1964. 25p.

Research

32.001.5

ROYAL INSTITUTE OF PUBLIC ADMINISTRATION. Register of research in political science. Prepared . . . for the Political Studies Association and the Public Administration Committee of the Joint Univ. Council for Social and Public Administration. London, the Institute, 1960-. Irregular. Mimeographed.

The 1960 *Register* (151p.) includes work for higher degrees completed during the session 1958-59 and currently in progress, but not research by members of staff (*Preface*). Sections: Politics and public administration—Political theory—Political and social history—Constitutional and administrative history. Suppt. 2: Additional entries and amendments for the University of Oxford. Entries consist of name, title of work, university and degree. No index.
The 1963 Register was the second issue. Annual supplements are to follow. That for 1964 (published [1966]), listing nearly 200 items, covers the session 1963/64.

Political Theory

320.1

SABINE, G. H. A history of political theory. 3rd ed., rev. and enl. London, Harrap, 1963. xii, 948p. 30s.

2nd ed. 1937.
The standard text-book. Gives acceptable short analyses of the major works concerned, with select bibliographies appended to chapters. The chief changes in the 3rd ed. are in chapters 33-35, on Marxism and dialectical materialism, Communism, and Fascism and national socialism Analytical index.

Immigration

325.1:016

GRAYSON, M. C., and HOUGHTON, V. P. Initial bibliography of immigration and race. [Nottingham], Univ. of Nottingham, Institute of Education, 1966. iii, 38p. Mimeographed.

About 400 items in 7 sections: 1. Introduction

—2. Psychology (3 sub-divisions)—3. Sociology—
4. Education (3 sub-divisions)—5. British government and United Nations publications—6. Dissertations—7. Miscellaneous. 68 journals cited.

325.1 (410)
INSTITUTE OF RACE RELATIONS. Coloured immigrants in Britain: a select bibliography based on the holdings of the library. . . . London, the Institute, 1965. 18p. Mimeographed.

About 200 items, including books, pamphlets and reprints, but not periodical articles, Parliamentary debates and bills. "It is hoped to fill these gaps in a later edition", states the foreword. Sections: Books and pamphlets (including reprints)—Unpublished works—Fiction, novels, etc. —Current periodicals (1. General—2. For immigrants (in English).) Items not available in the library of the Institute are marked with a cross.

325.1 (410)
SIVANANDAN, S., and SCRUTON, M., *comp.* **Register on research on Commonwealth immigrants in Britain.** London, Institute of Race Relations, 1967. [1], iii, 35p.

A *Preliminary check-list of research* was issued in 1966. To be biennial. It is planned to include items on Irish immigrants in the next issue.

The 1967 issue has entries for *c.* 150 unpublished thesis material and work in progress, in 19 sections (A-Z, from 'Area studies' and 'Associations and organisations' to 'Statistics' and 'Young people'). Entries supply short title, brief description, sponsor and/or publisher, commencing and completion dates. Unpublished theses, dissertations, etc., are indicated by asterisks. Author index.

Colonial Administration

325.35:016
Bibliographie d'histoire coloniale (1900-1930), publiée par les soins de A. Martineau, Roussier, Tramond. Premier Congrès International d'Histoire Coloniale. Paris, Leroux, 1932. xvi, 669p.

A series of contributions by specialists on the colonial achievements of their particular countries, with bibliographies appended. Omits Soviet Asia and India.

325.35:016
RAGATZ, L. J. A bibliography of articles, descriptive, historical and scientific, on colonies and other dependent territories, appearing in American geographical and kindred journals. Washington, Educational Research Bureau, 1951. 2v.

V. 1, originally published in 1934 (2v.), takes the bibliography to the end of 1934; v. 2, compiled by J. E. Ragatz, covers the period 1935-50.

—— **Colonial studies in the United States during the twentieth century.** London, Thomas, 1932. 48p.

Covers the period 1900-30, and has a bibliography.

—— **A list of books and articles in colonial history and overseas expansion published in the**

United States, 1900-30. Ann Arbor, Michigan, University Microfilms, 1939. 45p.

Supplemented by lists for 1931 and 1932 (1933-34. 41p.) and for 1933, 1934 and 1935 ([1936]. vi, 91p.).

325.35:016
ROYAL EMPIRE SOCIETY. Subject catalogue of the library of the Royal Empire Society, formerly the Royal Colonial Institute, by Evans Lewin. London, the Society, 1930-37. 4v.

Valuable for history, description, etc., of colonies and certain areas for which there are no adequate bibliographies.

See main entry at 941-44:016.

325.35 (02)
UNITED NATIONS. Progress of the non-self-governing territories under the Charter. New York, 1960-62. 6v. tables.

v. 1. *General review.* 1961. 7s.
v. 2. *Economic conditions.* 1961. 21s.
v. 3. *Social conditions.* 1961. 21s.
v. 4. *Educational conditions.* 1961. 10s. 6d.
v. 5. *Territorial surveys.* 1960. 39s.
v. [6]. *Table of contents and index.* 1962. 75c.
Covers the period 1946-57; 55 territories, under regions. V. 5 (vi, 476p.) is particularly detailed (*e.g.,* Mauritius, p. 143-56, covering economic, social and educational conditions, with 19 tables). The cumulative subject index in v. 6 (p. 5-60) is a good example of an analytical index.

The United Nations' *Non-self-governing territories: summaries of information transmitted* to the Secretary-General for the year 1960 (New York, U.N., 1963. viii, 349p. tables. 30s.), covering 56 territories in 4 regions, with statistics mainly for 1958/60, is the last in a series first issued in 1951 (covering information submitted in 1950). Data on economic, social and educational conditions.

325.35 (41-5):016
GREAT BRITAIN. COLONIAL OFFICE. Library. **Catalogue of the Colonial Office Library,** London. Boston, Mass., G. K. Hall, 1964. 15v. $875.

v. 1-2: *Author catalogue: pre-1950 accessions.*
v. 3-6: *Author and title catalogue: post-1950 accession.*
v. 7-8: *Subject catalogue: pre-1950 accessions.*
v. 9-13: *Subject catalogue: post-1950 accessions.*
v. 14-15: *Classified catalogue: post-1950 accessions.*

"All aspects of organisation and development of those countries which form or have formed part of the Commonwealth, are covered by this catalogue, which reflects the changing interests and activities of the Colonial Office over the past 300 years" (*Introduction*). This photolithographed edition consists of reproductions (21 per page) of card entries, except for v. 7-8, which are based on a sheaf catalogue. 187,000 card entries. There is no key to the classified catalogue (v. 14-15), which follows the Library of Congress classification. An invaluable catalogue of books, pamphlets, reports, official publications and periodical titles.

325.35 (41-5):016

GREAT BRITAIN. COLONIAL OFFICE and **CENTRAL OFFICE OF INFORMATION. The Colonies: a guide to material and information services** available to schools and to the public. London, H.M. Stationery Office, 1959. 36p. *Gratis.*

Succinct and helpful, though dated. Sections: 1. Publications (p. 5-14); annotated)—2. Films—3. Filmstrips. Lantern slides—4. Exhibitions and display material—5. Picture sets—6. Photoposters—7. Maps—8. Lecture services—9. Personal contacts (for students from the Colonies)—10. Information services.

325.35 (41-5) (02)

GREAT BRITAIN. COLONIAL OFFICE. The Corona library. London, H.M. Stationery Office, 1952-. illus., maps.

Basutoland, by A. Coates. 1966. 20*s.*
Bechuanaland, by B. A. Young. 1966. 20*s.*
British Guiana, by M. Swan. 1957. 25*s.*
Fiji, by Sir A. Burns. 1963. 30*s.*
Hong Kong, by H. Ingrams. 1952. 27*s.* 6*d.*
Jamaica, by P. Abrahams. 1957. 25*s.*
North Borneo, by K. G. Tregonning. 1960. 30*s.*
Nyasaland, by F. Debenham. 1955. 25*s.*
Sierra Leone, by R. Lewis. 1954. 25*s.*
Swaziland, by D. Barker. 1965. 20*s.*
Uganda, by H. Ingrams. 1960. 30*s.*

A series of well produced, illustrated volumes dealing with the United Kingdom's dependent territories (some now independent), the way their people live and how they are governed. Designed "to fill the place between official Blue Books on the one hand and the writings of occasional visitors on the other, to be authoritative and readable" (Series note).

325.35 (41-5) (02)

GREAT BRITAIN. COLONIAL OFFICE. An economic survey of the colonial territories. London, H.M. Stationery Office, 1952-55. 7v. maps.

See entry at 33 (41-5).

325.35 (41-5) (058)

GREAT BRITAIN. COLONIAL OFFICE. The colonial territories. London, H.M. Stationery Office, 1938-. (1961 to 1962. 1962. 8*s.* 6*d.*).

The Colonial Secretary's annual report to Parliament surveys the constitutional, administrative, economic and financial developments of the dependent territories. Each report includes statistical appendices, a diary of events of colonial interest and a list of Parliamentary and non-Parliamentary papers.

325.35 (41-5) (058.7)

The Colonial Office list. London, H.M. Stationery Office, 1862-. Annual. (1957. 35*s.*)

See entry at 354 (410).12.

325.35 (41-5) (083.4)

GREAT BRITAIN. COMMONWEALTH OFFICE. Dependent Territories Division. Digest of statistics. London, H.M. Stationery Office, 1965-. no. 57. Annual. (no. 58. August 1966).

See entry at 31 (41-5).

FOREIGN AFFAIRS

Bibliography

327:016

Current thought on peace and war: a quarterly digest of literature and research in progress on the problems of world order and conflict. Winter 1960-. New York, Institute for International Order, 1960-. No. 1-. Quarterly.

Issue no. 1 includes 386 abstracts; supplementary sources includes such items as conferences. Sections: Conflict and order in international relations—Framework of international relations —Force in international relations—East-West relations—Current crisis areas and issues—International economic stability—Institutions concerned with research. Each section ends with items of current research (author; title; place; date of completion). Index of authors and researchers.

V. 7, no. 1, 1967, has sub-title 'Crisis areas. World affairs digest' and carries 233 abstracts (each *c.* 300 words) from periodicals, newspapers and books in 6 sections, with readings appended to sections.

327:016

Foreign affairs bibliography: a selected and annotated list of books on international relations, 1919/1932-. New Yorker, Harper (subsequently Bowker), for the Council on Foreign Relations, 1933-.

1919-1932; edited by W. L. Langer and H. F. Armstrong. 1933.
1932-1942; edited by R. G. Woolbert. 1945.
1942-1952; edited by H. L. Roberts. 1955.
1952-1962; edited by H. L. Roberts and others. 1964. $20.

"Based largely on the annotated lists appearing quarterly in *Foreign Affairs*" (Foreword). The 1952 62 v. contains more than 9,000 entries in some 30 languages. Russian titles, in particular, have increased. Main sections: General international relations (p. 1-116)—The world since 1914 (p. 117-72)—The world by regions (p. 173-720). Brief (*c.* 15-word) critical annotations; many cross-references; author and title indexes. Covers international relations in the broadest sense, including recent history, economic, military, social and cultural affairs, and political developments in all countries. Restricted to books and collections of documents.

327:016

HARVARD LAW SCHOOL LIBRARY. Catalog of international law and relations. Cambridge, Mass., the Library, 1965-67. 20v.

See entry at 341:016.

327:016

International affairs. Published quarterly for the Royal Institute of International Affairs by the Oxford University Press, London, 1922-. v. 1, no. 1-. Quarterly. 37*s.* 6*d.* p.a.

About half of each issue is devoted to book reviews and a list of 'Other books received'. Thus v. 42, no. 4, October 1966 has signed reviews (p. 637-777) of *c.* 200 books, in sections (History

—International—Law—Military—Politics, economics and social; then regional sections). 'Other books received' (*c.* 70 items) is similarly grouped. Author index of books reviewed in each issue.

327:016

International information service. Chicago, Ill., Library of International Relations, 1963-. v. 1, no. 1-. Quarterly. ea. $3; $10 p.a.

About 3,500 abstracts p.a. Sections: General —Geography—History—Political factors (3 divisions)—Economic factors (6 divisions)—Social and cultural factors—International political and military factors—International economic and social factors—International organization and law (3 divisions)—Atlases, yearbooks, directories —Where to purchase magazines cited. Geographical index.

327:016

MOUSSA, F. Diplomatic contemporaine: guide bibliographique. Geneva, Centre Européen de la Dotation Carnegie pour la Paix Internationale, 1964. 199, [1]p. Sw. fr. 12.

400 entries, each with *c.* 100-word annotation. Part 1, Exposé méthodique et état des travaux (p. 13-56); part 2, Bibliographie commentée (A-Z authors, p. 57-192). Part 1 provides a classified arrangement of the items in part 2. Country index; list of reviews and annuals cited. Covers all aspects of diplomacy, including treaties, bilateral and multilateral diplomacy, such questions as protocol and diplomatic language, and diplomatic relations with Afro-Asian countries and the U.S.S.R.
Noted: *Guide to the study of international relations,* by J. K. Zawodny (San Francisco, Chandler Publishing Co. [1965]. xii, 151p.), with 520 entries.

327:016

ROYAL INSTITUTE OF INTERNATIONAL AFFAIRS. Library. **Index to periodical articles, 1950-1964** . . . Boston, Mass., G. K. Hall, 1964. 2v. $125 (U.S. & British Isles); $137.50 (elsewhere).

This Library, now the leading specialist collection in Britain dealing with international affairs from 1918 onwards, currently receives *c.* 600 periodicals. The *Index* is to *c.* 30,000 articles taken from these, for the period January 1950 to October 1964. Arranged by the Chatham House scheme of classification (classes A-H (general and subject), J-T (regions).) Preceding the index proper: list of principal periodicals indexed; guide to the classification scheme; geographic index; subject index.

327:016

The Universal reference system: political science, government and public policy series. v. 1: **International affairs.** New York, Universal Reference System; Oxford, Pergamon Press, 1965. xxxii, 1250p. $29.95; £10.

Compiled by the staff of the American Behavorial Scientist, and the first of a series of ten computer-produced bibliographies. Comprises a numerical list of 3,030 annotated items (212p.), a subject index (985p.) and an author index (8p.).

Makes no claim to completeness, and, indeed, includes no Chatham House publications. "It is difficult to decide for whom this expensive publication is intended. 3,030 books, pamphlets and articles are analysed ranging from Thucydides to George Kennan. When one considers that in an average year 800 books are received in this journal [*International affairs*] alone, one sees what a small sample has been taken. No criteria are given for the selection and several items of little value have been included" (*International affairs,* v. 43, no. 1, January 1967, p. 207).

327:016

The Yearbook of world affairs, 1947-. Under the auspices of the London Institute of World Affairs. London, Stevens, 1947-. Annual. (1967. 77*s.* 6*d.*).

Of value for its authoritative articles and annual survey of the literature. The 1967 has a survey of recent literature on the problem of economic expansion (more than 70 English-language books published usually in 1965 or 1966), as well as a reviews section ('Reports on world affairs'). Index of books reviewed.

327:016:016

CONOVER, H. F., *comp.* **A guide to bibliographic tools for research in foreign affairs.** 2nd ed., with a supplement. Washington, Library of Congress, 1958. iii, 145, 15p. $1.25.

First published 1956. 2nd ed. adds a suppt. of 15p.
An excellent annotated bibliography, with 351 main entries and much other material referred to in the annotations. "It contains bibliographies, manuals, indexes, surveys and other publications of value to the American librarian or student doing preliminary research on the political and economic scene abroad . . . Preference has been given to sources in the English language, although some foreign language material has been considered indispensable" (*Foreword*).
Sections: 1. General reference sources—2. Sources for international studies (serials carrying bibliographies on international affairs; related bibliographical serials; political science journals; current news journals; registers of research institutes and projects; surveys, yearbooks, directories; guides to statistics)—3. Specialized sources (international organizations; areas and countries). Indexes of authors' names and titles of journals, etc., and of subjects. There are few important omissions, but the work sorely needs updating.

Bibliographies on international relations and world affairs: an annotated directory, edited by E. H. Boehm (Santa Barbara, Cal., Clio Press, 1965. ii, 33p.) is a guide to bibliographies on world affairs, international law, foreign relations and area studies, theoretical studies, etc.; largely concerned with English-language material.

Dictionaries

327 (038)=00

HAENSCH, G. Wörterbuch der internationalen Beziehungen und der Politik, systematisch und alphabetisch. Deutsch, englisch, französisch, spanisch. Dictionary of international relations and politics, systematic and alphabetical . . . Munich, Hueber, 1965. xv, 638p. DM.34.50.

Also published by Elsevier (Amsterdam, etc.), 1965. 80s.

5,778 numbered entries in German, with English, French and Spanish equivalents. Systematically arranged in 11 sections, with sub-divisions (*e.g.,* VI. International negotiations and conferences. VI. 4. Phraseology (p. 292-9)). Differentiates between British and American English, Spanish usage in Spain and Latin America, German usage in Germany, Austria and Switzerland, and French usage in France, Belgium and Switzerland. Indexes in the four languages. *Babel* (v. 11, no. 4, 1965, p. 174) considers the dictionary specially useful "for any government translator".

G. Haensch's earlier *Internationale Terminologie* (Stuttgart, Müller, 1954. 180p.) covered 1,121 terms in the same four languages.

327 (038)=00
SCHWARZ, U., and HADIK, L. Stategic terminology: a trilingual glossary. New York, Praeger; London, Pall Mall Press, 1966. 157p.

See entry at 355.02 (038)=00.

Periodicals

327:05
MEYRIAT, J., ed. World list of international relations periodicals. Paris, International Studies Conference, 1951.

Arrangement is as in the *World list of social science periodicals,* under countries, A-Z. They are further grouped into four categories: original papers on international politics; original papers on international law; original papers on the problems of a specific world area; and notes, documents, texts, information and bibliographical material. Coverage of each periodical is briefly stated.

Organizations

327:061
CARNEGIE ENDOWMENT FOR INTERNATIONAL PEACE. Institutes of international affairs. New York, the Endowment, 1953. vii, 131p.

Describes the activities and usually lists the publications of 35 institutes in some 20 countries.

American agencies interested in international affairs (5th ed., compiled by D. Wasson (Published for the Council on Foreign Relations by Praeger, New York, London, etc., 1964. 200p. $5.50; 36s.) is a selected list of 293 organisations, with data on each (including publications). It includes chambers of commerce that promote commercial relations between the U.S. and other countries, and foreign information services.

History

327 (091)
RENOUVIN, P., ed. Histoire des relations internationales. Paris, Hachette, 1953-58. 8v. maps.

1: *Le moyen âge,* by F.-L. Ganshof. 1953.
2: *Les temps modernes.* I. *De Christophe Colomb à Cromwell,* by G. Zeller.
3: *Les temps modernes.* II. *De Louis XIV à 1789,* by G. Zeller.
4: *La révolution française et l'empire napoléonien,* by A. Fugier.
5: *Le XIXe siècle. I. De 1815 à 1871,* by A. Renouvin. 1954.
6. *Le XIXe. siècle. II. De 1871 à 1914,* by A. Renouvin. 1955.
7: *Les crises du XXe siècle. I. De 1914 à 1929.* 1957.
8: *Les crises du XXe siècle. II. De 1929 à 1945.* 1958.

A standard work that does not confine itself to political and diplomatic history but provides the economic, social and cultural setting. It also goes beyond European international relations. Chapter bibliographies.

327 (091)
ROYAL INSTITUTE OF INTERNATIONAL AFFAIRS. Survey of international affairs, 1920/23-. London, Oxford Univ. Press, for the Royal Institute of International Affairs, 1925-. tables, maps.

Pre-war series, 1920-1938, by A. J. Toynbee, and others. 1925-53. 17v.
War-time series, 1939-1946, edited by A. J. Toynbee. 1952-58. 11v.
Post-war series, since 1947, by P. Calvocoressi, and others. 1952-. Annual.
Consolidated index to the 'Survey of international affairs', 1920-1938, compiled by E. M. R. Ditmas. 1967. 272p. 100s.
Volumes in the war-time series deal with particular aspects over a period of years (e.g., *The Middle East, 1945-1950; The Far East, 1942-1946.* The post-war series consist of annual surveys. That for 1961 was published in 1965 (90s.). The surveys, by specialists in the various periods or regions, are characterised by their well-documented factual narratives and analytical indexes.

Reprints of o.p. Pre-war and War-time series are published by the Johnson Reprint Corporation, New York.

Biography

327 (092)
ACADÉMIE DIPLOMATIQUE INTERNATIONALE. Dictionnaire diplomatique, comprenant les biographies des diplomates, du Moyen Âge à nos jours; constituant un traité d'histoire diplomatique sur six siècles. Publié sous la direction de A.-F. Frangulis. Paris, A.D.I., [1954]. 1261p.

Entries vary in length from 2-3 lines to several pages (*e.g.,* Machiavelli: 9 columns, with 1 page of bibliography). Bibliographies are appended to articles on major figures, and some articles are signed. Living persons are included.

Documents

327 (093)
GREAT BRITAIN. FOREIGN OFFICE. British and foreign state papers, with which is incor-

porated Hertslet's "Commercial treaties", 1812/ 14-. London, H.M. Stationery Office, 1815-. Annual (v. 162: 1955-56. 1965. £12 12s.).

A valuable compilation, some of the documents not being readily available in any other publication. Coverage: treaties (including some to which Britain was not a treaty-party); constitutions; official correspondence concerning foreign affairs; other documents. Chronological list of documents precedes; subject and country index appended.

See also Great Britain. Treaty series, *at 341.24.*

327 (093)
ROYAL INSTITUTE OF INTERNATIONAL AFFAIRS. Documents on international affairs, 1928-. Edited by J. W. Wheeler-Bennett [and others]. London, Oxford Univ. Press, for the Royal Institute of International Affairs, 1929-.

Intended to accompany and supplement the *Survey of international affairs* (*q.v.*), although it can now be used independently, thanks to the notes prefacing each section. A collection of the available state papers, exchanges of notes, statements, speeches and other source material of a wide range of countries. Now annual (*e.g.,* 1961; selected and edited by D. C. Watts. 1965. 105s.).

Consolidated index to the 'Survey of international affairs', 1920-1938, and 'Documents on international affairs', 1920-1938 (1967. 100s.).

Diplomatic Archives

327 (093.2)
THOMAS, D. H., and CASE, L. N., *ed.* Guide to the diplomatic archives of Western Europe. Philadelphia, Univ. of Pennsylvania Press; London, Oxford Univ. Press, 1959. xii, 389p. 60s.

Essentially for the U.S. research worker using Western European archives; somewhat superficial descriptions of material. Chapters on Austria, Belgium, Denmark, France, Germany, Great Britain, Italy, Netherlands, Norway, Portugal, Spain, Sweden, Switzerland, Vatican City, Bavaria, League of Nations and United Nations, Public opinion and foreign affairs, Unesco. The chapter on Great Britain (p. 98-124) has a bibliography of 67 items. The longest chapter is that on Spain (p. 213-62). All contributors are American.

U.S. Department of State. Bureau of Intelligence and Research. *Foreign affairs research: a directory of governmental resources* ([2nd ed. Washington], 1967. vii, 83p. 35c.), previously issued in 1965, arranges sources by catchword title, A-Z, and includes bibliography and index.

Corps Diplomatique

327:354.11 (4/9)
Repertorium der diplomatischen Vertreter aller Länder seit dem Westfälischen Frieden (1648). Repertory of the diplomatic representatives of all countries since the Peace of Westphalia (1648). Zurich, Fretz & Wasmuth, etc. 1936-. v. 1-.

v. 1: 1648-1715, by L. Bittner and L. Gross. Berlin, Stalling, 1936.

v. 2: 1716-1763, by F. Hausmann. Zurich, Fretz and Wasmuth, 1950.
v. 3: 1763-1815. In preparation.
"Under each major country the representatives are listed by the country to which they are sent. For each man is given: his name, his capacity, the date of his mission, and the source of this information" (White, C. M., and others. *Sources of information in the social sciences* (1964), entry no. H 333).

327:354.11 (410) (058.7)
The Diplomatic service list. London, H.M. Stationery Office, 1966-. Annual. (2nd ed. 1967. 32s. 6d.).
See entry at 354.11 (410).

The London diplomatist list. London, H.M. Stationery Office, 1964-. 6 p.a. 26s. 6d. p.a.
See sub-entry at 354.11 (410).

Great Britain

327 (410) (091)
The Cambridge history of British foreign policy, 1783-1919. Edited by Sir A. W. Ward and G. P. Gooch. Cambridge, Univ. Press, 1922-23. 3v.

Modelled on the *Cambridge modern history.* A connected narrative based on official documents which gives the history of British foreign policy from the national point of view. Each volume has appendices of supporting documents and chapter bibliographies, and an index. Chapter 8 of v. 3 deals with the history of the Foreign Office during the whole period.

327 (410) (093)
GREAT BRITAIN FOREIGN OFFICE. Documents on British foreign policy, 1919-1939. London, H.M. Stationery Office, 1946-.

1st series, 1919-1929. v. 1-15 (covering 1919-February 1922). 1949-67.
2nd series, 1930-1938. v. 1-9 (covering 1930-1932). 1946-65.
3rd series, March 1938-September 1939. 1949-61. 10v. (v. 10 is the index).
Edited by the official historians, E. L. Woodward and R. Butler. A much more extensive collection, for the period, than that provided by *Documents on international affairs.* 2nd series, v. 9: *The Far Eastern crisis, 1931-1932* (lxv, 713p. 1965) reproduces 667 documents, with a tabular summary-index preceding (p. xiii-lxv): number; name of sender; date; main subject; page.
Series IA, to cover 1925 to 1929, began publication in 1966 with v. 1, *The aftermath of Locarno, 1925-1926* (105s.).

327 (410) (093)
TEMPERLEY, H., and PENSON, L. M., *ed.* A century of diplomatic blue books, 1814-1914. London, Cambridge Univ. Press, 1938. viii, 600p. (Reprinted London, Cass, 1966. 75s.).

Lists titles of all Parliamentary papers published between 1814 and 1914, bearing directly on British foreign policy, with historical introduction.

327 (410) (093)
VOGEL, R., *ed.* **A breviate of British diplomatic blue books, 1919-1939.** Montreal, McGill Univ. Press; Leicester, Univ. Press, 1963. xxxv, 474p. $10.50; 80s.

Continues the Temperley and Penson list. 1836 numbered items, chronologically arranged. Titles in full, with additional dates or notes, but no summary of contents. Analytical subject and country index, p. 437-74.

"United States documentary resources for the study of British foreign policy, 1919-1939", by D. C. Watt (*International affairs*, January 1962, v. 38, no. 1, p. 63-72) describes diplomatic papers in Washington and elsewhere.

Germany

327 (43) (093)
GREAT BRITAIN. FOREIGN OFFICE. Documents on German foreign policy, 1918-1945. London, H.M. Stationery Office, 1950-.

Documents from the archives of the German Foreign Ministry.
Series C (1933-37). The Third Reich: first phrase. v. 1-5 (1958-66): January 30th 1933-October 31st 1936. To be completed in 6v.
Series D (1937-45). v. 1-13. 1950-64. *The war years* begins with v. 8. V. 13: *The war years, June 23rd, 1941-December 11th, 1941* (1964. 60s.).

France

327 (44) (093)
La Politique étrangère de la France. Textes et documents 1966. Paris, La Documentation Française. *Notes et études documentaires*, 29th April 1967, nos. 3384-87. 307p.

Gives texts to which France was a party. Includes text of press conferences, speeches and interviews. Annexes: Relations des Conseils des Ministres. Subject and country indexes. Commendably quickly produced official publication.

U.S.S.R.

327 (47):016
HAMMOND, T. T., *ed.* **Soviet foreign relations and world Communism:** a selected, annotated bibliography of 7,000 books in 30 languages. Princeton, N.J., Princeton Univ. Press; London, Oxford Univ. Press, 1965. xxiv, 1240p. $25; £10.
See entry at 335.55:016.

Middle East

327 (5-015):016
Middle East record. Volume 1-: 1960-. Published for the Israel Oriental Society, the Reuven Shiloah Research Centre, by Israel Program for Scientific Translations, Jerusalem (London, Weidenfeld & Nicolson), [1962]-. tables, maps. (v. 2: 1961. 140s.).

"An annual account of the politics and international relations of the countries of the Middle East" (*Preface*, v. 1), and a development of the survey that has appeared during the past 13 years in *Hamizrah Hedadash* [The Near East]. Compilers regularly scan more than 200 newspapers, periodicals and official publications. Three parts: 1. The Middle East in world affairs—2. Relations between the countries of the Middle East—3. The countries of the Middle East. List of sources: name and subject indexes. Layout is reminiscent of *Keesing's Archives*. A considerable drawback is the time-lag: v. 2: 1961 appeared in 1966.

India

327 (540) (091)
INDIAN COUNCIL OF WORLD AFFAIRS. India in world affairs. [Bombay], Oxford Univ. Press, 1952 [i.e. 1953]-.

August 1947-January 1950: a review of India's foreign relations, from Independence day to Republic day, by K. P. Karunakaran. 1952 [i.e. 1953]. xi, 407p.
February 1950-December 1953: a review of India's foreign relations, by K. P. Karunakaran. 1958. viii, 266p.

India in world affairs, 1954-56, by M. S. Rajan (New York, Asia Publishing House, [1964]. xvi, 675p.), the third v. in the series, is a substantial volume. 12 chapters, including new chapters on India and the Commonwealth, and Foreign possessions in India. Appendices list foreign delegates visiting India, foreign countries visited by Indian delegates, foreign delegations visiting India, etc. Bibliography (general, and by chapters), p. 643-65; analytical index.

327 (540) (093)
—— **Documents on Indian affairs;** edited by Girja Kumar and V. K. Arora. Bombay, Asia Publishing House, [1965]. xxii, [1], 636p.

Part 1, Internal affairs; part 2, External affairs. 145 documents in 13 sections; documents (significant speeches, laws, etc.) appear chronologically in each section. Index for each part.

Africa

327 (66/69)
Année africaine. 1963-. Paris, Pedone, 1965-. Annual. (1964 v., published 1966. 65F.).

Produced jointly by the Centre des Hautes Études Administratives sur l'Afrique et l'Asie Moderne, the African section of the Centre d'Études des Relations Internationales de la Fondation Nationale des Sciences Politiques, and the Centre d'Études d'Afrique Noire de l'Université de Bordeaux.
"Deals mainly with external affairs of the territories of Africa south of the Sahara" (*International affairs*, v. 43, no. 3, July 1967, p. 601).

Canada

327 (71) (091)
CANADIAN INSTITUTE OF INTERNATIONAL AFFAIRS, Canada in world affairs. Toronto, Oxford Univ. Press, 1941-. v. 1-.

V. 1; *The pre-war years*, is followed by surveys covering, usually, two-year periods. V. 11: 1959 to 1961 (1965) consists of factual outlines of events by specialists, with ample footnote references. Detailed, non-analytical index.

For documents on the pre-war period, consult *Documents on Canadian foreign policy, 1917-1939,* selected and edited by W. A. Riddell (Toronto, Oxford Univ. Press, 1962. 860p. 108s.).

U.S.A.

327 (73) (091)
BEMIS, S. F., and **GRIFFIN, G. G. Guide to the diplomatic history of the United States, 1775-1921.** Washington, Government Printing Office, 1935. 979p.

Also valuable for international relations as a whole. Notes books and articles in many languages; source material, printed and manuscript; indexes collections of personal papers and authors.

327 (73) (091)
COUNCIL ON FOREIGN RELATIONS. The United States in world affairs, 1931-. New York, Harper [& Row], 1931-. Annual. (1965 v. 1966. $3.95).

Published since 1931 without interruption except for war years 1941-44. Aims to give "a concise, preliminary account of the international activities of the United States" (*Preface,* 1965 v.). The 1965 v. (published 1966) has 10 chapters; 53 sections. Footnote references to literature, preceded by list of periodicals and serials cited; chronology of major events (p. 389-409); analytical. Maps; cartoons; index.

327 (73) (093)
COUNCIL ON FOREIGN RELATIONS. Documents on American foreign relations, January 1938-. New York, Harper [& Row], 1939-. Annual. (1965 v. 1966. 76s.).

Introduced by the World Peace Foundation, Boston, in 1939, and carried forward since 1952 by the Council on Foreign Relations. The 1965 v. has 107 documents in 9 parts. Cumulative analytical index for 1961-1965 v.

Australia

327 (94)
AUSTRALIAN INSTITUTE OF INTERNATIONAL AFFAIRS. Australia in world affairs, 1950-55. Melbourne, Cheshire, 1957. vii, [2], 366p. maps.

10 well-documented contributions on the Australian Community, the International Community, the Pacific and Asian Community, and Australia and Suez. Partly-analytical index.

—— **1956-1960.** Melbourne, Cheshire, 1963. vi, 430p. 63s.

9 contributions, 5 of them concerning the Pacific and Asian community; footnote references. 7 black-and-white maps. Index.

Research

327.001.5
UNITED STATES. DEPARTMENT OF STATE. OFFICE OF EXTERNAL RESEARCH. External research: international affairs. A list of current social science research by private scholars and academic centers. [No.] 7.24-1965. [Washington], 1965. 104p. Annual.

Beginning in 1965, this annual includes both studies in progress and completed studies, previously issued separately. Name of issuing body varies.

The 1966 issue (7.25-1966. 111 pages) is in 19 sections, arranged A-Z by subjects, from 'Atomic energy' to 'Social conditions', some with subdivisions. It covers the period August 1965 through February 1966; c. 1,500 items.

PARLIAMENT

328 (4)
CAMPION, *Lord,* and **LIDDERDALE, D. W. S. European parliamentary procedure.** London, Allen & Unwin, for the Inter-Parliamentary Union, 1953. viii, [1], 270p. 30s.

Briefly describes "the systems of parliamentary procedure of certain Parliaments, mainly West European, associated in the Inter-Parliamentary Union" (*Foreword*). By countries, A-Z: Belgium, Denmark, Egypt, Finland, France, Ireland, Italy, Luxembourg, the Netherlands, Norway, Sweden and the U.K. 3 appended tables: constitutional data; dates and hours of sitting; committees. Index.

328 (41-44) (032)
WILDING, N., and **LAUNDY, P. An encyclopaedia of Parliament.** Rev. ed. London, Cassell, 1961. xi, 797p. 63s. (3rd rev. ed. 1968. xii, 912p. 84s.).

First published 1958.
Covers British and Commonwealth Parliaments, giving definitions of terms (*e.g.,* 'Closure'), background history (*e.g.,* 'Elizabeth I (1533-1603) and Parliament'), and notes on procedure, privileges and customs of Parliament. Lengthier articles have brief bibliographies, for further reading. The original ed. had 33 appendices, including a bibliography (p. 681-705). The revised ed. includes an updating supplement (p. 775-97). Both authors were members of the Federal and Southern Rhodesian parliaments.

Great Britain

328 (410):016
PALMER, J. Government and Parliament in Britain: a bibliography. London, Hansard Society, 1960. 42p.

A list of books about "Parliamentary Government as a working institution in our system of democracy" (*Preface*). Helpful brief annotations to many items. The 12 sections have introductions, cover central and local government, and include "Political biographies" (p. 31-39); "Some Parliamentary novels" (p. 39-41); and, "Further reading" (p. 41-42). The compiler is a Senior Library Clerk in the House of Commons Library.

328 (410) (03)
ABRAHAM, L. A., and **HAWTREY, S. C. A parliamentary dictionary.** 2nd ed. London, Butterworth, 1964. viii, 241p. 25s.

First published 1956.
An alphabetical guide to expressions in com-

mon usage in the Houses of Parliament, with explanation and comment. Understood to refer to House of Commons unless the context obviously requires otherwise. 'Speaker': 5½p. Cites acts and cases. No cross-references, but index. L. A. Abraham was formerly principal clerk of committees at the House of Commons, and S. C. Hawtrey, Clerk of the Journals, House of Commons. Whereas Wilding (*see at 328 (41-44) (03)*) includes historical aspects and pays some attention to other parliaments in the Commonwealth, Abraham-Hawtrey stresses current procedure in Parliament.

328 (410) (058.7)
Dod's Parliamentary companion for 1832-. London, Business Dictionaries, Ltd. 1832-. Annual. (1966. 30s.).

Formerly *The Parliamentary (pocket) companion*. Publisher varies.

Biographies of peers and members of the House of Commons; list of constituencies and votes cast at the most recent election; parliamentary terms and proceedings; list of ministers and officers of state; government and public offices; index.

Vacher's Parliamentary companion (London, Vacher, 1933-. 6 p.a., then quarterly. ea. 6s.; 20s. p.a.) gives more concise information more frequently. It gives an A-Z list of members of both Houses, with members' town addresses; constituencies and their members; and 'Principal government and public offices'.

328 (410) (058.7)
ROTH, A. The business background of Members of Parliament. London, Parliamentary Profile Services, Ltd., 1963. [4], xxviii, 240p. (1967 ed., by A. Roth and J. Kerbey. [4], xx, 412p. 36s.).

Part 1 lists M.P.s alphabetically (p. 1-101), with data on directorships, chairmanships and the like. Part 2 lists concerns in 19 classes (banks, investment trusts, insurance, manufacture, agriculture, advertising, etc.), with the names of relevant M.P.s.

The M.P.s' chart: parliamentary profiles, 1966-1967 session, by A. Roth, with J. Kerbey (London, Parliamentary Profile Services, Ltd., 1966. xx, 92p. 15s.) lists M.P.s alphabetically (p. 2-85), stating name, party, constituency, margin, position, political outlook, political history, when born, education, family, occupation, traits (*e.g.,* "small"; "balding"; "fruity voice").

In preparation, by the same publishers: *Lord on the board; The peer's chart.*

328 (410) (058.7)
"THE TIMES". House of Commons, 1966; with full results of the polling, biographies of members and unsuccessful candidates, photographs of all members, and a complete analysis, statistical tables and a map of the general election, October 1966. London, "The Times" Office, 1966. 319p. 45s.

Biographies appear under the name of the seats contested (p. 21-224). Portraits only of successful candidates. Statement of the party manifestos (p. 268-305). Index to candidates; index to constituencies.

328 (410) (091)
GREAT BRITAIN. HOUSE OF COMMONS. Members of Parliament: return of the names of every member returned to serve in each Parliament. London, H.M. Stationery Office, 1878-79. 2 pts.

"Compiled from writs and returns in the Public Record Office, checked with the books of parliamentary returns at the Crown Office" (Minto, J. *Reference books.* 1929. p. 65). Supplemented by *Return . . . for 1880 . . . with indexes to names . . . from 1705-1885* (1891); *1885-1900* (1901), etc.

The "Wedgwood report" (House of Commons. *Interim report of the Committee on House of Commons personnel and politics, 1264-1832.* (Command 4130), London, H.M. Stationery Office, 1931. 155p. 2s. 6d.) analyses the material available for listing M.P.s and suggests a scheme to fill all the gaps. Appendices give a list of Parliaments and information on Borough Records.

328 (410) (091)
HISTORY OF PARLIAMENT TRUST. The history of Parliament: the House of Commons, 1754-1790, [by] Sir Lewis Namier and John Brooke. Published for the History of Parliament Trust by H.M. Stationery Office, 1964. 3v. £22 1s.

v. 1. *Introductory survey, constituencies, appendices.*
v. 2. *Members, A-J.*
v. 3. *Members, K-Y.*

"With these three volumes, . . . the publication of the History of Parliament begins" (*General foreword,* v. 1). It is planned to cover the Westminster Parliament from 1264 to the present day. Other sections, similar in pattern, are in preparation.

V. 1 has tables, many references in the text and its own index. V. 2-3 consist of biographical studies plus political notes; 19 contributors. The article on Charles James Fox (v. 2, p. 455-61) is by John Brooke; it includes quotations from authoritative works and has 36 references. Well produced.

328 (410) (091)
JUDD, G. P., IV. Members of Parliament, 1734-1832. New Haven, Conn., Yale Univ. Press; London, Oxford Univ. Press, 1955. viii, 389p.

Attempts to show the relationship between the British ruling class ["a cohesive group . . . toughly knit"] and the House of Commons, 1734-1832 by a detailed statistical analysis of 5,034 M.P.s. 10 chapters (*e.g.,* 4. The age of members—5. Length of service—6. Social status and family background, etc.), followed by 'Check list of members' (p. 95-385). This last consists of 5,034 numbered entries (full name; dates of birth and death; position(s) held; parliamentary career (seat(s) and date(s)); sources (*e.g., D.N.B., G.E.C., Alumni Oxon.*), with many cross-references. Analytical index to chapters 1-10.

KEELER, M. F. The Long Parliament, 1640-1641. A biographical study of its members. Philadelphia, Pa., American Philosophical Society, 1956. ix, 410p.   328 (410) (091)

Three parts: 1. Portrait of a Parliament—2. Elections and returns—3. Biographical directory of the Parliament Men (p. 81-404), A-Z. Profuse footnotes (*c.* 20 per page). Index to part 1.

WEDGWOOD, J. C., *1st baron.* **History of Parliament, 1439-1509.** London, H.M. Stationery Office, 1936-38. v. 1-2.   328 (410) (091)

v. 1: Biographies of members of the Commons House, 1439-1509. 1936.
v. 2: Register of the ministers and of the members of both Houses, 1439-1509. 1938.
v. 3: Not yet published.
These 3 v. were intended to be the first of several series of analytical surveys from the 13th century onwards (*see* "Wedgwood report", above).

MAY, T. E., *1st baron Farnborough.* **Erskine May's Treatise on the law, privileges, proceedings and usage of Parliament.** 17th ed. Editor, Sir Barnett Cocks. London, Butterworth, 1964. xli, 1145p. 126*s.*   328 (410) (094)

First published 1844. "Erskine May" is not official but, next to the *Journals* of both Houses, it is accepted as the great secondary authority. The editor of the 17th ed. is Clerk of the House of Commons.
Books: 1. Constitution, powers and privileges of Parliament (chapters 1-11)—2. Practice and proceedings in Parliament: public business (12-33)—3. Proceedings in Parliament: private business (34-40). Chapter 33 (new): Representation in European Assemblies. Appendix: House of Commons Standing Orders relative to public business (1963). Table of cases; table of statutes. Analytical index, p. 1101-45. The 17th ed. is a thorough overhaul of the 16th ed. (1957), of which at least one hundred pages—one-tenth of the work—have become wholly obsolete through Parliament's most recent series of reforms" (*Preface*). Reviewed in *Times literary supplement,* no. 3284, 4th February 1965, p. 91.

For the historical development of parliamentary procedure, there are: Campion, G. F. M., *1st baron Campion. An introduction to the procedure of the House of Commons* (2nd ed. London, Macmillan, 1950. 348p.); and, complementary, from the historical viewpoint, to Erskine May,—Redlich, J. *The procedure of the House of Commons: a study of its history and present form* (London, Constable, 1908. 3v.).

Parliamentary Papers

BOND, M. F. The records of Parliament: a guide for genealogists and local historians. Canterbury, Phillimore, 1964. ix, 54p. illus. 10*s.* 6*d.*   328 (410) (094.5)

Reprinted from a series of articles in *The amateur historian,* v. 4. 6 subject sections: 1. Acts

of Parliament—2. Private Bill records—3. Parliamentary Papers—4. Judicial records—5. Records of debates—6. The House of Lords Record Office. Bibliography (p. 43-49); index. The author is Clerk of the Records, House of Lords.

FORD, P., and **FORD, G. A breviate of Parliamentary Papers, 1900-1916:** the foundation of the Welfare State. Oxford, Blackwell, 1957. xlix, 470p. 92*s.* 6*d.*   328 (410) (094.5)

———— **A breviate of Parliamentary Papers, 1917-1939.** Oxford, Blackwell, 1951. [1], xlviii, 571p. 65*s.*

———— **A breviate of Parliamentary Papers, 1940-1954:** war and reconstruction. Oxford, Blackwell, 1961. [1], 515p. 95*s.*

Each volume consists of summaries of selected Parliamentary Papers,—"the reports of committees, royal commissions and similar bodies in matters which have been, or might have been, the subject of legislation or have dealt with public policy" (*Introduction,* 1917-1939v.). The 1940-1954 v. is arranged in 16 sections (17 in the 1900-1916 v., which includes 'Irish Papers'): 1. Machinery of government—2. National finance—3. Monetary and economic policy, financial institutions—4. Agriculture and food supply—5. Trade and industry—6. Coal, fuel, power, water—7. Transport—8A. Post Office, telegraphy—8B. Broadcasting, the press—9. Inventions, patents, copyright—10. Labour—11. Social security—12. Health—13A. Housing—13B. Town and country planning—14. Education—15A. Population—15B. Social problems—16. Legal administration, police, law.

FORD, P., and **FORD, G. A Guide to Parliamentary Papers.** 2nd ed. Oxford, Blackwell. 1956. xiii, 79p. 7*s.* 6*d.*   328 (410) (094.5)

First published 1955.
This guide instructs the research worker as to "What Parliamentary Papers are, how to find them and how to use them" (*sub-title*). More useful for the serious researcher than for everyday use of current papers. Regrettably not indexed, but it is the only work of its kind; a valuable introduction to a complex subject.

———. **Select list of British Parliamentary Papers, 1833-1899.** Oxford, Blackwell, 1953, 165p. 35*s.*

A classified list of reports and other material "issued by commissions or similar bodies of investigation into economic, social and constitutional questions, and matters of law and administration". Valuable subject index. Over 4,500 papers listed; references are to the House of Commons' volume arrangement.

GREAT BRITAIN. HOUSE OF COMMONS. General alphabetical index to the Bills, Reports and Papers printed by Order of the House of Commons and to the Reports and Papers presented by Command, 1950 to 1958-59. London, H.M. Stationery Office, 1963. ii, 479p. 26*s.*   328 (410) (094.5)

Cumulates the sessional indexes of the period, and reference is to the volumes as arranged for the House of Commons. A-Z by subject, locality, etc.; many cross-references.

328 (410) (094.5)

GREAT BRITAIN. HOUSE OF COMMONS. General index to the Accounts and Papers, Reports of Commissioners, Estimates, etc., etc., printed by order of the House of Commons or presented by Command, 1801-1852. London, H.M. Stationery Office, 1853 (reprinted 1938).

—————**General alphabetical index to the Bills, Reports, Estimates, Accounts and Papers** printed by order of the House of Commons and to the papers presented by Command, 1852-1899. London, H.M. Stationery Office, 1909.

These cumulate the indexes published during the period. References are to House of Commons' volume arrangement.

'King's List' or the 'King catalogue'—*Catalogue of Parliamentary Papers, 1801-1900;* compiled by P. S. King (London, King, [1904]. viii, 317p.), with supplements for 1901-1910 ([1912]) and 1911-1920 ([1922])—is a poor tool. It lists, by subjects A-Z, over 10,000 items, but does not state session number, Command Paper number and the like.

Provisionally accepted for future publication by the Royal Historical Society: *List and index of Parliamentary Papers, 1700-1800,* edited by E. Wakstaff and A. T. Milne. This should supersede the *Catalogue of papers printed by order of The House of Commons, 1731-1800* (London, 1807; reprinted H.M.S.O., 1954).

328 (410) (094.5)

GREAT BRITAIN. HOUSE OF COMMONS. Library. **General index to the bills, reports and papers** printed by order of the House of Commons, and to the reports and papers presented by Command, 1900 to 1948/49. London, H.M. Stationery Office, 1960. 983p. £15 15s.

The essential index for Parliamentary Papers published in the first half of the twentieth century. Cumulates the sessional indexes of the period and refers to the House of Commons' volume arrangement. The alphabetical index (p. 3-802) is preceded by a table of volumes and papers indexed 1900-1948/49 (p. iv), and introductory notes (p. v-viii); p. 803-93: "Short titles of Bills, 1900-1948/49". Includes a select list of Chairmen of Committees in the index.

328 (410) (094.5)

Hansard's Catalogue and breviate of Parliamentary Papers, 1696-1834. Reprinted in facsimile, by P. Ford and G. Ford. Oxford, Blackwell, 1953. 220p. 50s.

A classified list, together with a breviate of the papers arranged under subject headings. This reprint includes a select list of House of Lords papers not in Hansard's Breviate. There is a very full index to the papers, and a helpful introduction.

328 (410) (094.5)

PARSONS, K. A. C. A checklist of the British parliamentary papers (bound set), 1801-1950. Cambridge, privately printed for the University Library, 1958. 15p.

Notes volume numbering for each year (*e.g.,* 1826 I-XXIX), with indication of volumes in more than one part and of large volumes likely to be shelved separately. Two appendices list Command Papers not printed or appearing in Lords or Commons set only. Includes only volumes covered by the Parliamentary [*i.e.,* sessional] indexes.

A guide to British parliamentary papers, by F. Rodgers and R. B. Phelps (Urbana, Univ. of Illinois Graduate School of Librarianship, 1967. 35, [i]p. (Occasional papers, no 82). $1) comprises three chapters, somewhat condensed, of a projected manual of British government documents, to act as a companion to Boyd and Rips' *United States government publications* (3rd ed. 1949). Items are described in 3 broad groups: 1. Journals, votes and proceedings—2. Bills, reports and papers—3. Acts of Parliament.

A numerical finding list of British Command Papers published 1833-1961/62, compiled by E. Di Roma and J. A. Rosenthal (New York, New York Public Library, 1967. [iii], 148p.) is "designed to help researchers ascertain the volume in the collected series of British Sessional Papers in which any particular Command Paper . . . appears" (Introduction).

A Chairman's index to reports of government-appointed committees is to be published in 1968 by the Library Association: Reference, Special and Information Section and Birmingham Public Libraries. It embraces the period 1941-67 and comprises 2,050 entries.

Parliamentary Debates

328 (410) 14

GREAT BRITAIN. HOUSE OF COMMONS. The Parliamentary debates. Fifth series. House of Commons: official report, 1909-. London, H.M. Stationery Office, 1909-.

Originally published as a private venture (Cobbett's *Parliamentary history of England from . . . 1066 to 12th August 1803.* London, Hansard, 1806-20. 36v., and its continuations). It became an official report in 1909: substantially *verbatim*.

Issued daily during the session; cumulated in bound volumes, with general detailed index (speakers and topics) to each session. A. J. P. Taylor. (*English history, 1914-1945,* p. 606) notes two limitations to Hansard. "The reporters do not include casual cries, unless these contributed to the progress of debate; hence, for instance, they omitted Amery's famous call to Greenwood on 2 September 1939. Nor was any record kept of the secret sessions held in both World Wars—unlike the French Chamber, which kept a secret record, published later."

The House of Commons *Journals,* published each session, are a record of what was *done* in the House of Commons, not what was said. They also record all papers laid before the House. The Journals constitute the authentic record of the proceedings of the House and primary authority on parliamentary procedure.

House of Commons' *Standing Committee debates* is issued daily when committees meet;—a verbatim report of proceedings in Standing Committee published by H.M.S.O. since 1919.

Also to be noted: *Standing orders of the House of Commons: Private business* (H.M.S.O., 1964) and *Standing orders of the House of Commons: Public business* (H.M.S.O., 1966).

328 (410) 14
GREAT BRITAIN. HOUSE OF LORDS. The Parliamentary debates. Fifth series. House of Lords: official report, 1909-. London, H.M. Stationery Office, 1909-.

Issued daily during the session cumulated and indexed similarly to the House of Commons *Debates*.
The *Journals* of the House of Lords, issued sessionally, are a record of what was done in the House of Lords, not what was said. Published since 1509.

328 (410)14:016
GREAT BRITAIN. HOUSE OF COMMONS. A bibliography of Parliamentary debates of Great Britain. London, H.M. Stationery Office, 1956. 62p. (House of Commons Library document no. 2.).

A bibliography of debates of both Houses of Parliament, including not only the standard sets of debates, both official and unofficial, but also information from diaries, etc. Helpful and evaluative notes are often provided, and a chronological plan assists quick reference. Debates in the Irish House of Commons are covered in an appendix.

Northern Ireland

328 (416)
NORTHERN IRELAND. HOUSE OF COMMONS. Parliamentary debates: official report, 7th June 1921-. Belfast, H.M. Stationery Office, 1921-. v. 1-.

Daily parts, followed by bound volumes. Each volume is indexed.

328 (416) 14
—— **THE SENATE. Parliamentary debates:** official report, 20th June 1921-. Belfast, H.M. Stationery Office, 1921-. v. 1-.

Daily parts, followed by bound volumes. Each volume is indexed.

Eire

328 (417)
EIRE. DAIL EIREANN. Diosbóireachtaí pairliminte: Parliamentary debates; tuairsig oifigiúil: official report, 9th September 1922-. Dublin, Stationery Office, 1922-. v. 1-.

Daily parts, followed by bound volumes. Each volume is indexed.

328 (417)
—— **SEANAD EIREANN. Diosbóireachtaí pairliminte: Parliamentary debates;** tuairsig

oifigiúil: official report, 11th December 1922-. Dublin, Stationery Office, 1922-. v. 1-.

Daily parts, followed by bound volumes. Each volume is indexed.

France

328 (44) (092)
ROBERT, A., *and others.* **Dictionnaire des parlementaires français,** comprenant tous les membres des Assemblées françaises et tous les ministres français, depuis le 1er mai 1789 jusqu'au 1er mai 1889. Paris, Bourloton, 1891. 5v.

A two-column, small-type biographical dictionary that is a convenient and valuable source (*e.g.,* Danton, v. 2, p. 253-55). No bibliographies. Continued by:

JOLLY, J., *ed.* **Dictionnaire des parlementaires français:** notices biographiques sur les ministres, sénateurs et députés français de 1889 à 1940. Paris, Presses Universitaires de France, 1960-. v. 1-. (v. 4. 1966. 24F.).

V. 1 includes lists of ministers, senators and presidents of the two Chambers and begins the politically-slanted biographical dictionary with the letter 'A'. V. 4: D (1966).

Africa

328 (6) 14
"Debates and proceedings of legislative (and legislative/advisory) bodies in Africa." Supplement to Standing Conference on Library Materials on Africa. *Library materials on Africa,* v. 4, no. 1, July 1966. [iii], 37p. Mimeographed.

The first draft of a list; to be distributed for librarians to check holdings and send additions and corrections.
Covers holdings of 14 libraries (9 in the U.K. and 4 in the U.S., plus microfilms at Nuffield College, Oxford). Arranged A-Z by countries; supplement (p. 1-3) precedes.

U.S.A.

328 (73) (091)
UNITED STATES. CONGRESS. Biographical directory of the American Congress, 1774-1961. . . . Rev. ed. Washington, U.S. Government Printing Office, 1961. 1863p. (85th Congress, 2nd session. House document no. 442). $11.75.

Chronological list of executive officers; list of delegates to the Continental Congress, 1774-88; list of Congresses (1st-86th, 1789-1961), with dates, officers and members (senators and representatives; biographies (p. 455-1863). 10,400 concise biographies (*e.g.,* George Washington: 42 lines—one sentence, the events being separated by semi-colons).
Supplemented by the sessional *Official congressional directory* (Washington, Government Printing Office, 1809-).

328 (73) 14
UNITED STATES. CONGRESS. Congressional record . . . March 4, 1873-. Washington, Government Printing Office, 1873-.

A daily record of the proceedings and debates, from the 43rd Congress onwards. Fortnightly indexes of (1) names and subjects (A-Z) (2) bills and resolutions (by bill numbers).

Preceded by *Debates and proceedings,* 1st-18th Congress, 1789-1824 (1834-56. 42v.); *Register of debates,* 18th-25th Congress, 1824-37 (1825-37. 14v. in 29); *Congressional globe,* 23rd-43rd Congress, 1833-73 (1834-73. 46v. in 108).

CQ Weekly report (Washington, Congressional Quarterly, 1943-. v. 1-) is an excellent guide to the working of Congress and its committees. Quarterly cumulating index; annual volume: *Congressional quarterly almanac.*

The American Erskine May is: *Sturgis standard code of parliamentary procedure,* by A. F. Sturgis (2nd ed. New York, McGraw-Hill, 1966. 283p. $4.95), first published in 1950.

33 ECONOMICS

Bibliographies

33:016

AMERICAN ECONOMIC ASSOCIATION. Index of economic journals. Homewood, Illinois, Richard D. Irwin, Inc., 1961-. v. 1-.

v. 1: 1886-1924; v. 2: 1925-1939; v. 3: 1940-1949; v. 4: 1950-1954; v. 5: 1954-1959 (1962).

A classified index (23 main classes) of articles, obituaries, bibliographies, etc. in 89 English-language economic journals. Includes marginal subjects such as agriculture, population, health, education, welfare, regional planning. V. 5 has *c.* 10,000 entries. Author and title index; topical index to classification schedules.

The American Economic Association's *Survey of contemporary economics* (1948-52. 2v.) and the American Economic Association and Royal Economic Society's *Surveys of economic theory* (1965-66. 3v.) are collections of review articles recording progress in specific economic subjects, with extensive references to the literature.

33:016

ASSOCIATED UNIVERSITY BUREAUS OF BUSINESS AND ECONOMIC RESEARCH. Bibliography of . . . publications of University Bureaus of Business and Economic Research. Eugene, Oregon, Bureau of Business Research, Univ. of Oregon, 1957-. v. 1-.

v. 1: 1950-1956 (1957. $2); v. 2: 1957 (1958. $1); v. 3: 1958 (1959. $2) . . . v. 8: 1963 (1964. $2). Originally *Index of . . . publications of Bureaus of Business and Economic Research.*

V. 8: 1963 (v, 78p.) has 534 entries for books and periodicals, in two sequences: publications by institutions; publications by subject or area, with sub-divisions. Author index; addresses of Associated University Bureaus.

33:016

Bibliography on income and wealth. v. 1, 1937/47-. International Association for Research in Income and Wealth. Cambridge, Bowes & Bowes (subsequently New Haven, Conn., the International Association), 1952-. (v. 8: 1957-1960. 1964. $12.50).

V. 8 has 2,735 annotated entries for books, pamphlets and periodical articles, on "the measurement of the income and wealth of nations". Items are selected for their critical and analytical value. The co-operative effort of scholars from nearly 40 countries and from international

organisations. Four main sections: 1. General—2. Discussion of concepts—3. International comparisons of national estimates—4. Estimates and analyses by countries. Annotations are in English, French or Spanish, according to the language of the original (if the latter is in German, etc., the annotation is in English). Soviet books and periodicals are not covered. Indexes of authors, geographic areas, and subjects (analytical).

V. 8, published in the U.S. only, is the last in the series. A periodical will take its place in the U.S.,—*Review of income and wealth.*

33:016

BRITISH COUNCIL. Economics: a select book list. London, Longmans, Green, 1963. 60p. 3s.

Prepared primarily for use overseas. Most of the books are by British authors or on some aspect of British economics. 772 numbered, unannotated items in classes A-S (A. Bibliographies —B. Encyclopaedias, dictionaries and atlases), plus "A select list of current periodicals' (44 titles). Author index.

The N.B.L. Reader's guide (fourth series no. 3), *Economics,* by R. L. Smyth (Published for the National Book League at the Univ. Press, Cambridge, 1960. 30p. 3s. 6d.) has 10-50-word concise annotations on *c.* 150 items, in ten sections. In each section elementary books come before more advanced texts, combining introductory surveys with outstanding contributions.

33:016

Business periodicals index. New York, Wilson, 1958-. v. 1-. 11 issues p.a., cumulating 3 times p.a. and annually.

Sub-title: "a cumulative subject index to periodicals in the fields of accounting, advertising, banking and finance, general business, insurance, labor and management, marketing and purchasing, office management, public administration, taxation, specific businesses, industries and trades".

Of the 117 journals indexed in the April 1964 issue, only 3 (*The economist, Operational research quarterly* and *Personnel management*) were British. About 35,000 entries p.a.

33:016

CHAMBRE DE COMMERCE ET D'INDUSTRIE DE PARIS. Bibliothèque. **Bibliographie: études et articles selectionnés.** Paris, 1931-. Monthly.

1931-49, as *Bibliographie d'ouvrages et d'articles sélectionnés.*

3 sections: subject index (yellow-tinted paper); geographical index (green-tinted paper); references (white paper). The references are classified into 7 groups, subdivided by topic and area: 1. Documents de référence, source—2. Situation politique et économique—3. Droit, économie politique—4. Organisation industrielle et commerciale—5. Finances publiques, fiscalité—6. Productions et marchés—7. Questions sociales. No cumulated indexes.

33:016

COMAN, E. T., Jr. **Sources of business information.** 2nd rev. ed. Berkeley, Los Angeles, California Univ. Press, 1964; London, Cambridge Univ. Press, 1965. xii, 330p. $8.50; 68*s.*

First published 1949 (New York, Prentice-Hall).

A standard work of reference for U.S. business libraries. The 2nd ed. has 4 introductory chapters on methodology of finding business sources, and 11 chapters on such subject fields as statistics, finance, automation, management and foreign trade. Systematic treatment within each chapter: bibliographies; handbooks, etc.; yearbooks and annual summary numbers of periodicals; trade magazines and the like; more comprehensive books and journals. Checklist at end of each chapter. Chapter 16, lists of basic reference books recommended for every business collection. Analytical index. (Similar entry in v. 1 of *Guide,* at 65:016.)

E. T. Coman, Jr. has contributed a survey of current and recent bibliographies of economics in *Library trends,* v. 15, no. 4, April 1967, p. 601-15; 104 references.

33:016

DAVINSON, D. E. **Commercial information:** a source book. Oxford, Pergamon Press, 1965. vii, 164p. 21*s.*

A survey in 14 chapters, with running commentary on publications. A superficial survey, with some serious omissions; woefully thin on statistical sources. Dates of publication not given. Appendix I: 'Services provided by foreign embassies in commerce and trade matters'; 2: 'Addresses of the principal organizations mentioned in the text'.

J. Bogardus's *Outline for the course in business and economics literature* (Rev. ed. New York, School of Library Service, Columbia Univ., 1964. 59p. (Library service K8252y)) is a classified checklist, first published in 1962, of *c.* 500 reference books and periodicals. Entries have annotations for use of students.

33:016

Documentation économique: revue bibliographique de synthèse, publiée avec le concours du Centre National de la Recherche Scientifique. Paris, Presses Universitaires de France, 1934-1939, 1947-. 6 p.a. 50F. (foreign, 55F.).

About 1,500 signed abstracts p.a., on perforated cards, 3 per page. 250-500-word abstracts, carried on to reverse of card, if necessary. Arranged in 9 main classes: 0. Références générales—1.

Économique publique. Statistique—2. Demographie—3. Conditions de l'activité économique—4. Activité économique—5. Monnaie et finances publiques—6. Relations économiques nationales—7. Communications et transports—8. Questions sociales. Each issue is devoted either to books or to periodical articles from *c.* 180 journals of many countries. Subject and author indexes per issue.

33:016

Economic abstracts: semi-monthly review of abstracts on economics, finance, trade and industry, management and labour. The Hague, Nijhoff, 1953-. v. 1-. 2 per month. D. Gld. 25 (foreign, D. Gld. 30) p.a.

Prepared by the Library of the Economic Information Service, Ministry of Economic Affairs, The Hague, with collaboration. About 3,000 120-word abstracts p.a. from U.S. Dutch, English, French, Italian, Spanish, Russian, etc. periodicals, pamphlets (reports) and books. English summaries are provided when abstracts are in languages other than English, French or German. Monographs are now (1966-) omitted and typography does not make for rapid perusal. Three main sections: Social sciences (60%)—Applied sciences (including Agriculture). Medicine. Technology (including Business economy and chemical industries) (38%)—The Arts. Architecture. Entertainment (including Town planning) (2%). U.D.C. numbers added. Detailed subject index in each issue. Annual (June-June) author index, including 'List of [*c.* 400] journals from which articles abstracted'. A valuable, fairly prompt service.

Not to be confused with the now defunct *Economic abstracts* (New York, Gradual School of Arts and Sciences, New York Univ., 1952-60. 6 p.a.) which published *c.* 1,200 signed abstracts p.a. of articles in *c.* 50 U.S. and European journals. Systematically arranged; no annual indexes.

33:016

GREAT BRITAIN. H.M. STATIONERY OFFICE. **Commerce, industry and H.M.S.O.:** a selection of government publications for the businessman. London, H.M.S.O., 1966. 31p. *Gratis.*

Annotated entries in 15 sections: For general reading and reference—Importing and exporting—Home industry and trade—Companies, finance and taxation—Industrial relations and manpower—Research and design—United Nations—O.E.C.D.—European Communities—E.F.T.A.—International Customs Tariff Bureau—International Customs Tariff Bureau—International Monetary Fund—Customs Co-operation Council—G.A.T.T.—H.M.S.O. catalogue service.

33:016

HALL, M., *and others, comp.* **A bibliography in economics** for the Honours School in Philosophy, Politics and Economics. 2nd ed. London, Oxford Univ. Press, 1959. 82p.

First published 1957.

Intended as a guide for those reading for higher degrees in economics. Sections: 1. Economic principles—2. Economic organization—3. Economic and social history—4. Statistics—5.

Currency and credit—6. Public finance—7. Economics of underdeveloped areas—8. Mathematics for economists. Further breakdown by topics. No index; no annotations. Periodical articles are included, but exact page-references are not given. About 1,800 items.

33:016

HARVARD UNIVERSITY. Graduate School of Business Administration. Baker Library. **The Kress Library of Business and Economics. Catalogue,** covering material published through 1776, with data upon cognate items in other Harvard libraries. Boston, Mass., Baker Library, Harvard Graduate School of Business Administration, 1940. x, 414p.

—— —— —— —— **Catalogue supplement,** covering material published through 1776 . . . Boston, Mass., Baker Library, . . . 1956. vi, 175p.

—— —— —— —— **Catalogue, 1777-1817,** giving data also upon cognate items in other Harvard libraries. London, Bailey Bros. & Swinfen, on behalf of the Baker Library, . . . 1957. [x], 397p. 80s.

—— —— —— —— **Catalogue, 1818-1848,** giving data upon cognate items in other Harvard libraries. Boston, Mass., Baker Library, . . . 1964. viii, 397p. 160s.

1940 v.: 7,279 items, including 23 incunabula; 6 locations. Supplement: 2,569 items, plus errata; 6 locations. 1957 v.: 7,085 items; 10 locations. 1964 v.: 7,642 items; 8 locations. Arranged chronologically by year, then A-Z by author. The 1957 v. has a narrower interpretation of "economics" than the previous volumes. The 1964 v. omits government publications except those of chamber of commerce and boards of trade, but it includes books and pamphlets in the main Baker Library.

33:016

HIGGS, H. — Bibliography of economy, 1751-1775. Prepared for the British Academy. Cambridge, Univ. Press, 1935. xxii, 744p. 75s.

6,740 numbered items, chronologically arranged by year of publication. Under each year, divisions are as follows: 1. General economics—2. Agriculture, etc., including the extractive industries—3. Shipping, navigation, etc.—4. Manufactures—5. Commerce—6. Colonies, British and foreign—7. Finance—8. Transport—9. Social conditions—10. Topography of economic interest—11. Miscellaneous. Indexes of authors and of anonymous titles.

33:016

INSTITUT FÜR WELTWIRTSCHAFT, Kiel University. [**Catalogues**]. Boston, Mass., G. K. Hall, 1966-.

Sachkatalog (Subject catalog). 1967. 83v. $6,500.
Regionenkatalog (Regional catalog). 1966. 52v. $4,000.
Personenkatalog (Biographical and bibliographical catalog of persons). 1966. 30v. $2,375.
Körperschaftenkatalog (catalog of corporations). 1966. 13v. $1,000.

Behördenkatalog (catalog of administrative authorities). 1966. 10v. $750.
Titelkatalog (title catalog). 1968. 15v. $1125.
Standortskartei der Periodika (catalog of periodical holdings). 1968. 10v. $675.
The Institut für Weltwirtschaft has one of the largest social science libraries in the world,—c. 900,000v. These catalogues consist of photolithographed reproductions of 4,369,000 well typed cards, 21 cards per page. They include many periodical articles. The *Standortskartei der Periodika* covers c. 19,000 titles, including newspapers.

33:016

International bibliography of economics. Prepared by the International Committee for Social Sciences Documentation. v. 1, 1952-. Paris, Unesco; then London, Stevens (subsequently Tavistock Publications) & Chicago, Aldine Publication Co., 1955-. (International bibliography of the social sciences).

V. 12: 1963 (lxxii, 470p.), published 1964, has 7,165 numbered items. 15 main classes: A. Preliminaries—B. Methods—C. General and basic works—D. History of economic thought—E. Economic history—F. Economic activity (with country divisions)—G. Organization of production—H. Production (goods and services)— I. Prices and markets—J. Money and finance—K. Income—L. Demand—M. Social economics and policy—N. Public economy (with country divisions)—O. International economics. Periodical articles are drawn from c. 2,000 periodicals. Author and subject indexes. 2-3 years' time-lag.

33:016

INTERNATIONAL MONETARY FUND and **INTERNATIONAL BANK FOR RECONSTRUCTION AND DEVELOPMENT.** Joint Library. **List of recent periodical articles.** Washington, 1947-. Monthly. Mimeographed. *Gratis.*

Each issue contains c. 350 references. Three main classes: 1. Economic theory—2. Descriptive economics. A. General; B. Geographical (divided by continents, then by countries)—3. International Monetary Fund, I.B.R.D., International Finance Corporation, International Development Association. Characterised by its prompt recording of worthwhile articles.

33:016

The Journal of economic abstracts. The American Economic Association. Cambridge, Mass., Harvard Univ., The Journal of economic abstracts, 1963-. Quarterly. ea. $1; $2.50 p.a.

Published co-operatively by the contributing journals under the auspices of the American Economic Association.
v. 1, no. 1 abstracts articles in 24 periodicals (28 issues) published in 16 countries and 8 languages, on pure and applied economics. In most cases abstracts are prepared by the author of the original article; location only of abstracter is given. About 2,000 200-word abstracts (mostly author abstracts) p.a. The classified contents list (19 sections, September 1967) that precedes gives a fair idea of coverage. Arranged under titles of journals, A-Z. Annual author index, but no

subject index. Decided time-lag of over one year. Academic appeal, as opposed to the commercial-world appeal of *Economic abstracts* (The Hague).

As from June 1966 includes the classified periodicals contents-listing that formerly appeared in the *American economic review*.

33:016
Keizaigaku bunken kihō. Quarterly bibliography of economics. Compiled by Keizai Shiryō Kyōgikai [Association for Documentation in Economics]. Tokyo, Yūhikaku, 1956-. v. 1, no. 1-. Quarterly.

About 15,000 references p.a., in 16 classes. Includes periodical articles in Japanese, Russian Chinese (only up to 1960), English, French, German, etc. Each issue carries author index and list of journals. "Best current Japanese bibliography of not only economics but also social sciences in general . . . " (*Guide to Japanese reference books* (1966), p. 143).

Preceded by the Osaka University of Commerce. Institute for Economic Research's *Bibliography of economic science* (Tokyo, Maruzen, 1934-39) in 4v. (1. *Public finance* (1919-1933)— 2-3. *Money and finance* (1919-1934, 1935)—4. *Commerce and industry* (1919-1936), a very full systematic listing (*c.* 120,000 items) of books and articles in periodicals published in Japan and major foreign countries (except the U.S.S.R.). Japanese sections are separate.

33:016
McNIERNEY, M. A., *ed.* **Directory of business and financial services.** 6th ed., rev. New York, Special Libraries Association, 1963. v, 187p. $6.50.

Supersedes W. Hausdorfer's *Handbook of commercial, financial and information services* (5th ed. 1956).

Annotated list of 1,560 U.S., Canadian and British business, economic and financial services that are printed periodically with regular supplements. A service, as distinct from newsletters and periodicals, is defined as "current information that is subject to constant or irregular change, often published in loose-leaf format; the service function consists in collecting widely scattered data that is [sic] assembled to meet the needs of a special group. It may be of a selective, interpretative character requiring the knowledge of experts". Exclude bank letters, brokerage letters, clipping services, mat services, market surveys, regional studies and government publications. 'Publishers and their business and financial services' (p. 1-148)—'General sources of business and financial information' (p. 149-50; bibliographies and directories)—Index of publishers, services and authors (including detailed subject index).

33:016
MOSSÉ, R., and **POTIER, M.** **Bibliographie d'économie politique, 1945-1960:** histoire des doctrines, statistique et économetrie, géographie économique, économie rurale, économie financière, travail, sociologie, démographie. Paris, Sirey, 1963. [vi], 124p. 16F.

Supplements in part A. Grandin's *Bibliographie générale des sciences juridiques, politi-ques, économiques et sociales de 1800 à 1925* (plus supplements, to 1950) (*see at 3:016*). R. Mossé founded *Documentation économique* (q.v.) in 1934.

About 2,000 entries for French books published 1945-60. No annotations, but references to reviews in *Revue économique, Revue d'économie politique* and *Bulletin analytique,* where relevant. Appendices list periodicals, series, official publications and those of banks and public bodies. Author index. Critically reviewed in *Bulletin des bibliothèques de France* (v. 8, no. 12, December 1963, p. 770-1).

33:016
PITTSBURGH. UNIVERSITY. Department of Economics. **Economics library selections.** Series **I. New books in economics.** Pittsburgh, Pa., 1964-. Quarterly. $12.50 per v. (academic libraries & individuals); $17.50 per v. (others), covering both series.

Continues Johns Hopkins University. Department of Political Economy. *Economics Library selections.* Series 1. *New books in economics.* March 1954-. Quarterly.

The Series 1, 1965, no. 3, September 1965 issue contains entries nos. 667-976 in 17 sections, plus author index. Final three sections: Bibliographies —Reference works—New journals. Evaluative annotations. A feature is use of code letter following each entry, indicating type of library for which the book is recommended (*e.g.,* A, for junior college library; B, for good college library; C, for university library; D, for university library emphasising graduate research; E. Alternative selections). Prices are given and total cost of items in categories A-D is stated.

Series 2: *Basic lists in special subjects* (1954-), issued by Johns Hopkins Univ., Dept of Economics up to 1963, comprises:

1. *International economics.* 1954.
2. *Statistics and econometrics.* 1955.
3. *A selected bibliography of economic reference works and professional journals.* 1956.
4. *Business fluctuations.* 1957.
5. *Economic theory and history of thought.* 1960.
6. *The economics of labor.* 1961.
7. *The economics of development and growth.* 1963.

Series 2, no. 3 is an annotated list of 164 books, 54 English-language and 31 foreign-language journals.

The University of Pittsburgh. Dept. of Economics' *Economics library selections. Cumulative bibliography, Series 1 and 2, 1954-1962* (New York, Gordon & Breach, 1965. x, 352p. $36) has 7,433 numbered citations of books contained in the 42 issues of the Johns Hopkins University's *Economics library selections.* For annotations the user is referred to the original series.

33:016
Referativnyĭ sbornik. Ekonomika promyshlen-nost'. Moscow, Akademiya Nauk SSSR, Institut Nauchnoĭ Informatsiĭ, 1953-. Monthly. £11 18s. p.a.

About 8,000 abstracts and references p.a.

Periodical articles from *c.* 1,400 journals in 72 countries. 7 main sections (also available separately): World economy. Economic position of countries—General economic problems and industrial organisation—Economy and organisation of production in heavy industry—Economy and organisation of production in consumer goods and food industry—Operational research —Organisation and financing of research. Manpower. Employment—Organisation of industrial manpower. More than 70% of the items in the first section are in languages other than Russian. Annual author and subject indexes.

33:016
Research index. Wallington, Surrey, Business Surveys, Ltd., 1965-. Fortnightly. £30 p.a.

An index to *c.* 80,000 articles and news items p.a., in *c.* 130 British business, economic and trade periodicals, and the national press. Section 1 (on pink paper): 'Industrial and commercial news' not dealing specifically with a particular company; A-Z by *c.* 150 topics; single-line entries. Section 2: 'Companies', arranged by companies, A-Z. Asterisk denotes articles of more than one page. Intended as a current-awareness service. Apart from covering periodicals not otherwise indexed, *Research index* is a corrective to other indexing services that often ignore company information in their selection of articles. No cumulations.

33:016
STEWART, C. F., and **SIMMONS, G. B.,** *comp.* **A bibliography of international business.** New York & London, Columbia Univ. Press, 1964. xiii, 603p. $15.

More than 8,000 items,—English-language books and periodical articles from 120 journals. Systematic order; 4 main classes (4: Nations and regions). Includes such subjects as banking, economic aid, industrial relations, transport, labour, nationalisation. Double entry, where relevant. No indexes. (Also entry in *Guide,* v. 1, at 65:016.)

33:016
Tropical abstracts; compiled from world literature on tropical and subtropical agriculture. Amsterdam, Royal Tropical Institute, 1946-. v. 1-. Monthly. Gl. 45 (90s.) p.a.

V. 21, 1966: 2,693 informative and indicative abstracts. Main sections: General—Products—Forestry—Animal husbandry—Fisheries—Economic and social aspects. Books (2 or 3 one-page reviews). U.D.C. numbers added. Index to v. 20, 1965 (received August 1966) consists of author index, subject index (p. 35-100), list of review articles and books.

33:016
World agricultural economics and rural sociology, April 1959-. Amsterdam, North-Holland Publishing Co., 1959-64; Farnham Royal, Bucks, Commonwealth Agricultural Bureaux, 1965-. Quarterly. 60s. p.a. to subscribers in C.A.B. contributing countries; 100s. to subscribers in other countries.

*See entry in Guide, v. 1, at 63:016;
added entry at 301 (-202):016.*

Encyclopaedias & Dictionaries

33 (031)=20
PALGRAVE, Sir **R. H. I. Palgrave's Dictionary of political economy;** edited by H. Higgs. London, Macmillan, 1925-26. 3v. (reprinted New York, Kelley, 1963; London, Cass, 1964. $75; £25).

First published 1894-96.
V. 1: A-E; v. 2: F-M; v. 3: N-Z. Each volume includes a supplement; general, analytical index in v. 3. Comprehensive signed articles (v. 3 has 129 contributors), with brief bibliographies. Sometimes bibliographies are extensive (*e.g.,* 'Physiocrats', v. 3, p. 103-8, includes a 2-column bibliography in small type). Still of value for biographical and historical data.

33 (031)=30
SELLIEN, R., and **SELLIEN, H.,** *ed.* **Dr. Gablers Wirtschaftslexikon.** 6. Aufl. Wiesbaden, Gabler, 1965. 2v. DM.116.

First published 1956.
16,000 entries; many of the articles (*e.g.,* 'Kybernetik') are extensive, signed and carry bibliographies. The standard and authoritative German dictionary of economics.

33 (031)=393
Bedrijfseconomische encyclopedie. Onder algemeene leiding van J. G. Stridiron. Utrecht, W. de Haan, 1947-52. 5v. illus., tables, maps.

v. 1: *Economie.* 1947.
v. 2: *Algemeene bedrijfseconomie.* 1948.
v. 3: *Bedrijfseconomie.* 1949.
v. 4: *Administratie (Boekhouding, calculatie en budgettering).* 1950.
v. 5: *Statistiek.* 1952.
An encyclopaedia of industrial economics. A Z subject sequence in each volume. Many contributors. Signed articles; short bibliographies appended. Profuse cross-references. V. 5 includes a general subject and name index.

33 (031)=40
ROMEUF, J., and **PASQUALAGGI, G. Dictionnaire des sciences économiques.** Paris, Presses Universitaires de France, 1956-58. 2v. diagrs.

International in scope. Articles are often signed and lengthy (*e.g.,* "Sécurité sociale", v. 2, p. 1008-22). Bibliographies are not invariably appended; when they are, they may cite periodical articles as well as books. About 400 biographies, excluding living economists. The article on G. M. Keynes, by Alain Barrère, runs to 2½ columns. V. 2 includes a list of contributors and their articles, and an index of authors cited. Adequate cross-references.

33 (038)=00
HERBST, R. Dictionary of commercial, financial and legal terms pertaining to trade and industry, including terms used in importing, manufacturing, distributing and marketing. 2nd ed. Lucerne, Thali. 1962-66. 3v. ea. Sw. fr. 98.50.

v. 1: *English-German-French.* 1962.
v 2: *Deutsch-englisch-französisch.* 1966.
v. 3: *Francais-anglais-allemand.* 1966.

First published 1955-65.

About 50,000 entry-words in each volume. Separate entries for different meanings of words. Compounds are entered under both parts, *e.g.*, 'Balance of trade'—also under 'Trade, balance of'). Good, compact layout and use of bold type and symbols. Many phrases (*e.g.*, 'Tag': 2½ cols.).

33 (038)=00

Kleines Aussenhandels Wörterbuch in acht Sprachen: deutsch, russisch, polnisch, tschechisch, englisch, französisch, spanisch, portugiesisch. Hrsg. vom Verlag "Die Wirtschaft". Berlin, Verlag "Die Wirtschaft", 1960. 304p.

1,275 numbered special terms for export, import, trade agreements, market research, publicity, fairs, banking, finance, customs and tariffs, transport, insurance and arbitration. "The book is mainly intended for business with capitalist countries" (*Preface*). Expressions found in general dictionaries are mostly omitted. The German terms and equivalents in 7 other languages extend over double pages; language keys; thumb index in 7 languages.

33 (038)=00

PAENSON, I., *comp.* **Systematic glossary, English-French-Spanish-Russian, of selected economic and social terms.** Oxford, Pergamon Press, 1963. xxxv, 414p. diagrs. Loose-leaf. £10.

See entry at 3 (038)=00.

33 (038)=00

SERVOTTE, J. V. Dictionnaire commercial et financier: français-néerlandais-anglais-allemand. 3. éd., rev. et augmentée. Brussels, Brépols, 1964. ix, 960p.

First published 1956.

About 12,000 entry-words (with many sub-entries) in French, followed by equivalents in Dutch, English and German, plus indexes in those three languages. In most cases entry-word and equivalents are followed by phrases in set order: word plus complement; word plus verb; word used as complement. Covers both British and U.S. English. Criticised in *Babel* (v. 12, no. 1, 1966, p. 50-2) for lack of categorisation of terms, omission of abbreviations and lack of balance in coverage of the four languages, although tribute is paid to the excellent reputation enjoyed by the dictionary "among businessmen, commercial correspondents, scholars and anyone wanting information on the right usage of words in commerce, finance, economics and law".

33 (038)=00

VAUGHAN, F. C., and **VAUGHAN, M. C. Glossary of economics,** including Soviet terminology. Amsterdam & Barking, Essex, Elsevier, 1966. viii, 201p. (Glossaria interpretum, G11). 65s.

1,669 entry-words in English/American, with French and German equivalents and a 17-page Russian supplement. Mainly terms in general industrial and labour economics, and applied microeconomic analysis, plus some accountancy, legal and banking terms. French, German and Russian indexes.

The European Economic Communities' *Terminological material: economic trends* (1967. 32s. 6d.) covers terms in German, French, Italian, Dutch and English, with an index in each language. This glossary is free to subscribers to the *Euratom dictionary: phraseological concordances* (Loose-leaf ed. 1964. German, French, Italian and Dutch).

33 (038)=20

GILPIN, A. Dictionary of economic terms. London, Butterworths, 1966. [7], 222p. 20s.

About 1,200 terms, with definitions and explanatory notes. Includes entries for propagators of doctrines (*e.g.*, Malthus, Marx), conferences and institutions (*e.g.*, Royal Economic Society; N.I.E.S.R.), slang expressions (*e.g.*, 'tired bulls') and Americanisms. Considered by *The economic journal* (v. 76, no. 3, September 1966, p. 712) to be "among the better buys".

J. R. Winston's slighter but long-lived *A dictionary of economic terms* (3rd rev. ed. London, Routledge, 1951. [i], 85p. 5s.) defines about 500 terms, with comment. Entries average 6-12 lines. First published in 1905.

33 (038)=20

GREENWALD, D., *ed.* **The McGraw-Hill dictionary of modern economics:** a handbook of terms and organizations. New York, London, etc., McGraw-Hill, 1965. xvii, [i], 697p. tables, diagrs., charts. $14.75; 118s.

Part 1, 'Terms' (p. 3-560), consists definitions of *c.* 1,300 frequently used modern economic terms, plus references to sources. Part 2, 'Organizations' (p. 563-697) describes the functions of *c.* 175 private, public and non-profit organisations, associations and research bodies concerned with economics and marketing. U.S. slant. Well produced. 8 contributors, but entries unsigned.

33 (038)=20

HANSON, J. I. A dictionary of economics and commerce. London, Macdonald & Evans, 1964. 401p. 35s. (2nd ed. 1967. [6], 432p. 35s.).

More than 4,000 entries, mainly concerned with terms in economic theory and applied economics. Reliable but not always up-to-date (*e.g.*, no entries for 'take-off' or 'production function'; out of date on Board of Trade). British slant. "Mainly useful to sixth-formers" (*Board of Trade journal*, v. 187, no. 3535, 18th December 1964, p. 1328).

The 2nd ed. contains 500 entirely new entries, many existing entries being revised and updated.

33 (038)=20

NEMMERS, E. E., and **JANZEN, C. C. Dictionary of economics and business.** Paterson, N.J., Littlefield, Adams, 1959 (reprinted 1960). [iii], 326p. $1.95.

About 4,000 very concise definitions (*e.g.*, Malthusian law of population: 1½ lines). Enters organisations under known abbreviated form, with cross-reference from the full form (*e.g.*, 'International Labour Office', under 'I.L.O.'; 'American Federation of Labour', under 'A.F.L.'). Primarily for use in U.S. colleges.

33 (038)=20

Pitman's Business man's guide: a comprehensive dictionary of commercial information. 13th ed. London, Pitman, 1957. iii, 483p. 20*s*. (14th ed. 1967. 32*s*.).

12th ed. 1949.
Definitions, some brief, some lengthy (*e.g.,* "Foreign exchange": 2¼ cols.; "Trustee": 8 cols.). Includes legal and office terms. Gives French, German, Spanish and Italian equivalents for the commercial terms defined. (Duplicate of entry in *Guide,* v. 1, at 65 (038)=20.)

Business terms, phrases and abbreviations (13th ed., edited by F. E. Perry. London, Pitman, 1966. [5], 232p. 12*s*. 6*d*.), first published in 1911, defines about 2,000 terms, with French, German, Spanish and Italian equivalents, but no index to these.

33 (038)=20

SELDON, A., and PENNANCE, F. G. — Everyman's dictionary of economics: an alphabetical exposition of economic concepts and their application. London, Dent, 1965. xxix, 449p. 25*s*.

About 500 entries by 13 contributors. A systematic layout of headings in 13 classes and a set of short bibliographies precede. Unsigned, extended definitions (*e.g.,* 'Mercantilism': 2p.; 'Sterling area': 1p.). Includes biographies (*e.g.,* Adam Smith: 1½p.) and institutions. Includes articles: 'Sources, statistical', 'Journals, economic'. Practical and up-to-date. Enables the user to distinguish between deflation, reflation, inflation and disinflation. Numerous cross-references. British slant. Cramped page. A handy reference tool for all types of library.

33 (038)=20

SLOAN, H. S., and ZURCHER, A. J. A dictionary of economics. 4th ed. New York, Barnes & Nobles, 1961. 371 p. $1.95.

First published 1949.
Defines and explains about 3,500 terms in economics, commerce, finance and banking. U.S. slant, entries being provided for U.S. law cases and the like. Definitions average about 6 lines. Many cross-references.

33 (038)=20

TAYLOR, P. A. S. A new dictionary of economics. London, Routledge & Kegan Paul, 1966. vii, 304p. 25*s*.

Concise, simple definitions of *c.* 2,500 terms, with numerous cross-references. Particularly good on institutions, national and international (*e.g.,* Overseas Development Institute) and government reports (*e.g.,* Radcliffe report: 2p.). Designed for business man and student. Good value, although critically reviewed in *Economica* (new series, v. 34, no. 134, May 1967, p. 228-9) for lack of reading references for many of the entries and lack of a section giving full titles of initials (*e.g.,* I.M.F., Unesco).

The concise commercial dictionary, by P. G. Osborn and S. T. Grandage (London, Sweet & Maxwell, 1966. 244p. 45*s*.) defines nearly 3,000 terms. Particularly handy for commercial-legal terms, Latin phrases, and for such terms as 'Fire insurance' and 'Debenture' (each ⅔ page). Appended dictionary of abbreviations.

33 (038)=30

EICHBORN, R. von. Wirtschaftswörterbuch. Düsseldorf, Econ-Verlag GmbH., 1961; London, Pitman, 1963. 2v. ea. DM.56; 105*s*.

v. 1: *Englisch-deutsch.* xvi, 923p.
v. 2: *Deutsch-englisch.* xvi, 1080p.
First published 1947.
About 25,000 main entry-words in each volume; many compounds and idioms (*e.g.,* 'Mortgage': 3 cols.; 'Förderung': 2½ cols.). Distinguishes between British and U.S. terminology (*e.g.,* 'Legal (Br.), lawful (U.S.)'). Where British or U.S. terms do not have their equivalent in German, an idiomatic translation is attempted. Genders of German nouns not shown. Fairly large type and good use of bold for the many sub-entries. A reliable and extensive business dictionary.

33 (038)=30

GUNSTON, C. A., and CORNER, C. M. Deutsch-englisches Glossarium finanzieller und wirtschaftlicher Fachausdrücke. 4. erw. Aufl. Frankfurt am Main, Knapp, 1962. 1060p. DM.49.80. (5th ed. 1967. 1122p. 100*s*.).

First published 1953.
About 15,000 main entries. Most terms are not merely translated; their precise application is stated in italics (*e.g.,* 'Gesetz=Law (*in the case of certain enactments*'). The 3rd ed. (1958. 814p.) was considered more reliable and certainly more extensive than anything else on the subject (*Babel,* v. 4, no. 4, 1958, p. 222), although the 4th ed. is criticised for mistranslations (*Babel,* v. 9, no. 3, 1963, p. 148-9). *International affairs* (v. 36, no. 1, January 1959, p. 137) suggests supplementing the 3rd ed. by an older work,—H. T. Price's *Deutsch-englisches Volkswirtschaftliches Wörterbuch* (Berlin, Springer, 1926-29. 2v.).
The 5th ed. (1967) reprints the text of the 4th ed plus a 160-page supplement. Reviewed in *International affairs,* v. 43, no. 4, October 1967, p. 811.

Ökonomisches Lexikon (Berlin, Verlag 'Die Wirtschaft', 1967. 2v. $23.60) is a German-German encyclopaedic dictionary of *c.* 15,000 economic terms, with numerous cross-references.

U. Becker's *Rechtswörterbuch für die gewerbliche Wirtschaft* (Frankfurt am Main, Knapp, 1966. 424p. DM.40) is particularly concerned with terms found in legal documents (*e.g.,* conditions of sale; tenders). Systematically arranged in subject chapters; German-English-French. Trilingual index; bibliography. Reviewed in *The incorporated linguist,* v. 6, no. 4, October 1967, p. 110.

33 (038)=30

RENNER, R., *and others.* **German-English economic terminology.** Munich, Hueber, 1965; London, Macmillan, 1966. 556p. DM.27.80; 63*s*.

7,000 terms, arranged in 25 sections (with subsections), ranging from general economics, currencies, banking and book-keeping, through bankruptcy, international trade, advertising and exhibitions, to transport, insurance and statistics, with a supplement on office equipment. Each section has English and German translation exercises. Highly recommended in *The incorporated linguist* (v. 5, no. 2, April 1966, p. 56-57), but thought scarcely adequate to the needs of a professional academic economist (*Economic journal*, v. 76, no. 304, December 1966, p. 998).

33 (038)=30=40
HAENSCH, G., and RENNER, R. Deutsch-französische Wirtschaftssprache. Terminologie économique allemand-français. 3. Aufl. Munich, Hueber, 1965. 456p.

The German-French counterpart of R. Renner's *German-English economic terminology*.

Other French and German economic dictionaries are F. Roepke's *Deutsch-französisch Glossarium* (4. aufl. Frankfurt am Main, Knapp, 1961. 464p. DM.28) and *Französich-deutsches Glossarium* (1964. 540p. DM.38.60; and *Fachwörterbuch für Wirtschaft, Handel und Finanzwesen . . . Französisch-deutsch, deutsch-französisch*, by R. Thomik, with E. Weinhold (Luxembourg, Peiffer; Paris, Dunod, 1963. xvi, 460p. NF.60).

33 (038)=393
BONS, A., and O'BEIRNE, D. R. Engels handelswoordenboek. Antwerp, Kluwer, 1957. 1172p.

A Dutch-English commercial dictionary; more than 32,000 Dutch entry-words (business, trade and legal terms), with English equivalents. (Duplicate of entry at 65 (038)=393.)

33 (038)=397
GULLBERG, I. E. Svensk-engelsk fackordbok för näringsliv, förvaltning, undervisning och forskning. Stockholm, Norstedt, 1964. xv, [1], 1246p. Sw. kr. 145.

A Swedish-English dictionary of technical terms used in business, industry, administration, education and research. About 130,000 entry- and sub-entry words; many are categorised. Lengthy entries under institutions ("Internationella": 36 columns). Many idioms, U.S. usage being distinguished from British. Good layout and typography, notably in use of bold and italic in sub-entries. The English-Swedish companion dictionary is in preparation.

33 (038)=40
DELATTRE, J., and VERNISY, G. de. Le vocabulaire baromètre dans la langage économique: dictionnaire anglais-française. Geneva, Librairie de l'Université: Georg, 1961. 152p.

About 750 entry-words; many idioms; colloquialisms (*e.g.*, 'zoom'; 'bearish').

Vocabulaire français-anglais et anglais-français de termes et locutions juridiques, administratifs, commerciaux, financiers et sujets connexes, by J. Jéraute (Paris, Pichon & Durand-Auzias, 1953. 415p.) is intended for French users. French-English, p. 9-181 (*c.* 8,500 entry-words); English-French, p. 185-414 (*c.* 12,000 entry-words). Terms are broadly categorised.

33 (038)=40
KETTRIDGE, J. O. French-English and English-French dictionary of commercial and

financial terms, phrases and practice. [2nd ed.] London, Routledge & Kegan Paul, 1949 (reprinted 1965). xii, 647p. 40s.

First published 1931 (xi, 647p.).
French-English, p. 1-324; English-French ("inverted counterpart" of English-French), p. 325-647. About 12,000 main entries in each half; appendices of conventional signs, French syllabification, abbreviations and conversion tables. Many phrases (*e.g.*, "actions": 3½ columns); also cautionary notes on usage in French and explanatory text in both languages (*e.g.*, "case of need"). Requires updating. (Also entered at 65 (038)=40.)
Noted: *Commercial French terms*, by R. C. M. Ransome (London, Pitman, 1965. vii, 85p. 12s. 6d.).

33 (038)=40
SERVOTTE, J. V. Dictionnaire commercial et financier, français-anglais, anglais-français. [Brussels], Marabout Service, 1959. 446, [1]p. *c.* 100s.

About 30,000 entries and sub-entries in the French-English section (p. 7-390), with English index of *c.* 7,000 words. Covers commercial, financial, economic and legal terms and phrases. Set order of entry: word followed by a complement; word followed by a verb; word as a complement to a substantive; word as a complement to a verb. 'Prix' has 137 sub-entries. Author is Sécretaire du Président de la Kredietbank.

33 (038)=40
SUAVET, T. Dictionnaire économique et sociale. 3. éd. revue. Paris, Éditions Ouvrières, 1965. 479p. maps, graphs. 19.95F.

See entry at 3 (038)=40.

33 (038)=50
EDLER, F. Glossary of mediaeval terms of business. Italian series, 1200-1600. Cambridge, Mass., Mediaeval Academy of Sciences, 1936. xx, 430p.

Glossary of *c.* 2,000 terms, each with some six examples of usage, on *O.E.D.* lines. Classified list appended. List of primary and secondary sources precedes.

33 (038)=50
MOTTA, G. Dizionario commerciale, inglese-italiano, italiano-inglese: economica-legge-finanza. Milan, Signorelli, 1961. x, [1], 1051p.

English-Italian, p. 1-515; Italian-English, p. 519-1051. About 15,000 main entries in each half. Many compounds and idioms (*e.g.*, "Account". 2½ columns; "Parts": 1). English nouns are categorised; stress in Italian not shown. Intended for Italian rather than British users. English terms are sometimes suspect. (Also entered in *Guide*, v. 1, at 65 (038)=50.)

Noted: *Glossario aziendale: italiano, inglese-inglese, italiano*, by G. Rossi (Milan, Etas Kompass. 1966. 393p.).

33 (038)=50
PAPI, G. U. Dizionario di economia. Turin, Unione Tipografico. Editrice Torinese, 1967. 1511p. L20,000.

An encyclopaedic dictionary of economics. The article 'Capitalismo' (p. 251-66) has 1¼ columns of bibliography, with many references in the text and footnotes; 'Monopolio': 2 columns, plus 1⅞ cols. of bibliography. Entries under countries deal wholly with monetary systems (*e.g.*, 'Regno Unito', p. 1154-83; in 22 sections, with two-fifth cols. of bibliography). 90 pages on Common Market. Excludes personal-name entries. Numerous cross-references. Bibliographies set solid and typographically unrelieved.

33 (038) = 50

SPINELLI, N. Dizionario commerciale, italiano-inglese, inglese-italiano . . . Ed. 1953 con un appendice. Turin, Lattes, 1953. [vii], 464, 683, 138p.

First published 1917.
Italian-English, p. 1-464 (including English abbreviations, p. 443-464); English-Italian, p. 1-683. 12-17,000 main entries in each half. Many compounds and idioms (*e.g.*, 'Account': 4 columns; 'Mercato': 2). Stress in Italian not shown. References from entry words in appendix to main entries. (Duplicate of entry in *Guide*, v. 1, at 65 (038) = 50.)

33 (038) = 60

MACDONALD, G. R. Spanish-English and English-Spanish commercial dictionary . . . 5th ed., rev. and enl. London, Pitman, 1944 (reprinted 1962). xiv, 950p. 30*s*.

Spanish-English, p. 1-394 (p. 395-418: Spanish verbs; abbreviations; weights and measures); English-Spanish, p. 419-940 (p. 941-50: place names, Christian names, etc.). About 20,000 entries in each half. By no means confined to commercial terms. (Duplicate of entry in *Guide*, v. 1, at 65 (038) = 60.)

L. A. Robb's *Dictionary of business terms, Spanish-English and English-Spanish* (New York, Wiley; London, Chapman & Hall, 1950. xii, 219p. 32*s*.) has *c*. 10,000 terms in each part. Terminology of 14 Central and Latin American countries, plus Spain, U.S.A. and Britain, is differentiated; *c*. 70 subject categories.

33 (038) = 60

SELL, L. L. Spanish-English comprehensive specialists' dictionary for insurance, finance, law, labor, politics, business. New York, McKay, 1957. xi. 650p.

More than 135,000 terms in English and Spanish. List of abbreviations, p. 643-50. The English-Spanish counterpart appeared in 1954 (New York, International Dictionary Co. 736p.).

33 (038) = 82

BRITISH IRON AND STEEL FEDERATION. Concise dictionary [of] commercial expressions. London, the Federation, 1961. 142p. *Gratis*.

An English-Russian, Russian-English dictionary, with about 2,000 entry-words in each half. Includes complete phrases. Many of the terms are not covered by the ordinary dictionaries.

33 (038) = 82

TELBERG, V. G. Russian-English glossary of economic and trade terms. 2nd ed., rev. and enl. New York, Telberg Book Corpn., 1965. iii, 106 1. $9.80.

The 1st ed. (1959) was largely based on V. T. Kolpakov's *Eksportnoiimportny-slovar'* (Moscow, 1954). This ed., a considerable enlargement, has 2,150 entry-words. Equivalents only. Concentrates on words and phrases occurring most frequently in Soviet writings on economics and commerce.

33 (038) = 956

Japanese-English dictionary of economic terms. Keizai yōgo Wa-Ei jiten. Tokyo, Tōyō Keizai Shinpōsha, 1963 (reprinted 1966). 626p.

"About 45,000 terms listed alphabetically in Hepburn romanization" (*Guide to Japanese reference books* (1966), p. 145). Appendix of English translations and abbreviations of the names of government departments, economic organisations and the like.

Noted: *English-Japanese dictionary of trade and industry* (Rev. ed. Tokyo, Kenkyūsha; London, Luzac, 1964. viii, 1068p. 60*s*.).

Periodicals

33 (05):016

BIBLIOTHEEK EN DOCUMENTATIE VAN DE ECONOMISCHE VOORLICHTINGDIENST. Catalogus van tijdschriften, 1965. The Hague, [1965]. [iv], 168p.; 1967 ed. 153p.

List of *c*. 1,900 current periodicals taken, as of 1st December 1964. Four sequences: (a) Titles, A-Z, plus note of frequency and code letters; (b) Code-letter entries plus full titles, as in (a); (c) Country and area index, sub-divided by subject. Many cross-references; (d) Subject index (subjects plus code letters). Spiral binding.

The Stockholm Handelshögskolan's *List econ. Lista över löpande utländska periodika inom nationalekonomi, företagsekonomi, ekonomisk geografi och statistik i svenska bibliothek* (Stockholm, 1963. [iv] 88 1. Sw.kr.15) is a mimeographed "list of current foreign periodicals in the field of economy, business administration, economic geography and statistics in Swedish libraries", compiled by Hans Baude.

33 (05):016

EUROPEAN ECONOMIC COMMUNITY. Commission. Library. **Catalogue général des périodiques.** 2. éd. [Brussels], Service des Publications des Communautés Européennes, 1965. 288p.

The main sequence is an A-Z list of 2,796 titles, noting frequency and the Commission Library's holdings. A second sequence shows the titles classified by subject. Subject index.

33 (05):016

HAMBURGISCHES WELT-WIRTSCHAFTS-ARCHIV. Abteilung Bibliothek. **Verzeichnis der laufenden Zeitschriften und Zeitungen** (ohne Jahresperiodika). 2. Aufl. Hamburg, HWWA. 1964. 2v.

Lists *c.* 3,000 periodicals and newspapers currently received. Entries give title (with translation of titles in uncommon languages), place of publication and, where appropriate, issuing body. V. 1 lists titles A-Z; v. 2 has separate lists of periodicals and newspapers, both under country of origin.

33 (05):016
HARVARD UNIVERSITY. Baker Library. **Statistical and review issues of trade and business periodicals.** 3rd ed. Boston, Mass., Baker Library, Graduate School of Business Administration, 1964. 23p. $1.

A-Z list of North American periodicals, noting the issues containing special statistical and annual review numbers, as well as issues containing specific subject surveys. No directories, buyers' guides or similar annual issues are listed unless they include industry statistics.

33 (05):016
Internationale Bibliographie der Fachzeitschriften für Technik und Wirtschaft. 4. Ausg. 1965 mit Stand Dezember 1964. Munich, Dokumentation der Technik, 1965. 2v.

Part of v. 1, section 10,—Industrie und Volkswirtschaft, Finanzen, Export (nos. 14127-15537) —provides a handy international working-list of economic periodicals. Entries state date of starting, frequency, price and publisher. V. 2 has indexes of titles, areas, subjects and publishers.

33 (05):016 (47)
HANDELSHÖGSKOLAN, Stockholm. Biblioteket. **Sovjetunion 1917-1964.** Förteckning över sovjetiska periodica av samhällsekonomiskt intresse i svenska bibliothek. Stockholm, Handelshögskolan, 1965. [iv], 99 l. Mimeographed. Unpriced.

"List of Soviet periodicals in the field of economics in Swedish libraries". Compiled by Ulla von Vegesack.

33 (05):016 (8=6)
SABLE M. H., *ed.* **Periodicals for Latin American economic development, trade and finance:** an annotated bibliography. Los Angeles, Univ. of California, Latin American Center, 1965. v, 72p. $2.50.

See entry at 33 (8=6) (05):016.

33 (05)/
The Economic journal: the quarterly journal of the Royal Economic Society. Cambridge, the Society, 1891-. v. 1, no. 1-. Quarterly. ea. 15s.

A valuable bibliographical tool, more than half the contents of each issue being devoted to reviews and lists of books and articles. The March 1966 (v. 126, no. 301) issue reviews 38 items (p. 85-151), has sections 'Recent periodicals and books' (p. 177-265, drawing on 129 journals) and 'New books' (p. 202-65: *c.* 500 items listed, with *c.* 100-word annotations for English-language books and shorter annotations for non-English books), and contents pages of 15 journals (p. viii-xi of advertisements).

The American economic review (American Economic Association. Evanston, Ill., Northwestern Univ., 1911-. 5 p.a.) is equally generous in reviews and bibliographies. The September 66, v. 56, no. 4, pt. 1 issue has reviews of 43 books (p. 881-978), 'Titles of new books' (p. 979-99; grouped by subjects) and the annual 'Sixty-third list of doctoral dissertations in American universites and colleges' (p. 1024-62; also grouped by subjects), as well as contents lists of journals. (As from June 1966 this contents listing has been transferred to *Journal of economic abstracts* (q.v.).)

Organisations

33:061 (4)
ECONOMIC COMMISSION FOR EUROPE. List of institutions in the field of applied economics in E.C.E. countries (scientific research institutes, universities and faculties of economics). [Geneva], United Nations, [E.C.E.], 1966. [i], [i], 107p. (E/ECE/615).

About 700 institutions in 28 countries; numbered entries under countries (A-Z). Entries state name of faculty, etc., university, address and major activities. Includes Eastern Europe and U.S.S.R., U.S.A. and Turkey. U.K. (p. 90-91): 8 scientific research institutions; 12 universities and faculties (economics).

Atlases

33 (084.4) (4/9)
GINSBURG, N. Atlas of economic development. Chicago, Univ. of Chicago Press, 1961. vii, 119p. tables, diagrs., maps. $5; $7.50.

48 black-and-white maps, plus text and tables. 8 sections, covering population (agriculture, minerals), transport, industries, etc. References to literature, p. 1-6. "The aim of the atlas is to increase understanding of the adjectives 'developed' and 'underdeveloped' as applied to countries and regions of the world" (*International affairs*, v. 38, no. 1, January 1963, p. 100). Page size (oblong): 10" × 14".

33 (084.4) (4/9)
HUMLUM, J. Kultur geografisk atlas. Atlas of economic geography. 5. udgave udarbejdet under medvirken of A. Krarup Morgensen. Bd. 1. Atlas. Copenhagen, Gyldendal, 1965. [xiv], 142p.

First published 1936; 4th ed. 1955.
The 4th ed. has 127 two-colour maps. Main headings: Geography of population—Agriculture —Livestock and animal products—Minerals and manufactures—Water power. Each page has very small maps of the world and of Europe, and more detailed maps of relevant areas. The *Geographical journal* (v. 122, pt. 1, March 1956, p. 120-1) praises the "great mass of accurate detail". No index. Page size 10¼" × 7½".

Noted: Jonasson, O., with B. Carlsund. *Atlas of the world commodities: production, trade and consumption; an economic-geographical survey* (Göteborg, Akademiförlaget Gumperts, [1961]. 81p. 25s.).

33 (084.4) (4/9)
JRO Weltwirtschaftsatlas. Atlas für Politik und Zeitgeschichte. Hrsg. Ernst Kremling. Bearb. Gustav Fochler-Hauke. Permanente Ausg. Munich, Jro-Verlag, 1957-. 2v. Loose-leaf. DM.348. Supplements DM.48 p.a.

The most detailed of economic atlases. When completed, will contain 576p. of maps (many of them folding) and 384p. of statistical data and text. V. 1 covers Europe and Africa; v. 2, the Far East, the Americas and world maps. A feature is the inclusion of coloured maps for individual countries showing physical features, communications, distribution of crops, minerals, etc. Section 101, in v. 2, covers the Caribbean and has a folding map (4p.) of the Caribbean-Mexico area, backed by data on each country and area, with a 40-line bibliography; foreign trade statistics (1963 or 1964); map of the Virgin Islands area; production and trade figures for Cuba, to 1962; map and statistics for the Dominican Republic; and statistics (1962 or 1963) for Haiti. 50% of these pages are dated 1966. Page size: 12" × 11 3/5".

Weltatlas: die Staaten der Erde und ihre Wirtschaft; edited by E. Lehrmann (Leipzig, VEB Bibliographisches Institut, 1952) has a German slant. Each economic map faces a corresponding location map on the same scale, avoiding overcrowding, of the economic map. Page size: 13" × 10".

33 (084.4) (4/9)
Oxford economic atlas of the world. Prepared by the Economist Intelligence Unit and the Cartographic Department of the Clarendon Press. 3rd ed. London, Oxford Univ. Press, 1965. viii, 286p. maps. 63s.

First published 1954; 2nd ed. 1959.
A revised and expanded ed. The coloured maps and supporting text and statistics (viii, 1-128p.) cover more than a hundred commodities, with increasing emphasis on fuel, power and industries. New maps show natural gas resources, distribution of petroleum refineries and aircraft production centres. Statistical data, in country index, are usually for 1958/60, wth pre-war figures for comparison. Map scales, usually 1:100M. to 1:400M., far too small for detailed location. Page size, 10" × 7½". "A concise reference volume of great value" (*The booklist*, v. 62, no. 1, 1st July 1966, p. 1012). For larger-scale maps, see Oxford regional economic atlases.
The Shorter Oxford economic atlas of the world (London, Oxford Univ. Press, 1966. [4], 128p. 30s.) has 128p. of coloured maps, with notes.

33 (084.4) (4/9)
VAN ROYEN, W., *and others.* **Atlas of the world's resources.** New York, Prentice-Hall; London, Constable, 1952-.

v. 1: *The agricultural resources of the world.* 1954. 84s.
v. 2: *The mineral resources of the world.* 1952. 70s.
v. 3: *Forestry and fishery resources* (not published).
V. 1-2 survey distribution and areas of production of particular commodities. Black-and-white maps, plus text data on occurrence, produc-

tion areas and methods, consumption, etc. Basic statistics; selected bibliographical references appended. Page size (oblong): 12½" × 15".

33 (084.4) (4)
NEUNDÖRFER, L. **Atlas sozialökonomischer Regionen Europas.** Hrsg. vom Soziographischen Institut an der Johann Wolfgang Goethe-Universität Frankfurt am Main. Baden-Baden, Lutzeyer (subsequently Nomos), [1961?]-. Loose-leaf.

Lfg. 1 consists of 36 maps, with facing and backing text and tables, covering Western Europe, including Scandinavia, plus Greece and Turkey. Lfg. 2:6 sheets (1964). To be in 100 maps. The 'elements' (agriculture, industry, movement of population, etc.) are dealt with in sets of 4 maps, each 1:4,000,000. Statistical data for c. 1950. Text and legends in 3 languages. Cumbersome page-size: 23" × 18".

J. Dollfus' *Economic atlas of Europe* (London, Murray, 1963. 48p. illus., maps. 32s. 6d.) has 27p. of maps in colour, mostly of Europe, on a scale of 1:12M. Each map illustrates an aspect of European economy (*e.g.,* power sources; transport; metal industry) and is described in the text. Page size: 9⅞" × 13". Originally published 1961; also French, German, Italian and Dutch editions.

33 (084.4) (47)
KISH, G., *and others.* **Economic atlas of the Soviet Union.** Ann Arbor, Univ. of Michigan Press; London, Cresset Press, 1960. 96p. maps. $10; 63s.

Four general maps of the Soviet Union (vegetation; administrative divisions; air lines; population distribution), plus maps of 15 regions, 4 per region: A. Agriculture and land use—B. Mining and minerals—C. Industry—D. Transportation and cities. Three-colour maps; regional map scales vary from 1:6M. to 1:12M. Bibliography (mainly of Russian sources), p. 88-89. Index-gazetteer to regional maps. Page size, 10¼" × 10¼".
A welcome supplement to the *Oxford regional economic atlas: the U.S.S.R. and Eastern Europe* (q.v), especially for the student. "The atlas would have been considerably improved by tighter editing and a certain degree of quantification of economic data" (*Economic geography*, v. 39, no. 1, January 1963, p. 93-94).

33 (084.4) (47)
Oxford regional economic atlas: the U.S.S.R. and Eastern Europe. Prepared by the Economist Intelligence Unit and the Cartographic Department of the Clarendon Press. London, Oxford Univ. Press, 1956 (reprinted with corrections, 1963). 142p. maps. 63s.

First published 1954.
Coverage includes the Mongolian People's Republic. 64p. of maps in colour; 48p. of notes and statistics; 25p. gazetteer. The maps deal with physical geography, agriculture, minerals, industries and human geography. Page size: 10" × 7½".

33 (084.4) (495)
KAYSER, B., THOMPSON, K., *and others.* . . . **Economic and social atlas of Greece.** Athens, [National Statistical Service], 1964. 74pl. Loose-leaf. 177s. 2d.

Text in Greek, English and French.

74 plates of maps (c. 200 in all; some in colour), covering population, agricultural crops and husbandry, industries, traffic, hotels, archaeological sites and foreign trade. Text and tables between map plates; figures up to 1962. Text in Greek, English and French. A well-produced atlas. Page-size (oblong): 17″ × 23¾″.

33 (084.4) (5-015)

Oxford regional economic atlas of the Middle East and North Africa. Prepared by the "Economist" Intelligence Unit, Ltd. and the Cartographic Department of the Clarendon Press. London, Oxford Univ. Press, 1960. viii, 135p. maps. 63s.

Coverage includes Somaliland Protectorate, French Somaliland and Somalia, Ethiopia, Sudan, Libya, Tunisia, Algeria and Morocco. 41 maps, some of them double-paged; supplementary notes and statistics, p. 65-120 (with figures only to 1956, although 1956 was a turning point in many respects in the Middle East). Index-gazetteer of about 4,000 names, p. 121-35; bibliography, p. vii-viii (literature; periodicals). Regional map scales, 1:4¼M.-1:11M. Some of the maps are crowded or poorly coloured; others (e.g., Sudan) are the reverse. Oil production and concessions are well mapped. Page size: 10″ × 7½″.

33 (084.4) (540)

Oxford economic atlas for India and Ceylon. Prepared by the Cartographic Department of the Clarendon Press. Bombay, etc., Oxford Univ. Press, Indian Branch, 1953. viii, 97, xxxvi p. maps.

97p. of maps in colour, with supporting statistical data.

An *Oxford economic atlas for Pakistan* was published in 1955.

33 (084.4) (6)

Africa: maps and statistics. Pretoria, Africa Institute, 1962-65. 10v. maps. ea. 75c.; R9 the set.

1. *Population.* 1962.
2. *Vital and medical aspects.* 1962.
3. *Cultural and educational aspects.* 1963.
4. *Transport and communication.* 1963.
5. *Energy resources, production and consumption.* 1963.
6. *Agriculture and forestry.* 1963.
7. *Livestock, farming and fishing.* 1964.
8. *Mining, industry and labour.* 1964.
9. *Trade, income and aid.* 1964.
10. *Political development.* 1965.

A total of 221p., including maps in English and Afrikaans. The aim is "to illustrate the more significant political, social and economic developments on the continent of Africa". No. 10 has maps and commentary, tables, an extensive bibliography (3p.) and a general index (9p.). Page size: 13½″ × 12⅓″.

Musiker (*Guide to South African reference books*, 4th ed., 1965, item 392) states that the work is to be completed in 12 parts, of which 8 had then been issued.

33 (084.4) (6)

Oxford regional economic atlas: Africa. Prepared by the Cartographic Department of the Clarendon Press. London, Oxford Univ. Press, 1965. 228p. maps, tables. 63s.

43p. of topographical maps, and 69p. of economic maps of the whole continent at 1:25,000,000. Notes and statistics (64p.); gazetteer of 48p. (c. 15,000 entries). Maps bled. Criticised in *Geographical journal* (v. 131, pt. 3, September 1965, p. 400-1) for indifferent colouring, overcrowding and out-of-dateness. Thus, economic and demographic maps show distribution for 1956; economic commentary is for the period 1953-60. A major omission in the acknowledgements: U.N. Economic Commission for Africa. Reviewed in *Africa*, v. 36, no. 1, January 1966, p. 97-98). Page size: 10″ × 7½″.

The Shorter Oxford atlas of Africa (London, Oxford Univ. Press, 1966. 100p. maps. 21s.) is based on the above, omitting the economic maps, notes and statistics.

33 (084.4) (689.1)

COLLINS, M. O., *ed.* **Rhodesia: its natural resources and economic development.** Salisbury, M. O. Collins (Pvt.), 1965. ii, 52p. illus., maps.

A series of maps on rectos, with text facing. The 34 good-quality maps are usually 1:2½M. and cover agriculture (2), climate (16), economic development (3) and natural resources (13). Gazetteer. p. 48-52. Page size (oblong): 14½″ × 17″.

33 (084.4) (73)

Rand McNally Commercial atlas and marketing guide. New York, Rand McNally. Annual. (97th ed. 1966. Service subscription, $55 p.a.).

Seven-eighths of this atlas is devoted to the U.S.A. Some 50 maps illustrate aspects of agriculture, communications, manufacturing, population, retail trade and transportation as they concern the whole country. Then follow maps and detailed statistics of each state, with particular emphasis on marketing areas, together with an index of cities, towns, counties, transportation lines, airports, banks and post offices and a further index of physical features. The main map of each state (25″ × 19″) varies in scale from Connecticut (1:342,000) to Texas (1:1,580,000). 12 pages are devoted to California. Apart from North America, the rest of the world is covered on small-scale maps and appears to be incidental to the main purpose of the volume. Gazetteer of c. 127,000 names, very largely U.S. cities and towns; grid references. Page size: 20¾″ × 14¼″.

Oxford regional economic atlas: United States and Canada (London, Oxford Univ. Press. 176p. maps. 35s.; 75s. 1967) has 128 pages of maps and an index-gazetteer listing 10,000 place-names. Page size: 10¼″ × 7¾″. Reviewed in *Geographical journal*, v. 133, pt. 4, December 1967, p. 583-4.

33 (084.4) (94)

Atlas of Australian resources. Canberra, Department of National Development, Regional Development Division. 1952-. maps. Loose-leaf.

First series, 1952-60 (2v.); Second series, 1962-.

ECONOMICS

The First series comprised 30 maps (29" × 17½") mostly at a scale of 1:6,000,000; ea. 5*s.* (paper), 6*s.* (linen strip), with a set of booklet commentaries, one per map. Covers all phases of Australia's agricultural, mineral, power, etc. resources and development.

The Second series consists of a replacement set of 30 maps (boxed set, 168*s.*; binder, £10 10*s.*). So far published: *Electricity* (1962); *Soils* (1963); *Population distribution and growth* (1964); *Mineral deposits* (1965). The *Electricity* map (1: 4,500,00) replaces the *Power and fuel* map in the First series and is more detailed, *e.g.,* on the functions of generating stations, with inset map showing electricity consumption. An article by T. W. Plumb and L. K. Hazlewood, "Planning the second series of the 'Atlas of Australian resources'", appeared in *Australian geographer,* v. 9, no. 5, 1965, p. 293-302.

—— —— **Index to Australian resources maps of 1940-59.** Canberra, the Department, 1961. 241p.

Contains references to published resources maps (issued either separately or included in other publications) covering all or part of the country. 'Resources maps' embraces maps known variously as 'special purpose', 'thematic', 'topic', etc. References state name of person or organisation compiling the map, date, title, publisher and approximate map scale (*Unesco bulletin for libraries,* v. 17, no. 3, May/June 1963, entry no. 175).

History

33 (091)
CARUS-WILSON, E. M. Essays in economic history: reprints edited for the Economic History Society. London, Arnold, 1954-62. 3v. 45*s.*

V. 1 contains reprints selected from the first twenty years of *Economic history,* 1926-41, and *Economic history review,* 1927-; articles substantially incorporated in later published work have not been included. "The aim of the present collection therefore is to make easily accessible in one volume a selection of those articles which have proved most in demand among students." Articles in v. 2-3 "range widely over a century of writing about economic history in a dozen different periodicals and one symposium".

Noted: *Index to economic history essays in Festschriften, 1900-1950,* by H. Schleiffer and R. Crandall (Cambridge, Mass., Harvard Univ. Press, 1953. 68p. $2.50) is arranged by broad subject headings; index of authors and proper names.

World surveys

33 (4/9) (02)
GREAT BRITAIN. BOARD OF TRADE. Hints to business men series. London, Board of Trade. *Gratis.*

About 60 individual country reports, revised biennially. The *Hints to business men visiting Dahomey* (1966. 31p.) has sections: General information—Travel—Hotels, restaurants and tipping—Postal, telegraph, telephone and telex facilities—Economic factors—Import and exchange control regulations—Methods of doing business—B.N.E.C. Africa—Useful addresses in Cotonou—Reading list (general; directories; statistics)—Board of Trade Export Credits Guarantee Department—Regional organisation of the Board of Trade. Map.

Revised editions and new titles are listed in *Recent additions to the Economics Division libraries,* Board of Trade Library Services (2 per month).

World economic comments is issued quarterly by the Board of Trade as part of the *Export service bulletin* (Daily. £10 10*s.* p.a.). The January to March 1968 issue (19 April 1968. 44p.) covers 111 countries A-Z, with *c.* 400 words of economic notes (plus exchange rates) on each; country index.

33 (4/9) (02)
Notes et études documentaires. Paris, La Documentation Française, Sécretariat Général du Gouvernement, Direction de la Documentation, 138F. p.a.

A wide-ranging series of monographs, political, constitutional, cultural and often economic surveys of various countries, as well as aspects of France itself. Thus *La situation économique de l'Algérie* (no. 3406-3407, 6th July 1967. 81p. tables, graphs, maps) is a comprehensive up-to-date survey in 3 pts.: Les aptitudes naturelles de l'Algérie au developpement économique—L'économie algérienne avant l'independance—L'économie algérienne après l'independance. 40 numbered tables, and numerous others; 6 maps. Bibliography, p. 81.

33 (4/9) (02)
UNITED STATES. DEPARTMENT OF COMMERCE. BUSINESS AND DEFENSE SERVICES ADMINISTRATION. Overseas business reports. Washington, Superintendent of Documents, 1962-. ea. 15*c.*; $13 (foreign, $18) p.a.

Supersedes *World trade information service* (1954-62. 5 pts.). Includes the following series: *Basic data on the economy of . . .; Establishing a business on . . .; U.S. trade with . . .; Investment in . . .;* and *Trade regulations . . .* *Basic data on the economy of the Republic of South Africa* (October 1966. 24p. 14 tables, map. (OBR 66-71), superseding OBR 63-3, provides concise data in 8 sections, with a bibliography of 27 items. *Establishing a business in France* (November 1966. 19p. tables. (OBR 66-76), superseding WTIS, pt. 1, no. 62-68, includes a bibliography. *U.S. trade with major world areas, January - September 1965-66* (December 1966. 16p.) consists entirely of tables. Valuable as brief, up-to-date statements. (The series is not listed in detail in the *Monthly catalog of United States government publications,* but only as a serial.) *International commerce* (weekly) announces new OBR titles and provides a half-yearly check-list (*e.g.,* 10th July 1967, p. 13-34).

The Department of Commerce also publishes a quarterly or half-yearly series of *Economic summaries* for some 82 countries, each 12-30p.; $1.50. Listed in the Department's *Semi-annual checklist* (*e.g.,* July 1967. 39p.), these reports are prepared on the spot by U.S. Foreign Service officials.

33 (4/9) (02)
WOYTINSKY, W. S., and **WOYTINSKY, E. S.
World commerce and governments;** trends and
outlook. New York, Twentieth Century Fund,
1955. lii, 907p. maps, diagrs.

Parts: 1. Trade—2. Transport—3. Governments.

————**World population and production;**
trends and outlook. New York, Twentieth
Century Fund, 1953. lxxii, 1268p. maps, diagrs.

Parts: 1. Man and his environment—2. World
needs and resources.—3. Agriculture—4. Energy
and mining—5. Manufactures.

These two volumes constitute "a statistical
picture of the collective resources, as well as the
economic performance and promise of the full
array of the nations of the world". Tables in the
first-named volume include figures, in most cases,
to 1952; in the second, to 1950. Each has a list of
sources and an index. *Annals of the Association
of American Geographers* (v. 46, no. 3, September 1956, p. 366-7) notes factual errors, stating
that *World population and production* "does not
profess to be more than a compendium and a
commentary only a single degree removed from
raw fact".

33 (4/9) (058)
BARCLAYS BANK D.C.O. Overseas survey . . .;
covering the trade and economic conditions which
prevailed during the year . . . in the overseas
territories in which the Barclays Group of Banks
is represented. London, Barclays Bank D.C.O.
Annual. illus., tables. *Gratis.*

A well illustrated economic survey of 45 countries and areas (1967 ed.), 20 of them are African
and 16 West Indian territories; satistics up to
1966.
Supplemented by a monthly *Overseas review.*
Barclays Bank D.C.O. also produces economic
surveys for individual countries at 2 or 3-yearly
intervals (e.g., *Libya; Sudan; Sierra Leone;
Ghana; Nigeria; Uganda; Kenya; Tanganyika;
Botswana, Lesotho and Swaziland; Zambia;
Malawi; Seychelles; Mauritius*).

33 (4/9) (058)
UNITED STATES. Department of Economic and
Social Affairs. **World economic survey.** New
York, United Nations, 1949-. Annual.

Initially as *World economic report,* a continuation of the League of Nations *World economic
survey* (1927-44. 11v.).
World economic survey, 1965 (1966), the 18th
issue, conforms to the pattern laid down since
1955; it contains a long-term study (pt. 1. The
financing of economic development) and a current
view (pt. 2. Current economic developments,
covering events of 1965 and early 1966 in three
major groups of countries,—developed market
economies; developing countries and centrally
planned economies). 93 tables; sources and notes.

33 (4/9) (083.4)
UNITED NATIONS. Statistical Office. **Current
economic indicators:** a quarterly statistical re-
view of developments in the world economy.
New York, United Nations, 1961-. v. 1, no. 1-.
Quarterly. ea. $1; $4 p.a.

Parts: 1. The world economy—2. The underdeveloped areas—3. Selected industrial countries
(Canada, France, Federal Republic of Germany,
Japan, U.K., U.S.A.). Each issue has a list of
principal published sources and notes on tables,
giving sources.

Developing countries

33 (4/9-77):016
HAZLEWOOD, A., *comp.* **The economics of
"under-developed" areas:** an annotated reading
list of books, articles and official publications.
2nd enl. ed. Published for the [Oxford Univ.]
Institute of Commonwealth Studies by Oxford
Univ. Press, London, 1959 (& reprints). xii, 156p.
10s. 6d.

First published 1954.
The 2nd ed. (1027 numbered items) adds *c.* 400
items for the period 1953 to early 1958. Asterisked
items are introductory. 30-word annotations; gives
contents lists of reports and additional references
in annotations. Index of authors and editors;
index of places. An excellent example of its kind.
Sequel:

*The developing nations: a guide to information
sources concerning their economic, political,
technical and social problems,* by E. G. ReQua
and J. Statham (Detroit, Michigan, Gale Research
Co., 1965. 339p. maps. $8.75) has *c.* 800 annotated
entries in 13 sections (1. Economic development,
p. 17-65; 2. Economic assistance, p. 69-98).
Author and title indexes. Expensive, compared
with Hazlewood; plenty of blank space.

The Ministry of Overseas Development Library's *Development index: list of periodical
articles* (1967-. Weekly (irregular) lists *c.* 20 articles per issue; arranged under subject headings,
A-Z.

33 (4/9-77):016
**INSTITUT UNIVERSITAIRE DES TERRI-
TOIRES D'OUTRE-MER,** Antwerp. **Recueil
bibliographique tiers-monde.** Antwerp,
I.U.T.O., 1964. iv, 157p.

About 1,000 items, classified by U.D.C., on the
developing countries. Lists books and especially
periodical articles in Western European languages.
330.114.2: Economic development, p. 9-41.
Material up to early 1963. Author index.
Appendix: 'Organisations and revues interested
in developing countries'.

33 (4/9-77):016
**ORGANISATION FOR ECONOMIC CO-OPERA-
TION AND DEVELOPMENT.** Development
Centre. **[Bibliographies.]** Paris, O.E.C.D., 1964-.
Mimeographed. *Gratis.*

Bibliographie sur l'Équateur. 1965. [iii], 85,
[4]p. 727 items.
Bibliographie sur la Guinée. 1965. iii, 46p.
c. 400 items.
Bibliographie sur l'Iran. 1965. xi, 305p. 2217
items.
Bibliographie sur le Pérou. 1965. iv, 211p. 1572
items.
Essai d'une bibliographie sur la Côte d'Ivoire.
1964. iv, 122p. *c.* 1,000 items.

Arrangement varies, but contents are usually grouped. Thus, *Bibliographie sur l'Iran* lists periodical articles and books in 11 classes. Appended: author index; list of chief journals cited; list of periodicals published in Iran. No annotations. Material up to 1964.

33 (4/9-77) (02)
INTERNATIONAL BANK FOR RECONSTRUC-TION AND DEVELOPMENT. [Economic development reports]. Baltimore, Md., Johns Hopkins Press; London, Oxford Univ. Press, 1951-.

Reports of General Survey Missions to various underdeveloped countries, organised by I.B.R.D. at the request of the governments concerned. These missions undertake a general review of the countries' economic potentialities and propose recommendations on long-term development programmes. Not all the reports are published by the Johns Hopkins Press (e.g., *Report on the economic aspects of Malaysia.* Kuala Lumpur, Government Printer, 1963. $2.50). Some of the series are the only reliable and lengthy economic surveys of the countries concerned. The reports run to 450-500 pages each and are supported by maps, tables and adequate indexes:

The basis of a development program for Colombia. 1952. 40s.
The economic development of British Guiana. 1953. 48s.
The economic development of Ceylon. 1953. 60s.
The economic development of Guatemala. 1952. 40s.
The economic development of Iraq. 1952. 40s.
The economic development of Jamaica. 1952. 40s.
The economic development of Jordan. 1957. 60s.
The economic development of Kuwait. 1965. 52s.
The economic development of Libya. 1960. 60s.
The economic development of Malaya. 1955. 60s.
The economic development of Mexico. 1953. 80s.
The economic development of Morocco. 1966. 68s.
The economic development of Nicaragua. 1953. 40s.
The economic development of Nigeria. 1955. 60s.
The economic development of the territory of Papua and New Guinea. 1965. 68s.
The economic development of Spain. 1963. 68s.
The economic development of Syria. 1955. 60s.
The economic development of Tanganyika. 1961. 68s.
The economic development of Uganda. 1962. 68s.
The economic development of Venezuela. 1961. 68s.
A public development program for Thailand. 1959. 48s.
Report on Cuba. 1951. 60s.
Surinam: recommendations for a ten-year development program. 1952. 40s.

33 (4/9-77) (083.4)
INSTITUT NATIONAL DE LA STATISTIQUE ET DES ÉTUDES ÉCONOMIQUES. Données statistiques. Paris, Imprimerie Nationale. Quarterly. ea. 10F; 35F p.a. (foreign, 44F).

Covers 17 non-European countries "d'expression française dont les échanges intéressent le plus souvent la 'Zone franc'". Excludes French West Indies and Réunion. Sections: Foreign trade (countries; commodities—Industrial production; mining; electricity—Transport—Prices—Money and credit—Public finance—External aid—Population.

33 (4/9-77) (083.4)
UNITED STATES. AGENCY FOR INTERNA-TIONAL DEVELOPMENT. Statistics and Reports Division. **A.I.D. economic data book** [series]. Washington, 1967-. tables, diagrs., maps. Loose-leaf.

Africa.
Far East.
Latin America.
Near East and South Asia.
Aims primarily "to serve the international programs and operational needs of the Agency . . . (*Preface*). The section on Jordan in the *Near East* volume consists of 9p., mostly tables giving 1961-1966 (prelim.) figures, and covering such matters as selected economic trends, central government finances, and balance of payments. Kept up to date by revised data sheets.

Europe

33 (4):016
ECONOMIC COMMISSION FOR EUROPE. Studies and other publications issued under the auspices of the Economic Commission for Europe, 1947-1966. New York, United Nations, 1967. viii, 81p. (E/ECE/642). $1.

Items in 11 sections: A. Work of the Commission as a whole—B. General economic problems—C. Agriculture—D. Energy—E. Housing, building and planning—F. Industry—G. Statistics—H. Timber—I. Trade—J. Transport—K. Water problems. Brief notes on subject scope of items and statement of language; no prices, but gives sales number. Subject index.

33 (4):016
ORGANISATION FOR ECONOMIC CO-OPERA-TION AND DEVELOPMENT. Catalogue of publications, 1966. Paris, O.E.C.D., 1966. 84p.

Lists publications on sale as at 30th June 1966. Includes o.p. items; some entries are annotated. Parts: 1. Economy—2. International trade and payments—3. Statistics—4. Development—5. Agriculture. Food. Fisheries—6. Energy—7. Industry—8. Manpower and social affairs—9. Education and science—10. General information. Index of titles and authors. Supplements to be issued until new catalogue in 1968.

33 (4):016
UNIVERSITÉ LIBRE DE BRUXELLES. Institut de Sociologie. **Bibliographie internationale d'économie régionale.** Brussels, the Institute, 1964. 757, [7]p. 690 Belg. fr.

About 4,000 briefly annotated entries for books and periodical articles on regional economics, 1945-60. Almost entirely concerned with 10 European countries, A-Z (Germany, England (p. 157-223), Belgium, Spain, France, Italy, Netherlands, Poland, Russia, Yugoslavia); short sections on Asia (p. 717-23), Australia and New Zealand (p. 725-9). Under each country, usual subdivisions: bibliography; demography; descriptions; theoretical studies; regional economics; statistical sources; regions. No index, but detailed contents list. To be kept up to date periodically.
English edition has title: *International bibliography on regional economy.*

DEWHURST, J. F., *and others.* **Europe's needs and resources:** trends and prospects in eighteen countries. New York, Twentieth Century Fund; London, Macmillan, 1961 (reprinted 1962). xxvi, 1198p. tables, charts, maps. 84s.

A compendium in 28 chapters, concentrating on post-war Western Europe,—the O.E.C.D. countries minus Yugoslavia and Turkey, plus Finland. 19 contributors. Covers aspects from population, manpower, output and expenditures to productivity, technology and economic integration. About 350 tables and 120 charts; no bibliography, but states sources of statistics; footnote references. Analytical index includes references to tables. No list of maps. Well produced.

A companion volume, also by J. F. Dewhurst and others, is: *America's needs and resources: a new survey* (New York, Twentieth Century Fund, 1955. xxix, 1148p. $10).

33 (4) (058)
ORGANISATION FOR ECONOMIC CO-OPERATION AND DEVELOPMENT. Economic surveys. Paris, O.E.C.D., 1953. Annual. ea. 5s.; 63s. the set.

Previously as *Economic conditions in member and associated countries,* and originally part of the O.E.E.C. annual report, 1949-52.
The 1965-66 series covers 22 countries: Austria; Belgium & Luxembourg; Canada; Denmark; France; Germany; Greece; Iceland; Ireland; Italy; Japan; Netherlands; Norway; Portugal; Spain; Sweden; Switzerland; Turkey; United Kingdom; United States; Yugoslavia.
The pamphlet on *Turkey* (1966. [i], 65p. 24 tables) has 3 parts: 1. Economy, trade, balance of payments. 1966 annual programme and budget —2. 'Development' policies—3. Prospects and conclusions. Statistical annex (1964 or 1965 figures). No index, bibliography or maps.

33 (4) (058)
UNITED NATIONS. ECONOMIC COMMISSION FOR EUROPE. Economic survey of Europe [in] 1946/47-. Geneva (then, New York), United Nations, 1948-. Annual.

In one volume up to the 1960v. Since then, in 2 parts. Latest pt. 1, The *European economy in 1965* (viii, 102p. 67 tables, 11 charts. 1966. 22s. 6d.) has 2 chapters: 1. Recent economic developments in Eastern Europe and the Soviet Union—2. Recent economic developments in Western Europe. Latest pt. 2: *Economic survey of Europe in 1965.* Pt. 2. *Incomes in postwar Europe: a study of policies, growth and distribution* (1967. v.p. $6.50; $8). This covers both Western and Eastern Europe; many tables; no index.
Kept up to date by the E.C.E.'s *Economic bulletin for Europe,* published in the 2nd, 3rd and 4th quarters of each year.

33 (4):061
UNITED NATIONS. List of institutions in the field of applied economics in E.C.E. countries. . . . Geneva, United Nations, 1966. [iii], 107p. (E/ECE/615). Mimeographed.

28 countries, A-Z. Entries under each fall into two categories: (*a*) research institutes specializing in, or at least partly carrying out, scientific research in problems of applied economics, and (*b*) economic universities or economic faculties of universities. For the U.S.S.R. (p. 78-89),—28 research institutes and 18 universities; for the U.K. (p. 90-91),—8 research institutes and 12 universities.

33 (4) (083.4)
ORGANISATION FOR ECONOMIC CO-OPERATION AND DEVELOPMENT. Main economic indicators. Paris, O.E.C.D., 1965-. Monthly, with quarterly supplements. ea. 9s.; 105s. p.a.

Replaces the O.E.C.D. bulletin, *General statistics* (last published January 1965).
Contains *c.* 1,500 major economic indicators appearing in nearly 300 statistical bulletins published by the 21 O.E.C.D. member countries. The quarterly supplements record industrial production and consumer price indices.
Retrospective coverage: *Main economic indicators, 1955-1964* (Paris, O.E.C.D., 1966. 459p. 32s.), with supplements, each covering a group of countries (*e.g.,* Supplement no. 6, February 1967, gives 1955/65 indicators for Japan, U.S.A., Austria, Italy, Netherlands and Sweden).

33 (4) (091)
The Cambridge economic history of Europe. Cambridge, Univ. Press, 1942-. v. 1-. illus., tables, maps.

v. 1: *The agrarian life of the Middle Ages.* 2nd ed., edited by M. M. Postan, xvi, 872p. 75s.
v. 2: *Trade and industry in the Middle Ages,* edited by M. M. Postan and E. E. Rich. 1952. xv, [1], 604p. 60s.
v. 3: *Economic organization and policies in the Middle Ages;* edited by M. M. Postan and others. 1963. xvi, 696p. 70s.
v. 4: *The economy of expanding Europe in the sixteenth and seventeenth centuries;* edited by E. E. Rich and C. H. Wilson. 1967. xxxii, 642p. 75s.
v. 5: In preparation.
v. 6: *The Industrial Revolution and after: incomes, population and technological change;* edited by H. J. Habbakuk and M. M. Postan, 1965. 2 pts. 105s.
The work was originally planned by Sir John Clapham and Eileen Power, the aim being to provide an authoritative survey of an aspect omitted from the Cambridge mediaeval and modern histories. General editors of the 2nd ed.: M. M. Postan and H. J. Habbakuk. V. 3 (critically reviewed in *The economist,* 11th May 1963, p. 547-8) has 8 chapters, each by a specialist; chapter bibliographics, p. 603-74. V. 6 is first of a group of 3 v. designed to cover the economic history of the Western world during and since the Industrial Revolution. The 2 pts. of v. 6 are by 12 contributors,—6 British, 4 U.S. and 2 French. Terminal date is the middle of the 20th century.

British Commonwealth

33 (41-44)
COMMONWEALTH ECONOMIC COMMITTEE. Commonwealth development and financing.

London, H.M. Stationery Office, 1961-. no. 1-. illus., tables, map.

1. *Canada*. 1961. o.p.
2. *Federation of Rhodesia and Nyasaland*. 1961. o.p.
3. *Pakistan*. 1961. 8s.
4. *New Zealand*. 1963. 7s. 6d.
5. *Nigeria*. 1963. 7s. 6d.
6. *Australia*. 1963. 7s. 6d.
7. *India*. 1963. 7s. 6d.
8. *Jamaica*. 1964. 7s. 6d.
9. *Uganda*. 1966. 7s. 6d.
10. *Malta*. 1966. 7s. 6d.
11. *Kenya*. 1967. 10s.

Sections of no. 9, *Uganda* (66p.): The economy in brief—Sources and uses of investment funds—Progress in main sectors. Summary. Bibliography of principal references.

British Colonies

33 (41-5)

GREAT BRITAIN. COLONIAL OFFICE. An economic survey of the colonial territories. London, H.M. Stationery Office, 1952-55. 7v. maps.

v. 1: *Central African and High Commission territories*. 1952. 25s.
v. 2: *East African territories*. 1954. 32s. 6d.
v. 3: *West African territories*. 1952. 25s.
v. 4: *West Indian and American territories*. 1953. 40s.
v. 5: *Far Eastern territories*. 1955. 27s. 6d.
v. 6: *Mediterranean and Pacific territories*. 1953. 20s.
v. 7: *Products of the colonial territories*. 1952. 42s.

Follows the pre-war annual surveys, the last of which was *An economic survey of the colonial empire*, 1937 (1940).

These regional volumes have sections on background, productive activities, finance and trade, and developments covering the period from 1938 onwards. V. 7 gives more detailed information on commodities in all territories. Now chiefly of historical value.

Great Britain

33 (410):016

SOCIETY OF INVESTMENT ANALYSIS. A bibliography for investment and economic analysis. London, the Society, 1965. [104]p. Ring binding.

A handy guide to c. 1,200 current economic items on both the national economy and individual industries, up to autumn 1964. Special classification scheme; classes 000-900. Two columns, one for title, the other for brief annotation. No indexes. Aims "to provide sufficient source material on any subject of prospective interest [*e.g.,* balance of payments; capital market] to the investment analyst or to anyone else undertaking a general study of industrial or economic conditions to enable him to produce a well informed assessment" (*Preface*).

33 (410) (058)

GREAT BRITAIN. H.M. TREASURY. Economic report on 1965. London, H.M. Stationery Office, 1966. 38p. tables, diagrs., graphs. 5s. Annual.

Issued as a supplement to *Economic trends,* no. 149, March 1966 (produced by Central Statistical Office), and so published from March 1963 onwards, annually. Previously (1947-62) as *Economic survey,* a Command Paper.

The 1965 *Report* has 6 main headings: 1. The course of the year—2. The balance of payments—3. Changes in demand—4. Production and manpower—5. Incomes, costs and prices—6. Monetary developments. Statistical appendix of 14 tables.

In February of each year the *National Institute economic review* (London, National Institute of Economic and Social Research, 1959-. Quarterly) is devoted to 'The economic situation: an annual review', with a calendar of economic events of the previous year and a statistical appendix.

33 (410) (083.4)

GREAT BRITAIN. MINISTRY OF LABOUR. Statistics on incomes, prices, employment and production. London, H.M.S.O., 1952-. no. 1, April 1952-.

See entry at 331 (410).

33 (410) (083.4)

LEWES, F. M. M. Statistics of the British economy. London, Allen & Unwin, 1967. 200p. tables. 30s.

Chapters: 1. Introduction—2. Labour—3. Production—4. Distribution and household spending—5. Transport—6. Companies—7. Finance—8. Overseas trade and payments—9. National accounting. Statistical tables up to 1964. Each chapter has an appended bibliography ('Publications'; 'Commentaries') of 2-5 pages. Author is Lecturer in Economic and Social Statistics, Univ. of Exeter.

33 (410) (083.4)

LONDON AND CAMBRIDGE ECONOMIC SERVICE. The British economy: key statistics, 1900-1964. London, Times Publishing Co. 1965. 28p. tables. 10s. 6d.

Published for the London and Cambridge Economic Service.

Plans to carry the eight tables currently published in the *London and Cambridge economic bulletin* back through 1900, with annual data as far as possible, "and for the same space of years to add 7 new tables of which 6 supplement existing tables,—those on Personal income and expenditure, for example, being supplemented by one on Taxation—and the last present some comparable series for the United States" (*The economic journal*, v. 75, no. 299, September 1965, p. 605-6). Indispensable as "an abstract and chronicle of our time". 15 tables. Sources indicated; explanatory notes; index to tables.

The survey covering 1960-66 (1967. 28p. 10s. 6d.) similarly has 15 tables for more than 200 economic and social series.

33 (410) (083.4)

MITCHELL, B. R., and DEANE, P. Abstracts of British historical statistics. Cambridge, Univ. Press, 1962. xiv, 513p. tables. 52s. 6d.

Restricted to economic statistics. Earliest figure is for 1199, "but for many topics continuous statistical material begins in the eighteenth century, and for most our starting point has been within the nineteenth century (*General introduction*). Less full on Ireland and eighteenth-century Scotland. 16 sections: 1. Population and vital statistics—2. The labour force—3. Agriculture—4. Coal—5. Iron and steel—6. Tin, copper and lead—7. Textile industries—8. Transport—9. Building—10. Miscellaneous production statistics—11. Overseas trade—12. Wages and standard of living—13. National income and expenditure—14. Public finance (4 pages of introductory text; 17 tables)—15. Banking and insurance—16. Prices. 194 tables; sources stated. Bibliography, p. 50-52, 499-502; analytical subject index. Well produced.

33 (410) (091)

CLAPHAM, Sir J. H. An economic history of modern Britain. Cambridge, Univ. Press, 1926-38. 3v. ea. 70s.

v. 1: *The early railway age, 1820-50.* 1926 (2nd ed., reprinted with corrections, 1939).
v. 2: *Free trade and steel, 1850-86.* 1932.
v. 3: *Machines and national rivalries (1887-1914); with an epilogue (1914-1929).* 1938.

A standard work. Ample footnote references to the literature throughout. Each volume has a detailed analytical index.

33 (410) (091)

The Economic history review. Published for the Economic History Society by Oosthoek, Utrecht, 1927-. v. 1, no. 1-. 3 p.a. 47s. 6d. p.a.

Mainly concerned with British and Netherlands economic history. V. 18, no. 2, August 1965 has articles on p. 225-396, and reviews and bibliography, p. 397-474. Reviews of 49 books (21 British, 16 other countries and 12 Low countries); periodical literature. V. 15, no. 3, April 1963, included the annual 'List of publications on the economic history of Great Britain and Ireland published in 1961', by J. Thirsk and F. M. L. Thompson (p. 610-34), noting more than 600 items, under: 1. Original documents—2. Books and pamphlets—3. articles in periodicals.

A key to earlier volumes: *Economic history review: an index of the first series, v. 1-18, 1927-48* (Utrecht, Oosthoek, [1965?]. 59p.).

33 (410) (091)

HANSON, L. W. Contemporary printed sources for British and Irish economic history, 1701-1750. Cambridge, Univ. Press, 1963. xxiii, [1], 978p. £10 10s.

"Planned and almost completed in its first stage by the late Henry Higgs who envisaged a series of volumes, of which the first, the Bibliography of Economics, 1751-1775, was published in 1935 . . . " (*Introduction*).

6,497 (numbered) + 15 items. Chronological order; under each year, regular sub-divisions (General (England, Scotland, Ireland)—Agriculture—Manufactures—Commerce—Colonies (internal affairs)—Finance—Transport—Social conditions, further divided. Titles are transcribed in full; bibliographical notes. Many official publications (Bills, proclamations, etc.). 66 library locations, including 5 in U.S.A. Index of titles (p. 715-931); general index (authors; subjects).

Scotland

33 (411) (047)

GREAT BRITAIN. SCOTTISH COUNCIL (Development and Industry). **Inquiry into the Scottish economy, 1960-1961:** report of a Committee . . . under the chairmanship of J. N. Toothill. Edinburgh, Scottish Council, [1961]. 203, lxxivp. 25s.

Aims "to review the present position and future prospects of the Scottish economy . . ., to draw conclusions and to make recommendations" (*Preface*). Covers industry, manpower, environment and regional development measures. 38 valuable appendices, with data on a wide range of subjects, from unemployment to climate. Index.

The Scottish Council (Development and Industry)'s *Scottish industry: an account of what Scotland makes and where she makes it* (1953 232p. illus., maps. 25s.) is edited by C. A. Oakley. The Scottish Council's *Natural resources in Scotland: symposium at the Royal Society of Edinburgh,* October 31 to November 2, 1960 (1961. ix, 796p. 105s.) consists of 51 specialised contributions, some with bibliographies appended.

Another co-operative effort is *The Scottish economy: a statistical account of Scottish life,* by members of the staff of Glasgow University; edited by A. K. Cairncross (Cambridge, Univ. Press, 1954. 336p. 30s.).

Annual surveys are available in '*The Glasgow Herald' trade review* (1966. 3s. 6d.) and the Clydesdale and North of Scotland's *Annual survey of economic conditions in Scotland.*

33 (411) (091)

MARWICK, W. H. "A bibliography of Scottish economic history, 1951-1962." In *Economic history review,* 2nd series, v. 16, no. 1, 1963, p. 147-54.

An evaluative running commentary. Sections: General—Medieval—The seventeenth century—The eighteenth century—The nineteenth and twentieth century.

Preceded by the author's contributions in *Economic history review,* 2nd series, v. 4, no. 3, 1952, p. 377-82, and v. 3, no. 1, 1931, p. 117-37.

Ireland

33 (415)

PRENDEVILLE, P. L. "A short bibliography of Irish economic history." In *Economic history review,* v. 3, no. 2, October 1931, p. 274-92; v. 3, no. 3, October 1932, p. 402-16; and v. 4, no. 1, October 1933, p. 81-90.

The three articles are respectively entitled "From the earliest times to the 16th century", "The seventeenth and eighteenth centuries", and "The nineteenth century". Running commentary.

Northern Ireland

33 (416)

ISLES, K. S., and CUTHBERT, N. **An economic survey of Northern Ireland.** Belfast, H.M. Stationery Office, 1957. xxv, 646p.

By the Professor of Economics and Senior Lecturer in Economics in the Queen's University of Belfast. Pts.: 1. The general level of prosperity —2. Factors controlling economic development—3. Economic considerations relating to policy. The standard work. No references or bibliography. 59 tables in statistical appendix; analytical index.

Annual economic review is published by *The Belfast newsletter.*

Eire

33 (417)

EIRE. NATIONAL INDUSTRIAL ECONOMIC COUNCIL. **Report on economic situation,** 1965. Dublin, Stationery Office, 1965. 77p. tables.

Text supported by 25 tables. Statistics up to 1964, with retrospective figures back to 1960. Appended tables, p. 55-77.

An annual economic survey is published by *The Irish times.*

England

33 (420) (091):016

HALL, H., *ed.* **A select bibliography for the study, sources and literature of English mediæval economic history.** Compiled by a Seminar of the London School of Economics under the supervision of Hubert Hall. London, King, 1914 (reprinted New York, B. Franklin, 1960). xiii, 350p. (Studies in economics and political science. Series of bibliographies, 41). 132s.

A classified bibliography of 3,200 items, with author and title index. Appended lists of learned social journals and of periodicals. Still of considerable value on manuscript sources.

33 (420) (091):016

WILLIAMS, J. B. **A guide to the printed materials for English social and economic history, 1750-1850.** New York, Columbia Univ. Press, 1926 (reprinted New York, Octagon Books, Inc.). 2v. $35.

About 7,500 selected entries—Pt. 1, 'Works of general reference' (including bibliographies and catalogues; encyclopaedias; local histories; biographies; in 11 sections)—pt. 2, Special subjects (economic theory; economic conditions and questions; industry; social and economic conditions and movements; social political theory and movements; sections 12-16). All items are briefly annotated. V. 2 includes author (plus brief title) and non-analytical subject indexes.

33 (424+427)

GREAT BRITAIN. DEPARTMENT OF ECONOMIC AFFAIRS. **The North West:** a regional study. London, H.M. Stationery Office, 1965. xii, 178p. tables, diagrs., map. 18s.

——— ———**The problems of Merseyside:** an appendix to 'The North West: a regional study'. London, H.M. Stationery Office, 1965. iv, 83p. tables. 8s. 6d.

The Merseyside report deals with the persistently high unemployment. 27 statistical tables compare with the North West region and the country as a whole.

——— ———**The West Midlands:** a regional study. London, H.M. Stationery Office, 1965. xii, 115p. illus., tables, maps. 12s. 6d.

6 chapters and summary; statistical appendix, p. 78-115 (36 tables on economic planning, population and employment); 20 maps, plus a folding map.

Wales

33 (429)

THOMAS, B. **The Welsh economy:** studies in expansion. Cardiff, Univ. of Wales Press, 1962. xiv, [i] 217p. tables, maps. 30s.

10 chapters, with 88 supporting tables and 18 graphs. Statistics up to 1958. Some footnote references. Analytical subject index, p. 205-16; index of names.

Welsh economic statistics: a handbook of sources, by A. Martin and J. P. Lewis (Cardiff, University College of South Wales and Monmouthshire, 1953. viii, 96p.) is a fairly comprehensive survey. A welcome feature is the extensive use of analytical entries where certain publications cover varied and unlikely items.

German Federal Republic

33 (43-15)

DEUTSCHE BUNDESBANK. **Report of the Deutsche Bundesbank** for the year . . . Frankfurt am Main, the Bank. Annual.

The 1966 report (vi, 164p. 1967) has two main parts (A. General. Economic trends and Central Bank policy—B. Explanation of the Deutsche Bundesbank's annual statement for 1966) and full supporting statistical tables.

Kept up to date by the *Monthly report of the Bundesbank* (1949-). This consists mainly of statistical tables, in 12 sections, preceded by survey articles. English edition is published about 3 weeks after the German.

33 (43-15)

Wirtschaft und Statistik. [Bonn], Statistisches Bundesamt. Monthly. ea. DM.7.20; DM.81.50 p.a.

About 50 pages of survey articles (economic survey; graphs on economic developments; economic indicators; price index) and 80-odd pages of statistical tables, with figures for previous months and years and cumulative statistical contents for the year,—a similar pattern to that of the U.S. *Current business.*

France

33 (44)

FRANCE. MINISTÈRE DE L'ÉCONOMIE ET DES FINANCES. Statistiques et études financières. Paris, Imprimerie Nationale, 1949-. no. 1-. Monthly. ea. 4F; 40F p.a. (with Supplément, 70F).

Consists of survey articles, with many tables and graphs, followed by a lengthy section of statistical tables.

The *Supplément* (1949-. Monthly) is devoted to a single article (*e.g.*, no. 216, December 1966: 'Balance des paiements de la France métropolitaine avec les divers pays étrangers en 1965'), supported by numerous tables.

The Bibliothèque de la Chambre de Commerce de Paris produces a biennial bibliography, *Economie régionale* (1957-).

Italy

33 (45)

BANCO DI ROMA. Review of the economic conditions in Italy. Rome, the Bank, 1947-. v. 1, no. 1-. 6 p.a.

V. 21, no. 1, January 1967 comprises 3 articles, 'Economic survey' (reviewing two months of economic activity in Italy), 2 book-reviews and a lengthy statistical section (p. 57-79; 11 main tables).

Spain

33 (46)

BANCO ESPANOL DE CREDITO. Anuario del mercado español. Madrid, the Bank. Annual.

A detailed regional analysis of the Spanish economy.

The most reliable guide to the social and economic history of Spain is *Historia social y económica de España y América*, edited by J. Vicens Vives (Barcelona, Editorial Teide, 1957-59. 4v. in 5).

Portugal

33 (469)

Bibliografia sobre a economia portuguesa. 1948/1949-. Lisbon, Institute Nacional de Estatística. Annual. (v. 12: 1960. 1967).

Annual bibliography of the Portuguese economy. V. 12 is compiled by A. D. Guerreiro.

U.S.S.R.

33 (47)

UNITED STATES. CONGRESS. Joint Economic Committee. **Current economic indicators for the U.S.S.R.** Washington, U.S. Government Printing Office, 1965. xii, 220p. 55c.

Continues *Dimensions of Soviet economic*

power (1962) and *Current economic indicators for the U.S.S.R.* (1964).

An impressive compilation of statistical material and interpretative articles. The best source for current Russian economic statistics in English. Includes a valuable bibliography of *c.* 700 recent Russian publications.

Geography, resources and natural conditions in the Soviet Union: an annotated bibliography of selected basic books in Russian, by C. D. Harris (Chicago, Dept. of Geography, Univ. of Chicago, 1962. 45p. Mimeographed) is an annotated list of 176 items in 11 sections; no index.

B. S. Wynar's article, "Pre-Soviet bibliographies on economics" (*The library quarterly,* v. 33, no. 3, July 1965, p. 258-69) covers general bibliographies, agriculture, industry, statistics and other subjects. 49 references; 3 tables.

Finland

33 (480)

FINLAND. MINISTRY OF FINANCE. Division for Economic Affairs. **Economic survey.** Helsinki, Akateeminen Kirkakauppa, 1948-. Annual.

Supplement to the annual Budget proposal. The 1966 issue surveys the economy in 1965 and 1966, with prospects for 1967. 95 tables, 3 graphs. Finnish, Swedish and English editions.

Norway

33 (481)

NORWAY. STATISTISK SENTRALBYRA. Okonomisk utsyn over året . . . Oslo, Statistisk Sentralbyrå. Annual.

Annual economy survey, with summary in English.

The 1966 survey (published 1967) has two main parts: world economic situation, and Norway (5 sections). Supporting tables, with retrospective figures. Appended list of 55 publications issued since the previous annual.

—— —— **Norges økonomi etter Krigen . . .** Oslo, Statistisk Sentralbyrå, 1965. 437p. N.kr.15.

The Norwegian post-war economy, 1946-63. 12 chapters, with summary in English. 88 tables and graphs. Footnote references.

Sweden

33 (485)

KONJUNKTURINSTITUTET, Stockholm. **The Swedish economy.** Stockholm, Konjunkturinstitutet. 3 p.a. ea. Sw.kr. 6.50; Sw.kr. 18 p.a.

Issues 1 and 2 of each year deal with the Swedish national budget. Issue 3 concerns the general economy, in 8 chapters. Many tables and graphs; sources and notes. In English.

The Svenska Handelsbanken, Stockholm, publishes an annual *Sweden's economy: an economic survey.*

Denmark

33 (489)
DENMARK. MINISTRY OF FOREIGN AFFAIRS. Economic survey of Denmark. Copenhagen, Schultz Forlag. Annual.

The 1966 economic survey (published 1966) has 8 sections (*e.g.,* 1. Main trends of the Danish economy in 1965 and 1966; 4. Agriculture; 7. Prospects of economic growth in the late 'sixties). 75 supporting tables and graphs. In English.

Switzerland

33 (494)
SWISS CREDIT BANK. The Swiss economy in . . . Zurich, the Bank. Annual. *Gratis.*

The 1965 issue, published 1966, has text in three sections: 1. General survey—2. Financial developments—3. Industry reports. Appendices: Economic indicators; Swiss stock and bond prices. Tables; graphs; bar diagrams.

The Union Bank of Switzerland's *Switzerland economic survey* (Zurich, the Bank) is also annual.

Asia

33 (5):016
UNITED NATIONS. ECONOMIC COMMISSION FOR ASIA AND THE FAR EAST. Guide to Asian economic statistics. Bangkok, E.C.A.F.E., 1957. 272p. Mimeographed. (E/CN.11/447).

19 subject groups, ranging from agriculture, forestry and fishing to national income. Annex (p. 271-2): 'List of main publications of international agencies which regularly or occasionally contain economic statistics for ECAFE countries'.

33 (5):016
————. ECAFE Library. **Asian bibliography.** January-June 1952-. Bangkok, [Economic Commission for Asia and the Far East], 1952-. v. 1, no. 1-. 2 p.a. Mimeographed.

A list of ECAFE Library's selected accessions dealing with Asia and the Far East. About 400 items in each issue; arranged by U.D.C., with area index; subject sub-divisions under areas. Includes many government and institutional publications. Titles of publications in Asian languages are translated.

33 (5) (058)
UNITED NATIONS. ECONOMIC COMMISSION FOR ASIA AND THE FAR EAST. Economic survey of Asia and the Far East, 1947-. Bangkok, 1948-. Annual. (1966 (published 1967). $3.50.).

Also issued as no. 4 of the quarterly *Economic bulletin for Asia and the Far East* each year. Pt. 1 of the 1966 issue: 'Aspects of the finance of development'; pt. 2: 'Current economic developments' (in individual countries). Appendix: 'Asian economic statistics', p. 221-82; '*Economic bulletin for Asia and the Far East':* index of articles.

Far East

33 (5-012) (058)
'Far Eastern Economic Review' . . . **yearbook.** Hong Kong, Far Eastern Economic Review, 1960-. illus., tables, graphs, maps. Annual. (1966. 22s.).

A mine of annual information on Asian countries, from Pakistan to Brunei and the Philippines (but not Russia in Asia). The 8th yearbook, 1967 reviews events in 1966, with prospects for 1967. Main sections: The region—Far Eastern round up (chronology, November 1965-November 1966)—Food and population—Regional co-operation—Trade & aid—Banking & finance—Business survey (by commodities)—Regional survey (p. 121-370; 26 countries, A-Z). Statistics up to 1965 and retrospective to 1962 or 1963. The information on China is particularly valuable as this is excluded in U.N. publications.

Supplemented by the weekly *Far Eastern economic review* (1946-) and its special supplements (*c.* 15 p.a.).

Southern Asia

33 (5-013) (051):016
BENKO, E. de, and **KRISHNAN, V. N. Research sources for South Asian studies in economic development:** a select list of serial publications. East Lansing, Mich., Michigan State Univ., 1966. 97p. (Asian Studies Center. Occasional paper no. 4).

Middle East

33 (5-015):016
A Cumulation of a selected and annotated bibliography of economic literature on the Arabic-speaking countries of the Middle East, 1938-1960. Cumulated at the School of Oriental and African Studies, University of London, from the bibliography prepared by the Economic Research Institute, American University of Beirut. Boston, Mass., G. K. Hall, 1967. 358p. $40.

Classified and annotated list of *c.* 9,600 entries (books, reports, monographs, official documents and ephemera), in English, French and Arabic. Mostly English-language material.

33 (5-015):016
A Selected and annotated bibliography of economic literature on the Arabic-speaking countries of the Middle East, 1938-1952. Beirut, American Univ. of Beirut, Economic Research Institute: Gedeon Press, 1954. ix, 199p.; annual supplements. 1955-.

Classified according to country, then by subject. Covers books, pamphlets, periodical articles and papers in English, French and Arabic. The term "economic" is liberally interpreted. The 1961 suppt. (*A selected and annotated bibliography . . . on the Arab countries of the Middle East*), published January 1963, has 252 briefly annotated entries, with author index.

33 (5-015) (058)
UNITED NATIONS. Department of Economic and Social Affairs. **Economic developments in**

the Middle East . . . New York, United Nations, 1955-. Biennial.

Supplement to *World economic survey* (q.v.). Annual (*e.g.,* 1954-1955) then biennial surveys. The latest, for 1961-1963 (1964. ix, 147p. $2), has chapters on agriculture, industry, petroleum and foreign trade and payments; statistical appendix; 73 tables. Sources given. "Middle East" includes the United Arabic Republic and the Sudan.

Preceded by *Economic developments in the Middle East, 1945 to 1954* (New York, United Nations, 1955. 236p. tables, maps).

China

33 (51):016
YÜAN, T'ung-li. **Economic and social development of modern China: a bibliographical guide.** New Haven, Conn., Human Relations Area Files, 1956. viii, 130, v, 87p.

About 2,500 entries for monographs and pamphlets published in English, French and German, 1900-55. Systematically arranged. Pt. 1: 14 sections (14. Reference books); pt. 2: Social development. No annotations; Index.

Communist China

33 (510):016
CHEN, N.-R. **The economy of Mainland China, 1949-1963:** a bibliography of materials in English. Berkeley, Cal., Committee on the Economy of China, Social Science Research Council, 1963. xxvii, 297p.

About 7,500 items, closely classified; mainly periodical articles. Part 1 consists of references to primary sources originating in Communist China (official documents; reports, speeches, etc.; semi-official and non-official publications, including editorials, articles and news reports). Part 2, materials published outside Communist China (including scholarly works and analyses, and reports). Includes translations of Communist Chinese publications. No annotations or index.

Noted: *Chinese economic statistics: a handbook for Mainland China,* by Nai-Ruenn Chen (Chicago, Aldine, 1966; Edinburgh Univ. Press, 1967. xxxi, 539p. tables, charts. 80s.) described in *Ad orientem* (catalogue 8, 1867) as a comprehensive compilation of statistics covering every aspect of the contemporary Chinese economy since 1949. . . ." Goes up to 1959 only. Bibliography, p. 499-514.

Japan

33 (52)
"THE ORIENTAL ECONOMIST". **The Japanese economic year book** . . . Tokyo, The Oriental Economist. Annual. (1966. 332p. $10; 80s.).

In English. Surveys the year's developments in individual commodity markets and industries. Includes a handy annual abstracts of Japanese statistics and a list of major companies.

The Japanese Government Economic Planning

Agency issues an annual *Economic survey of Japan* (Tokyo, Japan Times, Ltd.), kept up to date by the monthly *Japanese economic statistics* (1958-), now (March 1967-) *Economic statistics.*

The Bank of Japan publishes an annual *Economic statistics of Japan,* supported by its *Historical statistics of Japanese economy* (Tokyo, 1962. 107p.).

Saudi Arabia

33 (53)
SAUDI ARABIAN MONETARY AGENCY. **Annual report.** [Riyadh?], Research Department, Saudi Arabian Monetary Agency, Kingdom of Saudi Arabia, [1961?]-. Annual.

The *Annual report 1384-85 A.H.* (*1965*), the fifth, reviews developments during that fiscal year and discusses trends (General economy—Fiscal trends—Economic developments—Foreign trade —Balance of payments; etc.). 13 statistical tables.

India

33 (540)
INDIA. Government. **Economic survey.** . . . New Delhi, Government of India Press. Annual.

The 1963-64 survey, published 1964, has two main parts. Part 1 is a general review of developments in the preceding year, plus an assessment of future trends. Part 2 provides a more detailed analysis of developments in different sectors. Appendix of 27 statistical tables, plus graphs, in 7 sections.

"The economic history of India: a bibliographic essay", by D. T. Morris and B. Stein, appeared in the *Journal of economic history,* v. 21, June 1961, p. 179-207.

33 (540)
INDIA. Ministry of Finance. Department of Economic Affairs. **India pocket book of economic information,** 1966. [New Delhi], 1966. xvi, 282p. tables.

6th ed. 12 sections: 1. Natural resources—2. Political system—3. Economic framework—4. Financial institutions—5. Statistical tables (p. 13-184; figures to 1964/65)—6. Notes on the statistical tables—7. Five-year plans. . . . 11. Selected references (p. 268-72)—12. Miscellaneous information.

Pakistan

33 (549)
PAKISTAN. Ministry of Finance, Economic Adviser. **Pakistan economic survey** . . . Karachi, Manager of Publications. Annual. (1965-66. 1966. Rs.7.50).

The 1965-66 v. has statistics up to March 1965. 15 chapters, with 137 tables as well as graphs. Statistical section, p. 1-121. Some footnotes; index. Summary of main findings precedes.

A. H. Siddiqui's *The economy of Pakistan: a select bibliography* (Karachi, Pakistan Institute of

Development Economics, 1967. 42p.) covers books, articles and reports on the Pakistan economy published 1963-65. An earlier biblio-graphy (1963) covered 1947-62 publications.

Syria, Lebanon, Iraq

33 (567/569)

L'Economiste arabe. Étude mensuelle de l'écono-mie et les finances des pays arabe. Beirut & Damascus, Centres d'Etudes et de Documenta-tion Economiques, Financières et Sociales, 1958-. no. 1-. Mimeographed.

Covers the current economy of Syria, Lebanon and Iraq. Two main sections: economic and financial situation; documents. No. 109, January 1967 has many statistical tables, with figures up to November 1966 in some cases. No. 111, March 1967, is devoted to 'L'économie syrienne en 1966'.

Africa

33 (6)

UNITED NATIONS. Department of Economic and Social Affairs. **Economic survey of Africa since 1950.** New York, United Nations, 1959. xi, 248p. maps. tables.

Chapters: 1. Structural aspects—2. Growth trends—3. Development of external trade—4. Capital formation. Nearly 200 tables, with figures to 1957 (and in some cases, 1958), with full footnote source-references.

Supplemented by U.N. Economic Commission for Africa's *Industrial growth in Africa* (New York, United Nations, 1963. viii, 100p. tables, maps. $1.50), in 5 chapters with 99 tables, with statistics up to 1960), and particularly by its *Economic bulletin for Africa* (Addis Ababa, 1961-. 2 p.a.).

Economic survey of Africa, v. 1. Western sub-region. Republic of South Africa (Addis Ababa, United Nations, [1966?]. xi, 230, xvp. $3.50) has 150 tables, and footnote references. Section A, West Africa (8 countries) covers economic growth, 1950-1963, and planned development and structural change.

Tunisia

33 (611)

Economic yearbook of Tunisia. Tunis, Tunisian Union for Industry, Commerce and Handicraft, under the patronage of the Secretariat of State for the Plan and National Economy, 1964-. maps, tables. Annual. (1966-67 ed., published 1966).

Six main sections (thumb-indexed): 1. Political and administrative organisation—2. Basic data of the Tunisian economy—3. Plans and perspec-tive—4. Economic legislation and regulations—5. 'Repertory of articles' (*i.e.,* trade directory; p. 103-267)—6. Alphabetical index of names in section 5. Well produced. Also a French edition.

Africa South of the Sahara

33 (66/69):016

COMMISSION FOR TECHNICAL CO-OPERA-TION IN AFRICA SOUTH OF THE SAHARA. Inventory of economic studies concerning Africa south of the Sahara: an annotated read-ing list of books, articles and official publications. London, the Commission, [1960]. xi, 301p. 40s. Supplement no. 1-. 1963-.

1,377 items; 9 main areas, with subject divi-sions; author index. The economic studies in-clude official reports and periodical articles. Material published since 1945 and up to 1958 is included.
Supplement no. 1 (1963. 159p.) adds nearly 900 items.

33 (66/69) (087.7)

LANDSKRON, W. A. Official serial publications relating to economic development in Africa south of the Sahara. Cambridge, Mass, Center of International Studies, Massachusetts Institute of Technology, 1961. 44p.

Ghana

33 (667)

GHANA. CENTRAL BUREAU OF STATISTICS. Economic survey, 1965. Accra, Ministry of Information and Broadcasting, 1966. ix, 149p. tables, charts.

World economic conditions (p. 1-13); economic conditions in Ghana (p. 13-106). 112 tables; 5 charts.

A study of contemporary Ghana, edited by W. Birmingham and others, v. 1, *The economy of Ghana* (London, published for the Ghana Academy of Sciences by Allen & Unwin, 1966. 472p. tables, maps. 75s.) has 18 chapters in 5 sections, the work of 4 contributors. Bibliogra-phical note, p. 464-8 (running commentary); footnote references; non-analytical index. V. 2 has the title, *Some aspects of social structure.* 1967. 50s.).

South Africa

33 (680)

ANDREWS, H. T., *and others, ed.* **South Africa in the 'sixties:** a socio-economic survey. [Cape Town], South Africa Foundation, 1965. 233p. illus., tables, maps.

First published 1962. Part A, South Africa—land of opportunity (history; economic progress; economic structure; agriculture; minerals; manu-facturing industries); part B, The influence of South African race problems on economic de-velopment. A few footnote references. Appendix: 'A blueprint for the development of South West Africa.' Analytical index.

D. H. Houghton's *The South African economy* (Cape Town, Oxford Univ. Press, 1964. x, 261p.) includes a 'Select reading list' (p. 246-54), foot-note references, 16 maps and tables, and 26 statistical appendix tables. By the Professor of Economics at Rhodes University, Grahamstown, it is intended primarily for South African readers.

33 (680)
BARCLAYS BANK D.C.O. South Africa: an economic survey. London, the Bank, 1966. 87p. illus., tables, map.

An annual survey. Climate—Government and status—The economic structure—Population—Agricultural and pastoral production—Forestry—Fishing — Minerals — Industry — Communications—External trade—Customs and excise—Weights and measures—Currency, banking and finance—South African law—Taxation—Standards of living—Education—Immigration—South West Africa (p. 75-81). Statistics up to 1965.

Other annual surveys: the Standard Bank of South Africa, Ltd. (Johannesburg)'s *Annual economic survey of South Africa;* and, more strictly financial, the South African Reserve Bank (Pretoria)'s *Annual economic report.*

West Indies

33 (729)
Caribbean economic almanac, 1964-66. 2nd ed. Port of Spain, Economic and Business Research Information and Advisory Service, 1964. xii, 270p. tables. 49s.

First published 1962; biennial.
"Designed to give manufacturers and businessmen basic data needed to make full use of Caribbean markets and to provide research students with reliable material." Statistics are usually from official sources (with the source indicated). Covers Antigua, Barbados, Guiana, British Honduras, Dominica, Grenada, Guadeloupe, Jamaica, Montserrat, Netherlands Antilles, Puerto Rico, St. Kitts - Nevis - Anguilla, St. Lucia, St. Vincent, Surinam, Trinidad and Tobago, and the British Virgin Islands. Section of commodity data on petroleum and sugar, and a 16-page bibliography of Caribbean publications.

33 (729.2)
JAMAICA. CENTRAL PLANNING UNIT. Economic survey, Jamaica, 1966. [Kingston], 1967. [iii], 109p. tables, map.

Survey of economic activity—Overseas developments—National accounts—Balance of payments—External trade—Population and emigration—Agriculture—Mining—Manufacturing and processing—Construction and installation—Tourist trade—Electricity—Banking and finance—Retail prices—Central government receipts and expenditure—Legislation in 1966. Statistical tables usually for 1962/66 or 1963/66.

U.S.A.

33 (73):016
BERRY, B. J. L., and **HANKINS, T. D. A bibliographic guide to the economic regions of the United States:** a report prepared for the Commission on Methods of Economic Regionalization of the International Geographical Union. Chicago, Univ. of Chicago, Department of Geography, 1963. xvii, 101p. (Research paper no. 87). $4.

33 (73) (058)
The Economic almanac for 1940-: a handbook of useful facts about business, labor and government in the United States, Canada and other areas; with a brief glossary of terms used in business and economics. Washington, National Industrial Conference Board, [1940-]. tables. Annual (irregular).

The 1964 ed. (17th issue. xii, 698p.) has 24 sections (1. Population—2. Material resources—3. Labor—4. Productivity . . . 11. Manufacturing 12. Transportation . . . 17. Statistics of individual industries . . . 21. United States foreign trade—22. International financial position of the United States—23. International economic statistics—24. Canadian statistics). Glossary, p. 565-607. General index; Canadian index.

33 (73) (083.4)
ECONOMIC STATISTICS BUREAU, Washington. **Handbook of basic economic statistics,** 1947-. Washington, the Bureau, 1947-. Annual and monthly. $48 p.a.

A manual of basic economic data on industry, commerce, labour and agriculture. It is claimed that "the handbook is a compact compilation of more than 1,800 statistical series". Data are given back to 1913 or the first year thereafter for which figures are available. Both monthly supplements and annual volumes are cumulative.

33 (73) (083.4)
UNITED STATES. Department of Commerce. Office of Business Economics. **Survey of current business.** Washington, 1921-. Monthly. ea. 45c.; $6, $9.75 p.a.

Consists of a general survey and articles, with centre pages on blue-tinted paper: "Current business statistics". The December 1966 issue has statistics for 1963-65 and the first two quarters of 1966; annual indexes to sections, individual series, special articles and features. Subject index.
Business statistics: a weekly supplement to the 'Survey of current business' provides weekly and monthly data subsequent to those published in the latest monthly survey.

Latin America

33 (8=6):016
WISH, J. R. Economic development in Latin America: an annotated bibliography. New York & London, Praeger, 1966. xvi, 144p. 60s.

444 entries for books and periodical articles, mostly in English and usually briefly annotated. 6 chapters. Appendix A lists relevant information sources on Latin America; B highlights *c.* 10% of the items in the main sequence as being especially important.

33 (8=6):016
WILHELMS, C., and **ALMEIDA SEDAS, J. G. de,** *comp. and ed.* **Quellenverzeichnis zur Wirtschaftsstatistik Iberoamerikas.** Hamburg, [Insitut für Iberoamerika-Kunde], 1966. xvii, 199p.

215 numbered and annotated entries, chiefly

ECONOMICS

for official statistical publications and bank reports. Gives addresses of official statistical bureaux and institutes. Broad subject index, with country sub-divisions. Covers Latin America, Central America and the Caribbean area.

33 (8=6) (05):016
SABLE, M. H., *ed.* **Periodicals for Latin American economic development, trade and finance:** an annotated bibliography. Los Angeles, Univ. of California, Latin American Center, 1965. v, 72p. $2.50.

A selected list of 200 English- and foreign-language periodicals, published mainly in the U.S.A. and Latin America (but also in Western Europe), and available in the libraries of Harvard University, Massachusetts Institute of Technology or the University of California at Los Angeles. Covers general economics, business management, marketing and salesmanship, international and commodity trade, production, transportation, investment and finance, and industrial and labour relations. Part 1: General (nos. 1-54), with *c.* 50-word annotations; part 2, by countries or areas, A-Z. Title, subject and geographic indexes. Criteria for selection are not stated and there are surprising omissions in both parts.

33 (8=6) (058)
UNITED NATIONS. ECONOMIC COMMISSION FOR LATIN AMERICA. Economic survey of Latin America, 1948-. New York, United Nations, 1949-. tables, diagrs., graphs. Annual. (1965, published 1967. $5).

Discusses, with many supporting tables, salient features of the economic, industrial and trade development of the area as a whole, and their effects on different aspects of its economy. From 1954 each issue includes a country survey. The 1963 v. has 4 pts.: 1. The economic development of Latin America in recent years—2. Sectoral evolution (agriculture; manufacturing industry; transport; energy; housing)—3. Commodity trade and the balance of payments—4. The Cuban economy. 293 tables, with figures up to 1963 (estimated); sources cited; notes. No index.
A separate ECLA survey, *The Latin American economy in 1965,* was published in 1966 (51p. 5s. 6d.).

The *Economic bulletin for Latin America* (1956-. 2 p.a. $1.50 p.a.) supplements and brings up to date the annual *Economic survey.* It includes special articles (*e.g.,* v. 10, no. 1, March 1965 has an article on the recent activities of ECLA).

33 (910):016
HICKS, G. L., and McNICOLL, G. The Indonesian economy, 1950/1965: a bibliography. New Haven, Conn., Yale Univ., Southeast Asia Studies, [1967]. [ix], 248p.

1,270 unannotated entries in 27 sections (*e.g.,* 1. Bibliographies—2. Serials—3. Collected papers, symposia, etc.)—4. Economic history . . . 11. Agriculture—12. Mining and quarrying—13. Manufacturing industry . . . 16. Foreign trade . . . 23. Cooperatives . . . 25. Development plans and projects . . . 27. Economic assistance, etc.)

Many periodical articles. Author and subject indexes; list of *c.* 85 serials.

New Zealand

33 (931)
NEW ZEALAND. Government. **Economic review,** 1966. Wellington, Government Printer, 1966. 65p. tables.

An annual review. Part 1 is survey of economic conditions and trends during the past year and the outlook for 1966-67. Part 2 discusses the value of economic planning in a modern economy. The appendix analyses public authority expenditure in relation to total national expenditure in the post-war period.

Australia

33 (94)
AUSTRALIA. Government. **The Australian economy . . .** Canberra, Government Printer, 1956-. Annual.

The 1966 issue (27p.) is described as a survey that "chronicles our economic experience in 1965-66" (*Foreword*). Sections: Retrospect—The closing year—External account—Prospects abroad—The months to come. Tables.

33 (94)
AUSTRALIA. COMMONWEALTH BUREAU OF CENSUS AND STATISTICS. Digest of current economic statistics. Canberra, 1959-. Monthly.

The February 1967 (no. 78) issue is the first decimal currency issue. Coverage: production; trade; wages; retail prices; internal trade; building, etc.; finance; national accounts.

G. Palmer's *A guide to Australian economic statistics* (Rev. ed. Melbourne, Macmillan, 1966. xix, 324p. tables. $A5.50) analyses in detail all relevant statistics and includes a 14-page list of Australian statistical publications. Existing gaps in coverage of Australian published statistics are indicated.

Economic Geography

33:91:016
Geographical abstracts. C, Economic geography. London, Geo Abstracts, Department of Geography, London School of Economics, 1966-. 6 p.a. 54s. p.a.

About 1,200 indicative and informative abstracts p.a. Covers books, pamphlets, research papers, press notices and particularly periodical articles. A wide range of periodicals (*e.g., Agricoltura, Town and country planning, Fortune, Lloyd's Bank review*), including many foreign. Sections (increased to 17 in 1967): General—Historical—Agriculture—Forestry and fishing—Land use and resources—Minerals and energy—Manufacturing—Service industries (*e.g.,* grocery; shopping)—Transport, trade and tourist—Area studies and development—Urban studies—Regional planning—Economic regions. No indexes, but a comprehensive annual subject index to all four parts of *Geographical abstracts* was published in 1967.

33:91 (02)
CHISHOLM, G. G. Handbook of commercial geography. 18th ed., entirely rewritten by Sir D. Stamp. London, Longmans, 1966. xiii, 918p. maps, diagrs. 95s.

Chisholm's *Handbook* was first published 1889, and entirely rewritten for the 13th ed. (1937) by Sir Dudley Stamp (who died 1966).
A standard handbook that deals mainly with commodities, agricultural, mineral and manufactured (p. 123-311) and regional economic geography, by continents and countries (p. 312-873). Appendix of country statistics (p. 874-9). Statistics in text are usually up to 1963. Analytical index (p. 881-918), but no bibliography or references. Especially valuable for the study of commodities.

Economic Theory

330.1:016
BATSON, H. E., *comp.* **A select bibliography of modern economic theory, 1870-1929.** London, Routledge, 1930 (reprinted 1967). 224p. 40s.

About 2,000 entries. Pt. 1: Subject bibliography (annotated); pt. 2: Author bibliography (English authors; German authors; French authors), including periodical articles and reviews. Items not in the British Library of Political and Economic Science are asterisked. Index of authors.

W. Braeuer's *Handbuch zur Geschichte der Volkswirtschaftslehre; eine Bibliographisches Nachschlagewerk* (Frankfurt am Main, Klostermann, 1952. 224p.) is a bibliography of the history of economic doctrine, with emphasis on the writings of continental European economists.

330.1 (091)
GIDE, C., and RIST, C. A history of economic doctrines, from the time of the Physiocrats to the present day. Authorized translation by R. Richards. 2nd English ed., with additional matter from the latest French editions, translated by E. F. Row. London, Harrap, 1948 (and reprints). 800p. 21s.

First published 1915; the original work, *Histoire des doctrines économiques,* was first published in 1909.
The standard work. The 2nd ed. includes matter from the 7th French ed., 1947. Footnote references; analytical index.

Econometry

330.115
UNITED NATIONS. Statistical Office. **Input-output bibliography, 1955-1960,** by Charlotte E. Taskier. Harvard Economic Research Project. New York, United Nations, 1961. vi, 222p. Mimeographed. (ST/STAT/7).

About 2,000 references to books, chapters of books, articles, monographs, documents, doctoral theses, conference proceedings, etc. in 21 languages. 11 sections, including 8: 'National studies other than the United States' (p. 67-132) and 11: 'Critical reviews of input-output literature'. A number of items are annotated. Author and title index.

—— **Input-output bibliography, 1960-1963.** 1964. vii, 159p. $2. About 1,000 references, similarly arranged, in 23 languages.

—— **Input-output bibliography, 1963-1966.** 1967. vii, 259p. $3.50. About 1,500 references, similarly arranged.

331 LABOUR

331:016
International labour documentation. (New series). Geneva, International Labour Office, Central Library & Documentation Branch, 1949-. Weekly.

Initially a daily list; weekly from 1954.
About 1,200 indicative abstracts p.a. International coverage of books and periodical articles. 4 entries per page, to be cut into 5″ × 3″ cards, as required; not very manipulable for rapid reference. Computer-compiled subject index precedes. Quarterly indexes: personal author; corporate authors; international organisations document numbers; place names and dates of conferences; geographical.

Subject index to international labour documentation, 1957-1964 (Boston, Mass., G. K. Hall, 1968. 2v. $70 (U.S. and Switzerland); $77 elsewhere) cumulates entries from the above. It indexes references to more than 14,500 journal articles from *c.* 3,000 journals in the I.L.O. Library.

331:016
INTERNATIONAL LABOUR OFFICE. Library. **Bibliographie des sources de documentation sur le travail.** Bibliography of research sources on labour questions. Geneva, I.L.O., 1965. [i], vi, 129p. Mimeographed. (Bibliographical contributions, no. 24).

More than 1,500 entries. Six main sections (sub-divided by countries): Bibliographies—Conferences. Congresses—Dictionaries. Directories. Encyclopaedias (111 items)—History—Periodicals (674 items)—Statistics.

331:016
INTERNATIONAL LABOUR OFFICE. Publications of the International Labour Office, 1954-1965. Geneva, I.L.O., 1966. 64 p.

1953 ed. covers the period 1919 to 1953 inclusive; 1960 ed., 1944-60.
Sections: 1. Publications grouped by subject (subjects A-Z)—2. Periodicals—3. Documents and proceedings—4.Miscellaneous (including title

index and list of selected depository libraries for I.L.O. publications). Items in section 1 are annotated. The list does not include items not offered for sale.

The I.L.O. Central Library and Documentation Branch issued a *Subject guide to publications of the International Labour Office, 1919-1964,* in 1967 ([3], i, 478p.).

331 (038)=00
ASSOCIAZIONE INDUSTRIALE LOMBARDA.
Glossario del lavoro, italiano-francese-inglese-tedesco. Milan, the Association, 1964. [ix], 1335p.

About 20,000 Italian terms, with French, German and English equivalents across the double page. Many idioms; genders not stated. French, German and English indexes on tinted paper.

Labour

331 (083.4)
INTERNATIONAL LABOUR OFFICE. Year book of labour statistics. 1935/36-. Geneva, I.L.O.; London, Staples Press, 1936-. Annual. (1964. 45s. 6d.; 52s. 6d.).

Continues the statistical information included in the *I.L.O. year-book* published from 1931. Includes world figures on: employment; hours of work; consumer price indices and retail prices; family living studies; industrial injuries; unemployment; wages and labour income; social security; industrial disputes; and migration.

Supplemented and kept up to date by the quarterly *Bulletin of labour statistics* (1965-. v. 1. no. 1-. ea. 6s. 3d.; 21s. p.a.), replacing the monthly *International labour review: statistical supplement.* The *Year book* contains series for other countries than those in the *Bulletin,* as well as more detailed data. The *Supplement to the Bulletin of labour statistics* (April 1965-. 10 p.a.) provides the latest data available to I.L.O. since the latest issue of the *Bulletin.*

331 (410):016
GREAT BRITAIN. H.M. STATIONERY OFFICE. Government publications. Sectional list no. 21, revised to 31st August 1966: **Ministry of Labour.** London, H.M.S.O., 1966. 25p. *Gratis.*

Publications in eight groups, including 'Miscellaneous'. Entries for the 'Choice of careers' series (p. 2-6) and Reports of inquiries (p. 16-21).

331 (410) (083.4)
GREAT BRITAIN. INTERDEPARTMENTAL COMMITTEE ON SOCIAL AND ECONOMIC RESEARCH. Guides to official sources. No. 1: **Labour statistics.** 3rd ed. London, H.M. Stationery Office, 1958. vii, 78p. 5s.

First published 1948.
Describes the statistics collected by the Ministry of Labour and National Service, giving titles of publications in which those statistics can be found, plus period of coverage. A subject index to published sources of Ministry of Labour and National Service statistics is appended.

331 (410) (083.4)
GREAT BRITAIN. MINISTRY OF LABOUR. Statistics on incomes, prices, employment and

production. London, H.M. Stationery Office, 1962-. no. 1, April 1952-. Quarterly. ea. 20s.

8 parts:—A. General—B. Wages and salaries—C. Company profits, dividends, assets, etc.—D. Hours of work—E. Total working population—F. Prices—G. Production. Technical notes; index.

The monthly *Ministry of Labour gazette* (1893-) is a long-established source of labour statistics, particularly its 'Index of retail prices' (*i.e.,* cost-of-living index).

331 (6)
INTERNATIONAL LABOUR OFFICE. African labour survey. Geneva, I.L.O., 1958. xiv, 694p. (Studies and reports, new series, no 48). 30s.

16 chapters; many tables, with statistics up to 1957. Numerous appendices, p. 535-694 (*e.g.,* Appendix 2: Reference list of labour legislation). Bibliographies, p. 695-707, including "a short list of periodicals".
Deals with labour problems and policies in Africa south of the Sahara. The companion volume is:

——**Labour survey of North Africa.** Geneva, I.L.O., 1961. xiv, 473p. (Studies and reports, new series, no. 60). 24s.

Covers Morocco, Algeria, Tunisia, Libya and the United Arab Republic (*i.e.,* Egypt). Three appendices: a reference list of the principal labour legislation, additional tables, and a bibliography (p. 469-73).

Updated by the U.S. Department of Labor. Bureau of Labor Statistics' *Labor digests,* recent numbers of which concern African countries (*e.g.,* no. 93. *Labor conditions in Algeria;* no. 143. *Labor conditions in Republic of Zambia*).

The same Bureau has published a *Bibliography on labor in Africa, 1960 64* (Washington, U.S. Government Printing Office, 1965. v, 121p.).

Also noted: Friedland, W. H. *Unions, labour and industrial relations in Africa: an annotated bibliography* (New York, Cornell Univ. Center for International Studies, 1965. ix, 159p. $2).

331.001.5
ORGANISATION FOR ECONOMIC CO-OPERATION AND DEVELOPMENT. Register of research in the human sciences applied to problems of work and directory of relevant research institutions. Paris, O.E.C.D., 1962. 739p. 27s. 6d.

Prepared by O.E.C.D. with the help of national productivity centres. The 'Register' (p. 19-735) has data on organisations in Belgium, Denmark, France, Germany, the Netherlands, Norway, Sweden, Switzerland, and the U.K. (p. 577-735). 277 numbered entries, plus entries for universities and research institutes. Data include references to publications and to other bodies associated in the research. Subject index for each country section.

Labour force
331.024
See entry at 312 (4/5).

Industrial Relations

331.1/.2 (038)
UNITED STATES. BUREAU OF LABOR STATISTICS. Glossary of current industrial relations and wage terms. Washington, U.S. Government Printing Office, 1965. iii, 103p. (Bulletin no. 1438). 45c.

About 500 brief definitions of terms "likely to be encountered most frequently in reading about contemporary labor-management relations, wage procedures and Government labor policy in the United States, and by writers and supervisors in their employments". Definitions range from 15 to 150 words.

331.1:016
NEW YORK STATE SCHOOL OF INDUSTRIAL AND LABOR RELATIONS, Cornell University. **Library catalog.** Boston, Mass., G. K. Hall, 1967. 12v. $775 (outside U.S., $852.50).

Photolitho-offset reproduction of *c.* 210,000 cards, covering books and 80,000 pamphlets. A dictionary catalogue, including author and subject entries for selected articles from 150 periodicals, 1952-.
To be supplemented.

331.1 (410)
GREAT BRITAIN. MINISTRY OF LABOUR. Industrial relations handbook: an account of British institutions and practice relating to the organization of employers and workers in Great Britain; collective bargaining and joint negotiating machinery; conciliation and arbitration; and statutory regulation of wages in certain industries. Rev. [3rd] ed. London, H.M. Stationery Office, 1961. vi, 234p. 5s. 6d.

First published 1944.
Parts: 1. Organization within industry—2. Statutory and governmental provisions—3. Wages information. List of enactments and official publications, p. 226-8; detailed index.

Wages, Salaries

331.2:016
Employment relations abstracts. Detroit, Michigan, Information Service, Inc., 1950-. 24 p.a. Loose-leaf. $46.50.

About 6,000 abstracts p.a. in 20 thumb-indexed sections (6 groups: Employee-management relations—Human relations in employment—Labor economics—Government and management labor —Managerial organization—Labor movement and union structure). 112 journals (6 British) regularly abstracted, plus some books. Subject index (on salmon-tinted paper) for each issue, cumulating to half-yearly, with annual cumulation.

331.2 (410)
GREAT BRITAIN. MINISTRY OF LABOUR. Time rates of wages and hours of labour. London, H.M. Stationery Office, 1963. 308p. 21s.

Revised periodically.
Tables show the position, as at 1st April 1963, of minimum time rates of wages and standard working hours in the more important

industries and occupations. For current revisions see the Ministry of Labour's monthly *Changes in rates of wages and hours of work* (No. 1, May 1966-).

Careers

331.7 (038)=00
EUROPEAN ECONOMIC COMMUNITY. Commission. **Dictionnaire comparatif des professions** donnant lieu le plus souvent à migrations dans les pays de la Communauté Économique Européenne. 2. éd. [Brussels], Service des Publications des Communautés Européennes, [1965]. v.p.

Professions are classified and numbered (*e.g.,* 0. Agriculture—1. Mining—2/3. Manufacturing industries—4. Building and public works—5. Services (*e.g.,*catering trades)). Functions of individual professions are specified in French, German, Italian and Dutch across the double page (*e.g.,* Chef de cuisine).

331.7 (083)
INTERNATIONAL LABOUR OFFICE. International standard classification of occupations. Geneva, I.L.O., 1958. v, 236p.

"Developed to provide a basis for the international comparison of occupational data and to afford guidance to countries wishing to develop or improve their systems of occupational classification (*Preface*). The *I.S.C.O.* consists of 3 inseparable basic components, namely code numbers, titles and definitions. A decimal coding system. Not only the major, minor and unit groups of employment but also the 1,345 individual occupations are described and defined in some detail. Classified list of titles; A-Z index of occupational titles.

331.7 (083) (410)
GREAT BRITAIN. GENERAL REGISTER OFFICE. Classification of occupations, 1966. London, H.M. Stationery Office, 1966. xxxiv, 148p. 40s.

Sections: Summary of occupation orders and unit groups—Occupation unit groups, with short descriptions of contents (*i.e.,* definition of work; 27 orders; 211 groups (*e.g.,* woodworkers), specified—Alphabetical index for classifying occupations (p. 1-125; nearly 35,000 designations plus code number. Appendices: A. List of conventional codings—B. Social classes and socio-economic groups—C. Summary of industry groups.

331.7 (410):016
Cornmarket abstracts: a quarterly service for appointment officers, personnel managers, youth employment officers, careers masters, London, Cornmarket Press, 1967-. no. 1-. Quarterly.

The first issue, October/December 1966, has *c.* 450 indicative abstracts (10-50 words) from 68 journals, in 17 sections (General; A-Z by subjects, from Advertising, Agriculture and Armed forces to Retailing and Working overseas). Two lengthy sections, each with 29 sub-divisions: 'Industry' and 'Professions'. 'Selected new books and reports' lists *c.* 80 new books, citing location of reviews. Analytical subject index.

331.7 (410):016

NATIONAL BOOK LEAGUE. Careers: a selection of books giving ideas, advice and all the necessary information about careers, for young people, their teachers and parents. 2nd ed. London, N.B.L., 1965. 35p. 2s.

First published 1963.
An annotated list of 231 items. A general section, followed by careers, A-Z. Items are categorised (B=for boys; G=for girls; T=teachers' textbook). No index.

The Careers Research and Advisory Centre's *Basic books: a guide for schools with a sixth form* (London, C.R.A.C., 1966. 16p. 5s. 6d.) is particularly well annotated. Items are in 3 sections: 1. Books on further and higher education (A. General books—B. Books on particular courses—C. Periodicals)—2. Career books (similarly divided)—3. Books for careers-staff only (similarly divided).

The Library Association. County Libraries Group's *Reader's guide to books on choice of careers* (6th ed. London, the Association, 1966. 24p. 2s. 6d.) has some 250 books on c. 80 careers. No annotations or index.

331.7 (410) (02)

GREAT BRITAIN. MINISTRY OF LABOUR. Central Youth Employment Executive. **Careers guide:** opportunities in the professions, industry and commerce. 6th ed. London, H.M. Stationery Office, 1964. Loose-leaf. 15s. (bound, 8s. 6d.).

First published 1950. Each edition has subsequent amendment slips.
Consists of short pamphlets on c. 80 types of careers (*e.g.*, 1. Accountant; 82. Youth Employment Officer), stating type of work, qualities and educational qualifications required, training, opportunities and prospects, and where to obtain further information. A comprehensive guide for boys and girls entering careers direct from fifth and sixth forms after training. Does not list firms' industrial training schemes.

The Ministry of Labour's *Choice of careers* series comprises more than a hundred inexpensive pamphlets (1s. - 2s. 9d.) on various trades and professions (*e.g.*, no. 116. Civil aviation; no. 117. Teaching) and is more suited than the above for individual purchase.

331.7 (410) (02)

LONDON. UNIVERSITY. Appointments Board. **Careers for graduates:** a handbook of information. 2nd ed. London, Univ. of London, Athlone Press, 1963. viii, 220p. 12s. 6d.

First published 1955. Previously as *Appointments and careers for graduates and students.*
20 sections (20. Miscellaneous information, including grants and awards). Appendices: 1. Bibliography (general and by chapters, p. 195-202)—2. List of useful addresses (p. 203-83). Index. Intended for students, parents and teachers.

331.7 (410) (02)

MILLER, R. The Peacock book of careers for young girls. Edited by Susan Shaw. Harmondsworth, Middlesex, Penguin Books, 1966. xxix, 396p. 8s. 6d.

Arranged by careers A-Z. Under each, headings in bold (*e.g.*, Air hostess: Minimum qualifications—The work—Prospects—Training—Pay—Personal attributes). Other headings used, as appropriate: Further information—Grants—Related careers. Good layout.

Related guides: Women's Employment Federation. *Careers: a memorandum on openings and training for girls and women* (21st ed., rev. London, the Federation, 1966. 146p. 7s. 6d.), which has brief data on careers, plus addresses for further information; Women's Information and Study Centre. *Comeback: a guide for the educated woman returning to work* (London, the Centre, 1964. 41p. 3s. 6d.) has tabulated information (occupation; proportion of women; openings; basic training courses; refresher courses; part-time work), a list of publications (p. 32-34) and 'Some useful addresses'.

331.7 (410) (02)

WHEATLEY, D. E., *ed.* **Industry and careers:** a study of British industries and the opportunities they offer. London, Iliffe Books, 1961. xvi, 776p. 55s.

A valuable contribution on the structure of British industries, quite apart from data on careers. 3 introductory articles, followed by sections on industries (agriculture; mining and quarrying; food, drink and tobacco; etc.). On the General Post Office (p. 731-8) information covers scope and size, organization, technical work, recruitment and training, further education, recruitment, and scholarships. 'How to find out', p. 769-74. 96 pages of advertisements are appended. Well produced.

331.7 (410) (03)

EDMONDS, P. J., *ed.* **Careers encyclopedia:** a work of reference upon some 220 occupations, for teachers, parents, school-leavers, undergraduates and employment officials. 4th ed., completely rev. London, Macmillan & Cleaver, 1965. xv, 555p. (5th ed. 1967. xv, 567p. 25s.).

First published 1952.
Arranged by careers A-Z, from Accountancy to Youth leadership. Under each, notes on nature of work, age of entry, essential qualities, training, cost of training, examinations, social aspects, etc. Appendix 4: Some sources of information (p. 545-6). Index. Comparable with the Central Youth Employment Executive's *Careers guide* (q.v.), but gives more impression of the work involved, states C.R.A.C.'s *Basic books* (p. 8)
A 5th ed., 1967/68, covering c. 250 careers, appeared in 1967 (xv, 567p 25s.).

331.7 (410) (058)

Directory of opportunities for graduates, 1957-. London, Cornmarket Press, 1957-. Annual. (1967. 42s.).

Directory of opportunities for qualified and experienced men. London, Cornmarket Press. Annual. (1967/1968. 1967. 42s.). (Formerly *Directory of opportunities for qualified men*).

Directory of opportunities for school leavers, 1957-. London, Cornmarket Press, 1957-. Annual. (1966. 12s. 6d.; *gratis* to schools).

All three directories are advertising media: employers pay to be included. The first includes details of courses offered by firms to university graduates; the second has reference sections on career opportunities (under firms A-Z), post-graduate courses and professional associations. *Directory of opportunities for school leavers,* 1966, fullest of the three, has a valuable editorial section of articles. Its reference section covers trade associations, career opportunities (p. 158-413), professional associations and further education. 'Career opportunities' is by firms A-Z (for each firm: description; training; qualifications required; prospects; address of manager, or equivalent. 'The classified index' tabulates number of employees and vacancies, qualifications (*e.g.,* 'O' or 'A' levels), area (map code reference), 'boys or girls', age and page reference; training and alphabetical indexes.

331.7 (410) (058)
The Year book of technical education and careers in industry . . . ; edited by H. C. Dent. London, Black, 1957-. (10th annual issue, 1966. 50*s.*).

See entry at 378.96 (058).

Technical Training
331.86:016
Training abstracts service. London, Ministry of Labour, January 1968-. Monthly card service. 110*s.* p.a.

About 80 6″ × 4″ filing cards per month; abstracts average 400 words. Aims to bring together from a dozen abstracting services material that might otherwise escape notice, and to re-issue it in classified form (10 main classes); other items, abstracted by Ministry of Labour staff, are also fed into the system. No indexes.

331.86 (038)=20
GREAT BRITAIN. MINISTRY OF LABOUR. Glossary of training terms. London, H.M. Stationery Office, 1967. [i], 52p. 4*s.* 9*d.*

Defines *c.* 300 terms, including names of organisations. Different meanings are numbered. Occasionally quotes source. Appendices: 1. Abbreviations—2. List of sources used—3. Grouped items.

331.86 (4)
ORGANISATION FOR ECONOMIC CO-OPERATION AND DEVELOPMENT. Inventory of training possibilities in Europe. Paris, O.E.C.D., 1965. 896p. 52*s.* 6*d.*

Details of 1,662 European courses for trainees from developing countries. Major fields of training (1. Agriculture—2. Industry and commerce—3. Transportation—4. Health and sanitation—5. Public administration—6. Community development, social welfare and housing—7. Education—8. Economic development—9. Miscellaneous)—General information by countries (p. 775-831)—Bibliography (national, O.E.C.D. and international publications, p. 833-49).—Statistical summary. Index, by teaching establishments and by subject.

331.86 (410)
The Industrial training yearbook. 1967/68. London, Kogan Page, 1967. 499p. 50*s.*

A guide to government, university and professional bodies concerned with industrial training. Combines directory, encyclopaedia, a who's who and source book.

Industrial training research register, 1967 (London, H.M.S.O., 1967. 132p. 11*s.*) classifies and lists *c.* 250 current and recently completed research projects on or related to industrial training. Appendix gives addresses of research organisations; subject index.

Working Class Movements
331.88:016
DOLLÉANS, E., and **CROZIER, M. Mouvements ouvriers et socialistes:** chronologie et bibliographie. Paris, Éditions Ouvrières, 1950-56. 4v. in 5.

v. 1: *Angleterre, France, Allemagne, États-Unis (1750-1918),* by E. Dolléans and M. Crozier. 1950.
v. 2: *L'Italie (des origines à 1922),* by A. Leonetti. 1952.
v. 3: *L'Espagne (1750-1936),* by R. Lamberet. 1953.
v. 4: *La Russie,* by E. Zaleski. 1956. 2v.
Chapters in each volume carry a chronology and then unannotated lists of material—documents, autobiographies and biographies, official publications, periodicals, etc. V. 1 has an author index; not so v. 2-3. "Useful bibliographies . . . , though these are not always up to standard" (*Times literary supplement,* no. 3367, 8th September 1966, p. 810).

331.88:016
GULICK, C. A., *and others, comp.* **History and theories of working-class movements:** a select bibliography. Berkeley, California, Bureau of Business and Economic Research and Institute of Industrial Relations, Univ. of California, [1955]. xix, 364p.

Confined to material in English. Arrangement is by region and country, with appropriate subdivisions: United Kingdom (p. 1-140)—Latin countries—Germanic countries—N. Europe and Ireland—East and West Slavic, Baltic and Balkan countries — Asia — Oceania — Africa — Latin America—North America—International. Includes periodical articles; no annotations or index.

331.88:016
INTERNATIONAL COMMITTEE OF HISTORICAL SCIENCES. Répertoire internationale des sources pour l'étude des mouvements sociaux au XIXe et XXe siècle. Paris, Colin, 1958-. v. 1-.

v. 1: *La Première Internationale. Périodiques, 1864-1877.* 1958.
v. 2: ————. *Actes officielles du Conseil général et des Congrès.* 3 pts. 1960-63.
v. 3: ————. *Actes officielles des Fédérations et Sections nationales.* 1963.

An international catalogue of sources made possible by extensive international co-operation. The background, history and likely future of the *Répertoire* are described in *Bulletin d'informations, Association des Bibliothécaires Français,* no. 44, June 1964, p. 97-103.

331.88 (411)

McDOUGAL, I., *ed.* **An interim bibliography of the Scottish working class movement.** Edinburgh, Society for the Study of Labour History. Scottish Committee, 1965. [i], viii, 142p. 7s. 6d.

331.88 (44)

MAITRON, J., *ed.* **Le dictionnaire biographique du mouvement ouvrier français,** de 1789-1939. Paris, Éditions Ouvrières, 1964-. v. 1-.

1. *1789-1864. De la Revolution française à la fondation de la Première Internationale,* by R. Dufraisse and others. v.1: A-CZ. 1964.
2. *1864-1871. De la fondation de la Première Internationale à la Commune,* by M. Egrist, and others.
3. *1871-1914. De la Commune à la Grande Guerre,* by C. Chambelland, and others.
4. *1914-1939. De la première à la Seconde Grande Guerre Mondiale,* by C. Chambelland, etc.

According to the *Times literary supplement* (no. 3,367, 8th September 1966, p. 810) the first part, covering 1789-1864, contains 12,000 biographies. "Important source material for the writing of the biographies was provided by the 10,000 dossiers relating to the June 1848 Rising and the Paris Commune of 1871 kept in the archives of the War Ministry and never previously used for the purposes of historical research." Biographies are unsigned, but lists of works, bibliography and inconography, as appropriate, are appended. Article on P. J. Proudhon: p. 256-61 (⅔p. of bibliography).

Trade Unions

331.881 (038)

INTERNATIONAL CONFEDERATION OF FREE TRADE UNIONS. Glossary of trade union terms. Brussels, I.C.F.T.U., 1964. 156p. 5s.

Part 1: 'Glossary of trade union terms' (p. 5-130) defines *c.* 250 terms, with comment and cross-references. Part 2: 'Labour terms in four languages' (English-French-German-Spain; no reverse indexes; p. 131-9). The 6 appendices include a list of I.C.F.T.U. abbreviations.

331.881 (410)

CLEGG, H. A., *and others.* **A history of British trade unions since 1889.** Oxford, Clarendon Press, 1964-. v. 1-. tables.

v. 1: 1889-1910. ix, [1], 514p. 55s.
The only previous history of note is Sidney and Beatrice Webb's *History of trade unionism* (1894), the later editions of which (*e.g.,* 1920) added little of value. This scholarly continuation, to be in 3v., is a detailed survey with profuse footnote references and notes, and bibliography. Partly analytical index, p. 491-514.

V. L. Allen's *International bibliography of trade unionism* is due for publication in 1967, at 73s. 6d.

331.881 (410)

GREAT BRITAIN. MINISTRY OF LABOUR. Directory of employers' associations, trade unions, joint organizations, etc. London, H.M. Stationery Office, 1960. 177p. Loose-leaf. 21s. Amendments. 12s. 6d. p.a.

Employers' associations, sub-divided by type of industry (*e.g.,* textiles), p. 1-86; trade union federations, trade unions and other employees associations, p. 89-128; standing joint industrial councils, conciliation and arbitration boards, etc., p. 129-64. Gives name, address and telephone number in each case. Index at end of each main section.

PRIVATE FINANCE

332(032)

MUNN, G. G. Glenn G. Munn's Encyclopedia of banking and finance. 6th ed., revised by F. L. Garcia. Boston, Mass., Barkers Publishing Co., 1962. [iv], 788p. tables. $25.

First published 1924.
A standard U.S. reference work, and excellent on the U.S.A. Articles A-Z, from 'ABC agreements of the New York stock exchange' to 'Window dressing'. Longer articles have bibliographies (*e.g.,* 'Cotton': 2 cols. of text plus bibliography). Many cross-references and tables. Gives examples of forms (*e.g.,* wills, letter of credit); no biographies or country entries. Statistics up to *c.* 1961. Nothing on contemporary developments in the higher realms of international finance.

Handbuch der Finanzwissenschaft, hrsg. von W. Gerloff und F. Neumark (2. Aufl. Tübingen, Mohr, 1952-65. 4v.) is a comprehensive treatise, with chapter bibliographies.

332 (038)=00

HORN, S. F., *comp.* **Glossary of financial terms** in English/American, French, Spanish, German. Amsterdam, Barking (Essex), Elsevier, 1965. [viii], 271p. (Glossarium interpretum). DM.33; 60s.

2,278 numbered English/American terms, with equivalents and indexes in French, Spanish and German. Gives genders and includes phrases (*e.g.,* 'To write down the value of doubtful debts'). Bibliography, p. 270-1.

332 (038)=00

SWISS BANK CORPORATION. Petit dictionnaire financier et bancaire. Basle, Société de Banque Suisse, [1962]. 68p.

A single A-Z sequence of *c.* 750 terms and cross-references,—English, French and German terms, with French definitions and brief commentary. Different applications of terms are numbered.

The European Federation of Financial Analysts Societies' *List of definitions* (1965. 47p. 15s.) records the more important accountancy terms, and analytical concepts and ratios used by analysts in Belgium, Western Germany, France, the Netherlands, Switzerland and Britain, with definitions in English. French and German versions of the *List* are available.

332(100) (083.4)
INTERNATIONAL MONETARY FUND. International financial statistics. January, 1948-. London, H.M. Stationery Office, 1948-. Monthly. ea. $1.50; $10 p.a.

Contains data on the International Monetary Fund, the International Bank for Reconstruction and Development, international liquidity, interest rates, exchange rates, prices, changes in money, money supply and cost of living, international trade. 'Country pages', by *c.* 90 countries, A-Z (2p. per country). December 1966 issue has data up to October 1966 in some cases, and retrospectively usually to 1958. Valuable footnotes and country notes for financial history, *e.g.,* dates of re-valuation and devaluation of the franc.

Annual supplements (*e.g., Supplement to 1965/66 issues,* keyed to the October 1965 issue), give annual and quarterly data for the periods not covered in current monthly issues (*i.e.,* annual data for 1948-1957 and 1959, and quarterly data for 1957-1961).

Direction of trade, also a supplement—*see at* 382 (4/9) (083.4).

332 (410) (047)
GREAT BRITAIN. H.M. TREASURY. Committee on the Working of the Monetary System. Report. London, H.M. Stationery Office, 1959. viii, 375p. tables. (Cmnd. 827). 15*s.*

Chairman of Committee: Lord Radcliffe.

A basic survey. Chapters: 1. The background to post-war monetary policy—2. The objectives of monetary policy—3. The financing of the public sector—4. Financial institutions in the private sector—5. The work of the Bank of England—6. The influence of monetary measures —7. The management of the National Debt—8. International aspects of the monetary system—9. The status and organization of the Bank of England—10. Statistics (figures up to 1958)—11. The development of monetary institutions—12. Conclusions. Appendices. Analytical index, p. 361-75.

Supplemented by 4v. of minutes of evidence (London, H.M.S.O., 1959-60).

The outstanding and still valuable report on the working of the monetary system between the wars is the *Report of [the Macmillan] Committee on finance and industry. Minutes of evidence.* Index (London, H.M. Stationery Office, 1931. Cmd. 3897).

332 (410) (051)
Bank of England Quarterly bulletin. December 1960-. London, Economic Intelligence Department, Bank of England, 1960-. Quarterly.

Includes articles and an annex of statistics some of which are not available elsewhere. The December 1966 issue has 25 tables, with ample notes.

332 (410) (083.4)
GREAT BRITAIN. CENTRAL STATISTICAL OFFICE. Financial statistics. London, H.M. Stationery Office, 1962-. no. 1-. Monthly. ea. 10*s.* 6*d.*

10 sections: 1. Financial accounts—2. Ex-

chequer and central government—3. Local authorities—4. Public corporations—5. Banking and money supply—6. Other financial institutions—7. Companies—8. Capital issue and stock exchange transactions—9. Interest rates and security prices —10. Overseas finance. No. 58, February 1967 has 90 tables, with statistics up to mid-January 1967. Index.

Banking

332.1:016
SICHTERMANN, S. Schrifttum des Bank- und Kreditwesens von 1920 bis 1960, nach Stichworten geordnet. Frankfurt am Main, 1963-64. 305p.

Special issue of *Zeitschrift für das gesamte Kreditwesen.* 30,000 entries, arranged under subjects.

The Bank Deutscher Länder's *Bücher und Zeitschriften Verzeichnis* (Frankfurt am Main, the Bank, 1951-53. 1v. and suppt.) has as second supplement the Deutsche Bundesbank's *Bücher und Zeitschriften Verzeichnis* (Frankfurt am Main, the Bank, 1958).

Extensive bibliographies of the history of banking and credit in eleven European countries are appended (p. 355-480) to J. G. van Dillen's *History of the principal public banks* (London, Cass, 1934 (reprinted 1964). xii, 480p. 75*s.*). Includes "Modern bibliography of banking and currency (British Empire) from the XVth century to 1815", compiled under the direction of J. H. Clapham (p. 449-56).

332.1 (032)
THOMSON, W. Thomson's Dictionary of banking. 11th ed. by F. E. Perry and F. R. Ryder. London, Pitman, 1965. ix, 641p. tables. 105*s.*

First published 1912.

Notes much new legislation, and attempts "to expand the information of interest to those engaged in Executive and Trustee work" (*Preface* to the 11th ed.). Cites in full the appropriate sections of Acts, etc.; many cross-references. Some lengthy articles (*e.g.,* 'Proof of debts', p. 459-63; 'Bank rates', p. 63-67, giving Bank of England figures since 1829). Appendix 1. Scottish banking (p. 607-31)—2. Irish land laws in their relation to banking (p. 635-41). The standard short encyclopaedia of British banking.

The banker's vade-mecum is *Practice and law of banking,* by H. P. Sheldon and W.C.B. Drover (9th ed. London, Macdonald & Evans, 1962. xii, 650p. illus., tables, bibliog. 37*s.* 6*d.*).

Banklexikon: Handwörterbuch für das Bank- und Sparkassenwesen, by G. Müller and J. Löffelholz (5. neu. u. erw. Aufl. Wiesbaden, Gabler, 1963. xvi, 1638p. illus. DM.48) has shortish articles (*e.g.,* 'Liquidität': 2½ cols.; bibliography of 6 items) and many cross-references. Bibliography, p. 1627-38.

332.1 (038)=00
RICCI, J. Elsevier's Banking dictionary in six languages: English/American, French, Italian, Spanish, Dutch and German. . . . Amsterdam,

142

Barking (Essex), etc., Elsevier, 1966. [viii], 302p. 75s.

2,041 numbered entries in English/American, with equivalents and indexes in the other 5 languages. Includes phases such as 'mutilated cheque', 'token payment'.

332.1 (038)=00
SKANDINAVISKA BANKEN. Banking terms: French, German, Italian, Spanish, Swedish. Stockholm, the Bank, 1964. 66p. *Gratis.*

About 350 terms in English, with equivalents in French, German, Italian, Spanish and Swedish, but no indexes for terms in those languages. Gives genders and includes compounds (*e.g.,* 'revocable documentary credit', 'fully paid up share').

332.1 (058.7)
The Bankers' almanac and year book . . . London, Skinner, 1844. Annual. (121st year, 1965/66. 1966. 168s.).

The standard international banking reference book, with data on the principal banks of the world. The section on British banks (1965/66 ed., p. 1-310) gives details of directors, staffs, branches and accounts, with a geographical list of branches, plus supporting advertisements. International banks (p. 311-922), and banks of individual countries (by countries, A-Z); telegraphic addresses; insurances; exporters and importers. General and country indexes.

Polk's Bankers encyclopedia: the bank directory, 1898- (New York, Polk's Bank Encyclopedia Co., 1895-. 2 p.a., with monthly suppts.) is "a comprehensive, geographical listing of banks all over the world" (White, C. M., and others. *Sources of information in the social sciences* (1964), p. 169) and has the advantage of up-to-dateness.

332.1 (4/9)
BECKHART, B. H., *ed.* **Banking systems.** New York, Columbia Univ. Press; London, Oxford Univ. Press, 1954. 934p. tables.

A successor volume to *Foreign banking systems,* edited by H. P. Willis and B. H. Beckhart (New York, Holt, 1929), which is still valuable for its description and bibliographies of the period.
Covers the banking systems of 16 countries,— Australia, Brazil, Canada, Cuba, France, W. Germany, India, Italy, Japan, Mexico, the Netherlands, Sweden, Switzerland, U.S.S.R., U.K., United States. 19 contributors. Many tables, with figures to 1953 in some cases. Chapter bibliographies are extensive (*e.g.,* U.K. (p. 835-7): Government publications.—Banking history.—Banking system and theory.—Reviews). Detailed but not analytical index.

Banken der Welt. Kurzmonographie in deutscher und englischer Sprache, bearb. von K. Lanz (Frankfurt am Main, Knapp, 1963. 456p. DM.98) has articles on some 600 banks in 91 countries, under countries A-Z. Bank and town indexes. Bilingual: German on right-hand column, English on left-hand column of page.

The annual *European Banking gazetteer* (London, Manufacturers Hanover Trust) contains a list of banks represented in the main banking centres.

332.11 (410)
ACRES, W. M. The Bank of England from within, 1964-1900. London, printed for the Governor and Company of the Bank of England by Oxford Univ. Press, 1931. 2v.

The authoritative history. V. 2 includes a list of directories of the Bank, and of principal officials, 1694-1900, plus a 'List of the principal banks, pamphlets, &c. referred to in the text' (p. 633-40). General, analytical index in v. 2. Numerous footnote references to sources listed in v. 1, p. xv-xvi.

Another standard history is Sir J. Clapham's *The Bank of England: a history* [1694-1914] (Cambridge, Univ. Press, 1944. 2v. 63s.).

332.2
HORNE, H. O. A history of savings banks. London, Oxford Univ. Press, 1947. xv, 407p. ports., maps.

The standard work. Concerned with all the old savings banks now known as the Trustee Savings Banks and includes the history of the Post Office Savings Bank. Some biographical data; chronology (Appendix 1). Bibliography, p. 394-8; detailed index.

Currency

332.4/.5 (058)
PICK, F. Pick's Currency yearbook. New York, Pick Publishing Corpn., 1955-. Annual. (1966 ed. $50).

Sections (1966 ed.): Currencies (descriptions of 94 currencies, by countries A-Z)—The Eurodollar market—Gold—Descriptions of prices and movements in 36 international trading centres—Selected bibliography (p. 554)—Central bank directory. Analytical index.
Kept up to date by the monthly *Pick's World currency report* (1945-).

332.4/.5 (410)
MACKENZIE, A. D. The Bank of England note: a history of its printing. London, Cambridge Univ. Press, 1953. x, 163p. illus.

The only work concerned with the Bank of England note; covers the history of English banknote production up to the Second World War. Bibliography and index.

For continental Europe there is Hans Adler's *Handbuch der Banknoten und Münzen Europas* (Vienna, 1937. xxiii, 859. illus.; Nachträge. 1937-39. Loose-leaf). This gives details (including weights, size, fineness) of notes and coins of all European countries, with illustrations in every case. For the period this work is unique.

The classic work on the history of English coinage and paper money is: Feavearyear, A. E. *The pound sterling: a history of English money* (2nd ed., revised by E. V. Morgan. London, Oxford Univ. Press, 1963. 458p. 42s.), first published in 1931; critically reviewed in *Journal of the Institute of Bankers* (v. 84, pt. 3, June 1963, p. 223-7) for its inadequate references.

332 .4 (03)
DOURSTHER, H. Dictionnaire universel des poids et mesures anciens et modernes, contenant des tables des monnaies de tous les pays. Brussels, Hayez, 1840 (reprinted Amsterdam, Meridian Publishing Co., 1965). iv, 604p. 135s.).

See entry at 389.16 (03).

332.4 (03)
SEDILLOT, R. Toutes les monnaies du monde. Dictionnaire des changes. Paris, Sirey, 1955. 555p. 32F.

About 1,500 concise entries, arranged A-Z under countries and currencies, with definitions and historical accounts of monetary systems (*e.g.*, 'zloty': 1⅔p., with cross-reference from Poland).

332.4 (047)
BANK FOR INTERNATIONAL SETTLEMENTS. Annual report, 1930/31-. Basle, the Bank.

INTERNATIONAL BANK FOR RECONSTRUCTION AND DEVELOPMENT. Annual report, 1945/1946-. Washington, the Bank

INTERNATIONAL MONETARY FUND. Annual report, 1946-. Washington, the Fund.

International annual reports that cover monetary co-operation in breadth and in detail. As such they form perhaps the basic reference material on current monetary problems and developments.

World monetary reform: plans and issues; edited by H. G. Grubel (London, Oxford Univ. Press, 1964. xiii, 446p. 60s.), on international liquidity, is the best guide to the named plans of Keynes, Stamp, Bernstein, Triffin, Roussa, and so on.

332.4 (4/9)
UNITED STATES. Annual report of the Director of the Mint. Washington, U.S. Government Printing Office.

Contains annually a separate report on the world's monetary stocks of gold, silver and coins, and gives the coinage of nations and coins in circulation for all countries by denomination, weight, composition, diameter and thickness. A unique source.

332.4 (410)
GREAT BRITAIN. ROYAL MINT. Annual report of the Deputy Master and Comptroller for the year, 1870-. London, H.M. Stationery Office.

A mine of information on the coinage.

332.41
INTERNATIONAL MONETARY FUND. Schedule of par values. Washington, the Fund, 1946-. 2 p.a.

Gives for each country a schedule of par values in terms of gold (grains of fine gold per currency unit and currency units per troy ounce of fine gold) and U.S. dollars (currency units per

dollar and U.S. cents per currency unit) in a uniform manner to six significant figures. The schedule does not list exchange rates or specify the multiple rate systems maintained by some members of the Fund. (For details of these, see the Fund's *Annual Report on Exchange Restrictions* and monthly *International Financial Statistics.*)

332.45
Annual bullion review, 1936-. London, Samuel Montagu, [1937?]-. Annual.

Formerly *The annual bullion letter,* 1910-1935.
A concise review of the gold and silver market and production, London and world prices of gold, silver and sometimes other rare metals. Supporting tables.
The *Montagu monthly review. London financial markets* (London, Samuel Montagu, 1920-. v. 1, no. 1-. Monthly) was, until the end of 1964, *Samuel Montagu's Review of foreign exchanges.* It deals with bullion, foreign exchange, money and the stock exchange, and has tables on bullion prices, foreign exchange rates and selected stock market prices.

Balance of Payments

332.453 (02)
WASSERMAN, M. J., and **WARE, R. M. The balance of payments:** history, methodology, theory. New York, Simmons-Boardman, 1965. xi, 481p. $10.

A comprehensive, well-produced survey. Excellent bibliography, p. 412-27.

332.453 (038)
ORGANISATION FOR EUROPEAN ECONOMIC CO-OPERATION. Terminologie des échanges et paiements internationaux et de la comptabilité nationale français-anglais, anglais-français: glossaire et définitions. Terms used in international trade and payments and national accounts . . . Paris, O.E.E.C., 1958. 145, [i]p.

Compiled primarily for use of O.E.E.C.'s own translators. English-French, French-English; equivalents, with explanations. Terms are grouped, *e.g.*, 'Agreement' has sub-headings 'Commodity agreement', 'European Monetary Agreement' and 'Bilateral payments agreement' Bibliography appended.

332.453 (058)
INTERNATIONAL MONETARY FUND. Balance of payments yearbook, 1938, 1946, 1947-. London, H.M. Stationery Office, 1949-. Loose-leaf. Annual. (v. 16: 1959-63).

Continues the series of figures issued by the League of Nations, covering 1926 (1910, in a few cases) to 1938, and the United Nations, covering 1939 to 1945.
Sections: Introduction—Concepts and definitions—Summary statements: countries A-Z (79 countries or areas in v. 16). Information on countries is based partly on requirements laid down in the *Balance of payments manual* and partly on additional information supplied by countries. Since v. 5, in both loose-leaf and

bound form. The section on Italy (6p.) comprises 3 tables: 1. Basic global statement, 1959-65—2. Basic regional statistics, 1963—3. Analytic presentation, 1961- 3rd quarter 1964. Notes on tables (2½p.).

Inflation

332.571.2
ORGANISATION FOR EUROPEAN CO-OPER-ATION AND DEVELOPMENT. Library. **Bibliographie spéciale analytique. Inflation.** Paris, O.E.C.D., 1965. v, 84p.

About 100 items (books and periodical articles), with annotations averaging 200 words. Part 1, Inflation (generalities—theory; studies by countries and groups of countries); part 2, Anti-inflationary measures (sub-divided by countries). Annotations are normally in the language of the original item. With few exceptions, confined to the period 1960-65.

332.573
INTERNATIONAL MONETARY FUND. Annual report on exchange restrictions. Washington, the Fund, [1950]-. Annual.

The 17th annual report (1966. 632p.) has 2 parts, one general and the other consisting of country surveys (109 countries, A-Z). The section on Argentina (p. 31-43) covers such matters as imports and export payments, payments for invisibles, exports and import proceeds, and particularly changes during 1965. Important for its retrospective coverage.

Stock Exchange

332.6 (038)=00
THOLE, B. L. L. M., *comp.* **Elsevier's Lexicon of stock-market terms:** English/American-French-German-Dutch. Amsterdam, etc., Elsevier, 1965. [viii], 131p. 40s.

999 numbered English/American specialised terms relating to investment, bonds, shares and other securities, payments, coupons, dividends and conversions, etc., with equivalents and indexes in French, German and Dutch. Includes phrases (*e.g.*, 'Raise a dividend'; 'General meeting of shareholders'), and states genders.

332.61 (410) (02)
ARMSTRONG, F. E. The book of the Stock Exchange. 5th ed. London, Pitman, 1957. xi, 317p. 45s.

A handy reference book on the working of the Stock Exchange, as distinct from the many slighter works concerned with investment. Includes an 18p. glossary of Stock Exchange phraseology.

332.61 (410) (058.7)
The Stock Exchange official year-book, 1934-. London, Skinner, 1934-. 2v. Annual. (1966 ed. £10).

Preceded by *Burdett's Official intelligence* (1874-98) and *Stock Exchange official intelligence,* 1899-1933. Issued as 1v. prior to 1948.

A comprehensive list of public companies, utilities, corporations, etc. of the world, the securities of which are handled on the stock exchanges of Britain. Gives details of directors, history, structure, capital and dividends. Arranged in broadly classified sections. V. 1 (which has its own index) covers all group securities appearing in the *Stock Exchange official list,* except the commercial, industrial, etc. section—dealt with in v. 2. V. 2 also contains a classified list of all companies quoted on London and associated stock exchanges, and a complete index of both volumes (*c.* 30,000 entries in the 1966 ed.).

Retrospective financial data are given in *Stock exchanges, London and provincial: ten-year record of prices and dividends* (London, Mathieson, 1909-. Annual).

332.61 (410) (083.4)
Moodies Industries and commodities service. London, Moodies Services, Ltd. Loose-leaf. £20 p.a.

Three main sections, each updated at regular intervals: *General survey* (monthly): general economic and investment conditions, with forecast; graphs of trade, prices, wages, unemployment, gross domestic product, yields, weather, external indicators and international production. *Basic reviews* (frequency varies with subject). Each industry is dealt with under headings "Characteristics", "Long term prospects" and "Current review". Gives salient indicators and other charts, plus comparative statistics and division of revenue. *Statistical bulletin* (monthly & annual) covers production, prices, sales, stocks and trade in various industries and commodities for past seven years. Handy appended bibliography of statistical sources.

Not to be confused with the American Moody's Investor's Services, also loose-leaf.

332.61 (410) (083.4)
Moodies Security indices and chart service. London, Moodies Services, Ltd. Loose-leaf. £20 p.a.

Part 1 concerns the equity market as a whole; monthly sheets on equity prices, earnings, dividends and yields, the industrial market and industrial share prices compared with overseas countries. Part 2 covers particular industries and individual companies comprising those industries. Earnings, dividends and prices are charted over a period of twelve years.

Moodies quarterly *Investment handbook* (£13 13s. p.a.) has two parts (1. Leading industrial trustee companies—2. Financial and smaller companies) and covers *c.* 900 companies. It aims "to give rapid comparisons of company with companion using identical standards of measurement". Includes a transparent master graph and scale compiled from 60 representative shares, to compare with a graph of share prices for each individual company. Similar data are given in *Moodies Investment digest* (Annual. 21s.) which has details of 500 companies.

Moodies British company service is a card service covering 5,000 quoted companies.

332.61 (410) (083.4)
The Stock Exchange daily official list. London, Council of the Stock Exchange, 1843-. Daily. £60 p.a.

Cites the quotations for securities, together with the marks of business actually transacted. Government is given first, then commercial and industrial companies arranged in broad groups under various subject headings. The *List* constitutes a complete and official record of price movements from day to day, and is important not only in investment activities but also as the accepted basis for estate duty, probate valuations and investment holding values in balance sheets.

The Stock Exchange weekly official intelligence, 1882- (£14 p.a.) contains the official notices of the Council and various data, including "Dividends, shuttings and meetings". An important supplement, "Relief from United Kingdom income tax on dividends of overseas companies", is issued in January and July.

The *Northern Stock Exchange official list,* 1965- (Manchester, Council of Northern Stock Exchange, 1965-. £31 10s. p.a.) gives similar information to the London *List,* but is restricted to business done on the Northern Stock Exchange (Bradford, Huddersfield, Leeds, Liverpool, Manchester, Newcastle, Oldham and Sheffield).

332.63
FINANCIAL PUBLISHING CO. Consolidated tables of bond values . . . , showing net returns from 2.90 to 15% on bonds and other redeemable securities paying interest semi-annually. London, Routledge & Kegan Paul, 1921 (reprinted 1964). 100s.

Coupon rates are given at 3, $3\frac{1}{2}$, 4, $4\frac{1}{4}$, $4\frac{1}{2}$, $4\frac{3}{4}$, 5, $5\frac{1}{4}$, $5\frac{1}{2}$, 6, $6\frac{1}{2}$, 7, $7\frac{1}{2}$ and 8% and yield rates of 2.90%–7% by .10% and $\frac{1}{8}$%, 7.10%–10% by .10% to $\frac{1}{4}$%, 10.10%–15% by .10%, with maturities semi-annually to 50 years and then by 5-year periods to 100 years, to two decimal places.

332.66
"The Times" Book of prospectuses: statements for information and circulars to shareholders of public companies. Compiled from the records of the Share and Loan Department of the Stock Exchange, London, with the authority of the Council, London, Times Publishing Co., 1891-. 2 p.a., January-June, July-December.

Previously known as *Issues 1891-1910* and, later, *Prospectuses of public companies.*
The main body of the work is arranged first chronologically and then A-Z by the company issue of that date under the Stock Exchanges of London, Birmingham, Manchester and Dublin. Additional details of rights, issues, bonuses, auctions and the like, together with conversion offers. Index of companies A-Z.
"The Times" Issuing house yearbook (q.v.) supplies further details in a different order.

332.66
"The Times" Issuing house yearbook. 1948-. London, Times Publishing Co., 1948-.

Previously as the *Issuing house yearbook and financial ABC,* 1929-39, and in 1946-47 the *Issuing house yearbook.* The yearbook was not published for the years 1932 and 1933.
Three main lists: 1. The issuing houses in the U.K. in alphabetical order and under each house, the issue operations which it has carried out, arranged chronologically, usually for the past ten years.—2. A-Z list by London and provincial stockbrokers, followed by the issue operations of those firms chronologically.—3. A-Z list of issues by name of company.
For the complete prospectuses of issues by the companies, see *"The Times" Book of prospectuses.*

Investment

332.67:016
SOCIETY OF INVESTMENT ANALYSTS. A bibliography for investment analysis. London, the Society, 1965. 104p. 30s.

Systematically arranged; brief annotations for each entry. British and international publications only. Aims "to provide sufficient source material in any subject of prospective interest to the investment analyst or to anyone else undertaking a general study of industrial or economic conditions to enable him to produce a well-informed assessment". Reviewed in *Board of Trade journal,* v. 189, no. 3567, 30th July 1965, p. 231.

332.67 (02)
"INVESTOR'S CHRONICLE". Beginners, please: a series of extracts from articles under this title published recently by the *Investor's chronicle.* 2nd ed. London, Eyre & Spottiswoode, 1960. xxvii, 304p. 30s.

First published 1955.
An encyclopaedic dictionary of Stock Exchange idiom, with investors' glossary; index.

An investor's guide (London, The Financial Times, 1960. [7], 147p. 15s. 6d.), a succinct guide for the ordinary investor, is much more concerned with the tools of analysis than with description; it aims "to equip the ordinary amateur investor with something of the increasingly scientific approach of the professional". Includes a handy 8p. glossary of terms.

The investor's manual, 1961 (London, Kaye, 1961. 183p. 18s.) gives a ten-year record of *c.* 1,500 stocks and statistics on 130 leading British industrials. Incorporates *Stock Exchange highest and lowest prices and dividends, 1951-1960, Industrial securities handbook, A guide for shareholders* and *An investment ledger.* Latest ed.: 1964 (21s.).

Herbert Johnson's *Investment tables* (London, Mathieson, 1949) shows "the return per cent. per annum on the market price of stocks or perpetual debentures paying rates of interest varying (in $\frac{1}{4}$%) from 1 to 10 per cent. per annum" (sub-title).

332.67 (083.4)
LAWSON, G. H., and WINDLE, D. W. Tables for discounted cash flow, annuity, sinking fund, compound interest and annual capital charge calculations, with explanatory notes and examples. London, Oliver & Boyd, 1965. 102p. 10s. 6d.

Consists of five tables. Tables 1 and 2 accommodate all three variants of the Discounted Cash-Flow formula, namely, present value, rate of return and annuity method. Tables 3 and 4 are

the necessary tabulations for terminal value calculations, and Table 5 is the reciprocal of Table
3 and is the basic tabulation for the sinking fund
variation of the annual capital investment
criterion (*Introduction*).

Land & Property

333:016

DENMAN, D. R., *and others.* **Bibliography of
rural land economy and land ownership,
1900-1957:** a full list of works relating to the
British Isles and selected works from the United
States and Western Europe. Cambridge, Univ.
Press, 1958. xii, 412p.

A list of *c.* 6,500 works, first in classified order
(p. 1-259). 8 classes: A. History—B. General
works—C. Rural economy and—D. Land economy—
E. Estate economy—F. Research and education—
G. Reference works (bibliographies; periodicals;
statistics; statutes)—H. Foreign works (Danish,
French, German, Dutch and Italian), then under
authors (English; foreign—in chronological
order). Subject index.

333.22 (42)

HOSKINS, W. G., and **STAMP, L. D. The common lands of England and Wales.** London,
Collins, 1963. xvii, 366p. illus., maps. (The new
naturalist). 42*s.*

The authors were members of the Royal Commission on Common Land, 1955-58. 25 chapters
(1-7, by W. G. Hoskins; 8-25, on detailed regions,
by L. D. Stamp). Appendix: The commons of
England. County lists, p. 243-350 (name; acreage;
nature; rights ownership). Favourably reviewed
in *Geographical review,* v. 55, no. 4, October
1965, p. 583-4.

333.5

WALMSLEY, R. C., *and others.* **Rural estate
management . . . in England and Wales.** 4th
ed. London, Estates Gazette, 1960. xxvii, 760p.
65*s.*

First published 1948.
A compendium for agricultural landowners,
land agents, and students. Chapter bibliographies
are gathered together on p. 687-726. Analytical
index.

Co-operation

334:016

INTERNATIONAL LABOUR OFFICE. Library.
Bibliography on co-operation. Geneva, I.L.O.,
1958. ii, 128p. Mimeographed.

Parts: 1. Publications on co-operation (1945-
1958)—2. Selected list of books on co-operation
—3. Publications and documents of the International Labour Office on co-operation. Divisions
of pt. 1 are mainly geographical; pt. 2 covers A,
Generalities and B, Types of co-operation
(agricultural; consumers; credit and banking;
housing; insurance, marketing; production), with
country sub-divisions. About 1,500 entries,—"co-
operative literature as represented in the Library
of the I.L.O." (*Foreword*); no annotations.
Author and country indexes.

334:016

**INTERNATIONAL LABOUR OFFICE. Réper-
toire international des organisations coopéra-
tives.** International directory of co-operative
organisations. 11. éd. Geneva, I.L.O., 1958. xv,
213p.

128 entries, international and then under
countries, A-Z. In French and English. Data:
date of foundation; official publication; affilia-
tion; membership; turnover or volume of business (*e.g.,* budget; capital; reserves; claims paid).
Index in French, English and Spanish.

334 (410) (058.7)

The Co-operative directory. Compiled by the
Editorial Department of the Co-operative Union,
Manchester. Manchester, Co-operative Union,
Ltd., 1966. 440p.

First published 1887.
Directory information on distributive, wholesale, productive and special co-operative societies
in the British Isles (p. 2-388). Locality index. The
1966 ed. for the first time attempts to indicate the
main business carried on at any co-operative
branch of any co-operative society in the British
Isles. Locality index, p. 391-440.

334.1 (410)

Building societies year book: official handbook of
the Building Societies Association. London,
Franey, 1927-. Annual. (1966. 70*s.*).

Details of building societies include abridged
balance sheets of member societies; addresses of
branch offices and agents; list of members of the
Building Societies Institute.

*The Building societies who's who: a biographi-
cal directory of the home-owning and savings
movement throughout the world* (London,
Franey, 1951-. Annual.) includes brief entries for
those no longer living, and histories of the
principal societies.

Socialism

335:016

**STAMMHAMMER, J. Bibliographie des Social-
ismus und Communismus.** Jena, Fischer, 1893-
1909. 3v. (Reprinted Aalen, Zeller, 1964. 3v.
DM.250.).

An international bibliography (up to the end
of 1908) that aims at exhaustiveness. Author list
with subject index. 26,500 entries.

335 (038) = 30

EHLERT, W., *and others, ed.* **Wörterbuch der
Ökonomie Sozialismus.** Berlin, Dietz, 1967.
539p. tables, bar diagrs.

About *c.* 1,500 entries and numerous cross-
references. East German Communist slanted
(*e.g.,* article on 'Planung der Volkswirtschaft':
2$\frac{3}{4}$ col.). Entries for institutions, Ministries and
the like. No biographies; no bibliographies, although occasional references.

335 (091)

COLE, G. D. H. A history of Socialist thought.
London, Macmillan, 1953-60 (reprinted 1961-63
in 7v.). 5v.

v. 1: *Socialist thought: the forerunners, 1789-1850.*
v. 2: *Socialist thought: Marxism and Anarchism, 1850-1890.*
v. 3 *The Second International, 1889-1914* (forms v. 3-4 of reprint).
v. 4: *Communism and social democracy, 1914-1931* (v. 5-6 of reprint).
v. 5: *Socialism and Fascism, 1931-1939* (v. 7 of reprint).

Not a history of Socialism but of Socialist thought. Cole originally intended his history to go up to 1945, but he died in 1959 with this objective uncompleted. V. 1 has 26 chapters, a select bibliography (p. 317-32: chapter bibliographies preceded by general references), index of names and subject index.

335 (092)
OSTERROTH, F. Biographisches Lexikon des Sozialismus. Hannover, Dietz, 1960-. v. 1-. pl. (ports.).

v. 1: *Verstorbene Persönlichkeiten.*
Short biographies, averaging one page each, of *c.* 350 deceased Socialists connected with Germany. The biography of Karl Marx (p. 213-8) has 6 references appended. Index of *c.* 1,000 names. 48 pages of portraits.

Communism

335.55:016
HAMMOND, T. T., *ed.* Soviet foreign relations and world Communism: a selected, annotated bibliography of 7,000 books in 30 languages. Princeton, N.J., Princeton Univ. Press; London, Oxford Univ. Press, 1965. xxiv, 1240p. $25; £10.

Three main sections: Soviet foreign relations since 1917 (sub-divided into periods)—World Communism (regions and countries)—Special topics. Compiled by area and subject specialists. Much broader and deeper in scope than Kolarz. A judicious selection, with careful, frequently evaluative annotations. The leading ten items in each sub-section are marked 'A', and the next twenty, 'B'. Detailed index of authors and anonymous titles. Well produced.

J. Braunthal's *History of the International* (translated by John Clark. London, Nelson, 1967. 2v. illus. 95*s.*, 126*s.*) "will become as essential [for students of the European labour movement] as the late G. D. H. Cole's classic History of socialist thought" (*Times literary supplement*, no. 3,440, 1st February 1968, p. 105). V. 1 covers 1864-1914; v. 2, 1914-1943. Translated by John Clark.

Noted: Sworakowski, W. S. *The Communist International and its front organizations: a research guide and checklist of holdings in American and European libraries* (Stanford, Cal., Hoover Institution on War, Revolution and Peace, 1965. 493p. $10).

335.55:016
KOLARZ, W., *ed.* Books on Communism: a bibliography. 2nd ed. London, Ampersand, 1963. 568p. 30*s.*

Originally published 1959, edited by R. N.

Carew Hunt (although this is not stated). This ed. adds *c.* 700 new entries. About 2,500 annotated entries for English-language publications. Three main parts: 1. Studies of Communism in general and in the U.S.S.R. (sections 1-25)—2. Communism in other countries (26-50)—3. Official documents and publications (51-52). Addenda of selected titles for 1963. Annotations average *c.* 40 words; U.S. and British imprints given. Author-title index. *Bulletin des bibliothèques de France* (1966, no. 2, p. 157) complains of the confused arrangement of sections.

335.55:016
UNITED STATES. LIBRARY OF CONGRESS. Legislative Reference Service. **World Communism:** a selected annotated bibliography. Washington, 1964. 2v. (88th Congress. Senate. 2nd Section. Document no. 69). $1.20.

Part 1 (x, 394p.) comprises 3,059 numbered and annotated items in 14 main sections (1. A commentary on the bibliography—2. Bibliographies (nos. 1-90)—3. Indexes, guides, encyclopedias and other general reference aids (nos. 91-167). Part 2 (iii, p. 379-410) consists of section 15, Other literature on Communism (items. 3060-3202). Each part has an author index. Covers material in English only, up to the end of September 1963.

Public Finance
(*See also* 332.)

336 (4)
ORGANISATION FOR ECONOMIC CO-OPERATION AND DEVELOPMENT. National accounts statistics: expenditure, product and income, 1956-1965. Paris, O.E.C.D., 1967. 309p. tables.

In English and French. 4 parts: 1. Comparative tables—2. Tables by main country groupings (O.E.C.D. total; O.E.C.D. Europe; E.E.C.)—3. Tables by country (21 countries, including Canada, U.S.A., Japan and Turkey)—4. Rates of change for selected aggregates. Tables and explanatory notes. Previous v. covered 1955-1964 (1966).

336 (410)
GREAT BRITAIN. CENTRAL STATISTICAL OFFICE. Financial statistics. London, H.M. Stationery Office, 1962-. Monthly. ea. 10*s.* 6*d.*

Prepared in collaboration with the Statistics Divisions of Government Departments and the Bank of England, to bring together "the key financial and monetary statistics of the United Kingdom" (*Introduction*). 10 sections, including 10. Overseas finance. The no. 50, June 1966 issue has 91 tables and an index.

336.1 (4/9)
UNITED NATIONS. Department of Economic and Social Affairs. **Yearbook of national accounts statistics,** 1957-. New York, United Nations. 1958-. Annual. (1963, published 1964. $4.).

The *Yearbook* for 1963 gives (Part C) detailed estimates of national accounts for 76 countries and aggregate estimates of national income, mainly for the years 1956-62; expressed in native currency. Part D. International tables. The 1957 *Yearbook* covers the years 1950-56.

336.12 (410)
BRITTAIN, *Sir* **H. The British budgetary system.** London, Allen & Unwin, 1959. 320p. 25s.

A standard work. The composition of the budget is closely discussed item by item and is followed by a chapter on the national debt. Finally, the control of government expenditure by Parliament and the Treasury is explained in detail. Detailed index; no bibliography.

A. R. Prest's *Public finance in theory and practice* (London, Weidenfeld & Nicolson, 1960. 408p. 45s.) is more general in scope as a textbook, and includes chapters on U.S.A. and Canada.

Taxes

336.2 (4)
European taxation supplementary service. Amsterdam, International Bureau of Fiscal Documentation, 1963. 4v. Loose-leaf.

Section A-E: A. Corporate tax rates, by country—B. Individual tax rates, by country—C. Tax treaties concluded by European countries—D. Abstracts from official reports—E. Current bibliography on taxes over the world (monthly). Section E has 4 parts: 1. Official documents (covering 60 periodicals from 20 countries)—2. Books—3. Loose-leaf services—4. Periodicals (covering 220 periodicals from 70 countries).

The International Bureau of Fiscal Documentation also issues a series of loose-leaf guides to European taxation: v. 1, *Taxation of patent royalties, dividends, interest in Europe;* v. 2, *Corporate taxation in the Common Market,* as well as a *Bulletin for international fiscal documentation* ([1948?]-. Monthly).

336.21 (41-44)
GREAT BRITAIN. BOARD OF INLAND REVENUE. Income taxes in the Commonwealth. [New ed.] London, H.M. Stationery Office, 1958-60. 2v. Loose-leaf. 159s. Supplements. 1961-. (10th suppt. 1966. 42s.).

v. 1: *Africa, America.*
v. 2: *Asia, Australia, New Zealand and the Pacific Islands, Europe.*
Replaces the 1951-53 ed. and its annual supplements.
Summarises the income tax laws of the various Commonwealth countries. Information is given up to 1959 in most cases. The complementary work is:

————— **Income taxes outside the Commonwealth.** London, H.M. Stationery Office, 1956. 2v. 35s.; Supplements (4th supplement. 1960. 25s.).

Three parts: 1. U.S.A.; 2. Republic of Ireland; 3. Continental Europe (9 countries).

336.2 (410) (02)
CROYDON, C. H. Tolley's Income tax chart manual. London, Tolley. Annual. (1966-67. 21s.).

A valuable quick-reference guide to U.K. income tax that can be used by the non-specialist. The publisher also produces similar guides for Eire, the Channel Islands and Isle of Man, as well as guides to Corporation tax, Profits tax and Estate duty.

Other annual guides to income tax include *"Taxation" Key to income tax and surtax* (1966-67. 14s. 8d.), *Fieldhouse's Income tax simplified* (1966. 5s. 6d.), *Jordan's Income tax guide* (1965/6. 3s.) and *"Daily Mail" Income tax guide* (1966-67. 2s. 6d.).

The Commissioners of Inland Revenue *P.A.Y.E. tables* are *gratis.*

336.2 (410) (031)
WHEATCROFT, G. S. A., *ed.* **British tax encyclopedia.** [13th ed.]. London, Sweet & Maxwell, 1962-. 5v. Loose-leaf. £31 10s. Annual service, 168s.

First published 1921. Based on Konstam's *The law of income tax* (12th ed. 1952; suppts.).

V. 1 is a narrative treatise on the definition of income for tax purposes, taking clearly defined areas of income and discussing each separately, followed by a consideration of how each particular type of taxpayer is taxed. V. 2-5 contain the relevant statutory material, fully annotated. Because of the complex nature of legislation on income tax, plentiful and detailed cross-references are essential in a work of this kind; a high standard is reached in this encyclopaedia. Each v. has a full index to the complex work and its own tables of cases and statutes. V. 5 has consolidated tables of cases and statutes.

Simon's Income tax (2nd ed., edited by N. E. Mustoe. London, Butterworth, 1965. 5v. in 7. Loose-leaf and replacement v. £23. 117s. 6d. p.a.) devotes 3 v. to a narrative exposition of income tax law and practice; the rest contain relevant texts of statutes and statutory instruments, plus tables of statutes and cases. Not quite so extensive as *British tax encyclopedia,* but its different arrangement and method of indexing make it a useful alternative.

336.2 (410) (094)
HARRISON, *Sir* **E. R. A digest and index of tax cases;** being a judicial dictionary of the law. 6th ed. London, H.M. Stationery Office, 1949-. 2v. (v. 2, loose-leaf). 14th supplement. 1966. 22s. 6d.

Cases indexed are those reported in the official *Reports of tax cases, 1875-,* although other reports are included. V. 2 is a supplementary volume, updating v. 1. and cumulated by periodical addition and replacement by new sheets. Each volume has 3 sections: tables of tax cases, names of parties and subject matter. This last is arranged A-Z by subject and gives a brief account of each relevant case, plus judicial finding.

A similar *Index to tax cases* (London, Butterworth, 1873-1963. v. 1-40) has more numerous subject headings.

Butterworth's Income tax handbook; being the amended text of the income tax acts as operative during 1962/63- (London, Butterworth, 1962-. Annual. 1966-67. 42s.) is a handy-sized one-volume work that covers legal provision on income tax in a particular year. It includes provisions relating to capital gains tax and corporation tax.

336.24 / .25

TOASE, C. A., *comp.* **Licences and current official registers:** a brief guide to procedure, contents and inspection. London, Library Association (Reference, Special and Information Section: South Eastern Group), 1960. 52p. (Aids to reference service, no. 2).

Compiled to meet several types of inquiry: "1. The procedure for registration or for obtaining a licence, and in particular where to go and how much it costs.—2. Where and how registers and records of licences may be seen.—3. Where lists are published, or copies available in any form" (*Preface*). A most useful list, with full cross-references and notes on registration, contents and inspection, wherever applicable. Headings are arranged alphabetically, from "Accommodation addresses" to "Young persons under 18 street trading". Insert of *Corrections and additions* is dated February 1960.
A new ed. is in preparation.

Customs Tariffs

337.3

CUSTOMS CO-OPERATION COUNCIL. Nomenclature for the classification of goods in customs tariffs. [Brussels Nomenclature]. Brussels, the Council, 1965. Loose-leaf.

Contains the text of the Brussels Nomenclature, an internationally agreed standard system of classification of goods for customs tariffs, now used by many countries. A correlation table between the United Nations' Standard International Trade Classification, revised ('SITC Revised') and the Brussels Nomenclature ('BTN') is appended.

—— **Explanatory notes on the Brussels Nomenclature.** Brussels, the Council, 1966. 3v. Loose-leaf. £19 7s.

The official texts of the explanatory notes to the Nomenclature, essential for classifying many types of goods for tariff purposes. (Thus, under section II 13.03 there is a detailed description of "pectin substances", "pectinates" and "pectates"; under VI 38.01, "Artificial graphite" is stated as not covering retort carbon, sometimes incorrectly called artificial graphite. Supplementary notes indicate scope and contents of the statistical subheadings that the Council has recommended for insertion in tariffs or statistical nomenclatures operated by countries using BTN, to ensure correlation with SITC Revised).
The *Alphabetical index to the explanatory notes to the Brussels Nomenclature* (Brussels, 1955) (reprinted 1960). 3v. 95s. the set) refers to the previous ed. of the notes, but as each entry includes the BTN heading number, this can be used for reference instead.
A *Classification of chemicals in the Brussels Nomenclature* (Brussels, 1961. 9s. 6d.; new ed. 1967. 15s.) contains an A-Z list of c. 20,000

chemicals with their BTN heading classification numbers.

The Customs Co-operation Council has also published *Glossaire des termes douaniers internationaux* (Brussels, the Council, 1964. 60p.).

337.3

International customs journal. Brussels, International Customs Tariff Bureau. London, H.M. Stationery Office. Irregular. 60s. p.a.

Each number gives the customs tariff of a particular country (*e.g.,* Switzerland: no. 1, U.K.: no. 2, U.S.A.: no. 21). The *Journal* is kept up to date by new editions of each number (U.K. is now in its 23rd ed.) and also by supplements.

337.3 (410)

GREAT BRITAIN. H.M. CUSTOMS AND EXCISE. Tariff of the United Kingdom of Great Britain and Northern Ireland. London, H.M. Stationery Office, 1960-. Loose-leaf. Amendment service, 60s. p.a.

"Contains a statement of the duties of Customs and Excise chargeable on goods imported into or produced in the United Kingdom, of the related drawbacks and allowances[,] and of the prohibitions and restrictions in force" (*Introduction*). The schedule of duties is based on the Brussels nomenclature. Rates are shown in two columns: full rate, and preferential rate (for Commonwealth preference, Eire and EFTA). Also given for each items is a statistical key, including code number, statistical description and unit of quantity.
Complementary to the statistical key is the annual *Statistical classification for imported goods and for re-exported goods* (H.M.S.O., 1967. 12s. 6d.), the order and grouping of which follows the Standard International Trade classification, revised. A general survey of Customs regulations is given in *Customs regulation and procedure* (H.M.S.O., 1961. 9s.).

337.3 (73)

Custom house guide. New York, Import Publications, Inc., 1862-. Annual, with monthly supplement (*American import and export bulletin*).

A 2,000-page guide to U.S. customs regulations, including the complete tariff schedules, an A-Z list of 26,000 commodities (plus duty rates and item numbers), a lengthy section on ports (with details of concerns offering services to shippers), and internal revenue codes.

337.91 (4)

GREAT BRITAIN. BOARD OF TRADE. European Free Trade Association: compendium for the use of exporters. London, H.M. Stationery Office, 1965-. 240p. Loose-leaf. 12s. 6d.

Aims to set out and explain the rules of origin of the EFTA Convention, and to describe the formalities governing exports to the EFTA area (*Introduction*). Four sections: 1. A general description of the agreement origin rules and documentary evidence—2. Text of the Convention and Brussels Nomenclature headings—3. Forms—4. Bodies authorised to issue U.K. certificates of origin.

Production: Agriculture

338:63:016
Digest of agricultural economics. Oxford, Institute for Research in Agricultural Economics, Univ. of Oxford, 1957-. Quarterly. 21s. p.a.; ea. 5s.

See entry in the Guide, v. 1, *at 63:016.*

338:63:016
World agricultural economics and rural sociology, April 1959-. Amsterdam, North-Holland Publishing Co., 1959-64; Farnham Royal, Bucks., Commonwealth Agricultural Bureaux, 1965-. Quarterly. 60s. p.a. to subscribers in C.A.B. contributing countries; 100s. to subscribers in other countries.

As from 1965 prepared by the Commonwealth Bureau of Agricultural Economics, Oxford.

First half of 1967: 2,332 indicative and informative abstracts. Sections: 1. Agricultural policy —2. Agricultural products: supply, demand and prices—3. Marketing and distribution of agricultural products—4. International trade—5. Finance and credit—6. Economics of production —7. Co-operation—8. Education and training—9. Rural sociology—0. Research methods and techniques—R. Reference material (general; regional economic and social conditions; national economic and social conditions). News and views. Author, subject and geographical indexes in each issue.

338:63
FOOD AND AGRICULTURE ORGANIZATION. FAO commodity review. Rome, F.A.O., 1961-. tables. Annual. (1966. 15s.).

1966 v., based on information available to the F.A.O. up to 15th March 1966. Pt. 1: General review; pt. 2: Individual commodities (grains and rice; livestock products and oils; tropical export crops; other tree and field crops; agricultural raw materials; fisheries products; forest products). 73 tables; 21 charts.

338:63
FOOD AND AGRICULTURE ORGANIZATION. Production yearbook. Rome, F.A.O., 1948-tables. Annual. (1965. 35s.).

Pt. 1 of the F.A.O. *Yearbook of food and agricultural statistics.* The 1965 yearbook (v. 19, published 1966) contains 191 tables in 9 sections, with notes, and gives statistics for a ten-year period up to 1964. In English and French; table of contents in English, French and Spanish; Spanish glossary of terms in tables (by table no.), p. 521-66. For sources of prices, see 1960 v., p. 449-69.

The F.A.O. *Trade yearbook* (see at 382:63) forms pt. 2 of the *Yearbook of food and agricultural statistics.*

These two yearbooks are kept up to date by the F.A.O. *Monthly bulletin of agricultural economics and statistics,* 1952- (ea. 2s. 6d.; 25s. p.a.), which carries an article, a special feature and statistical tables of production, trade and prices in each issue.

338:63
FOOD AND AGRICULTURE ORGANIZATION. The state of food and agriculture. Rome, F.A.O., 1956-. diagrs., tables, charts. Annual. (1964. 30s.).

Sections (1964): 1. Summary—2. World outlook and review—3. Protein nutrition: needs and prospects—4. Synthetics and their effect on agricultural trade. 33 annex tables; 18 graphs. Information up to 15th July 1964. Each issue contains one or more special studies of problems of longer-term interest. In English and French, with Spanish glossary (of terms used in headings and notes). Conversion tables.

The 1965 issue is a review of the second postwar decade, 1955/64.

338:631.8
FOOD AND AGRICULTURE ORGANIZATION. Fertilizers: an annual review of world production, consumption and trade. Rome, F.A.O., 1953-. tables. Annual. (1965 v., published 1966. 12s. 6d.).

Sections: World output—Forms in which fertilizers are produced—World consumption— —International trade—Fertilizer prices—Review of production, consumption and trade, by continents and by countries. 28 appendix tables (detailed data for production, consumption and trade by countries, for a 6-year period). The 1965 v. contains, for the first time, data on the world nitrogen industry and on crop responses to fertilizers.

338:633
FOOD AND AGRICULTURE ORGANIZATION. World crop statistics: area, production and yield, 1948-64. Rome, F.A.O., 1966. [viii], 458p. tables, graphs. 35s.

80 computer-produced tables, in 14 groups, giving statistics for all the crops published annually in the F.A.O. *Production yearbook.* Trends are indicated by graphs for major crops —cereals, potatoes, groundnuts, tobacco, cotton, coffee and sugar—giving area, production and yield, by continents. List of countries (by continents or areas), p. 456-8. Oblong, with a 3-column page,—in English, French and Spanish.

338:633
COMMONWEALTH ECONOMIC COMMITTEE. Grain crops: a review of production, trade, consumption and prices relating to wheat, wheat flour, maize, barley, oats, rye and rice. London, published for the Commonwealth Economic Committee by H.M. Stationery Office, 1932-. Annual. (1966. iv, 222p. tables. 10s.).

The Commonwealth Economic Committee is now the Commonwealth Secretariat.

The main text (1966 v.) has 84 tables, with notes. Appendices on international policy, national policies affecting grain in certain countries, and duties and import restrictions on grain.

Kept up to date in the Commonwealth Secretariat's monthly *Grain bulletin,* with *Rice supplement.*

338:633.11
INTERNATIONAL WHEAT COUNCIL. World wheat statistics. London, the Council, 1955-. tables. Annual. (13th issue. 1967. 20s.).

Statistics of wheat and flour production, exports, imports and supplies, prices (producer and domestic, export and import), freight rates and inland transportation costs for wheat; usually for 3-year period, plus a 5-year average. The 1967 v. has 38 main tables (no. 37: wheat harvesting calendar), plus conversion tables.

The International Wheat Council also publishes an annual *Review of the world wheat situation* (*e.g.,* 1965/66, published [1967]) and *Trends and problems in the world wheat economy . . . 1950-1970* ([1966]. [1], vi, 39p.), which includes statistics up to 1966.

338:633.18

FOOD AND AGRICULTURE ORGANIZATION. The world rice economy in figures . . . 1909 to 1963. Rome, F.A.O., 1965. xiv, 134p. tables. (Commodity reference series).

19 tables: conversion factors; production; trade; utilization; prices. List of sources (production; trade; prices), p. 111-20. Headings in English and French; Spanish glossary of terms in tables, p. 123-34.

For current statistics, see the Commonwealth Economic Committee (now Commonwealth Secretariat)'s *Rice supplement* to its monthly *Grain bulletin*.

338:633.74

FOOD AND AGRICULTURE ORGANIZATION. Cocoa statistics. Rome, F.A.O., 1958-. Quarterly. ea. 3s. 9d.; 12s. p.a.

V. 10, no. 2 (April 1967) has 58 tables: general; producing countries; importing countries; special information (cocoa butter and cocoa powder: exports and imports). In English, French and Spanish.

World cocoa survey, by C. A. Krug and E. Quartey-Papafio (Rome, F.A.O., 1964. ix, [1], 242p. tables, maps., 20s.) deals with areas and individual countries. 5 appendices, including: 1. Sources of information (p. 214-6)—4. List of scientific names mentioned in cocoa literature—5. Conversion tables. Bibliography, p. 239-42; 35 black-and-white maps.

338:634

FOOD AND AGRICULTURE ORGANIZATION. Yearbook of forest product statistics, 1947-. Rome, F.A.O., 1948-. tables, graphs, maps. Annual. (1966. 12s. 6d.).

Compiled by Forestry and Forest Products Division of F.A.O. in collaboration with the Economic Commission for Europe. Covers 180 countries.

The 20th issue, 1966, gives production and trade statistics up to 1965 for coniferous and broad-leaved products, and products outside the forests, plus processed wood, pulp and pulp products. In English and French, with definitions of terms in English, French and Spanish. Conversion tables.

——**World forest product statistics:** a ten-year summary . . . 1954-1963. Rome, F.A.O., 1965. tables. 350p. 15s.

The first ten-year summary (1957) covered 1946-1955. Statistics of removals, production and trade for 170 countries. In English, French and (partly) Spanish. Definitions of terms in English, French and Spanish.

338:634.1/.8

COMMONWEALTH ECONOMIC COMMITTEE. Fruit: a review of production and trade relating to fresh, canned, frozen and dried fruit, fruit juices and wine. London, H.M.S.O., 1932-. tables. Annual. (1967. 40s.).

Prepared by the Commonwealth Secretariat, Commodities Section, as from 1967.

The 1967 v. has 157 tables in the main text, with statistics up to 1964 or 1965. 5 appendices.

Current developments are reviewed in the Commonwealth Secretariat's monthly *Fruit intelligence*.

338:637.1/.4

COMMONWEALTH SECRETARIAT. Commodities Division. **Dairy produce:** a review of production, trade, consumption and prices relating to butter, cheese, condensed milk, milk powder, casein, eggs, egg products and margarine. London, H.M. Stationery Office, 1932-. tables. Annual. (1967. 30s.).

Annual, 1936-.

The 1967 v. has 112 tables, with statistics up to 1966. Chapters on the commodities. Appendices (Government measures affecting dairy products in certain countries; Retail prices; Import duties and controls).

Kept up to date by the Commonwealth Secretariat's monthly *Intelligence bulletin,* covering dairy produce, eggs and poultry, and meat, and *Weekly dairy produce supplies*.

338:637.5

COMMONWEALTH SECRETARIAT. Commodities Division. **Meat:** a review of production, trade, consumption and prices relating to beef and veal, mutton and lamb, pig-meat, poultry-meat, offals, canned meat. London, the Secretariat, 1967. viii, 151p. tables. 30s.

The 17th post-war annual issue.

117 tables of statistics up to 1966. 3 appendices, on government measures, imports into the E.E.C., and import duties and controls.

Current developments are reviewed in the Commonwealth Secretariat's monthly *Intelligence bulletin*.

338:639

FOOD AND AGRICULTURE ORGANIZATION. Yearbook of fishery statistics, 1947-. Rome, F.A.O., 1948-. tables. Annual.

v. 16: *1963. Catches and landings.* 1964.
v. 17: *1963. Fishery commodities.* 1965.
v. 18: *1964. Catches and landings.* 1965.
v. 19: *1964. Fishery commodities.* 1965.
v. 20: *1965. Catches and landings.* 1966.
 27s. 6d.
v. 21: *1965. Fishery commodities.* 1966. 35s.

V. 21 brings up to date the annual statistics in v. 19. Production, imports and exports, by type (fish, fresh, chilled or frozen; fish products and preparations; fish, dried, salted or smoked;

crustaceans and molluscs, fresh, frozen, dried, salted; oils and fats; meals, solubles, etc.). V. 20: *1965. Catches and landings* has 3 sections: A. Summaries—B. By countries—C. By species. Maps and graphs.

Supplemented by *Bulletin of fishery statistics* (irregular).

338:639.2

COMMONWEALTH ECONOMIC COMMITTEE. Fish. London, H.M. Stationery Office, 1966. xiv, 212p. tables. (Reports of the Commonwealth Economic Committee. 41st report). 17s. 6d.

8 chapters: World fish resources—Conservation and regulation—The primary fishing industries—Treatment and the use of fish—International trade in fish and fish products—Consumption and markets—Commonwealth fisheries development —Summary and conclusions. 71 tables, with statistics up to 1964.

Production: Non-metallic Minerals

338:661/666

COMMONWEALTH SECRETARIAT. Commodities Division. **Non-metallic minerals:** a review of resources, production, trade, consumption and prices relating to sulphur, gypsum and anhydrite, asbestos, asphalt and bitumen, magnesite, graphite, mica and diamonds. London, Commonwealth Secretariat, 1967. vi, 170p. tables. 35s.

The Commonwealth Secretariat was previously the Commonwealth Economic Committee. Previous issue, 1964.

77 numbered tables, with statistics up to 1966. Appendix: tariff notes.

Production: Energy

338:662.6

COMMONWEALTH ECONOMIC COMMITTEE. Sources of energy: a review of consumption, resources, production, trade, stocks and prices relating to coal and lignite, petroleum, natural gas and hydro-electricity, and to nuclear power and other sources of energy. London, H.M. Stationery Office, 1966. viii, 185p. tables. 20s.

8 sections. Section [8]: New sources of energy (nuclear power; geothermal, tidal, wind and solar energy). 38 tables, with statistics up to 1964; 4 charts. No index.

The U.S. Bureau of Mines' *Minerals yearbook, 1965, v. 2: Mineral fuels* (Washington, U.S.G.P.O., 1967. vi, 465p. $2.50) has major sections on coal and petroleum and related products, and on such related products as helium, carbon black, peat, coke and coal chemicals, and natural gas liquids. Covers production, consumption, trade, prices, etc. for all countries. Numerous tables and graphs; no index.

338:662.6

UNITED NATIONS. World energy supplies, 1961-1964. 9th issue. New York, U.N., 1966. 99p. (Statistical papers, series J, no. 9). $2.

Annual data of production, trade and consumption in *c.* 170 countries for coal (including lignite),

coke, petroleum and derivatives, natural and manufactured gas, and electricity, with regional and global totals. Summary data also for 1954-64.

Production: Sugar

338:664.1

INTERNATIONAL SUGAR COUNCIL. Sugar year book, 1948-. London, the Council, [1949?]. Annual. (20th issue, 1966, published [1967]. 40s.).

Country tables, by countries A-Z; general tables (world production; imports; exports; stocks; consumption; etc.). Statistics relate to centrifugal sugar only (*i.e.,* sugar freed from liquid by means of a centrifugal machine). The 1966 v. has 364 pages of tables.

The International Sugar Council's monthly *Statistical bulletin* (ea. 10s.; 100s. p.a.) covers supply and demand, distribution, trade, consumption and stock.

F. O. Licht's *Internationales zuckerwirtschaftliches Jahr- und Adressbuch . . . Weltzuckerstatistik* (Ratzeburg, Licht) is the standard yearbook for the world's sugar economy (both sugarbeet and sugar-cane). It covers organization, production, imports, exports, plants and refineries, gives statistics, list sources and includes an English-German glossary, plus an atlas of sugar factories.

338:664.1

INTERNATIONAL SUGAR COUNCIL. The world sugar economy: structure and policies. London, the Council, 1963. 2v. tables, maps. 105s.

v. 1: *National sugar economies and policies.* 63s.

v. 2: *The world picture.* 42s.

V. 1 is divided into 7 pts., by continents and countries. Many tables, giving production, trade and consumption figures, and prices. Statistics up to 1962. Policies concern control of supplies, price regulations and the like. V. 2 has 2 pts.: world sugar; world sugar composition; world sugar trade; world sugar statistics (39 tables, 1957 or 1958 to 1962). Explanatory notes and sources.

Production: Vegetable Oils

338:665.3

COMMONWEALTH ECONOMIC COMMITTEE. Vegetable oils and oilseeds: a review of production, trade, utilisation and prices relating to groundnuts, cottonseed, linseed, soya beans, coconut and oil palm products, olive oil and other oilseeds and oils. London, H.M. Stationery Office, 1932-. Annual. (16th ed. 1967. 10s.).

1922-38, as *Oilseeds and vegetable oils.*

The 1967 v. gives production data up to 1964-65 and tabulated data up to 1964, with provisional information for a further year where available. 162 tables in main text. Appendices: 1. New supplies of vegetable oils—2. Margarine, compound cooking fat and soap—3. Whale oil.

Production and trade figures for the more important vegetable oils and oilseeds are currently reviewed in the Commonwealth Secretariat's *Tropical products quarterly*.

Production: Petroleum

338:665.5

AMERICAN PETROLEUM INSTITUTE. Petroleum facts and figures. New York, the Institute, 1928-. Annual.

Six sections: Production—Refining—Transportation—Marketing and utilization—Prices and taxation—General. Covers substantially all major statistics in the oil industry; particularly detailed for U.S.A. and Canada, with selected world data following. Also notes on geophysical activity; crude oil resources and production; refinery capacity; production of major refined oil products; major petroleum periodicals.

The British Petroleum Company, Ltd.'s *Statistical review of the world oil industry* gives a brief annual survey of reserves, production, consumption, trade, refining, tankers, energy, with an historical section and conversion factors. The 1966 issue (*gratis*) has 24 tables, with statistics for 1965 and 1966. Annual.

338:665.5

UNITED STATES. BUREAU OF MINES. International petroleum annual, 1965-. Washington, 1967-.

Previously *International petroleum quarterly*.
Largely statistical tables. Includes international petroleum statistics for 1965 (supply and demand; output; imports and exports; domestic demand) and for 1964 (final summary), as well as retail prices of gasoline, kerosene and lubricating oils by country, as of December 31, 1964 and 1965.

Production: Minerals

338:669

INSTITUTE OF GEOLOGICAL SCIENCES. Overseas Division, Mineral Resources Section. **Statistical summary of the mineral industry:** world production, exports and imports, 1960-1965. London, H.M. Stationery Office, 1967. iv, 417p. tables. 27s. 6d.

The Institute, formed in 1965 as part of the National Environment Research Council was previously 'Overseas Geological Surveys' and, prior to that, 'Colonial Geological Surveys'.
The latest in a series of six-year surveys. "No other statistical publication contains such detailed information on world trade in minerals and metals, etc." (*Chemical trade journal*, v. 150, no. 3912, 25th May 1962, p. 1063). The 1960-1965 v. deals with 59 major minerals or groups of minerals, A-Z (Abrasives—Zirconium minerals), plus 'Other minerals and metals'. 411 pages of tables, giving country-by-country coverage of production, imports and exports. List of 'Minerals produced in the Commonwealth and Sterling area', under countries A-Z (p. 412-5). Index of minerals.

338:669

Minerals yearbook, 1932/33-. U.S. Bureau of Mines. Washington, U.S. Government Printing Office, 1933-. tables. Annual. (1964 ed. 1966. 4v.).

v. 1: *Metals and minerals (except fuels)*. $4.75:
v. 2: *Mineral fuels (see at 338:662.6)*. $2.75.
v. 3: *Area reports: domestic*. $5.
v. 4: *Area reports: international*. $5.
V. 1 give systematic and statistical data on metals and minerals, A-Z, with many tables and references to the literature (*e.g.*, 'Magnesium': domestic (*i.e.*, U.S.) production; consumption and uses; stocks; prices; foreign trade; world review; technology.) Commodity index; world review index. While v. 1-2 and 4 have world coverage, v. 3 is confined to U.S.A. (by states, A-Z); no index. Preprints available on specific metals and minerals in v. 1 (at 10c.-15c.). A major statistical source on minerals.

Mineral trade notes (U.S. Bureau of Mines, 1935-. Monthly) has sub-title: "a monthly inventory of information from U.S. Government Foreign Service offices and other sources that may not otherwise be made available promptly." Each issue is largely a commodity review (minerals A-Z, sub-divided by country), plus 'Miscellaneous information'.

338:669

Mining annual review. London, "Mining journal". illus., diagrs., tables, maps. Annual. (1967. 30s.).

Title varies; previous title: "Mining journal" annual review.
The 1967 ed. has main sections: Metals and minerals (p. 9-99; 10 sections)—Technical progress reports (p. 101-97; 7 sections)—Countries (p. 199-311; 6 sections)—Progress of industrial countries (p. 313-91). Statistics up to 1966. Brief professional directory and buyer's guide. Indexes to manufacturers, companies and advertisers.

338:669.2/.8

AMERICAN BUREAU OF METAL STATISTICS. Year book . . . New York, the Bureau, 1920-. Annual. (45th annual issue, for 1965. 1966. $4.50; $4).

Gives production, consumption, distribution, principal producers, etc. of copper, lead, zinc, aluminium, gold and silver and other non-ferrous metals, especially tin.

338:669.2/.8

COMMONWEALTH ECONOMIC COMMITTEE. Non-ferrous metals: a review of resources, production, trade, consumption, stocks and prices relating to bauxite, aluminium, copper, lead, zinc, tin and cadmium. London, published for the Commonwealth Economic Committee by H.M. Stationery Office, 1963. vi, 214p. tables, charts. 12s. 6d.

General review (p. 1-33), covering production, trade, consumption and uses, prices; followed by 6 sections on the metals mentioned in sub-title. 91 tables; 7 charts.

World non-ferrous metal statistics (Birmingham, British Bureau of Non-ferrous Metals. Monthly) is more current. The December issue contains year's statistics. Coverage: copper, lead, zinc, aluminium, antimony, cadmium, tin,—production, trade, consumption, uses stocks. 40p. of tables; retrospective figures. The name of the Bureau was changed in July 1967 to 'World Bureau of Metal Statistics'.

Production: Textiles

338:677

COMMONWEALTH ECONOMIC COMMITTEE. Industrial fibres: a review of production, trade and consumption relating to wool, cotton, silk, flax, jute, sisal and other hemps, mohair, coir, kapok, rayon and other man-made fibres. London, published for the Committee by H.M. Stationery Office, 1948-. tables. Annual. (1966. 10s.).

First published 1933, as *Fibres.*
The 1966 v. (iv, 244p.) has 131 tables in the main text, with figures up to the 1964/65 seasons. 8 appendices on import duties, prices. No index.
Current developments are noted in the Commonwealth Secretariat's monthly *Wool intelligence.*

338:677.21

Cotton—world statistics. Bulletin of the International Cotton Advisory Committee. Washington, the Committee, 1947-. Quarterly. $4.50 p.a.

3 pts.: World tables (supply and demand; production; area and yield; imports and exports; stocks; prices; cotton yarn, cloth and rayon cloth: production, exports, imports)—Special tables (mill consumption; world's cotton-spinning spindles; looms in place; etc.)—Country tables (58 countries).
Annual *Special base book issue* (*e.g.,* April 1963, v. 16, nos. 9-10 (pt. 2). ii, 292p.).
Kept up to date by *Cotton: monthly review of the world cotton situation* (Washington, the Committee, 1947-.). V. 20, nos. 10-11 (May-June 1967) is an 'Annual review of the world cotton situation', with headings: General summary—Stocks—Acreage and production—Consumption—International trade—Balance of payments—Prices—Extra-long staple cotton situation—Competing fibres—Future prospects.

Production: Rubber

338:678

Rubber statistical bulletin. London, Secretariat of the International Rubber Study Group, 1946-. Monthly. ea. 8s.; 80s. p.a.

56 tables, covering production, trade, stocks and consumption, for natural rubber; natural latex; synthetic rubber; reclaimed rubber; natural, synthetic and reclaimed rubber; major sectors and end products. Table 56 (v. 21, no. 8, May 1967 issue): 'World position of natural rubber since 1900'.

Commodities

338.002.6 (038)

UNITED NATIONS. Department of Economic Affairs. **Glossary of commodity terms,** including currencies, weights and measures, used in certain countries of Asia and the Far East. Prepared by the Secretariat of the Economic Commission for Asia and the Far East. [Bangkok, United Nations], 1954. 121p. (E/CN.11/394) $1.50.

Part 1: Commodity terms (arranged A-Z; definitions, use, prevalence).

Part 2: Currencies, weights and measures in use in the region (A-Z by countries, from Afghanistan to Viet Nam: p. 94-106).

338.002.6 (083.4)

Commodity year book. New York, Commodity Research Bureau, 1939-. Annual. (1965. 386p. $16.45).

Statistical tables of 107 basic commodities, arranged A-Z. Statistics are mainly for the last 17 years, and the tables include world production, salient statistics, U.S. foreign trade and average price; as many as 20 different tables may appear under each product heading. Emphasis is on U.S. statistics, but the work has a wider use as a handy presentation of commodity trends.

338.002.6 (083.4)

GENERAL AGREEMENT ON TARIFFS AND TRADE. International Trade Centre. **Compendium of sources. Basic commodity statistics.** Geneva, G.A.T.T./I.T.C., 1967. [v], 232p. Mimeographed.

About 700-800 sources. Three main sections: A. General commodity sources—B. Agricultural commodities (1-13)—C. Metals and minerals (1-5, including 5. Petroleum). Includes annuals; for periodicals, gives price, publisher's name and address and a note on coverage. Many cross-references, but sorely lacks a commodity index.

338.002.6 (73)

SHERMAN, M. Industrial data guide. New York, Scarecrow Press, 1962. 368p. 82s.

Detailed guide to American industry. The three basic sources of information on all industrial products and fields of technology are: manufacturers; technical and scientific books, and periodical articles; and manufactured articles. The left-hand column of each 3-column page is a cross-section of the principal manufacturers; the centre column sub-divides the product, numbered and linked by number to the manufacturers; and the right-hand column lists the literature on each product (*e.g.,* the heading "Abrasives" lists 8 major manufacturers in col. 1, sub-divides the heading into 30 sub-headings, ranging from aluminium oxide to silicon carbide, in col. 2, and lists 1 book and 10 articles in col. 3. Appended list of publishers of books and journals cited in col. 3. A sort of digest of *Thomas' Register* and *Subject guide to books in print* (although obviously not as full as either), linked to various industrial products, A-Z.

Productivity

338.011:016

BAKEWELL, K. G. B. How to find out: management and productivity; a guide to sources of information arranged according to the Universal Decimal Classification. Oxford, Pergamon Press, 1966. x, 354p. facsims. 30s.

Relevant chapters: 3. Finding books on management and productivity—4. Using libraries —5. Dictionaries and encyclopaedias—6. Periodicals and abstracts—7. Management and productivity organizations—9. Some treatises and monographs on management and productivity.

Appendix 1. 'Statistics as an aid. . . .' Detailed index, listing authors, etc. of items cited. One of the better volumes in this series.

338.011:061 (410)
GREAT BRITAIN. NATIONAL ECONOMIC DEVELOPMENT OFFICE. Productivity: a handbook of advisory services. London, H.M. Stationery Office, 1967. 123p. 11s. 6d.

Lists (A-Z) 197 governmental and non-governmental organisations that are equipped to provide expert and practical services to firms in both manufacturing and distributive trades. Excludes firms of management consultants. A regional section notes services available in the main towns of the U.K. Subject index.

Noted: U.S. Labor Statistics Bureau. Labor Department. *Productivity: bibliography* (July 1966. iii, 129p. (Bulletin 1514). 65c.).

Industry

338.45:016
"Listing and bibliography of annual and less frequent inquiries into industry and distribution." In United Nations, *Statistical papers* (Statistical notes, series B, no. 23), 19 December 1958. 21p.

A list compiled by the U.N. Statistical Office, "of the annual and less frequent inquiries into industrial (mining, manufacturing, construction and gas and electricity producing) and distribution (wholesale, retail and related services) units that have been made by Governments" (prefatory note). The publications of 75 countries, the latter being arranged A-Z under continents or sub-continents. Publications include industrial censuses and go up to 1958.

338.45 (08)
GREAT BRITAIN. CENTRAL STATISTICAL OFFICE. Standard industrial classification. 2nd ed. London, H.M. Stationery Office, 1958. 35p. 2s. 6d.

The Standard Industrial Classification is used in arrangement of published statistics by Government Departments. The classification is based on industries and not on occupations. Libraries are classified thus: circulating, 820/6; government, 901/6; local authority, 906/3; university, 872; others, 899/4).
A separate *Alphabetical list of industries* (H.M.S.O., 1966. 9s.) lists c. 9,000 industries in A-Z order, with the appropriate classification numbers.

338.45 (4/9)
UNITED NATIONS. Statistical Office. Bibliography of industrial and distributive-trade statistics. [3rd ed.] New York, United Nations, 1967. iii, 139p. (Statistical papers, series M, no. 36, Rev. 3). $2.50.

First published 1963.
An annotated list of references to recent national enquiries. Arranged by continents, then countries, in tabular form, p. 3-113. For the purpose of the bibliography, "industry" covers mining, manufacturing, construction, and produc-

tion and distribution of electricity and gas; "distributive trades",—wholesale trade, retail trade and related personal services. Annex 2: 'List of divisions, major groups and groups of the International Standard Industrial Classification (ISIC).

338.45 (4/9)
UNITED NATIONS. Statistical Office. The growth of world industry, 1938-1961. New York, U.N., 1963-65. 2v. tables.

[1]. *National tables.* 1963. xvi, 849p. $10.
[2]. *International analysis and tables.* 1965. xiii, 345p.
The *National tables* cover 95 countries or areas and concern 18 mining, manufacturing and public utility industries that make up the industrial sector. The data in the second volume are "more complete in coverage and more comparable internationally" (*Foreword*).

338.45 (410)
GREAT BRITAIN. BOARD OF TRADE. Report on the census of production . . . , 1907-. London, H.M. Stationery Office, 1912-.

A detailed census of production is normally taken every five years, covering mining and quarrying, manufacturing, construction, gas, electricity and water. The simpler censuses for intervening years do not cover all establishments, and their main function now is to supplement the quarterly enquiries into fixed capital expenditure and stocks, the results of which appear in the *Board of Trade journal*.
The last census for which detailed results are published is that for 1958 (135 parts, of which 130 describe individual industries, 3 are summary tables and one consists of introductory notes, plus a separate A-Z index of products. A brief report on the censuses of 1959, 1960, 1961 and 1962 appeared in 1964. On earlier censuses, see the Interdepartmental Committee's *Guide to official sources,* no. 6, below.
The lengthy delay in publishing results of the full census is somewhat mitigated by the *Business monitor* (H.M.S.O.), which comprises nearly 70 different series, each on production statistics of a particular industry, and appears either monthly or quarterly.

338.45 (410)
GREAT BRITAIN. INTERDEPARTMENTAL COMMITTEE ON SOCIAL AND ECONOMIC RESEARCH. Guides to official sources. No. 6. **Census of production reports.** London, H.M. Stationery Office, 1961. x, 86p. 5s.

"A guide to the statistics prepared by the Board of Trade and published in the reports on the Censuses of Production and the Import Duties Act Inquiries for years from 1907 to 1958. The censuses for 1959, 1960 are also dealt with, though these inquiries had not been completed at the time of going to press" (*Introduction*). "Bibliography of associated publications", p. 69-71; specimen forms; index, p. 85-86.

338.45 (5)
ECONOMIC COMMISSION FOR ASIA AND THE FAR EAST. Industrial development in Asia and the Far East. Selected documents pre-

sented to the Asian Conference on Industrialization, Manila, 6-20 December 1965. New York, United Nations, 1966. 4v. tables. $22.75.

v. 1. *Progress and problems. Application of science and technology. Industrialization and foreign trade.* $5.
v. 2-3. *Individual countries.* $10.75.
v. 4. *Development of key indicators.* $7.
V. 2-3 covers 22 countries, A-Z, from Afghanistan to Viet-Nam, and including Australia, New Zealand, India, Pakistan and the Republic of China.
Many tables; data up to 1964. No indexes.

Prices

338.52 (410)
ROGERSON, B., *comp.* **Sources of prices.** Manchester, Commercial Library and Information Department, Manchester Public Libraries, [1960]. 8p. *Gratis.*

Under main subjects A-Z (further sub-divided) relevant periodicals are listed, with frequencies. A detailed subject index provides references to main subjects. Now out of date. A 2nd edition is planned.

Daily commercial report (London, Bagot and Thompson, Ltd., 1853-. 5 per week) gives current prices of metals, raw materials and foodstuffs.

Sources of U.S. prices of 6,800 commodities (arranged A-Z) appear in *Sources of commodity prices,* by P. Wasserman (New York, Special Libraries Association, 1960).

Business Concerns

338.7:016
ALEXANDER-FRUTSCHI, M. C., *comp.* **Small industry:** an international annotated bibliography. Glencoe, Ill., Free Press, 1960. xviii, [1], 218p.

At head of title-page: International Industrial Development Center, Stanford Research Institute.
1,133 numbered items, each with about 50 words of annotation. 8 sections, from 1. Economic and social characteristics of small industry and 2. Internal management problems of small industry, to 6. Specific industries (items 664-817), 7. Geographical areas and countries (items 818-1125), and 8. Bibliographies. Includes Chinese and other foreign language material; many cross-references. Author index; directory of publishers and periodical publications.

338.7 (092)
International businessmen's who's who, 1967; edited by W. J. Potterton. London, Burke's Peerage, Ltd., 1967. [v], 562p. 147s.

Claims to give biographical data on *c.* 6,500 business executives from some 60 of the world's largest countries. About 12 lines on each. By no means definitive (*e.g.,* no entries for Hambros, Clore, Wolfson, Ogilvie); slanted towards Britain, North America, Europe, Japan, Australia and New Zealand. Nevertheless, "a valuable addition to the small number of directories that give biographical information about leading business-

men" (*Board of Trade journal,* v. 193, no. 3674, 18th August 1967, p. 395).

338.7 (4/9)
Informations internationales. Paris, Société d'Éditions Économiques; Darmstadt, Verlag Hoppenstadt. Loose-leaf. £60 p.a.

Data on nearly 1,000 major and 12,000 associate and subsidiary companies in 19 countries. Each major company is described on a separate sheet. Sheets are arranged in order of business interest, then by country. Parallel texts in English, French and German. Annual classified index of main companies and an A-Z index of all companies.

338.7 (4):016
HENDERSON, G. P., *comp. and ed.* **European companies:** a guide to sources of information. 2nd ed. Beckenham, Kent, C.B.D. Research Ltd., 1966. xii, 168p. 70s.

First published 1962.
Has two main purposes: "(1) to list and describe sources of information on European companies and other forms of business enterprise; (2) to enable the user of foreign language sources to extract statistics and other basic information as easily as possible" (*Introduction*). Under countries (A-Z) are given details about the registration of companies, the principal legal forms of business enterprise, lists of stock exchanges and credit reporting services, and lists of directories, periodicals and services providing information on companies. Handy series of glossaries of financial terms in ten languages. Reviewed in *Board of Trade journal,* v. 192, no. 3646, 3rd February 1967, p. 269, which notes poor binding.

African companies: a guide to sources of information, a companion volume to the foregoing, is in preparation.

338.7 (4) (058)
Beerman's Financial year book of Europe. London, Beerman. Annual. (1966 ed. £10 15s.).

Basic data on *c.* 600 major commercial and industrial groups in Western Europe. Arranged by industrial groups (thumb-indexed: A. Finance —B. Services—C. Light industry—D. Heavy industry—E. Building—F. Oil and mines). Summary statements of capital and profits and of subsidiary and associated companies in each case. Clear presentation.

338.7 (4) (058.7)
Who owns whom . . . Continental ed. London, Roskill, 1961-. Annual. (6th ed.: 1966/67. 1966. £10).

v. 1: *France.*
v. 2: *Western Germany, Austria, Denmark, Norway and Sweden.*
v.3: *Belgium and Luxembourg, Holland, Italy and Switzerland.*
A directory of *c.* 63,000 parent, associate and subsidiary companies in Europe. 3 columns: associate and/or subsidiary; parent company; industrial classification of parent co. (code; key at end of volume). A new feature in the 6th ed. is inclusion of banks, finance and insurance companies. Introduction is in English, French and German.

338.7 (410)

The Directory of directors . . . A list of the directors of the principal public and private companies in the United Kingdom, with the names of the concerns with which they are associated. London, Skinner, 1880-. (1967 ed. 80s.).

Aims "to include the names of all directors of public companies and of those private companies with a paid up capital of more than £50,000." The 1966 ed. has c. 36,000 entries, arranged A-Z. An asterisk denotes membership of the Institute of Directors. Thumb-indexed; advertisements. May be used as an alphabetical index to directors given under companies in the *Stock Exchange official year-book* (q.v.).

338.7 (410)

Dun and Bradstreet's guide to key British enterprises: a selection of approximately 11,000 prominent firms and companies in the United Kingdom, both public and private, engaged in the primary, manufacturing and distributive trades, incorporating also the fields of transport and communication and a number of specialist service organizations, compiled from the business information files of Dun and Bradstreet Ltd. 4th ed. London, Dun & Bradstreet, 1967. xv, 1317p.

First published 1961.
For each firm is given full legal name, reference to parent company or group, H.Q. address, factory locations and branches, line of business and description of group or individual company activity, trade names, markets served, number of employees, date of formation and corporate structure, names of directors, telephone, telegram and telex numbers. The A-Z list of companies is followed by a classified list, with subject index and a list of parent companies, showing their constituent companies plus an index of these subsidiary companies.
For coverage, compare *Stock Exchange official year-book* (5,000 entries, including insurance, etc.), Exchange Telegraph Co.'s *Daily statistics service* (5,000), *Bradstreet's Register* (173,000; credit rating reports; not available to libraries), and the Registrar of Companies' index (350,000).

338.7 (410)

Exchange Telegraph Daily Statistics Service. London, Extel Statistical Services. Card service. £140 p.a.

Data on c. 5,000 quoted companies: date of registration, address, directors, bankers, auditors, description of company's activities, names of subsidiaries, capital details, dividend and interest dates, debentures particulars, comparative table (showing profits, percentage earned, dividends, allocations to reserves), balance sheets for 2-3 years, net asset value per share, liquid position, highest and lowest prices, earnings and dividend yield, annual report, dividend announcements and main points of Chairman's speech at annual meeting.
One card per company; revised cards incorporate new information or changes. Supplementary cards on such subjects as commodities (19 cards), countries (57 cards), British industries (24 cards), new issues and placings, British funds and capital issues.

An auxiliary card service (additional subscription), covering 1,700 companies, provides interpretative and other data that augment and extend the Daily Statistics Service. Other Extel services cover 250 European companies, 250 Australian companies and 500 North American companies.

338.7 (410)

GREAT BRITAIN. BOARD OF TRADE. Companies: geneal annual report. 1890-. London, H.M. Stationery Office, 1893-. Annual. (1964. 3s. 6d.).

Information on administration of the Companies Act, plus useful statistics on registration of companies during the past ten years by classes and by amount of nominal capital. Statistics of new companies registered appear each month in the *Board of Trade journal*.

The corresponding report for Northern Ireland (Belfast, H.M.S.O.) includes a list of newly registered companies.

————**Company assets, income and finance in 1963:** companies quoted on United Kingdom stock exchanges. London, H.M. Stationery Office, 1965. vii, 120p. 14s. 6d.

Previously published for 1960, 1957 and 1955.
The main table ranks quoted U.K. companies in order of assets. Data on each company's assets, liabilities, income, new capital, etc., 1963 or 1961-63. Various summary tables and A-Z list of companies. The 1960 ed. contains a rare list of non-quoted public companies.
A quarterly analysis of company accounts appears in the *Board of Trade Journal;* this includes statistics of appropriation of income, summary of balance sheets and sources and uses of capital funds. An article in *Economic trends,* no. 102, April 1962, p. 2-17, gives details for the period 1949-60, along with much other useful information on the income and finance of quoted companies.

338.7 (410)

Moodies British Company Service. London, Moodies Services, Ltd. Card service. £140 p.a.

Covers 5,000 quoted companies. Each company has a large card which is issued once a year, after publication of the accounts, and a small card re-issued cumulatively as soon as there is any news about the company to keep the large card up to date. The large card provides background information and a detailed analysis of figures measuring growth, efficiency and performance over last ten years. The small card includes earnings and dividends adjusted for new issues, balance sheet figures, tabulated details of dividends, a table of new issues, news items and the chairman's speech. A number of subject cards dealing with gold mining returns, taxation, traffic receipts and yield ratio are included. There is an alphabetical and classified index of companies issued in a loose-leaf binder.

338.7 (410)

Register of registrars, 1947-. Croydon, Day's Publications, 1948-. Annual. (1966. 2v. 100s.).

Includes a list of professional registrars and of firms providing transfer office facilities, plus a list of securities (including unit trusts) showing registration offices and requirements for registration of transfers.

338.7 (410)

The Times 300: a guide to the size of Britain's top companies [1965]-. London, The Times Publishing Co., 1965-. Annual. (1966. 5s.).

Aims "to provide annually in tabular form a number of measuring rods relevant to the size and performance of large British and European business groups". The companies are ranked in descending order of capital employed and details are included of net profit, turnover, number of employees and market capitalisation. There are also similar tables for major nationalized industries, clearing banks, overseas banks, building societies, insurance companies, unit trusts, investment trusts and the hundred leading European companies.

Similar publications are available for the U.S. (*Fortune*), France (*Entreprise*), Germany (*Maschine und Manager*), Italy (*24 Ore*) and Japan (*Time-Life International*).

338.7 (410)

Who owns whom (U.K. edition): a directory of parent, associate and subsidiary companies. 10th ed., compiled and published by O. W. Roskill. London, Roskill, 1967. vii, 1539p. 190s. Quarterly suppts., 20s. p.a.

9th ed. 1966.
70,000 entries. Four sections: 1. U.K. parent and associate companies showing subsidiary and associate companies—2. U.K. parent and associate companies, showing parent and associate companies—3. U.S. parent and associate companies, showing U.K. subsidiary and associate companies—4. Unit trusts, showing managers and trustees.

338.7 (410):016

BARKER, T. C., *and others.* **Business history.** London, Historical Association, 1960. 36p. 5s.

Three sections: 1. The study of business history (including: 'Sources', 'Treatment of the source material' and 'Methods of presentation')—2. Bibliography of business history (p. 23-29)—3. Business accounts, by B. S. Yamey.

338.7 (410) (091)

BUSINESS ARCHIVES COUNCIL. The first five hundred: chronicles and house histories of companies and organisations in the Business Archives Library. London, the Council, 1959. 22p.

——————— **Indexed sources for business history in London libraries and museums.** London, the Council, [1958]. 9p. Mimeographed.

338.7 (410) (093)

GREAT BRITAIN. NATIONAL REGISTER OF ARCHIVES. Sources of business history in reports of the National Register of Archives. London, the Register, 1964-. no. 1-. Mimeographed. Annual supplements.

No. 1 ([1], 16p.) lists *c.* 800 firms, A-Z, stating name, location and nature of industry. Supple-

ment 1 lists items indexed December 1, 1964—November 30, 1965 ([1], 12p.); supplement 2, items indexed December 1, 1965—November 30, 1966 [1], 29p.). Five-yearly cumulations are envisaged.

338.7 (410):347.736

GREAT BRITAIN. BOARD OF TRADE. Bankruptcy: general annual report. 1883-. London, H.M. Stationery Office, 1884-. Annual. (1964. 4s.).

Statistical tables include failures in principal trades and occupations, numbers of receiving orders by town and comparative annual figures for insolvency.

338.7 (420)

Daily list of new companies: a concise record of all companies registered in England. London, Information Bureau, 1898-. Daily. £60 p.a.

Information for each company includes name, registration number, date of registration, nominal capital, names and addresses of directors and/or secretary and, in some cases, purpose of company. In 1964, 48,315 companies were registered. Since May 1965, an alphabetical index of company names has been produced on a co-operative basis by eleven subscribing public libraries. Each library in turn indexes two months' issues and sends copies of this index to the other libraries. Unlike most Western countries, the United Kingdom has no officially published list of newly registered companies. Prior to 1962, the *Investor's Guardian* listed and indexed new companies.

338.7 (421)

GUILDHALL LIBRARY, London. **London business house histories:** a handlist. London, Corporation of City of London, [1965]. [ii], 156p. 1s. 6d.

Four sections: 1. Index of firms—2. 715 items, under trades, A-Z—3. Collective histories (items 716-33)—4. Archives (items 734-801). Addenda (7 items). Many of the items were issued privately and not to be found in standard bibliographies.

Compilation of a bibliography of Yorkshire business histories is nearing completion. It will contain *c.* 5,000 entries for 4,000 firms, and will be published by the Bradford Univ. Press, Reference Special and Information Section, Yorkshire Group.

338.7 (43)

Leitende Männer der Wirtschaft. 14. Aufl. Darmstadt, Hoppenstedt, 1966. xii, 1325p.

Lists 34,000 German business executives with full name, qualifications, date of birth and names of companies with which they are connected. Includes a useful list of abbreviations of business positions (*e.g.,* divisional manager, managing partner, authorised administrator), expanded in English, French and German.

Similar compilations are available for other countries, *e.g., Personen-Compass* (Austria), and alphabetical lists of directors can also be found in many financial yearbooks such as *Annuaire Desfossés* (France), *Svenska aktiebolag* (Sweden) and *Le recueil financier* (Belgium).

338.7 (73)

LARSON, H. M. Guide to business history:
materials for the study of American business
history and suggestions for their use. Cambridge,
Mass., Harvard Univ. Press, 1948. xxvi, 1181p.

4,904 numbered and annotated items in 7 parts
(87 sections): 1. General introduction—2. Historical background and setting of American
business—3. Business administrators, biographical and autobiographical books, pamphlets and
articles—4. The history of individual business
units—5. History of industries (p. 242-731)—6.
General topics in business history—7. Research
and reference materials. Detailed, analytical
index, p. 1057-1181. An excellent compilation,
with introductory notes for each section. A model
of its kind.

Restrictive Practices

338.89

**ORGANISATION FOR ECONOMIC CO-OPERA-
TION AND DEVELOPMENT. Glossaire de
termes relatifs aux practiques commerciales
restrictives.** Glossary of terms relating to restrict-
ive business practices. Paris, O.E.C.D., 1965. 95p.
9s.

60 terms are defined, with commentary (e.g.,
'Unfair competition': 25-word definition plus 1½p.
of commentary, including quotation from a
Convention of 1883). Four chapters. A. Terms
relating to economic concentration—B. Terms
relating to arrangements between enterprises—C.
Actions by enterprises—D. Other terms. Index.

Raw Materials

338.91 (03)

**JACKSON, N., and PENN, P. A dictionary of
natural resources.** Oxford, Pergamon Press,
1966. [v], 128p. 12s. 6d.; 21s.

Describes c. 1,000 'natural resources'—animals,
cereals, dyes and tannin, elements, fibres, food
and drink, fruit, gems, herbs, leather, medicinal,
minerals, nuts, oil, organic chemicals, perfume,
plants, resin, rocks, spices, trees, vegetables, wax
(A-Z), stating where chiefly grown or made, and
uses. Cross-references. Appended classified list
under categories as given above.

338.91 (41-44)

**COMMONWEALTH ECONOMIC COMMIT-
TEE.** Thirty-seventh report: **A review of Commonwealth raw materials.** London, H.M.
Stationery Office, 1958-60. 2v. 50s. (v. 1, 15s.;
v. 2, 35s.).

"The object of the enquiry is to show against
the background of world conditions the post-war
developments, other than those of a purely technical nature, in the production, consumption and
trade of Commonwealth raw materials and to
compare the post-war with the pre-war position"
(*Introduction,* v. 1). V. 1 deals with production,
consumption, trade, prices, Commonwealth
sources of energy, trends and developments; v. 2,
with the component countries. Several hundred
tables, with figures up to 1957. No general index.

338.91 (411)

Natural resources in Scotland: symposium of the
Royal Society of Edinburgh, October 31 to
November 2, 1960. Edinburgh, the Scottish
Council (Development and Industry), 1961. ix,
796p. 105s.

See sub-entry at 33 (411) (047).

338.91 (540)

**INDIA. COUNCIL OF SCIENTIFIC AND IN-
DUSTRIAL RESEARCH. The wealth of
India:** a dictionary of Indian raw materials and
industrial products. New Delhi, the Council,
1948-. illus., tables, graphs.

Raw materials. v. 1-7: A-PE. 1948-66, with
suppt. to v. 4: *Fish and fisheries* (1962).
Industrial products. v. 1-6: A-PI. 1948-65.

V. 5 of *Raw materials* completes the first half
of that series; it has 380 entries, 370 of them on
plant species, 7 on animals and 3 on minerals.
Each volume has its own index. References to
literature in the text, with appended list of books
and periodicals referred to. Many cross-references. Entries on plants give botanical description
and state use.

For each material in the *Industrial products*
series, development and present position, sources
and availability of raw materials, and manufacturing process and statistical data are indicated.
Chemistry and industry (no. 49, 3rd December
1966, p. 2038) takes exception to A-Z arrangement of entries; classification according to type
of industry (e.g., chemical; heavy engineering)
would have made the work more accessible to
the specialist reader.

338.91 (6)

**UNITED NATIONS EDUCATIONAL, SCIEN-
TIFIC AND CULTURAL ORGANISATION. A
review of the natural resources of the African
continent.** Paris, Unesco, 1963. 437p. map.
67s. 6d.

Covers topography and maps, geology (including mineral resources), geophysics, seismology,
hydrology and water resources, soils (including
soil conservation), flora and fauna (including
preservation of game-stocks). Includes list of
national parks, reserves and official and private
organisations connected with wildlife conservation. Large map. Reviewed in *New scientist,* no.
364, 7th November 1963, p. 340.

Economic Development

338.984 (058.7)

**OVERSEAS DEVELOPMENT INSTITUTE. De-
velopment guide:** a directory of development
facilities provided by non-commercial organisations in Britain. Published for the Overseas Development Institute by Allen & Unwin, London,
1962. [258]p. 25s.

198 numbered entries, arranged A-Z. Excludes
educational organisations and commercial concerns. About one page or more per entry: name;
address; telephone number; description of
objects and activities; publications; information;
advice; etc. (Commonwealth Agricultural Bureau:
3½p.; Outward Bound Trust: 1½p.). Index of
subjects (italicised) and catchwords (e.g., inverted

names of organisations). Each entry has been approved by the organisation concerned.

338.984.3:016

INTERNATIONAL BANK FOR RECONSTRUC-TION AND DEVELOPMENT. Selected readings and source materials on economic development: a list of books, articles and reports included in a small library assembled by the Economic Development Institute. Washington. I.B.R.D., [1962]. vi, 66p. Mimeographed.

394 numbered entries, arranged by broad subject headings, with author index. No annotations.

338.984.3 (02)

WATERSTON, A., *and others.* **Development planning:** lessons of experience Economic Development Institute, International Bank for Reconstruction and Development, Johns Hopkins Press, Baltimore, Md., 1965. xix, 706p. $10.75.

Two parts: 1. The development planning process—2. The organization of planning. 17 chapters; 10 appendices. Particularly valuable is appendix 3, 'National plans' (p. 586-643), covering 185 countries and areas, arranged A-Z. References are to plans that were in course of preparation, "as well as those whose preparation had been completed, by April 1, 1965, when the collection of information for the compilation terminated". Bibliography of works cited, p. 660-81; subject and name indexes.

Waterston mentions another recent bibliography: Yale Growth Center. *Bibliography of national economic development plans* (Preliminary version. New Haven, Conn., Yale Univ., 1965).

338.984.3 (4/9)

UNITED NATIONS. DAG HAMMARSKJOLD LIBRARY. Economic and social development plans: Africa, Asia and Latin America. New York, U.N., 1964. [v], 25p.

A bibliography of official documentation on economic and social planning in the developing countries of Africa (35 countries, A-Z), Middle East (8 countries, A-Z), Asia and Far East (18 countries, A-Z), Latin America (9 countries, A-Z) and the Caribbean (7 countries, A-Z). Includes periodic progress reports and evaluations of achievements.

338.984.3 (4/9)

────── **Economic and social development plans: centrally planned economies; developed market economies.** New York, U.N. 1966. v, 59p.

A sequel to the above bibliography. The 13 centrally planned economies are those of Eastern European countries, Mainland China, the Mongolian People's Republic, North Korea and North Vietnam. The 19 developed market economies are those of North America, Western Europe, Australia, Japan, New Zealand and South Africa. Informative notes on the history of plans under each country. Titles of plans are translated, if not in English or French. No annotations or index.

338.984.3 (4/9-77):016

HAZLEWOOD, A., *comp.* **The economics of development:** an annotated list of books and articles published 1958-1962. Published for the Oxford Univ. Institute of Commonwealth Studies by Oxford Univ. Press, London, 1964 [*i.e.* 1965]. 104p. 12s. 6d.

"An introduction to the dauntingly voluminous body of recent writings on economic development" (*Preface*). 732 items (many of them periodical articles), confined to English-language publications, each with 10-25 word expository annotations and usually priced. 12 classes, with sub-divisions (4. Area studies: (a) General—(b) Africa—(c) Asia—(d) Latin America and Caribbean—(e) Middle East. Cross references. Index of authors and editors; index of places.

A sequel to his *The economics of underdeveloped areas: an annotated reading list* (see at 33 (4/9-77):016).

338.984.3 (4/9-77):016

INSTITUT UNIVERSITAIRE DES TERRI-TOIRES D'OUTRE-MER, Antwerp. **Recueil bibliographique tiers-monde.** Antwerp, I.U.T.O., 1964. iv, 157p.

See entry at 33 (4/9-77):016.

338.984.3 (4/9-77) (02)

INTERNATIONAL BANK FOR RECONSTRUC-TION AND DEVELOPMENT. [Economic development reports]. Baltimore, Md., Johns Hopkins Press; London, Oxford Univ. Press, 1951-.

See entry at 33 (4/9-77) (02).

338.984.3 (4)

UNITED NATIONS. ECONOMIC COMMISSION FOR EUROPE. Economic survey of Europe in 1962. Pt. 2. Economic planning in Europe. New York, Nations, 1965. v.p. 12 tables, 11 charts. **$3.**

See entry at 33 (4) (058).

Poverty

339.12

PALTIEL, F. L. Poverty: an annotated bibliography and references. Ottawa, Canadian Welfare Council, 1966. x, 136p. $3.

704 well annotated entries in 17 sections (p. 1-85). Special attention drawn to poverty problems in rural areas; includes many non-Canadian references. Appendices: 1. Inventory (tabular) of research and action programmes actively conducted by welfare and social planning councils in Canada as of June 1965—2. [List of] Canadian periodicals and journals in health, welfare and social and behavioural sciences.

Distribution

339.8 (410)

GREAT BRITAIN. BOARD OF TRADE. Census of distribution and other services, 1961. Report. London, H.M. Stationery Office, 1963. 14 pts.

Previous reports, for 1950 and 1957.

All traders known to be engaged in retail distribution or in closely related service trades were asked to make statistical returns. Pt. 1: Establishment tables (7s.); pts. 2-13: Area tables; pt. 14 (ea. 3s.-7s.): Organisation tables (7s.).

Bibliographies

34:016

COLUMBIA UNIVERSITY. Law Library. **Dictionary catalog.** Boston, Mass., G. K. Hall, 1968. 28v. $2,230 (U.S.); $2,453 (outside U.S.).

705,000 entries, photolithographically reproduced from catalogue cards. Particularly rich in legal literature of the U.S. and the Commonwealth, and in documents and treatises on international law. Announced for publication in April 1968.

34:016

Current legal bibliography: a selected list of books and articles received by the Harvard Law School Library. October 1960-. Cambridge, Mass., Harvard Law School Library, 1961-. v. 1, no. 1-. 9 issues p.a. $3 p.a.; $15, including *Annual legal bibliography.*

Provides a comprehensive list of some 30,000 items annually,—periodical articles, monographs and contents of collected works. Main divisions: A. Common law jurisdictions—B. Civil law and other jurisdictions—C. General and comparative studies—D. Private international law—E. Public international law—F. International economic and social affairs—G. Roman law—H. Canon law. Subject and country sub-divisions.

The *Annual legal bibliography* (Cambridge, Mass., Harvard Law School Library, 1967-. v.1-) cumulates items in *Current legal bibliography.* V. 1 covers the period "July 1, 1965 through June 30, 1966". Subject index to the systematically arranged sequence.

34:016

HICKS, F. C. Materials and methods of legal research. 3rd ed. Rochester, New York, Lawyers Co-operative Publishing Co., 1942. 659p.

A detailed textbook of the method of legal research, giving an historical and descriptive account of all types of legal literature, American and English, and containing a table of regnal years and law terms, lists of British and American law reports, Anglo-American legal periodicals and Anglo-American legal abbreviations.

Comparable, more recent guides are: *Legal bibliography and the use of law books,* by A. S. Beardsley and O. C. Orman (2nd ed. Brooklyn, Foundation Press, 1947. xii, 653p.), and *Effective legal research: a practical manual of law books and their use,* by M. O. Price and H. Bitner (New York, Prentice-Hall, 1953. xiii, 633p.), but both lack Hicks's historical account of British material.

34:016

Index to foreign legal periodicals. General editor, K. Howard Drake. London, Institute of Advanced Legal Studies, in co-operation with the American Association of Law Libraries, 1960-. v. 1, no. 1-. Quarterly (the 4th quarter being a cumulated annual v.). 180*s.* p.a. (v. 7: 1966, 1967. £14 5*s.*).

A subject index to some 250 leading legal periodicals, covering international law (public and private), comparative law and municipal law of countries other than the U.S.A. and British Commonwealth countries, whose legal systems are based on common law. It is thus complementary to the *Index to legal periodicals* (*q.v.*). Lengthier book reviews are noted. Author and geographical indexes.

A five-yearly cumulation is contemplated.

A. P. Blaustein's *Manual on foreign legal periodicals and their 'Index'* (Dobbs Ferry, N.Y., published for the Parker School of Foreign and Comparative Law, Colombia Univ. by Oceana Publications, Inc., 1962. x, 137p. $9) is a guide to the 253 periodicals listed in the *Index to foreign legal periodicals* during its first year of publication.

34:016

Index to legal periodicals. 1908-. New York, Wilson, in co-operation with the American Association of Law Libraries, 1909-. Monthly.

Initially cumulated annually; three-year cumulations since 1926/28. Indexes *c.* 282 legal periodicals published in common-law countries. The monthly parts and the cumulated volume contain a subject and author index, a table of cases commented on, and an index of books reviewed (1940-), arranged under authors. Pronounced U.S. slant.

34:016

MARKE, J. J., *comp.* and *ed.* **A catalogue of the law collection at New York University,** with selected annotations. New York, Law Center of New York Univ., 1953. xxxi, 1372p.

"A guide to a working collection of legal material for the law student and legal researcher" rather than a bibliographical tool (*Introduction*). About 24,000 items, each usually with a 200-word annotation, citing forewords, reviews and other sources. Key to authorities cited, p. xvii-xxxi.

Sections: 1. Sources of the law—2. History of law and its institutions—3. Public and private law—4. Comparative law—5. Jurisprudence and philosophy of law—6. Political and economic theory—7. Trials—8. Biography—9. Law and literature—10. Periodicals and other serial publications (p. 1154-90)—11. Reference material (p. 1191-1214). Detailed sub-division. Subject and author indexes. The compiler is Librarian of the School of Law, New York University.

Also of value: Jacobstein, J. M., and Pimsleur, M.G., ed. *Law books in print; including books in English published throughout the world and in print as of December 1964* (Dobbs Ferry, N.Y., Glanville, 1965. 2v.; with supplements).

34:016

STOLLREITHER, K. Internationale Bibliographie der juristischen Nachschlagewerke. Frankfurt am Main, Klostermann, 1955. xiii, 595p.

A detailed survey that includes more general and also marginal-subject material (*e.g.*, in the fields of politics, economics, social sciences, sociology and statistics). The three main sections deal with the following: general reference material (bibliographies; other reference books, such as encyclopaedias); general legal reference books (bibliographies; encyclopaedias of law, manuals, dictionaries of legal terms, journals, etc.); special subjects (philosophy; comparative law; history of law; Roman law; canon law; civil law, etc.). The scope is truly international. The index (p. 469-595) has author, journal-title, subject and country entries.

34:016

Sweet & Maxwell's Guide to the legal profession. 6th ed. London, Sweet & Maxwell, 1963. x, 130p.

"Contains the information necessary to anyone wishing to become either a barrister or solicitor, or to study law at one of the universities" (*Publishers' preface*). Part *1*, Qualifications; part *2*, Books (p. 51-111: 4. Reading and choice of books—5. General law books and periodicals—6. The common law . . . 20. African law); part *3*, Suggested courses of reading (21. Bar examinations—22. Law Society examinations—23. London LL.B. examinations). A number of items have evaluative annotations.

34:016

SZLADITS, C., *comp.* **A bibliography on foreign and comparative law:** books and articles in English . . . Dobbs Ferry, New York, Oceana Publications, for the Parker School of Foreign and Comparative Law, Columbia Univ., 1955-. [v. 1]-. Supplement 1960/1961-. 1963-.

Chiefly concerned with foreign (*i.e.*, other than that of the common law jurisdictions) and private international law. V. 1 (1955. $15) has 13,742 entries up to 1952; v. 2 (1962. $15) has nearly 13,800 entries for the period 1953-59. Non-cumulative annual supplements (third suppt., covering 1963, published 1965).

34:016

SZLADITS, C. Guide to foreign legal materials, French, German, Swiss. New York, published for Parker School of Foreign and Comparative Law, Columbia Univ. by Oceana Publications, 1959. xv, 599p. $11.

French law, p. 3-116; German law, p. 118-330; Swiss law, p. 333-507. In the case of 'Swiss law', sub-division is: pt. 1, Sources of law; pt. 2, Repositories of the law (bibliographies; legislative materials and commentaries; case law; encyclopaedias and dictionaries; doctrinal writings; list of legal abbreviations). Many footnote references. Index of authors and titles; index to subjects. A guide for the common-law lawyer to the use of foreign legal materials,—laws, reports and books.

34:016

UNITED NATIONS EDUCATIONAL, SCIENTIFIC AND CULTURAL ORGANIZATION. Catalogue des sources de documentation juridique dans le monde. **A register of legal documentation in the world.** 2nd ed., rev. and enl. Paris, Unesco, 1957. 424p. 30*s*.

First published 1953.

Arranged A-Z under French name of country. The index to countries and territories has over 200 entries. Under "England and Wales" (p. 66-74), sub-headings: Legislation—Law reports—Centres of legal studies—Legal periodicals and reviews—Legal reference works and bibliographies. Range of material is naturally fuller in some countries than in others. Annotated entries.

34:016:016

FRIEND, W. L. Anglo-American legal bibliographies: an annotated guide. Washington, Library of Congress, Law Library, 1944 (reprinted 1966). xii, 166p. $10.

"Lists all classes of Anglo-American legal bibliographic materials except works devoted exclusively to American statutory materials, and library and publishers' catalogues" (*Special libraries,* v. 58, no. 1, January 1967, p. 64).

Libraries

34:026/027

WAY, D. J. The student's guide to law libraries. London, Oyez Publications, 1967. 58p. 7*s*. 6*d*.

Chapters: 1. The lay-out of a law library—2. The contents of a law library (p. 10-39; statutes, statutory instruments, reports, digests, unreported cases, text-books, periodicals, ministerial circulars) —3. How to tackle a given subject—4. Where to find your law library (London and provinces; local law soceties, etc.). 4 appendices, including list of current law reports and select list of precedent books. By the Sub-Librarian, Faculty of Law, University of Liverpool, and directed to the articled clerk, trainee legal executive or Bar student.

Dictionaries

34 (032)

BURROWS, *Sir* **R.,** *ed.* **Words and phrases judicially defined.** London, Butterworth, 1943-45. 5v. and corrective pocket-supplements to each v.

An alphabetical dictionary of words and phrases used in statutes or otherwise that have been defined or interpreted by the Courts in England or the Dominions. The relevant parts of the judgments are set out.

34 (032)

STROUD, F. Judicial dictionary of words and phrases. 3rd ed. London, Sweet & Maxwell, 1952-53. 4v.; Cumulative supplements (2nd. 1965. 50*s*.).

First published 1890.

A dictionary of words and phrases that have been interpreted by the judges, giving their interpretations. Statutory definitions not judicially interpreted are referred to. The 2nd cumulative suppt. goes up to 1st May 1964.

34 (032)

WHARTON, J. S. S. Wharton's Law lexicon; forming an epitome of the laws of England under statute and case law, and containing explanations of technical terms and phrases, ancient, modern and commercial, with selected titles relating to the civil, Scots and Indian law.

LAW

14th ed., by A. S. Oppé. London, Stevens and Sweet & Maxwell, 1949 (reprint of 1938 ed.). viii, 1081p.

A large dictionary of legal terms and phrases, with detailed explanations.

Smaller law dictionaries, with tables of legal abbreviations, law reports, etc.:
Mozley, H. N., and Whiteley, G. C. *Law dictionary*. 7th ed. London, Butterworth, 1962. [viii], 391p. 27s. 6d.
Osborn, P. G. *A concise law dictionary*. 5th ed. London, Sweet & Maxwell, 964, vii, 393p. 25s.
The Pocket law lexicon. 8th ed., by A. W. Motion. London, Stevens. 1951. viii, 419p.
Sturgess, H. A. C., and Hewitt, A. R. *A dictionary of legal terms, statutory definitions and citations*. 2nd ed. London, Pitman, 1940. vi, 313p.

34 (038)=30
BASEDOW, K. H. Wörterbuch der Rechts-sprache. Hamburg, Heldt, 1947-48. 2v.

v. 1: *Deutsch-Englisch*. 1948. 720p.
v. 2: *Englisch-Deutsch*. 1947. 616p.
The largest of the German and English dictionaries of legal terms. About 12,000 main entries in each volume; compounds, idioms, etc. are given separate lines. Two-column page,—one column for the entry-word, the other for its equivalent. Many idioms (*e.g.*, 'Writ': 3¼ cols.).

For the smaller library: Beseler, D. v. *Englisch-deutsches und deutsch-englisches Wörterbuch der Rechts- und Geschäftssprache* (2. rev. und erw. Aufl. Berlin, de Gruyter, 1947. iv, 223p.). Largely confined to equivalents; few idioms.

34 (038)=40
DALRYMPLE, A. W. French-English dictionary of legal words and phrases. 2nd ed. London, Stevens, 1948. [v], 130p.

—— **English-French dictionary of legal words and phrases.** 2nd ed. London, Stevens, 1951. v, 218p.

For the student and reader of French codes and French legal text-books and also for those "who may have occasion to deal with the intricacies of French law in general for professional and educational purposes" (*Preface to French-English dictionary*). Gives applications of terms, and idioms. The French-English part has *c.* 17,000 entries. No genders or pronunciation shown. Well printed.

T. A. Quemner's *Dictionnaire juridique, français-anglais, anglais-français* (Paris, Éditions de Navarre, 1963. 323p. 60F.) covers a wider field —law, finance, commerce, customs and excise, insurance, stock marketing and administration. According to *Special libraries*, v. 55, no. 3, March 1964, p. 189, it pays particular attention to differences between Anglo-American concepts and those prevailing in France.

34 (038)=82
TELBERG, I. Soviet-English dictionary of legal terms and concepts. New York, Telberg, 1961. iv, 111 1. $9.80.

About 2,000 Russian entry-words, with English equivalents.

Periodicals
34 (05):016
LONDON. UNIVERSITY. Institute of Advanced Legal Studies. **A survey of legal periodicals:** union catalogue of holdings in British libraries. 2nd ed. London, the Institute, 1957. ix, 82p. ([Institute] Publication no. 1).

First published 1949 as *A survey of legal periodicals held in British libraries*.
Records the holdings of 1026 legal periodicals (including year-books) in 76 libraries (41 of them in London), as against 54 lbraries in the 1st ed. These libraries range from national, academic and government libraries to professional and learned society libraries. Legislation and law reports are excluded. Dates of holdings given.

History
34 (091):016
GILISSEN, J., *ed*. **Introduction bibliographique à l'histoire du droit et à l'ethnologie juridique.** Bibliographical introduction to legal history and ethnology. Brussels, Éditions de l'Institut de Sociologie, 1965-. v. 1-. Loose-leaf.

To be completed in 6 v.

Roman Law
34 (37)
SASS, S. L., "Research in Roman law: a guide to the sources and their English translations". In *Library law journal*, v. 56, no. 3, August 1963, p. 210-33.

Main sections: 1. Sources in Roman law—2. English translations of Roman law sources—3. Dictionaries, encyclopedias and vocabularies (special praise for Berger, A. *Encyclopedic dictionary of Roman law*. Philadelphia, 1953)—4. Key to symbols for citing Roman law sources.
Another article by the same author appeared in *Library law journal*, v. 58, no. 2, May 1965, p. 130-59: "Medieval Roman law: a guide".

Eastern Europe
34 (4-11):016
Legal sources and bibliographies of Eastern Europe. New York, Praeger; London, Stevens, 1956-.

A series of national guides prepared by the Mid-European Law Project, Law Library, Library of Congress (*i.e.*, by emigrés):
Legal sources and bibliography of the Baltic States [Estonia, Latvia, Lithuania]; edited by V. Gsovski. 1964. $10; 70s.
Legal sources and bibliography of Bulgaria; edited by I. Sipkov. 1956.
Legal sources and bibliography of Czechoslovakia; edited by A. Bohmer and others. 1959.
Legal sources and bibliography of Hungary; edited by A. K. Bedo and G. Torzsay-Biber. 1956.
Legal sources and bibliography of Poland; edited by P. Siekanowicz. 1964.
Legal sources and bibliography of Romania; edited by V. Stoicoiu [1964]. $10; 70s.
The last-mentioned has 9 sections, including 8: "Bibliography of books and articles in foreign

languages", and 9: "List of principal laws, decrees, resolutions, etc., in effect in the People's Republic of Romania as of January 1, 1963". 1,589 numbered items (section 1-8).

Western Europe

34 (4-15):016
LONDON. UNIVERSITY. INSTITUTE OF ADVANCED LEGAL STUDIES. Union list of West European legal literature: publications held by libraries in Oxford, Cambridge and London. London, the Institute, 1966. viii, 426p. (Union catalogue no. 5). 45s.

Covers the holdings of 8 libraries. Sections: General reference material. General periodicals (p. 2-5)—Part A. Country sections (A-Z by countries and areas, p. 6-298; includes titles of periodicals as well as monographs)—Part B. Western Europe integration & co-operation (p. 299-378). General author, serial and subject indexes.

Commonwealth

34 (41-44):016
LONDON. UNIVERSITY. INSTITUTE OF ADVANCED LEGAL STUDIES. Union list of Commonwealth and South African law: a location guide to Commonwealth and South African legislation, law reports and digests held by libraries in the United Kingdom at May 1963. London, the Institute, [1963]. xi, 129p. 21s.

Previously as *Union list of Commonwealth law literature in libraries in Oxford, Cambridge and London* (1952).
Locations are given in 51 British libraries (29 of them in London) of the legislation, law reports and digests of cases of Commonwealth countries. Arranged by countries A-Z, from Aden to Zanzibar. Omits India and Pakistan. Dates of holdings of legislation and law reports are shown; subject index to law reports. Index to countries (and their provinces, etc.) precedes.

A guide to Commonwealth and colonial legislation . . . in the Lincoln's Inn Library; compiled from the catalogues of the library by Y. H. McGowan, assisted by S. Hodges (London, Lincoln's Inn Library, 1964. v, 48 l. Mimeographed) is arranged under countries and areas, A-Z, from Abyssinia to Zanzibar.

34 (41-44):016
Sweet & Maxwell's A legal bibliography of the British Commonwealth of Nations. 2nd ed. London, Sweet & Maxwell, 1955-.

   v. 1: *English law, to 1800.* 1955.
   v. 2: *English law, from 1801 to 1954.* 1959.
   v. 3: *Canadian laws and the laws of the North American colonies.* 1957.
   v. 4: *Irish law.* 1957.
   v. 5: *Scottish law.* 1957.
   v. 6: *The laws of Australia, New Zealand and their dependencies.* 1958.
   v. 7: *British Commonwealth, excluding the United Kingdom, Australia, New Zealand, Canada, India and Pakistan.* 1964. 84s.
   v. 8: *Indian and Pakistan* (in preparation).
V. 7 (first published in 1949) has 6 parts (1. Africa—2. The Middle East—3. Asia—4. Conti-

nental South America and the Southern Atlantic —5. Europe and the Mediterranean—6. Western Pacific), with detailed breakdown. Extensive analytical index (p. 419-59), by territory, subject and form of literature.

34 (41-44) (048)
English and Empire digest, with annotations: a digest of every English case reported from early times to the present day; edited by the Earl of Halsbury, Sir T. W. Chitty and others. London, Butterworth, 1919-30. 48v. (v. 45-48: Index). Cumulative supplements and replacement vols.

An arrangement of every English case reported in a law report or series of reports and of many cases decided in the Commonwealth countries. A note of the decision is always given, with references to all the reports of the case that have been published and references to later cases in which it has been judicially noticed. Cases are arranged systematically under broad subject headings. The work is being kept up to date by supplements, and volumes are being republished, incorporating up-to-date material (*e.g.,* Third cumulative suppt. (covering cases 1952-65). 1966 105s.; replacement v. 47 (Trusts and trustees, to Weights and measures). 1966. 75s.).

34 (41-44) (058)
Annual survey of Commonwealth law, 1965-. London, Butterworths, 1966-. Annual. (1965 v. 1966. 168s.).

The first of a series of annual volumes surveying legal developments throughout the British Commonwealth. 20 chapters, by specialists (*e.g.,* 1. Constitutional law—6. Contract—12. Company law and partnership—14. Taxation—20. Maritime law). Heavily footnoted. Tables of statutes and cases, p. xix-lxxviii. Analytical subject index; textual index.

34 (41-44) (091)
KEETON, G. W., *ed.* **The British Commonwealth: the development of its laws and constitutions.** London, Stevens, 1951-. v. 1-.

   v. 1. *The United Kingdom.* 1955. 2 pts. (pt. 1. 75s.; pt. 2, *Scotland,* replaced by v. 11).
   v. 2. *The Commonwealth of Australia.* 1952. o.p.
   v. 4. *New Zealand.* 2nd ed. 1967. 105s.
   v. 5. *The Union of South Africa.* 1960. Supplement. 1962. 123s.
   v. 6. *The Republic of India.* 2nd ed. 1964. 75s.
   v. 7. *The Dominion of Ceylon.* 1952. o.p.
   v. 8. *Pakistan.* 2nd ed. 1967. 97s. 6d.
   v. 9. *Malaya and Singapore, the Borneo Territories.* 1961. 90s.
   v. 10. *Ghana and Sierra Leone.* 1962. 75s.
   v. 11. *Scotland.* 1962. 105s.
   v. 12. *Tanganyika.* 1964. 75s.
   v. 13. *Uganda.* 1966. 90s.
   v. 14. *Nigeria.* 1967. 110s.; 55s.
A comprehensive survey. V. 1, pt. 1 covers England and Wales, Northern Ireland and the Isle of Man. For England, provides an analysis of the unwritten constitution and an account of the Welfare State. V. 14 has 24 chapters (with numerous footnote references to statutes), covering development of central and local government, public corporations, relations between the Federation and the regions; the Nigerian legal system.

LAW

Great Britain

34 (410):016

A Bibliographical guide to the law of the United Kingdom, the Channel Islands and the Isle of Man. London. Institute of Advanced Legal Studies, 1956. ix, 219p. (Reprinted Dobbs Ferry, N.Y., Oceana. $7.50).

Published jointly by the United Kingdom National Committee of Comparative Law and the Institute of Advanced Legal Studies, under the auspices of Unesco and of the International Association of Legal Science, with the support of the International Committee for Social Science Documentation.
"This bibliography . . . is selective and elementary" (*Preface*). Chapters are broken down into sections, each with a select bibliography appended. Final chapters (19-20) deal briefly with Roman law and canon law. Index of authors and editors; subject index.

34 (410):016

GREAT BRITAIN. TREASURY SOLICITOR'S DEPARTMENT. Catalogue of the legal library of the Treasury Solicitor. London, the Department, 1963. [189]p. Issued to Government Departments and legal bodies only.

"Intended purely as a guide and also to record the existence of the particularly early antiquarian books which are now rarely to be found outside the National and University Libraries" (*Introduction*). Author section (*c.* 1,400 entries); subject section (an asterisk indicates the standard work; law reports; periodicals.

34 (410) (091)

SELDEN SOCIETY. General guide to the Society's publications: a detailed and indexed summary of the contents of the Introductions, volumes 1-79; compiled by A. K. R. Kiralfy and G. H. Jones. London, Quaritch, 1960. iv, 168p.

V. 1 was published in 1887, and v. 79, in 1961. Detailed description of contents, p. 1-35; analytical index, p. 137-68. The Selden Society, whose aim is to study the history of law, prints, ancient records.

A bibliography of the Inns of Court and Chancery, compiled by D. S. Bland (London, Selden Society, 1965. xi, 75p.) comprises 862 numbered items, with many cross-references. 15 sections, including A. Manuscript sources—B. Histories, descriptions and general works—J. Drama—K. Literature; general—L. Libraries—M. Education—N. 19th-century reform—O. The legal profession. Indexes of authors, subjects and persons.

Scots Law

34 (411) (03)

Encyclopædia of the laws of Scotland; edited by Viscount Dunedin and others. Edinburgh, Green, 1926-. v. 1-. (v. 1-16. 1926-35).

——**Supplementary volume,** pts. 1 and 2, and Appendix; edited by J. F. G. Thomson. Edinburgh, Green, 1949-52. 3v. £10 10s.

No further volumes have been issued. The *Scottish current law yearbook* (*q.v.*) should be used to supplement the *Encyclopædia*.

34 (411) (03)

GIBB, A. D., and DALRYMPLE, A. W. Dictionary of words and phrases, judicially defined, and commented on, by the Scottish Supreme Courts. Edinburgh, Green, 1946. 382p.

". . . this is not a Scottish legal dictionary: it is not a rival to the excellent Bell [*Bell's Dictionary and digest of the laws of Scotland.* 7th ed. 1890]. It does not purport to include anything but the judges' explanations or definitions of the words which have happened to come under their notice. Further, it is to a very large extent concerned with lay words and expressions" (*Preface*).

34 (411) (038)

GIBBS, A. D. Students' glossary of Scottish legal terms. Edinburgh, Green, 1946. 95p.

Concise definitions (averaging *c.* 15 words) of *c.* 1,000 terms. "Concerned almost exclusively with legal expressions which are truly and exclusively lawyers' expressions" (*Introduction*). Adequate cross-references. Author was Regius Professor of Law in the Univ. of Glasgow.

34 (411) (058)

Scottish current law year book, being a complete statement of all the law from every source. 1948-. Edinburgh, Green, 1949-. (1965 v. 1966).

Annual cumulation of the monthly *Current law* (Scottish ed.). Sold only with *Scottish current law citator.* 1966. 180s. the 2v.

34 (411) (058.7)

The Scottish law list and legal directory for . . . , including correct and complete indices or lists of the judges and officers of the several courts of justice, of the advocates, Writers to the Signet, solicitors in the Supreme Courts, etc.; together with a list of the certificated practitioners in Scotland. Edinburgh, Scottish Law List. Annual. (1961. 17s. 6d.).

Sections: Edinburgh; Glasgow; Aberdeen; County; Accountants; County courts and county officials; Landowners' agents (followed by a list of charities in Scotland); English, Irish and foreign. General index precedes.

34 (411) (093)

STAIR SOCIETY. An introductory survey of the sources and literature of Scots law. Edinburgh, Stair Society, 1936. 486p.

The inaugural volume of the Stair Society, presenting the first comprehensive survey of the sources of Scots law which has ever been essayed. A complete guide, well documented and equipped with bibliographies. 38 contributions by specialists in 4 sections: Native sources—Non-native sources—Indirect sources—Special subjects.
Index, compiled by J. C. Brown (Edinburgh, Stair Society, 1939. 66p.), in two parts: index of cases cited; index of subjects.

34 (411) (094)

SCOTLAND. PARLIAMENT. The Acts of the Parliaments of Scotland, 1424-1707. 2nd rev. ed. Edinburgh, H.M. Stationery Office, 1966. lix, 191p. tables. 55s.

First published 1908.

The 1908 ed. contains a chronological table of all the Acts, the text of Acts of a public nature and still in force, and a digested index of those still in force. Omits local and personal Acts (Minto, J. *Reference books* (1929), p. 72).

Insert: *Index of short titles of the current Acts of the Parliament of Scotland, 1424-1707.* (1967. 4p. *Gratis*).

Ireland

34 (415) (058.7)

The Incorporated Law Society's Calendar and law directory for the year . . . Published by the authority of the Council of the Incorporated Law Society of Ireland. Dublin, Thom. Annual. (1961. 10s.).

Sections: Incorporated Law Society; Counsel; Solicitors; Northern Ireland; International; Notaries and commissioners; Costs.

34 (416)

NORTHERN IRELAND. The Statutes revised, Northern Ireland, A.D. 1226-1950 inclusive (as amended up to the end of 1954). Belfast, H.M. Stationery Office, 1956. 16v.

v. 1: *Legislation pre-1800.*
v. 2-8: *U.K. enactments, 1801-1920.*
v. 9-12: *U.K. enactments, 1921-1950.*
v. 13-6: *Northern Ireland enactments, 1921-1950.*

These volumes contain all the enactments affecting Northern Ireland, replacing material contained in almost 100 volumes.

Chronological table of the Statutes, 1226-1957, has been issued (1958) and an index is to be published.

The *Public General Acts* (Belfast, H.M.S.O.) have been published from 1921 onwards (*e.g.* 1965 v., published 1966. 50s.).

Statutory Rules and Orders of Northern Ireland, other than those of a local, personal, or temporary character, and also a classified list of local orders and an index appear annually (*e.g.* 1965 v., published 1966. 105s.).

There is also the *Index to the Statutory Rules and Orders in force on 31st December, 1964* (Belfast, H.M.S.O., 1965. 32s. 6d.).

34 (416):016

O'HIGGINS, P. A bibliography of periodical literature relating to Irish law. Belfast, Northern Ireland Legal Quarterly, Inc., 1966. xvi, 401p. 100s.

4,829 numbered entries, with interpolations. Arranged by subjects A-Z. About 120 periodicals are cited ('*l*' = leading article). Author and subject indexes.

34 (417) (093)

EIRE. ACHTANNA AN OIREACHTAIS. The Acts of the Oireachtais passed in the year . . . ; consisting of the Public General Acts and the Private Acts, with tables and index. Dublin, Stationery Office, 1922-. Annual. (1964, published [1966]. 25s.).

Irish and English texts on opposite pages.

Index to the legislation passed by the Oireachtais . . . 1922 to 1953 (Dublin, Stationery Office, 1955). Also, *Index to the Statutes, 1922 to 1958; with chronological tables . . .* (Dublin, Stationery Office, 1959).

The *Index to the Statutory Rules, Orders and Regulations,* for Eire, covers the period 1922-47 (Dublin, Stationery Office, [n.d.]. 3v.). Also, *Index to emergency powers orders* (Dublin, Stationery Office, 1943-54. 3v.).

English Law
Bibliographies

34 (420):016

GREAT BRITAIN. H.M. STATIONERY OFFICE. Government publications. Sectional list no. 57. Statute Law Committee. **Books and tables edited by the Statutory Publications Office.** London, H.M.S.O., 1962. [i], 7p. *Gratis.*

Sections: Statute law (with notes)—Subordinate legislation (with notes)—Alphabetical list of subject headings in Statutory Rules and Orders, and Statutory Instruments revised, which are obtainable as separate parts.

34 (420):016

Sweet & Maxwell's Guide to law reports and statutes. 4th ed., edited by W. Green. London, Sweet & Maxwell, 1962. 143p. 21s.

First published 1929.

Part 1: Enacted law (including editions of the statutes); part 2: Case law (columns: Reporter—No. and size of volumes—Period—Date of last edition). 'Abbreviations used' (*i.e.*, sources cited), p. 67-122; chronological list of the English law reports; table of dates of volumes and concurrent series of reports; Scottish reports after 1819.

A companion volume to *Where to look for your law.*

34 (420):016

Where to look for your law. 14th ed., edited by C. W. Ringrose. London, Sweet & Maxwell, 1962. vii, 239p. 12s. 6d.

First published 1908; 13th ed. 1960.

Sections: Subjects (A-Z, with many cross-references; under subjects, authors and dates of publications (U.S. items are so designated); items are asterisked if they are leading textbooks; p. 1-79)—Authors (A-Z: author, title, date, price; p. 81-169)—Command papers (A-Z under chairmen's names; *c.* 200 items; p. 170-9)—Current reports and periodicals (English, Scotch and Irish; p. 180-5)—Micro-card and micro-film productions—Law reports and their abbreviations (p. 187-237)—Table of regnal years. A valuable quick-reference guide.

34 (420):016

WILLIAMS, G. Learning the law. 7th ed. London, Stevens, 1963. ix, 218p.

First published 1945.

A handbook for the law student, to prepare him for reading textbooks. Contains much bibliographical information, particularly the chapters 'The mechanism of scholarship' (including a clear account of the law reports), 'Legal research' and 'General reading' (p. 203-15). Other chapters on 'Methods of study' and 'Technical terms'. Brief index.

Manuals

34 (420) (02)
Every man's own lawyer (Every man his own lawyer). [69th] centenary ed. London, Technical Press, 1962. v.p. 50s.

First published 1863; 68th ed. 1955.
A short elucidation of those parts of English law that are of most interest to the private citizen; written for non-specialist, and not intended as a means of avoiding solicitor's fees. The 69th ed. shows a substantial revision. 25 sections (1. Administration of the law—2. Personal rights and remedies—3. Mercantile and commercial law—4. Copyright, patents, designs and trade marks . . . 24. Ancient monuments and buildings of historic interest—25. Wagers, bets and gaming). Concise dictionary of legal terms (29p.). Footnote references. Index of *c.* 6,000 entries.

Newnes' Family lawyer; edited by D. Perkins (London, Newnes, [n.d.]. x, 894p. [1962].) has an even more popular appeal and is intended chiefly for the home library. Its eleven sections are enlivened by amusing and instructive line drawings. Not confined to strictly legal issues; background information on shares, weather and insurance are included. No footnote references. Index of *c.* 4,000 entries.

34 (420) (02)
STEPHEN, H. J. Commentaries on the laws of England. 21st ed. Editor-in-chief, L. O. Warmington. London, Butterworth, 1950. 4v., with cumulative supplement. (Supplement 1961. 1961. 12s. 6d.).

First published as *New commentaries.* 1841-45 (4v.).
v. 1: *Source of law and history of legal institutions; the law of property.*
v. 2: *The law of contract. The law of torts. Natural persons. Associations of persons.*
v. 3: *Civil procedure. Constitutional and administrative law.*
v. 4: *Criminal law.*
A text-book of long standing (18th ed. 1925), covering all the basic branches of English law.

Dictionaries

34 (420) (03)
JOWITT, W. A., *1st earl Jowitt.* **The dictionary of English law.** General editor, the late the Right Honourable the Earl Jowitt. Editor, Clifford Walsh. London, Sweet & Maxwell, 1959. 2v.

Claims to define and explain every English legal term, old and new. Terms derived from Scottish law and the civil law are included where they are of concern to the English lawyer. For each term etymology and translation (*e.g.,* of Latin tags) precedes definition and references to writers of authority; an historical outline of the subject is then followed by the modern application, together with the relevant statute, case or authority, plus frequent references to standard textbooks (see *Publisher's note*). Some bio-

graphies are included, with emphasis on legal careers or writings (*e.g.,* Bracton). Bibliography, v. 2, p. 1893-1905.

Law Reports

34 (420) (047)
All England law reports. London, Butterworths, 19361. Weekly, 180s. p.a.; including noter-up service, £10 7s. 6d.; bound v., £18 9s. ea. p.a.

A series of reports of decisions of all the courts; in suitable cases editorial notes are given, explaining the legal significance. Cases are speedily reported. Annual cumulative index and "noter-up" (*e.g.,* 1965, published 1966. 65s.); this also contains a table of cases, a table of statutes judicially considered, and a table of cases judicially noticed in later decisions.

34 (420) (047)
Weekly law reports. London, Incorporated Council of Law Reporting, 1953-. Weekly. 157s. 6d. p.a.

The series contains decisions of all courts, the most important of them being reported more fully in the *Law reports,* later. Here cases are reported speedily.
The annual cumulative index covering this series and the *Law reports* also contains tables of cases and statutes judicially considered.

34 (420) (047):016
MAXWELL, W. H., and **BROWN, C. R. A complete list of British and colonial law reports and legal periodicals.** 3rd ed. London, Sweet & Maxwell, 1937-46. 2v.

Gives the series of reports arranged according to countries and courts, with the number of volumes and period covered for reports and periodicals.

Yearbooks

34 (420) (058)
Current law. London, Sweet & Maxwell and Stevens, 1946-. Monthly, cumulated annually (*Current law year book,* with *Current law citator.* 1965 v. 160s.), and 5-yrly.

A survey by subject, believed to be complete, of all legal developments, legislation, decisions and literature. Full references to law reports, periodicals, etc., are given, and full indexes are provided, including case and Statute citators (*i.e.,* tables of earlier cases and Statutes affected by current development, legislative, judicial or literary). The making of orders, etc., under powers conferred by a Statute is shown in the citator.

Directories

34 (420) (058.7)
The Law list. London, Stevens, 1841-. Annual. (1967. 72s. 6d.).

A continuation of *The new law list,* by J. Hughes, 1798-1802, and *Clarke's law list,* 1803-1840.
Sub-title: "Published, so far as it relates to certified solicitors practising in England and Wales, by the authority of the Law Society". A

directory of law courts, judges, legal sections of government departments, barristers (with a list of barristers arranged by circuits) and solicitors in England and Wales (1966 ed., p. 1001-2472). In most cases full Christian names are given. An international section lists experts on foreign law practising in England, English lawyers practising abroad, etc.

History

34 (420) (091)

HOLDSWORTH, *Sir* **W. S. A history of English law.** Various editions. 1903-. v. 1-. London, Methuen, 1903-. v. 1-. (1966 reprint of v. 1-13. ea. 84*s*.).

v. 1: The judicial system. 7th ed.; revised by S. B. Chrimes [and others]. 1956. Index to v. 1-9, by E. Potton; v. 13 was published posthumously in 1953; v. 16 (1966) is the final v., devoted to the work of eminent lawyers between 1832 and 1875. A general index is in preparation.

The great history of English law; indispensable for detailed information.

Sources

34 (420) (093)

HOLDSWORTH, *Sir* **W. S. Sources and literature of English law.** Oxford, Clarendon Press, 1925. xii, 247p.

Based on 6 lectures delivered for the Council of Legal Education in 1924; a discussion of the contents and significance of the sources of English law since the Norman Conquest. Subjects: statutes, year-books, reports and abridgements, register of writs, textbooks and books of authority, developments outside common law —Star Chamber, Chancery, law merchant and the sphere of civilian practice.

34 (420) (093)

WINFIELD, *Sir* **P. H. The chief sources of English legal history.** Cambridge, Mass., Harvard Univ. Press, 1925 (reprinted 1962). xviii, 374p.

Based on a course of lectures delivered in the Harvard Law School in 1923, this essential guide discusses problems involved in the study of English legal history and equipment needed to face them; to each chapter is appended a critical list of printed sources and secondary works. Subjects: Existing bibliographical guides, Anglo-Saxon law, influence of Roman law on English law, statutes, Public Records, case law, abridgements, textbooks and books of practice.

Legislation

34 (420) (094)

Butterworth's Annotated legislation service (formerly Butterworth's Emergency legislation service, annotated: statutes supplements). London, Butterworth, 1939-.

An annotated edition of certain selected statutes of practical importance; some volumes are commentaries on individual statutes and, in fact, are monographs on the subjects they deal with. The latest index volume, to 1st January 1965 (London, Butterworths, 1966), contains alphabetical, chronological and classified lists.

34 (420) (094)

GREAT BRITAIN. Chronological table of the statutes, covering the legislation from 1235 to the end of 1966. London, H.M. Stationery Office, 1967. xii, 1269p. 105*s*.

Annual. Repeals are shown, but partial repeals do not always appear. Includes chronological table of the Acts of the Parliament of Scotland, 1424-1707, and of Church Assembly measures. Local and personal acts are not included after 1797. Entries relating to Ireland are subject to special rules.

34 (420) (094)

GREAT BRITAIN. Index to local and personal acts; consisting of classified lists of the local and personal and private acts and special orders and special procedure orders, 1801-1947. London, H.M. Stationery Office, 1949. viii, 1140p.

Repeals and amendments are shown, but the information about repeals, etc. prior to 1901 is not complete. An earlier ed., covering 1801-1890, contains Irish entries omitted from the 1801-1947 ed.

The local and personal acts themselves are published individually, with annual tables and index.

Supplementary index to the local and personal acts, 1948-1966: classified list of the local and personal acts (together with alphabetical and chronological lists) for the years 1948-1966 inclusive (Prepared in the Statutory Publications Office under the authority of the Statutory Law Committee. London, H.M.S.O., 1967. 228p. 50*s*.).

The Statutory Publications Office's *Chronological list of the local and personal acts, 1887-1947* also appeared in 1967 (200 p.).

According to J. L. Hobbs (*Local history and the library* (1962), p. 39), the best guides to earlier private acts are Vardon's *Index to local and personal and private acts* (1798-1840) and Bramwell's *Analytical table of private statutes* (1813. 2v.).

34 (420) (094)

GREAT BRITAIN. Index to the statutes in force . . . London. H.M. Stationery Office. Annual. (1966 ed. 1967. 2v. £10 10*s*.).

An analytical index of the public general statute law in force, with a table of statutes showing headings under which they are indexed. Omits pre-Union Scottish and Irish Acts. Certain acts of a local and personal character, printed amongst the public acts, are dealt with in an appendix. Appended chronological list of the Church Assembly measures.

34 (420) (094)

GREAT BRITAIN. The Public general acts and Church Assembly measures. London, H.M. Stationery Office, [1831-]. Annual (formerly sessional). (1965 ed. 1966. 2v. 126*s*.).

The public general acts (the current edition being published continuously since 1831) have been issued in various editions and formats, sessional or annual volumes dating from 1483; they are also published individually as they become law. Church Assembly measures have been included in the bound volumes since 1926.

34 (420) (094)
GREAT BRITAIN. The statutes revised, 1235-1948. 3rd ed. London, H.M. Stationery Office, 1950. 33v.

Gives the text of the public general acts as in force on December 31st, 1948. Repeals and amendments are shown. The Church Assembly measures are included.

Annotations to acts—directions for noting the amendments to the 3rd ed. of *Statutes revised* and to the annual volumes of statutes—has been published annually, covering the years 1949- (London, H.M.S.O., 1951-.).

34 (420) (094)
Halsbury's Laws of England; being a complete statement of the whole law of England, by the Rt. Hon. the Earl of Halsbury and other lawyers. 3rd ed., under the general editorship of the Rt. Hon. the Viscount Simonds. London, Butterworth, 1952-64. 43v. ea. 95s. Cumulative annual suppts. Current service (loose-leaf).

First published 1907-17; annual supplements. 2nd ed. 1931-42.

A complete encyclopaedia of English law, consisting of separate treatises on individual subjects arranged in alphabetical order (*e.g.*, 'Wills' (4 pts.), p. 839-1170). On many topics, Halsbury's *Laws* is the only convenient up-to-date source of information. V. 41-42, *General index;* v. 43, *Consolidated table of statutes.*

34 (420) (094)
Halsbury's Statutes of England. 2nd ed. Editor-in-chief, Sir R. Burrows. London, Butterworth, 1948-. Annual continuation v. and annual cumulative suppts.

v. 1-26, A-WILLS; v. 27, Tables of statutes and index; v. 28-, annual continuation v. (1948/49-); cumulative supplement (1966. 2v.). 44v., to 1965, £131 2s. 6d.

An annotated ed. of the statute law in force, arranged by topics A-Z ('Wills', v. 26, p. 1321-64; takes the Acts in turn, with notes). It reprints most of the Public General Acts, but a few that are of little interest to lawyers are omitted. A few local and personal acts, mainly those relating to London, are included. The titles are preceded by introductory notes.

Subordinate Legislation

34 (420) (094)
GREAT BRITAIN. Guide to government orders, indexing S.R. & O.s and S.I.s in force December 31, 1951-. London, H.M. Stationery Office, 1952-. Biennial. (1960. 126s.).

The guide is an index arranged systematically under broad subject-headings, A-Z. It shows the statutory powers under which instruments have been made and the instruments by which the powers have been exercised. Emergency legislation is omitted.

Previous to 1951, entitled *Index to statutory rules and orders and statutory instruments in force.* The *Daily list,* published by H.M.S.O., includes statutory instruments, and separate monthly and yearly lists are also published.

34 (420) (094)
GREAT BRITAIN. Statutory instruments. London, H.M. Stationery Office, [1891?]-. Annual.

Statutory rules and orders, until 1947.

The instruments are published, as made, during the year, and afterwards, in bound volumes. Local instruments, and those that have ceased to be in force by the time the bound volumes go to press, are not reprinted in them, but only listed. Certain instruments concerning the Colonies and made under the Royal Prerogative are printed in the bound volumes, as well as a numerical table, an index, a table of effects of the year's instruments on earlier legislation, and a classified list of local instruments.

34 (420) (094)
GREAT BRITAIN. The statutory rules and orders and statutory instruments, revised to December 31, 1948. London, H.M. Stationery Office, 1949-52. 25v.

An arrangement by subject of all the statutory instruments in force on December 31st, 1948. Certain instruments made under the Royal Prerogative and affecting the Colonies are included. Temporary instruments, including the Defence regulations, orders made thereunder, and certain rules of court, are omitted. Departmental legislation of Northern Ireland and Eire is omitted.

V. 25 contains a numerical table of instruments in v. 1-24, inclusive of those made in 1949-51, in operation on 31st December 1951, as well as a table showing the effect of instruments made in 1949-51 on earlier instruments.

Annual volumes of statutory instruments supplement the above since 1949. Individual instruments in these annual v. are tabulated by year and registration numbers or dates in *Numerical tables, S.R. & O. and S.I.* (q.v.); the effects (amendments, revocation, etc.) are recorded in *S.I. effects* (Annual. 1965 ed. 17s. 6d.). The latest tabulation is: *Table of government orders (combining the former S.I. effects and numerical table, S.R. & O. and S.I.) covering the general instruments to 31 December 1966* (London, H.M.S.O., 1967. vi, 642p. 84s.). A companion compilation is the *Index to governments orders in force on December 31, 1966. Subordinate legislation. The powers and their exercise.* (London, H.M.S.O., 1967. 1616p. 168s.).

Defence regulations printed as in force . . . , with an appendix showing statutory authorities for the regulations, is published annually by H.M.S.O.

34 (420) (094)
Halsbury's Statutory instruments; being a companion volume to Halsbury's *Statutes of England* London, Butterworth. 23v. & index. 1951-54 (and re-issues).

An annotated edition of all statutory rules and orders and statutory instruments in force, arranged by topics A-Z (Agriculture-Wills). It is being kept up to date by means of supplements; volumes containing much superseded matter are re-published, incorporating up-to-date matter. Not all instruments in force are reprinted in full.

German Law
34 (43):016

Bibliographie des deutschen Rechts in englischer und deutscher Sprache. Bibliography of German law in English and German. Eine Auswahl hrsg. von der Gesellschaft für Rechtsvergleichung. Mit einer Einführung in das deutsche Recht, von F. Baur. Karlsruhe, Müller, 1964. 584p.

A comprehensive selected bibliography, systematically arranged. Particularly full on the German Federal Republic and its Länder. Author and subject index. (Totok, W., and others. *Handbuch der bibliographischen Nachschlagewerke* (3. Aufl., 1966), p. 256.)

French Law
34 (44):016

DAVID, R. Bibliographie du droit français, 1945-1960. Établie par le Comité International pour la Documentation des Sciences Sociales sous la patronage de l'Association Internationale des Sciences Juridiques. The Hague, Mouton, 1964. 252p. (Maison des Sciences de l'Homme. Publications, série A. Bibliographies, 1). 35F.

Italian Law
34 (45):016

GRISOLI, A. Guide to foreign legal materials: Italian. Dobbs Ferry, N.Y., published for The Parker School of Foreign and Comparative Law, Columbia Univ., by Oceana, 1965. xv, 272p. $10.

Primarily for the common-law lawyer. Part 1, Sources of Italian law (chapters 1-6); part 2, Repositories of the law (1. Bibliographies—2. Legislative materials—3. Case law—4. Encyclopedias, form books and legal dictionaries—5. Doctrinal). Appendices: Current legal abbreviations; abbreviations of periodicals. Index to subjects; index to authors and titles.

Spanish Law
34 (46):016

FERNÁNDEZ DE VILLAVICENCES, F. and **SOLA CANIZARES, F. de. Bibliografía jurídica española.** Barcelona, Consejo Superior de Investigaciones Científicas, Instituto de Derecho Comparado, 1954. 127p.

Soviet Law
34 (47):016

AKADEMIYA NAUK SSSR. Institut Gosudarstva i Prava. **Literature on Soviet Law. Index of bibliography.** Moscow, Izd-vo Akademiï Nauk, SSSR, 1960. 279p.

English translation of *Literatura po sovetskomu pravu: Bibliograficheskiĭ ukazatel'* (1960).
Prepared by Soviet specialists for foreigners, indicating primary sources and treatises, states P. L. Horecky (*Russia and the Soviet Union* (1965), entry no. 612).

The Harvard Law School Library's *Soviet legal bibliography: a classified and annotated listing of books and serials published on the Soviet Union since 1917, as represented in the collection of the Harvard Law School Library as of January 1, 1965* (Cambridge, Mass., Harvard Univ. Press) is edited by V. Mostecky and W. E. Butler.

Scandinavian Law
34 (48):016

IUUL, S., *and others.* **Scandinavian legal bibliography.** Stockholm, etc., Almquist & Wiksell, 1961. 196p. (Acta Instituti Upsaliensis Jurisprudentiae Comparativae).

An evaluative bibliography, with added translation of titles in English. Deals with Scandinavian law in general, then with the law of Denmark, Norway, Iceland, Sweden and Finland.

Middle East Law
34 (5-015)

AZZAM, I. "The law in the Near and Middle East: basic sources in English." In *Law library journal*, v. 57, no. 3, August 1964, p. 234-40.

About 200 references (no annotations) in 5 main sections: 1. General works and treatises—2. Articles and essays—3. Periodicals—4. Composite works—5. Law in the individual countries (11, including Libya, Sudan and the United Arab Republic).

Chinese Law
34 (510):016

HSIA, Tao-Tai. Guide to selected legal sources of Mainland China: a listing of laws and regulations and periodical legal literature, with a brief survey of the administration of justice. Washington, U.S. Government Printing Office, 1967. viii, 357p. $2.

Two sections: 'List of statutory materials' ('Collection of law and decrees of the Central People's Government, September 1949 up to September 1954' and 'Collection of laws and regulations of the People's Republic of China, September 1954 to December 1963'); 'Selective list of periodical legal literature'. The compiler is Chief of the Far Eastern Law Division in the Library of Congress Law Library (*Library of Congress Information bulletin*, v. 26, no. 29, July 20, 1967, p. 468).

Indian Law
34 (540):016

ALEXANDROWICZ, C. H., *ed.* **A bibliography of Indian law.** London, Oxford Univ. Press, 1958. ix, 69p. 8s.

A list of c. 750 items in 14 sections (3. Legal encyclopaedias, digests and dictionaries). Considers all aspects of law, including court procedure and the legal profession. Directory of publishers; author index. No annotations.

South African Law
34 (680)

ROBERTS, A. A. A South African bibliography; being a bio-bibliographical survey and law-finder of the Roman and Roman-Dutch legal literature in Southern Africa; with an historical chart, notes on all judges since 1828, and other appendices. Pretoria, Wallach, 1942. 389p. R4.50.

A basic, annotated bibliography (p. 29-346; by authors A-Z), plus biographical notes on some of the authors. Judges, p. 347-84. Gives South African holdings of the works listed.

B. Beinart is preparing a revised ed. (Musiker, R. *Guide to South African reference books*. (4th ed., 1965), entry no. 82.)

United States Law

34 (73):016
ANDREWS, J. L., *and others.* **The law of the United States of America:** a selective bibliographical guide. New York, Univ. Press, 1965. vii, 100p. $4.

Compiled at the request of the International Association of Law Libraries.
Part 1: Primary and allied materials. Part 2: Text and secondary sources. Reference materials, p. 86-87. Annotated. Classified list of subject headings, following the system used by *Index to foreign legal periodicals*. No index.

34 (73):016
LONDON. UNIVERSITY. Institute of Advanced Legal Studies. **Union list of United States legal literature:** holdings of legislation, law reports and digests in libraries in Oxford, Cambridge and London. 2nd ed. London, the Institute, 1967. xii, 82p. 25s.

Covers federal and state statutes, the code of federal regulations, law reports and digests of cases. Treatises and periodicals are excluded, but reports of decisions of administrative tribunals and agencies are shown. Details of the years held are given. The leading law libraries of which holdings are listed range from national, government and academic to professional libraries.

34 (73):016
PRICE, M. "Anglo-American law". In *Library trends*, v. 15, no. 4, April 1967, p. 616-27.

A concise survey of current legal bibliographies. 46 references.

34 (73) (094)
United States code . . . 1964 ed. Prepared by the Committee on the Judiciary of the House of Representatives. Washington, U.S. Government Printing Office, 1965. 11v. & 3v. of indexes. Annual cumulative supplements (1. 1966. $6.75).

First published 1926.
Codifies general and permanent laws of the U.S. in force on 3rd January 1965. Arranged under broad subject headings (*e.g.*, defence, education), with sub-divisions. Statutes that have been amended are printed in amended form and notes provided. V. 12-14 comprise a popular name and general indexes.

Latin American Law

34 (8=6):016
UNITED STATES. LIBRARY OF CONGRESS. Law Library. **Index to Latin American legislation,** 1950 through 1960. Boston, Mass., G. K. Hall, 1961. 2v. $156.

30,900 catalogue cards, photolithographically reproduced. Covers the principal laws, decrees, regulations and administrative rulings of twenty Latin American republics. Arranged by country, then by subject and chronologically thereafter.

Legal Costume

34:391
HARGREAVES-MAWDSLEY, W. N. A history of legal dress in Europe until the end of the eighteenth century. Oxford, Clarendon Press, 1963. xii, 151p. illus 35s.

Chapters: 1. Italy, Spain and Portugal—2. France—3. Great Britain and Ireland—4. German-speaking countries, the Low Countries, Switzerland, Scandinavia, Hungary and Poland. Short glossary of terms, with line-drawings. Most of the illustrations are half-tones, not particularly clear or numerous, but backed by handy descriptions (*e.g.*, of the dress of chief of police in France). The 'Critical bibliography' (p. 121-9) covers manuscripts and books but is not annotated. Analytical index.

Legal Research

34.001.5
LONDON. UNIVERSITY. INSTITUTE OF ADVANCED LEGAL STUDIES. List of legal research topics completed and approved since 1935. 2nd ed. London, the Institute, 1961. vi, 27p. **Supplement,** 1961-July 1966. [1966]. v, 16p.

Prepared in co-operation with the Society of Public Teachers of Law.
Relates almost entirely to degrees of U.K. universities, but any Commonwealth degree notified has been included. Sections: Jurisprudence—Legal history—International law—Public law—Private law—Conflict of laws—Other systems of law (by countries or areas, A-Z).

——————**List of current legal research topics.** 14th ed. London, 1966. ii, 20p.

Entered under names of researchers, A-Z (name; university; degree; subject); 296 names. Detailed list of subjects.

Legal Aid

34.096
LAW SOCIETY. Legal aid handbook. 3rd ed. London, H.M. Stationery Office, 1966. [vii], 466p. Loose-leaf. 30s. Amendment service available. Supplement no. 1. February 1967. 2s.; no. 2. June 1967. 2s. 3d.

2nd ed. 1956.
Contents: Acts, regulations and orders, rules —Cost of successful unassisted parties—List of forms—The Legal Aid and Advice Schemes— Digest of notes for guidance of area and local committees published from time to time in the Law Society's *Gazette* which are of current application—Digest of *Gazette* statements—Criminal proceedings—Index, p. 451-66.

Jurisprudence

340.142:016
DIAS, R. W. M. A bibliography of jurisprudence. Being a companion to *Jurisprudence*, 2nd edition. London, Butterworths, 1964. viii, 234p. 30s.

An annotated list of *c.* 2,000 items in 20 sections. Near print. The compiler is a member of the Inner Temple and a barrister-at-law.

Medical Jurisprudence

340.6:016
BRITTAIN, B. P. Bibliography of medico-legal works in English. London, Sweet & Maxwell and F. B. Rothman, 1962. xx, 252p. *52s. 6d.*

Published under the auspices of the British Academy of Forensic Sciences.
1,432 authors are represented. Includes translations into English of foreign works and also publications in other languages by authors writing in English-speaking countries. Occasional brief annotations.

International Law

341:016
CLIFFORD-VAUGHAN, F. M. McA. A selective bibliography of works on international law. London and Paris, 1960. xxxii, 50p. Mimeographed.

763 items, systematically arranged (1. General—2. Sources of international law—3. Subjects of international law—4. International organisations—5. International public property (rivers, canals, etc.)—6. Pacific settlement—7. Security and war—8. Special (international penal law; international private law; etc.)). Included are some published theses and courses. A list of international periodicals and serials and an author index precede the bibliography. No annotations. Names of publishers are omitted from entries.

341:016
HARVARD LAW SCHOOL LIBRARY. Catalog of international law and relations. Cambridge, Mass., the Library, 1965-67. 20v. $1000.

A subject catalogue, entries being photolithographically reproduced from cards, 16 per page. Each volume has *c.* 1,000 pages, giving a total of *c.* 300,000 entries. An immense compilation, likely to be found in only a few large or specialised libraries.

341:016
UNITED NATIONS. Ways and means of making the evidence of customary international law more readily available: preparatory work within the purview of Article 24 of the Statute of the International Law Commission. Lake Success, New York, United Nations, 1949. vi, 114p.

A very good bibliography of the following sources of international law: state practice (including diplomatic documents), decisions of international tribunals and municipal courts, national legislation, decisions and opinions of international organizations, and of the Harvard University, Harvard Law School, Research in International Law.

341:016
ZAGAYKO, F. F. "Guide to a basic library on international law." In *Law library journal.* v. 53, 1960, p. 118-28.

About 300 items are listed, with emphasis on reference works and recent publications. Sections: 1. Basic reference tools—2. Sources of international law—3. Treaties—4. Periodicals—5. Short list of books recommended for first purchase (A. Treatises; B. Periodicals; C. Cases, reports, digests). Some annotations and footnote references. The compiler was International Law Librarian, Columbia University Law Library.

341 (038)=00
Dictionnaire de la terminologie du droit international. Publié sous le patronage de l'Union Académique Internationale. Tables en anglais, italien, espagnol, allemand. Paris, Sirey, 1960. xv, 755p.

A dictionary of terms used in international law as found in the texts of treaties, diplomatic correspondence and communications of international organizations. About 1,200 terms are dealt with; frequent citations from sources listed on p. xiii-xv. Appendix tables of terms in German, English, Spanish and Italian, with French equivalents that are entry-words in the dictionary proper, p. 651-755. Does not set out "to compete with or duplicate such publications as the *Wörterbuch des Völkerrechts . . ." (International affairs,* v. 36, no. 3, July 1960, p. 360-1).

341 (038)=30
SCHLOCHAUER, H.-J., *ed.* **Wörterbuch des Völkerrechts:** begründet von Karl Strupp. 2. Auf., völlig neu bearb. Berlin, de Gruyter, 1960-62. 3v. and index.

1st ed., edited by Karl Strupp, 1924-29. 2v.
A dictionary of international law. Very thoroughly compiled, all articles being signed, documented and systematically set out (*e.g.,* the short contribution on the Bretton Woods Conference, 1944, has three sections: History.—Objectives.—Outcome, and a bibliography of 6 items). Full cross-references. Each v. has 300-400 entries. The index v. contains tables of all entries in German, English and French and a table of leading cases in international law that are the subject of separate entries in v. 1-3. "An extremely useful tool for academic research as well as a handbook of great practical utility" (*International affairs,* v. 38, no. 1, January 1963, p. 87).

341 (058)
Annuaire français de droit international. Paris, Centre National de la Recherche Scientifique, [1956?]-. v. 1-. Annual. (v. 11: 1965. [1966]).

V. 11 has 12 survey-sections: Ouvrages généraux—Sources du droit international—Territoire et domaine international—Droit de la guerre; Forces étrangères—Arbitrage—Organisations internationales—Organisations européennes—Droits de l'homme—États nouveaux—Relations internationales—Droit international privé—Revues, annuaires, répertoires (v. 11, p. 1115-56). Appended (p. 1157-1219) is an excellent 'Bibliographie systematique des ouvrages et articles relatifs au droit international publié en langue française'. closely sub-divided; *c.* 2,000 items.

341 (058)
The British year book of international law,
1920/21-. London, Oxford Univ. Press, 1920-.
Annual. (1964 v. 1966. 90s.).

Issued under the auspices of the Royal Institute of International Affairs.
The 1964 v. has 8 contributions by specialists
(p. 1-335); many footnote references. Notes.
"Decisions of British courts during 1963-1964
involving questions of public or private international law" (p. 372-84). First-class reviews of
24 books (p. 385-426). Table of cases; analytical
index.
Index to v. 1-36, 1963 (160p. 45s.).

341.001.5
"Focus on world law". In *Intercom* (New York,
Foreign Policy Association), v. 9, no. 3, May/
June 1967, p. 26-71.

"A guide to current research in the field of
international law" (*Current geographical publications*, v. 30, no. 6, June 1967, p. 184).

International Organisations

341.1:016
**SPEECKAERT, G. P. Bibliographie sélective
sur l'organisation internationale, 1885-1964.**
[2. éd.]. Brussels, Union of International Associations, 1965. x, 148p. 21s.

First published 1956 as *International institutions and international organisations*.
Part 1: General (350 items: history; theory and
general studies; legal studies, etc.; yearbooks,
directories, periodicals, bibliographies). Part 2:
Individual organisations (730 titles on 214 individual international organisations, under French
titles, A-Z).

341.12:016
**HER MAJESTY'S STATIONERY OFFICE.
International organisations' and overseas
agencies' publications . . . :** supplement to
Government publications . . . London, H.M.S.O.,
1955-. Annual. (1966, published 1967. 1s. 6d.).

Part of H.M.S.O.'s annual *Government publications* up to and including 1954. (H.M.S.O. is
the official agent in the U.K. for publications of
international organisations and certain overseas
agencies.)
Lists the publications of international bodies
(A-Z), especially those of the United Nations and
its Specialized Agencies, the European Communities and O.E.C.D.; also a list of periodicals
and index. Kept up to date in H.M.S.O. *Daily
list* and *Monthly catalogue*.

341.12 (02)
COLLIARD, C.-A. Institutions internationales.
3. éd. Paris, Dalloz, 1966. xix, 747p. 20F.

2nd ed. 1963.
Intended for students of the Facultés de Droit
et des Sciences Economiques. A closely arranged
textbook, with 689 paragraphs. Chapter and
section bibliographies (*e.g.*, Federalism, p. 109-
37; bibliography of 2p.). Some 200p. are devoted
to a scholarly résumé of the historical evolution
of international rules and institutions. Data on

regional organisations, though the Warsaw Pact
and COMECON are dealt with cursorily. "A
very good reference book" (*International affairs*,
v. 42, no. 3, July 1966, p. 461).

League of Nations

341.121:016
**AUFRICHT, H. Guide to League of Nations
publications:** a bibliographical survey of the
work of the League, 1920-1947. New York,
Columbia Univ. Press, 1951. xix, 682p.

The most comprehensive bibliographical guide
so far available to League of Nations documents.
Entries are annotated. Does not pretend to be a
complete list, but all the important documents
are covered. Arrangement is systematic, with a
lengthy introduction prefacing each section. Appendices (p. 405-646) of basic League of Nations
documents; analytical subject index.

To supplement the coverage of Aufricht there
are two other sources: Carroll, M. J. *Key to
League of Nations documents placed on public
sale, 1920-1929*, and four supplements, 1930-1936
(Boston, World Peace Foundation; etc., 1930-
36); and Breycha-Vauthier, A. C. von. *Sources
of information: a handbook on the publications
of the League of Nations* (London, Allen &
Unwin, 1939).

341.121:016
**LEAGUE OF NATIONS. Catalogue of publica-
tions** issued by the League of Nations. Geneva,
1935. 312p.; Supplements.

The 1935 *Catalogue* gives the titles of all the
publications offered for sale up to the end of
May 1935. Four supplements cover the period 1st
June 1935 to 31st December 1945.

341.121 (091)
**WALTERS, F. P. A history of the League of
Nations.** Published under the auspices of the
Royal Institute of International Affairs. London,
Oxford Univ. Press, 1952. 2v. (1960 reprint in
1v. 30s.).

The standard work on the League of Nations.
An objective account. 67 chapters, taking the
narrative up to 1946. No bibliography, but a
rather general appendix note on sources, v. 2,
p. 816-7. Supported by a very good analytical
index.

United Nations

341.123:016
**"Bibliographical activities of international
organizations. Chapter 1: The United Nations."**
In UNESCO, Bibliographical services throughout
the world. 5th annual report, 1956 (Paris,
UNESCO, 1958), p. 149-62.

Particularly concerned with UNESCO bibliographies and publishing activities (p. 152-60) in
both 1956 and previous years. Followed by
briefer notes on bibliographies issued by F.A.O.,
W.H.O., I.C.A.O. and I.L.O.

341.123:016
BRIMMER, B., *and others.* **A guide to the use
of United Nations documents** (including refer-

LAW

ence to the Specialized Agencies and Special U.N. Bodies). Dobbs Ferry, New York, Oceana Publications, Inc., by arrangement with the New York Univ. Press, 1962. xv, 272p. charts. $7.50.

Designed "to be of assistance both to the researcher in United Nations materials and to the librarians dealing with United Nations documents collections" (*Introduction*). Part 1: Methods and problems of research (chapters: 1. The documentation system—2. The method of research (helpful advice on procedures for U.N. research, p. 56-78)—3. Research and the library —4. Research and the librarian. Part 2: Tools and guides (p. 131-232; chapters 5-9). The 7 appendices include organization charts. Bibliography (p. 268-9; no post-1955 references). Brief index (p. 270-2), to be used in conjunction with detailed table of contents. A thorough guide, though typographical layout is dull.
Supersedes C. C. Moor and W. Chamberlin's *How to use United Nations documents* (New York, Univ. Press; London, Cumberlege, 1952. iii, 26p.).

341.123:016
Current issues: a selected bibliography on subjects of concern to the United Nations. New York, United Nations, Dag Hammarskjold Library, December 1965-. no. 1-. Irregular. (ST/LIB/SER. G/2). nos. 1-2, ea. $1; no. 3, 75c.

Succeeds the United Nations Library (New York) *List of selected articles* (1949-63. Monthly). *See entry at 3:016.*

341.123:016
UNITED NATIONS. Department of Public Information. **Ten years of United Nations publications, 1945 to 1955: a complete catalogue.** New York, United Natons, Dept. of Public Information: Sales & Circulation Section, 1955. viii, 267p. Annual supplements. (*United Nations publications*, 1955-), 1956-.

"The purpose is to provide a convenient and comprehensive guide to the Official Records and publications and periodicals of the United Nations which have been issued since the beginning of the organization" (*Preface*). Lists cover the following bodies: Secretariat publications; official records of the General Assembly, Economic Council, Atomic Energy Commission, Disarmament Commission, Economic and Social Council, and Trusteeship Council. Only the addresses of Specialized Agencies are given. List of depository libraries.
United Nations publications, 1945-1965: a reference catalogue (New York, U.N., 1964. 71p.) has 17 sections (*e.g.*, 2. Economics, p. 13-36), with an appended list of United Nations periodicals.

341.123:016
UNITED NATIONS. Library, New York. Documents Index Unit. **United Nations documents index,** January 1950-: United Nations and Specialized Agencies documents and publications. Lake Success, New York, United Nations, 1950-. Monthly. 50s. p.a.

Latterly prepared by the Index section of the Dag Hammarskjöld Library.

Each issue consists of a checklist of numbered items, together with a subject index on tinted paper. Both the checklist and the index are cumulated annually.
It lists and indexes all documents and publications of the United Nations and all the printed publications of the International Court of Justice. It does omit restricted material and internal papers. Not confined to documents on sale, but includes mimeographed reports.

For United Nations publications issued prior to 1950, there is the incomplete series, *Check list of United Nations documents* (1949-). Fascicules have so far been issued as follows: pt. 4, no. 1-3. Trusteeship Council, 1947/49; pt. 5. no. 1-3. Economic and Social Council. 1946-49: pt. 6H, no. 1, Fiscal Commission. 1947-48.
The Dag Hammarskjold Library's *List of United Nations document series symbols* (New York, United Nations, 1965. iv, 139p. $2) gives a list of series symbols (with many cross-references) plus full names of bodies, and an index of subjects and bodies plus symbols.

341.123:016
UNITED NATIONS. United Nations official records, 1948-1962: a reference catalogue. New York, United Nations, 1963. 107p. 4s.

Items arranged in 10 sections (*e.g.*, Official records of the General Assembly; Official records of the Atomic Energy Commission; Official records of the Trusteeship Council). Appended list of U.N. depository libraries.

341.123 (02)
UNITED NATIONS. Office of Public Information. **Everyman's United Nations:** the structure, functions and work of the organization and its related agencies during the years 1945-1962. . . . 7th ed. New York, United Nations, 1964. x, [1], 638p. $5; 38s.

First published 1948; 6th ed. 1959.
Four parts: 1. Description and purposes of the United Nations—2. The work of the United Nations (p. 29-463; mentions publications)—3. Intergovernmental agencies related to the United Nations (*e.g.*, I.L.O.; International Monetary Fund)—4. A United Nations chronology for 1963. Appendices: U.N. information centres. Analytical index (*e.g.*, International Court of Justice: 2½ columns).
Kept up to date by the *U.N. monthly chronicle* ($3).

341.123 (058)
UNITED NATIONS. Office of Public Information. **Yearbook of the United Nations,** 1946/47-. New York, United Nations, 1947-. charts. Annual. (19th ed., 1965, published 1967. 168s.).

Part 1 deals with the general organisation of the U.N. and the issues facing it (*e.g.*, political and security questions; economic and social questions; legal questions; administrative and budgetary questions). Part 2: 'The intergovernmental organizations related to the United Nations'. Appendix includes text of Charter. Subject index; index of names.

341.123 (092)

Who's who in the United Nations: the authoritative, illustrated, biographical dictionary of key persons associated with the United Nations. Edited by C. E. Burckel. New York, Burckel, 1951. xii, 580p.

Nearly 1,700 entries, prepared in association with the U.N. Department of Public Information. Information as at late 1950.

Biographees were selected either because of (1) their positions in one of the organs of the U.N. and its specialised agencies, *e.g.,* permanent representatives and members of delegations to the U.N., members of the International Court of Justice, etc., (2) the significance of the functions which they are performing or have performed, *e.g.,* foreign ministers of the U.N. member countries and those persons who had a significant part in the conferences leading to the formal organization of the U.N., and who were still more or less active in public affairs. Some prominent U.N. workers were also included. Entries were based on a questionnaire and returned to the biographee for confirmation. Where this procedure was not possible, information was gathered from reliable sources and the entry prepared by the editorial staff.

341.16:001

UNITED NATIONS EDUCATIONAL, SCIENTIFIC AND CULTURAL ORGANIZATION. General catalogue of Unesco publications and Unesco sponsored publications, 1946-1959. Paris, Unesco, 1962. xvi, 217p. 5s. **Supplement.** 1964. xiv, 131p. 5s.

The parent list notes the latest edition of 2,681 numbered publications. Four parts in all; classified by U.D.C. The *Supplement,* similarly arranged, lists more than 1,300 publications issued 1960-63.

341.16:341.24 (038)

EUROPEAN COMMUNITIES. A glossary of legal terms appearing in the French texts of the treaties establishing the European Atomic Energy Community, the European Coal and Steel Community and the European Economic Community, and related documents. 2nd ed. London, H.M. Stationery Office, 1965. vi, 62p. spiral binding. 10s.

Entries for *c.* 100 terms in 4 columns: (1) the French expression; (2) the English translation normally adopted in the Community context; (3) identification of the document as published in French and of the passage in which the expression is to be found; (4) comments. Comments can be extensive (3p. in the case of 'Société'). Abbreviations of sources, p. v-vi.

J. Herbert's *Glossary of international treaties* (Amsterdam, Elsevier) was announced for publication in 1967. It will contain *c.* 2,000 entries in French, English, Italian, Spanish, Dutch, German and Russian, and is in the Glossaria interpretum series. It includes words and phrases in the NATO, Euratom, E.E.C., G.A.T.T., U.N.O., Unesco, W.H.O. and I.L.O. treaties and various Geneva conventions.

Regional Unions

341.17:016

Atlantic studies. Boulogne-sur-Seine, Atlantic Institute, 1964-. 2 p.a.

About 500 annotated items per issue. Covers political, economic, military and army control, social, juridical and cultural studies focused on the relations and co-ordination of policies covering 10 Atlantic countries, on their relations with other non-Communist nations, and on their relations with the Communist world. Projects of a purely national character are not listed. Includes studies in progress. Author and organisation indexes.

341.17:016

CONFERENCE ON THE ATLANTIC COMMUNITY, Bruges. **The Atlantic Community: an introductory bibliography.** Leyden, Sijthoff, 1962. 2v.

An annotated bibliography of 599 numbered items, under authors A-Z. One entry per page. Limited almost entirely to books and articles published since 1945 in the U.K., U.S., France, Germany, Austria, Switzerland and Italy which constitute a basic reading list for any study of the problems of the Atlantic Community. Subject index in v. 2.

341.17:016

PADELFORD, N. J. "A selected bibliography on regionalism and regional arrangements." In *International organization,* v. 10, no. 4, November 1956, p. 575-603. (Also available as an offprint.)

Nine sections, covering the Organization of American States, NATO, O.E.E.C., E.C.E., E.P.U., 'Regional organizations in the Soviet sphere', 'Middle Eastern regionalism', 'Regionalism in South and Southeast Asia', and 'The Pacific Region'. Includes official publications and periodical articles. No annotations.

"Inventory of lists, indexes and catalogues of publications and documents of intergovernmental organizations other than the United Nations" (*Unesco bulletin for libraries,* v. 21, no. 5, September/October 1967, p. 263-70) records, with document references, *c.* 250 Council of Europe, European Community, F.A.O., G.A.T.T., I.C.A.O., I.L.O., O.E.C.D., Unesco, W.H.O. and other organizations' catalogues, plus cross-references from titles.

341.17 (093)

PEASLEE, A. J. and XYDIS, D. P. International governmental organizations: constitutional documents. Rev. 2nd ed. The Hague, Nijhoff, 1961. 2v. 165s.

v. 1. *African Postal Union — International Maritime Consultative Organization.* 1961.
v. 2. *International Atomic Energy Agency — World Meteorological Organization.* 1961.

Texts of the basic constitutional documents of more than 100 international organisations, plus background information and select bibliographies, in most cases.

Europe

341.17 (4):016
COUNCIL OF EUROPE. Publications of the Council of Europe: catalogue, 1965. Strasbourg, the Council, 1965. 30p.

Ten sections: A. European treaty series—B. Consultative Assembly (records of proceedings; other publications)—C. Records of proceedings of the European Conference of Local Authorities—D. Political and economic surveys by the Secretariat—E. Human rights—F. Legal problems and criminology—G. Population and refugees—H. Public health—I. Partial agreement in the social field—J. Publications of the Directorate of Education and Scientific and Cultural Affairs on education, youth and cultural problems.

341.17 (4):016
EUROPEAN COMMUNITIES. Publications of the European Communities: catalogue, March 1964-July 1967. Luxembourg & Brussels. 119p. *Gratis.*

13 sections: 1. Official gazette—2. European Parliament—3. Court of Justice—4. Councils of Ministers—5. European Coal & Steel Community —6. European Economic Community (p. 59-90)— 7. European Investment Bank—8. European Atomic Energy Authority—9. Legal source of the European executives—10. Press and information service—11. Statistical Office—12. Economic and Social Committee—13. European schools. Gives prices and includes free items as well as those with limited distribution.
    The European Communities' Information Service's *A guide to the study of the European Communities* (Rev. ed. 1955) records official publications and also lists 150 books, pamphlets and articles.

R. Pryce's "The European communities, their work and publications" (*Aslib proceedings,* v. 14, no. 6, June 1962, p. 145-51) briefly describes the official sources of information available from the communities themselves, "and especially those concerning the work of the European Economic Community". Sections: Introductory material—Basic documents—The Common Market in action—Sources of further information—Discussion. The author is head of the London Office, Information Service of the European Communities.

341.17 (4):016
EUROPEAN COMMUNITIES. Service de Presse et d'Information. **Relevé bibliographique mensuel.** Monatliches veröffentlichungsverzeichnis. Brussels & Luxembourg. Monthly. Mimeographed.

Sections cover the E.E.C., European Community for Coal and Steel, Euratom, Press and information services, Statistical Office of the European Communities, Court of Justice of the European Communities, Journal, and works on European integration.

341.17 (4):016
EUROPEAN COMMUNITY. High Authority Library. **Ausgewaehlte Zeitschriftenaufsaetze. Articles selectionnés . . .** [Brussels?], the Community, [1957?]-. Monthly. Mimeographed.

No. 167 of 1966 lists *c.* 600 items arranged under 18 headings (*e.g.,* Integration—E.E.C.— E.C.S.C.—Mines—Coal—Iron and steel—Social problems—Automation—Economics and Finance —Miscellaneous). Contents list in German, French, Italian and Dutch.

341.17 (4):016
EUROPEAN COMMUNITY FOR COAL AND STEEL. High Authority Library. **Catalogue systematique des ouvrages, 1952-1962.** Brussels, [1962?]. 2v. Mimeographed.

A catalogue of 1285p., listing more than 10,000 items. Systematically arranged, with subject and author indexes. 8 main classes (1. General reference works—2. Economic policy. Statistics—3. Demography . . . 7. Telecommunications and communications—8. Social questions). Covers books and pamphlets; no annotations.

341.17 (4):016
EUROPEAN PARLIAMENT. Vierteljährliche methodische Bibliographie . . . Luxembourg, Directorate General of Parliamentary Documentation and Information, European Parliament, 1956-. v. 1, no. 1-. Quarterly.

'A quarterly classified bibliography', arranged in 10 main subject groups relating to the interests of the European Parliament,—political, economic, social, agricultural, transport, energy, etc. Each issue carries *c.* 700 entries.

341.17 (4):016
PAKLONS, L. L. Bibliographie européenne. Bruges, De Tempel for College of Europe, 1964. 218p.

A classified bibliography of almost 3,000 items, based on the stock of the library of the Postgraduate Institute of European Studies, College of Europe. Only separate works written on the specific subject of European integration are included, plus periodical articles of which the Library has received off-prints. For other periodical articles, the reader is referred to the bibliographies in the first section. Official publications of the Council of Europe and the European Communities are excluded. Entries are not annotated.

Bibliographie zur europäischen Integration, by G. Zellentin and E. Y. De Koster (2. rev. und erw. Aufl. Cologne, Europa-Union Verlag, 1965. 209p.) is annotated. First published in 1962, it has some six main sections, with bibliographies, reference works and periodical publications as final sub-divisions.

341.17 (4):016
PEHRSSON, H., and **WULF, H.,** *ed.* **The European bibliography.** Compiled by the European Cultural Centre, Geneva. Leyden, Sijhoff, 1965. [xi], 472p. D.fl. 42.50; 85s.

About 1,250 items, mainly books published 1945-63 on Europe as a whole. Each entry is annotated in English and French, and in the language of the book if it be German, Spanish, Italian or Dutch. 9 sections: 1. History—2. Europe and the world—3. General books—4. Art, letters and philosophy—5. Education—6.—Federalism—7. Politics and law—8. Economics—9.

Documentation (official publications of the European organisations and the I.L.O.). Author index.

341.17 (4) (02)
GROEBEN, H.v.d., and **BEOCKH, H.v. Handbuch der europäische Wirtschaft.** Baden-Baden, Nomos Verlag, 1958-. 10v. (*c.* 7000p.). Loose-leaf.

Sections: 1. Chronological list of events concerning European integration, the European Economic Community, and associated countries —2. European Free Trade Area—3. Euratom— 4-9. Coal and Steel Community, G.A.T.T., O.E.C.D., International Monetary Fund, World Bank, International Development Association, International Finance Corporation, European Parliament. Section 4 includes statistics, a directory of international organisations and their officers, name and subject indexes and a list of abbreviations. In German only, dealing with the E.E.C. in great detail; texts of treaties and agreements, plus official explanatory notes and extensive commentary.
Insertion of up-dating sheets is complicated by the many sections and various paginations.

341.17 (4):058
European year book. The Hague, Nijhoff, 1955-. Annual. (v. 12 (2 pts.): 1964. 1966. $29.10).

v. 1: 1948-53. 955.
Published under the auspices of the Council of Europe. Text in English and French.
Three main features: articles on aspects of European co-operation; texts of basic documents of the O.E.D.C., etc.; bibliography (list of publications of each organisation; general annotated bibliography on European co-operation, including periodical articles). V. 12 carries a brief contents-list of previous volumes.

Frontiers

341.222
UNITED STATES. Bureau of Intelligence and Research. Office of Research in Economics and Science. The Geographer. **International boundary studies.** Washington, U.S. Government Printing Office, 1961-. no. 1-. maps.

Previously prepared by the Office of the Geographer, Department of State. 77 studies have so far appeared. Listed in *Monthly catalog of United States government publications* as 'Official use. Not available'.
Finland - U.S.S.R. boundary (International boundary study no. 74. 19p. map) is the subject of abstract 67D/791, *Geographical abstracts D,* 1967, no. 4. This Study describes the boundary between the two countries, with historical background and details of agreements.

Aid

341.232:016
UNITED NATIONS EDUCATIONAL, SCIENTIFIC AND CULTURAL ORGANIZATION. International co-operation and programmes of economic and social development: an annotated bibliography; prepared by J. Viet. Paris, Unesco, 1961. 107p. (Reports and papers in the social sciences, no. 15). 7s. 6d.

341.232 (02)
KRUG, K., and **VENTE, R. E. Handbuch der Entwicklungshilfe.** Baden-Baden, Nomos Verlag, 1960-. 8v. Loose-leaf.

3 sections: 1. Developing countries (under each country: general survey; economic review; investment possibilities; statistics; agreements and treaties)—2. Countries giving aid (nature and amount of help given; public and private investment; agreements; reports; plans; private organisations concerned with aid. West Germany is covered in great detail)—3. International organisations and programmes: Europe, multilateral regional organisations, international agreements and conferences, private international institutions.
Probably the most detailed survey of international aid, covering many aspects both economic and technological. Although uneven in treatment, the first section gives much valuable information on individual countries; particularly helpful for those interested in overseas marketing and exporting. Texts of treaties. All in German only.

341.232 (058.7)
ORGANISATION FOR ECONOMIC CO-OPERATION AND DEVELOPMENT and **INTERNATIONAL COUNCIL OF VOLUNTARY AGENCIES. OECD - ICVA directory:** development aid of non-governmental, non-profit organisations. Paris, O.E.C.D., 1967. 1378p.

Pt. 1, Basic information about organisations (in 20 O.E.C.D. countries, plus I.C.V.A), p. 17-753; pt. 2, Country information: aid activity related to developing areas (141 areas in Africa, Asia, Europe, Latin America and Caribbean, Oceania). Data on more than 1000 organisations (name and address; telephone number; finance; staff; co-operating with . . .; publications; aims; activities).
Noted: *Directory of non-governmental organisations offering assistance in the developing countries* (Rome, Centre for Labour and Social Studies, 1964-).

341.232:061
ORGANISATION FOR ECONOMIC CO-OPERATION AND DEVELOPMENT. Development Centre. **Catalogue des instituts et programmes de formation en matière de développement, économique et social.** Paris, O.E.C.D., 1965. 258p.

341.232 (6)
UNITED NATIONS EDUCATIONAL, SCIENTIFIC AND CULTURAL ORGANIZATION. Institutions effectuant des travaux dans le domaine de la planification économique et sociale en Afrique . . . Paris, Unesco, 1966. 155p. (Reports and papers in the social sciences, no. 22).

Prepared for Unesco by the International Social Science Council and the Centre d'Analyse et de Recherches Documentaires pour l'Afrique Noire.
Comprises all aspects of social and economic development which generally fall under the heading of "technical assistance". Of 1,000 organizations involved, 300 figure in this work (U.S.A.: 51; France: 58; U.K.: 25). Data on organiza-

tions: name, address, telephone number, type of organization, date founded, purpose, officers. Data on study of particular area: project title or goal, period, finance, co-operation with other organizations, operational staff, reports on publications, etc.

341.232.1:016
NORTH ATLANTIC TREATY ORGANIZATION. Bibliography. Paris, NATO-OTAN, [1964]. 205p.

English ed. of the bibliography originally published in French, 1962.
A comprehensive, unannotated list of books and periodicals dealing with NATO. 12 chapters (1. North Atlantic Treaty—2. International agreements—3. Organization . . . 10. Selection of works (p. 185-201)—11. Selection of reviews on international affairs which regularly publish articles on NATO—12. Earlier bibliographies.
For fuller documentation, see Conference on the Atlantic Community, Bruges. *The Atlantic Community: an introductory bibliography* (Leyden, Sijthoff, 1962. 2v.).

341.232.1 (02)
NORTH ATLANTIC TREATY ORGANIZATION. NATO: facts about the North Atlantic Treaty Organization. Paris, NATO Information Service, 1962. ix, 320p. tables, diagrs., charts, map.

Pt. 1: History of the Alliance (up to 1961; covers structure and finances); pt. 2: Armed forces (co-ordination; co-operation; economic and financial problems, etc.). 26 maps, tables and charts. 21 appendices, including 21: Abbreviations.

Treaties

341.24:016
HARVARD UNIVERSITY. LAW SCHOOL. Library. **Index to multilateral treaties:** a chronological list of multi-party international agreements, from the sixteenth century through 1963, with citations to their text. V. Mostecky, editor. Cambridge, Mass., 1965. x, 301p. $13.

3,859 numbered items, 1596-1963. Entries state number, date, subject and sources. 'Subject and regional guide' (p. 253-301), listing each treaty under one or more of the following: topic, area (if regional), country or city, place of signature and date (if popularly so known), name of person(s) instrumental in drafting, and name of international organisation (in English) if the treaty is a charter, etc., of that organisation. "While the list is comprehensive for the period preceding 1960, it is necessarily incomplete for the most recent years because the texts of some treaties were not available in printed form at press time" (*Preface*).

341.24 (08):016
UNITED NATIONS. List of treaty collections. New York, United Nations, 1956. xv, 174p. *9s*.

Covers "collections published in and after the last two decades of the eighteenth century". Pts.: 1. General collections; 2. Collections by subject matter; 3. Collections by states (A-Z), listing collections, indexes, chronologies, special topics, treaties with special states. 698 items, annotated (contents; presence of index, etc.).

See also the valuable article by A. D. Roberts —"Searching for the texts of treaties", in *Journal of documentation* (v. 5, no. 3, December 1949, p. 136-63), and *Où trouver le texte des traités européens: bibliographie,* établie par Michel Roussier (Geneva, Carnegie Endowment, 1958. 54p. Sw. fr. 6).

For the historian: Myers, D. P. *Manual of collections of treaties and of collections relating to treaties* (Cambridge, Mass., Harvard Univ. Press, 1922. xlvii, 685p.). This has annotated entries arranged thus: general collections, by states; collections, by subject matter; and international administration. Subject index.

341.24 (08)
UNITED NATIONS. Treaty series: treaties and international agreements registered or filed and recorded with the Secretariat of the United Nations . . . 1946/47-. New York, United Nations, 1947-. v. 1-.

Texts are in the original languages, with English and French translations. Latest v., v. 539 (1965): 14 June 1965 - 22 June 1965, nos. 7819-7842.
Cumulative index to v. 1-100, 101-200, 201-300, 301-400 (1963), 401-450 (1966). This last index comprises (1) a chronological index and (2) a subject index.

The United Nations' *Statement of treaties and international agreements registered or filed and recorded with the Secretariat . . .* is issued monthly. Annexes record ratifications, accessions, prorogations, etc.

Preceded by:

LEAGUE OF NATIONS. Treaty series: publications of treaties and international engagements registered with the Secretariat of the League. Geneva, League of Nations; London, Harrison. 1920-46. 205v. General index, 1920-1946. Geneva, 1927-46. 9v.

341.24 (091)
TOSCANO, M. The history of treaties and international politics. 1. An introduction to the history of treaties and international politics: documentary and memoir sources. Baltimore, Johns Hopkins Press; London, Oxford Univ. Press, 1966. 685p. 108*s*.

English translation of *Storia dei trattati e politica internazionale. I, Parte generale* (Turin, Giappichelli, 1963), expanded ed. of *Lezioni di storia dei trattati e politica internazionale. I, Parte generale* (Turin, Giappichelli, 1958).
An indispensable, evaluative guide to the source material of 20th-century international history. Particularly valuable, states *International affairs* (v. 43, no. 3, July 1967, p. 537) on documents on the literature of World Wars I and II and memoir sources for the two wars. "The Italian side understandably receives great emphasis".

341.24 (410) (08)
GREAT BRITAIN. FOREIGN OFFICE. British and foreign state papers, with which is incorporated Hertslet's Commercial treaties. London,

Ridgway, 1841-. v. 1-. (v. 163: 1957-58. London, H.M. Stationery Office, 1966. £14.).

v. 1 (1841) covered 1812-14.
Items are chronologically arranged and consist of texts of agreements, treaties to which Great Britain was a partner, Orders in Council, appropriate acts of Parliament (*e.g.*, European Payments Union (Financial provisions), letters patent, etc. Chronological index precedes. Subject and country indexes. An important source, marred by its time lag.

341.24 (410) (08)
GREAT BRITAIN. FOREIGN OFFICE. Treaty series, 1892-. London, H.M. Stationery Office, 1892-. Annual.

Treaties to which the United Kingdom is a party and which have come into force are published as Command Papers in a special series. They have their Command number and their Treaty series number (beginning with no. 1 each year). They are published individually as presented to Parliament. Many treaties are published as Command Papers outside the Treaty Series when concluded but before they have come into force; when they have come into force, they are again published in the Treaty series with a different Command number.
General index to Treaty series, 1961-1964 (London, H.M.S.O., 1966. 200p. (Cmnd. 2871). 16s. 6d.) continues the series of indexes to these treaties (listed in H.M.S.O. *Sectional list no. 7: Treaty series, 1910-1962*).

341.24 (47):016
MARKERT, W., and **GEYER, D.,** ed. **Sowjetunion: Verträge und Abkommen.** Verzeichnis der Quellen und Nachweise 1917-1962. Cologne & Graz, Böhlau [for Arbeitsgemeinschaft für Osteuropaforschung], 1967. 611p. (Osteuropa-Handbuch). DM.78.

"Lists all known treaties, agreements and other documents having the force of contract or agreement, between the U.S.S.R. and other countries" (*International affairs*, v. 44, no. 2, April 1968, p. 352). Chronologically arranged; references to sources for each entry.

341.24 (6)
HERTSLET, *Sir* E. **The map of Africa by treaty.** 3rd ed., rev. and completed to the end of 1908 by R. W. Brant and H. L. Sherwood. London, H.M.S.O., 1909. 3v. and portfolio of maps. (Reprint in preparation. *c*. £35).

v. 1. *British colonies, protectorates and possessions in Africa.*
v. 2. *Abyssinia—Great Britain and France.*
v. 3. *Great Britain and Germany—United States. Appendix and index.*
Portfolio of 45 maps.
The aim "is to show how, by Treaty, Conquest or Cession, or under the name of a Protectorate, European Powers have succeeded at different times in obtaining a footing in various parts of the African Continent, and how those occupations have been greatly extended during the last few years . . ." (*Preface* to 1894 edition).

International Court of Justice

341.646:016
INTERNATIONAL COURT OF JUSTICE. Library. **Bibliography of the International Court of Justice.** The Hague, International Court of Justice, 1947-. no. 1-. (no. 21. 1967. 2s. 3d.).

A continuation of the lists published in chapter 9 of the *Yearbook* and *Annuaire* of the Court from 1946/47 to 1963/64, using the same grouping and continuing the numbering. No. 19: 1964-1965 (1966) lists items no. 6616-7122.

Noted: J. Douma's *Bibliography on the International Court, including the Permanent Court, 1918-64* (The Hague, Sijthoff, 1966. xxi, 387p. 80s.).

Disarmament

341.67:016
Arms control & disarmament: a quarterly bibliography with abstracts and annotations. Prepared by the Arms Control and Disarmament Bibliography Section, General Reference and Bibliography Division, Reference Department, Library of Congress. Washington, Library of Congress, 1964-. Quarterly. v. 1, no. 1-. Fall, 1964/65-. ea. 55c.; $2 (foreign, $2.50) p.a.

V. 1: 1451 items. Restricted to English-language material, plus translations. Includes official publications and covers *c*. 1,000 periodicals. Main sections: 1. The international political environment—2. The strategic environment—3. Institutions and means for the maintenance of peace—4. The historical background. About 3 months' time-lag. Each issue carries an author index. Annual cumulative author and subject indexes.

The quarterly *Disarmament and arms control* (Oxford, Pergamon Press, 1963-. v. 1, no. 1-. July 1963-. 40s. (individuals), £10 p.a. (libraries) carries an extensive bibliography, "Current literature and research". V. 1, no. 1 has 86 such items, some with annotations (journals and newspapers; books; index of names; disarmament research).

341.67:016
Current thought on peace and war: a quarterly digest of literature and research in progress on the problem of world order and conflict. Winter 1960-. New York, Institute for International Order, 1960-. no. 1-. Quarterly.

See entry at 327:016

341.67:016
Peace research abstracts journal. Clarkson, Ontario, Canadian Peace Research Institute, 1964-. v. 1, no. 1-. June 1964-. Monthly. $30 (individuals). $60 (institutions) p.a.

About 1,000 abstracts and references per issue. 100-200 word abstracts. International coverage. 10 sections: 1. The military situation—2. Arms control and disarmament—3. Tension and conflict—4. Ideology and issues—5. International institutions and regional alliances—6. Nations and national policies—7. Pairs of countries and crisis areas—8. International law, economies and diplomacy—9. Decision making and communications.

—10. Methods of study, and science and society. Monthly author index; quarterly subject index.

The economic consequences of disarmament: a collection of abstracts from the files of 'Peace research abstracts' . . . (Clarkson, Ontario, Canadian Peace Research Institute) was published in November 1964 (1, 58p. $1); author index.

341.67:016
UNITED STATES. DEPARTMENT OF STATE. Office of External Research. **Studies in progress or recently completed: arms control and disarmament.** Washington, 1963-. 2 p.a.

Compiled for the United States Arms Control and Disarmament Agency.
The November 1966 issue (ACD-8) contains 285 entries (usually annotated), under subjects A-Z (approaches and proposals — Collective security arrangements . . . Testing (nuclear weapons)—Verification). Also lists papers presented at recent meetings and conferences. Author and subject indexes.

341.67 (038)
UNITED STATES. ARMS CONTROL AND DISARMAMENT AGENCY. Glossary of arms control and disarmament terms, by R. W. Lambert. Washington, 1967. 66p.

341.67:061
UNITED NATIONS EDUCATIONAL, SCIENTIFIC AND CULTURAL ORGANIZATION. International repertory of institutions specializing in research on peace and disarmament. Paris, Unesco, 1966. 77p. (Reports and papers in the social sciences, 23). 6s.

1. Introduction—2. The United Nations and the Specialized Agencies: activities relating to peace research—3. International organizations—4. National institutions—5. Institutions promoting or reporting peace research. Appendix 2: List of research fields. Data (name; address; founded; structure; director; staff; fields represented; budget, sources of finance; main fields of research; other activities than research; publications; current research projects). Index.

Constitutions

342.4 (4/9)
PEASLEE, A. J., *ed.* **Constitutions of nations.** Rev. 3rd ed. The Hague, Nijhoff, 1965-. v. 1-. maps.

First published 1950 (3v.).
v. 1. *Africa.* 1965. 189s.
v. 2. *Asia, Australia and Oceania.* 1966. 2 pts. £11 11s.
The 3rd ed. is to be in 4v. Whereas in the 1st and 2nd eds. arrangement was A-Z by countries (v. 1: Afghanistan-Finland; v. 2: France-Poland; v. 3: Portugal to Yugoslavia), in the 3rd edition a more natural grouping by continents is used. V. 1. *Africa* gives summary translations of the constitutions of 36 African nations, of which only 4 appeared in the 2nd ed. (1956); bibliography, p. 1099-1100. V. 2 covers 36 countries, A-Z. The selective bibliography in pt. 2 (p. 1282-6) comprises in many cases books "indicated as appropriate by the governments in question" (*Foreword*).

342.4 (41-44):016
LIVINGSTON, W. S., *ed.* **Federalism in the Commonwealth:** a bibliographical commentary. Published for the Hansard Society by Cassell, London, 1963. xviii, 237p. 30s.

About 1,500 items (mainly books, but many references to periodical articles) surveyed in a running commentary. 11 contributions: general works; federalism in Canada, Australia, the West Indies, India, Palestine, Malaya, Nigeria, Rhodesia and Nyasaland. Index of authors cited. Apart from its main subject, is valuable for the broader study of comparative political institutions and processes.

342.4 (41-44) (02)
KEETON, G. W., *ed.* **The British Commonwealth:** the development of its laws and constitutions. London, Stevens, 1951-. v. 1-.

See entry at 34 (41-44).

342.4 (420)
HISTORICAL ASSOCIATION. English constitutional history: a select bibliography, by S. B. Chrimes and I. A. Roots. London, published for the Historical Association by Routledge, 1958. 39p. (Helps for students of history, no. 58). 4s.

Twelve sections, listing with brief annotations books and a selection of more important articles. Excludes works dealing with the internal organization of Scotland, Wales and Ireland or with any part of the British Commonwealth outside England.

Human Rights

342.7 (058)
UNITED NATIONS. Department of Social Affairs. **Freedom from arbitrary arrest, detention and exile.** Yearbook on human rights: first supplementary volume. New York, United Nations, 1959. vii, 249p.

Cites the basic laws of 55 countries; arrangement is A-Z by country.

342.7 (058)
UNITED NATIONS. Department of Social Affairs. **Yearbook on human rights** for 1946-. New York, United Nations, 1947-. v. 1-. Irregular. (1963 ed. 1967. $5.75).

The 1963 ed. includes relevant extracts from decisions of national and international courts for 96 States; texts and summaries of basic laws on human rights in Trust and Non-Self Governing Territories; and international agreements.

Criminal Law

343 (03)
SCOTT, *Sir H.,* *ed.* **The concise encyclopedia of crime and criminals.** London, Deutsch, 1961. 351p. illus. (pl.). 50s.

For the layman, by a former chief of Scotland Yard. 40 contributors. Includes biographies (*e.g.,*

John Howard, Sir Robert Peel, Al Capone) as well as entries for such subjects as Mafia, Mutiny on 'The Bounty', Espionage, and the argot of the underworld. Many cross-references. Bibliography, 'For further reading', p. 345-51. 96 plates.

343 (038)=00

ADLER, J. A., *ed.* **Elsevier's Dictionary of criminal science in eight languages:** English/ American — French — Italian — Spanish — Portuguese—Dutch—Swedish—German. Amsterdam, London, etc., Elsevier, 1960. xv, 1460p. £15 15s.

10,930 numbered English/American terms, with equivalents in the other 7 languages across the double page, and keys in those languages. Coverage: "the prevention, detection and suppression of crime, including the psychical state, physical conditions and special circumstances of lawbreakers, witnesses and victims" (*Preface*). Terms are categorised. The review in *Babel* (v. 9, no. 1-2, p. 110-1) notes mistranslations and omissions.

Criminology

343.9:016

ANDRY, R. G. **"Existing documentation services in criminology** and future needs, mainly with reference to the United Kingdom." *Aslib proceedings,* v. 17, no. 2, February 1965, p. 50-59.

A brief survey. Part A: 'Existing documentation services', covering research and library 'outlets'. Part B: 'Some suggestions for future requirements', with an enumeration of general needs (*i-x*).

343.9:016

CUMMING, *Sir* **J.** **A contribution towards a bibliography dealing with crime and cognate subjects.** 3rd ed. London, printed by the Receiver for the Metropolitan Police District, 1935. xv, [1], 107p.

First published 1914; 2nd ed. 1916.
Systematically arranged. Headings: History, nature, course of crime—Prevention, detention and trial—Reprieve, punishment, remedies, reformation. Includes periodicals; subdivision to country level under topics. Combined subject and geographical index; author index. Additions and errata, p. 89-90.

343.9:016

Excerpta criminologica: an international abstracting service. Amsterdam, Excerpta Criminologica Foundation, 1961-. 6 p.a. $31 p.a.

1966: 1,935 informative and indicative unsigned abstracts. 13 sections: 1. General—2. Biology. Psychology—3. Psychopathology. Psychiatry—4. Anthropology. Sociology. Social work—5. Special groups (sex; age; etc.)—6. Special offenses and non-criminal anti-social behavior—7. Prediction. Longitudinal studies—8. The victim—9. Prevention—10. Treatment of offenders—11. Resocialization—12. Penal law—13. Criminal procedure and administration of justice. Cross-references. V. 6, no. 6 (1966) includes annual subject index; list of journals abstracted (nearly 350, about 25% of them U.S.: 28 British titles), arranged by country; author index. International board of chief editors. Time-

lag: about 6 months. Each issue except the last of the year includes a special article. The major abstracting service in this field.

International bibliography on crime and delinquency (New York, National Research and Information Center on Crime and Delinquency, 1963-. v. 1, no. 1-. 3 p.a. $2.50 p.a.) is largely based on national and trade bibliographies, and library accessions lists. Each issue features a special bibliography either on a particular country or of a specific topic. Reviewed in *Unesco bulletin for libraries,* v. 18, no. 4, July/ August 1964, entry no. 235.

343.9:016

HOWARD LEAGUE FOR PENAL REFORM. **John Howard Library of Criminology and Penology. Catalogue,** 1963. London, the League, 1963. 82p. 3s. 6d.

A list of nearly 3,000 items in 8 main sections: 1. Social problems and social services—2. Crime and criminals—3. Child welfare and juvenile delinquency—4. Law and penal procedure—5. Treatment of offenders and penal institutions—6. Capital punishment—7. Biography and memoires—8. Miscellaneous: philosophy; psychology. Official journals and statistics received; journals and reviews received. Author index. The John Howard Library no longer exists.

343.9:016

INTERNATIONAL SOCIETY OF CRIMINOLOGY. **Éléments d'une documentation en criminologie. Selected documentation on criminology.** Paris, Unesco, 1961. 114p. (Reports and papers in the social sciences, no. 14). 7s. 6d.

1,158 numbered items. International section; country sections (A-Z, p. 27-105). The section on Yugoslavia has headings: Select bibliography—Criminal anthropology—Criminal psychology and psychiatry—Criminal sociology—Juvenile criminology—Legal medicine—Police science—Periodicals (items not numbered)—Repertory of institutions. Author index. In French and English.

Noted: "A bibliographical manual for the student of criminology", by T. Sellin and L. A. Savitz. In *Bulletin de la Société Internationale de Criminologie* (Paris), 1er semestre 1960, p. 81-122.

343.9:016

TOMKINS, D. L. C. **The offender: a bibliography.** Berkeley, Cal., Institute of Governmental Studies, Univ. of California, 1963. 268p. $7.50.

Three main parts: "the offender, who he is, what has contributed to his becoming an offender, and various methods of studying him" (*Preface*). Covers periodical articles, books (including analyticals), theses, government publications and reports for the period 1937 to early 1962. Entries, systematically arranged, are usually annotated. Author and subject index. (*College and research libraries,* v. 25, July 1964, p. 320).

—— **Probation since World War II: a bibliography.** Berkeley, Cal., Institute of Governmental Studies, Univ. of California, 1964. 311p.

343.9:016

"Topical bibliography of current technical literature [on criminology]". In *International review of criminal policy*. New York, United Nations, 1952-. 2 p.a.

International review, no. 19, June 1962, includes a bibliography on p. 147-217,—1,860 references to books, pamphlets and periodical articles, including separate contributions to symposia and the like. Sections: Criminology—Penal law—Penology—Criminal statistics—Juvenile delinquency—Criminal procedure—Judicial organisation and administration of justice—Police—Suppression of the traffic in persons, and related matters—Vagrancy—Historical studies—Personalities—Bibliographies.

343.9 (03)

SHEW, E. S. A companion to murder: a dictionary of death by poison, death by shooting, death by suffocation and drowning, death by the strangler's hand, 1900-1950. London, Cassell, 1960. xii, [1], 303p. 25s.

——A second companion to murder: a dictionary of death by the knife, the dagger, the razor . . . 1900-1950. London, Cassell, 1961. xiii, [1], 287p. 25s.

Both of these popularly written volumes consist of entries, alphabetically arranged. Entries for murderers (*e.g.,* W. H. Crippen: 4½p.), K.C.s and Q.C.s and such legal phrases as 'Diminished responsibility' (citing relevant Acts). V. 2 contains a list of the contents of both volumes, and each has a 'Table of murder', listing murderers under type of crime committed.

343.9 (05):016

SOCIAL SCIENCES DOCUMENTATION. Survey of criminological journals: a handlist of periodicals of interest to students of criminology, with their locations in certain London libraries. London, Institute for the Study and Treatment of Delinquency, 1958. [8]p.

Issued with the July 1958 number of *British journal of delinquency*. Offprint.
Pt. 1: Periodicals, with locations for 53 periodicals in 4 London libraries; pt. 2: Official serials, with locations for about 200 Commonwealth and foreign official report series in 3 London libraries.
Aslib Criminology Group is preparing a union list of periodicals (*Aslib proceedings,* v. 18, no. 9, September 1966, p. 234).

343.9 (411)

SCOTLAND. SCOTTISH HOME AND HEALTH DEPARTMENT. Criminal statistics, Scotland . . . : statistics relating to police apprehensions and criminal proceedings for the year . . . Edinburgh, H.M. Stationery Office. Annual. (1965, published 1966. (Cmmd. 3050). 7s. 6d.).

343.9 (42)

GREAT BRITAIN. HOME OFFICE. Criminal statistics, England and Wales . . . : statistics relating to crime and criminal proceedings for the year . . . London, H.M. Stationery Office. Annual. (1965, published 1966. (Cmmd. 3037). 25s.).

Five comparative tables, 1930-65; 26 annual tables for 1965. Graphs showing indictable offences, 1938-65. 11 chapters

Civil Law

347.7:016

BAYITCH, S. A. "Bibliographic sources of comparative common and civil law". In *Law library journal,* v. 55, no. 4, November 1962, p. 313-30.

326 items (books and periodical articles) surveyed in a running commentary. Sections: Comparative jurisprudence—Bibliographies—Descriptive works—Civil law compared—Sources of law—Substantive law—Procedural law—Areas of symbiosis.

Commercial Law

347.7

Digest of commercial laws of the world. New York, National Association of Credit Management, 1966-. 3v. Loose-leaf. Supply. service. $150.

Each volume covers a set of countries (*e.g.,* v. 1: Brazil, Chile, Egypt, El Salvador, Ireland, Italy, Japan, Lebanon, Mexico, Norway, Portugal, Peru and Uruguay). The complete series will embrace 58 countries. Each digest concerns such fields as contracts, agency and representation, forms of business organisation, bills of exchange and recognition of foreign judgment (*The C.R.R. courier,* v. 31, August 1966, p. 1).

Copyright

347.78

BOGSCH, A., *ed.* Design laws and treaties of the world, including references to the protection of works of applied art. Leiden, Sijthoff; Washington, Bureau of National Affairs, Inc., 1960. Loose-leaf. Annual supps.

"An English-language compilation of worldwide scope, of legislative and treaty provisions for the protection of designs" (*Foreword*). 1st instalment covers 12 countries, plus 8 multilateral conventions. Includes relevant provisions of copyright law, but for full texts refers to *Copyright laws and treaties of the world* (q.v.).

347.78

PINNER, H. L. World copyright: an encyclopedia. Leiden, Sijthoff, 1953-60. 5v.

Arranged by subjects alphabetically, then by country (v. 1-4: A-Z. 1953-58). V. 5, the index, includes notes on legislative amendments up to December 31, 1959.

Forms part of the series, *The protection of intellectual and industrial property throughout the world: a library of encyclopedias,* founded by H. L. Pinner and P. M. Dienstag. A further work in this series is H. L. Pinner's *World unfair competition law: an encyclopedia* (Leiden, Sitjhoff, 1965. 1024p. D.fl. 350).

347.78

UNITED NATIONS EDUCATIONAL, SCIENTIFIC AND CULTURAL ORGANIZATION. Copyright laws and treaties of the world. Paris, Unesco; Washington, Bureau of National Affairs, Inc., 1956-. Loose-leaf. Annual supplements.

"A compilation of the laws, orders, rules, regulations, conventions and treaties which establish, in and between the different countries of the world, the legal provisions for the protection of copyright" (*Explanatory notes*). All texts have been translated into English. The 85 countries covered are arranged alphabetically.

Air Law

347.81:016

INSTITUTE OF ADVANCED LEGAL STUDIES. Union list of air law literature in libraries in Oxford, Cambridge and London. London, Univ. of London, Institute of Advanced Legal Studies, 1956. [1], iv, 54p. (Institute of Advanced Legal Studies publication no. 4). 12s. 6d.

453 items, with locations in 22 libraries (20 in London; the others in Oxford and Cambridge). 5 sections: Books and pamphlets—International conferences and treaties—International organizations—Laws and regulations—Periodicals and reports. Subject index.

347.81 (094)

UNITED STATES. LIBRARY OF CONGRESS. Law Library. Air laws and treaties of the world: annotated compilation, compiled by William S. Strauss. Washington, 1961. vi, 1476p.

Issued by the House Committee on Science and Astronautics.

"The only comprehensive compilation of its kind ever published" (*Library of Congress Information bulletin*, v. 26, no. 22, 1 June 1967, p. 350, which mentions a later revision, also by W. S. Strauss in 1965 (3v. 4,483p.), issued by the Senate Committee on Commerce).

Magistrates' Courts

347.9

OKE, G. C. Oke's Magisterial formulist (a companion .volume to *Stone's Justices' Manual*) **Forms and precedents.** 16th ed. by W. Scott. London, Butterworth; Shaw, 1963. xxxvii, 994p. Supplementary v. and cumulative noter-up.

First published 1850.

Four parts: 1. Forms prescribed by 'Magistrates' Courts (Forms) Rules 1952-1963'—2. Magistrates' Courts Act, 1952 (and other related Acts)—3. Practice and miscellaneous forms—4. Felonies, misdemeanours and offences punishable on indictment and on summary conviction, and certain special matters (arranged A-Z, p. 148-990). Table of statutes (p. xiii-xxxvii) and index precede.

A companion compendium to *Stone's Justices' manual,* including forms and precedents for practical use that do not come before quarter sessions.

347.9

Stone's Justices' manual; being the yearly justices' practice . . . London, Butterworth, Shaw & Sons, 1842-. Annual. (98th ed. 1966. 2v. 142s. 6d.).

The 98th ed. brings statute law and case law to date to the end of 1965. Contains detailed information on the organisation and jurisdiction of magistrates' courts, followed by an alphabetical arrangement of the law, mainly criminal ("Offences, matters of complaint", p. 397-2860), applied to such courts. Appendices in v. 2 include forms and precedents, rules and general regulations. General index of 238p. Small print shows through thin, non-opaque paper.

Civil Proceedings

347.91/.95

The Encyclopædia of forms and precedents other than court forms. 4th ed. London, Butterworth, 1964-.

3rd ed. 1945-50, 20v. The 4th ed. is to be in 24v. (v. 7: COMMONS-EASEMENTS. 1966. 115s.).

Principles: "To provide a form for at least every ordinary transaction which occurs in practice and for all those except such as are purely academic. To present these forms in a simple and straightforward manner so that the nature and effect can be understood at a glance. To collect and arrange them so that they can be found with the utmost facility" (*Publishers' note*). Arranged by topics, A-Z. 'Landlord and tenant' occupies v. 11-12 (1966. p. 1-1593, with an index of 124p.). Each volume has a detailed, analytical index.

Atkin's Encyclopaedia of court forms in civil proceedings (2nd ed., by Lord Evershed and other lawyers. London, Butterworth, 1961-.). Arranged by topics, A-Z. Volumes do not appear in regular order (*e.g.,* v. 28. 1963; v. 21. 1966; v. 39. 1967). First published 1937 (16v.).

Canon Law

348 (03)

Dictionnaire de droit canonique, contenant tous les termes de droit canonique, avec un sommaire de l'histoire et des institutions de l'état actuel de la discipline. Publié sous la direction de R. Naz. Paris, Letouzey, 1935-65. 43 fasc. ea. 30F.

Includes biographies. Signed articles, many of them latterly by R. Naz. This dictionary will need replanning or correcting in the light of the reforms of the Second Vatican Council, states *Bulletin critique du livre français* (v. 19, no. 2, item no. 58949). Bibliographies appended to articles.

35 PUBLIC ADMINISTRATION

Bibliography

35:016

GREAT BRITAIN. MINISTRY OF OVERSEAS DEVELOPMENT. Library. Public administration: a select bibliography. [Rev. ed.] London, the Ministry, 1967. viii, 101p.

First published 1963; supplements, 1964, 1966.

The 1967 ed. (1,425 annotated entries) includes items published up to the end of 1966. Eight sections: 1. General and public administration—2. Public finance—3. Economic planning and development—4. Instruments of government (management; Civil Service)—5. Local government—6. Community development—7. Bibliographies (nos. 1318-63)—8. Periodicals (nos. 1364-1425). Index of authors.

35:016

International review of administrative sciences. Brussels, International Institute of Administrative Sciences, 1928-. v. 1, no. 1-. Quarterly.

The v. 32, no. 4, 1966 issue contains 'Bibliography—a selection' (p. 355-67), mostly of books (c. 65), with critical annotations and in author order, with periodical articles (c. 36) appended; also 'Publications of schools and institutes of public administration' (under continent and country; c. 12 items). International in scope.

35:016

SECKLER-HUDSON, C. Bibliography on public administration annotated. 4th ed. Washington, American Univ. Press, 1953. vii, 131p.

A well-produced reference guide to selected periodicals, pamphlets, revelant Government documents (mainly U.S.) and books. 1,100 annotated entries, systematically arranged in 11 sections; author index. The author is Chairman of the Department of Political Science and Public Administration at the American University.

35:016

UNITED NATIONS. Technical Assistance Programme. **International bibliography of public administration.** New York, United Nations, 1957. v, 101p. (ST/TAA/M/11).

A revised and expanded version of *Short international bibliography of public administration,* issued by the Technical Assistance Administration in 1953.

About 1,500 entries, the scope having been extended to include works in 12 languages. 26 sections, with author-alphabetical arrangement in each. Covers many types of administration, *e.g.,* section 6. 'Administration of non-self-governing territories'; 13. 'Organization and methods'; 14. 'Public finance' (p. 55-66); 18. 'Public works administration'. The final two sections cover 'Selected biographies and administrative histories' and 'Bibliographies'. Confined to books, some prices being given. No annotations or index.

35 (44):016

GOURNAY, B., *comp.* **Public administration.** New York, French Embassy, 1963. 207p. (French bibliographical digest. Series 2, no. 38).

Continues *Bibliographie de la fonction publique,* by H. Puget and others (1948. 212p.), covering 1900-47.

948 annotated items (writings on public administration in Metropolitan France, September 1944 to the end of 1958). Part 1, General studies (1-9. 8: Documentation in the administration). Part 2, The central administration (various departments and ministries). Author index. The English creaks somewhat.

Meetings

35.077

CREW, A. The conduct of meetings (Crew). 20th ed. by T. P. E. Curry and J. R. Sykes. London, Jordan, 1966. xxi, 234p.

First published 1910.

Four parts: 1. Meetings: general principles (chapters 1-10)—2. Public meetings (11)—3. Meetings of companies incorporated under the Companies Acts (12-22)—4. Meetings of local authorities (23). Appendix 1: Forms of notices of meetings of companies, agenda papers and minutes. Table of cases precedes. Detailed index, p. 221-34.

Civil Service

35.08 (410)

GREAT BRITAIN. H.M. TREASURY. Introductory factual memorandum on the Civil Service. London, H.M. Stationery Office, 1954. vi, 184p. 6s. **Chairman's report,** December 15th, 1953. 1955. 6s. 6d. (Cmd. 9613).

Authoritative description of the Civil Service, drawn up for the Royal Commission on the Civil Service.

The nearest approach to a study of the British civil service is R. K. Kelsall's *Higher civil servants in Britain, from 1870 to the present day* (London, Routledge & Kegan Paul, 1955. xvi, 232p.), which discusses only the administrative class, but is well documented.

Administrative Law

351 (410)

YARDLEY, D. C. M. A source book of English administrative law. London, Butterworths, 1963. 414p. xxxvi, 448p. 62s. 6d.

Deals with such matters as judicial control, tribunals and enquiries, Crown proceedings, public corporations, local government and the police. Appended bibliography (p. 425-39), some entries being annotated. Many citations of case law (tabulated, p. xxiii-xxxvi), but statutes and statutory instruments are also frequently referred to. Analytical index.

Police

351.74:016

International bibliography of selected police literature. Geneva, International Police Association (British section: Eastbourne, Sussex), 1962. [c. 100]p. Loose-leaf. 15s.

About 2,500 items, under countries A-Z (European countries plus Australia, Canada, Chile, Kenya and U.S.A.). Foreword and preface in English, French, Spanish and German. United Kingdom (c. 300 items) has sub-divisions: 1. Police history and biography—2. Personnel—3. Police organization, administration and operations—4. Investigation and field operations—5. Identification and laboratory technique—6. Traffic safety and investigation—7. Canine police—8. National police laws and regulations—9. Periodicals and journals (9).

351.74 (058.7)
International security directory: official year book of security, police and fire services. 6th ed. London, Security Gazette, Ltd., 1968. 389, xi p. 42*s*.

Police section (Interpol, p. 44-50; world police forces, p. 51-122)—Fire section (World fire brigades, p. 158-204)—Industrial security (addresses of industrial and commercial security departments, by countries, then area or town)—Supplies and sources.

351.74 (4/9):391
CRAMER, J. Uniforms of the world's police; with brief data on organization, systems and weapons. Springfield, Ill., C. C. Thomas, 1968. 199p.

351.74 (410) (058.7)
Police and constabulary almanac: official register for . . . London, Hazell, 1861-. Annual. (1965. 12*s*. 6*d*.; 16*s*.).

A directory of chief officials, superintendents, police and constabulary forces. Arranged under English counties, A-Z, then under Wales, Scotland, Northern England, Eire, Isle of Man, Channel Islands, etc. Handy appendices include motor index, list of persons authorised to grant motor licences, list of remand homes and approved schools, R.S.P.C.A. and N.S.P.C.C. branches. Advertisements.

Local Government

352:016
INTERNATIONAL UNION OF LOCAL AUTHORITIES. Bibliographia: new publications in the library of the I.U.L.A. The Hague, the Union, 1963-. no. 1-. 6 p.a.

About 100 items (usually annotated) per issue. Annotations are in the language of the original. Sections (A-Z): Economy—Education, arts, sport—Housing & building—Local government—Metropolitan areas—Planning—Public administration—Public finance—Public health—Social sciences—Social welfare—Traffic. No index.

352:016
LOGA: local government annotations service. London, Havering Public Libraries, 1966-. no. 1-. Monthly. 40*s*. p.a.

About 200 numbered abstracts per issue, from 90 periodicals; as from no. 6, covers relevant H.M.S.O. publications. Arranged under subject A-Z (from Accident prevention to Youth employment), with no index. Appended list of 'Books and pamphlets recently added to stock in the Reference Library' and 'Conferences and exhibitions'.

In 1967 the *Classified accessions list* and *Index to periodical articles*, previously restricted, became available from the Ministry of Housing and Local Government Library (ea. 6 p.a.; 45*s*. p.a.).

352 (4/9) (02)
HUMES, S., and MARTIN, E. M. The structure of local governments throughout the world. The Hague, Nijhoff, 1961. xxxvi, 449p. 72*s*.

A survey undertaken by the International Union of Local Authorities. Pt. 1 covers, in general terms, functions, units, elections, councils and staff; pt. 2 surveys 43 countries in detail. Chart shows pattern of local government. Monographs are promised, giving more detail on five countries.

352 (4/9) (058.7)
International municipal directory and buyers' guide (home and overseas). London, Municipal Engineering Publications, 1955. xvii, 376p.

Covers local government in the U.K., Commonwealth, Europe, North and Central America, South America and Asia. Chief officers are given for each municipality; also addresses of chambers of commerce, etc.

Great Britain

352 (410):016
GROSS, C. A bibliography of British municipal history, including gilds and Parliamentary representation. 2nd ed. Leicester, Univ. Press, 1966. xxxiv, 461p. 84*s*.

See entry at 941-201:016.

352 (410) (058.7)
The Municipal year book and public utilities directory, 1897-. London, Municipal Journal, Ltd., 1897-. Annual. (1967, published 1966. lxiv, 2046p. 147*s*.).

Sections: Introductory—General information including data on 34 subjects (*e.g.*, hospitals; water supply)—Main directory (county councils; London government; municipal corporations; U.D.C.s and R.D.C.s; Scotland, Ireland, Isle of Man)—Classified list of officers—Index. For municipalities, data on population, rates, departments, area, utilities (baths, markets, etc.), water supply, and historical background; followed by list of members of council, principal officers, date of council meetings, etc.

The *Local government manual and directory,* 1923- (London, Knight, Shaw, 1923-. Annual) is similarly arranged, but in tabular form and with separate sections for Catchment boards, Burial authorities, etc. It is confined to England and Wales.

352 (410) (083.4)
BARKER, W. Local government statistics: a guide to statistics on local government finance and services in the United Kingdom at August 1964; a research study. London, Institute of Municipal Treasurers and Accountants, 1965. xii, 13-160p. 30*s*.

15 sections (1. Population, area, living conditions . . . 15. General and regional reference (*e.g.*, *Annual abstract of statistics*). Directory of local authority societies, associations and publishers. Index.

352 (410) (092)
Who's who in local government. Edited by C. W. Scott-Giles. London, Municipal Publications, 1961. 161p. 50*s*.

Gives biographies of some 3,000 chief officers of local authorities in Great Britain.

352 (410):31

GREAT BRITAIN. INTERDEPARTMENTAL COMMITTEE ON SOCIAL AND ECONOMIC RESEARCH. Guides to official sources. No. 3: **Local government statistics.** London, H.M. Stationery Office, 1953. v, 34p.

Concentrates mainly on general and financial statistics. It includes references to some valuable statistics which are collected by the Institute of Municipal Treasurers and Accountants and by the Society of County Treasurers.

352 (410):336

INSTITUTE OF MUNICIPAL TREASURERS AND ACCOUNTANTS. Index to literature on the finance of local and public authorities, and related subjects, published between April, 1959 and March, 1964. Bexhill-on-Sea, Sussex, I.M.T.A., [1964?]. 34p. unpriced.

Second in a series of five-year indexes. First index (1959) covers the period September 1945 to March 1959. Includes all articles in *Local government finance* and *Telescope,* all I.M.T.A. lecture prints, study booklets and conference papers, and selected articles in *Accountancy* and *The accountant.* About 1000 entries, under subjects A-Z, from 'Abstract of accounts' to 'Working capital and balances'. Entry consists of title, author and source (first page only of articles).

352 (410):394.4

GARNER, J. F. Civic ceremonial: a handbook of practice and procedure. 2nd ed. London, Shaw, 1957. xi. 154p.

See entry at 394.4.

Scotland

352 (411)

The . . . County & municipal year book for Scotland. Coupar Angus (Perthshire), Culross, 1934-. (1966. 35s.).

Lists offices and staffs of Government departments and officials of county town and district councils, together with notes on institutions and national associations, and on Parliamentary matters.

352 (411)

Scottish municipal annual: a record of the facilities and services offered by local authorities in Scotland to those interested in industrial and commercial enterprise, 1932-. Glasgow, Guardian Society of Scotland, 1932-. Annual. (1964. 32s. 6d.).

Gives information on Scottish Departments, Boards, Corporations, etc. The main arrangement is alphabetical under burghs (197) and counties (33).

Eire

352 (417)

STREET, H. A. The law relating to local government. Dublin, Stationery Office, 1955. 1524p.

The most complete and comprehensive survey of Irish local government legislation.

England & Wales

352 (42) (03)

GOLDING, L. Dictionary of local government in England and Wales. London, English Universities Press, 1962. 446p. 25s.

About 1,000 entries—definitions and explanations, noting the duties of authorities (*e.g.,* 'Functions' (p. 159-66), including table showing main functions of 5 types of local authorities in England and Wales). Footnote references to statutes. Includes entries under names of reports (*e.g.,* Younghusband Report). Adequate cross-references; index.

352 (42) (091)

STEPHENS, *Sir* E., *comp.* The clerks of the counties, 1360-1960. [London], Society of Clerks of the Peace of Counties and of Clerks of County Councils, 1961. xiv, [1], 274p. illus. 84s.

Lists *c.* 2800 names, arranged A-Z according to counties, of those known to have held the office of clerk of the peace in the counties of England and Wales, 1360-1960, and the office of clerk of the County Council from 1889 to 1960 (p. 51-193). 7 columns, stating period of office, name, dates of birth and death, and biographical notes. 5 appendices. Index of names of clerks of the counties.

352 (42):34

MACMILLAN, H. P., *baron, ed.* **Local government law and administration in England and Wales.** London, Butterworth, 1934-41. 14v.; annual continuation v. 15-. 1940-; annual cumulative suppt. (*e.g.,* 1966. 150s.).

V. 14 of the main work is the index; v. 21. Educational supplement, has had 3 editions. There are also Emergency legislation supplements, 1941-.
The basic work.

352 (42):929.6

SCOTT-GILES, G. W. Civic heraldry of England and Wales. [Rev. ed.] London, Dent, 1953. xv, 440p. illus. 47s. 6d.

See entry at 929.6.014.

352 (420) (091)

REDLICH, J., and **HIRST, F. W. The history of local government in England.** London, Macmillan, 1958. xv, 261p.

A re-issue of Book 1 of *Local government in England* (1903), edited with introduction and epilogue by B. Keith-Lucas.
The best account of the development of local government in the 19th century. Excellent evaluative footnote references to the literature; bibliography, p. 253-6.

The massive *English local government, from the Revolution to the Municipal Corporations Act,* by Beatrice and Sidney Webb (London, Longmans, 1909-29. 11v.) was reprinted in 1963 (London, Cass). V. 1, *The parish and the county* (xxxiv, 664p.) has footnote references, an index of subjects (the entry 'Acts of Parliament' extends to 5 columns), index of authors and other persons, and index of places.

London

352 (421)

LONDON COUNTY COUNCIL. London statistics. London, L.C.C., 1890-. tables, maps. (New series, v. 1: 1945-54. 1957).

See entry at 31 (421).

U.S.A.

352 (73)

Book of the States. Chicago, Council of State Governments, 1935-. Biennial. $11 per v. (v. 16: 1966-1967. 1966).

Data on the individual States of the U.S.A., their executive, legislative and judicial offices, and on interstate and federal relations. Lists names of officials; statistics and other details (*e.g.,* State flowers; laws on marriage and divorce) in 8 sections. Two supplements appear in January and July of odd-numbered years, listing, respectively elective officials and legislators, and administrative officials (classified by functions).

Central Government

354 (4/9).11/.86

SPULER, B., *ed.* **Minister-Ploetz. Regenter und Regierungen der Welt.** Sovereigns and governments of the world. Würzburg, Ploetz.

v. 2, pt. 3: *Neuere Zeit, 1492-1918.* 1962.
v. 2, pt. 4: *Neueste Zeit, 1917/18-1964.* 1964. *Nachtrag, 1964/65.* 1966.
Arranged by countries (A-Z, German names). Details members of each cabinet, plus date of holding of office of each holder. The Supplement to v. 2, pt. 4 goes up to the Wilson Cabinet of 6th April 1966. Prefacing each volume is a list of countries in German, English, French and Spanish, plus native form, and of terms (numbered titles of offices) in the same languages.

Great Britain

354 (410):016

SEYMOUR-URE, C. "Bibliography on British central government and politics". In Bagehot, W. *English constitution* (London, Watts, 1964), p. 311-53.

354 (410) (02)

JENNINGS, *Sir* **I. Cabinet government.** 3rd ed. Cambridge, Univ. Press, 1959. x, 587p. 63s.

First published 1936.
A description of the central administration and its historical development during the last hundred years, in 15 chapters. Appendix 1: Governments ince 1835. Appendix 4: Biographical asnd bibliographical notes (p. 546-70). Covers material available up to the middle of 1957.

354 (410) (02)

MACKENZIE, W. J. M., and **GROVE, J. W. Central administration in Britain.** London, Longmans, Green, 1957. xvi, 487p.

A comprehensive factual manual of the work of the central government departments and of the various organs of administration directly subordinate to them. Each chapter is followed by a short bibliography.

A survey of development in recent years is available in the Royal Institute of Public Administration's *The organization of British Central government, 1914-1956: a survey by a study group . . .* ; edited by D. N. Chester, [and] written by F. M. G. Wilson (London, Allen & Unwin, 1957. 458p. 32s.).

354 (410).11/.86

The British imperial calendar and Civil Service list, 1809-. London, H.M. Stationery Office, 1809-. Irregular; now annual. (1967. 30s.).

Contents: royal households; public departments, England and Wales, Scotland, Northern Ireland; alphabetical list of officers; index to departments and sub-departments. In the case of officers, details are given of names, official positions, degrees and honours and salaries. The 1965 v. was the last to give individual salaries; thereafter salary scales of grades only are given.

354 (410).11/.86

Her Majesty's Ministers and heads of public departments. London, H.M. Stationery Office, 1950-. 5 p.a. ea. 3s.

Issued in February, April, July, October and December. Lists personnel down to Assistant Secretary level.

354 (410).11/.86

Know your Ministry: a description of government departments whose operations affect the conduct of business. London, Europa Publications, 1959. 248p.

A revised reprint of the series of articles which appeared in *The Midland Bank review,* August 1956 - August 1958. Chapters: The Treasury: public finance and the civil service—The Treasury: economic and financial policy—The Board of Trade—The Ministry of Agriculture, Fisheries and Food—The Ministry of Labour and National Service—Basic services (*e.g.,* G.P.O.)—Notes on other departments and statutory bodies (p. 215-27). References to official sources, p. 229-31; analytical index.

On the problem of keeping up to date on changes in government titles and functions, see C. A. Toase's note in *Library Association record,* v. 68, no. 11, November 1966, p. 405-6.

354 (410).11/.86

The New Whitehall series. London, Allen & Unwin, for the Royal Institute of Public Administration, 1954-.

The Colonial Office, by Sir C. Jeffries. 1956. 15s.
The Department of Scientific and Industrial Research, by Sir H. Melville. 1962. 25s.
The Foreign Office, by Lord Strang. 1955. 15s.
Her Majesty's Customs and Excise, by Sir J. Crombie. 1962. 30s.
The Home Office, by Sir F. A. Newsam. 1954 (2nd ed. 1955).
The Inland Revenue, by Sir A. Johnston. 1965. 20s.
The Ministry of Agriculture, Fisheries and Food, by Sir J. Winnifrith. 1962. 30s.

The Ministry of Labour and National Service, by Sir G. Ince. 1960. 25*s.*

The Ministry of Pensions and National Insurance, by Sir G. S. King. 1958. 18*s.*

The Ministry of Transport and Civil Aviation, by Sir G. Jenkins. 1959. 21*s.*

The Ministry of Works, by Sir H. Emmerson. 1956.

The Scottish Office, and other Scottish government departments, by Sir D. Milne. 1957.

The Treasury, by Lord Bridges. 2nd ed. 1966. 30*s.*

Each volume provides a clear and comprehensive exposition, with a list of ministers, etc., footnote references and an index.

Further volumes are in preparation on the Air Ministry, Post Office, Ministry of Health, and Admiralty.

354 (410).11
The Diplomatic Service list. London, H.M. Stationery Office, 1966-. Annual. (1967. 32*s.* 6*d.*).

Succeeds *The Foreign Office list* (1806-1965), following the formation of H.M.'s Diplomatic Service on 1st January 1965, by the merger of Foreign, Commonwealth and Trade Commissioner Services.

Five parts: 1. Home Departments—2. British Missions abroad—3. Consular districts—4. Chronological lists from 1946 (1966 v.) of Secretaries of State, Ministers of State, Permanent Under-Secretaries, Ambassadors and High Commissioners—5. Biographical notes and list of staff (1966 v., p. 135-317).

The Foreign Office and Commonwealth Office's *The London diplomatic list* (London, H.M. Stationery Office, 1964-. 6 p.a. 26*s.* 6*d.* p.a.) is an A-Z list of the representatives of foreign states and Commonwealth countries in London, with names and designations of the persons returned as composing the establishment of their respective offices. Appended list of national days.

354 (410).12
The Colonial Office list, 1862-1966. London, H.M. Stationery Office, 1862-66. Annual. (1966. 50*s.*).

1926-40, as *Dominions Office & Colonial Office list.*

Four parts: 1. The Colonial Office (functions and history; list of ministers and permanent under-secretaries; associations, institutions and committees)—2. Territories A-Z (32, plus 'Miscellaneous islands'; list of governors; concise data with short reading list on each territory)—3. Staff: 'Record of services' (career notes; p. 184-323 in 1966 v.)—4. Parliamentary and non-parliamentary papers of colonial interest issued during previous year. General index.

The Colonial Office is now part of the Commonwealth Office, and the *Colonial Office list* has been combined with the *Commonwealth Relations Office year book* to form the *Commonwealth Office list.* 1967- (q.v.).

354 (410).13
The Commonwealth Office year book. London, H.M. Stationery Office, 1967-. map. 65*s.*

Combines the previous *Colonial Office list* (1862-1966) and *Commonwealth Relations Office year book* (1951-1966).

Nine parts, including: 4. Member countries of the Commonwealth (p. 89-397)—5. Countries of the Commonwealth for whose external affairs Britain is responsible (p. 401-44)—6. Dependent territories of Commonwealth countries (p. 447-581)—7. Regional organisations. The section on Ceylon (p. 213-25) covers general data, history, constitutional development, constitution, government (with list of Cabinet, Parliamentary secretaries, judiciary, etc.), administration, ministries and government departments (with names of permanent secretaries) and diplomatic representation. Valuable statistics (*e.g.,* interim population figures). Analytical index.

354 (410).13
The Commonwealth Relations Office year book, 1951-. London, H.M. Stationery Office, 1951-66. Annual. (1966. 60*s.*).

As *The Commonwealth Relations Office list* from 1951 to 1965 (annually except in 1954).

In 6 parts; 59 chapters. Part 1, chapter 6: Organizations and societies concerned with various aspects of Commonwealth relations (p. 38-117). Part 4, chapters 25-50: Commonwealth countries (Australia—Zambia); chapter 51: Summary of Commonwealth data. Part 6 has miscellaneous chapters (*e.g.,* 55. Public holidays in the Commonwealth—58. A selection of recent official publications in the Commonwealth (p. 606-13)—59. List of articles printed in earlier editions. Chapter 48, on Southern Rhodesia (p. 551-60) covers general description, history, constitutional development, constitution, list of governors, governors, government departments, diplomatic representation overseas, diplomatic representation in Rhodesia. Partly analytical index.

The Commonwealth Relations Office year book has been combined with *the Colonial Office list* to form the *Commonwealth Office list.* 1967- (q.v.).

Scotland

354 (411)
GREAT BRITAIN. SCOTTISH OFFICE. Scottish administration. Rev. ed. Edinburgh, H.M. Stationery Office, 1967. viii, 91p. 8*s.*

First published 1950.

Describes Scottish administrative arrangements, with particulars of the scope of Government business transacted in Scotland. Does not deal with the work of Scottish local authorities. Parts: 1. Introduction—2. The Scottish Office—3. Statutory and other special departments, national institutions and Royal Commissions having functions in Scotland only—4. The law offices and the legal departments—5. Great Britain departments. 3 appendices.

Northern Ireland

354 (416)
MANSERGH, N. The government of Northern Ireland: a study in devolution. London, Allen & Unwin, 1936. 335p.

Pts.: 1. The demand for devolution—2. The Ulster question—3. Government in Northern Ireland—4. The merits and defects of devolution in the light of experience in Northern Ireland. Footnote references; list of authorities, p. 325-30. Subject and name indexes.

Eire

354 (417)

—— **The Irish Free State:** its government and politics. London, Allen & Unwin, 1934. 344p.

An analysis of "the peculiar virtues and vices which Representative Government has displayed in our country" (*Preface*). List of authorities, p. 335-9 (no publishers given).

354 (417)

KING, F. C., *ed.* **Public administration in Ireland.** Dublin, Parkside Press (v. 1-2); Civics Institute of Ireland (v. 3), 1944-54. 3v.

A basic work, covering all aspects of public administration in the Republic. There are no bibliographies, nor is there an index, but the lists of chapter headings are distinctive.

German Federal Republic

354 (43-15)

Die Bundesrepublik . . . Vereinigt mit *Handbuch für die Bundesrepublik Deutschland.* Berlin & Cologne, Heymann, 1953-. Biennial.

A directory of German Federal central and provincial government departments and officials, institutions, etc.

France

354 (44).11 / .86

Bottin administratif et documentaire . . . Paris, Société Didot-Bottin. maps. Annual. (169th year, 1966).

Two parts: 1. Administration (a directory of central and local government offices and officers, institutions and schools. Index of names on yellow-tinted paper). 2. Documentation (on pink-tinted paper), including regulations, tariffs and other tabular data. Advertisements.

Répertoire permanent de l'administration française au 1er janvier 1963 (22. éd. Paris, La Documentation Française. [iv], 362, lv p.), has a 55p. index of names.

Noted: *Bibliographie des almanachs et annuaires administratifs, ecclésiastiques et militaires français de l'ancien régime et des almanachs et annuaires généalogiques et nobiliaires du XVIIe siècle à nos jours,* compiled by G. Saffroy (1959. xvi, 110p.).

Italy

354 (45)

ITALY. PARLAMENTO. Camera dei Deputati. **Annuario parlamentare.** Rome, Tipografia della Camera dei Deputati, 1948-. Annual. (1966/67. [1966?]. 75s.).

Official directory of the Italian government, Chamber of Deputies and Senate, Judiciary, official agencies and associations. Analytical index.

U.S.S.R.

354 (47).11 / .86

INSTITUTE OF THE STUDY OF THE U.S.S.R. Key officials of the Government of the U.S.S.R. and Union Republics. Munich, the Institute, 1962. 111p.

Covers the period 1917 to February 1962. The principal executive departments and agencies of the Soviet Union are listed in order of formation and re-organisation, plus relevant dates. Index of personal names. (Reviewed in *Library of Congress Information bulletin,* v. 21, *no.* 41, 8th October 1962, p. 531.)

The U.S. Bureau of Intelligence and Research is producing a *Directory of Soviet officials* (Washington, Government Printing Office, 1966-. v.1-. (Intelligence reference aid, A 66-5)). Similar directories were issued in 1966 for Czechoslovak officials (144p.) and Polish officials (233p.).—Intelligence reference aids A 65-8 and A 66-2, respectively.

Norway

354 (481)

Norges statskalender . . . Oslo, Aschehoug, 1815-. Annual (irregular).

A detailed directory of Norwegian central and local government departments and officials. The name index in the 1967 ed. (p. 978-1116) runs to more than 20,000 entries.

Sweden

354 (485)

Sveriges statskalender . . . Uppsala & Stockholm, Almquist. Annual.

Directory of Swedish government departments and officials, associations, universities, etc.

Denmark

354 (489)

DENMARK. Kongelig Dansk Hof- og Statskalender. **Statshåndbog for kongeriget Danmark . . .** Copenhagen, Schultz, 1734-. Annual.

A detailed directory of Danish government departments and officials. The name index in the 1967 ed. (p. 1044-1256) runs to more than 50,000 names; index of government departments.

Netherlands

354 (492)

Staatsalmanak voor het Koninkrijk der Nederlanden. The Hague, Staatsdrukkerij en Uitgeverijbedrijf.

An official directory of Dutch government departments and officials. The name index has *c.* 20,000 entries; subject index.

Pyttersen's Nederlandse almanak (Zaltbommel, K. Drukkerij van de Garde N.V. 66th year, 1967) includes organisations as well.

Belgium

354 (493)

BELGIUM. Annuaire administratif et judiciaire de Belgique et de la capitale du royaume. Brussels, Bruylant. Annual.

A detailed directory of Belgian central and local government departments and officials. The 1966/67 ed. includes a list of Brussels streets and communes, faubourgs. Index of departments and subjects.

Communist China

354 (510).11/.86
UNITED STATES. DEPARTMENT OF STATE. BUREAU OF INTELLIGENCE AND RESEARCH. Directory of Chinese Communist officials. Washington, Government Printing Office, March 1966. 621p. Mimeographed. (Intelligence reference aid, A 66-8).

First published in 1960.
Identifies the leading Communist Chinese political, governmental and socio-cultural personalities. 9 sections (1. Political parties—2. Central government—3. National People's Congress . . . 9. Scientific organizations). Follows the Wade-Giles system of romanization of Chinese characters. The alphabetical name index "includes the Standard Telegraphical Code number for those individuals whose Chinese characters are available" (*Preface*).

Israel

354 (569.4).11/.86
ISRAEL. Government yearbook, 5711 [1950-51]-. English ed. Tel Aviv, Government Printer, 1950-. Annual. (5727:1966/67. 1967. 22s.).

Gives comprehensive data on the Government and its ministries, plus texts of principal legislation passed in the previous year. The statistical section is also published separately as *Statistical abstract of Israel* (q.v.) Select list of official publications.
The Hebrew edition includes a bibliography of books published in the previous year.

Americas

354 (7/8).11/.86
ORGANIZATION OF AMERICAN STATES. Chiefs of State and Cabinet ministers of the American republics. No. 4. Washington, Pan American Union, 1966. [iii], 34p. 25c.

Covers 21 republics, including the U.S.A.

U.S.A.

354 (73)
United States Government organization manual, 1935-. Washington, U.S. Government Printing Office, 1935-. Annual. (1966-67. Revised June 1, 1966. $2.)

Title and publisher vary. Originally irregular and loose-leaf.
"The official organization handbook of the Federal Government" (*Foreword*) and ranks with the U.S. *Congressional directory* as providing authoritative information on the federal government and changes in titles and functions of government departments and agencies. There is no comparable British publication. Main sections: Constitution of the U.S. (with amendments)—Legislative branch—Judicial branch—Executive branch—Supplemental information (*e.g.,* quasi-official agencies; selected multilateral international organizations—commonly used abbreviations; organization chart). Appended list of publications and list of names.

354 (73) (092)
UNITED STATES. DEPARTMENT OF STATE. The biographic register, revised as of June 30, 1966. [Washington, Government Printing Office], 1966. 602p. (U.S. Department of State. Department and Foreign Service series 126). $3.50.

Very brief biographical data on personnel of the U.S. Department of State, U.S. Foreign Service, U.S. Mission to the United Nations, Agency for International Development, Peace Corps, U.S. Arms Control and Disarmament Agency, U.S. Information Agency and Foreign Agricultural Service.

ARMED FORCES

Bibliographies

355:016
Air University Library index to military periodicals. Maxwell Air Force Base, Alabama, Air Univ. Library, 1949-. v. 1, no. 1-. Quarterly, with annual and triennial cumulative issues. Libraries only, on exchange basis. Distribution made by issuing office.

As *Air University periodical index,* 1949-62.
"A subject index to significant articles, news items and editorials appearing in 58 English-language military and aeronautical periodicals not indexed in readily available commercial indexing services" (*Preface*). The v. 17 annual cumulation, 1966, has *c.* 20,000 entries. 62 titles of periodicals are listed. Arranged A-Z authors, subjects in one sequence, with further subdivision as necessary, and finally A-Z by title. 'Aircraft industry and trade' (p. 28-32) has subdivision 'international aspects', further divided by country (Great Britain: 2 columns).

Militärwissenschaftliche Quellenkunde. Neuerwerbskatalog der Zentralbibliothek der Bundeswehr (Düsseldorf, Zentralbibliothek der Bundeswehr) is bi-monthly, with annual author and subject index.

355:016
COCKLE, M. J. D. A bibliography of English military books up to 1642. 2nd ed. London, Holland Press, 1957. xli, 268p. illus.

First published 1900 (xl, 268p.).
Entries nos. 1-166 consist of books in English, arranged chronologically; nos. 500-950 cover foreign books, arranged according to subjects A-Z (*e.g.,* art, military; cavalry and equitation), with final chronological order. Nos. 167-499 are not used. Index (p. 251-68) includes names of English printers.

Noted: Special Libraries Association. Military Libraries Division. *Military bibliographies,* no. 1-. New York, S.L.A., 1965-.

355:016
GREAT BRITAIN. MINISTRY OF DEFENCE. Libraries. Accessions to the Ministry of Defence libraries. London, Ministry of Defence Library (Central and Army). Monthly.

About 1,000 entries per month. Additions to stock are divided by 13 collections: 1. Service (historical and general)—2. Service (technical)—3. General—4. International relations, legal and public administration—5. Economics, management and industrial administration—6. Mechanical engineering and metallurgy—7. Electrical engineering and electronics—8. Aeronautical, automobile and marine engineering—9. Biology, medical and psychology—10. Mathematical and statistical—11. Computers and data processing—12. Other scientific and technical—13. Education and documentation. Items appear under both authors and subjects in one A-Z sequence in each of the 13 sections. Material in sections 1 & 2 (300 titles per month) includes reprints and extracts from journals, duplicated typescripts.

355:016:016

———— ———— ———— Index of book lists, 1968. London, Ministry of Defence Library (Central and Army), 1968. 22p.

An annual list, in two parts (1. Military; 2. Non-military, each A-Z by subjects), of booklists issued by the Library. Biographies and campaigns figure prominently as subjects. 1,739 book lists had been issued by May 1st, 1968.

355 (02)

EWING, L. L., and SELLERS, R. C., ed. The reference handbook of the armed forces of the world. Washington, Sellers & Associates, 1966. v.p. $14.95.

By countries A-Z (Afghanistan-Zambia). The section on Norway has headings: Defence budget. Population. Manpower in armed forces. Defense as percentage of gross national product—Army, navy and air force: manpower; general; equipment—Miscellaneous data (e.g., defence agreements; internal security forces). 6 appendices; no index.

Dictionaries

355 (03):016

CRAIG, H., Jr., comp. A bibliography of encyclopedias and dictionaries dealing with military, naval and maritime affairs, 1577-1965. 3rd ed., rev. and corrected. Houston, Texas, Fondren Library, Rice Univ., 1965. [ii], 101, xi l. Mimeographed.

First published 1960.
About 1,200 items, chronologically arranged. International coverage. Omits general encyclopaedias, biographical dictionaries, dictionaries for aeronautics, marine engineering and shipbuilding, textbooks and manuals with brief vocabularies, and sailing directions (Explanation). Some entries are annotated; sometimes the number of terms is stated. 'Works consulted and sources of information', p. x-xi. Author index.

355 (038)=20

UNITED STATES. JOINT CHIEFS OF STAFF. Dictionary of United States military terms for joint usage. Washington, U.S. Government Printing Office, 1964. vii, 249p. (JCS Pub. 1). Loose-leaf. $1.50.

About 3,000 current U.S. military terms for joint usage (p. 1-157). Appendix: NATO glossary

section (c. 2,000 terms, including a number appearing in the main dictionary, p. 159-249. (For fuller entry, see v. 1 of Guide to reference material (1966), p. 255.)

See also entries in v. 1 of the Guide (2nd ed.),
p. 255-6.

Periodicals

355 (05):016

UNITED STATES. DEPARTMENT OF THE AIR FORCE. Air University Library. Union list of military periodicals. Maxwell, Alabama, Air Univ. Library, Air Force Base, Alabama, 1960. viii, 121p. Available to libraries. Distribution made by issuing office.

An enlargement of the Air University Library's Union list of foreign military periodicals (1957).
About 1,000 titles, excluding periodicals published by regimental societies of purely local interest, annual reports, and other categories; 39 contributing libraries. Geographical index, p. 111-121. (Duplicate of entry in v. 1 of Guide at 623 (05):016.)

Other lists: U.S. Department of the Army. Army Library. Checklist of periodicals currently received in the Army Library (3rd ed. Washington, 1966. v, 82p.); Einaud, L., and Goldhammer, H. An annotated bibliography of Latin American military journals (Santa Monica, Cal., Rand Corporation, 1965. vi, 84p. Research Memorandum 4890).

Yearbooks

355 (058)

Brassey's Annual: the armed forces year-book, 1950-. London, Clowes, 1950-. illus., tables, diagrs., maps. Annual. (77th year, 1966. 84s.).

1886-1949, as Brassey's Naval and shipping annual (with some variation in title).
The 1966 v. has 32 contributions by specialists (e.g., 'The state of Britain's armed forces'; 'The French navy'; 'Progress with Polaris'; 'Some thoughts on panic in war'). Chapter 32 consists of a select list of works of service interest published 1965-66. Non-analytical subject index.

Quotations

355:808

HEINL, R. D. Jr. Dictionary of military and naval quotations. Annapolis, Md., U.S. Naval Institute, [1966]. xl, 367p. ports. $15.

Quotations from more than 1,400 individuals under 800 subject headings. A-Z; range extends chronologically from Homer to Liddell Hart. Gives source and date of quotation, where known and applicable. Index of authors of quotations. Library journal (v. 92, no. 8, 15th April 1967, p. 1606, 1608) complains that there is no list of the portraits scattered throughout the text in no discernible order. Reviewed in the Royal United Service Institution Journal, v. 112, no. 647, August 1967, p. 291.

Defence Policy

355.02 (038)=00

SCHWARZ, U., and HADIK, L. Strategic terminology: a trilingual glossary. New York, Praeger; London, Pall Mall Press, 1966. 157p. 45s.

Published under the auspices of the Graduate School of International Studies, Geneva.

About 400 English, French and German terms are defined in those languages, with supporting quotations from 29 authorities (*e.g.,* Clausewitz; *Dictionary of United States military terms . . .* (1964)). The English term and definition plus quotation(s) are followed by the French and German entries (normally supported by citations from authorities in those languages). French and German indexes (including equivalents); bibliography of authorities cited, p. 155-7.

British Army

355.1/.7 (410) (091)

FORTESCUE, Sir J. W. A history of the British Army. London, Macmillan, 1899-1930. 13v., with 6v. of maps.

Usually accepted as the standard work on British Army history. It suffers, however, from a lack of proportion: the majority of the volumes are devoted to the period between 1763 and 1810. Furthermore, it contains little or no information on the development of army organization and administration.

For army organization and administration, best sources are: Cruickshank, C. G. *Elizabeth's army* (1946); Firth, Sir C. H. *Cromwell's army* (3rd ed., 1931); Walton, C. *History of the British standing army, 1660-1700* (1894); Curtis, E. E. *The organization of the British Army in the American Revolution* (1926); Oman, Sir C. *Wellington's army* (1912); and Dunlop, J. K. *The development of the British Army, 1899-1914* (1938).

355.1/.7 (410) (091):016

NATIONAL BOOK LEAGUE. The British soldier: an exhibition of books, manuscripts and prints covering the last 250 years; organized by G. A. Shepperd, September-October 1956. London, N.B.L., [1956]. x, 54p. illus.

275 numbered items, with a supplementary list (Section 8) of 50 regimental histories, compiled by D. W. King. Sections 1-7 cover general aspects and periods, up to the Korean War of 1950-53. Chronological tables are provided. The major items are given annotated entries.

355.134 (4/9)

DORLING, H. T., with GUILLE, L. F. Ribbons & medals, naval, military, air force and civil. New ed., rev. and further enl. London, Philip, 1960. 296p. illus. (incl. 16 col. pl.). 25s.

First published 1916; 3rd ed. 1956.
Contents: Order of wearing—The V.C.—The George Cross—The George Medal—British orders—British decorations—Commonwealth war medals—Foreign countries, Belgium . . . Yugoslavia (p. 175-274), with description and black-and-white illustrations of leading medals. 16 coloured plates of British and foreign ribbons. Analytical index.

Decorations

355.134 (410)

CREAGH, Sir O'M., and HUMPHRIS, E. M., ed. The V.C. and D.S.O.: a complete record of all those officers, non-commissioned officers and men of Her Majesty's naval, military and air forces who have been awarded these decorations from the time of their institution; with descriptions of the deeds and services which won the distinctions, and with many biographical and other details. London, Standard Art Book Co. [1924]. 3v. ports.

". . . compiled from official publications and despatches, letters from commanding officers and other contemporary accounts, and from information from private sources" (*sub-title*).

355.134 (410)

GORDON, L. L. British orders and awards . . . Gnosall, nr. Stafford, the Author, 1959. x, 166, 4p.

See entry at 929.7 (410).

355.134 (410)

MAYO, J. H. Medals and decorations of the British Army and Navy. London, Constable, 1897. 2v. illus. (incl. col. pl.).

A detailed record of all British and Indian medals and decorations issued up to the date of publication. Reprints the official warrants and orders in full.

355.134 (410)

NORMAN, C. B. Battle honours of the British Army, from Tangier, 1662, to the commencement of the reign of King Edward VII. London, Murray, 1911. xxviii, 500p. illus., maps.

Notes on the battles for which honours have been awarded to British regiments. Records numbers taking part, casualties, etc.

The following deals with campaign medals only: Gordon, L. L. *British battles and medals: a description of every campaign medal and bar awarded since the Armada, with the historical reasons for their award and the names of all the ships, regiments and squadrons of the Royal Air Force whose personnel are entitled to them* (3rd rev. and enl. ed. Gosnall, nr. Stafford, the Author, 1962. xvi, 451p. illus.

Uniforms. Badges

355.14 (410)

EDWARDS, T. J. Regimental badges. 4th rev. ed., revised by A. L. Kipling. Aldershot, Gale & Polden, 1966. xxi, 378p. illus.

First published 1951.
An illustrated record of the cap badges of the regiments and corps of the British Army in use today, with notes on their origin. Does not include regimental crests. Section 1, Regular army; 2, Territorial army. Appendices; index.

More limited in scope are: Dawnay, N. P. *The badges of warrant and non-commissioned rank in the British Army* (London, Society for Army Historical Research, 1949. 64p. illus.), which gives a detailed historical record based entirely on official sources; and Cole, H. N. *Badges on battledress: post-war formation signs, and rank and regimental badges* (3rd rev. and enl. ed. Aldershot, Gale & Polden, 1953. xxx, 218p. illus.), which fills a gap.

355.14 (410)
LAWSON, C. C. P. A history of the uniforms of the British army, from its beginnings to 1760. London, Norman Military Publications (distributor: N. Vane), 1940-67. 5v. illus. (incl. col. pl.), tables. £13 6s.; ea. 45s.-63s.

An authoritative record, based on official records and warrants. V. 1-2 (1940-41), originally published by Peter Davies, have been reprinted (1962-63) by Norman Military Publications. V. 3 (1961) has a chapter on the American colonies and a bibliography. V. 4 (1966) covers the period *c*. 1797-1815. V. 5 (1967) introduces the foreign regiments in British service. Profusely illustrated (*e.g.*, v. 4 has 4 colour plates and 150 black-and-white drawings). Effective use of tables (*e.g.*, v. 4, p. 115-7, 'Scottish Fencibles': tabulated data:— regiment, date, facings, dress, lace, details, reference).

R. M. Barnes' *Military uniforms of Britain & the Empire, 1742 to the present time* (London, Seeley Service, 1960. 347p. illus. 42s.) gives strictly chronological treatment, to 1957. Emphasis is on overseas units. 16 coloured plates and numerous rather crudely shaded line-drawings; no bibliography. Definitely inferior to Lawson as a history.

355.14 (411)
BARNES, R. M., *and others.* **The uniforms and history of the Scottish regiments:** Britain— Canada — Australia — New Zealand — South Africa, 1625 to the present day. London, Seeley Service, [1956]. 351p. illus. (12 col. pl.), tables.

16 chapters, 12 of which cover the history, 1625-1954, by periods. Chapter 13: Early Scottish weapons; 14: The pipes; 15-16: Uniforms of the Scottish regiments. Appendices consist of abbreviated regimental histories (Scottish regiments of Britain, of Canada, Australia, etc.) noting H.Q. or depot, brief chronology, uniforms, battle honours, number of battalions in 1914-18, regimental march and motto, and affiliated or allied regiments. No bibliography. Index, giving names of regiments in capitals. 83 uniforms illustrated in colour on 12 plates; 26 line drawings.

Standards

355.15
EDWARDS, T. J. Standards, guidons and colours of the Commonwealth forces. Aldershot, Gale & Polden, 1953. xvi, 239p. illus. (15 col. pl.).

Provides a historical commentary on the official warrants, regulations and orders relating to regimental colours. Well documented, with excellent illustrations.

General Organisation of Forces

355.3 (410)
GREAT BRITAIN. MINISTRY OF DEFENCE. Army Department. **The Queen's Regulations for the Army,** 1961. London, H.M. Stationery Office, 1962. 653p. Loose-leaf.

Previous ed., 1955.
In 15 sections, with 37 appendices. Definitions, p. xvi. Analytical index.

Regulations for the Territorial and Army Volunteer Reserve, 1967 (London, H.M.S.O., 1967. 495p.) is also loose-leaf and has an analytical index.

The *Manual of military law, 1961* (10th ed. London, H.M.S.O.) is in 3 parts, loose-leaf. Part 3: The law of war on land.

355.3 (410)
The Army list. London, H.M. Stationery Office, 1814-. Annual. (1966. 52s. 6d.).

Frequency has varied. Preceded by *A list of general and field officers, as they rank in the Army, 1754-1868*. Now published for the Ministry of Defence, Army Department.
A list of serving officers arranged in corps and regimental order.

355.3 (73)
The Army almanac: a book of facts concerning the United States Army. [2nd ed.]. Harrisburg, Pa., Stackpole Co., [1959]. x, 797p. illus., maps.

An encyclopaedic dictionary of the organization and history of the component parts of the United States Army.

Operations of War
355.4 (084.4)
GREAT BRITAIN. MINISTRY OF DEFENCE. INSTITUTE OF ARMY EDUCATION. Visual Aids Section. **A map book for students of military history.** London, 1963-. Loose-leaf.

Intended to assist students in the reading of the set books and to assist tutors in presenting the subjects. 135 maps, usually in 2 or 3 colours. Sections: A. The American Civil War (some maps reproduced from the *West Point atlas*)—B. The campaign in North Africa (1964)—C. Wellington's campaigns (1965)—D. The campaign in Burma (1965)—E. Marlborough's campaigns (1967; gives 22 division insignias and a short book list)—F. The campaign in Italy (due in 1968). Supplementary sheets to follow. Page size (oblong): 10″ × 15″.

355.4 (4)
CHANDLER, D., *ed.* **A traveller's guide to the battlefields of Europe.** London, Evelyn, 1965. 2v. diagrs., plans. ea. 30s.

v. 1. *Western Europe.*
v. 2. *Central and Eastern Europe.*
V. 1 has 20 contributors; national sections deal with Belgium, Eire, France, Gibraltar, Great Britain, Holland, Portugal and Spain (subdivided by battlefields, A-Z). Glossary of military terms; campaign chronology; 30 plans and dia-

grams; bibliography (p. xiii). V. 2, covering 15 countries, has a similar pattern. For each battlefield: date; location; war and campaign; object of the action; opposing sides; forces engaged; casualties; result; nearby accommodation; suggested readings. Location categories, A-D (A: easily accessible and practically unchanged; D: difficult to reach and practically unrecognisable); 4 asterisks, if a very important action; 1 asterisk, if of minor significance.

Logistics

355.41 (038)=00

GERMANY. BUNDESMINISTERIUM FÜR VERTEIDIGUNG. Logistik Glossar. Englisch-französisch-deutsch, mit deutschen und französischen Register und Anhang: Abkürzungen. 2. Aufl. [Bonn], 1959. [71]p.

English-French-German glossary of logistics, with indexes in German and French. Appendix of abbreviations.

Military Geography

355.47:016

PELTIER, L. C., *comp.* **Bibliography of military geography.** [Washington], Military Geography Committee, Association of American Geographers, 1962. ii, 76 l. Mimeographed. $2.

"Compiled as an aid to students, teachers, research scholars and others who have an interest in military geography" (*Preface*). About 900 unannotated entries (many are for periodical articles). 6 main sections (with sub-divisions): 1. Military geography (including cartography)—2. Systematic military geography (*e.g.*, geology, geomorphology, climatology)—3. Historical—4. Topical (*e.g.*, geographic and environmental aspects of desert warfare)—5. Regional (divided by countries and areas). No index.

Regiments

355.486 (091)

CHICHESTER, H. M., and **BURGES-SHORT, G. The records and badges** of every regiment and corps in the British Army. [2nd ed.] Aldershot, Gale & Polden, [1900]. xv, 492p. illus. (incl. col. pl.).

An authoritative account of British regiments and corps, and their predecessors, up to 1900; includes detailed notes on badges, lists of unit histories, and information on uniforms, colours and standards.

355.486 (091):016

WHITE, A. S., *comp.* **A bibliography of regimental histories of the British army.** London, Society for Army Historical Research, with The Army Museum Ogilby Trust, 1965. viii, 265p. 105*s.*

About 2,500 briefly annotated entries. Sections: 1. General—2. Regular army—3. Departments, Corps—4. Auxiliary forces—5. Miscellaneous (*e.g.*, Women's corps; Disbanded regiments and corps). Entries note number of coloured plates. Appendix shows present-day titles of regiments. Index of names of regiments. The review in the

Times literary supplement (no. 3,333, 13th January 1966, p. 32) finds that "too few printed reminiscences and journals of regimental officers and other ranks are included". The compiler was for many years librarian of the War Office Library.

Air Force

358.4 (410) (058.7)

The Air Force list. London, H.M. Stationery Office, 1949-. Annual. (1966. 70*s.*)

Previously *The Monthly Air Force list,* February 1919-1939.
Arranged according to the various branches of the Royal Air Force; index of names; list of retired officers.

358.4 (410) (091)

LEWIS, P. Squadron histories: R.F.C., R.N.A.S. and R.A.F., 1912-59. London, Putnam, 1959. 208p. with 8p. of col. plates.

Very brief squadron histories (nos. 1-695), p. 11-124. 13 appendices, including: 1. Aircraft used as equipment or for service trials by squadrons (keyed to squadrons 1-695)—2. Aircraft specifications—3. Titles of squadrons . . . 7. Squadron and unit code lettering. Illustrations of flight-squadron markings appear on pages between p. 128 and 129.

358.4 (410) (094)

GREAT BRITAIN. MINISTRY OF DEFENCE. Air Department. **The Queen's regulations and Air Council instructions** for the Royal Air Force. 4th ed. London, H.M. Stationery Office, 1956. Loose-leaf.

In 16 sections; 35 appendices. Explanations of terms (4p.). No index or contents list.

—————**Manual of Air Force law.** 4th ed. London, H.M. Stationery Office, 1964. 2v. Loose-leaf. 60*s.*

Navy

359:016

GREAT BRITAIN. MINISTRY OF DEFENCE. Author and subject catalogues of the Naval Library, Ministry of Defence, London. Boston, Mass., G. K. Hall, 1967. 5v. $330 (U.S. and British Isles); $363 (elsewhere).

Claimed to be the world's largest collection of naval and maritime books, mainly devoted to naval and general history, voyages, hydrographic surveys and the like. Estimated 85,000 entries, photolithographically reproduced from cards. Entries include charts and maps.

359 (038)

NOEL, J. V., Jr. **Naval terms dictionary.** 2nd ed., revised by J. V. Noel, Jr. and T. J. Bush. New York, Van Nostrand, 1966. 377p.

First published 1952 (vi, 247p.).
About 6,000 entry-words, including naval slang, everyday technical and non-technical terminology, acronyms, code names and organisations, plus symbols applicable to the U.S. navy, and abbreviations (*e.g.*, of enlisted ratings). Considerably expanded and updated from 2nd ed.

359 (091):016

ALBION, R. G. Naval and maritime history: an annotated bibliography. 3rd ed. Mystic, Conn., Munson Historical Association, 1963. viii, 230p. $3; $5.

Published for the Munson Institute of American Maritime History. First published 1951 as *Maritime and naval history* (2nd ed. 1955).

An annotated list of items by more than 2,000 authors. Limited to books and periodicals in English. 7 major subject sections, with more than 70 sub-sections. "An indispensable companion to any writer on maritime subjects", comments E. G. R. Taylor (*The journal of the Institute of Navigation,* v. 17, no. 2, April 1964, p. 211).

British Navy

359 (410) (058.7)

The Navy list: containing the officers on the active list of the Royal Navy, April 1814-. London, H.M. Stationery Office, 1814-. Annual. (1967. 38s.).

Not published for sale between September 1939 and May 1949.

Cover sub-title: "containing lists of ships, establishments and officers of the Fleet".

Also: *The Navy list of retired officers, together with the Emergency list, 1965* (London, H.M.S.O., 1965. xvi, 272p. 27s. 6d.).

359 (410) (091)

CLOWES, *Sir* **W. L. The Royal Navy:** a history from the earliest times to the present. London, Sampson Low, 1897-1903. 7 v. illus., maps.

v. 7 has as sub-title ". . . to the death of Queen Victoria", and goes up to 1900. A most detailed work, and the standard history; full index, and many appendices of flag officers and of ships lost.

359 (410) (091)

LEWIS, M. A. The history of the British navy. London, Allen & Unwin, 1959. 260p.

First published 1957; reset ed. 1959.

A useful short account, set against a more general background. A short, critical bibliography is appended. Author was Professor of History, Royal Naval College, Greenwich.

The same author's *A social history of the Navy, 1793-1815* (London, Allen & Unwin, 1960. 467p. illus., maps, tables. 42s.) has footnote references and 'A list of contemporary sources quoted in the text', p. 444-6, apart from 32 plates and 14 tables. Analytical index; index of ships' names. Continued by *The navy in transition, 1814-1864: a social history* (London, Hodder, 1965. 287p. 42s.), which makes good use of W. R. O'Bryne's *The naval biographical dictionary: life and services of every living office* (1846),— "a solid book of reference" (*Encyclopædia Britannica* (11th ed.), v. 19 (1911), p. 312).

359 (410) (091)

NATIONAL MARITIME MUSEUM, London. **The commissioned sea officers of the Royal Navy, 1660-1815.** London, the Museum, 1954. 3v.

Provides a complete list of naval officers for the period covered.

359 (410) (091):016

MANWARING, G. E. A bibliography of British naval history: a biographical and historical guide to printed and manuscript sources. London, Routledge, 1930. xxii, 163p.

Pt. 1: Authors; pt. 2: Subjects. Brief entries (author-title-date), with analytical entries for Navy Records Society, Historical Manuscripts Commission. Calendars of State Papers, and entries for periodical articles.

An earlier list is: Callender, G. *Bibliography of naval history* (London, Historical Association, 1924-25. 2 pts.).

A select bibliography of naval history (1709-1893), compiled by Mary S. Coleman is listed in the Univ. of London School of Librarianship and Archives. *List of bibliographies and theses accepted for Part III of the University of London Diploma in Librarianship between 1936 and 1950.*

359 (410) (091):355.461

WARNER, O. Battle honours of the Royal Navy. London, Philip, 1956. 100p. illus.

A tabulated list of naval actions from 1588 to 1953, and details of single ship actions, listed alphabetically. Lists, with battle honours, follow of ships of the Royal and Commonwealth Navies now in commission, of Fleet Air Arm squadrons which have been in action, and of regiments with naval battle honours. A final section gives illustrations of ships' badges.

359 (410) (094)

GREAT BRITAIN. MINISTRY OF DEFENCE. Navy Department. **The Queen's Regulations for the Royal Navy.** Revised 1967. London, H.M. Stationery Office, 1967. Loose-leaf. 47s. 6d.

When completed it will supersede *The Queen's Regulations and Admiralty instructions for the government of Her Majesty's Naval Service* (1953).

Naval Medals

359:355.134

NATIONAL MARITIME MUSEUM, London. **British and foreign medals relating to naval and maritime affairs.** Arranged and indexed by the Earl of Sandwich. 2nd ed. London, H.M. Stationery Office, 1950. viii, 468p.

First published 1937; supplement, 1939.

The arrangement, "while following chronology as far as possible, [aims] to group the artists of the same schools together under their respective countries". There are specific sections for decorations, counters, coins, engraved medals, token coinage, medals given for life-saving, etc. Layout is on the column principle (Number; Reference; Place of action; Bar; Recipient; British ships engaged; Enemy ships captured, etc.; Notes). More than 2,000 entries. The index is in four sections: artists; general; personnel; ships.

Naval Dress

359:391 (410)

JARRETT, D. British naval dress. London, Dent, 1960. 148p. illus. 35s.

Four sections: 1. Before 1748; 2. 1748 to 1829; 3. 1830 to 1900; 4. After 1900. Profusely illustrated (86 plates and 19 line-drawings), many of the originals being in the National Maritime Museum. Illustrations also include badges. Detailed index. "A most interesting book for the general reader as well as a handbook for film and theatrical producers and for historical illustrations" (*The Naval review,* v. 49, no. 1, January 1961, p. 88).

From the National Maritime Museum itself comes: *The dress of the British sailor;* compiled by Admiral Sir Gerald Dickens (London, H.M. Stationery Office, 1957. 8p., with 24 plates. 3s.).

J. Moll's *Uniforms of the Royal Navy during the Napoleonic Wars* (London, Evelyn, 1965. [7], 43p. illus. 63s.) contains 20 coloured plates in the form of modern silhouettes and includes a bibliography.

Warships

359:623.82 (410)

MANNING, T. D., and WALKER, C. F. British warship names. London, Putnam, 1959. 498p.

An A-Z sequence of *c.* 20,000 entries, giving name, meaning or derivation, and a 1-2 line history. Ships of the same name are numbered under each name entry. When gaps occur in this enumerated sequence, the ships "do not qualify for inclusion", but the qualification, apart from that of British warships, is not stated. A history of names rather than of warships as such.

Naval Heraldry

359:929.6 (410)

WEIGHTMAN, A. E. Heraldry in the Royal Navy: crests and badges of H.M. ships. Aldershot, Gale & Polden, 1957. xviii, 514p. illus.

Arrangement is by names of ships, alphabetically. Diagrams of badges are accompanied by heraldic descriptions, origin and notes on historical background and battle honours.

36 SOCIAL RELIEF AND WELFARE INSURANCE

36:016

UNITED STATES. DEPARTMENT OF HEALTH, EDUCATION AND WELFARE. Catalogs of the Department Library. Boston, Mass., G. K. Hall, 1966. 49v. $3,150 (outside U.S., $3,465).

Author/title catalog. 29v. $1,930 (outside U.S., $2,123).
Subject catalog. 20v. $1,220 (outside U.S., $1,342).
The card catalogues of the Department Library contain *c.* 850,000 cards for books, pamphlets, congress proceedings, and federal, state and local documents. The *Author/title catalog* comprises *c.* 500,000 photo-offset produced cards, and the *Subject catalog, c.* 350,000.

36 (4/9) (058.7)

STANDING CONFERENCE OF VOLUNTARY ORGANISATIONS CO-OPERATING IN OVERSEAS SOCIAL SERVICE. Overseas service and voluntary organisations: a directory. London, National Council of Social Service, 1963. 64p. 4s.

Lists 59 organisations, giving address, purposes, overseas areas, services, and publications.

36 (410) (02)

CANS (Citizen's advice notes): a service of information compiled from authoritative sources. Cumulative edition, to 1967. London, National Council of Social Service, [1967]. Loose-leaf. 126s., including binder; suppts. 60s. p.a.

First published as *Notes on new emergency regulations,* 1939.
24 sections (*e.g.,* 1. Administration of justice . . . 18-19. Social services . . . 24. War pensions).

Summarises social legislation. Designed for use in Citizen's Advice Bureaux, but convenient as a popularised form of statutes and regulations. Supplements at intervals. A detailed index of 29 pages precedes.

36 (410) (02)

FAMILY WELFARE ASSOCIATION. Guide to the social services: a book of information regarding the statutory and voluntary services. London, the Association. Annual. (57th ed. 1968. 8s. 6d.).

Published as *How to help cases of distress,* 1895-1949.
The 55th ed. (xvii, 269p.) has 73 sections (1. Training for social work . . . 37. Family allowances . . . 73. Refugees) and a 'Book list' (p. 239-55), arranged by subject. Index.

36 (410) (02)

GREAT BRITAIN. CENTRAL OFFICE OF INFORMATION. Social services in Britain. Revised May 1966. London, C.O.I., 1966. 115p. illus. (Reference pamphlet no. 3). 10s. 6d.

Previous ed., 1964.
Contents: Introduction—The development of social services—Social security—Health and welfare services—Education—Youth services—Planning and housing—Employment—Treatment of offenders—Legal aid and advice—Voluntary organisations—Staffing the social services. Two appendices, including addresses of organisations (p. 102-8); reading list (p. 109-115; arranged in sections as above; includes many official reports). No index, but detailed contents list. Well produced.
The C.O.I. has also produced separate pamphlets on the *Health services in Britain* (1964) (see

at 362.1 (410)) and *Social security in Britain* (1964).

36 (410) (02)
NATIONAL COUNCIL OF SOCIAL SERVICE. Public social services: handbook of information. 12th ed. London, the Council, 1964. 190p. 16s.

First published 1917; 11th ed. 1961.
Coverage: social security, war pensions, public health, education, child care, housing, town and country planning, administration of justice. Includes Scotland and Northern Ireland. Index.

36 (410) (02)
NATIONAL COUNCIL OF SOCIAL SERVICE. Voluntary social services: a handbook of information and directory of organisations. Rev. ed. London, the Council, 1964. 160p. 12s. 6d.

First published 1928.
The directory of *c.* 300 organisations (p. 33-139) is preceded by classified lists of voluntary social service organisations (13 classes) and followed by an A-Z list of professional organisations, and 'Useful addresses'. Directory information: name and address; secretary; date of foundation; objects; activities; periodical. Index.

Additional information may be found in D. Hobman's *A guide to voluntary service* (London, H.M.S.O., 1964. 3s. 6d.) and *Some opportunities for voluntary social service in London* (New ed. London, N.C.S.S., 1965. 2s. 6d.; addendum 1966).

An "Annual charities review" appears in *The new law journal* (e.g., v. 116, 28th April 1966: "Digest of charities", p. 55-112, arranged A-Z, with descriptive notes).

36 (410) (02)
WILLMOTT, P. Consumer's guide to the British social services. Harmondsworth, Middlesex, Penguin Books, 1967. 287p. tables. 6s.

Concise information, with helpful tables (*e.g.,* table 17: Time-limits of claims for social security benefits). Chapters 3-8: 3. Children and young people—4. Marriage and family life—5. Special services for the elderly—6. The National Health Service—7. Other health and welfare services—8. Financial help and legal aid. Directory of organisations (by subjects, A-Z, p. 247-76). 'Useful sources of further information' (p. 277; a few standard works of references; also references to the literature in the text). Analytical index, in very small type. Favourably reviewed in *Bulletin of hygiene,* v. 42, no. 7, July 1967, p. 800-1.

Social Work

361/367:016
JOINT UNIVERSITY COUNCIL FOR SOCIAL AND PUBLIC ADMINISTRATION. Bibliography of social work and administration: a classified list of articles from selected British periodicals, 1930-1952. London, J.U.C.S.P.A., 1954. ix, 117p. 40s. Annual supplements.

Covers population, labour, social work, criminology, social psychology, leisure, and specific social services. Systematically arranged; 13 main classes. The main bibliography contains *c.* 6,000 entries, from 39 journals. No index. The *Thirteenth supplement, 1965* (1966) lists 725 items, from 43 journals. Subject index.

361/367 (03)
LURIE, H. L., *ed.* **Encyclopedia of social work.** New York, National Association of Social Workers, 1965. xxvii, 1060p. $13.

Continues *Social work year book,* issued by the Russell Sage Foundation (1929-. Biennial). 15th issue, 1965.
Contains 111 articles on the historical development and current problems in social work and social welfare, plus 94 biographies; also data on social welfare and demographic trends since 1790, with projection to 1980. Finally, a directory of governmental and voluntary social work and welfare agencies in the U.S., Canada and internationally.

361/367 (038)=00
LINGEMANN, E. Glossary of social work terms in English-French-German. 2nd ed. Cologne, Berlin, Heymanns Verlag, 1958. [vii], 142p.

First published 1956, compiled by A. Lorenzi.
Produced by the German National Committee of the International Conference of Social Work. About 2,500 terms, with equivalents, in 3 sequences: German-English-French (p. 3-57), English-French-German (p. 61-101), French-English-German (p. 105-42). Many sub-entries (*e.g.,* under 'Medical'—15). Genders not shown.

361/367 (038)=00
ZAPF, K. Wörterbuch der Sozialarbeit. Dictionary of social work . . . Cologne, Heymanns Verlag, 1961. xxxii, 463p.

Part 1 (p. 1-243) gives the German entry-word, with English, Dutch, French, Italian and Spanish equivalents across the double page. About 5,000 entry-words. Many compounds and some phrases. English, Dutch, French, Italian and Spanish indexes. Genders are shown.

361/367:378.9
UNITED NATIONS. Department of Social Affairs. **International directory of schools of social work.** New York, United Nations, 1955. 127p.

Lists 422 schools in 53 countries, but gives full details for only 318. Data: address, name of head, year of foundation, length of academic year, admission requirements, languages of instruction, number of staff and students, kind of training, field work, length of course, number of graduates in year, degrees and diplomas.

Trusts

361.8 (41-44)
KEELING, G. W., *comp.* **Trusts and foundations:** a select guide to organizations and grant-making bodies operating in Great Britain and the Commonwealth; edited by T. Landau. Cambridge, Bowes & Bowes, 1953. xiii, 194p. tables.

Data on nearly 1,000 educational, sociological

and other foundations, A-Z (name and address; officers; history; purposes; activities; conditions of membership; expenditure; capital and grants; publications). Excludes local authorities, universities, civic societies, and Scottish Common Good funds. Classified index (based on Dewey Decimal Classification) and alphabetical subject index. Bibliography appended. Now much dated.

Noted: National Council of Social Service. *Directory of grant-making trusts, 1968.* Edited by J. D. L. Booth (London, the Council, 1968. 544p. 80s.).

Social Welfare

362:016

"Selected bibliography on family, youth and child welfare". In *International social science review,* no. 9, April 1963, p. 69-79.

341 entries, not annotated, in 3 sections: 1. United Nations and Specialized Agencies—2. International organizations—3. National bibliographies (*i.e.,* national publications; 42 countries, A-Z). Appended annotated list of "Recent publications of the United Nations and the Specialized Agencies in the social field" (p. 80-87).
The no. 1 (1955) issue of *International social science review* carried a bibliography on the same subject. The *Review* ceased publication with no. 9.

362 (4/9) (058.7)

UNITED NATIONS. Department of Social Affairs. **International directory of nationwide organizations concerned with family, youth and child-welfare.** [New York?], United Nations, 1952. 289p.

Under countries A-Z, arranged in two sections: 1. Government agencies—2. National voluntary agencies. Directory information (*i.e.,* names and addresses) only.

362 (410) (02)

MOSS, J. Health and welfare services handbook: being a general guide to the health and welfare services administered by local authorities, together with National Insurance and National Assistance. 3rd ed. London, Hadden, Best, 1962. xvii, [1], 397p. 45s.

2nd ed. 1955.
Primarily a guide to legislation, but its 9 chapters include data on the various services. Prefatory tables of statutes, S.R.O.s and S.I.s and cases cited. Analytical index (p. 363-97).

362 (411) (02)

GREAT BRITAIN. SCOTTISH HOME AND HEALTH DEPARTMENT. Health and welfare services in Scotland. Report for . . . Edinburgh, H.M. Stationery Office. Annual. (1966. (Cmnd. 2984). 8s.).

The 1966 ed. has eight chapters (1. Current health problems—2. The young and the old—3. Local health authority services . . . 6. Hospital and specialist services—7. Staffing of the health service—8. Food safety and hygiene. Appendix 1: Research programmes in progress. 28 tables; 3 diagrams.

362 (421)

The Annual charities digest; being a classified digest of charities. London, Family Welfare Association and Butterworths, 1882-. Annual. (74th ed 1967. 18s. 6d.).

Until the 72nd ed., 1965, as *The Annual charities register and digest.*
An excellent, full and virtually complete list of national associations and societies that exist for the benefit and assistance of handicapped persons; also lists London charities. 31 sections (*e.g.,* 16. Homes and schools for children . . . 19. The homeless). Gives, in each case, objects, management and finance. Section 32: 'Miscellaneous information' (*e.g.,* Street collections, 1937-65). Index. Advertisements.

May occasionally be supplemented by *Low's Handbook to the charities of London, giving the objects, date of formation, office and secretaries of over 1,500 charitable and other beneficient institutions in and available for the Metropolis* (London, Newbery, 1836-. Annual (irregular). 1964-67 ed. 4s.).

362 (44)

LAROQUE, P., *ed.* **Social welfare in France.** Translated by P. Gaunt and N. Lindsay. Paris, La Documentation Française. [1966]. 984p. (Le monde contemporain).

Original French as *Les institutions sociales de la France.*
A detailed, systematic survey in 10 chapters (*e.g.,* chapter 3: Medicine, public health facilities and the campaign against social evils). Handicapped by lack of an index and bibliography.
A companion volume is: *Social security in France* (1965).

Health Services

362.1 (4/9)

WORLD HEALTH ORGANIZATION. World health statistics annual. Volume 3. **Health personnel and hospital establishments.** Geneva, W.H.O., 1966-. tables. Annual. (1967. 338p. 40s.).

Previously and up to 1961 as part 3 of *Annual epidemiological and vital statistics.* Consists largely of tables, with explanatory notes. Two parts: 1. Health personnel (medical and para-medical personnel; physicians)—2. Hospital establishments. Index of *c.* 200 countries or territories. In English and French.

362.1 (410)

GREAT BRITAIN. CENTRAL OFFICE OF INFORMATION. Health services in Britain. London, C.O.I., 1964. v, 68p. (Reference pamphlet no. 20). 5s.

Sections: Public health—The National Health Service—The School Health Service—Occupational health—Health services in Scotland—Health services in Northern Ireland—Medical research—Professional qualifications and training. 5 appendices, including 3. 'Selected reading list' (p. 57-62) of government and other publications, and 4. 'Health departments and organisations'. Detailed contents list; no index.

362.1 (73+71)

WASSERMAN, C. S., and **WASSERMAN, P. Health organizations of the United States and Canada;** national, regional and state: a directory of voluntary associations, professional societies and other groups concerned with health and related fields. New York, Cornell Univ. Graduate School of Business and Public Administration, 1961. iii, 191p. $10.

Very fully annotated directory of voluntary and unofficial bodies, arranged A-Z, with a subject index.

Hospitals

362.11:016

Hospital abstracts: a monthly survey of world literature, prepared by the Ministry of Health. London, H.M. Stationery Office, 1961-. v. 1, no. 1-. Monthly. ea: 7s. 6d.; 95s. p.a.

About 2,000 informative and indicative unsigned abstracts p.a. Aims "to cover the whole field of hospitals and their administration, with the exception of strictly medical and related professional matters" (prefatory note). 17 sections: Hospitals in general—Hospitals in Great Britain—Hospitals in other countries—Planning, design and construction—Equipment, fittings, furniture—Staff generally . . . Finance and accounting—Supplies and stores . . . Safety measures—The patient—Special departments—Special hospitals and units. Adequate cross-references. Includes notices of books. Author index and list of addresses of publications referred to, in each issue. Annual subject and author indexes.

362.11:016

Hospital literature index. Chicago, Ill., Library of the American Hospital Association, 1945-. Quarterly. $10 p.a.

2 p.a., 1945-61; annual and five-year cumulations.
About 17,500 references p.a. from English language literature. An A-Z author-subject index of literature about hospital administration, planning and financing, and administrative aspects of medical, paramedical, etc. fields. Includes references to significant books as well as periodical articles from c. 350 journals.

362.11(4/)

JETTER, D. Geschichte des Hospitals. Wiesbaden, Steiner, 1966-. v. 1-. (Sudhoffs Archiv. Beihefte).

v. 1. *Westdeutschland von der Anfängen bis 1850.* DM.74.

362.11 (410)

BRITISH MEDICAL ASSOCIATION. The hospital gazetteer. London, British Medical Association, 1960. viii, 163p. (1967 ed. 310p. 25s.).

An aid to doctors seeking junior appointments in British hospitals, including details of special departments, staff, accommodation and amenities. Arranged by regions, with an index of hospitals; also a summary of information on postgraduate degrees and courses of instruction.

362.11 (410)

The Hospitals year book: an annual record of the hospitals of Great Britain and Northern Ireland, incorporating "Burdett's Hospitals and charities". Founded 1889. London, Institute of Hospital Administrators, 1931-. Annual. (1967, published 1966. 95s.).

A detailed survey (1967 ed.: 1318p.) in 20 sections. Contains directories of Government departments, boards of governors, regional hospital boards, voluntary hospitals, contributory and provident schemes, local health authorities, executive councils, etc. Also, information on blood-transfusion services, bed and patient statistics, hospital finance, and similar useful material. Section 18, 'Reference information for the hospital administrator' (1967 ed., p. 557-955), includes legal notes, a list of statutory instruments, memoranda and circulars, summary of reports and 'Hospital literature—a short bibliography'. Section 20, 'Guide to hospital purchasing' (p. 997-1234). Alphabetical and "subject" indexes.

362.11 (411)

GREAT BRITAIN. SCOTTISH HOME AND HEALTH DEPARTMENT. Scottish hospitals directory. Edinburgh, H.M. Stationery Office, 1962. 45p. 3s. 6d.

Sections 1-5, by regions; sections 6-8, special types of institutions; section 9, blood transfusion. Index of names of hospitals (including grouping under types of clinics), p. 41-45.

362.11 (420)

CLAY, R. M. The mediaeval hospitals of England. London, Methuen, 1909 (reprinted Cass, 1966). 357p. illus. 63s.

The most valuable part of this history lies in appendix B, which is a list of nearly 800 houses for wayfarers, sick, aged, infirm, insane, and lepers founded before 1547, arranged by counties. Appended list of sources. Well produced. "It should be available in every historical and good general library" (*British medical journal,* no. 5,503, 25th June 1966, p. 1590).

362.11 (420)

PINKER, R. English hospital statistics, 1861-1938. London, Heinemann, 1966. xii, 162p. 25s.

Statistics for the census years 1861, 1891, 1911 and 1921, and for 1938, with commentary: number and average size of hospitals, bed provision and occupancy, average length of patients' stay, and voluntary hospital finance.

Convalescent Homes

362.16

KING EDWARD'S HOSPITAL FUND FOR LONDON. Directory of convalescent homes serving Greater London. London, the Fund, 1967. viii, 114, xxv p. 7s. 6d.

First published 1948.
Part 1: 'Convalescent homes situated within the four Metropolitan Hospital Regions and the Wessex Hospital Region, arranged alphabetically'

[by towns] (p. 1-98); part 2: Convalescent homes outside those regions but accepting patients from London. Those in the Metropolitan Hospitals Regions are approved by the Fund. Details include type of patient, number of beds, staff, visiting days, charges. Geographical, alphabetical, classified and children's indexes.

The King Edward's Hospital Fund for London also publishes a monthly *Time-table of out-patient clinics at hospitals in the Greater London area*. This gives details, including the departments and the days and hours of attendance, for some 350 hospitals (arranged alphabetically).

The complementary directory to that for Greater London is the British Hospitals Contributory Schemes Association's *Directory of convalescent homes serving the provinces (England and Wales)* (Annual. 1967. 7s. 6d.).

Rehabilitation

362.3/.4:016
AXFORD, W. A., *comp*. **Handicapped children in England**, their problems and education: books and articles published in Great Britain, from the 1944 Education Act to 1958. London, Library Association, 1959. 53p. (Special subject list no. 30).

See entry at 159.922.7:016.

362.3/.4:016
GRAHAM, E. C., and **MULLEN, M. M. Rehabilitation literature, 1950-1955**: a bibliographic review of the medical care, education, employment, welfare, and psychology of handicapped children and adults. New York, McGraw-Hill, 1956. 621p. $13; 97s. 6d.

Annotated entries for 5,214 books and periodical articles, largely American; subject arrangement, with author index. Supplemented by *Rehabilitation literature* (Chicago, National Society for Crippled Children and Adults, 1940-. Monthly).

Child Guidance

362.3 (058.7)
NATIONAL ASSOCIATION FOR MENTAL HEALTH. Directory of child guidance and school psychological services. London, The Association, 1966. 139p. 25s. Annual amendments, 1967, 1968.

Two lists of child guidance clinics, each under counties A-Z, sub-divided by towns, in England, Wales, Scotland.

The Disabled

362.4
GREAT BRITAIN. CENTRAL OFFICE OF INFORMATION. Reference Division. **Rehabilitation and care of the disabled in Britain.** London, C.O.I., 1965. [iv], 70p. illus., tables. (R.F.P. 4972/65).

Contents: Handicapped children—The elderly—The mentally disordered—The blind—The deaf and hard of hearing—The tuberculous—Pneumoconiosis—Other special groups (*e.g.*, spastics)—Rehabilitation and care of the disabled in Northern Ireland. Appendix 2: list of departments and organisations concerned with the handicapped; 3: Reading list (p. 67-70: statutes; annual reports; special (grouped as in contents)).

362.4
GREAT BRITAIN. MINISTRY OF LABOUR AND NATIONAL SERVICE. Standing Committee on the Rehabilitation and Resettlement of Disabled Persons. **Services for the disabled:** an account of the services provided for the disabled by Government departments, local authorities and voluntary organisations in the United Kingdom. 2nd ed. London, H.M. Stationery Office, 1961. v, 97p. illus. 8s. 6d.

Includes a brief history and bibliography. Appendix 1 is an annotated directory of voluntary organisations.

The Blind

362.41:016
AMERICAN FOUNDATION FOR THE BLIND. M. C. Migel Memorial Library. **Dictionary catalog of the M. C. Migel Memorial Library** . . . Boston, Mass., G. K. Hall, 1966. 2v. $100.

A catalogue of 23,000 photolithographically reproduced cards, on every phase of blindness. According to G. K. Hall *Annual Catalog*, "Typical subject headings include Preschool child, Reading, Public school classes, Space perception, Personality development, Counseling, Vocational guidance and placement, the Deaf-blind, and the War-blinded".

The Royal National Institute for the Blind Reference Library's *Works on blindness and associated subjects* (London, the Institute, 1962) had 1st suppt., 1964 and 2nd suppt. 1967.

362.41:016
LENDE, H. Books about the blind: a bibliographical guide to literature relating to the blind. New, rev. ed. New York, American Foundation for the Blind, 1953. vii, 357p.

First published 1940.
Sections (with sub-divisions): Work with the blind—Education of the young blind—Psychology in the field of blindness—Vocations and economic adjustment — Social adjustment — Literature and reading—Special groups (the blind veteran; the deaf-blind)—Biographies and autobiographies. About 4,200 entries, annotated, including coverage of periodical articles. Author index.

362.41 (058.7)
ROYAL NATIONAL INSTITUTE FOR THE BLIND. Directory of agencies for the blind in the British Isles and overseas. [Rev. ed.]. London, the Institute, in association with Gardner's Trust for the Blind, 1965. [1], ii, 179p. 10s. 6d.

A directory of local agencies in England, Scotland, Eire and Northern Ireland (noting types of blind persons catered for and availability of transport); agencies for the blind overseas. Also, list of periodicals in embossed type, list of letterpress periodicals dealing with welfare of the blind, and list of homes and hostels for the adult blind in England and Wales.

Hostels

362.52 (058.7)

LONDON COUNCIL FOR THE WELFARE OF WOMEN AND GIRLS. Hostels and residential clubs in London for professional and working women and girls. London, the Council. Annual. (1966. 3s. 6d.).

Covers the Greater London Boroughs, giving name of hostel, address, number and type of persons accommodated, charges, and conditions.

Old People

362.6 (410)

Old age: a register of social research. London, National Corporation for the Care of Old People, 1964. Loose-leaf. 20s.

A list of organizations (universities; research institutions; hospital authorities; Old People's Welfare Committees) and individuals engaged on research on old age. Each entry gives title, purpose, method, name of person or body in charge, and dates of research. Indexes of organizations and subjects.

Projects completed 1955-64 are listed in a separate publication with the same title (1965. 12s. 6d.).

362.6 (411)

SCOTTISH COUNCIL OF SOCIAL SERVICE, Inc. Scottish Old People's Welfare Committee. **Handbook of information on old people's welfare in Scotland;** edited by R. M. Murray. Edinburgh, Oxford, etc., Pergamon Press, 1965. iv, 118p. 3s. 6d.

Concise information, in 6 sections: 1. Financial and legal matters—2. Health—3. Welfare—4. Housing—5. Education—6. Legislation. Bibliography, p. 107-13 (sub-divided by subjects); detailed index.

Child Welfare

(See also 159.922.7 (058.7).)

362.7 (410)

GREAT BRITAIN. CENTRAL OFFICE OF INFORMATION. Reference Division. **Children in Britain.** Rev. ed. London, C.O.I., 1967. [iii], 53p. illus. (R.F.P. 5236/67).

Previously published 1964.

Sections: The development of child protection and welfare — Protective legislation — General services (p. 18-31)—Services for special groups (*e.g.,* mentally handicapped; young offenders). Appendix: Social service departments and organisations. 'Reading list' (p. 48-53; more than 200 items in 10 sections; includes many H.M.S.O. publications).

Freemasonry

366.1:016

WOLFSTIEG, A. Bibliographie der freimaurerischen Literatur. Leipzig, Hiersemann, 1911-26. 3v. & supplement. (Reprinted 1964. £38 10s.).

The main work (1911-13. 3v.) has *c.* 44,000 entries; the first supplement, edited by B. Berger (1926) adds a further 11,000.

366.1 (03)

BEHA, E. A comprehensive dictionary of Freemasonry. London, Arco, 1962. 207p. illus. 21s.

A popular dictionary, with some biographies (*e.g.,* Benjamin Franklin) and occasional line-drawings. Entries under names of Lodges and Masonic institutions. Definitions appear under the heading 'Definitions of Freemasonry'. Cross-references.

Clubs

367.2 (410)

The British club year book and directory. Brighton, British Club Year Book and Directory, 1961-. Annual. (1967. 105s.).

Gives addresses and brief details of 44,000 clubs in 50 categories (*e.g.,* motoring; athletics; also social, political and music), these being generally sub-divided into regions or counties. Strongest on sport and weakest on social and political fields (*e.g.,* no mention of Townswomen's Guilds or the Women's Institute). Appended is a handy 'Suppliers directory' for club secretaries. Reviewed in *The assistant librarian,* v. 58, no. 10, October 1965, p. 212.

Insurance

368:016

Insurance literature. New York, Special Libraries Association, Insurance Division, 1961-. 10 p.a.

Previously (1933-61) *Insurance book reviews. Bulletin.*

Covers books, pamphlets and proceedings; broad subject headings, with author and title index. "Confined almost exclusively to American and English publications" (Pendleton, O. W. *How to find out about insurance,* p. 11).

368:016

INSURANCE SOCIETY OF NEW YORK. Library. **Life insurance catalog** of the Library of the Insurance Society of New York. Boston, Mass., G. K. Hall, 1960. 352p. $27.

A subject catalogue on 7,400 cards, photolithographically reproduced. Covers all phases of insurance. Strong on histories of companies in the U.S. and abroad, and Insurance Department reports.

The Chartered Insurance Institute, London. Library. *Select list of useful books on insurance and related subjects* (1966. 9p. Mimeographed) records *c.* 160 items in 6 sections and gives prices, but no annotations.

The Library produces an annual *Books and pamphlets added to the Library . . .* (List no. 23: June 1st 1966 - March 15th 1967), with a supplement on fire hazards and processes of manufacture; also a *Select bibliography of reinsurance* (1967. 71p.).

SOCIAL RELIEF AND WELFARE INSURANCE

368:016

PENDLETON, O. W. How to find out about insurance: a guide to sources of information. Oxford, Pergamon Press, 1967. x, 196p. facsims. 21s.

U.D.C. order of chapters and even U.D.C. numbers for entries. 10 chapters: 1. Insurance in the modern world, with a note on careers—2. Organization of information: published sources, bibliographies, libraries—3. Encyclopaedias, dictionaries—4. Documents, research reports, lectures—5. Periodicals—6. Directories, statistical annuals, and periodicals—7. Associations, institutes, the insurance market—8. Education—9. History of insurance, illustrated by books and documents—10. Books (annotated bibliography of more than 100 of "the more useful and recently published books", p. 125-65). List of works referred to in text; index. The author was librarian, Chartered Insurance Institute. A valuable specialised guide.

368 (038)=00

CONFÉRENCE EUROPÉENNE DES SERVICES DE CONTROLE DES ASSURANCES PRIVÉES. International insurance dictionary. Berne, C.E.S.C.A.P., [1959]. xxxi, 1083p.

1,966 terms, in 11 languages (grouped in 3 columns across a double page: English, German, Dutch; French, Italian, Spanish, Portuguese; Danish, Swedish, Norwegian, Finnish). English terms are dealt with at entries no. 1-215, followed by definitions and explanations (nos. 221-259); French terms, nos. 301-588. Appendices: arbitrary symbols; abbreviations.

368 (038)=30

HEINZE, S. Fachwörterbuch der Versicherungswesens. Dictionary of insurance terms and phrases. Wiesbaden, Brandstetter, 1961. 2v. ea. 25s.

v. 1. *Deutsch-englisch.* 207p.
v. 2: *Englisch-deutsch.* 175p.
V. 2 has *c.* 3,000 main entries; many idioms. The work is a concise encyclopaedic dictionary of sorts, since it includes a few biographical entries and under 'Local health authority services' gives an explanation in English followed by a shorter one in German. 'Policy': 2 columns. An appendix lists insurance abbreviations.

368 (4/9) (058)

I.I.I. International insurance intelligence, incorporating the Insurance yearbook of Australia and New Zealand: an international yearbook of insurance companies' accounts. London, The Review (Insurance), Ltd., 1966-. £14 14s. per set of 4v.

A previous set of 17v. was published 1925-41; the new series will be 4v. p.a., covering accounts from 1964.
v. 1. *Northern Europe.* 1966.
v. 2. *Great Britain and Southern Europe.*
v. 3. *Africa, Australasia, Middle East, India, Pakistan, Japan and other Far East countries.*
v. 4. *Western hemisphere—Central America, U.S.A. and Canada, West Indies.*
V. 1 covers 10 countries, companies, being arranged A-Z under each.

368 (410) (058.7)

The Insurance directory & year book (Post magazine almanack): statistics and facts of ordinary life, industrial, life, fire, accident and marine insurance. London, Buckley Press. Annual. (126th year, 1966/67. 1967. 63s.).

Directory of insurance offices operating in the U.K. (including addresses of branch offices and their managers, and agents). States premium rates, statistical data. Includes a list of insurance brokers. General index precedes.

368.1 (058)

Stone and Cox Accident insurance year book. London, Stone & Cox. Annual. (1965. 45s.).

Covers a wide variety of types of accident insurance, from burglary to weather insurance. Introductory sections include articles. Reinsurance is also covered. Appended is a directory of insurance brokers.

368.23

Lloyd's Calendar. London, Lloyd's, 1898-. Annual. (1967. 18s.).

A compendium of information on shipping and marine insurance. Contents of the 1967 issue include: tidal predictions and tables (p. 25-179); Lloyd's insurance policies (p. 180-223); York-Antwerp rules (p. 249-56); Merchant Shipping Act (1964) (p. 257-67); Lloyd's Register of shipping (p. 189-299); Merchant Navy careers (p. 391-416); Lloyd's agents (p. 417-48); Aids to navigation (p. 481-504); Glossary of maritime and commercial terms (English, French, German, Greek, Italian, Spanish, Norwegian, p. 518-33); Seamarks of the world (p. 535-44); Principal lights around the coasts of Great Britain and the Republic of Ireland (p. 545-608); Weather news for mariners (p. 659-70); Advertisements; Index; Index to advertisements.

368.23 (038)

BROWN, R. H. Dictionary of marine insurance terms. London, Witherby, 1962. vi, 346p. (2nd ed. v, 346p. 38s. 6d.).

Concise definitions of *c.* 3,000 terms, including many shipping and commercial terms, and numerous abbreviations. Definitions vary in length from 25 words to half a page (*e.g.*, 'Valued policies'; 'Lloyd's Underwriters' Association'). The author is lecturer in marine insurance at the City of London College.

368.30 (038)

SACHS, W., and DRUDE, G., *ed.* **Lebensversicherungstechnisches Wörterbuch.** Deutsch-Englisch-Französisch-Italienisch-Spanisch. 2. Aufl. Karlsruhe, Verlag Versicherungswirtschaft, 1964. 308p.

A dictionary of actuarial and life insurance terms; *c.* 1,000 terms, with equivalents. Five sequences: German—English—French—Italian—Spanish; English—French—Italian—Spanish—German; French—Italian—Spanish—German—English; Italian—Spanish—German—English—French; Spanish—German—English—French—Italian.

368.30 (083.4)

Stone and Cox Ordinary branch life assurance tables, compiled from official sources. London, Stone & Cox, [1960]. Loose-leaf.

Lists assurance offices and gives company annual premium rates, etc., with figures up to 1959. A 40-page supplement of miscellaneous information provides explanations of various terms used, expectation of life tables, compound interest and discount tables (1% to 7%, etc.), notes on income-tax allowances and deductions, and the like.

Social Security

368.4:016

World bibliography of social security. Geneva, General Secretariat of the International Social Security Association, 1963-. v. 1, no. 1-. ea. $2.50; $10 p.a.

1960-63 published as 1 v. in 1964; continued quarterly.
More than 2,000 references p.a. for non-periodical literature as well as articles, plus notes on current social security legislation. Main headings: General — Sickness, maternity — Employment accidents, occupational diseases—Old age, disability, survivors — Unemployment — Family allowances—Other forms of social welfare. Subdivided by countries. Annual systematic subject index.

368.4 (05):016

INTERNATIONAL SOCIAL SECURITY ASSOCIATION. World list of social security periodicals. 2nd ed. Geneva, the Association, 1966. 59p. (Documentation series no. 3). $2.50.

First published 1963.
About 400 titles, covering social insurance, family allowances, social assistance and public social services. Arranged by country of publication, giving title, publisher, address, frequency, and whether printed. If summaries of articles are given in other languages, the language is indicated. No index of titles or subjects.

368.4 (4/9)

UNITED STATES. DEPARTMENT OF HEALTH, EDUCATION AND WELFARE. Social security systems throughout the world. Washington, 1964. 223p.

Details under countries: old age; invalids; widows and orphans; sickness and maternity; work injury; employment; family allowances.

368.4 (410)

GREAT BRITAIN. CENTRAL OFFICE OF INFORMATION. Social security in Britain. London, C.O.I., 1964. [ii], 38p. *Gratis.*

Contents: Introduction—The growth of social security provisions in Britain—Family allowances—National insurance—Industrial injuries insurance—War pensions—National assistance. 2 appendices; reading list, p. 36-38. Detailed contents; no index.

368.4 (410)

GREAT BRITAIN. H.M. STATIONERY OFFICE. Government publications. Sectional list no. 49, revised to 28th February 1967. **Ministry of Social Security.** London, H.M.S.O., 1967. 67p. *Gratis.*

Parts: 1. War pensions—2. National insurance, industrial injuries and family allowances —3. Supplementary Benefits Commission. Some entries are annotated.

368.4 (410):016

GREAT BRITAIN. INTERDEPARTMENTAL COMMITTEE ON SOCIAL AND ECONOMIC RESEARCH. Guides to official sources. No. 5: **Social security statistics.** Material collected by the Ministry of Pensions and National Insurance and the National Assistance Board. London, H.M. Stationery Office, 1961. viii, 171p. 8s.

The Committee's aim is "to indicate in detail what information is available and where it is to be found" (prefatory note). The first half of the guide gives details concerning national insurance, adjudication of claims, family allowances, war pensions, etc. The 'Subject index to published statistics', p. 87-136, is in column form (headings: Subject — Area — Period to which statutes relate—Issue in which statistics are published — Published in. Bibliographical references, p. vi. Appendix 9 (p. 165-6): 'Index to annual and other reports in the bound volumes of Parliamentary Papers'.

Youth Organisations

369.4 (4/9)

Yearbook of youth organisations. Munich, Unesco, 1954-. v. 1-.

V. 1: *Europe* (A-Z by countries), including also the international organizations. Details include objects and structure, with a list of publications. Loose-leaf; in English and French.
"When completed, this year-book will list 1,300 youth organizations, students' associations, youth departments of other organizations, and co-ordinating bodies for youth movements." (*Unesco bulletin for libraries*, v. 9, no. 4, April 1955, p. 80). No more published.

369.4 (410)

COOKE, D., ed. Youth organizations of Great Britain. London, Jordan, 1965. xv, 178p. 19s. 6d.

Chapters 3-7 consist of discursive accounts of the origin, history and aims of some 50 youth organizations, written by the youth organizations themselves and arranged by categories: 3. Some national voluntary associations within the Standing Conference (*e.g.,* Y.M.C.A.)—4. Preservice organisations (*e.g.,* Air Training Corps)— 5. Religious youth organisations (*e.g.,* Toc H)— 6. Political youth organisations (*e.g.,* The Young Socialists)—7. Some other youth organisations (*e.g.,* The Outward Bound Trust). Directory of youth organisations in 7 countries, p. 83-170. Index (nearly 200 entries).

Youth services in Britain (London, Central Office of Information, 1963. ii, 34p. (Ref. paper R.5506) *Gratis*) has 3 sections (Pattern of the youth services—Types of youth groups—Other organisations concerned with youth) and an appendix ('Notes on some leading youth organisations') (p. 16-32; 30 organisations described). Reading list, p. 33-4.

369.4 (410)
STANDING CONFERENCE OF NATIONAL VOLUNTARY YOUTH ORGANISATIONS. Annual report and directory . . . London, National Council of Social Service. Annual. (1964-65 ed. 1965). *Gratis*.

Includes a list of member organisations.

37 EDUCATION

(See also 159.922.7.)

Bibliographies

37:016
ALEXANDER, C., and BURKE, A. J. How to locate educational information and data: an aid to quick utilization of the literature of education. 4th ed. New York, Bureau of Publications, Teachers College, Columbia Univ., 1958. xvii. 419p.

First published 1935.

Scope is much wider than the title suggests, as considerable space is devoted to general information for students and research workers on use of libraries and bibliographical materials. Helpful chapters on publications of American educational associations and the U.S. Office of Education. Practical exercises are listed at end of each chapter. Index to subjects, forms of material, titles, authors, etc. Pronounced U.S. slant.

A. J. and M. A. Burke's *Documentation in education* (New York, Teachers College Press, 1967. xiv, 413p. $7.50) is a revision of the above work.

37:016
BLAUG, M. Economics of education: a selected annotated bibliography. Oxford, Pergamon Press, 1966. xiii, 190p. (Education libraries bulletin. Supplement 8). 42s.

792 well-annotated items in four sections: A. Developed countries (1-7)—B. Developing countries (1-5)—C. Bibliographies—D. Items received too late for classification. Includes much French and German literature. Index of authors; index of countries (not analytical). The compiler is Reader in the Economics of Education and head of the Research Unit in the Economics of Education, Institute of Education, Univ. of London.

37:016
British education index, August 1954 to November 1958-. Compiled jointly by the librarians of the Institutes of Education at Birmingham, Bristol, Cambridge, Durham, Exeter, Hull, Keele, Leeds, Leicester, London, Newcastle, Nottingham, Oxford, Reading, Sheffield, Southampton and Swansea. London, Library Association, 1960-. Termly parts, with 2-year cumulations. (v. 5: 1966-1967, parts and cumulation, 126s.; cumulation only, 105s.).

A subject index, with author key, to education articles in 50-60 British periodicals (including the *Yearbook of education*) and not confined to British education. Recent articles in certain non-educational periodicals (e.g., *History, Greece, Rome, Modern languages, Nature*), as well as *West African journal of education*, are included. About 2,000 items in the two-year cumulation. Adequate cross-references. Very few of the periodicals indexed are dealt with in the H. W. Wilson *Education index*.

"Ten years of indexing the *British education index* (1954-63)", by J. S. Andrews, appear in the *Library Association record,* v. 66, no. 5, May 1964, p. 203-6.

37:016
Bulletin signalétique. 20: Psychologie. Pédagogie. In *19-24: Sciences humaines. Philosophie* . . . Paris, Centre National de la Recherche Scientifique, 1961-. Quarterly. NF.80 (foreign, NF.85) p.a. (Section 20 separate, NF.30 (foreign, NF.35).

Formerly *Bulletin analytique. Philosophie* (v. 1-9. 1947-55); then *Bulletin signalétique. 19: Philosophie. Sciences humaines* (1956-60).

The *Pédagogie* part of Section 20 carried *c.* 3,000 indicative abstracts in 1966. Headings: 1. Pédagogie générale—2. Organisation de l'enseignement—3. Formation du personnel enseignant—4. Méthodes d'éducation—5. Techniques auxiliaires (moyens audio-visuels, machines à enseigner, etc.)—6. Domaine spéciaux de l'éducation (*e.g.*, children; adolescents; adults; handicapped)—7. Psychologie de la vie scolaire.

37:016
Education abstracts. 1949-. Paris, Unesco, 1949-. v. 1-. 10 p.a., then quarterly. ea. 3s. (v. 1-6 (nos. 1-64) reprinted New York, Kraus Reprint Corpn. $58.50; $65.)

Title changes: v. 1, nos. 1-6, *Abstracts ana bibliography*; v. 1, no. 7 to v. 3, no. 12, *Fundamental education abstracts*; v. 4, no. 1-, *Education abstracts*.

Not an abstracting service in the accepted sense. Each issue is a bibliographical survey of a particular theme,—an introductory essay followed by medium-length descriptive abstracts (*e.g.*, v. 9, no. 9, November 1957: "Encyclopaedias and dictionaries of education"). V. 15 (1963) issues have the following titles: "Primary education"; "History teaching"; and "Teaching comparative education"; v. 16: "Out-of-school education of young people"; "Agricultural education".

37:016
Education index. January 1929-. A cumulative subject index to a selected list of educational periodicals, proceedings and yearbooks. New York, Wilson, 1932-. 10 p.a., with cumulations every few months and annual, biennial and triennial.

The July 1965 - June 1966 volume indexes 199 journals, only about six of which are British (e.g., *British journal of educational psychology, Times educational supplement, Universities quarterly*). Indexing is on the usual Wilson dictionary system. About 45,000 entries and cross-references p.a.

37:016
INTERNATIONAL BUREAU OF EDUCATION. Annual educational bibliography. 1955-. Geneva, the Bureau, [1956?]-. Annual. (1965 v., published 1967. 17s.).

Cumulates the annotated bibliographies included in the quarterly *Bulletin* (1927-) of the International Bureau, and is, in fact, "a catalogue of the chief publications incorporated in the Bureau's Education Library during the year" (Kimmance, S. K. *A guide to the literature of education* (Rev. ed., 1961), p. 6). The *c.* 1,000 book items listed in the 1964 *Bibliography* (published [1966?]) are classified by U.D.C., with an author index. International in scope; helpful annotations. Author index.

The *Bibliography* is also available on thin paper, printed on one side, for mounting on cards,—the International Education Card Index Service.

37:016
INTERNATIONAL INSTITUTE FOR EDUCATIONAL PLANNING. Educational planning: a bibliography. Paris, the Institute, 1964. 131p. 10s.

About 550 entries (for books, periodical articles and documents), briefly annotated. The introduction notes that the literature is disturbingly thin on the relationship of education and educational planning to social development, as distinct from economic development. Sections: Existing bibliographies in educational planning—A. The purpose and value of educational planning—B. The preparation of educational planning—C. The organization and administration of educational planning—D. Case materials. Author index.

37:016
KIMMANCE, S. K. A guide to the literature of education. Rev. ed. London, Univ. of London, Institute of Education, 1961. [iv], 86p. Mimeographed. (*Education libraries bulletin*, Supplement 1). 5s.

First published 1958.
An excellent short guide to "the various types of printed material to be found in an education library, with selected examples of works . . . " (*Introduction*). Nearly 400 carefully annotated items: Bibliographies of education—Encyclopaedias of education—Dictionaries—Directories and yearbooks in education—Official publications (including legislation)—University and college calendars, prospectuses—Research—Educational organizations—Publications: Examining bodies —Periodicals—Library co-operation and bibliographical services—Textbooks: School—Classification schemes—Biographies in education—Abstracts—Education statistics. The 'Conclusion' (p. 71) mentions some gaps in the literature. Author and anonymous title index.

A much-expanded 3rd ed. is in preparation.

"Education", an up-to-date bibliographical survey by S. Forman and R. L. Collins in *Library trends* (v. 15, no. 4, April 1967, p. 648-69), concentrates on guides to the literature but includes encyclopaedias and catalogues of films. Tabulates points for an ideal system of bibliographical control for education. Cites 86 items in all, a list of these being appended.

37:016
LIBRARY ASSOCIATION. County Libraries Group. **Education.** 3rd ed. London, Library Association, 1966. 54p. (Readers' guides. New series, no. 92). 2s. 6d.

18 sections, including 'Bibliographies and periodical indexes', 'Guides to educational research' and 'Reference books'; *c.* 750 items. A number of entries are annotated. No index or introduction. Prices are given.

The National Book League's *Selected books on education* (1958; with Supplement, 1959. 13p. Mimeographed. 1s.) is an annotated author list of 91 items, including some Acts and Government reports. Also covers child psychology.

37:016
LONDON. COUNTY COUNCIL. Education Library. **Catalogue.** London, L.C.C., 1935. xxxvi, 847p.; First supplement, 1935-45. 1948. xxxv, 531p.

Covers not only works on education in a narrow sense, but background subjects, *e.g.*, music, literature, contained in this library for London educationists. Entries give author, title and date (but not publisher) and are annotated, with full analysis of contents of composite works and volumes of periodicals. A Dewey Decimal-classified catalogue, with subject and author indexes. Supplemented by periodically printed bulletins of selected additions.

Further supplements appeared in the *Education library bulletin* (nos. 1-12: Spring 1951-Spring 1957).

37:016
NATIONAL UNION OF TEACHERS. Library catalogue, July 1959. [New ed.] London, N.U.T., 1959. xxii, 308p. Supplement. 1960.

Previous ed., 1949.
Not restricted to education in the narrow sense, but includes works on background subjects covered by this library for N.U.T. members. Sections: Reference books—Classified list (based on Dewey) of books available on loan—Chronological lists of reports on departmental, interdepartmental select committees (titles only), governmental commissions, etc. Entries omit pagination. Author and subject indexes.

Recent accessions are recorded at intervals in the N.U.T. weekly journal, *The schoolmaster*.

37:016

Sociology of education abstracts. Liverpool, Sociology of Education abstracts, Department of Adult Education and Extra-Mural Studies, Univ. of Liverpool, 1965-. v. 1, no. 1/2-. Quarterly. 21s. p.a. (individuals); 42s. p.a. (institutions).

1965: 237 indicative and informative abstracts, arranged under authors A-Z. Content of abstract appears under set headings (in rubric): hypothesis; sample; instruments; findings; conclusion. The work of 31 abstractors. Education study area index (12 main headings),—annual. Annual list of journals from which abstracts taken (54 titles).

37:016

UNITED NATIONS EDUCATIONAL, CULTURAL AND SCIENTIFIC ORGANIZATION. Educational studies and documents. Paris, Unesco, 1953-. no. 1-.

This series includes the following bibliographies:
7. *Education for community development: a selected bibliography.* 1954. 2s.
13. *A bibliography on the teaching of modern languages.* o.p.
18. *Literacy teaching: a selected bibliography.* 1956. 2s.
19. *Health education: a selected bibliography.* 1956. 2s.
22. *Education clearing houses and documentation centres: a preliminary international survey.* 1957. 2s.
23. *An international list of educational periodicals.* 1957. 12s. 6d.
27. *Technical and vocational education in the United Kingdom: a bibliographical survey,* by R. C. Benge. 1958. 5s.
29. *Teaching about the United Nations and the Specialized Agencies: a selected bibliography.* o.p.
30. *Technical and vocational education in the U.S.S.R.: a bibliographical survey,* by M. I. Movshovich. 1959. 5s.
31. *An international bibliography of technical and vocational education.* 1959. 5s.
36. *Technical and vocational education in the U.S.A.* 1959. 5s.
44. *Education documentation centres in Western Europe.* 1962. 5s.

37:016

UNITED NATIONS EDUCATIONAL, SCIENTIFIC AND CULTURAL ORGANIZATION. International guide to educational documentation, 1955-1960. Paris, Unesco, 1963. 700p. 100s.

About 5,000 items. A guide to sources, intended for students and practitioners in the field as a means of promoting contact and collaboration. International sources, p. 15-23 (100 items); 95 countries and areas, A-Z, p. 25-600; 'foreign education' (p. 601-6). 'United Kingdom' (p. 469-95; 230 items): reference works; legislative and policy documentation; administration of the educational system; structure and organization; textbooks and instructional materials; education associations; educational journals; educational statistics; education biography; education libraries and museums; inter-availability of educational resources. Descriptions under headings, where applicable; annotated entries. Three-column index of 92 pages.
A subsequent 5-year volume was planned for publication in 1966-67.

37:016

UNITED STATES. DEPARTMENT OF HEALTH, EDUCATION AND WELFARE. Catalogs of the Department Library. Boston, Mass., G. K. Hall, 1966. 49v. $3,150 (outside U.S., $3,465).

See entry at 36:016.

37:016

WANDSWORTH PUBLIC LIBRARIES. Education: a guide to current literature. Compiled by E. W. Padwick. London, Wandsworth Borough Council, 1963. [vii], 98, xv p. Spiral binding. 7s. 6d.

About 1,200 items in 20 sections (Bibliographies—General reference books—Directories of schools—University calendars—Periodicals . . . Careers—Curriculum—Physical education). No annotations. Index of authors and subjects.

Encyclopaedias

37 (031)=20

MONROE, P., ed. A cyclopedia of education; edited with the assistance of departmental editors and more than 1,000 individual contributors. New York, Macmillan, 1911-13. 5v. illus.

A scholarly, comprehensive encyclopaedia with signed articles of varying, but sometimes considerable, length, each with a bibliography. V. 5 includes a subject index grouping articles under broad subject headings. Its date limits its usefulness, but many articles are still valuable in their own right and the work as a whole gives an excellent picture of early 20th-century educational thought in America.

37 (031)=20

RIVLIN, H. N., and SCHULER, H., ed. Encyclopedia of modern education. New York, Philosophical Library, 1943. xvi, 902p.

Initialled articles, mainly of medium length and on quite specific topics. Extensive cross-references. Short bibliographies for most articles. Covers all aspects of education and describes the educational systems of the main countries of the world. Much of the material is mainly relevant to American conditions, and the encyclopedia is too early for many important British topics resulting from the 1944 Education Act. Essentially for the layman.

37 (031)=20

WATSON, F., ed. The encyclopædia and dictionary of education; a comprehensive, practical and authoritative guide to all matters connected with educational principles and practice, various types of teaching institutions, and educational systems throughout the world. London, Pitman, 1921-22. 4v. illus.

Articles of varying length, usually initialled. Short bibliographies to most articles. A classified index is provided. In spite of the limitations of its age, it is still of value over a wide range of subjects.

37 (031)=30

Lexikon der Pädagogik. Berne, Francke, 1950-52. 2 pts. in 3v.

207

v. 1-2 (*Systematischer Teil*) constitute a dictionary of educational topics, A-Z; the 776 articles are signed and have adequate bibliographies. v. 3 covers the history of education, biographies (of about a thousand educationists, listing works by and on them), and a country-by-country survey. Appended list of contributors, with references to the articles written by them.

37 (031)=30
Lexikon der Pädagogik, hrsg. vom Deutschen Institut für Wissenschaftliche Pädagogik, Münster, und dem Institut für Vergleichende Erziehungswissenschaft, Salzburg. 2. unveränderte Aufl. Freiburg, Herder, 1960-64. 4v. and supplement.

First published 1930-32.
V. 1 has *c.* 300 contributors. Signed articles, including biographies. Most entries carry bibliographies (*e.g.,* 'Pädagogische Soziologie': 3½ columns, including ¾ column of bibliography; 'Spencer, Herbert': 1½ columns, including one-fifth column of bibliography). Many cross-references. V. 4 has an 83-page name and subject index. The Supplement, also the work of *c.* 300 contributors, has its own name and subject index. German slant.

Dictionaries

37 (038)=00
LAIDLER, F. F., *ed.* **A glossary in English, French, German, Spanish of terms used in home economics education.** London, Constable, 1963. 80p. 25*s.*

Compiled for the Fédération Internationale de l'Enseignement Ménager.
Brief definitions of English terms, A-Z, with tabulated equivalents and indexes in the other languages. Limited to *c.* 140 terms, many of which are educational (*e.g.,* "Public school") rather than domestic.

37 (038)=20
GOOD, C. V., *ed.* **Dictionary of education.** 2nd ed. New York & London, McGraw-Hill, 1959. xxvii, 676p.

First published 1945.
Dictionary, p. 1-612; education in Canada, England, France, Germany, Italy, p. 613-76. About 25,000 terms are defined, with cross-references. New terms have been added, others deleted, and new definitions given to some existing terms. Omits entries for persons and organisations.

37 (038) (410)=20
BARNARD, H. C., and **LAUWERYS, J. A.,** *comp.* **A handbook of British educational terms,** include an outline of the British educational system. London, Harrap, 1963. 210p. 15*s.*

"Primarily intended for readers in foreign or overseas countries who are interested in the British educational system and its institutions and history" (*Preface*). About 10-100 word definitions of *c.* 1,400 terms, including colloquialisms (under 'D': 'Divisional Executive'; 'Duke of Edinburgh Award'; 'dry bob'; 'debagging'); cross-references. Abbreviations, p. 206-10.

Periodicals

37 (05):016
LIBRARIANS OF INSTITUTES AND SCHOOLS OF EDUCATION. Union list of periodicals held in Institutes of Education libraries as at 31st May 1966. Newcastle-upon-Tyne, Librarians of Institutes and Schools of Education, 1966. [iv], 168p.

A computer-produced list of the periodical holdings of 22 libraries. About 1,500 periodicals. Excludes year books, annual proceedings of societies and the like. Brief statements of holdings (*e.g.,* 'current year'; 'one year only'; '1937-39 (incomplete)').

37 (05):016
LONDON. UNIVERSITY. INSTITUTE OF EDUCATION. Library. **Catalogue of periodicals in the library.** London, the Library, 1968. iv, 112p.

About 1,500 periodical titles. The main sequence is A-Z; a second sequence shows holdings by continent and country. Periodicals of British origin form only about 50% of the whole.

Scholars' guide to journals of education and educational psychology, by L. J. Lins and R. A. Rees (Madison, Wisconsin, Dembar Educational Research Series, Inc., 1965. [i], 150p. Spiral binding. $3.95) has data on 135 journals, A-Z. All the journals are American. Title and subject indexes.

37 (05):016
UNITED NATIONS EDUCATIONAL, SCIENTIFIC AND CULTURAL ORGANIZATION. Educational periodicals. [2nd ed.] Paris, Unesco, 1963. 260p. (International directories of education, 3).

First published 1957 as *An international list of education periodicals.*
Brief data (title, sub-title (if elucidatory), year founded, frequency, circulation, average number of pages per issue, language(s), publisher and address) on *c.* 5,000 current educational periodicals from 100 countries and areas. Pt. 1, International and countries, A-Z; pt. 2, A classified list of educational periodicals issued in the U.S.A. In English, French and Spanish. Title entries.
Other volumes in the Unesco 'International directories of education' series: 1. *Teachers' associations* (see at 371:061); 2. *Educational publishers* (1962; data on nearly 2,000 publishing firms from 82 countries).

Annuals

37 (058)
INTERNATIONAL BUREAU OF EDUCATION. International yearbook of education. Geneva, the Bureau, & Paris, Unesco, 1933-. Annual. (v. 27:1965. 48*s.*).

An annual world survey of educational progress (*c.* 90 national reports countries covered in the 1965 yearbook). Appendices list names of the chief officials in each country's Ministry of Education and give educational statistics.

The World year book of education. London, Evans, in association with the University of London Institute of Education and Teachers College, Columbia Univ., New York, 1931-. Annual. (1965. 70s.)

37 (058)

As *The Year book of education* until 1965; suspended 1941-47.

The 1965 year book, *The education explosion,* has 38 contributors. Section 1, Comparative and theoretical (13 chapters); section 2, Reports from countries (Europe, chapters 1-9; the Americas, 10-12; Asia, 13-17; Africa, 18-21). A few chapters have references appended. Tables; non-analytical index. The 1966 year book deals with *Church and state in education.*

Directories
37 (058.7)

Vacations abroad: courses, study tours, work camps. Paris, Unesco, 1948-. v. 1-. Annual. (v. 18: 1966. 10s.).

Gives the same type of detailed information as *Study abroad* (at 374.8 (058.7)), to which it originally formed a supplement.

Information on facilities offered (vacation courses, summer schools and seminars, study tours, hostels and camps, international voluntary work camps, etc.) by more than 960 institutions and organisations. International organisations first, then by countries (62), A-Z. Symbols indicate type of camp, financial assistance available, etc. Location index. Entries in English, French or Spanish; introduction trilingual.

Associations
37:061

UNITED NATIONS EDUCATIONAL, SCIEN-TIFIC AND CULTURAL ORGANIZATION. **An international directory of education associations.** Paris, Unesco, 1959. 91p. (Educational studies and documents, no. 34).

Contains information on 1,245 educational associations in 49 member-states of Unesco. "An education association is understood as a national or regional body of persons who work together solely in the field of formal or organized school education" (*Introduction*).

Official Publications
37:087.7

UNITED NATIONS EDUCATIONAL, SCIEN-TIFIC AND CULTURAL ORGANIZATION. **Sources of educational publications of an official nature.** *Education abstracts,* v. 8, no. 10, December 1956. 20p.

154 items, with brief annotations. 'International sources', 'Regional sources', then countries A-Z. For United Kingdom, for example, three sources are given: *Government publications.* Monthly list (H.M.S.O.), *B.N.B.,* and G. A. Baron's *Bibliographical guide;* for British territories, the Colonial Office *Monthly list,* Colonial reports; *Overseas education* (1929-. Quarterly); *Community development bulletin* (1949-. Quarterly); and *British book news.*

Tropical Areas
37 (213):016

LONDON. UNIVERSITY. INSTITUTE OF EDUCATION. **Catalogue of the Collection of education in tropical areas.** Boston, Mass., G. K. Hall, 1963. 3v. $140.

32,600 cards, photolithographically reduced, covering 7,000 books and 11,000 pamphlets. Arranged in one A-Z sequence of authors, subjects, localities and anonymous titles. Emphasis is on present and former British colonies, particularly in Africa. Includes allied fields such as anthropology, sociology, ethnology, religion, geography and history.

International
37 (4/9)

UNITED NATIONS EDUCATIONAL, SCIEN-TIFIC AND CULTURAL ORGANIZATION. **Unesco statistical yearbook,** 1963-. Paris, Unesco, 1964-. Annual. (3rd issue, 1965. 1966. 25s.).

The 1965 *Yearbook* (612p.) has 50 tables, covering 134 countries and areas. Subjects: population; education; libraries and museums; non-periodical publications; newspapers and other publications; paper consumption; film and cinema; radio broadcasting; television. The tables on education (p. 85-395) embrace educational institutions, public and private, for 1950, 1955, 1960, 1963 and 1964. 20 tables concern estimated enrolment, education at various levels and public expenditure. No statistics on special, adult and other education not classified by levels, but it is hoped to include these in later editions.

Supersedes the biennial *Basic facts and figures* (Unesco, 1952-62).

37 (4/9)

UNITED NATIONS EDUCATIONAL, SCIENTI-FIC AND CULTURAL ORGANIZATION. **World survey of education.** Paris, Unesco, 1955-66. 4v. £29 15s. 6d.

v. 1: *Handbook of educational organization and statistics.* 1955. 943p. 94s. 6d.
v. 2: *Primary education.* 1959. 1387p. 140s. (*See at 372 (4/9).*)
v. 3: *Secondary education.* 1962. 1482, xxiii p. 171s. (*See at 373 (4/9).*)
v. 4: *Higher education.* 1966. 1433, xxvii p. 190s. (*See at 378 (4/9).*)

V. 1 supersedes *World handbook of educational organization and statistics, 1952,* and has data on the educational systems of nearly 200 areas, arranged A-Z. Each country entry aims to include a descriptive text, statistics, a diagram of the school structure, a bibliography and a short glossary. The first of the three introductory chapters includes a table of illiteracy percentages. Cumulated glossary; general index. Bulky unbound volumes.

Great Britain
37 (410) (083.4)

GREAT BRITAIN. DEPARTMENT OF EDU-CATION AND SCIENCE. **Statistics of education** . . . Annual. (1965. 3 pts. 1966-67. 84s.)

Pt. **1** (1965) has 50 tables and includes 'A guide to sources of United Kingdom education statistics'. 3 main sections: 1. Education beyond compulsory school age—2. Schools—3. Finance. Part **2** has 89 tables, and charts. 7 main sections: 1. Population and numbers in school—2. Further education—3. Teachers—4. Award—5. School health service—6. School meals and milk.—8. Educational building. Part **3**, with 60 tables, has 6 main sections: 1. General Certificate of Education examinations—2. Certificate of Secondary Education examinations—3. School leavers during the academic year 1964-65—4. G.C.E. Advanced level results of students in further education—5. Flow of students with G.C.E. qualifications—6. Universities.

37 (410):087.7

ARGLES, M., and **VAUGHAN, J. E. British government publications concerning education:** an introductory guide. [2nd ed.]. Liverpool, Univ. of Liverpool, Institute of Education, 1966. 24p. 4s.

First published 1963.
A running commentary. A. Introduction—B. United Kingdom departments, committees, etc. which produce documents relating to education —C. Official literature of education (p. 7-22; England, Wales, Scotland, Northern Ireland, Isle of Man)—D. Appendix: Some important reports with their official designations. Lists series. No index.

37 (410):087.7

LIBRARIANS OF INSTITUTES OF EDUCATION. Union list of government publications relating to education (up to and including 1918). Leicester, Univ. of Leicester Institute of Education, 1959. 47p. Mimeographed.

The holdings of 14 libraries (excluding the University of London Institute of Education, whose holdings are to be listed separately). Sections: British government publications (p. 1-34: 'Bills and Acts of Parliament'; 'Command papers, Sessional papers, etc.'; 'Serial publications and miscellaneous non-parliamentary publications': (a) England, (b) Ireland, (c) Scotland, (d) Wales).—Foreign government publications (p. 34-35). Subject and author indexes. Items are stated in detail; adequate cross-references.

37 (410) (091)

HIGSON, C. W. J., *ed.* **Sources for the history of education:** a list of material (including school books) contained in the libraries of the Institutes and Schools of Education, together with works from the libraries of the Universities of Nottingham and Reading. London, Library Association, 1967. x, 196p. 96s. (72s. to members).

An unannotated list of 5,179 books on education (including textbooks and children's books) published up to 1870, and government publications up to 1918. Five sections, by periods and types. Locations in 17 libraries. Subject index; author index to government publications. The review in the *Times literary supplement* (no. 3,417, 17th August 1967, p. 747) notes that the collections concerned have been built up mainly since the war and could not claim to be exhaus-

tive. Manuscript material also needs to be recorded. Author is librarian of Univ. of Leicester School of Education.

37 (410) (092)

CHRISTOPHERS, A. An index to nineteenth-century British educational biography. London, Univ. of London, Institute of Education, 1965. xii, 88p. (Education libraries bulletin. Supplement 10). 20s.

Sections: 1. Collected biography (19 items)—2. Individual biography (450 numbered items, under biographees, A-Z). Subject index. Dates and very brief notes on careers of biographies are given in section 2. Includes many analyticals (*e.g.,* references to entries in *D.N.B.*). Helps to fill a gap. No annotations.

Scotland

37 (411)

GREAT BRITAIN. SCOTTISH EDUCATION DEPARTMENT. Education in Scotland in . . . : a report of the Secretary of State for Scotland. Edinburgh, H.M. Stationery Office, 1948-. Annual. (1965. Cmnd. 2914. 1966. 10s. 6d.).

Prior to 1947 was entitled *Education in Scotland: Report of the Committee of Council.* No full reports appeared for 1939-46.
Scottish counterpart of the Minister's report for England and Wales (*q.v.*). The 1965 report has 12 chapters and 33 statistical tables. Appendices include a list of statutory instruments and other papers.
The Scottish Education Department produces an annual *Educational statistics* (1966 v., published 1967. 16s. 6d.).

England & Wales

37 (42):016

GREAT BRITAIN. H.M. STATIONERY OFFICE. Government publications. Sectional list no. 2: **Department of Education and Science.** Revised to 31st December, 1965. London, H.M.S.O., 1966. 24p. *Gratis.*

Sections relating to education (p. 1-20): General—Primary and secondary education—Juvenile delinquency—Juvenile employment—Road safety — Further education — Teachers' pensions—Teacher training and supply—Scholarships and awards—Handicapped pupils and school health service—Milk and meals—Physical education — Wales — Finance — Pamphlets — Building bulletins—Film strips with lecture notes.

37 (42) (047)

GREAT BRITAIN. DEPARTMENT OF EDUCATION AND SCIENCE. Education in . . . ; being a report of the Department of Education and Science. London, H.M. Stationery Office, 1939-46; then Ministry of Education (1947-63).

Prior to 1928 was entitled *Report of the Board of Education for the year* . . . No issue for 1939-46; then Ministry of Education (1947-63).
The 1965 report has two parts: 1. A general survey—2. The year's events (sections: 1. The schools (England and Wales)—2. Further education (England and Wales)—3. The universities

(Great Britain)—4. Wales and Monmouthshire—5. Finance. 22 tables. Appendices (A-J) include list of publications. The 1950 report included an history survey for 1900-50.

37 (42) (091)

LOWNDES, G. A. N. The silent social revolution: an account of the expansion of public education in England and Wales, 1895-1935. London, Oxford Univ. Press, 1937. xii, 274p.

A standard work, dealing mainly with the development of elementary and secondary education during the period covered, but with a chapter on technical and further education. Extensive chapter bibliographies.

The most comprehensive history of elementary education is C. Birchenough's *History of elementary education in England and Wales, from 1800 to the present day* (3rd ed. London, Univ. Tutorial Press, 1938. xx, 572p.).

W. Boyd's *The history of Western education* (8th ed. London, Black, 1966. xii, 489p. 30s.) is a standard short history, ranging from ancient Greek education to that of the 20th century.

England

37 (420):016

BARON, G. A bibliographical guide to the English educational system. 3rd ed. London, Univ. of London, Athlone Press, 1965. 124p. 15s.

First published 1951.
19 chapters: 1. Reference books and lists—2. Periodicals—3. General—4. Primary education—5. Secondary education—6. Higher and further education—7. Youth clubs, youth centres and the youth service . . . 15. Approved schools—16. Teacher training institutions—17. The teaching profession—18. The universities—19. Miscellaneous. Annotated entries for chapters 1-2; otherwise in narrative form, with critical comments. Nearly 800 items. Index of authors, p. 99-121; no subject index. The author is Reader in Educational Administration, University of London Institute of Education.

37 (420) (091)

ARMYTAGE, W. H. G. Four hundred years of English education. Cambridge, Univ. Press, 1964. viii, 353p. 17s. 6d.; 32s. 6d.

Covers the period 1563-1963 in 12 chapters. Chapter notes, p. 270-324; refers to general sources used, p. vii-viii. Analytical index. The author is Professor of Education, Univ. of Sheffield.

See also: "Some books on the history of education in England", by W. E. Tate, in Univ. of London Institute of Education. *Education libraries bulletin*, no. 23, Summer 1965, p. 1-6.

Germany

37 (43):016

LIBRARIANS OF INSTITUTES AND SCHOOLS OF EDUCATION. Education in Germany: a union list of stock in Institute of Education libraries. Compiled by Miss J. V. Best. Rev. ed.

Southampton, Institute of Education, Univ. of Southampton, 1963. iii, 43p. Mimeographed. 2s. 6d.

France

37 (44):016

————Education in France: a union list of stock in Institute of Education libraries. Edited by J. V. Marder. Southampton, Institute of Education, Univ. of Southampton, 1965. iv, 59p. 3s.

U.S.S.R.

37 (47):016

APANASEWICZ, N., and ROSEN, S. M., *comp.* **Soviet education:** a bibliography of English-language materials. Washington, Department of Health, Education & Welfare, Office of Education, 1964. 42p. 20c.

An annotated bibliography of reference material published since the late 1950's, U.S. authors predominating; translations included. 281 titles in author index; also a classified sequence (78 subject categories).

The same two compilers have produced *Eastern European education: a bibliography of English-language materials* (Washington, U.S. Government Printing Office, 1966. 35p.), also for the Department of Health, Education & Welfare, Office of Education.

Japan

37 (52):016

KOKUSAI BUNKA SHINKOKAI. K.B.S. bibliography of standard reference books for Japanese studies, with descriptive notes. Vol. 5(B): Education. Tokyo, Univ. of Tokyo Press, 1966. xii, 186p. 24s.

Africa

37 (6).016

COUCH, M., *comp.* **Education in Africa: a select bibliography.** London, Univ. of London, Institute of Education, 1962-65. 2v. (*Education libraries bulletin.* Supplements 5, 9). 33s. 6d.

pt. 1. *British and former British territories in Africa.* 1962. x, 121p. 12s. 6d.
pt. 2. *French speaking territories (former French and Belgian colonies); Portuguese and Spanish territories; Ethiopia and Eritrea; Liberia; and general African references, 1962-1964.* 1965. xii, 116p. 21s.

Pt. 1 (*c.* 1,300 entries) excludes the Republic of South Africa. It is selected from the catalogue of the Library of the Department of Education in Tropical Areas of the Univ. of London, Institute of Education, and contains material listed to the end of 1961. General; then countries A-Z, with sub-divisions (*e.g.*, Nyasaland: General — Primary — Secondary — Higher — Adult — Women and girls) and final chronological order. Pt. 2 is similarly arranged; items starred were not available for checking by the compiler. Each pt. has a list of more than 200 periodicals cited.

The same Institute of Education's *African education abstracts* (January 1966-. No. 1-. 6 p.a.) covers teacher training, teaching media, higher education, research, science, mathematics, language, literature, history, art, adult education and general topics. The May 1967 (no. 3) issue (10 foolscap papers) has a 2-p. 'Information section'; 'Publications' comprises 54 items, with brief abstracts.

U.S.A.

37 (73) (058.7):016
KLEIN, B., *ed.* **Guide to American educational directories:** a guide to the major educational directories of the United States. New York, London, etc., McGraw-Hill, 1965. xii, [1], 337p. $22.50.

Arranged under subjects A-Z, from 'Advertising and public relations' to 'Zoology'. 'Bibliographies', p. 26-53; 'Biographies', p. 53-57. Entry under titles (e.g., *Guide to reference books*—but no mention of Winchell). States prices or if gratis. About 1,500 annotated entries; index of titles.

Latin America

37 (8=6) (058)
PAN AMERICAN UNION. Department of Educational Affairs. **Yearbook of educational, scientific and cultural development in Latin America.** Washington, P.A.U., 1966. 201p.

Educational Research

37.001.5:016
FOSKETT, D. J. How to find out: educational research. Oxford, Pergamon Press, 1965. viii, 132p. facsims. 15s.

Intended as "an explanation of the various types of publication and how to use them" and as complementary to Miss S. K. Kimmance's *Guide to the literature of education (Preface).* 3 of the 9 chapters deal with specific fields of research,—philosophy and sociology of education; administration; comparative education; history of education; psychology of education; teaching methods. References, p. 111-3; name and subject indexes; specimen pages from *British education index, Child development abstracts,* etc. A stimulating approach.

Also relevant: R. G. Astbury's "Educational research in the United Kingdom: agencies, guides" (*Library world,* v. 66, no. 783, September 1965, p. 76) and "Educational research in the United Kingdom: periodical literature" (*Library world,* v. 67, no. 788, February 1966, p. 240-3).

37.001.5:016
SCOTTISH COUNCIL FOR RESEARCH IN EDUCATION. Aids to educational research; comprising bibliographies and plan of research. Rev. ed. London, Univ. of London Press, 1954. vii, 39p.

First published 1949.
Includes bibliographies of material likely to be useful to research workers in education, including bibliographies of bibliographies, yearbooks, journals, encyclopaedias. Gives Scottish locations of periodicals.

37.001.5 (032)
HARRIS, C. W., and **LIBA, M. R.,** *ed.* **Encyclopedia of educational research:** a project of the American Education Research Association, a Department of the National Education Association. 3rd ed. New York, Macmillan, 1960. xlvii, 1564p. $25; 168s.

First published as *Ten years of educational research, 1918-27* (1928); 2nd ed. 1950.
Like its predecessor of the same title, edited by W. S. Monroe (2nd ed. 1950), the 3rd ed. provides a critical evaluation, synthesis and interpretation of reported studies in the field of education over a given period. "Planned not simply as a revision of earlier editions, but as a completely rewritten volume that would attempt to put into a new perspective the findings of research" (*Preface*). Entries A-Z, under broad headings. The entry for 'Vocational education' runs to nearly 9 pages and carries 55 references to material up to 1958. Does not supersede earlier eds. Some U.S. slant.
Can be kept up to date by the *Review of educational research* (1931-. 5 p.a.) (*q.v.*).

37.001.5 (047.1)
Review of educational research, 1931-. Washington, American Educational Research Association, 1931-. 5 p.a.

Each issue devoted to one of eleven particular subjects, *e.g.,* School plant and equipment, Teacher personnel, and in general a given subject is reviewed every 3 years. Each issue is divided into chapters that survey research during the period covered and conclude with a comprehensive bibliography. Updates Harris and Liba's *Encyclopedia of educational research* (q.v.).

37.001.5 (058)
NATIONAL FEDERATION FOR EDUCATIONAL RESEARCH IN ENGLAND AND WALES. Current researches in education and educational psychology . . . Slough, Bucks., the Federation. Biennial. (1961-63. 1965. 30s.).

Preceded by A. M. Blackwell's *A list of researches in education and educational psychology presented for higher degrees in the universities of the United Kingdom, Northern Ireland, and the Irish Republic, from 1918 to 1948* (1950); *A second list . . . for . . . 1949, 1950 and 1951* [1952]; *List of researches . . . [for] . . . 1952 and 1953* (1954); *List of researches . . . [for] . . . 1954 and 1955* (1956); and *List of researches . . . [for] . . . 1956 and 1957* (1958).
The 1961-63 v. records 940 numbered items under topics A-Z. Details under each entry: title of research; brief description; date of commencement; estimated duration; stage of progress (A-E); name and address for correspondence; research submitted for (degree); name and address of adviser/supervisor. Author index.

37.001.5 (058)
Pædagogica europæa: the European yearbook of educational research. Amsterdam, Elsevier, 1965-. v. 1-. (v. 1. 75s.).

Published with the support of the Council for Cultural Co-operation of the Council of Europe. V. 1 has 16 contributors; 13 original contributions (7 in English, 4 in French, 2 in German), based on empirical research (*e.g.*, "Educational psychology in the Soviet Union", p. 138-53, with 19 references and a resumé). The articles are followed by international and national reports. Intended for all who are involved in responsibility for the practice of education,—educators and administrators, scholars and research workers.

Theory
37.01

HILGARD, E. R. Theories of learning. New York, Appleton-Century-Crofts, 1948. vi, 400p. illus.

A scholarly introduction to the major current theories of learning. Extensive bibliography ('References and author index', p. 363-96).

A short history of educational ideas, by S. J. Curtis and M. E. A. Boultwood (4th ed. London, Univ. Tutorial Press, 1965. xii, 639p.) has 21 chapters, each with 'Suggestions for further reading'. Chapter 17: 'John Dewey (1859-1952)'. Footnote references; index of names and titles mentioned in text.

37.015 (038)=40
LAFON, R., *and others*. Vocabulaire de psychopédagogie et de psychiatrie de l'enfant. Paris, Presses Universitaires de France, 1964. xx, 604p. 48F.

See entry at 159.922.7 (038)=40.

Associations
371:061

UNITED NATIONS EDUCATIONAL, SCIENTIFIC AND CULTURAL ORGANIZATION. Teachers' associations . . . Paris, Unesco, 1961. 127p. (International directories of education, 1).

A directory of 1274 organisations (605 treated fully and 665, summarily) in 127 countries and territories. Based on replies to a questionnaire put out in 1959. Subject index. In English, French and Spanish.

Educational Systems
371 (4/9)
SASNETT, M. T. Educational systems of the world: interpretations for use in the evaluation of foreign credentials. [Los Angeles], Univ. of Southern California Press, 1952. 838p.

An outline of the educational systems of *c.* 80 countries at all levels from kindergarten to higher education, illustrated by block diagrams. Describes old and new systems where changes have taken place within previous 20 years or so. A bibliography is provided on each country.

371 (4)
COUNCIL FOR CULTURAL CO-OPERATION OF THE COUNCIL OF EUROPE. Education in Europe. Section 2. General and technical education. No. 5. School systems: a guide. Strasbourg, Council of Europe, 1965. 356p. illus., tables, diagrs. 17s. 6d.

A survey of school systems in 20 countries (United Kingdom treated as a single unit), A-Z. The section on the Netherlands (p. 207-27) gives a description of the school system, supported by diagrams, a list of terms, and statistics.

371 (410)
COLLEGE OF PRECEPTORS, London. Teachers' guide, 1965-66. London, College of Preceptors, 1965. viii, 815p. 32s. 6d.

Treats topics in A-Z order (*e.g.*, Administration—Audio-visual education—Books (p. 195-259), including educational magazines—Educational organisations—Educational organisations: who's who—Examining bodies—Higher education (p. 315-568)—Programmed learning . . . Teaching aids (p. 691-723)—Teaching overseas—Youth employment. Index; list of advertisers.

371 (420)
ASSOCIATION OF TEACHERS IN TRAINING COLLEGES AND DEPARTMENTS OF EDUCATION. Handbook on training for teaching. 4th ed. London, the Association and Methuen, 1964. xxi, 542p. maps.

First published 1954.
A guide for new entrants to the teaching profession. Aims to give in succinct form the fullest possible information about training for teaching in England and Wales. Main sections: Central Register and Clearing House, Ltd.—Area training organizations and their constituent colleges and departments (p. 4-481)—Specialist institutions — Proposed new training colleges. Appendices (lists of courses, qualifications, etc.); index.

371 (6)
SASNETT, M. T., and SEPMEYER, I. Educational systems of Africa: interpretations for use in the evaluation of academic credentials. Berkeley, Univ. of California Press, [1967]. xliv, 1550p. maps.

Report of a project sponsored by the Univ. of California, Los Angeles. Bibliography, p. 1510-50.

Vocational Guidance
371.048
See 331.7.

Methods of Instruction
371.3
DODD, W. E., and ENGLAND, A. Programmed instruction & teaching machines: an annotated bibliography. 2nd ed. Hanley, Stoke-on-Trent, Central Library, 167p. Mimeographed. 10s.

Bibliographies (general; vocational applications; language teaching; U.S. Office of Education sponsored research; list of programmes)—Abstracts and indexes—Periodicals—Information sources—Information references (p. 21-156; *c.* 2,000 items). Subject index.

371.3
GEE, R. D. Teaching machines and programmed learning: a guide to the literature and other sources of information. 2nd ed. Hatfield, Herts

County Council, Technical Library and Information Service, 1965. 128p. 15s.

First published 1963.
Contains more than 1,000 concisely annotated references to literature on teaching machines, programming and related aspects. Bibliography of programmed texts, and directories of manufacturers, suppliers of programmes, consultants, research and other organisations, films and periodicals. Index of authors, organisations and machines.

Audio-visual Aids

371.67
EDUCATIONAL FOUNDATION FOR VISUAL AIDS. Visual aids: films and filmstrips. London, the Foundation. Biennial. 8pts. ea. 2s. 6d.; index. 1s.

Covers current films, filmstrips and 2″ × 2″ slides of interest to schools. Details include publisher, date, price, age-group and 50-100 word description. Title and subject indexes. Each pt. is biennial, so that 4 pts. appear each year. Supplements appear in the January issue of *Visual education.*
The Educational Foundation for Visual Aids' *Educational films, 1946-66* (London, the Foundation, 1966. x, 130p. illus. unpriced) was produced in co-operation with N.C.A.V.A.E.

371.67
EDUCATIONAL MEDIA COUNCIL. The educational media index. New York, McGraw-Hill, 1964. 14v.

A comprehensive directory of non-book instructional material, each volume of which deals with a specific subject (*e.g.,* v. 10, Mathematics). Total coverage is *c.* 50,000 items. International in scope.
Supersedes *Educational film guide* (New York, H. W. Wilson, 1936-62. Annual, with irregular supplements), initially (1936-45) *Educational film catalog.* This listed 16-mm. films for use in schools, libraries, adult groups, etc.; arranged in A-Z and classified sequences, with annotations.

371.67
NATIONAL COMMITTEE FOR AUDIO-VISUAL AIDS IN EDUCATION. Survey of British research in audio-visual aids. London, the National Committee, 1965. 75p. (Experimental Development Unit report, no. 3). 15s.

371.67
UNITED NATIONS EDUCATIONAL, SCIENTIFIC AND CULTURAL ORGANIZATION. World film directory: agencies concerned with educational, scientific and educational films. Paris, Unesco, 1962. 66p.

Lists agencies in 133 countries and territories; arranged by regions.

———**Selected list of catalogues for short films and filmstrips.** Paris, Unesco, 1965. (Reports and papers on mass communication, no. 44).

Annotated list in 3 parts: 1. International and national catalogues; 2. Sources of materials other than those in pt. 1; 3. Films and filmstrips for particular subjects (*e.g.,* psychology, mental health, art, music).

Physical Education

371.7
The Physical education year book. London, Physical Education Association of Great Britain and Northern Ireland. Annual. (1966. 15s.).

Part 1 of the 1966 v. has 4 articles on development and research, a bibliography ('Research and recent literature') of 120 references and a survey ('Physical education in Australia and India). Part 2 deals with training in physical education, with a directory of colleges. Appendices include a list of sports organisations. Index to advertisers.

Special Schools

371.9 (420)
GREAT BRITAIN. DEPARTMENT OF EDUCATION AND SCIENCE. List of special schools, boarding houses for handicapped pupils, and institutions for further education and training of disabled persons in England and Wales. London, H.M. Stationery Office. Irregular. (List 42). (1963 ed. 4s. 6d.).

Title varies. Last issued 1963.
Includes day schools as well as boarding schools. Embraces the whole range of special schools, including hospitals. Arranged by type of school, then by county.

Primary Education

372 (4/9)
UNITED NATIONS EDUCATIONAL, SCIENTIFIC AND CULTURAL ORGANIZATION. World survey of education. v. 2. **Primary education.** Paris, Unesco, 1959. 1387p. 140s.

V. 2 has introductory chapters of a general nature (1. World survey of education, 1950-54; 3. The progress of primary education since 1930). The bulk (p. 61-1356) deals with individual countries, arranged A-Z under continent, etc. Select bibliography of 139 journals in primary education (p. 1362-6) and a glossary of terms. Analytical index.

Secondary Education

373 (4/9)
UNITED NATIONS EDUCATIONAL, SCIENTIFIC AND CULTURAL ORGANIZATION. World survey of education. v. 3. **Secondary education.** Paris, Unesco, 1961. 1482, xxiii p. 157s.

Deals with all types of education for young people between 12 and 18. Chapter 1: World survey of education, 1953-57; chapter 8: Secondary education periodicals (p. 149-59). Country surveys (A-Z, p. 161-1478; *c.* 200 countries and territories); a bibliography is usually appended (*e.g.,* U.S.A., p. 1377-8). Final section: 'Arab refugees from Palestine' (p. 1478-82). Index on blue-tinted paper.

373.5 (410)

The Education authorities directory and annual, 1909-. London, School Government Publishing Co., 1909-. Annual. (1966. 40s.).

A directory of education committees (including Scotland), secondary grammar schools, secondary modern schools, polytechnics, the universities, special schools and approved schools.

373.5 (410)

Education committees year book, 1903-. Published by "Education". London, Councils and Education Press, 1903-. Annual. (1966-67 ed. 1966. 42s.).

Similar in scope to *Education authorities directory,* but lists names of members of education committees (county council and county borough) and gives names, addresses and heads of all types of secondary schools. The 1966-67 ed. has a list of educational journals (p. 1019-27) and publishers.

373.5 (410)

The Girls' school year book: public schools. The official book of reference of the Association of Head Mistresses, 1906-. London, Black, 1906-. v. 1-. Annual. (1966. 21s.).

The counterpart to *Public and preparatory schools year book,* with similar information. Criterion for inclusion is possession of a governing body. Arranged by locality A-Z. Details include names of staff. Part 4: Careers (1966 ed., p. 499-675).

373.5 (410)

The Independent Schools Association year book. London, Black, 1957-. Annual. (1967. 25s.).

Details of the 'private' schools (*c.* 525) belonging to the Independent Schools Association. The 1966 ed. devotes p. 221-387 to careers, with particular attention to vocational training for girls. Index.

373.5 (410)

Paton's List of schools and tutors: an aid to parents in the selection of schools. London, Paton, 1898-. illus. Annual. (1966. 10s.).

Main divisions: Preparatory schools for boys; Boys' schools; Co-educational schools; Preparatory schools for girls; Girls' schools. Also lists of schools providing vocational courses, *e.g.,* nursing, horticulture. Information given usually includes a photograph of the school, name of principal, fees and a short description of scope and activities. Lists of scholarships and tutors and information about the professions are included. Alphabetical index of schools and principals. The lists of schools are not comprehensive.

373.5 (410)

Public and preparatory schools year book. The official book of reference for the Headmasters' Conference and of the Incorporated Association of Preparatory Schools, 1889-. London, Black, 1889-. Annual. (1967 ed. 30s.).

Pt. 1: A list of schools represented on the Headmasters' Conference arranged alphabetically by towns, with comprehensive information on each (*e.g.,* Governing bodies, names of staff (with qualifications), admission, fees, etc.). Pt. 4 gives similar information for preparatory schools, but arranged by county. Other sections give lists of tutors, university entrance requirements, careers information. Appendix of 'Book notes' (on educational books of the year).

373.5 (410)

Schools . . . : a directory of schools in Great Britain and Northern Ireland, arranged in order of their counties and towns; including statistical information regarding recognised public schools for boys, sections for tutors and career training courses and schools on the continent of Europe. London, Truman & Knightley, 1924-. v. 1-. illus. Annual. (44th ed. 1967 v. 15s.).

Geographical directory of schools in Great Britain—Boys' public schools (by columns)—Displayed announcements: Educational section (p. 351-840 in the 1967 v.; illustrations); Careers and vocational training section (p. 847-1019). Index to principals' names; index to displayed announcements.

373.5 (410)

The Schools of England, Wales, Scotland and Ireland: a book of reference for parents, principals and students, with scholarships, careers, and a continental section, and a directory of schools and colleges. Cheltenham, Burrow's Scholastic Bureau. Annual. (56th ed. 1967. 15s.).

Pt. 2: School announcements (arranged A-Z under counties; illustrations). Pt. 3: Special training for careers. Schools in France and Switzerland. Schools' equipment. Pt. 4: Directory of schools and colleges. Indexes.

373.5 (416)

NORTHERN IRELAND. MINISTRY OF EDUCATION. Local education authorities grant-aided schools and institutions of further education. Belfast, H.M. Stationery Office. Biennial.

373.5 (417)

EIRE. DEPARTMENT OF EDUCATION. List of national schools, arranged in alphabetical order. Dublin, Stationery Office.

Separate alphabetical list for each county.

373.5 (42)

GREAT BRITAIN. DEPARTMENT OF EDUCATION AND SCIENCE. List of independent schools in England and Wales recognised as efficient under Rule 16. London, H.M. Stationery Office, 1965. Irregular. (List 70). 8s.

Earlier editions as *List of primary and secondary schools in England and Wales . . .*
Lists all independent primary and secondary schools that applied for and received recognition as efficient. Arranged by counties; for each school gives names of responsible body, date from which recognised, head teacher, fees, number of pupils.

373.5 (42)
WALLIS, P. J. Histories of old schools: a revised list for England and Wales. Newcastle upon Tyne, Univ. of Newcastle upon Tyne, Dept. of Education, 1966. 98p. 10s.

A corrected and augmented reprint of a preliminary list in *British journal of educational studies* (November 1965; May & November 1966).
"Intended to provide scholars and students with a basic bibliography of the history of schools which existed in England and Wales before 1700; the references are selected, but are believed to be the best accounts available" (*Foreword*). About 2,000 entries, under English counties (A-Z); Wales and Monmouthshire (*e.g.,* Eton: 6 entries, including one bibliography). Cites more inclusive works (*e.g.,* county histories). Index of authors only. Good use of bold and italic.

Adult Education

374:061
UNITED NATIONS EDUCATIONAL, SCIENTIFIC AND CULTURAL ORGANIZATION. Adult education, 1966. Paris, Unesco, 1965. 156p. (International directories of education). 15s.

As *International directory of adult education* (1952).
Directory information (name and address; name of director; number of staff; objects; activities; publications) on 43 international organisations, and 900 agencies (183 official) in 86 countries (A-Z, p. 21-142). Subject index.

374 (410):016
KELLY, T., *ed.* **A select bibliography of adult education in Great Britain,** including works published to the end of the year 1961. 2nd ed. London, National Institute of Adult Education for Universities Council for Adult Education, 1962. xii, 126p. 42s.

First published 1952. The 1st ed. was supplemented by annual lists.
The 2nd ed. has been expanded to include not only the major items from the annual supplements "but also a great deal of other new material" (*Preface*). 1,195 items, usually annotated; 39 contributors. Four sections: 1. General (Yearbooks and dictionaries, encyclopaedias, periodicals, etc.)—2. The general and educational background—3. History and organisation of adult education—4. Theory and method. Author and subject indexes. The editor is Director of Extra-mural Studies in the University of Liverpool.

374 (410) (058.7)
NATIONAL INSTITUTE OF ADULT EDUCATION. Adult education . . . London, the Institute, 1952-. Annual. (1966. 10s.).

First published 1952-56 as *Adult education in the United Kingdom.*
Gives names, addresses and in many cases descriptions of agencies for adult education, plus titles of periodicals published (if any). Bibliography as insert.

Holiday Courses

374.8 (058.7)
UNITED NATIONS EDUCATIONAL, SCIENTIFIC AND CULTURAL ORGANIZATION. Study abroad: international guide; fellowships, scholarships, educational exchange. Paris, Unesco, 1948-. Annual. (v. 16. 1967. 20s.).

V. 16: information on more than 170,000 individual opportunities for subsidised study and educational travel abroad during 1967-68. Sections: Fields of study—International fellowship and scholarship programmes—Countries (A-Z by French names, p. 105-507)—Students abroad: a statistical analysis. Country and organisational index. Set subject - classification under countries (*e.g.,* 3. Science and technology; 5. Arts and literature). Trilingual: English, French, Spanish.

V. 18: 1966 of Unesco's *Vacations abroad: courses, study tours, work camps* appeared in 1966 (156p. 10s.).

P. Latham's *Holiday courses in Europe* (London, Blackie, 1964. 307p. 25s.) has 16 chapters, one per country (including 16. 'United Kingdom and Eire'). Appendix: Student travel, hotels, restaurants.

Higher Education

378:016
NATIONAL FOUNDATION FOR EDUCATIONAL RESEARCH IN ENGLAND AND WALES. Universities and university education: a select bibliography, compiled by J. P. Powell. Slough, Bucks, the National Foundation, 1966. viii, 51p. 15s.

1189 numbered items (including some duplicates) in 15 main classes: General—American universities—British universities—University history: general—History: institutions—Aims and functions — Curriculum — Teaching methods — Teaching aids—Teaching methods: special fields — Examinations — Libraries — Academic profession—Students—Study methods. Helpful notes and references under classes and their divisions. About 120 journals cited. Author index.

378 (038)
INTERNATIONAL FEDERATION OF UNIVERSITY WOMEN. Lexique international des termes universitaires. [Paris], Fédération Internationale des Femmes Diplômées des Universités, 1939. xvii, 755p.

Cover-title: "International glossary of academic terms."
Arrangement is alphabetical by country, 31 countries being covered; explanations of terms are given in French and English. Index of terms.

Glossaries of educational terms are also given in the Unesco *World survey of education* (see at 37 (02)) and in the *Dictionary of education,* edited by C. V. Good (see at 37 (032)).

378 (4/9)
UNITED NATIONS EDUCATIONAL, SCIENTIFIC AND CULTURAL ORGANIZATION. World survey of education. 4. Higher education. Paris, Unesco, 1966. 1433, xxvii p. 165s.

Consists of 200 national and international studies; dated received before the end of June 1964. Chapter 1: 'World survey of education, 1957 to 1961' (p. 15-42); 7: 'Selected bibliography on higher education' (p. 123-32). Country surveys are in A-Z order, with systematically arranged data (e.g., Portugal (p. 944-57): The educational system—The development of higher education—Glossary—Chart—University institutions—Institutions providing higher professional and technical training—Teacher training institutions—Trends and problems—Statutes (including reference data). 9 tables). Final section: 'Arab refugees from Palestine'. General index on blue-tinted paper.

378.001.5

KENDALL, M. Research into higher education: a bibliography. [2nd ed.] London, Univ. of London, Research Unit for Student Problems, 1964. 45p.

First published 1961 as *Bibliography of operational research into university and student problems.* Supplement, 1962.
394 concisely annotated entries in 10 sections (*e.g.,* 3. Social and economic background of students—4. Student life . . . 10. Follow-up studies of former students). Author index.

378.001.5

Research into higher education. Abstracts. London, Society for Research into Higher Education, Ltd., 1967-. v. 1, no. 1-. Quarterly.

Based on a regular survey of nearly 200 journals. "Intended for use by administrators, librarians, research workers, teachers and all who are interested in higher education" (*Preface*). V. 1, nos. 1-2: 114 signed abstracts in 9 sections: A. General, education and research—B. Architecture, buildings and equipment—C. Administration and organisation—D. The academic profession; staff—E. Students' background and characteristics—F. Selection and performance of students; careers—G. Teaching and learning situation; training—H. Curriculum—I. Types of student and instructor. Abstracts have rubric: aim/hypothesis; sample; instrument; results/findings.

378.001.5

SOCIETY FOR RESEARCH INTO HIGHER EDUCATION. Register of research projects in higher education. London, the Society, [1966]-. Loose-leaf.

Aims to be complete for projects in the U.K. and includes a few projects from abroad by workers who are members of the Society. Entries are in no particular order; no index.
Preceded by the Society's *List of members' research in progress as at December 1964* (18p. Mimeographed).

Universities

378.4 (4/9)

CHAMBERS, M. M., ed. Universities of the world outside U.S.A. Washington, American Council on Education, 1950. xvii, 924p.

Comparable to the American Council on Education's *American universities and colleges,* at 378.4 (73). Covers 2,000 institutions of higher education in over 70 countries outside U.S.A. Describes organization and operation of each institution, with statistics of teaching staff and student numbers, and the names of the chief administrative officers. A general index to institutions is provided.
Each country's section is prefaced by a handy introduction to its educational system as a whole, with a bibliography.

378.4 (4/9)

Index generalis: annuaire général des universités et des grandes écoles-académies, archives, bibliothèques, instituts scientifiques, jardins botaniques et zoologiques, musées, observatoires, sociétés savantes, 1919-39, 1952/53-1954/55. Paris, Dunod, 1920-39, 1953-55. Annual.

Title and publisher vary.
Six parts. Universities and other main teaching establishments; observatories; libraries and archives; scientific institutes and research centres; academic and learned societies; indexes. Arranged within sections A-Z by countries, except in the case of learned societies, which are arranged by subjects. Usually includes names of chief officers. *e.g.,* university professors and lecturers, chief librarians, chief officers of learned societies. Comprehensive name index of 105,000 entries and an index of places. Valuable for historical purposes.
Index generalis. France, 1958 (1959)—see at 378.4 (44).

378.4 (4/9)

INTERNATIONAL ASSOCIATION OF UNIVERSITIES. International handbook of universities and other institutions of higher education. 3rd ed., edited by H. M. R. Keyes. Paris, the International Association, 1965. 1034p. $13.50.

First published 1959.
Complementary to the *Commonwealth universities year-book* and *American universities and colleges* (qq.v.), in that it gives systematic information on some 140 universities in 100 countries outside the British Commonwealth and U.S.A. Arranged by countries A-Z. Compared with *World of learning,* it does not list names of professors and staff, but it has more descriptive information on admission requirements, degrees and diplomas. Brief entries for technical colleges and other professional schools. Index only of names of universities.

378.4 (4/9)

INTERNATION ASSOCIATION OF UNIVERSITIES. Liste mondiale 1965. [7. éd.] Paris, the International Association, 1965-. xvii, 384p.

First published 1952.
Notes more than 4,000 institutions of higher education in 132 countries and territories. Part 1, Institutions and national organisations (p. 1-316); part 2, International and regional organisations. Details: name, address, date of founding, name of general secretary, faculties. Gives addresses only of French écoles supérieures. Section on university vacations; appendix on the International Association. French and English texts.

Minerva. Jahrbuch der gelehrten Welt. Abteilung Universitäten und Fachhochschulen. 35. Jahrgang. Berlin, de Gruyter, 1966-. v. 1-.

378.4 (4/9)

First published in 1891 (covering 1891/92); suspended during the two World Wars. 33rd issue (1938) covered over Abt. 2, *Universitäten und Fachhochschulen*, omitting Abt. 1, *Forschungsinstitute* . . . 34th issue (1952-56), similarly.
V. 1 of the 35th issue (xxxiv, 1669p.), as in the 34th issue, deals with European institutions of higher learning, arranged under towns, by countries, A-Z. Data cover organisation, name of chancellor, vice-chancellor, etc., and of heads of faculties, degrees awarded and publications. A feature is the extensive name index (p. 1472-1669), which lists *c.* 40,000 names of academic staffs.
V. 2 will cover non-European countries.

The scientific and academic world, edited by F. E. Nord and M. K. Malhotra (Essen, Stifterverband für die Deutsche Wissenschaft, 1962. 243p.) is an English translation of *Weltverbundenheit der Wissenschaft* (1959). It covers more than 20 countries, including China and the U.S.S.R., and notes admission qualifications and student services as well as the usual directory data on universities.

Handbooks to universities of individual countries are listed in *Commonwealth universities yearbook, 1966*, p. 2215-8. The following titles are worth adding: *Handbook for higher educational institutions in the U.S.S.R.* (Washington, U.S. Department of Commerce, Joint Publications Research Service, 1965. [iv], 391p. $7); *Japanese universities and colleges, 1965-6, with major research institutes* (2nd ed. Tokyo, Japan Overseas Advertiser Co., Ltd., 1965. 475p. illus.).

The World of learning. 1947-. London, Europa Publications, 1947-. Annual. (17th ed., 1966-67. 1967. 150s.).

378.4 (4/9)

A directory of universities, colleges, libraries, learned societies, museums, art galleries and research institutes in more than 150 countries; preceded by a section on international scientific, educational and cultural organisations. Data include names of principal officials, a list of publications and number of students. The 17th ed. has been enlarged to include a new group, technological universities. Information on the U.S.S.R. is considerably expanded. New features: statement of the chief language of instruction (where not obvious) and length of academic year. Index of *c.* 16,000 institutions. but not of persons.

Europe

378.4 (4)

RASHDALL, H. The universities of Europe in the Middle Ages. New ed., edited by F. M. Powicke and A. B. Emden. London, Oxford Univ. Press, 1936 (reprinted 1942). 3v. illus. 147s.

v. 1. *Salerno. Bologna. Paris.*
v. 2. *Italy. Spain. France. Germany. Scotland, etc.*

v. 3. *English universities. Student life.*
First published 1895.
A scholarly account, heavily footnoted. Bibliographies precede accounts of individual universities (*e.g.*, Vienna, in v. 2: 1 page of bibliography). In v. 3 Oxford University occupies p. 1-273, with a 4-page bibliography. Appendices of documents and notes (*e.g.*, 'Paper universities', v. 2, p. 325-31). General index in v. 3, p. 497-558. Folding map.

Commonwealth

378.4 (41-44)

Commonwealth universities yearbook . . . : a directory to the universities of the Commonwealth and the handbook of their association. 1914-. London, Association of Commonwealth Universities, 1914-. tables, maps. Annual. (44th ed. 1967. 140s.).

Title varies; previously *The Yearbook of universities of the Commonwealth*. Publication suspended 1941-46.
Covers Commonwealth universities and university colleges; those for Eire and South Africa appear as appendices in the 1966 v. Main sequence: countries, A-Z; then towns A-Z. Under each university: principal officers; teaching staff; administrative and other staff; affiliated colleges, etc.; general information; statistics for the latest year. For each member of staff states degrees (with university of origin) and main fellowships. 7 appendices include details of university admission requirements and a short bibliography (general and reference books; reports; bibliographies; periodicals). General index; names index (*c.* 40,000 entries); end-paper contents-list.

Great Britain

378.4 (410)

BRITISH COUNCIL and ASSOCIATION OF COMMONWEALTH UNIVERSITIES. Higher education in the United Kingdom: a handbook for students from overseas and their advisers. London, Longmans, Green, 1936-. Biennial. (1966. 10s.).

Details of courses available to overseas students and of the educational system of which they form a part. 'Directory of subjects and facilities for study' (1966, p. 53-211; on green-tinted paper); addresses (p. 250-82); 'Other sources of information' (p. 8). Index; map.

378.4 (410)

COMMITTEE OF VICE-CHANCELLORS AND PRINCIPALS OF THE UNIVERSITIES OF THE UNITED KINGDOM. A compendium of university entrance requirements for first degree courses in the United Kingdom . . . (excluding part-time and external degree courses). London, Association of Commonwealth Univs., 1963-. Annual. (1697-68. 1966. 14s. 6d.).

Course requirements are tabulated across the double page (1966 ed. p. 12-213, including single honours tables, p. 19-151). Appendices: 1. Scottish universities—2. Addresses.

A more concise, popular compendium is the National Union of Teachers' *University & college entrance: the basic facts* (8th ed. London,

N.U.T., 1966. 119p. 5s. 6d.). Apart from the main section, 'The universities' (p. 19-103), has notes on student grants, training for teaching at college and university, and technological and further education. No index.

378.4 (410)
GREAT BRITAIN. UNIVERSITY GRANTS COMMITTEE. Returns from universities and university colleges in receipt of Treasury grant during the academic year 1963-1964. London, H.M. Stationery Office, 1965. (Cmnd. 2778). 6s. 6d.

A short annual account, followed by very comprehensive statistics, of university development and activities in England, Scotland and Wales.

The Committee on Higher Education's *Higher education*: report of a committee under the chairmanship of Lord Robbins, 1961-63 (London, H.M.S.O., 1963. 7v. (Cmnd. 2154). 126s.) consists of the *Report* and 5 appendices (1. The demand for places in higher education—2. Students and their education (2v.)—3. Teachers in higher education—4. Administrative, fiscal and economic aspects of higher education—5. Higher education in other countries (10 countries; 'Principal written sources', p. 300-6).

378.4 (410)
PRIESTLEY, B., *comp.* **British qualifications:** a comprehensive guide to educational, technical, professional and academic qualifications in Britain. Edited by P. Kogan. London, Deutsch, 1966. 1120p. 42s.

Deals with secondary school and further education examinations, university degrees and diplomas, membership of professional associations as well as 'Qualifications listed by trades and professions' (p. 386 - 1083; A - Z). Under Ceramics (p. 526-8) are noted relevant institutes and associations; university degrees and diplomas; college colleges; and the City and Guilds of London Institute examination. For employment officers, personnel managers and the like.

378.4 (410)
Which university? 1966-. London, Cornmarket Press, 1965-. Annual. (1966. 15s.).

Claims to describe every degree-level course and every university-level institution in the U.K. Intended for school leavers seeking a university place. Part 1 includes an index of courses available, with a chapter on steps to take for entrance to a university. Part 2 deals with colleges of advanced technology; part 3 is a classified list of courses offered by colleges other than those in parts 1-2.

378.4 (410) (083.2)
JACOBS, P. M. Registers of the universities, colleges and schools of Great Britain and Ireland. London, Univ. of London, Athlone Press, for the Institute of Historical Research, 1966. 50p. 10s.

Reprinted from *Bulletin of the Institute of Historical Research,* v. 37, November 1964, p. 185-232.

Arranged alphabetically by universities and by colleges; locations in 6 libraries. Very brief note on arrangement of registers; analytical entries for registers found in more inclusive works (*e.g.,* histories of schools).

Supplements "Bibliography of the registers (printed) of the universities, Inns of Court, colleges and schools of Great Britain and Ireland", by H. Raven-Hart and M. Johnston, in *Bulletin of the Institute of Historical Research,* v. 9, 1931-32, p. 19-30, 65-83, 154-70; agenda and corrigenda, v. 10, 1932-33, p. 109-13.

For calendars and other publications of individual British universities, see relevant sections of the annual *Commonwealth universities yearbook.*

Scotland

378.4 (414.3)
Glasgow University calendar . . . Glasgow, the University. Annual. (1966. 12s. 6d.).

Chief contents: History and constitution—officers—General information for students—Regulations regarding admission—Faculties (1966 ed., p. 119-485)—Higher degrees and research—Bursaries, scholarships, fellowships—Lists of awards. Appendices; general index.

378.4 (414.5)
Edinburgh University calendar . . . Edinburgh, Thin. Annual. (1966-1967. 1966. 12s. 6d.).

Chief contents: Admission—Faculties—Postgraduate study—Awards—Graduate lists. Class merit lists—Officials and staff of the university—Examinations. Index of subjects.

Ireland

378.4 (415) (092)
BURTCHAELL, G. D., and **SADLEIR, T. U.,** *ed.* **Alumni Dublinenses:** a register of the students, professors, and provosts of Trinity College, in the University of Dublin [1593-1860]. New ed. Dublin, Thom, 1936. xxiv, 905, 148p. illus. (pl.). 42s.

First published 1924 (covering 1593-1846).
Based on admission registers. Gives date and place of birth and father's name for more than 35,000 students. Is a reprint of the original, with supplement to 1860. Indispensable for Irish genealogical and biographical research.

Dublin. University. Trinity College. *A catalogue of graduates of the University of Dublin,* 1928- continues for contemporary graduates the work of Burtchaell and Sadleir. V. 6: 1931-1952 was published in 1952 (*i.e.,* 1955) at 10s.

The Dublin University calendar, 1966-7 (Dublin, Figgis, 1966). Chief contents: university and officers—Board, Council and committees—General information, degrees, admission, colleges charges and general regulations—Courses. Graduate studies and higher degrees—Prizes and other awards—Libraries, societies and other institutions—Names of students—Records (degrees, etc.). General index; index of officers.

The National University of Ireland. Calendar for the year 1966 (Dublin, Thom, 1967.) gives a list of officers and staff, data on studentships and regulations, and 1965 records of examination results, students who matriculated and degrees conferred.

The Queen's University of Belfast *Calendar, 1966-7* (Belfast, Boyd, 1966) gives a list of officers and staff, regulations, faculties, scholarships, etc., with directory and index.

London

378.4 (421)

University of London calendar . . . London, University of London. Annual. (1966/67 ed. 1966. 30s.)

Lists of officials and committee members are followed by an 'Historical note', the Principal's report for the previous year, text of the University of London Act, 1926, and details of faculties, boards, admission, etc. 'Schools and institutions' (1966/67 ed., p. 401-560); index of names (of staff), p. 562-644; general index.

Oxford

378.4 (425.72)

EMDEN, A. B. A biographical register of the University of Oxford, to A.D. 1500. Oxford, Clarendon Press, 1957-59. 3v. £27 6s.

"The primary purpose of this Register is biographical" (*Introduction,* v. 1). A scholarly work; c. 15000 entries. V.1 has a valuable introduction (p. xiii-xliii) and list of sources (p. xlvi-lvii). 2142 pages of biographies, with separate paragraphs for different stages of careers and quoting sources. The appendix to v. 3 contains "biographical notices of certain "English, Welsh and Irish graduates who are not known positively to have studied at Oxford or Cambridge . . ."; also an "Index of Christian names of 'Magistri' (to A.D. 1400 only).

Precedes, in point of coverage, Anthony à Wood's *Athenæ Oxonienses: an exact history of all the writers and bishops who had their education at the University of Oxford from 1500 to 1690....* (New [3rd] ed., with additions and a continuation by Philip Bliss. 4v. Rivington, 1813-20) and the more exhaustive compilations by J. Foster, *Alumni Oxonienses: the members of the University of Oxford, 1500-1714 . . .* (Oxford, Parker, 1891-2. 4v.) and its continuation, *Alumni Oxonienses . . . 1715-1886* (1888. 4v.).

The forthcoming *A bibliography of printed works relating to the University of Oxford,* by E. H. Cordeaux and D. H. Merry, will contain more than 10,000 entries under c. 500 headings.

378.4 (425.72)

Oxford University calendar for the year . . . Oxford, Clarendon Press. Annual. (1966. 42s.)

Part 1 includes class lists issued by public examiners and moderators for the 3 previous years, and lists of honorary degrees conferred over the previous 15 years. Part 2: 'The Colleges, Halls and other Societies',—not arranged A-Z but in order of seniority (not indicated in the contents; see *Times literary supplement,* no. 3351,

19th May 1966, leader on p. 455) 'Alphabetical list of members of the University' (1966 ed.: Men, p. 337-899; Women, p. 900-1048). Index of Colleges, Halls and Societies, with the number of members in residence. General index to part 1 only.

The historical register of the University of ...Oxford (1900) and its *Supplements,* for 1901-30 and 1931-50, are out of print.

Cambridge

378.4 (425.9)

EMDEN, A. B. A biographical register of the University of Cambridge, to 1500. Cambridge, Univ. Press, 1963. xl, 695p. 168s.

Identical in arrangement and scope of biographical notices with A. B. Emden's *A biographical register of the University of Oxford, to* A.D. *1500* (q.v.). Valuable introduction (p. xi-xxx: plan of *Register;* notes on colleges); list of sources (p. xxxiii-xl). About 7,000 entries,—asterisked if the name has been included in Venn's *Alumni Cantabrigienses,* v. 1. Many cross-references from variants of names. Entries cite authorities. Different stages of careers are punctuated by symbol ¶. Addendum; index of Christian names of 'Magistri' (to A.D. 1400 only), p. 689-95.

J. and J. A. Venn's *Alumni Cantabrigienses: a biographical list of all known students, graduates and holders of office to 1900.* Part 1, to 1751; Part 2, 1752-1900 (Cambridge, Univ. Press, 1922-27. 4v.; 1940-54. 6v.) lists only 4,650 names of scholars who entered the University before 1501. A reprint of the 2 pts. is available at £100. C. H. and T. Cooper's *Athenæ Cantabrigienses, 1500-1611* (Cambridge, Deighton Bell and Bowes & Bowes, 1858-1913; reprinted London, Gregg Press, 1967. £35) is more selective as well as being confined to a shorter period, and is comparable in these respects to Anthony à Wood's *Athenæ Oxonienses.*

378.4 (425.9)

The Annual register of the University of Cambridge for the year . . . Cambridge, Univ. Press. Annual. (1965/66 ed. 1966. 80s.)

Lists of University officials and offices are followed by Tripos lists (covering previous 5 years) and sections on individual colleges. A-Z list of members of the University (1965/66 ed., p. 615-1599),—but only A-Z for the surnames; the 16 columns of Smiths are arranged in order of seniority of their colleges. General index.

For previous records of Cambridge University, offices, distinctions, etc., see *The historical register of the University of Cambridge;* edited by J. R. Tanner (xii, 1186p. 1917. 40s.) and *Supplements,* from 1911 (1922-), now 5-yearly. Latest supplement, for 1961-65 (1967. 60s.).

378.4 (425.9)

PEEK, H. E., and HALL, C. P. The archives of the University of Cambridge: an historical introduction. Cambridge, Univ. Press, 1962. viii, 29p. pl. (facsims.). 25s.

A summary of the manuscript sources, with a bibliography of printed records appended.

Wales

378.4 (429)

UNIVERSITY OF WALES. Calendar for the academic year. [Aberystwyth, the University.] Annual. (1966-1967. 1966).

Chief contents: The Charter—Authorities, officers and members of the University—Pass lists (1965-66)—Lists of students awardships, fellowships, scholarships, prizes and distinctions, 1957-66—Approved departments and heads of such departments—Constituent colleges—Associated theological colleges—Regulations. Index.

Germany

378.4 (43)

Deutscher Hochschulführer. 1964-65. Hrsg. vom Verband deutscher Studentenschaften VDS. 40 Aufl. Bonn, 1964. 416p.

France

378.4 (44)

Index generalis. France, 1958: enseignement supérieur, recherche scientifique, observatoires. Paris, Klincksieck, 1959. 175p.

Plans for a complete 1958 revision of *Index generalis* were cancelled, and only the French section was published, on the same pattern as the parent work, with its own name index.

U.S.A.

378.4 (73)

AMERICAN COUNCIL ON EDUCATION. American junior colleges. 6th ed. Washington, the Council, 1963. 551p. $10.

First published 1940.

A companion volume to *American universities and colleges* (q.v.), with data on 650 accredited junior colleges; arranged by states.

378.4 (73)

AMERICAN COUNCIL ON EDUCATION. American universities and colleges. 9th ed. Washington, the Council, 1964. xv, 1339p. tables. $15.

First published 1928. Revised every 4 years.

Three main parts: 1. Higher education in the United States—2. Professional education in the United States—3. Institutional exhibits (p. 151-1243; individuals, universities and colleges, under States, A-Z; very detailed). Appendices include 3. Degree abbreviations; and 6. Summary list of the universities and colleges appearing in part 3, by State; level; type; control; enrolment; foreign students. The 9th ed. includes a new initial chapter on selecting a college and seeking admission. General index; institutional index.

The new American guide to colleges, by G. R. Hawes (3rd ed., completely rev. and enl. New York, Columbia Univ. Press, 1966. 597p. $8.95) compares more than 2,300 undergraduate colleges, using 53 criteria. Also noted: *Comparative guide to American colleges for students, parents and counselors,* by J. Cass and M. Birnbaum (New & enl. ed. New York, Harper & Row, 1966. xxxiv, [i], 725, [1]p.) .

Academical Dress

378.4:391 (4/9)

HAYCRAFT, F. W., *comp.* **The degrees and hoods of the world's universities and colleges.**

Completely revised and enlarged by E. W. E. Stringer. 4th ed. Cheshunt, Cheshunt Press, 1948. 159p. illus.

First published 1923; 3rd ed. 1927.

Short historical introduction. Main section gives under each country its universities and under each university its degrees and details of the shape and colours of its degree hoods. Separate sections for theological colleges and learned societies. Illustrations include a number of hoods in full colour and a section showing hood shapes. A comprehensive colour index is provided for locating any particular hood.

378.4:391 (4)

HARGREAVES-MAWDSLEY, W. N. A history of academical dress in Europe until the end of the eighteenth century. Oxford, Clarendon Press, 1963. xiii, 235p. illus. (21 pl.). 45s.

Chapters: 1. Italy, Spain, Portugal and Malta—2. France—3-4. Great Britain and Ireland—5. German-speaking countries, the Low Countries, Switzerland, Scandinavia, Hungary and Poland. A scholarly survey, with profuse footnotes. Glossary of terms (p. 190-5); critical bibliography (p. 196-210: A. Manuscripts—B. Printed books). Analytical index. Not very fully illustrated (coloured frontispiece and 21 black and white half-tones; 17 drawings), but descriptions are detailed.

378.4:391 (410)

SHAW, G. W. Academical dress of British universities. Cambridge, Heffer, 1966. vii, 120p. 35s.

Descriptions and diagrams of gowns, hoods, robes and caps worn by graduates and undergraduates. Index of universities and degrees, useful list of abbreviations of degrees (p. 13-16) which indicates, *e.g.,* which university grants a degree as Master of Dental Surgery. Illustrations are black and white, but may be supplemented by the coloured illustrations in *Academic dress of the University of Oxford* by D. R. Venables and R. E. Clifford (2nd ed. Oxford, Shepherd & Woodward, 1967. [2], 33p. col. ill. 5s. 6d.).

Universities: Modern Languages

378.94

STERN, E., *ed.* **Modern languages in the universities:** a guide to courses of study in five European languages at universities in the United Kingdom. 2nd rev. ed. London, Macmillan, 1965. vii, 376p. 30s.

The five languages are French (26 universities), German (24), Spanish (21), Russian (18) and Italian (13). Details on courses of study and admission to courses are given under each university. Final section: 'General schemes of studies with modern languages' (6 universities). A well-produced guide.

Technical Education

378.96:016

THE BACIE bibliography of publications in the field of education and training in commerce and industry. London, British Association for Commercial and Industrial Education, 1963-. v. 1-. (v. 1: March 1960-December 1962. 1963. 63s.).

Previously published in the quarterly *BACIE journal* (1947-).

V. 1 contains 1,022 indicative abstracts, each of *c.* 20 words, of periodical articles, pamphlets and some books. Sections: Training schemes—Education and training: descriptive—Training techniques—Executive development—Secondary and further education—Recruitment, selection, evaluation — Policy — Research — Miscellaneous. Subject index.

The same body has published a *BACIE register of programmed instruction in the field of education and training in commerce and industry* (v. 1: 1965. 1966. 40p.).

378.96:016

CIRF abstracts: ideas drawn from the current writings on vocational training for workers, supervisors and technicians. Geneva, CIRF (International Vocational Training Information and Research Centre), August 1961-. v. 1-. Looseleaf.

One or more pages per informative abstract. 15 sections: 1. Vocational training systems: general—2. Economic, technical and social aspects—3. Relationships between education and training—4. Organisation—5 to 11. Programmes—12. Trade descriptions—13. Teaching methods, examinations, research methods—14. Training facilities, equipment, teaching aids—15. Lists of publications, bibliographies.

378.96:016

Technical education abstracts from British sources. London, National Foundation for Educational Research in England and Wales, 1961-. v. 1, no. 1-. Quarterly. 63*s.* p.a.

V. 1, no. 1 (April 1961) covers September-December 1960 and carries some 250 informative abstracts, each of *c.* 150 words. 170 journals were initially covered, producing a wide range of topics. Each issue has author and title index and subject index. Decided time-lag. V. 5, nos. 1-4 appeared in January 1967, covering July 1964 - June 1965. *Nature* (v. 191, no. 4783, 1st July 1961, p. 21) has criticised the selection of so many abstracts from relatively few journals.

378.96 (058)

The Year book of technical education and careers in industry . . . ; edited by H. C. Dent. London, Black, 1957-. Annual. (11th issue, 1967. 50*s.*).

The 1967 *Year book* (xli, 1362p.) has four main sections: 1. Colleges, Department of Education and Science, councils, statutory and voluntary organisations—2. Careers in industry (p.

1007-1266; sub-divided by types of industry, 1-20: 21: Other careers)—3. Training schemes (statements by organising firms)—4. National apprenticeship agreements. List of H.M.S.O. pamphlets on careers; index to advertisers. Index proper precedes. An essential, well-established guide to technical courses and careers, but it contains no details of the 1966 White Paper on polytechnics. "Perhaps future editions of this admirable book of reference could include an annual review" (*Times literary supplement,* no. 3,398, 13th April 1967, p. 316).

378.96.001.5

NATIONAL FOUNDATION FOR EDUCATIONAL RESEARCH IN ENGLAND AND WALES. Technical education and training in the United Kingdom: research in progress, 1962-64. Compiled by J. Heywood with R. A. Abel. With a supplement, 1963-1964, of reported researches. Slough, Bucks., the Foundation, [1965]. v, 128p. tables. 21*s.*

Contents: Colloquium proceedings—Research abstracts (82) submitted for the Colloquium (p. 39-110)—Researches in technical education, 1963-64 (abstracts 83-132). Appendix: 'Research groups concerned with technical education'. Index.

Catholic Schools

379.77 (058.7)

Catholic schools in England and Wales. London, Catholic Education Council for England and Wales, 1954. 79p.

Complete survey of all Catholic schools in the country. Arranged first under diocese or archdiocese, then by following groups: Aided schools—All ages, Aided schools—Primary; Aided and special agreement secondary schools; Direct grant schools; Independent schools; Special schools. Gives address, name of head and number of pupils for each school.

379.77 (058.7)

The Directory of Catholic schools and colleges in Great Britain. London, Paternoster Publications, Sands & Co. 1935-. Annual. (29th ed. 1966).

Excludes maintained primary and secondary modern schools. Arranged in column form across double page. Directory of schools (by counties A-Z)—Directory of London schools (districts double page. Directory of schools (by counties) —Scholastic requisites—Classified buyers' guide Indexes to school advertisements, towns and counties.

38 COMMERCE. COMMUNICATIONS

Bibliographies

38:016

GREAT BRITAIN. HER MAJESTY'S STATIONERY OFFICE. Commerce, industry and H.M.S.O.: a selection of government publications for the businessman. London, H.M.S.O., 1966. 31p. *Gratis.*

See entry at 33:016.

38:016

UNITED STATES. DEPARTMENT OF COMMERCE. Publications. Washington, U.S. Government Printing Office, 1952. 795p. $2.75. Annual supplements.

The basic volume covers publications from 1790 to 1950. Annual supplements cumulate the weekly *Business service checklist.* Cites papers and articles in the Department of Commerce's four major periodicals, as well as individual publications of constituent bureaux (*e.g.,* Bureau of the Census; National Bureau of Standards).

Handbooks

38 (02)
STEPHENSON, J. Principles and practice of commerce. 5th ed., by H. O. Beecheno. London, Pitman, 1958 (and reprints). xiv, 674p. illus. diagrs. 30s.

First published 1916; 4th ed. 1951.
Sections: 1. General principles—2. Industry—3. Commerce—4. Trade—5. Exchange, banking and finance—6. Transport and insurance—7. Warehousing—8. Combines and monopoly—9. Commerce and the state. Contents have been brought up to date and condensed, by removing much historical information. No bibliographies analytical index. Probably the most comprehensive and useful general British manual. Gives many examples of forms and the like.

Trade Directories

38 (058.7):016
BIBLIOTHEEK EN DOCUMENTATIE VAN DE ECONOMISCHE VOORLICHTINGSDIENST. Catalogus van adresboeken. 3rd ed. The Hague, the Library, 1966. 208p.

Lists 1,400 directories, with place and date of publication and name of publisher. A code indicates whether the directory contains names of manufacturers, exporters, wholesalers, importers, retailers, agents and/or professions. Most entries are annotated. Arrangement is by continent, then by country, with an index of countries and subjects.
Kept up to date by entries in the 'Aanwinsten Bibliotheek EVD' section of *Economische voorlichting* (weekly).

Trade directories of the world (New York, Croner Publications, 1960. iii, 120p. Loose-leaf) is arranged by continent and sub-divided by country, then A-Z by title. For each title (*c.* 1,300), gives title, periodicity, pagination, price, brief note on scope, and publisher's name and address. No indication of date or edition and a number of defunct works are included. Index of trades and professions; index of countries.

Only 3 parts of *The reference manual of directories: an annotated list, index and guide to the directories of all countries,* compiled by G. P. Henderson (London, Jones & Evans' Bookshop, 1957-. Mimeographed) have appeared: pt. 7. *Canada* (1959. 25s.); pt. 11. *India, Pakistan, Ceylon, Burma* (1961. 20s.); pt. 14. *Australasia* (1957. 20s.). Publication of further parts is doubtful.

The U.S. Bureau of Foreign Commerce's *A guide to foreign business directories* was last published in 1955 (Washington, Government Printing Office. vii, 132p.). Pt. 1 lists country directories (general; special; local) under 79 countries, frequently with annotations. Pt. 2 lists international directories published in the U.S. by industry, trade or profession, A-Z. Subject indexes to pt. 1.

38 (058.7):016
Internationale Bibliographie der Fachadressbücher für Wirtschaft, Wissenschaft, Technik. 3. Ausg Munich-Pullach, Verlag Dokumentation, 1966. cxxiv p., 298 l. (Handbuch der technischen Dokumentation und Bibliographie. 5. Bd.). DM.88.

4,321 numbered entries in 11 sections (11. Industrie und Volkswirtschaft, Wirtschaftsadressbücher, nos. 3,278-4,321). Entries give title, publisher, date, pagination and price. Country, publisher and subject indexes.

38 (058.7):016
SMYTH, A. L. "Trades, professional and official directories as historical source material." In *The Manchester review,* v. 11, Autumn 1966, p. 39-58.

Includes a valuable "preliminary checklist" of about 500 directories in two parts (1. Commerce and industry—2. Public life), each with subdivisions. Manchester Reference Library's holdings and call numbers are given.

38 (058.7) (4/9)
Kelly's Directory of manufacturers and merchants, including industrial services. London, Kelly's Directories, 1880-. Annual. (1966-67. 160s.).

Previously as *Kelly's Directory of merchants, manufacturers and shippers.* . . .
The 80th ed., for 1966-67 has 3v. (4,202, 114p.):
v. 1: *Great Britain, Northern Ireland, Republic of Ireland* . . .
v. 2: *Europe, Africa, America, Asia, Oceania.*
v. 3: *Index to trades and services* . . .
V. 1 is in two main parts,—England, Scotland and Wales (excluding the London postal district), and London postal area. In each case alphabetical and classified trade directories are followed by a directory of exporters and importers. V. 2 has classified trades sections and general information notes, with maps, for countries of Europe and America; also French-English, German-English, Spanish-English lists of products and services (*c.* 3,000 terms in each list). The most comprehensive of British trade directories.

38 (058.7) (4)
SELKA, K. R., *ed.* **Europ Production, 1966.** Darmstadt, Europ Export Edition GmbH, 1966. 2,928p. [main section]. Annual.

Claims to contain "more than 450,000 entries of manufacturers in 17 European countries under some 10,000 article headings". Countries include the European Community, Austria, Bulgaria, Denmark, Finland, Hungary, Norway, Poland, Rumania, Sweden, Switzerland and Yugoslavia. Indexes of products in English, French, Italian, Spanish and German.

Bottin Europe, 1966 (Paris, Société Didot Bottin, 1966. 432, 877p. [main sections]) concerns only European Community countries. The first section gives details of Community and national organisations; the second lists products, with relevant manufactures, but in much less detail than *Europ Production.*

G. P. Henderson's *Current European directories* (Beckenham, Kent, CBD Research, Ltd.), due for publication in 1968 at 100s., is designed as a companion to *Current British directories*. It will cover general, town and specialised directories in all 34 countries of Europe, as well as international directories with European sections. Index of titles; subject index in English, French and German.

38 (058.7) (410)

Kelly's Directory of manufacturers and merchants, including industrial services. London, Kelly's Directories, 1880-. Annual. (1966-67. 1966. 160s.). v. 1.

See entry at 38 (058.7) (4/9).

38 (058.7) (410)

UK Kompass 1967. Register of British industry and commerce. London, Kompass Register, Ltd., 1967. 3v. £15 15s.

v. 1. *Indexes.*
v. 2. *Products and services.*
v. 3. *Company information.*

V. 1 has an index to names and addresses of 28,500 companies, and indexes (in English, French, German, Italian and Spanish) to 32,000 U.K. products and more than 1,000 services. V. 2 provides a breakdown of more than 33,000 products and services, classified under 30 trade groups and sub-divided into over 700 product tables and grids. V. 3 gives details of leading companies, under counties and towns, A-Z. Most companies have 50 or more employees; smaller companies are included when they are members of a group or are sufficiently specialised to warrant inclusion. The six-digit reference number is a vital part of this directory. Other symbols distinguish wholesalers from distributors, importers from exporters. Entries for companies that are members of the Confederation of British Industries are marked with an obelisk.

There are also Kompass registers for the following countries: Belgium—Luxembourg, Denmark, France, Italy, Netherlands, Spain, Sweden and Switzerland.—Liechtenstein.

38 (058.7) (410):016

HENDERSON, G. P., and ANDERSON, I. G. Current British directories, 1966-7. 5th ed. Croydon, Surrey, C.B.D. Research, Ltd., 1966. xii, 214p. 80s.

First published 1953.
About 2,000 entries in four parts: 1. Local directories—2. Specialized directories (nos. 401-1582)—3. International directories (a selection of international specialised directories published outside the British Isles; nos. 2001-2125)—4. Directories of the British Commonwealth and South Africa (nos. 3001-3281). Index; publishers' addresses. An important tool, but the perfect binding is inadequate for frequent handling.

British Rate and Data's *Directories and annuals* (London, MacLean & Hunter. Annual 1967. 10s. 6d.), lists directories and annuals by titles A-Z, with subject index. Information for each item includes publisher's name and address, month of publication, advertisement rates, details of format and sometimes print order. Wider in scope than *Current British*

directories, as non-directory annuals are also included. Although not as comprehensive in its listing of directories, it forms a useful complement because of its annual appearance.

38 (058.7) (415)

Thom's commercial directory. Dublin, Thom. Annual. (1965. 105s.).

Sections: Government departments—State-sponsored boards & companies—Professional associations—Trade associations—Trade unions and trade publications—Bank and kindred firms —Classified list of traders—Directory of companies—Classified list of manufacturers—Who's who in commerce and industry. Index to advertisers. Two new features: directory of companies; who's who in commerce. Thumb indexed.

O'Neill's Commercial who's who and industrial directory of Ireland (17th, 1963-64, ed. Dublin, Parkside Press. 105s.) includes an Irish directory of directors, specific industrial directory (sections 1-33), advertising and press, and 'General business information' (*e.g.,* handbook of Irish societies; industrial organisations; trade marks and trade names), and alphabetical index to industrial directory.

38 (058.7) (6)

Owen's Commerce & travel & international register . . . : Africa, Middle East & Far East, with international trade lists. London, Owen's Commerce & Travel, Ltd., 1954-. illus., maps. Annual. (1966. 72s. 6d.).

Title varies.
Arranged by areas, concentrating mainly on African and Middle East countries and territories. Aims to provide "the businessman, export manager, travel executive and general reader with a succinct survey of many countries of Africa, Middle East and Far East" (*Foreword*). Not merely a trade directory; gives statistical and other information as well (*e.g.,* 'Sudan' (1967 ed., p. 243-88) as a map, data on geography and population, on immigration and health requirements, provinces, principal newspapers, education, insurance companies, foreign trade, produce and agriculture, industry and development, and directory information ('Classified list of manufacturers, merchants, importers, exporters, etc.', p. 263-88)). Flagged sections.

G. P. Henderson's *African companies: a guide to sources of information* (Beckenham, Kent, CBD Research, Ltd.) is in preparation.

38 (058.7) (73)

Thomas' Register of American manufacturers . . . : a purchasing guide that aims to represent commercial manufacturers and primary sources of supply; for the direction of both domestic and foreign buyers. New York, Thomas Publishing Co., 1905-. Annual. $20 p.a.

The 1965 ed. has 5 v. : v. 1-3. Manufacturers classified by *c.* 70,000 products; v. 4. Alphabetical list of manufacturers, trademarks, commercial organizations; v. 5. Product finding guide to v. 1-3 and index of advertisers. An international purchasing directory.

38 (058.7) (73):016

KLEIN, B., *ed.* **Guide to American directories:** a guide to the major business directories of the United States, covering all industrial, professional and mercantile categories. 6th ed. New York, McGraw-Hill, 1965. xlv, 465p. $25.

First published 1956. Publisher varies.
Lists *c.* 3,350 industrial, professional and commercial directories by subjects, A-Z, with an index of titles. Describes the contents of each directory, stating periodicity, month of publication (if an annual), publisher and price.

38 (092)

World who's who in commerce and industry. 14th ed., 1966/67. Chicago, Marquis Who's Who, 1966. xv, 1556p. $27.50.

12th ed. 1962. As *Who's who in commerce and industry* (1936-59. 11 editions).
"Lists biographical records of nearly 25,000 individuals identified with commerce and industry, including the 10,500 whose career and familiar data are now first published in this book" (*Preface*). Some 15,000 names are also given of "business related biographies of *Who's who in America*" whose biographies are not included. The publishers stress that selection of biographees is made under carefully established selective standards. Appended A-Z list of 8,200 major companies, "with a roster of ranking executives".

Market Research
380.13:016

FANNING, D. Market research. London, Library Association, 1964. 22p. (Library Association Special subject list no. 44).

125 numbered entries, with occasional very brief annotations. Sections: Directories—Bibliographies—Market research—Motivation research —Industrial market research—Media research—Techniques and methods—General textbooks—Periodicals (nos. 106-25). Name and title indexes.

The Institute of Marketing's *Library catalogue: a list of books available for the use of the Institute's members and registered students* (Rev. ed. 1966. [i, 26]p.) contains *c.* 600 entries in 24 sections. Those in sections 1-23 are graded (1 to 4 stars) elementary and general introductory reading; useful, clearly written books classified (2-3 stars) according to the amount of material and design of detail shown; specialised works, advanced in theme and treatment. Appendix: Reference books'.

380.13:016

GENERAL AGREEMENT ON TARIFFS AND TRADE. International Trade Centre. **A bibliography of market surveys** by products and countries. Geneva, GATT, 1967. [i], xxi, 197p. $5.

Generally lists only marketing research reports issued since 1963. Two parts: 1. Market surveys by products, in SITC (Rev.) order; 2. National and area market surveys, by regions and their individual countries A-Z. Text in English, French and Spanish. Reviewed in *Board of Trade journal*, v. 193, no. 3,679, 22nd September 1967, p. 695.

380.13 (4)

WILLIAM-OLSSON, W. Marketing survey of the European Common Market. Stockholm, AB Exportbyran, 1960.

Gives identical statistical data for each of 241 administrative districts of the six member countries, under 34 headings. These last include area, climate, population, population density, age groups, details of towns of more than 10,000 inhabitants, occupations, places of work, number of employees in industry, service trades and agriculture, political groupings and living standards. List of statistical source material; 8 sketch maps, covering various aspects of living standards. Two wall maps, on economic conditions and population density respectively, accompany the work.

380.13 (410)

Great Britain: a "Geographia" marketing and media survey. London, Geographia, 1961. 26, 76p. 11 fldg. maps. 170s.

Divides the country into 11 provinces and 80 marketing regions, the latter based on circulation areas of evening newspapers. Geographical notes on each region as well as statistics of population (1961), retail outlets (1950) and advertising facilities. Summary tables (including ITV statistics) for each province, plus a map (47 × 37 cm.) showing regional and sub-regional boundaries. In some cases, the method of division seems highly questionable (*e.g.,* Warrington, is in the Manchester marketing region, whilst Oldham is not) and this is reflected in statistics and population and retail outlets.

Great Britain: a "Geographia" survey of manufacturing industry (London, Geographia, 1963. viii, 16p. 41 fldg. maps), based on the Census of Production, 1958, is primarily intended as a marketing aid. The first part covers 28 major industries (location on a 45 × 35 cm. map; graph for each). The second part shows, in maps (10 miles to 1"), graphs and statistical tables, distribution of industry within the major regions (further sub-divided into marketing areas).

M. K. Adler's *Directory of British market research organizations and services* (London, Crosby Lockwood, 1965. viii, 88p. 21s.) is in two sequences: pt. 1 lists market research facilities, A-Z and under each heading notes names of firms providing these services; pt. 2 lists market research organizations, with the services provided by each. Handy glossary of market research terms (p. 55-88). 2nd ed. 1967. 30s.

Noted: *England and Wales: statistical data for standard regions and administrative counties,* by W. William-Olsson (Stockholm, Almqvist & Wiksell, 1963).

Chambers of Commerce
380.15

CHAMBRE DE COMMERCE INTERNATIONALE. Annuaire mondial des chambres de commerce. [Paris], 1954-56. 2v. Loose-leaf.

Data on 3,400 chambers of commerce in more than 70 countries. Arranged by countries A-Z, then towns A-Z. Information on each chamber of commerce includes a list of publications. In

English and French, with a key for translation into German, Italian, Portuguese and Spanish.

Tourist Trade

380.8 (058.7)

Travel trade directory. London, Travel Trade Directory. Annual. (9th ed., 1966-67. 1966. 42s.).

Lists and locates "every kind of travel, tourism and transportation enterprise and official and representative body operating in and/or maintaining offices in the United Kingdom and Eire" (introduction). Sections: Travel and towns—Shipping—Coach rental—Car rental—Air—Rail—Who's who (personnel of managerial status)—Hotels and villas—Tourist and visa offices—Trade bodies—Clubs.

380.8 (083.4)

INTERNATIONAL UNION OF OFFICIAL TRAVEL ORGANISATIONS. International travel statistics, 1946-. Geneva, the Union, 1948-. Annual. (1964 ed. 1966. Sw.fr.40.).

Covers 93 countries and gives for each the number and nationality of visitors, arrivals by month, method of transport and estimates of tourists' receipts and expenditure.

IUOTO also publishes *Bibliographie touriste* (1957-. 3 p.a. 25s. p.a.), listing c. 900 items p.a.

The Organization for Economic Co-operation and Development produces an annual *Tourism in O.E.C.D. member countries* (1964 ed. Paris, O.E.C.D., 1965. 17s. 6d.), covering 20 countries.

Industrial Fairs

381.12

Messe und Ausstellung Kalendar, 1919-. Cologne, Messe und Ausstellungs-Gesellschaft, 1919-. 2 p.a. (1967. DM.14.).

Probably the fullest listing of fairs and exhibitions. Arrangement: 1. Germany, by town; 2. Other countries, by country and town; 3. Germany, chronologically; 4. Other countries, chronologically; 5. Subject list of all fairs and exhibitions; 6. Facilities for congresses and meetings in Germany. In German, English and French.

The *Board of Trade journal* (weekly) has a special quarterly supplement giving a classified list of trade fairs. Amendments and additions appear in the first issue of each calendar month.

1966 world exhibits (Athens, Graphointer Publications, 1966. 423p. $5.90.) is an annual, listing 1,500 trade fairs and exhibitions from 55 countries.

Foreign Trade

382 (038)

INTERNATIONAL CHAMBER OF COMMERCE. Incoterms, 1953; international rules for the interpretation of trade terms. Paris, I.C.C., 1953. 69p.

Parallel English/French text. Interpretations of terms such as "f.o.b.", "c.i.f.".

The I.C.C.'s *Trade terms, 1953* gives in the form of synoptic tables, definitions of the more important trade abbreviations used in 17 countries.

382 (058)

UNITED STATES. CHAMBER OF COMMERCE. Foreign Commerce Department. **Foreign commerce handbook:** basic information and a guide to sources, 1922/23-. Washington, Chamber of Commerce of the U.S., 1922-. Biennial (irregular). (14th ed. 1960.).

The 13th ed. (1959. [vi], 151p.) had four parts: 1. Foreign trade services—2. Information on major subjects—3. Bibliography, annotated (p. 87-129: reference books; leading indexes; books and pamphlets; periodicals; export business magazines)—4. Appendix (directory information).

382:061 (4/9)

GENERAL AGREEMENT ON TARIFFS AND TRADE (G.A.T.T.). **Manufacturing and trade associations, and product-promotion organizations** in 28 countries. Geneva, G.A.T.T., 1966. 93p.

Under each country are listed, in separate sequences, the leading chambers of commerce plus a selection of manufacturing or trading associations, and product research or promotion organizations.

The U.S. Department of Commerce's *A directory of foreign organizations for trade and investment promotion* (2nd ed. Washington, U.S.G.P.O., 1961. [iii], 108p. 35c.) describes the organizations abroad that are "actively engaged in promoting and facilitating trade and investment in the free world" (*Foreword*), with a note of their publications. Arranged under countries A-Z.

E.F.T.A. sources of information: a directory for exporters and importers (London, Federation of British Industries, 1962. v, 158p.) lists government and trade organizations, trade exhibitions, directories and sources of data and statistics for each of the 8 E.F.T.A. countries.

382:061 (410)

GREAT BRITAIN. BOARD OF TRADE. Statistics and Market Intelligence Library. **Trade associations and export groups:** a select list. Rev. ed. London, Board of Trade, 1966. v, 63p.

Previously as *Some trade associations, etc. in Britain,* issued by Board of Trade Export Services Branch.

Prepared mainly for use by Government offices, in Britain and overseas, concerned with promoting Britain's export trade. About 650 organisations listed (name; address; 'phone number)—"those with which the Board of Trade's export intelligence services have most frequently been in touch in the course of dealing with export enquiries". 22 groups, based on the main divisions of H.M. Customs and Excise's *Export list.* Subject index.

382:061 (410)

MILLARD, P. Trade associations and professional bodies of the United Kingdom. 3rd ed. Oxford, Pergamon Press, 1966. xlv, 372p. 60s.

First published 1962; 2nd ed. 1964.

"A trade association or professional body is defined as an organization or society which represents the interest and welfare, in the broadest sense, of any trade, industry or profession, collectively or individually, on a national or near-national scale" (*Introduction*). Also includes some local associations, particularly when their trades are historically associated with a particular area, but excludes regional branches of national bodies. Lists *c.* 3,000 organizations A-Z with addresses and telephone numbers and, in some cases, a brief statement of their aims. Indexed by subject and town. Then follow lists of chambers of commerce, trade, industry and shipping, as well as U.K. offices of international organizations. Considerably overlaps G. P. Henderson's *Directory of British associations*.

International

382 (4/9)

Common markets round the world; including trading groups, associations and other economic alliances. San Francisco, Bank of America, 1965. 92p.

Brings together concise information on the various economic groups of countries throughout the world. Arrangement is by region and each organization is considered under the headings "history", "objectives", "organization", "development" and accompanied by a sketch map showing member states. Handy summary tables giving countries and the organizations to which they belong.

382 (4/9)

EUROPEAN COMMUNITIES. Statistical Office. **Foreign trade statistics. Overseas associates.** Strasbourg & Luxembourg, European Community, 1965-. *c.* 12 pts. p.a. ea. 11*s.* 100*s.* p.a.

Quarterly import and export figures (cumulating throughout the year) for the 26 associated countries (mainly ex-colonies). About 6-10 countries figure in each part (*e.g.,* 1967, no. 1: Dahomey, Chad, Central African Republic, Gabon, Congo (Brazza), Mali. Headings consist of I.S.T.C. classification number, product-origin, quantity and value.

382 (4/9)

GENERAL AGREEMENT ON TARIFFS AND TRADE. International trade. Geneva, G.A.T.T., 1953-. Annual. (1965. 17*s.* 6*d.*).

Annual narrative account of world trade. Separate and critical examination of trade in primary commodities and in manufactures, trade of industrial areas and trade of non-industrial areas. Includes *c.* 40 statistical tables, many with data not elsewhere available or so presented.

The GATT *Compendium of statistics: internal trade statistics* (1967. [3], v, 150p.) has sub-title: "An analytical compilation of foreign trade statistics published by international agencies and national governments the world over, with an introduction on their use in market research."

382 (4/9)

INTERNATIONAL MONETARY FUND and **INTERNATIONAL BANK FOR RECON-** **STRUCTION AND DEVELOPMENT. Direction of trade:** supplement to *International financial statistics.* New York, I.M.F. and I.B.R.B., 1964-. Monthly (ea. $1); annual supplements (ea. $3). $10 p.a.

Originally (1950-) *Direction of international trade,* joint publication of the U.N. Statistical Office, I.M.F. and I.B.R.D. The annual supplements cover 1955-62 (1964), 1960-64 (1965) and 1961-65 (1966).

The November 1966 issue covers 67 countries, giving total trade (export and import) for each country with other countries and groups of countries. Statistics are cumulated throughout the year. The monthly country index shows the latest issue in which particular country data are published.

The *Annual 1961-65* provides (a) trade-by-country data for 1961-65 for 150 countries in $U.S., summary totals of those countries' trade with 19 areas, and comparisons of such totals with the total export and import data repeated monthly in *International trade statistics,* and (b) additions of these data into similar tables for the world and for 16 areas (*Introduction*).

382 (4/9)

UNITED NATIONS. Statistical Office. **World trade annual,** 1963-. New York, Walker, 1964-. 4v. Annual (3rd issue, for 1965. 1966. $160.).

v. 1. *Food. Beverages and tobacco. Crude materials, inedible, except fuels. Animal and vegetable oils and fuels.*
v. 2: *Mineral fuels, lubricants and related materials. Chemicals.*
v. 3. *Manufactured goods other than food, fuels, chemicals, machinery and transport equipment.*
v. 4. *Machinery and transport equipment. Commodities and transactions not classified according to kind.*

The U.N. International Trade Statistics Centre collects, verifies and standardizes detailed trade data from as many countries as possible. This is collected on tape in standard units of value (U.S. $) and quantity (metric tons) in terms of the 1312 S.I.T.C. items and published, as available, on a quarterly cumulative basis in the U.N. *Commodity trade statistics* (series D), of which there are *c.* 25 fascicules annually. Each fascicule contains the separate export and import figure of from 4 to 5 countries; a cumulative index covering 47 countries shows the fascicule number in which each of their quarterly returns appeared.

The *World trade annual* re-arranges the annual national figures so that under each commodity heading is tabulated the trade in that heading reported by each country—the country's total trade in the commodity, plus analysis of the total by countries of provenance (imports) or of destination (exports). The arrangement follows S.I.T.C. classification order, except that v. 1 contains S.I.T.C. sections 0, 1, 2, 4; v. 2, sections 3, 5; v. 3, sections 6, 8, and v. 4, sections 7, 9. Countries covered: U.S.A., Canada, Belgium - Luxembourg, France, Western Germany, Italy, Netherlands, U.K., Denmark, Norway, Sweden, Austria, Portugal, Switzerland, Iceland, Ireland, Greece, Turkey, Finland, Spain, Australia, Japan and Yugoslavia.

The U.N. *Yearbook of international trade statistics* (1950-) analyses the trade of each country but not in such detail and without giving countries of provenance and destination, except for total national trade figures. It does, however, cover 144 countries and territories (representing *c.* 98% of world trade). The 1964 v. (15th ed., published 1966. 86s. 6d.) covers 123 countries, accounting for over 80% of world trade (*Board of Trade journal*, v. 191, no. 3,626, 16th September 1966, p. 676).

382 (4/9):016
GENERAL AGREEMENT ON TARIFFS AND TRADE (G.A.T.T.). International Trade Centre. **International trade statistics: compendium of sources.** Geneva, G.A.T.T., 1967. v, 150p. Mimeographed.

Sub-title: "An analytical compilation of foreign trade statistics published by international agencies and national governments the world over, with an introduction on their use in market research". Contents: 1. Introduction— 2. Multinational statistical sources—3. Statistics for individual countries and territories (163, A-Z, Aden-Zambia). Includes national bank publications. Annotations state coverage, frequency, price and period. Many cross-references; no index.

———— **Basic commodity statistics: compendium of sources.** Geneva, G.A.T.T., 1967. 232p.

Three parts: general commodity sources; agricultural commodities; metals and minerals. Reviewed in *Board of Trade journal*, v. 193, no. 3,679, 22nd September 1967, p. 695. These two compendia give extensive bibliographical guidance to market researchers, librarians and statisticians.

Europe

382 (4):016
WILD, J. E., *comp.* **The European Common Market and the European Free Trade Association.** 3rd rev. ed. London, Library Association, 1962. 62p. (Special subject list no. 35). 9s. (members, 6s. 9d.).

750 entries (some of them annotated) in three sections: Books, pamphlets and reports— Periodical articles—Bibliographies, reading lists. Name and subject indexes. A new edition is much needed.

382 (4) (083.5)
ORGANISATION FOR ECONOMIC CO-OPERATION AND DEVELOPMENT. Foreign trade statistical bulletins. Paris, O.E.C.D., 1959-.

Series A: *Overall trade by countries.* Quarterly. ea. 12s. 6d.; 44s. p.a.
Series B: *Commodity trade: analysis by main regions.* Quarterly (ea. in 6 pts.). 72s. 6d. p.a.
Series C: *Commodity trade: detailed analysis by S.I.T.C. items.* 2 p.a. (ea. in 2 pts.). 84s. p.a.
Series A covers the foreign trade position of the 22 O.E.C.D. member-countries, expressed in values ($ U.S.). Series B provides breakdown by main commodity categories (based on S.I.T.C.

Rev.) and areas. Series C gives a complete breakdown by countries of origin and destination for a large number of commodities. An annual supplement provides further information on O.E.C.D. imports and exports for 93 S.I.T.C. items.

The European Communities, Statistical Office issues *Foreign trade: monthly statistics* (ea. 7s. 3d.) and a quarterly *Foreign trade: analytical tables* (in 2v. : exports; imports. ea. 15s.; 122s. p.a.) covering the trade of Common Market countries by commodity; statistics are cumulative throughout the year.

Commonwealth

382 (41-44)
COMMONWEALTH ECONOMIC COMMITTEE. Commonwealth trade . . . London, H.M. Stationery Office, 1949-. Annual. (1966 ed., published 1967. 15s.).

As *A review of Commonwealth trade* (1949). Part 1, General review (The Commonwealth in world trade; Commonwealth trading partners); part 2, The trade of Commonwealth countries (25 individual countries, including the U.K.). The 1965 ed. (1967) has 67 tables in the main text, with statistics for 1961-65, 15 appendix tables, and notes on tables.

Preceded by the Board of Trade's *Statistical abstract for the British Commonwealth* (v. 69 (1947) covered the ten-year period 1936-45) which continued *Statistical abstract for the British Empire* (1850-. 1865-; v. 68 covered the period 1929-38, publication being suspended during World War II).

382 (41-44)
GREAT BRITAIN. BOARD OF TRADE. The Commonwealth and the Sterling Area . . . Statistical abstract. 1889/1903-. London, H.M. Stationery Office, 1905-. Annual. (86th issue, 1965. 1966. 18s. 6d.).

Title varies. Originally (1850/63-) as *Statistical abstracts for the several colonial . . . possessions of the U.K.*
Subjects formerly covered included production, shipping and population; since World War II trade statistics (volume; direction) have occupied a predominant place, while others (*e.g.,* shipping) have been dropped completely. Includes data on world production, consumption and prices of selected commodity. Current issues give retrospective coverage for three years.
Later Sterling Area trade figures appear in quarterly articles in *Board of Trade journal*.

Great Britain

382 (410)
DOCK & HARBOUR AUTHORITIES' ASSOCIATION. Port statistics for the foreign trade of the United Kingdom. London, the Association, 1964-. 3 pts. Annual. ea. pt., 20s.

Part 1, arranged by trade groups (based on S.I.T.C. (Rev.)), covers the 20 principal ports for both exports and imports, by value and quantity. Part 2 has data on selected important commodities imported or exported at these ports, showing principal ports and industries concerned. Part 3 has data for individual ports (arranged geographically round the coasts of the U.K.) by commodity, showing volume and value. There is obvious overlap between *Port statistics,* and v. 5 of the Board of Trade's *Annual statement of the trade of the U.K.* But the three are "not strictly comparable because of the different emphases in their approaches" (*Board of Trade journal,* v. 192, no. 3,642, 6th January 1967, p. 18).

The National Ports Council's *Digest of port statistics, 1966* (London. 1966. 243p. illus., maps. 30s.) has 172 tables and associated notes on the major aspects of the British port transport industry for 1965. A major omission, states *Geographical journal* (v. 133, pt. 2, June 1967, p. 215-6), is the lack of time series.

382 (410)
GREAT BRITAIN. BOARD OF TRADE. Overseas trade accounts of the United Kingdom. January 1965-. London, H.M. Stationery Office, 1965-. Monthly. ea. 30s. £18 17s. p.a.

1848-. Previously (1950-64) as *Accounts relating to trade and navigation of the United Kingdom.*
Summary statistics of U.K. overseas trade, "compiled from the declarations made to H.M. Customs and Excise by importers and exporters or their agents, which are subject to verification by Customs officials" (*Note*). Tables: 1. Imports —2. Exports (produce and manufactures of the U.K.)—3. Exports of imported merchandise—4. Value of merchandise imported from and exported to each specified country—5. Imports of gold and coin—6. Quantities of certain imported goods entered for home use—7. Goods charged with duties of excise, etc. Index to imports and exports. Monthly issues give cumulative totals. Arrangement accords with the classification of goods in the *Statistical classification for imported goods and for re-exported goods* and the *Export list.*

382 (410)
GREAT BRITAIN. BOARD OF TRADE. Report on overseas trade. February 1950-. London, H.M. Stationery Office, 1950-. Monthly. ea. 4s.; 54s. p.a.

Presents the broad pattern of U.K. overseas trade in tabular statistical form, with a section on the overseas trade of other countries. The data are chiefly based on the more detailed statistics given in *Overseas trade accounts of the United Kingdom* (previously *Accounts relating to trade and navigation of the United Kingdom*). V. 18, no. 3, March 1967 has 14 tables and gives statistics up to January 1967; retrospective to 1956 or giving 1965 comparisons with 1966.

382 (410)
GREAT BRITAIN. H.M. CUSTOMS AND EXCISE. Annual statement of the trade of the United Kingdom with Commonwealth countries and foreign countries. London, H.M. Stationery Office, 1853-. 5v. Annual. (1963, published 1966. £38 5s.).

v. 1. *Summaries of import and export trade.*
v. 2. *Articles imported and re-exported, and trade in coin and bullion.*

v. 3. *Exports of U.K. produce and manufactures.*
v. 4. *Trade with individual countries.*
v. 5. *The foreign trade handled at each U.K. port.*

Eire

382 (417)
EIRE. CENTRAL STATISTICS OFFICE. Trade statistics of Ireland. Dublin, Stationery Office. Monthly. 1s. 3d. (Annual: Trade and shipping statistics. 1963 ed. 10s. 6d.).

The December issue of *Trade statistics of Ireland* gives annual figures.

England

382 (420)
CLARK, G. N. Guide to English commercial statistics, 1696-1782. London, Royal Historical Society, 1938. xvi, 211p.

Text covers Introduction ('Statistics based on the yield of the Customs before 1696')—The Inspectors-General of Imports and Exports—The Bills of Entry—The General Registers of Shipping—Note on the Port Books—Appendix of documents. 'Catalogue of statistical materials', by B. M. Franks (p. 151-206; headings: Commodities; Value or quantities; Imported or Exported; From; To; Period covered; Date of returns; Reference; Remarks). Index.

Africa

382 (6)
UNITED NATIONS. ECONOMIC COMMISSION FOR AFRICA. Foreign trade statistics of Africa. [Addis Ababa, [1963?]-.]. 2 p.a.

Series A. *Direction of trade.* ea. $1.50.
Series B. *Trade by commodity.* ea. $4.
Series A gives trade by country data in $1000. Series B provides cumulative half-yearly statistics on African commodity trade according to S.I.T.C. (Rev.), by regions and countries of provenance and destination in U.S. $1000. Imports and exports are analysed by sections, groups or subgroups. The January/June 1965 issue covered 12 African countries.

See also European Communities. Statistical Office. *Foreign trade statistics. Overseas associates,* at 382 (4/9).

Trade in Commodities

382:62
UNITED NATIONS. Economic Commission for Europe. **Bulletin of statistics on world trade in engineering products** in 1963-. New York, United Nations, 1966-. Annual. (1965 v., published 1967. $3). (ST/ECE/ENG/4).

Covers the exports of 28 countries, representing *c.* 99% of world trade in engineering products (from typewriters and machine tools to gas turbines and nuclear reactors); broken down into 80 product groups and 120 destinations, including also 12 regional sub-totals. Export data are expressed in U.S. $ million, on an f.o.b. basis. Explanatory notes, in English, French and Russian, precede tables.

382:63
FOOD AND AGRICULTURE ORGANIZATION. Trade yearbook. Rome, F.A.O., 1947-. v. 1-.

V. 18 (1964) has 119 tables in two main parts: 1. Value of agricultural trade; 2. Commodity trade, 1959-63. World coverage. Value, commodity and country notes in English, French and Spanish; headings in English and Spanish. Kept up to date by the F.A.O. *Monthly bulletin of agricultural economics and statistics* (1952-). The February 1967 (v. 16, no. 2) issue contains an article, commodity notes and 18 statistical tables (production; trade; prices); cumulative index for previous 12 months.

382:669.1
UNITED NATIONS. ECONOMIC COMMISSION FOR EUROPE. Statistics of world trade in steel . . . Geneva (later, New York), United Nations, 1961-. tables. Annual. (1965 v., published 1966. $1.).

Covers exports of semi-finished and finished steel products by regions and countries of destination. 25 exporting countries (Belgium-Luxembourg as one), A-Z.

382:677.31
COMMONWEALTH ECONOMIC COMMITTEE. Wool trade in wool and wool textiles, 1952-1963. London, H.M. Stationery Office, 1965. 195p. tables. 35*s.*

Continues the C.E.C.'s *World consumption of wool, 1950-53* and *Wool production and trade, 1952-56.*
Trade data on 69 countries, arranged A-Z under continents or regions. 268 tables in main text. The 13 appendices give comparative statistics for major trading countries; also import duties in selected countries.

Trade Agreements
382.4
Hertslet's Commercial treaties: a collection of treaties and conventions between Great Britain and foreign powers, and of the laws, decrees, Orders in Council, etc., concerning the same, so far as they relate to commerce, navigation, slavery, extradition, nationality, copyright, postal matters, etc. London, Stationery Office, 1827-1925. 31v. (Reprinted 1966. *c.* £500. v. 1-5, ea. £10; v. 6-31, ea. £18 10*s.*).

V. 22 is the general index to v. 1-21; v. 31, the general index to v. 22-30. Continued in *British and foreign state papers* (at 341.24 (08)).

382.4
Who's who in trade agreements, 1958. London, Rayment, 1958. 124p. 40*s.;* Quarterly supplements, June/September 1958-.

Lists A-Z the parties to trade agreements in force. The agreements themselves are listed in order of file number at the Registrar's Office. "Supplements note amendments to earlier agreements and additional agreements on which proceedings have commenced" (*Licences and current official registers,* compiled by C. A. Toase; loose insert).

382.4:016
GENERAL AGREEMENT ON TARIFFS AND TRADE. Secretariat. Information and Library Services. **G.A.T.T. Bibliography,** 1947/1953-. Geneva, G.A.T.T., 1954-. [i], 40, 8p. Annual supplements, 1955-; (12th supplement, January-December, 1966. [1967].).

Lists books, pamphlets, articles in periodicals, newspaper reports and editorials, including texts of lectures which refer to the General Agreement on Tariffs and Trade. Intended for reference for historians, researchers and students, on the operation of G.A.T.T. Omits G.A.T.T. Secretariat items (for which see G.A.T.T.'s *Publications* list, 1965-). The 11th supplement (covering 1965 & January 1966) has *c.* 850 items in 9 sections; mimeographed.

Imports
382.5 (410)
Croner's reference book for importers. New Malden, Croner Publications, Ltd. 200p. Looseleaf.

Usefully brings together current information on the general procedure for importing, import controls, exchange controls, purchase tax, marking, customs and excise, transhipment and insurance; detailed subject index.

Exports
382.6:016
GENERAL AGREEMENT ON TARIFFS AND TRADE. International Trade Centre. **A select bibliography for export promotion services in developing countries.** Geneva, G.A.T.T., 1966. v, 37p.

Aims to give assistance in the selection of important and relevant works to persons establishing or enlarging libraries of export promotion centres, or trade information centres in developing countries (*Introduction*).
Consists of 700 entries for books, directories and periodicals divided into two major sections, a functional section dealing with specialised aspects of trade and marketing, and a geographical section subdivided by regions and countries. Customs tariffs, trade and production statistics, and development plans are excluded.
The G.A.T.T. *Manual of export promotion technique* (1966. 218p.) examines the export techniques of 27 countries and describes the various national export-promotion boards, and the services and publications that they provide.

382.6 (410)
BRITISH MARKET RESEARCH BUREAU. Major British export markets. London, the Bureau, 1965. 253p.

Britain's major markets are defined as those to which over £100 million of goods were exported in 1964; data on 21 countries (including the U.K.). Statistics are simply presented and cover population, household amenities, private consumption expenditure, ownership of household durables, cars and telephones, advertising expenditure and foreign trade. For each country, statistics are similarly presented, using the same units; thus one can, for example, compare directly the gross national product, in total and per capita, of Australia and France.

There is some overlap with the International Advertising Association's *Concise guide to international markets,* 1966 (loose-leaf), but this covers more than 60 countries, with a much greater emphasis on advertising information.

382.6 (410)

The Mercantile year book and directory for exporters. London, Lindley Jones & Bro., Ltd., 1887-. Annual. (1966. 84s.).

This long-established directory provides a list of export merchants, buyers and consumers, with the overseas markets and the types of goods in which they are interested; an A-Z list of goods shipped, with names of appropriate merchants; overseas importers, with types of goods imported and British buying agency.

The Exporter's year book (London, Syren and Shipping, Ltd., 1917-. Annual. (1966. 65s.)), although primarily concerned with export documentation, gives for each country: principal towns, airport, banks, chamber of commerce, shipping, lines, holiday, currency, weights and measures, postal information and British representation. Kept up to date by *The merchant shipper* (monthly). More detailed information about exporting to particular countries (although part applies only to exporting from the U.S.A.) is given in the *Exporters' encyclopedia* (Dun and Bradstreet. Annual. $50).

Similar information appears in *Croner's Reference book for exporters* (New Malden. Croner Publications, 1967. 60s.), a loose-leaf publication kept up to date on a service basis.

382.6 (410):016

BROMLEY, D. W. What to read on exporting. 2nd ed. London, Library Association, 1966. 68p. (Special subject list no. 42).

First published 1963.

375 numbered items (plus interpolations), most of them annotated, in 16 sections. Covers items published to the end of September 1965. Prices are stated; gratis items included. Directory of publishers' addresses, p. 54-63. Author, title and subject index. A handy and timely list on the mechanics of foreign trade, finance, insurance, marketing, market research, advertising, packaging and commerce. 'Trade with individual areas', p. 32-48.

Postal Services

383 (038)=00

UNION POSTALE UNIVERSELLE. Bureau International. **Vocabulaire polyglotte du service postal international.** 3rd ed. Berne, U.P.U., 1961-64. 7 pts. ea. Sw. fr. 9.50. Supplements, 1963-.

First published 1954.

Definitions and equivalents for more than 1,000 terms in French, English, Spanish, Russian, Arabic and Chinese.

383 (4/9) (083.4)

UNION POSTALE UNIVERSELLE. Bureau International. **Statistique complète des services postaux,** 1958-. Berne, U.P.U., 1960-.

Every 3 years; in the years when the complete statistics are not published, an abridged version appears under the title *Statistique réduite des services postaux.*

383 (410)

GREAT BRITAIN. GENERAL POST OFFICE. Post office guide. London, H.M. Stationery Office, 1856-. Annual. (1967. 2s. 6d.). Monthly supplements.

Full details of inland and overseas services, including telephones, savings and remittances. Index.

————**Post offices in the United Kingdom and the Irish Republic,** excluding the London postal area. London, H.M. Stationery Office. 1966. 4s.

Gives correct postal and telegraphic addresses of more than 20,000 places in the British Isles (including Eire and the Channel Islands), *i.e.,* of every place at which there is a post office. Previous issue, 1964. *Postal addresses* (1966. 1s. 6d.) is an abridged version.

Supplemented by *London post offices and streets* (1966. 2s.).

383 (417)

EIRE. DEPARTMENT OF POSTS AND TELE-GRAPHS. Eolaí an Phoist. Post-office guide. Dublin, Stationery Office. 2 pts., issued in alternate years. Supplements to both pts. *Gratis.*

pt. 1. *General information: inland services.* Irregular (about once in 5 years). (1964. 1s. 6d.).

pt. 2. *Foreign services.* Annual (1964. 1s. 6d.).

Postage Stamps

383:656.835:016

LINDSAY, J. L., *26th Earl of Crawford.* **Catalogue of the philatelic library of the Earl of Crawford,** by E. D. Bacon, London. Philatelic Literature Society, 1911. x p., 924 col. Supplement. 1926; Addenda to Supplement. 1938.

Also published as v. 7 of *Bibliotheca Lindesiana,* with title *A bibliography of philately.* Lists monographs to 1908 and periodicals to 1906; an appendix lists all the periodicals in chronological order. One of the most complete bibliographies of any subject, not confined to books actually in the library; this collection is now in the British Museum.

For coverage of periodicals published January 1950 to date: "Index to current philatelic periodicals", in *The Stamp lover* (London. National Philatelic Society. 1950-. Bi-monthly). About 100 English-language journals are indexed: volume and page references are given, but not dates. Books are listed.

383:656.835:016

NEGUS, J. "A brief guide to sources of philatelic information." In *Philately,* v. 7(8), March/April 1959, p. 102-103; v. 7, no. 9, May/June 1959, p. 116, 121.

Surveys the major handbooks, bibliographies, and indexes to periodicals; does not cover stamp catalogues, or libraries as sources.

383:656.835 (032)

SUTTON, R. J., *comp.* **The stamp collectors' encyclopaedia.** 6th ed., revised by K. W. Anthony. London, Paul, 1966. 370p. illus., diagrs. 42*s.*

First published 1951.

About 3,000 brief entries, arranged A-Z,—philatelic terms (*e.g.,* 'Perforation': ½p. plus illustration), countries (*e.g.,* 'Italy': 17½ lines of postal history and general data), etc. Reproductions of three stamps at the head of each page. Appendices include a very brief glossary (p. 344-5) and an illustrated section on stamp recognition, with 123 examples.

383:656.835 (038)

PHILATELIC CONGRESS OF GREAT BRIT-AIN. A glossary of philatelic terms; edited by H. T. Graham. London, Blandford Press, 1951. 108p.

Pt. 1: A glossary of philatelic terms with some reference to postal history, compiled by a sub-committee of the Philatelic Congress of Great Britain; pt. 2: A glossary of technical terms relating to scientific methods as applied to philately, compiled by W. H. S. Cheavin.

383:656.835 (083.8)

GIBBONS, Stanley, Ltd. Priced postage stamp catalogue. London, Gibbons, 1865-. illus. Annual. (1st numbered ed. 1879).

pt. 1: *British Commonwealth, Ireland and South Africa.* 1968 ed. 1967. 35*s.*
pt. 2: *Europe and colonies.* 1968 ed. 1967. 60*s.*
pt. 3: *America, Asia and Africa.* 1968 ed. 1967. 50*s.*

Supplements appear in *Gibbons' Stamp monthly.*

The most important British stamp catalogue, more detailed than any except Robson Lowe (*q.v.*). From 1950 the illustrations in pts. 2-3 are reduced to three-quarters original size, but in pt. 1 they are still full-size. The stamps of Queen Elizabeth II's reign are brought together, with more details of varieties, in the *Elizabethan postage stamp catalogue* (1968 ed. 1967, 22*s.* 6*d.*).

Stanley Gibbons [simplified] whole world stamp catalogue is a single-volume world-wide catalogue, listing no varieties and suitable for children's libraries (Annual. 1968 ed. 1967. 40*s.*).

The most important American catalogue is: Scott Publications, Inc. *Standard postage stamp catalogue (the encyclopaedia of philately)* (New York, Scott, 1867-. illus. Annual. (1966 ed. 1966. $15). Supplements appear in *Scott's Monthly journal.*

Continental catalogues: (*a*) Yvert & Tellier. *Catalogue de timbres-poste* (Amiens, Yvert & Tellier, 1897-. 3v. illus. Annual). Title varies; supplements in *L'écho de la timbrologie* (monthly); (*b*) Zumstein. *Briefmarken-Katalog: Europa* (40th ed., 1957. Berne, Zumstein. 1956. Sw.fr.15.50). Supplements in *Berner Briefmarken Zeitung* (monthly).

383:656.835 (41-44)

LOWE, ROBSON, Ltd. The encyclopaedia of British Empire postage stamps. London, Lowe, 1948-. illus.

v. 1: *Great Britain and the Empire in Europe.* 2nd ed. 1952. o.p.
v. 2: *The Empire in Africa.* 1949. o.p.
v. 3: *The Empire in Asia.* 1951. 42*s.*
v. 4: *The Empire in Australia.* 1962. 84*s.*
v. 5: *America* (not yet published).

Includes handstruck stamps, postal stationery and local issues; bibliographies. The most detailed catalogue of British Empire stamps.

Supplements appear in *The philatelist* (monthly).

383:656.835 (410):016

STRANGE, A. M. A list of books on the postal history, postmarks and adhesive postage and revenue stamps of Great Britain. London, Great Britain Philatelic Society, 1964. 32p. 10*s.* 6*d.*

Entries grouped under 14 headings; no indexes.

Telephone, etc. Directories

384 (058.7) (4/9)

COCKX, A., and **STEKHOVEN, G. S. I.F.L.A.-I.A.T.U.L. telecode and telex address book:** telecode in 10 languages and international address book for libraries and documentation centres. 2nd ed. Sevenoaks, International Federation of Library Associations, 1966. 191p. 42*s.*

The telecode consists of about 50 three-letter code symbols for use in telex messages concerned with inter-library co-operation. This is followed by a directory of libraries and documentation centres arranged first geographically, then by name and then by "answer-back".

384 (058.7) (4/9)

International telephone directory, 1954-. Paris, International Telephone Directory, 1954-. Annual.

Covers 110 countries and is particularly valuable for its inclusion of some smaller countries about which there is a limited amount of directory information available. A-Z by countries, then classified by subject, each subject having the same classification number throughout. A table of international telephone charges appears on the first page of each national listing.

384 (058.7) (4/9)

Internationales Telex-Verzeichnis. 14th ed. Darmstadt, Telex-Verlag Jaeger & Waldmann, 1966. 3v. Annual.

Claims to include 168,749 telex subscribers from 112 countries and to be compiled from official information provided by the relevant national postal administrations and telecommunication companies. Subscribers are listed by country, first A-Z by name and secondly by town. V. 1 covers Europe and v. 2, the rest of the world. V. 3 contains a word list of answer-back codes in A-Z order, with full name and address of each subscriber (Australia, New Zealand and Germany have separate sequences).

384 (058.7) (4/9)

Marconi's International register. New York, Telegraphic Cable & Radio Registrations, Inc. (1967. 160*s.*).

Sections (1967 ed.): Alphabetical (name & address; principal codes; cable address)—Classified trade—South Africa supplement—Trade names, brands and trade marks—Legal—English, French, Spanish and German indexes of headings in the classified section—Cable address index—Code key.

384 (058.7) (4/9)

UNION INTERNATIONALE DES TELECOMMUNICATIONS. Official list of telegraph offices open for international service. 22nd ed. Geneva, Union Internationale des Télécommunications, 1965. 4v.

A list, compiled by computer, of about 350,000 telegraph offices throughout the world, giving name of country and territorial subdivision for each office. Valuable as a source of up-to-date gazetteer information. Quarterly supplements.

384 (058.7) (4/9)

World trade telex. Telex subscribers, classified according to trades . . . 8th ed. Darmstadt, Telex-Verlag Jaeger & Waldmann, 1965. v.p. DM.39.

7th ed. 1964.
Gives names and addresses of 149,348 telex subscribers in all the countries connected to an international telex network. Also an A-Z list of firms (by countries) with valuable information about the firms (*e.g.*, directors, capital, number of employees, manufacturing programme, export and import markets, and language of correspondence). Reviewed in *Telecommunication journal,* v. 33, no. 3, March 1966, p. 130.

384 (058.7 (4)

Teleurope: industry and commerce of the O.E.C.D. countries: export-import directory of the O.E.C.D. countries. . . 11th ed. Darmstadt, Teleurope, 1966. 2552p.

Annual. In 3 sections. The first lists firms by country, then name, with postal address, telegraphic address and trade classification symbol. The second lists firms by trade, then country, with postal and telegraphic addresses; indexes of trades in English, French, German and Spanish. Section three lists telegraphic addresses A-Z under country; following each address the beginning of the firm's name is stated, and reference to the first section gives full name and postal address. About 200,000 importers and exporters in the 21 O.E.C.D. countries as well as Finland are listed.

384 (058.7) (410)

GREAT BRITAIN. GENERAL POST OFFICE. [Alphabetical telephone directories]. London, G.P.O. Annual. 58 sections in 61 v.; also bound in 20 v., 101s.

Lists of subscribers covering Great Britain, Northern Ireland and the Isle of Man, but not the Channel Isles. The only general directory covering the whole country.

———— **Index to telephone directories.** London, G.P.O. Irregular. *Gratis.*

———— **[Classified telephone directories]:** London, G.P.O. 22v. Irregular (1966. ea. 3s. 6d.).

Published for the more populous areas only; gradually being replaced by classified sections in the alphabetical directories. Lists business-rate subscribers under trade headings arranged A-Z, but excludes barristers, and in London excludes certain retail trades.

———— **United Kingdom telex directory.**

The October 1966 issue (Supplement, January 1967) lists subscribers in two A-Z sequences: subscribers' names and answer-back code (on green-tinted paper).

384 (058.7) (410)

Sell's Directory of registered telegraphic addresses, with telephone numbers and classified trades. Epsom, Surrey, Business Dictionaries, Ltd. Annual. (82nd year, 1967. 97s. 6d.).

Three main sections: 1. Alphabetical list of firms (London; country)—2. Alphabetical list of telegraphic addresses (London; country); index to telex subscribers—3. Sell's classified trades list (the chief business concerns of the U.K. and Ireland in every trade). Special sections: Special list of contractors; trade marks and brands.

384 (058.7) (417)

EIRE. DEPARTMENT OF POSTS AND TELE-GRAPHS. Eolai telefóin. Irish telephone directory. Dublin, the Department, 1966. 2s. 6d.

Pt. 1, Dublin. A-Z names; code numbers only. Classified list of subscribers. Pt. 2, Rest of Eire. A-Z towns.

384 (058.7) (43)

Das Deutsche Branchen Fernsprechbuch der Firmen in der Bundesrepublik Deutschland und Berlin, 1965. 31. Aufl. Darmstadt, Deutscher Adressbuch-Verlag, 1964.

A classified arrangement, in 55 groups and under 40,000 entry-words, of manufacturers, service trades, wholesalers, retailers, exporters and handicraft workers as well as liberal professions, public authorities, economic organizations and scientific, technical, cultural and political institutions. Indexes in English, French, German and Spanish. Claims to include 1,600,000 names and addresses, plus telephone numbers.
A companion volume, *Das Deutsche Firmen Alphabet,* is an A-Z list by name of 500,000 German firms, giving address, telephone number and trade.

Adress- und Fernsprechbücher (Düsseldorf, Adressbucherverleger-Verband E.V. (1965. 64p.), official catalogue of the Germany directory-publishers association, lists general, specialized, local and telephone directories, with details of publication.

Transport

385/388 (091):016

DYOS, H. J. "Transport history in university theses, 1959-63". In *The journal of transport history,* v. 7, no. 1, May 1965, p. 54-86.

General history of transport—Sea transport—Ports, docks and harbours—Inland waterways—Road transport—Railway transport—Air transport. Covers 15 universities in the British Isles; 30 titles.

The previous list of university theses appeared in v. 4, no. 3, May 1960, p. 161-73.

ABC goods transport guide. 7s. 6d.

The May issue each year of *The journal of transport history* carries a "Transport bibliography" of *c.* 100 items in 2 sections: 1. Publications on the history of transport in British periodicals during the previous year (arranged under titles of journals)—2. Official publications referring to Great Britain and Ireland likely to become of historical importance. Excludes reports of official bodies.

385/388 (091):016
ROGERSON, I., *ed.* **History of transport.** Cheltenham, Gloucestershire Technical Information Service, 1965 (reprinted 1966). [ii], 46p. Mimeographed. (Bibliographical series, 4). *Gratis.*

—— **History of transport: a second list.** Cheltenham, Gloucestershire Technical Information Service, 1966. [ii], 24p. Mimeographed. *Gratis.*

The original compilation lists 300 books and some periodical articles. Four main sections, with sub-divisions: 1. General—2. Water transport—3. Land transport—4. Air transport. British slant; no annotations. Brief subject index; name index. The second list adds a further 200 items, similarly arranged, with name index.

385/388 (4)
UNITED NATIONS. ECONOMIC COMMISSION FOR EUROPE. Annual bulletin of transport statistics for Europe. 1949-. New York, United Nations, 1950-. Annual. (17th year, 1965. 1966. $2.).

The 1965 v. (1966) has a survey, 'Transport situation in Europe, 1960-1965', followed by 38 tables (general statistics; passenger transport; freight transport; networks; mobile equipment and staff), 4 charts and 3 appendices (1. Statistics of international goods transport (for 8 countries) —2. Definition of terms (p. 111-26; 153 headings) —3. Sources of information and coverage of statistics). Statistics for 27 countries. Addendum insert.

385/388 (410):656.022
ABC goods transport guide. London, Iliffe, 1954-. 2 p.a. (January and July). ea. 7s. 6d.

Road (home and international), rail, air, sea, canal; wharfingers, warehouses, plant hire (cranes, etc.). ABC list gives services under base town, indicating frequency and facilities available.

Railways

385 (4):016
HASKELL, D. C. A tentative check-list of early European railway literature, 1831-1848. Boston, Mass., Baker Library, Harvard Graduate, School of Business Administration, 1955. 192p.

4,171 items are listed chronologically, then A-Z under each year. Based on the Baker Library holdings, plus additional titles from 5 other libraries. Name and title index.

R. A. Peddie's *Railway literature, 1556-1830. a handlist,* by R. A. Peddie (London, Grafton, 1931. 79p.) lists 750 items in similar order, with index of names and of principal railway companies.

385 (4):656.022
Cook's Continental timetable. London, Cook. maps. Monthly. ea. 10s. 6d.

First published 1873.

Sub-title: "A simple guide to the principal rail services of Europe, North Africa and the Near East, with local steamer services in the North Sea, the Baltic and the Mediterranean". Sections: Passport and general information—International train services—Countries (France; Belgium and Holland; Switzerland; Italy; Spain and Portugal; Scandinavia; Germany; Austria; Yugoslavia; U.S.S.R./Eastern Europe; North Africa—steamship services).

385 (410):016
LEWTHWAITE, G. C. Branch line index: a list of articles on branch lines in Great Britain and Ireland which have appeared in the following magazines from their inception to the end of 1957: *Railway magazine, Trains illustrated, Railway world.* Leeds, Branch Line Society, 1960. 15p. 3s. 6d.; Supplement, 1958-62. 1963. 7p. 1s.

Articles from 1963 are indexed annually in *Branch line news.*

385 (410):016
OTTLEY, G., *with others, comp.* **A bibliography of British railway history.** London, Allen & Unwin, 1965. 683p. £10 10s.

A bibliography of 7,950 items, many of them annotated, with one location in 16 contributing libraries (particularly the British Museum) and private collections. Excludes children's books (usually), and highly technical books on specialized subjects, but includes spotter's books and some books which, while not specifically railway books, contains useful railway material. Detailed classification; main classes, A-T (*e.g.,* B. Railway transport at particular periods—C. Railway transport in particular areas . . . R. Research and study of railways and railway history . . . T. General directories, gazetteers, atlases, guide books, lists of stations, distance tables, timetables). Entries state number of illustrations. Lists and "genealogies" of railway companies as appendices. This comprehensive bibliography is supported by a very extensive author-title and subject index (p. 477-683). A model of its kind. Reviewed in *The engineer,* v. 223, no. 5,795, 17th February, 1967, p. 263.

G. Ottley is editing *Resources for the study of railways in the libraries and archives of the British Isles* for the Reference, Special and Information Section of the Library Association.

385 (410) (058.7)
CLINKER, C. R. Register of closed passenger stations and goods depots in England, Scotland and Wales. Harlyn Bay, Cornwall, the Author. 1964-66; Supplements, 1965-.

v. 1: *1830-1899.* 1966. viii, 42p.
v. 2: *1900-1964.* 2nd ed. 1964. viii, 131p.

Passengers no more by G. Daniels and L. A. Dench (Ian Allan, [1965]) lists passenger stations closed between 1919 and 1963, while H. C. Casserley's *Service suspended* (Ian Allan, [1951]) provides 60 illustrations of closed stations.

385 (410) (058.7)
Directory of railway officials & year book. 1894-. London, Tothill Press, 1894-. illus., maps. Annual. (1966-67 ed. 1966. 70s.).

"Compiled from official sources under the direction of the editor of *The railway gazette*" (title-page). Directory of railways and officials (British, p. 1-136); other countries of the world (A-Z), p. 137-428)—Locomotives and rolling stock—Oil engines—Transmission systems—Signalling—Electrified railways—Statistical and other information (including 'Railway bibliography', p. 639-46 (under 15 heads). General index; personal index to railway officials; index to advertisers; index to products advertised.

385 (410) (084.4)
British rail atlas and gazetteer. London, Ian Allan, 1965. 84p. 21s.

Maps on a scale of 8 miles to 1″ distinguish between the lines of each region by using distinctive colours. Indexes of stations, tunnels, summits, viaducts and major bridges. A companion work is *British railways pre-grouping atlas and gazetteer* (Ian Allan, [1958], 21s.), which shows the companies prior to 1923.

385 (410) (091)
CARTER, E. F. An historical geography of the railways of the British Isles. London, Cassell, 1959. x, 637p. 63s.

Aims at being a reference book on the histories of the various lines, some of them now extinct. Pt. 1, The railways of Great Britain; pt. 2, The railways of Ireland. Analytical index. No illustrations. Criticized in the *Railway gazette* (v. 112, no. 18, 29th April 1960, p. 505) for its "numerous errors, omissions, mis-statements, and contradictions. Most of the information seems to have been derived from secondary sources, and to have perpetuated their inaccuracies and inconsistencies."

385 (410) (091)
ELLIS, C. H. British railway history: an outline, from the accession of William IV to the nationalization of railways. London, Allen & Unwin, 1954-59. 2v. illus.

v. 1: 1830-1876. 30s.
v. 2: 1877-1947. 35s.
This constitutes the first general, popular history of the British railway companies (excluding those of Ireland). It carries copious references to the individuals concerned and includes mechanical and electric traction developments. Well illustrated.

385 (410) (091)
THOMAS, D. St. J., and CLINKER, C. R., ed. A regional history of the railways of Great Britain. Dawlish, David & Charles; London, Macdonald, 1960-. illus., facsims., tables, diagrs., maps.

v. 1: *The west country,* by D. St. J. Thomas. 3rd ed. 1966. 42s.
v. 2: *Southern England,* by H. P. White. 2nd ed. 1964. 42s.
v. 3: *Greater London,* by H. P. White. 1963. 42s.
v. 4: *North-east England,* by K. Hoole. 1965. 42s.
Each volume is self-contained. V. 4 has 44 good quality half-tone plates, 9 text illustrations, 8 regional maps, 1 folding map, plus author's notes and acknowledgements, p. 227-8.

385 (410):656.2
ABC rail guide and hotel guide. London, Skinner. Monthly. 8s. 6d.

Basically an alphabetical list of places in Great Britain which are served by railways, with information on fares and train times. Appended are Scottish, suburban, Irish and continental time-tables. The "Hotel guide" consists of advertisements.
For more detailed information, reference must be made to British Railways' regional timetables, in 8 bulky volumes (ea. 2s.-3s.), 2-3 monthly, with interim supplements, *gratis.*

385 (410):656.21
BRITISH TRANSPORT COMMISSION. Official hand-book of stations, including junctions, sidings, collieries, works, etc., on the railways of Great Britain and Ireland, showing the station accommodation, crane power, county, region, executive or company, and position. London, British Transport Commission, Railway Clearing House, 1956. 494p.

Data are given in column form; more than 30,000 entries. Includes private companies' sidings under the name of both the company and the place.
Supplemented by *Alterations in names of stations, opening of sidings, etc.* 1956-.

385 (410):91 (03)
Railway and commercial gazetteer of England, Scotland and Wales. 21st ed. London, McCorquodale, 1963. [vii], 716p. 85s

Lists about 46,000 places in Great Britain, stating population, distance from nearest railway station, distance of station from London and relevant London terminal, together with post offices, money-order offices and telegraph offices.

385 (421)
BARKER, T. C., and ROBBINS, M. A history of London transport: passenger travel and the development of the Metropolis. London, Allen & Unwin, 1963-.

v. 1. *The nineteenth century.* 1963. 40s.
Volume 1 of London Transport's official history, covering 'buses, trams, boats, and surface and underground railways. "Admirably written, excellently presented and backed by a wealth of information, facts and figures" (*Engineering*, v. 199, no. 5,156, 12th February 1965, p. 217). Contains nearly 70 pages of explanatory notes. Well documented.
To be completed in 2v.

Inland Waterways

386 (4)

Inland waterways series. London, & St. Ives (Hunts.) Imray, Laurie, Norie & Wilson, 1950-. illus., diagrs., maps, plans.

> *Inland waterways of Belgium,* by E. E. Benest. 1960. 35s.
> *Inland waterways of France,* by E. E. Benest. 1956. 36s. 6d.
> *Inland waterways of Great Britain and Ireland,* compiled by L. A. Edwards. 2nd ed. 1962. 45s.
> *Inland waterways of the Netherlands.* v. 1. *Southern Netherlands,* by E. E. Benest. 1966. 50s.; *North east Netherlands,* by E. E. Benest, 1968. 50s.

The volume *Inland waterways of France* (vii, 262p.) has tabulated 'Particulars of rivers and canals' (p. 39-252) (place; port, lock, etc.; km. distance (from start); Lock; km. from finish); Appendix of sketch plans of some of the principal watering junctions. (14p.); measured cross-sections of tunnels.

386 (410) (02)

BRITISH WATERWAYS. Inland cruising booklets. London, British Waterways Board, 1958-. 15v. ea. 3s. 6d.

> 1. *Llangollen Canal.*
> 2. *Trent Waterway.*
> 3. *Lee and Stort Navigations.*
> 4. *Staffordshire and Worcestershire Canal.*
> 5. *Shropshire Union Canal.*
> 6. *Oxford Canal.*
> 7. *Fossdyke and Witham Navigations.*
> 8, 9, 10. *Grand Union Canal.*
> 11. *Macclesfield Canal.*
> 12, 13. *Trent and Mersey Canal.*
> 14. *Severn Waterway.*
> 15. *Lancaster Canal.*

Each booklet includes a diagrammatic representation of the canal concerned, with parallel descriptive text; also brief history, charges, addresses and other handy data; illustrations and folding map of the waterway system. New editions of individual booklets are published irregularly.

Single-volume guides: British Canoe Union. *Guide to the waterways of the British Isles* (3rd ed. London, the Union, 1966. 270p. 21s.), with detailed descriptions of rivers, canals and lakes; L. A. Edwards' *Inland waterways of Great Britain and Northern Ireland* (2nd ed. London, Imray, Laurie, Norie & Wilson, 1962. xviii, 484p. 45s.), with systematic data on 138 numbered canals and rivers.

386 (410) (02)

The Canals of the British Isles; edited by C. Hadfield. Newton Abbot, Devon, David & Charles; London, Macdonald, 1950-. v. 1-. illus., maps.

> 1. *British canals: an illustrated history,* by C. Hadfield. 1950; rev. ed. 1959 (3rd imp., with extra illus.). 42s.
> 2. *The canals of south-west England,* by C. Hadfield. 1967. 30s.
> 3. *The canals of south Wales and the Border,* by C. Hadfield. 2nd ed. 1967. 50s.
> 4. *The canals of the north of Ireland,* by W. A. McCutcheon. [1965]. 42s.

> 5. *The canals of the east Midlands (including part of London),* by C. Hadfield. 1966.
> 6. *The canals of the west Midlands,* by C. Hadfield. 1966. 50s.
> 7. *The canals of the south of Ireland,* by V. T. H. and D. R. Delany. 1966. 50s.
> 8. *The canals of Scotland,* by J. Lindsay.

V. 6, *The canals of the West Midlands* has tabular data, notes on the principal engineering works, 16 plates, 20 text illustrations and diagrams, and an index; chapter notes, p. 297-313. V. 5-6 have valuable summary tables that detail the rise and fall of individual canals, several excellent maps of the completed canal networks and numerous photographs (*Geographical journal,* v. 133, pt. 2, June 1967, p. 216). V. 2 is to be the first of 2 v. to replace *The canals of southern England* (1955).

386 (410) (084.4)

The Canals book, 1967. Norwich, Norfolk, Dibb, 1967. 144p. maps. 5s.

The main feature is the wealth of large-scale maps (198 are numbered), showing depths of locks, etc. 'Canals and navigations', p. 22-138, giving detailed itineraries. Includes list of derelict and closed canals and navigations, hire craft on the canals and canal societies.

Waterways atlas of the British Isles, by J. Cranfield and M. Bonfiel (London, Cranfield and Bonfiel Books, 1966. 44p. 16s.) has 40 sketch maps similar to Ian Allan's two railway atlases (scale: 1" to 8 miles) and carries a gazetteer. An atlas for general reference and obviously not for use in detailed navigation. Indexes of towns, canals, rivers and hire-cruise bases.

Sea Transport

387:016

Books and the sea: a list of modern books on the sea and shipping. Compiled in collaboration with the National Maritime Museum, Greenwich. London, School Library Association, 1964. viii, 39p. 13s. 6d. (members, 9s. 6d.).

About 400-500 items, listed in groups with subdivisions: The high seas—Ships and vessels—Seamen—Sea arts and sciences—Maritime geography—Travel afloat. Items are asterisked if they contain footnotes and references to school material; obelisked if they contain a bibliography. Designations: 'J', for juniors; 'G', for the general reader; 'A', for more advanced reader. No annotations as such.

387 (261)

BONSOR, N. R. P. North Atlantic seaway: an illustrated history of the passenger services linking the old world with the new. Prescot (Lancs.), T. Stephenson, 1955. xxxii, 639p. illus., map. 57s. 6d. Supplement. 1960. p. 641-692. illus. 9s. 6d.

Histories of the companies and long lists of ships, with dates and technical details; lists of record crossings, and of "firsts and lasts". Full index of ships.

387:627.21 (410)

BIRD, J. The major seaports of the United Kingdom. London, Hutchinson, 1963. 454p. illus., tables, diagrs., maps. 105s.

A painstaking analysis, in 18 chapters, of "the physical environment, history, dock systems, markets and industries of the major British ports" (Church, M., and others, comp. and ed. *A basic geographical library* (1966), entry no. 930). Each chapter takes a group of ports, associated either by locality (*e.g.*, 'South Wales ports') or function (*e.g.*, 'General cargo ports'), as well as estuaries. Appendix: Report of the Rochdale Committee (1962). Chapter references; 107 maps and diagrams; 127 tables; 24 plates. Detailed index includes references to illustrations. Well produced.

387:656.022
ABC shipping guide. London, Skinner, 1953-. Monthly. 150*s*. p.a.

Formerly part of the *ABC world airways guide,* 1943-. Initially quarterly.

All the leading shipping lines of the world are listed alphabetically, with details of sailings and fares in respect of all their vessels for the next six months. Indexes to shipping lines, advertisers, and ports and destinations served.

Ports of call—see v. 1 of the *Guide to reference material,* at 656.6.022.

Road Transport

388.1 (058)
Passenger transport year book. Shepperton, Ian Allan, 1898-. Annual. (1966/67. 63*s*.).

Directory of manufacturers, lists of organisations, and detailed directories of bus and coach operators throughout the world. The British Isles section is also published separately as *Passenger transport: the little red book.*

388.1 (058)
Official ABC coach and bus guide, 1951-. Dunstable, Index Publishers, 1955-. maps. 2 p.a. (March and September, with supplement in May/June). ea. 10*s*.

Gives complete timetables and fares for regular coach services in Britain and on the continent; covers mainly long-distance services. Now includes international coach services, and coach/air and coach/boat connections.

There are also various regional guides (*e.g.*, London Transport's *Green Line coach guide*).

The British Road Services' *Directory* ([1965?]-. Loose-leaf) covers divisions, districts, groups and depots of the British Road Services, and includes Pickfords and Hay's Wharf services.

Air Transport

388.9 (091)
DAVIES, R. E. G. A history of the world's airlines. London, Oxford Univ. Press, 1964. xxx, 591p. 84*s*.

Detailed study, with maps, tables of airlines and their fleets, and photos. of 209 aircraft; select bibliog. pp. xxvii-xxx.

388.9:656.022
ABC world airways guide, 1934-. London, Skinner, 1934-. maps. Monthly. ea. 20*s*.

Formerly *ABC world airways and shipping guide. The ABC shipping guide* is now issued separately (see at 387.1:656.6.022).

Provides an index of fares, arranged under place A-Z, and a timetable of air services, numbered 23-2000 and also arranged A-Z, by name of service. Airline map section appended.

Supplemented by *ABC amendments service* (several monthly).

The *ABC air cargo guide.* 1958-. (London, Skinner, 1958-. Monthly. 5*s*. 6*d*.) gives schedules of regular routes, notes, import regulations, weights and dimensions, etc.

388.9:656.022
Airport times, 1964-. London, Airport Times, 1964-. Monthly. ea. 4*s*.

Abridged timetable of services within the British Isles and international services from and to the British Isles. Arranged alphabetically by town of departure, giving times, flight number, and class of aircraft, but not fares or other details. Simpler to use than the rather complex *ABC.*

388.9:656.022
Croner's Air transportation guide: a handy reference book and guide for all users of air transport, both for passengers and freight, by scheduled, non-scheduled and charter services. Compiled and edited by R. K. Bridges. Kingston upon Thames (then, New Malden), Croner, 1955-. 77*s*.; renewal 40*s*. p.a. Loose-leaf, with monthly supplements.

Describes services from London, but does not give timetables. Sections: 1. Addresses—2. Freight (general information; transshipment charges, freight charges, table of freight rates, groupage services, chartering, specialized services)—3. Passengers (air-sea interchange; baggage; children; credit travel; currency; fares; taxes; tickets) —4. Countries (climate; clothing; services; groupage services available; groupage rates; airport service charges; passport, visa and health regulations.

388.9:656.022
World airline record. Chicago, Roadcap and Associates. 1948-. Biennial. $29.50.

1st ed. as *Airline record.* Claims to list every scheduled airline in the world (over 300), giving history, routes (with map), traffic, finance, management, ownership, mergers, equipment and statistics. Checklist of airlines that have merged, ceased operations, or changed name, with references to earlier eds.

388.9:91 (03)
BRITISH EUROPEAN AIRWAYS. European gazetteer, 1966. [Ruislip, Middlesex, B.E.A., 1966]. [44]p.

"Primarily intended to help pinpoint the more popular resorts in relationship to the nearest BEA service" (introduction). About 650 entries, under countries A-Z. Data tabulated: Resort; B.E.A. gateway; onward by ('bus, etc.); Distance (miles); Time; Features (*e.g.*, spa; fishing; casino). Graphic symbols used.

Weights & Measures

Metric System

389.151

GREAT BRITAIN. NATIONAL PHYSICAL LABORATORY. Changing to the metric system: conversion factors, symbols and definitions, by P. Anderton and P. H. Bigg. London, H.M. Stationery Office, 1965 (reprinted with additions, 1966). 46p. 3s. 6d. (2nd ed. 1967. 4s. 6d.).

Contents: The International Systems of Units (SI)—Table 1: Conversion of common British units to equivalent values in SI units—Table 2: Conversion of specialized or obsolescent British units to equivalent values in SI units—Table 3: Conversion of common SI units to equivalent values in British units. 6 appendices, including bibliography (p. 45-46). Two indexes, one based on symbols of units, and the other on full names.

Units

389.16

AMIRAN, D. H. K., and **SCHICK, A. P.,** comp. and ed. **Geographical conversion tables.** Zurich, International Geographical Union, 1961. xxxvi, 315p. tables, map. Swiss fr. 20.

18 sets of tables, from 1. Basic conversion factors—2. Length—3. Area, to 15. Temperature—16. Pressure—17. Economic conversions (weights, etc. of commodities)—18. Weights, measures and currencies. Includes 10. Map scales—11. Slopes, angles, time—13. Global grid—14. The illumination of the globe. Text and table captions are in English, French, German, Russian and Spanish.

389.16

BRITISH STANDARDS INSTITUTION. British Standard conversion factors and tables. London, the Institution, 1959-62. 2 pts. (B.S.350: 1959-62). 40s. Amendments.

> pt. 1. *Basis of tables. Conversion factors.* 1959.
> 15s. Amendments PD 4850. 1963;
> PD 5023. 1963 (2s. 6d.); PD 5435. 1965.
> pt. 2. *Detailed conversion tables.* 1962. 25s.

Part 1 covers a wide range of conversion factors in metrology, mechanics and heat. Purely electrical units are not dealt with. Part 2 gives detailed conversions mostly to the nearest 6th significant figure.

389.16

CLASON, W. E., comp. **Elsevier's Lexicon of international and national units,** English/American — German — Spanish — French — Italian — Japanese — Dutch — Portuguese — Polish—Swedish—Russian. Amsterdam, London, New York, Elsevier, 1964. 75p. (Elsevier lexica). 27s.

299 English/American terms, with definitions, plus equivalents (but not indicating genders or plural forms) in 10 other languages. A second section lists units (300-368) used in different parts of the world, A-Z by 69 countries. 'Index of international and national units' (p. 61-72), covering 10 of the 11 languages in one A-Z sequence; 'Russian index . . .', p. 73-74. Appended is a bibliography of dictionaries, glossaries and vocabularies, and of textbooks. Reviewed in *The incorporated linguist,* v. 6, no. 2, April 1967, p. 53.

389.16

CUSSET, F. Tables complètes de conversion des mesures américaines, britanniques et métriques. Éd. rev. et completée. Paris, Blondel La Rougery, 1959. 230p.

Comprehensive: tables of length, surface, volume, capacity, flow, mass, force, energy, power, pressure, temperature, thermal units, moments of inertia, etc. Summaries, and chapter and page headings in 3 languages (English, French, German). A comparable work is:

F. Beigbeder's *Conversiones metrológicas entre los sistemas norteamericanos, inglés, métrico decimal, cegesimal y Giorgi* (Madrid, Ediciones Castilla, 1952. 765p). This compilation gives exhaustive tables of equivalents of length, surface, volume, pressure, energy, moments of inertia, viscosity, angles, etc. The 320 tables provide about 10,000 conversions.

The U.S. National Bureau of Standards' *Units of weight and measure (United States customary and metric): definitions and tables of equivalents* (Washington, G.P.O., 1960. ii, 62p. (NBS miscellaneous publications, 233) 40c.) gives exhaustive tables, but is much more restricted. For conversion from miles to km. it gives equivalents for each mile from 1 to 999. In the 1961 ed. (50c.) the units are defined in conformity with the 1959 agreement among the directors of National Standards Laboratories of English-speaking nations. New ed. 1967 [3], 251p. NBS miscellaneous publication, 286).

389.16

DOURSTHER, H. Dictionnaire universel des poids et mesures anciens et modernes, contenant des tables des monnaies de tous les pays. Brussels, Hayez, 1840. iv, 604p. (Reprinted Amsterdam, Meridian Publishing Co., 1965. 135s.).

Extremely full alphabetical list of units, with French, English and decimal equivalents; for monetary units gives French and English weights, content and value. About 10-20,000 different units in all. Invaluable on Asiatic, historical and obscure currencies or weights and measures (*e.g.,* Paolo; Ghersch; Platt; Batman; Line; Mud; Muck; Mun).

389.16

"The Economist" Guide to weights & measures; compiled by the Statistical Department of "The Economist." 2nd ed. London, "The Economist", 1962. 96p. 17s. 6d.

Conversion tables (monetary, linear and square measures, wages and salaries, etc.), currencies, and miscellaneous units of measure in use in Great Britain. Useful definitions appear under the heading 'Agricultural commodities' (*e.g.,* meat, cereals, woods). In the case of oil, the average density of the crude oil of 39 different countries is tabulated. Analytical index, with more than 1,000 entries.

389.16

GREAT BRITAIN. NATIONAL PHYSICAL LABORATORY. Units & standards of measurement employed at the National Physical Laboratory. London, H.M. Stationery Office, 1962-66. 4 pts.

> 1. *Length, mass, time-interval and frequency.* 3rd ed. 1962. 18p. 1s. 6d.
> 2. *Light.* 2nd ed. 1964. 10p. 1s. 6d.
> 3. *Electricity.* 2nd ed. 1962. 16p. 1s. 6d.
> 4. *Temperature.* 2nd ed. 1966. iv, 20p. 2s. 3d.
> References are appended.

389.16

NAFT, S., and SOLA, R. de. International conversion tables. Rev. and enl. by P. H. Bigg. London, Cassell, 1965. liii, 351p. 63s.

> First published 1961. Originally S. Naft's *Conversion equivalents in international trade* (1931). The English ed. has much additional material.
> Six sections: 1. Conversion factors—2. Conversion tables—3. Compound conversion factors—4. Special measures used in various industries, commerce and engineering (p. 173-282; arranged A-Z, from Automobiles and Aviation to Water conversion factors, Typographical point system and Clothing (sizes) and shoes): English, U.S. and continental (metric)—5. Geography of weights and measures (including A-Z list of 84 countries, with their units)—6. Other useful data (alphabets; chemical elements; electrical units; international standards; signs and symbols). Detailed contents list; no index. Key passages are in French, German, Italian and Spanish, as well as English.

389.16

UNITED NATIONS. Statistical Office. World weights and measures: handbook for statisticians. [Rev. ed.] New York, U.N., 1966. vi, 138p. tables, map. (Statistical papers, series M, no. 21. Rev. 1). $2.

> Provisional ed., 1955.
> Section 2 (p. 3-29): International systems and units of weights and measurements (metric system; relationships between the metric and the British systems; special measures (wood; shipping); energy and work; temperature; petroleum; numeration; time, *i.e.,* calendar systems). Section 3 (p. 30-102): National systems and units of weight, measure and currency (201 countries, A-Z). Index of weights and measures; index of currencies.

389.16 (091)

KISCH, B. Scales and weight: a historical outline. New Haven, Yale Univ. Press, 1965. xxi, 297p. Illus. $15. (Yale studies in the history of science and medicine, 1).

> "Devoted to the history of weighing; that is, to the idea of comparing as accurately as possible the mass of two objects" (*Preface*). Full bibliography, p. 265-281; indexes of names, places and subjects.
> F. G. Skinner's *Weights and measures: their ancient origins and their development in Great Britain up to A.D. 1855* (London, H.M. Stationery Office, 1967. xii, 117p. illus., tables, maps) is a Science Museum survey.

Standards

389.6 (100)

BRITISH STANDARDS INSTITUTION. Yearbook. Supplement: publications by international organizations. Annual. (1966. 7s. 6d.).

> Lists, in the same style as the *Year-book,* the Recommendations of the International Organization for Standardization (ISO), the publications of the International Electrotechnical Commission (IEC), and the International Special Committee on Radio Interference (CISPR), and the Specifications of the International Commission on Rules for the Approval of Electrical Equipment (CEE); subject index.

389.6 (410)

BRITISH STANDARDS INSTITUTION. British Standards. London, Crosby, Lockwood, 1903-32; British Standards Institution, 1932-. no. 1-.

> From 1903 to 1918 issued as reports, etc. of Engineering Standards Committee; from 1918 to 1931 known as British Standard specifications of the British Engineering Standards Association.
> Early standards were concerned with engineering products, but Standards now relate to all industries and products, and include methods of testing, terms, definitions and symbols, standards of quality, performance or dimensions, codes of practice, etc. Standards, drawn up by committees representing the industries concerned, are revised from time to time. Specific Standards appear in v. 1 of this *Guide* under the subject concerned.
> Collections of British Standards relating to certain subjects (*e.g.,* building; workshop practice) have been issued as British Standard Handbooks.

389.6 (410)

BRITISH STANDARDS INSTITUTION. British Standards yearbook. 1937-. London, the Institution, 1937-. Annual. (1967. 15s.).

> Title varies. Originally *Handbook of information.*
> Gives information on B.S.I. and its services but mainly (1967, p. 26-618) consists of a complete, annotated list of current British Standards, plus Handbooks, Codes of practice,—over 4,000 items. Lists of complete sets of British Standards maintained for reference in the U.K., and in overseas countries (p. 12-20). Excellent detailed subject index.
> Kept up to date by entries in *B.S.I. news* (monthly), which lists new and revised British Standards, Codes of practice, Amendments, etc. and also notes new work started and draft Standards circulated for comment, plus draft ISO and IEC Recommendations.

389.6 (43)

DEUTSCHER NORMENAUSSCHUSS. Normblatt-Verzeichnis. Berlin, Beuth-Vertrieb GmbH. Annual. (1963. DM.48.).

> The West German counterpart to the *British Standards yearbook.* The 1967 v. is the 50th anniversary issue.
> The Deutscher Normenausschuss publishes a bilingual list of *English translations of German Standards,* gratis. The 1967 ed. gives numbers and titles of more than 1800 DIN Standards available in English, with dates; U.D.C. subject index.

389.6 (44)

ASSOCIATION FRANÇAISE DE NORMALISA-TION. Catalogue des normes françaises. 24. éd., 1967-1968. Paris, A.F.N., 1967. 25F.

Main section consists of a numerical listing of French Standards under broad subject headings (*e.g.*, Railways and tramways); no annotations. Subject index.

389.6 (73)

STRUGLIA, E. J. Standards and specifications: information sources. A guide to literature and to public and private agencies concerned with technological uniformities. Detroit, Michigan, Gale Research Co., 1965. 187p. (Management and information guide series, no. 6). $8.75.

Annotated lists. Sections: 1. General sources and directories—2. Bibliographies and indexes

to periodicals—3. Catalogs and indexes to standards and specifications—4. Government sources [U.S.A.]—5. Associations and societies—6. International standardization—7. Periodicals concerned with U.S. and international standards. Author-title and subject indexes. Pronounced U.S. slant, but sections 4-5, occupying over half the book, should be of value to British users.

389.6 (73)

UNITED STATES. NATIONAL BUREAU OF STANDARDS. Standardization activities in the United States: a descriptive directory [by] Sherman F. Booth. Washington, U.S.G.P.O., 1960. iv, 210p. $1.75.

Detailed annotated directory of governmental and non-governmental agencies concerned with standards; subject index.

39 CUSTOM AND TRADITION

Costume

Bibliographies

391:016

COLAS, R. Bibliographie générale du costume et de la mode. Description des suites, recueils, séries, revues et livres français et étrangers relatifs au costume civil, militaire et religieux, aux modes, aux coiffures et aux divers accessoires de l'habillement. Avec une table méthodique et un index alphabétique. Paris, Colas, 1933. 2v. (Reprinted New York, Hacker Art Books. $30.).

The standard bibliography. 3,121 items, arranged A-Z by authors or anonymous titles. Full bibliographical data. Plates are listed separately for certain important works (e.g., *Galerie royale de costumes*). Frequently extensive and pertinent annotations. V. 2 contains an author and anonymous title index, plus a classified list, grouped by country, subject or form.

391:016

HILER, H., and HILER, M., *comp.* **Bibliography of costume:** a dictionary catalog of about eight thousand books and periodicals. Edited by H. G. Cushing, assisted by A. V. Morris. New York, Wilson, 1939. xl, 911p. (Reprinted New York, Blom. $18.50.).

Author, title, subject, editor, illustrator, engraver and other entries in one alphabet; *c.* 8,400 items. The fullest information, including non-evaluative annotation, is given in the author entry. "The items listed include books, periodicals and portfolios of plates dealing with dress, jewelry, and decoration of the body, in general and for special occasions, of all countries, times and peoples. . . . In addition to books on costume many books of travel, history and antiquities are listed since they include text or illustrations of costume value" (*Preface*).
"Still the most complete bibliography in the field" (Warwick, E., *and others. Early American dress* (1965), p. 391).

391:016

LIPPERHEIDE, F. J., *Freiherr von.* **Katalog der Freiherrlich von Lipperheide'schen Kostum-bibliothek.** Berlin, Lipperheide, 1896-1905. 2v. illus. (Reprinted London, F. Edwards, 1965. £31 10s.).

The catalogue of what was reputedly the largest collection of costume books ever formed. More than 5,000 entries, systematically arranged, with name and subject indexes. Includes background material (*e.g.*, travel books). Entries have full bibliographical details and are well annotated. "Like Colas, indispensable to advanced study of dress. A new, and vastly expanded edition is now in advanced stage of preparation" (Warwick, E. *Early American dress* (1965), p. 391).
A revised ed., with 4,500 new entries, was announced for 1967.

391:016

MONRO, I. S., and COOK, D. E. Costume index: a subject index to plates and illustrated text. New York, Wilson, 1937. x, 338p. Supplement. 1957. x, 210p.

Indexes illustrations of costume in 615 books; entries are under countries, types of people wearing costume, and specific articles. Locations in 33 libraries.
The supplement covers a further 347 titles.

391:016

VICTORIA & ALBERT MUSEUM, with THE COSTUME SOCIETY. Costume: a general bibliography, by P. Anthony and J. Arnold. London, The Costume Society, c/o The Victoria & Albert Museum, 1966. 49p. (Bibliography no. 1). 3s.

An annotated list of more than 400 books and journals, in 24 sections, "compiled for students who are beginning to study the history of costume" (*Introduction*). 12 of the 24 sections concern the ancient world and individual European countries (British Isles, p. 17-25) plus America. Others cover bibliographies; encyclopædias, glossaries and dictionaries; men's dress; children's dress; underwear; accessories; books for children. Deals with Western European costume in its historic sense only and excludes national dress.

"Other bibliographies, which will include earlier and rare books, will be compiled on such subjects as military uniform, national costume of different countries, religious costume, civil uniform, theatrical costume, fashion plates and accessories" (*Introduction*).

James Laver's *The literature of fashion: an exhibition arranged . . . for the National Book League* (London, Cambridge Univ. Press for the N.B.L., 1947. 64p. illus.) has 265 annotated entries, plus a list of bibliographies and catalogues. It includes pictures, drawings and prints. Period and subject divisions.

Readers' guide to books on costume (London, Library Association, County Libraries Section, 1961. 20p. (New series, no. 62). 1s.) contains *c.* 300 items, systematically arranged, with occasional annotations. Excludes books in foreign languages; sections on theatrical costume and accessories. A short list of books for children is appended.

Dictionaries

391 (03)

LELOIR, M. Dictionnaire du costume et de ses accessoires, des armes et des étoffes, des origines à nos jours. Paris, Gründ, 1951. x, 435p. illus. (incl. col. pl.).

Many short entries, particularly detailed on French aspects. Very fully illustrated (*e.g.,* on p. 380, 23 types of shako are shown). Entries consist of historical notes with brief descriptions of types.

391 (03)

PICKEN, M. B. The fashion dictionary: fabric, sewing and dress as expressed in *The language of fashion.* New York, Funk & Wagnalls, 1957. xiv, [1], 397p. illus.

First published as *The language of fashion* (1939).

"A quick and ready reference for more than 10,000 words" (*To the reader*). Concerns wearing apparel, sewing, accessories and the making of them. Grouped by subjects. The entry under 'Sleeves', for example, occupies 5½ columns, describes some 50 types of sleeve and has 11 line-drawings. In all 207 plates and numerous rather small line-drawings. Index of illustrations (*c.* 1,000) grouped under such headings as 'Embroidery', 'Laces', 'Stitches', 'Wigs'.

391 (03)

PLANCHÉ, J. R. A cyclopaedia of costume; or, Dictionary of dress, including notices of contemporary fashions on the continent; and a general chronological history of the costumes of the principal countries of Europe, from the commencement of the Christian era to the accession of George the Third. London, Chatto & Windus, 1876-79. 2v. illus. (some col.).

The dictionary forms v. 1 and covers a great variety of costumes, material, armour, etc., from lace, hood, sleeves, pin and wimple to crozier,

helmet, gauntlet and sword; many quotations; some footnote references. V. 2 is a history from 53 B.C. to A.D. 1760. Despite its age, it is still valuable for details of costume of the medieval and Renaissance periods.

391 (03)

WILCOX, R. T. Folk and festival costume of the world. New York, Scribner, 1965; London, Batsford, 1966. [240]p. illus. $6.95; 45s.

111 plates, each with 6-8 black-and-white drawings, with facing pages giving descriptive captions (colours, materials and uses of costumes depicted). Fairly comprehensive international coverage; countries and areas A-Z, with some peculiarities ('Africa' is treated as one area; 'Anatolia' is separate from 'Turkey'; other headings: 'Bedouins', 'Bible lands', 'Gypsies', 'Tyrol'); U.S.A., pl. 95-105. Bibliography of 1½p.; brief index.

391:069

HUENEFELD, I. P. International directory of historical clothing. Metuchen, N.J., Scarecrow Press, 1967. x, 175p. $5.

A directory of historical societies and museums in the U.S.A., Canada and Europe that own various kinds of dress (regional, ecclesiastical, military) and accessories.

History

391 (091)

BOUCHER, F. A history of costume in the West; translated by John Ross. London, Thames & Hudson, 1966. [4], 441p. illus. 168s.

Translation of *Histoire du costume en occident, de l'antiquité à nos jours* (Paris, Flammarion, 1965).

A particularly well-illustrated history, arranged chronologically by periods from prehistory to 1964. 1,150 photogravure illustrations, 352 of them in colour, and many of them reproduced from paintings; descriptive captions. 12 chapters, each with short bibliography appended. General bibliography (p. 423), 4 sections: 1. Bibliographies —2. General studies—3. Dictionaries and manuals —4. Reviews. Glossary, p. 425-36. Index carries notes and has references to the illustrations. Index, partly analytical, p. 437-41. Favourably reviewed in *Times literary supplement,* no. 3,409, 29th June 1967, p. 572.

Of the series, *The costume of the western world* (planned by the International Publishing Co., Amsterdam, and issued in England by Harrap), only 6 of the planned 30v. have been published: Laver, J. *Early Tudor, 1485-1558;* Blum, A. *The last Valois, 1550-1590;* Reynolds, G. *Elizabethan and Jacobean, 1558-1625:* Thienen, F. V. *The great age of Holland, 1600-1660;* Blum, A. *Early Bourbon;* Reade, B. *The dominance of Spain, 1550-1660.* Available in 1 v.: Laver, J., ed. *The Tudors to Louis XIII.* (London, Harrap, 1952. 63s.). (Costume of the western world, v. 3). Illustrations are throughout taken from contemporary works of art.

391 (091)

BRUHN, W., and **TILKE, M. A. A pictorial history of costume:** a survey of costume of all periods and peoples from antiquity to modern times, including national costume in Europe and non-European countries. Tübingen, Wasmuth; London, Zwemmer, 1955, 74p. illus. (some col.).

Based on the German edition *Das Kostümwerk* (1941). 200 colour plates illustrate about 4,000 costumes up to the end of the 19th century.

M. Tilke's *Costume patterns and designs: a survey of costume patterns and designs of all periods and nations, from antiquity to modern times* (London, Zwemmer, 1956. 49p. with 128 pl. 105s.) was planned as a supplement to Bruhn and Tilke. Many of the 128 plates are in colour, explanatory text preceding. The drawings are mostly to the scale 1 : 10.

391 (091)
HANSEN, H. H. Costume cavalcade. London, Methuen, 1956. 160p. illus. (some col.). 25s.

Translated from the Danish *Klaededragtens kavalkade* (1954). Covers world costume from ancient times to the 1950s; 685 very good coloured illustrations, with sources; fills a gap for the small library unable to afford the more expensive works. Bibliography, p. 156.

391 (091)
KELLY, F. M., and SCHWABE, R. Historic costume: a chronicle of fashion in Western Europe, 1490-1790. 2nd ed. London, Batsford, 1929. xv, 305p. illus. (some col.).

First published 1925.
The illustrations are from R. Schwabe's careful drawings. Includes patterns and a bibliography.

The same authors' *A short history of costume and armour, chiefly in England, 1066-1800* (London, Batsford, 1931. 2v. illus.) is particularly valuable on armour.

391 (091)
LESTER, K. M., and OERKE, B. V. An illustrated history of those frills and furbelows of fashion which have come to be known as: **accessories of dress.** Peoria, Ill., C. A. Bennett, Inc., [1940]. viii, [1], 587p. illus. (incl. pl.).

In 6 parts (43 chapters): 1. Accessories worn at the head (*e.g.,* hat, veil, wig, earrings, comb; and toilet accessories)—2. Accessories worn at the neck, shoulders and waist (*e.g.,* cravat, shawl, girdle)—3. Accessories worn on the feet and legs (shoes, hose, garters, gaiters, etc.)—4. Accessories worn on the arm and hand (bracelet, ring, gloves, etc.)—5. Accessories carried in the hand (*e.g.,* umbrella, handkerchief, muff)—6. Accessories used on the costume (*e.g.,* buttons, embroidery, fur, braid). 59 plates; 644 illustrations in text (mostly half-tone). Chapter references; bibliography, p. 577-9. Index to illustrations; index, partly analytical, to text. A mine of information.

391 (091)
NORRIS, H. Costume and fashion. London, Dent, 1927-38. v. 1-3, 6. illus. (some col.), maps.

v. 1: *The evolution of European dress through the earlier ages.* 2nd ed. 1931. xv, 300p. 36s.
v. 2: *Senlac to Bosworth, 1066-1485.* 1927. xxvii, 485p. 45s.
v. 3 (in 2 pts.): *The Tudors.* [1485-1547; 1547-1603]. 1938. xx, 832p. 70s.

v. 6: *The nineteenth century,* by H. Norris and O. Curtis. 1933. xii, 264p. o.p.
v. 4 and 5 not published owing to the death of the author; they were to have covered the Stuart and Hanoverian periods. It would have been the most comprehensive and ambitious work of its kind; includes patterns. Coverage is mainly British. According to Brian Reade (*British book news,* no. 180, August 1955, p. 1149), this work is marred by the nature of the illustrations —reproductions from freehand drawings and "colour plates after somewhat fancy paintings". Nor is the terminology wholly reliable.

391 (091)
RACINET, A. Le costume historique: cinq cents planches, trois cents en couleurs, or et argent, deux cents en camaïeu. Paris, Firmin-Didot, 1886. 6v. illus. (some col.).

V. 1 is general in coverage, including a list of plates, bibliography (p. 141-65) and glossary (p. 169-256). V. 2-6 provide a period and national survey in four parts; pt. 1 deals with ancient times; pt. 2, with Oceania, Africa, America, etc.; pt. 3, Byzantium, etc.; pt. 4, Europe. No general index. Very full, although old-fashioned in style. The many illustrations range from hair styles and furniture to armour.

391 (091)
TRUMAN, N. Historic costuming. London, Pitman, 1936 (reprinted 1945). xii, 152p. illus. (incl. col. pl.).

28 chapters; a chronological survey, from 550 B.C. to A.D. 1910. The numerous keyed black-and-white illustrations in the text and summaries at the end of chapters are features. Particularly of value for theatrical producers and designers, covering civil, ecclesiastical and military dress.

Another work that links costume with the theatre is Iris Brooke's *Western European costume . . . and its relation to the theatre* (London, Harrap, [1939-40]. 2v. illus. (incl. pl.). V. 1 covers 13th-16th century; v. 2, 17th-19th century. 32 coloured plates, 176 black-and-white illustrations in all. Aims "to give some of the more usual styles and fashions worn since the theatre commenced to be a leading interest in Western Europe" (*Introduction*). No bibliographies; index in v. 2.

National Costume

391 (411)
DUNBAR, J. T. History of Highland dress: a definitive study of the history of Scottish costume and tartans, both civil and military, including weapons; with an appendix on Early Scottish dyes, by Annette Kok. Edinburgh & London, Oliver & Boyd, 1962. xii, 248p. illus. (some col.). 105s.

16 chapters, including 'Women's costume', 'The costume of the clans', 'Early Highland military uniform', 'Firearms', 'The powder horn and sporran', 'Plaid brooches'. Many quotations; occasional footnote references. Frontispiece and 58 plates (some in colour). The index has references to the plates.

391 (411)

INNES, *Sir* T., of Learney. **The tartans of the clans and families of Scotland.** 7th ed. Edinburgh & London, Johnston & Bacon, 1964. iv, 300p. illus. (some col.). 30s.

First published 1938.

The standard work, by the Lord Lyon King of Arms. Introduction (p. 1-67)—The Highland dress and how to wear it (p. 67-81)—Flags and banners—116 illustrations (in colour) of tartans and historical sketches of 114 clans and families (p. 72-295). Index.

The author is also editor of a more specialized work: Adam, F. *The clans, septs, and regiments of the Scottish highlands* (4th ed. Edinburgh, Johnston, 1952. viii, 624p. illus. (some col.). 42s.). This has a list of dependent clans, showing the tartans they use.

391 (415 + 411)

McCLINTOCK, H. F. **Old Irish and Highland dress,** and that of the Isle of Man. With chapters on pre-Norman dress, as described in early Irish literature, by F. Shaw, and on early Tartans, by J. Telfer Dunbar. 2nd & enl. ed. Dundalk, Dundalgan Press, 1950, [18], 141; [6], 87p. illus.

First published 1943.

Book 1 deals with old Irish dress ('References in contemporary English and continental writings', p. 74-94, and Isle of Man, p. 127-30); 56 illus.; detailed index. Book 2, 'Old Highland dress and tartans' has footnote references and a detailed index; 'Early tartans', p. 63-79; 20 illus.

391 (420) (03)

CUNNINGTON, C. W., CUNNINGTON, P., and **BEARD, C. A dictionary of English costume.** London, Black, 1960. vi, [1], 281p. col. front., illus. 40s.

Concise definitions of some 3,000 items of costume and accessories from 900 to 1900 A.D., indicating date (or period) and relevant sex for each. 303 clear line-drawings. Glossary of materials, p. 248-280. List of modern equivalents of obsolete 16th and 17th-century colour names. About a sixth of the text may be attributed to the late Charles Beard, states the *Preface*.

391 (420) (091)

BROOKE, I. English costume . . . London, Black, 1935-50. 7v. ea. 16s.

English costume of the early Middle Ages: the 10th to the 13th centuries.
English costume of the later Middle Ages: the 14th and 15th centuries.
English costume in the age of Elizabeth: the 16th century.
English costume of the seventeenth century. 2nd ed. 1950.
English costume of the eighteenth century, by I. Brooke and J. Laver.
English costume of the nineteenth century, by I. Brooke and J. Laver.
English children's costume since 1775.

A popular series that aims to be a useful guide and not a serious text-book. Uniform pattern. Thus, *English costume of the seventeenth century* has 89 pages, with 40 pages of illustrations (8 in colour), with descriptive text facing; treatment is chronological, by 10-year periods. No index.

391 (420) (091)

CUNNINGTON, C. W., and **CUNNINGTON, P. Handbook of English mediaeval costume.** London, Faber, 1952. 192p. illus. 60s.

———— **Handbook of English costume in the sixteenth century.** London, Faber, 1954. 224p. illus. 42s.

———— **Handbook of English costume in the seventeenth century.** 2nd ed. London, Faber, 1967. 222p. illus. 50s.

———— **Handbook of English costume in the eighteenth century.** London, Faber, 1957. 443p. illus. 63s. (New ed., by C. Willett and P. Cunnington, 1964. [*i.e.* 1965] 443p. 70s.).

———— **Handbook of English costume in the nineteenth century.** London, Faber, 1959. 606p. illus. 84s. (Rev. ed. 1966 [*i.e.* 1967]. 606p. 84s.).

A valuable series progressively more fully documented. Particularly detailed for the 19th century, in which year-by-year changes in fashion are shown. The carefully-drawn illustrations are based on contemporary sources; glossaries; bibliographies. The final volume has 247 black-and-white illustrations, with coloured frontispiece, a glossary of materials (p. 570-5), a bibliography of sources (p. 576-81) and a detailed, analytical index.

391 (420) (091)

CUNNINGTON, C. W., and **CUNNINGTON, P. The history of underclothes.** London, Joseph, 1951. 266p. illus.

Chronological treatment in 13 chapters (1: Medieval period; 2-13, periods 1485-1939). 119 black-and-white illustrations. Bibliography of primary and secondary sources, p. 259-60. Detailed but non-analytical index.

391 (420) (091)

CUNNINGTON, P., and **LUCAS, C. Occupational costume in England,** from the eleventh century to 1914 . . . London, Black, 1967. 427p. illus. (incl. pl.).

15 chapters on different professions (*e.g.,* Transport; Police; Firemen; Medical profession). Bibliography and list of museums, p. 395-403; sources of figures (299 references, by chapters). Analytical index to text and illus.

391 (73)

WARWICK, E., and *others.* **Early American dress:** the Colonial and Revolutionary periods. New York, Blom, 1965. 428p. illus., maps. (History of American dress, v. 2). $17.50.

Based on *Early American costume* (1929), by E. Warwick and H. C. Pitz. A chronological survey in 9 chapters, from the founding of the colonies to the United States of 1790. Costume of men and women are given separate treatment in chapters 2-7. Chapter 8: 'Children in North America, 1785-1790'; 9: 'Frontier life'. Well produced; careful drawings from original sources. The major items in the bibliography (p. 389-98) are given evaluative annotations; analytical index (p. 399-425).

R. T. Wilcox's *Five centuries of American costume* (London, Black, 1963. 207p. 40s.) is considered (*Times literary supplement,* no. 3373, 20th October 1966, p. 965) to be "a superficial skimming of European fashion with American interpolations"; illustrations are "often inaccurate in detail and in caption". Bibliography, p. 203-7. No index.

391.1

WAUGH, N. The cut of men's clothes, 1600-1900. London, Faber & Faber, 1964. 160p. illus., diagrs. 50s.

A chronological survey, in three main periods: 1600-1680, 1680-1800, 1800-1900. Includes quotations from contemporary sources. Bibliography (*c.* 35 books; 4 journals); list of museums with costume collections (p. 157). List of artists, engravers and illustrators. Index (accessories and detail, *e.g.,* buttons; cravat; ruffles). 29 plates and frontispiece; 42 cutting diagrams; 27 tailors' patterns.

391.2 (420)

CUNNINGTON, C. W., and **CUNNINGTON, P. English women's clothing in the nineteenth century.** London, Faber & Faber, 1937. xx, 460p. illus. (some col.). 105s.

10 chapters, chronologically arranged by year. Minute description of fashions (*e.g.,* 1833: Introduction; general survey—Dresses: day; evening—Outdoor garments; mantles; mantlets; shawls—Accessories; gloves; shoes). Glossaries, p. 429-40; authorities, p. 441-2; chronological table, p. 443; note on English museums containing 19th century costumes, p. 444-6. Detailed index, p. 447-60. 80 excellent collotype illustrations; also half-tones and diagrams in text.

—— ——**English women's clothing in the present century.** London, Faber & Faber, 1952. 312p. illus. (some col.). 73s. 6d.

69 plates (3 in colour) and many line-drawings in the text. Glossary of textiles, p. 294-6.

391:34

HARGREAVES-MAWDSLEY, W. N. A history of legal dress in Europe until the end of the eighteenth century. Oxford, Clarendon Press, 1963. xii, 151p. illus. 35s.

See entry at 34:391.

391:378.4 (4)

HARGREAVES-MAWDSLEY, W. N. A history of academical dress in Europe until the end of the eighteenth century. Oxford, Clarendon Press, 1963. xiii, 235p. illus. (21 pl.). 45s.

See entry at 378.4:391 (4).

391.3 (420)

CUNNINGTON, D., and **BUCK, A. Children's costume in England,** from the fourteenth to the end of the nineteenth century. London, Black, 1965. 236p. col. front., illus. 42s.

One chapter per century; many contemporary quotations. Deals with children from infancy to the age of *c.* 16. Particularly rich in illustrations:

frontispiece, 32 plates (only 1 in colour) and many contemporary line-drawings in the text (nearly one per page). Bibliography, p. 226-9 (manuscript sources; printed manuscripts and books; dress and domestic economy; journals; secondary sources). Non-analytical index, with references to plates.

Hair

391.5

CORSON, R. Fashions in hair: the first five thousand years. London, Peter Owen, 1965. 701p. illus. 130s.

Includes beards, wigs, and ornaments (*e.g.,* combs). Chronological arrangement, 2700 B.C. to 1964 A.D.; very fully illustrated (2,500 line-drawings, plus reproductions from contemporary sources); detailed index. Bibliography, p. 678-86.

Regalia

391.7

TWINING, E. F. T., *baron.* **European regalia.** London, Batsford, 1967. xvii, 334p. illus. (incl. pl.). £12 12s.

11 chapters: 1. Crown and Empire—2. Crown and the West—3. Church and crown—4. Crowns of princes and sovereign dukes—5. Crown miscellany—6. Sceptres—7. Orbs—8. Swords—9. The lesser ornaments—10. Anointing vessels—11. Royal obsequies. Appendix: Record of royal tombs which have been opened and found to contain regalia. Footnote references; select bibliography, p. 310-1. Analytical index, covering the 96 plates, illustrations and footnotes. A handsome volume. The author's *A history of the crown jewels of Europe* (1960) is a companion work.

Marriage

392.5:016

ALDOUS, J., and **HILL, R. International bibliography of research in marriage and the family, 1900-1964.** Minneapolis, Univ. of Minnesota Press, 1967. 508p. $15.

Nearly 13,000 citations in 6 sections. KWIC index; classified index; author and periodical lists. "Substantially valuable to social scientists", notes *Library journal,* v. 92, no. 8, 15th April 1967, p. 1001, pointing out that the compilers relied heavily on *International bibliography of sociology, Psychological abstracts* and *Sociological abstracts,* "obviating the need for searching there".

392.5 (094)

GREAT BRITAIN. GENERAL REGISTER OFFICE. Abstract of legal preliminaries to marriage in the United Kingdom and the other countries of the British Commonwealth of Nations, and in the Irish Republic. London, H.M. Stationery Office, 1951. v, 189p.

"In most cases states the position as it was in the latter part of 1947" (*Preface*). For each country gives titles of laws; banns and licences; marriageable age; prohibited degrees; residential qualifications; consent for minors; by whom and at what times marriages may be solemnized;

places at which they may be solemnized; fees.

The G.R.O.'s *The official list for 1957,* Part 1, *List of Registration Officers* (London, H.M.S.O., 1967. 230p. 23s.) is published by the authority of the Registrar-General pursuant to section 73(2) of the Marriage Act, 1949.

Nicknames
392.91

FRANKLYN, J. A dictionary of nicknames. London, Hamilton, 1962. xx, 132p. 18s.

See entry at 929.2.09:392.91.

Death Rites
393

NATIONAL ASSOCIATION OF FUNERAL DIRECTORS. Year book and directory. London, the Association. Annual (1966. 20s.).

Lists cemeteries, crematoria, mortuaries, registrars of deaths, embalmers.

Inn Signs
394:659.13

LARWOOD, J., pseud. [*i.e.,* H. D. J. van Schevichaven], **and HOTTEN, J. C. English inn signs;** being a revised and modernized version of "History of signboards", with a chapter on the modern inn sign, by Gerald Millar. London, Chatto & Windus, 1951. xv, 336p. illus.

This edition is confined to inn signs, although earlier editions (1866-1907) included tradesmen's signs (now covered in part by Sir Ambrose Neal's *Signboards of old London shops* (1947). Brief bibliography, p. 316.

Public Festivals
394.2

See at 398.33.

Holidays
394.26

Bank and public holidays throughout the world. New York, Morgan Guaranty Trust Company of New York, 1920-. Annual. *Gratis.*

Lists holidays both chronologically and by countries (over 200 states and countries in the 1966 ed.); notes on Saturday closing of banks in the U.S.A. and elsewhere.

394.26

HAZELTINE, M. E. Anniversaries and holidays: a calendar of days and how to observe them. 2nd ed. Chicago, American Library Association, 1944. xix, 316p.

First published 1928.
Pt. 1: Calendar of events, dates of birth; pt. 2: Books about holidays, special days, and seasons; pt. 3: Books about persons referred to in the calendar. Not confined to American holidays and persons. Classified and general indexes.

Official Ceremonies
394.4

GARNER, J. F. Civic ceremonial: a handbook of practice and procedure. 2nd ed. London, Shaw, 1957. xi, 154p. 22s. 6d.

First published 1953, by F. G. and J. F. Garner.
The 2nd ed. has the following chapters: 1. Historical notes—2. The office of mayor—3. The legal position of the mayor—4. Ceremonial position of the mayor—5. Ceremonies and functions — 6. Civic insignia — 7. Ceremonial officers. Appendices include "Rules for flying flags on civic buildings". Index, but no illustrations.

Etiquette
395

POST, E. P. Emily Post's Etiquette. 11th ed., revised by Elizabeth L. Post. New York, Funk & Wagnall, 1965. [xxv], 107p. illus.

First published 1922.
Standard U.S. etiquette. Legislates for every conceivable occasion, with understanding and humour. 84 chapters in 15 pts.: 1. The art of conversation—2. Correspondence—3. As others see you—4. Advice to travellers—5. Formal entertaining—6. Informal entertaining—7. Special occasions — 8. Weddings — 9. Invitations — 10. Cards and calls—11. Protocol in official circles —12. Good manners for every day—13. On how to dress—14. The well-appointed house—15. Family life. Analytical index. Examples of letters, invitation cards, menus, laying out a table.

Lady behave: a guide to modern manners, by A. Edwards and D. Beyfus ([4th] rev. & enl. ed. London, Cassell, 1957. xi, [i], 338p. illus. 21s.), possibly the nearest British equivalent to Emily Post, is modern, practical and reasonably comprehensive, amusing as well as informative. Examples of invitation cards, etc. Appendix: 'How to address titled people' (p. 307-19). Analytical index.

395 (410)

FAWCETT, F. B. Court ceremonial and book of the court of King George the Sixth: a handbook of ceremonial at the Court of King George VI, with all necessary information regarding royal functions and ceremonies. London, Gale & Polden, 1937. xi, 161p. illus.

Presentation at Court, investitures, coronations, and other ceremonial; functions of the various officers of the Household; dress regulations, order of precedence, and other Court etiquette.

395 (420)

WILDEBLOOD, J., and BRINSON, P. The polite world: a guide to English manners and deportment from the thirteenth to the nineteenth century. London, Oxford Univ. Press, 1965. xiv, 291p. illus. (incl. pl.). 45s.

A detailed analysis of etiquette and polite behaviour, quoting sources. Coverage ranges from salutations (bowing, shaking hands, removing the hat) to use of the fan, walking and sitting, spitting and sneezing. Useful in historical drama production as well as social history. Footnote references. 16 plates; 12 illustrations in text. Analytical index.

Use of Titles

395.6/7 (410)
HEYWOOD, V. British titles: the use and misuse of the titles of peers and commoners, with some historical notes. 2nd ed. London, Black, 1953. xi, 188p.

First published 1951 (xi, 188p.).
Chapters: 1. The Royal House—2. The Peerage—3. Courtesy titles—4. The Baronetage—5. The Knightage—6. The Privy Council—7. The great officers of state—8. The Prime Minister—9. Miscellaneous—10. The law—11. The churches—12. Forms of address.
A most useful guide, providing information not readily available elsewhere (*e.g.,* in the chapter on the Peerage, such topics are discussed as: life-peers; female succession to an earldom; abeyance; mistakes in patents; etc.).

395.6/.7 (420)
Titles and forms of address: a guide to their correct use. 13th ed. London, Black, 1966. xi, 164p. 15*s.*

First published 1918.
Confined to English titles, including those of the church and civic dignitaries. Abbreviations (p. 1-23); 'Some pronunciations of proper names' (p. 24-37). Text proper cover royalty, peerage, etc., the armed services, the law, decorations and honours, the universities and government services. Analytical index.

L. G. Pine's *Written and spoken guide to titles and forms of address* (Kingswood, Elliot, [1959]. 124p. 10*s. 6d.*) has some supplementary material and a little on foreign titles.

395.6/.7 (5)
AUSTRALIA. DEPARTMENT OF EXTERNAL AFFAIRS. Asian forms of address. Canberra, the Department, [1964]. [iii], 22p.

Explains the order of names used in 16 Asian countries (A-Z, including Indonesia) and the meaning of the forms of address and titles most commonly used. "Meant mainly to help Australians in their contact with Asian students and Asian visitors to this country" (introduction).

Women and Society

396:061
NATIONAL COUNCIL OF WOMEN OF THE UNITED STATES. International directory of women's organizations. New York, Research and Action Associates, 1963. 216p. Loose-leaf.

Describes 275 international and U.S. organizations comprised predominantly or exclusively of women. "Information about the organizations includes their correct titles, acronyms, names of principal elected officers, names and addresses of principal staff officers, membership statistics, organizational structures, meeting schedules, and publications" (*Library of Congress information bulletin,* v. 23, no. 1, 6th January 1964, p. 10).

396:061 (410)
GREAT BRITAIN. CENTRAL OFFICE OF INFORMATION. Reference Division. **List of women's organizations in Britain.** London, Central Office of Information, 1959. iii, 27p.

Lists 123 organizations, classified as: international; British (6 sections): feminist and general, political, professional, social, philanthropist, religious, and sporting. Gives secretary's name and address, date of foundation, objects membership, other member country (if any), and official journal. Alphabetical index of organizations.

Gypsies

397:016
BLACK, G. F. A gypsy bibliography. London, Quaritch, for the Gypsy Lore Society, 1914. vii, 226p. (Gypsy Lore Society Monographs, no. 1).

A preliminary edition was issued in 1909 (139p.). 4,577 items in author order, with subject index.

397:016
LEEDS. UNIVERSITY LIBRARY. Brotherton Library. **Catalogue of the Romany Collection** formed by D. U. McGrigor Phillips and presented to the University of Leeds. Edinburgh, Nelson, for the Brotherton Collection, 1962. xii, [1], 227p. 21*s.*

20 sections, including drawings and paintings, photographs, gramophone records, letters, playbills and press cuttings. International coverage. Section 1. Bibliographies and other general works; 2. Official documents. 1234 numbered items, each with brief bibliographical description. Index.

397:016
LIVERPOOL. UNIVERSITY. LIBRARY. A catalogue of the gypsy books collected by the late Robert Andrew Scott Macfie. Liverpool, Univ., 1936. 178p.

Brief author catalogue only; appendix of songs and music.

Folklore

Bibliographies

398:016
AMERICAN FOLKLORE SOCIETY. Abstracts of folklore studies. Austin (Texas), Univ. of Texas Press, 1963-. v. 1-. $3 p.a.

International in coverage, with about 1,000 indicative and informative abstracts in 1966. Arranged in order of the titles of periodicals abstracted, with subject index in each issue; cumulated index to v. 1-2 (1965). The September issue (1964-) includes an extensive bibliography of books and articles.

398:016
Bibliographie internationale des arts et traditions populaires. International folklore bibliography. Internationales volkskundliche Bibliographie . . . Années 1939/41-. Basle, Commission Internationale des Arts et Traditions Populaires, 1949-.

Continues *Internationale volkskundliche Bibliographie* (Berlin, published for the Verband Deutsche Vereine für Volkskunde by de Gruyter, 1919-41. v. 1-13: 1917-36), which itself continues from 1917 the *Catalogus van Folklore in de Koninklijke Bibliotheek* (The Hague, Drukkerij "Humanitas", 1919-22. 3v. in 2). Published by the Commission Internationale de la Philosophie et des Sciences Humaines and subsequently as in imprint, with Unesco help.

V. 5 (1959. xvi, 728p. Basle, Krebs) lists 11,405 items published in 1952/54, with supplement for previous year. Systematically arranged; universal coverage. Author and subject indexes. A geographical index would help considerably.

398:016
BONSER, W. A bibliography of folklore, as contained in the first eighty years of the publications of the Folklore Society, London, published for the Folk-Lore Society by W. Glaisher, 1961. xv, 126p. 30s.

2626 entries; a classified index to *Folk-lore record; Folk-lore journal, Folk-lore* and the Society's extra publications, 1878-1957. Classes A-P: A. General topics—B. Folklore of the British Isles—C. Folklore of other countries and races—D. Mankind—E. Human activities—F. Natural history—G. Natural phenomena—K. Calendar customs—L. Religious folklore & the supernatural—M. Miscellaneous aspects of folklore — N. Narrative folklore — P. Folklore in literature and art. Brief notes explain or expand titles of articles. Indexes: authors; topography of the British Isles; foreign countries, races and tribes; subjects.
Preceded by N. W. Thomas. *Bibliography of anthropology and folklore* (London, Nutt, for the Folk-Lore Society, 1906-7. 2v.).

398:016
CLEVELAND PUBLIC LIBRARY. John G. White Department. **Catalog of folklore and folk songs.** Boston, Mass., G. K. Hall, 1964. 2v. $105.

24,200 cards photolithographically reproduced on 1157 pages. The White collection is international in scope and embraces "folk tales, riddles, proverbs (the largest body of proverbs in the U.S.), folk songs and ballads, fables, chapbooks and medieval romances; works on superstition, magic and witchcraft; and studies of folk habits, beliefs and customs" (G. K. Hall, *Annual catalog of reference works, May 1968,* p. 12).

Dictionaries
398 (031)
Funk and Wagnalls' Standard dictionary of folklore, mythology and legend. M. Leach, editor. New York, Funk & Wagnalls, 1949-50. v. 1-2.

Short signed articles under specific headings on phrases, motifs, gods, etc., and 52 long articles on broad subjects (*e.g.,* Dance, p. 276-96; subdivided by countries, etc.; tabulated data, *e.g.,* for ceremonial clowns). International scope (*e.g.,* articles on Finnish folklore, p. 380-7, with numerous references in text and at end; Slavic folklore, p. 1019-1025, with more than 2½p. of biblio-

graphy). Some biographies (*e.g.,* Hans Andersen). Emphasis on American and American Indian cultures. Headings not distinctive.
A v. 3, to contain index and bibliography, has yet to be published.

398 (031)
Handwörterbuch der Sage, hrsg. von W.-E. Peuckert. Göttingen, Vandenhoeck & Ruprecht, 1961-. Lfg. 1-.

To be completed in 8v. (*c.* 45 Lfg.).
Encyclopaedia of mythology and folklore. Well-documented articles, arranged by themes, A-Z.

398 (032)
ROBINSON, H. S., and **WILSON, K. The encyclopaedia of myths & legends of all nations.** Rev. ed. London, Edmund Ward, 1962. xi, 244p. 25s.

Originally published New York, Doubleday, 1950.
Arranged by races; brief accounts useful for identification. Indexes of names and subjects.

Europe
398 (4) (03)
INTERNATIONAL COMMISSION ON FOLK ARTS AND FOLKLORE. International dictionary of regional European ethnology and folklore. Chief editor, A. Hultkranz. Copenhagen, Rosenkilde & Bagger, 1960-. v. 1-.

Published under the auspices of the International Council for Philosophy and Humanistic Sciences.
v. 1: *General ethnological concepts.* 1960.
v. 2: *Folk literature (Germanic),* by L. Bødker. 1965. (See entry at 398.2 (*43*).)
Entries in v. 1 are arranged A-Z (usually the English word), with references appended (*e.g.,* 'Folk culture': 2½p., 15 references). Entries consist of definition, comment (plus quotation) and references. French, Spanish, German and Swedish equivalents of entry words are added. Bibliography, p. 251-82.

398 (410)
BRAND, J. Brand's Popular antiquities of Great Britain. Faiths and folk-lore: a dictionary of national beliefs, superstitions and popular customs, past and current, with their classical and foreign analogues, described and illustrated. Forming a new edition of "The popular antiquities of Great Britain", by Brand and Ellis, largely extended, corrected and brought down to the present time, and now first alphabetically arranged by W. C. Hazlitt. London, Reeves & Turner, 1905. 2v. illus. (Reprinted New York, Blom; London, Blond, 1967. 112s. 6d.).

Brand's original work, *Observations on popular antiquities,* was published in 1777; a new ed., by Sir Henry Ellis, appeared in 1813.
In the Hazlitt edition, the editor makes his own comments and retains many illustrative passages from the obscurer Elizabethan and Jacobean writers. Entries A-Z (from Abbot of Bon Accord to Yule log), and far easier to use than Brand's *Observations.* Reviewed in *Times*

literary supplement, no 3,417, 17th August 1967, p. 749.

398 (411)
McNEILL, F. M. **The silver bough**: a four-volume study of the national and local festivals of Scotland. Glasgow, Maclellan, 1957-. v. 1-. illus.

> v. 1: *Scottish folk-lore and folk-belief.* 1957.
> v. 2: *A calendar of Scottish national festivals, Candlemas to Harvest Home.* 1959.
> v. 3: *A calendar of Scottish national festivals, Hallowe'en to Yule.* 1961.
> To be completed in 4v, v. 2-4 dealing with the festivals in calendar order. V. 1 carries a very short bibliography; that in v. 2 is a little fuller (but authors and titles only). The latter is well illustrated and carries many quotations. The review of v. 2 in *Scottish studies,* v. 4, 1960, p. 219-22 refers to it as "a valuable compendium of information".

398 (415)
Ó SÚILLEABHÁIN, S. **A handbook of Irish folklore.** Dublin, published by the Educational Co. of Ireland, Ltd., for the Folklore of Ireland Society, 1942. xxxi, 699p. (Reprinted London, Jenkins. 1963. 105s.).

> "The main purpose of this book is to serve as a guide for collectors of Irish oral tradition" (*Instructions to collectors*). 14 chapters, from 1. Settlement and dwelling, to 13. Popular oral literature and 14. Sports and pastimes. No index, but a detailed contents list (p. xix-xxxi); no sources. A mine of information and also, because of the many questions listed, a guide for further research.

398 (429)
JONES, T. G. **Welsh folklore and folk-custom.** London, Methuen, 1930. xx, 255p.

> "Whenever possible, sources have been indicated, and a bibliography and glossary of terms [p. 236-42] are added" (*Preface*). Includes many beliefs reported from oral tradition. Considerably shorter than:

RHYS, J. **Celtic folklore: Welsh and Manx.** Oxford, Clarendon Press, 1901. 2v.

> A pioneer treatment of Welsh folklore, with a useful list of bibliographical references appended.

398 (429)
OWEN, T. M. **Welsh folk customs.** Cardiff, National Museum of Wales, 1959. 258p. with 16p. of plates. 10s. 6d.

> At head of title-page: National Museum of Wales. Welsh Folk Museum.
> Chapters: 1. The Christmas season—2. Candlemas and the movable festivals—3. May and midsummer — 4. Harvest and winter's eve — 5. Birth, marriage and death. The catalogue of 567 items (p. 186-255) and selected bibliography (p. 256-8) follow. "The text provides an integrated study of the subject based on the literature, on replies to questionnaires and on information collected in the field" (*Foreword*). Well documented.

398 (43) (03)
ERICH, O. A., and BEITL, R. **Wörterbuch der deutschen Volkskunde.** Leipzig, Kröner Verlag, 1934. viii, 864p. illus., maps.

> A compact dictionary of German folklore, with many concise unsigned articles and often short bibliographies (*e.g.,* 'Neujahr': 4p.; 10 lines of bibliography; 'Märchen': nearly 3p.; ¼ col. of bibliography). Many cross-references.
> *Atlas der deutschen Volkskunde* (Hrsg. M. Zender. Marburg, Elwert, 1959-66), an atlas of German folk tradition, is a post-war series of 48 maps. (The pre-war series, 1937-40, consisted of 120 maps.) The maps are mostly on a scale of 1:2 M., with some at 1:4 M. Particularly valuable is the 975-page commentary on birth, marriage and death customs, etc. Reviewed in *Geographical journal* (v. 133, pt. 3, September 1967, p. 412-3), which mentions that atlases of folk culture are in active preparation, thanks to the German example, in Finland, the Low Countries, Austria, Sweden, Switzerland, Hungary, Poland and Russia.

398 (47):016
AKADEMIYA NAUK SSSR. Institut Russkoĭ Literatury (Pushkinskiĭ Dom). **Russkiĭ fol'klor: bibliograficheskiĭ ukazatel', 1917-1944.** Sostavila M. Ya. Mel'ts. Pod red. A. M. Astakhovoĭ i S. P. Luppova. Leningrad, the Academy, 1966. 683p.

> A bibliography of 5,140 items, systematically arranged, on Russian folklore. Entries include textbooks; references to reviews. Many cross-references. Name and locality indexes; index of periodical titles.

———— **Russkiĭ fol'klor: bibliograficheskiĭ ukazatel', 1945-1959.** Leningrad, the Academy, 1961. 401p.

> Bibliography of 2,905 entries, setting the pattern, in coverage and arrangement, for the retrospective list above.

Asia

398 (5-013):016
KIRKLAND, E. C. **A bibliography of South Asian folklore.** Bloomington, Indiana Univ. Press, 1966. xxiv, 291p. (Indiana Univ. folklore series, 21).

> A bibliography of nearly 7,000 items, "covering all categories of folklore and publications in all languages for South Asia" (*Ad Orientem. Catalogue 9,* 1967, entry no. 1078).
> Noted: Jain, S. K. *Folklore of India and Pakistan: a complete catalogue of publications in English language, compiled from up-to-date sources, with short notes and annotations.* (Regina. Regina Campus Library, Univ. of Saskatchewan, 1965. 39l. $1.).

398 (52)
KOKUSAI BUNKA SHINKOKAI. **K.B.S. bibliography of standard reference books for Japanese studies,** with descriptive notes. V. 8. **Manners and customs, & folklore.** Tokyo, K.B.S., 1961. [vii], 101p. 20s.

243 numbered and annotated entries, in 15 sections: 1. Dictionary and bibliography — 2. History of social life—3. Folklore—4. Dwellings, clothes and food—5. Family and social organization — 6. Life cycles — 7. Popular beliefs and superstition—8. Festivals—9. Annual functions —10. Children's play, toys and dolls—11. Tea ceremony, flower arrangement—12. Legend and folktale—13. Folklore of the Loochoo Islands—14. Folklore of the Ainu—15. Periodicals. Titles and authors (or editors), as well as publishers, are given in romanised form and then in Japanese characters. No index.

398 (54)

SEN GUPTA, S. A bibliography of Indian folklore and related subjects. Calcutta, Indian Publications, 1967. 196p. (Indian folklore series, no 11). 57*s*.

Reprinted from *Folklore* (Calcutta), v. 6, no. 7, July 1965—v. 8, no. 5, May 1967.
About 5,000 entries for English-language publications on the folklore of India and Pakistan.

North America

398 (7)

HAYWOOD, C. A bibliography of North American folklore and folksong. 2nd rev. ed. New York, Dover, 1961. 2v. maps. 100*s*.

First published 1951.
v. 1. *The American people north of Mexico, including Canada.*
v. 2. *The American Indians north of Mexico, including the Eskimos.*
About 40,000 items in all, closely classified. V. 1 has 5 parts: general, regional, ethnic, occupational and miscellaneous bibliography. V. 2: 1. General bibliography (folklore; music; dance; arrangements; recordings)—2. Bibliography of the various culture areas. Particularly full index in v. 2,—p. 1161-1292 (each page of *c.* 220 lines); index supplement of composers, arrangers and performers. Reviewed in *Journal of the American Musicological Society* (v. 11, no. 1, Spring 1964, p. 109-10), which considers the close classification to be of great value.

Latin America

398 (8=6):016

BOGGS, R. S. Bibliography of Latin American folklore. Washington, Latin American Bibliographical and Library Association; New York, Wilson, 1940. x, 109p.

Annotated list of 794 books and periodical articles in 15 sections.
Supplemented by references scattered throughout the annual "Folklore bibliography", in *Southern folklore quarterly,* March issue, 1941-.

Children's Lore

398-053.2

OPIE, I., and OPIE, P. The lore and language of schoolchildren. Oxford, Clarendon Press, 1959. xviii, [i], 417p. illus., maps. 38*s*.

"The present study is based on the contributions of some 5,000 children attending seventy

schools, primary, secondary modern and grammar, in different parts of England, Scotland and Wales, and one school in Dublin" (*Preface*). Riddles, topical rhymes, nicknames, pranks, street games, superstitions and other traditions of children aged 6-14. Geographical, first-line and general indexes. 11 distribution maps. Fully illustrated by examples.

Folk Literature

398.2

AARNE, A. The types of the folktale. 2nd revision, translated and enlarged by Stith Thompson. Helsinki, Suomalainen Tiedeakatemia, Academia Scientiarum Fennica, 1961. 588p. (FF communications no. 184).

First published 1910.
Covers "Europe, west Asia, and the lands settled by these peoples", and is supplementary to Stith Thompson's wider-ranging *Motif-index.*

398.2

EASTMAN, M. H. Index to fairy tales, myths and legends. 2nd ed. Boston, Faxon, 1926. ix, 610p. Supplement. 1937. ix. 566p. 2nd supplement. 1955-58. 6v.

About 30,000 references in an alphabetical analytical index, with list of books analyzed; geographical list; bibliography of books on the art of story telling. Supplement has short subject list. Includes some modern stories.

398.2

THOMPSON, S., ed. Motif-index of folk-literature: a classification of narrative elements in folk tales, ballads, myths, fables, mediaeval romances, exempla, fabliaux, jest-books, and local legends. Rev. ed. Copenhagen, Rosenkilde & Bagger; Bloomington, Indiana Univ. Press, 1955-58. 6v.

First published, Bloomington, 1932-36. 6v.
A systematic thematic index, covering a vast collection of folk-literature; references and some source material are cited. An indispensable study of the subject. A-Z index and list of sources.
The scope of the revised ed. is extended to include Icelandic sagas, early Irish literature, and oral tales of India. V. 6, as before, provides a detailed alphabetical index of motifs.

398.2 (43)

BODKER, L. Folk literature (Germanic). Copenhagen, Rosenkilde & Bagger, 1965. 365p. (International dictionary of European ethnology and folklore, v. 2).

Entries in A-Z order. Covers the folk literature of the German-speaking part of Europe, including Scandinavian and Dutch. Entries comprise etymological note, definition, comment and references to the literature (*e.g.,* 'Märchen', p. 184-8, with 8 lines of references; 'Lied', p. 184-8, with 8 lines of references; 'Lied', with nearly a page of references). Many cross-references. Bibliography, p. 335-65 (by authors, A-Z, with chronological index).

Handwörterbuch des deutschen Märchens, hrsg. . . . von L. Mackensen. Berlin, de Gruyter, 1930-. v. 1-. (Handwörterbücher zur deutschen Volkskunde, Abt. 2).

398.2 (43)

v. 1-2: A-G. 1930-40.
Encyclopaedia of the Germany fairy tale. Includes biographies as well as articles on types and motifs. Well documented. Incomplete.

398.2 (44)
DELARUE, P. Le conte populaire français: catalogue raisonné des versions de France et des pays de langue française d'outre-mer: Canada, Louisiane, îlots français des États-Units, Antilles Françaises, Haïti, Île Maurice, La Réunion. Publié sous le patronage du Musée National des Arts et Traditions Populaires, avec le concours de la Commission Internationale des Arts et Traditions Populaires et du C.N. de la R.S. Paris, Éditions Érasme; Maisonneuve et Larose, 1957-64. 2v.

A systematically arranged catalogue. The section 'Contes merveilleux' is sub-divided by types, of which § 325 is 'Le magicien et son élève, ou l'apprenti magicien' (p. 279-92). V. 2 has a supplement on 'Le conte français d'Amérique du nord' (p. 711-27). Brief bibliographical notes accompany entries. No indexes.

398.2 (= 8)
HARKINS, W. E. Bibliography of Slavic folk literature. New York, King's Crown Press, Columbia Univ., 1953. 28p. 7s.

194 numbered items in 4 sections: General and comparative Slavic—East Slavic—West Slavic—South Slavic. Aimed at teachers as well as students, and librarians. Russian cyrillic characters are not romanised. Brief but comprehensive.

Metrical Romances

398.22
BORDMAN, G. Motif-index of the English metrical romances. Helsinki, Suomalainen Tiedeakatemia, Academia Scientiarum Fennica, 1963. 134p. (FF communications no. 190).

Systematic thematic index (*e.g.*, V, Religion), following Stith Thompson's method of classification and enumeration. Excludes prose pieces. Bibliography, p. 13-15. Excellent analytical index, p. 104-34.

398.22
FLETCHER, R. H. The Arthurian material in the Chronicles especially those of Great Britain and France. 2nd ed., expanded by a bibliography and critical essay for the period 1905-1965, by L. S. Loomis. New York, Burt Franklin, 1966. ix, 335p.

First published 1906.
Aims to show what Arthurian material is contained in the European chronicles, especially in those of Great Britain and France. Treats more than 200 chronicles, ranging from mid-6th to end of 16th century. 12 chapters (*e.g.*, 3. Geoffrey of Monmouth, p. 43-115). Numerous footnote references to the literature. Supplementary bibliography, 1905-65, p. 333-5.

Noted: *Bulletin bibliographique des études arthuriennes* (Paris, Société Internationale Arthurienne, [1949?]-. v. 1-. (v. 16. 1964. 174p.); Parry, J. J., and Schlauch, M. *A bibliography of critical Arthurian literature . . . 1922-35* (New York, Modern Language Association of America, 1931-36. 2v.), supplemented by lists (now annual) in *Modern language quarterly*.

398.22
FLUTRE, L.-F. Tables des noms propres avec toutes leurs variantes figurant dans les romans du Moyen Age, écrits en français ou en provençal et actuellement publiés ou analysés. Poitiers, Centre d'Études Supérieurs de Civilisation Médiévale, 1962. xvi, 324p.

Two pts.: 1. Noms de personnes et êtres animés ou personnifiés (p. 1-187)—2. Noms géographiques et ethniques (p. 191-313). Appendix and addenda. List of sources, p. ix-xvi. Good use of bold face.

Popular Superstitions

398.3:016
ROBINSON, M. W. Fictitious beasts: a bibliography. London, Library Association, 1961. 76p. illus. (Library Association bibliographies, no. 1). 14s. 8d. (11s. to members).

349 annotated items, in 2 main sections: 1. General (classical; medieval and Renaissance; modern)—2. Beasts (*e.g.*, dragon; mermaid; sea-serpent; unicorn). Restricted to European beliefs and confined to printed books and to the English view of the subjects, from the earliest times to the present day. Excludes manuscripts and foreign-language material, although Latin and French works in the earlier periods are cited when no translations are available. Two other omissions: deliberate inventions and traditional beasts used in fiction. Includes periodical articles; analytical entries (*e.g.*, for Aristotle's works). Index of authors and subjects. 14 illustrations.

398.3 (02)
ACKERMANN, A. S. E. Popular fallacies: a book of common errors explained and corrected, with copious references to authorities. 4th ed. London, Old Westminster Press, 1950. xv, 843p.

Excludes superstitions; a hotchpotch of curious information, not always authoritative but frequently useful.

398.3 (03)
RADFORD, E., and RADFORD, M. A. Encyclopaedia of superstitions. [2nd ed.], edited and revised by Christina Hole. London, Hutchinson, 1961. 384p. 35s.

First published 1948.
A popular rather than an authoritative work, but it helps to fill a gap. States the superstition and then gives a country-by-country survey of practice or observance; distinguishes between superstitions and customs. Occasional footnote references; select bibliography (author list), p. 371-6; detailed index. The approach is largely British.

398.3 (43)
Handwörterbuch des deutschen Aberglaubens, hrsg. unter besonderer Mitwirkung von E. Hoffmann-Krayer und Mitarbeit . . . von H. Bächtold-Stäubli. Berlin, de Gruyter, 1927-42. 10v. (Handwörterbücher zur deutschen Volkskunde, Abt. 1).

An encyclopaedia of German superstitions and popular beliefs. Contains about 2,500 lengthy, signed and usually well-documented articles. V. 10 is the comprehensive index.

Calendar Festivals

398.33
CHAMBERS, R., *ed.* **Book of days:** a miscellany of popular antiquities in connection with the calendar. London, Chambers, 1862-64 (in parts); various re-issues (*e.g.,* Lippincott, 1891). illus.

"A bridge between the early formal accounts of the folklore, history and customs connected with the holidays and saints' days and those written in the simpler style of today." Many curious facts are assembled in calendar order, although not all are relevant to the calendar. Useful for finding anniversaries of events on particular days; includes dates of births and deaths. British and European slant. Detailed index.

There are three similar works by W. Hone: *The every-day book* (London, Tegg, 1826-27. 2v.); *The table book* (1827-28. 2v.); *The year-book* (1832). The first two were re-issued in 3v. in 1831, and new editions of all three works were published in 1874.

398.33 (4)
MEYER, R. E. Festivals: Europe. New York, Washburn, 1954. xii, 328p.

Material is grouped under 21 countries (including Turkey), arranged A-Z. In each case the country's festivals are surveyed and then listed by months. Very full index.

398.33 (4-015)
SPICER, D. G. Festivals of western Europe. New York, Wilson, 1958. xi, 275p.

Covers 12 countries (excluding Great Britain); under each country entries are in calendar order. Indexes of countries and festivals. Much fuller descriptions than Meyer's *Festivals: Europe,* but covering fewer countries. Bibliography.

398.33 (410)
FOLK-LORE SOCIETY. British calendar customs. London, Glaisher, 1936-. illus.

England, by A. R. Wright; edited by T. E. Lones. 3v. 1936-40. (v. 1: Movable festivals; v. 2-3: Fixed festivals). ea. 30s.
Orkneys and Shetland; edited by M. M. Banks. 1946. 21s.
Scotland; edited by M. M. Banks. 3v. 1937-41. (v. 1: Movable festivals; v. 2-3: Fixed festivals). ea. 30s.
A volume on Wales is in preparation.
Arranged in calendar order; lists of authorities.

Indexes to the *England* and *Scotland* series are in v. 3 of each series.

398.33 (410)
HOWARD, A. Endless cavalcade: a diary of British festivals and customs. London, Barker, 1964. xiv, 300p. 30s.

Calendar arrangement; includes fairs and sporting events. Well illustrated; bibliography, p. 285-287, but no specific references for individual events. Full index.

398.33 (410)
HUNT, C. British customs and ceremonies: when, where, and why; an informative guide. London, Benn, 1954. 208p.

Alphabetical arrangement of places, with descriptions of the ceremonies; customs not confined to one place (*e.g.,* All Fool's Day) are included in the main sequence; excludes fairs and sporting events. Full index. No references.

398.33 (410)
TRENT, C. The BP book of festivals and events in Britain. London, Phoenix House, 1966. 160p. illus. (some col.). 25s.

Contents are arranged by regions, then towns: Midland England — London — Home counties — Northern counties—Wales—Scotland—Ireland—The festival calendar (month; place; event). Festivals include the Shakespeare Festival, Glyndebourne, Aldeburgh Festival, Haslemere Festival. Good half-tone illustrations, about 1 per page; 22 coloured plates. No index.

398.33 (420)
SPICER, D. G. Yearbook of English festivals. New York, Wilson, 1954. xxv, 298p. map. $5; 37s. 6d.

Part 2: Chronological survey; part 2: The Easter cycle. In calendar order gives very readable, rather popularised accounts of current festivals, thus supplementing Chambers' *Book of days.* Glossary; bibliography; indexes of customs, counties and regions.

394.2 (420)
WHISTLER, L. The English festivals. London, Heinemann, 1947. 241p. illus.

The calendar festivals described in some detail, with helpful bibliographical footnotes. An appendix indexes carols in several collected volumes.

Riddles

398.6
TAYLOR, A. A bibliography of riddles. Helsinki, Suomalainen Tiedeakatemia, Academia Scientiarum Fennica, 1939. 173p. (FF communications no. 126).

Intended as a guide to the literature of the European traditional riddle. 10 sections: General bibliography of riddles — General works on riddles — Collections of riddles (p. 17-140: 896 numbered items) — Anagrams — Arithmetical riddles—Biblical riddles—Catechetical questions — Paradoxes — Rebus — Studies in individual riddles. Has only a few titles of Old English riddles and of contemporary Latin riddles. Occasional evaluative notes. Index of names.

Singing Games
398.8
GOMME, A. B. The traditional games of England, Scotland and Ireland, with tunes, singing-rhymes and methods of playing according to the variants extant and recorded in different parts of the Kingdom. New York, Dover, 1964. 2v. illus. ea. $2.50, 20s.

Unabridged reprint of *Dictionary of British folk-lore* (London, Nutt, 1894-8. 2v.).
More than 600 games are listed (A-Z), described and analysed. Rhymes are given in full, with local versions. 'Memoir on the study of children's games', p. 458-531. The standard authority.

Nursery Rhymes
398.83
The Oxford dictionary of nursery rhymes; edited by I. and P. Opie. Oxford, Clarendon Press, 1951 (reprinted with corrections, 1952). xxvii, 467p. illus. (incl. pl.). 42s.

Contains entries on more than 500 rhymes and songs traditionally handed on to young children. Entry is usually under the most prominent word or subject; information is given on the history of each rhyme, parallels and first appearance, source and variations. The illustrations are taken from drawings on old ballad sheets.
Index of notable figures; index of first lines.
A similar dictionary is stated to be projected of skipping rhymes, schoolboy rhymes, rhymes used in street games, and so forth.

G. F. Northall's *English folk-rhymes: a collection* of traditional verses relating to places and persons, customs, superstitions, etc. (London, Kegan Paul, Trench, Trübner, 1892. xii, 565p.), has 17 subject sections (*e.g.,* 11. Games—12. The almanac—13. Weather), plus 18. Additions and corrections. Many quotations; references to sources. Sources, p. ix-xii.

Proverbs
398.9:016
BONSER, W., *ed.* **Proverb literature:** a bibliography of works relating to proverbs, compiled from material left by the late T. A. Stephens. London, Glaisher for Folk-lore Society, 1930. xx, 496p. port.

4,004 items, with brief annotations. Arrangement is by languages (including dialects) and also countries. Some periodical articles are included. London locations of books are given. The index covers authors, anonymous titles and subjects.

398.9:016
MOLL, O. E. Sprichwörterbibliographie. Frankfurt am Main, Klostermann, 1958. xvi, 630p. DM.98; DM.106.50.

Lists some 9,000 items under languages, subdivided chronologically; covers collections of proverbs and works on their history, psychology, form and use. Includes periodical articles. Gives library locations for some books. Wide scope, including, for example, Lamb's essay on popular fallacies.

398.9 (02)
TAYLOR, A. The proverb, and **An index to the proverb.** Hatboro, Pa., Folklore Associates; Copenhagen, Rosenkilde & Bagger, 1962. 223, 105p.

Reprinted from the editions of 1931 (Cambridge, Mass., Harvard Univ. Press) and 1934 respectively.
The text has 4 parts: 1. The origin of the proverb—2. The content of proverbs—3. The style of proverbs (dialogue, epigrammatic, etc.) —4. Proverbial phrases, Wellerisms and proverbial comparisons. Footnote references; many examples. The catchword index has *c.* 1,250 entries. Bibliography, p. 102-5.

398.9 (03)
ARTHABER, A. Dizionario comparato di proverbi e modi proverbiali italani, latini, francesi, spagnoli, tedeschi, inglesi e greci antichi. [New ed.] Milan, Hoepli, 1952. xvi, 892p.

First published 1929.
1,483 proverbs, in their Italian form, are arranged alphabetically by key-word, followed in each case by French, Spanish, German, English, etc. equivalents. Indexes to the Latin, French, Spanish, German, English and ancient Greek forms of the proverbs. Usefully supplements language dictionaries for this type of idiom.

G. Ilg's *English proverbs* (Amsterdam, Elsevier), in preparation, will consist of *c.* 600 entries in English, with equivalents in French, German, Dutch, Italian, Spanish and Latin. A similar collection of German proverbs is also in preparation.

398.9 (03)
CHAMPION, S. G. Racial proverbs: a selection of the world's proverbs arranged linguistically. 2nd ed. London, Routledge, 1950 (reprinted 1964). cxxx, 767p. map. 60s.

First published 1938.
Sub-title: "with authoritative introductions to the proverbs of 27 countries and races". Introductions to particular language sections are by folklore specialists. The selection comprises more than 26,000 proverbs, taken from nearly 200 languages and arranged in translated form, by keywords under language headings. List of authorities cited (21p.). Four indexes: linguistic and geographical, subject-matter, race and alternative chief-word indexes.

398.9 (03)
DAVIDOFF, H. A world treasury of proverbs from twenty-five languages. London, Cassell, 1953. 492p.

Includes more than 15,500 proverbs, arranged in alphabetical order of subject. Index of authors, but not of key words. Does not give precise references and in many cases gives no attribution. List of sources, p. 5-6.

398.9 (03)
LIPPERHEIDE, F. F. v. Spruchwörterbuch.
Sammlung deutscher und fremder Sinnsprüche,
Wahlsprüche, Inschriften. Berlin, Haude &
Spenersche Verlagsbuchhandlung, 1962. viii,
1069p.

First published 1907. The 1962 ed. is a reprint.
About 31,300 proverbs (25,000 German; 700
Greek; 700 Latin; 250 Italian; 630 French; 1100
English; 1500 Biblical, apart from 800 in minor
languages). The German translation of non-
German proverbs is followed by the original.
Reviewed in *Bulletin des bibliothèques de France*,
v. 8, no. 2, February 1963, p.*638.

398.9 (03)
**MALOUX, M. Dictionnaire des proverbes,
sentences et maximes.** Paris, Larousse, 1960.
xvi, 628p. 35s.

More than 10,000 proverbs, arranged under
topics, A-Z (Abnégation-Zèle), then by language
of the original (all are translated into French).
Under 'Pauvreté': 41 proverbs from 20 languages
(10 are French in origin). Catchword index, p.
561-628. Bibliography, p. xiii-xvi.

398.9 (03)
**STEVENSON, B. E. Stevenson's Book of prov-
erbs, maxims and familiar phrases.** New
York, Macmillan, 1948; London, Routledge,
1949. viii, 2957p.

Contains more than 73,000 proverbs, maxims
and phrases. Subject arrangement, with dates;
index of keywords. Overlaps considerably with
Stevenson's *Book of quotations*. Gives precise
citations; international in scope.

Scots Proverbs
398.9 (411)
**CARMICHAELL, J., comp. The James Carmich-
aell collection of proverbs in Scots;** edited by
M. L. Anderson. Edinburgh, Univ. Press, 1957.
vii, 149p. illus.

Contents : Introduction—Text—Notes—Glossary. 1,868 items, with MS. source and dates.

A. Hislop's *The proverbs of Scotland, collected
and arranged, with notes, explanatory and illustrative, and a glossary* (Glasgow, Porteous &
Hislop, 1862. ix, [i], 372p.) has first an A-Z
sequence of more than 2,000 proverbs, with
explanations, if required, and then a classified
sequence.

English Proverbs
398.9 (420)
**APPERSON, G. L. English proverbs and prover-
bial phrases:** a historical dictionary. London,
Dent, 1929. x, 721p.

Arranged alphabetically under first significant
word. The use of each proverb in literature is
indicated. Form of entry: proverb; various applications; date; quotation (with author and date).
List of sources, p. vii and viii.

398.9 (420)
COLLINS, V. H. A book of English proverbs,
with origins and explanations. London, Longmans, 1959. x, 144p. 12s. 6d.

"A collection of the chief proverbial sayings
that are current today" (*Preface*). Gives date of
earliest use (marked 'R') or the "record of the
date of an adumbration of what later crystal-
lised into and became established as a proverbial saying" (marked 'A'). Examples of usage.
Arrangement is alphabetical by the main catchword; catchword index. List of sources, p. ix.

398.9 (420)
**SMITH, W. G., comp. The Oxford dictionary of
English proverbs.** 2nd ed., revised by Sir P.
Hartley. Oxford, Clarendon Press, 1948. xxxii,
740p. 48s.

First published 1935.
Contains more than 11,000 entries, arranged
alphabetically under the first significant word.
Cross-references from other key words, but not
necessarily from the first word of the proverb.
Gives sources and users, arranged chronologically, with dates. A list of collections of proverbs,
p. xxix-xxxi; also a useful introduction by J. E.
Heseltine on "Proverbs and pothooks; proverbs
and proverb literature". The 1st ed. carried an
index.

The older store-house of English (and foreign)
proverbs, *Lean's Collectanea*, by V. S. Lean
(Bristol, Arrowsmith, 1902-4. 4v. in 5), is classified in various ways, by country, calendar,
subject-matter, etc.

398.9 (420)
**TILLEY, M. P. A dictionary of the proverbs in
England** in the sixteenth and seventeenth cen-
turies: a collection of the proverbs found in
English literature and the dictionaries of the
period. Ann Arbor, Univ. of Michigan Press;
London, Oxford Univ. Press, 1950. xiii, 854p.
front. $15; 120s.

Subject entry, items being arranged A-Z thereunder, citing sources; bibliography of works
quoted, p. 769-802. Indexes of significant words
in proverbs (p. 809-54); and a Shakespeare index
p. 803-8), giving exact references. About 11,780
proverbs are listed.

Welsh Proverbs
398.9 (429)
EVANS, J. J. Welsh proverbs: in English and
Welsh. Llandyssul, Cardiganshire, Gomerian
Press (J. D. Lewis & Sons, Ltd.), 1965. [4], 59p.
8s. 6d.

Parallel Welsh and English text.

German Proverbs
398.9 (43)
**KREMER, E. P. German proverbs and prover-
bial phrases,** with their English counterparts.
Stanford, Cal., Stanford Univ. Press; London,
Oxford Univ. Press, 1955. viii, [1], 116p.

Arrangement is by the first significant word of
the German proverb; the English version follows.
Bibliography, p. 116.

G. Ilg's seven-language *Deutscher Sprich-
wörter* (Amsterdam & London, Elsevier) is in
preparation.

See also F. F. v. Lipperheide's *Spruchwörter-buch,* at 398.9 (03).

French Proverbs

398.9 (44)

ILG, G. **Proverbes français,** suivis des équivalents en allemand, anglais, espagnol, italien [et] néer-landais. Amsterdam & London, Elsevier, 1960. xii, 97p. (Glossaria interpretum G4). 30s.

607 French proverbs, with English, German, Italian, Spanish and occasionally Latin equivalents. If equivalents are only approximate, this is stated. 27 subject groups (*e.g.,* End and means; Cause and effect; Justice). Alphabetical catch-word index (p. 81-97), poor for catchwords other than French.

Proverbes et dictons français, by J. Pineaux (3. éd. Paris, Presses Universitaires de France, 1960. 128p. (Que sais je? no. 706) is a study of French proverbs and sayings in 6 chapters (*e.g.,* 2. Les ouvrages consacrés à l'études des proverbes —3. L'utilisation des proverbes dans la iittéra-ture). Many examples; no index. Short biblio-graphy, p. 126.

Italian Proverbs

398.9 (45)

GIUSTI, G., and CAPPONI, G. **Dizionario dei proverbi italiani.** Milan, Veronelli, 1956. xxxiv, 483p.

Full index.

Spanish Proverbs

398.9 (46)

SAINZ DE ROBLES, F. C. **Refranero español.** Introducción, selección y notas. 4. ed. Madrid, Aguilar, 1962. 550p.

A study of the Spanish proverb, with numerous examples.

A collection of Spanish proverbs and aphor-isms, with equivalents in Latin, French, Italian, English and German: *Diccionario de aforis-mos, proverbios y refranes . . .,* by J. Sintes Pros (3. ed. Barcelona, Editorial Sintes, [1961]. 595p.).

Chinese Proverbs

398.9 (51)

SCARBOROUGH, W. **A collection of Chinese proverbs.** 2nd ed. Shanghai, Presbyterian Mission Press, 1926. vi, 381, xiv p. Reprinted New York, Paragon Book Reprint Corp., 1964. $12.50.

Grouped under broad headings, with a topical index. Proverbs in Chinese script, with trans-literation and translation.

Japanese Proverbs

398.9 (52)

BUCHANAN, D. C. **Japanese proverbs and sayings.** Norman, Oklahoma, Univ. of Oklahoma Press, 1965. xvii, 280p.

Some 2,500 proverbs and idioms illustrative of Japanese psychology and culture. Arranged alphabetically under 56 subjects, with transiter-ated and translated titles, explanation, and some-times English proverbial equivalent. Index of subjects.

American Proverbs

398.9 (73)

TAYLOR, A., and WHITING, B. J. **A dictionary of American proverbs** and proverbial phrases, 1820-1880. Cambridge, Mass., Belknap Press of Harvard Univ. Press, 1958. xxii, [1], 418p. $9.50.

Arranged alphabetically by keyword, with full references to book and page. Includes proverbs used by American authors of the period, even if the proverbs are not American in origin. Criti-cized in the *Times literary supplement* (no. 2,998, 14th August 1959, p. 468) as casting too wide a net in its interpretation of what constitutes a proverb and a proverbial phrase. A 10-page bibliography of texts and reference works (p. xiii-xxii).

9 GEOGRAPHY. BIOGRAPHY. HISTORY

9 (03)

BOUILLET, M. N. Dictionnaire universel d'histoire et de géographie . . . Refondu sous la direction de L. G. Gourraigne. 34. éd. Paris, Hachette, 1914. ii, 2237p.

Fairly comprehensive for biography (giving the titles of leading works in the case of writers) and geography. The latter includes entries under countries (listing counties, départements, etc., with chronologies of reigns and the like) as well as places. A compact volume, containing some 3 million words.

908 AREA STUDIES

(See also 33 (4/9).)

908 (4/9):016

AMERICAN UNIVERSITIES FIELD STAFF. A select bibliography: Asia, Africa, Eastern Europe, Latin America. New York, A.U.F.S., 1960. ix, 533, [1]p. $4.75. **Supplement, 1961.** 1963. $1.

7,544 numbered items, some with annotations, in the main volume. The supplement adds a further 500, published June 1959 - June 1961. Mostly English-language books and periodicals, for the U.S. college student and general reader; concentrates on the humanities, omitting the social sciences. Subject sub-divisions: Religion and philosophy—History and description—Fine arts—Language and literature—Drama. Major regions are further divided geographically into countries, followed by the subject sub-divisions. Entries marked 'A' (about 10% of the whole) are recommended for first consideration; those marked 'B' (a further 20%) are recommended as next priority. Indexes of authors and of titles.

908 (4/9) (02)

GREAT BRITAIN. ADMIRALTY. Geographical handbook series. [London], Admiralty, Naval Intelligence Division, 1941-46. 58v. illus., diagrs., maps, tables.

Germany. 4v. 1944-45.	*Turkey.* 2v. 1942-43.
Luxembourg. 1944.	*Iraq and the Persian*
France. 4v. 1942.	*Gulf.* 1944.
Corsica. 1942.	*Syria.* 1943.
Italy. 4v. 1944-45.	*Palestine and Trans-*
Spain and Portugal. 4v	*jordan.* 1943.
1941-45.	*Indo-China.* 1943.
Norway. 2v. 1942-43.	*Tunisia.* 1945.
Denmark. 1944.	*Morocco.* 2v. 1941-42.
Iceland. 1942.	*Algeria.* 2v. 1943-44.
Netherlands. 1944.	*French West Africa.* 2v.
Belgium. 1944.	1943-44.
Greece. 3v. 1944-45.	*French Equatorial Africa*
Dodecanese. 1941.	*and Cameroons.* 1942.
Albania. 1945.	*The Belgian Congo.*
Jugoslavia. 3v. 1944-45	1944.
China proper. 3v.	*Netherlands East Indies.*
1944-45.	2v. 1944.
Western Arabia and	*Pacific Islands.* 4v.
the Red Sea. 1946.	1943-45.
Persia. 1945.	

Originally available for official use only. Whilst the purpose of these handbooks is primarily naval, the contents "are by no means confined to matters of purely naval interest. For many purposes (*e.g.*, history, administration, resources, communications, etc.) countries must necessarily be treated as a whole, and no attempt is made to limit their treatment exclusively to coastal zones" (*Preface*). Packed with information and obsolete only in certain respects, the volumes provide excellent background material and carry numerous maps; bibliographies; analytical indexes.

Länderlexikon (2., völlig neubearb. Aufl. Hrsg. vom Hamburgischen Welt-Wirtschafts. Archiv. Hamburg, Verlag Weltarchiv GmbH, 1962-. v. 1- illus., maps, tables) is arranged by country groups, with systematic treatment of each country, plus a short bibliography. First published in 3v., 1953-60.

908 (4/9) (02)

Handbooks to the modern world. London, Blond, 1966-. illus., maps.

Western Europe: a handbook; edited by J. Calmann. 1967. 147s.
Africa: a handbook; edited by C. Legum. Rev. & enl. ed. 1966. 126s.
Asia: a handbook; edited by G. Wint. 1966. 147s. (*See at 908 (5) (02)*.)
Latin America and the Caribbean: a handbook; edited by C. Veliz. 1968. 168s.

Each volume is a compendium of information on general issues in the area and the particular countries concerned; contributed by a team of specialists; chapter bibliographies; 20-37 maps per volume. *Times literary supplement* (no. 3,417, 17th August 1967, p. 740) describes Western Europe as aiming to combine a good deal of information already in *Whitaker's Almanack, Annual register* and *Statesman's year-book* and queries how long will the book be useful as a work of reference in a rapidly changing world.

Further titles in preparation: *The Soviet Union and Eastern Europe, The Middle East, North America,* and *Australia and New Zealand.*

908 (4/9) (02)

UNITED STATES. DEPARTMENT OF THE ARMY. Area handbooks. Washington, U.S. Government Printing Office, 1957-.

Prepared by Foreign Areas Studies Division, Special Operations Research Office, The American University, Washington, D.C.

Volumes so far published, in U.D.C. order.

Germany. 1960. 2nd ed.	*Cyprus.* 1964. $2.
1964. $4.	*Syria.* 1966. $1.25.
Korea. 1965. $2.75.	*Malaysia and Singa-*
Japan. 1961. 2nd ed.	*pore.* 1966. $2.75.
1964. $3.25.	*Thailand.* 1963 (re-
Saudi Arabia. 1967.	printed 1967). $2.50.
$1.25.	*Cambodia.* 1967. $1.75.
India. 1965. $2.50.	*Vietnam.* 1965. $2.
Nepal. 1965. $1.25.	*South Vietnam.* 1967.
Pakistan. 1958. Rev. ed	$1.75.
1966. $3.25.	*Laos.* 1968. $2.

U.A.R. (Egypt). 1957. Rev. ed. 1965. $1.25.

Republic of Sudan. 1960. 2nd ed. 1964. $2.

Ethiopia. 1960. 2nd ed. 1964. $2.50.

Morocco. 1966. $1.50.

Algeria. 1965. $1.50.

Liberia. 1965. $1.50.

Nigeria. 1961. 2nd ed. 1964. (Official use. Not available. Sent to depository libraries.

Senegal. 1964. $1.50.

Republic of Congo (Léopoldville). 1962. Distribution by distributing office.

Kenya. 1967. (Official use. Not available. Sent to depository libraries.).

Dominican Republic. 1967. $2.25.

Brazil. 1965. $3.50.

Peru. 1966. $2.50.

Colombia. 1961. 2nd ed. 1964. $2.

Ecuador. 1966. $3.

Venezuela. 1964. $1.75.

Indonesia. 1965. $2.50.

The *Area handbook for Pakistan* (1958. Rev. ed. 1966. xii, 607p. 11 illus., 22 tables, maps. $3.25) has 30 chapters in 4 sections: 1. Social background—2. Political background—3. Economic background—4. National security. Bibliography (by sections; each: 'Recommended further reading'; 'Other sources used'), p. 571-607, lists items in English, including periodical articles and unpublished theses. Detailed contents list; no index.

908 (4/9) (02)

Worldmark encyclopedia of the nations: a practical guide to the geographic, historical, political, social & economic status of all nations, their international relationships and the United Nations system. 2nd rev. and enl. ed. Edited by M. Y. Sachs. New York, Worldmark Press, Inc., 1963. 5v. illus., maps. $49.95. (3rd ed. 1967. 5v. $59.95).

First published in 1v., 1960.

The 2nd ed. is similarly arranged to the 1st ed. Volume titles: *Europe—Americas—Asia & Australia—Africa—United Nations.* 135 maps; 600 tables. The *United Nations* volume includes a general, analytical index and bibliography (p. 266-9). Systematic coverage of each country with bibliography. "It probably would be most useful in small and medium-sized collections where official handbooks and statistical works are unavailable" (*Library journal,* v. 88, no. 20, 15 November 1963, p. 4356). Frequent revision is clearly called for.

908 (4/9) (058)

The Europa year book. 1959-. London, Europa Publications, 1959-. 2v. (1968. £14; ea. 150s.).

v. 1. *International organisations. Europe.*

v. 2. *Africa, the Americas, Asia, Australasia.*

The title is now a misnomer. V. 1 covers the same ground as the former loose-leaf *Europa* (1926-58). *Orbis,* also loose-leaf (1938-58) is replaced by v. 2. For each country an introductory survey and then data on statistics, constitution, government, political parties, legal system, religion, press, publishers, radio and television, finance, trade and industry, transport and tourism, atomic energy and universities. Contains more directory information than does the *Statesman's year-book.* Its accuracy has been questioned (*International affairs,* v. 37, no. 1, January 1961, p. 32).

908 (4/9) (058)

The International year-book and statesmen's who's who. 1953-. London, Burke's Peerage, 1953-. map, charts. Annual. (1968. 189s.).

Three parts: 1. International organizations. Organization of Foreign Ministries of great powers (charts)—2. States of the world (A-Z, p. 81-622)—3. Biographical section (p. 1-853). The information in part 2 is similar to that in the *Statesman's year book* (*e.g.,* Peru: Constitution and government—Legal system—Area and population—Currency—Finance—Banks—Production, industry and commerce — Communications — Newspapers—Atomic energy—Education and religion—National flag (description)); it lacks the bibliographies in *S.Y.B.* Part 3 has nearly 10,000 biographies (*e.g.,* De Valera: 45 lines). Entries are based on replies to questionnaires and the draft is submitted to the biographee before publication.

908 (4/9) (058)

The Statesman's year-book: statistical and historical information of the states of the world for the year . . . London, Macmillan, 1864-. tables, maps. Annual. (1966-67. 1966. 63s.).

Contents of the 1966/67 ed.: Comparative statistical tables (figures up to 1965), p. xv-xxviii —Part 1. International organizations (p. 3-52)— Part 2. The Commonwealth (grouped geographically, p. 55-567)—Part 3. The United States of America (with sub-divisions for individual states, p. 569-786)—Part 4. Other countries (A-Z, p. 789-1629)—Index (p. 1633-1732). Two topical maps by Bartholomew. Systematically arranged data on each country (*e.g.,* Italy: constitution & government; area and population; religion; education; social welfare; justice; finance; defence; production; commerce; communications; money; banking; weights and measures; diplomatic representatives; books of reference (statistical information; unofficial); national library (address)). The index has *c.* 10,000 entries ('Coffee products of' has 67 country entries).

The handiest, cheapest and most accurate of the international year books.

Developing Countries

908 (4/9-77):016

Bibliographie über Entwicklungsländer. Bearb. von der Forschungsstelle der Friedrich-Ebert-Stiftung in Zusammenarbeit mit dem Institut für Selbsthilfe und Sozialforschung. Hannover, Verlag für Literatur und Zeitgeschehen, 1961-. v. 1-. 2 p.a.

Preceded by *Literatur über Entwicklungsländer* (Hannover, Verlag für Literatur und Zeitgeschehen, 1961-63. 2v. and 2 suppts.), covering 1950-59 and 1960 publications in German, English, French and Russian.

The developing nations: a guide to information sources concerning their economic, political, technical and social problems, by E. G. ReQua and J. Statham (Detroit, Gale Research Co., 1965. 339p. $8.75) is an annotated list of English-language books, articles, reports, conference papers, general reference sources, bibliographies and directories, agencies and institutions. Author and title indexes.

EUROPE

908 (4):016
COUNCIL FOR CULTURAL CO-OPERATION OF THE COUNCIL OF EUROPE. Books dealing with Europe: bibliography for teachers. Strasbourg, Council of Europe, 1965. 67p.

About 250 annotated entries for books and pamphlets (mostly in English, French and German). Aimed chiefly at helping teachers to find background materials (*Preface*). Sections: Geography—History—Philosophy—Culture (5 divisions, including Painting, Architecture and Sculpture)—European integration—Education—The teaching of European civics—Europe and the world—Textbooks and other works for the young. No index.

908 (4):016
UNITED STATES. LIBRARY OF CONGRESS. European Affairs Division. **Introduction to Europe:** a selective guide to background reading. Washington, Library of Congress, 1950. 201p.

A well annotated bibliography. Arrangement is primarily by areas and, by countries, with subsections on land and people, history, the contemporary political and economic scene, and cultural aspects. Author index.

———— **Supplement,** 1950-1955; compiled by H. Conover. Washington, Library of Congress, 1955. iii, 181p.

Issued by the General Reference and Bibliographical Division of Library of Congress. Annotations average some 10 lines each; 491 items, including some periodical articles; annotations cite further works. Index of authors and anonymous titles.

908 (4-011):016
The American bibliography of Slavic and East European studies for 1956-. Bloomington (and later, London), Indiana Univ. Press, 1957-. Annual. (1963, published 1966. 26s. 6d.).

Aims to include all books and periodical articles written by Americans in this field. 11 sections, sub-divided by country. Author index. 1961 v.: 1,863 entries.

908 (4-011):016
JOHANN GOTTFRIED HERDER INSTITUT, Marburg. Bibliothek. **Alphabetischer Katalog.** Boston, Mass., G. K. Hall, 1964. 5v. $320 (U.S. & West Germany).

The Herder Institute Library was set up in 1950, "for the purpose of scholarly research on those countries in which German and Slavic peoples lived in proximity for many centuries" (*Foreword*), and is the reference library of the largest West German institute for East Central Europe (*c.* 70,000 v., including 1,100 current periodicals).
The catalogue consists of 63,400 cards, photolithographically reproduced. Valuable for its coverage of East Germany, Estonia, Latvia, Lithuania, Poland and Czechoslovakia. Omits items on the natural sciences, medicine and technology.

908 (4-012):016
Südosteuropa - Bibliographie. Munich, Süost-Institut, 1956-. v. 1-. Five-yearly, each in 2 pts.

v. 1: *1945-1950.* 1956-59. 2 pts.
v. 2: *1951-1955.* 1960-62. 2 pts.
v. 3: *1956-1960.* 1964-. pt. 1-.
Countries covered: Czechoslovakia, Hungary, Yugoslavia, Albania, Bulgaria and Rumania. Aspects: physical features, population, history, economy, science and culture. Author indexes. V. 1, pt. 1: *Slowakei, Rumänien, Bulgarien* (1956. iii, 91p.) lists 1,589 items; separately published works are asterisked. Periodical articles from 24 journals.

Commonwealth

908 (41-44):016
CARNELL, F., *comp.* **The politics of the new states:** a selected annotated bibliography, with special reference to the Commonwealth. Published for the Institute of Commonwealth Studies by Oxford Univ. Press, London, 1961. xvi, 171p. 12s. 6d.

1,599 numbered items (books, and articles from 67 journals) in 21 chapters. (21: Bibliographies and other sources, items 1558-99). Annotations, where given, average *c.* 30 words. Asterisked items form a basic reading list. "This bibliography has grown out of the practical requirements of teaching in this field" (*Introduction*). Considered (*Times literary supplement,* no. 3121, 22nd December 1961, p. 919) an invaluable work of reference for students of Commonwealth affairs. *International affairs* (v. 38, no. 4, October 1962, p. 510) has reservations on the scope of the bibliography. It certainly requires updating.

908 (41-44):016
HORNE, A. J. **The Commonwealth today:** a select bibliography on the Commonwealth and its constituent countries. London, Library Association, 1965. 107p. (L.A. Special subject list no. 45). 24s. (18s. to members).

720 numbered and annotated items,—"books published in recent years and still in print today" (*Preface*). Includes some year books but only a few government publications. Arranged on a geographical basis (The Commonwealth in general—The Commonwealth in Africa . . .); Britain omitted. Author index. A handy book-list within its self-imposed limits.

908 (41-44):016
NATIONAL BOOK LEAGUE. **Commonwealth reference books and bibliographical guide.** London, N.B.L., 1965. 54p. 2s.

About 700 items, many with brief annotations. 'Commonwealth bibliography' (p. 3-18) is divided into general and then country (A-Z) sections (*e.g.,* India: current national bibliography; retrospective bibliography (7 items)). 'Commonwealth reference books' (p. 18-54) is divided by continents or regions and major countries (*e.g.,* Canada: atlases and gazetteers; biographies; dictionaries; directories; encyclopaedias; handbooks; travel books). No index.

J. E. Flint's *Books on the British Empire and Commonwealth: a guide for students* (London,

Oxford Univ. Press on behalf of the Royal Commonwealth Society, 1868. vi, 66p. 12s. 6d.) is an unannotated list of c. 1,500 items published since 1940, arranged by countries; no index. 'Some useful bibliographies', p. 65-66.

908 (41-44):016
ROYAL EMPIRE SOCIETY. Subject catalogue of the library of the Royal Empire Society, formerly the Royal Colonial Institute, by E. Lewin. London, the Society, 1930-37. 4v. (Reprinted London, Dawsons Pall Mall Press, 1967. ea. £16; £60.).

v. 1: *British Empire generally, and Africa.*
v. 2: *Australia, New Zealand, South Africa, General voyages and travels, Arctic and Antarctic.*
v. 3: *Canada, Newfoundland, West Indies, Colonial America.*
v. 4: *Mediterranean dependencies, Middle East, India, Burma, Ceylon, Malaya, East Indies, Far East.*
v. 5: *Biography catalogue of the Library of the Royal Commonwealth Society,* by Donald H. Simpson (London, R.C.S., 1961. xxiii, 511p. 115s. 6d.)—see at 92:016.

Arranged geographically under subjects and in chronological order. Indicates pamphlets and periodical articles as well as books. The fine library of the Royal Empire Society (now Royal Commonwealth Society) was damaged in the bombing of London and the catalogue no longer strictly applies to it. It remains an indispensable bibliography.

908 (41-44) (02)
GREAT BRITAIN. CENTRAL OFFICE OF INFORMATION. Commonwealth fact sheets. London, C.O.I. maps. ea. 8d.

A series of 4 to 8-page pamphlets, revised at intervals. Latest editions:

Antigua. 1966.
Bahamas. 1966.
Basutoland (*Lesotho*) 1964.
Bermuda. 1965.
British Guiana (*Guyana*). 1965.
British Honduras. 1963.
British Solomon Is. Prot. 1965.
British Virgin Is. 1966.
Brunei. 1964.
Cayman Islands. 1964.
Ceylon. 1964.
Cyprus. 1963.
Falkland Is. Dependencies. 1966.
Fiji. 1967.
Ghana. 1966.
Gibraltar. 1965.
Gilbert & Ellice Is. 1963.
Hong Kong. 1966.
India. 1963.
Jamaica. 1965.
Kenya. 1965.
Malawi. 1966.
Malta. 1966.
Mauritius. 1966.
New Hebrides. 1965.
Nigeria. 1963.
Pakistan. 1963.
Pitcairn. 1967.
Rhodesia. 1965.
Seychelles. 1965.
Sierra Leone. 1965.
Tanzania. 1965.
Tonga. 1965.
Trinidad and Tobago 1963.
Uganda. 1965.
Zambia. 1966.

The pamphlet on Rhodesia (1965. 8p.) has sections: General—History—Constitution and government—Social services—The economy. Reading list. Good 2-colour map.

C.O.I. Reference pamphlets on overseas affairs cover similar ground in more detail. Recent issues:
71. *Guyana.* 1966. 5s.
72. *Botswana.* 1966. 5s.
73. *Lesotho.* 1966. 5s.
74. *Barbados.* 1966. 4s. 6d.

The pamphlet on Barbados ([vii], 26p. illus. map) has sections: Introduction—The land and people—History—Constitutional development—Economic progress. Appendix: Some facts and figures. Reading list, p. 26.

908 (41-44):026/027
HEWITT, A. R. Guide to resources for Commonwealth studies in London, Oxford and Cambridge; with bibliographical and other information. London, Athlone Press, for Institute of Commonwealth Studies, Univ. of London, 1957. viii, 219p.

Includes a concise survey of library resources by subjects (p. 50-68), bibliographies and works of reference (p. 72-90), and notes on individual collections (p. 93-179). An excellent example of its kind.

908 (41-44) (058)
The British Commonwealth year book, 1962/63. London, MacGibbon and Kee, 1963. xix, 614p. 70s.

As *Commonwealth co-operation* and then *The Empire and Commonwealth yearbook* (London, Neame, for the Empire Economic Union), 1952-59; title changed to *The British Commonwealth year book* with the 9th ed. (for 1961 [1960]).
Part 1: The Commonwealth; regional organisations, etc.—2. Europe and the Mediterranean. Asia. Africa. America (p. 71-492)—3. Raw materials and commodities (p. 495-602). Statistical and other concise data, on the lines of the *Statesman's year book*. Index, p. 609-14. No more published.

908 (41-44):087.7
HARVARD UNIVERSITY. Baker Library. **A finding-list of British Royal Commission reports on the British Dominions.** [2nd ed.]. Prepared under the direction of A. H. Cole. Cambridge, Mass., Harvard Univ. Press, 1939. 134p.

First published 1935.
About 1,000 items, under 19 subject headings. Omits Ireland, British India and Crown Colonies.

Great Britain

908 (410):016
GREAT BRITAIN. CENTRAL OFFICE OF INFORMATION. Reference material on United Kingdom home affairs available from the Central Office of Information. London, C.O.I., 1967. [i], 11p.

A price list of papers, pamphlets and fact sheets prepared by the Reference Division, C.O.I. The list of papers, pamphlets and short notes is followed by 'Fact sheets on Britain', 'Notes on science and technology in Britain' and 'Reference material on sale' from H.M.S.O.

908 (410) (02)

BRITISH ASSOCIATION FOR THE ADVANCE-MENT OF SCIENCE. [Scientific surveys]. London, the Association, etc., 1949-. illus., maps.

Each volume is a 200-300 page survey, stressing geographical, social, economic and other aspects of the city and district in which a meeting of the British Association has been held. Each is a co-ordinated collection of essays by specialists, short bibliographies being usually appended to contributions. Recent volumes:

1949. *A scientific survey of North Eastern England.* London, the Association. 10s.
1950. *Birmingham and its regional setting.* Birmingham, Cornish. 15s.
1951. *A scientific survey of South Eastern Scotland.* London, the Association. 15s.
1952. *Belfast in its regional setting: a scientific survey.* London, the Association. 21s.
1953. *A scientific survey of Merseyside.* Liverpool, Univ. Press. 21s.
1954. *The Oxford region: a scientific and historical survey.* Oxford, Univ. Press. 21s.
1955. *Bristol and its adjoining counties.* Bristol, Wm. George's Sons. 30s.
1956. *Sheffield and its regions: a scientific and historical survey.* Sheffield, A. B. Ward. 30s.
1957. *A view of Ireland: twelve essays . . .* Dublin, Eason. 21s.
1958. *The Glasgow region: a general survey.* Glasgow, Univ. Press. 30s.
1959. *York: a survey, 1959.* York, Local Executive Committee. 15s.
1960. *The Cardiff region.* Cardiff, Univ. of Wales Press. 21s.
1961. *Norwich and its region.* Norwich, Jarrolds. 20s.
1962. *Manchester and its region.* Manchester, Univ. Press. 30s. Index. 2s.
1963. *The North East of Scotland.* Aberdeen, Central Press. 22s. 6d.
1964. *A survey of Southampton and its region.* Southampton, Univ. Press. 31s. 6d.
1965. *The Cambridge region.* London, the British Association. 30s.
1966. *Nottingham and its region.* Nottingham, Univ. of Nottingham for the British Association. 70s.
1967. *Leeds and its region.* Leeds, Austick, for the British Association. 35s., 50s.

908 (410) (02)

GREAT BRITAIN. CENTRAL OFFICE OF INFORMATION. Britain: an official handbook. London, H.M. Stationery Office, 1946-. illus., tables, maps. Annual, from 1954. (1968. 36s.).

Originally compiled only to be sent overseas; first placed on sale in 1954.
Attractively produced, with excellent summaries of institutions and life in Britain. Sections (1967 ed.): 1. The land and the people—2. Government—3. Law and order—4. Defence—5. Social welfare—6. Education—7. Planning and housing—8. The churches—9. Promotion of the sciences and the arts—10. The national economy —11. Industry—12. Agriculture, fisheries and forestry—13. Transport and communications—14. Finance—15. Trade and payments—16. Labour—17. Sound and television broadcasting—18. The press—19. Sport. Section bibliographies, p. 488-515, including many C.O.I. Reference pamphlets and other government publications, are "only intended to be a guide to further reading on the subjects covered . . .". Publishers and prices are given. Detailed analytical index. A model of what such an official handbook should be.

Scotland

908 (411):016

FESTIVAL OF BRITAIN. Scottish Committee. **Catalogue of an exhibition of 20th century Scottish books** at the Mitchell Library, Glasgow. [Glasgow], Scottish Committee of the Festival of Britain, 1951. 310p.

Arranged by subject: History; Towns and countryside; Language and literature; Customs and folk-lore, etc. Scottish periodicals, year-books and directories are also listed.

908 (411):016

LIBRARY ASSOCIATION. County Libraries Group. **Readers' guide to books on the face of Scotland.** 2nd ed. London, Library Association, County Libraries Group, 1964. 35p. (New series no. 76). 2s. 6d.

First published 1949.
Unannotated list of c. 450 items. Sections: Periodicals and annuals—Guide books and gazetteers—General works—7 regions—Famous towns—Geology—Archaeology—Roads and railways—Architecture—Climbing and walking—Natural history and field sports. List of publishers' addresses; prices given. Out of print books included if still worthwhile. No index.

908 (411):016

British humanities index . . . Regional lists. **Scotland.** London, Library Association, 1954-. Annual. (1965, published [1966]. 68, [7]p. 25s.).

See entry at 941.1:016.

908 (411):016

MEIKLE, H. W., *and others, comp.* **Scotland: a select bibliography.** London, Cambridge Univ. Press for National Book League, 1950. 39p. (National Book League Book list. Second series).

Intended as a brief guide for students to the history, literature, customs and institutions of Scotland.

908 (411) (02)

The Third statistical account of Scotland. Edinburgh, Oliver & Boyd, 1951-53; Glasgow, Collins, 1958-. illus., maps.

The intention in each volume, undertaken through the efforts of the Scottish Council of Social Service, is to present a comparative view of the way of life of the people of Scotland in the 20th century. In the tradition of Sir J. Sinclair's *The statistical account of Scotland* (Edinburgh, Creech, 1791-99. 21v.) and *The New statistical account of Scotland* (Edinburgh, Blackwood, 1845. 15v.). Parts (chronologically arranged):

Ayrshire, edited by J. Strawhorn and W. Boyd. 1951. 20s.
The county of Fife, edited by A. Smith. 1952. 20s.
The county of East Lothian, edited by C. P. Snodgrass. 1953. 20s.

The city of Aberdeen, edited by H. Mackenzie. 1953. 20s.

Glasgow, edited by J. Cunnison and J. B. S. Gilfillan. 1958. 50s.

The county of Dunbarton, edited by M. S. Dilke and A. A. Templeton. 1959. 42s.

The county of Aberdeen, edited by H. Hamilton. 1960. 42s.

The county of Lanark, edited by G. Thomson. 1960. 42s.

The county of Argyll, edited by C. M. Macdonald. 1961. 42s.

The county of Banff, edited by H. Hamilton, 1961. 42s.

The counties of Peebles and Selkirk, edited by J. B. P. Bullock and J. M. Urquhart. 1964. 42s.

The counties of Moray and Navin, edited by H. Hamilton. 1965. 42s.

The Stewartry of Kircudbright and the county of Wigtown, edited by J. Laird and D. G. Ramsay. 1965. 42s.

The county of Stirling, edited by R. C. Rennie; *The county of Clackmannan,* edited by T. C. Gordon. 1966. 84s.

The city of Edinburgh, edited by D. Keir. 1966. 105s.

In *The counties of Peebles and Selkirk* (399p. 21 pl. 1 ¼" fldg. map), the account of each county begins with a general description (physical environment, history, occupations, culture and way of life), followed by descriptions of the social parishes by local inhabitants. Reviewed in *Scottish geographical journal,* v. 82, no. 3, December 1966, p. 207.

Ireland

908 (415):016

EAGER, A. R. A guide to Irish bibliographical material; being, A bibliography of Irish bibliographies and some sources of information. London, Library Association, 1964. xiii, 392p. 96s. (72s. to members).

3,803 numbered items, broadly classified by the Dewey scheme. Is more than a list of bibliographies, since it includes works that are not bibliographies *per se* but are standard or representative works. Articles in periodicals and newspapers, and unpublished material and work in progress are also recorded. Biography, history and topography occupy one-third of the whole. Very occasional annotations. Author and subject indexes.

Reviewed in *Library Association record,* v. 66, no. 8, August 1964, p. 371.

908 (415):016

EIRE. NATIONAL LIBRARY OF IRELAND, *comp.* **Books on Ireland:** [a] list. Dublin, O Lochlainn, 1953. 45, [1]p.

An earlier list (*Select list of books relating to Ireland*) was published in 1942 (28p.).

9 sections: 1. Directories and year books—2. Description—3. History (with sub-divisions)—4. Social and economic—5. Ulster question—6. The Irish abroad—7. Irish language and literature—8. Anglo-Irish literature—9. Art and music. Some of the 300 items are annotated; no prices are given. No index.

Neither the above, nor the Library Association. County Libraries Section. *Face of Ireland* (1951. 16p. Readers' guide, new series, no. 10) has the scope of the older bibliography published by the New York Public Library—*List of works relating to Ireland, the Irish language and literature . . .* (1905. 122p.)—3,750 items.

Northern Ireland

908 (416) (058)

NORTHERN IRELAND. GENERAL REGISTER OFFICE. The Ulster year book: the official year-book of Northern Ireland. Belfast, H.M. Stationery Office, 1926-. illus., maps. Triennial. (13th, 1966-1968. 1967. 10s.).

None published 1938-46. As from 12th issue, prepared by the Northern Ireland Information Service.

Provides "statistical and other information on Northern Ireland and its people; their social conditions, health, education and industries; and the administrative activities of Departments concerned with central and local government services" (*Preface*). 18 sections; section bibliographies, p. 342-50. Index. Similar in layout to *Britain: an official handbook.*

To be published in future as an annual.

Eire

908 (417) (02)

EIRE. DEPARTMENT OF EXTERNAL AFFAIRS. Facts about Ireland. Dublin, the Department, 1963. [ii], 102, [1]p. illus., tables, maps.

An attractive pocket-sized compendium, with some of the many illustrations in colour. Main sections: Geography. History—Constitution. Government—Finance. Natural resources and economy. Trade—Health and social services—Literature and culture. Theatre. Art and architecture—Irish scientists—Diplomatic missions and representation. 'Some books on Ireland', p. 99-102 (History and description—Literature and art—Economics, government and directories).

908 (417) (02)

EIRE. SAORSTÁT EIREANN. Irish Free State: official handbook. Dublin, Talbot Press, 1932. 324p.

Although published 36 years ago, this handbook remains the best and most complete survey of very many aspects of political, social and cultural life in Eire. Each section has been written by the leading authority in its subject at that time and has its own separate bibliography. Well indexed.

Wales

908 (429):016

LIBRARY ASSOCIATION. County Libraries Section. **Face of Wales.** [New ed.] London, the Association, 1958. 32p. (Readers' guides, New series, no. 41).

A selective check-list, unannotated, of works mainly topographical, relating to Wales and the Border Marches.

908 (429) (02)

Celtic studies on Wales: a survey. Prepared for the meeting of the Second International Congress of Celtic studies held in Cardiff, 6 to 13 July 1963, and published on behalf of the Board of Celtic Studies of the University of Wales. Edited by Elwyn Davies. Cardiff, Univ. of Wales Press, 1963. xix. [4], 182p. illus.

Celtic archaeology and art—Welsh history and historians—Studies in the Welsh laws—Literature —Language and linguistics. Includes a list of the publications of the Board of Celtic Studies. No index.

908 (429) (047)
GREAT BRITAIN. SECRETARY OF STATE FOR WALES. Wales, 1966. London, H.M. Stationery Office, [1967]. iv, 162p. tables, maps. (Cmnd. 3208). 12s. 6d.

Annual report. 12 sections: 1. Introduction— 2. Planning—3. Employment and industrial development—4. Agriculture, fisheries, forestry and rural industries—5. Education—6. Research and archaeology—7. Health, housing and public services—8. Social services—9. Communications —10. Defence—11. Information services—12. Cultural activities. No index. Includes Monmouthshire.

Germany

908 (43):016
GERMAN INSTITUTE, London. Selective list of books on German politics, economics, social science and modern history, available in the German Institute. London, the Institute, [1966?]. [42]l. Mimeographed.

About 350 unannotated items. Concentrates on post-World War II Germany. Intended only as a general introduction to the subject. Sections: General information—Politics—Economics (including biographical literature)—Agriculture— Sociology—Modern German history—Contemporary history.

908 (43):016
Schrifttum über Deutschland 1918-1962. Ausgewählte Bibliographie deutscher Publikationen. Bearb. in Gemeinschaft mit dem Forschungsinstitut der Deutschen Gesellschaft für Auswärtige Politik durch Inter Nationes, Bonn. Wiesbaden, Steiner, 1962. 306p. (2nd ed. 1964. 292p. DM.18).

A selective list of German publications (with some non-German items) on Germany. Systematically arranged. Pt. 1, General: 1918-1945; 1945-1962 (c. 2,500 items). Pt. 2, Subjects, A-M (M. Publications in 43 foreign languages). Annotations, chiefly for items in pt. 1; prices given. Author index.

German Democratic Republic

908 (43-11):016
EPSTEIN, F. T., comp. **East Germany: a selected bibliography.** Washington, Library of Congress, 1959. vii, 55p. ([2nd ed.], compiled by A. H. Price. 1967. 133p. $1.).

A highly selective guide (325 items) to general background sources on East Germany published

1947-58. Sections: General reference aids— History—Demography—Politics and government —Law and justice—Economics—Social conditions—Intellectual life—Religious groups—U.S. official publications and pronouncements on the Soviet Zone of Germany. Indexes: Monographs and articles; Periodicals. Preference is given to material in English, but a great deal of literature in German is also included (*International affairs,* v. 36, no. 3, July 1960, p. 417).

908 (43-11) (03)
GERMANY. BUNDESMINISTERIUM FÜR GESAMTDEUTSCHE FRAGEN. SBZ von A bis Z. Ein Taschen- und Nachschlagebuch über die Sowjetische Besatzungszone Deutschlands. 10. uberarb. u. erw. Aufl. Bonn, Deutscher Bundes-Verlag, 1966. 605p.

First published 1953.
Alphabetical sequence of entries, p. 9-517. Includes biographies (e.g., 'Ulbricht': ⅔ col.) and articles on aspects of East Germany (e.g., 'Wirtschaft': 8p., including a chart); entries for abbreviations; many cross-references. Chronological table, 1945-66. 'Literatur-Hinweise' (p. 582-605: 769 items in 13 sections. 13, Nachschlagewerke. Zeitschriften).

908 (43-11) (058)
Handbuch der Deutschen Demokratischen Republik; hrsg. vom Deutschen Institut für Zeitgeschichte in Verbindung mit dem Staatsverlag der Deutschen Demokratischen Republik. [1963]-. [Berlin], Staatsverlag der D.D.R., [1964]-. tables, maps. Annual.

Previously as *Jahrbuch der Deutschen Demokratischen Republik,* 1956-61.
A survey of many aspects of East German life, —government, internal and foreign policy, economy, health, education, culture, sport. Includes a directory of organisations and some statistical tables.

German Federal Republic

908 (43-15) (02)
ARNTZ, H. Facts about Germany. 6th ed. [Bonn], Press & Information Office of the Federal Government of Germany, 1966. 396p. illus., tables, map. DM.10.90.

A pocket-sized compendium in 7 parts (65 sections): Background — Policy — Economy — Social life—Education—Culture—Chronology. 48p. of good illustrations; folding map; statistics up to 1963. Includes East Germany.

908 (43-15) (058)
Deutschland-Jahrbuch, 1949-, hrsg. von K. Mehnert und H. Schulte. Essen, Rheinisch-Westfälisches Verlagskontor, 1949-. diagrs., maps. Irregular.

The first volume (1949) covered the post-war period towards the end of 1948; the second volume (1953) covers 1948-52.
Sections: 1. Government, law, politics—2. Economy—3. Social life—4. Church, education, science—5. Art and culture. Detailed subdivision; 64 contributors to the 1953 volume. Obituary: lengthy bibliographies; subject index.

Berlin

908 (431.5)

ZOPF, H., and HEINRICH, G., *ed.* **Berlin-Bibliographie** (bis 1960). In der Senatsbibliothek Berlin. Berlin, de Gruyter, 1965. xxxi, 1012p. (Veröffentlichungen der Historischen Kommission zu Berlin, beim Friedrich-Meinecke-Institut der Frei Universität Berlin. Bd. 15. Bibliographien. Bd. 1).

About 20,000 unannotated entries. Three main sections: A. Allgemeine Bibliographien, Bibliothekskataloge, Nachschlagewerke und biographische Lexika—B. Brandenburg-Preussen—C. Berlin (p. 47-812: 1. Allgemeines; 2. Ortskunde und Beschriebung; 3. Statistik; 4. Geschichte; 5. Kulturgeschichte; 6. Berlin als Behördenstadt; 7. Wirtschaft; 8. Natur; 9. Vororte und Verwaltungsbezirkes. Name and subject indexes. Well produced.

Austria

908 (436) (03)

BAMBERGER, R., and MAIER-BRUCK, T. **Österreich Lexikon.** Vienna, Österreichischer Bundesverlag, 1966. 2v. illus., tables, plans.

An encyclopaedic dictionary devoted to Austria. Includes biographies (*e.g.,* Dollfuss: $\frac{2}{3}$ col., including portrait; 7 references). 'Wien': v. 2, p. 1257-66, including $\frac{1}{2}$ col. of bibliography. 3-page bibliography at end of v. 2, with a 16-page physical atlas in colour, mostly on a scale of 1:800,000.

908 (436) (058)

Österreichisches Jahrbuch . . . nach amtlichen Quellen; hrsg. vom Bundespressedienst. Vienna, Druck und Verlog der "Österr. Staatsdruckerei." tables. Annual.

The 1964 volume (36. Folge) has sections on foreign policy, administration and organisation, press, education, art and sport, social services, economy, transport, agriculture, regions and 'Austria in figures' (statistics for 1963 and 1964). Many tables. Full contents list; no index.

Czechoslovakia

908 (437)

KUHN, H. **Handbuch der Tschechoslowakei.** Munich, Lerche, 1967. 1021p. DM.142.

Four parts: 1. Area and population—2. State structure (13 sections, on parties, associations, press, schools, colleges, academies, churches, etc.) —3. Parties and organisations—4. Administration: government, high schools, churches, theatre, music, scientific libraries, museums, national galleries, etc.

A short, popular introduction: *Czechoslovakia today: a panoramic view,* compiled and edited by V. Straka (Prague, Artia, [1965?]. 192, 78, [2]p.), with 78p. of illus.

Czechoslovakia: a bibliographic study, by R. Sturm (Washington, Library of Congress, Slavic and Central European Division, 1967. xii, 157p. $1) is a running commentary, with a list of citations.

Poland

908 (438):016

POLAND. COMMISSION NATIONALE DE BIBLIOGRAPHIE. **Bibliographie sur la Pologne:** pays, histoire, civilisation. 2. éd. Warsaw, Panstwowe Wydawnictwo Naukowe, 1964. 300p.

Prepared by the Polish Librarians' Association; sponsored by Unesco.
Entries for 1,574 books and periodicals in the humanities and social sciences, in 13 sections. Items are in Polish and Western European languages, with annotations in French. Appended supplement for 1960-63.

All about Poland (London, Swiclerski, 1967) is advertised as the English ed. of an encyclopaedic guide first published in Warsaw. It comprises more than 1,200 pages, with 1,000 illustrations.

Hungary

908 (439.1) (058)

Hungary 66. Hungary, Pannonia Press, [1966?]. 403p. illus., tables.

The first in a series of yearbooks in Russian, English, French, German and Spanish editions. Aims to summarise figures and facts on the history, economy, social, political and culture life of Hungary. Who's who, p. 326-41. No index. Well produced.
Information Hungary, edited by F. Erdei, is due for publication by Pergamon Press, Oxford, in 1968 (1144p. illus., maps) at *c.* £12.

France

908 (44):016

PEMBERTON, J. E. **How to find out about France:** a guide to sources of information. Oxford, Pergamon Press, 1966. xvi, 199p. illus., facsims., maps. 27s. 6d.

A running commentary; not restricted to works of French origin. "Aims to serve as a point of departure for every type of enquiry concerning France" (*Preface*). 17 chapters, in Dewey order (1. National bibliographies and encyclopedias—2. Philosophy and religion—3. Government, society and the press . . . 7. Dictionaries . . . 10. Music—11. Theatre, drama, cinema—12. Literary history . . . 16. Geography and travel—17. Archaeology, biography and history. 34 facsimiles from pages of items discussed. Index of subject and forms only. Dates and publishers of items are not given.

Noted: Taylor, A. C. *Bibliography of published theses on French subjects deposited in university libraries of the United Kingdom, 1905-1950* (Oxford, Blackwell, 1964. 45p. 20s.).

908 (44) (02)

Panorama de la France. Paris, La Documentation Française, 1967. xvi, 1213p. tables, diagrs., maps. 60F.

A detailed survey. Sections: Geography—Population—Institutions—Economy—Social and religious life—Cultural life—Education—Information—Relations with the world (*e.g.,* aid to underdeveloped countries). Appended data (p. 1187-1210) include the text of the constitution, addresses of French ministries. Contents list, but no index.

Les institutions publiques de la France (1959-61. 2v.), *Les institutions sociales de la France* (1963) and *Social welfare in France* (1961) are in the same series.

908 (45)

HASSALL, W. O. A select bibliography of Italy: A thousand books about Italy, its geography, population, cities and regions, its language, literature and history, its social, economic and political life, its art and music. London, Aslib, 1946. 82p.

Subject arrangement; very occasional notes; no index. An appendix describes special collections in England (see also *Journal of documentation,* v. 1, no. 2, September 1945, p. 63-71).

908 (45) (02)

GARDNER, E. G., *ed.* **Italy: a companion to Italian studies.** London, Methuen, 1934. x, [1], 274p. map.

11 chapters by the editor and four specialists on the history, literature and art of Italy up to the Fascist revolution. Each chapter has a bibliography. Partly analytical index.

Noted: Centro Italiano di Ricerche e Documentazione. *Italia, 1966. Annuario dell'economia, della politica, della cultura* (Milan, 1966. 1191p. $18.50).

Malta

908 (458.2):016

BEELEY, B. E., *comp.* **A bibliography of the Maltese Islands:** provisional draft. Durham, Durham Colleges in the Univ. of Durham, Department of Geography, 1939. 30p. map. Mimeographed.

664 items, including dissertations, periodical articles, government publications. Pt. 1: 'List of some collections of material on the Maltese Islands'.

908 (458.2) (058)

The Malta year-book for the year 1951-. St. George's Bay (subsequently St. Julian's Bay), St. Michael's College Publications, [1953]- illus., maps. Annual.

A compendium, with main sections on history, government, statistics, education, general information, societies and organisations, and special activities; tourist and sports supplements. 'A list of some books on Malta'; directory information.

Spain

908 (46):016

HISPANIC SOCIETY OF AMERICA, New York. Library. **Catalogue of the Library** of the Hispanic Society of America. Boston, Mass., G. K. Hall, 1966. 10v. $675.

211,000 photolithographed catalogue cards on 10,048 pages. The Library contains more than 100,000 v. on the cultures of Spain, Portugal and colonial Hispanic America. Stresses art, history and literature; includes music, social customs, regional costumes, description and travel, but excludes Indian subjects.

908 (46) (02)

Spain. [Madrid?], Spanish Information Service, 1962. 282p. illus., graphs. 100 pesetas.

Two main parts: 1. The eternal Spain (geography; history; Spaniards and Spanish society)— 2. The Spain of today (political and administrative organization; foreign policy; culture; economy; law and justice; labour; other aspects of present-day society (*e.g.,* sport; public health and social work)). Some of the illustrations are in colour; statistics up to 1961. Contents list, but no index. Attractively produced.

Portugal

908 (469):016

HISPANIC SOCIETY OF AMERICA, New York. Library. **Catalogue of the Library of the Hispanic Society of America.** Boston, Mass., G. K. Hall, 1966. 10v. $675.

See entry at 908 (46):016.

Russia

908 (47):016

HORECKY, P. L., *ed.* **Russia and the Soviet Union:** a bibliographic guide to Western language publications. Chicago & London, Univ. of Chicago Press, 1965. xxiv, 473p. $8.95.

Sponsored by the Coordinating Committee for Slavic and East European Library Resources (COCOSEERS), under the chairmanship of Alexander Dallin.

1,966 numbered items; 31 contributors. 9 main sections: 1. General reference aids and bibliographies—2. General and descriptive works—3. The land—4. The people: ethnic and demographic features—5. The nations: civilizations and politics—6. History—7. The state—8. The economic and social structure—9. The intellectual and cultural life (language; literature; folklore; history of thought and culture; religion; education and research; the fine arts; music, theatre and cinema). Evaluative annotations, sometimes with further references. Asterisked items are available as paperbacks. Author and title index. A standard bibliography.

The companion work edited by Horecky is: *Basic Russian publications: an annotated bibliography on Russia and the Soviet Union* (Chicago, Univ. of Chicago Press, 1962. xxvi, 313p. $6.50). Its 1,396 annotated entries are the work of 32 contributors. Science and technology are omitted in both volumes.

908 (47):016

LHÉRITIER, A. "Bibliographie des travaux parus en France concernant la Russie et l'U.R.S.S.". In *Cahiers du monde russe et soviétique,* v. 4, no. 1-2, January/June 1963. p. 150-200.

974 numbered items, systematically arranged. Mainly periodical articles; author index.

A further article in v. 6, no. 3, July/September 1965 issue (p. 437-65): "Les thèses concernant la Russie et l'U.R.S.S. soutenues en France de 1888 à 1964"—295 items in subject groups, with subdivisions, plus author index.

908 (47):016

MAICHEL, K. Guide to Russian reference books. Stanford, Cal., Hoover Institution on War, Revolution and Peace, Stanford Univ., 1962-. v. 1-.

v. 1: *General bibliographies and reference books.* 1962. $5.

v. 2: *History, historical sciences, ethnography, geography.* 1964. $12.

v. 3: *Social sciences, religion, philosophy, military science, library science.*

v. 4: *Humanities (Literature, Language, Music, Fine Arts).*

v. 5: *Science, technology and medicine.*

v. 6: *Supplementary material and cumulative index.*

V. 2, edited by J. S. G. Simmons, with 1,436 numbered items (plus interpolations), embraces the history of the U.S.S.R., world history, auxiliary historical sciences (*e.g.*, archaeology; genealogy and heraldry; numismatics; palaeography), ethnography, geography and geology. Systematically arranged; admirably annotated. Includes periodical articles and a few items not published in the U.S.S.R. Russian words are transliterated throughout. Author, title and subject index. Excellent use of bold face.

908 (47) (032)

McGraw-Hill Encyclopedia of Russia and the Soviet Union. Editor, Michael T. Florinsky. New York & London, McGraw-Hill, 1961. xiv, [1], 624p. illus., diagrs., tables, maps. 183*s*.

"The object of the Encyclopedia is to present, within the relatively brief space of a single volume, a mass of useful information on Russia before and after the revolution of 1917" (*Editor's Preface*). 91 contributors, the lengthier articles being signed. The article on Konsomol runs to 3 columns, with a bibliography of 3 items; that on Stalin runs to 2 columns, with a bibliography of 5 items. Bibliographies are confined to English-language material. Very well illustrated, with more than 400 illustrations, diagrams, maps, etc. Its main weakness, according to *Library journal,* v. 87, no. 2, 15th January 1962, p. 210-1, is neglect of the pre-Soviet period. Strong in biography, economics and technology; weak in factual detail, cross-references and geographical coverage (Neiswender, R. *Guide to Russian reference and language aids* (1962), p. 37-38). The editor is Professor of Economics, Columbia University.

908 (47) (032)

Die UdSSR: Enzyklopädie der Union der Sozialistischen Sowjetrepubliken; hrsg. [von] W. Fickenscher unter Mitwerkung von H. Becker, R. Rompe, W. Steinitz, u.a. Leipzig, Verlag Enzyklopädie, 1959. 1104p. illus., ports., maps. DM.36.

A German translation of the supplement (v. 50, published 1957) on the U.S.S.R. to the 1st ed. of the *Bol'shaya sovetskaya entsiklopediya* 1927-47). Incorporated into the translation are the latest available statistics. Name and subject indexes.

Information U.S.S.R., edited and compiled by Robert Maxwell (Oxford, London, etc. Pergamon Press, 1962. xii, 982p. illus., maps, tables. £10) is largely (p. 1-763) is translated from v. 50: *SSSR* (1957) of the *Bol'shaya sovetskaya entsiklopediya* and reproduces its ideological slant.

908 (47) (032)

UTECHIN, S. V. Everyman's Concise encyclopaedia of Russia. London, Dent, 1961. xxvi, 623p. illus., maps. (Everyman's Reference library). 30*s*.

Contains more than 2,000 entries. Of these more than 600 concern geography, 325—history and politics, 165—the arts, and only 145 deal with economic matters. Biographical sketches; references to literature appended to entries. The review in the *Times review of industry* (v. 15, no. 175, August 1961, p. 17) finds the bibliographical references very useful; but "the reader would like to find more information in the encyclopaedia itself" and calls for a statistical appendix. According to *International affairs* (v. 37, no. 4, October 1961, p. 522), its main weakness is a certain lack of selectivity and balance. The author is Senior Research Officer in Soviet Studies, London School of Economics. His views are, on the whole, anti-Communist. (See review in *Times literary supplement,* no. 3,138, 20th April 1962, p. 265.)

Estonia

908 (474.2):016

UNITED STATES. LIBRARY OF CONGRESS. Estonia: a selected bibliography; compiled by Salme Kurt. Washington, Library of Congress, 1958, iv, 74p.

Intended for the non-specialist, with preference given to titles in English, and secondarily to titles in French and German. Subject arrangement; author and title index.

Ukraine

908 (477) (03)

KUBIJOVYČ, V., *ed.* **Ukraine: a concise encyclopaedia.** Toronto, for the Ukrainian National Association by the Univ. of Toronto Press, 1963-. v. 1-. illus., tables, maps. (v. 1. $37.50.).

Translation of an encyclopaedia published in the Ukraine, 1949.

A systematic survey to be published in 2v. V. 1 covers general information, physical geography, natural history, population, ethnography, language, history, culture and literature. V. 2 is to cover law and government, religion, the arts, national economy and Ukrainians abroad. Scholarly; rich in bibliographies, tables and statistics, but poor illustrations.

Finland

908 (480):016
AALTONEN, H., *comp.* **Books in English on Finland:** a bibliographical list of publications concerning Finland until 1960, including Finnish literature in English translation. Turku, Univ. Library, 1964. 276p. (Publications of Turku Univ. Library. 8).

4,912 numbered items plus *c.* 140 in the appendix ('A selected list of books published from 1961 to 1963 inclusive'). Includes official publications (*e.g.,* United Nations) and analyticals. 19 sections (1. General works and geography, travel)—2. History—3. Biographies—4. Economic conditions . . . 11. Literature . . . 14. Pure sciences, physics and chemistry . . . 18. Bibliographies (no. 4775-4812)—19. Periodical publications. Dictionaries, general and special, nos. 3647-3707). Includes periodical articles; some cross-references. Index of persons; index of anonymous publications. No subject index.

A short bibliography on Finland, compiled by E. K. Neuvonen (Turku, Univ. Library, 1955. 38p.) (Publications of Turku Univ. Library, 7) is a new and much enlarged edition of a list published in 1936 and later in *The Finland year book:* a selection of publications concerning Finland in English, French, German, Italian and Dutch. 13 sections.

908 (480) (02)
Introduction to Finland, 1963. Porvoo, Helsinki, Werner Söderström Oiakeyhtio, 1963. 201p. illus.

First published 1960, in English, French, German and Spanish eds.
A collection of 16 articles on selected topics rather than a comprehensive survey of Finnish affairs. Main sections: Geography and politics (6 articles, plus 'Notes and statistics')—Economics (5 articles, plus 'Statistical tables')—Cultural and religious life (5 articles, plus 'Notes and statistics')—Biographical notes (p. 253-76; past and present; portraits)—'A bibliography on Finland' (sections; p. 277-83). Index.
A new edition is in the press.

Norway

908 (481):016
GRONLAND, E. Norway in English: books on Norway and by Norwegians in English, 1936-1959. A bibliography, including a survey of Norwegian literature in English translation from 1742 to 1959. [Oslo], Norwegian Univ. Press, 1961. 152p. (Norsk bibliografisk bibliothek. Bd. 19).

4,500 items, systematically arranged. Covers all major aspects, including language, literature, history, social life and science. Subject index. Compiled by a librarian of the University of Oslo.

908 (481) (058)
The Norway year book, 1967. 7th ed., edited by E. Tveterås. Oslo, Tanum, 1966. 478p. $8.

Contributions cover many aspects of Norway: natural conditions; history, government, administration; international relations; religion; public instruction; social conditions; science, literature, arts; travel, sports; natural resources; industries; transport; foreign trade, banking. Up-to-date and informative. Not over-detailed; articles rather than tables and lists of facts and figures. Selective index.
A popular reference annual on Norway is *Hvem-hva-hvor: Aftenpostens oppslagsbok* 1936-40, 1946-. (Oslo, Chr. Schibsteds Forlag, 1935-39, 1945-). This follows the pattern of the Danish *Hvem-hvad-hvor* [who-what-where] (*q.v.*).

Sweden

908 (485):016
SVENSKA INSTITUTET FÖR KUTURELLT. Information about Sweden: a bibliography of publications available at the Swedish Institute, Stockholm. Stockholm, the Institute, 1964. iv, 45p.

About 300 items in 18 classes (subject classes: C. Religion—E. Education—F. Swedish language —G. Literature—H. Fiction. Essays—I. Fine arts. Music. Theatre. Film—K. History—L. Biographies—M. Ethnography—N. Geography. General information—O. Political science—P. Industry. Technology—Q. Economy—R. Physical education. Sport—S. Defence—V. Medicine). No annotations; prices stated. Subject index.

908 (485):016:016
OTTERVIK, G., *comp.* **Bibliografier.** Kommenterad urvalsförteckning med särskild hänsyn till svenska förhållanden. 3 uppl. Lund, Bibliothekstjänst, 1966. Sw.kr.85.

Basically a bibliography of Swedish bibliographies. More than half of the *c.* 2,000 items emanate from Scandinavia, and many of those from Sweden. Thus, of the 141 entries under 'Geografi' (area studies), 82 concern Sweden. Arranged according to the Swedish library classification. Concisely annotated. Author and anonymous title index. Reviewed in *Library Association record* v. 69, no. 10, October 1967, p. 307.

908 (485) (02)
SVENSKA INSTITUTET FÖR KULTURELLT. Facts about Sweden. Stockholm, the Institute, [1964]. [ii], 52, [ii]p. illus., tables, graphs.

Sections: History — Government — Defense — Religion — Judiciary — Education — Social welfare—Economy—Finance—Labor market—Standard of living—Culture—Sport—The country and the people—Information services—Annual fairs and other events—Booklets on Sweden published by the Swedish Institute (p. 52).

31 (485) (058)
När-var-hur: aktuell uppslagsbok. Årg. 1-, 1945-. Stockholm, Svenska Samlingsverk, 1944-47; Bokförlaget Forum, 1948-. Annual. (Årg. 22, 1966. 1965. Sw.kr.15.50, 17.50.).

När-var-hur,—when—where—what. A yearbook of current Swedish affairs.

908 (485-017):016

MARKLUND, E. Övre Norrland i litteraturen: en bibliografi över Norrbottens och Västerbottens län. Utg. av K. Engström. Goteborg, [Univ.], 1963. xv, 698p. (Acta Bibliothecae Universitatis Gothoburgensis, v. 6).

9,199 numbered, unannotated items, including many periodical articles, on the northern half of Sweden. Sections: Bibliography & librarianship—General works — Religion — Education — Folk literature—Fine arts—Archaeology—History—Biography—Genealogy—Topography (p. 183-265)—Travels—Maps and cartography—Social sciences, law, statistics—Economics (p. 377-529)—Sports and games—Warfare—Science (p. 543-679)—Public health.

Denmark

908 (489):016

AHNFELT-RONNE, V., and **PEDERSEN, J. V. Denmark; literature, language, history, society, education, arts: a select bibliography.** Copenhagen, the Royal Library, 1966. 151p. D.kr.15.

A select bibliography of books and periodical articles in English published during 1950-65. Excludes theses and purely scientific works on specialised subjects. 25 subject headings. Five-yearly supplements are promised, if there is a demand.

908 (489) (02)

DENMARK. ROYAL DANISH MINISTRY OF FOREIGN AFFAIRS. Press and Information Department. **Denmark: an official handbook.** 13th ed. Copenhagen, Krak, 1964. [iv], 889p. illus., tables, map.

An excellent illustrated handbook. 26 subject sections (*e.g.*, 1. The monarchy. Symbols. National anthems—2. Land and people—3. Foregin affairs . . . 11. Education (p. 237-312) . . . 20. Trade and industry (p. 433-537) . . . 24. Science. Research. Technology (p. 563-641)—25. The arts (p. 643-787—26. Bibliography (classified on Dewey lines; p. 804-27). Detailed index (p. 828-89) that differentiates type and length of treatment (*e.g.*, A=Article; C=Comment(s); H=Historical reference(s)). An admirable example of its kind.

908 (489) (058)

Hvem-hvad-hvor: Politikens aarbog [årbog], 1934-. Copenhagen, Politikens Forlag, 1933-. Annual.

Hvem-hvad-hvor (who—what—where) acts as a Danish *Whitaker's Almanack,* but is far more popular in tone and less detailed; it gives far more space to Danish and Scandinavian topics and far less to other countries. Certain features appear regularly (*e.g.*, events and obituaries of the year), but many articles are special to each issue. Each volume has an index which includes references to articles in previous volumes. General index to v. 1-25: *Stikordsregister over samtlige 25 årgange* (1958. 112p.). Articles are all well illustrated with drawings, diagrams and colour plates which generally appear simultaneously in other Scandinavian works.

Iceland

908 (491.1)

Iceland 1966: handbook. Editors, J. Nordal and V. Kristinsson. Reykjavik, Central Bank of Iceland, 1967. xi, 390p. illus., maps, tables. 50s. First published 1926.

Statistical and factual material, primarily. 11 sections. 'Selected list of books on Iceland in foreign languages' (p. 362-75). Analytical index

Netherlands

908 (492) (02)

NETHERLANDS. Government Information Service. **Digest of the Kingdom of the Netherlands.** The Hague, the Service, 1963. 6 pts. illus.

Previous ed. as *Digest of the Netherlands.* The 6 parts are:
Education, arts and sciences. [1962]. D.fl.3.30.
Constitutional organization. [1962]. D.fl.3.30.
Social aspects. [1963]. D.fl.3.30.
Economy. 3rd ed. 1964. D.fl.3.30.
History and politics. 3rd ed. 1964. D.fl.3.30.
Social insurance. 1966 reprint. D.fl.1.

Greece

908 (495):016

AMERICAN SCHOOL OF CLASSICAL STUDIES AT ATHENS. Catalogue of the Gennadius Library. Boston, Mass., G. K. Hall, 1965. 7v. $425 ($467.50, outside U.S.).

About 100,000 cards, photolithographically reproduced. A library of nearly 50,000 v. on Greece. According to the publishers, areas of particular strength include: Renaissance editions of classical and Byzantine authors and of Greek grammars; early modern Greek literature; the beginnings of classical archaeology (1750-1825); travellers to the Greek East (to 1900); Greek Bibles and the Orthodox Church; early printed materials on Turkish history; Greece under Turkish domination; Greek War of Independence (including Byroniana); the early Kingdom of Greece; and the "Eastern Question".

908 (495):016

BAXEVANIS, J. E. Modern Greece: a bibliography. Chicago, Argonaut, 1964. 400p. $7.50.

A bibliography of *c.* 6,500 books, periodical articles and pamphlets, many of them not previously recorded. Covers items in Greek, French, German and Italian as well as English.

Yugoslavia

908 (497.1):016

ANDONOV-POLJANSKI, H., *comp. and ed.* **Britanska bibliografija za Makedonija. British bibliography on Macedonia.** Skopje, Archives of the Socialist Republic of Macedonia, [1966?]. 512p.

Annotated bibliography of *c.* 4,000 items, including Blue books and articles in *The Times,* and covering all periods, to date. The review in *the Times literary supplement* (no. 3385, 12th January 1967, p. 30) notes lack of a subject index and the execrable paper.

908 (497.1) (02)
YUGOSLAVIA. SAVEZNA NARODNA SKUPS-TINA. Facts about Yugoslavia. Zagreb, S.N.S., 1966. 135p. illus., tables, map.

A pocket-sized compendium, with data and statistics for 1964 and 1965. Sections: The land—Population—Historical background of the Yugoslav peoples—Government and social system—Political and social organization—Principles of foreign policy—The national economy—Social welfare—Cultural life—Sport.

Bulgaria

908 (497.2):016
PUNDEFF, M. V. Bulgaria: a bibliographic guide. Library of Congress, Reference Department, Slavic and Central European Division. Washington, U.S. Government Printing Office, 1965. ix, 98p. 55c.

Part 1, Bibliographic survey (p. 3-55) is a running commentary (1. General reference works—2. Land and people—3. Language and literature—4. History—5. Politics, government and law—6. Economy and social conditions—7. Intellectual life). Part 2, Bibliography, is an A-Z author listing of the 1,243 items previously discussed. Based primarily on holdings of Library of Congress and other American libraries; location symbols.

Rumania

908 (498):016
FISCHER-GALATI, S. A. Rumania: a bibliographic guide. Library of Congress, Reference Department, Slavic and Central European Division. Washington, 1963. viii, 75p. 45c.

Part 1, Bibliographic survey (p. 1-34) is a running commentary (1. General reference works—2. The land—3. The people—4. History—5. Politics and government—6. Law and justice—7. Social conditions—8. Economics—9. Religion—10. Intellectual life—11. Language and literature). Part 2, Bibliography, is an A-Z author listing of the 748 items previously discussed. Library of Congress locations and *National union catalog* symbols given. The items are almost all monographs plus periodical titles; mostly in Rumanian; also, the most important publications in other languages.

Asia & Africa

908 (5/6):016
LONDON. UNIVERSITY. SCHOOL OF ORIENTAL AND AFRICAN STUDIES. Library catalogue. Boston, Mass., G. K. Hall, 1963. 28v. $1600.

554,000 catalogue cards, photolithographically reproduced. A comprehensive catalogue (author, subject and title entries) of material (including periodical articles and analyticals from other collective works) on all aspects of Asia, Oceania and Africa, but excluding the purely scientific, medical and technical. Available as a set or in 14 sections: Author catalogue—Title index—Subject catalogues (General. Africa. Middle East. South Asia. Southeast Asia and Pacific Islands. Far East)—Catalogue of manuscripts and microfilms—Chinese catalogues (Titles. Authors. Subjects)—Japanese catalogue—Catalogue of periodicals and series (included in the Author catalogue). Also available in 14 sections (*e.g.,* Middle East. 2v. £70).
To be supplemented.

Islamic World

908 (5/6=927):016
AL-HAJRASI, S. M. Guide bibliographique des ouvrages de référence. Bibliographical guide to reference works. Cairo, National Commission for Unesco of the United Arab Republic, 1965. 130p.

A guide to reference books in the Arab world. An Arabic ed. is also available.

908 (5/6=927):016
Index islamicus, 1906-1955: a catalogue of articles on Islamic subjects in periodicals and other collective publications; compiled by J. D. Pearson and J. F. Ashton. Cambridge, Heffer, 1958 (reprinted 1961, with minor corrections). xxxvi. 895p. 105s. **Supplement,** 1956-60. 1962. 63s. **2nd supplement,** 1961-1965. 1967.

The main volume has more than 26,000 entries drawn from 510 periodicals, as well as *Festschriften,* other collective works and congress proceedings; The 1962 Suppt., compiled by J. D. Pearson, comprises 7,296 items. Aims to cover the whole field of Islamic studies, pure science and technology alone being excluded. Not confined to Islamic countries of North Africa and the Near and Middle East, but includes items of Islamic interest from other countries. Classified arrangement, with main divisions: General works and bibliography—Religion and theology—Law—Philosophy and science—Art—Geography—Ethnology and history—Language—Literature—Education. Author index.

908 (5/6=927) (032)
RONART, S., and RONART, N. Concise encyclopaedia of Arabic civilization. Amsterdam, Djambatan, 1959-66. 2v. maps.

v. 1. *The Arab East.* 1959 (reprinted 1967). 110s.
v. 2. *The Arab West.* 1966. 105s.
Does not claim to be a scholarly work by an Orientalist. "What we aimed at was to serve all those who wish to understand the convictions, attitudes and reactions of the Arabic people" (*Preface*). V. 1 covers the Arabian Peninsula, Egypt, Iraq, Jordan, Lebanon and Syria. 'Kuwait': 4p., including tables on oil production and royalties. Biographies are included ('Salāh al-Dīn': 1½p.); adequate cross-references. No bibliographies, but 'Reading suggestions' (p. 588-9). Diacriticals shown. 20 maps.
V. 2 covers Morocco, Algeria, Tunisia, Libya and the Sudan.

ASIA

908 (5):016
Asian bibliography. Bangkok, U.N. Economic Commission for Asia and the Far East. Library, 1952-. v. 1, no. 1-. 2 p.a.

A selective list of the ECAFE Library's book accessions dealing with Asia and the Far East.

Titles of publications in Asian languages are translated. About 500 items per issue on 33 areas (A-Z), with subject sub-divisions (*e.g.,* Hong Kong: Agriculture. Administration—Audit— Budget — Education — Fisheries — History — Immigration — Police — Public service — Public works—Trade—Water transport).

908 (5):016
ASSOCIATION OF BRITISH ORIENTALISTS. A select list of books on the civilizations of the Orient. Prepared by the Association of British Orientalists and edited by W. A. C. H. Dobson. Oxford, Clarendon Press, 1955. xii, 76, [4]p.

Arranged by broad areas (each with introduction), sub-divided by countries and then by subjects (including Oriental languages). Coverage is Near, Middle and Far East, from ancient to modern times. Appended list of Oriental studies in British universities.

Noted: Embree, A. T. *Asia: a guide to basic books* (New York, Asia Society, 1966. 57p.).

908 (5):016
Behavior science bibliographies. New Haven, Conn., Human Relations Area Files, 1949-.

The following bibliographies, usually annotated, on Asia and the Far East, have appeared:
Southeast Asia, by J. K. Irikura. 1956. (*See at 908 (5-012):016.*)
Selected bibliography on the geography of Southeast Asia, by K. J. Pelzer. 1949-56. 3v. (1. *Southeast Asia*—general. 1949—2. *The Philippines.* 1950—3. *Malaya.* 1956). (*See at 915-012:016.*)
Economic and social development of modern China: a bibliographical guide, by T'ung-li Yüan. 1956. 2 pts. (*See at 33 (51):016.*)
Annotated bibliography of Afghanistan, by D. N. Wilber. 2nd ed. 1962. (*See at 908 (581):016.*)
Annotated bibliography of Burma. F. N. Trager, editor. 1956. (*See at 908 (591):016.*)
Japanese and Chinese language sources on Burma: an annotated bibliography. F. N. Trager, editor. 1957.
Bibliography of Indonesian peoples and cultures, by R. Kennedy. 2nd rev. ed. 1962. (*See at 908 (910):016.*)
Selected bibliography of the Philippines. Prelim. ed. F. Eggan, director. 1956. (*See at 908 (914):016.*)

908 (5):016
"Bibliography of Asian studies". In *The Journal of Asian studies.* Ann Arbor, Michigan, Association for Asian Studies. Annual.

1936-40, as *Bulletin of Far Eastern bibliography,* 1941-56, as "Far Eastern bibliography", in *Far Eastern quarterly.* Cumulated annually from 1946. Now forms the September issue of *The Journal of Asian studies* each year.
V. 25, no. 5, September 1966 (vi, 322p.) has *c.* 20,000 entries; 24 areas (*e.g.,* India, p. 198-278). 'Southeast Asia' has sub-divisions: Periodicals— General and miscellaneous—Bibliography— History—Geography, description and travel—

Economics—Social sciences—Politics and government—Education, study and teaching—Arts, language and literature. Includes Philippines and Indonesia. Author index.

Tōyōshi kenkyū bunken ruimoku [Annual bibliography of Oriental studies], 1934- (Kyoto, Kyoto Jinbun Gakkai, 1935-. Annual since 1957) lists *c.* 5,500 books and articles p.a. on Oriental studies (excluding Japan) in Japanese, Chinese and Korean, and in European languages. Author index.

908 (5):016
GARDE, P. K. Directory of reference works published in Asia. Paris, Unesco, 1956. xxvii, [1], 139p.

1,619 works of ready reference (general and special encyclopaedias and dictionaries, bibliographies, directories and yearbooks, atlases and gazetteers, and statistical annuals) arranged by U.D.C., with country sub-division. Confined to Afghanistan, Burma, Cambodia, Ceylon, China, Hong Kong, India, Indonesia, Japan, Laos, Malaya, Pakistan, Philippines, Singapore, Thailand and Viet-Nam. Author and anonymous title, subject, and language-dictionary indexes.

908 (5):016
NEW YORK. PUBLIC LBRARY. Dictionary catalog of the Oriental Collection of the New York Public Library, Reference Department. Boston, Mass., G. K. Hall, 1960. 16v. $960.

Contains some 318,000 entries for about 65,000 volumes. The Arabic, Indic and Ancient Near East holdings of the Oriental Collection are the largest in the U.S.A. "Other outstanding features are the comprehensive holdings of Japanese technical and scientific periodicals, a unique collection of linguistic works, and a fine collection in the field of Oriental religions, especially of Islam and Buddhism". The bibliography is made up of photolithographed card-catalogue entries —printed, typed and hand-written, 21 to the page, and by no means as legible as the photolithographed edition of the British Museum *General catalogue.* This is, nevertheless, a major tool in its field.

908 (5):016
Orientalische Bibliographie. 1887-1911, 1926. Begrundet von A. Müller. Bearb. und hrsg. von L. Scherman. Berlin, Reuther, 1888-1922, 1928. 25v. & 1 pt. (reprinted 1965. £135.).

Comprehensive annual bibliography of books, pamphlets, periodical articles and reviews covering the whole field of Oriental studies. "With this publication the series of German orientalist bibliographies reached its zenith" (Pearson, J. D. *Oriental and Asian bibliography* (1966), p. 134).

Predecessors are: J. T. Zenker's *Bibliotheca Orientalis,* 1846-71 (reprinted 1966); *Wissenschaftlichen Jahresberichte über die morgenländischen Studien,* 1859-81; Friederici's *Bibliotheca Orientalis,* 1876-83; and *Litteraturblatt für orientalische Philologie,* 1883-86.

908 (5):016

PEARSON, J. D. Oriental and Asian bibliography: an introduction, with some reference to Africa. London, Crosby, Lockwood, 1966. xvi, 261p. 35s.

Three parts: 1. Producers of the literature (Oriental, Asian and African studies, and interested organisations)—2. The literature and its controls (manuscripts; reference books; periodicals; general bibliographies; bibliographies of parts of Asia; select bibliographies)—3. The storehouse of the literature (libraries in Britain, U.S.A., U.S.S.R., etc.). Appendix B lists (authors, A-Z) c. 300 works referred to in the text, with page references; index. Valuable as a general approach.
This introductory volume is to be followed by individual regional volumes.

908 (5):016

ROYAL ASIATIC SOCIETY OF GREAT BRITAIN AND IRELAND. Library. **Catalogue of printed books published before 1932** in the library of the Royal Asiatic Society. London, the Society, 1940. vii, 541p.

An author list, giving title, place and date. Gazetteers are listed in an appendix, and periodicals are listed to 1939. Books in Chinese and Siamese are excluded, as are pamphlets and Bibles.

908 (5) (02)

SPULER, B., ed. Handbuch der Orientalistik. Leiden, Brill, 1952-. v. 1, pt. 1-.

v. 1. *Ägyptologie.* pts. 1-2. 1952, 1959.
v. 2. *Keilschriftforschung und alte Geschichte Vorderasiens.* pts. 1, 3, 4. 1957-66.
v. 3. *Semitistik.* 1964.
v. 4. *Iranistik.* pts. 1, 3. 1955-58.
v. 5. *Altaistik.* pts. 1, 3. 1963-64.
v. 6. *Geschichte der islamischen Länder.* pts. 1-3. 1952-59.
v. 7. *Armenische und kaukasische Sprachen.* 1963.
v. 8. *Religion.* pts. 1, 2. 1961-64.
Ergänzungsband. 1(1), 3, 5. 1951-64.
A comprehensive treatise on the languages, history and culture of the countries of Asia, by specialists. Chapter bibliographies; name indexes to each part.

908 (5) (02)

WINT, G., ed. Asia: a handbook. New York, Praeger, [1966]; London, Blond, 1967. xiii, 856p. $25; 147s.

81 essays by 60 contributors of international standing, predominantly British. All but 5 of the essays have bibliographies. Covers countries east of Afghanistan, including Soviet Asia and Hong Kong. *The booklist* (v. 63, no. 18, 15th May 1967, p. 953-61) finds the factual material rather brief and compressed. "The overall flavor is that of a symposium or an anthology of articles from learned journals." 22 well-drawn maps; analytical index.

908 (5) (043)

BLOOMFIELD, B. C., ed. Theses on Asia accepted by universities in the United Kingdom and Ireland, 1877-1964. London, Cass, 1967. xi, 127p. 63s.

2571 numbered entries; 25 universities. Arranged by areas: Asia—Near and Middle East—Centra Asia—South Asia—South-East Asia—Far East—Oceania. Index of authors .

908 (5) (058)

Asian annual: the "Eastern world" handbook. London, Foreign Correspondents, Ltd., 1954-. Annual. (1966. 25s.).

The major part of the 1966 v. covers countries A-Z (p. 15-124), systematically (*e.g.,* Afghanistan: Geography and climate—Area and population—Constitution—Representatives abroad—Foreign representation — Agriculture — Forests — Minerals—Industry—Development—Five-year plans —Community development—Currency and banking—Exchange control—Foreign trade—External aid—Communications—Education). Sections follow on aid to Asia, the Asian Development Bank and so on.

Far East

908 (5-011) (058)

Owen's Commerce & travel & international register . . . : Africa, Middle East & Far East, with international trade lists. London, Owen's Commerce & Travel, Ltd. illus., maps. Annual. (1966. 72s. 6d.).

See entry at 38 (058.7) (6).

South-east Asia

908 (5-012):016

AMERICAN INSTITUTE OF PACIFIC RELATIONS. Books on South-east Asia: a select bibliography. Rev. ed. New York, the Institute, 1960. 69p.

First published 1950, and edited by J. F. Embree. The 1960 revision includes supplements for the period June 1956 to April 1960.
A list of recent outstanding works on the history and political, social and economic problems of the area in general, and of Burma, Indochina, Indonesia, Malaya, Singapore and British Borneo, the Philippines, and Thailand. List of articles in American Institute of Pacific Relations periodicals.

908 (5-012):016

EMBREE, J. F., and DOTSON, L. O. Bibliography of the peoples and cultures of mainland Southeast Asia. New Haven, Yale Univ. Press, 1950. xxxiii, 821p. (Yale Univ. Southeast Asia Studies).

An extensive bibliography, with critical annotations, of c. 12,000 books and periodical articles in western languages on racial history, ethnology, cultural history, social studies, language and literature. Arranged under country and topic. No author index.

J. K. Irikura's *Southeast Asia: selected, annotated bibliography of Japanese publications* (New Haven, Conn., Human Relations Area Files, 1956. xii, 544p. (Behavior science bibliographies)) has 965 entries.

908 (5-012):016
HOBBS, C., *comp.* **Southeast Asia: an annotated bibliography** of selected reference sources in Western languages. [2nd ed.], rev. and enl. Washington, Library of Congress, Reference Dept., Orientalia Division, 1964. v, 180p. $1.

Previously published 1952.

535 numbered and systematically annotated items (mostly published 1952-63) in 7 sections: 1. Southeast Asia—general—2. Burma—3. Thailand—4. Cambodia, Laos and Vietnam—5. Malaysia—6. Indonesia—7. Philippines. Evaluative annotations. Index of authors, titles and selected subjects.

The School of Oriental and African Studies, Univ. of London issued the mimeographed *The Far East and South-East Asia: a cumulated list of periodical articles* between 1954 and 1965. This had four annual cumulations, May 1954 - April 1958 and was thereafter monthly until it ceased with the June 1965 number.

Bibliographies of bibliographies of the area: *Bibliographies of Southeast Asia and the Pacific areas,* by E. J. Frei (Quezon City, Bibliography Society of the Philippines, 1958. 33p.); *South and Southeast Asia: a bibliography of bibliographies,* by G. R. Nunn (Honolulu, Hawaii, East-West Center Library, 1966. 59 l.).

908 (5-012) (093.2)
INSTITUTE OF ASIAN ECONOMIC AFFAIRS. Union catalogue of documentary materials on South-East Asia. Tokyo, the Institute, 1964. 5v. £22 6s.

v. 1. *General and South-East Asia in General.*
v. 2-3. *India.*
v. 4. *Other countries in Asia.*
v. 5. *Index.*

South Asia

908 (5-013):016
DUTTA, R. Guide to South Asian material in the libraries of London, Oxford & Cambridge. 2nd ed. Cambridge, Univ. of Cambridge, Centre of South Asian Studies, 1966. [3], 18 l. 5s.

Designed for the use of students pursuing modern South Asian studies, this *Guide* is the outcome of an explanatory surveys made of libraries in connection with the national union catalogue of South Asian material under preparation at the Centre of South Asian Studies. Valuable details of resources in 39 libraries: London (non-university libraries) (8), London (university libraries) (8), Oxford (4), Cambridge (19).

908 (5-013):016
PATTERSON, M. L. P., and **INDEN, R. B.,** *ed.* **South Asia: an introductory bibliography.** Chicago, Ill., Syllabus Division, Univ. of Chicago Press, 1962. xxxvi, 412p. $3.

4,369 numbered, unannotated items, in 6 main sections: A. General—B. History (p. 19-103)—C. Social structure and organization (p. 104-70)—D. Political and economic structure; political, economic and social change (p. 171-286)—E. Religion and philosophy (p. 287-324)—F. Literature, science and the arts (p. 328-72). Chronological, topical and geographical sub-divisions. Countries involved are India, Pakistan, Ceylon and Nepal. Excludes works in South Asian languages; no cross-references. Author and title index.

908 (5-013):016
UNITED STATES. LIBRARY OF CONGRESS. Orientalia Division. **Southern Asia:** publications in western languages; a quarterly accession list. Washington, Library of Congress, 1952-. v. 1, no. 1-. Quarterly. $2 p.a.

A list of all books in western languages (1945-) and a selected list of periodical literature (July 1951-). Country coverage: India; Pakistan; Ceylon; Tibet; Nepal; Bhutan; Burma; Thailand; Indochina; Malaya; Indonesia; Philippines.

Beginning with the issue for April 1956 (v. 5, no. 2), as *Southern Asia accessions list,* includes monographs in certain lanuages of South Asia bearing an imprint of 1946 or later.

908 (5-013):016
WILSON, P. "A survey of bibliographies on Southern Asia". In *Journal of Asian studies,* v. 18, no. 3, May 1959, p. 365-76.

An annotated list. Sections: Periodically published bibliographies—Southern Asian areas (Indonesia; Philippine Islands; Mainland southeast Asia; India, Pakistan, Ceylon, Nepal)—General selective bibliographies—Humanities—Archaeology, History, Geography—Social sciences—Natural sciences—Government publications—Periodicals and newspapers—Theses—Bibliographies of bibliographies.

908 (5-013):091
WAINWRIGHT, M. D., and **MATTHEWS, N.,** *comp.* **A guide to Western manuscripts and documents in the British Isles relating to South and South East Asia.** London, Oxford Univ. Press, 1965. xix, 532p. 100s.

List of 80 manuscript depositories in London (p. 1-258); England, excluding London (p. 259-357); Wales and Monmouthshire; Scotland; Northern Ireland; Eire; Papers in private ownership (not deposited); Addenda. Omits the India Office Library colections; "to have included these would at least have doubled the size of the work" (*Preface*). Detailed index, p. 473-532. Well produced. "An indispensable source of reference" (*Times literary supplement,* no. 3,297, 6th May 1965, p. 357).

Middle East

908 (5-015):016
ETTINGHAUSEN, R. A selected and annotated bibliography of books and periodicals in Western languages dealing with the Near and Middle East, with special emphasis on medieval and modern times. Washington, Middle East Institute, 1952. [ii], viii, 111p. (American Council of Learned Societies; Committee on Near East Studies). **Supplement,** 1954. p. 112-137.

A select, classified, annotated list of the best books in western languages on the Near and

Middle East, intended for use in colleges and public libraries.

908 (5-015):016
JERUSALEM. HEBREW UNIVERSITY. Economic Research Institute. **A selected bibliography of articles dealing with the Middle East.** Jerusalem, the Institute, 1954-. v. 1-.

V. 1 (1954) cover 1939-1950, v. 2-3 (1955-59), 1951-54 and 1955-58 respectively.
The selection is based on articles in periodicals available in the Hebrew University and elsewhere in Israel, but the majority are in English. Primary arrangement is by area, 'Middle East' including Egypt and the Sudan, but excluding Israel. Sub-division is by subject. V. 3 includes a section on Israel-Arab relations. Total of 3,446 entries in v. 1-3.

908 (5-015):016
The Middle East journal. Washington, Middle East Institute, 1946-. Quarterly. ea. $2; $7.50 p.a.

V. 21, no. 1, Winter 1967 (144p.) includes a detailed chronology (p. 64-85), 12 book reviews, plus 'Recent publications' and 'Forthcoming books' (p. 110-28), and a 'Bibliography of periodical literature' (p. 129-140; items 18485-18884), with headings: Geography—History (medieval)—History and politics (modern)—Economic conditions — Social conditions — Science, philosophy and religion—Language—Literature and arts — Law — Philosophy — Biography—Miscellaneous—Book reviews (items 18682-18884).

908 (5-015) (05)
LJUNGGREN, F., and **HAMDY, M. Annotated guide to journals dealing with Middle East and North Africa.** Cairo, American Univ. in Cairo Press, 1964. 107p.

908 (5-015) (058)
The Middle East and North Africa: a survey and directory of Aden (South Arabia), Algeria, Chad, Cyprus, Ethiopia, French Somaliland (Djibouti), Iran, Iraq, Israel, Jordan, Kuwait, Lebanon, Libya, Mali, Mauritania, Morocco, Muscat and Oman, Niger, the Persian Gulf States, Saudi Arabia, Somalia, Spanish North Africa, the Sudan, the Syrian Arab Republic, Tunisia, Turkey, the United Arab Republic (Egypt) and the Yemen, with geographical, historical and educational surveys, concise information about political, industrial, financial, cultural and educational organisations, and Who's who in the Middle East and North Africa. London, Europa Publications, 1948-. maps. Annual. (14th ed. 1967-68. 1967. 120s.).

Three main parts: 1. General survey—2. Territories, A-Z (1966/67 ed., p. 95-790)—3. Who's who (p. 791-897). The section on the Sudan (p. 587-616) has 24 sections, gives statistics for 1964 and up to September 1965, and carries a bibliography. General select bibliographies, p. 898-903 (Books on the Middle East; Books on North Africa; periodicals). End-paper map in colour. A valuable compendium. *Africa report* (v. 11, no. 3, March 1966, p. 51), reviewing the 1965/66 ed., notes absence of statistical tables on national defence and foreign aid. *International affairs* (v.

43, no. 3, July 1967, p. 623-4) praises it for including chapters on the five major African organisations.

908 (5-015):061
LJUNGGREN, F., and **GEDDES, C. L.,** *ed*. **An international directory of institutes and societies interested in the Middle East.** Amsterdam, Djambatan, 1962. 159p.

Data on 351 institutes in 47 countries. Arranged under countries A-Z. Data: name, address, history, purpose and fields of interest, administration, membership, academic staff, degrees conferred, meetings, library and publications. Index of serial publications; index of institutes and societies.

North-eastern Asia
908 (5-018):016
KERNER, R. J. Northeastern Asia: a selected bibliography: contributions to the bibliography of the relations of China, Russia and Japan, with special reference to Korea, Manchuria, Mongolia and Eastern Siberia, in Oriental and European languages. Berkeley, Univ. of California Press, 1939. 2v. (Publications of the Northeastern Asia Seminar of the Univ. of California).

Extensive, though uneven, bibliography of selected printed works on the relations of China, Russia and Japan and on other subjects related thereto: Bibliography, periodicals, dictionaries, geology, geography and travel, archaeology, history, government and politics, military and naval affairs, economic and social conditions, religion and philosophy, frontier problems, international relations. Author index precluded by lacks of funds.

The *Author-title catalog* and *Subject catalog* of the East Asiatic Library, Univ. of California, Berkeley, is due for publication in Spring 1968 by G. K. Hall, Boston, Mass. It comprises *c.* 315,000 cards, photolithographically reproduced. The *Author-title catalog* occupies 13v. ($865; $951.50, outside the U.S.) and the *Subject catalog,* 6v. ($390; $429, outside the U.S.). The Library is particularly strong in Chinese, Korean and Japanese material.

China
908 (51):016
CORDIER, H. Bibliotheca Sinica: dictionnaire bibliographique des ouvrages relatifs à l'Empire chinois. 2. éd. Paris, Guilmoto, 1904-08. 4v. **Supplément.** Paris, Geuthner, 1922-24. (Reprinted, with 1961 index, New York, B. Franklin, 1965. *c.* £50.).

50,000 entries in main work; 20,000 in supplement. "The only reasonably complete bibliography for China in any European language" (Ad Orientem, *Catalogue* no. 6 (1966), p. 99). Classified; no annotations. Pt. 1 (in v. 1-3): La Chine proprement dit—pt. 2. Les étrangers en Chine (in v. 3)—pts. 3-5 (v. 4). Relations des étrangers avec les chinois. Les chinois chez le peuples étrangers. Les pays tributaires de la Chine. An author index, lacking in all previous editions and printings, was published separately in New York, 1953 (reprinted 1961).

908 (51):016
LUST, J., with EICHHORN, W. Index sinicus: a catalogue of articles relating to China in periodicals and other collective publications, 1920-1955. Cambridge, Heffer, 1964. xxx, 663p. 168*s*.

19,734 numbered, unannotated items. "Collective publications" comprises memorial volumes, symposia and the like, and proceedings of congresses and conferences. "Intended as a contribution towards filling the gap between Cordier's *Bibliotheca Sinica,* the supplementary volume of which covered works published up to 1924, and the monthly list of periodical articles on *The Far East and South-East Asia*" [1954-65], and as a supplement to T. L. Yuan's *China in Western literature* (qq.v.). Includes important reviews and obituary notices as well as substantial articles. Similar pattern to *Index Islamicus.* 27 classes, classes 2-20 being subjects and 21-27, areas (21. Manchuria—22. Mongols and Mongolia—23. Tibet—24. Sinkiang and Central Asian countries —25. Hsi-Hsia—26. Hong Kong—27. Macao). 'Tibet' is subdivided: General—Tibetan studies. Bibliography—Description. Travel—Tibetan and related languages—Literature—History. Foreign relations—Social conditions—Folklore—Communications—Religion—Art. Music. Dancing—Sciences and Medicine.

Chinese periodicals are covered in *Index to learned articles, 1902-1962;* compiled in the Fung Ping Shan Library, Univ. of Hong Kong by Ping-Kuen Yu (1963. xxxi, 573p. 170*s.*).

908 (51):016
Revue bibliographique de sinologie. 1. année, 1955-. Paris, Mouton, 1957-. v. 1-. Irregular. (v. 3: 1957. 140*s.*)

Abstracts of periodical articles and notices of books, covering Chinese history, sociology, anthropology, art, language and literature, and philosophy. Includes numerous Chinese and Japanese items. Systematically arranged and well indexed.

908 (51):016
SINGAPORE. UNIVERSITY. Library. **Catalogue of the Chinese Collection of the University of Singapore Library;** [compiled] by Chiang Chen-Yu. Singapore, Univ. of Malaya Press, 1956-65. 2v.

In Chinese.

Noted: Institute of Asian Economic Affairs. *The union catalogue of Chinese literature on modern China* (Hong Kong, the Institute, 1967-68. 8v. *c.* £88). This lists 35,000 selected titles published in China, 1912-65, and held by 22 libraries in Japan (locations given). V. 1-3: Social science—v. 4: Natural science—v. 5-6: Humanities—v. 7: Author index—v. 8: Index by items.

908 (51):016
TENG, SSU:YÜ, and BIGGERSTAFF, K. An annotated bibliography of selected Chinese

reference works. Rev. ed. Cambridge, Mass., Harvard Univ. Press, 1950. x, 326p. (Harvard-Yenching Institute studies, v. 2).

First published 1936.

908 (51):016
YUAN, Tung-Li. China in Western literature: a continuation of Cordier's *Bibliotheca Sinica.* New Haven, Far Eastern Publications, Yale Univ., 1958. xix, 802p.

About 15,000 items—"a record of virtually all books concerning China published in English, French and German between the years 1921 and 1957" (*Foreword*). 28 sections: 1, Bibliography and reference (p. 10); 2-21, subject sections; 22-28, regions (26. Taiwan (Formosa); 27. Hong Kong; 28. Macao). Appendix 1: Serial publications (p. 695-715); 2: Addenda. No annotations. The compiler was formerly Head Librarian of the National Library, Peking.

By contrast, C. O. Hucker's *China: a critical bibliography* (Tucson, Arizona, Univ. of Arizona Press, 1962. x, 125p. $3.50) is highly selective. Described as an indispensable guide (*Journal of Asian studies,* v. 22, no. 3, May 1963, p. 321), it is the first of four reference guides to Western literature on Asia being prepared by the Oriental Studies Staff of the Univ. of Arizona.

908 (51) (03)
COULING, S. The encyclopaedia Sinica. Shanghai, Kelly & Walsh, 1917. viii, 633p. (Reprinted 1965. 80*s.*).

A scholarly work still of considerable value. Articles A-Z, with short addenda and corrigenda. A mine of information (*e.g.,* on 'Names'); 'Han Dynasty', including list of rulers with names in Chinese characters as well as in romanised form). Biographies; many cross-references. Author was one-time Honorary Secretary and Editor, North-China Branch, Royal Asiatic Society.

Communist China

908 (510):016
BERTON, P., and WU, E. Contemporary China: a research guide. Edited by H. Koch, Jr. Prepared for the Joint Committee of the American Council of Learned Societies and the Social Sciences Research Council. Stanford, Cal., Hoover Institution on War, Revolution and Peace, Stanford Univ., 1967. xxix, 695p. $22.50.

2226 numbered and usually annotated items. 4 pts.: 1. Bibiographies and indexes (p. 1-104); 2. General reference works (p. 105-225); 3. Selected documentary material (p. 226-332); 4. Selected serial publications (p. 333-584; *e.g.,* J.R.P.S. series, p. 413-30). Appendix A: Research libraries and institutions; surveys, directories, catalogues and references. B: Dissertations and theses. Subject index; author-title index. A valuable guide.

908 (510):016
LINDBECK, J. M. H. "Research materials on Communist China: United States government sources". In *Journal of Asian studies,* v. 18, no. 3, May 1959, p. 357-63.

Material is noted under the department, etc., concerned: Library of Congress (newspapers; periodicals; books; current acquisitions; photo-duplication service), Department of State, U.S. Information Agency; Department of Agriculture; National Library of Medicine; Bureau of the Census, Department of Commerce.

Contemporary China: a bibliography of reports on China published by the United States Joint Publications Research Service; edited by Richard Sorich (prepared for the Joint Committee on Contemporary China of the American Council of Learned Societies and the Social Science Research Council. New York, Readex Reprint Corpn., 1961. [iii], 99, [i]p.) conveniently lists the numerous JPRS translations of articles in Chinese press and serial publications. Category list; subject index. These and subsequent translations are also listed in the *United States Government publications: monthly catalog.*

908 (510) (02)
Handbook on People's China. Peking, Foreign Languages Press, 1957. 236p. (London, Collet's. 6*s.*).

Gives detailed facts and figures, plus more general background information on Communist China, its social and economic development, especially since 1949.

908 (510) (058)
Communist China yearbook. 1962-. Hong Kong, China Research Associates, [1963?]-. Annual.

"Our first attempt to meet the pressing need for systematic and continual information on Communist China. . . . It contains no information of pure propaganda nature" (*Foreword,* 1962 ed.). The 1962 ed. covers the period January 1961 to the end of the first quarter of 1962, in 7 parts (pt. 7: Foreign relations, p. 443-584). Detailed contents; no index.

The Union Research Institute's *Communist China, 1964* (Hong Kong, 1965. 2v. Mimeographed. HK$27 (32*s.*)) is the tenth in a series of annual volumes covering events in Communist China. V. 1: Agriculture—Communications and transportation — Domestic affairs — Domestic trade—Finance—Industry—Legal affairs—Scientific and technological development. V. 2: Cultural affairs—Education—Literature and art —Foreign affairs—Foreign trade—Military affairs—Overseas Chinese affairs—Party affairs —Youth League affairs and youth movements.

Hong Kong

908 (512.317)
Hong Kong: report for the year . . . Hong Kong, Government Press, illus., maps. Annual. (1966, published 1967. 22*s.* 6*d.*).

22 chapters (*e.g.,* 1. Review: the social services 2. Employment—3. Financial structure . . . 9. Social welfare . . . 18. Geography and climate . . . 21. History—22. Constitution and administration). 45 statistical and other appendices (1966 v. has statistics for 1966), including 'Leading newspapers and magazines' (English; Chinese, p. 336). Analytical index. Well produced.

A bibliography was last appended in the 1963 report. A revised edition appeared separately in 1965: Braga, J. M. *A Hong Kong bibliography* (Hong Kong, Government Printing Department. HK$1).

Manchuria

908 (518):016
BERTON, P. A. Manchuria: an annotated bibliography. Washington, Library of Congress, Reference Department, 1951. xii, 187p.

843 items in various languages, particularly Japanese.

Korea

908 (519):016
COURANT, M. Bibliographie coréenne. Tableau littéraire de la Corée, contenant la nomenclature des ouvrages publiés dans ce pays jusqu'en 1890 ainsi que la description et l'analyse detaillées des principaux d'entre ces ouvrages. Paris, Leroux, 1894-96. 3v. **Supplément** (jusqu'en 1899). 1901. illus. (pl.). (Reprinted 1968. *c.* £55.).

3821 entries, often annotated .V. 1: Enseignement, Études des langues, Confucianisme, Littérature—v. 2: Mœurs et coutumes, Histoire et géographie—v. 3: Sciences et arts, Religions, Relations extérieures .Index.

908 (519):016
HAZARD, B. H., Jr., *and others, comp.* **Korean studies guide.** Berkeley, Los Angeles, Univ. of California Press, 1954. xii, 220p. maps.

491 annotated entries in 17 classes (*e.g.,* 1. Libraries, general bibliographies—2. Reference materials—3. Geography—4. Art and archaeology. . . 16. Education—17. Special reference materials and addenda. 3 appendices include a glossary. Indexes of titles and authors.

——**Russian supplement** . . . , by R. L. Backus. Berkeley, etc., 1958. xii, 211p.

893 annotated entries.

908 (519):016
SILBERMAN, B. S. Japan and Korea: a critical bibliography. Tucson, Arizona, Univ. of Arizona Press, 1962. xiv, 120p.

Items no. 1616-1933 concern Korea. An annotated and graded guide for the student and non-specialist.

908 (519) (058)
Korean annual. Seoul, Hapdong News Agency, 1963-. Annual.

The 1966 *Annual* has sections: Chronology—Government—International relations—National economy—Social affairs—Culture—General information—Laws and documents—Who's who (p. 432-87)—Statistics (p. 488-530). Index.

The Korean National Commission for Unesco's *Unesco Korean survey* (Seoul, Dong-a Publishing Co., 1960. 936p. illus.) has the same comprehensive scope as the Japanese National Commission for Unesco's *Japan: its land, people and culture* (q.v.). It has bibliographies.

Japan

908 (52):016

BORTON, H., *and others.* **A selected list of books and articles on Japan** in English, French and German. Rev. and enl. ed. Cambridge, Mass., Harvard Univ. Press, for the Harvard-Yenching Institute, 1954. xiv, 272p.

First published 1940.

1,781 items, many of them concisely annotated, sometimes critically. Includes material up to 1952. Systematic arrangement in 14 classes: Bibliographies—Reference works—Periodicals—Geography—History—World War II and Occupation 1941-52—Economics—Government and politics —Sociology and ethnology—Education and journalism—Mythology, Religion and philosophy —Language—Literature—Art. The analytical index (p. 223-72) covers titles, authors, editors, translators and subjects.

908 (52):016

CORDIER, H. Bibliotheca Japonica: dictionnaire bibliographique des ouvrages relatifs à l'Empire japonais rangés par ordre chronologique jusqu'à 1870, suivi d'un appendice renfermant la liste alphabétique des principaux ouvrages parus de 1870 à 1912. Paris, Leroux, 1912. xii p., 762 col. (Publ. de l'École des Langues Orientales Vivantes, 5 sér., v. 8). (Reprinted 1968. 120s.).

Pioneer and still standard list of materials for Japanese studies. About 3,500 items.

908 (52):016

Guide to Japanese reference books. Nihon no sankotosho. Chicago, American Library, 1966. xii, 303p. $10.

Nihon no sankotosho was first published 1962; this is an English translation of the 2nd ed. (1965).

2,375 code-numbered items, systematically arranged in 19 classes (A-U), with sub-divisions. Entries consist of author's name, romanised and then in Japanese characters, followed by title, similarly treated, with English translation. Most entries are annotated. Author, anonymous title and subject index. Confined to books published in Japan and in Japanese, with a few exceptions, plus indexing and abstracting services. Reviewed in *Library Association record,* v. 69, no. 5, May 1967, p. 178.

More or less complementary in language coverage is the Kokusai Bunka Shinkokai's *A classified list of books in Western languages relating to Japan* (Tokyo, Univ. of Tokyo Press, 1965. ix, 316, 124p. 100s.), a record of books acquired by the K.B.S. up to the end of October 1962.

Twelve doors to Japan, by J. W. Hall and R. V. Beardsley (New York, McGraw-Hill, 1965) includes a valuable bibliography, p. 587-623.

908 (52):016

KOKUSAI BUNKA SHINKOKAI, *comp.* **K.B.S. bibliography of standard reference books for Japanese studies,** with descriptive notes. Tokyo, Kokusai Bunka Shinkokai (and, latterly, Univ. of Tokyo Press), 1959-.

v. 1: *Generalia.* 1959.

v. 2: *Geography and travel.* 1962.
v. 3: *History and biography.* 1963-64.
v. 4: *Religion.* 1963 (reprinted 1966). *See at* 299.52:016.
v. 5: *Philosophy, science and education.*
v. 6(A): *Language.* 1961.
v. 6(B): *Literature.* pt. 1. 1962.
v. 7(A): *Arts and crafts.* 1959.
v. 7(B): *Theatre, dance and music.* 1960.
v. 8: *Manners and customs, & folklore.* 1961.

Each volume has c. 200-300 evaluatively annotated entries, systematically arranged. Titles, authors and imprint in Japanese characters as well as romanised. Indexes of authors and editors (romanised, then in Japanese characters). Otherwise text is in English.

908 (52):016

SILBERMAN, B. S., *comp.* **Japan and Korea: a critical bibliography.** Tucson, Arizona, Univ. of Arizona Press, 1962. xiv, 120p.

1,933 numbered items (including some duplicates). Japan (nos. 1-1615), sections: Introductory works. Bibliographies; select; general. Journals—Land and people—Language (including dictionaries)—History (p. 7-28)—Religion and philosophy—Japanese art—Literature—Political patterns—Social organization and structure—Education—Economic patterns—Population. Introduction to each section. Author and anonymous title index. An annotated and graded guide for the student and non-specialist.

908 (52) (02)

Japan handbook, 1966: a wealth of useful data on Japan for everyday reference. 2nd ed. Tokyo, Rengo Press, 1966. xlii, 216p. tables, maps.

Sections: 1. Geography—2. History—3. Education. Religion—4. Government—5. Agriculture—6. Finance—7. Trade—8. Labor—9. Industries—10. Transport & telecommunications—11. Miscellany (National anthem. Medicine. Military code. Health insurance . . .)—12. Statistical section (p. 76-166)—13. Treaties (with U.S.A., Korea). Detailed analytical index of 40 pages.

908 (52) (02)

JAPANESE NATIONAL COMMISSION FOR UNESCO. Japan: its land, people and culture. [Tokyo], Printing Bureau, Ministry of Finance, 1958. 1,077p., with 5 maps, illus., tables. (Rev. ed. 1964).

Covers all aspects of Japanese life, including health problems, economy, literature, fine arts, recreation and tourism. No bibliographies. Appendices: Conversion table of weights and measures; Comparative chart of important historical events. Index (which could be more detailed), p. 1059-74; location of places, p. 1074-77.

908 (52) (03)

[SERICHI, I., and BONMARCHAND, G.] Dictionnaire historique du Japon. Tokyo, Librairie Kinokuniya, 1963-. fasc. 1-. (Publications de la Maison Franco-Japonaise).

fasc. 1: A. xviii, 107p.

Planned for publication in c. 20 fascicules. Fasc. 1 has 345 fully annotated entries that cover subjects ranging from biography, place names, individual journals, agricultural produce to the dance, musical instruments, porcelain and 'Ameda shinkō' (Buddhism). Romanised form of name-entry, followed by Japanese characters (also given for special names and terms). References appended to each entry. Sources, p. viii-ix. Well produced.

Taiwan (Nationalist China)

908 (529)

China yearbook. 1957/1958-. Taipei (Taiwan), China Publishing Co., 1958-. illus., charts, maps. Annual. (18th ed. 1964/1965. 1965. NT.$150; U.S.$5.).

Previously (1952/53-1956/57) *China handbook,* which continues that issued (1st ed. 1943) issued by the Ministry of Information of the Kuomintang Government.

The 18th ed. covers July 1963-June 1964. 10 parts: 1. General information—2. Government and its functions—3. National defense—4. International affairs—5. National economy—6. Social affairs—7. Education and culture—8. Chinese Communist régime (p. 552-604)—9. Chronology—10. Who's who (Nationalist Chinese only) (p. 644-815; obituaries, p. 815-7). Appendix.

Saudi Arabia

908 (53):016

MACRO, E. L., *comp.* **Bibliography of the Arabian Peninsula.** Coral Gables, Florida, Univ. of Miami Press, 1958. xiv, 80p.

2,380 titles of books and articles, with emphasis on travel, politics and oil.
Bibliography on Yemen and notes on Mocha (Coral Gables, Florida, Univ. of Miami Press, 1960. vii, 63p.) is by the same compiler. It has 894 entries; notes on Mocha, p. 31-63.

India

908 (54):016

BRITISH COUNCIL. British books on India: a selection written between the eighteenth century and the present day, showing something of the contribution made by British scholars to Indian studies. London, British Council, 1961. 142p. *Gratis.*

A catalogue of an exhibition of about 1,300 British books on Indian subjects. 16 main classes, arranged A-Z, ranging from 'Agriculture and forestry' to 'Topography and travel', and including 'Linguistic and literary studies including language dictionaries', 'Maps' and 'Medicine and medical history'. 'History' occupies pages 50-77. No annotations, but titles are given in full. No index.

908 (54):016

PATTERSON, M. L. P., and **INDEN, R. B.,** *ed.* **Introduction to the civilization of India, South Asia:** an introductory bibliography. Chicago, Ill., Univ. of Chicago, The College, 1962. 448p. $3.

Lists 4,369 publications on India, Pakistan, Ceylon and Nepal, mostly in English. Six major sections: General—History—Social structure and organization—Political and economic structure

and political, economic and social change—Religion and philosophy—Literature, science and the arts.

908 (54):026/

SUTTON, S. C. A guide to the India Office Library; with a note on the India Office records. London, H.M.S.O., 1967. xii, 12p. illus. (incl. pl.), facsims. 27s. 6d.

First published 1952.
The account of the India Office records, a new feature, "will be useful until the full guide to the Records, now being prepared, is completed . . . Indispensable for all serious orientalists" (*Times literary supplement,* no. 3442, 15th February 1968, p. 166).

908 (540):016

Index India: a quarterly documentation list of articles, editorials, notes and letters, etc., from periodicals and newspapers published in English . . . Jaipur, Rajasthan Univ. Library, 1967-. v.1, no. 1-. Quarterly. 140s. p.a.

World English-press coverage on India and matters Indian. V. 1, no. 1 indexed 6,500 items from *c.* 375 publications.

908 (540) (02)

The Gazetteer of India: Indian Union. v. 1: Country and people. Delhi, Publications Division, Ministry of Information and Broadcasting, 1965. xii, 657p. maps. Rs. 22.50; 45s.

Previous ed. as *The Imperial gazetteer of India, 1907-9* (26v.) (see at *915.4 (083.86)*).
This edition is to be in 4v. (v. 2. History and culture; v. 3. Economic structure; v. 4. Administration and public welfare). There is a possibility that State gazetteers will follow. V. 1 has 10 chapters. Each chapter and, where necessary, each section of a chapter is by a specialist. Chapters: 1. Physiography—2. Weather and climate—3. Geology—4. Flora—5. Fauna—6. The people—7. Languages—8. Religions (78p., the longest)—9. Social structure—10. Social life (20p. only). Index. "For all its faults, the *Country and people* volume probably contains a wider range of useful information than any other work of comparable length" (*Journal of Asian studies,* v. 26, no. 2, February 1967, p. 318).

908 (540) (058)

India: a reference annual . . . Compiled by the Research and Reference Division, Ministry of Information and Broadcasting. [New Delhi], the Ministry, 1953-. Annual.

The official handbook. The 1965 ed. has 30 sections (*e.g.,* 1. The land and the people—2. National symbols—3. Government . . . 8. Health . . . 15. Finance . . . 20. Industry . . . 29. Important events of 1964—30. General information (awards, etc.), and appendices. Select bibliography, p. 548-67.
Much more detailed than *India . . . : an annual review* (London, Information Service of India. illus, tables, maps), whose 1966 ed. [1967]. x, 161p. 3s. 6d.) has a foreword and 21 articles on aspects of Indian life (*e.g.,* 'Food for millions'; 'Tribal societies in India'; 'New trends in Indian films'). 'Facts and figures' (p. 129-61), with

statistics usually for 1964 or 1965. Well illustrated; no index.

908 (540) (058)
"The Times of India" directory and year book, including Who's who. Bombay & London, "The Times of India" offices (Bennett, Coleman & Co.), 1915-. tables, map. Annual. (1965-66. [1966]. 80s.).

Published as *Indian year-book,* 1915-47, and as *The India and Pakistan year-book and who's who,* 1948-51.
Facts and figures on the Indian Union and its States. Statistics (1965-66 v.) up to 1963/64. Includes classified trades directories. 'Who's who in India' (p. 1176-1270): nearly 1,500 entries.

The *Hindustan year-book and who's who, 1966* (34th year of issue. Calcutta, S. C. Sarkar, 1966. 612, 226p. Rs.6; 20s.) has two main parts: 1. General, administrative, economic, industrial and agriculture; 2. States and territories (who's who, p. 166-196). Statistics for 1964, 1965, etc.

Ceylon

908 (548.7):016
KULARATNE, E. D. T., and **SILVA, M.,** *comp.* **A select list of books and other publications on Ceylon.** Colombo, Ceylon Library Association, 1965. 56p.

Systematically arranged: Culture and religion—Sociology and anthropology—Law, politics and government—Fine arts—Description and travel—History and antiquities . . . — Biography. List of works in Tamil and of government publications, appended.

Noted: *A bibliography of Ceylon; its land, people, history and culture: a systematic guide in Western languages,* compiled by H. A. I. Goonetileke (Library Association thesis, 1964. 4v.); and *Some books on Ceylon: a selected and partially annotated bibliography, including a short section on the Maldive Islands,* compiled by J .J. Hediger (Ithaca, N.Y., Cornell Univ. Press, 1964. 130p.).

908 (548.7) (058)
Ceylon year book . . . Colombo, Department of Census and Statistics, 1948-. illus., maps. Annual. (1966. Rs. 7.50.).

The 15th issue, for 1963 (published 1964) has 23 chapters. Aims to be a convenient source of information on the history, geography, general economy and governmental activities. The first issue is retrospective to 1938. For detailed statistics, see *Statistical abstract of Ceylon* (at 31 (548.7)).

Pakistan

908 (549):016
ABERNETHY, G. L., *comp.* **Pakistan: a selected, annotated bibliography.** 2nd ed., rev., with a supplement for the period February 1957 to February 1960. New York, American Institute of Pacific Relations, 1960. ii, 39p. 75c.

First published 1957.
The main bibliography has three parts: Books.—Government of Pakistan publications—

Periodical articles (18 classes). Annotations average about 25 words in length.

G. B. Moreland's *Star and crescent: a selected and annotated bibliography of Pakistan, 1947-1957* (Karachi, Institute of Public and Business Administration, Univ. of Karachi, 1958. 36p.) is confined to books.

A. R. Ghani's *Pakistan: a select bibliography* (Lahore, Pakistan Association for the Advancement of Science, 1951. xxii, 339p.) has 9,000 selected references (books, pamphlets, articles) in 8 chapters. Omits education, architecture, archaeology, languages, literature, art, folklore. These were to be covered in a subsequent volume.

908 (549):016
SIDDIQUI, A. H. A guide to reference books published in Pakistan. Karachi, Pakistan Reference Publications, 1966. 41p.

Lists more than 400 English-language reference works published in Pakistan between the date of the partition (1947) and the end of 1965, and relating mainly to Pakistan. A few entries are briefly annotated. Arranged A-Z by subject; author index. (*Library of Congress Information bulletin,* v. 26, no. 37, 14th September 1967, p. 629).

908 (549) (058)
Pakistan . . . Karachi, Pakistan Publications. Annual. tables.

Pakistan, 1963/64 [1964?]. 185p. R4) has two main parts: 1. The Centre (*i.e.,* Central government). Law and administration—Economic survey—Public services—Welfare—Pakistan and the world. 2. Provinces (East Pakistan—West Pakistan). Statistical tables up to 1963/64. No index.

The *West Pakistan year book,* 1963 (Lahore, Directorate of Publications, Research and Films, Information Department, 1963) is illustrated and has 51 sections (15. Statistics).

Iran

908 (55):016
ORGANISATION FOR ECONOMIC CO-OPERATION AND DEVELOPMENT. Development Centre. **Bibliographie sur l'Iran.** Bibliography on Iran. Paris, O.E.C.D., 1965. xi, 305p. Mimeographed. *Gratis.*

2,217 numbered items (without annotations) in 11 sections: 1. General conditions—2. Law and politics—3. Demographic and social structures—4. Agriculture and land reform—5. Mining, crafts and industry—6. Oil—7. Communications and transport—8. Foreign trade, balance of payments —9. Economic situation and structures—10. Planning and development—11. Technical co-operation. Author index; 'List of the principal newspapers and periodicals quoted'; 'List of periodicals published in Iran'. "Completes and brings up to date the very useful study made by François Barrès: 'Les publications sur l'Iran en langues francaise et anglaise dans quelques bibliothèques parisiennes (depuis 1945)' " (*Introduction*).

Bibliography of Iran. Coronation ed., compiled by G. Handley-Taylor (London, Bibliography of Iran, 1967. xviii, 34p. 25s.) contains *c.* 350 items. Annotations consist of bibliographical details only. Arranged A-Z by authors; no index. Annual supplements, 1968-, have been announced.

908 (55):016

WILSON, *Sir* **A. T. Bibliography of Persia.** Oxford, Clarendon Press, 1930. x, 253p.

Basic bibliography of works in European languages on the history, achaeology, geography, etc., of Persia, standard translations of Persian works, bibliographies and writings on Persian literature, religions, etc. Arrangement: alphabetical, by author.

"A bibliography of bibliographies on Iranian studies," by Iraj Afshar (in *Iranica*, v. 1, January 1963. 217p.) lists nearly 300 bibliographies and has indexes of persons, meetings, periodicals consulted, and a list of libraries consulted and specialising institutions; annotations in Iranian (*Unesco bulletin for libraries*, v. 18, no. 6, November/December 1964, entry no. 389).

908 (55) (058)

Iran almanac and book of facts, 1967. [6th ed.] Tehran, Kucheh Kalkhali, 1967. 800, [1]p.

First published 1961.
Five chapters: 1. History and geography—2. National affairs—3. Foreign relations—4. Economic aspects—5. Social and cultural life. Appendices include a "Who's who" (p. 735-87; *c.* 450 entries), telephone directory, and 'Bibliography of Iran' (p. 797-8; plus suggested readings and sources).

Turkey

908 (560):016

BIRGE, J. K. A guide to Turkish area study. Washington, Committee on Near Eastern Studies, American Council of Learned Societies, 1949. xii, 240p. tables.

A running commentary, in 13 chapters (1. Sources of general information—2. The geography of Turkey . . . 5. History . . . 7. Social organization in Turkey . . . 11. Religion—12. Art —13. Music). Bibliography of *c.* 600 items, p. 145-184.

Syria

908 (569.1):016

UNITED ARAB REPUBLIC. NATIONAL LIBRARY, Cairo. **A bibliographical list of works about Syria.** 2nd ed. Cairo, 1965. 192, 166p. (Bibliographical lists of the Arab world, no. 3). 25s.

First published 1961.

Israel

908 (569.4):016

Palestine and Zionism: a bibliography of books, pamphlets and periodicals. New York, Zionist Archives and Library, 1946-. Monthly, cumulating annually and triennially.

Supersedes the Library's 'Recent materials on

Zionism and Palestine' and its 'Articles on Zionism and Palestine in recent periodicals'. Layout is similar to that of the *P.A.I.S. bulletin*, with author, title and subject entries.

908 (569.4)(058)

The Israel yearbook . . . In co-operation with the Economic Department of the Jewish Agency, incorporating *The Palestine yearbook and Israel annual.* [Tel Aviv], Israel Yearbook Publications, Ltd. Annual.

The 1965 v. has chapters on finance, research, science and culture, investment and development, foreign trade, the legal system, petroleum, agriculture and other aspects.

Soviet Central Asia

908 (57):016

Bibliography of recent Soviet source materials on Soviet Central Asia and its borderlands (including the Middle East). London, Central Asian Research Centre, 1957-. no. 1-. 2 p.a.

Issued as supplements to *Central Asian Review* and initially incorporated into that journal.
Entries, usually annotated, are for books and periodicals and cover the six Muslim Soviet Socialist Republics, borderlands (Afghanistan, India, Pakistan, Persia, Tibet, etc.) and, since 1960, the Middle East (including United Arab Republic), and are so arranged.

908 (57):016

SINOR, D. Introduction à l'étude de l'Eurasie Centrale. Wiesbaden, Harrassowitz, 1963. xxiv, 371p.

4,403 numbered items in 3 pts.: 1. Les langues et les peuples (L'Ouralien. L'Altaïque)—2. L'histoire (p. 191-346: L'Antiquité. Le Moyen Âge. L'époque mongole. L'époque de la décadence)—3. Notes sur l'ethnographie. Introduction to sections and very brief running commentary. Author and anonymous title index.

Noted: *Soviet Central Asia: a bibliography,* by R. A. Pierce (Berkeley, Cal., Center for Slavic and East European Studies, 1966. 3v.), v. 1: 1558-1866; v. 2: 1867-1917; v. 3: 1917-1966.

Afghanistan

908 (581):016

WILBER, D. N. Annotated bibliography of Afghanistan. 2nd ed. New Haven, Conn., HRAF Press, 1962. xii, 259p. (Behavior science bibliographies). (3rd ed. 1967. *c.* 60s.).

First published 1956.
About 1,300 items (books and periodical articles) in 9 sections: general sources of information; reference books; geography; history; social organisation; social evolution and institutions; political and economic structure; language and literature; art and archaeology. A supplement records items published between 1956 and June 1962. Author index.

M. Akram's *Bibliographie analytique de l'Afghanistan. 1. Ouvrages parus hors de l'Afghanistan* (Paris, Centre de Documentation Universitaire, 1947. iii, 6, 504, iiip. Mimeographed) notes *c*. 2,000 works, periodical articles and manuscripts.

908 (581) (058)
"The Kabul times" annual, 1967-. Kabul, "Kabul Times" Publishing Agency, 1967-. illus., tables, maps. Annual.

Factual, statistical and administrative data. 'Provinces' (p. 94-152) includes names of officials. Bibliography, p. 156-8; Who's who, p. 159-74. Text of constitution of Afghanistan.

Indochina

908 (59):016
CORDIER, H. Bibliotheca Indosinica: diction-naire bibliographique des ouvrages relatifs à la Péninsule Indochinoise. Paris, Imprimerie Nationale, 1912-32. 5v. (Publications de l'École Française d'Extrême-Orient, v. 15-18 bis). (Re-printed 1968. £30 2s.

V. 1: *Birmanie, Assam, Siam, Laos;* v. 2: *La Péninsule Malaise;* v. 3-4: *Indochine Française;* v. 5: *Index,* by M.-A. R. Cabaton.
A bibliography of *c*. 20,000 items covering all fields, of works in European languages. The pioneer and still standard bibliography for Indo-China, Burma and Malaya.

Bibliographie critique des œuvres parus sur l'Indochine française . . . , by R. Auvade (Paris, Maisonneuve et Larose, 1965. 154p. 16F.) covers only 150 items, nearly all in French, but it does give a brief and objective analysis of each item. Reviewed in *Bulletin critique du livre français,* v. 20, no. 7, July 1965, entry no. 64412).

Burma

908 (591):016
TRAGER, F. N., *ed.* **Annotated bibliography of Burma.** Prepared by the Burma Research Project at New York University. New Haven, Conn., HRAF Press, 1956. viii, 230p. (Behavior science bibliographies). $5.75.

1,018 numbered items, most entries being annotated; lengthy annotations for basic works. 6 sections: 1. Bibliographies—2. Books, pamph-lets and other separates—3. Periodicals—4. Burma official, selected publications by the Government of Burma—5. Serials cited—6. Topical bibliography (21 sections), p. 193-230.

Japanese and Chinese language sources on Burma: an annotated bibliography. F. N. Trager, editor (New Haven, Conn., HRAF Press, 1957. x, 122p.) is the companion piece, with 229 entries.

Noted: Htar, K. T. *Select bibliography of books on British Burma, 1826-1948,* a University College School of Librarianship thesis (*Univ. of London theses and dissertations accepted for higher degrees, 10 October 1966 - 30 September 1967* (1967), p. 59).

Thailand

908 (593):016
CHULALONGKORN UNIVERSITY, Bangkok. Central Library. **Bibliography of material about Thailand in Western languages.** Bang-kok, [the University], 1960. vii, 325p. 35s.

Includes "books, periodical articles, pamphlets, mimeographed documents, microfilms, and films concerning the fields of philosophy and religion, social sciences, language and literature, pure science and applied science, arts and recreation, history, travel and biography" (*Preface*). Classed arrangement; no index.

908 (593):016
MASON, J. B., and **PARISH, H. C. Thailand bibliography.** Gainesville, Florida, Department of Reference and Bibliography, Univ. of Florida Libraries, 1958. vii, 247p. (Bibliography series, no. 4).

"This first comprehensive bibliography devoted solely to the Kingdom of Thailand (Siam) con-tains over 2,300 references, many annotated, to books, articles, and documents in nine European languages" (*Far East digest* (Institute of Pacific Relations), no. 135, June 1958, p. 27-28). Biblio-graphies (p. 1-2)—Books, pamphlets, theses and government publications (p. 3-103)—Thai language studies and dictionaries—Articles (p. 120-232). No annotations; no index.

908 (593) (02)
Thailand: facts and figures, 1966. Bangkok, Department of Technical and Economic Co-operation, National Development, [1967]. [ix], 130p. illus., maps, tables.

Pt .1, Some facts (p. 1-77); pt. 2, Some figures (p. 81-130), for 1957-66, usually. Sources stated. 75 tables. No index. Well produced.

908 (593) (058)
THAILAND. Office of the Prime Minister. **Thai-land: official year book.** Bangkok, Government Printing Office. illus., tables, map. Annual. (1964. 40 Baht; $2).

The 1964 v. has 15 chapters: Government—Foreign affairs—National defence—Social wel-fare measures—Medical and health services—The administration of justice—National economy—Trade and finance—The mass media—Educa-tion—Religion—Arts and culture—Sports—Tourism. General index.

Thailand: aspects of landscape and life, by R. L. Pendleton with R. C. Kingsbury and others (New York, Duell, Sloan & Pearce, 1962. xv, 321p. illus., tables, diagrs., maps. $10) has 10 chapters, each with a bibliography ('Major sources') and footnote references. 26 maps; 51 half-tone illus-trations; statistics up to 1956. The volume is an American Geographical Society handbook.

Noted: Thailand. Department of Technical and Economic Co-operation. *Thailand: facts and figures, 1965* (Bangkok, 1965. 138p. illus., maps).

Malaya

908 (595):016
CHEESEMAN, H. R., *comp.* **Bibliography of Malaya;** being a classified list of books, wholly or partly in English, relating to the Federation of Malaya and Singapore. London, published for the British Association of Malaya, by Longmans, Green, 1959. xi, 234p.

About 5,000 entries for books and periodical

articles, some with brief annotations. Covers Malaya from 17th century up to 1957. 20 classes, arranged A-Z, from 'Agriculture, forestry and horticulture' to 'Second World War in Malaya', 'Trade and economics' and 'Travel'. 'Bibliographies and lists', p. 30-35; 'Fiction', p. 66-77. Author index.

University of Singapore. Library. *Catalogue of the Malaysia/Singapore Collection* (17,000 cards photolithographically reproduced; classified, with supporting author sequence) is to be published by G. K. Hall, Boston, Mass., in January 1969.

908(595):016

LIM, B., *comp.* **Malaya: a background bibliography.** *Journal of the Malayan Branch, Royal Asiatic Society,* v. 35, pts. 2 & 3 (nos. 198/199), 1962. v, 199p.

About 4,000 unannotated entries, covering the Federation of Malaya, the States of Singapore and Brunei, and the colonies of Sarawak and North Borneo. Compiled at the National Library of Australia, Canberra, in 1956. Lists books, parts (*e.g.,* chapters) of books, pamphlets, periodical articles, etc. 8 main sections, with sub-divisions: 1. Bibliographies—2. General and descriptive—3. History—4. Constitutional development—5. Administration—6. Economic conditions—7. The Malayan people—8. Parties and politics. Gives locations in the Commonwealth National Library, Canberra, the British Museum, London School of Economics, etc. No index.

908 (595) (058)

Malaysia: official year book . . . Kuala Lumpur, Government Printer. illus., tables, maps. Annual. (v. 3: 1963. 1964).

Spine title: "Baku Rasmi Tahunan".
22 chapters (1. An introduction to Malaysia—2. The people—3. His Majesty's Government—4. Government in the States . . . 10. Transport and communications . . . 17. The rubber industry . . . 20. Social services). 4 appendices, including 'Statistics' (p. 495-542).

The Singapore year book (Singapore, Government Printing Office. illus., tables, maps. Annual. (1964, published 1966) is the Government's annual report. It has 20 sections. Bibliography (sectionalised), p. 394-400.

Cambodia

908 (596)

FISHER, M. L. Cambodia: an annotated bibliography of its history, geography, politics and economy since 1954. Cambridge, Mass., M.I.T. Center for International Studies, 1967. 66p.

Vietnam

908 (597):016

MICHIGAN STATE UNIVERSITY. Vietnam Project. **What to read on Vietnam:** a selected annotated bibliography. 2nd ed., with a supplement covering the period November 1958 to October 1959. New York, Institute of Pacific Relations, 1960. 73p.

First published 1959.

Laos

908 (598):016

LAFONT, P. B. Bibliographie du Laos. Paris, École Française d'Extrême-Orient, 1964. 269p. map.

About 4,000 entries, some with brief annotations. 23 sections (General—Geography—Geology and paleontology . . . Languages and writings—Literature—Law . . . Economy, finance, labour — Education — Travel — Miscellaneous —Bibliographies (p. 233-4). Appendix: books in Lao, Siamese, Vietnamese and Russian. Index of authors; index of authors of compte-rendus.

AFRICA

908 (6):016

AFRICAN BIBLIOGRAPHIC CENTER. African affairs for the general reader: a selected and introductory bibliographical guide. New York, African-American Institute, 1967. 210p. $5.

More than 1,700 items. A well-annotated list of periodicals plus annotated entries for *c.* 1,600 books, pamphlets and articles, in subject (A-Z) and area sequences. Titles suitable for elementary and primary schools are listed. Indexes of authors and titles.

The Center's *A current bibliography on African affairs* (New York, Greenwood Periodicals, Inc., 1963-. Monthly. ea. $2.25; $20 p.a.) includes book reviews, commentary section, forthcoming publications section and, as from August 1967, original bibliographies and bibliographical essays.

908 (6):016

Afrika-Bibliographie. Verzeichnis des wissenschaftlichen Schrifttums in deutsche Sprache. 1960/61-. Bonn, Schroeder, 1963-. Annual. (1962, published 1964. DM.13.).

Compiled by R. Thoden for the Wissenschaftlicher Ausschuss der Deutschen Afrika-Gessellschaft. 1960/61 v.: 83p.; 1962 v.: 148p. Confined to German-language material.

908(6):016

BLOOMFIELD, B. C., and **McKEE, M.,** *comp.* **Africa in the contemporary world.** London, National Book League, 1967. 30p. 1s.

189 numbered items, with brief evaluative annotations, arranged under countries within 5 regions. A general section precedes. Appendix (p. 30): African literature: a list of some leading African authors. Prices are given; most of the books listed are in print. No index. Aims "to provide the intelligent general reader with a selection of reading matter in the English language" (*Preface*).

908 (6):016

HARVARD COLLEGE LIBRARY. Widener Library shelflist number 2: Africa. Classification schedule; classified listing by call number; alphabetical listing by author or title; chronological listing. [Cambridge, Mass.], 1965. 794p. £10.

Lists *c.* 10,000 primary works on history,

civilisation and government, general geography and travel, general social and economic conditions, religious affairs and the various races of the African countries and adjacent islands.

908 (6):016
HOLDSWORTH, M. Soviet African studies, 1918-1959: an annotated bibliography. London, Royal Institute of International Affairs, 1961. 2v. Mimeographed. ea. 12s.

> pt. 1. *General functional studies.*
> pt. 2. *Regional studies.*
> Analyses Soviet writing on Africa up to the end of 1958; well annotated. Items published in 1959 are listed only. Pt. 1 covers general symposia, politics, sociology, geography, ecology, travel, economics, language, folklore and literature (282 numbered entries); pt. 2, entries no. 283-498. Both pts. include author and subject indexes.

Supplemented by the Central Asian Research Centre's *Soviet writing on Africa, 1959-61: an annotated bibliography* (London, R.I.I.A., 1963. viii, 93p. 6s.).
For information on later and current Soviet writing on Africa, see *Mizan* (6 p.a.) and *Mizan. Supplement A: Middle East and Africa, Soviet and Chinese press reports* (6 p.a.). (London, Central Asian Research Centre. Monthly), as from July 1960.

908 (6):016
INTERNATIONAL AFRICAN INSTITUTE. Africa bibliography series: ethnography, sociology, linguistics and related subjects. Compiled by Ruth Jones. London, the Institute, 1958-.

———————**African abstracts:** a quarterly review of ethnographic, social and linguistic studies appearing in current periodicals. London, the Institute, 1950-. 42s. p.a.

See entry in v. 1 of Guide to reference material (2nd ed. 1966-) *at 572.9(6):016.*

908 (6):016
LONDON. UNIVERSITY. SCHOOL OF ORIENTAL AND AFRICAN STUDIES. Library Catalogue. Boston, Mass., G. K. Hall, 1963. 28v. $1600.

See entry at 908 (5/6):016.

The School of Oriental and African Studies' *Index Africanus* is in preparation.

908(6):016
STANDING CONFERENCE ON LIBRARY MATERIALS ON AFRICA. United Kingdom publications and theses on Africa, 1963-. Cambridge, Heffer, 1966-. Annual. ea. 25s.

The 1963 volume contains 1,260 numbered items (books, periodical articles, some newspaper articles and references in Hansard). Theses are listed separately (p. 83-88). Arrangement of entries in the main sequence is A-Z by countries ('Commonwealth' appears between 'Chad' and 'Congo'), following a general section. Index of authors.

908 (6):016
UNITED STATES. DEPARTMENT OF THE ARMY. Heaquarters. **Africa, its problems and prospects:** a bibliographic survey. Washington, 1962. vi, 197p. fldg. map. (Rev. ed. 1967. 226p.).

More than 1,000 annotated entries. Six sections: 1. Strategic implications of environment—2. The spectrum of Africa: the past and present—3. Regional Africa—4. Africa by country and territory (p. 81-154)—5. Source materials (p. 155-70)—6. Appendixes (political divisions; chronology; etc.). Covers material up to 1962, including periodical articles. No index.

908 (6):016:016
GARLING, A., *comp.* **Bibliography of African bibliographies.** Cambridge, African Studies Centre, 1968. 13p. Mimeographed. 7s. 6d.

About 900 items, with locations in 7 Cambridge libraries. Arranged by regions and their countries. States number of entries in each bibliography.

Noted: International Conference on African bibliography. *Survey of current bibliographical services on Africa* (London, International African Institute, 1967. [133]p.).

908 (6):016:016
TAYLOR, A. V. African studies research: a brief guide to selected bibliographies and other sources for African studies. [Preliminary ed.]. Bloomington, Indiana Univ., African Studies Program, 1964. n.p.

A valuable select list in five parts: 1. Basic bibliographies and general works of reference—2. Special bibliographies—3. List of works, by countries—4. List of works, by subjects—5. Guide to bibliographical archives and special collections. This bibliography is preliminary to one in preparation by Indiana Univ. Press.

908 (6) (02)
JUNOD, V. I., and **RESNICK, I. N.,** *ed.* **The handbook of Africa.** New York, New York Univ. Press, 1963. 472p. tables, maps. $10.

A compendium that aims "to provide comparable factual information on each of the fifty-odd political units of Africa, and to provide basic source material by a thorough process of footnoting. No attempt is made either to interpret or analyze the data" (*Introduction*). Countries are arranged A-Z, with notes and references. It claims to give as complete a factual picture of the social, political and economic life of those countries as possible, high lighting gaps, weakness and uncertainty in the information now available. Appendices: 1. Colonial policies in Africa—2. Regional groupings—3. Metropolitan aid to Africa—4. British and French trade and marketing systems—5. Tables of measures and currency, No index.

Whereas Junod and Resnick is a compendium of basic data for the scholar, *Africa: a handbook to the continent,* edited by C. Legum (2nd rev. and enl. ed. New York, Praeger, 1965. xii, 558p. illus., maps. 126s.) is a collection of essays and commentary by more than 40 specialists for the ordinary reader. It claims to lie "between Lord Hailey's invaluable *African survey* (written by an expert for experts) and John Gunther's, now alas outdated, *Inside Africa* (written by a non-expert for non-experts" (*Preface*). The section on Togo (p. 264-6) has divisions: General—Political development—Economic situation—Basic information. In most cases short bibliographies are appended (*e.g.*, South Africa: 49 items). Analytical index. First published 1963.

908 (6) (02)

Meyers Handbuch über Afrika. Hrsg. und bearb. von der Fachredaktion der Bibliographischen Instituts. Mannheim, Bibliographisches Institut, 1962. 779p. illus., tables, maps. 779p. 42*s.*

The main part (p. 11-512) consists of a general survey (natural features, native and non-native population, history, industry, transport, education and science). 'Länderlexikon' (p. 513-703) gives systematic data on 53 countries and areas (*e.g.*, Libya: area and population; natural features; economy; transport; state and administration; education and religion; history). Biographies ("Führende Männer), with portraits, p. 700-37. Bibliography, p. 738-45, systematically arranged, like the text, and mainly general surveys. Index, p. 747-79.

Die Länder Afrikas (Bonn, Schroeder, for Deutsche Afrika-Gesellschaft, 1958-) is a series of regional monographs, particularly valuable on small African countries on which literature is at present meagre. Nearly 30 titles, ranging in length from 78p. (*Uganda*) to 304p. (*Nigeria*). The monograph on South Africa is in its 2nd ed. Each is by a specialist and includes statistical tables, folding maps, bibliography and index. Quality varies. Reviewed in *Geographical journal*, v. 133, pt. 1, March 1967, p. 85-86.

908 (6):026/027

"Collections of Africana". In *Unesco bulletin for libraries*, v. 15, no. 5, September-October, 1961, item 356; v. 16, no. 1, January/February 1962, item 53; v. 17, no. 2, March/April 1963, item 139; v. 18, no. 4, July/August 1964, item 263.

A far from complete descriptive list of some libraries or other institutions which have important collections of Africana. The United Kingdom is represented only by the London School of Economics. Details: name and address; size of collections on African subjects; special subject field covered; bibliographical publications, if any; any special projects in progress or planned; facilities (inter-library lending, etc.).
See also entry at 908(6):016.

908 (6):026/027 (410)

COLLISON, R. L. W., *comp.* **The SCOLMA directory of libraries and special collections on Africa.** 2nd ed. London, Crosby Lockwood, 1967. [iv], 92p. 35*s.*

First published 1963.
SCOLMA is The Standing Conference on Library Materials on Africa. 160 numbered entries for libraries and collections in the British Isles (including Eire), arranged under towns A-Z.

Data: address; technical services; publications; availability; hours; description of libraries or stock. Prefatory notes (p. 1-4) on SCOLMA and its publications, 'Other projects' and 'Area specialisation project' (June 1966). Excellent index of subjects and titles of publications.

908 (6):026/027 (73)

DUIGNAN, P. Handbook of American resources for African studies. Stanford, Cal., Stanford Univ.: Hoover Institution on War, Revolution and Peace, 1967. xiv, 218p.

Notes on 95 library and manuscript collections, 108 church and missionary libraries and archives, 95 art and ethnographic collections, 26 private U.S. collectors and 4 business archives. Lengthy entries in some cases (*e.g.*, Peabody Museum, p. 110-6). Index of names of bodies, countries, subjects, etc.

908 (6):043

STANDING CONFERENCE ON LIBRARY MATERIALS ON AFRICA. Theses on Africa accepted by universities in the United Kingdom and Ireland. Cambridge, Heffer, 1964. 74p. 13*s.* 6*d.*

1,142 theses, presented in 1920-62. Arranged by region and country, with broad subject divisions, where applicable. Notes on availability of items. Continued in SCOLMA's *United Kingdom publications and theses on Africa, 1963-* (q.v.).

Library of Congress. African Section. *A list of American doctoral dissertations on Africa* (Washington, Library of Congress, 1962. 69p.) is an author list of more than 700 items, with subject index.

Boston University Libraries' *List of French doctoral dissertations on Africa, 1884-1961* (Boston, Mass., G. K. Hall, 1966. 336p. $19 (U.S.); $20.90 (outside U.S.) records 2,918 titles, arranged by country or area; author and subject index.

A comparable German list is J. Koehler's *Deutsche Dissertationen über Afrika. Ein Verzeichnis für die Jahre 1918-1959.* Mannheim, Bibliographisches Institut. Bonn, Schroeder, 1962. DM.14).

908 (6) (05):016

CONOVER, H., *comp.* **Serials for African studies.** Washington, General Reference and Bibliography Division, Reference Department, Library of Congress, 1961. viii, 163p. $1.

Expansion of the list of periodicals in *Research and information on Africa: continuing sources* (1954) (see at 908 (6):016).
2,082 numbered entries, arranged A-Z under latest form of title. Omits official reports of departments and certain other categories. Locations in 43 U.S. libraries. Frequency, earlier title(s), and the occurrence of illustrations, maps, etc., are noted in entries. Not by any means confined to serials published in African countries. Bibliographical sources (annotated), p. 145-7; General index, p. 149-54; Index of organizations, p. 155-63.

908 (6) (05):016
DUIGNAN, P., and GLAZIER, K. M., *comp.* **A checklist of serials for African studies.** Stanford, Cal., Hoover Institution on War, Revolution and Peace, Stanford Univ., 1963. vi, 104p. (Hoover Institution. Bibliographical series, 13). $3.

1,417 numbered items, in two parts: 1. African serials (items 1-1221)—2. African newspapers (items 1222-1417). Includes monographic series, some annual reports of institutions, yearbooks and directories, ephemeral publications, newsletters, bulletins, missionary magazines, statistical journals, government debates and gazetteers. Excludes most government departmental annual reports, geological and meteorological series, and book or pamphlet series. Gives dates of holdings of the various libraries of Stanford University. Modelled on Conover's *Serials for African studies* (q.v.), but entries are less detailed, even if more up to date.

908 (6):05/A
Africa: journal of the International African Institute. London, Oxford Univ. Press, 1928-. v. 1, no. 1-. Quarterly. ea. 15*s.*; 45*s.* p.a.

V. 37, no. 2, April 1967 contains four articles, 'Notes and news', signed reviews of 22 books (p. 229-48) and 'Bibliography of current publications' (p. 249-60). The bibliography comprises *c.* 450 items (mainly periodical articles) in 11 sections: 1. General. Miscellaneous—2. Ethnography. Anthropology. Sociology—3. History. Archaeology—4. Religion. Philosophy. Cosmology. Witchcraft—5(a). Language. Linguistics. 5(b). Books in African languages—6. Economic and social studies. Development—7. Government. Administration. Political studies—8. Law—9. Education—10. Arts. Literature. Folklore—11. Health. Medicine. Nutrition.
Offprints of 'Notes and news' and the 'Bibliography', in a form suitable for filing and classification, are available, each at 10*s.* p.a.

908 (6) (058)
Owen's Commerce & travel & international register . . . : Africa, Middle East & Far East, with international trade lists . . . London, Owen's Commerce & Travel, Ltd., 1954-. illus., maps. Annual. (1966. 72*s.* 6*d.*).

See entry at 38 (058.1) (6).

908 (6):061
INSTITUT AFRICAIN DE GENÈVE. Institut Universitaire des Hautes Études Internationales. **Répertoire des principales institutions s'intéressant à l'Afrique Noire.** Geneva, the Institute, 1964. v.p. Loose-leaf.

A directory of some 200 archival collections, libraries, information centres, scientific associations and the like concerned with tropical Africa, in Europe and the U.S.

908 (6 = 40) (02)
L'Afrique d'expression française. D.O.M. et T.O.M. de la République Française. 6. éd. Paris, Europe/France Outremer, 1966. 264p. illus., tables, maps. (1967. 42F.; 44F.).

Forms no. 435, April 1966 issue of *Europe/ France Outremer,* and is published annually.
Data on 21 independent states of Africa, arranged A-Z (Algeria-Tunisia). In each case: political and administrative organisation; diplomatic corps; finance and economy; trade; development plans; social organisation; miscellaneous information, including short bibliography. Statistical data included.
The monthly *Europe/France Outremer* (1923-. 90F (France), 100F (foreign) p.a.), itself a handy illustrated record of progress in French-speaking Africa, has special issues on specific countries (*e.g.,* no. 436, May 1966: *Cameroun;* no. 437, June 1966: *Algérie un an après*; no. 438-439, July/August 1966: *Madagascar*).

North Africa

908 (61) (058)
Annuaire de l'Afrique du nord. Algérie—Maroc —Tunisie—Libye. Tome 1-: 1962-. Aix en Provence, Centre de Recherche sur l'Afrique Mediterranéenne, 1964-. maps. Annual. (1963 v., published 1965. 160*s.*).

Includes selected documents and a bibliography of books and articles published during the year. The 1964 v. (1966) has contents: Études — Chroniques — Chronologie — Document — Chronique scientifique — Comptes rendus — Bibliographie—Index—Tables de matières. The 1965 v. has an extensive 'Bibliographie critique' (p. 841-1056) in two sequences,—authors (A-Z) and systematic (6 classes with sub-divisions), with a similarly arranged Arabic section (p. 1019-56). Covers books and periodical articles, political, military, economic, educational, cultural, etc. aspects, plus societies.

Libya

908 (612):016
HILL, R. W. A bibliography of Libya. Durham, Durham Colleges in the Univ. of Durham, Department of Geography, 1959. 100p.

A list of some 2,000 books and periodical articles, to 1957. Five sections: A, Bibliographies, periodicals and maps; B, General studies; C, Environment studies; D, Historical and political studies; E, Human and economic studies. 43 subsections. United Nations and British government publications are included. Italian sources are well represented. No index.

908 (612):026/027
WARD, P., *ed.* **A survey of Libyan bibliographical sources.** [?], the Author, 1964. iii, 20p. Mimeographed.

Sponsored by the Oasis Oil Co. of Libya.
Describes in some detail facilities offered by libraries, archives and the sources of information in Libya, for the research worker, professional librarian and general reader (*Introduction*). The survey covers embassies, universities, oil companies and so on (p. 1-16). Details of facilities offered include publications. Appendices: 1. Material on Libya—2. Arranging Libyan material —3. Castle museums—4. Periodicals in Libya— 5. Private libraries—6. Bookshops.

United Arab Republic (Egypt)

908 (621/623):016

MAUNIER, R. Bibliographie économique, juridique et sociale de l'Égypte moderne (1798-1916). Cairo, Société Sultanieh d'Économie Publique, 1918. xxxii, 372p. 6,695 entries.

908 (621/623):016

PRATT, I. Modern Egypt: a list of references to materials in New York Public Library, 1929. v, 320p. 6,000 entries. Reprint in preparation.

908 (621/623) (058)

UNITED ARAB REPUBLIC. The year book. [Cairo, U.A.R., Director General, Information Department.] illus., maps. Annual.

Originally as *The U.A.R. yearbook*, 1959. As from the 1962 ed. confined to Egypt only.
The 1964 ed. has 28 sections (*e.g.*, 1. The land the people—2. Internal policy—3. Foreign policy . . . 13. Scientific research . . . 19. Social welfare . . . 25. The Suez Canal . . . 28. The Qaltara Depression). Statistics up to 1963. Pocket-sized.

Sudan

908 (624):016

El NASRI, A. R., *comp.* **A bibliography of the Sudan, 1938-1958.** [London?], Oxford Univ. Press, for Univ. of Khartum, 1962. x, 171p. 35s.

Continues R. H. Hill's *A bibliography of the Anglo-Egyptian Sudan* (1939). 2,763 items, the largest section being on Government and politics. Agriculture, anthropology, economics, history, language and literature, medicine also figure. The compiler is librarian of the Univ. of Khartum.
Supplemented by "Sudan bibliography, 1959-1963", by A. Ibrahim and A. R. El Nasri, in *Sudan notes and records*, v. 46, 1965, p. 130-66.

908 (624):016

HILL, R. L. A bibliography of the Anglo-Egyptian Sudan, from the earliest times to 1937. London, Oxford Univ. Press, 1939. 213p. 20s.

About 5,000 items, on all aspects of knowledge. History, p. 113-52, includes Biography and Genealogy, and is arranged under periods. Indexes of persons and subjects.

908 (624) (058)

Sudan almanac, 1965-66 [: an official handbook]. Compiled by the Central Office of Information, Republic of the Sudan. Khartoum, Government Printing Office, 1965-66. 313p. chart, map. 2s.

First published 1948. Biennial (irregular).
The 1965-66 issue has 26 sections, including 3. History and ethnography—4. Religion—5. Geology, geography and climate—6. The Nile—7. Executive and legislature—8. Local government . . . 16. Wild life—17. Education . . . 19. Transport . . . 22. Press and publications (including newspapers and magazines) . . . 25. Sports—26. Weights, measures and money conversion tables.

Ethiopia

908 (63):016

MATTHEWS, D. G., *comp.* **A current bibliography on Ethiopian affairs:** a select biblio-

graphy from 1950-1964. Washington, African Bibliographic Center, [1965]. iii, 46p.

Based on *Ethiopia, 1950-1962,* compiled by D. G. Matthews in early 1963, and *Ethiopian survey* (January 1964), compiled by A. P. Delaney, which supplements it.
Also noted: Matthews, D. G. *Ethiopian culture: a bibliographic research guide* (Washington, African Bibliographic Center, 1966. 17p. $4).

Morocco

908 (64):016

Informations bibliographiques marocaines. Rabat, Bibliothèque Générale et Archives, [?]-. 24 p.a. *Gratis.*

About 3,000 systematically arranged items p.a. on political administrative and social aspects of Morocco and North Africa. Includes periodical articles and documents.

Africa South of the Sahara

908 (66/69):016

CARTRY, M., with **CHARLES, B. L'Afrique au sud du Sahara: guide de recherches.** Paris, Fondation Nationale des Sciences Politiques, 1963. 85 l. Mimeographed.

About 950 entries for books and periodical articles, mostly in French. Parts: 1. Les ouvrages fournissant des données de base et de bibliographie (généralités; cadre géographique; donnés demographiques; donnés économiques; histoire de l'Afrique Noire; sociétés et civilisations)—2. Contexte traditionnel et changements sociaux—3. La vie politique, partis et effectifs—4. Idéologies. Some annotations, especially for items in part 1; brief introductions under headings.

Afrika-Schrifttum. Literature on Africa. Études sur l'Afrique. Bibliographie deutschsprachiger wissenschaftlichen veröffentlichungen über Afrika südlich der Sahara (Wiesbaden, Steiner, 1966-. v. 1-.) is devoted to German-language material, but on Africa south of the Sahara. Covers geography, ethnology, linguistics, tropical medicine, geology and botany. V. 1 (688p.) refers to c. 650 journals. Reviewed in the *Geographical journal*, v. 133, pt. 3, September 1967, p. 375-6.

The CARDAN card service (1966-), joint venture of the Centre of African Studies, Cambridge (CAS) and the Centre d'Analyse et de Recherches Documentaires pour l'Afrique Noire, Paris (CARDAN), covers current literature in the social sciences on Black Africa south of the Sahara. Each subscriber receives c. 7,000 cards p.a. and a cumulative index. Three types of card are distributed: (1) cards with abstracts (A.C.; quarterly; £11 p.a.), covering periodical articles, symposia, mimeographed material and conference proceedings; (2) index cards (D.C.; quarterly; £11 p.a.) for periodical articles that are too short or ephemeral to merit abstracting; (3) cards for books and other major works (B.C.; annual). The annual cumulative subject index embraces all three categories. It is hoped to extend coverage beyond European languages to Chinese and Japanese. (See SCOLMA. *Library materials on Africa*, v. 5, no. 2, November 1967, p. 52-53).

908 (66/69):016
CONOVER, H. F., *comp.* **Africa south of the Sahara: a selected, annotated list of writings.** Washington, General Reference and Bibliography Division, Reference Department, Library of Congress, 1963. vi, 354p. $2.25.

Replaces two earlier Library of Congress bibliographies: *Introduction to Africa* (1952) and *Africa south of the Sahara . . . 1951-56* (1957). Covers all Africa except Mediterranean-littoral countries (Morocco, Algeria, Tunisia, Libya, Egypt) and includes the Sudan, Ethiopia and Somalia (previously in *North and Northeast Africa, 1951-1957;* compiled by H. F. Conover (1957. v, 182p.).

2,173 numbered entries, mostly for English-language material; excellent evaluative annotations have references to a further 1,000 items. Main sections: General (nos. 1-478)—West Africa—French-speaking Africa (general)—Former French West Africa—East Africa—Rhodesia and Nyasaland (Federation)—South Africa—Congo (Leopoldville) — Portuguese Africa — Spanish Guinea. The 'Congo (Leopoldville)' section has sub-divisions: Bibliography—General—History—Politics—Economics (including population)—Social sciences—Ethnology and linguistics—Missions, education and arts. Subject, locality, author and anonymous title index. "The best single-volume bibliography available" (Bloomfield, B. C., and McKee, M. *Africa in the contemporary world* (1967), p. 6).

908 (66/69):016
GLAZIER, K. M. Africa south of the Sahara: a select and annotated bibliography, 1958-1963. Stanford, Stanford Univ., Hoover Institution on War, Revolution and Peace, 1964. iv, 65p. $1.50.

Describes 150 "important works published or revised during the last few years" (*Preface*). Selection is based on leading reviews, which are cited in each case. Limited to books in English or translated, and still in print. Arranged by authors, A-Z. Title and subject indexes.

908 (66/69):016
HOOVER INSTITUTION ON WAR, REVOLUTION AND PEACE. United States and Canadian publications on Africa. 1961-. Stanford, the Institution, Stanford Univ., 1963-. Annual (1964 v. 1967). (Hoover Institution. Bibliographical series).

Preceded by Library of Congress, General Reference and Bibliography Division. *United States and Canadian publications on Africa in 1960* (1963).
Lists books, pamphlets and periodical articles on Africa south of the Sahara.

908 (66/69):016
LANDSKRON, W. A. Official serial publications relating to economic development in Africa south of the Sahara: a preliminary list of English-language publications. Cambridge, Mass., Center for International Studies, Massachusetts Institute of Technology, 1961. 44 l.

Essentially a list of latest issues of annual or quarterly reports (1958-60) published in 28 African states and areas by government or government-sponsored bodies.

908 (66/69):016
NORTHWESTERN UNIVERSITY, Evanston, Ill. Library. **Catalog of the African Collection** of the Northwestern University Library. Boston, Mass., G. K. Hall, 1963. 2v. $120.

28,300 cards, photolithographically reproduced on 1,350 pages. Author catalogue (with entries for serials), primarily on Africa south of the Sahara, with special stress on the Congo and former British and German colonies. Fields covered range from Anthropology, Linguistics and History to Economics, Education and Trade to Health and Demography.

908 (66/69):016
United States and Canadian publications on Africa in 1960. Washington, Library of Congress, 1962; 1961-. Stanford, Cal., Hoover Institution, Stanford Univ., 1963-. Annual. (1963 v. (1964). 25s.).

Excludes Morocco, Algeria, Tunisia, Libya and Egypt. Pt. 1, Works on Africa in general; pt. 2, Works dealing with specific regions. The 1963 v. covers 1,572 numbered items (books and periodical articles). No annotations. Author index.

908 (66/69):016:016
SOUTH AFRICAN PUBLIC LIBRARY, Cape Town. **A bibliography of African bibliographies covering territories south of the Sahara.** 4th ed. (rev. to November 1960). Cape Town, 1961. iv, 79p. (Grey bibliographies, no. 7). 21s.

First published in *South African libraries,* October 1942 and January 1943.
About 1,100 items, adding more than 350 items and omitting a very few superseded items. Entries are closely classified by U.D.C. and include a number of analyticals (*e.g.*, "hidden" bibliographies) and theses. Occasional notes. Items in Africaans, German, Portuguese, etc., are included.
Addenda in the *Quarterly bulletin of the South African Library.* A suppement to the 4th ed. is in preparation.

908 (66/69) (02)
HAILEY, M., *1st baron Hailey.* **An African survey,** revised 1956: a study of problems arising in Africa south of the Sahara. Issued under the auspices of the Royal Institute of International Affairs. London, Oxford Univ. Press, 1957. xxvi, [2], 1676p. maps. 168s.

First published 1938.
24 chapters: 1. The physical background—2. The African peoples—3. The African languages—4. Population records—5. Political and social objectives—6. Systems of government—7. The non-European immigrant communities—8. The administration of African affairs—9. Law and justice—10. Direct taxation—11. The land—12. Agriculture and animal husbandry—13. Forests—14. Water supply and irrigation—15. Soil conservation—16. Health—17. Education and cultural agencies—18. Economic development in

Africa—19. Projects of economic development—20. The problems of labour—21. Co-operative institutions—22. Minerals and mines—23. Transport and communications—24. The organisation of research. Numerous footnote references. The encyclopaedic treatment is enhanced by a detailed analytical index (p. 1617-76). 11 maps. "Perhaps the most important reference book (and certainly the best-known) published on Africa" (Bloomfield, B. C., and McKee, M. *Africa in the contemporary world,* p. 7).

According to H. F. Conover (*Africa south of the Sahara* (1963), p. 4), a new edition of the *Survey* was in progress in 1962.

A complementary survey, although somewhat condensed, is *Tropical Africa,* by George H. T. Kimble (New York, Twentieth Century Fund, 1960, 2v. illus., maps. $15). v. 1: *Land and livelihood;* v. 2: *Society and polity.* "Kimble's detachment . . . enables him to take broader sweeps if not always to probe as deeply" (*International affairs,* v. 37, no. 2, April 1961, p. 253). Consists of working papers by 40 contributors. Reviewed in *Geographical review,* v. 51, no. 3, July 1961, p. 447-9.

West Africa

908 (66):016

JOUCLA, E. A. **Bibliographie de l'Afrique occidentale française.** [2. éd.]. Paris, Société d'Éditions Géographiques, Maritimes et Coloniales, 1937. 2, 704p.

First published 1912.
Covers books, papers, official documents, periodicals, maps and charts. An author list, with several subject indexes.

908 (66):016:016

RYDINGS, H. A. **The bibliographies of West Africa.** Ibadan, Nigeria, Ibadan Univ. Press on behalf of the West African Library Association, 1961. 36p. tables. 5s.

50 bibliographies of West Africa, presented first in a running commentary, with excellent critical annotations, and then in tabulated, summary form (Item no.; Country, etc.; Author, etc.; Period covered; No. of entries; Arrangement; Scope and limitations; Indexes). Includes general bibliographies of Africa and serial bibliographies. Countries: Mauritania, Senegal, French Sudan, French Niger, Ivory Coast, Dahomey, Portuguese Guinea, Liberia, Gambia, Sierra Leone, Ghana, Nigeria. Author index.

908 (66) (058)

West African annual, 1964/65. 2nd ed. Edited by L. K. Jakande. Lagos, John West Publications, Ltd., 1964. xv, 337p. maps. 63s.

First published 1962.
A compendium of information on 15 countries, A-Z (Cameroun—Upper Volta), preceded by a general survey of West Africa. No bibliographies or index; statistics outdated (1959 figures).
The annual *Guid' Ouest Africain,* 1948- (Paris, Diloutremer; Dakar, Agence de Distribution de Presse) covers Senegal, Mauritania, Mali, Ivory Coast, Haute-Volta, Niger, Dahomey, Togo and

Guinea, and includes directory information, maps and town plans.
Le Guid' Cameroun and *Le Guid' Afrique Equatoriale* are also in the Les guides d'outremer series.

French Sahara

908 (661):016

BLAUDIN DE THÉ, C., and MOULIAS, -. **Essai de bibliographie du Sahara français** et des régions avoisinantes. 2. éd. Paris, Arts et Métiers Graphiques, 1960. 259p.

First published 1959.
Published with the co-operation of Organisation Commune des Régions Sahariennes. Part 1, *Les territoires du sud de l'Algérie . . . ,* by Lieut. Moulias, revised and completed by Lieut. Thinières, has entries 1-2,372 in 16 sections. Part 2, by C. Blaudin de Thé, takes the title of the work and has entries 2373-9301, in 20 sections (1. Voyages et explorateurs—2. Sciences naturelles—3. Sciences humaines—4. Varia . . . 17. Voies et moyens de communications—18. Organisations et mise en valeur du Sahara). Author index; list of 89 French journals cited.

Mali

908 (662):016

BRASSEUR, P. **Bibliographie générale du Mali** (anciens Soudan français et Haut-Sénégal-Niger). Dakar, Institut Français d'Afrique Noire (IFAN), 1964. 461p. map. (Institut Français d'Afrique Noire, Catalogues et documents. 16). 115s.

4,902 numbered items, often annotated. Includes many references to periodical articles. 6 main sections: 1. Sources (cartes; périodiques; bibliographies—sources manuscrites; sources imprimées)—2. Le Soudan—3. Milieu physique—4. Milieu humain—5. Mise en valeur—6. Biographies (nos. 4651-4873). Author, locality and subject (non-analytical) index.

Noted: "Mali: a bibliographical introduction", by C. H. Cutter, in *African studies bulletin,* v. 9, no. 3, December 1966, p. 74-87.

Sierra Leone

908 (664):016

LUKE, H. C. **A bibliography of Sierra Leone,** preceded by an essay on the origin, character and peoples of the colony and protectorate. 2nd ed. London, Oxford Univ. Press, 1925. [viii], 230p.

First published 1910.
1,103 items. An authoritative bibliography, the author being Colonial Secretary at the time.

Gambia

908 (665.1):016

GAMBLE, D. P. **Bibliography of the Gambia.** Bathurst, Government Printer, 1967. xi, 154p. 20s.

Guinea

908 (665.2):016

ORGANISATION FOR ECONOMIC CO-OPERA-TION AND DEVELOPMENT. Development Centre. **Bibliographie sur la Guinée** . . . Paris, O.E.C.D., 1965. [i], iii, 46 l. Mimeographed. *Gratis.*

Lists *c.* 400 items. Sections: Reference works (including analyticals, *e.g.,* for *Worldmark encyclopedia*)—General—Regional geography—Socio-cultural geography — History — Sociology — Political science—Law. Public administration—Foreign relations—Economics. Economic conditions—Development plans—Housing—Banking. Money. Credit—Commerce. Industry—Agriculture. Fisheries—Labour—Demography—Education—Guinean periodicals (21 titles). Covers books, official publications and periodical articles. Occasional explanations of titles. No index or annotations.

Liberia

908 (666.2):016

SOLOMON, M. D., and **D'AZEVEDO, W. L.,** *comp.* **A general bibliography of the Republic of Liberia.** Evanston, Ill., Northwestern Univ., 1962. 68p.

More than 2,000 unannotated entries for books and periodical articles. Four sections: individual authors; anonymous title or corporate author entries; official documents; maps, etc.

908 (666.2) (058)

The Liberian yearbook for 1956-. [Monrovia], 'Liberian Review', [1955?]-. tables. Annual.

The 1962 ed. (272p.) has 21 chapters (1. The land and people—2. Government and administration—3. The interior administration . . . 7. Government finance—8. Projects in education . . . 11. Public utilities—12. Agriculture and forestry . . . 17. Social organizations. Clubs & associations . . . 19. Religious organizations—20. The press & radio broadcasting—21. Bibliography on Liberia (p. 268-72), including official publications.

Ivory Coast

908 (666.8):016

ORGANISATION FOR ECONOMIC CO-OPERA-TION AND DEVELOPMENT. Development Centre. **Essai d'une bibliographie sur la Côte d'Ivoire.** Paris, O.E.C.D., 1964. [i], iv, 122 l. Mimeographed. *Gratis.*

1. Monographs (1.1: Authors, A-Z—1.2: Titles (*i.e.,* anonymous items), A-Z)—2. Articles (similarly arranged). About 1,000 items. Annexes include list of libraries and books consulted (p. 110); list of periodicals cited; and list of French organisations that are working or have operated in the Ivory Coast. No index or annotations.

Ghana

908 (667):016

JOHNSON, A. F., *comp.* **A bibliography of Ghana, 1930-1961.** London, published for the Ghana Library Board by Longmans, 1964. xiii, 210p. 42*s.*

Is in some respects a continuation of A. W. Cardinall's standard work, *A bibliography of the Gold Coast* (Accra, Government Printer, [1932]. xxiii, 384p.).

2,608 numbered items (no annotations) under 44 headings (*e.g.,* Bibliographies—Newspapers—Directories—Geography—Maps—Geology and climate . . . History—Politics and government: 20th century . . . Economics, trade and finance . . . Poetry—Plays—Government publications (Gold Coast; Ghana; Great Britain)). Continued by bibliographies produced by the Padmore Library, Accra.

Bibliography of Ghana, 1957-1964, compiled by G. M. Pitcher (Kumasi, the Library, Kwame Nkrumah Univ. of Science and Technology, 1962. [iii], 111p. 18*s.*) had a 1st ed. in 1960; it then covered 1957-1959. About 700 briefly annotated entries for books and periodical articles under 26 headings. Author and anonymous title index.

Noted: *The culture of Ghana: a bibliography*; compiled by E. Y. Amedekey (London, Library Association, 1966. xiv, 634p. Thesis.

908 (667) (058)

Ghana year book. 1960-. Accra, Ghana Graphic Co. (subsequently 'Daily Graphic'), [1960?]-. Annual.

Contents includes 'Ghana at a glance'; National assembly; list of officials; directory of banks, colleges and schools; diplomatic missions and representatives; trade directory (on yellow-tinted paper); organisations; personalities (1966 ed., p. 191-253). Index; no list of contents.

Nigeria

908 (669):016

HARRIS, W. J., *comp.* **Books about Nigeria:** a select reading list. 3rd ed. Ibadan, Univ. Press, 1962. 46p. (4th ed. 1963. 52p. 5*s.*).

First published 1959.
The 3rd ed. lists *c.* 350 items, with brief annotations. 15 sections: 1. Reference works—2. Periodicals—3. Natural history—4. Education—5. Food and health . . . 8. Biography and travel . . . 11. Law—12. Economics—13. Fine arts—14. Literature—15. Official publications. Author and name index.

908 (669):016:016

DIPEOLU, J. O. Bibliographical sources for Nigerian studies. Evanston, Ill., Northwestern Univ. Press, 1966. 26p.

About 130 annotated entries. Sections: General bibliographies — Geography — Agriculture and Botany—Anthropology, Ethnology & Sociology—Education—History, Politics and Government—Economics—Fine arts—Language and Literature—Government publications—Addenda.

908 (669) (02)

The Nigeria handbook. London, Crown Agents for the Colonies, for the Government of Nigeria; Lagos, Government Printer, 1953. x, 339p. illus., maps.

The first post-war official handbook to Nigeria. Excellent and detailed, covering cultural as well as administrative aspects. Appendix of official statistics and information; bibliography, p. 272-88.

The *Nigeria year-book* (Lagos, Nigerian Printing & Publishing Co.) (1963. 2*s.* 6*d.*), includes a trades directory.

Equatorial Africa

908 (67):016

BOGAERT, J. **Sciences humaines en Afrique noire: guide bibliographique (1945-1965).** Brussels, Centre de Documentation Économique et Sociale Africaine (CEDESA), 1966. x, 226p. Belg. fr. 400.

Published with the support of the Ministère de l'Education Nationale et de la Culture.

Two parts, each with sub-divisions: 1. Bibliographies générales et ouvrages généraux de référence et d'information—2. Bibliographies specialisées et ouvrages par matières. 1,494 numbered and annotated items, plus interpolations. A selection, based on contributions by libraries, especially the Bibliothèque de l'Université à Kinshasa (Congo). Author, geographical and subject indexes. List of works consulted, p. ix-x. Well produced.

908 (67):016

INTERNATIONAL AFRICAN INSTITUTE. **Select annotated bibliography of tropical Africa.** New York, Twentieth Century Fund, 1956. [511p.]. Mimeographed.

About 3,000 entries, usually annotated. 1. Geography—2. Ethnography—3. Sociology and linguistics—4. Administration and government—5. Economics—6. Education—7. Missions—8. Health. Covers books and articles. No index.

Congo

908 (675):016

HEYSE, T. **Bibliographie du Congo Belge et du Ruanda-Urundi** (1939-1951). Brussels, Camperhout, 1953. 2v. (Cahiers belges et congolais, no. 4-7, 9-12, 16-21).

The basic bibliography on the Congo. 854 pages in all, dealing with specific aspects, *e.g.,* geology and mines, agriculture, communications, economy, history, culture, etc.

Supplemented by *Documentation générale sur le Congo et le Ruanda-Urundi,* edited by T. Heyse and J. Berlage (Brussels, Camperhout, 1960. 95p.) (Cahiers belges et congolais no. 34).

T. Heyse's survey of bibliographies, general and special, appeared in *Archives, bibliothèques et musées de Belgique* (v. 31, no. 2, 1961, p. 107-14; v. 32, no. 2, 1962, p. 177-90. There is also his *Biographie et documentation générale sur le Congo* (Brussels, A.R.S.O.M., 1962. p. 48-56).

Études congolaises, v. 4, March 1963 (iii, 130p.) is devoted to "Bibliographie générale des articles et ouvrages politiques sur la République du Congo-Léopoldville" (1959-1962).

908 (675) (031)

Encyclopédie du Congo belge. Brussels, Éditions Bieleveld, [1950-53]. 3v. illus., diagrs., maps.

An encyclopaedic survey, by various contributors. Systematically arranged. V. 1 covers history, prehistory, peoples, geology, climate, soils, botany and agriculture; v. 2, forestry fauna, fishing, stockbreeding, minerals; v. 3, public health, agricultural diseases, applied entomology, economics and industry, transport, electricity, water supply, tourism, political administration and judiciary, finances, land tenure, mining, etc. Statistics are given up to 1948. A general index is also included in v. 3 (p. 847-60).

East Africa

908 (676) (058)

The Year book and guide to East Africa . . . : Kenya, Uganda, Tanganyika, Zanzibar, Portuguese East Africa, Mauritius, Seychelles, etc. London, Hale, 1950-. maps, plans. Annual. (1966. 12*s.* 6*d.*).

Published as part of the *South and East African year-book and guide,* 1901-49.

The first half (1965 ed., p. 19-172) provides basic data on each territory (history, administration, geography, climate; financial, production, trade and population statistics). The second half (p. 173-312) consists of travel sections, describing routes, and supported by maps, town plans and an atlas of 16 p. of coloured maps (Bartholomew). Advertisements included.

Southern Africa

908 (68) (03)

ROSENTHAL, E., *comp. and ed.* **Encyclopaedia of Southern Africa.** 3rd ed. London, Warne, 1965. viii, 628p. illus. pl., maps. 42*s.* (4th rev. ed. 1967. viii, 636p. 45*s.*).

First published 1961.

Covers the Republic of South Africa, Rhodesia, Zambia, Malawi, S.W. Africa, Mozambique, Basutoland, Swaziland and Bechuanaland. 23 main articles (on Afrikaans literature, Battles, Birds, Climate, Diamond industry, Geology, Insects, Plants, Rugby football, etc.) are signed. About 5,000 entries, including biographies (Smuts: 2½ cols.; Kruger: 2¾ cols.). No bibliographies. 10 colour plates (*e.g.,* of national and historical flags); 22 maps. Choice of persons for inclusion shows the affect of South Africa's apartheid policy, although some living non-whites are included. A mine of information at a popular level.

908 (68) (058)

The Year book and guide to Southern Africa . . . : Republic of South Africa, South West Africa, Rhodesia, Zambia, Malawi, etc. London, Hale, 1950-. illus., tables, maps. Annual. (1966. 15*s.*).

Published as part of the *South and East African year-book and guide, 1901-49.*

Coverage includes Basutoland, Bechuanaland, Swaziland and Southern Angola. The first half (1966 ed., p. 21-322) provides basic data on the administration and economy (including statistics) of each territory. The second half (p. 323-704) consists of 21 travel sections, describing routes and supported by maps, 19 town plans. Advertisements included.

As from 1967 the title will be *Guide to Southern Africa* (London, Hale. 21s.), with emphasis on the tourist rather than the immigrant viewpoint. Publication is to be twice yearly.

South Africa

908 (680):016
MENDELSSOHN, S. **Mendelssohn's South African bibliography** . . . With a descriptive introduction by I. D. Colvin. London, Kegan Paul, 1910. 2v. illus. (Facsimile ed. London, Holland Press. 1957).

An annotated catalogue, systematically arranged, of the Mendelssohn Library, and other works relating to South Africa prior to 1910, including official publications, periodical articles and maps.
"A revised edition which will include books published up to 1925 is being prepared at the South African Public Library" (Musiker, R. *Guide to South African reference books* (4th ed., 1965), p. 2).

908 (680):016
MUSIKER, R., *comp.* **Guide to South African reference books.** 4th rev. ed. Cape Town & Amsterdam, Balkema, 1965. x, 110p. R2.50.

First published 1951, edited by M. E. Green.
497 numbered, annotated entries. Aims "to include the more important reference books on South African topics" (*Introduction*), and with certain exceptions is limited to books published in the Republic of South Africa. Excludes subject bibliographies (for which see *A bibliography of African bibliographies* (at 908 (66/69):016:016). Scope of this edition has been extended to include South West Africa and the then Basutoland, Bechuanaland and Swaziland. The evaluative annotations carry references to further material. Author, anonymous title and subject index. A basic guide.
R. Musiker has also compiled a *Guide to sources of information in the humanities* [in Southern Africa] (Potchefstroom Univ. in collaboration with the South African Library Association, 1962. iv, 100, ii p.; *Supplement.* 1965. ii, 25p.).

908 (680) (058)
SOUTH AFRICA. BUREAU OF CENSUS AND STATISTICS. **Official year book of the Union,** and of Basutoland, Bechuanaland Protectorate and Swaziland. Pretoria, Government Printer, 1910-. Annual.

A valuable source of statistical and descriptive data. The latest year book, no. 30 (1960) is much reduced .It contains only descriptive material, and needs to be supplemented by the *Statistical year-book* ([1964]-. *See at 31 (680)*).

State of South Africa: pictorial, social, economic, financial, statistical (Johannesburg, Da Gama Publications, 1957-. illus., tables. Annual.) provides a handy and up-to-date comprehensive survey, with statistical tables and directory information, but is no real substitute for the pre-1960 *Official year book*. Analytical index.

Botswana, etc.

908 (681/688):016
CAPE TOWN. UNIVERSITY. SCHOOL OF LIBRARIANSHIP. **Bibliographical series.** Cape Town, School of Librarianship.

The series (listed in South African Public Library, Cape Town. *A bibliography of African bibliographies* (at 908 (66/69:016:016) includes area bibliographies:
Bibliography of Basutoland; compiled by J. Te Groen. 3rd ed. 1964. viii, 30p.
Bibliography of Bechuanaland; compiled by P. E. Stevens. 1949. v, 27p.
South West Africa [1919-1946]: a bibliography, by F. J. Welch. 1946. v, 33p.
South West Africa, 1946-1960: a selective bibliography, by E. J. Roukens de Lange. ix, 51p.
Swaziland: a bibliography, compiled by J. Arnhem. 1950 (reprinted 1963). ii, 20, [v]p.
Zululand and the Zulus: a bibliography, compiled by M. H. Galloway. 2nd imp. 1963. 12p.

South West Africa

908 (688)
SOUTH AFRICA. Republic. DEPARTMENT OF FOREIGN AFFAIRS. **South West Africa survey, 1967.** Pretoria, Government Printer, 1967. 190p. illus., tables, maps. R2.50 (overseas, R3.10.).

"Sets out primarily to describe South Africa's achievements in the Territory in the economic, social and political spheres" (*Introduction*). Sections: Geographical features—Population groups—Historical background . . . Government and administration—The economy of South West Africa (p. 59-107)—Education—Health—Housing. 4 annexures. Footnote references. South African viewpoint.

South West Africa; compiled by Theo de Jager; edited by Brigitte Klaas (Pretoria, State Library, 1964. [ii], 216p. R3) is a bibliography of more than 1,948 items, arranged under authors A-Z.

Central African Federation

908 (689):016
CENTRAL AFRICAN FEDERATION. National Archives, *comp.* **A select bibliography of recent publications** concerning the Federation of Rhodesia and Nyasaland. Salisbury, Federal Information Department, [1960]. 13p. *Gratis.*

Sections: General and descriptive (general; history and biography)—Politics and economics—Farming—Geology, flora and fauna—Anthropology and ethnography—Some newspapers. periodicals and journals—Official periodical publications—Government publications on special topics. About 250 entries, some of them very briefly annotated. No index.

908 (689) (02)
CENTRAL AFRICAN FEDERATION. **Handbook to the Federation of Rhodesia and Nyasaland.** Edited by W. V. Brelsford. London, Cassell, for the Federation Information Department, 1960. [v], 803p. illus., maps. tables. 63s.

A detailed compilation, with statistics to 1958. 45 chapters and appendices (including a list of newspapers and periodicals, and a list of learned societies).

Zambia
908 (689.4) (02)

ZAMBIA. Information Services. **A handbook to the Republic of Zambia.** Lusaka, Government Printer, [1965?]. vi, 153p. illus., map.

Sections: Introduction—The land and the people—Historical survey—Geography—Population—The government—Defence—Public finance — Customs and Excise — Immigration — The economy—Agriculture—Natural resources—Development of the community—Living conditions — Communications — Tourism — Miscellaneous —Statistical appendices (figures up to March 1965).

Malawi
908 (689.7):016

BROWN, E. E., and others. **A bibliography of Malawi.** New York, Syracuse Univ., 1965. v, 161p. (Syracuse Univ. Eastern African bibliographical series, no. 1). 36s.

Lists nearly 2,500 items. "We have endeavoured to make the bibliography as complete as possible" (*Preface*). Arranged under subjects A-Z (Agriculture—Zoology; Bibliography, p. 29-32; Biography, p. 33-37), preceded by a general section. Includes government publications.

Malagasy Republic
908 (691):016

GRANDIDIER, G. **Bibliographie de Madagascar.** Paris, Comité de Madagascar, etc., 1906-57. 4v.

1. *1500-1905.* 1905-6. 2v.
2. *1904-1933.* Paris, Société d'Éditions Géographiques, 1935.
3. *1934-1955.* Tananarivo, Institut de Recherche Sciéntifique, 1957.
23,003 items in author order. Author and subject indexes.

908 (691) (03)

RAJEMISA-RAOLISON, R. **Dictionnaire historique et géographique de Madagascar.** Fianarantsoa, [Librarie Ambozontany], 1966. 383p. maps.

Mauritius
908 (698.2):016

TOUSSAINT, A. and ADOLPHE, H. **Bibliography of Mauritius** (1502-1954), covering the printed record, manuscripts, archivalia and cartographic material. Port Louis, Esclapon, 1956. xvii [1], 884p.

8,865 items in 6 main groups, with chronological sub-division. Includes material on Mauritius printed abroad as well as Mauritius imprints and manuscripts. Index of authors and anonymous titles.

Annual supplements are issued regularly in the *Annual report* of the Archives Department. The annual reports of the Mauritius Institute also include a list of books and pamphlets relating to Mauritius acquired during the year.

AMERICAS
Canada
908 (71):016

CAMPBELL, H. C., ed. **How to find out about Canada.** Oxford, Pergamon Press, 1967. xiv, 248p. facsims. 30s.

A running commentary in 15 chapters (Dewey classification order): 1. General guides to Canadian achievement (bibliographies and catalogues; encyclopedic works; museums, libraries and archives; newspapers and general periodicals) —2. Canadian thinkers and religious writers—3. Canadian social and political structure—4. Canadian education—5. Canadian economics and business—6. Language—7. Science in Canada—8. Technology in Canada — 9. Medicine — 10. Canadian art—11. Sports and pastimes—12. Literature—13. Geography—14. Biography—15. History. Detailed index of subjects, authors and anonymous titles. 33 facsimile reproductions of pages. Not always up to date, but a valuable guide. Editor is Chief Librarian, Toronto Public Libraries.

908 (71):016

GARIGUE, P. **A bibliographical introduction to the study of French Canada.** Montreal, Department of Sociology and Anthropology, McGill Univ., 1956. 133p.

2,984 numbered items, covering books, periodical articles and theses. 9 sections (with subdivisions): 1. General historical studies—2. The human geography of French Canada—3. The social institutions—4. French-speaking groups outside the Province of Quebec—5. Social changes and social problems—6. Cultural characteristics—7. The educational system—8. Special problems in the study of French Canada—9. Bibliographies (nos. 2950-84). No index.

908 (71):016:016

TANGHE, R., comp. **Bibliography of Canadian bibliographies.** Toronto, published in association with the Bibliographical Society of Canada, Univ. of Toronto Press; London, Oxford Univ. Press, 1960. [6], 206p. $10; 80s.

1,665 numbered items. Sections: General bibliographies—Current bibliographies—Collective bibliographies—Author bibliographies—Newspapers. Reviews—Manuscripts—23 subject classes (in Dewey order). Occasional brief annotations; location of MSS. and microforms given. Index of compilers; index of authors. Added title-page in French.

——**Supplement, 1960 and 1961.** Toronto, Bibliographical Society of Canada, 1962. 24p.

——**Supplement, 1962 and 1963.** Toronto, Bibliographical Society of Canada, 1964. 27p.

908 (71) (031)

Encyclopedia Canadiana. [Rev. ed.]. Editor in chief, J. E. Robbins. Ottawa, the Canadiana Company, Ltd., 1965. 10v. illus., maps, plans. $149.50.

First published 1957-58. 10v.
About 700 contributors; longer articles are

signed. Articles are generally short. Selective biographies (*e.g.,* James Wolfe: 1½ cols., including one illus. and 5 items of bibliography). History of Canada is scattered by topic (*e.g.,* Church history; Economic history; Military history). Census figures for population of Provinces but population figures for individual places are largely lacking. Individual subjects (*e.g.,* Accidents, Accountancy) are considered within a Canadian framework. English-Canadian and French-Canadian topics have separate, parallel treatment when required, but always in English. Series of articles, *e.g.,* on immigrants ('Czech origin, people of', etc.). Valuable geographical articles (*e.g.,* 'Baffin Island': nearly 5p.; signed; 5 illus., 1 map, bibliography of 5 items, 4 of them periodical articles). Well illustrated (*c.* 1 per page); small maps (no scale); town plans. V. 10 includes an 'Atlas of Canada' by C. S. Hammond & Co.,— 32p. with an index gazetteer *c.* 8,000 entries. No general index; cross-references by means of asterisks. The layout suggests a popular rather than a scholarly work.

An older encyclopaedia is *The encyclopedia of Canada* (General editor, W. S. Wallace. Toronto, University Associates of Canada, 1935-37 (reprinted 1940, 1948). 6v. illus., maps. Newfoundland supplement. 149). This covers all aspects of Canada. Articles are not signed, although each v. has a short list of contributors of special articles. Some plates and occasional maps; no bibliographies. Bulked by large type and featherweight paper.

908 (71)(058)
CANADA. DOMINION BUREAU OF STATISTICS. The Canada year book, 1905-: official statistical annual of the resources, history, institutions and social and economic conditions of Canada. Ottawa, Queen's Printer, 1906-. tables, maps. Annual. (1966. $7.).

Also available in French. Published as the *Statistical abstract and record,* 1886-88; and *The statistical year-book of Canada,* 1890-1905. The 1966 v. has 27 chapters (27. 'Official sources of information and miscellaneous data'), a chronology of Canadian history from 1497, an index of special articles in previous editions, and a bibliography ('Books about Canada', p. 1121-36).

The Dominion Bureau's *Canada: the official handbook of present conditions and recent progress* is a popular illustrated annual (1930-). *Canada, one hundred, 1867-1967* (1967. vii, 501p. $2) is the enlarged centennial volume issued in place of the 1967 official handbook. It is fully illustrated, with some colour plates, and has a bibliography (p. 480-7). Analytical index.

Canadian annual review for 1965 (Toronto, Univ. of Toronto Press, 1966. xvi, 569p.   ) has four main parts: Parliament and politics (including the Provinces, p. 120-201)—External affairs and defence—The national economy—Life and leisure; with titles of books cited in text, obituaries and an analytical index.

Canadian almanac and directory for the year 1847- (Toronto, Copp Clark, 1847-. Annual. 121st ed. 1968. $13.75) resembles Whitaker's *Almanack* in content but has more directory information.

908 (714 + 719):016
COOKE, A., and CARON, F., *comp.* **Bibliographie de la Péninsule du Québec - Labrador** . . . Centre d'Études Nordiques, Université Laval, Quebec. Boston, Mass., G. K. Hall, 1967. 2 v. $145 (U.S. and Canada); $159.50 (elsewhere).

Bibliography of *c.* 10,000 card entries, photolithographically reproduced, with a bilingual topical and regional index in v. 2. Covers monographs, periodical articles and manuscripts, and especially theses and private papers. The index contains *c.* 60,000 entries.

908 (714) (058)
Annuaire du Québec. Québec yearbook. 1964-1965. 47. éd. Ministère de l'Industrie et du Commerce, Bureau de la Statistique du Québec. 1965. xvi, 736p. illus., tables, maps, plans. $3.

Five chapters (24 parts): 1. The milieu—2. Human milieu—3. The resources of the Québec economy—4. Trade—5. Finance. Footnote references. 'Books published in the French language from 1960 to 1964', p. 169-85.

Mexico

908 (72):016
Handbook of Latin American studies. Gainesville, Florida, Univ. of Florida Press, 1936-. v. 1-. Annual. (v. 28. 1966. $20).

See entry at 908 (8=6):016.

908 (72) (02)
Mexico, 1966: facts, figures and trends. [3rd ed.] Mexico City, Banco Nacional de Comercio Exterior S.A., 1966. [vii], 272, [1]p. illus., tables.

First published 1960; 2nd ed. 1963.
Attractively illustrated, with 30 illus. in colour. Three main parts: 1. The Mexican and his homeland (chapters 1-4)—2. The national economy (5-12)—3. Society and culture (13-17). Bibliography of further reading, in 3 parts, as for text, p. 271-2. No index.

908 (72) (03)
Diccionario Porrua de historia, biografia y geografia de México. Mexico, Editorial Porrua, S.A., 1964. xxix, [1], 1721p maps. (2nd ed. 1965).

Unsigned articles, A-Z, with brief references (*e.g.,* Porfirio Díaz: 2½ columns, 2 references; Popacatépetl: 1½ columns, 1 reference; Maximilian of Hapsburg: 4 columns, 7 references). Numerous cross-references. Supplement, p. 1629-1709. 10 maps, poorly coloured.

Enciclopedia de México (Mexico, Insituto de la Enciclopedia de México, 1966-. v. 1-. illus., pl. maps) is to be published in 10v. V. 1 (xv, 606 cols.): A—Bravo, has many brief entries. 'Aztecas' occupies cols. 861-98, is signed and has 2″ of bibliography. About one black-and-white illus. per page.

Caribbean

908 (729):016
Current Caribbean bibliography: an annual list of publications. Port of Spain, Caribbean Commission Central Secretariat, 1951-. v. 1-.

Last cumulation: v. 9-11 (1959-61), pt. 1 published 1964. Pt. 2, the index, was never published because of the folding up of the Caribbean Commission. Plans are being made by the Caribbean Regional Library to resume publication with an issue for 1967. (See *Library of Congress Information bulletin*, v. 26, no. 27, 6th July 1967, p. 425.)

Covers publications issued in the French, British, Dutch and U.S. possessions in the Caribbean. Entries are classified by U.D.C., with an author, subject and title index, as well as a chronological index.

Caribbean studies (Puerto Rico, Institute of Caribbean Studies, Univ. of Puerto Rico, 1961-. v. 1, no. 1-. Quarterly) carries 'Book reviews' (*c.* 6 long reviews per issue), 'Book notes' and 'Current bibliography'. The latter has *c.* 800 entries per issue and covers books, pamphlets and articles of value to Caribbeanists. The area is defined as comprising the Antilles, Yucatán, British Honduras, Central America, Panama, Colombia, Venezuela and the Guianas.

908 (729):016

Handbook of Latin American studies. Gainesville, Florida, Univ of Florida Press, 1936-. v. 1-. Annual. (v. 28. 1966. $20.).

See entry at 908 (8=6):016.

908 (729) (02)

The Caribbean who, what, why: Jamaica, Trinidad and Tobago, Barbados, British Guiana, British Honduras, Windward Islands, Leeward Islands. 2nd ed. [Kingston?], L. S. Smith, 1965. 844p.

First published for 1955-56, as *British Caribbean, who, what, why.*

Detailed information on each area (*e.g.*, Jamaica, p. 41-207: General description; political constitution; trade and commerce; education; agriculture; industry; medical and health; civil aviation; etc.). The biography section is divided by categories (*e.g.*, Banking); section on companies; index of advertisers.

908 (729) (058)

The West Indies and Caribbean year book. London, Skinner, 1927-. illus., tables, maps. Annual. (1967, published 1966. 63s.).

Title varies; initially the *West Indies year book,* 1926/27-.

Covers 28 areas and island groups; includes Venezuela, Colombia and the Guianas. A mine of information on each area (*e.g.*, 'Cuba' (1966 ed., p. 546-55) has sections on history, administration and legislature, local government, economy, trade, public services, education, hotels, newspapers, etc., plus a business directory, maps, 3 illustrations, and tables). Shipping, air, port and trade information; gazetteer and index to maps.

908 (729:492) (02)

KRUYTHOFF, S. J. The Netherlands Windward Islands . . . : a handbook of information . . . 3rd ed. Oranjestad, Aruba, 1964. 133p. illus., tables, maps.

A well-illustrated compendium, covering history, administration, flora and fauna, St. Maarten, industries, Saba, St. Eustatius, airmail tariffs, historical episodes and persons of distinction, folklore. Bibliography, p. 130.

Jamaica

908 (729.2):016

DELATTRE, R. A guide to Jamaican reference material in the West India Reference Library. Kingston, Institute of Jamaica, 1965. [iii], 76, [1]p.

Annotated bibliography of *c.* 300 items. Sections: General bibliography—A. Retrospective bibliography, including library catalogues—B. Current bibliography. Maps, prints, films, etc.—C, D. Periodicals & newspapers (guides & lists; indexes and abstracts)—E. Biography—F. Directories, handbooks, yearbooks, etc.—G-N. Special subjects (education; history; language and literature; law; music; science; sociology; etc.). Closely classified; many cross-references. Includes Caribbean as well as purely Jamaican sources. Author index. Locations given in three libraries.

908 (729.2):016

JAMAICA LIBRARY SERVICE. Jamaica: a select bibliography. [Kingstown], Jamaica Independence Festival Committee, 1963. vi, 115p.

Aims at including "the most important publications dealing with all aspects of Jamaica" (*Foreword*). Collected from the holdings of the library of the University of Jamaica, the West India Reference Library of the Institute of Jamaica and the Jamaica Library Service. About 1,000 items under 17 headings (including Bibliography, Biography and Current periodicals; Dewey classes). Author index.

908 (729.2) (058)

The Handbook of Jamaica for . . . ; comprising historical, statistical and general information concerning the island, obtained from official and other reliable records and compiled by the Jamaican Information Service. Kingston, Jamaica, Government Printing Office, 1881-. tables, maps. Annual. (1964. 10s.).

First published 1881; not published 1940-45.

The 1964 v. covers geography, population, meteorology, politics, agriculture, communications and transport, literature and art, industries, etc. as well as directory information and bibliographies (*e.g.*, government publications on sale, p. 703-17; principal newspapers and periodicals, p. 717-8).

Trinidad & Tobago

908 (729.87)

The Trinidad and Tobago year book, 1865-. Port of Spain, Trinidad, Yuille's Printerie, 1865-. Annual. (100th year, 1965-66, published 1965).

A comprehensive year book; includes a classified trades directory, complete civil list, directory of companies, churches, institutions, clubs and the like, and the text of regulations (*e.g.*, stamp duties), as well as statistical data. Detailed general index.

U.S.A.

908 (73):016

America: history and life—a guide to periodical literature. Santa Barbara, Cal., Clio Press, July 1964-. v. 1, no. 1-. Quarterly.

See entry at 973:016.

908 (73):016

UNITED STATES. LIBRARY OF CONGRESS. General Reference and Bibliography Division. **A guide to the study of the United States of America:** representative books reflecting the development of American life and thought. Prepared under the direction of Roy P. Basler. Washington, Government Printing Office, 1960. xv, 1193p. $7.

6,487 numbered and annotated items, annotations averaging about 100 or more words. 32 chapters: Literature (1607-1955)—Language— Literary history and criticism—Biography and autobiography—Periodicals and Journalism— Geography—The American Indian—History (chapters 8-12)—Travel and Travelers—Population—Society—Communications—Science and Technology — Medicine—Entertainment—Sports and Recreations—Education—Philosophy and Psychology — Religion — Folklore — Music — Art and Architecture—Land and agriculture— Economic life—Constitution and government— Law and justice—Politics—Books and Libraries. Index (p. 1091-1193) of authors, subjects and titles.

Selected items of Americana published up to 1875 are listed in: American Studies Association. Committee on Microfilm Bibliography. *Bibliography of American culture, 1493-1875;* compiled and edited by David R. Weimer (Ann Arbor, Michigan, Univ. Microfilms, 1957. xvi, 228p. $3.50). This is systematically arranged; no indexes.

Latin America

908 (8=6):016

BAYITCH, S. A. Latin America: a bibliographical guide to economy, history, law, politics and society. Coral Gables, Florida, Univ. of Miami Press, 1961. xv, 335p. (Univ. of Miami School of Law, Interamerican legal studies). $12.50.

About 10,000 unannotated entries; includes periodical articles. 5 parts: 1. Introduction—2. General information on Latin America—3. Fundamentals and backgrounds—4. Guide, by subjects (A-Z, p. 40-86)—5. Guide, by countries (20 countries, Argentina—Venezuela, divided by subjects A-Z). Subject index, with country-subdivisions. List of *c.* 400 periodicals and other serials scanned, p. ix-xiv.

Noted: Bayitch, S. A. *Latin America and the Caribbean: a bibliographical guide to works in English* (Coral Gables, Univ. of Florida Press; Dobbs Ferry, N.Y., Oceana Publications, 1967. xxviii, 943p. $30), which emphasises economic, political and legal aspects.

908 (8=6):016

GEOGHEGAN, A. R. Obras de referencia de América Latina: repertorio selectivo y anotado de enciclopedias, diccionários, bibliografías, repertorios biográficos, catálogos, guías, anuarios, índices. Buenos Aires, the Author, 1965. xxiii, 280p.

Published with the assistance of Unesco.

2,693 numbered, annotated items, classified by U.D.C. Includes periodical articles and is not confined to items published in Latin America. Brief annotations. Analytical index of authors, subjects and areas, p. 249-80.

908 (8=6):016

Handbook of Latin American studies. Gainesville, Florida, Univ. of Florida Press, 1936-. v. 1-. Annual. (v. 28. 1966. $20.).

V. 1-13 were published by Harvard Univ. Press, Cambridge, Mass.

A comprehensive annual annotated bibliography, latterly "prepared by a number of scholars for the Hispanic Foundation in the Library of Congress" (*sub-title*). Each volume has *c.* 5,000 entries, nearly all with 50-70 word annotations, sometimes evaluative and sometimes signed. Subject and author indexes; full list of periodicals scanned.

As from v. 26 coverage was reorganised so as to cover *Humanities* and *Social sciences* in alternate years. Thus, v. 26 (1964) covers *Humanities;* v. 27 covers anthropology, economics, education, geography, government and international relations, law and sociology (25 sections, with area and country sub-divisions). V. 27 has 4,264 numbered entries, plus numerous interpolations. Nearly 600 journals are cited. The 66 contributing editors are all from U.S.A., but there are 5 foreign corresponding editors. A feature of recent volumes (v. 22 (1960-)) is the inclusion of special articles (*e.g.,* v. 27: "Latin American studies in Japan"). Author and subject indexes to v. 1-28 (1936-66) are planned.

908 (8=6):016

HISPANIC AND LUSO-BRAZILIAN COUNCILS, London. **Author and subject catalogues of the Canning House Library.** Boston, Mass., G. K. Hall, 1966. 5v. $245 (U.S. and British Isles); $269.50 (elsewhere).

57,000 photolithographed entries reproduced from author and subject cards representing *c.* 35,000 books, mainly of 20th and 19th-century origin. Covers all but highly technical subjects. The Hispanic catalogue (45,800 entries) is reproduced in 4 v.; the Luso-Brazilian catalogue (12,600 entries), in 1 v.

908 (8=6):016

HISPANIC AND LUSO-BRAZILIAN COUNCILS, London. **Latin America:** an introduction to modern books in English concerning the countries of Latin America. 2nd ed., rev. London, Library Association, 1966. v, 41p. 10s. (7s. 6d. to members).

First published 1960.

329 numbered items, with brief notes on some items. The most generally important items are indicated, in descending order, by 3, 2 or 1 asterisks. 'General books' including periodicals; sections on individual countries (A-Z) follow. Does not include British, French, Dutch, etc.

possessions in the West Indies. Aims to help librarians to select books on Latin America, written in English and still obtainable, for a relatively modest expenditure. Prices given. Author index.

908 (8=6):016
HISPANIC SOCIETY OF AMERICA. Library. **Catalogue of the Library** of the Hispanic Society of America. Boston, Mass., G. K. Hall, 1962. 10 v. $675.

211,000 cards, photolithographically reproduced. "The Society's library contains over 100,000 volumes, covering the cultures of Spain, Portugal and colonial Hispanic America. Emphasis is on the art, history and literature of these countries, including music, social customs, regional costumes, and description and travel, but excluding Indian subjects" (G. K. Hall & Co. *Annual catalogue of reference works, May 1967,* p. 28). Author and subject catalogue; excludes manuscripts, books printed before 1701, and most periodicals.

Widener Library shelflist number 6: *Latin America and Latin American periodicals* (Cambridge, Mass., Harvard Univ. Press, 1966; London, Oxford Univ. Press, 1967. 2v. £26) records 25,546 items in three sequences: v. 1, Classified listing by call number; v. 2, Alphabetical listing by author or title; chronological listing. Periodicals, v. 1, p. 649-75 (c. 1,500 titles). Computer-produced.

908 (8=6):016
PAN AMERICAN UNION. Columbus Memorial Library. **Index to Latin American periodical literature, 1929-1960.** Boston, Mass., G. K. Hall, 1962. 8v. $350.

About 250,000 catalogue cards (authors, subjects and other secondary entries), photolithographically reproduced. Indexes articles from more than 3,000 periodicals, these being mostly of Latin American origin.
A supplementary volume for 1961-1965 is in preparation (2v. $85), indexing articles from c. 800 periodicals.

———— **Indice general de publicaciones periódicas latino-americanas. Humanidades y ciencias sociales.** Index to Latin American periodicals. Humanities and social sciences. v. 1: 1961- Boston, Mass., G. K. Hall, 1962-. Annual. (v. 3: 1963. 1965. $16.).

V. 3: 1963 has c. 4,900 entries, author, title and subject entries. Beginning with v. 4: 1964, the index will be issued quarterly, with a cumulative author index. V. 5: 1965 (1967) draws on c. 200 periodicals.

908 (8=6):016
OKINSHEVICH, L. *comp.* **Latin America in Soviet writings: a bibliography.** Edited by R. G. Carlton. Baltimore, Md., Johns Hopkins Press for Library of Congress, 1966. ea. $15; $25 the set.

v. 1: *1917-1958.*
v. 2: *1959-1964.*
Prepared under the auspices of the Hispanic Foundation, Library of Congress.

V. 1 lists more than 3,800 titles and v. 2, nearly 5,000, by country under broad subjects in the fields of politics and government, languages and literatures, foreign relations, travel, society and social conditions, international economic relations, and economic conditions and policies. Also lists Soviet translations of works by Latin American authors. Author and subject indexes. Each entry is translated and, where necessary, annotated. Further suppts. will possibly be five-yearly. Reviewed in *Inter-American review of bibliography,* v. 17 (4), October/December, p. 434-5. Reflects Soviet interest in Latin America since the Cuban revolution of 1959.

908 (8=6):016
SABLE, M. H. A guide to Latin American studies. Los Angeles, Calif., Latin American Centre, Univ. of California, 1967. 2v. $25.

5,024 numbered, annotated entries. Intended to facilitate research at the undergraduate and graduate level in any discipline and/or professional field related to Latin America. Also serves as a guide for locating specialists mentioned. The *Preface* identifies gaps in the literature. Coverage (mostly post-1950): books, periodicals and periodical articles, pamphlets, government documents, theses and conference proceedings. 50-100-word articles. Arranged under broad subject headings, A-Z (*e.g.,* 'Area studies'; 'Bibliographies'; 'Dictionaries'; 'Reference books'; 'Foreign trade'), with subject, country or form subdivisions. Author and analytical subject indexes in v. 2 (p. 635-780). To be used in conjunction with the annual *Handbook of Latin American studies.* Large format. Adversely reviewed in *International affairs,* v. 44, no. 1, February 1968, p. 173.

908 (8=6) 026/027
LONDON. UNIVERSITY. INSTITUTE OF LATIN AMERICAN STUDIES. Guide to Latin American collections in London libraries. London, the Institute, 1967. [20]p.

A directory, noting library stocks and facilities for users, of 28 libraries in London, arranged A-Z by name. Ranges from the Bank of England library and the Royal Anthropological Society library to those at the British Museum and Victoria and Albert Museum. Intended primarily for students and research workers attached to the Institute of Latin American studies.
The Institute has also produced *Theses in Latin American studies at British universities, in progress and completed, 1966/1967.* [1967]. 12p.

908 (8=6) (058)
The South American handbook, 1924-: an annual traveller's guide to the countries and economics of South America, Central America, Mexico, Caribbean and West Indies. London, Trade and Travel Publications, Ltd., 1924-. tables, maps. Annual. (43rd ed., 1967. 20s.).

Initially as *Anglo-South American handbook,* 1921-22.
Data on each of the 23 countries concerned, covering physical features, climate, principal products, industry, natural resources, government, foreign trade, transport, currency, and weights

and measures. Leading cities are described separately. Thus, the part on 'Cuba' (1967 ed., p. 809-19) has sections: general information; the people; communications; Havana (4 pages, including plan); economy; hints for visitors. 8 coloured maps (Philip) and index precede. Appendices on insurance, steamship services, etc.

908 (8＝6):061
HILTON, R., *ed.* **Handbook of Hispanic source material and research organizations in the United States.** 2nd ed. Stanford, Cal., Stanford Univ. Press, 1956. xiv, 448p.

First published 1942.
'Hispanic' covers Spain, Portugal and Latin America, as well as the Southern U.S. states up to the time of U.S. annexation. Comprehensive subject coverage—social and natural sciences, fine arts and humanities. Organizations are arranged by states and cities, with name index. The editor was Director of Hispanic American Studies, Stanford University.

Noted: U.S. Library of Congress. Hispanic Foundation. *National directory of Latin Americanists: biobibliographies of 1,884 specialists in the social sciences & humanities* (Washington, 1966. 351p.).

Brazil

908 (81):016
JACKSON, W. V. **Library guide for Brazilian studies.** Pittsburgh, Univ. of Pittsburgh Book Centers, 1964. xiii, 194p. map.

Chapters: 1. Introduction—2. General materials—3. Humanities—4. Social sciences—5. Science and technology—6. Cooperative development of resources—7. Conclusions. Bibliography of 125 items (p. 83-99). 5 appendices, including '2. Union list of selected Brazilian periodicals in the humanities and social sciences'. Claims to be "a thorough review of the existing literature of library resources" (*Introduction*). Index of libraries.

908 (81) (02)
WRZOS, C. B. R., *ed.* **Brazilian information handbook** for 1967. 12th year of issue. Rio de Janeiro, [the Editor?], 1967. 185p. illus. 10*s*.

A pocket-book of handy data, especially for the tourist. Concise political and economic information; notes on towns; directory, etc.

908 (81) (031)
Grande enciclopédia portuguesa e brasileira . . . [pt. 2]. Lisbon & Rio de Janeiro, Editorial Enciclopédia, [1964?]-. v. 1-. illus., maps.

v. 1 [1968]: A—CALAD.
This part of the *Grande enciclopédia* deals with Brazil only. To be completed in 4v. On pt. 1 (1935-60. 40v.) see *Guide* (1959) at 030.1＝69.

Argentina

908 (82) (031)
SANTILLÁN, D. A. de. **Gran enciclopedia argentina:** todo lo argentino ordenado alfabeticamente, geografía e historia, toponimias, biografías, ciencias, artes, letras, derecho, economía,

industria y comercio, instituciones, flora y fauna, folklore, léxico regional. Buenos Aires, Ediar, 1956-64. 8v. & Apendice. illus., maps.

A well-illustrated encyclopaedia which is devoted solely to the Argentine Republic. Particularly useful as a gazetteer and as a national biographical dictionary. The encyclopaedia also functions as a dictionary and includes regional terms. Portraits (often rather small), facsimiles and some coloured illustrations support the text. Maps of provinces are given, but not town plans (*e.g.,* of the city of Buenos Aires). The article on the province and city of Buenos Aires runs to 36 pages. Biographies of writers (*e.g.,* Alberdi) list the authors' works, but do not note material on the writers. Bibliographies are not usually appended to articles. The *Apendice* comprises mainly biographies and entries under places. Complementary to the *Diccionário histórico argentino* (1953-4. 6v.), although there is some overlap.

Peru

908 (85):016
ORGANISATION FOR ECONOMIC CO-OPERATION AND DEVELOPMENT. Development Centre. **Bibliographie sur le Pérou** . . . Paris, O.E.C.D., 1965. [ii], 4p., 211 l. Mimeographed. *Gratis.*

1,561 numbered, unannotated items in 7 sections: 1. Reference works—2. General works—3. Social structures—4. Administration, law and politics—5. Economic situation and policy—6. Economic activities—7. Commerce and commercial policy. Index of authors; list of periodicals published in Peru (165 titles).

908 (85) (031)
TAURO, A. **Diccionario enciclopédico del Perú.** Lima, Editorial Mejía Baca, [1966-67]. 3v. illus. (some col.), maps. $88.

Covers the history, geography, flora and fauna, culture, institutions, etc. of Peru. Numerous biographies (*e.g.,* 'Sucre': 4½ cols.) (including contemporaries) and entries under places ('Cuzco': 7 cols. of gazetteer information, history; includes illustration of coat of arms). Numerous small line-drawings (including portraits); half-tones (a few in colour). V. 3 carries addenda. No bibliographies or lists of sources. Lists major works by Peruvian writers.

Colombia

908 (86) (02)
Quick Colombian facts. 5th ed., edited by E. C. Leiva. Bogotá, Instituto Colombiano de Opinión Pública, 1965. 315p. tables, map.

First published 1955.
A pocket-sized guide to information, much of it directory data (on municipalities, universities, etc.) and statistics (economy; press; minerals; trade; etc.).

Ecuador

908 (866):016
ORGANISATION FOR ECONOMIC CO-OPERATION AND DEVELOPMENT. Development Centre. **Bibliographie sur l'Équateur** . . . Paris, 1965. [2]p., 3, 85 l. 4p. insert as suppt.

671 numbered, unannotated items in 7 sections: 1. Reference works—2. General works—3. Social structures—4. Administration, law and politics— 5. Economic situation and policy—6. Economic activities—7. Commerce, commercial policy. Index of authors; list of periodicals published in Ecuador (56 titles), as insert.

OCEANIA

908 (9):016

O'REILLY, P. "Bibliographie de l'Océanie . . ." In *Journal de la Société des Océanistes* (Paris, Musée de l'Homme), [1946?]-.

The 19th instalment of this bibliography, by P. O'Reilly and R. Heyum, appeared in v. 19 (1963), p. 327-91, listing *c.* 900 items in 13 sections (history and geography, ethnology, linguistics, economic life, culture, art and literature). Areas chiefly concerned: Oceania, Micronesia, Melanesia, Polynesia. No index.

Patrick O'Reilly has also compiled *Bibliographie méthodique, analytique et critique de la Nouvelle-Calédonie* (Paris, Musée de l'Homme, 1955. 361p.); *Bibliographie méthodique, analytique et critique des Nouvelles-Hébrides* (Paris, Musée de l'Homme, 1958. 304p.), both in the Publications de la Société des Océanistes series, nos. 4 and 8 respectively; and *Bibliographie de Tahiti et de la Polynésie française* (Paris, Société des Océanistes, Musée de l'Homme, 1967, xv, 1046p.) in 14 sections (reviewed in *Times literary supplement,* no. 3449, 4th April 1968, p. 336).

The *Dictionary catalog of printed books,* The Mitchell Library, Public Library of New South Wales, Sydney, is due for publication in mid-1968 by G. K. Hall, Boston, Mass. (38v. $2,400, U.S.A. & Australia; $2,640, elsewhere). It comprises 631,000 cards, photolithographically reproduced. The publishers describe the Mitchell Library as "the foremost single collection of documentary materials relating to the Australasian and South Pacific region, including the East Indian archipelago and Antarctica".

Indonesia

908 (910):016

KENNEDY, R. Bibliography of Indonesian peoples and cultures. Rev. and enl. ed. by T. W. Maretzki and H. Th. Fischer. New Haven, Conn., Southeast Asian Studies, Yale Univ., by arrangement with Human Relations Area Files, 1962. xxii, 207p.

Reprint of a bibliography (1945) which at the time gave extensive coverage of books and periodical articles on Indonesia. Subjects: anthropology and sociology, archaeology, linguistics, acculturation, geography, colonial administration, education, economics and history. No index.

908 (910) (02)

NUGROHO. Indonesia: facts and figures. Djakarta, Terbitan Pertjobaan, 1967. xxxiv, 608p. tables, maps. Mimeographed.

See entry at 331 (910),

Philippines

908 (914):016

EGGAN, F., and HESTER, E. D. Selected bibliography of the Philippines, topographically arranged and annotated. Prelim. ed. New Haven, Conn., Human Relations Area Files, 1956. vi, 138p.

Annotated bibliography of 900 items in 23 sections. Entries for items that together form a fairly comprehensive account of the history, culture, resources and economy of the Philippines are asterisked.

More recent: Houston, C. O. Jr. *Philippine bibliography: an annotated preliminary bibliography of Philippine bibliographies since 1900* (Manila, Univ. of Manila, 1963. [ii], 69, 23p. $3.25),—155 entries.

908 (914) (03)

GALANG, Z. M., ed. Encyclopedia of the Philippines. Manila, E. Floro, [c. 1950-58]. 20v. illus., maps, facsims. £80.

Systematically arranged: v. 1-2. Literature; v. 3-4. Biography; v. 5-6. Commerce and industry; v. 7-8. Art; v. 9. Education; v. 10. Religion; v. 11-12. Government and politics; v. 13-14. Science; v. 15-16. History; v. 17-18. Builders; v. 19-20. General information. Includes bibliographies.

The Philippines: a handbook of economic facts and general information (Manila, Department of Foreign Affairs in co-operation with National Economic Council, [1966]. 170p. illus., graphs. has 4 parts: 1. General information—2. Agriculture and natural resources—3. Philippine industry—4. Infrastructure. Appendices: statistical tables; brief trade directory.

Australian Territories

908 (92/95)

AUSTRALIA. DEPARTMENT OF TERRITORIES. Annotated bibliography of select government publications on Australian territories, 1951-1964. Canberra, 1965. 55p.

About 700 briefly annotated items. 1. General (A-Z, authors)—2. Australian territories (A-Z: Christmas Island, Cocos (Keeling Islands), Nauru, Norfolk Island, Northern Territory, Papua and New Guinea. Includes processed material. No index.

New Zealand

908 (931):016

HARRIS, J., comp. Guide to New Zealand reference material. 2nd ed. Wellington, New Zealand Library Association, 1950. xiii, 114p.; Supplements no. 1-2. 1951-57.

First published 1947.
A well-annotated list of more than 100 entries. Sections: General reference—Bibliographies and libraries—Philosophy—General science—Physical science and technology . . . History and sociology —Local history . . . Fine arts. Language. Literature. Includes analytical entries.

Supplement no. 1 (1951. 29p.) and no 2 (1957. 36p.) were both compiled by A. G. Bagnall.

908 (931):016:016
NEW ZEALAND LIBRARY ASSOCIATION. A bibliography of New Zealand bibliographies. Prelim. ed. Wellington, the Association, 1967. 58p. 10s.

Lists under subject headings 315 bibliographies concerned with aspects of New Zealand.

908 (931) (031)
McLINTOCK, A. H., *ed.* **An encyclopaedia of New Zealand.** Wellington, Owen, Government Printer, 1966. 3v. illus., pl., tables, maps. 150s.

Signed articles by *c.* 350 contributors, usually with references (*e.g.,* 'Otago province': 6½p., 4 maps, 6 references; 'Welfare services': 4p., 5 references). Some 700 biographies, including 'Expatriates—biographies' (v. 1, p. 575-604). The 500 maps are a feature. 96 plates in all, with 3, 4 or 6 illustrations per page; also numerous small text illustration. Analytical index, v. 3, p. 713-843. Well produced.

The *Oxford New Zealand encyclopaedia* (London, Oxford Univ. Press, 1965. xii, [4], 376p. illus., maps. 48s.) is designed both as a self-contained one-volume reference book for New Zealand and as a companion to the *Oxford junior encyclopaedia* (Rev. ed. 1964. 12v. and index). Shortish, unsigned articles, without references (*e.g.,* Sedden, R. J.: 2 cols., including portrait; 'Maori arts and crafts': 5 cols., 3 illustrations). About 100 contributors. Cross-references, plus references to the *OJE*.

908 (931) (058)
New Zealand official yearbook. Wellington, Department of Statistics, 1892-. illus., tables, graphs, maps. (Annual). (71st issue, 1966. 21s.).

A detailed survey in 41 chapters (1964 ed.): Physiography, demography and social characteristics (chapters 1-10)—Transport and communications (11-12)—Production (13-20)—Trade, prices, consumption (21-24)—Finance (25-31)—Labour (32-37)—General (38-41). Appended: statistical summary (p. 1109-32), with data up 1963 and retrospective to 1912 or 1913. 'Latest statistical information', p. 1197-1224 (on green-tinted paper). Analytical index, p. 1225-57. The select bibliography in the 1966 ed. (p. 1107-30) is sub-divided by subject.

Australia

908 (94 + 931) (03)
The modern encyclopaedia of Australia and New Zealand. General editor, V. S. Barnes. Sydney, Horwitz Publications and Grahame Book Co., 1965. 1199p. illus., pl.

Facts and figures on all aspects of Australia and New Zealand, plus Papua—New Guinea. Concisely written articles, A-Z, with short bibliographies appended to the more important. Articles not signed; 23 advisers and contributors. Contains biographies (including contemporaries); entries for public institutions, local flora and fauna. 54p. chronology of principal events and a 'Quick reference' section. Appendix of statistical data up to and including 1963. Section of coloured illustrations, though a dearth of text illustrations. No index, but plentiful cross-references. Attractively produced.

908 (94) (03)
The Australian encyclopaedia. [2nd ed.]. Editor-in-chief, Alec H. Chisholm. Sydney, London [etc.], Angus & Robertson, 1958. 10v. illus. £45; £A50.

First published 1925-26. 2v.
Founded on the 1st ed., but hardly any of it has remained untouched. Work begun 1950. About 4,500 contributors; nearly all articles are initialled. Where an article is taken over from the 1st ed., both the original author's and the reviser's initials are given. Index of initials in v. 1. Articles are of good length, and some are very full indeed, *e.g.,* a series on the Aborigines, v. 1, p. 3-106.

Serle's *Dictionary of Australian biography* (1949. 2v.) was used as the starting point for biographies, but the *Encyclopaedia* has more than twice Serle's 1,030 entries. Serle excludes persons still living in 1943, and many little-known pioneers. No living persons are given entries in the *Encyclopaedia,* although they may be mentioned to complete a family history. All places with 1,000 or more inhabitants are given, and also smaller places of historical interest, and natural features. 1954 census figures, and frequently earlier ones as well, to show growth or decline.

More than 2,000 illustrations, mostly on plates (64 coloured). Maps are the weakest feature: there are 8 coloured maps of the separate States and of the continent as a whole, giving very meagre information, and other simple maps in the text. No street plans for Canberra, Sydney, etc.—only sketch maps of the metropolitan areas and surrounding districts.

Bibliographies, when given, are up to about a third of a column in length and usually confined to books in English, but scientific articles often have references to periodical literature and sometimes include material in foreign languages. Some cross-references; v. 10 is the general index. The list of shipwrecks, together with an account of the 1956 Olympic Games, have been placed at the beginning of v. 10.

908 (94) (03)
The Australian junior encyclopaedia. New [2nd] ed. Editor, Charles Barrett; revision editor, R. P. C. Bower. Sydney, Australian Educational Foundation, 1958. 3v. illus. £A11 10s.

First published 1951.
Fairly long signed articles on broadly grouped topics, *e.g.,* Geography, History, Aborigines, Cities and Government, with sub-divisions. No bibliographies. Many illustrations, with several colour plates and maps. In proportion to its size, it is far more richly illustrated than *The Australian encyclopaedia,* with which it has no connection. V. 3 ends with 'First steps in learning', 'The Queen's tour of Australia', 'Sport and recreation', 'Famous people in Australian history', and a general index of some 3,850 entries.

908 (94) (058)
AUSTRALIA. COMMONWEALTH BUREAU OF CENSUS AND STATISTICS. Official year book of the Commonwealth of Australia. Canberra, Government Printing Office, 1908-. tables, maps. Annual. (No. 51: 1965. 1965. 20s.).

V. 1 covers 1788-1907. Largely a statistical

work, but has historical and other material, including a chronological table of events since 1788. The 1965 year book has 31 detailed chapters. Appended: 'Diary of principal economic events, 1964-65', 'Chronological table, 1955 to 1965', 'Statistical summary, 1901-02 to 1964-65', 'List of special articles and miscellaneous matter contained in previous issues', 'General index' (p. 1327-52), 'Printed publications issued by the Central Office of the Commonwealth Bureau of Census and Statistics'.

The *Official year book* is also available in 12 parts, ea. 2s.

A popular version of the *Official year book* is *Australia: official handbook* ([Canberra, Australian News and Information Bureau]). The 1965 issue (331p.) is well illustrated, with maps, and includes in its 14 sections contributions on history, physical features, population, government, etc. Brief index.

The individual States also issue year books.

Papua, New Guinea

908 (95)

The Handbook of Papua and New Guinea. 5th ed. Sydney, Pacific Publications, 1966. iv, 440p. illus., maps, plans.

First published 1954.
Sections: Geography — History — People — Method of government—Law and justice—Finance and taxation—Commerce, trade and banking—Primary and secondary industries—Communications and transport and land policy—Agriculture—Forestry—Health and medical services—Education—Religion and missions. Directory (p. 249-340). Index to place names. General index.

An *Encyclopaedia of Papua and New Guinea,* to comprise two—possibly three—large volumes, is in preparation for publication in 1968. It is being produced in association with the University of Papua and New Guinea (Ad Orientem. *Catalogue nine,* 1967, p. 139).

Pacific Islands

908 (96):016

TAYLOR, C. R. H., *comp.* **A Pacific bibliography:** printed matter relating to the native peoples of Polynesia, Melanesia, and Micronesia. 2nd rev. and enl. ed. London, Oxford Univ. Press, 1965. xxx, 692p. 160s.

First published 1951 (xxix, 492p.).
More than 16,000 references (to periodical articles as well as books), classified by island groups and by subjects. Covers every island group of Polynesia, Melanesia and Micronesia, and includes New Zealand. According to Ad Orientem *Catalogue nine, 1967* (p. 147), over 13% of the entries concern the Maori, over 5%, Hawaii and 4%, the Fiji Islands.

908 (96):016:016

LEESON, I. A bibliography of bibliographies of the South Pacific. Melbourne & London, Oxford Univ. Press, 1954. 72p.

Published under the auspices of the South Pacific Commission.
Divided first by geographical area and secondly by subject. Includes bibliographies in periodicals; omits bibliographies the contents of which are covered by more important texts on the same subject.

908 (96) (058)

Pacific Islands year book and who's who. 9th ed. Sydney, Pacific Publications Pty., Ltd., 1963. 496, 196p. illus., tables, maps, plans. $A5.

First published 1932. 10th ed. [1968]. $A7.80.
General and introductory sections (history, administration, industries, etc.), p. 7-64; island groups and territories (5 groups: Polynesia, Micronesia, Melanesia, Malaysia and non-tropical islands), p. 65-478. General index; index of place names. Appendix: 'Who's who in the Pacific Islands' (156p.; *c.* 1,500 biographees). 80 maps, plus 5 folding maps.

Handbook of Fiji (2nd ed. Sydney, Pacific Publications, 1965. 272p. illus., tables, maps. $A1.50) is a companion volume to *The handbook of Papua and New Guinea* (at 908 (95)). First published 1962, it has 17 sections, directory information and a detailed index.

Hawaii

908 (969)

HAWAII. UNIVERSITY. Sinclair Library, Honolulu. **Dictionary catalog of the Hawaiian Collection.** Boston, Mass., G. K. Hall, 1963. 4v. $215.

68,000 cards, photolithographically reproduced on 3,278 pages, representing the world's largest and most complete collection of Hawaiiana: more than 42,000 items. Includes Hawaiian government documents since 1915, and over 1,500 Hawaiian serials.

Arctic, Antarctic

908 (98/99)

DARTMOUTH COLLEGE LIBRARY, Hanover, N.H. **Dictionary catalogue of the Stefansson Collection on the Polar Regions.** Boston, Mass., G. K. Hall, 1967. 8v. $470 (outside U.S., $517.).

About 120,000 photolithographed cards, representing *c.* 20,000 v., *c.* 20,000 pamphlets and many manuscript items. "The major emphasis of the Collection is now historical coverage, with primary concern for the history of Polar exploration."

The Polar bibliography, produced by Science and Technology Division, Library of Congress, for the Department of Defence, Washington (v. 1-3. 1956-59), consisted of abstracts of unclassified reports and other documents prepared by military agencies or their contractors since 1939. Subject and individual author indexes.

908 (98):016

Arctic bibliography. Prepared by the Arctic Institute of North America, with support of Government agencies of the United States and Canada. Washington, U.S. Government Printing

Office, 1953-. v. 1-. Annual (now biennial). (v. 12. 1965. $5.)

V. 1-12 carry 76,725 signed abstracts of papers, etc. covering all aspects of the Arctic, the result of exploration and scientific investigation. Of the 7,276 papers abstracted in v. 12, 3,360 are in English, 3,165 in Russian, 493 in Scandinavian languages, 112 in German and 140 in French, etc. 2,548 of the papers were published in 1962 and 3,610 in 1961. Arrangement is by authors, A-Z. The subject and locality index to v. 12 has c. 35,000 entries (p. 967-1392). Aspects of Greenland covered: botany; construction; geology; inland ice; meteorology.

908 (99):016
Antarctic bibliography. Prepared at the Library of Congress and sponsored by the Office of Antarctic Programs, National Science Foundation, 1965-. v. 1-. Annual. (v. 2: 1966. 1967. $4.25.).

V.1 comprises abstracts of and references to 2,000 items published primarily between 1962 and 1965. 13 main subject groups, covering all pertinent topics. Represents holdings of Library of Congress, 8 other government agencies and the American Geographical Society.

An earlier listing is the U.S. Navy Department Bureau of Aeronautics' *Antarctic bibliography* (Washington, Government Printing Office, 1951. 147p. maps. $1.25),—5,500 items, systematically arranged, with author index.

A guide to Antarctic information sources (Washington, Science Communication Inc., 1962. iv, 47 l. $1.50) gives comprehensive coverage. 3 sections: Topic finder list—Directory of Institutions—Publications list. Reviewed in *Polar record*, v. 12, no. 76, January 1964, p. 83-84.

91 GEOGRAPHY, EXPLORATION, TRAVEL

Bibliographies

91:016
AMERICAN GEOGRAPHICAL SOCIETY. Research catalogue of the American Geographical Society. Boston, Mass., G. K. Hall, 1962. 15v. and map suppt. $865 (outside U.S., $951.50).

v. 1-2.	*General.*
v. 3.	*Regional. North America.*
v. 4-5.	*United States.*
v. 6.	*Mexico, Central America, Bermuda, West Indies, South America.*
v. 7.	*South America.*
v. 8-10.	*Europe.*
v. 11.	*Africa.*
v. 12-13.	*Asia.*
v. 14.	*Australasia.*
v. 15.	*Polar regions, Oceania, Tropics.*

More than 200,000 entries (21 card-entries per page; 10,436p.). A photolithographic reproduction of the A.G.S. Library's card catalogue. The library is the largest geographical library in the Western hemisphere and its *Research catalogue* is particularly strong in periodical articles. The

Map supplement ([i], 24p.) is merely a map key to the classification scheme used.
Kept up to date by *Current geographical publications* (*q.v.*).

91:016
Bibliographie géographique internationale, 1891-. Paris, Colin (now Centre National de la Recherche Scientifique), 1891-. v. 1-. Annual. (v. 69: 1963. 1965. 54F.).

Published under the auspices of the International Geographical Union, with the aid of Unesco. Title varies. Issues covering 1891-1914 were published as part of the *Annales de géographie*.
The 1963 v. has c. 10,000 entries and sub-entries from c. 1,200 periodicals (listed p. 9-31), plus books, etc. (Relative coverage: France, 660 numbered entries; Italy, 406; Spain, 127; U.S.A., 204; British Isles, 214. Arrangement: A. *Partie générale* (p. 33-233) (Méthodes et enseignement. Histoire des sciences géographiques. Histoire des découvertes géographiques. Géographie historique . . . Géographie humaine. Bibliographies. Annuaires. Glossaires. Congrès. Biographies. B-F. *Partie régionale* (p. 234-919) (continents, then countries, sub-divided: general; bibliographies; physical geography; human geography; economic geography; regional studies). More than 100 contributors. B1, France, has appended subject index, the only section so favoured. Author index; detailed contents list. List of periodicals. About 2-3 years' time lag.

91:016
CHURCH, M., *and others, comp. and ed.* **A basic geographical library:** a selected and annotated book list for American colleges. Washington, Association of American Geographers, Commission on College Geography, 1966. xi, 153p. At nominal cost to interested individuals or institutions.

Aims to be a standard list of books that "according to the best available opinion, are of special excellence or of positive value to the student of geography", and primarily to offer guidance to the college librarian (*Introduction*). 1,343 numbered entries, plus numerous interpolations, with concise, often critical annotations. Very largely English-language items. Parts: 1. General works and aids (items 1-95)—2. Geographical methods (*e.g.,* cartography; photogrammetry; regional planning)—3. Thematic geography (*e.g.,* agricultural; military). No map series mentioned. Index of authors, editors and translators, but none of anonymous titles (*e.g.,* of periodicals and year books) or subjects. A basic list that should be in libraries of all levels. Very favourably reviewed by C. D. Harris in *Geographical review*, v. 57, no. 3, July 1967, p. 448-9, but criticised in *Vestnik Moskovskogo Universiteta. Seria geografiya,* 1967, no. 1, p. 111-3, for poor representation of basic Russian items.

91:016
COX, E. G. A reference guide to the literature of travel, including voyages, geographical descriptions, adventures, shipwrecks and expeditions. Seattle, Univ. of Washington, 1935-49. 3v. (Univ. of Washington Publications in language and literature. v. 9-10, 12).

v. 1: *The old world*. 1935. $6.
v. 2: *The new world*. 1938. $8.
v. 3: *Great Britain*. 1949. $10.

Source material is covered up to 1800. Entries, usually annotated, are arranged chronologically under area or subject. V. 3 includes chapters on maps and charts, general reference books, and bibliographies. A v. 4 was projected, "with which will be combined items that missed printing in the preceding volumes" (*Preface* to v. 3). Indexes of personal names in v. 2 (covering v. 1-2) and v. 3.

Noted: Kinauer, R., *comp. Lexikon geographischer Bildbände* (Vienna, Hollinek, 1966. xi, 463p. 123s.), a bibliography of illustrated geography books.

91:016

Current geographical publications: additions to the *Research catalogue of the American Geographical Society*, 1938-. New York, American Geographical Society, 1938-. v. 1-. 10 p.a. Mimeographed. $3.75 p.a.

About 5,500 entries p.a., covering books (with some analytical entries for chapters or sections), periodical articles, maps and atlases. Three sections: 1. General (by subjects)—2. Regional—3. Maps (a selection, listed as from v. 27, no. 9, November 1964). The Photograph suppt., listing illustrations in the books and periodicals scanned, ceased with the December 1952 issue. Titles in non-English languages are not translated, but titles of English, French, etc., summaries of periodical articles are given. Annual indexes: subject index (using classified groups); author and regional, A-Z.

91:016

Documentatio geographica. Geographische Zeitschriften- und Serien-Literatur. Bearb. und hrsg. vom Institut für Landeskunde. Bad Godesberg, the Institute, 1966-. 6 p.a., cumulated annually. DM.48 p.a.

Previously (1954-65) as *Westermanns Geographische Bibliographie* (10 p.a.), which listed *c.* 400 items per issue and made a feature of references to reviews.

In its present form, carries *c.* 5,000 entries p.a., very largely periodical articles. Systematically arranged; no references to reviews. Annual author, subject heading, regional and classified indexes are promised. The 1966 cumulation (2v.) appeared in 1967.

Contents of German-language geographical journals and monograph series are listed in Berichte zur Deutschen Landeskunde. *Verzeichnis der geographischen Zeitschriften, periodischen Veröffentlichungen und Schriftenreihen Deutschlands und der in den letzteren erschienenen Arbeiten.* Bearb. von R. D. Schmidt und C. Streumann. Sonderheft 7, 1964. (Bad Godesberg, Bundesanstalt für Landeskunde und Raumforschung Selbstverlag. [ix], 303p.). Lists the contents of the *Petermanns Mitteilungen Ergänzshefte*, 1-270 (1860-1963), p. 150-64. Name index; list of journals; list of institutions (under locality); 'Regional register'.

91:016

EDWARDS, K. C., and **CRONE, G. R. Geography in Great Britain, 1956-60.** A report submitted to the XIXth International Geographical Congress, Stockholm, August 1960. London, Royal Geographical Society, 1960. 15p.

A systematic survey, citing published books and papers, map series, etc. Sections: Research and publications (1. Physical geography—2. Human geography—3. Historical geography—4. Cartography and surveying—5. Regional geography—6. Methodology); Societies and institutions [and their publications]. Reprinted in the *Geographical journal*, v. 126, pt. 4, December 1960, p. 427-41.

91:016

Geographical abstracts. London, Geo Abstracts, Department of Geography, London School of Economics. pts. A-D. 180s. p.a.

A. *Geomorphological abstracts.* 1960-. Now 6 p.a. 36s. p.a.
B. *Climatology, biogeography and cartography.* 1966-. 6 p.a. 36s. p.a.
C. *Economic geography.* 1966-. 6 p.a. 54s. p.a. *See entry at 33:91:016.*
D. *Social geography.* 1966-. 6 p.a. 54s. p.a. *See entry at 308 (4/9):016.*

Geomorphological abstracts (quarterly, 1960-63) takes over from the British Geomorphological Research Group's *A bibliography of British geomorphology,* edited by K. M. Clayton (London, Philip, 1964. x, 211p. 18s.). *Geomorphological abstracts. Index, 1960-1965* (1966. 371p. 50s.) has a subject entries with more than 22,000 entries (an average of *c.* 7 entries per abstract) as well as a subject index. Sections A-D produced *c.* 5,000 abstracts in 1966.

The computer-produced *Geographical abstracts. Index 1966* (1967) had *c.* 40,000 entries. A valuable new abstracting service, drawing on many sources. Near print; titles of periodical articles are not underlined and do not stand out sufficiently for rapid scanning.

91:016

Geographisches Jahrbuch, 1866-. Gotha, Perthes, 1866-. v. 1-. Annual (irregular).

Later volumes were published by VEB Hermann Haack, Geographisch-Kartographisch Anstalt. Not published 1944-47, or since 1956.

An important bibliographical year-book, covering a different geographical area with each issue. Thus, v. 60 (1950) is entitled: *Erforschung der Polargebiete, 1932-47* by L. Breitfuss (xvi, 320 p.); v. 61, pt. 1 (1954): *Vorderindien, Ceylon, Tibet, Nepal, 1926-53,* by E. Reiner (vii, 186p.); v. 61, pt. 2 (1956): *Die Mongolei (1938-1954); Nordostchina (1927-1953); Vorderindien, Ceylon, Tibet, Nepal (Ergänzungen); Neuseeland (1938-1952).* Items (book and periodical articles) are not annotated, but each section has an introductory survey. None issued since 1956.

Indexes for 1866-1936 appear in v. 40 and 52. Wright and Platt's *Aids to geographical research* (2nd ed., 1947) also gives contents (p. 52-57, 273-4) up to v. 58, pt. 1 (1943).

91:016

LONDON. UNIVERSITY. INSTITUTE OF EDUCATION. Handbook for geography teachers. Prepared by the Standing Sub-Committee in Geography. 5th ed. General editor, M. Long. London, Methuen, 1964. xv, 534p. 22s. 6d.

First published 1955.
Compiled by 18 contributors and 32 reviewers. 13 sections, including: 3. Indoor geography (atlases, globes, maps)—4. Visual aids—5. Geographical societies and other organizations—6. Book list for the primary stage—7. Book list for the secondary stage (p. 258-357)—8. Book list for teachers and sixth forms (p. 358-474)—9. Geography in literature, exploration and travel —10. Official publications—11. Addresses of publishers. Annotations. No index. 'Bibliographies' (p. 466-7) omits *New geographical literature and maps.*

The Unesco *Source book for geography teaching* (London, Longmans, for Unesco, 1965. xv, 254p. diagrs.) devotes chapter 8 to 'Sources of documentation' (p. 201-54), covering periodicals, bibliographies (an improvement on the *Handbook* list), 'A succinct international bibliography', teaching material, international statistics and 'A select list of helpful addresses'.

910:016

NATIONAL BOOK LEAGUE. Books on geography: an exhibition of books available in the United Kingdom. Prepared for the General Assembly and 20th Congress of the International Geophysical Union. Selected by a Committee of Geographers acting on behalf of the Programme Committee. London, N.B.L., 1964. 51, [5]p. 2s.

818 numbered items, with some blanks. Books exhibited were in print July 1964. Sections 1-14: 1-8, subject sections (*e.g.,* economic geography, climatology)—9. Regional geography . . . 11. Glossaries and bibliographies. 12. Atlases (by publishers, A-Z, nos. 407-82)—13. Teaching of geography in schools (nos. 483-768)—14. Exploration and travel. No index.

Noted: *Basic readings in geography* (3rd ed. Syracuse Univ., Department of Geography, 1960. 61p. Mimeographed), "an annotated list of important materials and reference sources recommended especially for the advanced student of geography" (Church, M., and others, comp. *A basic geographical library* (1966), entry no. 7).

91:016

National geographic magazine. Cumulative index. v. 1: **1899-1946.** Washington, National Geographic Society, 1952. ii, 656p.

Subject, title (of article) and author index, p. 1-593; index of maps, including large maps issued as special supplements, p. 594-656. Of particular value as a source for illustrations.

——**National geographic index, 1947-1963** inclusive. With lists of expeditions, researches and awards. Washington, N.G.S., 1964. 398p.

Similarly arranged to the main work. The map index (p. 333-98) is on blue-tinted paper.

91:016

New geographical literature and maps. 1951-. London, Royal Geographical Society, 1951-. v. 1, no. 1-. 2 p.a. 40s. p.a.

Previously (1913-51) included as accessions lists in the *Geographical journal.*
About 1,000 entries per issue. V. 3, covering the more important accessions to the Library and Map Room, 1961-65, has *c.* 10,000 entries, a considerable increase (1951-55: *c.* 4,500). All articles in 20 of the principal British and overseas geographical periodicals are included, and a selection from 250 other titles. Also available as galley proofs on gummed paper to libraries, for cataloguing purposes.
Short notes on books which it has not been possible to review in *Geographical journal.* Layout of entries, with good use of bold face, is calculated to provide maximum facility of reference, although no indexes, cumulative or otherwise, are provided. Features: annual 'List of completed theses in geography' (published since 1960); 'List of periodicals added to the Library' (in each issue). All new atlases and maps received in the Map Room are listed. An essential tool for British libraries in this field.

910:016

Referativnyï zhurnal. Geografiya. Moscow, Proizvodstvenno-Izdat. Kombinat VINITI, 1957-. diagrs. maps. Monthly. £23 16s. p.a.

Included in *Geologiya i geografiya,* 1954-56.
About 3,000 indicative and informative abstracts p.a. Headings: Theory and general subjects of physical and economic geography—Cartography—Period of evolution of man—Oceanology. Hydrology. Glaciology (with author index)—Meteorology and climatology (with author index) — Biogeography — Conservation. Regionalism—Geography of the U.S.S.R.—Geography of Europe outside U.S.S.R.—Geography of Asia outside U.S.S.R.—Geography of Africa—Geography of America, Australia, Oceania and Antarctic. Annual author, subject and geographical indexes.
11 separate parts are available. (For details see v. 1 of *Guide* (2nd ed), at 551.4:016.)

91:016

VINGE, C. L., and VINGE, A. G. U.S. government publications for research and teaching in geography and related social and natural sciences. Totowa, N.J., Littlefield, Adams, 1967. 360p.

A revision of the monograph published by the National Council for Geographic Education in 1962.
Includes entries taken from the *Monthly catalog of United States government publications,* arranged by government department.

91:016

WRIGHT, J. K., and PLATT, E. T. Aids to geographical research; bibliographies, periodicals, atlases, gazetteers and other reference books. 2nd ed., completely revised. New York, published for the American Geographical Society by the Columbia Univ. Press, 1947. xii, 331p. (American Geographical Society Research series no. 22).

First published 1923.

A valuable tool that badly needs revising. 1,174 numbered items. Annotations are detailed and evaluative. Contents: Introduction—General aids—Topical aids—Regional aids (by areas and countries) and general geographical periodicals. Detailed index of the items listed.

C. D. Harris's *Bibliographies and reference works for research in geography* (Chicago, Univ. of Chicago Press, Dept. of Geography, 1967. 89p. Mimeographed) serves as a supplement to Wright and Platt.

C. S. Minto's *How to find out in geography* (Oxford, Pergamon Press, 1966. xiii, 99p. illus., facs. 10s. 6d.) lists c. 650 books, periodicals and atlases considered suitable for undergraduate readers. The chapters are in Dewey classification order, to stress different aspects of geography. Omits guides. Very brief index. For beginners. *Concise guide to the literature of geography;* edited by J. Burkett and prepared by students of the School of Librarianship, Ealing Technical College (London, Ealing Technical College, 1967. 47p. 7s. 6d.) is a wide-ranging introduction, with annotated entries on bibliographies, societies, periodicals, reference material, maps and atlases, and storage and retrieval of geographical information. Index.

Manuals

(See also Guide (2nd ed.), v. 1, at 551.4 (021/022).

91 (021)
Géographie universelle: publiée sous la direction de P. Vidal de la Blache et L. Gallois. Paris, Colin, 1927-48. 15v. in 23. illus., maps.

v. 1: *Les îles britanniques* (A. Demangeon). 1927.
v. 2: *Belgique, Pays-Bas, Luxembourg* (A. Demangeon). 1927.
v. 3: *États scandinaves. Régions polaires boréales* (M. Zimmermann). 1933.
v. 4: *Europe centrale* (E. de Martonne). 1931. 2v.
v. 5: *États de la Baltique. Russie* (P. Camena d'Almeida). 1932.
v. 6: *La France (France physique)* (E. de Martonne). 1942.
  —*(France économique et humaine).* A. Damangeon). 1947-48. 2v.
v. 7: *Méditerranée. Péninsules méditerranéennes* (M. Sorre, etc.). 1933-34. 2v.
v. 8: *Asie occidentale* (R. Blanchard). *Haute Asie* (F. Grenard). 1929.
v. 9: *Asie des moussons* (J. Sion). 1928-29. 2v.
v. 10: *Océanie* (P. Privat - Deschanel). *Régions polaires australes* (M. Zimmermann). 1930.
v. 11: *Afrique séptentrionale et occidentale* (A. Bernard). 1939. 2v.
v. 12: *Afrique équatorial, orientale et australe* (F. Maurette). 1938.
v. 13: *Amérique septentrionale* (H. Baulig). 1935-36. 2v.
v. 14: *Mexique et Amérique centrale* (M. Sorre). 1928.
v. 15: *Amérique du sud* (P. Denis). 1927. 2v.

Each volume is by an authority. Covers economic, human and social geography. Chapter bibliographies are a feature, but a general index to the whole work is lacking. For the larger reference library.

Also for the large library is an older work, still valued for its scope and detailed treatment: *Nouveau dictionnaire de géographie universelle,* by Louis Vivien de Saint-Martin and Louis Rousselet (Paris, Hachette, 1877-95. 7v.; Supplément 1-2. 1895-1900. 2v.). It covers physical, political and economic geography, ethnology and historical geography, and carries bibliographies.

91 (021)
Géographie universelle Larousse. Ouvrage publié sous la direction de Pierre Deffontaines avec la collaboration de Muriel Jean-Brunhes Delamarre. Paris, Larousse, 1958-60. 3v. illus., diagrs., maps, plans, tables. 242F.

1. *L'Europe péninsulaire.* 1958. 84F.
2 *Afrique. Asie péninsulaire. Océanie.* 1959. 84F.
3. *Extrême Orient. Plaines eurasiatiques. Amérique.* 1960. 84F.

63 contributors, roughly one per country. Lavishly illustrated (1,804 black-and-white and 84 excellent coloured illustrations). 16 double-page coloured maps and 194 black-and-white maps, although the latter are at times (*e.g.,* economic maps) overcrowded. Bibliographies appended to contributions on countries run usually to 6-10 items. V. 3 includes an index of place names for the whole work. A stimulating visual aid to the study of geography, illustrations occupying about the same amount of space as text. The text shows some unevenness of treatment. Thus, while the orogenesis of the Appennines is fairly discussed, the structure of the Alps scarcely receives a mention. West and Central Africa could have been treated in greater detail. Reviewed in *Geographical review,* v. 51, no. 4, October 1961, p. 604.

The *Larousse encyclopedia of world geography* (London, Hamlyn, [1964]. 736p. illus., maps. 105s.) is adapted from the *Géographie universelle Larousse.* It has 820 black-and-white maps and illustrations (86 in colour). Contributors are not stated; illustrations are poorly placed. 30% of text devoted to European countries, 10% to North America. No cross-references in text; no bibliographies (or even sources, for statistics). Recommended (*The booklist,* v. 63, no. 1, September 1966, p. 3), not for use as a library reference book but for home reading and as secondary geographical material in public, college and secondary school libraries.

91 (021)
Geographies for advanced study. Editor, S. H. Beaver. London, Longmans, Green, 1953-. illus., diagrs., maps.

A reliable series, more up-to-date and detailed as well as better illustrated than the more extensive Methuen Advanced geographies series (volumes of which tend to be reprinted without changes). Chapter references and analytical index to each.

(a) *Geography of population,* by J. Beaujeu-Garnier. 1966. 45s.
Geomorphology, by B. W. Sparks. 1960. 37s. 6d.
Human geography, by A. V. Perpillou. 1965. 50s.
Statistical methods and the geographer, by S. Gregory. 1963. 30s.
The tropical world, by P. Gourou. 4th ed. 1966. 30s.

(b) *A regional geography of Western Europe*, by F. J. Monkhouse. 1959. 50s.

The Western Mediterranean world, by J. M. Houston. 1964. 63s.

The British Isles, by L. D. Stamp and S. H. Beaver. 4th ed. 1954. 46s. 6d.

Central Europe, by A. F. A. Multon. 1961. 50s.

The Soviet Union, by G. Jorré. 2nd ed. 1961. 40s.

The Scandinavian world, by A. C. O'Dell. 1957. 45s.

Malaya, Indonesia, Borneo and the Philippines, by C. Robequain. 2nd ed. 1958. 42s.

Land, people and economy in Malaya, by Ooi Jin-Bee. 1963. 45s.

West Africa, by R. J. H. Church. 5th ed. 1966. 60s.

An historical geography of South Africa, by N. C. Pollock and S. Agnew. 1964. 30s.

North America, by J. W. Watson. 1963. 57s. 6d.

The Polar world, by P. D. Baird. 1964. 37s. 6d.

West Africa is by the Professor of Geography in the University of London. It has 89 maps and diagrams and 114 plates. Individual countries (part 3) are covered on p. 177-526. Chapter bibliographies, footnote references; detailed, non-analytical index. An earlier edition was translated into Russian.

91 (021)
Methuen's Advanced geographies. London, Methuen.

A series of standard text-books, usually adequately equipped with maps and chapter bibliographies. Tend to be reprinted rather than revised. But some of the volumes are outstandingly good (*e.g., Ireland*, by T. W. Freeman (3rd ed. 1965), considered in *Geographical journal*, v. 132, pt. 2, June 1966, p. 274-5, to be "the only comprehensive geography of Ireland"). In U.D.C. order:

Maps and diagrams, by F. J. Monkhouse and H. R. Wilkinson. 2nd ed. 1963. 42s.

Map projections, by G. P. Kellaway. 2nd ed. 1953. 15s.

The skin of the earth, by A. A. Miller. 1953. 21s.

Coastal and marine morphology, by A. Guilcher. 1958. 42s.

Climatology, by A. A. Miller. 9th ed. 1961. 30s.

The earth's problem climates, by G. T. Trewartha. 1962. 60s.

Plant and animal geography, by M. I. Newbigin. 3rd. ed. 1950. 30s.

Geography in the twentieth century, by G. Taylor. 3rd. ed. 1957. 50s.

Urban geography, by G. Taylor. 2nd ed. 1951. 45s.

A geography of Europe, by G. W. Hoffman. 2nd ed. 1961. 75s.

An economic geography of Great Britain, by W. Smith. 2nd ed. 1953. 63s.

Ireland, by T. W. Freeman. 2nd ed. 1960. 40s. 3rd ed. 1965. 65s.

Wales, by E. G. Bowen. 1957. 50s.

Germany, by R. E. Dickinson. 2nd ed. 1961. 65s.

France, by H. Ormsby. 3rd ed. 1964. 50s.

A geography of Italy, by D. S. Walker. 2nd ed. [1967]. 63s.

A geography of Spain and Portugal, by R. Way. 1962. 45s.

Asia, by Sir L. D. Stamp. 10th ed. 1959. 60s.

South-east Asia, by C. A. Fisher. 1964. 84s.

The Middle East, by C. A. Fisher. 5th ed. 1962. 50s.

Japan, by G. T. Trewartha. 2nd ed. 1965. 84s.

India and Pakistan [including Ceylon], by O. H. K. Spate. 2nd ed. 1957. 90s.

Africa, by W. Fitzgerald. 10th ed. 1967. 63s.

West Africa, by J. C. Pugh and W. B. Morgan. 1965. 63s.

South Africa, by M. Cole. 1961. 105s.

Anglo-America, by P. Griffin, and others. 1963. 63s.

North America, by Ll. R. Jones and P. W. Bryan. 10th ed. 1954. 36s.

Canada, by G. Taylor. 3rd rev. ed. 1957. 45s.

South America, by E. W. Shanahan. 4th ed. 1963. 30s.

Australia, by G. Taylor. 7th ed. 1959. 42s.

91 (022)
Focus. New York, American Geographical Society, 1950-. v. 1, no. 1-. Monthly. ea. 50c.

Earlier sub-title: "presenting a brief, readable, up-to-date survey of a country, region or resource [*e.g.*, Water; Uranium], helpful in understanding current world events". V. 17, no. 10, June 1967: *South Africa* consists of a folder of 6 pages, with 6 maps, 2 graphs and a brief bibliography of 8 items. Sections cover environment, history, industrialisation, agriculture, mineral wealth, transport, and the people. 50 titles in this series are still in print.

Encyclopaedias

91 (031)=82
GRIGOR'EV, A. A., *ed.* **Kratkaya geograficheskaya entsiklopediya.** Moscow, Gos. Nauchnoe Izd-vo "Sovetskaya Entsiklopediya", [1960]-66. 5v. illus., maps.

"A concise geographical encyclopaedia", covering economic and physical geography, as well as touching on geology, geophysics, biology, economics, ethnography, etc. V. 1 has 3,500 entries, some 300 poor illustrations (including 50 coloured), 26 excellent coloured maps and 80 maps in the text. The signed article on Ghana in v. 1 runs to 5 columns, has 3 maps, 2 illustrations and 8 lines of bibliography. Russian slant. The A-Z sequence concludes in v. 5, which has a supplement of articles, reference tables of geographical data and biographical notes on explorers, geographers and the like (*e.g.*, Stamp, Mortonne, Mackinder), with reference back to the main sequence for mentions in articles. Essentially, though not solely, a high-quality gazetteer. Detailed appraisal in *Geographical review*, v. 58, no. 1, January 1968, p. 161-2.

91 (032)
STAMP, *Sir* L. D., *ed.* **Longman's dictionary of geography.** London, Longmans, 1966. xv, 492p. 85s.

Aims to serve as a companion to the textbook of the student, and a source of basic information for the citizen (*Preface*). An encyclopædic dictionary, including biographies of geographers; entries for countries, towns, states, mountains, rivers, etc., for terms in geomorphology, geology, commodities, for societies, journals and awards. Population figures to 1960/61. Quotes 9 standard sources, including Chisholm and *Glossary of geographical terms* Appendix: 'A selected bibliography of geographical books' (in print February 1965), p. 483-92. Well produced. A handy compendium that supplements the general encyclopædia.

91 (033)

The Geographical digest . . . Edited by H. Fullard. London, Philip, 1963-. tables, maps. (Annual). (1967. 10s. 6d.).

Concise data on recent changes in the world, of interest to geographers, *e.g.*, political, administrative and place-name changes; statistics of population, production and trade; new sources of raw materials; engineering projects; communications; exploration; discovery and survey (including space research); major geographical catastrophes. The 1967 issue cites statistics for 1964 or 1965 and gives some sources and footnotes.

J. Laffin's *New geography, 1966-67* (London, etc., Abelard-Schumann, 1967. 237p. 25s.) is a more casual selection of data on current topics. About 200 entries, for subjects and areas, A-Z, from 'air transport' and 'Aden' to 'weather forecasting' and 'Zambia'. Predominantly economic data. Gives 'snippet' information (*British book news*, no. 321, May 1967, p. 385). Index has grouped headings. Aims to be two-yearly.

Dictionaries

91 (038)=00

BONACKER, W. Karten-Wörterbuch: eine Verdeutschung fremdsprachiger Kartensignatur-Bezeichungen . . . 2 erw. Aufl. Berlin-Friedenball, Spiegel Verlag P. Lippa, 1957. xxiv, 288p.

First published 1941.
A polyglot glossary of terms (physical features, etc.) occurring on maps. No less than 56 languages are covered, including Breton, Cambodian, Osset and Tatar. Under each language about 450 words are given in the native tongue, first transliterated, then in the original script, with the German meaning and notes on pronunciation of the original. Some 21,000 terms are so covered.

91 (038)=00

GREAT BRITAIN. WAR OFFICE. Geographical Section, General Staff. **Short glossaries.** London, 1943-. 30v.

The following short glossaries have been published:
Albanian. 2nd ed. October 1946.
Bulgarian. Provis. ed. May 1943.
Chinese. January 1943.
Czech and Slovak. July 1943.
Danish. Provis. ed. May 1943.
Dutch. Provis. ed. May 1943.
Estonian. Provis. ed. July 1943.
Finnish. May 1943.
French. May 1943.
German. May 1943.
Greek. May 1943.
Hungarian. July 1943.
Icelandic. March 1944.
Indo-Chinese. February 1945.
Italian. May 1943.
Japanese. Provis. ed. July 1943.
Latvian. Provis. ed. July 1943.
Lithuanian. Provis. ed. July 1943.
Malay. Provis. ed. and 1st ed. August 1943.
Norwegian. Provis. ed. May 1943.
Persian. Provis. ed. July 1943.
Polish. July 1943.
Portuguese. Provis. ed. May 1943.
Rumanian. May 1943.
Russian. May 1943.

Serb and Croat. May 1943.
Spanish. May 1943.
Swedish. Provis. ed. May 1943.
Thai (Siamese). October 1943.
Turkish. July 1943.
Coverage: terms usually found in maps. The term or abbreviation is followed by romanized form and meaning. Less extensive than the R.G.S. *Glossaries (q.v.)* so far as the range of terms is concerned.

91 (038)=00

ROYAL GEOGRAPHICAL SOCIETY. Permanent Committee on Geographical Names for British Official Use. **Glossaries.** London, the Society, 1942-. v. 1-.

1. *Modern Greek.* 1942.
2. *Russian.* 1942.
3. *Albanian.* 1943.
4. *Serbo-Croat and Slovene.* 1943.
5. *Romanian.* 1944.
6. *Thai (Siamese).* 1944.
7. *Turkish.* 1945.
8. *Japanese.* 1954.
9. *Arabic.* 1961.
10. *Vietnamese.* 1963.
11. *Hebrew.* 1964.

A series of glossaries of terms (physical features, etc.) and abbreviations occurring on maps, charts, etc. of the country concerned. The word is given in native form, then romanized, with the English meaning and note on application. V. 9-11 are duplicated and unpriced; v. 9-10 are no longer available.

91 (038)=20

MONKHOUSE, F. J. A dictionary of geography. London, Arnold, 1965. v, 344p. diagrs., maps. 35s.

3,400 entries, selected on the basis of usage and arranged A-Z. Gives specific, factual information on terms, plus etymology and cross-references rather than mere definitions. Supported by 225 maps and well-drawn diagrams. The critical review in *Geographical review* (v. 57, no. 1, January 1967, p. 134-6) notes errors and omissions, and that in the *Times literary supplement* (no. 3,331, 30th December 1965, p. 1218) asks for whom the book is intended and hints at a lack of balance in the entries. The author is Professor of Geography at the University of Southampton.

91 (038)=20

MOORE, W. G. A dictionary of geography: definitions and explanations of terms used in physical geography. 4th rev. ed. London, Black, 1967. [viii], 246p. illus. (incl. pl.), diagrs., maps. 30s.

First published 1949 (Penguin Books).
Clear definitions of c. 2,000 terms, including some peculiar to certain countries. Includes "a generous sprinkling of climatological and meteorological terms" (*Note to the first edition*). Entries vary in length from 8 words ('fluvial') to one page (*e.g.,* 'Monsoon'). Very numerous cross-references; no bibliographies.

A. Knox's *Glossary of geographical and topographical terms* (London, Stanford, 1904. 432p.) still has value.

91 (038)=20

STAMP, *Sir* **L. D.,** *ed.* **A glossary of geographical terms;** prepared by a Committee of the British Association for the Advancement of Science. 2nd ed. London, Longmans, 1966. xxxi, 539p. 75s.

First published 1961.

Covers physical, human, economic and political geography. Various definitions, drawn freely from leading works with acknowledgements, are given, with 'Comment' added, if called for. Thus the entry on 'Isolation' (p. 261) cites definitions from the O.E.D., Mill and the *Meteorological glossary,* followed by a comment of 15 lines, including two references. Includes foreign terms (*e.g.,* 'Liwa'). The 2nd ed. introduces some new terms and re-defines others; also adds entries in the field of mathematical geography. Appendices: 1, Greek and Latin roots commonly used in construction of terms. 2, List of words in foreign languages which have been absorbed into English literature. 3, Some stratigraphical terms. No illustrations or diagrams. 'List of standard works to which reference is made under abbreviated titles', p. xix-xxvi.

91 (038)=30

FISCHER, E., and **ELLIOTT, F. E. A German & English glossary of geographical terms.** New York, American Geographical Society, 1950. vii, 111p. (American Geographical Society Library series 5).

Attempts to include the terms that the geographer is most likely to encounter; specialized terms in related sciences have been omitted. Geomorphology is included, since in Germany geomorphology is regarded as an integral part of geography. Short biographies of eminent geographers; entries on peoples and races. Considered (White, C. M., etc. *Sources of information in the social sciences,* entry B 369) particularly valuable for its definitions in physical and mathematical geography. Chief source books, p. iv-v.

91 (038)=40

DAINVILLE, F. de, with **GRIVOT, F. Le langage des géographes:** termes, signes, couleurs des cartes anciennes, 1500-1800. Paris, Picard, 1964. [xxi], 384p. illus., facsims., maps.

Three main parts: 1. Géographie astronomique —2. Géographie naturelle—3. Géographie historique. Index of terms, abbreviations, signs and colours. Sources, p. xiii-xviii.

91 (038)=40

INSTITUT GÉOGRAPHIQUE NATIONAL. Lexique anglais-français des termes appartenant aux techniques en usage à l'Institut Géographique National. Paris, the Institute, 1956-58. 2 pts. in 3v.

pt. 1, v. 1: Géodesie et nivellement; topographie; photogrammetrie; cartographie; optique; photographie générale; mécanique; chimie; physique; navigation. 1956.
pt. 1, v. 2: Liste des abréviations anglaises et américaines; liste de grandeurs et de l'unités, avec leurs définitions; tableaux d'équivalents d'unités; tableaux de transformation; annexes sur les projections. 1958.
pt. 2: Reproductions et tirages. 1958.

91 (038)=82

TELBERG, I. Russian-English geographical encyclopedia. New York, Telberg Book Co., 1960. 142 l. map. $9.80.

Based on entries in the 2nd ed. of M. S. Bodnarskiĭ's *Slovar' geograficheskikh nazvanii* [Dictionary of geographical names] (Moscow, 1958).

A. Sarna's *Russian-English dictionary of geographical terms* (New York, Telberg Book Co., 1963-64. 2v. ea. $9.80) is based on terms and definitions in *Kratkaya geograficheskaya entsiklopediya* (1960-64. v. 1-4). Most of the terms could be found in any good general or scientific Russian-English dictionary. "If the padding were cut out the result might make a very useful appendix to a real dictionary" (*The incorporated linguist,* v. 4, no. 1, January 1965, p. 25).

Periodicals

91 (05):016

HARRIS, C. D. An annotated world list of selected current geographical serials in English; with an appendix of major periodicals in various languages regularly providing English summaries of articles, or periodicals partly in English and partly in other languages. Chicago, Illinois, Department of Geography, Univ. of Chicago; [London, Royal Geographical Society], 1960. 14p. 2s. 6d.

Contents: A. Key international periodicals—B. Other scholarly serials, listed by country (14 countries)—C. Periodicals for the general reader —D. Bibliographies (nos. 42-45)—E. Appendix (31 titles). 76 titles in all, with 10-40 word annotations (main features; reviews carried, etc.).

"Current geographical serials, 1960", by C. D. Harris and J. D. Fellman, in *Geographical review,* v. 51, no. 2, April 1961, p. 284-9, gives a broad analysis of 420 geographical serials.

91 (05):016

HARRIS, C. D., and **FELLMAN, J. D.,** *comp.* **International list of geographical serials.** Chicago, Ill., Univ. of Chicago Press, 1960. lix, 189p. (Chicago Univ. Department of Geography. Research paper 63). $4.

1,637 numbered entries arranged by area; international periodicals are followed by country sections, arranged by countries, A-Z. "A comprehensive inventory of all known geographical serials, both those currently published and those no longer active (closed)" (*Introduction and explanation*). 47 sources of the titles listed are given on p. ix-xii. Index of titles, including cross-references.

The Royal Geographical Society's *Current geographical periodicals: a hand-list and subject index of current periodicals in the Library of the Royal Geographical Society* (London, the Society, 1961. 19p.) lists about 700 titles, alphabetically by title. A supplement (p. 16) notes geographical bibliographies, library accessions lists and cartographical bibliographies; subject index, p. 17-19.

Répertoire des principaux périodiques d'interêt géographique cités dans la 'Bibliographie géographique internationale' (Paris, Éditions du Centre National de la Recherche Scientifique, 1966. 74p.) lists *c.* 900 titles and gives addresses of publishers.

91 (05):016
HARRIS, C. D., and **FELLMAN, J. D. A union list of geographical serials.** 2nd ed. Chicago, 1950. xix, 124p. (Univ. of Chicago. Department of Geography. Research paper no. 10).

First published as *A comprehensive checklist of serials of geographical value.* pt. 1 (March 1949).
Over a thousand numbered titles are listed and arranged geographically (international: then by regions and countries). In the case of four libraries—Library of Congress, American Geographical Society, University of Chicago, and the Royal Geographical Society—complete holdings are noted. 81 libraries in all are drawn upon (2 in Britain, 4 in France and 75 in the U.S.A.). Holdings show imperfect runs. Title index.

C. D. Harris has recently produced *An annotated list of selected current geographical serials of the Americas and the Iberian peninsula* (Chicago, 1967. 16p.).

Directories

91 (058.7)
Orbis geographicus, 1964/66 . . . World directory of geography. Compiled and edited on behalf of the International Geographical Union, in co-operation with the national committees, by E. Meynen. Weisbaden, Steiner, 1964-66. 2 pts.

First issued in 1952, on the occasion of the International Geographical Congress, Washington. The 1960 issue is a special suppt. to *Geographisches Taschenbuch, 1960/61.*
Pt. 1 of the 1964/66 issue deals with the I.G.U. and with geographical and cartographical societies, institutes and agencies. Pt. 2 is a directory of *c.* 3,000 geographers (name; date of birth, degrees; present post; private address), under countries A-Z, with a name index.

The *Geographisches Taschenbuch und Jahrweiser für Landeskunde* (Weisbaden, Steiner, 1949-) is slanted towards Western Germany. It lists German institutes, organisations, geographical research workers, German surveying and mapping services, as well as geographical data and articles, plus lengthy lists of books, maps and articles and several folded coloured maps.

A Geographer's reference book (Published by the Geographical Handbook Committee. Sheffield, Geographical Association, 1955. 222p.), primarily for teachers of geography, has initial chapters on university geography departments in Great Britain and British institutions and societies of importance to the geographer. Later chapters: 'Current sources of reference material and statistics', and finally (p. 99-194), 'Some new developments in world resources', with bibliographies. Now somewhat dated.

Announced for publication: *A reference hand-book of geography,* by Muriel Lock. This is to contain basic information on professional bodies and on special geographical classification schemes, etc., as well as noting the leading subject literature.

91 (058.7)
World directory of geographers. New York, International Geographical Union, 1952. 167p.

Questionnaires on which this directory was based were sent to 60 countries. Pt. 1: Index of geographers; lists the names of 3,517 geographers in alphabetical order, noting (when made available) year of birth, present position, permanent mailing address, and regional and special interests. Pt. 2: Index of interests; is arranged alphabetically (a) by subjects, and (b) by countries. The directory was prepared with the financial assistance of Unesco and appears in English and French editions.

Gazetteers

91 (083.86)
Chambers's World gazetteer and geographical dictionary, edited by T. C. Collocott and J. O. Thorne. Rev. ed. Edinburgh, Chambers, 1965. viii, 806p. 37*s.* 6*d.*

First published 1954.
About 12,000 entries. "The normal layout of articles is: heading (in heavy type); pronunciation, if given (in italic type); alternative title or variants, if any (in small capitals); derivation, if interesting; location; description; population (where relevant); historical note (where relevant)." (*Preface*). Emphasis is on Britain (*e.g.,* Birmingham, England: 140 lines; Birmingham, Alabama: 5½ lines). The supplementary index gathers "cross-references in the form of variant names or alternative spellings, as well as references to information occurring in the main body of the text". The rev. ed. includes a digest of recent developments.

91 (083.86)
The Columbia Lippincott Gazetteer of the world; edited by Leon E. Seltzer, with the Geographical Research Staff of Columbia University Press and with the co-operation of the American Geographical Society. New York, Columbia Univ. Press; London, Oxford Univ. Press, 1952. x, 2148p. 2nd printing. New York, Columbia Univ. Press, 1962, x, 2172p. $65.

The last Lippincott gazetteer was published in 1905. "While the emphasis is on the modern world, the ancient world has not been neglected. For the United States—every county and every incorporated place in the 1950 census . . . ; for China—the seat of every county . . . ; for France every village of over 2,000 persons, as well as the capital of every canton; for the Soviet Union —every city, workers' settlement or town, and country seat" (*Preface*). Gives co-ordinates or distance to nearest larger town, plus historical, political and economic information. Some 130,000 entries; fairly balanced treatment (*e.g.,* Birmingham, England: 32 lines; Birmingham, Alabama: 26½ lines).
The 2nd printing (1962) contains a 36-page supplement, identifies the new nations and major

politico-geographical developments since 1952, and includes 1960 U.S. census figures. The supplement is available separately.

91 (083.86)

LANA, G., *and others, comp.* **Glossary of geographical names in six languages,** English/French/Italian/Spanish/German and Dutch. Amsterdam, etc., Elsevier, 1967. viii, 184p. (Glossarium interpretum, 12). D.fl. 27.50; 55s.

The 'Basic table' comprises 4,372 numbered entries and cross-references. The entries consist of the English form of place name, followed by variants (if any) in the other 5 languages. Apart from place names proper, names of some countries, counties, regions, waterways and rivers also figure. The index is a single A-Z sequence of all forms and variants given in the 'Basic table'. This glossary is a help where variants exist, but there is little point in having entries where no variants are known (*e.g.,* Accrington, Margate, Manchester). Critically reviewed in *Babel,* v. 13, no. 3, 1967, p. 188-9, and in *Geographical journal,* v. 133, pt. 4, December 1967, p. 566-7 .

91 (083.86)

ROYAL GEOGRAPHICAL SOCIETY. Permanent Committee on Geographical Names for British Official Use. **List [of names].** New series. London, the Society, 1953-.

1. *Poland* (1953).
2. *Persia* (1955).
3. *Czechoslovakia* (1958).
4. *Bulgaria* (1959).
5. *Tibet* (1967).
6. *Bahrain* (1962).
7. *Kuwait and the Neutral Zone* (1962).
8. *Mongolia* (1965).
9. *Former Izmail 'skaya oblast'* (1965).
10. *Administrative divisions of Ethiopia* (1966).
11. *Armenian SSR* (1966).
12. *Moldavian SSR* (1966).

These supersede the original series, published 1925-38. In each case official forms of names, arranged alphabetically, are given with geographical co-ordinates, an indication of their position relative to the administrative centre of the district, and a note of any superseded forms of names.

91 (083.86)

"The Times" Index-gazetteer of the world. London, "The Times" Publishing Co., Ltd., 1965. xxxi, 964p. £10.

About 345,000 geographical locations (countries, towns, villages, rivers, mountains and other geographical features), with co-ordinates and map references to the *c.* 198,000 locations given in the Mid-century edition of "The Times" Atlas of the world. The remaining locations have wavy lines in place of the map references. Geographical equivalents in some 50 languages, p. vii-xxviii. Does not give reference to the volume in which the map occurs; some omissions are noted in *The booklist,* v. 64, no. 10, 15th January 1968, p. 553-5.

91 (083.86)

UNION POSTALE UNIVERSELLE. Dictionnaire des bureaux de poste. 5. éd. Berne, Bureau International de l'Union Postale Universelle. 1951. 2 v.

About 300,000 entries. An alphabetical tabulation of locations, stating county, state or province and country. Prefatory information includes the names of countries in their own and other languages.

A comparable work, kept up to date by supplements is: International Telecommunication Union. *Official list of telegraph offices open for international traffic* (22nd ed. Geneva, the Union, 1966. 2v.). This contains about 280,000 entries.

91 (083.86)

UNITED STATES. BOARD ON GEOGRAPHIC NAMES. Gazetteers. Washington, Government Printing Office, 1955-.

A world series of gazetteers of official standard names and by far the fullest of their kind. Entries state co-ordinates, identify the feature in general terms (*e.g.,* island, point) and source of name. Gazetteer no. 83. *France* (1964. 2v.) contains *c.* 100,000 entries. Limited distribution, unpriced, as from no. 69. Many earlier volumes are o.p.

1. *British East Africa.* 1955.
2. *Madagascar,* [etc.].
3. *Jordan.*
4. *Bolivia.*
5. *Hong Kong,* [etc.].
6. *Chile* (2nd ed. 1967).
7. *British West Indies.*
8. *Albania* (2nd ed. 1961).
9. *Burma.*
10. *British Borneo.*
11. *Greece.*
12. *Japan.*
13. *Indonesia,* [etc.].
14. *Antarctica* (2nd ed. 1966).
15. *Mexico.*
16. *British Honduras.*
17. *Rhodesia and Nyasaland.*
18. *Costa Rica.*
19. *Iran.*
20. *Angola.*
21. *Uruguay.*
22. *China.* 2v.
23. *Italy,* [etc.].
24. *Hawaiian Islands.*
25. *Nicaragua.*
26. *El Salvador.*
27. *Honduras.*
28. *Haiti.*
29. *Southwest Pacific.*
30. *Cuba* (2nd ed. 1963).
31. *South Atlantic.*
32. *Indian Ocean.*
33. *Dominican Republic.*
34. *French West Indies.*
35. *Paraguay.*
36. *Ecuador.*
37. *Iraq.*
38. *Puerto Rico, the Virgin Islands,* [etc.]. 1958.
39. *South Pacific.* 1957.
40. *Australia.*
41. *Libya.*
42. *U.S.S.R.,* [etc.]. 7v. 1959.
43. *Germany: Soviet Zone & East Berlin.*
44. *Bulgaria.*
45. *Egypt and the Gaza Strip.*
46. *Turkey.* 1960.
47. *Germany: Federal Republic & West Berlin.* 2v.
48. *Rumania.*
49. *Ceylon.*
50. *Portugal and Cape Verde Islands.* 1961.
51. *Spain and Andorra.*
52. *Hungary.* 1961.
53. *Denmark and Faroe Island.*
54. *Arabian Peninsula.*
55. *Yugoslavia.*
56. *Venezuela.*
57. *Iceland.*
58. *Southern Vietnam and the South China Sea.*
59. *Gabon.* 1962.
60. *Cameroun.*
61. *Republic of Congo (Brazzaville).*
62. *Finland.*
63. *Rio Muni, Fernando Po,* [etc.].
64. *Central African Republic.*
65. *Chad.*
66. *Austria.*
67. *Pakistan.*
68. *Sudan.*
69. *Laos.*
70. *Mainland China.* 1963.
71. *Brazil.*
72. *Sweden.*
73. *Belgium.*
74. *Cambodia.*
75. *North Korea.*
76. *Zanzibar.*

77. *Norway*, [etc.].
78. *Kenya*. 1964.
79. *North Vietnam*.
80. *Republic of Congo*
    (*Leopoldville*)
81. *Tunisia*.
82. *Uganda*.
83. *France*. 2v.
84. *Burundi*.
85. *Rwanda*.
87. *Upper Volta*. 1965.
88. *Senegal*.
89. *Colombia*.
90. *Ivory Coast*.
91. *Guinea*.
92. *Tanzania*.
93. *Mali*.
94. *Guatemala*.
95. *South Korea*.
96. *Burma*. 1966.
97. *Thailand*.
98. *Togo*.
99. *Niger*.
100. *Mauritania*.
101. *Sierra Leone*.
102. *Ghana*. 1967.

91 (083.86)

Webster's Geographical dictionary: a dictionary of names of places, with geographical and historical information and pronunciations. [Rev. ed.] Springfield, Mass., Merriam; London, Bell, 1955 (& revised reprints, *e.g.*, 1966. 90*s*.). xxxi, 1293p. 24 maps.

First published 1949.
About 40,000 place-names, with pronunciation, pertinent geographical information and adequate cross-references. Ancient and medieval place-names are included and the lengthy prefatory material carries tables of geographical terms in various languages (pp. xx–xxv). Entries are usually brief (*e.g.*, Birmingham, England: 10½ lines; Birmingham, Alabama: 9 lines). Minimum population of towns and villages included: 1,500 for U.S.A. and Canada; 3,000 for South Africa; 5,000 for the British Isles, Australia, New Zealand and most of Latin America; 10,000 for Western and Central Europe, Argentina and Brazil; 20,000 for India and the Philippines; 25,000 for U.S.S.R., China and Japan. Designed primarily for the North American user (*e.g.*, Portsmouth, England: 6 lines; Portsmouth, Virginia: 13 lines).
Revision in post-1955 reprints is minor, *e.g*, new census figures; changed names of African territories.

91 (083.86):016

"Preliminary list of reference material dealing with geographical names". In *World cartography*, v. 6, 1958 [i.e., 1960], p. 55-69.

Lists "gazetteers, geographical dictionaries, indexes to atlas or map series, and other publications dealing with geographical names" received in the United Nations Library up to 1959. 724 numbered items, arranged A-Z by country of publication, with index of countries and territories. Gives title, publisher, place of publication, date, language, and number of pages listing place-names (*i.e.*, excluding pages of maps, etc.).
See also "List of national authorities dealing with geographical names", in *World cartography*, v. 7, 1962, p. 17-18, and a further list of authorities in Aurousseau, M. *The rendering of geographical names* (Hutchinson, 1957), p. 113-28.

History of Geography

91 (091)

DICKINSON, R. E., and HOWARTH, O. J. R. The making of geography. Oxford, Clarendon Press, 1933. [vi], 264p. illus. (pl.).

Chapters 1-15 deal with historical aspects. Chapters 16-20: The development of physical geography—The development of human geography—The development of biogeography—The regional concept—Summary and conclusions. Appended is a selected list (p. 254-8) of books and articles which deal specifically with the history of geography, general and by chapters. Standard works are mentioned in the text proper. Detailed index. "The best general history of geography" (Church, M., and others, comp. and ed. *A basic geographical library* (1966), entry no. 188).

91 (091) "—"

BESNIER, M. Lexique de géographie ancienne. Paris, Klincksieck, 1914. xx, 893p.

At each entry is given the ancient name, the modern one when established, references to the sheets of the *Atlas antiquus* of A. van Kampen (London, Macmillan, 1908), and to principal published authorities. Individual monuments and parts of towns are not included and relatively more space is given to obscure than to famous places.
Dictionnaire de géographie ancienne et moderne . . . , by P. Deschamps (Paris, Maisionneuve et Larose, 1964, viii, 1594; ii, 208p.), originally published in 1870 and functioning as a supplement to Brunet's *Manuel*, lists nearly 8,500 ancient place-names, Greek and Latin.
J. G. T. Graesse's *Orbis Latinus oder Verzeichnis der wichtigsten lateinischen Orts- und Ländernamen*. 2. Aufl. Neubearb. von F. Benedict (Berlin, Schmidt, 1909. vii, 348p.) lists medieval Latin place-names and (in the first ed.) their modern equivalents.

91 (091) "—"

THOMSON, J. O. History of ancient geography. Cambridge, Univ. Press, 1948 (reprinted 1965). xi, 427p. illus. maps. 108*s*.

12 chapters, ending with the 5th century A.D. A scholarly survey of the beliefs and theories about the cosmos, heavens and earth, by the one-time Professor of Latin in the University of Birmingham. Profuse footnote references, but with citations drastically curtailed. Notes on books, etc., p. 392-4. 66 illustrations in the text and maps. Detailed index. Very readable; "the definitive work on the legacy of classical geographers" (Parry, J. H. *The age of reconnaissance* (1963), p. 347).

An older worker still of value is H. F. Tozer's *A history of ancient geography* (2nd ed., with additional notes by M. Cary. Cambridge, Univ. Press, 1935. xxxv, 387p. o.p.), a follow-up of E. H. Bunbury's classic *History of ancient geography* (1879; 2nd ed. New York, Dover, 1959. 2v. $12.50).

91 (091) "04/14"

KIMBLE, G. H. T. Geography in the Middle Ages. London, Methuen, 1938. xi, 272p. illus.

A survey in 10 chapters, with 20 illustrations, by the then Lecturer in Geography at the University of Reading. Numerous footnote references. The select bibliography (p. 245-57) contains of a valuable list of texts and another of secondary material, including periodical articles.

GEOGRAPHY

Biography

91 (092)

CRONE, G. R. Modern geographers: an outline of progress in geography since A.D. 1800. London, Royal Geographical Society, 1959. 56p., with 7 pl. and map.

The development of geographical theories in the last 150 years, outlined in a series of biographical sketches of leading geographers, from Humboldt to Mackinder and Bowman.

Urban Geography

91-203:016

SOMMER, J. W. Bibliography of urban geography, 1940-1964. Hannover, N.H., Dartmouth College, Department of Geography, 1966. vii, 94p. (Geography publications at Dartmouth, no. 5).

1,310 numbered items arranged by major world areas (Great Britain, nos. 308-502) then by authors, A-Z. Aims "to bring together the scholarly periodical literature" (*Introduction*) and draws upon 77 serials, chiefly in English or French. Author index and a generalised subject index.

Travel

910.2

ROYAL GEOGRAPHICAL SOCIETY. Hints to travellers. London, the Society. v. 1. 11th ed. 1935. v. 2. 11th ed. 1938 (reprinted 1944).

First published 1854.
v. 1: Survey and field astronomy (instruments; calculations; geographical surveying and mapping).
v. 2: Organization and equipment. Scientific observation. Health, sickness and injury.
A practical manual, now partly superseded but still of considerable value.

The medical chapters in the *Hints* are replaced by J. M. Adams' *A traveller's guide to health* (London, Hodder & Stoughton, for R.G.S., 1966. 189p. illus. 12s. 6d.), primarily designed for the small scientific expedition that has no doctor. Valuable also to the explorer, mountaineer and even tourist. Appendices contain suggestions for further reading. Reviewed in *The lancet,* no. 7,464, 17th September 1966, p. 624.

Exploration

910.3:016

CIVICA BIBLIOTECA BERIO, Genoa. Raccolta Colombiana. **Catalogo della Raccolta Colombiana.** Civica Biblioteca Berio. Boston, Mass., G. K. Hall, 1963. 151p. $30 (U.S. & Italy).

3,100 catalogue cards, photolithographically reproduced,—the catalogue of the Columbus Collection, Berio Civic Library. One of the largest collections on the voyages and discoveries of Columbus and other early explorers of the Western hemisphere.

910.3 (084.4)

Atlas istorii geograficheskikh otkrytiĭ i issledovaniĭ. Moscow, Glavnoe Upravlenie Geodezii i Kartografii, 1959. 198p. R30.

Historical atlas of geographical discovery and exploration. 92 pages of maps showing routes taken by explorers of all nationalities in all parts of the world. "Stress is on the territory of the U.S.S.R. and on the exploits of Russian travelers and navigators" (*Guide to Russian reference books,* by K. Maichel. v. 2 (1964), item F172).

910.3 (084.4)

DEBENHAM, F. Discovery and exploration: an atlas-history of men's journeys into the unknown. London, Hamlyn, 1960. 272p. illus., maps. 42s.

A well illustrated book for older children. Arranged by continents. Recommended in *Geographical journal* (v. 127, pt. 3, September 1961, p. 347) for the plotting of itineraries and adequate portrayal in maps. Many well chosen and unusual illustrations. Brief biographies of explorers. Includes a gazetteer section, "Books about explorers and exploration" (p. 246-51), a general, analytical index and a map index. Brief biographies of explorers.

910.3 (091)

BAKER, J. N. L. A history of geographical discovery and exploration. 2nd ed. London, Harrap, 1937.

First published 1931.
Quotes original sources; liberal maps; valuable bibliographies; full index. The standard work on the subject.

Noted: Zavatti, S. *Dizionario degli esploratori e delle scoperte geografiche* (Milan, Feltrinelli, 1967. vi, 360 p. maps. L.800). Brief documented biographies of travellers and explorers (especially Italian), with 25 maps of routes and a chronology. Reviewed in *Geographical journal,* v. 133, pt. 4, December 1967, p. 570.

Bibliography, documentation, terminology (v. 3, no. 2, March 1963, p. 40) mentions that a working group of the International Commission for Maritime History "is continuing the *Bibliography of the History of Discoveries* in the form of a *Bibliography of the History of the Great Ocean Routes".*

910.3 (091)

BEAZLEY, Sir C. R. **The dawn of modern geography:** a history of exploration and geographical science. London, Murray, 1897-1906. 3v. (Reprinted Gloucester, Mass., Peter Smith, 1964. 3v. $35).

Part 1 deals with the period "from the conversion of the Roman Empire to A.D. 900, with an account of the achievements and writings of the early Christian, Arab and Chinese travellers and students". Part 2 covers the period from the close of the 9th to the mid-13th century (c. A.D. 900-1266). Part 3: 1260-1420, with an appendix on the leading manuscripts of the principal texts in pts. 2 and 3, and an analytical index. Numerous footnote references. A detailed, scholarly study.

Expeditions

910.4

TEREK, E. Scientific expeditions. Jamaica, N.Y., Queens Borough Public Library, 1952. xvii, 176p.

Lists major scientific expeditions, with data on purpose personnel, equipment, sponsorship and the like; bibliography of source material and index of members and sponsors of expeditions (Murphey, R. W. *How and where to look it up,* p. 642).

Shipwrecks

910.45
HOCKING, C. Dictionary of disasters at sea during the age of steam; including sailing-ships and ships of war lost in action, 1824-1962. London, Lloyd's Register of Shipping.

Due for publication 1968.
The result of more than 15 years of research. Describes in narrative form every known ship loss of consequence.

Tropics

91 (213):016
UNITED STATES. DEPARTMENT OF THE ARMY. Natick Laboratories. **An inventory of**

geographic research of the humid tropic environment. Dallas, Texas Instruments, Inc., 1965-66. 2v.

> v. 1. *KWIC index: Humid tropic environment literature.*
> v. 2. *Compendium and appendices.*

V. 2 is described in *Geographical journal* (v. 133, pt. 3, September 1967, p. 408) as an exhaustive guide and bibliography, sponsored by the Office of the Chief of Research and Development Department of the Army, Earth Sciences Division.

K. H. Stone's *A bibliography of bibliographies on the geography of the tropical region* (Athens, Ga., Univ. of Georgia, Department of Geography, for the Geographic Section, Organization for Tropical Studies, 1966, [iii], 8 l. Mimeographed) lists *c.* 110 items, under authors A-Z. Includes periodical articles; no annotations. May be followed by a 'second phase' bibliography, "preferably annotated, of principal works on the region and its parts" (*Preface*).

912 ATLASES & MAPS

(On Cartography, see Guide (2nd ed.) v. 1, *at 528.9.)*

912 (4/9)
Atlante internazionale del Touring Club Italiano. 9. ed. Milan, Consociazione Turistica Italiana, 1956. 2v. (maps and index). L. 52,000.

First published 1927; 8th ed. 1951; the 9th ed. is termed "edizione del sessantennio".
The 9th ed. is made up of separately issued double maps—93 maps on 173 plates, with 154 large-scale insets. The maps are well designed and well produced, particularly useful for location purposes. Relief is by hachuring and shading in light buff and almost the maximum number of names have been inserted on some plates. The British "R.G.S. II" system has been largely followed in transliterating non-Roman scripts, making the large index (*Indice dei nomi.* 1956 [1957]. 257p.) of *c.* 250,000 entries convenient for English readers. On the reverse of maps are notes on sources, glossaries of appropriate topographical terms, etc. "One of the most elaborate, detailed and cartographically superior of world atlases" (Church, M., and others, comp. and ed. *A basic geographical library* (1966), entry no. 43. Page size: 20" × 14⅛".

912 (4/9)
Atlas général Larousse. Paris, Larousse, 1959. [v], 456p. maps, tables. 99.50F.

Contains 431 maps and insets in colour, 183 town plans, 250 statistical tables (figures, to 1957) and an index-gazetteer with 55,000 entries. Physical, political, geological, historical and economic maps are followed by the index-gazetteer which is studded with tiny town plans of selected cities; appended are more than 50 pages of historical notes and 30 pages of statistics. Intended particularly for the student and general reader. The

review in the *Scottish geographical magazine,* December 1959, p. 186, calls for two main improvements: greater legibility through less liberal use of bold type, and greater accuracy. Hill shading is good but some of the special maps, particularly in concentrated areas like the North African coast, are too crammed with details. A scale of 1:1M is often used. Page size, 11⅞" × 7⅝".

912 (4/9)
L'Atlas historique et géographique Vidal-Lablache. Nouv. éd. Paris, Colin, 1951. 130p. of maps and 31p. of index.

First published 1894.
The 1936 [4th] edition carried more maps and a considerably larger index-gazetteer than the 1951 edition. Two parts: 1. Cartes historiques (ancient, medieval and modern history). 2. Cartes géographiques (including physical, political, economic, communications, ethnogeographical, etc. maps).
385 maps, including insets; index gazetteer of 32,000 names (1936 ed.: 420 maps; index gazetteer of 69,500 names). Page size: 14½" × 10".

912 (4/9)
Atlas international Larousse politique et économique. Publié sous la direction de I. du Jonchay et de S. Rado. Nouv. éd. ent. ref. et mise à jour. Paris, Larousse, 1966. 272p. maps. 249F.

First published [1950].
92p. of maps. The 45 pages of political maps are designed to show propinquity of neighbouring countries (*e.g.,* Common Market countries). As a result some countries are never shown in their

entirety except on a very small scale (*e.g.,* Italy, Brazil, Alaska). Some overcrowding. The 47 pages of economic maps cover agriculture and industries of continents, plus communications. Text and all annotations are in French, English and Spanish, with German, Russian and Chinese added for captions. The maps are followed by 300 statistical tables (with data for 1938-64) and an index-gazetteer of *c.* 30-35,000 entries. Page size, 20″ × 13⅛″. (Partly based on review in *The assistant librarian,* v. 60, no. 10, October 1967, p. 228.)

912 (4/9)
Atlas mira. [A. N. Baranov and others, editors]. Moscow, Glavnoe Upravlenie Geodezii i Kartografi MVD, SSSR, 1954. 280 pl. of maps. (2.izd. 1967. [xii], 250p. £30).

A finely produced world atlas. The U.S.S.R. is covered in great detail (54 maps), ranging from a general map (1:10M. scale) to regional maps (1:1½M.); but other countries are also quite well recorded. The majority are physical maps, showing relief by means of a wide range of hypsometrical tints, with contours in brown and in some cases oblique shading into violet. Railways, in red, are a prominent feature. Some general political and communications maps are included. Page size 19″ × 13″. Its usefulness to non-Russian readers is limited by the fact that all names are transliterated or translated into Russian, and an attempt is made to render names phonetically.

—— **Ukazatel' geograficheskikh nazvanii.** Moscow, 1954, v. 272p.

The gazetteer or index of geographical names in the *Atlas mira;* contains rather more than 200,000 names.
An *English translation to 'Atlas mira'* of all map titles and legends in this atlas was made by V. G. Telberg (New York, Telberg Book Co., 1956. 87p.).
An octavo version (page size, 7¾″ × 4½″) of the *Atlas mira* (1963 ed.) contains 165 maps and a 128-page gazetteer listing *c.* 100,000 names.

Atlas mira does not include economic maps. These are found to some extent in *Geograficheskii atlas dlya uchitelei srednei shkoly* (2nd ed. 1959) (*q.v.*) and, for pre-war maps, in *Bol'shoi sovetskii atlas mira* (v. 1. 1937) (*q.v.*).

The 2nd ed. of *Atlas mira* (1967) has 250p. of maps. It incorporates results of Russian surveys of ocean floors. Maps are unhinged and do not open flat, as in the 1954 ed. The price includes an index-gazetteer, to be published separately. Page size, 19¼″ × 12¼″.

912 (4/9)
Bertelsmann Atlas international. Gütersloh, Bertelsmann, 1963. 252, 240p. maps. DM.176.

252 pages of maps, with physical maps preponderating. Scales range from 1:2M. to 1:60M. (world). Central Europe is favoured with a scale of 1:800,000. Glossary, in German, English and French. 240p. of index-gazetteer (165,000 entries). Names of places in native form, followed by German. Page size, 12″ × 16″. "Perhaps the most outstanding of recent German world atlases"

(Church, M., *and others, comp. and ed. A basic geographical library* (1966), p. 5).

912 (4/9)
Bol'shoi sovetskii atlas mira [Great Soviet atlas of the world]. Moscow, Nauchno-izdatel'skii Institutom Bol'shogo Sovetskogo Atlasa Mira, 1937. v. 1. 168 pl. of maps.

Planned in 3v. V. 2 was apparently published in 1939, but only v. 1 is referred to in the article on geographical atlases in the 2nd ed. of the *Bol'shaya sovetskaya entsiklopediya* (v. 5, p. 542-3). The maps in v. 1 are equally divided into pt. 1, Maps of the world (plates 1-83), and pt. 2, Maps of the U.S.S.R. (plates 84-168). Complementary to the maps in the *Atlas mira* in that it has only a few physical maps of the U.S.S.R., but a number of economic, geological, etc. maps. No gazetteer.
A translation of the titles and legends of the Great Soviet atlas, volume 1, by A. Perejda and V. Washburne, appeared in 1940 (Ann Arbor, Michigan, Edwards. 168p.).

912 (4/9)
Cart actual: topical map service. Budapest, Cartactual, 1965-. no. 1-. Quarterly.

Each issue consists of a portfolio of maps, in black and white, or black and brown, well drawn, with clear lettering. Records recent changes of names of administrative divisions, new railways, new cities and boundaries. Thus v. 3, no. 10, 1967 (no. 2) has 50 maps showing new Soviet railway lines and reservoirs, new Belgian motorways, present-day Soviet boundaries, towns and changes of geographical names in Belorussia and Uzbekistan, and the new seaport of Ashdod, Israel. Subtitle and text in English, French and German. Invaluable in its field, though it sometimes anticipates events.

912 (4/9)
Cassell's New atlas of the world: the world in physical, political and economic maps, with statistics and index. Edited by Harold Fullard. London, Cassell, 1961. xviii, 130pl. of maps, 104p. of gazetteer. 105s.

Copyright: George Philip & Son, Ltd.
The regional maps are mainly political, with various scales (British Isles, 1:1M; U.S.A., 1:2½M; Central and East Africa, 1:8M; Latin America, 1:12½M). There is only one double-page map of the Middle East, plus a one-page map of Palestine, whereas the U.S.A. is given 5 double-pages. Economic and other maps follow (pl. 99-130); these include commodity world-distribution maps (pl. 116-30). Statistical data are shown by means of bar diagrams, etc. Index gazetteer of more than 66,000 entries, giving page references and co-ordinates. Page size, 13¼″ × 9¼″.

The Caxton world atlas, edited by W. Gordon East (London, Caxton Publishing Co., 1960. 532p., with 773pl. and maps. £13 15s.) also has maps by Philip. It is a profusely illustrated geographical text-book *cum* atlas. The text has a separate index of some 4,500 entries. 773 illustrations, including 32 colour plates. 104 maps of various scales and sizes; the inset sketch-maps are too small and generalized for serious use by students. Index-gazetteer of more than 60,000 names. Reviewed in *The geographical journal,* v. 126, pt. 3, September 1960, p. 359. Page size, 16" × 11".

912 (4/9)

The Edinburgh world atlas, of modern geography. 5th ed. Edinburgh, Bartholomew, 1967. [4], 108, 51p. maps. 45s.

First published 1949. Also published with *Everyman's Encyclopaedia* (1958 and 1959), and issued as *The Advanced atlas of modern geography* (*e.g.,* 7th ed. Edinburgh, Oliver & Boyd, 1963).
108 pages of maps. World maps (1-27): geology, physiography, vegetation, population, temperature, rainfall and oceanography, economic development, ethnology, routes of commerce. Area maps are physical. Maps of the British Isles are 1:1¼M.; those of Europe, 1:3M.; North America, 1:5M.; Russia, China, Japan, etc., 1:6M. The general index-gazetteer has *c.* 24,000 entries, with "hour" co-ordinates and page references. Page size 15" × 10". Excellent cartography.

Neither *The Citizen's atlas of the world* (10th ed. Edinburgh, Bartholomew, 1952), with its 200 pages of political maps of index-gazetteer of *c.* 95,000 names, nor *The Columbus atlas; or, Regional atlas of the world* (Edinburgh, Bartholomew, 1954), with its 160 pages of maps (large physical) and its index-gazetteer of *c.* 50,000 names, is now in print.

912 (4/9)

Encyclopaedia Britannica world atlas: political-physical maps, world distributions and world political geography, geographical summaries, geographical comparisons, glossary, index to political-physical maps. Chicago & London, Encyclopaedia Britannica, Inc., 1965. xiv, 416p. £10 10s.

First published 1949.
125 pages of political-physical maps, by C. S. Hammond. 508 maps in all, including thematic and conurbation maps. Various scale; some maps are fold-out. Poor coverage of British Isles (only 1 double-page spread), but U.S.A. (p. 16-125) is well covered. Text includes 'World geographical summaries', statistical data and a glossary. Index-gazetteer (*c.* 78,000 entries) includes population figures. Criticised in *The geographical journal* (v. 132, pt. 4, December 1966, p. 581-2) for adopting the much used and somewhat outdated maps produced by the Istituto Geografico de Agostini, featured in *Goldmanns grosser Weltatlas* (1963). Page size, 15" × 11".

912 (4/9)

The Faber atlas. Edited by D. J. Sinclair. 4th rev. ed. Oxford, Geo Publishing Co., Ltd., 1964 (rev. reprint, 1966). xi, 154, 44p. maps. 39s. 6d.

First published 1956.
An attractive small-sized atlas, 154 pages of physical maps, etc. Map scales usually 1:1¼M. - 1:40M. Main regional maps are good examples of layer colouring and hill shading. Includes a number of world resources maps and regional maps of land use, geology, population, as well as

some town plans. Nearly one-half of the maps concern Europe and nearly one-quarter, Britain. Index-gazetteer of *c.* 25,000 names. Page size, 12" × 8½".

912 (4/9)

Fiziko-geograficheskiĭ atlas mira. Moscow, Akademiya Nauk SSSR i Glavnoe Upravlenie Geodezii i Kartografii GGK, SSSR, 1964. 298p. maps. £20.

249 pages of physical maps, excellently coloured. Three main sections: natural features (including geology, climate, soil, vegetation) of the world as a whole (pl. 2-76; scales, 1:60M., (pl. 78-190; scales, 1:17½M., 20M., 25M., etc.); U.S.S.R. (pl. 192-249; scales, 1:15M., 20M., 35M., etc.), including climate, hydrological, etc. maps. Page size 20" × 13". Reviewed in *The geographical journal,* v. 132, pt. 1, March 1966, p. 157.
Soviet geography, v. 6, no. 5/6, May/June 1965, is a special issue of 403p., devoted to a translation of the legend matter and explanatory text of the above atlas.

Geograficheskiĭ atlas dlya uchiteleĭ srednei shkoly (Moscow, GUGK MVD SSSR, 1955 (2nd ed., 1959). 191p. illus., maps)—'Geographical atlas for secondary-school teachers'—has 156 pages of maps and charts (U.S.S.R.: 61p.), mainly physical. Index-gazetteer of *c.* 30,000 entries. Considered (Maichel, K. *Guide to Russian reference books,* v. 2, p. 209) the Soviet counterpart of such smaller medium-sized atlases as *Bartholomew's Advanced atlas* and *Goode's World atlas.*

912 (4/9)

Goldmanns grosser Weltatlas. Die Umwelt des Menschen. Astronomie, Geologie, Geographie, Klimakunde, Wirtschaft, Bevölkerungskunde. Hrsg. von L. Visintin [and others]. Völlig überarb. und erg. Neuaufl. Munich, Goldmann, 1963. vi, 332p. maps. DM.190.

Previously published 1955.
222 pages of maps. The physical maps are particularly good and well coloured, but the political maps, which are smaller, are of indifferent quality. Many small thematic maps; inset town plans; data on country accompanies maps. Index-gazetteer of *c.* 110,000 entries. Page size, 16" × 11¼".

912 (4/9)

Goode's World atlas. Edited by Edward B. Espenshade, Jr. 12th ed. Chicago, Rand McNally, 1964. xii, 288p. maps, diagrs. $9.95.

First published 1922, as *Goode's School atlas.* The 12th ed. is a revised reprinting of the 11th (1960).
The 11th ed., with 168p. of maps, has a greatly improved appearance, light contour colouring and pronounced hill-shading being used. Clear contour lines; conurbations shown in red. Mainly physical maps, often 1:4M. scale, with a variety of special maps. World maps, p. 1-48; North America, p. 49-87; Europe, p. 102-37 (including Eurasia), as well as 16 plans of cities and environs, and physiographic, land use, vegetation, minerals, languages, population and rainfall maps. 'A pronouncing index of over 30,000 geographical names' (p. 173-288) states page, name,

pronunciation, region, latitude and longitude. On maps, names are often given in native form as well as in English. Page size, $11'' \times 9\frac{1}{2}''$.

912 (4/9)

Grande atlante geografico. 5. ed. Novara, Istituto Geografico de Agostini, 1959. 323p. maps. 100s. (6th ed. 1965-66. 3v.).

232 coloured plates. "Fine physical and economic maps. The large number of world maps showing distribution of physical, cultural and economic features makes this atlas of special interest to the student" (Church, M., and others, comp. & ed. *A basic geographical library* (1966), entry no. 44). 91-page index-gazetteer of 100,000 names. Page size, $16\frac{3}{4}'' \times 11\frac{1}{4}''$.

V. 1 contains geographical and historical maps; v. 2 is a compendium of general geography and commentaries on the historical maps; v. 3 covers history of exploration (*Bollettino della Società Geographica Italiana,* series 9, v. 8, nos. 4-8, 1967, p. 235-62).

912 (4/9)

Der Grosse Bertelsmann Weltatlas. Herausgeber: Kartographisches Institut Bertelsmann; Leitung: W. Bormann, Güterloh, Bertelsmann, 1961. xxxii, 120 pl., 185, 52p. maps. DM.88.

The main sequence of maps (100 pl.) is usually on a scale of 1:5M., and consists chiefly of physical maps, with political maps of continents. The supplementary sequence (20 pl.) deals with 'Mitteleuropa' on a scale of 1:1M., this region including the Netherlands and marking conurbations (published in an English ed. as *Atlas of Central Europe* (London, Murray, 1963), *q.v.*). Hill shading is rather heavy. The index-gazetteer of 185 pages, with 52 supplementary pages for 'Mitteleuropa', has *c.* 150,000 entries. Entries are given for some places not on the maps; these are located in terms of the nearest town on the map, with distance and compass direction. End-paper key-maps. The introduction provides pronunciation keys for various languages and also a glossary (native language, with German equivalents, p. xxv-xxxi). Compares favourably with some post-war one-volume atlases for number and quality of maps and size of gazetteer. Page size, $12\frac{1}{2}'' \times 9\frac{1}{2}''$.

A revised and updated American version of this atlas appeared as the *McGraw-Hill international atlas* (1964) (*q.v.*).

912 (4/9)

Der Grosse Brockhaus Atlas. Erdkunde, Wirtschaft, Geschichte. Wiesbaden, Brockhaus, 1960. 40, 664p. illus., maps. DM.83; 155s.

This atlas accompanies the 16th ed. of *Der Grosse Brockhaus* and also *Der Neue Brockhaus* (1960). 5 sections: 'Welt und Mensch' (statistical data, etc.), p. 1-40; 'Karten zur Erdkunde' (375 coloured maps, covering topography, geology, vegetation, climate, anthropology and economy of the major regions; also historical maps), p. 1-280; 'Bilder zur Erdkunde', p. 281-392; 'Atlas zur Weltgeschichte: Karten und Bilder', p. 391-464; 'Namenverzeichnis' (index-gazetteer of about 60,000 names). Many of the 375 coloured maps are double-page; about 50 of them deal with

Germany. Town plans are included. Scales for regional maps up to 1:550,000; other scales; 1:1¼M. (1:4M. for U.S.A.). Makes a dumpy volume; page size, $9\frac{1}{2}'' \times 6''$.

912 (4/9)

Der Grosse JRO Weltatlas. Luxusausgabe. Mit 128 vielfarbigen Landkartenseiten mit über 150,000 Namen, sowie einem ausführlichen Läderlexikon, farbigen Bildern aus aller Welt, Spezialkarten, einer Flaggentafel, zwei Registern und einer Schallplatte. 21. Aufl. der Volksausg. Munich, JRO Verlag, 1961. v.p. DM.68.

First published 1949.

128 pages of politico-physical maps, with special emphasis on German-speaking Europe. Index-gazetteer of more than 150,000 names. Includes thematic maps, coloured illustrations, country data and statistics, and even a gramophone record. Page size, $17\frac{1}{4}'' \times 12\frac{1}{2}''$.

The 'Permanentausgabe' has 178 pages of politico-physical maps, 160 pages of illustrations, an index-gazetteer of *c.* 178,000 names and a larger format ($18'' \times 15''$). DM.150.

912 (4/9)

Haack Grosser Weltatlas. Gotha & Leipzig, VEB Hermann Haack, Geographisch-Kartographische Anstalt, 1967-. maps.

When completed, will comprise 118 maps, chiefly topographical. 36 maps published, to date. Of high standard. Scale mostly 1:3M., 1:6M. or 1:9M. (Germany, 1:300,000 or 1:750,000). The first large-scale representation of the DDR. A location atlas rather than an analytical tool (*Geographical journal,* v. 134, pt. 1, March 1968, p. 156). Page size, $13'' \times 11''$.

912 (4/9)

Hamlyn's New relief world atlas. Edited by S. Carpenter. London, Hamlyn, 1966. 205p. maps. 30s.

144 pages of maps, including 32 colourful regional maps and 34 large-scale detailed maps, plus sea-floor relief. Claims to be the first atlas to use exclusively special shaded relief which has a three-dimensional effect (obtained by photographing from models), but many of these heightened relief maps have previously appeared in *The "Reader's digest" Great world atlas (q.v.).* Well balanced territorially, with good coverage of Balkans and the Suez and Panama Canals. But *The cartographic journal* (v. 4, no. 1, June 1967, p. 55-56) finds landforms poorly represented. Index-gazetteer: 25,000 names; countries are not stated in entries. Page size, $12'' \times 8\frac{1}{2}'''$. "Better value than most in its price range" (*Geographical journal,* v. 133, pt. 4, December, 1967, p. 582).

912 (4/9)

The Hammond Ambassador world atlas. 2nd ed. Maplewood, N.J., Hammond, 1961 (1966 reprint). xii, 352p. maps, plans. $14.95.

First published 1954; annual revised reprints of 2nd ed.

320 pages of maps, mainly political, plus numerous black-and-white street maps. Two features: clearly marked political subdivisions and the index-gazetteer, with its 100,000 entries.

charts and data tables. 30% of the maps concern the U.S.A. The 1966 reprint has a larger format; page size, $15\frac{3}{4}'' \times 11\frac{3}{4}''$.

The Hammond *Citation world atlas* (New perspective ed. New York, Hammond, 1966. xii, 352p. maps. $7.95) is an attractive smaller atlas, with an index-gazetteer of *c*. 22,000 entries. Of the 320 pages of maps, p. 186-320 concern the U.S.A. Page size, $12\frac{1}{4}'' \times 9\frac{1}{2}''$.

912 (4/9)

International map of the world on the millionth scale: report for 1966. New York, United Nations, Department of Economic and Social Affairs, 1968. iii, 96p. (ST/ECA/SER.D/6). $2.

Section 1: Work of the United Nations [and its specialized agencies], ICAO and UNESCO, relating to the map; 2: Status of publication of IMW sheets. The latter section includes an index map showing status of publication and consists largely of a table (p. 11-90) of published sheets, with an alphabetical index. Parts of the world still not mapped on IMW sheets include Canada, Greenland, Alaska, Spitzbergen, Franz Josef Land, Madagascar, New Zealand (North Island), island groups in the Pacific, and parts of the U.S.A. and South Africa.

The IMW sheets are normally produced by various governments for the territories under their jurisdiction. For the most part layer tints are used for altitudes, conforming to a greater or less extent to a standard scheme; particularly valuable for general reference and comparative purposes. About 90% of the world is now mapped in this series.

912 (4/9)

The Library atlas. 8th ed. Edited by H. Fullard and H. C. Darby. London, Philip, 1967. xxiv, 88, 208p. maps. 63*s*.

176 pages of physical maps; 32 pages of economic maps, including distribution of production and natural resources. For each continent there are also vegetation, rainfall and soil maps. Climate graphs. Index-gazetteer of more than 50,000 entries. Page size, $11'' \times 9''$.

About 80% of the maps in *The Library atlas* and *The University atlas* (12th ed. Edited by H. Fullard and H. C. Darby. London, Philip, 1967. 176p. maps. 45*s*.) are identical. Page size, $11'' \times 9''$.

The Record atlas (Edited by H. Fullard. 27th ed. London, Philip, 1967. [vii], 128, 130p. 42*s*.) has 128p. of detailed political, etc., maps and a gazetteer of *c*. 60,000 names. Lettering on maps varies in quality. A good cheap atlas for locating places. Page size, $11'' \times 9''$.

912 (4/9)

McGraw-Hill International atlas. Edition Kartographisches Institut Bertelsmann, under the direction of W. Bormann. New York, McGraw-Hill, 1964. xii, 20, 20, 20, 252, 188, 52p. maps. $59.50.

A revised and updated American edition of the *Grosser Bertelsmann Weltatlas* (1961) (*q.v.*).

126 plates of coloured physical maps (mostly double-page spreads), plus thematic maps. Emphasis on Europe (pl. 10-45) and Central Europe (pl. 101A-111). Scales are mutually comparable throughout the atlas. Shows the 1937

boundaries of Germany in relation to Poland and Czechoslovakia. Text in German, English and French. Index-gazetteer of *c*. 150,000 names. Reviewed in *The booklist,* v. 62, no. 8, 15th December 1965, p. 378-82.

912 (4/9)

Meyers Duden-Waltatlas (Taschenatlas) Hrsg. vom Kartographischen Institut Meyer in Gemeinschaft mit dem Dudenredaktion, Mannheim, Bibliographisches Institut, 1962. 736p. tables, maps. DM.16.80.

174 maps. Includes a star atlas and an historical atlas. 140 pages of geography text. Index-gazetteer of *c*. 34,000 names. Page size, $13'' \times 8\frac{3}{4}''$.

Meyers Grosser physicher Weltatlas (Mannheim, Bibliographisches Institut, Kartographisches Institut Meyer, 1965-.) is to be completed in 8v. (ea. DM.18.80) before 1969:

Atlas zur Biogeographie.
Atlas zur Bodenkunde. 1965.
Atlas zur Geologie. 1968.
Atlas zur Geomorphologie.
Atlas zur Himmelskunde.
Atlas zur Klimatologie.
Atlas zur Orographie.
Atlas zur Ozeanographie. 1968.

912 (4/9)

National geographic atlas of the world. Enl. 2nd ed. M. B. Grosvenor, editor-in-chief. Washington, National Geographic Society, 1966. 343p. maps. $18.75 (limp); $24.50 (bound).

First published 1963.

Double-page maps on p. 8-179. Political, with light hill shading. This enables a great many names to be recorded on the maps; very clear lettering. Many inserts, for conurbations, islands and the like. The map sequence starts with world maps (p. 8-19), then U.S.A. (p. 20-43); Europe, p. 82-117. Main communications and fathom lines shown. Descriptive accounts and statistical data precede the individual maps. Index-gazetteer (p. 183-343) of *c*. 150,000 place-names, with grid references. Has much to recommend it as a fairly large atlas, moderately priced. Two drawbacks: the map extends to the edge of the sheet in each case; irritating variation in map scales (*e.g.,* Germany: 24 miles to $1''$; Switzerland and N. Italy: 21 miles to $1''$; Greece and the Aegean: 26 miles to $1''$). Opens well. Page size, $25'' \times 19''$.

912 (4/9)

The Oxford atlas. Edited by Sir Clinton Lewis and J. D. Campbell, with the assistance of D. P. Bickmore and K. F. Cook. Rev. reprint. London, Oxford Univ. Press, 1966. p. 9-96, xxiv, 93p. maps. 70*s*.

First published 1951.

112 pages of physical and physical-political maps in 6 colours, as against 88 pages in the original ed. New approach; shows relief with layer colour in light tints without contours. For its size, gives a good coverage at relatively large scale (*e.g.,* British Isles (p. 22-30), 1:1M.; France, 1:2M.; and large areas of Africa, 1:8M.), thanks to many double-page spreads. 24 pages of natural and human distribution maps. Index-gazetteer of

more than 50,000 names. Page size, $15\frac{1}{2}'' \times 10\frac{1}{2}''$.

The *Concise Oxford atlas;* prepared by the Cartographic Department of the Clarendon Press, under the general editorship of D. P. Bickmore, with historical information and contemporary notes by T. K. Derry (2nd ed. London, Oxford Univ. Press, 1958. 120p. of maps, 168p. of gazetteer. 30s.) was first published in 1952. The 2nd ed. has additional maps, more recent information in the notes and a gazetteer with some 40,000 names. This atlas gives special emphasis to Great Britain. Page size, $10'' \times 7\frac{1}{2}''$.

The *Oxford junior atlas* (London, Oxford Univ. Press, 1964. iii, 7p. with 48 maps. 6s.), also prepared by the Cartographic Department of the Clarendon Press, is described as "a definite improvement on the general quality of junior atlases", though critically reviewed in *The cartographic journal,* v. 2, no. 1, June 1965, p. 47. Page size, $10\frac{1}{4}'' \times 7\frac{1}{2}''$.

912 (4/9)

Pergamon General world atlas. General editor, S. Knight. Produced by the Cartographic Department of the Pergamon Press. Oxford, Pergamon Press, 1966. [i], 128p. maps. 21s.

87 pages of physical and human geography maps in 6 colours. More than 90 thematic maps, covering climate, population, soils, etc. Good clear lettering. 39 pages of index-gazetteer, with more than 20,000 entries in 2 colours; gives co-ordinates. Page size, $10\frac{3}{4}'' \times 8\frac{1}{2}''$. Remarkably cheap and attractive. Europe and Britain-oriented (18 pages of maps on Britain).

The *Pergamon World atlas* (Oxford, Pergamon, 1968. 525p. maps. £20) has 200p. of physical maps, *c.* 400 thematic maps and an index-gazetteer of 150,000 entries. Based on a Polish world atlas. Page size, $16'' \times 12''$.

912 (4/9)

Prentice-Hall World atlas. Edited by J. E. Williams. 2nd ed. Englewood Cliffs, N.J., Prentice-Hall, 1963. vii, 96, 41p. diagrs., maps. $9.25.

Originally prepared in the Geographisches Institut und Verlag, Vienna. 96 pages of maps, mainly physical-political, with a good selection of thematic maps (world and regional). Good, clear cartography and lettering, and well-balanced territorial coverage. Index of only 20,000 names. Page size, $12'' \times 8\frac{1}{2}''$.

912 (4/9)

Rand McNally New cosmopolitan world atlas. Chicago, Rand, McNally, 1965. xl, 236, 124p. illus., maps. $16.95.

First published 1949 as *Rand McNally cosmopolitan world atlas.*

175 pages of political and special maps (p. 76-125: U.S.A.). Special section of historical maps; 'Geographical and historical facts about the United States', p. 189-232. Considered (*Library journal,* v. 89, no. 22, 15th December 1964, p. 4894, 4896) inferior to the *National Geographic atlas.* Gazetteer of 82,000 entries. Page size: $14\frac{1}{2}'' \times 11\frac{1}{4}''$.

The *Odyssey world atlas* (New York, Odyssey Press, 1966. 317p. $19.95) has 147p. of maps (42

of them on U.S.A.; 22, Europe) and includes thematic maps; 127p. index-gazetteer (*c.* 105,000 entries). A location atlas (*The booklist,* v. 64, no. 3, 1st November 1967, p. 281-8).

912 (4/9)

The "Reader's digest" Great world atlas. London, "Reader's Digest" Association, 1961. 179p. illus., maps. (3rd revision. 1964. 183p. 84s.).

Planned under the direction of Frank Debenham.

Three main sections: 'The face of the world' (p. 5-28: 11 orthographic maps of continents and larger regions, with heightened colouring and hill-shading); 'The countries of the world' (p. 29-100: 47 reference maps by George Philip, Ltd., showing relief by subdued hyposometrical tints); and 'The world as we know it' (p. 101-44: text, illustrations, diagrams and maps). Topics in this last section range from 'Outer space: The boundless sky' to 'The earth's treasures', 'Bird migration', 'What the world is eating' and 'Weather chart'. Two index-gazetteers (British Isles; world), with about 25,000 entries and grid references. Reviewed in *Geographical journal,* v. 127, no. 3, September 1961, p. 378-9. No maps showing the world's main seaways or scheduled air routes. Page size, $16'' \times 10\frac{3}{4}''$.

912 (4/9)

STIELER, A. Stieler's Atlas of modern geography. 10th ed. Gotha, Perthes, 1930. [v], 336p. and 108 pl.

The best-known of the larger German pre-war atlases, containing 108 plates of maps—263 maps. Relief by brown hachures, often not very revealing; political boundaries by ribbons of colour; the name plates extremely detailed, sometimes crowded. Its principal use is therefore locational, the index containing about 300,000 entries, some in German forms.

An enlarged international edition was appearing in 1938, but was never completed. Page size, $15\frac{1}{4} \times 9\frac{1}{4}''$.

Andrees allgemeiner Handatlas (8. Aufl. Hrsg. E. Ambrosius. Bielefeld, Velhagen, 1930. 2v.) is another well-known, pre-war German atlas. Mainly political, it includes some fine physical as well as thematic maps. V. 2 constitutes the index-gazetteer.

912 (4/9)

"The Times" Atlas of the world. Mid-century ed., edited by J. Bartholomew. London, "The Times" Publishing Co., 1955-59. 5v. ea. 105s.

v. 1: *The world; Australasia; Far East.* 1958.
v. 2: *South-west Asia and Russia.* 1959.
v. 3: *Northern Europe.* 1955.
v.4: *Southern Europe and Africa.* 1956.
v. 5: *The Americas* [including the Pacific Ocean]. 1957.

Previous ed. (1920-22. 2v.), as *"The Times" Survey atlas of the world.* 120 plates in all, primarily physical-political maps, each volume carrying 24 double-page plates, mounted on hinges. Excellent cartography, by Bartholomew. Relief shown by layer colours, contours being drawn. Arterial and main roads and international airports in red. Names are in 'local official' form for countries with Roman alphabets. Most important areas are on the scale of 1:1M. V. 3 has scales 1:850,000 (British Isles); 1:1M. and 1:2½M. Inset maps of islands and cities. 150-ft. fathom line shown. Key map on back of double-page plates. Each volume has its own index-gazetteer. A total of more than 200,000 places, etc. are indexed. (See also *"The Times" Index-gazetteer of the world,* at 91 (083.86)).

Binding in 5 separate volumes does distribute the weight, but allocation of areas to particular volumes is a difficulty. Thus v. 3, *Northern Europe,* includes S.W. France, Corsica, Czechoslovakia (but not Hungary) and Switzerland; v. 2, *South-west Asia and Russia,* includes India, Pakistan and the Indian Ocean. Page size, 21¼" × 13".

"The Times" Atlas of the world. Comprehensive ed. (1967. xliii p., 123pl., 272p. £10 10s.) is a 1-v. ed. Maps are not hinged. Index-gazetteer of more than 200,000 place-names. New names for recently created African states. Card insert for map legends, saving 1½". Special maps of moon, etc., international glossary, as in *Times Index-gazetteer.* Page size, 19¾" × 13".

912 (4/9)
The Whitehall atlas. Cartographic editor, Harold Fullard. London, Stanford, 1960. vi, 208, 174p. 63s.

Originally published as *Atlas van de Westerse Beschaving* (Amsterdam, Elsevier).
Reference maps, p. 1-128; physical maps, p. 129-43; statistical information, p. 161-76; economic maps, p. 177-208; gazetteer of more than 50,000 names, with geographical coordinates; list of alternative spellings of place names. The 251 maps and insets, by Philip, of various sizes and scales (*e.g.,* England 1:1M.; Egypt, 1:4M.; Italy, 1:5M.; British East Africa, 1:8M.), cover geology, volcano and earthquake zones, climate, ethnography, vegetation, economics, soils and land use. Usefully supplements the larger atlases. Page size, 11" × 8¾".

912 (4/9)
The World book atlas. Chicago, Field Enterprises Educational Corporation, 1966. xx, 392p. maps. $29.95.

First published 1963. Revised annually.
Intended to be used in conjunction with the *World book encyclopedia,* and for students. 200 pages of physical, political and historical maps (U.S.A.: p. 156-213), by Rand, McNally. Conurbations on special inset maps. Population tables (p. 228-80) include Canadian and U.S. 1960 census details. Gazetteer has *c.* 80,000 entries. Page size: 14" × 11".

Bibliographies

912 (4/9):016
AMERICAN GEOGRAPHICAL SOCIETY. Map Department. **Index to maps in books and periodicals.** Boston, Mass., G. K. Hall, 1967. 10v. $650; $715 (outside U.S.).

160,000 photolithographed entries reproduced from cards. Arranged A-Z according to subjects and geographical areas in one sequence; within each geographical area, sub-division is chrono-

logical. Entries state title and scale of maps, with full citation of the article or book containing the map.

912:016
Bibliographie cartographique internationale, 1936-. Paris, Colin, 1938-. Annual (irregular). (1963 v., published 1965. 41.13F.).

Issued under the auspices of the Comité National Français de Géographie and the Union Géographique Internationale, with the co-operation of Unesco and the Centre National de la Recherche Scientifique. The geographical societies of some twenty countries collaborate in its production.
The 1963 v. lists 2,946 numbered items, arranged under continents and countries, preceded by a section on world maps and atlases, charts and globes. It includes maps published in 54 countries, and states scale, map-sheet size and if coloured. The brief subject index (well over 500 unspecified entries under 'Villes') needs to be used in conjunction with the author index. List of more than 1,000 map producers and publishers.

912 (4/9):016
BRITISH MUSEUM. Catalogue of printed maps in the British Museum: accessions. London, Trustees of the British Museum, 1884-. Annual. (pt. 102. 1966).

First published in 1884. Pt. 1 contained A-L only; M-Z entries were incorporated into the catalogue of 1885.
Supplements the basic *Catalogue of the printed maps, plans and charts in the British Museum;* compiled by R. K. Douglas (London, 1885. 2v.).
The British Museum *Catalogue of printed maps, charts and plans,* published in photolithographic form in 1967 is in the same format as the *General catalogue of printed books.* It records the holdings of the British Museum up to 1964 15v. £135). *World* and *London* excerpts (qq.v.) are available separately.

912 (4/9):016
BRITISH MUSEUM. World: an excerpt from the British Museum *Catalogue of printed maps, charts and plans.* Photolithographed ed. to 1964. London, Trustees of the British Museum, 1967. [i]p., cols. 335-806. 54s.

About 5,500 entries. Arrangement: General atlases—General maps and charts—Subjects (A-Z, from Agriculture to Zoology). Appendix: Bibliographies. Biographies. Cartography. Catalogues. . . .

912 (4/9):016
DESTOMBES, M., *ed.* **Mappemondes, A.D. 1200-1500.** Catalogue préparé par la Commission des Cartes Anciennes de l'Union Cartographique Internationale. Amsterdam, N. Israel, 1964. xxxii, 332p. pl. (facsims.). (Monumenta cartographica vetustioris aevi, v. 1).

Chapters: 1. Les mappemondes médiévales—2. Liste des mappemondes antérieures à l'an 1200—3. Catalogue des mappemondes contenues dans des manuscrits, A.D. 1200-1500—4. Catalogue des mappemondes manuscrits isoleés et globes terrestres, A.D. 1200-1500—5. Pièces métalliques, XVᵉ siècle—6. Liste des mappemondes, A.D. 1200-1500—5. Pièces métalliques, XVᵉ siècle—6. Liste des mappemondes, A.D. 1200-1500 décrites dans les volumes [chapters] 2-4. General bibliography, p. 255-80. Index of authors, cartographers, etc.; list of locations and collectors.

912 (4/9):016
GREAT BRITAIN. DIRECTORATE OF OVERSEAS SURVEYS. Catalogue of the maps published by the Directorate of Overseas (Geodetic and Topographical) Surveys. Tolworth, Surrey, the Directorate, 1960. n.p. index-maps. 10s.

49 sections of text, each followed by index maps showing the principal map series (geology, soils, land-use, vegetation, population, etc., as well as topographical) issued by the Directorate. Scales are mostly between 1:25,000 and 1:125,000. Details: scale; D.S.O. number; standard series description; title; edition; date; price per sheet; remarks. Coverage is of colonial territories, mainly.

The Directorate also issues an *Annual report* which includes index maps. The Catalogue itself is supplemented by monthly *Map additions lists*.

912 (4/9):016
INTERNATIONAL CIVIL AVIATION ORGANIZATION. I.C.A.O. aeronautical chart catalogue. Catalogue O.A.C.I. des cartes aéronautiques. Catálogo O.A.C.I. de cartes aeronáuticas. Montreal, I.C.A.O., 1951. maps. Loose-leaf. Supplements to date.

A world list of the charts conforming with I.C.A.O. standards.

The sheets of the World aeronautical chart (WAC) vary in size (*e.g.,* British Guiana, 19½"×29"; Canary Islands, 18½"×25"; Cairo, 20½"×31½") but are uniformly on a scale of 1:1M. (also 1:½M. for certain areas). Sheets are produced nationally. Thus, those for Canada are published by the Department of Mines, Ottawa; those for France and French overseas territories, by the Institut Géographique National. Civilian airfields are shown. On the back of each sheet is a key map.

Co-ordination of the International map of the world on the millionth scale (IMW) and the World aeronautical chart (WAC) is being studied.

912 (4/9):016
"New atlases and maps: additions to the Map Room". In *New geographical literature and maps.*

Each six-monthly issue lists c. 150 atlases and maps, arranged under world and major regions, and then by countries. Gives scale and sheet size, plus price in the case of O.S., D.O.S. and Bartholomew map sheets. (*Main entry at 91:016.*)

The Cartographic journal (1964-. 2 p.a.) devotes *c.* 3 pages per issue to "Recent maps" (arranged by areas); also a section "Recent literature" (arranged by subjects),—*c.* 80 items per issue.

912(4/9):016
RV-Katalog über deutsch und ausländische Landkarten, Reiseführer, Atlanten und Globen. . . . Stuttgart, Reise- und Verkehrsverlag. Loose-leaf.

Probably the leading map trade-catalogue. Takes the form of monthly *Kartenbrief über neue Landkarten und Reiseführer* and special *Sonderverzeichnis.* Helpful features are the details given of new parts of map series and atlases, and the index maps. German material predominates, but little of major importance is missed. The section on Great Britain (12p.) covers motor maps and atlases, tourist, commercial and physical maps, guides, hotel guides, Ordnance Survey maps, geological and historical maps, national atlases, the Survey gazetteers, special areas, town plans; London (maps, guides, etc.); Ireland.

A shortened version, *Der Kleine RV Katalog.* Landkarten, Reiseführer, Globen, Atlanten aus aller Welt (Stuttgart, Reise- und Verkehrsverlag, [1966]. 96p.

The *Stanford reference catalogue,* to appear later in 1968 (London, Stanford. Loose-leaf. 30s. p.a.; 10s. p.a. for bi-annual bulletin) will present Stanford's *International map bulletin.*

912 (4/9):016
SALISHCHEV, K. A. "Nationalatlanten". In *Petermanns geographische Mitteilungen,* 1960, 1st quarter, p. 77-88.

Examines and compares 23 national atlases, stating scales and noting inclusion of non-physical and non-political maps, amount of text-matter, etc. Criteria are laid down for the types of map to be included in a national atlas.

A parallel study is: *Atlas nationaux: histoire, analyse, voies de perfectionnement et d'unification.* Rédigé à la demande de la Commission des Atlas Nationaux de l'Union Géographique Internationale sous la direction du Prof. K. A. Salichtchev (Moscow, Akad. Nauk SSSR, 1960. 148p. 4 diagrs., 3 maps, 9 tables. R. 650). This surveys the contents of the national atlases of Finland, Russia, Egypt, Czechoslovakia, Italy, Tanganyika, India, Canada, Belgian Congo, Australia, Sweden, France, U.S.A., Morocco, Poland and Israel.

A further article by K. A. Salishchev: "Die heutigen Regionalatlanten und die Tendenzen ihrer Entwicklung", in *Petermanns geographische Mitteilungen,* 1963, 1st quarter, p. 57-73.

World cartography (New York, United Nations, Department of Economic and Social Affairs. No. 8, 1967. 108p. $2) reports on cartographic activities in 24 countries in Latin America, Africa and the Middle East.

912 (4/9):016
UNITED STATES. DEPARTMENT OF THE ARMY. Foreign maps. Washington, Department of the Army, 1956. [iv], 270p. maps, tables. (Technical manual no. 5-248). (2nd ed. 1963. 286p.).

11 chapters, 10 of which deal with regions and countries. Omits the American continent, Africa (other than North Africa), much of the Far East, and Spitzbergen. Confined to official maps, the section on the British Isles (p. 151-7) deals with O.S. and G.S.G.S. maps. Glossary of mapping terms, p. 261-5. Very helpfully illustrated by 148 black-and-white and coloured specimen maps; 35 tables.

Dated, but still useful: W. Thiele's *Official map publications: a historical sketch, and a bibliographical handbook of current maps and mapping services in the United States, Canada, Latin America, France, Great Britain, Germany, and certain other countries* (Chicago, American Library Association, 1938, xvi, 365p.). Index of places, forms (*e.g.*, charts) and issuing bodies. The Americas are given detailed treatment.

912 (4/9):016
UNITED STATES. LIBRARY OF CONGRESS. A list of geographical atlases in the Library of Congress, with bibliographical notes. Washington, Library of Congress, 1909-. v. 1-. (v. 6. 1963. $5.25).

v. 1-4 (1909-20), compiled by P. L. Phillips; v. 5-6 (1958-63), compiled by C. E. LeGear.
V. 6, covering titles 7624-10254, covers nearly 2,500 articles received 1956-60, including *c.* 800 Oriental publications. Arranged by continent and country. Author lists and topographical indexes in v. 2-6, with cumulated index to v. 1-4 in v. 4. Entries sometimes have biobibliographical notes, often extensive. V. 5 deals with world atlases, special and general. While v. 6 records atlases of Europe, Asia, Africa, Oceania, the Polar regions and Oceania, v. 7 is to deal with the Western hemisphere and individual countries of North and South America. V. 8 will form an integrated author list and index, according to *Special Libraries*, v. 55 (3), March 1964, p. 184.

A *Bibliography of terrestrial, celestial and maritime atlases published in the Netherlands,* edited by C. Koeman (5v. ea. *c.* £22 10*s.*), is in preparation.

912 (4/9):016
WALSH, S. P., *comp.* **General world atlases in print:** a comparative analysis. [2nd ed.] New York & London, Bowker, 1966. 66p. $3; 24*s.*

Evaluates 29 general-purpose English-language world atlases. Based on the "collected findings and evaluations of the most competent reviewing authorities" (*Foreword*). Criteria cover cost; age suitability; authority; scope, contents and arrangement; supplementary material (*e.g.*, illustrations); indexing; accuracy and up-to-dateness; types of maps; methods of indicating relief; format and scale. The atlases are examined in detail, arranged by number rating. The highest number ratings are given to *The Times atlas, McGraw-Hill international atlas, World book atlas, National geographic atlas* and *Rand McNally new cosmopolitan atlas.* Title index.

912 (4/9):016
Zumstein Katalog, mit Register. Munich, Zumsteins Landkartenhaus. Annual. (1965. DM.16.50)

An annual catalogue of maps (with index maps of series), town plans, atlases, globes and guide books. World coverage, with emphasis on Germany. Index (on tinted paper) of places, subjects, etc.; also advertisement pages. More convenient to use than *RV-Katalog.*

912 (4/9):016:016
DRAZNIOWSKY, R. "Bibliographies as tools for map acquisition and map compilation."

In *The cartographer,* v. 3, no. 2, December 1966, p. 138-44.

A brief survey of 52 bibliographies, including leading publishers' catalogues, library accessions lists and more inclusive bibliographical aids. Appended list of the 52 items. A valuable checklist.
Another version of this article appeared in *Library trends,* v. 15, no. 4, April 1967, p. 710-7.

912 (4/9):026
DE PARIS, P. M. Library resources in the Greater London area. No. 1, **Maps.** London. Library Association, Reference and Special Libraries Section (South Eastern Group), 1953. 12p.

Contents: Special map collections—Map collections in general libraries—Map collections in special libraries—Conclusions (with notes on minimum requirements for an adequate collection of sheet maps. Appendix: Some sources of information on current maps.

This brief account may be contrasted with an extensive survey of North American resources:— *Map collections in the United States and Canada: a directory* (New York, Special Libraries Association, 1954. 170p.). The scope and nature of the holdings of each library is indicated. Arrangement of libraries is alphabetical, under states in the case of U.S.A., and under provinces in the case of Canada. A map shows locations.

The British Cartographic Society's Map Group is considering compilation of a nation-wide guide to map resources.

Europe

912 (4)
Euroatlas. Strassen- und Reiseatlas. Road and travel atlas . . . [Physical ed.] Berne, Kümmerly & Frey, 1961. 96 pl. of maps, 56p. of text. DM.16.80, 19.80.

Clearly drawn sectional maps of Western and Northern Europe, mostly at 1:1M. (Alps, 1:$\frac{1}{2}$M.). Legend in German, French, English and Italian. 56p. of index and explanatory notes.

Other recommended road atlases: *Europa-Autoatlas* (Stuttgart, Hallwag (London, Philip), 1965. 124p. maps. 33*s.*), with 92 pages of coloured maps, covering Europe except Poland and Roumania; scale, mainly 16M:1"; 54 town plans; *Shell-Europa Atlas* (Stuttgart, Mairs Geographischer Verlag (London, Philip), 1965. 278p. maps. 28*s.* 6*d.*), with 198 1:1$\frac{1}{4}$M. maps.

The Michelin sectional maps are usually at a scale of 3.15M:1",—France (sections 51-87; ea. 3*s.* 6*d.*); Germany (sections 202-6; ea. 4*s.* 6*d.*); Belgium (sections 1, 2, 4, 6; ea. 4*s.* 6*d.*); Holland (sections 1, 6, 5; ea. 4*s.* 6*d.*); Switzerland and N. grid references. Separate transparent overlay at 6.3M:1",— Spain and Portugal (sections 42-43; ea. 4*s.* 6*d.*); and at 8M:1",—Portugal (section 37; 4*s.* 6*d.*).

912 (4-015)
DOLLFUS, J. Atlas of Western Europe. Paris, Société Européenne d'Études et d'Informations; London, Murray, 1963. 48p. illus., maps. 32*s.* 6*d.*

27p. of maps; 17p. of text (explanatory notes) and illustrations; list of place-names and equivalents. Data on population, language, industry, farming, administrative divisions, etc. provided so as to encourage a European rather than a purely national attitude in users. The review in *Scottish geographical magazine* (v. 79, no. 2, September 1963, p. 124-5) complains that many maps are cluttered with too much special detail and that the standard of cartography is variable.

912 (4-015)

Historisch-geographisches Kartenwerk. Britische Inseln, Frankreich, Belgien, Niederlande, Luxemburg. Unter Leitung von Edgar Lehmann; bearb. von Wolfgang Schmeer [u.a.]. Leipzig, Verlag Enzyklopädie, 1960. ii, 53p.; 28 pl. of maps.

191 maps on 28 plates. Those for Great Britain occupy plates 2-9 and cover economic and historical changes, population, Ireland, London, agriculture, mining and industry, and communications. Those for France (pl. 10-17), Belgium, Netherlands and Luxembourg (18-25) are followed by others on the whole area (26-27) and 'Colonial problems' (28). The booklet includes an index-gazetteer and a subject index. Map-plate size, 16″ × 11″.

912 (4-0191)

Atlas of Central Europe. London, Murray, 1963. 20p. of maps, 2, 52p. illus. 42s.

Originally a self-contained section of the German edition of the *Grosse Bertelsmann Weltatlas.*

The 20p. of coloured maps, almost all 1:1M., cover Benelux, West Germany, Austria, Switzerland, East Germany, lower half of Danube, and parts of Czechoslovakia, N. Italy and Poland. Conurbations shown. Glossary of German geographical terms; index of English equivalents of names. Gazetteer of c. 37,000 names, with grid references. Page size, 12¾″ × 9½″.

Great Britain

912 (410)

The Atlas of Britain and Northern Ireland. Planned and directed by D. P. Bickmore and M. A. Shaw. Oxford, Clarendon Press, 1963. xii, 200p. of maps; 22p. of gazetteer. £26 5s.

Standard scale is 1:2M., enlarged by 1:1M and 1:½M. for regions, and reduced to 1:8M. for small distribution maps. The 1:2M. and 1:1M. maps are used for physical geography, agriculture, fisheries, industry, demography, housing, administrative boundaries, communications and trade. Up to 12 printing colours used. Many fascinating and unusual maps (*e.g.*, new factory building, 1948-1958). L. Dudley Stamp calls the atlas "a landmark in the history of British cartography", with originality and freshness of approach as the most striking feature (*The geographical journal*, v. 129, pt. 4, December 1963, p. 506-7). But he complains that the maps have an obsession with circles, and that some maps attempt too much. The detailed analysis in *The geographical review*, v. 54, no. 2, April 1964, p. 295-8 points out that several resources are

ignored, *e.g.*, education, health, culture, history, scenery. The gazetteer has c. 15,000 entries, with grid references. Separate transparent overlay at 1:2M. Page size, 20½″ × 15½″.

912 (410)

Bartholomew's Road atlas of Great Britain, fifth-inch to mile. 20th ed., with new town plans and improved road information. Edinburgh, Bartholomew, 1967. 112p. 15s.

First published 1943.

Map sections are on the fifth-inch scale; district maps (London, Liverpool, Manchester, Birmingham, Glasgow and Edinburgh), on half-inch scale. 27 throughway town plans. The well-coloured maps are on p. 2-96. 16-page gazetteer-index of over 4,000 place-names. Maps on end-papers provide a 1:3M. key: motorway supplement insert has 7 maps (fifth-inch).

An article, "Motoring maps", in *Which* (3rd July 1963, p. 196-203) compares leading maps and gives as 'best buys': Ordnance Survey ¼″ series, 5th series (ea. 5s. 6d.); Bartholomew's Road atlas; A.A. road books; ESSO road maps (ea. 6d.). "In general Michelin maps [covering England, Wales, Scotland and Northern Ireland; ea. 5s.] . . . present far more information of value to motorists than do British maps—width and straightness of road, length, scenic value . . . in a clear and liberal way".

912 (410)

GREAT BRITAIN. ORDNANCE SURVEY. [Maps]. Chessington, Surrey, Ordnance Survey.

The principal current O.S. series in wide use are the 1″:1 mile (7th series. 190 sheets (now 189). ea. 5s. 6d. - 8s. 6d. (completed in 1961; revised at the rate of c. 12 p.a.); 8 tourist area maps, with layer tints and hill shading, ea. 6s.-15s.), ¼″:1 mile (17 sheets, England, Wales, Scotland, ea. 4s. 6d. - 7s. 6d.; for motorists); 1:625,000 (England, Wales, Scotland on 2 sheets; topographical, geological and thematic maps; ea. 5s. - 12s. 6d.) and archaeological and historical maps (*see at 941 (084.4).*

"The origins of the Ordnance Survey of Great Britain", by R. A. Skelton (*The geographical journal*, v. 128, pt. 4, December 1962, p. 415-30) has 17 illustrations (mostly facsimiles) and 12 references.

J. B. Harley's *The historian's guide to Ordnance Survey maps* (London, published for the Standing Conference for Local History by the National Council of Social Service, 1964. 51p. maps, facsims. 5s.) is reprinted from *The amateur historian,* with additional material. 5 main sections: 1. The 1″ : 1 mile maps of England and Wales—2. 6″ and 25″ maps of England and Wales—3. The town plans and small-scale maps of England and Wales—4. The period maps of the Ordnance Survey—5. The Ordnance Survey maps of Scotland.

912 (410)

GREAT BRITAIN. ORDNANCE SURVEY. National planning maps of Great Britain, 1:625,000. Chessington, Ordnance Survey, 1944-58. 2v. maps. 12s. 6d.

v. 1: *Scotland;* v. 2: *England and Wales.* Each

volume has 25 maps, plus a base map.

This series of maps (33½″ × 24½″) covers Great Britain in north and south sheets, sheet 1 covering Scotland and the northern part of England, and sheet 2, the remainder of England and Wales, on a scale of *c*. 10 miles : 1″. This scale provides a convenient wall map of the whole country and also a reference atlas that can be bound in sheet form. The base map shows main roads, rivers, railways, principal towns and villages. The special maps fall into categories: population; administrative areas; geology (solid; drift; economic minerals; limestone); topography and physical features; rainfall; agriculture (vegetation; land utilization; land classification; types of farming); communications (roads; railways); industries (coal and iron; iron and steel; electricity; gas and coke). The maps are available separately. 20 of them are published for the Ministry of Housing and Local Government, at 12*s*. 6*d*., and the other 5 at 5*s*. Explanatory texts (*Land classification; Average annual rainfall;* etc.) are available at 1*s*. to 2*s*. 6*d*. each.

A detailed description of the atlas appears in *Government information and the research worker,* 2nd ed., edited by R. Staveley and M. Piggott (London, Library Association, 1962, p. 174-83).

912 (410)
The National Trust atlas, showing plans of historic, architectural & scenic interest in England, Wales and Northern Ireland. London, National Trust, 1964. [121], [21]p. maps. 25*s*.

An atlas—"a guide to *situation,* not a Guide Book. It is so designed that the traveller consulting it is able to discover at a glance what interesting places lie within his reach" (*Explanatory notes*). 60 Bartholomew maps (30 double papers); index of *c*. 6,000 places.

912 (410)
"The Reader's digest" Complete atlas of the British Isles, including Great Britain, England, Wales and Scotland, with the Orkney and Shetland Islands, North Ireland, the Channel Islands . . . Isle of Man and the Republic of Ireland. London, Reader's Digest Association, 1966. 230p. maps. 110*s*.

Four sections: 1. The nature of the land (p. 5-22; physical maps)—2. The country we live in (p. 23-68; physical maps)—3. The fabric of a nation (p. 69-158; a great variety of subjects, *e.g.,* agriculture, transport, industry, bird migration, folklore, place-names; text; small maps; illustrations)—4. Places in the British Isles (gazetteer, p. 159-213: *c*. 35,000 names). According to the reviewer in *Scottish geographical magazine* (v. 83, no. 2, September 1967, p. 143-4), contains a wealth of miscellaneous information, "and some of the attempts to deal with difficult material are interesting and attractive. But the total presentation reflects the publisher, who is not noted for the ability to distinguish between the significant and the trivial."

912 (410)
ROYAL GEOGRAPHICAL SOCIETY. Reproductions of early maps. 7. Early maps of the British Isles, A.D. 1000 - A.D. 1579. London, R.G.S., 1962. 35*s*.

Collotype facsimiles of 20 manuscript and printed maps, from the Cotton World map of *c*. A.D. 1000 to the general map in Saxton's *Maps of England and Wales* (1579), with introduction and notes by G. R. Crone. 15 collotype plates in portfolio, 21″ × 16½″.

912 (410):016
CHUBB, T. The printed maps in the atlases of Great Britain and Ireland; a bibliography, 1579-1870 . . . with an introduction by F. P. Sprent and biographical notes on the map makers, engravers and publishers, by T. Chubb, assisted by J. W. Skells and H. Beharrel. London, Homeland Association. 1927. xvii, 479p. illus. Facsimile reprint. London, Dawsons Pall Mall, 1966. £10 10*s*.

Chapters: The atlases of England and Wales—The atlases of Scotland—The atlases of Ireland—Biographical notes. Arrangement of items in the three main chapters is chronological. Contents of atlases are analyzed, with bibliographical notes.

Usefully supplemented by atlases listed in *The Harold Whitaker Collection of county atlases, road-books and maps presented to the University of Leeds,* by Harold Whitaker (Leeds, Brotherton Library, 1947. 142p.).

For a full list of county maps, consult the bibliography to chapter 8 of *Maps and mapmakers,* by R. V. Tooley (2nd ed. London, Batsford, 1952).

County atlases of the British Isles, 1579-1850, compiled by R. A. Skelton and others (London, Map Collectors' Circle, 1964-. pt. 1 (1579-1611). p. 1-44; pt. 2 (1612-1646), p. 45-88. Map collectors' series, nos. 9, 14. 105*s*. p.a. (10 nos. p.a.)) will eventually replace Chubb's *Printed maps* and "be the definitive reference on the county cartography of the British Isles prior to the expansion of the official surveys" (*The geographical journal,* v. 130, pt. 3, September 1964, p. 433).

912 (410):016
GREAT BRITAIN. ORDNANCE SURVEY. The Ordnance Survey catalogue. Chessington, Surrey, O.S., 1967. 39p. *Gratis.*

A detailed price list, with a folding key map of the 1:1¼M. scale. Covers 1:25,000, 1″ (7th series), ½″, ¼″ (5th series), 1:1M. and smaller scale maps; 1:625,000 maps; archaeological and historical maps; facsimile reproductions of old maps; administrative area maps; Geological Survey, Soil Survey and Land Use Survey maps; maps of Ireland, Isle of Man and Channel Islands; 1:1,250 and 1:2,500 plans; 6″ maps; etc. Index.

Also notes on the National Grid Reference System, map scales and dimensions. Index maps, including insert index-map to the 1:25,000 series.

Kept up-to-date by the Ordnance Survey's monthly *Publication report,* also *gratis.* This lists new and revised O.S. map sheets (small, medium and large-scale) published during the previous month. (There is also a quarterly Geological Survey *Publication report.*)

912 (410):016
GREAT BRITAIN. PUBLIC RECORD OFFICE. Maps and plans in the Public Record Office.

1. British Isles, *c.* 1410-1860. London, H.M. Stationery Office, 1967. xv, 648p. 105*s.*

Classified into general groups, then into parishes. Maps of London are arranged under the City and Metropolitan Boroughs as of 1964.

Scotland

912 (411):016

ROYAL SCOTTISH GEOGRAPHICAL SOCI-ETY. The early maps of Scotland, with an account of the Ordnance Survey. 2nd ed., rev. Edinburgh, Royal Scottish Geographical Society, 1936. 171p.

Smaller-scale maps (arranged chronologically). —Miscellaneous maps (by subject: agricultural, railway, geological, etc.)—The larger-scale maps of Scotland (arranged by counties)—Early instruments for charting and map-making—The Ordnance Survey—The town-plans of Scotland (A-Z by towns). Bibliography (p. 149-55).
A valuable list. Abbreviations indicate the chief libraries where the maps may be seen.
The 3rd ed. is due in 1968.

Scotland on the map: an exhibition of maps. (Glasgow, Royal Scottish Geographical Society, [1956]. 24p.) lists 131 items, with annotations.

J. G. Bartholomew's *Survey atlas of Scotland* (Edinburgh, Geographical Institute, 1912. 23p.) contains 68 maps and plans; general scale, $\frac{1}{2}''$ to 1 mile.

912 (414.5)

An Atlas of Edinburgh. Compiled by the Edinburgh Branch of the Geographical Association. Edinburgh, City Litho Co., 1964 (reprinted 1965). 39, 5p. illus., diagrs., maps. 10*s.*

A well-produced atlas, the maps being interspersed with half-tone illustrations, graphs and drawings. 34 contributions on aspects of Edinburgh and S.E. Scotland. Social data mapped and analysed include population (ward figures), rooms per house, student population, and accessibility. Included is an excellent map of house types. The *Scottish geographical magazine* review (v. 82, no. 3, December 1966, p. 210) finds use of 6 different scales excessive and the page size (15" × 10") abnormal.

Northern Ireland

912 (416)

NORTHERN IRELAND. ORDNANCE SURVEY. The Ordnance Survey maps of Northern Ireland. Belfast, Ministry of Finance, 1962. v, 24p. illus., maps.

A descriptive catalogue.

Eire

912 (417)

EIRE. ORDNANCE SURVEY. Catalogue of the maps and Ordnance Survey publications. Rev. ed. Dublin, Stationery Office, 1949.

—— ——**Catalogue of small scale maps and charts,** 1st August 1956. Dublin, Stationery Office, 1956.

England and Wales

912 (42)

BARTHOLOMEW, J. The survey atlas of England & Wales. 2nd ed. Edinburgh & London, Bartholomew, 1939. xii, 81 pl. of maps, 24p.

Still a valuable reference-atlas for England and Wales, illustrating "the physical features, geology, climatology, population and political divisions of the country" (*sub-title*). The physical maps, on a scale of $\frac{1}{2}''$ to 1 mile, show relief by layer colouring, with roads in brown. Town plans are included.
The "Short general index to towns and villages" contains about 10,000 entries. The prefatory material carries a bibliography, "The cartography of England and Wales", arranged chronologically and going up to 1937.

London

912 (421)

Bartholomew's Reference atlas of Greater London, covering the whole Metropolitan Police area, with larger-scale maps for Central London and index for quick location of over 59,000 names. 12th ed. Edinburgh, Bartholomew, 1963. xxxiii, 156 pl. of maps, 301p. 50*s.* (13th ed. 1967. xxxvii p., 164 pl. of maps. 340p. 84*s.*).

11th ed. 1961.
A convenient-sized and comprehensive atlas. The 156 plates of maps in colour, cover the 1,000 square miles of the old Greater London area mostly on a scale of 4" to 1 mile, with Central London at 10" to 1 mile. Page size, $9\frac{1}{4}'' \times 6''$.
The 13th ed. has locations for over 62,000 names.

Geographers' Master atlas of Greater London (Sevenoaks, Kent, Geographers' Map Co., Ltd., 1967. 160 pl. of maps. 287p. 57*s.* 6*d.*) covers much the same ground as Bartholomew on a scale of 3" to 1 mile. The whole of the Greater London area is included, and boundaries and names of G.L.C. boroughs are marked. Index of streets at end.

912 (421)

Geographia London map directory: a street atlas and London and its surrounds. London, Geographia, 1964. xvi, 194 pl. of maps, 81p. 210*s.*

Slightly larger coverage than Bartholomew, with a consequent increased index to 62,000 names. The scale is also slightly larger: $4\frac{1}{2}''$ to 1 mile for the inner area and 3" to 1 mile for the outer. Large-scale; 10" maps of City but not West End. Overall size is $13\frac{1}{2}'' \times 10\frac{1}{2}''$, making it less portable than Bartholomew. Maps are in colour, and the larger scale gives a greater clarity to small features and congested areas. Useful selective marking of street numbers on the more important streets.

E. Jones, Professor of Geography at the London School of Economics, discusses the projected new London atlas in the *Geographical journal* (v. 131, pt. 3, September 1965, p. 330-43). The basic scale is to be 1:50,000, with 1:25,000 for the central area only.

912 (421):016

BRITISH MUSEUM. London: an excerpt from the British Museum Catalogue of printed maps, charts and plans. Photolithographic ed. to 1964. London, Trustees of the Brtiish Museum, 1967. [ii]p., 202 cols. 30s.

About 2,500 entries. Arrangement: General atlases—General plans—Administrative divisions —Commercial, industrial and professions—Communications—Disease and medical (A-Z)—Public services—Religion—Sociology—General views— Particular plans and views—London: City— London: Environs. Appendix: Catalogues, dictionaries, etc. Topographical index.

Wales
912 (429)

DAVIES, M. Wales in maps. Cardiff, Univ. of Wales Press, 1951. 111p. maps.

97 black - and - white maps, on the left-hand page, with commentary facing it, written in simple language for school use. The maps cover physical geography, history, agriculture and settlement, commerce and industry, population.

A national atlas of Wales is in preparation at Aberystwyth.

O. C. Evans's *Maps of Wales and Welsh cartographers* (London, The Map Collectors' Circle, 1965. 22p. of text; 20 illus.) describes the regional maps of Wales from Saxton's *Maps* (1579) to the late 19th century. This is v. 2, no. 13 of the Map Collectors' Circle publications (105s. p.a. for nos. 11-20).

Germany
912 (43)

Atlas östliches Mitteleuropa. Hrsg. von Th. Kraus, E. Meynen, H. Mortensen, H. Schlenger. Bielefeld, Velhagen & Klasing, 1959. 2v. maps.

Covers East Central Europe from the Baltic to the Moravian Gate and from the Elbe to the eastern boundary of Poland. The boundaries of Germany are those prior to World War II. 68 plates of physical, historical and economic maps, some in 11 colours. A pocket contains sheets of the pre-war 1:300,000 Übersichtkarte, covering the former German territories. Page size, 21½″ × 14½″. See review in *Geographical journal,* v. 126, pt. 1, March 1960, p. 69. Legends in English and French are in a separate volume.

912 (43)

Der deutscher Planungsatlas. Hannover, Akademie für Raumforschung und Landesplanung, in Verbinding mit Dienststellen der Länder, 1951-. maps.

The official atlas of the Federal Republic of Germany, including an *Atlas von Berlin* (v. 1. 1962). 256 sheets (unbound and unnumbered) were published between 1953 and 1959. V. 2: *Niedersachsen und Bremen* (the first to be published), consists of 90 sections, with scales 1:800,000 to 1:1,600,000. A wide range of topics is covered, from physical maps, to economic, agricultural, industrial and cultural maps. The 101 maps of Berlin (v. 9. 1962) are particularly good, covering geology, vegetation, population, transport, etc.

The *Shell Atlas [Deutschland], mittlerer und westlicher Teil, 1:500,000* (Stuttgart, Mairs Geographischer Verlag) had its 33rd ed. in 1966. Some explanatory notes are in English and French as well as German.

The *Deutscher Generalatlas* (Stuttgart, Mairs Geographischer Verlag, 1967-) is on a scale of 1:200,000 for the Federal Republic (pl. 14-118); town plans follow (pl. 120-150); maps of Europe, 1:4½M. (pl. 151-160). Index-gazetteer, p. 162-423 (c. 60,000 entries). Folding maps.

Austria
912 (436)

Atlas der Republik Österreich. Hrsg. von der Kommission für Raumforschung der Österreichischen Akademie der Wissenschaften unter der Gesamtleitung ihres Obmannes Hans Bobek. Vienna, Kartographische Anstalt Freytag-Berndt und Artaria, 1961-. maps. fasc. 1-.

To consist of 85 major maps, 1:1M. 12 sections —general, topographical, climate, hydrology, soil, flora and fauna, economy, population, agriculture and forestry, industry, power, mining, trade, transport and communications, culture. Also inset maps and plans. Pt. 1 (1961. ÖS.285), the first of 5 annual pts., had 19 plates. Page size, 28¾″ × 18½″.

Czechoslovakia
912 (437)

Atlas Československé Socialistické Republiky. [Prague], Ústřední Správa Geodézie a Kartografie, 1966. 16p. 58 pl. of maps, [9]p. Kčs. 230.

58 maps covering geology, geomorphology, climate, biogeography, population, mining, industries (chemicals; textiles), agriculture, transport, trade, housing, health, social security, education and culture of Czechoslovakia. Scale mainly 1:100,000. Excellent colouring. Headings and explanatory notes on maps in Czech, English and Russian. Index-gazetteer of c. 5,500 names. Page size, 19½″ × 17½″.

Poland
912 (438)

Atlas świata Państwowe Wydawnictwo Naukowe. Warsaw, P.W.N., [1963?-].

The national atlas of Poland, produced by the Institute of Geography of the Polish Academy of Sciences, Warsaw. To consist of c. 200 topographical maps and c. 300 thematic maps, illustrating demographic, climate and economic data. Scale, 1:10M.—1:12½M. 4v. in 8.

France
912 (44)

Atlas de France. 2. éd. Comité National de Géographie. Paris, Éditions Géographiques de France, 1951-59. 80 pl. of maps. £21 17s. 6d.

First published 1933-45.
The 2nd ed. has its 80 sheets divided as follows: Géographie physique (26)—Biogéographie (8)— Géographie économique (29)—Géographie

humaine et géographie politique (17). Where information was unchanged, plates were repeated from the 1st ed. Each sheet may contain various maps. Thus, sheet no. 80, Santé publique, comprises 14 maps, showing incidence of major diseases, etc. in France. Distributions are mainly shown by départements, in flat tints. More important maps are in 4 sheets at 1:1M. No index gazetteer. Page size, 20″ × 15½″.

Regional atlases (of which 18 are projected): *Atlas de la France de l'Est* (Nancy, Berger-Levrault, 1960-) in 6 sections,—physical, demographic, rural, industrial, communications and culture. Scale, mainly 1:700,000; page size, 14″ × 16″; *Atlas du Norde de la France* (Paris, Berger-Levrault, 1961. 74 pl. of maps, with text). Scales, 1:400,000 and 1:800,000; page size 14¼″ × 23¾″; *Atlas de Paris et de la Région Parisienne* (Paris, Berger-Levrault, 1967) has 963p. of text and *c.* 400 maps on 87 pl. Page size, 27″ × 21½″.

The best known map sheet series is the Carte de France (Paris, Institut Géographie National), with main scales at 1:25,000, 1:50,000 and 1:100,000.

The Carte Michelin sectional road maps cover Africa (particularly North Africa) and Western Europe, as well as France (1:200,000).

912 (44):016
INSTITUT GÉOGRAPHIQUE NATIONAL, Paris. **Catalogues des cartes de l'I.G.N. Cartes en service.** Paris, the Institut, 1964. Monthly supplements.

Lists mainly maps of France and French-speaking Africa, the West Indies and Oceania. Sections A-Z (Cartes terrestres, A-X; Cartes aéronautiques, Y; Cartes en relief, Z). Includes town plans; states map sizes. Key maps.

Italy

912 (45)
DAINELLI, G. Atlante fisico-economico d'Italia. Milan, Consociazione Turistica Italiana, 1940. xvii p. with 82p. of maps.

A finely produced national atlas, covering geology, climate and rainfall, population and vital statistics, agriculture and forestry, industry, communications, etc. 508 maps and 82 tables. Many of the maps are small, the scale being 1/2.5M. for larger maps.
Note illustrative, the accompanying explanatory text on each map or set of maps, appeared separately (1940. 147p.). It carries a subject index.

Spain

912 (46)
Nuevo atlas de España. Madrid, Aquilar, 1961. 455p. maps, illus., tables, graphs.

An excellent reference atlas of maps and illustrations, in 4 sections: general (physical, political and economic maps, at 1:3,250,000); historical; regional; provincial (at 1:600,000), including Spanish colonies (*e.g.,* Fernando Po). 'Síntesis geográfia - estadística', p. 21-95. Gazetteer, p. 395-455,—*c.* 30,000 entries, with grid references.

More up-to-date geographical data appear in the Instituto Geográfico y Cadastral's *Reseña geográfica del Atlas nacional de España* (Madrid, 1965. 227p.).

The *Atlas national de España* itself (Barcelona, Editorial Teide, S.A.) has been announced for 1968, at $70. It consists of a place-name index (over 40,000 references), 28 plates of general maps of Spain (28.8″ × 20.8″) and 100p. of thematic maps (30″ × 20.8″), with transparent overlay.

Portugal

912 (469)
GIRÃO, A. de A. Atlas de Portugal: continente, ilhas adjacentes e provincias ultramarinas. 2. ed. Coimbra, Instituto de Estudos Geográficos, Faculdade de Letras, [1958]. 43 pl. of maps.

Published in commemoration of the quincentenary of the death of Prince Henry the Navigator. The 43 plates of maps (scales, 1:1M. to 1:5M.) cover geology, drainage, climate, population, agriculture, industries, communications, trade, dialects and the overseas provinces. Text and captions in Portuguese and English. Plate size, 17″ × 12″.

Portuguese Possessions

912 (469-44)
Atlas de Portugal ultramarino et das grandes viagens portuguesas de decobrimento e expansão. Lisbon, Ministério das Colonias. Junta das Missões Geográficas e de Investigações Colónias. 1947. [v]p., 110 maps, [ii]p.

110 large and clear maps, using a minimum of colour, covering the Portuguese possessions. Scales are usually 1/1M. to 1/2M. Geology, mineral deposits, economy, etc. are covered.

U.S.S.R.

912 (47)
Atlas SSSR. Moscow, Glavnoe Upravlenie Geodezii i Kartografii MVD SSSR, 1962. 185p. maps. R.15.

Previous eds., 1947, 1954, 1955.
General atlas of the U.S.S.R. in 3 main sections: physical maps of major regions (62p.; 1:3M. or 4M., with a few at 1:8M.); maps of natural conditions (30p.; geology, tectonics, minerals, geomorphology, climate, soils, etc.); economic (52p.; population, electric power, industries, agriculture; also economic map of each major region). Index-gazetteer of *c.* 27,000 names.

The school atlas, *Geograficheskiĭ atlas SSSR dlya 7-go i 8-go klassov sredneĭ shkoly* (3rd ed. Moscow, GUGK MVD SSSR, 1956. 76p.) has 60p. of maps, including economic, geological, meteorological, agricultural and other special maps of the U.S.S.R., with 16 pages of text, including a short gazetteer.

A physical map of European U.S.S.R., *SSSR-Evropeiskaya chast'* (1:2½M.) is available on 4 sheets (ea. 24⅛″ × 34″; 10s.); and a physical map of U.S.S.R. as a whole, *Fizicheskaya karta SSSR* (1:5M.), for schools, on 4 sheets (ea. 28⅛″ × 38⅝″; 10s.).

Atlas sel'skogo khozyaistva SSSR (Moscow, GUCK MVD SSSR, 1960. 308p. R.15), though nominally an agricultural atlas, is perhaps the most noteworthy regional atlas of the U.S.S.R. Its 297 plates of maps include many on physical geography. Reviewed in *The geographical review,* v. 52, no. 3, July 1962, p. 417.

912 (47):016

Kartograficheskaya letopis'. Organ Gosudarstvennoï bibliografii SSSR. 1931-1940, 1946-. Moscow, Vsesoyuznaya Knizhnaya Palata, 1931-.

An annual annotated bibliography (initially quarterly), listing all separately published maps and atlases issued in the U.S.S.R., and particularly of the U.S.S.R. Indexes of names, places, and titles (tourist maps).

The best survey in English of Soviet maps and atlases is that in K. Maichel's *Guide to Russian reference books,* v. 2 (1964), entries no. F127-F174.

Finland

912 (480)

Suomen kartasto. Atlas of Finland. Atlas över Finland, 1960. Suomen Maantieteellinen Seura. Helsinki, Kustannuososakeyhtiö Otava, 1960. [viii]p., 39 pl. of maps.

A new edition of the Geographical Society of Finland's *Atlas of Finland,* first published in 1899. The only country to have produced 4 editions of its national atlas.

39 double plates of special maps of excellent quality; scales, 1:1M., 1:6M., etc. 455 maps, covering altitudes and depths, geodesy and mapping, geology, climate (34 maps), hydrology, fauna, flora, vegetation zones, forests and peatlands, population (37 maps), arable area, agriculture (64 maps), forestry, industry, foreign trade and harbours, traffic, inland trade, co-operative movement, finance, education, health and medical care, history, elections, geographic regions, communications. There are even maps showing distribution of dentists, blue-and-grey-eyed people, Norwegian lemmings, and sausage factories. Largest scale, 1:1M. (population maps); usually each double-plate has several small maps. No subject index, although there is a detailed contents list in Finnish, English and Swedish. Legends are also trilingual. Page size, $18'' \times 13\frac{1}{2}''$. Reviewed in *Geographical journal,* v. 129, pt. 1, March 1963, p. 111-2.

Separate 'Explanatory notes' in Finnish (1962. 122p.) describes and supplements the maps. An English edition of this has been promised.

Norway

912 (481)

Cappelens Norge atlas. Redigert av K. Gleditsch, F. Isachsen og A. Røhr. Oslo, Cappelens, 1965. v.p. maps.

A physical atlas of Norway, consisting largely of sectional maps (pl. 8-64), at a scale of 1:400,000, with 3 special maps (pl. 4-7) at 1:150,000. Index-gazetteer of 115p. (*c.* 45,000 names). Page size, $12'' \times 9\frac{1}{2}''$.

Sweden

912 (485)

Atlas över Sverige. Svenska Sällskapet för Antropologi och Geografi. Stockholm, Generalstabens Litografiska Anstalts Förlag, 1953-.

Being issued in 75 fascicules. When completed will contain 150 full-size coloured maps, with descriptive texts. Some 130 fascicules were issued by 1967. A regional atlas of Sweden, covering geology, meteorology, mineral deposits, climatology, soil, vegetation, population, agriculture, trade and port traffic.

Denmark

912 (489)

Atlas over Danmark. Atlas of Denmark. Udgivet af det Kongelige Danske Geografiske Selskab. Copenhagen, Hagerup (subsequently Reitzels Forlag), 1949-61. 2v. illus., maps.

1. *Landskabsformerne* (The landscapes). 1949. 32p.; explanatory booklet. 129p.
2. *Befolkningen* (The population). 1961. 2p., 10 double pl., 1 pl., 2p.; explanatory booklet. 124p.

V. 1 has many sectional maps, with text and indexes to types of landscape, in Danish and English. V. 2 consists of population maps, 1:200,000, each dot representing 25 persons. The booklets include illustrations and bibliographies. Page size of maps, $22'' \times 15''$.

Netherlands

912 (492)

Atlas van Nederland. Nederland, Topografische Dienst. The Hague, Staatsdrukkerijen Uitgeverijbedrijt, 1965-. maps. Loose-leaf.

29 plates issued by mid-1966. Excellent examples of colour printing by Topografische Dienst, Delft. General scale, 1:600,000; regional soil maps, 1:200,000. 17 sections. One map, topical because of the Common Market, shows character and details of the gas supply, differentiating the 3 sources (coke ovens, natural gas; and residue gas from refineries). Reviewed in *The geographical journal,* v. 132, pt. 3, September 1963, p. 439-40.

Belgium

912 (493)

Atlas de Belgique. Atlas van Belgie. Brussels, Comité National de Géographie, 1954-. £35 5s.

A well-produced atlas. Sheets so far produced include coverage of climate, flora and fauna, agriculture and forestry, population and industries. The size of the map page is generous (*c.* $25'' \times 15''$) and coloration excellent. Brief explanatory data on reverse of maps.

Switzerland

912 (494)

Atlas der Schweiz. Editor-in-chief, E. Imhof. Wabern-Bern, Verlag der Eidgenössischen Landestopographie, 1965-. Lfg. (8 pl.)—. maps. Loose-leaf.

General scale (double-spread): 1:½M., with large-scale topographical maps at 1:50,000 of Aletsch Glacier and other selected areas. Will comprise more than 300 coloured maps on *c.* 90 double-sized plates. Topographical relief plates from the *Schweizerischer Mittelschulatlas.* Explanatory notes and statistical tables accompany each map. Good choice of colours for contours, rocks, snowfields and glaciers. Reviewed in *The geographical journal,* v. 132, pt. 1, March 1966, p. 156-7. Page size, 20″ × 15″.

Roumania
912 (498)

VICTOR, T., *ed.* **Atlas geografic Republica Socialista România.** Bucharest, Editura Didactică şi Pedagogică, 1965. 109 maps. 108s.

A compendium of information on Roumania, expressed in terms of maps and graphs; covers livestock, agriculture, climate, geology, industry, international trade, relief forms, mining, hydrology, population density, communications, types of lakes and towns, etc. Double-page maps, 1:1,750,000; single-page maps, 1:2,500,000. Reviewed in *Geographical journal,* v. 133. no. 2, June 1967, p. 270-1.

Arab World
912 (5/6=927)

Atlas of the Arab world and the Middle East. London, Macmillan, 1960. [ii], 60, [8]p. illus., maps. 35s.

About a hundred coloured maps on 40 pages, with a further 20 pages of 42 illustrations, and an index with some 4,000 names. The maps, by Djambatam of Amsterdam, are general (covering North Africa and the Middle East: physical; climate; vegetation; population; air routes; minerals; history) and regional. Thus the maps of Iraq show main crops, agricultural regions and irrigation, climatic types, precipitation, temperature, minerals, industries and oil concessions, as well as including a large physical map. Scales range from 1:4M. to 1:13M.
Geographical journal (v. 126, pt. 4, December 1960, p. 551) finds this atlas more attractive than the *Oxford regional economic atlas: the Middle East and North Africa,* but less reliable and accurate in its information: it has too many minor errors. Page size, 13⅓″ × 9⅔″.

Asia
912 (5):016

GOSLING, L. A. P. **Maps, atlases and gazetteers for Asian studies:** a critical guide. New York, Univ. of the State of New York, 1965. vi, 27p. Typescript. (Occasional publication no 2, Foreign Area Materials Center, Univ. of the State of New York). 10s.

Middle East
912 (5—011)

BRAWER, M., and KARMON, Y. **Atlas of the Middle East.** Tel Aviv, Yavneh Publishing House, 1964-. 40, 40p. (2nd ed. 1967).

Maps, p. 1-40; text in Hebrew. Maps cover geology, agriculture, population, pipe lines and physical features.

South-east Asia
912 (5—012)

Atlas of South-east Asia, with an introduction by D. G. E. Hall. London, Macmillan, 1964. 84, [7]p. 50s.

Coverage: Philippines, Indonesia, Singapore, Malaya, Thailand, Indochina, Burma. Maps, by Djambatan, Amsterdam, p. 2-60, cover physical, political, economic, climate, population, agriculture, communications and other aspects. 6 town plans (*e.g.,* Rangoon). Photogravure illustrations, p. 61-84; index of *c.* 6,000 entries.

China
912 (51)

TING, Wên-chiang, *and others, ed.* **Chung Kuo fîn shêng hsin-t'u** [New provincial atlas of China]. 5th rev. ed. Shanghai, Shên-pao Kuan, 1948. 2, 94, [2]p. 58 pl. of maps.

Sectional location maps; city plans; thematic maps. Page size, 11⅘″ × 8⅝″. In Chinese.
The 1934 ed. included a 180-page index gazetteer. The U.S. Board on Geographic Names has published a *Gazetteer of Chinese place names based on the index to V. K. Ting atlas* (Washington, Army Map Service, 1944. lxxix, 229p.).

Communist China
912 (510)

China: provisional atlas of Communist administrative units. Central Intelligence Agency. Washington, U.S. Department of Commerce, Office of Technical Services, 1959. ix p., 29 pl. of maps, 14p.

Three general maps of Communist administrative units and one of railways and selected roads are followed by maps (5-29) of provinces on a scale of 1:1½M. to 1:5M. These latter maps originally appeared in *The provincial atlas of China* (Shanghai, Ti-t'u ch'u pan she, 1956). The Chinese characters on the maps and legends are translated. Map index and legend for plates 5-29, with table of areas and populations.

Japan
912 (52)

Teikoku's Complete atlas of Japan. Tokyo, Teikoku-Shoin Co., Ltd., 1964. 56p. (Rev. ed. 1968).

Large-scale maps of conurbations and districts, as well as thematic maps—climate, geology, industry, land utilisation, mining, national parks, physical features, population, soil and transport. Index-gazetteer of *c.* 4,000 names.

India
912 (540)

National atlas of India. Preliminary Hindi ed. Edited by S. P. Chatterjee. Dehra Dun, Ministry of Education and Scientific Research, 1957. [ii], 8 p., 26 pl. of maps.

26 sheets of maps, most of them with several inset maps; standard scale for main maps, 1:5M. English and Hindi text. Coverage: administrative, physical, climate, geographical, forest, cash crops,

milch cattle, working cattle, railway, airways, education, archaeological sites, Page size, 30″ × 26″, almost maximum size for an atlas. Called "an outstanding national atlas" by Sir L. Dudley Stamp (*Geographical journal,* v. 125, pt. 1, March 1959, p. 96-97), who adds that "work is already in hand on a large atlas which will involve over 300 plates and which will probably extend into the period of the Third Five-Year Plan [1961/66]".

This latter, the National Atlas Organisation's *National atlas of India* (Calcutta, Survey of India, 1959-) has loose-leaf maps (1:1M.) covering administration, physical geography, population, transport, etc. Page size, 22″ × 15½″.

S. P. Chatterjee's "Our national and regional atlases" appeared in *Bombay geographical magazine,* v. 14, no. 1, December 1966, p. 39-57, with maps.

Turkey

912 (560)
Türkiye atlasi. Istanbul, Milli Eğitim Basimevi, [1961]. 23 double pl. 150s.

Publication of the Faculty of Letters, University of Istanbul.

The first national atlas of Turkey. No explanatory text. 87 maps and diagrams, mostly based on original research, but some are compilations or are taken from other sources. Thus, the 44 small maps on climate are based on data of the General Directorate of Meteorology.

Israel

912 (569.4)
Atlas of Israel: cartography, physical geography, history, demography, economics, education. Jerusalem, Department of Surveys, Ministry of Labour, and the Bialik Institute, the Jewish Agency, 1956-. maps. Loose-leaf.

A fine piece of cartography, map scales being normally 1:¾M. to 1:2M. Some ninety maps have so far been issued. Sections (ea. 32s. 6d.): 1. Cartography (14 maps)—2. Geomorphology (7)—3. Geology (3)—4. Climate (5)—5. Hydrology (3)—6. Botany (2)—7. Zoology (3)—8. Landscape evolution (3)—9. History (15)—10. Population (6)—11. Settlements (7)—12. Agriculture (12)—13. Industry and commerce (11)—14. Communications (3)—15. Services (education, health, postal and cultural facilities). Town plans are included. In Hebrew. Page size, 19⅞″ × 15⅝″. Reviewed in *Scottish geographical magazine,* v. 79, no. 1, April 1963, p. 60.

An English edition is planned after completion of the Hebrew ed.

Africa

912 (6)
Africa: maps and statistics. Pretoria, Africa Institute, 1962-65. 10v. maps. ea. v. 75c.; R9 the set.

See entry at 33 (084.4) (6).

912 (6)
The Shorter Oxford atlas of Africa. Prepared by the Cartographic Department of the Clarendon Press. Oxford, Clarendon Press, 1966. 96p. maps. 21s.

Based on the *Oxford regional economic atlas: Africa* (1965) (*see at 33 (084.4) (6)*).

48 pages of topographical maps; gazetteer of c. 18,000 names. The whole continent is mapped at 1″ : 50, 33 or 25 miles.

912 (6):016
UNITED NATIONS. ECONOMIC COMMISSION FOR AFRICA. United Nations Regional Cartographic Conference for Africa, 1-12 July 1963, Nairobi, Kenya. v. 2: **Proceedings** of the Conference and technical papers. New York, U.N., 1966. x, 332p. illus., diagrs., maps. (E/CONF. 43/106).

v. 1: Report of the Conference.

v. 2, pt. 2: Reports by governments and international organizations on their activities for the African continents (p. 41-174), *e.g.,* Michelin road maps of Africa (submitted by France); report on cartographic activities in Sierra Leone (submitted by Sierra Leone). A general section, covers aerial photography, photogrammetry and topographical mapping (*e.g.,* progress report on the compilation of the *Atlas du Maroc,* submitted by Morocco).

Noted: *A preliminary bibliography of African atlases,* by R. E. Dahlberg (New York, Special Libraries Association, Geography and Map Division. *Bulletin* no. 59, March 1965, p. 3-9).

Morocco

912 (64)
Atlas du Maroc. Comité de Géographie du Maroc. Rabat, Institut Scientifique Chérifien, 1956-. maps.

11 sections (25½″ × 20″) so far published. A series of loose maps, with explanatory handbooks, each of 30-40 pages. 150-200 maps are envisaged on some 54 separate topics, to cover physical, human and economic geography, from topography, climate and geology to disease vectors and economic development. Sheets usually carry 2 maps apiece with scales 1:100,000, 1:200,000 and 1:500,000, and cover forestry, cattle-breeding, rural development, distribution of diseases, and railways. Reviewed in *Scottish geographical magazine,* v. 77, no. 2, September 1961, p. 124-5.

Central & Southern Africa

912 (66/69):016
SCIENTIFIC COUNCIL FOR AFRICA SOUTH OF THE SAHARA. Cartes topographiques de l'Afrique au sud du Sahara. London, Commission for Technical Co-operation in Africa South of the Sahara, 1955. [vii], 40p.

A bibliography of topographical maps, arranged in seven sections, the first being general and the others regional. Prominence is given to scales. Atlases are included.

————**Cartographie de l'Afrique au sud du Sahara.** 2e partie, **Cartes spéciales.** London, Commission for Technical Co-operation in Africa South of the Sahara, 1955. [x], 70p.

A bibliography of special maps, arranged in

seven sections, the first general and the others regional, followed by smaller groupings. Scales are stated; maps included.

These two bibliographies are the revised text of the bibliography published in 1953.

The C.S.A. (Scientific Council for Africa) and the Commission for Technical Co-operation in Africa are sponsoring an *International atlas of West Africa,* in English and French. Basic scale, 1:5M. 48 maps, physical and thematic. Descriptive notes; general index. The first section of 8 map sheets appeared in April 1968. Page size, $21\frac{1}{8}'' \times 30\frac{3}{8}''$.

Sierra Leone

912 (664)

Atlas of Sierra Leone. Freetown, Survey and Lands Department; London, Stanford, 1953. [1]p., 16 maps, iv p.

Four general maps are followed by maps of Sierra Leone (5-16), covering climate, soil, medical facilities, tribal distribution, postal facilities, agricultural products, population density, mineral deposits, geology, physical geography, and towns (Freetown, Bonthe, Bo, Magburaka).

Appendices consist of a gazetteer of towns, etc., a gazetteer of physical features, chiefdom names, statistical data, and a map list.

J. I. Clarke's *Sierra Leone in maps* (London, Univ. of London Press, 1966. 119p. 20s.) contains 51 black-and-white maps (usually 1:30M.), with explanatory text facing each map. Headings: A. General—B. Physical environment, flora and fauna—C. Society and settlements—D. Economy —E. History. Bibliography, p. 115-9, including many periodical articles.

Congo

912 (675)

Atlas général du Congo. Brussels, Académie Royale des Sciences d'Outre-Mer, 1948-63. maps. £77 10s.

A comprehensive atlas, with explanatory text. Covers many aspects of the Republic (latterly: aviation; magnetic declination; medical establishments; hydroelectric power plants and lines, electoral parties, volcanology, frontiers of Ruanda-Urundi, and population density and distribution in Équateur province). The Carte electorale du Congo (sheet 625. 1961) is at 1:5M.; size: $18'' \times 17\frac{1}{2}''$.

Uganda

912 (676)

Atlas of Uganda. Uganda, Lands and Surveys Department. Kampala, Government Printer, Uganda, 1962. 83p. maps. 80s.

40 pages of coloured maps (mostly 1:1,500,000), sometimes 12 to a page, each accompanied by explanatory text. Ranges from external communications, physical geography, climate, flora and fauna, human geography, rural economy, industry and trade, to history. Town plans of Kampala and Jinja. Brief gazetteer. Page size: $19\frac{1}{4}'' \times 20\frac{1}{2}''$.

Kenya

912) (677)

Atlas of Kenya: a comprehensive series of new and authentic maps prepared from the National Survey and other governmental sources, with gazetteer and notes on pronunciation and spelling. Nairobi, Survey of Kenya, 1959. 4 l., 45 pl. of maps, 3 l.

Maps cover geology, physical features, soil, meteorology, agriculture, population, economy, administration and history. Scales, 1:1M. to 1:3M. Town plan of Mombasa; interesting reproductions of early maps. Gazetteer of 1,500-2,000 names. Reviewed in *Geographical journal,* v. 127, pt. 4, December 1961, p. 554. Page size: $20'' \times 18''$.

Tanganyika

912 (678.2)

Atlas of Tanganyika, East Africa. 3rd ed. Tanganyika, Department of Lands and Surveys. Dar-es-Salaam, Government Printer, 1956. 29p. of maps. 60s.

2nd ed. 1948 (*Atlas of the Tanganyika territory*).

29 plates of maps (uniformly 1:3M.), covering physical geography, biogeography, human geography, industry and commerce, and town plans. Appended are a statistical section and gazetteer. A transparent population overlay is provided for use with the individual maps. Page size, $22'' \times 23''$

South Africa

912 (680)

TALBOT, A. M. and **TALBOT, W. J. Atlas of the Union of South Africa.** Pretoria, Government Printer, 1960. [9], lxiv, 177p. maps, tables. £12 12s.

Prepared in collaboration with the Trigonometrical Survey Office and under the aegis of the National Council for Social Research. English and Afrikaans text.

All the maps (about 700), except for a few relief, geological and vegetation maps, are black and white. Sections: 1. Relief, geology, mining, soils, vegetation and fisheries—2. Climate and water resources—3. Population—4. Agriculture —5. Industries and occupations—6. Transportation—7. External trade. Effective use of dot maps to show such details as the number of eggs (1 dot = 50,000 dozen) sold by European farmers, 1945/60, or the phosphorus content of natural pastures in winter, 1933-1935. A scale of 1:8M. is used for most maps. Page size, $17\frac{1}{2}'' \times 22\frac{1}{2}''$.

The Automobile Association of South Africa's *Road atlas and touring guide of Southern Africa* (2nd rev. ed. Johannesburg, the Association, 1963. 200p. illus., maps, plans) includes "detailed diagrams of the entrances and exits for over 200 towns" (Musiker, R. *Guide to South African reference books* (4th ed., 1965), p. 65).

Rhodesia

912 (689.1)

COLLINS, M. O., *ed.* **Rhodesia: its natural resources and economic development.** Salisbury, M. O. Collins (Pvt.), 1965. ii, 52p. illus., maps.

See entry at 33 (084.4) (689.1).

Canada
912 (71)

Atlas of Canada. Ottawa, Department of Mines and Technical Surveys, Geographical Branch, 1957 (published 1959). 110 pl. of maps. Looseleaf. (London, Stanford, £18.).

110 sheets, consisting of 450 maps. (Sheets can be purchased separately at 50c.; 5s.) Coverage: historical; bathy-orographical; geological and climatic; demographic, social and economic. A high standard of mapping; exhaustive gazetteer. (Reviewed by L. D. Stamp in *Geographical journal,* v. 126, pt. 2, June 1960, p. 241-2). Sheet sizes, $21'' \times 16\frac{1}{2}''$ to $16\frac{1}{2}'' \times 25''$. Both French and English edtiions are available.

912 (711)

British Columbia atlas of resources. Editors: J. D. Chapman and D. B. Turner; cartographic editors: A. L. Farley and R. I. Ruggles. Vancouver, B.C., British Columbia Natural Resources Conference, 1956. vii, 92p. (loose-leaf), 48p. of maps.

"This is perhaps the finest regional atlas yet produced in North America, and it ranks high among the leading regional atlases of the world." (*Geographical review,* v. 48, no. 1, January 1958, p. 133-4). Pt. 1: Geographical characteristics; pt. 2: Resources use; pt. 3: Map indexes and gazetteer.

Economic atlas of Manitoba, edited by T. R. Weir (Winnipeg, Department of Industry and Commerce, Province of Manitoba, 1960. v, 81p.) is another outstanding regional atlas, with more than a hundred maps. Page size, $23'' \times 17\frac{1}{4}''$.

U.S.A.
912 (73)

National geographic atlas of the fifty United States. Washington, National Geographic Magazine, 1960. 13 pl. of maps, 32p. $6.75 to members only.

Consists of 13 ten-colour double-page maps, each $19'' \times 25''$, together with 1 facsimile. The states of Alaska and Hawaii are included. The 32-page index-gazetteer lists more than 30,000 names.

The first 4 sheets of the *National atlas of the United States of America* were reported in *Library of Congress Information bulletin,* v. 26, no. 10, 9th March 1967, p. 187. The project is being undertaken by the U.S. Geological Survey, with an advisory group to assist. The complete volume is scheduled for publication late in 1968. Map sheets (ea. $1-$1.50) cover physical features, environmental conditions, history, agriculture, economy, and socio-cultural and administrative aspects, plus U.S. world-relationships.

These United States: our nation's geography, history and people (Pleasantville, Reader's Digest

Association, 1968. 236p. maps) has maps for each State (with c. 45,000 locations), maps illustrating cultural geography, physical and economic aspects; descriptive text (with index); index-gazetteer (*Library of Congress information bulletin,* v. 27, no. 10, 7th March 1968, p. 140).

Latin America
912 (8=6)

Map of Hispanic America, on the scale of 1:1,000,000. American Geographical Society. Washington, Government Printing Office, 1922-45. 923p. maps.

107 sheets (ea. $2.50) covering the entire subcontinent south of the U.S.A. Topographical maps. Supported by an excellent index-gazetteer, giving geographical co-ordinates for c. 150,000 places.

The A.G.S. has also published a comprehensive *Catalogue of maps of Hispanic America* (1930-33. 4v.). The listing is continued in *A catalogue of Latin American flat maps, 1926-1964,* edited by P. V. Monteiro (Austen, Institute of Latin American Studies, Univ. of Texas, 1967). Reviewed in *Geographical journal,* v. 134, pt. 1, March 1968, p. 158.

Brazil
912 (81)

Atlas do Brasil (geral e regional). [2nd ed.] Rio de Janeiro, Instituto Brasileiro de Geografia e Estatística. 1959. 165p. illus., diagrs., maps.

97 pages of maps, general and regional. The regional maps (c. 1:3M. to 1:8M.) deal with relief, climate, vegetation, population, economic production and transport. All maps are accompanied by explanatory text. A few well-chosen photographs. "More in the nature of a geographical sketch than a detailed analysis" (*Scottish geographical magazine,* v. 79, no. 1, April 1963, p. 60). Page size: $21'' \times 15''$.

Colombia
912 (86)

Atlas de economía colombiana. Bogotá, Banco de la República, Departamento de Investigaciones Económicas, 1959-60. 2 pts. maps, tables, graphs.

pt. 1. *Aspectos físico y geográfico.*
pt. 2. *Aspectos político, humano y administrativo.*
Despite the specific title, this is a general atlas covering the physical, political, cultural and administrative structure of Colombia, with a short geographical text, statistical tables and graphs. Page size, $15\frac{1}{4}'' \times 11''$. Very favourably reviewed in *The geographical review,* v. 52, no. 3, July 1962, p. 432.

Pacific Islands
912 (9)

KENNEDY, T. F. A descriptive atlas of the Pacific Islands: Australia, Polynesia, Melanesia, Micronesia, Philippines. Wellington, Reed, 1966. 65p. maps.

Grey, black-and-white maps only, illustrating each of the principal island groups. Concise supporting text. Page size: $9\frac{1}{4}'' \times 7''$. Reviewed in *Geographical journal*, v. 133, pt. 2, June 1967, p. 242-3.

Indonesia

912 (910)

Atlas nasional seluruh dunia untuk sekolah landjutan. Djakarta & Bandung, Penerbit Ganaco n.v., 1960. 71 p. of maps.

A general commercial atlas of Indonesia, intended for school use. 22 of the plates are devoted to Indonesia "and are useful in giving current political divisions and nomenclature". (*The geographical review*, v. 42, no. 3, July 1962, p. 422, which comments very favourably).

New Zealand

912 (931)

McLINTOCK, A. H., *ed.* **A descriptive atlas of New Zealand.** Wellington, R. E. Owen, Government Printer, 1959 (reprinted 1960). xxi, 110p. with 48 pl. of maps. illus.

An atlas of 48 plates, with scales 1:1M. to 1:3,200,000, covering geology, economy, population, land utilization, climate, physical and political geography. A map of Antarctica is included (p. 84-85); also inset town-plans. 24 full-page illustrations. Index-gazetteer has *c.* 18,000 entries; analytical index to text commentary. Page size, $12'' \times 10''$.

Australia

912 (94)

Atlas of Australian resources. Canberra, Department of National Development, 1952-. maps. Loose-leaf.

See entry at 33 (084.4) (94).

Arctic

912 (98)

SWITHINBANK, C. W. M. Ice atlas of Arctic Canada. Ottawa, Canadian Defense Research Board, 1960. 67p.

"Mapped and charted data . . . for 324 stations between Northern Alaska and Western Greenland, showing symbolically the number of months of five types of ice cover ("concentration") and of four degrees of difficulty of navigation" (Church, M., and others, comp. and ed. *A basic geographical library* (1966), entry no. 1317). Bibliography appended.

"Ice atlases", by T. Armstrong, in *Polar record*, v. 12, no. 77, 1964, p. 161-3. illus. (pl.), briefly reviews eight current ice atlases, including the *Ice atlas of Arctic Canada.*

Antarctic

912 (99)

Antarctic maps and surveys, 1900-1964. Text by G. D. Whitmore. New York, American Geographical Society, 1965. 4p. of text, 11 pl. of maps. (Antarctic map folio series, folio 3). $5.

11 plates, each containing 2 or 3 maps. Extent of maps or photographic cover is shown by 2-5 colours. Reviewed in *The cartographic journal*, v. 4, no. 1, June 1967, p. 54-55. Page size, $17'' \times 11''$.

The A.G.S. Antarctic map folio series (1965-) has now reached folio 9, *Magnetic and gravity maps of the Antarctic* (1968. $4).

912 (99)

Atlas Antarktiki. Moscow, Glavnoe Upravlenie Geodezii i Kartografii, 1966-. v. 1-. (v. 1. R.30).

V. 1 consists of 225 pages of maps; v. 2, the text, was expected late in 1967.

V. 1 is in 3 parts (introductory; general geographical; regional) and includes geological, climate and ice cover, as well as depicting the history of explorations. Alphabetical index of place names. Claims to be the first complete atlas of the Antarctic. "It is without doubt the most exciting cartographic document which has ever been produced in the Soviet Union" (*Cartographical journal*, v. 4, no. 1, June 1967, p. 54), although the pages devoted to map and photographic cover compare unfavourably with the A.G.S. Antarctic map folio series, folio 3 (*q.v.*). Page size, $24'' \times 15\frac{1}{2}''$. Index-gazetteer of *c.* 5,000 place-names.

Soviet geography: review and translation, special issue, v. 8, no. 5-6 (p. 261-507) consists of a translation of introduction and legends on maps in v. 1.

912 (99):016

UNITED STATES. LIBRARY OF CONGRESS. Reference Department, Map Division. **Selected maps and charts of Antarctica:** an annotated list of maps of the South Polar regions published since 1945. Compiled by Richard W. Stephenson. Washington, Library of Congress, 1959. vi, 193p.

495 numbered items, arranged by issuing bodies or cartographers. Index of places and issuing bodies; date index; index arranged by scales.

914/919 REGIONAL GEOGRAPHY AND GUIDES

Guide Books

914/919 (026)

BAEDEKER, K. Handbook[s] for travellers. Freiburg, Baedeker; London, Allen & Unwin.

This famous series began when Karl Baedeker took over the Rheinreise in 1828. Noted for

concise, detailed and carefully evaluated descriptions that always have the wellbeing of the tourist in mind (*e.g.,* "The renaissance stonework at the top of the campanile is particularly worthy of study—477 steps; beware of crumbling masonry"; cited in *The listener*, v. 73, no. 1879, 1st April 1965, p. 490-1), with a wealth of maps, town plans and panoramas. Although many of the pre-1945 series have never been revised, a number of them still have value (e.g., *Egypt and the Sudan* (8th ed., 1929. 495p.; *Switzerland* (28th ed. 1938. lviii, 568p.)).

Some 15 post-1945 guides deal with areas of West Germany; a few have been translated into English (*Berlin* (7th ed. 1965); *Cologne and Bonn, with environs* (1961); *Frankfurt and the Taunus* (1951); *Munich and its environs* (2nd ed. 1960); *Northern Bavaria* (1951); *Southern Bavaria* (1953)). Others include: *Great Britain* (1966-67. 3v.); *Tyrol and Salzburg* (14th ed. 1961). This last has 24 maps, 3 town-plans, 4 panoramas and nearly 180 pictorial sketches (considered "seldom communicative" by the *Times literary supplement*, no. 3,802, 24th March 1961, p. 191).

The Baedeker 'Autoreiseführer' are intended mainly for motorists, but are less detailed than their Michelin "Guides verts" counterparts. Some have English editions, 'Autoguides': *Austria* (1958); *France, including Corsica* (1961); *Spain and Portugal* (1960); *Benelux* (1958); *Switzerland: official handbook of the Automobile Club of Switzerland* (2nd ed. 1967).

A more recent 'Touring guides' series includes: *Austria* (due Autumn 1967); *France* (1961); *Italy; Spain and Portugal; Scandinavia; Benelux; Switzerland* (due Autumn 1967); *Yugoslavia*. Volumes on *Germany* and *Turkey* are in preparation.

914/919 (026)
Blue guides. Editor, S. Rossiter; advisory editor, L. R. Muirhead. London, Benn, 1918-. maps, plans.

Concentrate on Western European countries; well furnished with data, coloured maps and town plans, though less detailed and stylistic than Baedeker. Average price is *c.* 50s., but some smaller volumes (*e.g.*, Florence, Venice, Majorca are available as 4s. 6d.-6s. paperbacks).

Scotland (5th ed. 1967. 50s.)	*Florence.* 10s.
Edinburgh. 12s. 6d.	*Southern Italy, with Sicily and Sardinia.* 40s.
Ireland. 40s.	
England (7th ed. 1965. 55s.)	*Northern Spain.* 50s.
	Southern Spain. 52s. 6d.
London (9th ed. 1965. 25s.)	*Majorca, Minorca, with Ivizá.* 7s. 6d.
Oxford and Cambridge. 7s. 6d.	*Denmark.* 40s.
North West France. 42s.	*Holland.* 35s.
South of France. 42s.	*Belgium and Luxembourg.* 35s.
Paris. 21s.	*Bernese Oberland and Lucerne.* 21s.
Northern Italy. 50s.	*Greece* (1967. 70s.).
Venice. 4s. 6d.	*Athens and environs.* 25s.
Rome and Central Italy. 55s.	

914 (026)
Europa Touring. Guide automobile d'Europe Motoring guide to Europe. Automobilführer von Europe. [New ed.] Berne, Hallwag, 1967. x, 984p. maps.

Revised annually.
Main sections: Towns (A-Z; with town plans main roads only; advertisements for hotels)—

Text (descriptions of places, under countries, in alphabetical order of national automobile plates). 92 double-paged maps, beginning with N.E. France. Gazetteer and index.

914/919 (026)
Fodor's Modern guides. London, Neame (subsequently MacGibbon & Kee), 1953-. illus., maps, plans.

Revised annually and a wide-ranging series, like the Nagel guides. Attractive modern format; half-tone illustrations. Cartography, less good. Volumes (usually 15s., paperback; 25s. - 30s., cased), in U.D.C. order:

Guide to Europe	*Holland*
Men's guide to Europe	*Belgium and*
Women's guide to Europe	*Luxembourg*
	Switzerland
Britain and Ireland	*Greece*
Germany	*Yugoslavia*
Austria	*Japan and East Asia*
France	*India*
Italy	*Guide to the Caribbean*
Spain and Portugal	*Bahamas and Bermuda*
Moscow	*South America*
Scandinavia	*Hawaii*

914/919 (026)
Les Guides bleus. Paris, Hachette.

The 'Guides bleus' proper are detailed guides on the Baedeker pattern, covering France in *c.* 20v.; other volumes deal with Western and Southern European countries (*Allemagne; Autriche; France; Guide littéraire de France; Italie; Espagne; Portugal, Madère, Açores; Pays nordique; Hollande; Suisse; Grèce; Yougoslavie*) as well as areas of French-speaking Africa and West Indies (*Afrique Centrale, les république d'expression française; Afrique occidentale française; Maroc; Antilles. Guyanne*) and the Middle East (*Israël; Turquie*).

The 'Guide bleus illustrés' deal with smaller areas, often capital cities and their environs (*Londres et ses environs; Paris et sa proche banlieu; Châteaux de la Loire; La Côte d'Azur; Megève, Saint Gervais et leurs environs; Rouen; Rome; Sicilie; Iles Baléaires; Bruxelles et ses environs; Genève et ses environs; Athènes . . . ; Istanbul et des environs; Dakar, Saint-Louis et leurs environs; Brazzaville, Léopoldville, Pointe-Noire; New York et ses environs; Rio de Janeiro et ses environs*).

The 'Hachette world guides' are also published in English (*Paris in a week; Italy; Spain; Portugal, Madeira, Azores; Greece; Turkey; Lebanon; Israel; The Middle East*).

914/919 (026)
Guides Michelin. Paris, Services de Tourisme Michelin. illus., maps.

"Les guides rouges", issued annually (at Easter), deal primarily with hotels and restaurants, garages and service stations, giving town plans, exact location of hotels and street-traffic direction. *France* (1967 ed. 1068p. 22s. 6d.) is noted for its astringent allotting of 1, 2 or 3 stars for outstanding cuisines. English editions (London, Dickens Press): *Germany* (1967. 18s.); *France* (1966 ed. 25s.); *Paris* (1967 ed. 3s. 6d.).

French eds. include *Italie* (10th ed. 1965); *Espagne* (1966); *Benelux* (1965). Noted for meticulous accuracy. The Michelin *France* has data (based on users' letters as on reports by Michelin agents (incognito or otherwise) on nearly 4,000 towns.

"Les guides verts" are mainly concerned with sight-seeing, that on Paris being a model of its kind. 16 of these deal with regions of France. Five, those on *Brittany, Châteaux de la Loire, French Riviera. Paris* and the *Pyrenees* are available in English, like the annual *Camping in France*. They are to be used in conjunction with the 1:200,000 Michelin maps.

"Les guides verts" are also available in French and English editions on *Austria, Italy* and *Switzerland* (English ed., ea. 15s.). French eds. only: *Algérie-Sahara; Maroc*.

914/919 (026)
Nagel's guide series. Geneva, Nagel (London distributor: Muller), 1949-.

Supplements the 'Guide bleu' and 'Blue guide' series by covering countries in Asia, Africa and the Americas. Published in English, French, German, Italian, Spanish, Swedish, Danish, etc. Some Guides bleus (*e.g. Turquie* (1965) are also marked as 'Les guides Nagel'. The latest volume, *China* (1967. 126s.) has notes on history, geography, culture, economy, etc., 92 p. of plans, and 29 maps in colour. Volumes, in U.D.C. order:

Europe. 1956
Six little states of Europe. 1961
Great Britain and Ireland. 1953
Germany. 1965 ed.
Austria. 2nd ed. 1958
Czechoslovakia. 1959
Poland. 1964
Hongrie. 1957
France. 3rd ed. 1956
Paris and its environs. 1950
Côte d'Azur and Italian Riviera. 1961
Italy. 4th ed. 1956
Florence. 1959
Rome. 1963
Venice. 1959
Spain. 1953
Balearic Islands. 1961
Portugal. 1956
U.S.S.R. 1965
Moscow and environs;
Leningrad and environs. 1958
Scandinavia. 1958
Finlande. 1953
Norvège. 2nd ed. 1956
Suède. 2nd ed. 1956
Danemark. 2nd ed. 1956
Islande. 1953
Holland. 2nd ed. 1963
Belgium-Luxembourg. 1950
Switzerland. 1954
Yugoslavia. 1954
Rumania. 1967
China. 1967
Japan. 1964
Cyprus. 1964
Israel. 1965 ed.
Morocco. 1953
Congo belge. 1959
Canada. 1955
Mexico. 1960
Brazil. 1955.

914 (026)
ROYAL AUTOMOBILE CLUB. The Royal Automobile Club 1966 continental handbook & guide to Europe. Western section. London, R.A.C., 1966. illus., maps, plans. 17s.

Pink section (p. 1-64) gives general information; white section (p. 65-708) has data on individual countries (including F.I.A. affiliated clubs, hotel tariffs, notes on food and drink, motoring and traffic, plus descriptive gazetteer). Appendix comprises a glossary, first-aid hints, catalogue of maps and guides and an index. Supplement: distance chart, conversion tables, etc. Many town plans, showing one-way streets. Atlas (32p. of coloured maps). Atrractively produced.

————**Guide to Eastern Europe,** 1967. London, R.A.C., 1966. 160p. illus., maps, plans. 7s. 6d.

A companion volume, covering Bulgaria, Czechoslovakia, Greece, Hungary, Poland, Roumania, Turkey, Yugoslavia and U.S.S.R., plus a résumé of motoring regulations applying to East Germany. Albania not included because information is very limited. Map references to the atlas in the R.A.C. *Continental handbook.*

Europe

91 (083.86) (4)
Duden-Wörterbuch geographischer Namen. Europa (ohne Sowjetunion). Mannheim, Bibliographisches Institut, [1966]. 740p. DM.32.

About 28,000 entries for names of localities, mountains, landforms, rivers, seas, lakes and administrative units in European countries except the Soviet Union. Pronunciation of entry-words is given, based on the International Phonetic alphabet. Very brief description and location. Entry is under German form of name (*e.g., Elsass*, not Alsace; *Fünfkirchen*, not Pécs), with cross-references only from earlier forms of names. Map-grid references. Reviewed in *Times literary supplement,* no. 3,413, 27th July 1967, p. 680.

Great Britain

914.1 (02)
The County book series. Edited by Brian Vesey-Fitzgerald. London, Hale, 1947-56. 44v. illus., maps.

The 44 volumes, each by a different author, consist of 36 on English counties, 6 on Scotland and 2 on Ireland. As descriptive material they seek to capture the spirit of the region rather than to serve as detailed guide-books. Each has references to sources and an analytical index and is well illustrated.

914.1 (02)
Regions of the British Isles; edited by W. G. East. London, Nelson, 1960-. illus., maps.

Northern England, by A. E. Smailes. 1960. 50s.
The Highlands and islands of Scotland, by A. C. O'Dell and K. Walton. 1962. 50s.
The East Midlands and the Peak, by G. H. Drury. 1963. 50s.
Lancashire, Cheshire and the Isle of Man, by T. W. Freeman, and others. 1966. 63s.

The series, to be in 14v., is designed to provide a comprehensive and detailed survey of the physical and economic geography of the British Isles. Other volumes are to deal with: Southeast England; Wessex; Southwest England; the Bristol region; the Eastern lowlands of England; the West Midlands; Yorkshire; Wales; Southern Scotland; and Ireland. The first volume covers the four most northerly counties of England, has nearly 70 line-maps, 46 plates and valuable selected chapter references (p. 303-14).

914.1 (026)
**ROYAL AUTOMOBILE CLUB. The Royal Auto-
mobile Club guide and handbook.** London,
R.A.C., 1904-. Annual since 1946. (1967. 17s. 6d.)

Lists 5,500 R.A.C.-appointed, approved or
recommended hotels, motels, guest houses and
restaurants, plus detailed tariff charges; arranged
A-Z by place; appointed hotels have a star classification. Also lists 8,500 garages and service
stations. The directory covers England, Scotland
and Wales, with a separate list for Ireland. About
100 town plans; 64 pages of two-colour road
maps. Data on R.A.C. and A.A. telephone boxes,
ferries, hills (with gradients), and much else. The
1967 ed. includes revision of mileages between
neighbouring towns.

"The Reader's Digest"—A.A. book of the road,
incorporating the Ordnance Survey four miles to
the inch series (London, 'The Reader's Digest'
Association, with the A.A., 1966. 408p. illus.,
diagrs., maps. 63s.) comprises town plans, strip
maps of key roads, 4" folding maps ('The British
Isles by road', p. 137-264), a gazetteer of 24,000
place-names, 'Roadside recognition' (p. 337-89),
and notes on first aid and law for the motorist.

914.1 (026)
The Shell and BP guide to Britain; edited by G.
Boumphrey. London, Ebury Press in association
with G. Rainbird, 1964. xxxii, 808p. illus., maps.
30s.

An admirably and fully illustrated description
of the counties of England, Wales and Scotland
in 48 sections, preceded by a general introduction.
The section on Somerset (p. 33-48; 4 illus.) considers geology and scenery, industries, flora and
fauna, archaeology and architecture; 'Some
houses and gardens open to the public'; 'Books
for further reading'; 'Gazetteer' (description of
43 places A-Z best worth seeing, some of them
asterisked). 32-page road and a 12 miles:1" physical atlas, based on the Ordnance Survey map.
Index of names; key map on end-papers. No
town plans. A weighty volume, for the motorist
rather than the walker.

G. Grigson's *The Shell country alphabet*
(London, Joseph, in association with G. Rainbird,
1966. 400p. illus. (incl. col. pl.), maps. 30s.) has
c. 700 entries (e.g., 'Barrows': 2p. plus reference
to illustrations; 'Turner, J. M. W.' : ½p.). Preceded by classified index (e.g., 'Artists of the
countryside', 'Boundaries and divisions of the
land').

914.1 (058.7):016
HENDERSON, G. P., and **ANDERSON, I. G.
Current British directories, 1966-7.** 5th ed.
Croydon, Surrey, C.B.D. Research, Ltd., 1966.
xii, 214p. 80s.

See entry at 38 (058.7) (410)

914.1 (083.86)
**BARTHOLOMEW, J. G. Gazetteer of the Bri-
tish Isles.** 9th ed. reprinted 1963, incorporating
a summary of the 1961 census. 1963 (reprinted
1966). xxxi, 763p. maps. 50s.

The standard, current gazetteer of the British
Isles. The 1966 reprint does not include the atlas

of 47 pages. New and amended entries are differentiated. Pt. 1: Introductory and statistical; pt. 2:
Gazetteer of the British Isles, "containing over
90,000 place-names, with location, postal, railway and other information". Most of the entries
are limited to one line, giving location, population and size. Brief etymological dictionary of
place names.

Included are country seats (e.g., Acton Castle:
Huntingdon House) and landmarks of all kinds.
Under the entry word "The" are 2½ columns of
entries which might otherwise be overlooked.
Pronunciations are given for place-names which
are difficult to pronounce (e.g., Llangollen).

*Cassell's Gazetteer of Great Britain and Ire-
land, being a complete topographical dictionary
of the United Kingdom* (London, Cassell, 1894-
98. 6v. illus. 60 maps) follows the plan used by
Samuel Lewis in his *Topographical dictionary*
(see at 942 (03)). This is the most recent gazetteer
of the British Isles to give entries of more than
a couple of lines. The topographical details are
useful and are not restricted to antiquities. The
maps are not very good and the illustrations are
small and picturesque in style.

914.1 (083.86)
**GREAT BRITAIN. ORDNANCE SURVEY
OFFICE. Gazetteer of Great Britain;** giving
the positions of all the names shown on the Ordnance Survey quarter-inch maps in terms of the
National Grid. Chessington, Ordnance Survey,
1953. 147p. 12s. 6d.

Lists more than 40,000 place-names.

914.1 (083.86)
**The Railway and commercial gazetteer of Eng-
land, Scotland and Wales** (19th edition), containing a complete list (arranged in alphabetical
order) of every railway station, town, village,
hamlet and place in Great Britain, showing the
distance from London to each railway station
and the distance by road from the station to the
town, village, hamlet, parish and place; with the
locality, population (from last census), line of
rail, nearest railway station, distinguishing post
offices, money order and telegraph offices, and
the "through rate" routes for merchandise, passengers and parcels to, from or through London
and all parts of the Kingdom by various railways.
London, McCorquodale, 1938. xii, 722p. 42s.

About 45,000 entries.

Scotland
914.11 (026)
**AUTOMOBILE ASSOCIATION. Road book of
Scotland,** with gazetteer, itineraries, maps and
town plans. 3rd post-war ed., rev. London, A.A.,
1964. 283, v, 2-36p. maps.

First published 1953.
Chief contents: the itineraries (270; p. 50-97).
preceded by key map and through-route maps;
gazetteer information on more than 2,000 towns
and villages (p. 98-283); Bartholomew road atlas
of Scotland (⅛" : 1 mile); short glossary.

914.11 (026)
The Shell guide to Scotland, by M. McLaren.

London, Ebury Press, in association with G. Rainbird, 1965. 496p. illus., maps. 50s.

A well illustrated description, with more than 1,250 entries in the extensive 'Gazetteer'. 32 coloured plates, apart from numerous black-and-white illustrations. Gazetteer entries are considered (*Times literary supplement*, no. 3328, 9th December 1965, p. 1662) to favour country against town and, perhaps, the north and east Lowlands against the south and west; particularly weak on architecture. 8 two-colour 15 miles : 1″ maps; no town plans. A weighty volume, for the motorist rather than the walker.

Compared unfavourably (*Geographical journal*, v. 132, pt. 2, June 1966, p. 274) with the A.A. *Road book of Scotland,* which is much cheaper and has 30 pages of pleasant, informative text 5 miles : 1″ maps, plus a map showing west coast ferry routes.

914.11 (083.86)
GROOME, F. H. Ordnance gazetteer of Scotland; a graphic and accurate description of every place in Scotland. New ed., with census appendix, 1901. Edinburgh, Jack, 1901. 1762p. illus. map.

Still of considerable value for its detailed treatment (*e.g.,* "Glasgow", p. 652-729) and bibliographies, although the references to the contemporary Ordnance Survey sheets for location no longer apply. The gazetteer is followed by a general survey of Scotland (physical features; geology; agriculture; population; industries, etc.).

914.11 (083.86)
JOHNSTON, W., and JOHNSTON, A. K. Gazetteer of Scotland, including a glossary of the most common Gaelic and Norse names. Edinburgh & London, Johnston, 1937. 330p. maps. (2nd ed. 1958. 248p. and 24 maps.)

The gazetteer gives, in general, the same information as Bartholomew's *Survey gazetteer of the British Isles (at 914.1 (03)),* and sometimes less. Lists of parliamentary constituencies, ferries, Scots peerage, golf courses. 24 pages of coloured maps at about 8 miles to the inch.

914.11 (083.86)
GREAT BRITAIN. GENERAL REGISTER OFFICE, Edinburgh. **Place names and population. Scotland:** an aphabetical list of populated places, derived from the census of Scotland. Edinburgh, H.M. Stationery Office, 1967. 190p. 27s.

List of *c.* 10,000 places, showing 1961 Census population figures (p. 10-104). 7 appendices, including: 1. Cities, large burghs, small burghs and burgh wards: population, 1961—2. Civil parishes: population, 1961.

914.11:413.11
JOHNSTON, J. B. The place-names of Scotland. 3rd ed., enl. London, Murray, 1934. xvi, 335p. 15s.

First published 1892.
The alphabetical list of place-names (p. 75-326) is preceded by sections on Celtic names, Norse names, English names, Roman, Norman and purely modern names, and ecclesiastical names. A short bibliography and an index to names not on the list are appended.
Scottish studies (1957-. v. 1, no. 1-) runs a series, 'Notes on Scottish place-names' (*e.g.,* 27. *Thurso,* p. 171-6; 15 references, in v. 10, pt. 2, 1966).
Regional lists include:
The place names of Aberdeenshire, by W. McC. Alexander (Aberdeen, Third Spalding Club, 1952. 419p.).
Place-names of West Aberdeenshire, by J. Macdonald (Aberdeen, New Spalding Club, 1899. xxviii, 347p.).
Places and place-names round Alyth, by J. Meikle (Paisley, Gardner, 1925. 203p.).
Place names of Argyll, by H. C. Gillies (London, Nutt, 1906. xxvi, 273p.).
The place-names of Arran, by R. Currie (Glasgow, John Smith, 1908. 95p.).
Place-names of Dumbartonshire, by J. Irving (Dumbarton, Bennett & Thomson, 1928. iii, 61p.).
The place-names of Dumfriesshire, by Sir E. Johnson-Ferguson (Dumfries, Courier Press, 1935. xxxiv, 140p.).
Place names of Elginshire, by D. Matheson (Stirling, Mackay, 1905. 208p.).
The place-names of Fife and Kinross, by W. J. N. Liddall (Edinburgh, Green, 1896. xiv, 58p.).
The place-names of Galloway, their origin and meaning considered, by Sir H. Maxwell (Glasgow, Jackson, 1930. xlvi, 278p.).
Place-names in Glengarry and Glenquoich, and their associations, by E. C. Ellice (2nd ed., rev. London, Routledge, 1931. xii, 163p.).
Hawick place names: a study of their origin and derivation, by W. S. Robson (Hawick, Hood, 1947. 82p.).
Place names, Highlands and Islands of Scotland, by A. MacBain (Stirling, MacKay, 1922. xxxiii, 381p.) Gaelic Society of Inverness. *Transactions,* 1871/2-1934/6.
Place-names of Lewis and Harris, by D. MacIver (Stornoway, 'Gazette' office, 1934. 102p.).
Gaelic place-names of the Lothians, by J. Milne (London, McDougall's Educational Co., 1912. 51, 44, 30p.).
Orkney Antiquarian Society. *Proceedings,* v. 1-15. 1923-39.
Place-names of Ross and Cromarty, by W. J. Watson (Inverness, Northern Counties Printing & Publishing Co., 1904. lxxxvi, 302p.).
Place-names of Rousay, by H. Marwick (Kirkwall, Macintosh, 1947. vii, 95p.).
Place-names of Shetland, by J. Jakobsen (London, Nutt, 1936. 273p.).
Place-names of Skye and adjacent islands, with lore, mythical, traditional and historical, by A. R. Forbes (Paisley, Gardner, 1923. 495p.).
The place-names of Stirlingshire, by J. B. Johnston (2nd ed. Stirling, Shearer, 1904. ix, 65p.).
Place-names of West Lothian, by A. Macdonald (Edinburgh, Oliver & Boyd, 1941. xi, 179p.).

914.11:413.11
MACKENZIE, W. C. Scottish place-names. London, Kegan, Paul, 1931. xi, 319p.

Arranged under subjects: hills, rivers, isles, etc., with extensive notes following each chapter, giving sources, variations, etc.

914.11:413.11

WATSON, W. J. History of the Celtic place-names of Scotland, being the Rhind Lectures in Archaeology (expanded) delivered in 1916. Edinburgh, Blackwood, 1926. xx, 558p.

Published under the auspices of the Royal Celtic Society.

914.11:413.11:016

ROYAL SCOTTISH GEOGRAPHICAL SOCIETY. Bibliography of the place-names of Scotland; compiled by G. Walker. Edinburgh, the Society, 1945. 19p. Typescript.

See also Hancock, P. D., *comp. A bibliography of works relating to Scotland, 1916-1950* [1960], v. 2, p. 278-80, for the more recent material on Scottish place-names.

Ireland

914.15 (026)

AUTOMOBILE ASSOCIATION. Road book of Ireland, with gazetteer, itineraries, maps & town plans. London, A.A., 1965. 270, v, 2-32p. maps, plans.

Gives touring information on *c.* 3,000 towns and villages. Chief contents: itineraries (with key map and through-route maps); gazetteer (p. 76-270), with town plans; Bartholomew road atlas of Ireland ($\frac{1}{8}''$: 1 mile): 32 pages of coloured maps.

Noted: Royal Irish Automobile Club. *Official gazetteer of Ireland* (Dublin, 1948).

914.15 (026)

Shell guide to Ireland, by Lord Killanin and M. V. Duignan. London, Ebury Press, 1962. viii, 478, [8]p. illus., maps. 45s. (2nd rev. ed. 1967. 50s.).

"A general guide, with particular attention to antiquities and items of historic and artistic interest" (*Preface*). Historical introduction; 'Gazetteer' (p. 39-461, A-Z; *e.g.,* 'Tara': 2¼ cols.). Appendices: A. Fishing in Ireland—B. Irish golf clubs—C. The Irish language and Irish place-names—D. Glossary (p. 474-5)—E. 'A short bibliography of books on Ireland' (p. 476-8). 17 coloured plates; over 200 black-and-white drawings in the text; 6 rather poor quality black-and-white maps, locating all places mentioned in the 'Gazetteer'.

914.15:413.11

HOGAN, E. Onomasticon Goedelicum locorum et tribuum Hiberniae et Scotiae: an index, with identifications, to the Gaelic names of places and tribes. Dublin, Hodges, 1910. xvi, 695p. map.

Bibliography, p. xi-xiv.

Regional lists include:
County of Clare Irish names explained, by J. Frost (Limerick, McKern, 1906. 66p.).
The place-names of Decies, by P. Power (London, Nutt, 1907. xxvii, 503p. maps).
The place-names of Westmeath, by P. Walsh (Dublin, the Editor, 1915. pt. 1 (viii, 116p.).
The place names of County Wicklow, by L. Price

(Dublin, Dublin Institute for Advanced Studies, 1945-58. 6 pts.

See also Ulster Place Name Society *Bulletin* (1952-. v. 1-) and "List of books on place names" in R. I. Best's *Bibliography of Irish philology,* 1913, p. 19-21; 1942 ed., p. 9-17.

914.15:413.11

JOYCE, P. W. The origin and history of Irish names of places. Dublin, Gill, 1869-71 (v. 1-2); London, Longmans, Green, 1898-1913. 3 v. (Reprinted. Dublin, Talbot Press).

The best guide to Irish place-name study, giving location, derivation and meaning of each name. V. 1-2 give systematic treatment, each chapter having an alphabetical index of places; there is also an index of root words. V. 3 is an A-Z list of place-names, with Irish forms and translations, usually not dealt with in v. 1-2.

914.16 (058.7)

Belfast and Northern Ireland directory, 1967. 87th ed. Belfast, Century Newspapers, Ltd., [1966?]. [viii], 124, 2262p. 65s.

Directory information on government departments and local boards; Belfast streets; alphabetical list; professions and trades; counties, towns and villages (p. 1776-2220); limited companies.

914.16 (083.86)

NORTHERN IRELAND. GENERAL REGISTER OFFICE. Census of population of Northern Ireland, 1961. Topographical index. Belfast, H.M. Stationery Office, 1962. 189p. 25s.

Eire

914.17 (026)

IRISH TOURIST BOARD. Illustrated Irish guide. Dublin, the Board, [1965?] 501p. illus., maps.

Covers Eire only. Contents: General aspects (fauna and flora; archaeology . . . ; 'A selection of books on Ireland' (p. 41-43); glossary)—Province of Leinster (Dublin, p. 54-78)—Province of Munster—Province of Connacht—Province of Ulster. Compact and well illustrated. Not enough large-scale maps; no detailed map of Dublin. Index of places.

England & Wales

914.2 (02)

FELLOWS, A. England and Wales: a traveller's companion. 2nd ed. London, Oxford Univ. Press, 1964. xx, 419p. illus. (pl.), maps. 30s.

First published 1937.
The main text, in 15 chapters, is virtually unaltered, although chapter bibliographies have been updated. But the invaluable Appendix of places of interest has been completely revised, enlarged and much simplified (*Amateur historian,* v. 6, no. 6, winter 1965, p. 208). Sub-divisions within each county on early man, Roman, early Christian and Saxon times, strip lynchets, churches, chapels, monasteries and cathedrals,

houses, castles, windmills, bridges and museums. Well illustrated; 33 plates, 2 maps.

914.2 (026)
AUTOMOBILE ASSOCIATION. Road book of England and Wales, with gazetteer, itineraries, maps & town plans. 4th ed. London, A.A., 1965. 532, vp., p. 2-60. maps, plans.

Giving touring information on more than 6,000 towns and villages. Chief contents: 830 itineraries (p. 40-152), with key map and through-route maps; gazetteer (p. 153-532), with small town-plans; place index; Bartholomew's road atlas of England and Wales ($\frac{1}{4}"$: 1 mile; 60 pages of 2-colour maps).

914.2 (083.86)
GREAT BRITAIN. GENERAL REGISTER OFFICE. Census, 1961, England and Wales. Index of place names. London, H.M. Stationery Office, 1965. 2v. 100s.

An index of place names was first produced in the series of census in 1831. In 1955 published as a separate double volume in the 1951 series of census publications.
Lists more than 65,000 place-names recorded in the 1961 census, including "the names of some 25,000 places, such as villages, hamlets and localities without legally defined boundaries, for which the populations have not been, or in most cases, could not be ascertained" (introductory). Headings: Name; Description; Administrative county; Borough, urban district, etc.; Number of registration district; P.S.D. or P.S.B. code number; Population, 1961.

914.2 (083.86)
GREAT BRITAIN. LORD CHANCELLOR'S DEPARTMENT, County Courts Branch, *comp.* **Index to the parishes, townships, hamlets & places** contained within the districts of the several County Courts in England & Wales, 10th ed. London, H.M. Stationery Office, 1966. [iii], 253p. 45s.

About 40,000 entries: name—county—town where county court located. Entries are grouped in lines of ten. Includes the names of places still used locally, although they are no longer administrative areas.

England

914.20 (02)
The King's England. Edited by Arthur Mee. New ed., rev. and reset. London, Hodder & Stoughton, 1966-. illus., maps.

First ed. 1936-53. 40v.
One volume per county (combined v. for Bedfordshire and Huntingdonshire, Hampshire and the Isle of Wight, Leicestershire and Rutland; 3v. for the Yorkshire Ridings), plus introductory v., *Enchanted land*). In each v. the places described are arranged A-Z, historical, architectural and biographical notes being included. Aims at conveying the atmosphere of each place and tends to repeat popular legends rather than historical facts. Folding map, with key.

914.20:413.11
ANDERSON, O. S. The English hundred-names. Lund, Ohleson; Gleerup, 1934-39. 3v.

The first volume (1934) is general in coverage, with entries A-Z. Bibliography, p. iii-xiii; index of *c*. 400 hundred-names.
The second and third v. (1939)—*The South-eastern counties* and *The South-western counties* —also have entries A-Z, a short bibliography and index of *c*. 450 hundred-names each.

914.20:413.11
EKWALL, E. The concise Oxford dictionary of English place-names. 4th ed. Oxford, Clarendon Press, 1960. li, 546p. 50s.

First published 1936.
Has entries for about 15,000 place-names, giving details of county, earliest linguistic forms and variant derivations. Includes "what may be called the chief English place-names" and most of the towns listed in Bartholomew's *Gazetteer*. Pattern of entry: name; county; forms with date; authorities; comments. Includes a valuable introduction, with a list of works consulted (p. xxxiv-xlvii).
Incorporates many additions and corrections to the 3rd ed. (1947).

The same author's *Etymological notes on English place-names* (Lund, Gleerup; Copenhagen, Munksgaard, 1959. 110p. (Lund studies in English, 27)) deals with 80 elements. Appendix (p. 102-3): Some notes on London street-names; bibliography, p. 104-6; index of names, p. 109-10.

914.20:413.11
EKWALL, E. English river names. Oxford, Clarendon Press, 1928. xcii, 488p.

"The intention is to collect and deal with names of more general interest and importance" (*Preface*). The lengthy introduction on English phonology is followed by a bibliography (pp. xi-xxx). Pattern of entry: name, location: geographical function, if any (*e.g.,* boundary); authorities; comments on origin. "The index omits names found in the text in their alphabetical place; also names mentioned indirectly by way of illustration are generally not included."

914.20:413.11
ENGLISH PLACE-NAME SOCIETY. [Publications.] London. Cambridge Univ. Press, 1924-. v. 1-. ea. usually 42s.

v. 1: *Introduction to the Survey of English place-names,* by A. Mawer and F. M. Stenton. 1924. 2 pts. o.p.
v. 2: *Buckinghamshire,* by A. Mawer and F. M. Stenton. 1925. o.p.
v. 3: *Bedfordshire and Huntingdonshire,* by A. Mawer and F. M. Stenton. 1926. o.p.
v. 4: *Worcestershire,* by M. Mawer, and others. 1926. o.p.
v. 5: *The North Riding of Yorkshire,* by A. H. Smith. 1928. o.p.
v.6-7: *Sussex,* by A. Mawer, and others. 1929-30. o.p.
v. 8-9: *Devon,* by J. E. B. Gover. 1931-32.
v. 10: *Northamptonshire,* by J. E. B. Gover. 1933.
v. 11: *Surrey,* by J. E. B. Gover, and others. 1934.

v. 12: *Essex*, by P. H. Reaney. 1935.

v. 13: *Warwickshire*, by J. E. B. Gover, and others. 1936.

v. 14: *The East Riding of Yorkshire and York*, by A. H. Smith. 1937.

v. 15: *Hertfordshire*, by J. E. B. Gover, and others. 1938.

v. 16: *Wiltshire*, by J. E. B. Gover, and others. 1933.

v. 17: *Nottinghamshire*, by J. E. B. Gover, and others. 1933.

v. 18: *Middlesex, apart from the City of London*, by J. E. B. Gover, and others. 1942.

v. 19: *Cambridge and Ely*, by P. H. Reaney. 1943.

v. 20-22: *Cumberland*, by A. M. Armstrong, and others.

v. 23-24: *Oxfordshire*, by M. Gelling.

v. 25-26: *English place-names elements*, by A. H. Smith. 1956.

v. 27-29: *The place-names of Derbyshire*, by K. Cameron. 1959. 3v.

v. 30-37: *West Riding of Yorkshire*, by A. H. Smith. 1961-3. 8v.

v. 38-41: *Gloucestershire*, by A. H. Smith. 1964-5. 4v. ea. 42s.

v. 42-43: *Westmorland*, by A. H. Smith. 1967. 2v. 105s.

Each volume contains a list of place-names of one county, arranged by hundred, with full notes on linguistic forms and derivations. Field names and street names are also analysed. Entries brings to light, valuable archaeological, historical and etymological evidence. "Though always of a high standard, the volumes of the English Place-Name Society have become increasingly thorough over the past forty years" (*Nature*, v. 206, no. 4987, 29th May 1965, p. 860).

The following concern English counties that are not covered by the English Place-Name Society series:

The place-names of Berkshire, by W. W. Skeat. Oxford, Clarendon Press, 1911. 118p.

Cheshire place-names, by S. Potter. Liverpool, 1955. 26p. (reprinted from Trans. Hist. Soc. Lancs. & Cheshire).

Cornish names: an attempt to explain over 1,600 Cornish names, by T. F. G. Dexter. London, Longmans, 1926. 90p.

Place-names of Dorset, by A. Fägersten. Uppsala, Appelberg, 1933. xxiii, 334p.

Place-names of Durham, by C. E. Jackson. London, Allen & Unwin, 1916. 115p.

"Saxon land-charters of Hampshire, with notes on place- and field-names", by G. B. Grundy, *Archaeological journal*, series 1-4, v. 78 (1921), 81 (1924), 83 (1926), 84 (1927), 85 (1928), with index.

The place-names of Herefordshire: their origin and development, by A. T. Bannister. Cambridge, Univ. Press, 1916. xx, 231p.

The place-names of the Isle of Man, with their origin and history, by J. J. Keen. Douglas, Manx Society, 1925-29. 2v. (xxiv, 645p.).

The place-names of the Isle of Wight, by H. Kökeritz. Uppsala, Appelberg, 1940. 306p.

The place-names of Kent, by J. K. Wallenberg. Uppsala, Appelberg, 1934. xx, 626p.

Place-names of Lancashire, by E. Ekwall. Manchester, Chetham Society, 1922. xvi, 280p.

A handbook of Lancashire place-names, by J. Sephton. Liverpool, Young, 1913. xi, 256p.

The place-names of Lancashire, their origin and history, by H. C. Wyld and T. O. Hirst. London, Constable, 1911. xxiv, 400p.

"Leicestershire place-names", by A. C. Wood. *Trans. Philological Society*, 1917-20, p. 57-78.

The place and river names of the West Riding of Lindsey, Lincolnshire, by T. B. F. Eminson. Lincoln, Ruddock, 1934. 288p.

An attempt to ascertain the true derivation of the names of towns and villages, and of rivers, and other great natural features of the county of Norfolk, by G. Munford. London, Simpkin, 1870. xii, 239p.

Place-names of Northumberland and Durham, by A. Mawer. Cambridge, Univ. Press, 1920. xxxviii, 271p.

"Records of the past in Rutland place-names", by G. Phillips. *Rutland magazine*, v. 1, 1904, p. 245-58.

Shropshire place-names, by E. W. Bowcock. Shrewsbury, Wilding, 1923. 271p.

Place-names of Somerset, by J. S. Hill. Bristol, St. Stephen's Press, 1914. vii, 373p.

Notes on Staffordshire place-names, by W. H. Duignan (London, Frowde, 1902. xix, 178p.

The place-names of Suffolk, by W. W. Skeat. Cambridge, Antiquarian Society, 1913. x, 130p.

The place-names of Wiltshire, their origin and history, by E. L. Ekblom. Uppsala, Appelberg, 1917. xviii, 187p.

Worcestershire place-names, by W. H. Duignan. London, Frowde, 1905. xi, 185p.

914.20:413.11

REANEY, P. H. The origin of English place-names. London, Routledge & Kegan Paul, 1960. x, 277p. 32s.

Includes chapters on 'The Celtic element', 'The English element', 'The French element', 'Latin influence', 'Field-names', 'Street names'. 'For further reading', consisting of chapter readings, p. 243-5. 3 maps; index of subjects; index of place-names (about 4,000 place-names). Abbreviations for names of counties, etc., are freely used, giving much compact information.

English place-names, by K. Cameron (London, Batsford, 1961. 256p. illus. 30s.) deals with various aspects of English place-names in 20 chapters. Bibliography, p. 229-32; indexes of place-names, street-names and field-names (p. 233-56) contain *c.* 6,000 entries.

914.20:413.11:016

ROBERTS, R. J. "Bibliography of writings on English place-names and personal names". In *Onoma* (Louvain), v. 8, 1958/59, no. 3, p. 1*-82*.

Attempts to record all relevant publications up to 1959. Includes Isle of Man and Channel Islands. 1,223 items (books, periodical articles and contributions to Festschriften) in 3 main sections: 1. General works on English onomastics —2. Place names (national surveys; special topographical features; historical studies; names of doubtful location; local studies (grouped by areas, not countries, items no. 374-1060); etc.)—3. Personal names. Index of personal names; index of names. Notes, reviews of books. "Includes much for the local historian and the genealogist" (*Library Association record*, v. 66, no. 5, May 1964, p. 228).

London

914.21 (058.7)

The Post Office London directory for 1967, with sectional street plan on a scale of approximately 4 inches to a mile (with Central London on a scale of 6 inches to a mile), in a special case. 168th annual publication. London, Kelly's Directories, Ltd., 1967. xxxii, 2743p. maps. 120s., or in 2v., 140s.

First published 1800 (*New annual directory*).
5 main sections: Official (government offices, etc.), city and municipal, law, postal, ecclesiastical; Private residents ("an alphabetical list with addresses of the occupiers of selected private houses and flats"), Post Office London index to buildings, etc.; Streets; Alphabetical (commercial and professional); Classified trade and professions (more than 10,000 classifications, A-Z). Invaluable.

Kelly's local London, provincial and other directories are listed in G. P. Henderson's *Current British directories* (at 38 (058.7) (410)).

914.21 (083.86)

EKWALL, E. Street-names of the City of London. Oxford, Clarendon Press, 1954. xvi, 209p. map. 25s.

Includes "practically all street names found before 1500 and some recorded even later" (*Preface*). Introduction discusses elements, chronology, etc. Scholarly and thorough etymological study, quotes many medieval records. Street map c. 1600.

H. A. Harben's *Dictionary of London; being notes topographical and historical relating to the streets and principal buildings in the City of London* (London, Jenkins, 1918. xxiv, 641p.) remains invaluable for both early and later street-names.

914.21 (083.86)

LONDON COUNTY COUNCIL. Names of streets and places in the administrative county of London, including the names of blocks of dwellings, parks and open spaces, showing postal districts with delivery office numbers, localities, metropolitan boroughs, Parliamentary constituencies, county electoral divisions and municipal map- and Ordnance sheet-references, together with particulars of Orders made since 1856 relative to street names and numbers. 4th ed. London, L.C.C., 1955. ii, 870p.

An A-Z tabulation. Appendix (p. 851-70): Names abolished since 1st August 1949, with present names.

———— **Naming and numbering of streets and buildings** . . . : decisions of the Council, 1st October 1948-. London, L.C.C. (now Greater London Council), 1949-. Monthly. Mimeographed.

Serves as a supplement to the L.C.C. *Names of streets and places.* Changes of name and number, and new names; each issue is arranged by boroughs, with no index or cumulations. Does not give the areas or map references of *Names of streets and places.* Now covers the new Greater London area.

Wales

914.29 (083.86)

DAVIES, E., *ed.* **A gazetteer of Welsh place-names.** Prepared by the Language and Literature Committee of the Board of Celtic Studies of the University of Wales. Cardiff, Univ. of Wales Press, 1957. xxxvii, 118p. (3rd ed. 1967. 15s.).

Cover title: *Rhestr o enwau lleaedd. A gazetteer of Welsh place-names.* Text of introduction is in Welsh and English.

"The primary purpose of the list is to serve as a guide to the orthography of Welsh place-names; any usefulness it may have as a gazetteer is a secondary matter" (*Introduction*). Not exhaustive but attempts to include the Welsh names of all towns and parishes and the chief natural features, villages, railway stations and post offices; farm-names are usually only given if they have historical, biographical or literary interest.

The 4,500 place-names in the gazetteer section are keyed to the National Grid 1" map, with four-figure references. Glossary, p. xxxii-xxxv.

Flintshire place-names, by E. Davies, also published by the Univ. of Wales Press, Cardiff, on behalf of the Board of Celtic Studies there (1959. xi, 184p. 15s.), contains c. 2,000 entries and references. In Flintshire place-name nomenclature is bilingual. "The meaning of many names has defied explanation" (*Preface*). Bibliography, p. ix-x.

914.29:413.11

CHARLES, B. G. Non-Celtic place-names in Wales. London, University College, 1938. xvii, 326p. (London mediaeval studies. Monograph no. 1).

Considers, in the manner standardized by the English Place-Name Society, place-names of English, French, Flemish and Scandinavian origin "when their history is known or old forms have been found for them".

The place-names of Wales, by T. Morgan (2nd and rev. ed. Newport, Mon., Southall, 1912. [iv], 262p), first published 1887, gives meanings of place-names, the majority being derived from purely Celtic sources. No etymology or index, place-names being arranged A-Z under counties.

914.29:413.11

THOMAS, R. J. Enwau afonydd a nentydd Cymru. Cardiff, Univ. of Wales Press, 1938. xxii, 235p.

An authoritative treatment of the great wealth of Welsh river-names, with a full list of sources consulted.

914.29:413.11

WILLIAMS, I. Enwau lleoedd. Liverpool, H. Evans, 1945. [viii], 64p.

A popular handbook of Welsh place-names arranged by subject (*e.g.* mountains, valleys, lakes, woods, etc.).

Germany

914.3 (083.86)

MÜLLER, F. Müllers grosse deutsche Ortsbuch; vollständiges Gemeindelexikon mit den neuen

336

Postleitzahlen. 15. vollständiges uberarb. und erw. Aufl. Wüppertal-Barmen, Post- und Ortsbuch-verlag, 1965. 1225p.

Revised at intervals of 3-4 years.
A gazetter of more than 125,000 places in both West and East Germany, and including former German territory that is now Polish. 2-line entries, with map references for each locality in the Federal Republic, based on Mair's Deutsche Generalkarte, 1 : 200,000. This edition has postal zip codes.

914.3:413.11
BACH, A. Deutsche Namenkunde. 2. stark erw. Aufl. Heidelberg, Winter, 1952-56. 3v.

v. 2: *Die deutsche Ortsnamen.* 1953-54. 2 pts. maps.

See entry at 929.2.09 (43).

914.3:413.11
BAHLOW, H. Deutschlands älteste Fluss- und Ortsnamen erstmalig gedeutet aus verschollenem Wortgut europäischer Vorzeitvölker (mit gesamt-register). Hamburg, 1962-63. 2v. in 1.

——**Deutschlands geographisches Namenwelt:** etymologische Lexikon der Fluss- und Ortsnamen alteuropäischer Herkunft, Frankfurt/Main, 1965. xvi, 554p.

France

914.4 (083.86)
Dictionnaire de communes: France métropoli-taine. Départements d'outre-mer. Rattachements et statistiques. 31. éd. Paris, Berger-Levrault, 1968. x, 942p.

About 40,000 entries, stating département (or smaller unit), existing (or nearest) postal, tele-graph and telephone facilities, transport facilities, number of houses and population.

Similar gazetteers are available in J. Meyrat's *Dictionnaire national des communes de France. Renseignements P.T.T. et S.N.C.F.* (18 éd., entièrement refondue et mise à jour au 1965. Paris, Michel, 1965, 1281p.), and the *Bottin des communes. Dictionnaire général des communes, principaux hameaux, écarts et lieux-dits, France métropolitaine, Union Française d'outre-mer* (et Paris, Didot-Bottin.

An older gazetteer-dictionary, still of use, is P. Joanne's *Dictionnaire géographique et admini-stratif de la France et de ses colonies* (Paris, Hachette, 1890-1905. 7v. illus.).

914.4:413.11
DAUZAT, A., and ROSTAING, Ch. Dictionnaire etymologique des noms de lieux en France. Paris, Larousse, 1963. xii, 738p. 29F.

Nearly 30,000 entries. Conjectural forms of place-names are asterisked. Many cross-references and abbreviations. List of principal authors and works cited, p. ix.

914.43 (03)
Dictionnaire de Paris. Paris, Larousse, 1964. 592p. illus. 80.80F.

An A-Z dictionary of events, institutions, monuments and customs, by some 20 specialists. 500 illustrations, including reproductions of documents. Very readable. Reviewed in *Bulletin critique du livre française,* v. 19 (7-8), no. 223-224, July/August 1966, entry no. 60603).

Italy

914.5 (026)
TOURING CLUB ITALIANO. Guida d'Italia del Touring Club Italiano. Milan, Touring Club Italiano. maps, plans.

First published 1914-29.
An excellently produced series of guides, on Baedeker lines, each with some 400-500 pages and supported by folding maps, town plans and a bibliography.
1: *Piemonte.* 1940.
2: *Torino e Vale d'Aosta.* 7th ed. 1959.
3. *Lombardia.* 7th ed. 1954.
4: *Milan e Laghi.* 1956.
5: *Véneto.* 4th ed. 1954.
6: *Venézia e dintorni.* 1951.
7: *Venézia Tridentina.* 5th ed. 1958.
8: *Venézia Giúlia.* 1963 ed.
9: *Liguria.* 4th ed. 1952.
10: *Emilia e Romagna.* 4th ed. 1957.
11: *Toscana.* 3rd ed. 1959.
12: *Firenze e dintorni.* 4th ed. 1964.
13: *Marche.* 3rd ed. 1962.
14: *Umbria.* 4th ed. 1966.
15: *Lázio.* 3rd ed. 1964.
16: *Roma e dintorni.* 1960. (also in English. Hachette Blue guides).
17: *Abruzzi e Molise.* 3rd ed. 1965.
18: *Campánia.* 3rd ed. 1963.
19: *Nápoli e dintorni.* 1960 ed.
20: *Púglia.* 3rd ed. 1962.
21: *Lucánia e Calábria.* 1938.
22: *Sicilia.* 1953.
23: *Sardegna.* 3rd ed. 1952.

Spain

914.6 (083.86)
Diccionario geográfico de España. Madrid, Ediciones del Movimiento, 1956-61. 17v.

"The fullest information about Spain yet co-lected in a single work" (*Times literary supple-ment,* no. 3,176, 11th January 1963, p. 28). In gazetteer form, entries A-Z, often containing very detailed information. Questionnaires were sent out to all the towns and villages of Spain, to be answered by the local authorities.

U.S.S.R.

914.7:016
"Geography". *In* Maichel, K. *Guide to Russian reference books,* v. 2-. Edited by J. S. G. Sim-mons (Stanford, Cal., Hoover Institution on War, Revolution and Peace, Stanford Univ., 1964), p. 189-227.

An excellently annotated bibliography of *c.* 300 items under headings: Bibliographies of bibliographies—General bibliographies—Selec-tive bibliographies—Bibliographies of disserta-tions—Institutional bibliographies—Bibliogra-phies of periodicals—Abstracts and indexes—

Regional physical geography bibliographies—Special subject bibliographies—Cartography, geodesy, maps and atlases—Administrative regions—Encyclopedia (Grigor'ev)—Dictionaries and gazetteers—Biography and portraits—Handbooks.

Noted: Harris, C. D. *Geography, resources and natural conditions in the Soviet Union: an annotated bibliography of selected basic books in Russian* (Chicago, Department of Geography, Univ. of Chicago, 1962. 45p. Mimeographed).

914.7:016
UNITED STATES. LIBRARY OF CONGRESS. Reference Department. **Soviet geography: a bibliography.** Washington, Library of Congress, 1951. xx, 668p.

4,421 numbered entries, covering books, periodical articles, maps, etc. Pt. 1: Geography, by subject: pt. 2: administrative, natural and economic regions. Author index; no annotations; Library of Congress press marks.

914.7 (083.86)
SSSR. Administrativno-territorial'noe delenie Soyuznykh respublik na 1-e oktyabrya 1938-. Moscow, 1938-. Biennial (irregular). (12th ed. 1963). (Inf.-statisticheskiĭ otdel pri Sekretariate Prezidiuma Verkhovnogo Soveta SSSR).

'The U.S.S.R. Administrative-territorial divisions of the Union Republics as of 1st October 1938-'. The 1963 ed. tabulates *c.* 15,000 administrative units, arranged under oblasts. Population of leading towns is given. Map.

Norway

914.81 (026)
Norge rundt: Aftenpostens turist- og reisehåndbok. 2. utvidede, reviderte og ajourførte utg. Oslo, Chr. Schibsteds Forlag, 1957. 335, iii, 37, 104p. (Aftenpostens håndbokserie).

A good guide book to Norway. The bulk of the text is arranged A-Z by places, but there are also maps of Norway (1 : 1M.) (derived from the general map published for the general rail, bus, ship and air timetable *Rutebok for Norge*), coloured reproductions of the arms of Norwegian towns, a list of some 8,000 places, with condensed information about postal and telephonic communications, transport, district, map references, etc; finally, tabular information about counties, towns, rural districts, mountains, waterfalls, lakes, rivers and islands with statistics of populations, areas, lengths, heights, etc.

The English ed., *Tourist in Norway: travel guide & gazetteer* (Oslo Chr. Schibsteds Forlag, 1958. 370p. (Aftenposten's handbooks) N. kr. 17.50) omits the maps and tables, but adds some 65 pages of material useful to the foreign tourist (practical hints; suggested itineraries). The translation is very good.

914.81 (083.86)
Norge. Oslo, Cappelens Forlag, 1963. 4v. illus., diagrs., maps. N.kr.780.

v. 1. *Land og folk.*
v. 2-3. *Geografisk leksikon.*
v. 4. [*Atlas*].
An authoritative and very well produced geography, geographical encyclopaedia and atlas of Norway. V. 1 is a regional and systematic geography of Norway (415 pages of text, 50 coloured plates, 287 black-and-white illustrations). V. 2, the geographical encyclopaedia, describes more than 35,000 places, arranged A-Z, in words, 3,000 pictures, statistics, maps and diagrams. V. 4 has a 64-page atlas, the maps being mostly at the scale of 1 : 400,000; gazetteer, with more than 60,000 entries. Enthusiastically reviewed in *The geographical review,* v. 55, no. 1, January 1965, p. 129-30.

Sweden

914.85:016
"Geografi. Sverige". In Ottervik, G., *comp. Bibliografier* (Lund, Bibliothekstjänst, 1966), p. 160-8.

Lists about 80 area-study bibliographies of Sweden, particularly of counties and towns.

Denmark

914.89 (026)
TRAP, J. P. Danmark. 5. udg., redigeret af Niels Nielsen, Peter Skautrup og Povl Engelstoft. Copenhagen, Gad, 1953-. v. 1, pt. 1-. illus., maps.

Standard historical, geographical, statistical description of Denmark. Detailed and well illustrated. The arrangement is by *amter* (counties), and within each *amt* by *købstæder* (municipalities), *herreder* (rural districts) and *sogne* (parishes). As well as a social and historical treatment for each place, there are excellent descriptions of all important buildings, both old and new. V. 1, pt. 1, is a general introduction, *Landet og folket;* v. 1, pt. 2, and v. 3, pt. 1 & 2 deal with Greater Copenhagen; and v. 3, pt. 3 with Copenhagen administrative county (*i.e.,* the area outside the city) and Roskilde administrative county. The remaining volumes published to date deal with individual *amter,* obtainable either as complete volumes or in separate parts.

914.89 (026)
Turist- og rejsehåndbogen Danmark rundt. Udarbejdet i samarbejde med Turistforeningen for Danmark og Forenede danske motorejere. 8. udg. Copenhagen, Politikens Forlag, 1959. 384p. illus., maps. (Politikens håndbøger, 31).

A guide book to Denmark published by the Copenhagen daily *Politiken.* It provided the model for *Norge rundt* (*q.v.*) published by the Oslo daily *Aftenposten;* the two books are very similar in layout and appearance. The Danish work does not, however, contain any tabular section. It may be supplemented by a series of special guides published by *Politiken,* e.g. *Swovene omkring København* (Woods around Copenhagen), *Museumsfører for Storkøbenhavn* (Guide to the museums of Greater Copenhagen), etc., and *Hvem byggede hvad?* (Who built what?) an architectural guide book to Denmark of some 440p. by Harald Langberg (1952). *Politiken* publishes various tourist maps, and also *Kort over*

København og omegn (Atlas of Copenhagen and district) which is excellent and, like *Danmark rundt,* very frequently revised.

For English-speaking visitors there is *Tourist in Denmark: travel guide.* (Under the auspices of the National Travel Association of Denmark. 4th rev. ed. Copenhagen, Politikens Forlag, 1959. 224p. 11*s*. 6*d*.) This is abridged and translated from the main work. For the capital there is a separate publication, *Tourist in Copenhagen and Northern Zealand* (4th printing, 1959. 64p.).

Rejsehåndbogen Danmark (8. udg. Udarbejdet med bistand af Turistforeningen for Danmark. Copenhagen, Gad, 1955. 341p.) is, compared with the *Politiken* series, a very sober work, unillustrated, apart from its maps, and not so frequently revised. It is sound, however, and supplements *Danmark rundt* because it is arranged in 170 routes, and not alphabetically by places.

Switzerland
914.94 (02)

Geographie der Schweiz in drei Bänden. Berne, Kümmerly & Frey, 1961-.

v. 2: *Alpen,* by G. Gutersöhn. Pt. 1, *Wallis, Tessin, graubünden* (1961. 64 illus. and black-and-white maps; 16 tables; 5 coloured maps (1 : 50,000, etc.); 469 references); pt. 2, *Waadt, Freiburg, Bern . . .* (1964. 63 illus. and black-and-white maps; 16 tables; 6 coloured maps; 473 references). Index to each v.

"The volumes yet to be published will complete what must remain for many years, the standard work of geographical scholarship in Switzerland" (*Scottish geographical magazine,* v. 79, no. 1, April 1963, p. 58).

914.94 (083.86)

KNAPP, C., *and others, ed.* **Geographisches Lexikon der Schweiz,** mit dem Beistande der Geographichen Gesellschaft zu Neuenburg. Neuchâtel, Attinger, 1902-10. 6v. illus., tables, graphs, maps.

A gazetteer dictionary of Switzerland, with many thousand entries and a profusion of illustrations and good maps. The article on Switzerland itself occupies v. 4, p. 627-770 to v. 5, p. 1-428, and is in 12 sections.

A Jacot's *Schweizerisches Orts-Lexikon mit Verkehrskarte* (19. Aufl. Lucerne, Bucher, 1957. 392p.) is a gazetteer with *c*. 70,000 very brief entries; much use of graphic symbols.

Noted: *Dictionnaire des localités de la Suisse. Schweizerisches Ortschaftenverzeichnis, 1960 . . .* (Berne, Eidgenossisches Statistisches Amt, 1967, 415p.).

Yugoslavia
914.97:016

MILOJEVIC, B. Z., *comp.* **Geography of Yugoslavia:** a selective bibliography. Washington, Library of Congress, 1955. xvii, 79p.

Contents: Climatology—Hydrography—Geomorphology—Plant and animal geography—

Human geography: general studies—Economic and transportation geography — Settlements, urban geography and the origin of population—Political geography—Regional and physical geography—Historical geography and the history of geography. Author index.

South-east Asia
915-012 : 016

PELZER, K. J. Selected bibliography on the geography of Southeast Asia. New Haven, Conn., Southeast Asia Studies, Yale Univ., 1949-.

v. 1. *Southeast Asia, general.* 1949. (700 entries).
v. 2. *The Philippines.* 1950. (1,000 entries).
v. 3. *Malaya.* 1956. (2,250 entries).

Intended as a companion to *Bibliography of the peoples and cultures of Mainland Southeast Asia,* by J. F. Embree and L. G. Dotson (1950) (*see at* 908 (5-012:016), but with emphasis on physical, cultural, economic and political geography. V. 1-3 list a total of *c*. 4,000 items. Arranged by subject; no author index. Volumes covering Indonesia, Burma, Siam and Indochina were due to follow.

China
915.1:016

ANTE, R. "JPRS: a source for geographical literature on China." In *Geographical review,* v. 52, no. 3, July 1962, p. 442-4 .

Notes on the translations of Chinese geographical material issued by the U.S. Joint Publications Research Service (JPRS). Examples are given. The *Monthly catalog of United States government publications* lists more recent translations.

Noted: *The geography of China: a selected and annotated bibliography,* edited by T. Herman (New York, Univ. of the State of New York, State Education Dept., Foreign Area Materials Center, 1967. 44p.).

Japan
915.2:016

HALL, R. B., and **NOH, T. Japanese geography:** a guide to Japanese reference and research materials. Ann Arbor, Univ. of Michigan Press, 1956. x, 128p.

At head of half-title page: Center for Japanese Studies. Bibliographical series number 6.

11 sections: 1. Bibliographies—2. Encyclopedias, dictionaries and gazetteers and travel guides—3. Yearbooks, collections of statistics and censuses—4. Sets and collections—5. Periodicals—6. Atlases, maps, cartography and air-photo coverage—7. History of Japanese geography—8. Regional geography—9. Historical and cultural geography—10. Economic geography—11. Regional descriptive geography. 1,254 annotated entries, giving author's names ın Japanese characters as well as in English, and titles, transliterated, in Japanese characters and translated. Appendix: List of publishers, with characters.

The *K.B.S. bibliography of standard reference books for Japanese studies, with descriptive notes.* V. 2, *Geography and travel* (Tokyo, Kokusai Bunka Shinkokai, 1962. [ix], 164p.) comprises 284 numbered and well-annotated entries in 12 sections (12. Periodicals). Author index.

915.2 (026)

Japan: the official guide. Edited by Tourist Industry Bureau, Ministry of Transportation. 8th postwar rev. ed. [Tokyo], Japan Travel Bureau, 1961. lxxiii, 1,015p. maps. $6.50 (outside Japan).

First published 1914.

A detailed pocket guide-book, describing 38 routes. 15 sections; bibliography, p. 857-96. 62 maps and town plans; vocabulary, p. 897-911; index, p. 920-1015.

India, etc.

915.4 (026)

LOTHIAN, *Sir* A., *ed.* **A handbook for travellers in India, Pakistan, Burma and Ceylon.** 20th ed. London, Murray, 1965. cii, 632p. maps, plan. 55s.

A Baedeker-type guide, with maps and town plans. The lengthy introductory section (p. i-cii) gives general hints and information, and data on history and administration. In the guide section, India occupies the bulk, arrangement of material being on the route principal; Pakistan, Kashmir, Burma and Ceylon sections are followed by a directory and index.

India

915.4 (083.86)

The Imperial gazetteer of India. New ed. Oxford, Clarendon Press, 1907-9. 26v.

v. 1-4. *The Indian Empire* (1. Descriptive—2. *Historical*—3. *Economic*—4. *Administrative*).
v. 5-24. *Gazetteer* (A-Z).
v. 25. *Index.*
v. 26. *Atlas,* by J. G. Bartholomew. Rev. ed. 1931. 17s. 6d.
The latest edition (*The Gazetteer of India: Indian Union.* Delhi, 1965-) is to be in 4v. (*See at 908 (540) (02).*)

Africa

916:016

SOMMER, J. W. Bibliography of African geography, 1940-1964. Hanover, N.H., Dartmouth College, Department of Geography, 1965. viii, 139p. Spiral binding. (Geographical publications at Dartmouth, no. 3). $2.

Aims "to bring together scholarly periodical literature on Africa from the discipline of geography" (introduction). 1,725 entries in 4 main sections: 1. Human geography—2. Economic geography—3. Physical geography—4. General Africana. List of 58 journals (primarily in English or French) used as sources; also a list of 19 journals that did not have entries on Africa. Author index.

South Africa

916.8:413.11

SOUTH AFRICA. PLACE-NAMES COMMITTEE. Amptelike plekname in die Unie en Suidwes-Afrika (Goedgekeur tot einde 1948). Official place names in the Union and South West Africa. Approved to end [of] 1948). Pretoria, Government Printer, 1952. 376p.

916.8:413.11

UNION OF SOUTH AFRICA. DEPARTMENT OF EDUCATION, ARTS AND SCIENCE. Amptelike plekname in die Unie en S.W.A. [Suidwes-Afrika]. Lys name goedgekeur sedert 31.1.1952-10.7.57. [Cape Town], 1957. [84]p.

Official place-names in the Union of South Africa and South-West Africa approved between 31st January 1952 and 10th July 1957. Supplements the above list.

Canada

917.1:016

CANADA. DEPARTMENT OF MINES AND TECHNICAL SURVEYS. Geographical Branch. **Bibliography of periodical literature on Canadian geography, 1930-1955.** Ottawa, the Department, 1958-. pt. 1-. (Canada. Geographical Branch. Bibliographical series, no. 22). 50c. per pt.

Published under the auspices of the International Geographical Union, with the concurrence of Unesco and the French Centre National de la Recherche Scientifique. This bibliography represents part of Canada's contribution to the *Bibliographie géographique internationale.*
Pts. 2- deal with separate provinces (*e.g.,* pt. 2: Prairie Provinces. 1959. 25p.; pt. 6: Northern Canada. 1959. 36p.).

917.1:016

CANADA. DEPARTMENT OF MINES AND TECHNICAL SURVEYS. Geographical Branch. **A selected list of periodical literature on topics relating to Canadian geography** for the period 1930-1939. Ottawa, 1954. iv, 97p. (Bibliographical series no. 11). 50c.

—————— **A selected list . . .** for the period 1940-1950. 2nd ed. Ottawa, 1956. vi, 131p. (Bibliographical series no. 9).

——————. **Selected bibliography of Canadian geography** with imprint 1951. Ottawa, 1952. vi, 52p. (Bibliographical series no. 8, pt. 3).

Systematic arrangement; a general section is followed by sections for provinces, with breakdown by topics. The 1940-1950 list includes the titles of the 55 periodicals indexed. No indexes. The *Selected bibliography* is published annually (*e.g.,* 1961, published 1964. 85p. 75c.).

917.1 (083.86)

CANADA. DEPARTMENT OF MINES AND TECHNICAL SURVEYS. Geographical Branch. **Gazetteer of Canada: British Columbia.** 2nd ed. Ottawa, the Department, 1966. xviii, 741p. $7.50.

First published 1953 by the Canadian Permanent Committee on Geographical Names, as one of a series planned to cover all the provinces. This original series (1952-62) is being replaced by another published by the Department of Mines and Technical Surveys.

The British Columbia v., by far the largest to date, lists *c.* 35,000 place-names, with brief description or identification, location and co-ordinates.

917.1:413.11
SEALOCK, R. B., and SEELY, P. A. Bibliography of place-name literature: United States and Canada. 2nd ed. Chicago, Ill., A.L.A., 1967. 362p. $7.50.

See entry at 917.3:413.11.

Mexico & Central America
917.2 (026)
HANSON, E. P. The new world guides to the Latin American republics . . . 3rd ed., completely rev. New York, Duell, Sloan and Pearce, 1950. 3v. illus., maps.
See entry at 918 (026).

U.S.A.
917.3:016
McMANIS, D. R. Historical geography of the United States: a bibliography, excluding Alaska and Hawaii. [Ypsilanti], Michigan, Eastern Michigan Univ., 1965. vi, 249p.

"Includes general, topical, regional and state bibliographies, and references on the United States as a whole and by regions and states" (*Library trends,* v. 15, no. 4, April 1967, p. 707).

917.3 (026)
American guide series, compiled by the Federal Writers' Project. Various publishers, 1937-1950.

The only detailed guide-books for the United States. Over 150 volumes, covering states, cities, regions and certain special subjects. Much local history is included; well illustrated.
13 State guides are still in print: Florida, Idaho, Indiana, Michigan, New York, North Dakota, Ohio, Pennsylvania, South Carolina, Virginia, West Virginia, Wyoming (New York, Oxford Univ. Press. 45s.-52s. 6d.); North Carolina (Univ. of North Carolina Press. 40s.).
A complete list of the series is given in Baer, E. A. *Titles in series* (1953), nos. 492-660.

917.3 (026)
Mobil travel guides. New York, Simon & Schuster. 7v. Revised annually. ea. $1.95.

The 7v. cover: California and the West; the Northeastern States; the Great Lakes area; the Middle Atlantic States; the Northwest and Grand Plains States; the Southeastern States; Southwest and South Central Area. Roughly comparable to the Guides Michelin, red series.

917.3:413.11
SEALOCK, R. B., and SEELY, P. A. Bibliography of place-name literature: United States and Canada. 2nd ed. Chicago, Ill., A.L.A., 1967. 362p. $7.50.

First published 1948.
Lists 3,599 books and periodical articles, arranged by state, province and such regions as New England and Mississippi Valley. States region, meaning, spelling and pronunciation. Author and subject indexes.

917.47 (026)
HART, H. H. Hart's guide to New York City. New York, Hart; London, Muller, 1964. 1331p. illus., maps.

A detailed guide; more than 200 sections A-Z ('After the theatre', 'Air taxi', 'Airline terminals' to 'World's Fair' and 'Wrestling'). Hotels, p. 594-690; Restaurants, p. 979-1119. 64-page coloured map section in middle, giving location of actual shops, clubs, etc., in Fifth Avenue, Park Avenue, etc. Index, p. 1293-1328.

Latin America
918 (026)
HANSON, E. P. The new world guides to the Latin American republics. Sponsored by the Office of the U.S. Co-ordinator of Inter-American Affairs . . . E. P. Hanson, editor-in-chief; R. B. Platt, editor. 3rd ed., completely rev. New York, Duell, Sloan and Pearce, 1950. 3v. illus., maps.

v. 1: *Mexico, Central America and the West Indies.*
v. 2: *Andes and West coast countries.*
v. 3: *East coast countries.*
"Very useful for condensed information about the countries of South and Central America" (Barton, M., with Bell, M. V., comp. *Reference books.* 6th ed., 1966. p. 32). Includes bibliographies and lists of maps.

Brazil
918.1 (03)
Dicionário geografico brasileiro, com mapas e ilustrações dos estados e territorios. Rio de Janeiro, Globo, [1966]. 559p. maps. (Enciclopedias e dicionarios Globo).

Philippines
919.14:016
HUKE, R, E. Bibliography of Philippine geography, 1940-1963: a selected list. Hanover, N.H., Dartmouth College, Department of Geography, 1964. 84p. $1.50.

Designed to supplement v. 2 of K. J. Pelzer's *Selected bibliography on the geography of southeast Asia* (at 915-012:016). Lists more than 1,200 items.

New Zealand
919.31 (026)
The New Zealand guide, superseding Wise's N.Z. index to every place in New Zealand: a comprehensive gazetteer, geographical reference and travel guide. Compiled by Edward Stewart Dollimore. Dunedin, Wise, 1957. xiii, 923, [1]p. map.

Gazetteer ('Every place in New Zealand'), p. 1-882. Entries give location and relation to nearest large town, etc., as a minimum. Fuller entries (*e.g.,* 'Wellington', p. 841-4) describe facilities, state origin of name and include historical and even biographical notes. Adequate cross-references. Appendices (p. 883-923) Mountains (giving heights); 'General information section'; 'A New Zealand travel guide'. A map shows principal districts, but is hardly in keeping with the detailed text; no bibliography. Well produced.

Noted: Reed, A. W. *A dictionary of Maori place names* (Wellington, Reed, 1961. 144p.).

Antarctic

919.9 (083.86)

ROBERTS, B. "Antarctic gazetteers". In *Polar record*, v. 12, no. 76, January 1964, p. 84-86.

Brief description of those produced in Australia, France, Britain, New Zealand, the U.S. and the U.S.S.R.

92 BIOGRAPHY

Bibliographies

920:016

ARNIM, M. Internationale Personalbibliographie. 2. verb. und stark verm. Aufl. Leipzig (later Stuttgart), Hiersemann, 1944-63. 3v.

First published 1936, covering the year 1850-1935 (25,000 entries).

The 2nd ed. extends to the 1950s. (v. 1-2. 1944-52; v. 3, ed. by G. Bock and F. Hodes, covering the period 1944-59, with supplement to v. 1-3. 1963.) and has *c.* 90,000 entries, with emphasis on German writers, but nevertheless international.

An index to bibliographies of individual authors. Valuable for singling out 'hidden' bibliographies contained in books, biographical dictionaries (*e.g.,* Kürschner) bio-bibliographies (*e.g.,* Poggendorff; Goedeke), periodical articles, Festschriften, etc. 2 or 3 references, on average, per entry, and more for the more important writers (*e.g.,* G. B. Shaw: 7, plus 1 reference in v. 3.). Because these bibliographies are often appended to biographical material, this work serves as a key of sorts to biographical data.

Because of entries omitted from the 2nd ed., the 1st ed. should still be used.

92:016

Biography index: a cumulative index to biographical material in books and magazines. New York, Wilson, 1946-. v. 1-. Quarterly, with annual and triennial cumulations. Service basis.

V. 1-7 (1946-67): 1946-64.

Based on 1,600 periodicals regularly indexed in the Wilson indexes, works of collective biography (completely analysed), a select list of legal and medical periodicals, and obituaries of national and international interest from the *New York times.* The main section is alphabetical by biographee; the entry gives full name, dates, nationality, occupation. The second section is a subject index to the professions and occupations of biographees. Portraits are indicated when they appear in connection with indexed material. All biographees are American unless otherwise stated. Separate sub-heading, where appropriate, —"Juvenile literature".

92:016

CHEVALIER, C. U. Répertoire des sources historiques du moyen âge. Bio-bibliographie. Nouv. éd. refondue, corr. et augm. Paris, Picard, 1905-07 (reprinted 1960). 2v. 525F.

First published 1877-86.

Universal in coverage, with limitations regarding Slav, Hungarian and Scandinavian countries.

Valuable particularly for its inclusion of many obscure people occurring in medieval history. Arrangement is alphabetical by name of person (French form of name). Entries give the briefest of biographical data and consist in the main of references to sources—books, periodical articles and other published documents.

For main entry, *see at* 94 "04/":016.

92:016

HYAMSON, A. M. A dictionary of universal biography of all ages and of all peoples. 2nd ed. London, Routledge, 1951. xii, 680p.

First published 1916.

A finding-list of *c.* 110,000 biographies contained in the 23 most comprehensive biographical dictionaries and encyclopaedias, *e.g., D.N.B.,* the *Annual register.* Of these 23 dictionaries only the *D.N.B.* and *D.A.B.* are completely indexed. "The work covers all countries and all generations. An endeavour has been made to include every one whose work or whose memory [has] survived until today." Does not include living persons. Entries, usually single-line, include name, nationality, country of adoption, profession, dates (where known) and a coded reference to the work or works in which a fuller biography can be found.

L. B. Phillips' *The dictionary of biographical reference, containing over 100,000 names; together with a classed index of the biographical literature* (New ed., corr. and augm. with supplement to date . . . London, Low, 1889. xiv, 1038p.) indexes some 40 biographical dictionaries, etc. Reprinted Graz, Akademie Druck und Verlagsanstalt, 1964. ÖS 1560.

92:016

OETTINGER, E. M. Bibliographie biographique universelle. Dictionnaire des ouvrages relatifs à l'histoire de la vie publique et privée des personnages célèbres de tous les temps et de toutes les nations . . . enrichi du répertoire des bio-bibliographies générales, nationales et spéciales. Brussels, Stienon, 1854. 2v.

A bibliography of *c.* 45,000 separately published works relating to the life and career of prominent men and women of all countries, from the earliest times.

92:016

RICHES, P. M., *comp.* **An analytical bibliography of universal collected biography,** comprising books published in the English tongue in Great Britain and Ireland, America and the British Dominions. London, Library Association, 1934. ix, 709p.

Single-line entries: essentially a finding list. An analysis of "every volume of collected biography [written in Engish] that could be traced up to the end of 1933 . . . aims at gathering together, under the names of the persons written about, those short lives published in collected form that are now almost unknown to the student; . . . main purpose [of the work] is to assist students and research workers in History and its many branches".

Pages 1-541: Analytical index of biographies arranged alphabetically—name, dates, short description and reference to main work (56,000 entries). Other sections include bibliography of the 3,000 volumes analysed for main entries, chronological and occupation index of biographees, author and subject bibliography of biographical dictionaries.

Golland, K. S. *Biographies for children: a select list* (4th ed., edited by R. W. Thompson. London, Borough of Havering Libraries, 1967. 123p. Mimeographed. 25s.), first published 1960, has *c.* 3,000 entries and includes analyticals and an author, short-title index. Critically reviewed in *Library Association Record*, v. 70, no. 1, January 1968, p. 24-25.

92:016

SLOCUM, R. B., *ed.* **Biographical dictionaries and related works: an international bibliography.** Detroit, Michigan, Gale Research Co., 1967. xxiii, 1058p.

A bibliography of *c.* 4,800 collective biographies (who's who's, directories, registers), portrait and biography indexes, catalogues, dictionaries of anonyma and pseudonyma, etc., published since 1500. In 3 sections: universal biography; foreign and U.S. national biography by area; and foreign and U.S. national biography by vocation. Some entries are annotated. Author, title and subject indexes. Bibliography, p. xix-xxiii.

Biographical dictionaries: Universal

92 (100)

CHALMERS, A. **The general biographical dictionary;** containing an historical and critical account of the lives and writings of the most eminent persons in every nation, particularly the British and Irish; from the earliest accounts to the present time. New ed., rev. and enl. London, Nichols, 1812-17. 32v.

First published [1761-1767?].
An account of persons of all nations, eminent for genius, learning, public spirit and virtue, with a preference, as to extent of narrative, to those of our own country." Discursive entries.

92 (100)

Chambers's Biographical dictionary. New ed., edited by J. O. Thorne. Edinburgh, Chambers, 1961. viii, 1,432p. 70s.

First published 1897.
The 1961 edition, which contains 15,000 entries, has been completely revised and re-set. Every entry has been scrutinized and the layout is more systematic. Criterion for inclusion: "Is he (or she) likely to be looked up?" The policy "of clothing the bare facts with human interest and critical observation" has been continued. Biblio-

graphies are compressed and not entirely satisfactory. Subject index, p. 1398-1432. A good up-to-date one-volume work.

92 (100)

GRIMAL, P., *ed.* **Dictionnaire des biographies.** Paris, Presses Universitaires de France, 1958. 2v. illus.

A universal biographical dictionary (v. 1, A-J; v. 2, K-Z). About 6,000 entries and 128 photogravure plates. Confined to deceased persons. Contributions are signed; 21 contributors, apart from the editor. Bartok: $1\frac{1}{2}$ columns; Rilke: $1\frac{1}{2}$ columns; Sir Humphry Davy: 2 columns; Colette: 1 column. Brief bibliography and, usually, iconography are appended to entries. 'Abréviations et ouvrages les plus souvent cités', v. 1, p. ix-xii. Greek names used as entry words are given in transliterated and original form.

92 (100)

HEINZEL, E. **Lexikon historischer Ereignisse und Personen in Kunst, Literatur und Musik.** Vienna, Hollinek, 1956. xxvi, [1], 782p. illus. (17 pl.).

See entry at 93 (032).

92 (100)

HOEFER, J. Ch. F. **Nouvelle biographie générale,** depuis les temps les plus reculés jusqu' à nos jours, avec les renseignements bibliographiques et l'indication des sources à consulter . . . sous la direction de M. le Dr. [J. Ch. Ferdinand] Hoefer. Paris, Didot, 1852-66. 46v. (Reprinted Copenhagen, Rosenkilde & Bagger, 1963-. 46v. ea. D.kr. 78.).

Originally *Nouvelle biographie universelle*, but, as the result of a legal action taken by the owners of Michaud (*q.v.*), the title was changed.

Concise articles for 52,420 eminent living men as well as for important deceased persons omitted from Michaud. A popular work; for scholarship does not compare with the older work. No original work was involved in the compilation of Hoefer, for many of the articles were condensations of entries contained in other bibliographical works published by Firmin Didot, while others are taken in their entirety or were extracts or abridgements of articles taken from Michaud.

Published in weekly parts, 10 making a volume.

92 (100)

JÖCHER, C. G. **Allgemeines Gelehrten-Lexicon** . . . Leipzig, Gleditsch, 1750-51 (reprinted Hildersheim, Georg Olms Verlagsbuchhandlung, 1960-61). 4v.

————— **Fortsetzung und Ergänzungen** . . . von Johann Christophe Adelung [u.a.] Leipzig, Gleditsch, etc. 1784-1897 (reprinted Hildersheim, Georg Olms Verlagsbuchhandlung, 1960-61). 7v. (A-ROMULEUS).

A universal biographical dictionary, covering all periods up to about 1750, and particularly valuable for the Middle Ages. For writers, works are listed. The layout of the basic four volumes is congested and titles only of works are cited. The supplementary volumes (facsimile reprint, have a more generous layout and works are listed in paragraph form, with date and place of publication (*e.g.,* Drummond of Hawthornden: 16 lines of biography; ½ column, giving details of six works). A minor feature is the inclusion of cross-references from initials (used as noms-de-plume) to full names.

92 (100)

MICHAUD, J. F. Biographie universelle, ancienne et moderne. Nouv. ed., publiée sous la direction de M. [Joseph François] Michaud.

First published 1811-1862. 85v. (Initially 1811-1828, 52v., but two major supplements, in 3v. (mythology) and 30v., were added.) New ed. 1843-65. 45v. Paris, Desplaces. (Michaud died in 1858 and was succeeded as editor by Ernest Desplaces.) Reprint of 1843-65 ed. Graz, Akademie Druk- und Verlagsanstalt, 1964. ÖS42,820.)

Although it is in some respects dated, the work is still useful because of the high standard of scholarship of the contributors. (300 writers collaborated in the compilation of the work.) Lengthy, signed articles, with adequate bibliographical information.

One serious defect of the first edition was that many of the entries had strong royalist and Catholic bias. This was to a large degree corrected in the second edition, although it still occurs in some of the earlier volumes. The English articles are not entirely satisfactory, for there are many errors of fact and some "inadequacy of treatment", but with all its shortcomings "there is no book where [the] errors are so few in proportion to the great extent of the work." (R. C. Christie.)

For a detailed account of the history and development of *Michaud,* particularly its law suit with Firmin Didot on the question of literary copyright and the publication of *Hoefer,* see p. 204-210 of an article by R. C. Christie in the *Quarterly review,* v. 157, January 1884.

92 (100)

The New Century cyclopedia of names; edited by C. L. Barnhart with the assistance of W. D. Halsey. New York, Appleton-Century-Crofts, Inc., 1954. 3v.

". . . information about proper names having importance in the English-speaking world . . . the most frequently used English and native spellings and pronunciations, as well as the essential facts about more than 100,000 proper names of every description—persons, places, historical events, plays and operas, works of fiction, literary characters, works of art, mythological and legendary persons and places, and any other class of proper names of interest or importance today."

A completely revised edition of the original *Century cyclopedia of names* which formed v. 11 of the *Century dictionary* (1914).

Supplements in v. 3 include chronological table of world history, rulers, chiefs of state, etc. arranged by country.

92 (100)

OETTINGER, E. M. Moniteur des dates. Biographisch — genealogisch — historisches Welt — Register enthaltend die Personal—Akten der Menschheit . . . von mehr als 100,000 geschicht-lichen Persönlichkeiten aller Zeiten und Nationen von Erschaffung der Welt bis auf den heutigen Tag. . . . Leipzig, Denicke, 1866-73; Hermann, 1873-82. 9 v. (Reprinted Graz, Akademie Druck- und Verlagsanstalt, 1964. 1038p. ÖS4100.)

More than 100,000 very brief biographical entries for historical persons of all times and nations. No bibliographies.

92 (100)

THOMAS, J. Universal pronouncing dictionary of biography and mythology. 5th ed. Philadelphia & London, Lippincott, 1930. xii, 2550p.

First published 1870.
Comprehensive for all countries and for all times. Stress is laid on the correct pronunciation of names and the preface discusses this in some detail. The work derives largely from such works as Michaud's *Biographie universelle (q.v.),* etc. Articles are usually brief, with references.

Appendix 1: Vocabulary of Christian names, with their equivalents in the various European languages; Appendix 2: Disputed or doubtful pronunciations.

92 (100)

Webster's Biographical dictionary: a dictionary of names of noteworthy persons, with pronunciations and concise biographies. Springfield, Mass., Merriam; London, Bell. 1953 (reprinted 1966). xxxvi, 1697p. 105*s.*

First published 1943.
Universal in scope but "intended primarily for English-speaking users", and the choice of entries reflects this. Information presented concisely. Length of entries "is no measure of the relative importance of the person treated but rather an indication of editorial judgment of material likely to prove useful to consultants". Includes living people, "upwards of 40,000 persons". Pronouncing list of pre-names (p. 1628-68). Thumb index. Less than one-third overlap with *Chambers's Biographical dictionary.*

Biographical dictionaries: Contemporaries

92 (4/9)

Current biography, 1940-. New York, Wilson, 1940-. illus. Monthly, except August, $6 p.a. annual v. $8 p.a.

Current biography contains longish, readable articles on the life and work of people in public life. Sources of the information for the articles are newspapers, magazines, books and the biographees themselves. References are given at the end of each article. Brief obituary notices, with a reference to the *New York times* obituary, are given for persons whose biographies have previously appeared.

An annual volume cumulating the monthly issues and giving the year's entries in one alphabetical sequence is published,—called *Current biography yearbook since* 1955. Sketches are revised prior to printing and any necessary changes made in the entries. Each annual volume contains a professional index, a supplement listing the biographies of the women and an obituary. The

1950 volume contains a cumulative index for 1940-50; the 1960 volume contains a cumulative index for 1951-60, and the 1967 v., a cumulative index for 1961-67.

920 (4/9)
HANDLEY-TAYLOR, G., *comp.* **Dictionary of international biography:** a biographical record of contemporary achievement. London, Dictionary of International Biography Co., 1963-66. v. 1-3. (v. 3. 1966. 105*s.*).

V. 1 has *c.* 4,000 biographical entries, citing 39 other biographical reference works. V. 3 (1966) has more than 7,000 entries and, for the first time, includes the addresses of all biographees. Selection of entries in each volume seems haphazard, and no editorial policy is stated.
4th ed. (1967), compiled by E. Kay, has more than 10,000 entries.

92 (4/9)
The International who's who. London, Europa Publications. Annual. (31st ed., 1967-68. 150*s.*).

First published 1935.
The 31st ed. contains nearly 14,000 authoritative biographies. Method of selection: persons of international standing from every country are asked personally for details of their career and experience, and the press of the countries is constantly scrutinized to get up-to-date information about rising personalities as well as established figures. In many cases information is given for persons for countries where no national *Who's who* exists. Entries give name, title, dates, nationality, education, profession, career, politics, works (scientific, literary, etc.), address, telephone number.
The 31st ed. (xix, 1449p.) includes a list of persons who have died since the previous edition.

92 (4/9)
VAPEREAU, G. Dictionnaire universel des contemporains, contenant toutes les personnes notables de la France et des pays étrangers . . . 6. éd. Paris, Hachette, 1893, iii, 1629p.; Supplément. 1895. ii, 103p.

A useful feature of the work is that each page carries parallel entries which refer back to persons treated in previous editions, the number of which is quoted.

920 (4/9)
Who's who in international organizations, 1963. Brussels, Union of International Associations, 1963. 80p. 7*s.* 6*d.* (Available only to purchasers of the *Yearbook of international organizations.*)

An index to the 10,500 individuals named in the 1962-63 edition of the *Yearbook of international organizations.*

92 (4/9)
Who's who in world Jewry.

See entry at 296 (092).

92 (4/9)
World biography. 5th ed. Bethpage, New York, Institute for Research in Biography, Inc., 1954. viii, 1215p.

First published 1940 as *Biographical encyclopedia of the world.*
Covers the "world's notable living artists, writers, scholars, scientists, physicians, jurists, lawyers, religious leaders, educators, philosophers, musicians, statesmen, business heads and military figures . . . selected without political, ideological or racial preference". Full detailed entries; states specializations, but does not list works. Claimed to be "the largest and most comprehensive international encyclopaedia of contemporary biography".
The 3rd ed. (1946) had its 18,000 entries arranged in 13 categories, with many portraits and an alphabetical index.

Europe

92 (4)
Who's who in Europe: dictionnaire biographique des personnalités européennes contemporaines, par E. A. de Maeyer. Edition 1, 1964-1965. Brussels, Éditions de Feniks, [1964]. [xiii], 2680p. (1966-1967 ed. 1967. xlvi, 2928p.).

About 30,000 biographies of contemporaries in 25 countries. Entries are *c.* 15-25 lines in length. Covers politicians, writers, scholars, scientists, doctors and the like. No entry for Harold Wilson. Appended list of abbreviations and list of pseudonyms, 'double names'.

92 (4-011) (03)
Who's who in Central and East-Europe, 1935/36: a biographical dictionary containing about 10,000 biographies of prominent people from Albania, Austria, Bulgaria, Czechoslovakia, Danzig, Estonia, Finland, Greece, Hungary, Latvia, Liechtenstein, Lithuania, Poland, Rumania, Switzerland (including the League of Nations), Turkey and Yugoslavia. Edited by Stephen Taylor. 2nd ed. Zurich, Central European Times Publishing Co., Ltd., 1937. 1275p.

First published 1935.
Now dated and partly superseded by works covering specific countries (*e.g.,* Austria, Liechtenstein, Switzerland) but still valuable because it contains biographical material not available elsewhere.

92 (4=8)
Kleine slavische Biographie. Bearb. von Helene Auzinger [u.a.]. Weisbaden, Harrassowitz, 1958. viii, 832p.

About 3,000 concise biographies of Slavs, past and present, who have been prominent in the life and culture of their countries. Compiled by the editor and six other members of the Slavisches Seminar, Munich University, each compiler specializing in a particular country. Titles of works (with any German translations), compositions, etc., are given for writers, musicians and the like. Lenin is included, but not Stalin or Molotov. A handy bibliography of important reference books and standard works is appended (p. 809-32); this is sub-divided into "Ostslaven" (Russia; the Ukraine), "Westslaven (Czechoslovakia; Poland; etc.), and "Sudslaven" (Bulgaria, Yugoslavia), then by country and subject or form of material.

Commonwealth

92 (41-44):016

NATIONAL BOOK LEAGUE. Commonwealth biography. London, N.B.L., 1966. 22p. 4s.

An annotated reading list of 105 items, prepared for the Commonwealth in Books exhibition at New Zealand House in October 1966. 15 sections: Africa: General—Australia—Canada—Ghana—Guyana—Hong Kong—India—Kenya—Malawi—Malaysia—Mauritius—New Zealand—Nigeria—Southern Rhodesia—Zambia. All the books were in print in October 1966.

92 (41-44):016

ROYAL COMMONWEALTH SOCIETY. Biography catalogue of the Library of the Royal Commonwealth Society, by Donald H. Simpson. London, Royal Commonwealth Society, 1961. xxiii, 511p. 115s. 6d.

"The aim has been to list all the Library's biographical material. Books published up to the autumn of 1960 and periodicals to the close of 1959 have been included" (*Preface*). Some 12,000 entries for over 6,500 individuals, embracing periodical articles and analytical entries from volumes of collective biography, as well as books and pamphlets. The main sequence, 'Individual biographies' (p. 1-388) is followed by 'Collective biography and country indexes' (p. 388-431), 'Addenda' (p. 433-5) and 'Supplementary list of authors' (p. 441-511). "The men and women included are, in the main, those born in, or actively connected with, countries of the Commonwealth, and persons in the United Kingdom who have been of significance in Imperial affairs" (*Preface*). There are also numerous entries for explorers and travellers of many countries. Items asterisked represent books or periodicals destroyed by enemy action but inserted for their bibliographical value. Entries include full name, dates of birth and death and a brief description of the biographee; they indicate the presence of portraits and illustrations.

Great Britain

92 (410):016

HANHAM, H. J. "Some neglected sources of biographical information: county biographical dictionaries, 1890-1937." In *Bulletin of the Institute of Historical Research*, v. 34, no. 89, May 1961, p. 55-66.

There are two types of county biographical dictionary, the illustrated volume of local worthies and the county *Who's who*. Unfortunately the value of all types of such dictionaries is diminished at present by the fact that there is no complete set in existence. The Press-Gaskell series, Pike's New Century series, and county *Who's who* are briefly described. Appended is a summary of libraries' holdings arranged under English counties A-Z, followed by Wales, Scotland and Ireland. Usually only one major library holding is given per title.

92 (410):016

MATTHEWS, W., *comp.* **British autobiographies:** an annotated bibliography of British autobiographies published or written before 1951.

Berkeley, Univ. of California Press, 1955. xiv, 376p.

6,654 entries for persons "born in the British Isles" and "naturalised British subjects". Arranged alphabetically, anonymous works under the first word of the title. Subject and locality index of biographees.

92 (410):016

MATTHEWS, W., *comp.* **British diaries:** an annotated bibliography of British diaries written between 1442 and 1942. London, Cambridge Univ. Press, 1950. xxxiv, 339p.

Diaries arranged chronologically by date of first entry.

". . . includes diaries written by Englishmen, Scotsmen, Welshmen and Irishmen in the British Isles, in Europe, and on the high seas, and also the diaries of American and other travellers in the British Isles, so far as they have been published in England and in English." Diaries in manuscript form are recorded, with locations. Author index, p. 313-39.

92 (410) (03)

Celebrities of the century: being a dictionary of men and women of the nineteenth century; edited by L. C. Sanders. New and rev. ed. London, Cassell, 1890. vi, 1077p.

Although superseded for its main entries by those in the *D.N.B.* it is still useful for the lesser personalities of the 19th century and also for foreign persons.

The 40 principal contributors are listed at the beginning of the book. Only the main entries are signed, with initials, by the contributors. The purpose of the entries is "utility rather than completeness".

92 (410) (03)

The Dictionary of national biography. London, Oxford Univ. Press.

The latest editions of the Dictionary are:
1. *The Dictionary of national biography, from the earliest times to 1900.* 1908-09 re-issue (and reprints). 22v. (2 alphabetical sequences; 29,120 articles; more than 600 contributors; 30,500p.). £65.
2. *The Dictionary of national biography, 1901-1911.* 1920. 3v. in 1. 2088p. 63s.
3. *The Dictionary of national biography, 1912-21.* Edited by H. W. C. Davis and J. R. H. Weaver. 1927. xxvi, 623p. 63s. Includes cumulative index for 1901-1921.
4. *The Dictionary of national biography, 1922-1930.* Edited by J. R. H. Weaver. 1937. xiv, 962p. 63s. Includes cumulative index for 1901-30.
5. *The Dictionary of national biography, 1931-1940.* Edited by L. G. Wickham Legg. 1949. xvi, 968p. 70s. Includes cumulative index for 1901-1940.
6. *The Dictionary of national biography, 1941-1950.* Edited by L. G. Wickham Legg and E. T. Williams. 1959. xxi, 1031p. 120s.
Contains biographies of 725 men and women who died between 1st January 1941 and 31st December 1950. In a number of cases no bibliography is given, sources being stated as 'Personal information; private knowledge' by the

contributor. Upwards of 300 contributors. Appended (p. 989-1031) is a 'Cumulative index to the biographies contained in the supplements of the Dictionary of National Biography 1901-1950'.

7. *The Concise dictionary of national biography. Being an epitome of the main work and its supplement. Part 1. From the beginnings to 1900* (1903; 1953 imp. [vi], 1503p. 65s., which includes corrigenda (p. 1457-1503) not published elsewhere). Acts as an index to the main work and also as an independent reference work. It summarizes entries, usually 1/14th of the original length.

8. *The Dictionary of national biography. The concise dictionary.* Part 2. *1901-1950; being an epitome of the twentieth-century 'Dictionary' down to the end of 1950.* 1961. [vi], 528p. 45s.

History. The Dictionary of national biography, the largest of all the national biographical dictionaries, owes its existence to George M. Smith of the London publishing firm of Smith, Elder and Co. Smith's first intention was to produce "an improved and extended cyclopaedia of universal biography on the plan of the *Biographie universelle"* [of Michaud], but Leslie Stephen advised that a work on such a scale was impracticable and suggested "the production of a complete dictionary of national biography which should supply full, accurate and concise biographies of all noteworthy inhabitants of the British Islands and the Colonies (exclusive of living persons) from the earliest historical period to the present time". This alternative plan was adopted and Leslie Stephen was appointed editor in the autumn of 1882.

The work "appeared in 63 quarterly volumes [reduced to 21 in later reprints] between 1885 and 1900: v. 1-21 [1882-1889] under the editorship of Leslie Stephen, v. 22-26 [1890-1891] under the joint editorship of Leslie Stephen and Sidney Lee, and v. 27-63 [1891-1900] under the sole editorship of Sidney Lee. In order to include notable persons who died during the progress of the work a Supplement in 3 volumes, 64-66, [later v. 22 of the reprint] was published in 1901-1902, the date of Queen Victoria's death, 22nd January 1901, being taken as its limit. These 66 volumes were reprinted with corrections, on thinner paper in 1908 and 1909 and re-issued in 22 volumes".

In 1917 the *Dictionary* was presented by the family of George M. Smith to the Oxford University Press who have continued to publish it since that time.

Scope. "It is believed that the names include all men and women of British or Irish race who have achieved any reasonable measure of distinction in any walk of life. . . . No sphere of activity has been consciously overlooked; [includes] early settlers in America . . . natives of these islands who have gained distinction in foreign countries [and] persons of foreign birth who have gained eminence in this country." The biography of Queen Victoria constitutes virtually a work in itself.

The articles are signed and contributed by persons considered to be an expert on the life and career of the biographee. Bibliographies are given and the sources of the information on which the article is based are quoted.

A completely revised edition is not being undertaken by the publishers, but any corrections or alterations which arise as the result of current historical investigation are published by the Institute of Historical Research of the University of London in its *Bulletin.*

Reviews of the decennial volume for 1931-1940, together with a discussion of the bibliographical intricacies of the whole work, appear in the *Times literary supplement,* 16th December 1949, p. 819; *Times,* 3rd November 1949, and *Library Association record,* v. 60, no. 6, June 1958, p. 181-91.

The decennial volume for 1941-1950 reveals a slightly more liberalised selection policy at work. It includes a biography of J. B. Hobbs, whereas the main work omitted W. G. Grace.

The Concise dictionary. Part 2. *1901-1950* (1961) has been the subject of some criticism. A. J. P. Taylor (*English history, 1914-1945,* p. 606) finds it "not wholly free from the editorial outlook of Oxford academics" and instances the omission of E. D. Morel and Ronald Firbank. Length of epitomized entries is fairly well balanced (*e.g.,* 'Asquith': $\frac{1}{2}$ col.; 'Chamberlain, Arthur Neville': 1. col.; 'Baldwin': about 1 col.; 'Lloyd George': 2 cols.), although Thomas Hardy receives well short of a column, against Meredith's $1\frac{1}{2}$ columns. Bernard Shaw is given rather more than a column; Eric Blair (George Orwell), a mere 7 lines. Writers are less generously treated than men of affairs,—apparently a *D.N.B.* tradition (see review in *The Listener,* v. 67, no. 1,710, 4th January 1962, p. 36). A new feature is the 'Select subject index' (p. 485-528). This includes entries for subjects such as 'General strike (1926)', 'Hymns', 'Local government', 'London, Architecture in', 'Newspapers and periodicals', 'Trade unions' and 'Type faces', followed by the names of the persons prominently associated with the subject and included in the *Concise dictionary.* Omissions occur in the biographies cited in this index. Under 'Newspapers and periodicals', for instance, *The times* (2 editors), *The daily telegraph* (1 editor) and *The morning post* (1 editor) are passed over (see *The times,* 14th December 1961, p. 16).

92 (410) (03)

Dictionary of national biography. Corrections and additions. Cumulated from the *Bulletin of the Institute of Historical Research,* University of London, covering the years 1923-1963. Boston, Mass., G. K. Hall, 1966. iv, 212p. $25 (U.S. and British Isles); $27.50 (elsewhere).

1,300 entries, photographically reproduced by offset. A cumulation, A-Z, of 'Corrections and additions' to *D.N.B.* appearing in the *Bulletin,* v. 1 (1923)-36 (1963). A number of corrections and additions are signed; corrections by the staff of the *Bulletin* are in square brackets. The entry 'Sir Robert Howard (1626-1698)' runs to $2\frac{1}{4}$ columns of corrections and additions. As no revision of the *D.N.B.* is likely to be published for many years, this cumulation is an essential supplement to the main work.

92 (410) (03)

EMDEN, A. B. A biographical register of the University of Cambridge, to 1500. Cambridge, Univ. Press, 1963. xl, 695p. 168s.

See entry at 378.4 (425.9).

BIOGRAPHY

92 (410) (03)
EMDEN, A. B. A biographical register of the University of Oxford, to A.D. 1500. Oxford, Clarendon Press, 1957-59. 3v. £27 6s.

See entry at 378.4 (425.72).

92 (410) (03)
MUSGRAVE, Sir W., comp. Obituary prior to 1800 (as far as relates to England, Scotland and Ireland), compiled by Sir William Musgrave . . . and entitled by him "a general nomenclator and obituary, with reference to the books where the persons are mentioned and where some account of their character is to be found." Edited by Sir G. J. Armytage. London, Harleian Soc., 1899-1901. 6v. (Harleian Society publications, nos. 44-49).

A finding list of obituaries contained in some 90 works, MSS., collections, etc. British families only. The great majority of the works indexed are in the British Museum. Brief entries: name, description, date of death, place of residence, source of information.

The scope of the work makes it an invaluable supplement to the *D.N.B.*

A supplementary finding list is: *An Index to the biographical and obituary notices in the Gentleman's magazine", 1731-1780* (London, British Record Society, 1886-91. viii, 677p. (Index Society publications, no. 15)). This has single-line entries: name, residence, year and volume number of the *Magazine.*

92 (410) (03)
PRATT, A. T. C., ed. People of the period: being a collection of the biographies of upwards of six thousand living celebrities. London, Beeman, 1897. 2v.

Useful supplement to Boase (*see* at 92 (420)(03)) to whom reference should be made for persons of the late Victorian era. Entries for authors and composers list their principal works.

92 (410) (03)
WARD, T. H., ed. Men of the reign: a biographical dictionary of eminent persons of British and colonial birth who have died during the reign of Queen Victoria. London, Routledge, 1885. iv, 1028p. (Reprinted Graz, Akad. Druk- und Verlagsantalt, 1964. ÖS1140; $45.).

A concise biographical dictionary which also includes persons of foreign birth closely identified with England. Largely extracted (but rewritten) from the 11 editions of *Men of the time* (see entry for *Who's who*) but supplemented by other sources, e.g., *The Times, Annual register,* many professional journals, etc.

The principle of selection has been to include anyone who has achieved sufficient distinction in public life "to make himself felt among his contemporaries". About 3,000 entries.

92 (410) (03)
Who was who . . . : a companion to *Who's who,* containing the biographies of those who died during the period . . . London, Black, 1929-.

1897-1915. 5th rev. ed. 1967. 84s.
1916-1928. 4th rev. ed. 1967. 84s.

1929-1940. 1940. 2nd rev. ed. 1967. 84s
1941-1950. 1952. 84s.
1951-1960. 1961. 84s.

Further volumes are to appear decennially. The 1951-1960 v. has c. 8,500 entries.

"The entries are for the most part as they last appeared in Who's who, with the dates of death added and in some cases further additional information to bring them up to date. . . . In a few instances the details are included of a biographee whose death occurred before 1951" (*Preface*).

Regarding omissions, see annotation to *Who's who.*

92 (410) (03)
Who's who: an annual biographical dictionary, with which is incorporated "Men and women of the time". London, Black, 1849-. Annual. (1968. 36, viii, 3416p. 168s.).

Scope. An authoritative dictionary of contemporary biography, the aim being "to furnish in as compact a form as possible a series of biographical sketches of eminent living persons of both sexes, in all parts of the civilized world". The criterion of selection is that of "personal achievement or prominence, and of a man's or woman's interest to the public at large or to any important section of that public".

History. Published originally by Baily Bros. and later by Simpkin, Marshall, Kent, it was in its early days mainly lists of names under various headings, e.g., Royal Household, House of Commons, etc. without any individual biographical details. It continued in this style until it was bought by A. & C. Black in 1896. The following year it became *Who's who.* 49th year, 1897 (first year of new issue, edited by Douglas Sladen). Its aim now was "to include all the most prominent people in the Kingdom, whether their prominence is inherited, or depending upon office, or the result of ability which singles them out from their fellows in occupations open to every educated man and women". In 1899 the title became *Who's who, 1899; an annual biographical dictionary.* In 1901 it incorporated *Men and women of the time,* adjusted its title and has appeared in this style ever since.

A concurrent biographical dictionary, *Men of the time,* first appeared in 1852, published by David Bogue. With its third edition in 1856 it included entries for women, although this was not recognized in the title of the work until the 13th edition of 1891, when it appeared as *Men and women of the time.* From the 5th edition in 1862 until the 14th and last edition in 1895, it was published by Routledge. Black's bought the copyright in 1900 and, as stated above, incorporated it into *Who's who,* the first joint edition appearing in 1901. Adam Black was editor, 1900-1936.

Compilation. Initially a questionnaire is sent to a person chosen for inclusion and thereafter a proof of the entry is submitted annually to the biographee for revision. Death removes the entry to the appropriate volume of *Who was who* (*q.v.*), but others disappear from the pages of *Who's who* for a variety of reasons, e.g. proofs not returned, no longer of public interest, etc. As these persons will not appear in *Who was who,* it is therefore necessary for all editions of *Who's who* to be retained for a complete record.

As A. J. P. Taylor observes (*English history, 1914-1945*, p. 606), "The entries are produced by the individuals included and are therefore not always accurate. Sometimes there are mistakes, sometimes—as with previous marriages—deliberate omissions". On the other hand, "It cannot be stated too emphatically that inclusion in *Who's who* has never at any time been a matter for payment or of obligation to purchase the volume" (*Preface*).

"The centenary of *Who's who*", in *The bookseller*, 10th July 1948, deals with the origin and development of the work.

92 (410) (03)
WILSON, *Sir* **A. T.,** and **McEWEN, J. H. F. Gallantry:** its public recognition and record, in peace and in war, at home and abroad. London, Oxford Univ. Press, 1939. xvii, 498p.

20 chapters on various awards, particularly the Albert Medal and the Edward Medal. Notes are given on the actions performed by those who were awarded medals. Bibliography (p. xvii); analytical index.

Scotland

92 (411) (03)
A Biographical dictionary of eminent Scotsmen; originally edited by Robert Chambers. New ed. revised under the care of the publishers. With a supplemental volume, continuing the biographies to the present time, by the Rev. T. Thomson, with numerous portraits. Blackie, 1855. 5v.

The original edition (4v.) covered the period up to 1834, but for this edition the stereotypes were revised and reprinted, bringing the information up to 1855. V. 5 contains additional entries and is up to 1855.

The work contains entries for living persons and dates from the earliest times.

For 'Works on clan and family history and Scottish personalities', consult Hancock, P. D., comp. *A bibliography of works relating to Scotland, 1916-1950.* v. 2, p. 37-91.

92 (411) (03)
Scottish biographies, 1938. London & Glasgow, Thurston, 1938. xii, 808p.

The first publication of a *Who's who* in Scotland.

Ireland

92 (415) (03)
CRONE, J. S. A concise dictionary of Irish biography. Rev. and enl. [2nd] ed. Dublin, Talbot Press, 1937. viii, 290p.

First published 1928.

Brief entries of "notable Irish men and women in every sphere of activity". Indispensable as a biographical guide.

R. Hayes's *Biographical dictionary of Irishmen in France* (Dublin, Gill, 1949. 332p.) first appeared serially in the Irish periodical, *Studies.* An Appendix (p. 327-32) lists Irish noble families surviving in France.

92 (415) (03)
Thom's Irish who's who: a biographical book of reference of prominent men and women in Irish life at home and abroad. Dublin, Thom, 1923. 266p.

Contains some 2,500 biographies.

A. R. Eager devotes p. 223-73 of his *A guide to Irish bibliographical material* (1964) to Irish biography, collective and individual. He cites a "List of names of Irish biographies in the 'D.N.B.' 2nd supplement, v. 1-3", in *Irish book lover*, v. 3, 1912, 205-7; v. 4, 1913, p. 80-82, 116-17; and A. Webb's *A compendium of Irish biography* (Dublin, Gill, 1878), "invaluable, never wholly superseded", listing 478 authorities consulted.

England

92 (420):016
STAUFFER, D. A. The art of biography in eighteenth-century England: bibliographical supplement. Princeton, N.J., Princeton Univ. Press; London, Oxford Univ. Press, 1941. 2v.

Contents: Subject and author index of biographies and autobiographies written or translated in England, 1700-1800 (p. 1-278); Chronological table of the most important biographical works in England, 1700-1800 (p. 285-293).

92 (420):016
STAUFFER, D. A. English biography before 1700. Cambridge, Mass., Harvard Univ. Press; London, Cambridge Univ. Press, 1930. xvii, 392p.

Considers "historically and critically the art of English biography from the earliest times to the year 1700".

Bibliography: pt. 1. Subject and author index of English biographies before 1700. Full titles are given under the names of the authors; cross references are given for the subjects of the biographies. Anonymous works are described under the subjects of the lives, p. 287-366.

Chronological table of the most important English biographies before 1700, p. 373-79.

92 (420) (03)
BOASE, F. Modern English biography; containing many thousand concise memoirs of persons who have died since the year 1850, with an index of the most interesting matter. Truro, Netherton & Worth, 1892-1921. 3v. and 3 supplementary v. (Reprinted London, Cass, 1965. 6v. £42.).

A most valuable work, supplementing the *D.N.B.*, particularly for the lesser-known personalities of the 19th century. Each volume contains an analytical index to the entries. About 30,000 short biographical sketches of persons who died between 1851 and 1900. Notes source of portraits (photographs), lists published works, theatre performances and other facts sometimes omitted in larger works of reference, states the *Times literary supplement* leader (no. 3,330, 23rd December 1965, p. 1189-90). Draws on obituaries and notices in *The times, Illustrated London news* and other journals, as well as local newspapers, records, etc., and so has a greater coverage of national and local celebrities who died in the latter part of the 19th century than *D.N.B.* (q.v.).

The sub-title of the supplement varies, stating the scope as covering those "who have died during the years 1851-1900."

92 (420) (03)
Who's who in history. Oxford, Blackwell, 1960-. v. 1-. illus., geneal. tables.

v. 1: *British Isles, 55* B.C. *to 1485*, by W. O. Hassall. 1960. 27s. 6d.
v. 2: *England, 1485-1689*, by C. R. N. Routh. 1961. 30s.
v. 3: *England, 1603-1714*, by C. P. Hill. 1965. 42s.

The work on the British Isles is to be completed in 4 volumes, under the general editorship of C. R. N. Routh. V. 4 is to cover late Georgian and Victorian England, by B. Rees and E. W. Gladstone.

"Intended to interest and instruct the amateur" (*Introduction*). Each volume has some 200 entries, arranged chronologically, and "includes a large number of secondary people whose influence on their times modern scholarship has come to recognize". The aim is to make each volume a portrait of its age. V. 3 contains c. 200-300 biographies (Cromwell: 5½p., portrait and 6 references). Under each entry reference is made to the standard biographies and also to relevant passages in *They saw it happen* (Oxford, Blackwell, 1957-60. 4v.), an anthology of eye-witnesses' accounts of events in British history, 55 B.C.-1940 A.D. V. 1 of *Who's who in history* includes 32 plates and other illustrations based on contemporary sources, as well as royal family pedigrees. Each volume has a detailed alphabetical index.

London

92 (421) (03)
KENT, W. London worthies. London, Heath Cranton, 1939. xiv, 421p. illus.

350 entries; both living and deceased persons. Very personal approach, both in persons selected and in the entry itself. (William Caxton, 4 columns; Christopher Wren, 8 columns; John Burns (friend of the author), 9 columns). "A topographical even more than a biographical work", not restricted to those born in London. Presumably criterion of inclusion is an association with London. Anecdotal; should be used critically.

92 (421) (03)
Who's who in the city, 1964: a guide to the men in the City of London, with their occupations, biographical notes and livery companies. London, City Press, [1965?]. [ii], 171, [ii]p.

About 1,200 brief biographies of the *Who's who* type. States directorships, chairmanships, memberships of livery companies, and the like.

Channel Islands

92 (423.4) (03)
BALLEINE, G. R. A biographical dictionary of Jersey. London, Staples Press, [1948]. 715p.

Approximately 300 biographies, not confined to persons born on the island. No living persons included. Lengthy, informative articles, usually documented.

Appendices: Non-Jerseymen who have left their mark on Jersey history (p. 616-73); Persons incorrectly claimed as Jerseymen (p. 674-5); 4, Brief bibliography of Jersey history, p. 696-701); abbreviations. Also, chronological index of biographies (p. 705-7); classified index of biographies (p. 709-15).

Who's who in the Channel Islands, 1967 (St. Helier, Jersey, Channel Islands Publishing Co., 1967. xxx, 154p. ports. 105s.) comprises nearly 1,200 biographies in Jersey, Guernsey, Alderney and Sark. Has a foreword on Channel Island family names, by F. Le Maistre. Small but clear portraits; map.

Wales

92 (429) (03)
HONOURABLE SOCIETY OF CYMMRO-DORION. Y bwygraffiadur Cymreig hyd 1940. [Editors. 1943-47, Sir J. E. Lloyd; 1943-53, R. T. Jenkins]. London, Hon. Soc. of Cymmrodorion, 1953. liv, 1110p.

In Welsh. Supersedes all previous Welsh biographical dictionaries. Modelled on *D.N.B.* Contributors number about 300. The work covers period A.D. 400-1940 and contains some 3,500 biographies, of which about 200 are articles on the history of important Welsh families. Biographies are of Welshmen and others who have contributed to Welsh history or to the Welsh way of life in Wales or elsewhere.

The key (p. xxix-liv) to the abbreviations used is a valuable source of further biographical material. A list of pseudonyms forms another appendix.

92 (429) (03)
—— **The dictionary of Welsh biography** down to 1940. London, the Society; Oxford, Blackwell, 1959. lviii, 1,157p. 126s.

Based on the Welsh ed. of 1953.
3,500 signed articles, covering all periods and walks of life. For inclusion, the biographee or at least one of his parents had to be born within Wales. "The present English edition is not a mere translation of the Welsh volume. The intervening years have enabled the Editors to pick up the fruits of later research and to make many corrections" (*Preface*). There is an appendix of additional biographies.

It is planned to publish supplements to each edition at approximately ten-year intervals. The Welsh and English editions of the first supplement (1941-50) are expected shortly.

92 (429) (03)
Who's who in Wales. 3rd ed. London, Belgravia Publications, 1937. xliv, 259p.

Dated, but contains some concise information not easily obtainable elsewhere.

92 (429.35)
Flintshire County Library. Bibliography of the county of Flint. Part 1, Biographical sources. 1953.

See entry at 942.935.

Germany

92 (43) (03)

Allgemeine deutsche Biographie: hrsg. durch die Historische Commission bei der Königliche Akademie der Wissenschaften. Leipzig, Duncker & Humblot, 1875-1912. 56v.

v. 1-45: A-Z.
v. 46-55: Nachträge bis 1899, ANDR-Z (A-AD, in v. 45).
v. 56: General index to the whole work.

The standard German biographical dictionary. Lengthy, authoritative signed articles (about 23,600 in all) containing bibliographies. Includes persons who died before 1899.

Neue deutsche Biographie (q.v.) is largely based on this work.

92 (43) (03)

Biographisches Jahrbuch und deutscher Nekrolog 1896-1913: . . . hrsg. von A. Bettelheim. Berlin, Reimer, 1897-1917. 18v.; Index to v. 1-10. 1908.

Each volume records the death of prominent Germans during the year under review. Alphabetically arranged, with lengthy, signed obituaries containing bibliographies for the more prominent subjects and short notices of the less prominent. Title was changed with the volume for 1914-1916 to *Deutsches biographisches Jahrbuch*. A useful supplement to *Allgemeine deutsche Biographie*. A cumulative index, compiled by Georg Wolff covering the years 1896-1905 (v. 1-10), was published in 1908.

92 (43) (03)

Deutsches biographisches Jahrbuch; hrsg. von Verbande der Deutschen Akademien. Stuttgart, Deutsche Verlags-Anstalt. 1925-1932.

v. 1, 1914-16 (published 1925), v. 2, 1917-20 (published 1928), v. 3, 1921 (published 1927), v. 4, 1922 (published 1929), v. 5, 1923 (published 1930), v. 10, 1928 (published 1931), v. 11, 1929 (published 1932).

The 1923 volume contains a cumulative index to v. 1-5 (1914-23 inclusive). General format and structure of the work as in *Biographisches Jahrbuch* (q.v.). Each volume is a complete alphabetical sequence, with signed articles and bibliographies. The work also contains short, unsigned obituaries.

A comprehensive illustrated biographical record of the Nazi movement is available in: *Das deutsche Führerlexikon, 1934/35* (Berlin, Stollberg, 1934. 552p.). Official organizations are listed in a separately paged section (148p.). A rare work.

92 (43) (03)

Kürschners deutscher Gelehrten-Kalender 1961. 9. Ausg., hrsg. von Werner Schuder. Berlin, de Gruyter, 1961. 2v. DM.140.

First published 1925.
The 9th ed. (2,567 pages) has *c.* 17,000 concise biographical entries for scholars in German-speaking countries. V. 1: A-N; v. 2: O-Z und Register. V. 2 includes an obituary list of about 1,700 names, a 'Festkalender' and a classified list of entries, arranged A-Z by classes.

The complementary annual covering belles lettres is *Kürschners deutscher Literatur-Kalender* (1897-), an A-Z list of living German, Austrian, Swiss and other German-language writers abroad, noting published works and addresses. Obituary notices appended.

92 (43) (03)

Neue deutsche Biographie: hrsg. von der Historischen Kommission bei der Bayerischen Akademie der Wissenschaften. Berlin, Duncker & Humblot, 1953-.

v. 1-7. A-HARTMANN. 1953-65.

First projected in 1925, the work is largely based on the *Allgemeine deutsche Biographie* (q.v.). Includes all who have had an influence on German history and culture and is not confined to the present-day geographical frontiers of Germany. Austrians, Dutch and Swiss are included if they satisfy this condition. The entries, which are signed, include bibliographies and details of portraits. Each volume contains an index referring to the appropriate entries in the relevant volume of the *A.D.B.* V. 4 includes articles on Albrecht Dürer by Hans Jantzen (10½ columns, with ½ column of bibliography, including sources for illustrations), Erasmus (11 columns, with 1 column of bibliography) and Friedrich Engels (13 columns; 1 column of items by Engels; ¼ column of material on Engels).

92 (43) (03)

RÖSSLER, H., and FRANZ, G. Biographisches Wörterbuch zur deutschen Geschichte. Unter Mitarbeit von Willy Hoppe. Munich, Oldenbourg, 1952. xlviii, 968p. geneal. tables.

A compact and well-balanced biographical dictionary of deceased German celebrities, "history" being interpreted in a wide sense to cover statesmen, politicians, scientists, medical men and artists. Articles are signed and brief bibliographies (1 to 4 items) are appended. Hindenburg, Brahms and Moltke each receive 2½ columns; Hitler, 2 columns; Mommsen, 1 column. Collected biographies are listed on p. 962-6; agenda and corrigenda, p. 967-8. Cross-references from the same authors' *Sachwörterbuch zur deutschen Geschichte* (1958) (see at 943 (03)).

92 (43) (03)

Wer ist wer? Das deutsche Who's who. 15. Ausg. von Degeners *Wer ist's?* Berlin-Grunewald, Arani Verlags-GmbH., 1966.

v. 15, pt. 1. *Bundesrepublik Deutschland und Westberlin.* xii, 2292p.
pt. 2. *Sowjetische Besatzungszone. Ost Berlin.* 384p.

Founded on *Wer ist's?*, first published in 1905. The West Germany part has *c.* 25,000 biographies; the East Germany part, *c.* 5,000 entries. Entries vary in length from 2 lines to ½ col. (*e.g.,* Ulbricht).

92 (43) (03)

Who's who in Germany: a biographical dictionary containing about 12,000 biographies of prominent people in and of Germany, and 2,400 organizations. Edited by H. G. Kliemann and S. S. Taylor. New York, Intercontinental Book &

Publishing Co., Ltd.; Munich, Oldenbourg, 1964. 2v. (2120p.) DM.130.

First published 1955; 2nd ed. 1960.
About 12,000 entries. " . . . published in English in order to be of use to people throughout the world . . . contains the biographies of nearly all significant personalities which represent the Federal Republic at home as well as abroad." Concise, factual entries. Business and industry well represented.
Appendices: Nobel Prize winners born in Germany; Knights of the Order "Pour le mérite" for Sciences and Arts born in Germany. Also, separately paged 'Directory of organizations, associations and institutions' (145p.).

East Germany
92 (43-11) (03)
GERMANY. Federal Republic. BUNDESMINIS-TERIUM FÜR GESAMTDEUTSCHE FRAGEN. SBZ-Biographie. Ein biographisches Nachschlagebuch über die Sowjetische Besatzungszone Deutschlands. 3. Aufl. Bonn, 1964 (reprinted 1965). 406p.

About 2,500 entries (with separate paragraphs for parts of entry). Gives publications, if any. Walter Ulbricht: 1 column. Narrow format for double column.

See also *Wehr ist wer?* (at 92 (43) (03), pt. 2.

Luxembourg
92 (435.9) (03)
MERSCH, J. Biographie nationale du pays de Luxembourg, depuis ses origines jusqu'à nos jours. Luxembourg, Imprimerie de la Cour Victor Buck, 1947-. fasc. 1-. illus., ports.

fasc. 1-14. 1947-66.
Not arranged alphabetically; a series of lengthy and scholarly contributions on prominent persons, famous families, etc. Thus, fasc. 9 (1958-60. 280p.) includes 'Les rois du Pays-Bas, grand ducs de Luxembourg', by Jules Mersch (p. 30-280). Footnote references; quotations from primary sources.

92 (435.9) (03)
Who's who in Belgium and Grand Duchy of Luxembourg . . . 2nd ed., edited by F. Michielsen and S. S. Taylor. [New York], Intercontinental Book & Publishing Co., Ltd., 1962. xxiii, 1343p. $20.

See entry at 92 (493) (03).

Austria
92 (436) (03)
Neue österreichische Biographie, 1815-1918; begrundet von Anton Bettelheim [u.a.]. Vienna, Amalthea-Verlag, 1923-, v. 1-. ports.

Abt. 1: *Biographien.* v. 1-13 (1923-59).
Abt. 2, Bd. 1: *Bibliographie zur Neuen österreichische Biographie,* by H. Bohatta. 1925.
Title changed with Abt. 1, Bd. 10 (1957) to *Grosse Österreicher. Neue Österreichische Biographie ab 1815.*

Abt. 1 is planned to appear in about 25 v. *Bibliographie* (Abt. 2, Bd. 1) lists 2,337 biographical sources.

92 (436) (03)
Österreiches biographisches Lexikon, 1815-1950. Hrsg. von der Österreichischen Akademie der Wissenschaften. Unter der Leitung von Leo Santifaller, bearb. von Eva Obermayer-Marnach. Graz-Cologne, Böhlaus, 1957-. v. 1-. ea. ÖS 252.

V. 1-3 (Lfg.. 1-15) (1957-65): A-KNOLL.
Each volume contains about 2,000 biographies, giving fairly concise biographical data, with bibliographies. Covers personalities of the Austro-Hungarian Empire which was dissolved in 1918. The entry for Count Julius Andrassy runs to 1½ columns, including bibliography (works by: 2½ lines; material on: 10½ lines, including a reference to *Neue deutsche Biographie*); that for Hofmann von Hofmannsthal, 4½ columns (works by: ½ column; material on 1¾ columns). Frequently cited works are listed on p. xxi-xxix, v. 1. Good, clear layout.
To some extent continues C. von Wurzbach's *Biographisches Lexikon des Kaiserthums Oesterreich* (Vienna, Zamarski, 1865-91. 60v.), which goes forward from 1750.

92 (436) (03)
Who's who in Austria . . . a biographical dictionary containing about 4,000 biographies of prominent personalities from and in Austria. 5th ed., edited by R. Bohmann and S. S. Taylor. Vienna, Intercontinental Book & Publishing Co., Ltd., 1964. 856p. ÖS 364.

First published 1955.
The 5th ed. includes c. 1,000 biographies that appear for the first time. Appended 'Directory of organizations, institutes, associations and enterprises'. Also a 'Residential directory', an index showing the home address of personalities dealt with.

Czechoslovakia
92 (437) (03)
KUHN, H., and BÖSS, O., ed. Biographisches Handbuch der Tschechoslowakei. Munich, Lerche, 1961. xiii, 640p.

"Systematische Abteilung' (p. 1-120) arranges names of biographies under types of organisation, —political, governmental, trade unions, associations, cultural and journalistic, scientific, university, ecclesiastical, etc. 'Biographische Abteilung' (p. 121-640) is arranged by biographies, A-Z,— c. 3,000 entries.

Poland
92 (438) (03)
AKADEMJA UMIEJETNOSCI (subsequently Polska Akademja Umiejetności), Cracow. Polski slownik biograficzny. Cracow, Nakladem Polskiej Akademja Umiejetności (now Polska Akademia Nauk, Instytut Historii Wydawn. Zakladu Narodowego im Ossolinskich). 1935-. v. 1-. iłlus.

v. 1-10, pt. 4 (1935-64): A-JAROSINSKI.
The definitive dictionary of Polish biography. V. 1 to v. 7, pt. 1 (A-Frankowski) were published

1935-48. Publication was resumed in 1958; to be completed in 20 v. Scholarly, signed articles, eventually covering some 25,000 Poles of all epochs, as well as foreigners who have played an important part in Polish affairs (*Polish facts and figures*, no. 628, 22nd August 1959, p. 7). Articles include references to sources.

Hungary

92 (439.1) (03)

FEKETE, M,, *ed.* **Prominent Hungarians**, home and abroad. Munich, Aurora Publications, 1966. 334p.

Usual *Who's who* information on more than 3,200 "notable living Hungarians or Hungarian-born politicians, artists, writers and scientists, . . . regardless of whether they live inside or outside Hungary" (*Preface*). Appendices: New members of the Hungarian Academy of Science—Honours list, 1965—Abbreviations.

V. 1 (A-K. *c. 75s.*) of a new Hungarian biographical dictionary, edited by A. Kenyeres, appeared in 1967 (Budapest). It has *c.* 1,200 portraits of biographies. V. 2 is in active preparation, according to Ad Orientem. *Catalogue ten, 1967,* entry no. 3107.

France

92 (44) (03)

Dictionnaire biographique français contemporain. 2. éd. Paris, Pharos, Agence Internationale de Documentation Contemporaine, [1954]. 708p. illus.; Suppléments 1-2: 1955-1956.

First published 1950.
Includes Frenchmen and others who by living in France have identified themselves with French life. Entries are usually documented.

92 (44) (03)

Dictionnaire de biographie française. Paris, Letouzey, 1929-. v. 1-.

v. 1-10 (1929-65): A-DESPLAGNES.
Editors, successively: M. Jules Balteau, Michel Prévost, Marius Barroux and Roman d'Amat. The *Dictionary of national biography* has been taken as one of the models on which the work has been based. Work began before the first World War (see entry for Balteau in v. 5 of the *Dictionnaire*) but the first fascicule was not issued until 1929. V. 1 was completed in 1933. The work is to be completed in 20v., the volumes containing 6 fascicules of 128p. each.
Lengthy, authoritative signed articles with good bibliographies and/or sources used for the compilation of the articles. Persons included are:
(1) outstanding Frenchmen and women from Metropolitan France and her dependant territories from the earliest times—their life, work and influence,
(2) the work and career of foreigners who have played an important part in the life of France.
No living persons are included.

92 (44) (03)

Nouveau dictionnaire national des contemporains. 4. éd. Paris, Les Éditions du Nouveau Dictionnaire National des Contemporains, 1966. [iv], [1], 784p. ports.

First published [1962], covering 1961/62.
About 2,000 entries, each with character sketch and, usually, a portrait. 'Jules Romains': 1¾ cols.; Jean Anouilh: ¾ col. (no portrait). 'Index professionel' arranges names of biographies under vocational categories, A-Z. Alphabetical list of names precedes.

92 (44) (03)

Who's who in France . . . Dictionnaire biographique des principales personnalités de France, des départements et territoires français d'outre-mer, des états africains d'expression française, de la République malgache, des français notables vivant à l'étranger et des étrangers notables résidant en France. 8. éd. Paris, Lafitte, [1967]. 116, 1436p. 160F.

First published 1953, covering 1953-1954; then biennially.
Modelled on *Who's who*. The 8th edition contains about 18,000 entries (Mauriac: ½ column; de Gaule: 1 column). *Who's who* type of information (date of birth, parentage; marriage; education; professional career; works (for writers); decorations; recreations; membership of clubs, etc.; address). Official French decorations—4 pages of coloured illustrations. Obituary. Larger format (10½″ × 8¼″). Clear sansserif type—much more legible than the muddy presswork in *Who's who.*

Italy

92 (45) (03)

Chi è? Dizionario biografico degli italiani d'oggi. 7. ed. Rome, Scarano, 1961. 714p.

First published 1928.
Who's who style of entry, except that the biographies are compiled by the editor and not by the biographees. About 7,000 entries. Lists works, with dates.

A fuller contemporary survey is: *Panorama biografico degli italiani d'oggi;* a cura di G. Vaccaro (Rome, Curcio, 1956. 2v.), containing some 25,000 entries.

A remarkable retrospective biographical work is the *Enciclopedia biografica e bibliografica italiana* (Milan, Istituto Editoriale Italiano, 1936-. illus.), planned in 48 series, each dealing with a special category (*e.g., Ser. 6, Poetesse e scrittrici.* 1941-42. 2v.). Contributions have been made to 12 of the series.

92 (45) (03)

COSENZA, M. E. Biographical and bibliographical dictionary of the Italian Humanists and of the world of classical scholarship in Italy, 1300-1800. 2nd ed., rev. and enl. Boston, Mass., G. K. Hall, 1962. 5v. $350; $385.

First produced 1954 in microfilm form by the Renaissance Society of America.

92 (45) (03)

Dizionario biografico degli italiani. Rome, Istituto della Enciclopedia Italiana fondata da Giovanni Treccani, 1960-. v. 1-.

v. 1-8 (1960-66): A-BEREGAN.
The Italian equivalent to the *Dictionary of national biography.* To be completed in 40

volumes, issued at the rate of 2 p.a. Designed to include some 40,000 biographies, from the 5th to the 20th century, excluding living persons. There are more than 300 contributors to v. 1, which contains numerous long, scholarly, signed articles (*e.g.,* Pope Adrian I, by O. Bertolini: 20 columns of text, with 2 columns of bibliography). The review in *Times literary supplement,* no 3077, 17th February 1961, p. 102, notes "some exceptionally long articles, packed with the results of first-hand research, on comparatively minor characters".

92 (45) (03)
Who's who in Italy, 1957-1958. A biographical dictionary containing about 7,000 biographies of prominent people in and of Italy, and 1,400 organizations; edited by Igino Giordani and Stephen S. Taylor, Milan, Intercontinental Book & Publishing Co.; London, Tiranti, 1958. xvi, 1,137p.

Entries, where possible, are based on questionnaires. In English, "to facilitate its consultation and use throughout the world . . . Contains biographies of nearly all significant Italian personalities, representing the most active segment of the Country, both in Italy and abroad. Length of a biography is in no way related to the importance of the personality referred to" (*Preface*). Pt. 1: Biographies (p. 1-992); pt. 2: Directory of organisations, associations, undertakings (p. 993-1137).

Malta

92 (458.2) (03)
Malta Who's who, 1965: a biographical dictionary. 2nd issue. Valetta, Progress Press Co., [1965?]. xiv, 263p.

First published 1964.
Usual *Who's who* information on *c.* 1,000 prominent Maltese, including those "who have made their homes overseas yet wish to retain a link with the land of their birth" (*Foreword*). Abbreviations; obituary.

Spain

92 (46) (03)
ESPERABÉ DE ARTEAGA, E. Diccionario enciclopédico ilustrado y crítico de los hombres de España. Madrid, Artes Gráficas Ibarra, [1956]. 530, [1] p. ports.

Contains about 3,000 entries, ranging in length from 3-4 lines to 5 pages (*e.g.,* for Unamuno y Jugo). Includes the eminent living as well as the dead, although more space is devoted to the figures of the last century. Addenda are given at the end of each letter of the alphabet concerned. Typography is good but the portraits are very small and poor. Articles are unsigned and carry no bibliographies.

The best general source for Spanish and Hispanic-American biography is probably the *Enciclopedia universal ilustrada europeo-americana* and its supplements.

92 (46) (03)
Who's who in Spain . . .: a biographical dictionary containing about 6,000 biographies of prominent

people in and of Spain and 1,400 organitzations [*sic*]. Edited by S. Olives Canals and S. S. Taylor. New York, Intercontinental Book & Publishing Co., Ltd., 1963. xv, 998p.

Who's who information, with sub-entry headings (date of birth; marriage; education; career; awards; publications; membership; address) in bold type. General Franco: ¾ col.; Damaso Alonso: 2½ cols. (1 col. of writings). 'Directory of organizations, associations and institutes', by categories, p. 929-98.

Portugal

92 (469) (03)
Quem é alguém (Who's who in Portugal). Dicionário biográfico das personalidades em destaque do nosso tempo, 1947-. Lisbon, Portugália Editora, [1947]-.

The 6th ed. (1955. 674p.) contained some 3,000 entries, which vary in length from 3 or 4 to about 35 lines. Writers' major works are listed.

Russia

92 (47) (03)
Russkiĭ biograficheskiĭ slovar'. Izd. Imp. Russkago Istoricheskago Obshchestva. St. Petersburg, "Kadima", 1896-1918. 25v. (Reprinted New York, 1962-63. £280.)

The largest and most important of the Russian biographical dictionaries; published by the Russian Imperial Historical Society. Biographies of *c.* 40,000 persons who died before 1893. Many lengthy signed articles with bibliographies.

I. M. Kaufman's *Russkie biograficheskie i biobibliograficheskie slovari* (New ed. Moscow, Gos. Izd. Kul't. Lit., 1955) is a list of Russian biographical and bio-bibliographical dictionaries up to 1954.

U.S.S.R.

92 (47) (03)
LEWYTZKYJ, B., and **MÜLLER, K. Sowjetische Kurzbiographien.** Hannover, Verlag für Literatur und Zeitgeschehen, 1964. 343p. (Schriftenreihe des Forschungsinstitut der Friedrich-Ebert-Stiftung).

About 2,500 short biographies of leading party and government officials and leading figures in non-governmental bodies. Part 1 is a directory, with names under Republics and organisations; part 2 gives biographies, A-Z ('Personalia, Titel und Ämter'). 'A. N. Kossygin': ½ col. Dates given for all appointments. German transliteration of surnames; some misprints. Appendix updates to February 1964. No explanatory list of abbreviations and acronyms occurring in text. Reviewed in *College and research libraries,* v. 26, no. 4, July 1965, p. 332-3.
A separate volume for notables in science and cultural activities is in preparation.

92 (47) (03)
OSTEUROPA INSTITUT, Munich. **5,000 Sowjetköpfe.** Gliederung und Gesicht eines Führungkollektivs. Unter Mitwirkung von Otto Böss und Günter Schäfer. Hrsg. von Hans Koch. Cologne,

Deutsche Industrieverlags-GmbH, 1959. xiv, 862p.

The biographical dictionary proper (718p.) is preceded by lists (142p.) of members of the U.S.S.R. Academy of Sciences and similar bodies, of ministers and other officials. The dictionary is a Soviet *Who's who* necessarily based on secondary sources—the information available in Soviet periodicals and newspapers. The review in *LLU translations bulletin* (v. 2, no. 1, January 1960, p. 42-43) notes that David Oistrakh is included, but not Igor Oistrakh; "L. D. Landau, but not E. M. Lifshits, A. F. Ioffe, but not A. V. Ioffe. Artem I. Mikoyan but not M. I. Gurevich". The I.S.O. system of transliteration is used, so that "Krushchev" will be found under "Chruscev".

92 (472) (03)
UNITED STATES. DEPARTMENT OF COMMERCE. Office of Technical Translations. Joint Publications Research Service. **Biographical information from the Bol'shaya Sovetskaya Entsiklopediya, Yezhegodnik** (Great Soviet Encyclopedia. Annual). Washington, 1963. [ii], 162p. $3.

A translation of 'Biographic notes' from the 1962 annual (p. 585-623), comprising *c.* 650 short notices.

The best current tool for Russian and Soviet Russian biography for readers of Russian is probably the *Bol'shaya sovetskaya entsiklopediya* (2nd ed. 1949-58) and its annuals (1957-).

92 (47) (03)
Who's who in the U.S.S.R., 1965-66: a biographical dictionary, containing about 5,000 biographies of prominent personalities in the U.S.S.R. Edited by A. Lebed, H. E. Schulz and S. S. Taylor. New York & London, Scarecrow Press, 1966. 1189p. $25; £10 10s.

First published 1962, covering 1961-62.
The 1965-66 ed. comprises *c.* 5,300 potted biographies of Soviet political and military leaders, scientists, artists, athletes and other public figures, listing notable speeches, theses and publications, if any (titles usually in Russian only). Krushchev: no entry; Brezhnev: 1 col. Appendix 3: Deceased since the 2nd ed. went to press. Poorish printing. Prepared by the Institute for the Study of the U.S.S.R., Munich, which published a *Biographic directory of the U.S.S.R.* in 1958 (ix, 782p.).
A 3rd ed. is to be published in 1968.
The Institute for the Study of the U.S.S.R. publishes a monthly *Porträts der UdSSR Prominenz* (1960-. Mimeographed. ea. 25c.; $15 p.a.). English translation began in 1965. The service covers *c.* 165 biographies p.a.

Baltic States
92 (474) (03):016
BALYS, J. P. "**Baltic encyclopedias and biographical dictionaries**". In *The Quarterly journal of the Library of Congress,* v. 22, no. 3, July 1965, p. 270-3.

Notes on 26 encyclopaedias and biographical dictionaries concerned with Lithuania, Latvia and Estonia.

Finland
92 (480) (03)
Kuka kukin on (Aikalaiskirja). Who's who in Finland: henkilotietoja nykypolven suomalaisista, 1960. Helsinki, Otava, 1960. 1,098p.

About 5,000 entries, covering Finnish contemporaries; supplementary biographies, p. 1081-4. Obituary, p. 1085-98. Entries vary in length from 2½ lines to 1 column (*eg..,* U.K. Kekkonen: ⅔ column). In Finnish only.

A Finnish *Who's who* in Swedish is *Vem och vad? Biografisk handbok, 1957* (Helsingfors, Schildt, 1957. 656p.), first published 1920. This contains some 2,300 biographies. Obituary, p. 639-51; abbreviations, p. 652-6.

Norway
92 (481):016
ANDRESEN, H. Norsk biografisk oppslags litteratur; katalog utarb. for Norsk Slektshistorisk Forening. [Oslo], Cammermeyer, [1945]. 219p.

A bibliography of Norwegian biographical sources, prepared for the Norwegian Genealogical Society. 3,409 items, systematically arranged, with place and subject index.

92 (481) (03)
Hvem er hvem? 9. utg., utgitt av Bjørn Steenstrup. Oslo, Aschehoug, 1964. 685p. N.kr.160.

First published 1912.
The Norwegian *Who's who.* The 9th ed. contains *c.* 4,000 biographies, and an obituary list.

92 (481) (03)
Norsk biografisk leksikon. Oslo, Aschehoug, 1923-. v. 1-.

v. 1-15 (1923-66): A-SØRBRØDEN.
Includes Norwegian men and women—both living and dead—from the earliest times. Well-documented entries. The work is produced by the editorial board with the collaboration of outside contributors. A useful feature is the provision of outline family trees when several members of a family have articles devoted to them.

H. Andresen's *Norsk biografisk oppslags-litteratur* (Oslo, Cammermeyer, [1945]. 218p.) is a systematically arranged bibliography of Norwegian biographical sources, with locality and subject index.

On Scandinavian biographical dictionaries, see *Nordisk tidskrift för bok- och biblioteksväsen,* v. 42, no. 1, 1955, p. 1-11.

Sweden
92 (485) (03)
Svenska män och kvinnor: biografisk uppslagsbok. Stockholm, Bonnier, 1942-55. 8v. ports.

A biographical dictionary of Swedish men and women, including living persons. Articles are usually signed (with initials). The portraits are numerous, averaging one or two per page. Many cross-references but no bibliographies, although writers' works are given.

A useful substitute for *Svenskt biografiskt lexikon* (*q.v.*), though less scholarly, pending completion of the latter.

92 (485) (03)

Svenskt biografiskt lexikon. Under red. av Erik Grill. Stockholm, Bonnier, 1918-. v. 1-.

V. 1-16 (1918-66): A-GEHLIN.

Includes prominent Swedish men and women from the earliest times and also those associated with the country for a long time. V. 1-10 included living persons, but these were excluded from v. 11 onwards.

To date, about 3,300 entries have been published. Signed, well-documented articles, some written by the editorial staff responsible for the work, others by independent experts. The work is under the editorial supervision of Person-historiska Instituet (the Institute of Biography), Stockholm, but is printed by Albert Bonniers Forlag at their own expense.

92 (485) (03)

Vem är det? Svensk biografisk handbok, 1967. Redaktör Sten Lagerström. Stockholm, Norstedt, 1966. xv, 1069p.

First published 1912.
The Swedish *Who's who*, containing 9,400 short, factual biographies. Goes up to 1st July 1966. Obituary, 1958-1966. Neatly produced; sanserif type. Many abbreviations.

Denmark

92 (489):016

ERICHSEN, B., and KRARUP, A. Dansk personalhistorisk bibliografi. Systematisk fortegnelse over bidrag til Danmarks personalhistorie (i tilslutning til Bibliotheca Danica). Copenhagen, Gads, 1917. 806p.

Danish biography index of periodical articles as well as books.
The same authors' *Dansk historisk bibliografi* has as v. 3, *Personalhistorie* (see at 948.9:016).

92 (489) (03)

Dansk biografisk leksikon. Grundlagt af C. F. Bricka, redigeret af P. Engelstoft under medvirkning af S. Dahl. Copenhagen, Schultz, 1933-44. v. 1-26; Supplement, v. 27. 1944.

A revised and enlarged edition of *Dansk biografisk leksikon,* udg. af. C. F. Bricka (1887-1905. 19v.).
Lengthy and well-documented articles are signed by the contributors. Includes living persons.

92 (489) (03)

Kraks blå bog, 1965: 7220 nulevende danske mænd og kvinders i evnedsløb. Copenhagen, Krak, [1965]. 1359p.

First published 1910. Annual.
The 1965 ed. contains the usual *Who's who* information on 7,220 living Danish men and women, with separate paragraphs under each entry for 1. Family; 2. Posts; 3. Career. Includes a list of publications, where appropriate. List of abbreviations; list of those covered in the 1964 v.

who had since died. The 1959 v. carried an index to entries in v. 1-49, 1910-58.

Netherlands

92 (492) (03)

Nieuw Nederlandsch biografisch woordenboek. Onder redactie van P. C. Molhuysen, Dr. P. J. Blok, Dr. L. Knapper, Fr. K. H. Kossmann. Leiden, Sijthoff, 1911-37. 10v.

Each volume is a complete A-Z sequence and contains lengthy authoritative articles. Index references are to columns, not pages. Each volume contains a cumulative index to the work at that stage and v. 10 has an index to the complete work.

92 (492) (03)

Who's who in the Netherlands, 1962/1963: a biographical dictionary containing about 4,000 biographies of prominent personalities from and in the Netherlands. Edited by S. S. Taylor and M. Spruytenburg. New York, Intercontinental Book & Publishing Co., Ltd., 1962. 987p.

The usual *Who's who* information, with headings for sub-entries (birth; parentage; education; career; publications; recreations; membership; address; telephone number) in bold, for easy reference. Appended: 'Directory of organizations, institutes, associations and enterprises' (p. 835-987).

92 (492) (03)

Wie is dat? 1956. Biografische gegevens van Nederlanders die een vooraanstaande plaats in het maatschappelijk leven innemen met vermelding van adressen. [Dutchmen who occupy a leading place in the social life of the country, with a record of their addresses.] 6. uitg. The Hague, Nijhoff, 1956. 703p.

First published 1931.
Entries compiled from information supplied by the biographees give full name, profession, date and place of birth, education, career, publications, address. Predominance of professional persons; few women or nobility and gentry.

Belgium

92 (493):016

DHONDT, J., and VERVAECK, S. Instruments biographiques pour l'histoire contemporaine de la Belgique. 2. éd. Louvain, Nauwelaerts, 1964. 88p. (Centre Interuniversitaire d'Histoire Contemporaine. Cahiers, 13).

A survey for sources for Belgian biography. 5 chapters, on universal and Belgian biographical dictionaries and collections, sources confined to a particular period, province, region or town, and biographical sources of a professional nature (*e.g.,* clergy, artists). 294 numbered items, the more important being annotated. Indexes of places, persons and catchwords.

92 (493) (03)

ACADÉMIE ROYALE DES SCIENCES, DES LETTRES ET DES BEAUX-ARTS DE BELGIQUE. Biographie nationale. Brussels, Bruylant-Christophe (subsequently Bruylant), 1866-. v. 1-.

v. 1-28 (1866-1944).

v. 29-33: Supplément 1-5 (1957-66).

The Belgian *D.N.B.* Long, signed obituaries by specialists (*e.g.,* Cardinal Mercier, by A. Simon: 21½ columns, including 1 column of bibliography (sources; works on); Henri Pirenne, by F. L. Ganshof: 52⅔ columns, with sub-headings, and 1 column of bibliography). Each of the supplementary volumes has a separate A-Z sequence and list of contributors.

Supplemented by obituary notices in the *Annuaire de l'Académie Royale.* The Academy also produces a valuable *Index biographique des membres, correspondants et associés . . . de 1769 à 1963* (2. éd. Brussels, Palais des Académies, 1964. 299p.), with numerous 4-5 line entries and references to notices in the *Annuaire, Bulletin beaux-arts,* etc. Entry-words for living persons are in bold.

92 (493) (03)

Who's who in Belgium and Grand Duchy of Luxembourg: a biographical dictionary containing about 7,000 biographies of prominent people in and of Belgium and the Grand Duchy of Luxembourg. 2nd ed., edited by F. Michielsen and S. S. Taylor. [New York], Intercontinental Book & Publishing Co., Ltd., 1962. xxiii, 1343p. $20.

First published 1959.

The usual *Who's who* information, with headings for sub-entries (birth; marriage; education; career; awards; membership; address; telephone numbers) in bold, for easy reference. Appended: 'Directory of organizations, institutes, associations and enterprises' (p. 1181-1341).

Switzerland

92 (494) (03)

Schweizer biographisches Archiv. Redaktion, W. Keller. Zurich, EPI, Verlag Internationaler Publikationen (v. 1-4); H. Börsigs Erben (v. 5-6), 1952-58. 6v. ports.

Short, factual biographies of people prominent in the public life of Switzerland. Each volume has a separate A-Z sequence. The entries, which are based on a questionnaire, are in the native language of the biographee. Most of the entries have an illustration of the biographee and these appear in a separate section at the back of each volume. V. 6 has biographical entries on p. 9-129, plus 384 portraits on p. 133-228.

Apart from its own index, v. 6 has a cumulative index to biographies and portraits in all 6v.

The *Historisch-biographisches Lexikon der Schweiz. Dictionnaire historique et biographique de la Suisse* (Neuchâtel, 1921-34. 7 v. and 2 supplements) contains many signed biographical articles, with bibliographies and illustrations. A lengthy section, 'Personengeschichte', is included in H. Barth's *Bibliographie der Schweizergeschichte* (see at 949.4:016).

92 (494) (03)

Who's who in Switzerland, including the Principality of Liechtenstein, 1966-1967: a biographical dictionary containing about 3,900 biographies of prominent people in and of Switzerland (includ-

ing the Principality of Liechtenstein). [6th ed.] Geneva, Nagel, [1966]. 696p. 1955. xiv, 620p.

First published 1952; 5th ed., for 1964-1965 (1964).

Who's who information (personal; education; career; publications; honours; membership of societies, etc.; address) on outstanding Swiss citizens at home and abroad. Appended classified list of public organizations, societies, etc. arranged under the following headings: Culture; Religion; State and Community; Trade, Finance and Industry.

Greece

92 (495) (03)

Poios einai poios, eis tēn Hellada: biographiko lexiko. Athens, Ekloges, 1958. 407p.

A who's who in Greece, in Greek. About 1,500 entries. Exact dates, not merely years, are given for appointments, etc. An obituary for the period 1st January-15th November 1958 follows.

Hellēnikon Who's who (Athens, 1962. 576p.; 2,500 entries) has been noted.

Mega Hellēnikon biographikon lexikon, begun in Athens, 1958, "promises to some extent to be the Greek equivalent to the great national biographies" (*The Library quarterly,* v. 32, no. 4, October 1962, p. 319). 4v. had been published by 1962.

Yugoslavia

92 (497.1) (03)

Ko je ko u Jugoslaviji: biografski podaci o jugoslovenskim savremenicima. Belgrade, Sedona Sile, 1957. 810p.

"Who's who in Yugoslavia: biographical notes on present-day Yugoslavs." The first *Who's who* for Yugoslavia since 1928. Nearly 6,000 entries. Entries vary considerably in length, but are generally short and factual; anti-Titoists are omitted. Reviewed in *International affairs,* v. 34, no. 4, October 1958, p. 540.

Arab World

92 (5/6=927) (03)

Who's who in the Arab world, 1965-1966. Beirut, Publitec Editions, [1966?]. 319p. 189s. (2nd ed. 1967-1968. £12).

1st ed. Possibly to be annual.

About 1,500 entries for personalities in the U.A.R., Syria, Iraq, Jordan, Saudi Arabia, Kuwait, Bahrain and Qatar. Separate section for each country.

Asia

92 (5) (03)

The Asia who's who. Hong Kong, Pan-Asia Newspaper Alliance, 1957-. Annual. (3rd ed. [1960?]. xii, 939p. 90s.)

First published 1957.

The 3rd ed. has *c.* 5,000 concise biographies, arranged A-Z under country. 19 countries in the main section, Afghanistan to Vietnam. 'China' is represented by the Taiwan régime. The four Communist countries—the People's Republic of China, North Korea, North Vietnam and Outer

Mongolia—are relegated to the appendix. Chinese, Japanese, Korean and Vietnamese names appear in both English and native forms.

92 (5) (03)
BEALE, T. W. An Oriental biographical dictionary, founded on material collected by the late T. W. Beale. A new ed., rev. and enl., by H. G. Keene. London, W. H Allan, 1894. viii, 434p. (Reprinted New York, Kraus Reprint, 1965. 126s.).

More than 5,000 entries. Omits Anglo-Indians (for whom see *D.N.B.*) and Chinese. Name in Arabic, etc., characters follow transliterated form. Entries vary in length from 2 words to 1 column ('Alamgir I (Aurangzib)': nearly 1 col.). Numerous cross-references. Gives lists of works and members of dynasties.

Middle East
92 (5—015) (03)
Who's who in the U.A.R. and the Near East . . . 24th ed., edited by J. E. Blattner. Cairo, ["Who's Who in the U.A.R. and the Near East"], 1959. 664p. ports.

No subsequent annual issues, apparently. Title varies. The 21st ed., for 1955, has the title *Who's who in Egypt and the Near East.*
Coverage: United Arab Republic, the Sudan, Iran, Libya, Cyprus, the Lebanon, Jordan, Iraq, Saudi Arabia, India, Pakistan, Ceylon, Indonesia, Ethiopia and Aden. Directory and general information (p. 19-228) precedes the biographical section (p. 229-664), in English or French. Many entries are slight (*e.g.*, 1½ lines, giving only name, description, address and telephone number). Portraits are small and poorly reproduced.

China
92 (51):016
WU, Wên-Chin. Leaders of twentieth-century China: an annotated bibliography of selected Chinese biographical works in the Hoover Library. Stanford, Cal., Stanford Univ. Press, 1956. vii, 106p. (Hoover Institute and Library Bibliographical series, 4).

About 500 items, covering material published up to 1954. Sections: 1. General collective biographies—2. Biographies of political figures—3. Biographies of military figures—4. Biographies of intellectuals—5. Biographies of industrialists and business men—6. Biographies of overseas Chinese—7. Directories and school yearbooks—8. Serials. Appendix: Publisher's list. Chinese books only, with authors and titles in Chinese characters as well as in romanized forms. Titles are not translated, but the descriptive annotations meet this deficiency. Hoover Library pressmarks are given.

92 (51) (03)
BOORMAN, H. L., with **HOWARD, A. C.,** ed. **Biographical dictionary of Republican China.** New York, Columbia Univ. Press, 1967-. v. 1-.

v. 1: AI-CH'Ü. 1967. $20.
v. 2: DALAI-MA. 1968. 180s.
V. 1 contains 150 essay-biographies on persons

living and dead who were prominent during the Republican period 1911-49. It includes entries for Chang Kai-shek (p. 319-38; 1 page of bibliography) and Chou En-lai. 'General bibliographical reference works' (p. 481-2). Most of the personages will be drawn from political, military, economic and academic spheres. Chinese characters follow romanized form of entry name To be completed in 5v. "Unfortunately, specific reference data are not supplied for the entries; until they appear in the fifth and final volume, the reader will be forced to reserve judgement on the validity of sources used" (*The China quarterly,* no. 32, October/December 1967, p. 171). Well produced.

A. W. Hummel's *Eminent Chinese of the Ch'ing period* (Library of Congress. Washington, Government Printing Office, 1943-44. 2v.) covers the period 1644-1912. Signed contributions; references to sources.
H. A. Giles' *A Chinese biographical dictionary* (London, Quaritch, 1898. xii, 1022p. Reprinted New York, Paragon Book Gallery, 1964. 2v.) deals with the period from earliest times up to the 1911-12 Chinese revolution. 4,000 entries. It lacks references to sources. A supplementary index, by J. V. Gillis and Yü Ping-Yüeh, appeared in 1936 (Peiping).

92 (51) (03)
PERLEBERG, M. Who's who in modern China, from the beginning of the Chinese Republic [*i.e.,* 1912] to the end of 1953. Over two thousand detailed biographies of the most important men who took part in the great struggle for China, including detailed histories of the political parties, government organizations, a glossary of new terms used in contemporary Chinese, together with a double index in Chinese and English and two charts. Hong Kong, Ye Olde Printerie, Ltd., 1954. xii, 429p.

Aims to provide, without taint of propaganda, unbiased information about the present and past rulers of Nationalist and Communist China. 2,019 entries, including deceased persons, *e.g.,* Sun Yat-sen. Sections follow on the Nationalist Government (p. 268-288) and the Central People's Government (p. 290-334).

92 (51) (03)
Who's who in China. Shanghai, The China Weekly Review, [1950]. 6th ed. 263p. illus.

Work originally began in 1940, was interrupted by the war, and recommenced in 1946. Difficulties of publication made the material largely out-dated but it was decided to publish this edition, as it was thought that the work was a "worthwhile historical record and that foreign scholars and students of China will find much of the material of interest and use".
Largely, but not entirely, superseded by Perleberg, M. *Who's who in modern China* (*q.v.*).

Communist China
91 (510) (03)
BARTKE, W. Chinaköpfe. Kurzbiographien der Partei- und Staatsfunktionäre der Volksrepublik

China. Hanover, Verlag für Literatur und Zeitgeschehen, 1966. viii, 454p. (Schriftenreihe des Forschungsinstituts der Friedrich-Ebert-Stiftung B. Historisch-politisch Schriften.)

Three parts: 1. Personalia, Titel und Ämter (c. 500 entries; p. 1-353)—2. Die Organization der Chinesichen Führungsapparates—3. Die personelle Besetzung des Partei- und Staatsapparates und der Organisationen. Names in Chinese characters and romanized form. Details include posts held and career. Bibliography of sources, 453-4. Up to 1949 the Biographical service of the Union Research Institute was used; chief sources, post-1949: *People's daily* (Peking) and New China News Agency. Reviewed in *International affairs,* v. 44, no. 1, January 1968, p. 176.

92 (510) (03)
Who's who in Communist China. Hong Kong, Union Research Institute, 1966. [1], v, 754p. 135s.

1,200 biographical sketches of professors, artists and writers, youth leaders and the like. Titles of Chinese works in both English and Chinese characters. Chou En-lai: 10½ cols. Includes biographies of persons who died recently, because of their posthumous influence on events. But no member of the Chinese Communist Party who died before 1949 is included. Major sources stated, p. iii. 9 appendices, including lists of members of Committees, Councils, etc.

Hong Kong
92 (512.317) (03)
Hong Kong who's who: an almanac of personalities and their history, 1958-1960. Rola Luzzatto, editor & publisher; Rennie Remedios, assistant editor. Hong Kong, the Editor, 1959. 288, [19]p.

"Short biographical information on the most prominent citizens of Hong Kong, both men and women . . . Government Officials, Consuls, Financial and Industrial Leaders, Writers, Artists, Social Workers and the Clergy" (*A final word from the editor*). About 9,000 biographies, entries varying in length from 4 lines to 1 page. Names are given in Chinese characters, if appropriate. Index of biographies; classified index (8 categories).

Japan
92 (52):016
KOKUSAI BUNKA SHINKOKAI. K.B.S. bibliography of standard reference books for Japanese studies, with descriptive notes. v. 3. **History and biography.** Tokyo, Univ. of Tokyo Press, 1963-. pt. 1-. ea. pt. 20s.

Only 2 pts. of v. 3, to be in 3 pts., have so far been published.

92 (52) (03)
The Japan biographical encyclopedia & who's who . . . Tokyo, Rengo Press, Japan Biographical Branch Department. Irregular. (3rd rev. ed.: 1964-65. 1963. $30.).

First published 1958.
The 1964-65 edition contains biographies of 15,200 prominent Japanese, past and present.

Names are given in Japanese characters as well as in romanized forms. Appendices: Name index; Chronology; Glossary (miscellaneous data: table of emperors, era names, etc.); Foreign service; Cabinets of Japan; Transition (obituary; additional information).

Noted: Japanese Politics Economy Research Institute. *Who's who of contemporary Japan, 1963* (Tokyo, Fiji Book Co. (distributors), 1963. 466p. $20).

India
92 (540):016
JAIN, S. K., *comp. and ed.* **A bibliography of Indian autobiographies,** including journals, diaries, reminiscences and letters, etc. Regina, Saskatchewan, Regina Campus Library, Saskatchewan Univ., 1965. 39p.

265 items, arranged under autobiographees, A-Z. Aims to record only important books in the case of particularly famous men (*e.g.,* Gandhi, Nehru, Tagore); "otherwise I have tried to note every Indian biography" (*Introduction*). Includes biographies of personalities born in India but who lived abroad.

92 (54) (03)
BUCKLAND, C. E. Dictionary of Indian biography. London, Sonnenschein, 1906. xii, 494p.

"The main facts of the lives of about 2,600 persons—English, Indian, foreign, men or women, living or dead—who have been conspicuous in the history of India, or distinguished in the administration of the country, in one or other of its branches, or have contributed to its welfare service and advancement by their studies and literary products, or have gained some special notoriety." The entries date from 1750 "when the English power in India was being established". It is still useful for the period covered and is not entirely superseded by any other work.
Bibliography is appended, together with a list of the reference works consulted by the compiler of the *Dictionary.*

92 (540) (03)
"The Times of India" directory and year book, including Who's who. Bombay & London, "The Times of India" offices (Bennett, Coleman & Co.), 1915-. tables, map. Annual. (1965-66. [1966]. 80s.)

The *Who's who* section in the 1965/66 annual (p. 1176-1270) comprises c. 1,300 short, factual biographies (Mrs. Gandhi: 1¼ cols.). States publications, films, etc. produced but without dates.

Noted: *Men of education in India* (*distinguished Who's who*) (New Delhi, Premier Publications, 1965. 344p.) and *Who's who in India* (New Delhi, Guide Publications, 1967. 182p.).

Pakistan
92 (549)
Biographical encyclopedia of Pakistan. [Lahore], Biographical Research Institute, Pakistan, for International Publishers (Pakistan), Ltd., 1965. [xii], 936, xix, 547, xv p. ports., map. £10 10s.

First published 1955.

Biographical data on important figures in present-day Pakistan. The main part has entries for *c.* 3,000 personalities in 12 sections (*e.g.:* Founders and pioneers—Government and the Services—Public and social life—Law and justice . . . Land and farming. The diplomatic corps). The supplement, for Lahore, Sargodha, Khairpur and Hyderabad divisions, has 7 sections. Index to each part. One or more small and poorly reproduced portraits per entry.

Turkey

92 (560) (03)

Who's who in Turkey, 1960; compiled and edited by Afsin Oktay. Ankara, Cyclopedic Publications, [1959]. vii, 192p.

First published 1958.
Nearly 1,500 biographies of "men and women who have been making Turkish history and who are likely to make more of it" (*Preface* [to 1st ed.]). Gives usual *Who's who* information, including telephone number. Menderes: $\frac{2}{3}$ column; Zorlu: 1 column.
Supplemented by *Current events and biographies* (Monthly. July 1960-. v. 1, no. 1-.).

Osman Nebioglu's *Who's who in Turkey.* (U.S. Department of Commerce, Office of Technical Services, Joint Publications Research Service, 1963. 1067p. Mimeographed. (JPRS 20,490). $11.70) has *c.* 5,000 entries. It notes works by writers, plus dates.

Lebanon

92 (569.3) (03)

Who's who in Lebanon, 1963-64. Dictionnaire biographique des principales personnalités du Liban et des étrangers notables y résidant. Beirut, Editions Publitec, 1964. 465p.

To be biennial.
Half of this 1st edition gives the text of decrees and is a directory of government officials, firms and other organisations. About 1,700 biographies, p. 257-465, with headings for sub-entries (date of birth, family, education, career, publications, honours, membership, etc.) in bold.

Israel

92 (569.4) (03)

Who's who: Israel, 1966-67. [12th ed.] Tel-Aviv, Mamut, 1966. 45p., 692 cols., p. 693-958. illus.

Previous titles: *Palestine and Transjordan Who's who,* 1945; *Palestine personalia,* 1947; *Who's who in the State of Palestine,* 1949 and 1952. Present title, 1955-. Part 1, Personalia (containing *c.* 2,500 biographies); part 2, Public bodies and enterprises (municipalities; political parties; institutions . . .). Preceding pt. 1 is a directory of officials ('Knesset and Government departments').

An *Entsiklopedyah la-halutse ha-yishuv u-bonav* (Tel Aviv, Hotsa'ah, Sifriyat Rishonism (10v., completed in 1959) has been noted). It has "biographies of some 3,000 persons who were active in the propagation of the Zionist idea and in the founding of the Republic of Israel" (*Library of Congress Information bulletin,* v. 18, no. 37, 14th September 1959, p. 562).

Malaysia

92 (595) (03)

The Who's who in Malaysia, 1965 (KDN 1334). Edited and published by J. Victor Morais. Petaling Jaya, Malaysia, Solai Press, [1965]. lxxvii, 490p. ports.

Previous ed. 1963.
More than 3,500 entries, mostly with portraits. The *Who's who* proper, with its supplement (p. 1-476) is preceded by 4 sections,—Who's who in the Malayan, Sarawak, Singapore and Sabah governments. Notes on the territories; members of the Senate and House of Representatives; Representatives abroad; Diplomatic Corps; National organisations.

Africa

92 (6) (03)

SEGAL, R., and others. Political Africa: a who's who of personalities and parties. London, Stevens, 1961. ix, [1], 475p. map. 50s.

'Personalities' (A-Z), p. 1-288; 'Parties' (under countries or areas, A-Z, from Algeria to Zanzibar), p. 291-475. Cross-references from each country to the relevant names in the 'Personalities' section. The biographical data are often the only information easily available for many of the 400 African personalities included. Lengthy entries (*e.g.,* Kenyatta—$3\frac{1}{2}$ columns). Segal tries to assess the importance of the personalities concerned. The 'Parties' section describes more than 100 parties, their history, aims, etc., with cross-references to entries in the "Personalities" section. No index or bibliographies. The volume presents Africa at the end of March 1961, with later details included at page-proof stage, and does not claim to be objective.
Updated but not superseded by S. Taylor's *The new Africans* (q.v.).

R. Segal's *African profiles* (Rev. ed. Harmondsworth, Middlesex, Penguin Books, 1963. 406p. map. 7s. 6d.), first published 1962, is based on the accounts in *Political Africa,* but re-grouped under areas. Name and subject index.

Rolf Italiaander's *The new leaders of Africa* (Englewood Cliffs, N.J., Prentice-Hall, 1961. xiv, 306p. illus.) contains 28 biographies.

92 (6) (03)

TAYLOR, S., ed. The new Africans: a guide to the contemporary history of emergent Africa and its leaders; written by fifty correspondents of Reuters News Agency. London. Hamlyn, 1967. 504p. illus., ports., maps.

Covers 33 countries, A-Z. The section 'Congo Democratic Republic (Kinshasa)', p. 75-107, includes 24 potted biographies (p. 92-107), with 13 portraits. Data up to 1966. About 600 biographies in all. Small but clear photolitho portraits. Well produced.

Sudan

92 (624) (03)

HILL, R. A biographical dictionary of the Sudan. The 2nd ed. of *A biographical dictionary of the Anglo-Egyptian Sudan* (1951). London, Cass, 1967. xvi, 409p. 90*s*.

The 1st ed. contained "over 1,900 short notices of people who have died before 1948 and who have contributed, each after his fashion, to the story of the Sudan; . . . not a dictionary of national biography in the accepted sense [but] a record of the human contribution to Sudan history" (*Preface to the first edition*). The 2nd ed. seems to be a reprint of the original text, plus an addendum: 'Notes and corrections', p. 395-409, and a new introduction. Not confined to persons who lived in the Sudan. 'Glossary of ranks, titles and other designations', p. ix-xvi.

The Directory of the Republic of the Sudan, 1963. 5th ed. (London, Diplomatic Press) includes a 'Who's who in the Sudan'.

Nigeria

92 (669) (03)

Who's who in Nigeria: a biographical dictionary. Lagos, Nigeria, Nigerian Printing & Publishing Co., Ltd., 1956. 278p. illus.

" . . . the first publication of its kind which has been attempted in Nigeria on a country-wide scale. It includes the biographies of more than 1,500 prominent people in the day to day life of the country."
Later editions have not been traced.

East Africa

92 (67) (03)

Who's who in East Africa, 1965-66. Nairobi, Marco Publishers (Africa), Ltd., [1966]. [vi], 154, 103, 123, 9p. ports. 80*s*.

Previous ed., 1963/64.
About 5,000 biographical sketches of personalities (African, Asian and European) in Kenya, Tanzania and Uganda. Numerous portraits (*c.* 2 per page). More than 70% of the entries in the 1963-64 ed. have been revised and *c.* 1,000 new entries added.

Material for a dictionary of East African biography has been collected by the librarian of the Royal Commonwealth Society. It comprises data on and references to more than 5,000 persons connected with East Africa prior to 1900.

Congo

92 (675)

INSTITUT ROYAL COLONIALE BELGE. Biographie coloniale belge. Brussels, the Institute (subsequently the Academie Royale des Sciences Coloniales), 1948-. v. 1-. ports.

V. 1-5 (1948-58) each have a separate A-Z sequence of biographies of deceased persons. Not confined to Belgians connected with the Congo (*e.g.,* Leopold II) but includes entries for Livingstone, Stanley and others. More than 2,000 biographies in all, v. 4-5 each carrying cumulative biographee and author indexes to previous volumes. All entries are signed, dated and documented (normally with a bibliography; sometimes with references as well). Corrigenda and addenda to earlier volumes appear in v. 4-5.

92 (675) (03)

ARTIGUE, J. Qui sont les leaders congolais? 2. éd. Brussels, Éditions Europe-Afrique, 1961. 377p.

First published 1960.
Brief biographies of more than 800 Congolese personalities,—senators, deputies, ministers, provincial representatives, clergy, chieftains, leading syndicalists, officials and journalists. A few single-line entries. Appendices include a list of sources used, acronyms and addenda.

Southern Africa

92 (68) (03)

ROSENTHAL, E., *comp.* **Southern African dictionary of national biography.** London, Warne, 1966. xxxix, 430p. 65*s*.

About 2,500 biographies of deceased persons of note. Covers the Republic of South Africa, S.W. Africa, Rhodesia, Malawi, Mozambique, Swaziland, Botswana and Lesotho. Gives brief assessments of achievements and place in history. Smuts: 2¾p. Prefatory classified list (p. vi-xxxix) of biographees under categories, A-Z (*e.g.,* Social work; Literature; Medicine; Lawyers; Legislators; Sport).

The same compiler has produced an *Alphabetical index to the biographical notices in South Africa, 1892-1928* (Johannesburg, [Public Library], 1963. 114p.).

92 (68) (03)

Who's who of Rhodesia, Mauritius, Central and East Africa, 1966 (supplement to the *Who's who of Southern Africa*). Johannesburg, Wootton & Gibson, Pty., Ltd., 1966. 207p. ports. 30*s*.

First published 1961 as *Who's who of the Federation of Rhodesia and Nyasaland, Central and East Africa, incorporating* The Central and East African who's who (first published 1953). Now incorporated in *Who's who of Southern Africa,* but also available separately.
About 1,500 concise biographies, plus many portraits. Obituary; list of abbreviations.

92 (68) (03)

Who's who of Southern Africa, including Mauritius, and incorporating "South African who's who" and "Central African who's who". 50th ed. Johannesburg, Combined Publishers, 1966. viii, 1237p. 120*s*.

Annual. First published 1907. Title changed from *South African who's who* in 1959 (43rd ed.).
South African biographies, p. 85-958 (*c.* 7,000); South West African section biographies, p. 963-1015; Rhodesian, Central and East African section, p. 1019-1194 (available separately at 60*s*.); Mauritius, p. 1201-23. Obituary; list of abbreviations. Official directory precedes.

South Africa

92 (680):016

USHPOL, R. A select bibliography of South African autobiographies. [Cape Town], Univ. of Cape Town, School of Librarianship, 1958. iv, [2], 48p. Mimeographed.

143 numbered and annotated items, arranged alphabetically by authors. Annotations often give chapter headings or leading phases of the writer's career. Occupations and vocations index; p. 36-40; index of titles, p. 4-48.

Noted: Olivier, Le R. *Versamelde suid-Afrikaanse biografies: 'n bibliographie* (Cape Town, Univ. van Kaapstad, Skool van Biblioteekwese, 1963. 71p. R.125).

Mauritius

92 (698.2) (03)

Dictionnaire de biographie mauricienne. (Dictionary of Mauritian biography.) Directeur de publication, A. Toussaint. Port Louis, Société de l'Histoire de l'Île Maurice, 1941-. v. 1-.

v. 1. (*i.e.,* pts. 1-16). 1941-45. 502p. A-Z index. 693 entries.
v. 2. (*i.e.,* pts. 17-25). 1945-52.
v. 3. (*i.e.,* pts. 26-). 1964-.

The work is "Planned . . . to include about fifteen hundred notices, dealing with all those who, identified with Mauritius, whether by birth, adoption or temporary connection, played a part worth recording in the history of Mauritius." No living persons. Entries in French or English (depending on the country of origin of the person concerned) are signed and documented and indicate where portraits of the person are to be found.

V. 2 contains a provisional list of persons it is intended to include in future parts of the dictionary. Cumulative indexes to the whole work are published irregularly. Pt. 27 (January 1965) contains 25 biographies (p. 793-824), signed and with bibliography and iconography appended.

Canada

(*See also 92 (73) (031).*)

92 (71):016

MATTHEWS, W., *comp.* **Canadian diaries and autobiographies.** Berkeley, Univ. of California Press, 1950. [iii], 136p.

Covers both British and French Canada and includes published and unpublished documents.

92 (71) (03)

Biographies canadiennes-françaises. 20. éd., edited by J. A. Fortin. Montreal, the Editor, 1965. 1347, [1]p. ports.

First published 1920.
Nearly 1,000 entries,—twice as many as its predecessors. In no particular order, except that Governor-Generals, Lieutenant-Generals, Prime Ministers and Ministers come first. Includes deceased (*e.g.,* Sir François-Charles Langelier). Information conveniently given in short paragraphs. A good portrait accompanies each biography. Index of names.

Vedettes (Who's who en française) (4 éd. Montreal, La Société Nouvelle de Publicité, 1962) is considered a more important biographical source for prominent French Canadians. First published 1952.

92 (71) (03)

The Canadian who's who, with which is incorporated "Canadian men and women of the time": a biographical dictionary of notable living men and women. v. 10: 1964-1966. Toronto, Trans-Canada Press, 1966. viii, 1237p. $37.

First published 1910. Annual, with half-yearly supplement.
More than 8,000 biographies. Concise, factual entries. Claims to be the only *Who's who* in Canada in which no one has paid for inclusion. Biographees are categorised in an appended section (p. 1198-1228), ranging from Accountancy to Transportation and traffic. Abbreviations listed. The semi-annual biographical service (1) adds entries received too late for inclusion in the main work; (2) corrects information contained in the original entry.

92 (71) (03)

Dictionary of Canadian biography. Dictionnaire biographique du Canada. Edited by G. W. Brown, M. Trudel and A. Vachon. Toronto, Univ. of Toronto Press, 1966-. v. 1-.

v. 1: *1000 to 1700.* 1966. 100s. Planned in 20v., spread over 20 years. The product of very extensive historical research and unique cooperation between French and English Canadians. Each volume covers a specific period of history, with biographies arranged A-Z in each. (V. 2 is to cover 1701-40). V. 1 is self-contained and lists 117 contributors and contains 594 articles ranging from 200 to *c.* 10,000 words each in length. 65 of the biographies are of Indians. The biography of Jean Talon, the longest, runs to *c.* 13,000 words; ⅓rd col. of bibliography. Includes many obscure figures. Index to v. 1 includes names mentioned only in the biographies of others, plus references to the biographees (main article in bold type). General bibliography, p. 685-71. Preceding the biographies proper are several valuable introductory articles on early Canada (*e.g.,* 'The Indians of North-eastern North America'; 'Glossary of Indian tribal names') and an extensive bibliography of manuscripts and printed sources. An excellent introduction to early Canadian history. Well produced, on good white paper.
There is a parallel French edition, *Dictionnaire biographique du Canada.*

92 (71) (03)

ROBERTS, C. G. D., and **TUNNELL, A. L.,** *ed.* **A standard dictionary of Canadian biography:** the Canadian who was who, 1875-1937. Toronto, Trans-Canada Press, 1934-38. 2v.

v. 1: *1875-1933.* 1934. 562p. (409 entries).
v. 2: *1875-1937.* 1938. xvii, 478p.
Eminent Canadians who died between 1875-1937. Signed, documented entries; average length: 1-2,000 words. The length of the entry "does not always indicate the importance of the subject but has been determined by the amount of useful, available, authentic source-

material". In the main the biographies are Canadian, but also included are some who were born in Canada but achieved distinction elsewhere and others who were born abroad yet significantly affected Canadian life. In these cases emphasis has been placed on the Canadian phase of their life. Entries for authors list their most important works.

V. 2 contains index to entries in v. 1.

Although further volumes were projected none has yet been published.

92 (71) (03)
WALLACE, W. S. The Macmillan dictionary of Canadian biography. 3rd ed., rev. and enl. New York & London, Macmillan, 1963, [ix], 822p. 90s.

First published 1926.

Modelled on *D.N.B.* More than 5,000 concise entries; no living persons. Ranges from the earliest times to those who died before 1961. The most comprehensive Canadian biographical dictionary. Principle of selection: ". . . to include only those names which seemed most likely to be the object of enquiry, [*e.g.*] all those who have held important offices of state." In this edition an attempt has been made to extend the usefulness of the *Dictionary* as a guide to Canadian authors. Entries are documented (*e.g.,* John Galt: 1 page; lists chief works and 5 items on Galt). List of sources, p. vii-viii. The compiler is Librarian Emeritus of the University of Toronto.

92 (71) (03)
Who's who in Canada, 1964-65: an illustrated biographical record of men and women of the time. 52nd year of issue. Associate editors, Hugh Fraser and Herbert E. Barnett. Toronto, International Press, Ltd., [1964]. [46] 1631p. ports. $27.50.

Who's who information on *c.* 3,000 personalities; 1 or 2 portraits per page. Preceding the biographies: Abbreviations—Obituary—Index of biographies.

Mexico
92 (72) (03)
GARCÍA RIVAS, H. 150 biografías de mexicanos ilustres. 2. ed. Mexico, Editorial Diana, 1964. 262p.

First published 1964.

Arranged by periods: Mexico indigena (6 biographies)—La conquista (16)—La colonización (10)—El virreinato (27)—La independencia (28)—Mexico independante (22)—La reforma (18)—El Porfiriato (11)—La revolución (12). Prominent figures are allotted about 2 pages (*e.g.,* Porfirio Díaz, p. 235-5; Quetzalcóate, p. 14-15; Agustín de Iturbide, p. 157-8). Index of names.

Caribbean
92 (729) (03)
The Caribbean who, what, why: Jamaica, Trinidad and Tobago, Barbados, British Guiana, British Honduras, Windward Islands, Leeward Islands. 2nd ed. [Kingston?, Jamaica], L. S. Smith, 1965. 844p.

First published for 1955-56, as *British Caribbean, who, what, why.*

The biography section is divided by categories (*e.g.,* banking).

92 (729) (03)
Personalities: Caribbean, Bahamas, Bermudas; compiled and edited by O. L. Levy. Kingston, Jamaica, Personalities, Ltd., 1966. 835p. ports.

More than 5,000 biographies (Bustamante: 1¼ cols.), arranged A-Z in 10 areas; Bahamas, Barbados, British Honduras, Guyana, Jamaica (p. 221-551), Cayman, Turks & Caicos Is., Netherlands Antilles, Puerto Rico, Trinidad & Tobago, Windward & Leeward Is. Appended: 'Modes of addressing'; Abbreviations.

Cuba
92 (729.1)
PERAZA SARAUSA, F. Diccionário biográfico cubano. Gainesville, Florida, 1965-. v. 1-. Mimeographed. (Biblioteca del bibliotecario). ea. $5.

v. 1-12 (1951-66).

V. 1-8: 4,667 entries, many of them 1-2 lines (names, etc.; position). V. 7 has addenda. 'Personalidades urbanas, 1959' and a general index. V. 8: 'Personalidades cubanas (Cuba en el exilio)'. V. 12 has 180 biographies and a general index to v. 1-12 (p. 62-100).

Jamaica
92 (729.2) (03)
Who's who in Jamaica, 1963: an illustrated biographical record of outstanding people in Jamaica. Kingston, Jamaica, Who's who (Jamaica), Ltd., [1964?]. 430p. ports. (1966 ed. 1967. 424p.)

Biographical data on *c.* 3,000 Jamaicans and other persons connected with the island. Some small portraits. Obituary; abbreviations.

U.S.A.
92 (73):016
KAPLAN, L., *and others.* **Bibliography of American autobiographies.** Madison, Univ. of Wisconsin Press, 1961. xiii, 372p. $6.

Lists 6,377 autobiographies published before 1945. Like *British autobiographies,* compiled by W. Matthews (1955; at 92 (410):016), is arranged alphabetically by authors, anonymous works appearing under the first word of the title. Subject index of biographees. Excludes diaries, for which see *American diaries,* compiled by W. Matthews (1945; see below).

92 (73):016
KLINE, J., *comp.* **Biographical sources for the United States.** Washington, Library of Congress, 1961. v, 58p. 40c.

An annotated list of 163 collective biographies "dated principally from 1945 to 1960" [and] "presented as a guide to current biographical information about living Americans, especially those who have made notable contributions to the arts and professions, to business and corporate enterprise, and to military and civilian affairs" (*Preface*). Three main sections: General; Regions and States (with sub-divisions); Special and professional groups (alphabetically by groups—Aeronautics, Anthropologists, Armed Forces, Artists, Athletes, Authors, etc.). Index of authors, anonymous titles, and subjects.

92 (73):016

MATTHEWS, W., *comp.* **American diaries:** an annotated bibliography of American diaries written prior to the year 1861. Berkeley, Univ. of California Press, 1945. xiv, 383p.

Covers . . . "the English-speaking world of America". Diaries are arranged chronologically by date of first entry, covering the years 1629 to 1860. Manuscript diaries have been excluded.

92 (73) (03)

Appleton's Cyclopaedia of American biography; edited by J. G. Wilson and J. Fiske. New York, Appleton, 1888-1900. 7v. illus.

v. 1-6: A-Z, supplement, A-Z; analytical index. 1888-1889.

v. 7: Supplement, A-Z; pen-names, nick-names, soubriquets; list of deaths in v. 1-6; analytical index. 1900.

The aim was to include all noteworthy persons of the American continent by providing entries for "above 15,000 prominent native and adopted citizens of the United States, including living persons, from the earliest settlement of the country." Also included are about 1,000 men of foreign birth closely identified with American history.

V. 7 includes nearly 2,000 additional persons who had become prominent since the publication of the main work. Long articles, signed; for scholarship and authority the corresponding entries in the *D.A.B.* (*q.v.*) have superseded Appleton which, however, contains many useful articles for persons not dealt with elsewhere.

Illustrated, many facsimiles of signatures, with occasional full-length portraits.

92 (73) (03)

The Concise dictionary of American biography, edited by J. G. E. Hopkins. New York, Scribner, 1964. London, Oxford Univ. Press, 1965. viii, 1273p. $22.50; 150s.

Abridges the 14,870 biographies in the original *D.A.B.* and is thus limited to eminent Americans who died before 1941, plus suppts., on a reduction scale of 1:14. Lengths of entries vary from 2 line-identifications to several pages (George Washington: 2p.), in an attempt to preserve the flavour of the original biography in the longer articles (*e.g.,* interpretation of character and estimation of influence on American society). Occasional revisions of articles. Praised for admirable editing (*Library journal,* v. 91, no. 8, 15th April 1965).

92 (73) (03)

Dictionary of American biography. Under the auspices of the American Council of Learned Societies. New York, Scribner; London, Oxford Univ. Press, 1928-37. 20v. and index; Supplement

1: edited by H. E. Starr. 22v. Reprinted (new format), New York, Scribner; London, Oxford Univ. Press, 1943. 21v.; 1946. llv. (on thin paper).

—— **Supplement** 1; edited by H. E. Starr. 1944. Numbered v. 21.

—— **Supplement** 2. R. L. Schuyler, editor; E. T. James, assistant editor. 1958. viii, 745p. Numbered v. 22.

V. 1-3 edited by A. Johnson; v. 4-7, edited by A. Johnson and D. Malone; v. 8-20, edited by D. Malone.

In the main work there are 13,633 articles by 2,243 contributors who are listed in the volume to which they contribute. Signed articles (by initials); bibliographies.

The need had long been felt for an authoritative national biography of comparable standard with the *Dictionary of national biography,* but no organization in the country had the resources necessary to carry out the task. The idea was given a further impetus in 1919 with the founding of the American Council of Learned Societies. After some preliminary discussions dating from 1920, a committee was formed in 1922 and in 1924 the American Council urged the publication of a work with the following recommendations:

"that the title should be the *Dictionary of American biography;* that the character of compilation should be kept up as nearly as possible to the level maintained in the *Dictionary of national biography;* that the articles should be based as largely as possible on original sources; should be the product of fresh work; should eschew rhetoric, sentiment, and coloring matter generally, yet include careful characterization; should be free from the influence of partisan, local or family prepossessions, striving to the utmost for impartial and objective treatment; should study compression and terseness; and should be written as largely as possible by the persons most specifically qualified, though the minor notices should be prepared 'in the office'. It was agreed that references to sources of information should be appended to the articles; that living persons should be excluded; that in the main compilation should be confined to American citizens, or, in the colonial period, to those having a corresponding position."

The *Dictionary* includes "in general only those . . . who have made some significant contribution to American life in all its manifold aspects". The length of an article has not been determined solely by the relative importance of the person, but also by the amount of available authentic material, by the nature of his career and by the completeness of biographies already published.

It is narrower in scope than *Appleton's Cyclopaedia* (*q.v.*), which includes Canada and Latin America, and not so inclusive as the *National cyclopaedia of American biography* (*q.v.*) which, being less selective, has many lesser known personalities, but the *D.A.B.*'s articles are more scholarly and authoritative.

The *Index* consists of 6 indexes:

1. Alphabetical list of biographees, with contributors' names.

2. Alphabetical list of contributors, with biographies written by them.
3. Birth place of biographees, arranged by (a) state, (b) foreign countries.
4. Schools and colleges attended by biographee.
5. Occupations of biographees.
6. Topics: an analytical index which includes "distinctive topics about which there are definite statements and discussions".

Compiled by the publishers and not by the authors of the *Dictionary*.

Supplement 1 [to December 31st, 1935] "includes, in addition to memoirs of persons whose death occurred too late for inclusion in alphabetical order, a certain number of memoirs which failed to be included in the earlier volumes. . . . Contains no biographies of persons whose deaths occurred later than 31st December, 1935". 652 memoirs by 358 contributors.

Supplement 2 contains 585 biographies of persons who died during the five-year period 1936-1940 inclusive—the latest date at which, in the editor's judgement, a considered opinion may be given. 451 contributors.

92 (73) (03)
Directory of American scholars: a biographical directory. Edited by the Jaques Cattell Press. 4th ed. New York, Bowker, 1963-4. 4v. ea. $15.

First published 1942 (lv.).
v. 1: *History.* 1963.
v. 2: *English, speech, and drama.* 1963.
v. 3: *Foreign languages—modern and classical, linguistics, philology.* 1963.
v. 4: *Philosophy, religion and law.* 1964.

Published with the co-operation of the American Council of Learned Societies.

Each volume has *c.* 5,000 brief entries. V. 1 has biographies of 6,700 college and university teachers and individuals prominent as editors, authors, researchers, etc. Because of overlapping disciplines, the 4 volumes are linked by cross-references. *American men of science,* also edited by Jaques Cattell (10th ed. 1960-62. 5v.), is linked with this *Directory*.

92 (73) (03)
International celebrity register. U.S. ed. Editor-in-chief, C. Amory. New York, Celebrity Register, Ltd., 1959. v, 864p. ports. $26.

About 2,000 biographies, each with a portrait and written in journalistic vein. 'Celebrity' does not mean, for example, accomplishment in the sense of true or lasting worth—rather it often means simply accomplishment in the sense of popular, or highly publicized, temporary success" (from the 'Four hundred' to the 'Four thousand'). Mainly U.S., but embraces international personalities. Statements by biographees are frequently included.

92 (73) (03)
The National cyclopaedia of American biography, being the history of the United States as illustrated in the lives of the founders, builders and defenders of the republic, and of men and women who are doing the work and moulding the thought of the present time. New York, White, 1892

"Aim of the work [which began in 1888] is to exemplify and perpetuate, in the broadest sense, American civilization through its chief personalities [by providing] biographical sketches of all persons prominently connected with the history of the nation." Includes "rulers, statesmen, soldiers, persons noteworthy in the church, at the bar, in literature and science, and the professions [and] also those who have contributed to the industrial and commercial progress and growth of the country".

A special feature has been to provide entries for young persons not normally included in a work of this kind who are not yet prominent in the life of the nation but for whom it is anticipated information will be sought in the future.

The work has a complicated structure:

(1) *National cyclopaedia.* v. 1-35, 1892-1935. (In progress). Lengthy entries, illustrations (some full page) with facsimile signatures and occasionally a sketch of the biographee's home. Covers living and dead persons, eminent and not so eminent. For each volume entries are grouped according to the work and career of the person, and there is a general alphabetical index. No bibliographies.

(2) *Current series volumes.* 1930-. (In progress). Style and arrangement of entries similar to the main work.

(3) *Index volume.* 1892-. (In progress). A loose-leaf cumulative volume containing analytical author and topic indexes to the complete *Cyclopaedia,* i.e., main work and current series volumes. Pt. 1, v. 1-30; pt. 2, v. 31-39; and pt. 3, current series volumes (1930 to date), are revised as new volumes appear and require cumulative indexing.

An additional work, indispensable as a classified index to the *Cyclopaedia,* is:

(4) *White's Conspectus of American biography: a tabulated record of American history and biography.* 2nd rev. and enl. ed. New York, White, 1937. 455p.

92 (73) (03)
UNITED STATES. DEPARTMENT OF STATE. The biographic register, revised as of June 30, 1966. [Washington, Government Printing Office], 1966. 602p. (U.S. Department of State. Department and Foreign Service series 126). $3.50.

See entry at 354 (73) (092).

92 (73) (03)
Who knows—and what—among authorities, experts and the specially informed; with a roster of collected general authorities and a location index "keying" 12,000 selected knowers to 35,000 subjects chosen for entry in it. Rev. ed. Chicago, Ill., Marquis, [1954]. 907p. [with gaps].

First published 1949.

A companion volume to the same publisher's *Who's who in America.* The 12,000 American specialists are listed alphabetically. The indexes, etc. appear on yellow tinted paper: 'The roster of selected subject authorities' (subjects A-Z, with specialists' names, p. 831-50); 'Selected information sources' (p. 851-59); and 'The "Keying" locator index' (p. 870-907). Biographical data covers specialization, date of birth, education, honours, career, publications, present position, association memberships, and address.

92 (73) (03)

Who was who in America, v. 1: 1897-1942. A companion volume to "Who's who in America". Chicago, Ill., Marquis, 1943 (3rd printing, 1950). x, 1369p.

Contains 27,458 entries removed from v. 1-21 of *Who's who in America* because of the death of the biographees. Covers personalities from the Civil War onwards.

——, **v. 2: 1943-1950.** Chicago, Ill., Marquis, 1950. 654p. $10.50.

Contains 8,500 entries removed from v. 22-26 of *Who's who in America.*

——, **v. 3: [1949-1961].** Chicago, Ill., Marquis—Who's who, 1960. 959p. $20.

Contains 12,828 entries, withdrawn from v. 26-31 of *Who's who in America,* pronunciation of surnames being given as necessary (*e.g.,* Dulles). Addendum (p. 952-9) notes "deaths or dates of deaths or other revisions received after the main body of the volume had gone to press".

The detailed entries in the 3v. are largely auto-biographical, "having been prepared from information originally supplied by the biographees, approved personally—and frequently revised—before publication in a Who's who during the subject's lifetime".

92 (73) (03)

Who was who in America. Historical volume, 1607-1896. Chicago, Ill., Marquis Who's who, 1963. 670p. $26.

Precedes the 3v. of *Who was who in America* for 1897-1942, 1943-1950, 1951-62.

Biographies of 13,300 individuals, both of the U.S. and other countries, "who have made contributions to, or whose activity was in some way related to the history of the United States". Includes sketches of some persons who died before 1607 and many others not listed in *Who was who in America.* Appendices contain chronological lists of the principal officers of the Federal government, of first governors, etc.

92 (73) (03)

Who's who in America: a biographical dictionary of notable living men and women. Chicago, Ill., Marquis, 1899-. v. 1-. Biennial. (v. 34: 1966-1967. 1966. $32.50.)

V. 34: 1966-67 has *c.* 60.000 entries.

An authoritative dictionary of contemporary biography, including "the best known men and women in all lines of useful and reputable achievement—names much in the public eye, not locally but generally". An asterisk following an entry indicates that the published data could not be confirmed.

The biographees fall into two groups:
(1) those selected because of their special prominence or distinction in certain fields;
(2) those included arbitrarily on account of their official position or public standing.

Includes not only American citizens but all persons of any nationality likely to be of interest to Americans.

Supplemented by:
Who was who in America (*q.v.*). 2v. For all persons deleted because of death.
Current biographical reference service. Monthly.
Indices and necrology (including 'Non-current listings', and vocational-geographical index, the latter covering v. 26 onwards only). 1952-58. 3v.
Ten-year cumulative index, 1939-1949. Cumulative index for 1951-1955.

Not all entries are carried forward, and in these instances a reference is given to the volume in which they last appeared.

The Monthly supplement and international who's who: current biographical reference service began in December 1939 and ceased in August 1959.

Marquis also publishes regional biographical dictionaries: *Who's who in the East (and Eastern Canada): a biographical dictionary of noteworthy men and women of the Middle Atlantic and Northeastern States and Eastern Canada* (10th ed. 1965. $27); *Who's who in the Midwest (and Central Canada)* . . . (10th ed. 1966. $27); *Who's who in the South and Southwest* . . . (9th ed. 1965. $26); and *Who's who in the West (and Western Canada)* . . . (10th ed. 1966. $27).

92 (73) (03)

Who's who in colored America: an illustrated biographical directory of notable living persons of African descent in the United States. 7th ed., edited by G. J. Fleming and C. E. Burckel, New York, C. E. Burckel & Associates, 1950. xvi, 648p.

About 3,000 entries; based on questionnaire to biographees.

1st ed. (1927) stated that eligibility for inclusion was "based on achievement as recorded by public opinion or substantiated by actual existence of work accomplished".

Biographees, who mostly reside in the United States (although some are working or serving abroad), are of two kinds:

(1) "those whose level of position automatically includes them, *e.g.,* judges, religious leaders, etc.
(2) those whose personal achievement and learning, unique experience or association, public following, activity in the public interest, or leadership position, make them the kind of persons about whom others may have important reason to know more."

Appendix A: Geographical distribution of biographees (in 41 states and other territories); Appendix B: Vocational distribution.

92 (73) (03)

Who's who of American women (and women of Canada): a biographical dictionary of notable living women of the United States of America and other countries. 4th ed. (1966-1967). Chicago, Ill., Marquis Co., 1965. 1298p.

First published 1958; 3rd ed.: 1964-1965 (1963).

The 4th ed. has 22,200 entries, of which 9,900 appear for the first time. Data cover name; status (marital, etc., as indicated by the biographee herself); occupation; education; birthplace and date of birth; parentage; education; honours;

BIOGRAPHY

family; career; association, board and club memberships; politics or religion; publications; address. Names asterisked also appear in the current *Who's who in America.* "Like all invitational biographical dictionaries, this suffers somewhat from the inflated egos of a certain percentage of the entrants' submitting their own information" (*Library journal,* v. 88, no. 20, 15th November 1963, p. 4356). Vocational percentage of entries: Educators (college and secondary): 12.4%; Club, Civic/Religious leaders: 11.2%; Business Executives: 8.6%; Librarians/Curators: 6.4%; etc. Includes Joan Sutherland but not Margot Fonteyn among the non-Americans.

According to *Library of Congress Information bulletin* (v. 18, no. 16, 20th April 1959, p. 226), a separate vocational-geographical index is to be published.

Latin America

92 (8=6) (03)

Who's who in Latin America: a biographical dictionary of notable living men and women of Latin America; edited by R. Hilton. 3rd ed. California, Stanford Univ. Press; Chicago, Marquis, 1945-51. 7v.

First published 1935 (1,000 entries); 2nd ed. 1940 (1,500 entries).

Previously in one sequence, the 3rd ed. (8,000 entries) is arranged on a regional basis, which diminishes ease of reference if the country of the biographee is not known. Includes entries for 20 republics; "qualification for admission . . . is residence, not nationality".

pt. 1: *Mexico.* 1946. (2nd printing, 1947). xiii, 130p.
pt. 2: *Central America* (*i.e.,* Costa Rica, El Salvador, Guatemala, Honduras, Nicaragua and Panama). 1945 (2nd printing, 1947). xiii, 130p.
pt. 3: *Colombia, Ecuador and Venezuela.* 1951. xvii, 149p.
pt. 4: *Bolivia, Chile, Peru.* 1947. xviii, 209p.
pt. 5: *Argentine, Paraguay and Uruguay.* 1950. xvii, 258p.
pt. 6: *Brazil.* 1948. xxii, 269p.
pt. 7: *Cuba, Dominican Republic and Haiti.* 1951. xvii, 77p.

Brazil

92 (81) (03)

COUTINHO, A. Brasil e brasileiros de hoje. Rio de Janeiro, Editorial Sul Americana, S.A., 1961. 2v. ([viii], 727, 650p.).

Who's who information on *c.* 7,000 living Brazilians. Lists authors' works. Janio de Silva Quadros: 12 lines only.

92 (81) (03)

Quem é quem no Brasil: biografias contemporaneas. v. 4, 1955. São Paulo, Sociedade Brasileira de Expansão Comercial, Ltda., 1955. 740, xxxviii p. ports.

First published 1948.
The Brazilian *Who's who.* Entries are classified into categories.

92 (81) (03)

Who's who in Brazilian economic life: an annual biographical dictionary of men and women representing a vital force in Brazil's drive for economic development. São Paulo, Sociedade Brasileira de Publicações Culturais e Econômicas, [1967]. 672, 39, 40p. ports.

About 900 biographies, mostly with portraits. *Who's who* type of information, position and address being given first. Includes an obituary and a list of leading banks, holding companies and industrial firms in Brazil.

Argentina

92 (82) (03)

Quién es quién en la Argentina: biografias contemporaneas. 8. ed. Buenos Aires, Kraft, 1963. xvi, 1050p.

First published 1939.
Who's who information on *c.* 7,000 Argentines. Lists authors' works, with dates. Appended directory of business firms and institutions. Small sanserif type; heavily abbreviated.

Chile

92 (83) (03)

Diccionario biográfico de Chile. 12. ed. (1962-1964). Santiago, Empresa Periodística Chile, [1966?]. lii, 1545p.

First published 1936-37. Biennial (irregular).
Who's who information; short, factual entries; type set solid. Addenda, p. vii-lii.

Peru

92 (85) (03)

Pequeño diccionario histórico-biográfico del Perú. Suscintas biografias de personajes ilustres. Lima, Field Ediciones, 1961. 175, [2]p. $20.

Pocket-sized dictionary of *c.* 500 deceased personalities, *e.g.,* Bolívar; Sucre; Pachacutec Inca. Length of entry: *c.* 25-150 words. Bibliography.

Noted: Paz-Soldán, J. P., ed. *Diccionario biográfico de peruanos contemporaneos* (Lima, Gil, 1917. 439p.).

Colombia

92 (861) (03)

OSPINA, J. Diccionario biográfico y bibliográfico de Colombia. Bogotá, Editorial de Cromos (v. 2-3, Editoria Aquila), 1927-39. 3v. ports.

Covers the period from the Spanish conquest 1536) to the present day. The 1927 v. has 89 contributors. Some articles are signed. Length of articles varies from 2 lines to 1 page. Lists works by writers. Bibliography, p. 10-11. Some portraits,—small and poorly reproduced.

92 (861) (03)

Quién es quién en Colombia. 3. ed. Bogotá, Oliverio Perry s Cia, 1961. 387p. ports.

First published 1944 as *Quién es quién en la Gran Colombia.*

367

About 3,000 entries of the *Who's who* type, usually with small portrait. Arranged under categories, A-Z (Abogados; Artistas; Aviadores; Eclesiasticos; Medicos; Militares; Odontologos; etc.), with A-Z index. Includes list of members of the Government and of Congress, 1962-64.

Venezuela, etc.

92 (86/87) (03)
Quién es quién en Venezuela, Panamá, Ecuador, Colombia. Con datos recopilados hasta el 30 de junio de 1952. Bogotá, Perry, [1952]. liii, 1074p. port.

A *Who's who* of the four republics concerned, in four alphabetical sequences, each with an index. Four separate country lists are also provided of relevant pseudonyms, professions (A-Z under each country) and obituary. The portraits are numerous—2 or 3 per page—but they are small and vary in quality.

British Guiana

92 (881) (03)
Who is who in British Guiana, 1945-1948; edited by C. N. Delgh and V. Roth. 4th ed. Georgetown, Daily Chronicle, 1948. 845p. illus.

First published 1937.
Short, factual entries, with the information presented in tabular form. Upwards of 3,000 entries; 517 illustrations. Data are based on questionnaire submitted to all who were on the register of jurors.
Classified list of professions, trades and occupations of biographees, p. 575-646.

Pacific Area

92 (9) (03)
Pan-Pacific who's who: an international reference work. A biographical encyclopedia of men and women of substantial achievement in the Pan-Pacific area: Alaska, Australia, British Columbia, California, Canal Zone, China, Hawaii, Japan, New Zealand, Oregon, Philippines, Washington. 1940/41 ed., edited by G. F. M. Nellist. Honolulu, Hawaii, Honolulu Star-Bulletin, Ltd. 815p.

The purpose is to make the work "fully representative of men and women of all races and creeds who, in various fields of endeavour, have contributed in some substantial measure to the material and cultural advancement of the Pan-Pacific area". Index to biographees by country (p. 793-815).
The 1940-41 ed. incorporates v. 6 of *Men of Hawaii.*

Philippines

92 (914) (03)
VILLARAEL, H. K. Eminent Filippines. Manila, National Historical Commission, 1965. xxvi, 294p. illus. (National Historical Commission. Publication, 1).

New Zealand

92 (931) (03)
SCHOLEFIELD, G. H., *ed.* **A dictionary of New Zealand biography.** Wellington, New Zealand Department of Internal Affairs, 1940. 2v.

Modelled on the *D.N.B.*, the entries are for persons, not necessarily resident in New Zealand, "who had significance in the history of the Dominion" from roughly 1840 onwards. 95 per cent of the entries are the work of the editor; the others are signed by the contributors. Entries are documented. Short glossary of Maori words. Bibliography, v. 1, p. xviii-xix.
Work was sponsored by the National Historical Committee as an official New Zealand centennial publication.

92 (931) (03)
Who's who in New Zealand. 8th ed., edited by G. C. Petersen. Wellington, A. H. & A. W. Reed, 1964. 305p. 60s. (9th ed. 1968).

First published 1908; 7th ed. 1961. To be published henceforth at three-yearly intervals.
Who's who information on c. 3,000 personalities, p. 55-303. Preceded by official list, list of Governors of New Zealand, general elections, 1960 and 1963, the universities, etc. Obituary (p. 304-5) covers the period since the previous edition.

Australia

92 (94) (03)
ALEXANDER, J. A., *ed.* **Who's who in Australia:** an Australian biographical dictionary and register of titled persons; with which is incorporated Johns's "Notable Australians" 16th ed. Melbourne, Colorgravure Publications (a division of *The Herald*), 1959. 896p.

First published 1906.
Factual and brief entries (occasionally very brief—2 or 3 lines) are compiled "from matter supplied by the subjects". 18,500 biographies, some 2,300 included for the first time.

92 (94) (03)
Australian dictionary of biography. General editor, Douglas Pike. Melbourne, Univ. Press; Cambridge, Univ. Press, 1966-. v. 1-.

v. 1-2: 1788-1850 (A-H; I-Z). 1966-67. ea. 120s.
4v. are planned for 1851-90 and probably 6v. for 1891-1938,—some 6,000 articles in all, by c. 2,000 contributors, plus a 'Biographical register' maintained by the Australian National University (a leading supporter of the whole project) to preserve details of many individuals not selected for entry but worth recording. A general index will follow completion of the three sections. V. 1 contains 500 entries by c. 250 authors; v. 2 brings the total up to 1,116—convicts, administrators, explorers, miners, etc. Admiral Wm. Bligh (of the *Bounty*): 7½ cols., including 6 references (periodical articles, etc.) and 2 references to historical records. V. 2 has nearly 300 contributors. A production of high standard. Reviewed in the *Commonwealth journal*, v. 9, no. 6, December 1966, p. 279-80. "It is the great merit of the *Australian Dictionary of Biography* [unlike the *D.N.B.*] that it offers a genuine cross-section of society" (*Times literary supplement*, no. 3,435, 28th December 1967, p. 1263).

92 (94) (03)
SERLE, P. Dictionary of Australian biography. Sydney, Angus & Robertson, 1949. 2v.

Modelled on the *D.N.B.*, the volumes contain 1,030 biographies of Australians or men [the work includes 42 women] who were closely connected with Australia, who died before the end of 1942 . . . Average length of the biographies is about 640 words. Entries are authoritative, detailed and well-documented. Reviewed in *Historical studies, Australia & New Zealand,* v. 4, no. 16, May 1951, p. 378-81.

92 (94) (03)
Who's who in Australia: an Australian biographical dictionary and register of titled persons; with which is incorporated Johns's "Notable Australians". 18th ed. Melbourne, Colorgravure Publications, [1965]. 951p.

First published 1906.
The 19th ed. has more than 8,500 entries. Appendices: holders of the V.C.; titles, baronetage, knightage in Australia; mode of addressing persons of title and official position; wearing of orders and decorations.

The *National register short list* (Canberra, History Department, Australian National Univ., 1959. [1], 108p. Mimeographed.) is a list of some 4,000 names, arranged alphabetically. Entries give name in full, dates, profession and references. List of sources, including periodical articles, p. 1-3. "The Register has been built up since 1954 from entries in the older biographical dictionaries, from encyclopaedias, directories, newspapers, journals, books and theses as they came to hand. Names covered by Percival Serle's *Dictionary of Australian biography* have not been included" (prefatory note).

Polynesia

92 (96) (03)
Pacific Islands year book and who's who. 9th ed. Sydney, Pacific Publications Pty., Ltd., 1963. 654p. maps, plans.

First published 1932.
156-page section, 'Who's who in the Pacific Islands', with *c.* 1,500 entries, plus addenda (including 'Deceased during compilation').

Tahiti, etc.

92 (962.1) (03)
O'REILLY, P., and **TEISSIER, R. Tahitiens:** répertoire bio-bibliographique de la Polynésie française. Paris, Musée de l'Homme, 1962. xvi, 535p. illus. (Publications de la Société des Océanistes, no. 10). 100F. **Supplément.** 1966. iv, 104p. (Publications . . . , no. 17).

The main work mentions more than 6,000 names in *c.* 700 separate articles, for the period 1765 onwards. Includes list of governors and commandants; table of professions, list of ships, etc. 'Gauguin': p. 164-72, including 2 cols. of bibliography; Queen Pomaré IV: p. 367-73 (including Descendance — Iconographie — Bibliographie).
Companion works by P. O'Reilly: *Calédoniens: répertoire bio-bibliographique de la Nouvelle-Calédonie* (Paris, Musée de l'Homme, 1953. x, 308p. (Publications . . . , no. 3)); *Hébridais: répertoire bio-bibliographique des Nouvelles-Hébrides* (Paris, Musée de l'Homme, 1957. x, 292p. (Publications . . . , no. 6.)).

929 GENEALOGY. HERALDRY

929:016
GATFIELD, G. Guide to printed books and manuscripts relating to English and foreign heraldry and genealogy; being a classified catalogue of works of those branches of literature. London, Mitchell & Hughes, 1892. 646p. (Reprinted New York, Gale Research Co., 1967. $19.50.)

A classified list of more than 17,500 books, periodicals and manuscripts, arranged under such headings as Heraldry, Arms, Crests, Mottoes, Seals, Pedigrees, Royalty [and other social classes], Wills, Sepulchral monuments, Flags, Orders and Family histories, with some subdivisions by country. Index of subjects. This work is valuable for its scope, but is poorly planned.

929:016
NEWCASTLE-UPON-TYNE. CENTRAL PUBLIC LIBRARIES. Catalogue of books and tracts on genealogy and heraldry in the . . . Libraries. Newcastle-upon-Tyne, Doig, 1910. 68p.

Supplements Gatfield up to 1910. Arranged in Dewey order; headings: Families, Registers, Names, Epitaphs, Heraldry, Titles, Orders, Arms, Crests, Seals and Flags.

GENEALOGY

929.1 / .5:016
NEWBERRY LIBRARY, Chicago. **Genealogical index.** Boston, Mass., G. K. Hall, 1960. 4v. $275.

417,000 cards, photolithographically reproduced. Arranged under surnames A-Z. Includes many analytical entries from town and county histories and registers, as well as published family histories.

929.1 / .5 (4 / 9)
Almanach de Gotha: annuaire généalogique, diplomatique et statistique, 1863-1944. Gotha, Perthes, 1763-1944. Annual.

The first sections (in the later editions divided into reigning houses in Europe and elsewhere, mediatized ruling families and other princely lines) are an important source of information on that branch of genealogy.

929.1 / .5 (4 / 9)
The International year-book and statesmen's who's who. London, Burke, Ltd., 1953-. Annual.

Pt. 1 includes a section: Reigning royal families of the world, Europe, Asia and Africa.
Main entry is at 908 (4/9) (058).

929.1/.5 (4/9)
SIRJEAN, G. Encyclopédie généalogique des maisons souveraines du monde. Paris, the Author, 1959-. (v. 12. 1966. 42F.).

V. 1-9. *Lignées souveraines.*
v. 1: *Les Mérovingiens.* 1959.
v. 2: *Les Carolingiens.* 1959.
v. 3: *Les Capétiens directs.* 1959.
v. 4: *Les Valois.* 1960.
v. 5: *Les Bourbons.* 1961.
v. 6: *La IVᵉ maison d'Orléans.* 1961.
v. 7: *Les Bonaparte.* 1961-2. 2 pts.
v. 8: *Les illégitimes.* 1963.
v. 9:
V. 10-. *Branches cadettes.* 1964-.

Genealogical data, particularly on French royal houses. A general volume (1960) includes 6 extensive tables (each 15 columns) covering the leading European royal houses from A.D. 1 to 1960.

929.1/.5 (4/9)
STOKVIS, A. M. H. J. Manuel d'histoire, de généalogie et de chronologie de tous les états du globe depuis les temps les plus reculés jusqu'à nos jours. Leiden, Brill, 1888-93. 3v. (Reprinted Amsterdam, 1966. £38.).

v. 1. *Asie. Afrique. Amérique. Polynésie.* 574, lxxxi p.
v. 2-3. *Les états de l'Europe et leurs colonies.* viii, 548p.; xxix, 967p.
Comprises historical summaries of states, fiefs, etc., with lists of sovereigns and elected rulers, and hundreds of skeletal genealogies.

Europe

929.1/.5 (4)
Genealogisches Handbuch des Adels, bearb. unter Aufsicht der Ausschusses für adelsrechtliche Fragen der deutschen Adelsverbände in Gemeinschaft mit dem Deutschen Adelsarchiv. Glücksburg/Ostsee, subsequently Limburg a.d. Lahn, Starke, 1951-. illus.

Four series:
Fürstliche Häuser, v. 1-7 (1951-64).
Gräfliche Häuser, A, v. 1-4 (1952-62); B, v. 1-2 (1953-60).
Freiherrliche Häuser. A, v. 1-5 (1952-63); B, v. 1-3 (1954-63).
Adelige Häuser. A, v. 1-7 (1953-65); B, v. 1-6 (1954-64).
Covers European royal and princely houses, countly, baronial and noble families respectively. A successor, at least in part, to *Almanach de Gotha,* which ceased publication in 1944. The *Genealogisches Handbuch* does not, however, include the valuable diplomatic section of the *Almanach de Gotha (Library Association record,* v. 54, no. 1, January 1952, p. 24).

929.1/5 (4)
ISENBURG, W. K. P. Stammtafeln zur Geschichte der europäischen Staaten. 2. verb. Aufl., hrsg. van Frank Baron Freytag von Loringhoven. Marburg, Stargardt, 1953-57. 4v.

v. 3-4 have the title *Europäische Stammtafeln . . .*

A valuable source for genealogical tables. V. 4 contains 160 such tables, one per page. The last 7 of these are concerned with British families,—Walpole, Stanhope, Peel, Londonderry, Pitt, Fox and Newcastle. Detailed indexes.

929.1/.5 (4)
PRYCE, F. R. A guide to European genealogies, exclusive of the British Isles; with an historical survey of the principal genealogical writers. 1965. xlvii, 271p. (Library Association thesis).

An index of 11,300 European families contained in 11 major genealogical compilations, from Père Anselme to Prinz von Isenburg (*q.v.*). Gives references from all titles and lists locations of the works indexed, in 196 British libraries. Includes an annotated bibliography of other important compilations.

Great Britain

929.1/.5 (410):016
CAMP, A. J. "Collections and indexes of the Society of Genealogists". *The genealogist's magazine,* v. 13, no. 10, June 1961, p. 311-7.

Describes the "great card index" (about 3 million references), Boyd's Marriage index, the Collection of heraldic illustrations, and Irish wills and pleadings, 1569-1909.

In the same issue of *The genealogist's magazine* (p. 317-9) appears 'Work in progress, 1961', a brief survey of "what work of genealogical importance and interest is being undertaken at the present time, not only in the Society itself but also outside".

929.1/.5 (410):016
HAMILTON-EDWARDS, G. Tracing your British ancestors: a guide to genealogical sources. London, Joseph, 1967. 265p. illus. 30s.

Valuable on the material at the Public Record Office, on the consolidated indexes of wills and administrations to 1857, and on Prerogative Court of Canterbury inventories. Excellent 37-page bibliography, arranged under the section headings,—"probably the best yet to appear in any book" (*Library journal,* v. 92, no. 13, July 1967, p. 2552). Reviewed in *The genealogists' magazine,* v. 15, no. 9, March 1967, p. 335.

Tracing your ancestors, by A. J. Camp (the Director of Research, Society of Genealogists) (London, Foyle, 1964. 78p. 4s.) is an admirably condensed survey of sources, with references to the literature and specimens.

Noted: *Directory for the genealogist and local historian,* edited by M. Pinhorn (London, Phillimore, 1964. [ii], 24p. 5s.).

A basic list of books on British genealogy and heraldry, by P. W. Filby, was due to be published by the American Library Association in 1966.

929.1/.5 (410):016
KAMINKOW, M. J. A new bibliography of British genealogy, with notes. Baltimore, Md., Magna Charta Book Co., 1965. xvii, 170p.

1,783 numbered items, the more important being annotated. 8 parts: 1. General works (bibliography; manuals and introductions; indexes to pedigrees; other indexes; guides, calendars, indexes, etc. to manuscript collections; guides to microfilm holdings; library directories)—2. Periodicals, including newspapers—3. Particular subjects (A-Z, 'Army' to 'Wills')—4. English counties (A-Z)—5. Ireland—6. Scotland—7. Wales—8. Islands (including West Indies). Addenda. Index (authors, series, etc.). "The main aim has been to list books that have not been listed elsewhere, and to indicate where to look for a list of those that have" (*Introduction*). Considered (*The genealogists' magazine*, v. 15, no. 7, September 1966, p. 255-7) "one of the most important genealogical bibliographies published during recent years, and largely replaces H. G. Harrison's *Select bibliography of English genealogy* which, published in 1937, is now considerably out of date". This review also notes errors under pt. 3, 'Navy'.

The same author has more recently compiled *Genealogical manuscripts in British libraries: a descriptive guide* (Baltimore, Md., Magna Charta Book Co., 1967. x, 140p. $7.50).

929.1 / .5 (410):016
MANCHESTER CORPORATION. Public Libraries. **Reference library subject catalogue;** edited by G. E. Haslam. **Section 929: Genealogy.** Manchester, Manchester Public Libraries, 1956-58. 3v.

v. 1: *Pedigrees and family histories.* 1956. 88p. 12s. 6d. (see *Guide*, p. 424).
v. 2: *Parish registers and wills.* 1957. 91p. 17s. 6d. (see *Guide*, p. 424).
v. 3: *Personal and place names; epitaphs; heraldry; flags.* 1958. 87p. 20s.
The 3 volumes contain entries for 1,457, 1,216 and 1,407 items respectively and are in Dewey classified order, with author index and index of places. Items are occasionally given bibliographical notes. If a work comprises several volumes, individual titles or coverage are given. "The emphasis is, rightly on Lancashire and Cheshire, but the collection is national in scope." (F. R. Pryce, in *Library Association record*, v. 5, no. 8, August 1957, p. 287).

929.1 / .5 (410):016
MARSHALL, G. W. The genealogist's guide. Guildford, Billing, 1903. xiii, 880p. (Reprinted New York, Genealogical Publishing Co., 1967. $15.).

An index to printed pedigrees of families having three generations in male line, arranged by family surnames, A-Z. "A remarkably accurate index" (*Library journal*, v. 92, no. 13, July 1967, p. 2552). The preface (p. vii-xiii) cites a number of other works recommended as useful. The reprint has a new introduction by A. J. Camp. Should be supplemented by J. B. Whitmore's *A genealogical guide* (1953) (*q.v.*).

According to M. J. Kaminkow (*A new bibliography of British genealogy* (1965), item 34), R. Sims' *Manual for the genealogist* (2nd ed. Edinburgh, Avery, 1888. xx, 542p.) is still a valuable guide to genealogical sources, "as it contains

more detailed reference to archives than any of the modern works".

G. W. Marshall also compiled *An index to the pedigrees contained in the printed Heralds' visitations . . .* (London, Hardwicke, 1866.) See note at 929.2 (42).

929.1 / .5 (410):016
SOCIETY OF GENEALOGISTS. Genealogists' handbook. 4th ed., edited by P. Spulford and A. J. Camp. London, the Society, 1967. 40p. 3s.

3rd ed., 1961.
A concise guide to sources for the beginner in genealogical research. Primarily designed to assist those working on families of British descent that do not appear in print. Sections: Reference books (p. 6-7)—Somerset House—Census—Parish registers—Nonconformist and other registers—Wills—Professional and educational records—The Society of Genealogists (p. 16-23)—The Public Record Office—Local Record Offices—The British Museum—The College of Arms—Visitations — Heraldry — Scotland — Wales — Ireland — Emigrants and immigrants. No index.

Introducing genealogy, by A. J. Willis (London, Benn, 1961. 95p. 8s. 6d.), a reconstruction and expansion of the author's *Genealogy for beginners* (1955), is on similar lines, but includes a bibliography (p. 77-83) of 58 items.

929.1 / .5 (410):016
SQUIBB, G. D. Visitation pedigrees and the genealogist. London, Phillimore, 1965. 48p. 12s. 6d.

An almost exact reprint of the articles in *The genealogists' magazine*, v. 13, 1960-61, p. 225-36, 266-74.
By the Norfolk Herald Extraordinary, and an expert evaluation. Appended list of pedigrees in printed visitations which purport to be copies or collations of original visitations, and a bibliography of printed lists of disclaimers. Indexes of visitations and names.

929.1 / .5 (410):016
UNITED STATES. LIBRARY OF CONGRESS. American and English genealogies in the Library of Congress. 2nd ed. Compiled under the direction of the Chief of the Catalog Division. Washington, 1919 (reprinted 1967). 1332p. $22.50.

Prelim. ed. 1910.
Lists some 7,000 families. Thousands of cross-references. "Although out of date, is of supreme importance for any genealogical researcher" (*Library journal*, v. 92, no. 5, 15th March 1967, p. 1144).

American and English genealogies in the Library of Congress, compiled by Dr. and Mrs. C. K. Jones (1954), consists of 67 cards, "micro-carded from Library of Congress card copy".

929.1 / .5 (410):016
WHITMORE, J. B., *comp.* **A genealogical guide:** an index to British pedigrees, in continuation of Marshall's "Genealogist's guide (1903)". London, Walford, 1953. 658p.

Previously published in 4v., without final addenda, as v. 99, 101, 102 and 104 of the Harleian Society Publications (1947-53).

"The best general reference guide" (A. D. Roberts, *Introduction to reference books.* 3rd ed., 1956. p. 169).

Ireland

929.1/.5 (415)
FALLEY, M. D. Irish and Scotch-Irish ancestral research: a guide to the genealogical records, methods and sources in Ireland. Evanston, Ill., the Author, 1962. 2v.

v. 1: *Repositories and records.*
v. 2: *Bibliography and family index.*
Deals comprehensively with every phase of record searching in the U.S. and in Ireland (where research is virtually impossible because of the destruction of records in 1922). Includes sources of Irish material not in Ireland. "Easily the best Irish genealogical work ever to have been published" (*Library journal,* v. 88, no. 114, August 1963, p. 2884).

A simple guide to Irish genealogy, compiled by W. Clare. 3rd ed., rev. by R. Clare. Irish Genealogical Research Society (Canterbury, Kent, Achievements, Ltd., 1967. 45p. 15s.) comprises a survey of sources and repositories, 'Irish genealogy: a concise list of references, books on printed records' (p. 31-36) and 'A select bibliography of Irish family history' (p. 36-45).

Genealogical atlas of Ireland, by D. E. Gardner and others (Salt Lake City, Deseret Book Co., 1964.) is compiled from Philips' *Handy atlas of the counties of Ireland* (1885) and Samuel Lewis's *Atlas of the counties of Ireland.* It lists the various records and their whereabouts and has an extensive 40-page gazetteer.

England & Wales

929.1/.5 (42)
GARDNER, D. E., and SMITH, F. Genealogical research in England and Wales. Salt Lake City, Utah, Bookcraft Publishers, 1956-65. 3v. illus., facsims., maps.

V. 1 (1956) has the following chapters: 1. Brief historic and economic background—2. Family sources . . . —3. Cemeteries, burial grounds and churchyards—4. Civil registration of births, marriages and deaths—5. Examples of civil registration—6. The census records of England and Wales—7. How to trace place and family in the 1841 and 1851 census records—8. Street and local addresses in the 1851 census returns—9. The parish and its administration—10. The parish registers—11. Laws relating to the keeping of parish registers—12. How to use parish registers—13. Bishop's transcripts and their value—14. Marriage licences and the intention to marry—15. The Nonconformists, their history and records—16. The Jews in Great Britain and the Commonwealth—17. The Roman Catholics and their records—18. Surnames. Given names. Dialect.
V. 2 (1959): 1. Planning research and recording research results—2. An introduction to probate records—3. Wills, administrations and inventories—4. Probate calendars or indexes and act

books—5. Miscellaneous probate records—6. Examples of the value of probate records—7. Naval and military records. Merchant shipping records. Churches on foreign soil—8. Historical events related to genealogical research—9. The counties of England and Wales.
V. 3 (1965) includes a discussion of apprentice and freeman records; reading early English script; Chancery proceedings, schools and university registers; poll books; feet of fines; inquisitions post-mortems, and manor court rolls.

Gathers together a mass of data, simply explained; many footnote references and facsimiles. Each volume has an analytical index. Chapter 9 of v. 2, "The counties of England" (p. 195-307) is supported by numerous black-and-white maps, but the lettering on these is far from clear in many cases, and there is no gazetteer. "Contains the most up-to-date guide to the whereabouts of the genealogist's main series of records that there is" (*Genealogist's magazine,* v. 13, no. 11, September 1961, p. 345). The same review states that on probate records it is "undoubtedly the best that has ever appeared in print".

A genealogical atlas of England and Wales, compiled from original maps; compiled by D. E. Gardner and others, appeared *c.* 1960 (Salt Lake City, Deseret Book Co. 88p. maps).

929.1/.5 (420)
WAGNER, *Sir* A. R. English genealogy. Oxford, Clarendon Press, 1960. xii, 397p. 55s.

"About two thirds of the book deals with the social and historical background and the subject matter of English genealogy. The rest is concerned with the study, literature and technique of the subject and the nature of the record evidence on which they rest" (*The purpose of this book*). Chapter 10, 'The study and literature of genealogy' (p. 304-58) is particularly valuable. Many footnote references. Index, p. 377-99. "Concerned rather with the peerage and gentry than with the 'common man' " (Willis, A. J. *Introducing genealogy,* p. 82).

929.1/.5 (424)
HIGGS, A. H., and WRIGHT, D., *comp.* **West Midlands genealogy:** a survey of the local genealogical material available in the public libraries of Herefordshire, Shropshire, Staffordshire, Warwickshire and Worcestershire. London, Library Association (West Midlands Branch), 1966. vii, 101, xiii p. 10s.

Arranged by counties (general; individual places). Includes: directories; poll books and electoral registers; local newspapers and periodicals; parish registers; wills; census returns; assessments of rentals, etc.; ecclesiastical records; family papers; pedigrees, etc.; indentures; lists of jurors. Effective and inexpensive; "a model of what can be done" (*The genealogists' magazine,* v. 15, no. 7, September 1966, p. 258-9).

Germany, etc.

929.1/.5 (43\
BIRD, J. "Some sources for German genealogy and heraldry". In *The genealogist's magazine,* v. 13, no. 5, March 196ᴜ, p. 143-4.

Brief annotations.

929.1 / .5 (44)
—— **"Some sources for French genealogy and heraldry"**. In *The genealogist's magazine*, v. 13, no. 8, December 1960, p. 237-8.

Brief annotations.

929.1 / .5 (45)
"Some sources for Italian genealogy". In *The genealogist's magazine*, v. 14, no. 3, September 1962, p. 66-68.

Bibliographical works and general reviews—Genealogy—Heraldry.

929.1 / .5 (492)
"Some sources for Dutch genealogy". In *The genealogist's magazine*, v. 14, no. 1, March 1962, p. 24-27.

U.S.A.

929.1 / .5 (73):016
American genealogical index. F. Rider, editor; . . . published by a committee representing the cooperating subscribing libraries. Middletown, Conn., 1942-52. 48v. ea. $10.

Begun in 1936 as a surname card index (cf. *Preface*). V. 48 completes the first series. Continued by series 2:

American genealogical-biographical index to American genealogical, biographical and local history materials. F. Rider, editor. Middletown, Conn., Godfrey Memorial Library, 1952-. v. 1-. ea. $10.

It is estimated that series 2 (47v. by 1964) will contain references to more than 12 million "untraceable" Americans. Indexes not only genealogies and family histories but "also books of early vital records of towns, churches, sects, etc.," with exact bibliographical citation (White, C. M., and others. *Sources of information in the social sciences*, item B358).

929.1 / .5 (73):016
STEVENSON, N. C. Search and research: the researcher's handbook. A guide to official records and library sources for investigators, historians, genealogists, lawyers and librarians. Rev. ed. Salt Lake City, Utah, Deseret Book Co., 1959. 364p. $2.95.

Preliminary chapters deal with types of material. The sources are very largely American; p. 63-323 are concerned with U.S. states (alphabetically arranged) and Canada; p. 323-46: England and Wales, Scotland, Northern Ireland and Eire; p. 346-56: Foreign libraries and archives; p. 356-60: Heraldry, history, geography and paleography.

The bulk of *The handy book for genealogists: state and county histories, maps, libraries, bibliographies of genealogical works, where to write for records, etc.*, by G. B. Everton and G. Rasmuson (3rd ed. Logan, Utah, Everton, 1957. 1,205p. maps. $2.50.) is concerned with the U.S.A.; other countries (Belgium-Wales), p. 177-205.

929.1 / .5 (73):016
UNITED STATES. LIBRARY OF CONGRESS. American and English genealogies in the Library of Congress. 2nd ed. . . . Washington, 1919 (reprinted 1967). 1332p. $22.50.

See entry at 929.1 / .5 (410):016.

929.1 / .5 (73):016
WHITMORE, W. H., *ed.* **The American genealogist;** being a catalog of family histories. 5th ed. Albany, N.Y., Munsell, 1900. 406p. (Reprinted Detroit, Mich., Gale, 1967. $18.).

First published 1862 as *A handbook of American genealogy*.
A transcript of the title-pages of books and pamphlets on family history published in America, 1771-1900.

Index to American genealogies, and to genealogical material contained in all works such as town histories, county histories, local histories, historical society publications, biographies, historical periodicals and kindred works, alphabetically arranged (5th ed. rev., improved and enl. Albany, N.Y., Munsell, 1900. Supplement, 1908. 352,107p. (Reprinted Detroit, Michigan, Gale Research Co., 1967. $18) is a companion work to Whitmore's *The American genealogist*. It comprises *c*. 57,500 entries.

Family histories

Great Britain

929.2 (410):016
THOMSON, T. R. A catalogue of British family histories. 2nd ed. London, Murray, 1935. 202p.

First published [1928].
An A-Z list of British families of whom histories exist, with details. Though not including "biographies, printed pedigree sheets, reprints from genealogical magazines, peerage claims or works produced in America", it supplements both Marshall's *Genealogist's guide* and Whitmore's *Genealogical guide*.

929.2 (410) (02)
BURKE, A. P. Family records. London, Harrison, 1897. xi, 709p. illus.

Supplementary to Burke's *Landed gentry* and *Peerage*. Covers families without title or estate but distinguished by ancestry or service or fortune. Gives drawings of arms which have official authority.

Scotland

929.2 (411):016
EDINBURGH. PUBLIC LIBRARIES. Scottish family histories: a list of books for consultation in the Reference Library, George IV Bridge. 3rd ed. Edinburgh, Libraries and Museums Committee, 1958. [ii], 68, [i]p.

2nd ed. 1955.
Arranged A-Z by the most popular form of the family name (dukes of Argyle, under Campbell). Author—title—date only. Some analyticals. A list of thirty useful general works on genealogy and kindred subjects is prefixed.

929.2 (411):016

STUART, M. Scottish family history: a guide to works of reference on the history and genealogy of Scottish families. Edinburgh, Oliver & Boyd, 1930. [x], 386p.

The first part, by Sir James Balfour Paul, is entitled "How to write the history of a family"; the second and main part consists of an alphabetical list of families, with references to books, pamphlets, periodical articles and collections. Also included is a section, "Miscellaneous lists of names of persons".

929.2 (411) (02)

ADAM, F. The clans, septs and regiments of the Scottish Highlands. 4th ed., rev. by Sir T. Innes of Learney. Edinburgh, Johnston, 1952. viii, 624p. and 56 p. of pl. illus.

First published 1908.
A standard, well-documented account of the history and structure of the clan system, Highland dress and heraldry, clan septs and dependents. Includes 112 coloured plates of tartans, a list of the clans in order of precedence, and a clan map of Scotland.

929.2 (411) (02)

FERGUSON, J. P. S., *comp.* **Scottish family histories held in Scottish libraries.** Edinburgh, Scottish Central Library, 1960. xii, [1], 194p. 25*s*.

A list of some 2,000 works held in 77 Scottish public, county, university and special libraries. Includes MSS. and typescript papers, pedigrees and genealogical charts. Analytical entries; adequate cross-references. Arranged by family names, A-Z. Appendix (p. 189-94): 'A selection of general works dealing with Scottish family history'.

929.2 (411) (02)

INNES, *Sir* **T.,** of Learney. **The tartans of the clans and families of Scotland.** 7th ed. Edinburgh & London, Johnston & Bacon, 1964. iv, 300p. illus. (some col.). 30*s*.

See entries at 391 (411).

929.2 (411) (02)

STEWART, D. C. The setts of the Scottish tartans, with descriptive and historical notes. London, Oliver & Boyd, 1950. 125p. illus.

Illustrates the setts (or tartan patterns) of 261 different tartans, mainly in diagrammatic colour strips. The standard work on tartan design.

Ireland

929.2 (415)

BURKE, *Sir* **J. B. Burke's Genealogical and heraldic history of the landed gentry of Ireland.** 4th ed., edited by L. G. Pine. London, Burke's Peerage, 1958. xxxvi, 778p. illus.

Previous editions: 1899, 1904, 1912.
The number of families included in the 4th ed. is much smaller than in the 3rd ed., "partly by the natural disappearance of old landed families from the Irish scene, partly by inability to obtain information from many of those to whom we write", as well as from considerations

of the size of the volume (*Preface*). Illustrations of arms, in black and white.

929.2 (415)

HOWARD, J. J., and **CRISP, F. A.,** *ed.* **Visitation of Ireland.** Privately printed, 1897-1917. 6v. illus.

V. 4-6 were edited by F. A. Crisp alone. Pedigrees, with arms, facsimiles of signatures, etc. are shown of prominent Irish families from about 1800.

929.2 (415)

MacLYSAGHT, E. Irish families, their names, arms and origins. Dublin, Hodges Figgis, 1957. 366p. illus., map.

The main sequence is alphabetical by family name, ignoring prefixes "O" and "Mac"; it deals with names and origins. Plates (1-27) illustrate Irish family arms, with descriptive captions. The bibliography is in 2 parts: 1. Irish family histories (p. 316-31): 2. General (including 'Periodicals containing much material for family history'); County, diocesan and local histories, p. 331-6. The author is Chairman of the Irish Manuscripts Commission and was formerly Chief Herald of Ireland.

929.2 (415)

——**More Irish families.** Galway & Dublin, O'Gorman, 1960. 320p. illus., maps. 45*s*.

'More Irish families', p. 17-243, extending the coverage of the basic work. Bibliography (p. 285-90): (a) 'Family histories': supplementary list; (b) 'The Irish abroad'.

929.2 (415)

——**Supplement to 'Irish families'.** Dublin, Helicon Press, 1964. 163p. 40*s*.

The third and last volume. The series includes the vast majority (more than 2,500 in all) of Irish surnames—"not only Gaelic, but also names of non-Irish origins which have become numerous in Ireland" (*Preface*). Pt. 1 (p. 9-155) deals with names not covered in the 2 previous volumes; pt. 2 (p. 157-63) gives additional information on 56 names in those volumes.

929.2 (415)

O'HART, J. Irish pedigrees; or, The origin and stem of the Irish nation. 5th ed. Dublin, Duffy, 1892. 2v.

Family trees are traced down to the 16th century.

England & Wales

929.2 (42)

HOWARD, J. J., and **CRISP, F. A.,** *ed.* **Visitation of England and Wales.** Privately printed, 1893-1921. 21v. illus.

V. 10-21 were edited by F. A. Crisp alone. Pedigrees, with facsimiles of signatures, are shown of prominent English and Welsh families from about 1800.

A supplementary work by the same editors is entitled *Visitation of England and Wales. Notes* (Privately printed, 1896-1821. 21v. illus.); v. 3-21 were edited by F. A. Crisp alone. Pedigrees, reprints of deeds, grants of arms and letters are shown of prominent families from about 1800.

An index to the pedigrees contained in the printed Heralds' visitations, by G. W. Marshall (London, Hardwicke, 1866. viii, 164p.) is arranged under name of family and gives source. A list of the books referred to in the 'Index', p. v-vii.

Germany
929.2 (43):016

Familiengeschichtliche Bibliographie, hrsg. unter dem Schutze der Arbeitsgemeinschaft der deutschen familien- und wappenkundlichen Vereine, 1900-. Leipzig, etc., Zentralstelle für Deutschen Personen und Familiengeschichte, 1928-. v. 1-.

Systematically arranged bibliography of German personal and family history. V. 1 covers 1900-1920. Volumes thereafter sometimes consisted of annual lists bound together. V. 6, pt. 3 consists of an index for 1897-1937.

Family Names
929.2.09

WEEKLEY, E. Surnames. 3rd ed. London, Murray, 1936. xxii, 364p.

First published 1916.
Chapters 13-14 deal with French and German surnames respectively. The bibliography (p. xv-xviii) has the following sections: A: Books on names. B: Sources for medieval names. C: Sources for modern surnames. D: Dictionaries quoted. Detailed index.

Great Britain
929.2.09 (410)

EWEN, C. H. L'E. A history of surnames of the British Isles: a concise account of their origin, evolution, etymology and legal status. London, Kegan Paul, 1931. 508p.

A "short bibliography" (p. 429-36: general; then by languages alphabetically), is followed by an index of names and elements and an "index of matters".

929.2.09 (410)
GUPPY, H. B. Homes of family names in Great Britain. London, Harrison, 1890. lxv, 601p.

A section on "The distribution in alphabetical order of general, common and regional names" is followed by an analysis under the names of English counties arranged alphabetically and under Wales and Monmouthshire. An appendix deals with Scottish family names.

929.2.09 (410)
HARRISON, H. Surnames of the United Kingdom: a concise etymological dictionary. London, Morland Press, 1912-18. 2v.

Form of entry: Surname—Language—Meaning—Etymology—Supporting quotation (if available). The "Forespeech" mentions other works in the field which the author used with advantage. V. 2 has an etymological appendix of the principal foreign names found in British directories.

929.2.09 (410)
REANEY, P. H. A dictionary of British surnames. London, Routledge & Kegan Paul. 1958. lix, 366p.

"All names included are known to survive" (*Preface*). About 10,000 entries (c. 20,000 family names), with adequate cross-references. The useful introduction carries a list of abbreviations (p. li-lix) which serves as a bibliography. Each entry includes variants, sources, and origin of the surname, with derivatives. Excludes first and local names.

B. Cottle's *The Penguin dictionary of surnames* (Harmondsworth, Middlesex, Penguin Books, 1967. 334p. 6s.) has entries for 8,000 first, local, nickname and occupational English, Irish, Scots and Welsh names.

Scotland
929.2.09 (411)

BLACK, G. F. The surnames of Scotland; their origin, meaning and history. New York, New York Public Library, 1946. lxxii, 838p.

Reprinted from the *Bulletin of the New York Public Library*, August 1943-September 1946.
". . . includes a number of early personal names which did not become surnames, but nevertheless have a special interest of their own" (*Preface*). An appendix provides a glossary of obsolete or uncommon Scots words occurring in the dictionary of names. Prefixed is a list of the principal works referred to (p. lix-lxxi), some 350 titles in all.
The standard dictionary of Scottish surnames.

Ireland
929.2.09 (415)

KELLY, P., *ed.* **Irish family names;** with origins, meanings, clans, arms, crests and mottoes; collected from the living Gaelic and from authoritative books, manuscripts and public documents; edited with introduction, notes and Gaelic script. Chicago, Ill., O'Connor & Kelly, 1939. 136p. illus.

929.2.09 (415)
WOULFE, P., *ed.* **Sloinnte gaedheal is gall:** Irish names and surnames; collected and edited with explanatory and historical notes. Dublin, Gill, 1923. xlvi, 696p. (Reprinted 1967. $17.50.).

About 7,000 entries, under Irish (Gaelic) form; index shows English forms. Bibliography and a valuable essay on the Irish name system. Although largely superseded by MacLysaght, "for the average genealogist seeking information on a particular family, Woulfe is still indispensable for most libraries" (*Library journal*, v. 92, no. 22, 15th December 1967, p. 4493).

929.2.09 (415)
MacLYSAGHT, E. A guide to Irish surnames. Dublin, Helicon, Ltd., 1964. 248p. 12s. 6d.; 21s.

About 2,500 surnames, A-Z, with origin, location and page references to MacLysaght's *Irish families,* where the names are more fully discussed. 'Bibliography of Irish family histories', p. 207-47 (*c.* 800 items, based on the list compiled by E. Mack and M. Hewson, printed in *Irish families* (1957), with subsequent additions by E. Mack.

England & Wales
929.2.09 (42)
BARDSLEY, C. W. A dictionary of English and Welsh surnames, with special American instances. London, Frowde, 1901. xvi, 837p.

Completed after the author's death. County locations are given for surnames. Very easy to refer to, despite the compact three-columned page.

929.2.09 (420):016
ROBERTS, R. J. "Bibliography of writings on English place-names and personal names". In *Onoma* (Louvain), v. 8, 1958/59, no. 3, p. 1*-82*.

Section 3. Personal names (items no. 1061-1223: books, periodical articles and contributions to Festschriften). Index of personal names.

Main entry at 914.20:413.11:016.

England
929.2.09 (420)
FRANSSON, G. Middle English surnames of occupation, 1100-1350; with an excursus on toponymical surnames. Lund, Gleerup; London, Williams & Norgate, 1935. 217p. (Lund Studies in English, no. 3).

This work supplements to some extent the standard earlier work: *Onamasticon Anglo-Saxonicum: a list of Anglo-Saxon proper names, from the time of Beda to that of King John,* by W. G. Searle (Cambridge, Univ. Press, 1897. lvii, 601p.).

929.2.09 (420)
MATTHEWS, C. M. English surnames. London, Weidenfeld & Nicolson, 1966. 359p. 42*s.*

Deals with *c.* 2,500 surnames under the chapter headings 'Occupational names', 'Nicknames', 'Names of relationship', 'Local news'. "Hardly touches on the large subjects of surname distribution and local variation" (*Preface*). Bibliography, p. 313-6. Appendix: 'Classified lists of surnames', including 4. A selection of pre-Conquest personal names. Analytical index of surnames.

929.2.09 (420)
REANEY, P. H. The origin of English surnames. London, Routledge & Kegan Paul, 1967. xix, 415p. maps. 50*s.*

Aims to give "a general account of the development of English surnames, their classification, changes in pronunciation and spelling, and the gradual growth of hereditary family names" (*Preface*). 17 chapters; index of subjects, 357-9; index of surnames, p. 360-415 (*c.* 6,500 names). Bibliography, p. xvii-xix. A companion to the author's *Dictionary of British surnames* (q.v.).

Isle of Man
929.2.09 (428.9)
MOORE, A. W. Manx names; or, The surnames and place-names of the Isle of Man. 2nd ed., rev. London, Stock, 1903 (cheap ed. 1906). 261p.

1st ed. 1890 (*The surnames and place-names of the Isle of Man.* xi, 372p.).
Pt. 1: Surnames (Celtic origin; Scandinavian origin; exotic names; names obsolete before written records); Appendix A: Obsolete Christian names; B: Nicknames. Pt. 2: Place-names (Celtic; Scandinavian). Index of surnames; index of place-names.

Germany
929.2.09 (43)
BACH, A. Deutsche Namenkunde. 2. stark erw. Aufl. Heidelberg, Winter, 1952-56. 3v.

v. 1: *Die deutschen Personennamen.* 1952-53. 2 pts.
v. 2. *Die deutschen Ortsnamen.* 1953-54. 2 pts. maps.
v. 3: *Registerband,* bearb. von D. Berger. 1956.
V. 1-2 provide a systematic study of German personal and place names. In each case pt. 1 deals with phonetics, form, syntax, formation and meaning; pt. 2, with historical, geographical, sociological and psychological aspects. Both v. 1 and v. 2 have subject indexes.

Noted: Gottschald, M. *Deutsche Namenkunde: unsere Familiennamen nach ihrer Entstehung und Bedeutung.* 3. verm. Aufl., besorgt von E. Brodführer (Berlin, de Gruyter, 1954. 630p.).

929.2.09 (43)
BRECHENMACHER, J. K. Etymologisches Wörterbuch der deutschen Familiennamen. 2. von Grund auf neubearb. Aufl. der "Deutschen Sippennamen". Limburg an der Lahn, Starke, 1957-63. 2v. DM.160.

France
929.2.09 (44)
DAUZAT, A. Dictionnaire étymologique des noms de famille et prénoms de France. Paris, Larousse, 1951. 604p.

Contains about 24,000 family-name entries, giving variants, origin and meaning, indicating locality and period. A list of the 14 leading works on the subject is included.

Portugal
929.2.09 (469)
NASCENTES, A. Dicionário etimológico da lingua portuguesa. Rio de Janeiro, 1932-52. 2v.

V. 2 (389p.) deals with proper names.

Russia
929.2.09 (47)
BENSON, M., *comp.* **Dictionary of Russian personal names,** with a guide to stress and morphology. Philadelphia, Pa., Univ. of Pennsylvania Press; London, Oxford Univ. Press, 1964. v, 175p. 2nd ed. 1968. 188p. 57*s.*

Indicates stress in *c.* 23,000 selected surnames. A special section lists surnames of famous people in which the stress differs from the generally accepted one. Bibliography, p. 173-5.

U.S.A.

929.2.09 (73)

SMITH, E. C. Dictionary of American family names. New York, Harper, 1957. 244p.

"Lists alphabetically many of the common surnames in this country [U.S.A.], and includes notes on the origin of each. The introduction explains the process of surname formation." (*Library of Congress Information bulletin*, v. 16, no. 30, 29 July 1957, p. 393).

Nicknames

929.2.09:392.91

FRANKLYN, J. A dictionary of nicknames. London, Hamilton, 1962. xx, 132p. 18*s.*

Limited to *c.* 2,000 nicknames of persons, stating usage, source and, sometimes, century. Reverse index ('the names, states, mental and physical characteristics, places of nativity and other peculiarities that attract the nicknames, terms of address, and terms of reference recorded . . .'; *e.g.,* 'Bus-conductor, female: clippy'). Index of sources, p. 132; references to sources, p. x-xx.

Personal Names

929.2.09:413.13:016

SMITH, E. C. Personal names: a bibliography. New York, New York Public Library, 1952. 226p. (Reprinted New York, Gale Research Co., 1967. $9.)

Reprinted from *Bulletin of the New York Public Library*, 1950-51.
A classified bibliography of 3,415 references; includes periodical articles. Library locations. Each source is evaluated as 'good', 'fair' or 'poor'. Detailed index.

929.2.09:413.13 (091)

YONGE, C. M. History of Christian names. New ed., rev. London, Macmillan, 1884. cxliii, 476p. (Reprinted New York, Gale Research Co., 1967. $13.50.)

First published 1863.
A survey of Christian names from Hebrew, ancient Persian, Greek, Latin, Celtic, Teutonic and Slavonic sources. A glossary, which precedes the survey, gives the meanings of these forenames and acts as an index. Still a standard work on the subject.

929.2.09:413.13 (410)

LOUGHEAD, F. H. Dictionary of given names, with origins and meanings. 2nd ed., rev. and corrected. Glendale, California, A. H. Clark, 1957. 248p. $6.

First published 1933.
Includes a prefatory bibliography of 6 pages.

929.2.09:413.13 (410)

PARTRIDGE, E. Name this child: a dictionary of modern English and American given or Christian names. 3rd ed., rev. and much enl. London, Hamilton, 1951. 296p.

First published 1936; 2nd ed. 1938 (x, 233p.).
A dictionary of modern English given names, p. 25-287; adds variants and diminutives, origin and notes on use. An appendix (p. 291-6) provides "a list of obsolete and extremely obsolescent given names". Previous works in the field are briefly noted on p. 7.

929.2.09:413.13 (420)

WITHYCOMBE, E. G., *comp.* **The Oxford dictionary of English Christian names.** 2nd ed. Oxford, Clarendon Press, 1950. 340p. 18*s.*

Includes all names found in England since the fourteenth century, giving etymology, meaning and earliest usage. Although it contains many valuable historical names, it is occasionally uneven and does not wholly supersede C. M. Yonge's *History of Christian names (q.v.).*

929.2:09:413.13 (429)

DAVIES, T. R., *comp.* **A book of Welsh names.** London, Sheppard Press, 1952. 72p. 7*s. 6d.*

Welsh Christian names, arranged alphabetically. Gives sex and derivation, and notes early examples. Lists of gods, heroes, saints and founders of tribes.

929.2:413.13 (43)

GOTTSCHALD, M. Die deutschen Personennamen. 2. verb. Aufl. Berlin, de Gruyter, 1955. 151p.

Bibliography, p. [4].

929.2.09:413.13 (44)

AUDEBERT, A. Dictionnaire analytique des prénoms. Paris, Calmann-Lévy, 1956. 229, [3]p. Fr. fr. 500.

Has about 400 entries. For each forename gives variants and diminutives, appropriate saint's day, brief biography of the saint or other famous person(s) bearing the forename, and also (in italics) the character of persons with this name. Appended are a calendar of saints, etc., and a list of sources (1 page).

929.2.09:413.13 (46)

GOSNELL, C. F. Spanish personal names; principles governing their formation and use which may be presented as a help for cataloguers and bibliographers. New York, Wilson, 1938. xi, 112p.

Bibliography of sources, p. 89-101.

Parish Registers

929.3 (410)

SOCIETY OF GENEALOGISTS. A catalogue of parish register copies in the possession of the Society of Genealogists. Rev., enl. ed. London, the Society, 1963. 70l. Mimeographed.

First published 1937.
"This list is intended to fill the gap until the new National Index of Parish Register Copies,

now nearing completion, is ready" (*Introduction*). It is hoped to be "the first step towards publishing in parts a complete catalogue of the Society's library". 10 sections: 1. England and Wales—2. Scotland—3. Ireland—4. Roman Catholics—5. Nonconformist—6. Friends (Quakers)—7. French churches—8. Dutch churches—9. Overseas—10. Extracts. About 350 entries (Parish—County—Date), under first name of parish, A-Z (except when the first name is a geographical prefix, *e.g.*, North, South, Upper, Lower, Great, Little). MF = Microfilm; asterisk denotes availability for loan.

929.3 (42)

SOCIETY OF GENEALOGISTS. National index of parish registers: a guide to Anglican, Roman Catholic and Nonconformist registers before 1887, together with information on marriage licences, bishop's transcripts and modern copies. [New ed.] London, the Society, 1966-.

First published 1939.
This new ed. is to be in 11 regional v. for England and Wales, of which v. 5 is the first to appear: *South Midlands and Welsh Border, comprising the counties of Gloucestershire, Herefordshire, Oxfordshire, Shropshire, Warwickshire and Worcestershire;* compiled by J. D. Steel, with others (1966. xxiv, 300p. 32*s*. 6*d*.). For each county,—general information; parish list (A-Z by parishes). 'National record repositories and libraries', p. xx-xxii.
V. 1 will be entitled *Sources of births, marriages and deaths before 1837;* v. 10-11 will cover North Wales and South Wales respectively.

Wills

929.3:347.67

BRITISH RECORD SOCIETY. Index library: calendars and indexes of wills and administrations in prerogative and consistory courts, inquisitions post-mortem in Chancery, marriage licences, etc. Edited by W. P. W. Phillimore, G. S. Fry and others. London, the Society, 1888-. v. 1-.

Volumes in this series are listed in *Texts and calendars,* edited by E. L. C. Mullins (1958; see at 942:016). V. 79: *Wills at Chelmsford, v. 2,* was published in 1961 (70*s*.).

Phillimore's *Parish register series: marriages* (1896-1927) is listed in Minto, J. *Reference books* (1929), p. 220-1.

929.3:347.67

CAMP, A. J. Wills and their whereabouts; being a thorough revision and extension of the previous work of the same name by B. G. Bouwens. Bridge Place, near Canterbury, Kent, published for the Society of Genealogists by Phillimore & Co., Ltd., 1963. xix, 137p. 21*s*.

B. G. Bouwen's *Wills and their whereabouts* was published 1939; 2nd ed. 1951.
Preliminary pages on testamentary procedure, on making will abstracts, on courts having jurisdiction throughout England and Wales, and the Principal Probate Registry. Locations in England (by counties A-Z; p. 1-99); the Channel Islands; Ireland; the Isle of Man; Scotland (p. 104-11) and Wales. Index of courts and places.

929.3:347.67

PHILLIMORE, W. P. W., and **THRIFT, G.,** *ed.* **Indexes to Irish wills.** London, Phillimore, 1909-20. 5v.

The 5 volumes are arranged on a diocesan basis:
1. *Ossory, 1536-1800. Leighlin, 1652-1800. Ferns, 1601-1800. Kildare, 1661-1800.*
2. *Cork & Ross, 1584-1800. Cloyne, 1621-1800.*
3. *Cashel & Emly, 1618-1800. Waterford & Lismore, 1645-1800. Killaloe & Kilfenora, 1653-1800. Limerick, 1615-1800. Ardfert & Aghadoe, 1690-1800.*
4. *Dromore, 1678-1858. Newry & Mourne, 1727-1858.*
5. *Derry, 1612-1858 & Raphoe, 1684-1858.*

HERALDRY

Bibliographies

929.6:016

COPE, S. T. Heraldry, flags, and seals: a select bibliography, with annotations, covering the period 1920 to 1945. London, Aslib, 1948. 55p.

An offprint from the *Journal of documentation* (v. 4, no. 2, June 1948, p. 92-146). It includes books and periodical articles, and is arranged in an alphabetical sequence of authors. There is an index of subjects. The annotations are excellent.

929.6:016

GATFIELD, G. Guide to printed books and manuscripts relating to English and foreign heraldry and genealogy. London, Mitchell & Hughes, 1892. 646p.

See entry at 929:016.

Manuals

929.6 (02)

BOUTELL, C. Boutell's Heraldry; revised by C. W. Scott-Giles and J. P. Brooke-Little. London, Warne, 1966. xii, 329p. illus. (incl. col. pl.).

Compiled mainly from Boutell's *The manual of heraldry* (1863) and *English heraldry* (1867). Rev. eds., 1954, 1958, 1963.
An armorial classic. Chapters on the 'grammar' of armoury (*i.e.*, the tinctures and emblems in use), complemented by accounts of the orders of chivalry, corporate and national arms, plus notes on heraldic authorities and sources. Combined glossary and index. The 1966 revision has an enlarged section on ecclesiastical heraldry and a completely rewritten chapter on 'Commonwealth and foreign heraldry'. Arrangement of text and the illustrations (which include 28 col. pl.) are far superior to those in Fox-Davies' *Complete guide to heraldry* (1909).

929.6 (02)

FOX-DAVIES, A. C. A complete guide to heraldry. Rev. ed. London, Nelson, 1949 (reprinted 1961) xii, 647p. illus. (of coats of arms).

First published 1904 as *The art of heraldry.* Fox-Davies died 1928. Rev. ed., edited by C. A. H. Franklyn.

An authoritative and comprehensive work. Arranged in systematic, short chapter form. Comprises the history of armory, a detailed description of the treatment of charges used, regalia, seals, badges, cadency, the law of armorial bearings, and the artistic employment of heraldry. Each chapter is lavishly illustrated (in all 16p. of coloured pl.; nearly 800 drawings); subject and name indexes.

A revised and expanded ed. by J. P. Brooke-Little has been announced.

929.6 (02)

FRANKLYN, J. Shield and crest: an account of the art and science of heraldry. 3rd ed. London, MacGibbon & Kee, 1967. xviii, 521p. illus. (incl. col. pl.). 105s.

First published 1960.
A notable grammar of heraldic practice, with splendid examples in colour of shields and crests current in the 20th century. The blazonry and charges are described in great detail and with particular regard to their original use and meaning. Descriptions of plates are unhelpfully relegated to end of text. A good index of proper names, but some of the charges are given only under general headings, e.g., fish, flower.

The 3rd ed. has c. 24 pages of extra information, chiefly enlargements of existing sections; some extra illustrations. Almost every page reset. "One of the standard textbooks of heraldry in English in the 20th century" (*Times literary supplement*, no. 3,413, 27th July 1967, p. 693).

929.6 (02)

GAYRE of Gayre and **Nigg, R. Heraldic standards and their ensigns.** Edinburgh & London, Oliver & Boyd, 1959. xix, 132p., with 16 col. pl.

The aim is to clarify and illustrate the various types of heraldic ensigns. Claims to be the first book devoted to the heraldic flag. 1. The pennon —2. The lance pennon—3. The personal banner —4. The guidon—5. The heraldic standard—6. The streamer—7. The heraldic household badge —8. The gonfallon or gonfallion—9. Heraldic vanes—10. Banderoles and helm-streamers—11. The armorial or heraldic flag. Footnote references; 53 figures; detailed index.

929.6 (02)

HOPE, W. H. St. J. Heraldry for craftsmen and designers. London, Hogg, 1913. 425p.

Valuable for contemporary illustrations of medieval heraldic art, brasses, seals, etc.

929.6 (02)

WOODWARD, J., and **BURNETT, G. A treatise on heraldry, British and foreign,** with English and French glossaries. 2nd ed. Edinburgh, Johnston, 1896. 2v. illus. (66 col. pl.).

First published 1892.
The best English survey of continental heraldic practice. The illustrations are excellent. It covers the origin, history, and practical application of armory. V. 2 contains an index of proper names and subjects. This treatise serves as an introduction to Rietstap's *Armorial général* (q.v.).

Dictionaries

929.6 (03)

PALLISER, Mrs. B. Historic devices, badges and war-cries. London, Sampson Low, 1870. iv, 435p. illus.

A wealth of information on British and foreign heraldic symbolism. Arranged A-Z, with index.

929.6 (038)=00

STALINS, G. F. L., baron, and others. **Vocabulaire-atlas héraldique** en six langues, français, English, deutsch, espagnol, italiano, nederlandsch. Paris, Société du Grand Armorial de France, 1952. 119p. illus.

At head of title-page: Académie Internationale d'Héraldique.
Three parts: pt. 1, the six-language vocabulary, arranged to correspond and to be a key to the drawings (or parts of them), in pt. 3 and consecutively numbered 1-529; pt. 2, an A-Z index of the terms in pt. 1 and the corresponding drawings in pt. 3; pt. 3, the black-and-white plates (p. 75-119), numbered 1-23.

929.6 (038)=20

GOUGH, H., and **PARKER, J. Glossary of terms used in heraldry.** New ed. Oxford, Parker, 1894. xxviii, 659p. illus. (Reprinted Detroit, Michigan, Gale Research Co., 1966. $14.50.)

First published 1847.
Still considered the best glossary for general use; numerous cross-references. Two excellent features are the many small illustrations (over 1,000), and the full index. A short bibliography precedes.

Europe

929.6 (4)

GAYRE of Gayre and Nigg, R., ed. **The armorial who is who,** 1961/1962-: a register of armorial bearings in current use, with the names and addresses of the bearers and the authority for their use. Edinburgh & London, The Armorial, 1962-. illus. (incl. pl.). Biennial. (2nd ed.: 1963/1965. 1965. 63s.).

The 2nd ed. has a main section: 'Arms of the Chiefs of Royal Houses and Houses of Sovereign Rank, Consorts of Sovereigns, and the Prince and Grand Master of the Sovereign Military Order of Malta' (name; degrees, etc.; address(es); arms; crest; motto; grant). Alphabetical list follows, with addenda and list of abbreviations.

929.6 (4)

KOLLER, F., and others. **Armorial universel.** Brussels. Éditions de la Librairie Encyclopédique, 1951-. v. 1-. (v. 1. Belg. fr. 1,000).

Authors are given as 'F. Koller et A. Schillings et un comité international'.
A sequel of sorts to J. B. Rietstap's *Armorial général,* but no evidence of the publication of v. 2, due to appear during 1951 (*Preface*, v. 1), has been traced. V. 1 gives brief entries, describing arms, device and badge, with a very brief historical note on the family concerned, occasionally. Arranged A-Z by family names. 26 contributors, covering 29 countries.

929.6 (4)

LOUDA, J. European civic coats of arms. Edited by D. Morrah. London, Hamlyn, 1966. 265p. illus. (pl.). 10s. 6d.

The origin and development of civic coat of arms — Changes and their meaning — Civic heraldry overseas—Glossary. 320 plates (4 per page), plus brief description, Aachen-Zwickau. Index to illustrations.

929.6 (4)

RIETSTAP, J. B. Armorial général; précédé d'un dictionnaire des termes du blason. 2. éd. Gouda, van Goor, 1884-87; Paris, Dupont, 1904; Institut Héraldique, 1905-14; Hague, Nijhoff, 1926-34. 2v. and Supplements. (Reprinted London, Heraldry Today, 1965. £15 15s.)

First published 1861.
The standard encyclopaedia of European arms. The entries are arranged A-Z by families. Individual coats of arms are not illustrated. Supplements, with illustrations, were issued by V. and H. Rolland, Paris, Dupont, 1904; Institut Héraldique, 1905-14; and Hague, Nijhoff, 1926-54. 7v. Each volume contains entries A-Z. *Table de supplément*, by H. Rolland (Lyons, 1951. 190p.).
Plates illustrating the arms in the original work of Rietstap were published under the title *Armoiries des familles contenues dans l'Armorial général* (Paris, Institut Héraldique Universel, 1903-12; Hague, Nijhoff, 1938. 6v.). The plates are arranged in one A-Z sequence. 3rd ed. of these plates, by V. and H. Rolland, entitled *General illustrated armorial* (Lyon, Sauvegarde Historique. 6v.), 1953. Reprinted as *Illustration to the 'Armorial général' of J. B. Riestap* (London, Heraldry Today, 1967. 3v. £25).

Commonwealth

929.6 (41-44)

GREAT BRITAIN. COMMONWEALTH OFFICE. British Commonwealth coats of arms. [London, Commonwealth Office], 1956-. ea. 10s. 6d.

Single leaves, with excellently coloured illustrations, heraldic description and date of grant by Royal Warrant. 25 so far issued, Bahamas—Uganda.

Great Britain

929.6 (410)

BURKE, Sir J. B. The general armory of England, Scotland, Ireland and Wales; comprising a registry of armorial bearings from the earliest to the present time. London, Harrison, 1884. lxxix, 50, 1185p. illus. (Reprinted London, Clowes, 1961. 147s.).

First published 1842.
The 1884 edition contains dscriptions of about 60,000 coats-of-arms. The work is in dictionary form, the entries being under the name of the family or corporation. The illustrations are confined to the arms of the English and Welsh dynasties. There is an index of mottoes which includes the names of the families concerned.

The romance of heraldry, by C. W. Scott-Giles (Rev. ed. London, Dent, 1965. xiii, 234p.

illus. 55s.) relates the development of British heraldry to the chief historic events.

929.6 (410)

DE LA BERE, Sir I. The Queen's orders of chivalry. London, Kimber, 1961. 212p. illus. 36s.

Chapters 1-10 deal with the histories of the various orders. Later chapters cover investitures and presentation of insignia; order of precedence of insignia; wearing of insignia on formal occasions; foreign orders, decorations and medals; and return and replacement of insignia. 20 halftones; also, line-drawings.

929.6 (410)

FOX-DAVIES, A. C. Armorial families; a directory of gentlemen of coat-armour. 7th ed. London, Hurst & Blackett, 1929. 2v. illus. (22 col. pl.).

First published 1895.
Introductory chapter on the abuse of arms. The entries are in A-Z order, by families. Only those arms which are officially recorded are included. Full heraldic descriptions are given, with accounts of the recent bearers of the arms. The work is well illustrated and there is an index of quarterings.

929.6 (410)

————— **The book of public arms:** a complete encyclopaedia of all royal, territorial, municipal, corporate, official, and impersonal arms. London, Jack, 1915. xx, 877p. illus. 35s.

First published 1894.
Arranged in A-Z order of entries, this work is still the current authority. Each entry gives a full description of the arms, crest, and motto borne, together with the date of the grant, where such exists.

929.6 (410)

MOULE, T. Biblioteca heraldica Magnae Britanniae: a bibliography of heraldry, genealogy, nobility, knighthood and ceremonies from 1469-1821. 1822. xxiii, 668p. (Reprinted New York, Barnes & Noble, 1966. $15.).

A classic bibliography of 810 items, arranged chronologically. Includes lists of visitations and the principal foreign books on genealogy and heraldry. The reprint is less unwieldy than the original.

929.6 (410)

PAPWORTH, J. W., and MORANT, A. W. W. Papworth's Ordinary of British armorials. Reproduced from the original edition of 1874. London, Tabard Publications, 1961. xxii, 1,125p. 126s.

Photolithographed reproduction of *An alphabetical dictionary of coats of arms* (1874), with a new introduction.
Encyclopaedic; not superseded. May be called Burke's *General armory* in reverse. Arms are listed, A-Z, under the heraldic charges. Description of each coat-of-arms is followed by name of family to which it belongs. Index of the charges described. According to *Genealogists' handbook* (4th ed. 1967, p. 30), Papworth's

380

Ordinary, like Burke's *General armory,* is "both inaccurate and incomplete", despite the fact that it is indispensable for identifying coat of arms.

929.6 (410)
TREMLETT, T. D. The "New dictionary of British arms". In *The genealogist's magazine,* v. 13, no. 10, June 1961, p. 320-323.

The main classes of material in the medieval section of the forthcoming *New dictionary* are: 1. Seals; 2. Rolls of arms; 3. Monumental heraldry. Although it will cover a very wide field (armory (name and blason) and ordinary (blason and identification)), it will still not include direct abstracts from the official record.

929.6 (410)
WAGNER, *Sir* A. R. The records and collections of the College of Arms. London, Burke, 1952. 87p. front.

A survey of the history and resources of the College by one of its officers. Contains a bibliographical account of the records compiled by the former heralds in their private and official capacities. A catalogue of the heralds' visitations is included.

929.6 (411)
INNES, *Sir* T. Scots heraldry: a practical handbook of the historical principles and modern application of the art and science. 2nd ed., rev. and enl. Edinburgh, Oliver & Boyd, 1956. xxiv, 258p. illus. (col. pl.).

First published 1934.
The standard work on the Scottish practice of armory. Includes a bibliography: 'Guide to further study of Scottish heraldry' (p. 234-8).

Noted: Court of the Lord Lyon. *Roll of Scottish arms;* edited by Lt.-Col. Gayre of Gayre & Nigg and Reinold Gayre of Gayre & Nigg. Edinburgh, The Armorial, 1964 [1965]-. (pt. 1, v. 1: A-G. 177p. 105*s.*).

929.6 (411)
PAUL, *Sir* J. B. An ordinary of arms contained in the Public Register of all arms and bearings in Scotland. Edinburgh, Green, 1903. xxiv, 428p.

First published 1893.
The Scottish equivalent of Papworth's *Dictionary,* the entries being under the heraldic charges. There is an index of family names.

929.6 (42)
SCOTT-GILES, C. W. Civic heraldry of England and Wales. [Rev. ed.] London, Dent, 1953. xv, 440p. illus. 45*s.*

First published 1933.
Contains introductory chapters on the history and use of the emblems most commonly employed. The entries are arranged, under counties, in a sequence of county councils, cities, county boroughs, urban and district councils. Full heraldic descriptions are given, together with the date and emblematic origin of each grant. There are indexes of mottoes and subjects.

929.6 (420)
WAGNER, *Sir* A. Heralds of England: a history of the office and College of Arms. London, H.M. Stationery Office, 1967. xvii, 609p. illus. (of coats of arms), ports. £21.

An authoritative account, sumptuously printed and illustrated. Reviewed in *'The times' Saturday review,* 22nd January 1968, p. 21.

Ecclesiastical Heraldry

929.6:28
WOODWARD, J. A treatise on ecclesiastical heraldry. Edinburgh, Johnston, 1894. xiii, 7, 580p. illus. (36 pl.).

The most comprehensive work in this aspect of heraldry. It embraces British and continental armory, including that of colleges. Many of the plates are in colour. Index of persons and places.

Naval Heraldry

929.6:359
WEIGHTMAN, A. E. Heraldry in the Royal Navy: crests and badges of H.M. ships. Aldershot, Gale & Polden, 1957. xviii, 514p. illus. 30*s.*

Crests and badges of more than 300 ships, A-Z (H.M.S. *Abercrombie - Zodiac*). For each ship: badge; description of badge; origin; battle honours; history of the ship. Half-tone and text illustrations.

Crests

929.6.014
FAIRBAIRN, J. Fairbairn's Book of crests of the families of Great Britain and Ireland. 4th ed., rev. and enl. by A. C. Fox-Davies. Edinburgh, Jack, 1905 (and reprints). 2v. illus. (pl.).

First published 1859.
V. 1 contains the index of surnames together with one of mottoes (with translations), a key to the plates, and a dictionary of heraldic terms. The second volume contains the plates.

Mottoes

929.6.019
ELVIN, C. N. A book of mottoes borne by the nobility, gentry, cities, public companies, etc. Translated and illustrated, with notes and quotations. Reproduced from the original ed. of 1860. London, Heraldry Today, 1963. xii, 230p. 31*s.*

Many annotations, but no details of dates or authorities. Often gives the address as well as name of family associated with each motto. Reviewed in *The genealogists' magazine,* v. 15, no. 4, December 1965, p. 149.

Nobility

Europe

929.7 (4)
Annuaire de la noblesse de France et de l'Europe. 89e volume (117e année). Paris, "Le Nobiliaire". [1960]. 719, [1], [2]p. front.

Founded in 1843; first English ed., 1953.

This 89th edition has been considerably revised. Sections: 2. Les maisons souveraines d'Europe—3. Les anciennes maisons souveraines d'Europe—4. Titres de ducs et de princes français portés en France—5. Les maisons ducales et princières de France—6. Nomenclature des maisons ducales et princières d'Espagne—7. Les maisons nobles de France et d'Italie—8. Tablettes historiques et généalogiques—9. Les familles titrées et nobles de Belgique—10. Les familles titrées et nobles du Pays-Bas—11. Les ephemerides de la noblesse—12. L'ordre souverain de Malte—13. La société de Cincinnati—14. La légion d'honneur (Americains d'élite decorés de la Légion d'Honneur)—15. Le Sang Royal. Index of families cited, p. 715-9.

The latest international ed. in English has the title *The royalty, peerage and aristocracy of the world* (*Annuaire de la noblesse de France*) (90th v. London, Annuaire de France, [1966]. xiv, 730p. 150s.). Four parts: 1. The royal and sovereign reigning houses of Europe—2. The princely and ducal houses of Europe—3. The titled nobility of the kingdom of Belgium—4. List of the principal foreign orders—5. The foremost families of the U.S.A.

929.7 (4)

RUVIGNY AND RAINEVAL, *9th marquis of*. **The titled nobility of Europe:** an international peerage or "Who's who" of the sovereigns, princes and nobles of Europe. London, Harrison, 1914. lxxii, 1598p. illus. (of coats of arms).

Contains accounts of existing titles and biographies of living members of many families in one A-Z sequence, with an index of surnames, variations and lesser titles. Coverage is somewhat uneven, many minor titles (especially of barons) being omitted, and some national entries (*e.g.,* French, Spanish) being slight.

The same author's *The nobilities of Europe* (London, Melville, 1909-10. 2v.) includes brief notes on the history of the nobility in various countries, with lists of Britons ennobled abroad or having held certain foreign orders, and of foreign nobles who have become British subjects.

Commonwealth

929.7 (41-44)

BURKE, *Sir* **J. B. A genealogical history of the dormant, abeyant, forfeited, and extinct peerages of the British Empire.** New ed. London, Harrison, 1883. xii 642p. (Reprinted London, Burke's Peerage, 1964. 105s.).

Useful for ancestry and descendants of peers; but personal details should be taken from Cokayne (*q.v.*).

Previous editions of the *Dictionary of the peerages of England, Scotland and Ireland, extinct, dormant and in abeyance* appeared in 1831, 1840 and 1846, edited by John Burke.

A genealogical and heraldic history of the extinct and dormant baronetcies of England, Ireland and Scotland, by J. and J. B. Burke (2nd ed. London, 1844) has been reprinted (London, Burke's Peerage, 1964. 652p. armorial illus. 105s.).

929.7 (41-44)

HAYDN, J. The book of dignities; containing lists of the official personages of the British Empire, civil, diplomatic, heraldic, judicial ecclesiastical, municipal, naval and military . . . with the sovereigns and rulers of the world, the orders of knighthood of the United Kingdom and India. 3rd ed. London, W. H. Allen, 1894. xxviii, 1170p.

Based on R. Beatson's *A political index* (3rd ed. 1806. 3v.), which contains some fuller lists.

An invaluable compilation. Important offices are listed from their beginnings, others from 1760. For sovereigns, officers of state and bishops, Haydn is superseded by the Royal Historical Society's *Handbook of British chronology* (1939) (*see at 941:930.24*).

Great Britain

929.7 (410)

BURKE, *Sir* **J. B. Burke's Genealogical and heraldic history of the landed gentry.** 18th ed., edited by P. Townend. London, Burke's Peerage, 1965-. illus. (v. 1. 1965. £12 12s.).

1st ed., *Burke's Genealogical . . . history of commoners* (1833-38. 4v.); 2nd ed., *Landed gentry of Great Britain and Ireland,* with an index of about 100,000 names (1843-49. 3v.).

The 18th ed. is to be in 4v., each arranged A-Z. V. 1 contains biographical sketches of *c.* 600 distinguished families of England, Scotland and Wales; 500 armorial illustrations; index of families. Gives brief biographical sketch of present head of family; name of wife and children (if any); lineage; arms (both illustration and description); seat. Perhaps one-half of the families are no longer landowning.

American families with British ancestry are included in the 1939 ed., p. 2539-3021, published separately in 1948 as *Burke's Distinguished families of America: the lineages of 1,600 families of British origin now resident in the United States of America.*

There is also: Burke, *Sir* J. B. *A genealogical and heraldic history of the colonial gentry* (London, Harrison, 1891-95. 2v. illus.).

929.7 (410)

BURKE, *Sir* **J. B. Burke's Genealogical and heraldic history of the peerage, baronetage, and knightage.** London, Burke's Peerage, 1826-. illus. (of coats of arms). Irregular. (104th ed. 1967. xcvi, 3059p. £16 16s.)

Generally known as Burke's *Peerage.* The original title was *Genealogical and heraldic dictionary of the peerage and baronetage of the United Kingdom.*

Contents include, besides occasional articles, the royal lineage (with a comprehensive repertorium of collaterals), tables of precedence, orders, decorations and medals, peerage, baronetage, orders of knighthood and knightage, spiritual lords, Privy Council and companionage. The 103rd ed. includes three prefatory articles, on the House of Lords, the nobility and the princes of Great Britain.

929.7 (410)

[COKAYNE, G. E.] **The complete peerage of England, Scotland, Ireland.** Great Britain and the United Kingdom, extant, extinct or dormant. London, St. Catherine Press, 1910-59. 13v. in 14. £73 10s.

The previous ed. (1887-98. 8v.) and v. 1-5 of this edition have the title: *Complete peerage of England, Scotland, Ireland, Great Britain and the United Kingdom, extant, extinct, or dormant.*
Excellent biographical data, giving fully, yet concisely, particulars of parentage, birth, honours, officers, public services, politics, marriage, death and burial of every holder of a peerage; well documented. Includes pedigrees. Throws valuable light on the whole history of the House of Lords.
According to the *Genealogist's magazine* (v. 17, no. 10, June 1961, p. 319), there is "progressively less hope of the supplementary and index volume of the *Complete peerage* being printed".

929.7 (410)

Debrett's Peerage, baronetage, knightage and companionage. London, 1713-. illus. Annual. (163rd year. London, Kelly's Directories, Ltd., 1965. £12 12s.)

Editors and publishers vary. Sub-title, 1966: "Comprises information concerning persons bearing hereditary or courtesy titles, privy councillors, knights, companions of the various orders, and the collateral branches of peers and baronets."
1966 ed., pt. 1: Peerage (including Royal family; royal warrant holders), p. 33-1167; pt. 2: Baronetage, knightage and companionage.
As compared with Burke's *Peerage*, this is less useful for genealogical enquiries, as the lineage is not set out in full; only the relationship of existing collaterals and a brief conspectus of the history of the title is shown; and dates are generally restricted to year only. On the other hand, the issue of female collaterals is included.

929.7 (410)

Kelly's Handbook to the titled, landed and official classes, 1880-. London, Kelly's Directories, 1880-. Annual. (93rd ed., 1967. 126s.).

Entries in the 93rd ed., arranged alphabetically in the main sequence (p. 113-2151; addenda) consists of short biographies. Preceded by A-Z list of royal warrant holders; abbreviations; general table of precedence; wearing of orders, decorations, etc.; forms of epistolary address; the Royal family. The object is to cover those who have a definite position, (1) from hereditary rank; (2) from a title or order; (3) as Members of Parliament; (4) as members of the higher grades of the diplomatic, naval, military, air, clerical, legal, colonial, or civil services of the State; (5) as Deputy Lieutenants and Justices of the Peace . . . , Royal Academicians and presidents of learned societies; (6) as landed proprietors; (7) as distinguished members of the dramatic, literary and artistic world; (8) as leading members of the British commercial world. Unevenly printed.

929.7 (410)

Knights Bachelor, 1953-1954: a list of the existing recipients of the honour of knighthood, together with a short account of the origin, objects and work of the Imperial Society of Knights Bachelor by G. W. Wollaston. 22nd ed. London, Imperial Society of Knights Bachelor, [1954]. 385p. pl., tables.

929.7 (410)

——Supplement: **Knights Bachelor** 1964-65. 20th ed. [1965]. 182p. illus. Private circulation.

Both works contain a separate unpaged illustrated appendix—"The armorial bearings of a few knights bachelor".

929.7 (411)

The Scots peerage, founded on Wood's edition of Sir Robert Douglas's Peerage of Scotland; containing an historical and genealogical account of the nobility of that kingdom. Edited by Sir J. B. Paul. Edinburgh, Douglas, 1904-14. 9v. illus. (of coats of arms).

Contains biographies in narrative form not only of title-holders but of all offspring in the male line. A very comprehensive name index is contained in v. 9.

929.7 (415)

BURKE, *Sir* J. B. **Burke's Genealogical and heraldic history of the landed gentry of Ireland.** [New ed.]. Edited by L. J. Pine. London, Burke, 1958. xxxvi, 778p.

First published 1899.
A supplement to the 1912 ed. (the latest available) is provided in the 15th, centenary ed. (1937) of *Burke's Landed gentry,* which carries an Irish supplement.

Italy

929.7 (45)

Elenco ufficiale della nobiltà italiana. Rome, Presidenzi del Consiglio dei Ministri, Consulta Araldica del Regno, 1934. 1033p.

Appended 'Dizionario dei predicati della nobiltà italiana' (p. 931-1033).

Russia

929.7 (47)

IKONNIKOV, N. **La noblesse de Russie.** 2. éd. Paris, [the Author], 1957-62. 20v. & index. Supplements 1-5. 1963-66. Mimeographed.

Sub-title: 'Éléments pour servir à la reconstitution des registres généalogiques de la Noblesse, d'après les actes et documents disponibles complétés grâce au concours dévoué des nobles russes'. Arranged A-Z (v. 1: A-Bestorijev. [xi], 563, 11p. List of sources, p. [xi]).

U.S.A.

929.7 (73)

BURKE, *Sir* J. B. **Burke's Distinguished families of America:** the lineage of 1,600 families of British origin now resident in the United States of America. London, Burke, 1947. iv, 494p. illus. (pl.).

In 1939 a new feature was introduced into Burke's *Landed gentry (q.v.)* and for the first time

American families of British descent were included. This feature is now issued separately.

Arrangement is alphabetical, with two addenda. More than 200 heraldic illustrations in colour. 59 plates.

Titles

929.7:395.6/.7

HEYWOOD, V. British titles: the use and misuse of the titles of peers and commoners, with some historical notes. 2nd ed. London, Black, 1953. xi, 188p.

Titles and forms of address: a guide to their correct use. 13th ed. London, Black, 1966. xi, 164p. 15s.

See entries at 395.6/.7.

Orders & Decorations

929.71 (4/9)

WEHRLICH, R. Orders and decorations of all nations, ancient and modern, civil and military. Washington, Quaker Press, 1965. [vii], 328, [8]p. illus. (pl.). $20.

Arranged under countries, A-Z, with U.S.A. first. In each case the order is briefly described, with history, plus statement on badge, star and ribbon and note (if any). Black-and-white reproductions, with the exception of 1 col. pl.

Most of the 195 illustrations in J. Mericka's *Orders and decorations;* edited by D. Morrah. Translated by B. Golová. (London, Hamlyn, 1967. 316p. 63s.) are coloured, although they are small. No cross-reference from text to illustrations; references and bibliography (p. 109); glossary (p. 309-11); index.

929.71 (4)

HIERONYMUSSEN, P. Orders, medals and decorations of Britain and Europe in colour. Translated from Dutch by C. H. Colquhoun. London, Blandford Press, 1967. 256p. illus. (incl. col. pl.). 35s.

Originally as *Europaeiske ordner i farver* [European orders in colour] (Copenhagen, Politikens Forlag, 1966).

The 80 coloured plates (450 photographs) of orders, medals and decorations of 28 European nations are preceded by an introductory essay and followed by an encyclopaedia of orders (date of institution; to whom it may be given; classes; whether or not returnable on death of holder). "An excellent general guide in a comparatively small volume" (*Times literary supplement,* no. 3,414, 3rd August 1967, p. 713).

929.71 (41-44)

JOCELYN, A. Awards of honour: the orders, decorations, medals and awards of Great Britain and the Commonwealth, from Edward III to Elizabeth II. London, Black, 1956. xx, 276p. illus. (20 col. pl.).

17 chapters: Introduction and definitions; Orders; Miscellaneous honours; Regimental honours; Medals; Decorations; Life-saving medals; Naval, military and air decorations; Campaign medals, 1793-1955; Polar exploration

medals; Long service and good conduct medals; Good shooting medals; Royal Societies' medals; Indian, dominion and colonial decorations and medals; Empire and colonial police medals; Medical and nursing services' decorations; Miscellaneous decorations. The 20 colour-plates consist of mounted reproductions of medals and ribbons. Detailed index, p. 265-76. Page size, $12\frac{1}{2}'' \times 10''$.

929.71 (410)

GORDON, L. L. British orders and awards: a description of all orders, decorations, long service, coronation, jubilee and commemoration medals, together with historical details concerning knighthood, service ranks and similar information. [Gnosall, nr. Stafford, the Author], 1959. x, 166, 4p.

Pt. 1, Medals (13 sections; descriptions: obverse, reverse, size, ribbon, etc.; notes; includes 'Orders awarded to ladies only'); pt. 2 (p. 101-60): History of medals—Knighthood and chivalry—Naval and military notes, 1840-60—Military ranks. No illustrations; index. 4 pages of addenda and corrigenda.

Flags

929.9 (4/9):016

COPE, S. T. Heraldry, flags and seals: a select bibliography. London, Aslib, 1948. 55p.

See entry at 929.6:016.

929.9 (4/9):016

SMITH, W., *comp. and ed.* **The bibliography of flags of foreign nations.** Flag Research Center, Winchester, Mass. Boston, Mass., G. K. Hall, 1965. 163p. $33.

3,200 entries for printed material and manuscripts on many types of flags. In two parts: 1. Topical entries (*e.g.,* naval, military, international, religious, provincial, municipal, organisational) —2. Geographical entries, A-Z.

929.9 (4/9) (02)

BARRACLOUGH, E. M. C., *ed.* **Flags of the world.** [2nd rev. ed.] London, Warne, 1965. x, 325p. illus. (incl. pl.). 50s.

First published 1897; rev. ed. 1961, edited by H. G. Carr.

18 chapters arranged similarly to the sequence in Campbell and Evans. Includes flags of merchant ship, yacht, corporations and public bodies; signal flags (the international code). 340 flags in full colour; more than 400 text drawings. The 1965 ed. covers the flags of Malawi, Zambia, Kenya, Malaysia, the French African republics, the personal flags of Queen Elizabeth, and the U.S.A. state flags.

929.9 (4/9) (02)

CAMPBELL, G., and **EVANS, I. O. The book of flags.** 5th ed. London, Oxford Univ. Press, 1965. xi, 124p. illus. (incl. 15 col. pl.).

First published 1950.

16 chapters, chapters 1-8 dealing with British flags, 9-15 with flags of the Commonwealth and other nations, and 16, 'International flags'. Ap-

pendix 1: 'Days for hoisting flags on Government buildings'. Apart from the 15 colour plates, there are many line-drawings. Sources, p. viii.

The observer's book of flags, by I. O. Evans (Rev. ed. London, Warne, [1966]. 208p. illus. (incl. 80 col. pl.), 5s.) is pocket sized and good value for its price. Each of the 80 colour plates reproduces 3 to 6 or more flags, and there are also 74 line-drawings. Discusses origin and development of the world's flags.

929.9 (4/9) (02)

GREAT BRITAIN. ADMIRALTY. Flags of all nations. New ed. London, H.M. Stationery Office, 1955-. v. 1-. illus., diagrs. Loose-leaf.

Previous ed. 1932. To be published in 3v.
v. 1: *National flags and ensigns.* 1955. Reprinted, with Amendments and changes since 1955. 1965. xviii, 230p. o.p.
v. 2: *Standards of rulers, sovereigns and heads of state; flags of heads of ministries and of naval, military and air force officers.* 1958. x p. with 217 col. pl. 150s. Amendment no. 1. June 16, 1961. 20s.; Change no. 1. November 9, 1962. 22s. 6d.
V. 3 is to follow, covering flags of all public bodies, badges of territories, colonies, etc., and badges of public departments when used to deface national flags or ensigns.
Arrangement in v. 1 is by countries, A-Z, following general and British Commonwealth sections. Illustrations are well coloured and Admiralty bunting pattern numbers are stated. Very little text.

929.9 (4/9) (02)

KANNIK, P. A handbook of flags. London, Methuen, 1958. 203p. illus. (col. pl.).

Originally published in Denmark, 1956. Colour reproductions of 861 official flags of the present time, including those of individual states of Germany, Russia and the United States; also some 80 national coats of arms. Historical and descriptive notes, but limited to recent years. The Great Britain section includes several rarely depicted departmental badges, *e.g.,* British Ocean Weather Ships, Northern Lights Commissioner's flag.

929.9 (41-44)

GREAT BRITAIN. COLONIAL OFFICE. Flags, badges and arms of His Majesty's Dominions beyond the seas and of territories under His Majesty's protection. London, H.M. Stationery Office, 1932-. Loose-leaf pl.

Earlier ed. 1910.
Pt. 1, Flags and badges (ea. 7s. 6d.); pt. 2, Arms (ea. 10s. 6d.).
"Contains colour illustrations of the flags, flag badges and—where they exist—coats of arms (the last with full heraldic description and date of Royal Warrant, etc.)" (see Royal Commonwealth Society. *Library notes.* New series, no. 23. November 1958, p. 1-2). 36 loose plates with 20 half-page-size inserts; well coloured. Kept up to date by single sheets of new or amended designs (*e.g., Flag badge: Queen's Representative in State of Singapore.* 1961.). A new edition is long overdue.

929.9 (410)

PERRIN, W. G. British flags; their early history, and their development at sea; with an account of the origin of the flag as a national device. Cambridge, Univ. Press, 1922. xii, 207p. illus.

Chapters: 1. The origin of the flag and its development up to the end of the 13th century—2. Early English, Scottish and Irish flags—3. The Union flags and jacks—4. Flags of command—5. Colours of distinction—6. Flag signals—7. Ceremonial and other usages. 13 coloured illus.; analytical index.

93 HISTORY

Bibliographies

93:016

The American Historical Association's Guide to historical literature. Chairman, Board of editors, George Frederick Howe. New York, Macmillan, 1961. xxxv, 962p. $16.50.

A complete revision of *Guide to historical literature,* edited by G. M. Dutcher and others (1931). More selective and less fully annotated than the 1931 ed. (still of value) on Western European history, but more extensive on other continents. Primarily intended "to serve those students or teachers who know English . . .". About 20,000 items (bibliographies, libraries and museum collections; encyclopaedias and works of reference; geographies, gazetteers and atlases; anthropologic, demographic and linguistic works; printed collections of sources; shorter and longer general histories; histories of periods, areas and topics; biographies; government publications; publications of academies, universities and learned societies; periodicals). Includes periodical articles. Nine sections: 1. Introduction and general history—2. Historical beginnings—3. The Middle Period in Eurasia and North Africa 4. Asia since early times—5. Modern Europe (p. 383-645)—6. The Americas (p. 646-744)—7. Africa (p. 745-69)—8. Australasia and Oceania (p. 770-89)—9. The world in recent times (p. 790-854). Sub-division by countries and subjects. Marginal subjects covered include literature, politics, economics, law, culture, art and philosophy. Very brief (*c.* 12-word) annotations. About 225 contributors (90% of them U.S.). Analytical index, p. 855-962. A valuable tool; clear layout.

93:016

Annual bulletin of historical literature. 1911-. London, Historical Association, 1912-. no. 1-. Annual. (no. 49. 1965. 7s. 6d.).

No. 49, dealing mainly with the publications of 1963, has running commentary on *c.* 700 items.

12 sections, each prepared by a specialist: 1. General—2. Prehistory—3. Ancient history—4. The earlier Middle Ages, 500-1200—5. The later Middle Ages, 1200-c. 1500—6. The 16th century —7. The 17th century, 1603-1713—8. The 18th century, 1713-1783—9. The 19th century, 1783-1914—10. Europe and the wider world—11. American history—12. The 20th century, 1914-1963. Highly selective; books are mostly in English and stress British material. Author index. General index, v. 1-12: 1911-22 (1923).

93:016
FRANZ, G. Bücherkunde zur Weltgeschichte, vom Untergang des römischen Weltreiches bis zur Gegenwart. Unter Mitwirkung von L. Alsdorf [u.a.]. Munich, Oldenbourg, 1956. xxiv, 544p.

More than 7,000 entries, sometimes briefly annotated or detailing contents. Omits works in Asiatic languages and on the B.C. era. The work of 23 contributors, all German-speaking. Systematically arranged; pt. 1. 'Allgemeiner Teil' (classes A-G); pt. 2. 'Die Länder der Welt' (Europe, p. 54-362; Germany, nos. 852-1092a). European and German slant. Index of names.

93:016
FREWER, L. B. Bibliography of historical writings published in Great Britain and the Empire, 1940-1945. Oxford, Blackwell, 1947. xx, 346p.

Edited for the British National Committee of the International Committee of the Historical Sciences.
5,315 items, systematically arranged; classes A-T, arrangement being by areas, periods, etc. Index of persons; index of places. Covers books and periodical articles, based on some 120 journals. Continued, for books and pamphlets, by:

LANCASTER, J. C., *comp.* **Bibliography of historical works issued in the United Kingdom, 1946-1956.** London, Univ. of London, Institute of Historical Research, 1957. xxii, 388p.

Compiled for the 6th Anglo-American Conference of historians in London, 1957. About 7,400 entries, systematically arranged. No annotations; no indication of maps or illustrations. Single entry; author index only.

KELLAWAY, W., *comp.* **Bibliography of historical works issued in the United Kingdom, 1957-60.** London, Univ. of London, Institute of Historical Research, 1962. xvi, [i], 236p. 30s.

Follows the previous pattern. 3,801 items.

—————— **Bibliography of historical works issued in the United Kingdom, 1961-1965.** London, Univ. of London, Institute of Historical Research, 1967. xiv, 298p. 35s.

4,883 items, covering all aspects of history. Main sections: General—World history—European history (British history, nos. 1682-3940)—Byzantium, the Crusades and the Middle Ages—Asia; Africa; America; Australasia and Pacific Islands.

Annual duplicated supplement available from Institute of Historical Research.

93:016
HEPWORTH, P. How to find out in history: a guide to sources of information for all. Oxford, Pergamon Press, 1966. xiv, 242p. facsims. 20s.

Aims at "describing sources of information on history and its allied subject biography, and methods of approach to them" (*Preface*). 5 chapters: 1. General considerations—2. Universal biographical and historical works—3. Europe in general. The United Kingdom. The British Commonwealth (p. 72-130)—4. Individual countries (under continents)—5. The fringe of biography and history (*e.g.,* chronology; maps; heraldry; flags; genealogy)—6. The sources of history. 63 facsimiles. A handy bibliographical survey for beginners, marred by an inadequate index (no individual works are indexed). Critically reviewed in *The assistant librarian,* v. 60, no. 7, July 1967, p. 147-8.

93:016
Historische Zeitschrift. Sonderheft 1-: Literaturberichte über Neuerscheinungen zur ausserdeutschen Geschichte. Munich, Oldenbourg, 1962-.

Sonderheft 1 ([v], 779p.) surveys publications, 1945-58 on 11 countries and areas: Scandinavia, Italy (Middle Ages), Hungary, Poland, Soviet Russia, Russia and the Soviet Union, Latin America, South Asia, Japan, England and France (Middle Ages). 1965. *Sonderheit 2* (author and anonymous title index. [v], 619p.) surveys more than 3,000 publications, 1945-1962 or 1963, on the following: 1. Netherlands (general; Middle Ages)—2. Belgium—3. England (Middle Ages; p. 108-259: 607 items footnoted, with running commentary as text)—4. Ireland—5. France (Modern period; p. 277-427)—6. U.S.A. (p. 428-546)—7. China (p. 547-68). Author and anonymous title index. Contributions are by international specialists. *Sonderheft 2* is reviewed in *Times literary supplement,* no. 3350, 12th May 1966, p. 399.

93:016
International bibliography of historical sciences, 1926-. Washington, London, Paris, etc., for the International Committee of Historical Sciences, 1930-. v. 1-. Annual. (v. 32: 1963. Paris, Colin, 1966).

Published with the assistance of Unesco and under the patronage of the International Council for Philosophy and Humanistic Sciences.
V. 32: 1963—7,874 items. Selected classified lists, noting reviews (but otherwise uncritical) of books and articles in most languages. Quality of selection has varied; particularly valuable for countries without national bibliographies.

93:016
INTERNATIONAL COMMITTEE OF HISTORICAL SCIENCES. Bibliographie internationale des travaux historiques publiés dans les volumes de "Mélanges", 1880-1939. . . . **International bibliography of historical articles in Festschriften and miscellanies.** Établie avec le

concours des comités nationaux sous la direction de H. Nabholz par M. Rothbarth et U. Heffenstein. Paris, Colin, 1955. xi, 443p.

—————— 1940-1950 . . . Paris, Colin, 1965. 448p. 90F.

Subject grouping of articles and studies. Limited to Festschriften, etc. published in Europe, but items are international in scope, covering ancient, medieval and modern history.

Supplement, for France only, in *Bibliographie annuelle de l'histoire de France* . . . Année 1964 (1965), p. lv-lxi: "Liste des mélanges dépouillés de 1953 à 1964".

93:016

Jahresberichte der Geschichtswissenschaft; im Auftrage der Historischen Gesellschaft zu Berlin, hrsg. von F. Abraham, J. Hermann, E. Meyer, [etc.] 1-36. Jahrgang., 1878-1913. Berlin, Mittler, 1880-1916. 36v.

Essential guide to the historical literature of the period. Not exhaustive for writings in countries other than Germany.

93:016

LANGLOIS, C. V. Manuel de bibliographie historique. Paris, Hachette, 1901-04. 2 pts.

Still valuable, particularly for French material, Pt. 1: "Instruments bibliographiques." Pt. 2: "Histoire et organisation des études historiques".

93:016

LONDON. UNIVERSITY. Institute of Education. **Handbook for history teachers.** General editors: W. H. Burston and C. W. Green. London, Methuen, 1962. xiv, [1], 716p. 25s.

Intended as "a general work of reference for teachers of history in primary and secondary schools of all kinds" (*Joint editorial preface*). Pts.: 1. The teaching of history—2. School books (subdivided by forms, countries, periods and subjects)—3. Visual material—4. Select bibliographies (p. 397-716). Running commentary, for the most part; annotated entries for pt. 1 and much of pt. 3; cross-references. The select bibliographies are compiled by an impressive range of specialists.

93:016:016

COULTER, E. M., and GERSTENFELD, M. Historical bibliographies; a systematic and annotated guide. Berkeley, Cal., Univ. of California Press, 1935. 206p. (Reprinted New York, Russell, 1965. $6.50.).

Carefully selected and well-annotated lists arranged regionally under subjects; out of date in many sections.

An article on current bibliographies of the historical sciences, by E. Zimmermann, appeared in the *Zeitschrift für Bibliographie*, v. 2, no. 3, 1955, p. 198-213.

Manuals

93 (02)

Clio. Introduction aux études historiques. Nouv. [2., 3.] éd. Paris, Presses Universitaires de France, 1947-53. v. 1-13.

Publication began in 1934.

v. 1-9 are summaries of various periods of history, ancient, medieval and modern (to 1919).

v. 10: *Histoire de l'art.* 1949-50. 2 pts.

v. 11: *Textes et documents d'histoire.* pts. 2, 4. 1937, 1939.

v. 12: *Atlas historique. Antiquité. Moyen Âge. Temps modernes.* 1936-37. 3 pts.

v. 13: *Chronologie des civilisations.* 1949.

Particularly valuable for continental, especially French, history. v. 12, *Atlas historique,* is inferior to Philip's *Historical atlas,* the maps being in black and white only.

93 (02)

Helps for students of history. Edited by C. Johnson, H. W. V. Temperley and J. P. Whitney. S.P.C.K., 1918-24; Historical Association, 1950-.

A valuable series of booklets, written by experts, each giving an outline of the subjects, selective bibliographies and critical appraisals. New editions and additional titles are being issued by the Historical Association, which took over the series in 1949.

Recent titles:

no. 61. *British history since 1926,* by C. L. Mowat. 1960. 5s.

62. *County records,* by F. G. Emmison and I. Gray. 1961. 5s.

63. *Overseas expansion and the British Commonwealth,* by W. P. Morell. 1961. 5s.

64. *Local history from Blue Books,* by W. R. Powell. 1962. 6s.

65. *Guides to sources of illustrative material for use in teaching history,* by G. Williams. 1962. 8s. 6d.

66. *The history of the Church,* by O. Chadwick. 1962. 6s.

67. *Medieval European history,* by R. H. C. Davis. 1963. 5s.

68. *Modern European history,* 1494-1788, by A. Davies. 1967. 5s.

69. *English local history handlist,* edited by F. W. Kuhlicke and F. G. Emmison. 1965. 8s. 6d.

70. *The use of medieval Chronicles,* by J. Taylor. 1965. 5s.

93 (02)

History of mankind: social and cultural development. London, Allen & Unwin, 1963-. v. 1-. illus., maps.

v. 1. Section 1: *Prehistory,* by J. Hawkes; 2: *Beginnings of civilization,* by C. L. Woolley. 1963. 52p. of half-tone illustrations.

v. 2. *The ancient world* [1200 B.C. - A.D. 500], by L. Pareti and others. Translated from the Italian. 1965. 3 pts. ea. 42s.

v. 6. *The twentieth century,* by C. Ware and others. Section 1: Introduction. The development and application of scientific knowledge; 2-4: The transformation of societies. 2 pts. 1966. 168s.

V. 6, pt. 2, has chapter bibliographies, p. 1319-63 and an analytical index. According to *Nature* (v. 207, no. 5000, 28th August 1965, p. 905-6), v. 2 falls between two stools: "the purely objective and factual presentation with full bibliographical references; and the theory of developmental processes throughout the world".

93 (02)
The McGraw-Hill illustrated world history.
Edited by E. Wright and K. M. Stamp. New
York, McGraw-Hill, [c. 1964]. 529p. illus. (incl.
pl.), ports., maps. $15.

A popular general survey in 40 chapters, with
very brief chapter bibliographies. Most of the
contributors are British. According to *The booklist* (v. 62, no. 5, 1st November 1965, p. 234-7),
40% of the text is devoted to the last two
centuries, with emphasis on political events. 32
coloured plates; 17 historical maps (considered
clearer and more readable than those in Shepherd's *Historical atlas*). For public and school
libraries.

The *Larousse encyclopedia of ancient and
medieval history* (General editor, M. Dunan.
Translated from French. London, Hamlyn, 1963.
413p. illus. (incl. 32 col. pl.), maps. New ed.,
1965. 30s.) and *Larousse encyclopedia of modern
history from 1500 to the present day* (General
editor, M. Dunan. Translated from French.
London, Hamlyn, [1965?] 448p. illus. (incl. 35
col. pl.), maps. 30s.; 84s.) are essentially picture
books. "The McGraw-Hill survey is more convenient for reference; the Larousse has the more
recherché illustrations" (*Times literary supplement*, no. 3,284, 4th February 1965, p. 85).

93 (02)
PLOETZ, K. Auszug aus der Geschichte. 26.
Aufl. Würzburg, A. G. Ploetz-Verlag, 1960. xx,
1707p.

A systematic summary of history up to 1960;
in 6 main periods, with country divisions, then
chronologically. The latest period, 1914-60,
includes coverage of cultural aspects (science;
philosophy and religion; film, radio and television; literature; music; art). A feature is the
detailed author and subject index (p. 1624-1707),
with c. 12,000 entries.

93 (02)
Propyläen-Weltgeschichte. Eine Universalge-
schichte. Hrsg. von G. Mann and A. Heuss. Berlin, IM Propyläen Verlag, 1960-64. 10v. illus.,
facsims., maps.

1. *Vorgeschichte. Frühe Hochkulturen.*
2. *Hochkulturen des mittleren und östlichen
   Asiens.*
3. *Griechenland. Die hellenistische Welt.*
4. *Rome. Die römische Welt.*
5. *Islam. Die Enstehung Europas.*
6. *Weltkulturen. Renaissance in Europa.*
7. *Von der Reformation zum Revolution.*
8. *Das neunzehnte Jahrhundert.*
9. *Das zwanzigste Jahrhundert.*
10. *Der Welt von Heute.*
International team of contributors. Each
volume has good half-tone illustrations, maps,
chronology, name and subject index.
Supplementary v. 11, *Summa historica. Die
Grundzüge der welthistorischen Epochen* (1965.
735p. 70 illus., 64 tables. DM.90) includes an
extensive bibliography, p. 545-687; v. 12, *Bilder
und Dokumente zur Weltgeschichte* (1965, 574p.
1,072 illus. (43 in colour). 10 facsims., 7 maps.
DM.150) provides the illustrative record.

Libraries
93:026/027
**CLARK, G. K., and ELTON, G. R. Guide to
research facilities in history** in the universities
of Great Britain and Ireland. 2nd ed. Cambridge,
Univ. Press, 1965. 55p. 7s. 6d.

"One chief purpose . . . was to stress the
existence of places other than the well-known
research centres at London, Cambridge and
Oxford" (*Preface*). Facilities at 36 universities
(A-Z, Aberdeen-York) are systematically noted
(*e.g.*, specialisations; suitable libraries in neighbourhood; MS collections; microfilms of historical material; postgraduate courses not leading
to a research degree; to whom the student should
apply for information or admission).

Encyclopaedias
93 (031)
Historische W.P. encyclopedie. Hoofredactie:
Ph. de Vries [en] Th. Luykx. Uitg. onder
auspicien van de Winkler Prins Stichting.
Amsterdam, Elsevier, 1957-59. 3v. illus., ports,
maps.

Signed articles by more than a hundred contributors on all periods of world history, with
bibliographies. Emphasis is on the history of the
Netherlands and Belgium and their colonial
possessions. Biographies are included. About
2,100 pages in all; some 13,000 entries, a number
of the contributions being lengthy (*e.g.*, on
World War II). About 900 half-tone illustrations;
105 maps, 72 of them in colour.

93 (031)
Sovetskaya istoricheskiï entsiklopediya. Moscow,
Sovetskaya Entsiklopediya, 1961-. v. 1-.

v. 1-4: A-DVIN. 1961-63.
To be completed in 12v.: c. 25,000 articles.
Prepared with the assistance of foreign specialists.
More than one-third of the text is concerned with
the history of the U.S.S.R. and over 40% of the
remainder deals with Asia, Africa and Latin
America. Includes biographical entries; bibliographies, sometimes extensive, chronologies,
maps, diagrams and statistical tables accompany
articles.

93 (032)
**HEINZEL, E. Lexikon historischer Ereignisse
und Personnen in Kunst, Literatur und Musik.**
Vienna, Hollinek, 1956. xxvi, [1], 782p., with 17
pl.

A source book on historical events and persons, as depicted in art, literature and music.
About 1,500 entries, covering such subjects and
persons as the Counter-Reformation, Battle of
Naseby, the German War of Liberation (1809,
1813-15); Napoleon I (p. 523-31); Abraham
Lincoln (1 page); Charlotte Corday. Full cross-
references.

93 (032)
**LANGER, W. L. An encyclopedia of world
history,** ancient, medieval and modern, chronologically arranged. Rev. ed. Boston, Houghton,
1948. 1270p. (3rd ed. London, Harrap, 1956.).

First published 1940.

A new version of Ploetz's *Manual of universal history* (1925). Brief summaries, arranged chronologically, of events up to 1945, with some attention to economic and social developments, and with emphasis on the 18th and 19th centuries. The 3rd ed. carries an appendix covering events since 1945. Outline maps, genealogies and full index.

Theses

93 (043):016

Historical research for university degrees in the United Kingdom, 1930-. London, Univ. of London, Institute of Historical Research, 1931-. Annual.

Issued since 1932 as *Theses supplement, no. 1-*, to the *Bulletin of the Institute of Historical Research*, v. 10 (1932-33)-. Covers all universities in the U.K. "Theses completed" has been issued since no. 15 (1954) separately from "Theses in progress". The 1966 ed. of the latter (*Bulletin . . . Theses supplement* no. 27, May 1966. v, 92p.) lists 1,733 numbered items, arranged by periods and areas, with author index.

For British historical theses presented before 1930, see lists in *History* (Historical Association), 1920-29.

93 (043):016

KUEHL, W. F. Dissertations in history: an index to dissertations completed in History Departments of United States and Canadian universities, 1873-1960. Lexington, Ky., Univ. of Kentucky Press, 1965. 249p. $12.50.

An author list of 7,635 doctoral dissertations from some 80 universities. Extensive subject index. Reviewed in *College and research libraries*, v. 27, no. 4 July 1966, p. 316.

Periodicals

93 (05):016

BOEHM, E. H., and **ADOLPHUS, L.,** *ed.* **Historical periodicals:** an annotated world list of historical and related serial publications. Santa Barbara, Cal. & Munich, Clio Press, 1961. xix, 620p. $27.50.

"All-inclusive rather than evaluative" (*Introduction*). Covers about 5,000 serial publications in four categories: A. History (all periods, and prehistory); B. Auxiliary historical disciplines; C. Local history; D. Related fields and general publications ("if they contain more than 20 per cent historical material or are otherwise recommended as worthy of inclusion" (*Introduction*)). Longer entries, usually given to items in categories A-B only, note title, sub-title, frequency, date of starting, date of most recent volume examined, publisher or sponsoring institution, editor, subject coverage, language, inclusion of summaries, indexes and tables of contents, and subscription rates. Numerous minor typographical errors. Remarkably wide coverage, including even monograph series (*e.g.*, Rolls series), but far from exhaustive. Needs to be supplemented, like Caron and Jaryc, by international and national lists.

93 (05):016

CARON, P., and **JARYC, M. World list of historical periodicals and bibliographies.** Oxford, etc., International Committee of Historical Sciences, 1939. 391p.

The original list of 3,103 periodicals is supplemented by annual additions in the *International bibliography of historical sciences*, v. 16, 1947-. A useful selection, but far from exhaustive for British periodicals and publications of societies.

93 (05):016

WESTDEUTSCHE BIBLIOTHEK (*formerly* Preussische Staatsbibliothek). **Bibliographie historischer Zeitschriften, 1939-1951,** bearb. Heinrich Kramm, Marburg, Rasch, 1952-54. 3v.

v. 1: Deutschland, Österreich, Schweiz; v. 2: Grossbritannien, Irland, Niederlande, Belgien, Luxemburg, Frankreich, Portugal, Spanien, Italien; v. 3: Norwegen, Schweden, Dänemark, Finnland, Tschechoslowakei, Ungarn, Jugoslawien, Rumanien, Bulgarien, Griechenland, Polen, Baltische Länder, Sowjetunion.

Details (from their first issue) of historical periodicals current between the years 1939 and 1951 in the countries listed. Lists arranged under: General history; bibliography; auxiliary sciences; pre-history, archaeology, classical history; legal, social and economic, military, cultural, ecclesiastical, local history; foreign policy. Indexes of titles and places of publication.

93 (05)=20/

The American historical review. New York, Macmillan Co., 1895-. Quarterly. $10 p.a.

Three-quarters of this periodical is regularly devoted to reviews and lists. Thus, the January 1967 issue (v. 72, no. 2, p. 411-805) has four authoritative articles (on the 18th century) as well as the presidential address (p. 425-522), signed reviews of 259 books (p. 523-756) and a list of 'Other recent publications' (p. 757-800). The reviews average 300-400 words in length and the books dealt with cover all periods and countries: General (13)—Ancient (7)—Medieval (24)—Modern Europe (97)—Near East (4)—Africa (13)—Asia and the East (18)—Americas (83). 'Other recent publications' embraces books and articles. The July issue indexes all books received or listed during the year. Cumulative index every 10 years.

93 (05)=20/

Bulletin of the Institute of Historical Research. London, Athlone Press, 1923-. 2 p.a. 30s. p.a.

The November 1965 issue (v. 38, no. 98) contains 4 articles, including one in a series, 'Bibliographical aids in research' (20. 'The British in South America: an archive report', p. 172-91). Also, 'Notes and documents'; 'Historical news'; 'Summaries of theses'; 'Historical manuscripts—migration'; Index.

Theses supplement to the *Bulletin:* see at 93 (043):016.

93 (05)=20/

The English historical review. London, Longmans, Green, 1886-. Quarterly. 84s. p.a.

The April 1967 issue (v. 82, no. 323) devotes p. 225-341 to 4 authoritative articles (two are mediaeval and two, 19th-century studies) and 'Notes and documents' (two items, both on mediaeval subjects). The remaining half consists of signed reviews of 10 books (p. 342-64). 'Short notices' of 126 books (signed, 300-400 word shorter reviews, p. 365-445) and a list of 'other publications'. Annual author index of books reviewed. Cumulative index irregularly.

93 (05) ⇒ 30/
Historische Zeitschrift. Munich, Oldenburg, 1859-. 6 p.a.

Three-quarters of this long-respected journal is devoted to reviews and notices. The April 1967 issue (Bd. 204, Heft 2), p. 265-528, has signed reviews of 43 works (p. 429-525), sub-divided by periods and countries, and notices ('Anzeigen und Nachrichten') of 88 other items (books and articles) (p. 429-525), International coverage. Book review index. Cumulated indexes to v. 1-56, 57-96, 97-130.
On *Historische Zeitschrift. Sonderheft 1-*, see entry at 93:016.

93 (05) = 40/
Revue historique. Paris, Presses Universitaires de France, 1876-. Quarterly. 72F. p.a.

The January/March 1967 issue (276p.) has 6 articles (p. 1-182), 4 of them on France, and includes 'Quelques sources récentes pour l'histoire de la Second Guerre Mondiale', by J. Bariéty (p. 63-98). Signed reviews of 25 books (p. 183-232); short reviews of 31 books (p. 233-49); 'Recueils périodiques et sociétés savantes' (p. 250-61); Chronique (dissertations, etc.). Insert: 'Liste des livres reçus au Bureau de la Réduction' (8p.).

Illustrations

93 (084.1)
PARMENTIER, A. E. E. Album historique, publié sous la direction de E. Lavisse. Paris, Colin, 1897-1907. 4v.

v. 1. *Le moyen âge.*
v. 2. *La fin du moyen âge.*
v. 3. *Le 16e et le 17e siècles.*
v. 4. *Le 18e et le 19e siècles.*
"Valuable illustrations and portraits showing costume, furniture, manners and customs, civil and military life" (Minto, J. *Reference books* (1929), p. 233.

See also *Propyläen-Weltgeschichte.* v. 12. *Bilder und Dokumente* (1965), at 93 (02).

93 (084.1)
WILLIAMS, G. A., *comp.* **Guide to sources of illustrative material for use in teaching history.** London, Historical Association, 1962 (reprinted 1965). 94p. (Helps for students of history no. 65). 8s. 6d.

Section 1: Sources of material (governmental and other institutions; libraries, museums and art galleries; commercial firms; producers and distributors of films and of filmstrips)—2: Reference books (on sources of illustrations, etc.)—3. Types of material (illustrated books and periodicals;

historical atlases; wall-maps; old maps; wall pictures and wall charts; photographs, postcards, aerial photographs; lantern slides and transparencies; demonstration models and model figures; records and other original material. Sections 4, 5 and 6 (Periods of history—Subjects —Material relating to particular users) are virtually indexes to sections 1 and 3). Libraries, firms, producers and distributors in section 1 are European and U.S.; specialisations are stated.

Historical Atlases

93 (084.4)
L'Atlas historique et géographique Vidal-Lablache. Nouv. éd. Paris, Colin, 1951. 131p. of maps and 31p. of index.

See entry at 912 (4/9).

93 (084.4)
dtv-Atlas zur Weltgeschichte. Mainz, Taschenbuch Verlag, 1965-. v. 1-. maps.

1. *Von den Anfängen bis zur Französischen Revolution.* 2nd ed. 1965. 295p.
V. 2, due for publication in 1968, will cover the period from the French Revolution to date, and will contain 105 maps in colour offset on the major political, economic and international problems of the period; chronology; 36-page index.

Penguin Books are to produce an English edition (*Times literary supplement*, no. 3413, 27th July, 1967, p. 664).

93 (084.4)
Grosser historischer Weltatlas. 3.-2. Aufl. Munich, Bayerischer Schulbuch-Verlag, 1953-. v. 1-. maps.

1. *Vorgeschichte und Altertum;* ed. by H. Bengston and V. Milojčič. 3rd ed. 1958. (*See entry at 931 (084.4).)
2. *Mittelalter.*
3. *Neuzeit;* ed. by J. Engel. 2nd ed. 1957. (*See entry at 931 (084.4).)
V. 1 covers prehistory and antiquity up to 1200 A.D. and has accompanying text volume (*Erläuterung.* 1954). V. 2 has not yet been published.

93 (084.4)
MEER, F. van der. Atlas of Western civilization. English version by T. A. Birrell. 2nd rev. ed. Princeton, N.J., & London, Van Nostrand, 1960. 240p. illus., maps. 85s.

First published 1954 (Amsterdam, Elsevier).
"This atlas is primarily intended for those who are prepared to browse long and meditatively over maps" (*Preface*). 54 coloured maps, fully supported by a running commentary and 976 photogravure illustrations. Four main sections: 1. The three roots (Hellas; Rome; Christ)—2. Mediaeval Christendom—3. National civilizations and their expansion—4. From European to Atlantic world. Page size, 14" × 10½".
Shorter atlas of Western civilization, by F. van der Meer and G. Lemmens (London, Nelson, 1967. 224p. illus., maps. 30s.) has 19 coloured maps, 9 plans and 244 half-tone illustrations. The small-scale maps are definitely subordinate to illustrations and text.

93 (084.4)

MUIR, R. Muir's Historical atlas, ancient, medieval and modern; comprising *Muir's Atlas of ancient and classical history* and Muir's *Historical atlas, medieval and modern.* [9th ed.], edited by R. F. Treharne and H. Fullard. London, Philip, [1963], 8, xvi, 24p.; 112 col. pl. of maps. 40s.

First published 1927.

Coverage is 1500 B.C. up to post-World War II developments in Europe, Africa, India, and the Near and Middle East. A sound atlas for senior forms of secondary schools, and for colleges and universities (Treharne, R. F. *Bibliography of historical atlases* (1939), p. 11, on the 7th ed.). Page size, $11'' \times 8''$.

93 (084.4)

PUTZGER, F. W. Historischer Weltatlas. Jubiläumsausgabe. 85. Aufl. in Zusammenarbeit mit der Kartographischen Anstalt von Velhagen und Klasing, neu hrsg. von A. Hansel und W. Leiserung. Bielefeld, Velhagen & Klasing, 1963. 146 pl. of maps, 24p. of index. DM.14.80.

First published 1877.

Good, clearly coloured maps, a number of them folding. Covers pre-history, ancient history, the Middle Ages, and particularly modern Europe, to date. Page size, $10'' \times 7''$.

93 (084.4)

Rand McNally Atlas of world history; edited by R. R. Palmer. Chicago, Rand McNally, 1957. 216p. maps.

120 maps, of which 75 are coloured; commentary on pages between maps; index-gazetteer of 8,000 entries, as against some 24,000 in W. R. Shepherd's *Historical atlas.* Good coverage for the 19th and 20th centuries (to 1950). "Certainly the best world historical atlas yet produced in this country [U.S.A.] . . . Nonetheless, because of its greater number of maps and indexed names, libraries will continue to depend heavily on Shepherd's work as a historical reference atlas" (*Geographical review*, v. 49, no. 4, October 1959, p. 596). Bibliography, p. 192. Page size, $10\frac{3}{4}'' \times 7''$.

93 (084.4)

SHEPHERD, W. R. Shepherd's Historical atlas. 9th ed., containing all the maps of the seventh edition and a new supplement of historical maps for the period from 1929 to 1964, prepared for the Atlas by C. S. Hammond & Company. London, Philip (sole distributors in the British Commonwealth, excluding Canada), 1965. xii, 226, 115p. maps. 115s.

First published 1911.

Modelled on Putzger's *Historischer Schulatlas* (*q.v.*). The 9th ed. contains 226 pages of well coloured, clear maps and plans, with instructive comments covering the period 1450 B.C. - A.D. 1965. About 15% of the maps concern the U.S. Index of 115 pages (*c.* 28,000 entries). 'Acknowledgements' (bibliography), p. iv-vi.

One of the best historical atlases in English. "Suitable for senior forms of secondary schools and for colleges and universities" (Treharne, R. F. *Bibliography of historical atlases* (1939), p. 9).

93 (084.4)

TOYNBEE, A. J., and MYERS, E. D. Historical atlas and gazetteer. *A study of history*, v. 11. Issued under the auspices of the Royal Institute of International Affairs. London, Oxford Univ. Press, 1959. x, [1], 257p. maps. 42s.

Consists of (i) a gazetteer of all place-names mentioned in v. 1-10 and in the appendix to v. 11 of *A study of history*, consisting of brief locations with occasional notes; (ii) an atlas (p. 88-202) of 103 black-and-white maps, some of them double-paged; (iii) an index to the place-names in the atlas. The maps are in five groups, the first giving synoptic views of civilizations and higher religions, the others illustrating primary, secondary and tertiary civilizations (up to 1955) in the Old World, and civilizations in the New World. Tends to concentrate on the Mediterranean and Southern Asian axes of civilization. Some of the mechanical tints used as shading patterns are confusing on the smaller-scale maps but usually the lettering and presentation are admirable. Page size, $9\frac{3}{8}'' \times 7\frac{1}{4}''$.

93 (084.4)

VRIES, S. de, *and others.* **An atlas of world history.** London, Nelson, 1965. 183p. illus., maps. 50s.

Translated from Dutch; originally as *Elseviers historische atlas* (Amsterdam, Elsevier, 1963).

64 pages of coloured maps (beginning with 8 pages of maps of Great Britain from 1st to 20th century), followed by 6 pages of black-and-white sketch maps (battlefields, *e.g.*, Waterloo; growth of towns, *e.g.*, Rome, London). Preceded by 301 black-and-white half-tone illustrations with succinct linking commentary. Index to maps. The coloured maps are in pastel shades and clearly lettered. Page size: $10\frac{1}{4}'' \times 7\frac{1}{2}''$.

93 (084.4)

Westermanns Atlas zur Weltgeschichte: Vorzeit/ Altertum, Mittelalter, Neuzeit; hrsg. von H.-E. Stier [u.a.]. Braunschweig, Westermann, 1956. [6]p., 160p. of maps. (4. Aufl. [1963?]. DM.24.80).

Contains more than 400 excellently coloured maps, including many town plans. Coverage goes up to 1953; balanced treatment (pre-history and ancient history: p. 1-44; medieval history: p. 45-91; modern history: p. 93-160). No index-gazetteer.

The 3 parts are available separately.

93 (084.4):016

TREHARNE, R. F., *comp.* **Bibliography of historical atlases and hand-maps** for use in schools. London, Bell, for Historical Association, 1939. 24p. (Historical Association Pamphlets no. 114).

104 items, with critical annotations. Sections: A. Class atlases—B. Hand-maps (for class use)—C. Reference atlases and hand-maps. Names and addresses of publishing firms; no index.

Manuscripts

93:091:016

HALE, R. W., Jr., ed. Guide to photocopied historical material in the United States and Canada. Ithaca, New York, published for the

American Historical Association, by Cornell Univ. Press, 1961. xxxiv, [1], [241p.].

11,137 items; more than 300 locations. Arranged under country or area concerned, preceded by more general material (*e.g.*, 'General Collections', 'Bibiographies, General', 'Reference, General', 'Ancient world'). Predominantly U.S.A. (items 3238-11092, subdivided by States, etc.). Bibliography, p. xxi-xxv.

The *Bodleian quarterly* carries equivalent lists for Britain.

Historiography

930
BARZUN, J., and GRAFF, H. F. The modern researcher. New York, Harcourt, Brace, 1957. xiii, 386p.

Deals with methods of research and report writing, emphasizing problems of historical research and historical writing. Chapter 4, 'Finding the facts'; chapter 5, 'Verification'. 'For further reading', p. 355-67 (including guides and bibliographies, general; A-Z by subjects; no annotations). Analytical index, p. 368-86.

930
BLOCH, C., and RENOUVIN, P. Guide de l'étudiant en histoire moderne et contemporaine. Paris, Presses Universitaires de France, 1949. viii, 144 p.

Three parts: Les instruments de travail— L'accès aux documents (p. 53-98; manuscript and printed sources; libraries, general and special, in France)—L'instruction au travail personnel. Intended for the French student. No index.

930
FUETER, E. Geschichte der neueren Historiographie. 3. vermehrte Aufl. von Dietrich Gerhard u. Paul Sattler Munich, Oldenbourg, 1936. 670p. (Handbuch der mittelälterlichen u. neueren Geschichte, Abt. 1. Allgemeines).

First published in 1911; 3rd ed. contains only minor alterations and marginal cross-references. French translation, by E. Jeanmarie, as *Histoire de l'historiographie moderne* (Paris, Alcan, 1914. 785p.), contains some corrections and additions.

A fundamental work on the historiography of the period from the Renaissance to *c.* 1870, containing biographical sketches of European and American historians and brief evaluations of their work.

E. Bernheim's *Lehrbuch der historischen Methode und der Geschichtsphilosophie* (7th ed., Munich, 1914) is an exhaustive study of historical criticism and method. Reprinted New York, Franklin, in 2v.

A. von Brandt's *Werkzeug des Historikens* (Stuttgart, Kohlhammer, 1958) is a serviceable introduction for students who can read German.

930
GOOCH, G. P. History and historians in the nineteenth century. [2nd ed.] rev., with a new introduction. London, Longmans, Green, 1952. 547p.

First published 1913. The 2nd ed. has additional footnotes and an introduction on recent historical studies.

A detailed and scholarly survey, by a specialist in the period.

Supplemented by *Some modern historians of Britain: essays in honor of R. L. Schuyler;* edited by H. Ausubel, and others (New York, Dryden Press, 1951).

A history of historical writing, by J. W. Thompson and B. J. Holm (New York, Macmillan, 1942. 2v.) includes several chapters on British historiography. There are many small errors and the judgments are sometimes open to question. Valuable footnote references; index of names.

A history of historical writing, by H. E. Barnes (2nd rev. ed. New York, Dover, 1962; London, Constable, 1963. xiii, [i], 440p. $2.25; 18s.), first published in 1937, is a running commentary in 15 chapters, each with 'Selected references' appended. Detailed index of authors and titles, etc., p. 407-40.

930.1:016
RULE, J. C., comp. Bibliography of works in the philosophy of history, 1945-1957. The Hague, Mouton, 1961. vii, [i], 87p. (*History and theory. Studies in the philosophy of history.* Beiheft 1). D.Gl.9.

1,307 unannotated entries, covering theories of history, historiography, method of history, and related disciplines (*e.g.,* economics psychology and sociology). Excludes non-Western books and articles, and also Marxist interpretation of history. Chronological list (books; articles), p. 1-74; indexes of subjects and names.

930.1:016
NOWICKI, M., *comp.* Bibliography of works in the philosophy of history, 1958-1961. The Hague, Mouton, 1964. [v], 25p. (*History and theory. Studies in the philosophy of history.* Beiheft 3).

1,500 unannotated entries, similarly arranged.

Also projected as Beihefte is a series of special bibliographies on various philosophers of history such as Arnold Toynbee, J. Orteaga y Gasset, B. Croce and Charles Beard.

930.2
CLARK, G. K. Guide for research students working on historical subjects. Cambridge, Univ. Press, 1958. 56p. 5s. 6d.

"This Guide was written to help research students when starting work on historical subjects in the University of Cambridge . . ." (*Preface*). Chapters (p. 7-38): 1. Introductory—2. The objects of research —3. The choice of subject —4. The equipment needed —5. Reviewing the evidence —6. Presenting the evidence —7. The researcher's notes —8. Conclusion. Appendices: 1. Books on historical research (p. 39-40); 2. The search for materials (p. 40-51; libraries; bibliographies and catalogues; primary evidence, records, etc); 3. Working tools (p 51-56).

930.2

LANGLOIS, C. V., and **SEIGNOBOS, C. Introduction to the study of history;** translated by G. G. Berry. London, Duckworth, 1898 (reprinted 1926). xxvii, 350p.

Original ed. entitled *Introduction aux études historiques* (Paris, Hachette, 1898).

A straightforward English translation of a still basic work on historical method; chapters on criticism of documents and on historical reconstruction from source material. The English edition provides a more detailed table of contents and an index.

930.2

SAMARAN, C. L'histoire et ses méthodes. Paris, Gallimard, 1961. xiii, [iii], 1771, [1]p. tables. (Encyclopédie de la Pléiade, 11).

Contributions from many distinguished historians; pronounced French slant. Deals in detail with types of historical evidence, including archaeological remains and repositories such as libraries, museums, archives and discography. Well documented (e.g., Archéologie mediévale, p.275-328; bibliography of 5½p.). Chronological table, p.1541-1647. Name index, p. 1651-1717.

Dates

(See also 941:930.24; 942:930.24)

930.24

COLLISON, R. L. W., Newnes' Dictionary of dates. 2nd rev. ed. London, Newnes, 1966. 428p. 35s.

Frst published 1962.

"I have tried to follow the present vogue for facts and allusions many of which relate to scientific and technological achievements rather than wars and battles, and for cultural and sociological leaders in preference to field-marshals and admirals" (*Preface*). The dictionary of dates (p. 11-278) covers persons, institutions, battles, countries (listing chief dates in their history), towns, newspapers, etc.,—usually 2-line entries. The list of anniversaries, covering people and events (p. 281-428) is arranged in calendar order, some 10 birth or death dates and 6 dates of events being cited for each day, on the average.

In the 2nd ed. some entries have been replaced by others on more topical events and developments, and other entries are amplified or otherwise amended.

930.24

HAYDN, J. Dictionary of dates and universal information relating to all ages and nations. By the late Benjamin Vincent, rev. and brought up to date. 25th ed., continuing the history of the world to midsummer 1910. London, Ward, Lock, 1910. xii, 1614p.

First published 1841.

A dictionary of miscellaneous subjects, arranged alphabetically. Each subject is treated chronologically (*e.g.*, entries for "Coroner", in which some statutes relating to coroners are mentioned; "Mexico", in which about 200 events from 1503 onwards are recorded; and "Tele-

phone", a list of events in the history of the telephone). Includes statistical data. Index, p. 1549-1605.

Everyman's dictionary of dates, compiled by C. Arnold-Baker and A. Dent; revised by A. Butler (London, Dent, 1964. xxiv, 455p. (Everyman's Reference library). 25s.) similarly consists of single subject articles, over 8,000 in all, mentioning some 36,000 dates and going up to the present day. No index. 5th ed., rev. by A. Butler, 1967 (xxiv, 541p.).

930.24

KELLER, H. R. Dictionary of dates. New York, Macmillan, 1934. 2v.

v. 1: *Old World (Europe, Africa, Asia and Australasia), World War, Peace Conference, League of Nations,* [etc.].

v. 2: *New World, including the Arctic and Antarctic.*

Arrangement is by countries and then chronological. No index.

930.24

LITTLE, C. E. Cyclopedia of classified dates, with exhaustive index. New York, Funk & Wagnalls, 1900. viii, 1454p.

Primary arrangement is by countries alphabetically, then by period (*e.g.*, 1831-1880; 1880-1892), then by subject (army, navy; art, science, nature; births, deaths; church; letters; society; state; miscellaneous), each subject being finally arranged by date. Coverage is up to 31st December 1894. A valuable feature is the detailed index (p. 1163-1454).

930.24

MAS-LATRIE, L., *comte de.* **Trésor de chronologie, d'histoire et de géographie,** pour l'étude et l'emploi des documents du moyen âge. Paris, Palme, 1889. [vi], vi p., 2,300 col., ii p.

This massive work provides for the world (excluding America) a basic chronological structure. Chapters on and tables of the various eras are followed by lists of saints and fathers of the church (the latter being a table of contents and index to Migne's *Patrologia*), of popes, cardinals, councils and emperors. Lists of rulers and ecclesiastics for the countries of Europe, Asia and Africa, with natural emphasis on France.

Reprint in preparation.

A less systematic, but still standard, work is: *Art de vérifier les dates* (1750. 4th rev. ed., 1818-44. 44v.).

Sir H. Nicolas's *The chronology of history* (New ed. London, Longman, 1838. xxiv, 406p. (The Cabinet cyclopaedia: History) is still a useful handbook for the research student, being a compendium of basic information on chronological problems: eras, calendars, dates of popes and councils, etc.

930.24

PETERS, A. Histoire mondiale synchronoptique. Version française sous la direction de Robert Minder . . . Basle, Éditions Académiques de Suisse, 1963. table, with index of 61p.

Synoptic tables, forming a chronological strip 15 metres long, showing development—political, social, religious, philosophical, economic, technical, literary and artistic—of the world. Includes Far Eastern culture. Good use of colour. "Should be in every library" (*Bulletin des bibliothèques de France,* v. 8, no. 6, June 1963, p. *427-*429.

930.24
STEINBERG, S. H. Historical tables, 58 B.C. - A.D. 1965. 8th ed. London, Macmillan, 1966. x, 261p. 15s.

First published 1939.
Chronologically arranged, usually in 10 or 15-year periods, and usually in 6 parallel columns across the double page,—under areas for the left-hand page (*e.g.,* 1475-1484: Western Europe—Central, Northern and Eastern Europe—Countries overseas)—and under broad subjects for the right-hand page (*e.g.,* Ecclesiastical history—Constitutional and economic history—Cultural life). No index.
Supplemented and complemented by A. Mayer's *Annals of European Civilization, 1501-1900 (see at* 94:930.24).

Public Records

930.25:016
INTERNATIONAL COUNCIL ON ARCHIVES. Archivum. Fascicule bibliographique, no. 1. **Bibliographie analytique internationale des publications relatives à l'archivistique et aux archives.** Paris, Presses Universitaires de France, 1964. viii, 192p. 20F.

A list of 2,885 publications on archival works and archives that appeared in 1958 and 1959. Supplements the bibliographies published in the preceding volumes of *Archivum.* According to *Unesco bulletin for libraries,* v. 19, no. 2, March-April 1965, entry no. 74, this bibliographical issue is to appear regularly.

930.25:016
LANCASTER, C., *ed.* **Archives, 1956-60.** London, Library Association, [1963]. [100]p. (British Records Association. Occasional publication, no. 1). 3s.

Reprinted from *Five years' work in librarianship, 1956-1960* (London, Library Association, 1963). Preceded by "Archives, 1948-1955", by R. Ellis, in *Five years' work in librarianship, 1951-1955* (1958) p. 343-94.
Six sections: 1. Introduction—2. National bodies—3. Ecclesiastical bodies—4. Local authorities—5. Universities, institutions and societies—6. British commonwealth archives (p. 497-535). 14 references.

Also of value: "Writings on archives, current research and historical manuscripts", compiled by G. Quimby and F. B. Evans, in *American Archivist,* v. 30, no. 1, January 1967, p. 129-65.

930.25 (02)
BOUARD, A. de. Manuel de diplomatique française et pontificale. Paris, Picard, 1929-52. 2v. 3 folders, plates.

The most recent study on French and Papal diplomatic; 3v. of text planned; v. 1, Diploma-tique générale; v. 2, L'Acte privé; v. 3, L'Acte public [not published, to date].

For an excellent introduction to the study of diplomatic, see *La diplomatique,* by G. Tessier (Paris, Presses Universitaires, 1952. ("Que sais-je?" series)).

930.25 (02)
JENKINSON, *Sir* **H. A manual of archive administration.** New ed. London, Lund, Humphries, 1965. xxii, 261p. illus., diagrs. 36s.

First published 1922; 2nd ed. 1937 (the 1965 re-issue adds a 7-page introduction and a substantial and authoritative bibliography covering 1937-65).
The standard work in English on the theory and practice of archive keeping and archive making. Pt. 1 defines the word "archives" and discusses general principles; pt. 2 deals with the history and classification of archives and with the duties of the archivist; pt. 3 is devoted to the special problem of "modern archives"; pt. 4 is concerned with the making of archives and is of value to the administrator and the clerk as well as to the archivist. A more recent work on the subject is Brenneke, A. *Archivkunde: ein Beitrag zug Theorie und Geschichte des Europäischen Archivwesens* (Leipzig, 1953).

Information on current work on archives is kept up to date in "Bibliographie analytique internationale des publications relatives à l'archivistique et aux archives" in *Archivum* (Paris, 1952-).

Introduction to the resources of European archives: *Guide international des archives.* t.1: *Europe* (League of Nations, Institut International de Coopération Intellectuelle, 1934) with its supplement: "Bibliographie sélective des guides d'archives," compiled by R.-H. Bautier, in *Journal of documentation,* v. 9, no. 1, March 1953, p. 1-41.

930.25 (02)
SCHELLENBERG, T. R. Modern archives: principles and techniques. Melbourne, Cheshire; London, Angus & Robertson, 1956. xv, 248p.

The author is Director of Archival Management, National Archives, Washington.
Pt. 1, Introduction—2. Record management—3. Archival management. A mass of information carefully arranged (see review in *Journal of documentation,* v. 13, no. 2, June 1957, p. 81-83). Examples are largely but not entirely drawn from American policy and practice. Footnotes (by chapters), p. 237-41.
Schellenberg's more recent *The management of archives* (New York & London, Columbia Univ. Press, 1965. xvi, 383p. 86s.) includes a short glossary and a selective bibliography (p. 373-6).

930.25 (038)
HERBERT, J., *ed.* **Elsevier's Lexikon of archive terminology,** French—English—German—Spanish—Italian—Dutch. Compiled and arranged on a systematic basis by a committee of the International Council of Archives. Amsterdam, London, etc., Elsevier, 1964. [viii], 83p. 25s.

175 terms in French, plus explanation, and

equivalents in the other 5 languages. 6 sections: 1. Les documents d'archives—2. Structure des archives—3. Instruments de travail—4. Conservation des archives—5. Opérations techniques du traitement des archives—6. Utilisation des archives et reproduction documentaire. 6 language indexes.

930.25 (038)
UNITED STATES. GENERAL SERVICES ADMINISTRATION. National Archives and Records Service. **Glossary of records terminology.** Draft. [Washington], 1956. ii, 31p.

An attempt to standardize professional terminology for those engaged in archival and records management. About 350 terms are defined, a number of more general library terms (*e.g.,* 'alphabetico-subject filing system'; 'oversize documents') being included. Full cross-references.

ARCHAEOLOGY

Bibliographies

930.26:016
Annuario bibliografico di archeologia (opere e periodici entrati in Biblioteca con la data di pubblicazione del 1952 (anno 1)—. A cura di Cesare d'Onofrio. Istituto Nazionale di Archeologia e Storia dell'Arte. Modena, Società Tipografica Modenese, 1954-. v. 1-. Annual. ea. L.4,000.

v. 6: 1957 (published 1960) has 2,514 numbered, annotated and systematically arranged entries. 14 classes, with country, subject, etc., sub-divisions: 1. Archeologia cristiana e bizantinologia—2. Architettura e topografia—3. Arti minori e industria—4. Ceramica—5. Epigrafia—6. Filologia—7. Numismatica—8. Pittura e mosaico — 9. Preistoria e protoistoria — 10. Religione. Etnologia—11. Scavi e notizie archeologiche (1. Generalia; 2. Africa e Oriente; 3. Grecia e Italia; 4. Europa (tranne Grecia e Italia): items 1864-2091)—12. Scultura—13. Storia. Vita pubblica e privata—14. Varia. Author and subject indexes. A list of the 600 periodicals from which articles are taken (or abstracted) appears on p. 5-14.

930.26:016
Archäologische Bibliographie. Beilage zum Jahrbuch des Deutschen Archäologischen Instituts. Berlin, de Gruyter, 1913-. Annual. (1962 v. 1964. DM.22.).

A comprehensive bibliography of high standing. V. 72: 1957 (published 1958) listed 4,005 items in three main sections: 1. General—2. Regional—3. Subject (sub-divided A-I, K). Author index. Publication is reasonably prompt. The Deutsches Archäologisches Institut. Römische Abteilung. Bibliothek's *Katalog der Bibliothek des Kaiserlich Deutschen Archäologischen Instituts in Rom* (Rome, Löscher; Berlin, de Gruyter, 1913-32. 2v. in 4) and *Supplement 1. Ergänzungen zu Band 1 für die Jahre 1911-1925* (1930) precedes and supplements the above.

930.26:016
Art and archaeology technical abstracts. Published at the Institute of Fine Arts, New York Univ., for the International Institute for Conservation of Historic and Artistic Works, London, 1966-. v. 6, no. 1-. Quarterly. 150s. p.a.

Formerly (v. 1-5, 1955-65) *I.I.C. abstracts.*
About 2,000 indicative and informative signed abstracts p.a. Abstracts articles from *c.* 200 journals. Sections: A. General methods and techniques—B. Paper—C. Wood—D. Textiles—E. Paintings—F. Glass and ceramics—G. Stone and masonry—H. Metals—I. Animal and vegetable products. Each no. has a bibliography supplement (*e.g.,* v. 6, no. 1: "The preservation of natural stone, 1839-1965: a bibliography", by S. Z. Lewin, p. 185-277; 341 annotated items; name index).

930.26:016
Bibliographie annuelle de l'Age de la Pierre Taillée (paléolithique et mésolithique). Publiée sous la direction de R. Vaufrey avec le concours de l'Unesco. Paris, Bureau de Recherches Géologiques, Géophysiques et Minières, Service d'Information Géologique, 1955/56-. no. 1-. Annual. (no. 5. 1960. 5F.).

Heading: "Union Internationale des Sciences Préhistoriques et Protohistoriques".
About 1,500 references p.a. Of the 6 sections, 5: Archéologie; 6. Gisements archéologiques et paléontologiques (sub-divided by continents and countries, are largely an index to sections 1-4 (1. Généralités—2. Géologie quaternaire—3. Paléontologie quaternaire—4. Paléontologie humaine). A monthly card-service is also available.

930.26:016
BLECK, R.-D. Bibliographie der archäologisch-chemischen Literatur. Weimar, 1966. 253p. Mimeographed. (Jahresschrift des Staatlichen Museums für Ur- und Frühgeschichte Thuringens).

2,139 numbered items on scientific investigation of artistic and cultural products of all periods, chemical preservation processes and the history of chemical technology.

930.26:016
COWA surveys and bibliographies. Cambridge, Mass., Council for Old World Archaeology, 1957-. Series 1-. Biennial. (Series 2. 1960-1. $18 (personal); $25 (institutional); areas ea. $2.).

Each series comprises 22 area reports on the archaeology of the entire Old World from palaeolithic to recent times. Areas 1-8 cover Europe; 9-14, Africa; 15-20, Asia; 21, Pacific Islands; 22, Australia. Each area report covers the last 2-3 years of archaelogical activity in the area, and consists of a survey of current work and an annotated bibliography of the more important books and articles. Thus, British Isles: Area 1, no. 2, 1960 has a 13-page report and a briefly annotated list of 128 numbered items. Editor-in-chief, Donald Freeman Brown.

Preceded by *Recent publications in Old World archaeology* by Hallam L. Movius, jr. (Cambridge, Mass., Peabody Museum, 1948-55. nos. 1-8).

930.26:016

GAUDEL, P., *comp.* **Bibliographie der archäologischen Konservierungstechnik.** Bergung. Restaurierung. Konservierung. Nachbildung. Materialkunde. Berlin, Lichterfelde, 1960. 212p.

About 600 annotated entries in 5 sections on the recovery, restoration, conservation and copying of archaeological remains. Some annotations are lengthy. Author index; list of abbreviations for the 62 sources cited.

930.26:016

LAVALLEYE, J. Introduction aux études d'archéologie et d'histoire de l'art. 2. éd. Louvain, Nauwelaerts, 1958. 276p.

First published 1946 (210 p.).

930.26:016

LONDON. UNIVERSITY. Preedy Memorial Library. **Catalogue of books on archæology and art** and cognate works belonging to the Preedy Memorial Library and other collections in the University Library. London, Univ. of London, 1937. xviii, 437, 25p.

Two sections: *1.* Archaeology and ancient art (general headings; then under the earliest civilizations of the classical East, followed by continental divisions and their various national areas); *2.* Art.
Books, maps and plans, and periodical titles are included; about 10,000 items in all. Detailed index, p. 377-437; supplement of 25p.

930.26:016

PEABODY MUSEUM OF ARCHAEOLOGY AND ETHNOLOGY, Harvard University. **Author and subject catalogues of the Library.** Boston, Mass., G. K. Hall, 1963. 53v. $3,500; outside U.S.A., $3,850.

The author catalogue comprises *c.* 300,000 cards; the subject catalogue, *c.* 315,000 cards. The Library has more than 80,000 books, serials and pamphlets in many languages. The photolithographed card catalogue runs to 29,302 pages.

930.26:016

Répertoire d'art et d'archéologie: dépouillement des périodiques et des catalogues de ventes, bibliographie des ouvrages d'art français et étrangers, 1910-. Paris, Morancé (subsequently Mouton), 1910-. v. 1-. Annual. (v. 67: 1963. 1967).

Now published under the auspices of the Comité International d'Histoire de l'Art et Bibliothèque d'Art et d'Archéologie de l'Université de Paris. Subsidised by Unesco. V. 67: 1963 contains 12,385 entries, often very briefly annotated, for books and particularly periodical articles (in *c.* 1,000 periodicals from 41 countries). 5 main periods, plus 'Généralités' and 'Islam, Inde, Extrême-Orient', sub-divided by subject and then country. Index of artists' names; index of authors. 'Généralités' includes a section, 'Topographie, Urbanisme, Monuments historiques, Archéologie et Fouilles' (sub-divided by country). The first main period, 'Antiquités' (nos. 2666-5271 in v. 67) has sections 'Généralités—Égypte—Proche Orient —Eurasie—Grèce—Rome'.

930.26:016

ROUNDS, D. Articles on antiquity in Festschriften; the ancient Near East, the Old Testament, Greece, Rome, Roman law, Byzantium: an index. Cambridge, Mass., Harvard Univ. Press, 1962. xx, [i], 560p. $20.

10,000 items, covering all periods from the end of the Neolithic Age onwards (excepting only the New Testament period). Arranged under authors and subjects, with numerous cross-references from more inclusive headings (*e.g.,* 'Sculptors'; 'Sculpture'). Appendix, 'Dealing with Festschriften' (p. 549-60). Critically reviewed, with notes on omissions and errors, in *Library journal,* v. 33, no. 2, April 1963, p. 210-2.

Manuals

930.26 (02)

DÉCHELETTE, J. Manuel d'archéologie préhistorique, celtique et gallo-romaine. [1. éd.-2 éd.] Paris, Picard, 1924-34. 6v. illus., maps.

v. 1: *Archéologie préhistorique.* 1924. 2 pts.
v. 2-4: *Archéologie celtique ou protohistorique.* 2nd ed. 1924-27.
v. 5-6–: *Manuel d'archéologie galloromaine,* by A. Grenier. 1931-. (v. 1-4. 1931-60).
This basic work forms part of the *Manuel d'archéologie et d'histoire d'art,* published by Picard. Other works in the series:
Contenau, G. *Manuel d'archéologie orientale, depuis les origines jusqu'à l'époque d'Alexandre.* 1927-47. 4v.
Jéquier, G. *Manuel d'archéologie égyptienne.* 1924. v. 1; continued by:
Vandier, J. *Manuel d'archéologie égyptienne.* 1952-. v. 1-. (*see at 930.26(32)*).
Picard, C. *Manuel d'archéologie grecque.* 1935-54. 4v.
Cagnat, R., and Chapot, V. *Manuel d'archéologie romaine.* 1916-20. 2v.
Enlart, C. *Manuel d'archéologie française, depuis les temps mérovingiens jusqu'à la Renaissance.* 1924-32. 2v.

930.26 (02)

EBERT, M. Reallexikon der Vorgeschichte, unter Mitwirkung zahlreicher Fachgelehrter, hrsg. von M. Ebert. Berlin, de Gruyter, 1924-32. 15v., illus., maps.

An authoritative encyclopaedia on prehistory, the signed articles (A-Z) being by specialists. Important articles carry lengthy bibliographies and even the shortest entries have references. 'Kupferzeit (Europa)': v. 7, p. 185-191 in 11 sections; 10 lines of blibliography, plus references in the text. Each volume has about 130 plates and maps, the text referring to these in detail. Includes ancient history of various countries. V. 15, the index volume, has *c.* 60,000 entries.

930.26 (02)

Handbuch der Archäologie, im Rahmen des "Handbuchs der Altertumswissenschaft"; begründet von W. Otto, fortgeführt von R. Herbig. Munich, Beck, 1939-50. 3v.

Forms Abteilung 6 of the monumental *Handbuch der Altertumswissenschaft.* First published 1897.

930.26 (02)

LEROI-GOURHAN, A., *and others.* **La pré-histoire.** Paris, Presses Universitaires de France, 1966. 366p. illus. (Nouvelle Clio: l'histoire et ses problèmes, no. 1).

3 parts: 1. La documentation (sources (*i.e.,* sites, with commentary); bibliographies (455 items: reviews, series, congresses; manuals, treatises and general works — Europe, Asia, Africa, America, Oceania and Australia, Methodology, art; no annotations)—2. Nos connaissances —3. Problèmes et directions de recherche. Footnote references; index. 54 small but clear illustrations.

930.26 (02)

Lexikon der alten Welt. Hrsg. von C. Andresen [and others]. Zurich, Artemis Verlag, 1965. 3,524 col. illus., maps, charts. DM.280.

Not strictly limited to classical antiquity, like the *Oxford classical dictionary;* includes material on the Orient when related to Western culture and also on early Christianity. 237 signed articles, with up-to-date bibliographies; numerous cross-references. Includes chronologies, German translations of Greek and Latin quotations, extensive list of abbreviations, list of place-names, plus map references; index of Greek and Latin terms, with German equivalents (*College and research libraries,* v. 27, no. 4, July 1966, p. 316).

930.26 (02)

MÜLLER-KARPE, H. Handbuch der Vorgeschichte. Munich, Beck, 1966-. v. 1-. illus. (incl. pl.), maps.

To be published in 5 v. (1. *Altsteinzeit—2. Jungsteinzeit—3. Kupferzeit—4. Bronzezeit—5. Früheisenzeit.*
V. 1 (xi, 391p. 274 plates. DM.85.) is a detailed and well-documented survey in 10 chapters. Chapter 11: 'Verzeichnisse und Register' lists abbreviations for sources cited and has subject, name and locality indexes.

Encyclopaedias & Dictionaries

930.26 (032)

COTTRELL, L., *ed.* **The concise encyclopædia of archæology.** London, Hutchinson, 1960. 512p. illus., maps. 50s.

The concise encyclopaedia (p. 33-500) consists of *c.* 600 unsigned articles by 48 contributors. Articles, which include some biographies, vary considerably in length (10½ lines on Machu Picchu; ½ column on Charles Darwin; 5 columns on Dead Sea Scrolls). Compiled to help the intelligent amateur; no entries under Mommsen, Niebuhr, Russia or London; inadequate cross-references; no index. "For further reading", p. 501-9. 16 pages of coloured illustrations; 160 monochrome illustrations and outline maps. A French translation was published in 1962.

930.26 (032)

Dictionnaire archéologique des techniques. Paris, Éditions de l'Accueil, 1963. 2v. illus. (incl. pl.), maps.

Techniques are dealt with A-Z in signed

articles by 38 contributors. Covers the ancient civilisations of Central America, Peru and Bolivia, China, Central Asia, Mesopotamia, Egypt, Greece, Rome and Central Europe. The article 'Écriture' is divided by areas (*e.g.,* America, Far East, India, Egypt), p. 388-410; 27 illustrations, including facsimiles (with sources); references in text. 'Métallurgie', p. 622-75. 10 black-and-white maps. Bibliography at end of v. 2 (p. 1081-4).

930.26 (032)

FILIP, J. Enzyklopädisches Handbuch zur Ur- and Frühgeschichte Europas. Unter Mitwirkung zahlreicher Fachgelehrter u. wissenschaftl. Institutionen. Stuttgart, Kohlhammer, 1966-. v. 1-. illus. (incl. pl.), tables, maps. (v. 1: A-K. DM.94.).

To be in 2v. V. 2 (L-Z und Nachträge) due in Summer 1967.
Many short articles on the prehistory and early history of Europe, some of them signed; references appended. Helpful entries under 'Inventaria archeologia', 'Izvestija'. 'Bretagne': 5 cols.; 'Kroatien': 6 cols., listing publications produced locally; 'England': nearly 4 cols., with ½ col. of bibliography. Numerous good line-drawings; 40 plates appended.

930.26 (038)

STEWART, J. Archaeological guide and glossary. 2nd ed. London, Phoenix House, 1960. xi, 237p. illus. 25s.

First published 1958.
Four sections (Prehistory—Roman—Houses—Castles), each arranged A-Z. About 700 terms are defined; 28 half-tone illustrations. Adversely criticized in the *Times literary supplement* (no. 3047, 22nd July 1960, p. 470) because of misprints, mistakes, faults in coverage and rather crude line-drawings. Has a decided British slant.

Terms used in archaeology: a short dictionary, by Christopher Trent (London, Phoenix House, 1959. 62p.) provides a single alphabetical sequence of about 350 terms and is intended "to give as clear a definition as possible of the terms likely to be encountered in reading books about archaeology or in listening to lectures. Intended primarily for the layman" (*Preface*).

Periodicals

930.26 (05):016

BRUNS, G., and others, *ed.,* **Deutsches Archäologisches Institut. Zeitschriftenverzeichnis.** Wiesbaden, Steiner-Verlag, 1964. 327p. DM.85.

Catalogo dei periodici della biblioteca dell' Istituto Nazionale di Archeologia e Storia dell' Arte. A cura de C Tanfani e F. Roselli (Rome, Palombi, 1947. 70p.) lists 1,250 titles of periodicals. Supplemented by *Indici dei periodici attivi* (Modena, Società Tipog. Editrice Modenese, 1956. 24p.).

Archaeological Discoveries

930.26 (091)

DANIEL, G. E. A hundred years of archaeology. London, Duckworth, 1959. 344.

A valuable discussion of significant discoveries and developments, 1840-1940, in prehistoric archaeology. Chronological table of main events; bibliography of secondary works, references to original material being given in footnotes to the text.

China

930.26 (31)
Archaeology in China. Cambridge, Heffer, 1959-. v. 1-. illus., maps.

v. 1: *Prehistoric China,* by Chêng Tê-k'un. 1959. 42*s.* Supplement: *New light on prehistoric China.* 1966. 30*s.*
v. 2: *Shang China,* by Chêng Tê-K'un. 1960. 84*s.*
v. 3: *Chou China,* by Chêng Tê-K'un. 1963. 84*s.*
v. 4: *Han China.*
v. 5: *Six-dynasties China.*
v. 6: *T'ang China.*
v. 7: *Sung China.*
v. 8: *Ming China.*
Planned in 8 volumes. V. 1 has good illustrations, the text being further supported by figures, maps and charts. There is a list of Chinese characters, an index and a selective, up-to-date bibliography. Reviewed in *Pacific affairs,* v. 32, no. 4, December 1959, p. 427.
V. 4-8 are in preparation.

Egypt

930.26 (32):016
Annual Egyptological bibliography. Bibliographie égyptologique annuelle, 1947-. Leiden, Brill, 1948-. Annual (pt. 15: 1961. 1963. D.fl.45).

Compiled by Jozef M. A. Janssen for the International Association of Egyptologists. Arranged alphabetically by authors. The 1963 volume (published 1968) has items 63,001-63,617. Monographs are differentiated by means of a symbol. If the original is in English, the annotation is also in English; if the original is in any other language, the annotation is in French. No subject index, but indexes for the year 1947-1956 were published in 1960 (xviii, 476p. 72*s.*).

I. A. Pratt's *Ancient Egypt: sources of information in the New York Public Library;* compiled under the direction of R. Gottheil (New York, New York Public Library, 1925. xv, 486p.) is a classified list of *c.* 10,000 items. *Supplement, 1925-1941* (1942. 340p.).

930.26 (32):016
PORTER, B., and **MOSS, R. L. B.** Topographical bibliography of ancient Egyptian hieroglyphic texts, reliefs and paintings. London, Oxford Univ. Press, 1927-51. 7v. maps, plans. o.p.

v. 1. *The Theban Necropolis.* 2nd ed. 1960-64. 2 pts. ea. £10.
v. 2. *Theban temples.* 1929. 63*s.*
v. 3. *Memphis (Abû Rawâsh to Dahshûr).* 1931. 63*s.*
v. 4. *Lower and Middle Egypt, Delta and Cairo to Asyût.* 1934. 63*s.*
v. 5. *Upper Egypt, sites.* 1937.

v. 6. *Upper Egypt, chief temples (excluding Thebes).* 1939. 63*s.*
v. 7. *Nubia, the deserts, and outside Egypt.* 1951.

930.26 (32):016
PRATT, I. A., *comp.* **Ancient Egypt: sources of information** in the New York Public Library. New York, Public Library, 1925-42. 2v.

A classified, unannotated list, with author index, of 17,500 books and periodicals in the New York Public Library, covering the period down to the conquest of Egypt by the Arabs in 639 A.D. The main volume covers material acquired up to 1924; the supplement, 1925-41. A reprint of the 2v. is in preparation at *c.* £10.

Noted: Lichtheim, M. "Ancient Egypt: a survey of current historiography", in *American historical review,* v. 69, no. 1, October 1963, p. 30-46.

930.26 (32) (02)
VANDIER, J. V. Manuel d'archéologie égyptienne. Paris, Picard, 1952-. v. 1-.

v. 1: *Les époques de formation.* Pt. 1: La préhistoire; pt. 2: Les trois premières dynasties. 1952. 2v.
v. 2: *Les grandes époques.* Pt. 1: L'architecture funéraire; pt. 2: L'architecture religieuse et civile. 1954-55. 2v.
v. 3: *La statuaire.* 1959. 2v. 78.50F.
v. 4: *Bas-reliefs et peinture: scènes de la vie quotidienne.* 1964. 2v. 80F.
Published under the auspices of the Centre National de la Recherche Scientifique. Continues G. Jéquier's *Manuel d'archéologie égyptienne* (Paris, Picard, 1924. v. 1).
An illustrated guide to the study of the monuments and artifacts of ancient Egypt, dealing only incidentally with its religion, literature and history.

930.26 (32) (03)
POSENER, G. A dictionary of Egyptian civilization. [Translated from the French by A. Macfarlane . . .]. London, Methuen, 1962. x, 324p. illus., maps. 48*s.*

Translation of *Dictionnaire de la civilisation égyptienne* (Paris, Hazan, 1959).
A small dictionary with signed articles, ranging from brief entries to essays (*e.g.,* on hieroglyphics; mummifying). Profusely illustrated—315 clear illustrations, of which 145 are in colour. Many cross-references. Index of names; general index.

930.26 (32) (092)
Who was who in Egyptology: a biographical index of Egyptologists; of travellers, explorers and excavators in Egypt; of collectors and dealers in Egyptian antiquities; of consuls, officials, authors and others whose names occur in the literature of Egyptology, from the year 1700 to the present day, but excluding persons now living, by Warren R. Dawson. London, Egypt Exploration Society, 1951. x, 172p. 20*s.*

Sources of information are quoted in entries: (1) other published works—biographies, periodical articles, society transactions, etc.; (2) unpublished material—diaries, correspondence, notebooks, etc. (3) direct personal enquiry. The main works (77 in all) used by the compiler are listed.

Palestine

930.26 (33) (02)

VAUX, R. de. Ancient Israel: its life and institutions. Translated by J. McHugh. London, Darton, Longman & Todd, 1961. xxiii, 592p.

Originally as *Les institutions de l'Ancien Testament* (Paris, Les Éditions du Cerf, 1958-60. 2v.).
Four main parts: 1. Family institutions—2. Civil institutions—3. Military institutions—4. Religious institutions (p. 271-517). Bibliography (updated to 1961 in the English translation), p. 519-52 (small type). Analytical, 3-column index, p. 552-67; index of Semitic forms; index of Biblical references. Scholarly and well produced.

930.26 (33) (084.4)

KRAELING, E. G., ed. Historical atlas of the Holy Land. New York, Rand, McNally (U.K. & British Commonwealth distributors: London, Vane) 1959. 88p. illus., maps. 25s.

A short account of the finding of the Dead Sea Scrolls, followed by 22 coloured maps, many of them spread over double pages, plus insets. The maps are political, overprinted on physical base maps, the relief features rarely showing through. The maps are followed by a condensed history of the Holy Land, consisting essentially of illustrations and comments on them. An index to the maps (but not to places mentioned in the text) is appended. Reviewed in *Geographical journal*, v. 127, pt. 1, March 1961, p. 126. Page size, 10″ × 6½″.

India

930.26 (34):016

Annual bibliography of Indian archæology, 1926-. Leiden, Kern Institute, 1958-. Irregular. (v. 20: 1962-63. 1966. 75s.).

Published with the aid of the government of India, the government of Ceylon, the Netherlands Organization for Pure Research (Z.W.O.) and the Netherlands Institute for International Cultural Relations.
V. 15 has a lengthy introduction (p. xiii-xci) which reviews explorations, excavations and archaeological activities in India, Pakistan, Ceylon, Further India, Indonesia, Afghanistan and Central Asia. The bibliography (4,192 items) is in five sections and includes commemorative and obituary notices, as well as notes, an index and appended half-tone plates.

930.26 (34 (032)

DOWSON, J. Classical dictionary of Hindu mythology and religion, geography, history, and literature. London, Trubner, 1879 (and reprints). xix, 411p.

Compared with J. Garrett's *Classical dictionary of India*, is more concerned with the strictly classical period of Indian history and religion.

Gives many very brief entries, indicating pronunciation. Sanskrit index; general index. All characters are romanized.

930.26 (34) (032)

GARRETT, J. A classical dictionary of India, illustrative of the mythology, philosophy, literature, antiquities, arts, manners and customs, etc., of the Hindus. Madras, Higginbotham, 1871. xii, 793, [iv], 160p.

Attempts to do for ancient India what Sir William Smith did for the classical world. Entries are fairly full and there are a number of quotations. A list of works quoted or referred to appears on p. ix-x.

Mesopotamia

930.26 (352):016

Bibliographie analytique de l'Assyriologie et de l'archéologie du Proche-Orient. Leiden, Brill, 1956-. v. 1-.

v. 1, section A: *L'archéologie, 1954-1955*. 1956.
v. 1, section PH: *La philologie, 1954-1956*. 1957.
v. 2, section A: *L'archéologie, 1956-1957*. 1960.
The sections on archaeology are in 3 pts.: General bibliography; Bibliography by regions; notices of publications appearing before 1954 and 1956, respectively. The section of v. 1 on philology also has 3 pts.: General bibliography; Systematic bibliography (7 classes, with subdivisions); notices of publications appearing before 1954. Each of the sections has an author index.

I. A. Pratt's *Assyria and Babylon: a list of references in the New York Public Library* (New York, Public Library, 1918. vi, 143p.) lists 2,750 items.

Noted: Council of Europe, Strasbourg. Council for Cultural Co-operation. *Assyriology: European research resources* (1968. 32p. 10s.).

930.26 (352) (084.4)

BEEK, M. A. Atlas of Mesopotamia: a survey of the history of civilisation of Mesopotamia from the Stone Age to the fall of Babylon. Translated by D. R. Welsh. Edited by H. H. Rowley. London, Nelson, 1962. 164p. illus., maps. 70s.

Text, on the civilisations of Sumeria, Assyria and Babylonia, is interspersed with illustrations and maps. 296 photogravure illustrations; 22 good maps, with overlay text. Biblical references, p. 162; index, p. 153-61. Criticised in *The geographical journal* (v. 128, pt. 4, December 1962, p. 523) for paucity of air photographs "or photographs of scale-model reconstructions of cities and buildings—so stimulating a feature of [*Atlas of the*] *Classical world*". Page size, 13½″ × 10″.
Also published in German and in Dutch.

Persia

930.26 (355)

PRATT, I. A. List of works in the New York Public Library relating to Persia. New York, Public Library, 1915. vi, 151p.

2,750 items. A reprint is in preparation.

Classical Antiquities

930.26 (37/38):016

L'Année philologique: bibliographie critique et analytique de l'antiquité gréco-latine. Fondée par J. Marouzeau . . . 1924/26 . . . Paris, Société d'Éditions 'Les Belles Lettres', 1928-. Annual. (v. 36. *Bibliographie de l'année 1965 et complément d'années antérieurs.* 1967. 117s. 6d.).

A continuation of J. Marouzeau's *Dix années de bibliographie classique . . . 1914-1924* (Paris, 1927. 2v.).

Each annual volume consists of 2 pts.: Authors and works (arranged by authors, A-Z)—Specific aspects. This latter includes 4. 'Antiquités', A. 'Archéologie' (p. 349-459)—*c.* 1,500 annotated items. Four indexes: to collections, ancient authors, humanists, and modern authors.

930.26 (37/38):016

Fasti archeologia: annual bulletin of classical archaeology. International Association for Classical Archaeology. Florence, Sansoni, 1946-. v. 1-. illus. (pl.). (v. 17: 1962. 1965).

V. 17 contains 8,083 indicative and informative abstracts in 6 main sections (with regional, etc. sub-divisions): 1. General—2. Prehistoric and classical Greece—3. Italy before the Roman Empire—4. The Hellenistic world and the Eastern provinces of the Roman Empire—5. The Roman West—6. Christianity and late antiquity. Profuse cross-references. 3 indexes: authors, ancient and modern; geographical names; subjects. A valuable tool.

Also noted: Breccia, A. E. *Avviamento e guida allo studio della storia e delle antichità classiche* (Pisa, 1950. 377p.).

930.26 (37/38) (02)

Handbuch der Altertumswissenschaft; begründet von I. von Müller, erweitert von W. Otto, fortgeführt von H. Bengtson. Munich, Beck, 1887-.

A massive co-operative work of the highest importance. Monographs, by specialist writers which are constantly being revised and some of which are still in preparation, cover the whole field of classical antiquity. Numerous footnote references and detailed index to each volume. Sections so far issued (many now o.p., but some reprinted), listed under the current numeration, are:
1. Abt.: *Einleitende und Hilfdisziplinen.*
2. Abt.: 1. Teil: *Griechische Grammatik;* 2. Teil: *Lateinische Grammatik.*
3. Abt.: 1. Teil: *Geschichte des alten Orients;* 2. Teil: *Hellenische Landeskunde;* 3. Teil: *Geographie von Italien;* 4. Teil: *Griechische Geschichte;* 5. Teil: *Römische Geschichte.*
4. Abt.: 1. Teil: *Griechische Staatskunde;* 2. Teil: *Römische Privatalterturmer;* 3. Teil: *Heerwesen und Kriegführung der Griechen und Römer.*
5. Abt.: *Geschichte der Philosophie, Naturwissenschaften und Religion.*
6. Abt.: *Handbuch der Archäologie.*
7. Abt.: *Geschichte der griechischen Literatur.*
8. Abt.: *Geschichte der römischen Literatur.*
9. Abt.: *Lateinische Literatur des Mittelalters.*
10. Abt.: *Rechtsgeschichte des Altertums.*
12. Abt.: *Byzantinisches Handbuch.*
10. Abt., 3 Teil iv, was published in 1966

930.26 (37/38) (02)

LAURAND, L. Manuel des études grecques et latines. Nouv. éd. entièrement refondue par A. Lauras. Paris, Picard, 1948-58. 4v. illus., maps.

Previous edition, 1946-50.
1. *Grèce: Géographie, histoire, institutions grecques. Littérature grecque. Grammaire historique grecque.* 12. éd. 1956.
2. *Rome: Géographie, histoire, institutions romaines. Littérature latine. Grammaire historique latine.* 1958.
3. *Compléments, atlas, tables.* 7. éd. rev. et corrigée. 1948.
4. *Pour mieux comprendre l'antiquité classique; pédagogie; linguistique.* 1958.
Contains a mass of concise information on all aspects of the classical world, systematically arranged into short paragraphs and well indexed. Sources and bibliographies are frequently given. The 'Petit atlas d'histoire', in v. 3, consists of small black-and-white maps and is a feature done better elsewhere.

930.26 (37/38) (02)

PLATNAUER, M., *ed.* **Fifty years of classical scholarship.** Oxford, Blackwell, 1954. xvi, 431p. illus. 21s. 6d.

14 chapters (8 on Greek, 6 on Latin scholarship; from Homer to 'Silver Latin poetry'); 17 contributors. Literature, history and philosophy are the main themes. Footnote references are appended to chapters. The chapter, 'The Greek historians', by G. H. Griffith (p. 150-92), has 128 footnote references (p. 177-92). No index.

Noted: *History of classical scholarship, from the beginnings to the end of the Hellenistic age* (London, Oxford Univ. Press, 1968. 330p. 63s.).

930.26 (37/38) (031)

DAREMBERG, C., and **SAGLIO, E. Dictionnaire des antiquités grecques et romaines,** d'après les textes et les monuments, contenant l'explication des termes qui se rapportent aux mœurs, aux institutions, à la religion . . . et en général à la vie publique et privée des anciens. Paris, Hachette, 1873-1919. 5v. and index. illus. (Reprinted, 1962-63. £225.)

Scholarly and well documented, covering all phases of ancient Greek and Roman life, customs and institutions. Excludes biography and literature. Signed articles. Useful indexes of authors, Greek words, Latin words, and subjects. Excels possibly even Pauly-Wissowa's *Reallexikon* in presentation of material; "is still an unequalled source of reference on many topics such as arms, dress, furniture, ceramics, cultural practices, sport, architecture, deities, etc." (Ad Orientem. *Books on Africa and the Orient. Catalogue five.* 1966, entry no. 1963).

930.26 (37/38) (031)

PAULY, A. F. von, and **WISSOWA, G. Pauly's Real-Encyclopädie der classischen Altertumswissenchaft.** Neue Bearbeitung begonnen von G. Wissowa, fortgeführt von W. Kroll und K. Mittelhaus, unter Mitwirkung zahlreicher Fachgenossen, hrsg. von K. Ziegler. Stuttgart. Metzler, 1894-1967. Supplement 1-. 1903-.

Published in 2 series running concurrently. *1. Reihe* covers A-Q (24v. in 32 pts.; completed 1963); *2. Reihe*, R-Z (9v. in 17 pts.; completed 1967). *Supplement-Bänden* 1-10, 1903-65.

An indispensable work of scholarship for any large general library. Comprehensive signed articles, with adequate bibliographies, cover every aspect of classical literature, history, geography, antiquities and civilisation. The article 'Ptolemain als Geograph' in Suppt. 10 extends to p. 679-834, with bibliography p. 819-34. 2 columns, lines numbered in tens for easy cross-reference.

Der Kleine Pauly. Lexikon der Antike auf der Grundlage von Pauly's Real-Encyclopädie der classischen Altertumswissenschaft unter Mitwirkung zahlreicher Fachgelehrter, bearb. und hrsg. von K. Ziegler und W. Sontheimer (Stuttgart, Druckenmüller, 1964-. v. 1-) is to be a condensation in 4v. V. 1 (1,558 cols.) is the work of 99 contributors (mostly German). Signed articles; that on Aristophanes runs to nearly 5 columns (as against 23 in the original), with 10 lines of references. Supplement, col. 1519-58. Well produced.

930.26 (37/38) (031)
SMITH, *Sir* W. **Dictionary of Greek and Roman biography and mythology.** London, Murray, 1880. 3v. illus.

The period covered is from the earliest times to the fall of the Western Empire in A.D. 746.

A one-volume adaptation and revision is: *A classical dictionary of Greek and Roman biography, mythology and geography,* revised throughout and in part re-written by G. E. Marindin (London, Murray, 1894. vi, 1018p. illus., maps). The period covered is from the earliest times to the fall of the Western Empire in A.D. 746. Short entries; no authorities cited *in situ.* An appendix cites the most important reference works consulted.

—— **Dictionary of Greek and Roman geography.** London, Murray, 1854-57 (reprinted 1873-78). 2v. illus., maps.

—— *and others, ed.* **Dictionary of Greek and Roman antiquities.** 3rd ed., rev. and enl. London, Murray, 1890-91 (and reprints). 2v. illus.

First published 1842; 2nd ed. 1848.
Signed articles; references in text; gives etymology. Complementary to the *Dictionary of Greek and Roman biography and mythology.*

These three works, though much dated and partly, at least, superseded by Pauly and others, are still of value.

930.26 (37/38) (032)
The **Oxford classical dictionary;** edited by M. Cary [and others]. Oxford, Clarendon Press, 1949. xx, 971p. 60s.

Modelled on Lübker's *Reallexikon* (8th ed. 1914), and designed to cover the same ground as the older dictionaries of Sir William Smith. 6 editors; 3 assistant editors; 161 contributors. More space is given to biography and literature, less to geography, and the bibliographical information is restricted to the more important and standard works.

Articles are signed and normally short but there are numerous comprehensive subject surveys which go beyond the general terminal date of 337. Most useful, but many changes on the editorial board have caused some omissions and inconsistencies.

Sir P. Harvey's *Oxford companion to classical literature* (1937; see *Guide* (1959) at 87 (03)) has been considered more practical for ready reference purposes.

The New century classical handbook, edited by C. B. Avery (New York, Appleton-Century-Crofts; London, Harrap, 1962. xv, 1162p. 84s.) has *c.* 6,000 unsigned entries; gives pronunciation but no etymology. No citations. Nearly 100 half-tones; amateurish text-illustrations. The *Times literary supplement* (no. 3,220, 14th November 1963, p. 929) considers Sir W. Smith, Robert Graves (*The Greek myth.* 1955) and the *Oxford classical dictionary* quite adequate for all general purposes. The *Handbook's* most useful function "is over historical biography, and even here it is alarmingly uncritical".

930.26 (37/38) (032)
SEYFFERT, O. A dictionary of classical antiquities: mythology—religion—literature—art; rev. and ed. Henry Nettleship and J. E. Sandys. London, Allen & Unwin, 1957. vi, 716p. illus. 30s.

Founded on Seyffert's *Lexikon der classischer Altertumskunde* (1882). The 1957 edition is a reprint of the 3rd edition (1894) of the English translation.

A standard small-scale work, compact, yet readable. Adequate cross-references; some references to sources; general index.

Harper's Dictionary of classical literature and antiquities; edited by H. T. Peck (2nd ed. New York, Cooper Square Publishers, 1897 (reprinted 1902). xv, 1701p.), includes biography and has many cross-references and good, small illustrations.

930.26 (37/38) (032)
WARRINGTON, J. Everyman's Classical dictionary, 800 B.C. - A.D. 337. London. Dent, 1961. xxxvii, 537p. 20s.

Claims to supplant Sir William Smith's *Smaller classical dictionary* (revised by H. E. Blakeney and J. Warrington. London, Dent, 1956. xxiv, 352p.). "Hundreds of articles are supplied on persons and subjects ignored by the old volume" (*Preface*). Articles vary in length from about 8 words to 2 pages (*e.g.,* on Heracles). For writers, the articles cite the "best" editions and translations. According to the *Times literary supplement,* no. 3106, 8th September 1961, p. 592, it is conspicuously less well planned and somewhat less reliable than the *Oxford companion to classical literature.*

930.26 (37/38):05
SOUTHAN, J. E., *comp.* **A survey of classical periodicals:** union catalogue of periodicals relevant to classical studies in certain British libraries. London, Univ. of London, Institute of Classical Studies, 1962. xii, 181p. (*Bulletin* supplement no. 13). 30s.

Details the holdings of 51 libraries (19 in London). About 600 titles, including yearbooks. References from earlier to later titles. Some entries give fuller details of imperfect runs. Volume number given as well as date, whenever possible.

The *Bulletin* of the Institute of Classical Studies also includes a report on 'Research in classical studies for university degree in Great Britain and Ireland' (section A, Work in progress; section B, Work completed), arranged under universities, A-Z.

930.26 (37/38) (084.4)
HEYDEN, A. A. M. van der, and **SCULLARD, H. H.,** *ed.* **Atlas of the classical world.** London, Nelson, 1959. 221, [1]p. illus., maps. 70s.

"Not intended primarily for professional scholars" (*Foreword*).

70 coloured maps, plus insets; 475 photogravure plates, including many air photographs. The atlas is a companion volume to the *Atlas of the Bible* and the *Atlas of the early Christian world*. It illustrates the centuries from prehistoric Greece to the decline of the Roman Empire before the barbaric immigrations of the 4th century. Information is presented in three ways: maps, giving religious, economic, military, literary, artistic and political statistics; illustrations (line-drawings and photographs); descriptive articles, covering geography, history and culture. Maps include town plans and a number have lengthy legends; scales are not often indicated. 24 pages of index. Well produced. Page size, $13\frac{1}{2}'' \times 10''$.

Shorter atlas of the classical world, compiled by H. H. Scullard and A. A. M. van der Heyden (London, Nelson, 1962 [*i.e.,* 1963]. 239p. illus., maps. 15s.) is not a mere abridgement. Prof. Scullard has provided a new 40,000-word account of the Greek and Roman civilisations. But the chief features are the 200 or so excellent illustrations of landscape and culture. The 10 coloured maps occupy a rather inconspicuous place. Reviewed in *The geographical journal,* v. 129, pt. 3, September 1963, p. 372.

930.26 (37/38) (084.4)
Murray's Small classical atlas; edited by G. B. Grundy. 2nd ed. London, Murray, 1917. xxiii p., 14 pl. of maps.

First published 1904.
Excellent maps by Bartholomew, with coloured relief, double-page spread and hinged. The 14 plates deal with the Roman Empire, Egypt, Greece, Asia Minor, the principal battlefields in Greek and Roman history, and Palestine. Index-gazetteer, p. v-xxiii. Page size, $13\frac{1}{2}'' \times 9''$.

930.26 (37/38) (084.4)
THOMSON, J. O. Everyman's Classical atlas, with an essay on the development of ancient geographical knowledge and theory. [New ed.]. London, Dent, 1961. lxx p., 56 pl. of maps, p. 59-125. illus. 18s.

First published as *Everyman's Atlas of ancient and classical geography,* 1907; rev. ed. 1952.
The text consists of the essay, together with notes on some of the battlefields of antiquity.

The 56 maps (by Bartholomew) and 5 sketch maps are of various sizes and scales. The index-gazetteer carries some 3,500 entries and is followed by 29 pages of illustrations. The small page size ($8'' \times 5''$) is not enhanced by the 1" margin for maps and much white space for the illustrations.

Rome

930.26 (37):016
BORRONI, F. "Il Cicognara": bibliografia dell' archeologia classica e dell'arte italiana. Florence, Sansoni, 1954-. v. 1-. facsims.

v. 1: *Opere bibliografiche citate.* 1954-55. 2 pts.
v. 2: *Archeologia classica.* 1957-65. pts. 1-5.
A large-scale bibliography, with some annotations.

V. 1 has 8 sections (1. Bibliografica; 2. Cataloghi di biblioteche d'arte e di libri d'arte; 3. Enciclopedie, lessici e dizionari; 4. Estetica; 5. Orazione, accademiche, dissertazioni, conferenze; 6. Poemetti didascalici e sulle arti; 7. Tecnica; 8. Conservazione e restaure), with an author and subject index and index of facsimiles. Section 5, Musei, occupies a considerable portion of v. 2, pt. 2. V. 2, pt. 5 deals with architecture, painting, plastic arts, ceramics, vases, mosaic, metal work, glass, ivory, tapestry, etc. Items are numbered in each section (*e.g.,* v. 2, pt. 5, items 10297-12416), final arrangement being chronological.

930.26 (37) (02)
SANDYS, Sir J. E., *ed.* **A companion to Latin studies.** 3rd ed. Cambridge, Univ. Press, 1921. xxxv, 891p. illus., maps. (Reprinted New York, Hafner, 1963. $17.50.).

First published 1910.
A detailed guide which, despite its age, is still valuable; on the same pattern as Whibley's *Companion to Greek studies* (*q.v.*). Chapters are by specialists; sections and chapters carry bibliographies. Four indexes: persons, deities and races; places, rivers and mountains; scholars and modern writers; Latin words and phrases. 141 illustrations; 2 maps.

A comparable, smaller work is: *Companion to Roman history,* by H. S. Jones (Oxford, Clarendon Press, 1912. xii, 472p. illus. (80 pl.), maps. (80 pl.). This also has section and/or chapter references, and three indexes: general; Latin terms; Greek terms, now o.p.

Also o.p. is: *A topographical dictionary of ancient Rome,* by S. B. Platner; completed and revised by T. Ashby (Oxford, Univ. Press, 1929. 632p. illus.).

930.26 (37) (032)
NASH, E. Pictorial dictionary of ancient Rome. London, Zwemmer. 1961-62. 2v. illus., maps, plans. £21 the set (not sold separately).

Sponsored by the Deutsches Archäologisches Institut.
Essentially a pictorial record (v. 1, 674 halftones; v. 2, 664) of the city of Rome's ancient monuments and buildings, with brief descriptions and bibliographies. Thus, the entry on Fornix Fabianus occupies p. 398-400, has 4 illustrations, 6 lines of description and a biblio-

graphy of 26 items. V. 1 has general bibliography, p. 9-12; pictorial sources, p. 12-13. Scholarly. New and rev. ed. 1968. £21.

Greece

930.26 (38) (02)
WHIBLEY, L., *ed.* **A companion to Greek studies.** 4th ed., rev. Cambridge, Univ. Press, 1931. xxxviii, 790p. illus., maps. (Reprinted New York, Hafner, 1963. $17.50).

First published 1905.
A comprehensive handbook designed primarily for the student of Greek literature and providing information on every aspect of Greek life and culture, including geography, fauna and flora, agriculture and housing, etc. Chapters by specialists.
Four indexes: persons, deities and races; places; scholars and modern writers; Greek words and phrases.

930.26 (38) (032)
DEVAMBEZ, P., *and others.* **A dictionary of ancient Greek civilization.** Translated from French. London, Methuen, 1967. 496p. illus. (Methuen's Dictionaries of the arts). 90s.

Translation of *Dictionnaire de la civilisation grecque* (Paris, Hazan, 1966).
More than 750 concise articles, arranged A-Z. Covers Greek life and thought from the earliest times to the Roman conquest. More than 400 good illustrations. Adversely reviewed in *Times literary supplement,* no. 3,428, 9th November 1967: "The treatment prefers omission to compression and easiness of reading to precision".

Great Britain

930.26 (410):016
Archaeological bibliography for Great Britain & Ireland, 1950/51-. London, Council for British Archaeology, 1949-. Annual. (1965 v. 1967. 20s.).

Previously as *Archaeological bulletin for the British Isles,* 1940/46, 1947, 1948/49, itself succeding the Reports of the Congress of Archaeological Societies. Covers archaeology in a wide sense, with material from earliest times to A.D. 1600, and a selection of 17th-century items; also industrial archaeology. The 1964 v. is in 2 parts: 1. A topographical section under country, period and subject headings; 2. A bibliography containing articles from periodicals (57 general and *c.* 100 local), books and monographs. Subject index, partly analytical.
As *British archaeological abstracts . . .* 1967-. (1968-. Annual).

The Council for British Archaeology also publishes a quarterly *Current and forthcoming offprints in archaeology in Great Britain and Ireland,* and a *Calendar of excavations* during each summer.

930.26 (410):016
BONSER, W. A Romano-British bibliography (55 B.C. - A.D. 449). Oxford, Blackwell, 1964. 2v. 168s.

9,370 items, closely classified; 15 classes and 666 sub-divisions. Classes: 1. General topics—2. History—3. Army, fleet and defence—4. Social and economic—5. Religion—6. Geography—7. General archaeology—8. Numismatics—9. Art—10-15. Regions of England, Scotland and Wales. 'Periodicals and collective works abstracted': 253 items. No annotations, but brief explanatory notes sometimes follow title, and presence of maps and plates is indicated. V. 2 consists of indexes: author; subject; personal names; place-names (a) England, (b) Scotland, (c) Wales and Monmouthshire. A valuable compilation for the period, particularly in view of the time-lag in publishing *Writings on British history.*

930.26 (410):016
COUNCIL FOR BRITISH ARCHAEOLOGY. British archaeology: a book list. [Rev. ed.] London, the Council, 1960. 43p. 5s. 6d.

Replaces the 1949 list (*British archaeology: a book list for teachers*).
About 1,200 items in three main sections: periods, from the palaeolithic to the Industrial Revolution; regional books, covering England, Scotland and Wales; and books for children, with a short selection of original studies of a more elementary nature. No annotations, except for series such as those of the Royal Commission on Historical Monuments; no index.

930.26 (410):016
GOMME, G. L., *and others.* **Index of archaeological papers,** 1665-1890. Constable, 1907. xi, 910p.

Prepared for the Congress of Archaeological Societies and the Society of Antiquaries of London. Continued annually for the years 1891-1910 under the same auspices (Constable, 1892-1914). The main work is an index under authors to articles in 94 journals of archaeological and historical content. The supplements include further indexes of subjects and places mentioned, referring back to the author sequence.
The series is incomplete on the historical side, many local societies having been omitted, and it is superseded for 1901 onwards by Mullin's *Guide to the historical publications of the societies of England and Wales* (see at 942:016) and Milne's *Writings on British history,* 1934- (see at 941:016) and, for the more strictly archaeological material, by the *Archaeological bulletin for the British Isles,* subsequently *Archaeological bibliography for Great Britain & Ireland* (q.v.).

930.26 (410):016
GREAT BRITAIN. H.M. STATIONERY OFFICE. Government publications: Ancient monuments and historic buildings. Sectional list no. 27, revised to 30th September 1965. London, H.M.S.O., 1965. 14p. *Gratis.*

Lists in particular Ministry of Public Building and Works' Official guides and Royal Commissions on Ancient and Historical Monuments and Constructions' Inventories and reports. Includes o.p. items.

The Ministry of Public Building and Works' *Excavations: annual report* covers pre-historic, Romano-British and medieval excavations in general and then; in detail, by counties A-Z (1967 ed. London, H.M.S.O., 1968. 44p. pl. 3s. 6d.).

The Council for British Archaeology's monthly *Calendar of excavations*, 1951-, lists sites on which work is to be done and where amateur assistance is invited.

930.26 (410) (02)
BRITISH MUSEUM. Department of British and Medieval Antiquities. **Guide to Anglo-Saxon and foreign Teutonic antiquities.** London, British Museum, 1923. xii, 179p. illus., pl.

——— **Guide to the antiquities of Roman Britain.** [3rd ed.] London, British Museum, 1964. [8], 82p. illus., pl., maps. 7s.

First published 1922.
A short general introduction is followed by sections dealing with various aspects of life in Roman Britain, each illustrated by objects in the Museum's collections. 27 plates; bibliography.

——— **Later prehistoric antiquities of the British Isles.** London, British Museum, 1953. x, 81p. 6s.

Describes and illustrates the collections belonging to the Neolithic, Bronze and Early Iron Ages, with a general introduction to each period.

930.26 (410) (02)
COLLINGWOOD, R. G., and **MYRES, J. N. L. Roman Britain and the English settlements.** 2nd ed. Oxford, Clarendon Press, 1937. xxvi, 515p. maps. 38s.

A standard, well-arranged volume of the Oxford History of England. It is not written in collaboration, Collingwood being solely responsible for Roman Britain and Myres for the English settlements. The descriptive bibliography (p. 462-89) is of great value.

930.26 (410) (02)
COLLINGWOOD, R. G., and **WRIGHT, R. P. The Roman inscriptions of Britain.** Oxford, Clarendon Press, 1965-. v. 1-. illus. (incl. pl.).

v. 1. *Inscriptions on stone.* £12 12s.
A finely produced work, with details of 2,400 inscriptions; entries arranged under regions and counties, then towns. In each case, a reproduction of the original plus transcription and translation. 'Milestones' are covered in items 2219-2400. Short glossary and translation of military terms; index of sites. Bibliography (p. xix-xxxiii): A. Abbreviations of periodicals and serial works—B. Manuscript sources—C. Separate works—D. Museum catalogues.

930.26 (410) (02)
GREAT BRITAIN. MINISTRY OF WORKS. Illustrated regional guides to ancient monuments in the ownership or guardianship of the Ministry of Works. London, Edinburgh, H.M. Stationery Office. 6v. illus., maps.

v. 1: *Northern England,* by Lord Harlech. 3rd ed. 1959. 4s. 6d.
v. 2: *Southern England,* by Lord Harlech. 2nd ed. 1952. 7s.
v. 3: *East Anglia and the Midlands,* by Lord Harlech. 2nd ed. 1955. 7s.

v. 4: *South Wales and Monmouthshire,* by Sir C. Fox. 3rd ed. 1954. 5s.
v. 5: *North Wales,* by Lord Harlech. 2nd ed. 1954. 5s. 6d.
v. 6: *Scotland,* by V. G. Childe and W. D. Simpson. 4th ed. 1961. 7s. 6d.
Written by specialist authorities, the volumes have brief but valuable introductions arranged by period, followed by county lists giving a short account of each monument, the nearest railway station and the hours of admission for the public.

930.26 (410) (02)
Regional archaeologies. General editor, D. M. Wilson. London, Cory, Adams & Mackay, 1965- illus., maps.

South West Scotland, by J. G. Scott. 1967. 16s.
Roman frontiers of Britain, by D. R. Wilson. 1967. 16s.
The Severn basin, by K. S. Painter. 1967. 16s.
Wessex, by P. J. Fowler. 1967. 16s.
Yorkshire, by I. H. Longworth. 1965. 15s.
North Wales, by K. Watson. 1965. 15s.
South Wales, by C. Houlder and W. H. Manning. 1967. 16s.
A series of attractively illustrated little books (ea. *c.* 80-90p.), covering the most famous sites and intended for schools, students and local (mainly amateur) archaeological groups. The volume on North Wales has 49 half-tones and text-drawings, plus small maps, and includes a gazetteer of sites (p. 73-87), list of museums and a reading list, plus index. 1″ O.S. map references. A volume on London is due shortly.

930.26 (410) (02)
WOOD, E. S. Collins' Field guide to archaeology. London, Collins, 1963. 384p. illus. (incl. pl.), maps. 25s.

A practical guide in 4 parts: 1. General background—2. Field antiquities—3. The technical and legal aspects of archaeology—4. Aids and suggestions (1. Following up; 2. Sites to visit; 3. Books to read, p. 333-9). 59 half-tones; 189 maps and line-drawings. Regional maps. Index of places; index of subjects. "The most lucid and factual guide to British field-archaeology that has appeared . . ." (*Times literary supplement,* no. 3200, 28th June 1963, p. 479).

Ordnance Survey. *Field archaeology: some notes for beginners* (4th ed. London, H.M.S.O., 1963 [*i.e.,* 1964]. vii, 176p. diagrs. (Ordnance Survey. Professional papers, new series, no. 13. 10s.) gives period-by-period treatment, from pre-Roman times to the Industrial Revolution, and includes a bibliography.

930.26 (410):061
HARCUP, S. E., *comp.* **Historical, archaeological and kindred societies in the British Isles:** a list. London, Univ. of London, Institute of Historical Research, 1965. [3], 53p. 7s. 6d.

See entry at 941:061.

930.26 (410):061
WOOD-JONES, R. B., *comp.* **Directory of societies and public bodies concerned with historic buildings and ancient monuments.** Reprinted

from *Transactions* of the Ancient Monuments Society, v. 7, 1959, p. 125-34. [10]p.

930.26 (410) (084.3)
GREAT BRITAIN. ORDNANCE SURVEY. Historical maps.

See entry at 941 (084.3).

Scotland

930.26 (411)
FEACHEM, R. A guide to prehistoric Scotland. London, Batsford, 1963. 223p. illus., maps. 35*s*.

A list of the various types of ancient monument in Scotland, with an introductory essay. 'The gazetteer' (p. 25-190) is arranged by places A-Z, under the following heads: Early settlements—Chambered tombs—Henge monuments—Stones and cairns—Cup-and-ring markings—Homesteads—Hill-forts and settlements—Brochs—Duns—Cranmogs. Grid refs to 1″ map (7th ed.); road numbers; nearest large town. Index to monuments, p. 215-23.

930.26 (411)
GREAT BRITAIN. MINISTRY OF WORKS. Ancient monuments in Scotland: a list, corrected to 30th September 1966. London, H.M. Stationery Office, 1967. 50p. 6*s*. 6*d*. Suppt. no. 1. 1968. 8*d*.

Lists names of ancient monuments and historic buildings protected under the Ancient Monuments Acts, or otherwise, in the case of what is now the Ministry of Public Building and Works. Arranged under counties A-Z, individual monuments being surveyed by types.

930.26 (411)
GREAT BRITAIN. ROYAL COMMISSION ON THE ANCIENT MONUMENTS OF SCOTLAND. Reports and inventories. Edinburgh, H.M. Stationery Office, 1909-.

1: *Berwick.* 1909. o.p.
2: *Sutherland.* 1911. o.p.
3: *Caithness.* 1911. o.p.
4-5: *Galloway.* 1912-14. 2v. o.p.
6: *Berwick.* Rev. issue. 1915.
7: *Dumfriesshire.* 1920. o.p.
8: *East Lothian.* 1924. o.p.
9: *Outer Hebrides, Skye and the Small Isles.* 1928. o.p.
10: *Midlothian and West Lothian.* 1929. o.p.
11: *Fife, Kinross and Clackmannan.* 1933. o.p.
12: *Orkney and Shetland.* 1946. 3v. o.p.
13: *City of Edinburgh.* 1951. 45*s*.
14: *Roxburghshire.* 1956-. 2v. 105*s*.
15: *Selkirk.* 1957. 67*s*. 6*d*.
16: *Stirlingshire.* 1963. 2v. £12 12*s*.
17: *Peeblesshire.* 1967. 2v. £10 10*s*.
The descriptions are arranged by parish. With the 7th Report, the format was changed from octavo to quarto, to the great improvement of the numerous illustrations and plans. Up to 1938 monuments erected up to 1707 were included; in that year the Commissioners were empowered to cover those up to 1815, and in 1948 the terminal date was left to the Commissioners' discretion.

930.26 (411)
LACAILLE, A. D. The Stone Age in Scotland. London, Oxford Univ. Press, for Wellcome Historical Medical Museum, 1954. 345p. illus., maps. 30*s*.

The first authoritative work to deal with both the geological and the archaeological evidence bearing on the earliest colonization of Scotland by man. Extensive bibliography and index.

A short guide to Scottish antiquities was published for the National Museum of Antiquities, Scotland, by H.M. Stationery Office (1949).

Ireland

930.26 (415) (02)
EVANS, E. Prehistoric and early Christian Ireland—a guide. London, Batsford, 1966. xii, [2], 241p. illus. (incl. pl.), maps. 45*s*.

The archaeological background (p. 5-40)—Gazetteer (of the more remarkable sites, p. 41-214; arranged under counties, A-Z); glossary (p. 215-21); bibliography (p. 223-30); index of monuments and illustrations; non-analytical subject index. The author is Professor of Geography, Queen's University, Belfast.

930.26 (415) (02)
MACALISTER, R. A. S. The archæology of Ireland. 2nd ed. London, Methuen, 1949. xx, 386p. illus.

In addition to a general index, has an index of Irish topography (arranged by counties, followed by towns alphabetically) and an index of authorities cited. The latter gathers together the footnote references and serves as an informal bibliography (p. 383-6).

930.26 (416)
NORTHERN IRELAND. MINISTRY OF FINANCE. Archaeological Survey of Northern Ireland. **An archaeological survey of County Down.** Belfast, H.M. Stationery Office, 1966. xxiv, [1], 483p. illus. (incl. pl.), tables, diagrs., maps, plans. 147*s*.

A handsome volume, with 213 plates. Contents: General information—Prehistoric monuments and antiquities—Early Christian and medieval monuments and antiquities—Later monuments—Church plate—Coins and tokens. Select bibliography (p. 458); primary sources (p. 459); glossary; analytical index.

England & Wales

930.26 (42)
GREAT BRITAIN. MINISTRY OF PUBLIC BUILDING AND WORKS. Ancient monuments in England and Wales: a list . . . corrected to 31st December 1963. London, H.M. Stationery Office, 1965. 154p. 15*s*. 3rd suppt., corrected to 31st December 1966. 1967. 8p. 1*s*. 6*d*.

A topographical list of scheduled ancient monuments, *c*. 2,000 in all, some relatively modern. Marginal symbols indicate who is in charge of each monument, those monuments revealed by aerial photography, those now used for ecclesiastical purposes and those now inhabited as dwellings.

England

930.26 (420)

COLVIN, H. M., *ed.* **The history of the King's Works.** London, H.M. Stationery Office, 1963. 2v. and portfolio of plans. illus.(incl. pl.). £12 12*s.*

An exhaustive history of all public buildings for government, defence, royal pleasure and worship in England from before the Norman Conquest to 1485. Separate portfolio of folding plans of Dover Castle, Tower of London, Westminster Palace and Windsor Castle.

930.26 (420)

The County archaeologies. General editor, T. D. Kendrick. London, Methuen, 1930-37. illus., maps. *Sussex,* 25*s.;* others, o.p.

Berkshire, by H. Peake. 1931.
Cornwall and Scilly, by H. O'Neill Hencken. 1932.
Kent, by R. F. Jessup. 1930.
Middlesex and London, by C. E. Vulliamy. 1930.
Somerset, by D. P. Dobson. 1931.
Surrey, by D. C. Whimster. 1931.
Sussex, by E. C. Curwen. 1937.
Yorkshire, by Frank and H. W. Elgee. 1933.

Valuable regional surveys extending to the Norman Conquest, except for the Sussex volume, which ends with the Roman period. Sussex also omits the archaeological gazetteer which lists the antiquities of the county under parish with bibliographical references; such gazetteers, except for Berkshire and Surrey, do not aim at completeness.

930.26 (420)

GREAT BRITAIN. ROYAL COMMISSION ON THE ANCIENT AND HISTORICAL MONU- MENTS . . . OF ENGLAND. Inventories. London, H.M. Stationery Office, 1910-.

Buckinghamshire. 1912-13. 2v. o.p.
Dorset. v. 1: West. 1952. 63*s.*
Essex. 1916-23. 4v. o.p.
Herefordshire. 1931-34 3v. o.p
Herefordshire. 1931-34. 3v. o.p.
Huntingdonshire. 1926. 52*s.* 6*d.*
London. 1924-30. 5v. o.p. (*See at* 942.1 (02).)
City of Cambridge. 1959. 2v. 105*s.*
Middlesex. 1937. o.p.
City of Oxford. 1939. 45*s.*
St. Albans Cathedral guide. 1952. 2*s.* 6*d.*
Westmorland. 1936. o.p.
City of York. v. 1. 1962. 52*s.* 6*d.*

Profusely illustrated and detailed accounts, arranged by parish, each monument inspected and checked on the spot by a member of the staff of the Commission. Before 1946 only monuments erected before 1714 were included; the coverage is now extended to 1850.

930.26 (420)

THOMAS, N. A guide to prehistoric England. London, Batsford, 1960. 268p. illus. 30*s.*

Covers the major pre-Roman earthworks of

England. Glossary of archaeological terms, p. 31-34; gazetteer, by counties alphabetically, p. 37-255. Under county division is into Neolithic, Bronze Age, Iron Age, etc. Ordnance Survey 1″ sheet references are given. Bibliography, p. 257-62; index to sites. 69 illustrations.

930.26 (428.9)

MANX MUSEUM AND NATIONAL TRUST. The ancient and historic monuments of the Isle of Man: a general guide, including a selected list, with notes. Douglas (Isle of Man), Manx Museum and National Trust, 1958. 49p. illus. map, tables. (3rd ed. 1967. 48p. 1*s.* 6*d.*).

Contents: The early history of the Isle of Man —Suggestions for further reading (p. 17)—The Ancient Monuments Administration in the Isle of Man—Illustrations (p. 19-30)—Map of sites —The ancient and historical monuments of the Isle of Man: a selected list, with notes (p. 31-47) —Alphabetical index to sites.

Wales

930.26 (429)

GREAT BRITAIN. ROYAL COMMISSION ON ANCIENT AND HISTORICAL MONU- MENTS IN WALES AND MONMOUTH- SHIRE. Inventories. London, H.M. Stationery Office, 1911-.

1: *Montgomery.* 1911. o.p.
2: *Flintshire.* 1912. o.p.
3: *Radnorshire.* 1913. o.p.
4: *Denbighshire.* 1914. o.p.
5: *Carmarthenshire.* 1917. o.p.
6: *Merionethshire.* 1921. o.p.
7: *Pembrokeshire.* 1925. o.p.
[8]: *Anglesey. 1937.* 126*s.*
[9]: *Caernarvonshire.* 1956-64. 3v. £12 15*s.*

V. 1-7 issued as folios: with v. 8 format and style were brought into line with the English and Scottish volumes. No date limit was given to the Welsh Commission but only with the Anglesey volume was the 18th century systematically covered and nothing erected later than 1850 is included. Arranged by parishes, with numerous illustrations and maps.

930.26 (429)

GRIMES, W. F. The prehistory of Wales. Cardiff, National Museum of Wales, 1951. xvii, 288p. 15*s.*

A full, one-volume survey of the prehistory of Wales. It is arranged in two parts—a descriptive guide to the successive cultures, and a descriptive catalogue of the collections at Cardiff.

The Cambrian Archaeological Association has published: *A hundred years of Welsh archaeology,* edited by V. E. Nash-Williams (1949).

France

930.26 (44):016

GANDILHON, R., and **SAMARAN, C. Bibliographie générale des travaux historiques et archéologiques,** publiés par les sociétés savantes de la France. Période 1910-40. Paris, Imprimerie Nationale, 1944-. v. 1-.

See entry at 944.1/.9:016.

930.26 (44):016

LASTEYRIE du SAILLANT, R. C., *comte de.* **Bibliographie générale des travaux historiques et archéologiques,** publiés par les sociétés savantes de la France depuis les origines jusqu'à 1885. Paris, Imprimerie Nationale, 1888-1918. 6v.

See entries at 944.1 / .9:016.

930.26 (44):016

MONTANDON, R. **Bibliographie générale des travaux palethnologiques et archéologiques** (époques préhistorique, protohistorique et gallo-romaine). Paris, Leroux, 1917-38. 5v. & 3 suppts.

Continued since 1952 in the *Bulletin de la Société préhistorique française.*
The main work has more than 30,000 entries.

930.26 (44):016

RUELLE, Ch.-E. **Bibliographie générale des Gaules.** Répertoire systématique et alphabétique des œuvres, mémoires et notices concernant l'histoire, la topographie, la religion, les antiquités et le langage de la Gaule jusqu'à la fin du Ve siècle. Suivi d'une table alphabétique des matières. 1re période: Publications faites depuis l'origine de l'imprimerie jusqu'en 1879 inclusivement. Brussels, Éditions Culture et Civilisation, 1964. xiv, 1731p. Belg. fr. 1350.

Reprint of the original ed. (Paris, 1886). No. more published.
12,000 entries.

Russia

930.26 (47)

AKADEMIYA NAUK SSSR. Institut Istorii Material'noĭ Kul'tury. **Sovetskaya arkheologicheskaya literatura: bibliografiya 1941-1957.** Sostavili N. A. Vinberg [and others]. Moscow, Izdat. Akad. Nauk SSSR, 1959. 773p. R.25.90.

8,765 items, a comprehensive bibliography of archaeological literature (books, periodical articles, chapters of books and some dissertations) published in the U.S.S.R. In 2 pts., 1941-55 and 1956-57. Classified arrangement in each sequence within 6 groups (General; European U.S.S.R.; Caucasus; Central Asia and Kazakhstan; Siberia and the Far East; and literature on foreign archaeology and translated literature), with further sub-division by period or subject.
Preceded by Akademiya Nauk SSSR. Bibliothek. *Sovetskaya arkheologicheskaya literatura, 1918-1928* (1931) and, published subsequently, *Sovetskaya arkheologicheskaya literatura, 1929-1940* (1965).
Current Russian writings on archaeology are listed in *Novaya sovetskaya literatura po istorii, arkheologii i etnografii* (Moscow, 1934-). See entry at 947:016.

Noted: Field, H. *Bibliography of Soviet archeology and physical anthropology, 1936-1967* (Coconut Grove, Florida, 1967. viii, 21p.).

Sweden

930.26 (485)

Swedish archaeological bibliography. Stockholm, Svenska Arkeologiska Samfundet, 1951-. v. 1-.

v.1, covering 1939-48, edited by S. Janson and O. Vessberg. 1951.
v. 2, covering 1949-53, edited by C. Callmer and W. Holmqvist. 1957.
v. 3, covering 1954-59, edited by W. Odelberg and H. Thylander. 1965.
V. 2 consists of a descriptive bibliography and history of archaeology in both Sweden and other countries, and an author index. A record of work published by Swedish archaeologists.

Islam

930.26 (5/6=927)

PEARSON, J. D., and **RICE, D. S.,** *comp.* **Islamic art and archaeology:** a register of works published in the year 1954. Cambridge, Heffer, 1956. iii, 38p. Mimeographed. 10s.

—— —— **Islamic art and archaeology:** a register of works published in the year 1955. Cambridge, Heffer, 1960. iii, 65p. Mimeographed. 10s.

See entries at 7 (5 927) in Guide (1959)

Asia

930.26 (5)

CONTENAU, G. **Manuel d'archéologie orientale** depuis les origines jusqu'à l'époque d'Alexandre. Paris, Picard, 1927-47. 4v. illus.

v. 1-3. *Histoire de l'art.* 1927-31.
v. 4. *Les découvertes archéologiques de 1930 à 1939.* 1947.
V. 1 (Notions générales—race, chronologie, langage, écriture, religions, etc.; histoire de l'art —art archaïque d'Elam et de Sumer) has 357 illustrations and chapter bibliographies p. 491-521. Index in v. 3 covers v. 1-3.

Southern Africa

930.26 (68)

GOODWIN, A. J. H. **The loom of prehistory:** a commentary and a select bibliography of the prehistory of Southern Africa. Cape Town, South African Archaeological Society, 1946. 151p.

J. D. Clark's *The prehistory of Southern Africa* (Harmondsworth, Penguin Books, 1959. xxvi, 341p. illus. (incl. pl.), diagrs., tables, maps. 6s.) includes an extensive bibliography, p. 315-30. The same author's *Atlas of African prehistory,* (Chicago, Ill., Univ. of Chicago Press, 1968. 62p. maps. £14 12s.), compiled under the auspices of the Pan-African Congress on Prehistory, contains 12 base maps of ecology and paleo-ecology and 38 transparent overlays. Page size, 17" × 20".

S. E. Holm's *Bibliography of South African pre- and pro-historic archaeology* (Pretoria, Van Schaik, 1966. xxv, 144. R.525) has 1,151 annotated entries, mostly for the area of the Republic of South Africa. Makes good use of extracts from and references to reviews, but hardly any post-1960 titles are included. Reviewed in *Africa,* v. 37, no. 4, October 1967, p. 499.

Americas

930.26 (7/8):016

Abstracts of New World archaeology. 1959-. Washington, Society for American Archaeology, 1960-. v. 1-. Annual. (v. 1. $3.50.)

V. 1 contains 676 indicative and informative abstracts of books, periodical articles and theses in 28 sections. Section 1, 'General', embraces bibliographical sources; surveys, summaries and distributions; history and rôle of archaeology; theory and scope of archaeology; methods, techniques and identifications; exhibition catalogues; miscellaneous. Sections 2-28 deal with countries and regions, working from north (Arctic) to south. Author index.

Mexico
930.26 (72)

BERNAL, I. Bibliografía de arqueología y etnografía: Mesoamérica y norte de México, 1514-1960. Mexico, Instituto Nacional de Antropología e Historia, 1962. 634p. maps.

About 14,000 items on the pre-Spanish conquest civilisations of Mexico and Central America. Main subject sections: common cultural areas; pre-ceramic periods; codices, chronology and general inscriptions of regional groups; relations with other world areas; history of science, literature; bibliography and biography. Author index. (Based on review in *College and research libraries*, v. 24, no. 4, July 1963, p. 321.)

Archaeology of Religions
930.26:2

See: Cabrol, F. *Dictionnaire d'archéologie chrétienne et de liturgie,* at 27 (031).

Finegan, J. *The archeology of world religions,* at 291.8.

Klauser, T., ed. *Reallexikon für Antike und Christentum,* at 291 (031).

Epigraphy
930.271

CAGNAT, R. Cours d'épigraphie latine. 4. éd. Paris, Fontemoing, 1914. xxvii, 504p.

First published 1885.

Strongly recommended as a "textbook" of Roman epigraphy (*Encyclopædia Britannica* (11th ed.), v. 14, p. 638). Bibliography, p. xix-xxvii.

Palaeography
930.272:016

LONDON. UNIVERSITY. Library. The Palaeography Collection in the University of London Library: an author and subject catalogue. Boston, Mass., G. K. Hall, 1968. 2v. $105 (U.K. and British Isles); $115.50 (elsewhere).

A collection primarily concerned with material for the study of the manuscript book in Greek, Latin and Western European languages. The author catalogue comprises *c.* 10,800 cards; the subject catalogue, *c.* 13,100 cards. Due for publication May 1968.

930.272 (37)

STEFFENS, F. Paléographie latine: 125 facsimilés en phototypie, accompagnés de transcriptions et d'explications avec un exposé systématique de l'histoire de l'écriture latine. Éd.

française, d'après la nouvelle éd. allemande par R. Coulon. Paris, Champion, 1910. xl, 125p. 125 pl.

Standard work for the study of Latin palaeography and diplomatic. Examples of papal, imperial and private documents; book hand and court hand. Transcript and detailed notes for each plate.

930.272 (37)

THOMPSON, *Sir* E. M. An introduction to Greek and Latin palaeography. Oxford, Clarendon Press, 1912. xvi, 600p. facsims.

Standard work in English on palaeography of Western Europe. Deals with alphabets, writing materials, forms of books, abbreviations; Greek section: book and cursive hands; Latin section: majuscule, national and minuscule hands, English book and court hand. Court hands in continental countries are not dealt with.

Will be superseded by the series of Oxford Palaeographical handbooks, edited by R. W. Hunt, C. H. Roberts and F. Wormald. *Greek literary hands, 350* B.C.-A.D. *400,* by C. H. Roberts (Oxford, Clarendon Press, 1956. 30*s.*), has so far been published.

Information on recent publications in the field of palaeography and MS. studies to be found in the Library Association's *Year's work in librarianship,* 1928-50 (chapter entitled "Palaeography and manuscripts"), subsequently *Five years' work in librarianship,* 1951/55-.

930.272 (42)

DENHOLM-YOUNG, N. Handwriting in England and Wales. Cardiff, Univ. of Wales Press, 1954. xi, 102, [33]p. illus. (pl.) 30*s.*

An introduction to the study of palaeography, with bibliography and annotated plates for students beginning their research on some aspect of English or Welsh history or literature. Emphasis is on the period from the coming of the Caroline minuscule to the 17th century. Sections on types of hands are supplemented by valuable guidance on particular problems and on the use of palaeography in the criticism of texts.

930.272 (420)

GRIEVE, H. E. P. Examples of English handwriting, 1150-1750, with transcripts and translations. Chelmsford, Essex Education Committee, 1954. [iv], ii, 33p. 28 pl. (Essex Record Office Publications, no. 21). (2nd ed. 1959. 13*s.* 3*d.*).

Pt. 1: From Essex parish records; pt. 2: From other Essex archives.

So far the only work on the palaeography of local records in England. Transcripts and notes for all documents reproduced. Valuable guidance for the beginner in reading local records.

930.272 (420)

HECTOR, L. C. The handwriting of English documents. 2nd ed. London, E. Arnold, 1966. 136p. illus. (pl.).

First published 1958.

Six chapters: 1. The equipment of the writers—2. The equipment of the reader—3. Abbreviation—4. Scribal conventions and expedients—5. English handwriting from the Conquest to 1500—6. English handwriting since 1500. Transcripts of passages represented in plates; bibliography, p. 132-3 (works asterisked contain transcribed facsimiles); index.

930.272 (420)
JENKINSON, *Sir* H. The later court hands in England, from the 15th to the 17th century, illustrated from the Common Papers of the Scriveners' Company of London, the English Writing Masters and the Public Records. Cambridge, Univ. Press, 1927. 2v.

Pt. 1: Text; pt. 2: Plates.
Standard work on English hands of the 15th, 16th and 17th centuries, containing (pt. 1) valuable study on various aspects, bibliography, and transcripts and notes for the plates in pt. 2. Alphabets in pt. 2.

930.272 (420)
JOHNSON, C., and JENKINSON, *Sir* H. English court hand, A.D. **1066-1500,** illustrated chiefly from the Public Records. Oxford, Clarendon Press, 1915. 2v.

Pt. 1: Text; pt. 2: Plates.
Standard work on English medieval chancery, exchequer and legal hands, containing (pt. 1) valuable study on various aspects and bibliography, development of individual letters, abbreviations, and transcripts (where necessary), with detailed notes for the plates in pt. 2.

ANCIENT HISTORY

Bibliographies

931:016
PETIT, P. Guide de l'étudiant en histoire ancienne. Nouv. éd. Paris, Presses Universitaires de France, 1962. viii, 208p. 8F.

A well documented guide. Sections: Histoire ancienne — L'acquisition des connaissances fondamentales —La connaissance des textes anciens —Les sciences dites auxiliaires (*i.e.,* archaeology, geography, numismatics, papyrology) —Le travail personnel (research methods). Indexes of ancient authors, geographical names, peoples and subjects, and modern authors. Material up to 1958 is included; articles in periodicals are cited. About 1,800 items.

A comparable German work is H. Bengston's *Einführung in die alte Geschichte* (2. durchgesehene und ergänzte Aufl. Munich, C. H. Beck'sche Verlagsbuchhandlung, 1953. viii, 197p.). This has 9 chapters, with sub-divisions and bibliographies appended. 4. Aufl. 1962. 205p.

Noted: Merkel, E., ed. *Bibliographie zur alten Geschichte* (Frankfurt an Main, Klostermann, 1965-. v. 1-), v. 1: 1945-1965.

931 (02)
The Cambridge ancient history. Cambridge, Univ. Press, 1923-39. 12v. and 5v. of plates. v.

1-2, o.p., v. 3-12, 84*s.* to 90*s.* per v.; plates, 45*s.* to 63*s.* per v. Rev. ed. 1961-.

The history as a whole was planned by J. B. Bury. V. 1-6, edited by J. B. Bury, S. A. Cook, F. E. Adcock; v. 7-11, edited by S. A. Cook, F. E. Adcock, M. P. Charlesworth; v. 12, edited by S. A. Cook, F. E. Adcock, M. P. Charlesworth, N. H. Baynes. Plates prepared by C. T. Seltman.

v. 1: *Egypt and Babylonia, to 1580* B.C.
v. 2: *The Egyptian and Hittite Empires, to c. 1000* B.C.
v. 3: *The Assyrian Empire.*
v. 4: *The Persian Empire and the West.*
v. 5: *Athens, 478-401* B.C.
v. 6: *Macedon, 401-301* B.C.
v. 7: *The Hellenistic monarchies and the rise of Rome.*
v. 8: *Rome and the Mediterranean, 218-133* B.C
v. 9: *The Roman Republic, 133-44* B.C.
v. 10: *The Augustan Empire, 44* B.C. - A.D. *70.*
v. 11: *The Imperial peace,* A.D. *70-192.*
v. 12: *The Imperial crisis and recovery,* A.D. *193-324.*

A standard work, each chapter by a specialist. The aim of the editors was to produce a work of scholarship for professional students which would yet be intelligible to the general reader. The volumes of plates, illustrating the arts and cultures of the ancient peoples, are particularly valuable: maps are included in the text volumes, which have reliable and extensive bibliographies.

The revised ed. of v. 1-2 is being issued in separate chapter-facsicules (ea. 3*s.* 6*d.*-10*s.* 6*d.*) as they are ready. Fascicules 1-66, 1961-68.

Chronology of the ancient world, by E. J. Bickerman, Thames and Hudson (London) 1968. (50*s.*) is largely devoted to tables and charts showing the different cycles of civic and solar time, and to a lengthy list of events in the ancient world. Analytical index.

Historical Atlases

931 (084.4)
Grosser historischer Weltatlas, 1. Teil: **Vorgeschichte und Altertum.** 2. verbesserte Aufl., hrsg. von H. Bengston & V. Milojčiv̆. Munich, Bayerischer Schulbuch-Verlag, 1954. 2v. (Karten; Erläuterungen).

44 pages of clear and comprehensive maps of which the value is enhanced by the accompanying explanatory volume (125 columns). Includes some excellent town plans and an index of about 4,500 names. There is no comparable English publication.

General entry at 93 (084.4).

931 (084.4)
McEVEDY, C. The Penguin atlas of ancient history. . . . Harmondsworth, Middlesex, Penguin Books, 1967. 96p. maps. 15*s.*

Covers Europe, the southern coast of the Mediterranean and the Near East, up to the 4th century A.D. The atlas (p. 16-92) consists of 2-colour maps on the right-hand page and text facing. Clearly marked maps. Index, p. 93-96.

931 (084.4)

Muir's Atlas of ancient and classical history. 2nd ed., edited by G. Goodall and R. F. Treharne. London, Philip, 1956. 8p; 96p. of maps; 32p.

First published 1938.
96 pages of maps, with insets; index gazetteer of about 12,500 names.

Everyman's Atlas of ancient and classical geography (Rev. ed. London, Dent, 1952. ix, 256p.) has 80 pages of maps, with an historical dictionary of place names (p. 1-217). The index-gazetteer (p. 221-56) gives longitude, latitude and map-page references. First published 1907; 3rd ed. 1961 (lxx, 125p. 18s.).

Ancient Geography

931:91

CARY, M. The geographical background of Greek and Roman history. Oxford, Clarendon Press, 1949. vi, 331p. maps. 30s.

The opening chapter gives a concise account of the Mediterranean environment as a whole; succeeding chapters deal regionally with the various parts of the ancient world, including the Near East. Footnotes carry copious and exact references. Reviewed by E. G. R. Taylor in *Geographical journal*, v. 114, pt. 1-3, September 1949, p. 83-84.

India

934 (02)

The Cambridge history of India. v. 1: **Ancient India,** edited by E. J. Rapson. Cambridge, Univ. Press, 1935. xxiv. 736p. and 34 plates; map in pocket.

An authoritative, factual account, with chapters by specialists. Chapter bibliographies (p. 653-96); footnote references; chronology, 2500 B.C. - A.D. 89.

934 (02)

The Cambridge history of India. Supplementary v.: **The Indus civilization,** by Sir M. Wheeler. Cambridge, Univ. Press, 1953. xi, 98, xxiv p. illus. (pl.). 22s. 6d.

Designed to replace the now superseded account in v. 1 of the main work, it provides a straightforward factual survey of the prehistory of India based on the actual evidence available at the time of writing. Excellent plates, but no bibliography apart from references in footnotes.

934:930

PATHAK, V. S. Ancient historians of India: a study in historical biographies. London, Asia Publishing House, 1966. xi, [iv], 184p. 20s.

Running commentary on historical works; many footnotes. Chapters: 1. The beginnings of historical traditions—2. The *Harshacharita*—3. The *Vikramānikadeva-charita*—4. The *Vikramānkābhyutlaya*—5. The *Prithraraja-vijava*—6. History in historical narrative. Bibliography (p. 173-7); index.

Greece & Rome

937 (02)

History of the Greek and Roman world. General editor, M. Cary. London, Methuen, 1934-. maps.

To be published in 7v.
v. 1: *A history of the Greek world from 776 to 479 B.C.,* by H. T. Wade-Grey, is still in preparation.
v. 2: *A history of the Greek world from 479 to 323 B.C.,* by M. L. W. Laistner. 3rd ed. 1957. 45s.
v. 3: *A history of the Greek world from 323 to 146 B.C.,* by M. Cary. 2nd ed. 1951 (reprinted 1962). 45s.
v. 4: *A history of the Roman world from 753 to 146 B.C.,* by H. H. Scullard. 3rd ed. 1961. 50s.
v. 5: *A history of the Roman world from 146 to 30 B.C.,* by F. B. Marsh. 3rd ed. (reprinted 1964). 48s.
v. 6: *A history of the Roman world from 30 B.C. to A.D. 138,* by E. T. Salmon. 5th ed. 1966. 50s.
v. 7: *A history of the Roman world, A.D. 138-337,* by H. M. D. Parker. 2nd ed. rev. by B. H. Warmington. 1958. 45s.

MEDIAEVAL and MODERN HISTORY

Dictionaries

94 (03) /2

HABERKERN, H., and WALLACH, J. F. Hilfswörterbuch für Historiker. Mittelalter und Neuzeit. 2. neubearb, und erw. Aufl. Berne, Francke, 1964. 678p. Sw. fr. 75.

About 20,000 terms in many languages connected with medieval and modern history are briefly defined. In A-Z order, with numerous cross-references, particularly from a term in one language to its equivalent in German (*e.g.,* from 'Lag' and 'Danegeld' to 'Gilde' and 'Dänengeld'). Many entries for Latin terms; also for such English terms as 'District Councils', 'Boroughs', 'Town Council', 'Overseers', 'Parliament' (1½ cols.), 'Vestry' (¾ col.). Gives country of origin. No bibliographies.

Atlases

94 (084.4)

MUIR, R. Muir's Historical atlas, medieval and modern. 10th ed., edited by R. F. Treharne and H. Fullard. London, Philip, 1964. xvi, 96, 24p. maps. 37s. 6d.

96 pages of maps, some in colour; arranged chronologically from 'The realms of civilisation, c. 200 A.D.' to 'Africa, 1964'. Index-gazetteer of c. 12,000 names. Page size, 11" × 9". "Excellent for general purposes" (Davis, R. H. C. *Medieval European history,* p. 7).

MEDIAEVAL HISTORY

Bibliography

94 "04/14" :016

CHEVALIER, C. U. Répertoire des sources historiques du moyen àge. Nouv. éd. refondu, corr. et augm. Paris, Picard, 1894-1907 (reprinted 1959-60). 4v. 919F.

First published 1877-1903. Two parts: *Bio-bibliographie* (1877-86); nouv. éd., 1905-07. 2v. *Topobibliographie* (1894-1903 (1959 reprint). 2v. 390F.).

"One of the most important bibliographical monuments ever devoted to the study of medieval history," containing "an enormous mass of useful information" (*Encyclopædia Britannica*, 11th ed. (1910-11), v. 6, p. 114), but without evaluation. The *Bio-bibliographie* (see entry at 92:016) has entries under the "names of all the historical personages alive between the years 1 and 1500 who are mentioned in printed books", etc. *Topobibliographie*, arranged by place and topic, endeavours to do the same for places, institutions and the like. "Though very useful, this is by no means so complete as the *Bio-bibliographie*" (*op. cit.*).

94 "04/14":016
DAVIS, R. H. C. Medieval European history: a select bibliography. London, for the Historical Association by Routledge & Kegan Paul, 1963. 47p. (Helps for students of history, no. 67). 5*s*.

An evaluative, running commentary on *c.* 600 items. Sections: General surveys—Historical atlases—Transition from the ancient world—The Barbarian invasions of the fifth century—The Franks . . . Islam — Slavonic Europe — Feudal society—Agrarian history—Industry and commerce—Towns—Thought and literature in Western Europe—Art and architecture. Index of authors. Assumes some knowledge of French and also a little German.

94 "04/14":016
HALPHEN, L. Initiation aux études d'histoire du moyen àge. 3. éd. rev., augm. et mise à jour par Y. Renouard. Paris, Presses Universitaires de France, 1952. xv, 205p.

First published 1940.
3 pts.: 1. Première orientation (Les grandes synthèses historiques; Les atlas et les grands ouvrages de consultation; Comment construire ses lectures)—2. L'accès aux documents (Les grands recueils de documents historiques; Le déchiffrement et l'interpretation des documents historiques; Les documents littéraires et archéologiques—3. La recherche historique (L'enquête bibliographique (p. 134-58); Les archives et les bibliothèques de manuscrits (p. 159-84); La présentation des résultats). Index of authors and countries. An invaluable handbook.

94 "04/14":016
MEDIEVAL ACADEMY OF AMERICA. Progress of medieval studies in the United States of America. Buletin. Boulder, Colorado, Univ. of Colorado, 1923-. no. 1-.

Title varies. *Bulletin* no. 24 (1957. $2) has title: *Progress of medieval and Renaissance studies in the United States and Canada.*
Contents of *Bulletin* no. 24: 'Papers read at meetings of learned societies'; 'Items of special interest'; 'Books in press'; 'List of active medieval and renaissance scholars' (a list of books, periodical articles, arranged by authors, alpha-

betically); 'Doctoral dissertations'; Obituary; 'Index by fields of interest'.

H. F. Williams' *An index of mediaeval studies published in Festschriften, 1865-1946, with special reference to Romantic material* (Berkeley & Los Angeles, Univ. of California Press, 1951. x, 651p. $4) covers more than 5,000 items, taken from *c.* 500 Festschriften.

International guide to medieval studies: a quarterly index to periodical literature (Darien, Conn., American Bibliographic Service, 1961-. v. 1, no. 1-) is complementary to the above two compilations; it also indexes book reviews.

94 "04/14":016
PAETOW, L. J. A guide to the study of medieval history. Rev. ed. prepared under the auspices of the Medieval Academy of America. London, Kegan Paul, 1931. xix, 643p. (Reprinted New York, Kraus, 1964).

First published 1917. 552p. 2nd ed. adds material published between 1917 and 1928.
Valuable guide to bibliographies, printed sources and secondary works for the history of medieval Europe and its Eastern neighbours. Pt. 1: Numbered list of books arranged by subject under the headings: Bibliography, Reference, Auxiliary Studies, Modern works, Collections of sources. Pts. 2 & 3, arranged by topic, each containing an introduction, recommendations for reading, and a bibliography referring to pt. 1.
A new edition is in preparation.

94 "04/14":016
POTTHAST, A. Bibliotheca historica Medii Aevi: Wegweiser durch die Geschichtswerke des europäischen Mittelalters bis 1500. 2. verb. u. verm. Aufl. Berlin, Weber, 1896 (reprinted 1955). 2v.

First published 1862.
The most complete guide in existence (though not free from error) to the printed sources (excluding records) for the history of medieval Europe, 400 - *c.* 1500. Pt. 1, Lists of the great general collections and the collected *Scriptores* for each country, Pt. 2, List of the printed works of individual medieval authors, arranged alphabetically by author.

A new work, designed to supersede Potthast, has the title *Repertorium fontium historiae Medii Aevi*: primum ab A. Potthast, nunc cura collegii historicorum e pluribus nationibus emendatum et auctum. It is sponsored by the Istituto Storico per il Medio Evo; Istituti di Archeologia, Storia, e Storia dell'Arte in Roma; Medieval Academy of America; and other bodies). V. 1: *Series collectionum* (£10) and v. 2: *Fontes, A-B* (£12 10*s.*) appeared in 1962 (Rome, Istituto Storia Italiano por il Medio Evo). V. 1 gives the contents of all the collections of narrative sources; v. 2 is the first part of a detailed description of sources, A-Z (*c.* 15,000 entries). The entry 'Abaelardus' (3 cols.) has sub-headings for manuscripts, medieval translations, editions, modern translations and commentaries. Preceding the A-B sequence is a general list of sources (p. 3-46) and list of journals cited (p. 49-87).

94 "04/14":016

WILLIAMS, H. F. An index of mediaeval studies published in Festschriften, 1865-1946, with special reference to Romantic material. Berkeley, Univ. of California Press, 1951. x, 165p.

Aims to list all material found in *c.* 500 Festschrift volumes "dealing with the art, customs, history, language and literature and science of Western Europe from about the 5th century to the first years of the sixteenth". Author and subject indexes.

94 "04/14" (02)

The Cambridge medieval history. Planned by J. B. Bury; edited by H. M. Gwatkin, J. P. Whitney, J. R. Tanner, C. W. Previté-Orton and Z. N. Brooke. Cambridge, Univ. Press, 1911-36. 8v. and portfolios of maps.

> v. 1. *The Christian Roman Empire and the foundation of the Teutonic kingdoms.* 1911.
> v. 2. *The rise of the Saracens and the foundation of the Western Empire.* 1913.
> v. 3. *Germany and the Western Empire.* 1922.
> v. 4. *The Eastern Roman Empire (717-1453).* 1923. 2nd ed., as *The Byzantine Empire.* 1966-67. 2v. ea. 140s.
> v. 5. *Contest of Empire and Papacy.* 1926.
> v. 6. *Victory of the Papacy, 1929.*
> v. 7. *Decline of Empire and Papacy.* 1932.
> v. 8. *The close of the Middle Ages.* 1936. 75s.
> Portfolios of maps for v. 1-8 (86 maps.).

"By far the most useful and comprehensive work in English" (Davis, R. H. C. *Medieval European history,* p. 5). A closely packed survey, each chapter being an authoritative statement by a scholar of repute. An important feature of each volume is the very full bibliography.

The new v. 4, in 2v. (xl, 1168p.; xlii, 517p.) is considerably expanded, with 42 plates, 18 maps, numerous tables; general and chapter bibliographies (p. 808-1041; p. 377-476); analytical indexes.

The Shorter Cambridge medieval history, by C. W. Previté-Orton (Cambridge, Univ. Press, 1952. 2v. illus., maps, general tables) incorporates some up-to-date material. Unlike the parent work, it has illustrations, but no bibliographies.

94 "04/14" (05)

Speculum: a journal of mediaeval studies. Cambridge, Mass., Mediaeval Academy of America, 1926-. v. 1, no. 1-. Quarterly. $12 per v.

The January 1967, v. 42, no. 1, issue (232p.) has 8 scholarly articles, historical or literary in scope (p. 1-129); signed reviews of 42 items (p. 130-221); 'Bibliography of American periodical literature' (p. 226-7); 'Books received' (p. 228-32).

94 "04/14" (058.7)

GALLAIS, P., *and others.* **Répertoire international des médiévistes.** Poitiers, Centre d'Études Supérieures de Civilisation Mediévale, 1965. 713p.

First published as *Répertoire des médiévistes européens.* (1960).
Information (name; position; address; specialisation; publications since 1959) about 3,530 medievalists throughout the world. Indexes of

places of residence and of special subjects and fields of interest. (Based on *Unesco bulletin for libraries,* v. 20, no. 3, May/June 1966, entry no. 182.)

94 "04/14" (084.4)

McEVEDY, C. The Penguin atlas of medieval history. Harmondsworth, Middlesex, Penguin Books, 1961. 96p. maps. 10s. 6d.

Atlas, p. 14-90: 39 black-and-white maps on recto, with notes facing. Aims to show the unfolding of medieval history in Europe and the Near East as a continuous story. Period covered: A.D. 362-1478. Three maps for A.D. 528. Clear lettering. Page size (oblong), 9" × 7".

94 "04/14" (084.4)

Westermanns Atlas zur Weltgeschichte. Teil 2. **Mittelalter.** Hrsg. von H.-E. Stier [u.a.]. 4. Aufl. Braunschweig, Westermann, 1956. 47p. of maps.

Part 2 of a well-known historical atlas, and lacking all the physical maps (in part 1); also, has no index-gazetteer. Nevertheless, "more enterprising and more stimulating (and extremely learned)" than Muir's *Historical atlas, medieval and modern* (Davis, R. H. C. *Medieval European history,* p. 7).

94 "04/07"

CECCHELLI, C. Bibliografia del mondo barbarico. Rome, Ruffolo, 1954. 2v. illus.
> v. 1. *Generalità.*
> v. 2. *Le grande stirpi. Popoli diversi.*

A bibliography covering the Dark Ages. 4,831 numbered entries, some with annotations, systematically arranged. V. 2 deals with individual races and tribes. Numerous small illustrations. No index, but full contents-list.

94 "11/12"

ATIYA, A. S. The Crusade: historiography and bibliography. Bloomington, Indiana Univ. Press, 1962; London, Oxford Univ. Press, 1963. 170p. 32s. 6d.

Annotated bibliography of 1,500 items, covering Eastern as well as Western sources.

Noted: Mayer, H. E. *Bibliographie zur Geschichte der Kreuzzüge* (Hannover, Hahn, 1965. 2. unverändte Aufl. xxxii, 272p. DM.36), with 5,362 items.

The Widener Library (Harvard College Library) Shelflist, *Crusades* (Harvard Univ. Library, Cambridge, Mass., 1965 [xiii], 23, [1], 19, [1], 19p.) consists of classified, author (or title) and chronological listings of more than 1,000 items.

Renaissance

94 "14/15"

Bibliographie internationale de l'Humanisme et de la Renaissance. Geneva, Droz, 1966-. v. 1-.

> v. 1. *Travaux parus en 1965.* xii, 285p. 42F.
> A list of 3,199 items. Reviewed in *Bulletin critique du livre français, 1967,* entry no. 69589.

MODERN HISTORY

94 "15/19" (02)

The New Cambridge modern history. Cambridge, Univ. Press, 1957-. v. 1-.

Advisory Committee: Sir George Clark, J. M. Butler, J. P. T. Bury, and the late E. A. Benians. To be completed in 14 volumes. Volumes so far published:
1. *The Renaissance, 1493-1520*; edited by G. R. Potter. 1957.
2. *The Reformation, 1520-1559*; edited by G. R. Elton. 1958.
5. *The ascendency of France, 1648-88*; edited by F. L. Carsten. 1961.
7. *The old régime, 1713-63*; edited by J. O. Lindsay. 197.
8. *The American and French revolutions, 1763-93*; edited by A. Goodwin. 1965. 50s.
9. *War and peace in an age of upheaval, 1793-1830*; edited by C. W. Crawley. 1965. 50s.
10. *The zenith of European power, 1830-70*; edited by J. P. T. Bury. 1960. 40s.
11. *Material progress and world-wide problems, 1870-1898*; edited by F. H. Hinsley. 1965. 40s.
12. *The shifting balance of world forces, 1898-1945*. 2nd ed. Edited by C. L. Mowat. 1968. 1st ed. 1960.

Re-appraisals by specialists of the periods covered by the *Cambridge modern history* (1902-26. 13v. and atlas). No bibliographies, but v. 10 contains ample footnotes and has a 52-page index. The 1960 ed. of v. 12 was criticized for thin treatment of the post-1920 years: World War II, post-1917 Russia, Hitler's Germany and De Gaulle were not dealt with.

The series has been criticised by Professor Butterfield (*Contemporary review*, v. 207, no. 1197, p. 194-8) for excessive emphasis upon political history and concentration on the west of Europe; the chapter approach tends to cut up the sequence of national histories.

"The New Cambridge Modern History follows the precedent of the older series in not giving footnote-references for the statements in the text except on occasions when they seem to be called for" (*General introduction*, v. 1). The omitted bibliographies appear in:

A bibliography of modern history, edited by J. Roach (Cambridge, Univ. Press, 1968. xxix, 388p. 30s.) is closely related to the *New Cambridge modern history*. The 6,040 entries (usually unannotated) are very largely the work of the *c.* 200 contributors to *NCMH*. 3 main sections: A. 1493-1648 (to be used with v. 1-4 of *NCMH*); B. 1648-1793 (with v. 5-8); C. 1791-1945 (with v. 9-12). 195 sections, with brief introductions and many itemised cross-references. Cites many collections of published series "and those books are noted which contain useful bibliographies" (*Introduction*). The main emphasis is on books in English mostly published prior to 1961; more than 80% of items concern Europe, and 75%, Western Europe. Analytical subject-index.

94 "15/19" (084.4)

The Cambridge modern history atlas. 2nd ed. Cambridge, Univ. Press, 1924. 229p. and 141 pl. of maps.

The introduction (p. 1-118) is followed by an index of marginal references to maps and an index of local names in the introduction. The gazetteer (p. 145-229) gives map number, latitude and longitude. Some of the maps, which include insets, were specially drawn for this atlas. The period covered is 1490-1910.

94 "15/19" (084.4)

Grosser historischer Weltatlas . . . 3. Teil: Neuzeit. Hrsg. von J. Engel. Munich, Bayerischer Schulbuch-Verlag, 1953-. v. 1-.

V. 3 covers the period 1477-1954, with emphasis on European and German history. Maps (p. 109-200) are chiefly political, but some cover economic subjects, population and the like (*e.g.,* maps showing voting in Germany, 1871, 1880 and 1912); gazetteer of 15,000 entries.

94 "15/18" (084.4)

POOLE, R. L. Historical atlas of modern Europe, from the decline of the Roman Empire; comprising also maps of parts of Asia, Africa and the New World connected with European history. Oxford, Clarendon Press, 1902. viii, 328p. 90 pl. of maps.

Based on Menke's ed. of Spruner's *Hand-Atlas* (1880), with additional material from Longnon's *Atlas historique de la France* (1885-89) and new maps for the British Isles, Byzantine, Asian and Colonial history. Each plate is accompanied by a note by an authority. Period dealt with: A.D. 285-1897, with a supplementary map on South Africa just previous to 1900. No index.

94 "15/17":016

DAVIES, A. Modern European history, 1494-1788: a select bibliography. London, Historical Association, 1966. 39p. (Helps for students of history, no. 68). 5s.

Replaces the bibliography (Helps . . . , no. 55) published in 1953.

A list, with some brief commentary on sections, of *c.* 200 items (including periodical articles). 19 sections, 8 on general aspects (*e.g.,* 'The Age of the Renaissance'; 'The seventeenth century revolutions') and 11 on countries. Aims "to introduce the student to some of the best secondary works available, and the original authorities and rare books are not included" (*Preface*). Preference given to works in English. Items asterisked are available as paperbacks. No author index.

94 "17/19":016

Historical abstracts: a quarterly, covering the world's periodical literature, 1775-1945; edited by E. H. Boehm. Vienna, Universität Historisches Seminar, and New York, 640 West 153rd Street, 1955-. Quarterly.

An attempt to provide abstracts of articles on political, diplomatic, economic, social, cultural and intellectual history. 1775-1945, appearing in periodicals throughout the world, from June 1954. Excludes articles of limited local interest and those on the history of other subjects.

V. 12 (1966): 3,516 signed indicative abstracts. Pt. 1, General; 2. Topics (international relations; wars and military history; World War I; World War II; political history; social & cultural history; economic history; religions and churches; sciences and technology); 3. Area or country. Profuse cross-references. 'Bibliographical news'.

Annual subject and author indexes. five-year indexes, v. 1-5, 6-10 (1963-5), ea. $37. The abstracts are to be used with care; they are not always reliable.

H.A. Bulletin (published by *Historical abstracts*, $2-$6 p.a.), designed for the use of individual students rather than for research workers and teachers, is a reprint to Pt. 1 of *Historical abstracts*, plus 'Bibliographical news'. Author and subject indexes.

94 "17/19" (02)
Oxford history of modern Europe. Oxford, Clarendon Press, 1954-. tables, maps.

> v. 2. *The struggle for mastery in Europe, 1848-1918*, by A. J. P. Taylor. 1954. 42s.
> v. 2. *The Russian Empire, 1801-1917*, by H. Seton-Watson. 1967. 50s.
> v. 12. *Spain, 1808-1939*, by R. Carr. 1966. 63s.

Under the general editorship of Allan Bullock and F. W. D. Deakin. The series is to be in 16 v., to cover European history, 1789-1945. A separate author for each volume, giving more cohesion than the *New Cambridge Modern History* chapter-approach. V. 1-2 are to deal with international relations; v. 3-4, with the history of ideas; v. 5-16, with individual countries or sections of Europe. V. 8, by Raymond Carr (xxix, 766p. 8 maps) has a 'Bibliographical index' that assembles all references in the text, and a 'Bibliographical essay' (p. 703-14) in 15 sections, with a valuable running commentary. Analytical index.

94 "17/19" (058)
The Annual register: a review of public events at home and abroad for the year, 1758-. London, 1761-. v. 1-. tables, graphs, maps. Annual. (1966. Longmans, Green, 1967. 126s.).

Various publishers. The idea of providing a broad grouping of the chief movements of each year originated from Edmund Burke, Dodsley being the first publisher (*Encyclopedia Britannica* (11th ed.), v. 4, p. 826). Present title: *The Annual register of world events: world events in 1966*; edited by Sir Ivison Macadam.

15 sections: 1. History of the U.K.—2. The Commonwealth—3. International organizations —4. The Americans—5. The U.S.S.R. and Eastern Europe—6. Western and Central Europe —7. The Middle East—8. Africa (excluding Commonwealth)—9. East and South East Asia (excluding Commonwealth)—10. Religion—11. Science—12. Law—13. The arts—14. U.K. finance, trade and industry—15. Documents and reference (including obituary and chronology). Analytical index, mostly places and persons. Well produced.

World events, being the annual register of the year . . . (London, Longmans; subsequently Harmondsworth, Penguin Books) was a paper-backed pocket ed. of *The annual register* for the years 1959, 1960 and 1961 (1961-62. 10s.; 10s.; 15s.).

94 "17/19" (084.4)
PALMER, A. W. A dictionary of modern history, 1789-1945. New ed. London, Cresset Press, 1962. 364p. (Penguin reference books). 5s.

For school use; "intended as an aid to study, not a substitute for it" (*Preface*). About 800-900 very selective entries A-Z, from Aaland Islands to Zulu War, 1879. Includes biographies (*e.g.,* 'Smuts': ⅔p.) as well as events (*e.g.,* 'French Revolution': 2½p.) and parties (*e.g.,* Communist Party': nearly 2p.). Internal cross-references.

Noted: *Wörterbuch der Zeitgeschichte seit 1945* ([Stuttgart?], Kröner, 1967. viii, 465p. tables. DM.17.50).

94 "18/19" (084.4)
GILBERT, M. Recent history atlas, 1870 to the present day. Cartography by J. R. Flower. London, Weidenfeld & Nicolson, 1966. [v], 121p. maps. 15s.

121 black-and-white maps, depicting "not only wars and battles, but also treaties, alliances, population problems and political confrontations . . ." (*Preface*). Map on p. 121: 'American preparedness since 1960'. No text apart from that given on the maps themselves, although much interesting detail and information is conveyed. The review in *International affairs* (v. 43, no. 2, April 1967, p. 428) instances the maps depicting the causes of World War II in Europe. Page size, 13¼" × 10".

A. Boyd's *An atlas of world affairs* (Maps by W. H. Bromage. 5th ed. London, Methuen, 1964. 160p. maps. 8s. 6d.), first published 1957, has 70 black-and-white maps in the style of J. F. Horrabin's pre-war *Atlas of current affairs*, with double-page spread for map and explanation facing. Index of c. 2,500 places and subjects. Suffers from not being sufficiently up to date.

94 "19/"
Keesing's Contemporary Archives: weekly diary of world events. Bristol, Keesing, July 1931-. Weekly. Loose-leaf. 140s. p.a. Name index. 20s.

Covers events from 1st July 1931, with a 35-page synopsis of 1918-31 as a supplement to v. 1. Weekly loose-leaf summary of national and international news, abstracted from news agencies' reports, official sources and the principal newspapers of each country. Sources of each report are quoted, enabling reference to full reports in other publications, but precise details of dates and pages are not given. Reproduces speeches and texts of documents, often in full; statistical tables; maps. Each report refers directly to the previous report on the same subject.

A fortnightly index cumulates frequently, eventually forming a volume index usually covering two years; most entries are under countries. As from 1959 maps are indexed under their subjects as well as under the separate heading 'Maps'. Also from 1959, a quarterly index of names (additional 20s. p.a.), cumulating annually and biennially.

Unbiased and authoritative; the best news digest.

Keesing's is of Dutch origin and has been published in 4 countries, but the English ed. now has no connection with the others: *Keesing's Historisch archief* (Amsterdam, July 1931-); *Les Archives contemporaines, système Keesing* (Brussels, July 1931 - May 1940); *Keesing's Archiv der Gegenwart* (Vienna, July 1931-; suspended March 1945-1949).

Facts on file the index of world events. October/November 1940-. (New York, Facts on File, Inc., 1940-. Weekly. Loose-leaf. $120 p.a.) is a comparable weekly loose-leaf service, with annual bound volumes, and five-year indexes, but it is less detailed and more popular in style than *Keesing's.*

Facts on File also publishes *News dictionary . . .: an encyclopedic summary of contemporary history.* New York, 1964-. Annual. $4.75; ($6.75).

94 "19":016
INSTITUTE OF CONTEMPORARY HISTORY (The Wiener Library). **Quarterly select list of accessions.** London, Winter 1965/66-.

The Summer 1967 issue (8p.) has *c.* 170 entries, systematically arranged: Political and social sciences—Historiography—International relations —Race relations—Concentration camps—Jewry —Churches in the modern world—Biography— World War I—World War II—Countries. Jewish angle.

This accessions list also appears in *Journal of contemporary history.*

The Institute of Contemporary History and Wiener Library's *Catalogue of work in progress on contemporary European history* (1967. 14p.) has 16 headings (International affairs; countries, A-Z). Brief descriptions of work in progress, if not clear from title, plus note of university and date for completion.

Europe

940:016
BROMLEY, J. S., and **GOODWIN, A.,** *ed.* **A select list of works on Europe and Europe overseas, 1715-1815.** Edited for the Oxford Eighteenth-Century Group. Oxford, Clarendon Press, 1956. xii, [1], 132p.

Mainly books, with some periodical titles. Ten of the 27 chapters deal with general aspects; chapters 11-25, with specific countries; chapters 26-27, with geographical aspects and biographical dictionaries. No index or annotations, but items of "specific usefulness as introductions to some larger subject" (*Preface*) are asterisked. Includes material in German, French, Italian, etc.

940:016
BULLOCK, A., and **TAYLOR, A. J. P.,** *ed.* **A select list of books on European history, 1815-1914.** 2nd ed. Edited for the Oxford Recent History Group. Oxford, Clarendon Press, 1957. [vii], 79p.

First published 1949.

16 sections, nos. 4-16 dealing with specific countries, sub-divided by aspects or periods. Omits Great Britain. No annotations or index. Books are in English and other Western languages.

940:016
RAGATZ, L. J. A bibliography for the study of European history, 1815 to 1939. Ann Arbor, Michigan, Edwards, 1942. xiv, 272p.

1st suppt., 1943; 2nd suppt., 1945.

Includes books and articles in main languages arranged by subject under: pt. 1, Europe as a whole; pt. 2, individual countries; pt. 3, international relations. No indexes.

940 (093.2)
THOMAS, D. H., and **CASE, L. M.,** *ed.* **Guide to the diplomatic archives of Western Europe.** Philadelphia, Univ. of Pennsylvania Press; London, Oxford Univ. Press, 1959. xii, 389p.

See entry at 327 (093.2).

940:930.24
MAYER, A. Annals of European civilization, 1501-1900. London, Cassell, 1949. xxii, 457p.

"Annals" (p. 43-305)—arranged chronologically; under each year countries or areas (British Isles; Low Countries; Northern Europe; Central Europe; Latin Europe; Slavonic Europe) are sub-divided by subjects A-Z and then into events.

"Summaries" (p. 309-457)—arranged A-Z by subjects (*e.g.,* Literature) which are sub-divided chronologically. The 41 subjects (with country divisions in the case of Literature and Painting) include Academies, Chemistry, Libraries, Newspapers, Periodicals, Physics, etc.

An index of names and an index of places precede (p. 1-42).

Chronology of the modern world, 1763 to the present time, by N. Williams (London, Barrie & Rockliffe, 1966. xiii, 923p. 60s.), arranges events under each year, subdivided by month. Verso page covers political events (arranged by months), A-M; recto page tabulates 12 categories (*e.g.,* P. Science, technology, discovery, etc.—Q. Scholarship—U. Literature—V. Statistics—Z. Births and deaths). Analytical index, p. 713-923; *c.* 18,000 entries. According to *Library journal* (v. 92, no. 13, July 1967, p. 2553), best on the political side; "many errors have crept into the index" and criteria for including certain events are puzzling.

World Wars I & II

940.3 + 940.53:016
Bücherschau der Weltkriegsbücherei. Stuttgart, Weltkriegsbücherei/Bibliothek für Zeitgeschichte, 1929-. Quarterly.

A bibliography of books and periodical articles on World Wars I and II in all their aspects; also covers current developments of a military nature and study of atomic warfare. The 1961 v. (1963) lists *c.* 10,000 items annually and latterly issued in annual volumes (that for 1959 was published in 1961). Valuable, although tendentious in its pre-1939 form. Annual author and anonymous-title index.

The volume for 1961 (Jahrgang 33), has the title *Jahresbibliographie Bibliothek für Zeitgeschichte. Weltkriegsbücherei,* Pt. 1, 'Neuerwerbungen der Bibliothek' (p. 2-508), is systematically arranged; pt. 2, 'Forschungs- und Literaturberichte' (p. 509-627), consists of four special contributions (*e.g.,* 'Indochina War, 1945-54').

G. K. Hall (Boston, Mass.) plan to publish the *Systematischer Katalog* (20v. $1340 (U.S. & W. Germany); $1474 (elsewhere)) and *Alphabetischer*

Katalog (11v. $725 (U.S. and W. Germany); $797.50 (elsewhere) of the Bibliothek für Zeitgeschichte by 31st October 1968. Over 500,000 cards will be photolithographically reproduced.

940.3+940.53:016
GREAT BRITAIN. H.M. STATIONERY OFFICE. Government publications. Sectional list no. 60, revised to 31st May 1967: **Histories of the First and Second World Wars.** London, H.M.S.O., 1967. 18p. *Gratis.*

First World War, 1914-1918—History of the Second World War (military, civil and medical series). Many of the entries are annotated.

940.3+940.53:016
HORNING, J. "Les deux guerres mondiales". In *Bulletin des bibliothèques de France,* v. 9, no. 2, December 1963, p. 463-87.

Evaluates the principal sources (both publications and institutions) for the study of recent history, particularly of World Wars I and II. Cites more than 170 publications.

L. Morton's "Sources for the history of World War II" (in *World politics,* v. 13, no. 3, April 1961, p. 435-53) has a running commentary on ten types of sources (records; manuscript histories;; reference works; official publications; memoirs and biography; etc.). U.S. slant.

British collections on World Wars I and II are noted in *Repositories in Great Britain* (London, Imperial War Museum, Foreign Documents Centre, 1966. [3], 6p. *Gratis*).

940.3+940.53:016
INTERNATIONAL COMMISSION FOR THE TEACHING OF HISTORY. Les deux guerres mondiales: bibliographie sélective. Brussels & Paris, Brépols, 1964. 246p. illus.

About 1,800 entries, some of them annotated. Three main sections: '1914-1918: bibliographie sélective', by J. de Launay (p. 93-105: general works; chronologies; diplomatic history; military operations; life and conditions within States; memoirs and biographies; periodicals; bibliographies; illustrated works)—'1919-1939: histoire des origines de la deuxième guerre', by E. Anchieri (p. 107-59)—'1939-1945: histoire de la deuxième guerre mondiale', by H. Michel and J-M. d'Hoop (p. 161-243). Includes a few films and gramophone records.
English translation by Pergamon Press as *The two world wars* (1965. 50s.).

940.3:016
GUNZENHÄUSER, M. Die Bibliographien zur Geschichte des Ersten Weltkrieges. Literaturbericht und Bibliographie. Frankfurt am Main, Bernard & Graefe Verlag für Wehrwesen, 1964. 63p. (Schriften der Bibliothek für Zeitgeschichte Weltkriegsbücherei. Heft 3).

Notes 450 items. Two sections: 1. Literaturberichte (p. 9-26; a running commenting on the numbered items in section 2)—2. Bibliographie (A. Activity in the special library field; B. Special bibliographies on the history of World War I; C. Historical science and general resources). Author index.

940.3:016
NEW YORK PUBLIC LIBRARY. Subject catalog of the World War I Collection. Boston, Mass., G. K. Hall, 1961. 4v. $165.

61,300 photolithographed card entries for works in many languages, periodicals and pamphlets.

940.53:016
"Bibliographie". In *Revue d'histoire de la deuxième guerre mondiale.* Paris, Presses Universitaires de France, 1950-. Quarterly. 23F. p.a.

The July 1967 issue (17th year, no. 67) includes review articles (p. 51-114) and 'Bibliographie' (p. 115-28), listing *c.* 250 books and periodical articles. Includes material in Russian, Polish, etc. Some items are very briefly annotated. Four sections (with subdivisions): 1. Généralités—2. Situation internationale avant la geurre—3. La geurre—4. La vie intérieure des états.

940.53 (02)
History of the Second World War: United Kingdom, Civil Series; edited by Sir K. Hancock. London, H.M. Stationery Office, 1949-.

——: **United Kingdom, Medical Series;** edited by Sir A. S. Macnalty. London, H.M Stationery Office, 1952-.

——: **United Kingdom, Military Series;** edited by J. R. M. Butler. London, H.M. Stationery Office, 1952-.

British official history of the origins, conduct and conclusion of World War II. Of the 28v. planned for the Civil series, 27 have been published; of the 21 planned for the Medical series, 19 are available; and of the 33 planned for the Military series, 28 are available. See H.M.S.O. *Sectional list no. 60: Histories of the first and second World Wars* (1967).

On the official histories of World War II, see 8th report of the Select Committee on Estimates (1956-57). Lists of Commonwealth and U.S. series appeared in *Library Association record,* v. 60, no. 5, May 1958, p. 166-7. For the U.S. angle,—Price list 50, American history (44th ed. Washington, U.S. Government Printing Office, 1961. *Gratis*)—indexed under 'World war, 1939-45' and *United States army in World War II: master index* (Washington, U.S.G.P.O., 1960. 145p. 75c.). Other, parallel official histories, are being compiled for Poland, etc.
The Imperial War Museum, London, has issued a number of mimeographed subject lists (e.g., *The North African Campaign.* 1961. 43p.; *The invasion of Normandy.* 1959. 7, 5, 11, 42p.), supplemented by its monthly *Accessions list.*

For diplomatic aspects, consult the series of *Documents on British foreign policy, 1919-39* (H.M.S.O., 1946-. See at 327 (410) (093).); *Documents on German foreign policy, 1918-45* (H.M.S.O., 1949-.); *Documenti diplomatici italiani,* nona serie 1939-43 (Rome, Libreria dello Stato, 1954-.); and *Foreign relations of the United States.* Diplomatic papers: The Soviet Union, 1933-39. (Washington, Government Printing Office, 1952).

A general guide to printed materials for the history of the Second World War is badly needed.

Noted: "Quelques sources récentes pour l'histoire de la Seconde Guerre Mondiale", by J. Bariéty, in *Revue historique,* January/March 1967, p. 63-98.

940.53 (02)
JOSLEN, H. F. Orders of battle, Second World War, 1939-1945. London, H.M. Stationery Office, 1960. 2v. 126*s.*

Prepared for the Historical Section of the Cabinet Office; based on official documents. Sub-title for both volumes: 'United Kingdom and colonial formations and units in the Second World War, 1939-1945'.
V. 1, pt. 1: Divisions (Appendix 1, Composition and war establishment of divisions)—2. Armoured, cavalry, tank, motor machine-gun brigades and support groups—3. Infantry brigades. V. 2, pt. 4: Parachute and airlanding brigades—5. Colonial brigades—6. Miscellaneous brigades—7. GHQ, Army Group, Army and Corps Troops—8. British units which served on the Indian establishment and in Indian formations—9. British units in the colonies and Faroe Islands. Supplement: Formations and units engaged in the Battle of El Alamein, 23rd October 1942, and the Assault-landing in Normandy, 6th/7th June 1944. Index.

Eastern Europe

940 (-011):016
KERNER, R. J. Slavic Europe: a selected bibliography in the Western European languages, comprising history, languages and literature. Oxford, Univ. Press, 1918. [ii], xxiv, 402p. (Harvard Bibliographies. Library series, v. 1).

Select list of basic works on various aspects of Slavonic life, in Western languages. The few bibliographies with Slavonic titles listed contain references to bibliographies and sources in western languages. Arrangement is ethnological rather than by country.

A handbook of Slavic studies: a selected bibliography in Western European languages, comprising history, languages and literatures, edited by L. I. Strakhovsky (Cambridge, Mass., Harvard Univ. Press, 1949. xxi, 753p.) is mainly concerned with historical aspects. Chapters are by specialists, with selected bibliographies appended. Numerous footnote references; comparative chronology (p. 675-722).

940 (-011):016
MILLER, L. H. "East European history". In *Library trends,* v. 15, no. 4, April 1967, p. 730-44.

A condensed bibliographical survey, concentrating on current coverage, especially of Russian historical literature (national and regional bibliographies; periodicals; etc.). Briefer notes on Finnish, Czeck, Bulgarian bibliographical services

are followed by paragraphs on periodicals and bibliographies in non-Slavic languages.

Commonwealth

941-44:016
MORRELL, W. P. British overseas expansion and the history of the Commonwealth: a select bibliography, 3rd rev. ed. London, Historical Association, 1961. 40p. (Helps for students of history, no. 63). 5*s.*

Originally edited by A. P. Newton (1929).
Consists of 8 sections, 1-7 covering generalities and individual areas, and 8, 'Oceanic enterprise and sea-power'. About 350 items, with brief annotations.

941-44:016
NATIONAL BOOK LEAGUE. Commonwealth history. London, N.B.L., 1965. 44p. 2*s.*

An annotated reading list of 263 items, prepared for the Commonwealth Book Exhibition at Marlborough House in October 1965. 9 sections: General — Africa — Australia—Canada—The Far East—India, Pakistan and Ceylon—The Mediterranean—New Zealand—The West Indies. All the books were in print in September 1965. No index.

941-44:016
PARKER, J. Books to build an empire: a bibliographical history of English overseas interests, to 1620. Amsterdam, N. Israel, 1965. viii, 290p. maps.

The sub-title is more to the point than the title. A narrative survey of 207 books and editions, with a handy check-list (p. 242-65). Well printed and production. Nothing new as a bibliographical survey, states the review in *The mariner's mirror* (v. 52, no. 4, November 1966, p. 400) but the book "will be useful to university students and librarians".

941-44 (02)
The Cambridge history of the British Empire. General editors (originally), J. H. Rose, A. P. Newton, E. A. Benians. Cambridge, Univ. Press, 1929-. v. 1-2, 4-8.

v. 1.: *The old Empire, from the beginnings to 1783.* 1929. 90*s.*
v. 2: *Growth of the new Empire, 1783-1870.* 1940. 87*s.*
v. 3: *The Empire-Commonwealth, 1870-1919;* edited by E. A. Benians. 1959. 105*s.*
v. 4: *British India, 1497-1858;* edited by H. H. Dodwell. 1929. o.p.
v. 5: *Indian Empire, 1858-1918, with chapters on the development of administration, 1818-58;* edited by H. H. Dodwell. 1932. o.p.
v. 6: *Canada and Newfoundland.* 1930. 90*s.*
v. 7, pt. 1: *Australia.* 1933. o.p.; v. 7, pt. 2: *New Zealand.* 1933. o.p.
v. 8: *South Africa, Rhodesia and the Protectorates.* 1936; 2nd ed. 1963. 105*s.*
On similar lines to the *Cambridge modern history,* each volume containing some 20-30 chapters by specialists. Social, economic and cultural aspects are touched upon. The lengthy, valuable bibliography appended to each volume is divided into pt. 1, Collections of MSS. in public and private archives and official papers and publications, and pt. 2, Other works.

941-44 (02)

MANSERGH, N. Survey of British Commonwealth affairs: problems of external policy, 1931-1939. Issued under the auspices of the Royal Institute of International Affairs London, Oxford Univ. Press, 1952. xx, 481. 63s.

Parts: 1. From Empire to Commonwealth: the years of transition—2. The external policies of the Dominions, 1931-9—3. The Commonwealth and the War. Footnote references; bibliography of sources, p. xii. Analytical index.

941-44 (02)

—— **Survey of British Commonwealth affairs: problems of wartime co-operation and postwar change, 1939-1952.** Issued under the auspices of the Royal Institute of International Affairs. London, Oxford Univ. Press, 1958. xvi, 469p. 65s.

A comprehensive yet very readable survey. Footnote references; bibliography of sources, p. xiii-xiv. Analytical index. The author is Smuts Professor of the History of the British Commonwealth in Cambridge University.

941-44 (093)

GREAT BRITAIN. PUBLIC RECORD OFFICE. Calendar of State Papers, Colonial. London, H.M. Stationery Office, 1860/1963-. v. 1/43-. (Reprinted 1965. ea. £10 10s.; £11 5s.).

v. 1, 5, 7, 9-43. *America and West Indies,* 1574 . . . 1737. 1860-1963.
v. 2-4. *East Indies, China and Japan,* 1513-1616; 1616-1621; 1622-24. 1862-78.
v. 6, 8. *East Indies, China and Persia,* 1625-1629; 1630-1634. 1884, 1892.
V. 41-43 (1954-63) are available in the original edition (84s.; 63s. 110s.). The series is being continued.
The *America and West Indies* volumes include much material relating to French, Dutch and Spanish settlement in those areas.

941-44(093)

GREAT BRITAIN. PUBLIC RECORD OFFICE. The records of the Colonial and Dominion Offices; by R. B. Pugh. London, H.M. Stationery Office, 1964. vi, 119p. facsims. (Public Record Office handbooks, no. 3). 10s. 6d.

Designed to introduce the searcher to a large mass of public records,—the Colonial Office and Commonwealth Relations Office (previously Dominions Office) groups. Three sections; the first describes administrative arrangements for handling Commonwealth relations; the Second describes the records that these administrations have created, particularly during the last century or so; the third has brief notes in the classes that make up this complex. Annotated list of record classes, p. 57-119.

941-44 (093)

MANSERGH, N., *ed.* **Documents and speeches on British Commonwealth affairs, 1931-1952.** Issued under the auspices of the Royal Institute of International Affairs. London, Oxford Univ. Press, 1952. 2v.

Of necessity a selection; some parts of docu-

ments and speeches have been omitted. The collection begins with the Statute of Commonwealth and ends with the proclamation of Queen Elizabeth II. 22 sections.

—— **Documents and speeches on Commonwealth affairs, 1952-1962.** Issued under the auspices of International Affairs. London, Oxford Univ. Press, 1963. xxi, 775p. 84s.

226 documents, in 4 main parts: 1. Constitutional structure and membership—2. External policies: foreign affairs, defence and trade—3. Economic and social policies—4. The Commonwealth: organization and purposes. Index.

Guide to the principal Parliamentary Papers relating to the Dominions, 1812-1911, by M. I. Adams and others (Edinburgh & London, Oliver & Boyd, 1913 viii, 190p.) charts the preceding century.

941-44:930

WINKS, R. W., *ed.* **The historiography of the British Empire-Commonwealth.** Durham, N.C., Duke Univ. Press; London, Transatlantic Books, 1966. xiv, 596p. $12.50; 100s.

21 essays by different hands (*e.g.,* South Africa, by L. M. Thompson, p. 212-36; British Central Africa, by G Shepperton, p. 237-47; British West Africa, by H. M. Wright; p. 261-78; British East Africa, by G. Bennett, p. 248-60). Final essay: "Commonwealth literature: developments and prospects". Footnote references. Detailed index (p. 529-96) of authors, anonymous titles and subjects.

Great Britain

Bibliographies

941:016

ANDERSON, J. P. The book of British topography: a classified catalogue of the topographical works in the library of the British Museum relating to Great Britain and Ireland. London, Satchell, 1881. xvi, 472p. (Reprinted Amsterdam, 1966. 90s.).

Nearly 14,000 items, with full titles of works, but no annotation or pagination. Contents: Catalogues — General topography (including England and English counties, A-Z)—Wales (general; regional; counties, A-Z) — Scotland (general; counties, A-Z) — Ireland (general; counties, A-Z)—Addenda—Index of places and subjects. The "General topography" section includes such topics as antiquities, directories, islands, railways and views.

941:016

Bibliography of British history. Tudor period, 1485-1603; edited by Conyers Read. 2nd ed. Issued under the direction of the American Historical Association and the Royal Historical Society of Great Britain. Oxford, Clarendon Press, 1959. xxviii, 624p. 63s.

First published 1933 .
"An exhaustive survey of the material in print has been made to 1st January 1957, but many entries have been made for books and

articles appearing since that date (*Preface to second edition*). 6,543 numbered entries, most of them annotated. Author and subject index, p. 545-624.

—— **Stuart period, 1603-1714;** edited by G. Davies . . . Oxford, Clarendon Press, 1928. x, 459p.

3,858 numbered entries, most of them annotated, in 16 sections. A new edition is in preparation.

—— **The eighteenth century, 1714-1789;** edited by S. Pargellis and D. J. Medley. Oxford, Clarendon Press, 1951. xxvi, 642p.

4,558 numbered entries, most of them annotated.

These 3v. provide a continuation of Gross's *Sources and literature of English history . . . to about 1485* (see at 942:016). The Tudor volume has been criticized for inaccuracies and the third volume for lack of balance.

The starting point for advanced work. As selected, annotated bibliographies, they cover both primary and secondary (contemporary and later) source material, pamphlets and periodical articles. History is interpreted in a wide sense, covering political, constitutional, military and naval, religious, economic, social, literary, art and science aspects, as well as local and colonial history, voyages and travels. Each volume carries an index of authors and specific subjects.

New editions are planned, with further volumes covering the period 1789-1914.

The first of a series of 'Bibliographical handbooks' on British history, sponsored by the Conference on British Studies (in the U.S.A.) is *Tudor England, 1485-1603,* edited by M. Levine (London, Cambridge Univ. Press, 1968. xii, 116p. 25s.). It has over 2,350 references to printed sources, essays, monographs, biographies and articles. Four other volumes are in preparation.

941:016
BONSER, W. An Anglo-Saxon and Celtic bibliography (450-1087). Oxford, Blackwell, 1957. xxxvii, [1], 574p. 126s.

11,975 items, drawn from 422 periodicals, collected works, etc. Sections: 1. General topics and historical source material—2. Political history—3. Local history—4. Constitutional history and law.—5. Social and economic history—6. Ecclesiastical history and religion—7. Geography and place-names—8. General culture—9. Archaeology—10. Numismatics and seals—11. Epigraphy—12. Art. Closely classified; outline of classification scheme, but no indexes.

941:016
BONSER, W. A Romano-British bibliography (55 B.C. - A.D. 449). Oxford, Blackwell, 1964. 2v. 168s.

See entry at 930.26 (410).

941:016
GROSE, C. L. A select bibliography of British history, 1660-1760. Chicago, Univ. of Chicago Press, 1939. xxv, 507p. $9.

Compared with the *Bibliography of British history (q.v.),* supplements Davies on the Stuart period and is not entirely superseded by Pargellis and Medley. 3,801 entries. Classified by periods: General (1660-1760); 1660-88; 1689-1714; 1715-60, and sub-divided by broad subjects under each period. Outstanding items are asterisked. The annotations provide well-informed comments. Author and subject index.

941:016
LIBRARY ASSOCIATION. County Libraries Group. **Readers' guide to books on medieval Britain.** 2nd ed. London, L.A., the Group, 1964. 23p. (Readers' guides. New series, no. 82). 2s. 6d.

First published 1940.
A checklist of c. 300 entries in 17 sections; occasional annotations; no index. Includes biography, early texts, literature and art, heraldry, war.
Other L.A. County Libraries Group Readers' guides (ea. 2s. 6d.): no. 100. *Hanoverian Britain* (2nd ed. 1968); no. 84. *Victorian Britain* (2nd ed. 1965). *Tudor and Stuart Britain* is in preparation.

941:016
MOWAT, C. L. British history since 1926: a select bibliography. London, Historical Association, 1960. 32p. (Helps for students of history, no. 61). 5s.

Four sections: 1. Bibliographies and general references—2. Before the War, 1926-39 (16 sub-sections, including 'Political biographies and memoirs')—3. The War years, 1939-1945—4. Since 1945 (7 sub-sections). Deliberately excludes military and diplomatic history of World War II. Some annotations and occasional running commentary. No index. Author is Professor of History, University College of North Wales, Bangor.

941:016
NATIONAL BOOK LEAGUE. Mirror of Britain; or, The history of British topography: catalogue of an exhibition held at 7 Albemarle Street, London, W.1, 29 May-6 July 1957. London, N.B.L., 1957. 91p.

266 items, arranged chronologically in sections: General surveys—County histories—Towns and villages—Buildings, parks and gardens—Regional studies and scenery—Tours—Roadbooks, maps and district guides—Poems—Maps. Fairly full transcripts of title pages, plus annotations for the more important items, and name of library lending the item. Appendices: Some sources of reference on British topography (p. 57-58); current books (subdivided as in the main sequence; p. 59-89). Author and illustrations index.

941:016
STOCKHAM, P., *with others, comp.* **British local history:** a select bibliography. London, Dillon's Univ. Bookshop, [1964] [ii], 80p.

An unannotated list of c. 1,500 books in 36 main sections, with some introductory section notes. Designed "to give some idea of the great range of books available at both a local and national level" (introduction). County and country approach, p. 1-31; subjects, A-Z (p. 31-

76); maps (p. 76-79); periodicals (p. 79-80). Subjects: Archaeology—Bibliographies—Building—Castles—Chronology—Crafts and craftsmen—Customs and folklore—Dialect—Domestic life—Ecclesiology—Genealogy—Heraldry — Historical geography and topography—Land and inclosures—Law—Local government and administration—Manorial life—Money, rates and taxes—Palaeography—Philanthropy—Place names—Population and social studies—Records and archives—Social history—Towns—Travel and communications—Village and farm—Windmills. Entries indicate presence of illustrations and bibliographies; also prices (in bold). No index.

Readers' guide to books on sources of local history (3rd ed. London, Library Association, 1964. 30p. (Readers' guides, new series, no. 78). 2s. 6d.) lists *c.* 300 items, a few with annotations, under 29 subjects, A-Z, following a general section. Introductory notes on some subjects. No index.

941:016
Writings on British history, 1934-: a bibliography of books and articles on the history of Great Britain from about 450 A.D. to 1914, published during the year 1934[-39], with an appendix containing a select list of publications in 1934[-39] on British history since 1914. Compiled for the Royal Historical Society by A. T. Milne. London, Cape, 1939-. Annual for years 1934-39.

The volume for 1939 was published in 1953.
An exhaustive bibliography, entries being grouped under "General works" and then under periods, with subject sub-division. No annotations, but entries for books carry references to reputable reviews. Detailed subject and author indexes.

—— **1940-1945** . . . London, Cape, 1960. 2v. 105s.

12,380 numbered entries. "The aim . . . is to provide, as in previous volumes of the series, exhaustive lists of books and articles published on British history during the period covered" (*Introduction*). V. 1 covers general works and period histories to 1714; v. 2 covers later periods to 1914, with the Appendix, p. 775-87. A list of bibliographies to be consulted for publications relating to British history not included in the *Writings* appears on p. 10-11.

Writings on British history, 1901-1933, edited by H. H. Bellot, is being published in 5v. (v. 1-3. 1968). V. 1 (105s.) covers auxiliary sciences and general works; v. 2 (63s.), *The Middle Ages, 450-1485;* v. 3 (105s.), *The Tudor and Stuart periods, 1485-1714.* V. 4 (2 pts.), *The eighteenth century, 1714-1815* is in the press; v. 5 (2 pts.), *1815-1914* is in preparation. Volumes covering publications of 1946 onwards are in preparation at the Institute of Historical Research.

941:016:016
HUMPHREYS, A. L. A handbook of county bibliography; being a bibliography of bibliographies relating to the counties and towns of Great Britain and Ireland. London, Humphreys, 1917. x, 501p.

A detailed and invaluable guide. The 6,000 bibliographies are arranged under counties, A-Z,

the general works being followed by those on the individual towns and villages. The entries include manuscript and periodical sources. Full bibliographical details are given. Detailed index (p. 399-500) of authors, personal names, places, and subjects, which gives full data under each entry as well as page references. Annotations are occasional and brief.

941 (026):016
FORDHAM, *Sir* **H. G. The road-books and itineraries of Great Britain, 1570 to 1850:** a catalogue. Cambridge, Univ. Press, 1924. xiv, 72p.

A chronological survey, without annotations. There is an index of names of authors, publishers and printers,

The author has also compiled a *Hand-list of catalogues and works of reference relating to carto-bibliography and kindred subjects for Great Britain and Ireland, 1720 to 1927* (Cambridge, Univ. Press, 1928. 25p.); chronological arrangement; author index.

941 (032)
STEINBERG, S. H. *ed.* **A new dictionary of British history.** London, E. Arnold, 1963. vi, [i], 407p. 30s.

Successor to *A dictionary of British history,* edited by J. A. Brendon (1937). 11 contributors; signed articles. Covers the countries that are, or were at one time, members of the Commonwealth (unlike Brendon). Excludes all purely biographical entries (these formed more than 50 % of entries in Brendon). Few bibliographical references; liberal cross-references. Brief coverage of political, constitutional, legal, ecclesiastical and economic aspects of British history.

941:061
HARCUP, S. E., *comp.* **Historical, archaeological and kindred societies in the British Isles:** a list. London, Univ. of London, Institute of Historical Research, 1965. [iii], 53p. 7s. 6d.

A-Z list of *c.* 850 societies states name, date of founding, secretary's address and publications. Topographical index (under England, Channel Islands, Isle of Man, Wales and Monmouthshire, Scotland, Ireland); Select list of subjects (arts and crafts; Economic and social history; Folklore and dialect; Heraldry and genealogy; Medicine; Naval and military history; Numismatics; Religion; Science and technology).

941 (084.3)
GREAT BRITAIN. ORDNANCE SURVEY. Historical maps.

The following archaeological and historical maps are available as both flat maps and as folded map and text in book form:
Ancient Britain. North and South sheets. 1951. 1:625,000. ea. 7s. 6d.; 12s. 6d.
Neolithic Wesex. 1932. o.p.
Neolithic South Wales. 1936. o.p.
Map of Southern Britain in the Iron Age. 1:625,000. 7s. 6d.; 17s. 6d.
Map of the Trent Basin (neolithic). 1933. o.p.
Celtic earthworks of Salisbury Plain. 1933. o.p.

Map of Roman Britain. 3rd ed. 1:1,000,000. 7s. 6d.; 12s. 6d.

Map of Hadrian's Wall. 1964. 2″ : 1 mile. 7s. 6d.; 10s.

Britain in the Dark Ages. 1:1,000,000. 7s. 6d.; 17s. 6d.

Monastic Britain. North (1950) and South (2nd ed. 1954) sheets. 1:625,000. ea. 7s. 6d.; 12s. 6d.

Seventeenth century England. 1930. o.p.

941 (084.3)

RODGER, E. M., *comp.* **The large-scale county maps of the British Isles, 1596-1850:** a union list, compiled in the Map Section of the Bodleian Library. Oxford, Bodleian Library, 1960. xx, 52p. 7s. 6d.

818 entries, with 25 locations (7 of the libraries being national or copyright libraries); entries 819-32 cover lost or uncompleted surveys. The period taken is that between the work of the Tudor cartographers and that of the Ordnance Survey. Arrangement is by countries, etc. (England, Wales, Islands, Scotland, Ireland), subdivided by counties; final arrangement is chronological. Details given: date, engraver(s), number of sheets, scale, location. Index of personal names. The review in *Scottish geographical magazine* (v. 77, no. 2, September 1961, p. 125-6) notes that three-quarters of the entries concern England, "but in Scotland, and perhaps more, in Ireland, there are several gaps in the list".

941 (084.3)

ROYAL GEOGRAPHICAL SOCIETY. Early maps of the British Isles, A.D. 1000 - A.D. 1579. London, the Society, 1961. 15 pl., with separate 'Introduction and notes'. (Reproductions of early maps, 7). 35s.

Collotype facsimiles of 20 manuscript and printed maps, with introduction and notes by G. R. Crone (32p.; bibliography, p. 30-31). The maps, states the prospectus, "have been chosen to illustrate the development of the map of the British Isles from the Cotton world map of circa A.D. 1000 to the general map in Christopher Saxton's county atlas of England and Wales, A.D. 1579". Page size, 21″ × 16½″.

Other available maps in the series 'Reproductions of early printed maps' and 'Reproductions of early manuscript maps' on Britain:

2. *English county maps.* 1932. 21 sheets, 25″ × 19½″, with memoir. 105s.

6. *Gough map of Great Britain.* 1959. 2 sheets, 23½″ × 25½″, in colour, with memoir. 50s.

941 (084.3):016

GREAT BRITAIN. PUBLIC RECORD OFFICE. Maps and plans in the Public Record Office. London, H.M.S.O., 1966-.

v. 1. *British Isles,* c. *1410-1860.* 1967. xv, 648p. 105s. (See entry at 912 (410):016.)

4,173 items; detailed descriptions of manuscript maps.

941 (091):016

GREAT BRITAIN. H.M. STATIONERY OFFICE. Government publications. Sectional list no. 17 (revised to 30th November 1965): **Publications of the Royal Commission on Historical Manuscripts.** London, H.M. Stationery Office, 1966. 30p. *Gratis.*

Mainly a list of the H.M.C. reports, which are of two kinds: Commissioners' Reports to the Crown and Inspectors' Reports to the Commissioners. It is in the latter that the historian will find his material. The *22nd Report* (1946) gives locations of MS. collections at the end of World War II. Alphabetical list and chronological summary of reports appended.

The *Bulletins* of the National Register of Archives add much information about private and semi-private collections not covered by RCHM reports.

941 (091):016

GREAT BRITAIN. HISTORICAL MANU-SCIPTS COMMISSION. Guide to the reports on collections of manuscripts of private families, corporations and institutions in Great Britain and Ireland issued by the Royal Commissioners on Historical Manuscripts. Part 1, **Topographical guide.** London, H.M. Stationery Office, 1914. 2 pts. o.p.

An index of places referred to in the various manuscripts reported on, 1870-1911, plus a list of reports published and a scheme of numbering the reports.

A *Topographical guide* to reports issued since 1911 is in preparation.

941(091):016

—— —— **Guide to the reports of the Royal Commission on Historical Manuscripts, 1911-1957.** Part 2, **Index of persons.** Edited by A. C. S. Hall London, H.M. Stationery Office, 1966. 3v. £10 10s.

Continues the *Index of persons* (2v.) that formed Pt. 2 of the *Guide . . . 1870-1911* (London, H.M.S.O., 1935-38), being a cumulated index of all persons mentioned in the individual-volume indexes to the H.M.C.'s reports.

Great Britain: Records

941 (093):016

DAVIS, G. R. C. Medieval cartularies of Great Britain: a short catalogue. London, Longmans, Green, 1958. xxi, 182p.

Pt. 1, Cartularies of religious houses (p. 2-137); pt. 2, Secular cartularies. 1,344 entries, with a bibliographical description of each; if an item is asterisked, it has been deposited on loan. Arrangement in pt. 1, under England and Wales, and Scotland, is A-Z by locations. Effective use of bold type. Indexes: 1. Present owners, etc., of MSS. (corporate; private); 2. Former owners, etc., of MSS. Described in the *Annual bulletin of historical literature* (no. 44 (1960), p. 15) as "an indispensable guide to the location of monastic and other chartularies", in public or private ownership.

941 (093):016

GREAT BRITAIN. H.M. STATIONERY OFFICE. Government publications. Sectional list no. 17, revised to 31st July 1967: **Publications of the Royal Commission on Historical Manuscripts.** London, H.M.S.O., 1967. 31p. *Gratis.*

Details of series, followed by 'Alphabetical list' and 'Chronological summary of Reports' [1870-1967].

941 (093):016

GREAT BRITAIN. H.M. STATIONERY OFFICE. Government publications: Sectional list no. 24 (revised to 31st July 1965). **Record publications.** London, H.M. Stationery Office, 1965. 62p. *Gratis.*

An invaluable, though frequently overlooked, guide to the great series of documents on British history published by the Stationery Office. Complete lists of available (priced) and o.p. works. Includes: 1. Public Record Office calendars, etc. (Chancery records; State Papers: England, Scotland, Ireland; Researches in foreign archives)—2. P.R.O. lists and indexes—3. P.R.O. Privy Council registers—4. Rolls series—5. Publications of the Record Commissioners, etc.—6. Scotland —7. N. Ireland—8. Ireland—9. Works in facsimile. Micro-opaque cards. Miscellaneous publications. Index.

The P.R.O. *Annual report of the Keeper of Public Records* (formerly Deputy Keeper) is of particular value.

The P.R.O. Rolls series,—*Rerum Britannicarum Medii Aevi Scriptores, or Chronicles and memorials of Great Britain and Ireland during the Middle Ages*—consisting of 99 individual works (253v.) plus the unpublished no. 18, v. 2-, was reprinted by Kraus Reprint Ltd. in 1965 ($4,750).

941 (093):016

GREAT BRITAIN. HISTORICAL MANUSCRIPTS COMMISSION. NATIONAL REGISTER OF ARCHIVES. List of accessions to repositories in . . . London, H.M. Stationery Office, 1958-. Annual. (1966 v., published 1967. 102p. *8s. 6d.*).

The 1964 volume lists accessions under 129 repositories (record offices, public libraries, etc.), by names, A-Z. Types of records deposited, with dates, are stated. Country (England, Scotland, Ireland and Wales) and county index.

941 (093):016

GREAT BRITAIN. PUBLIC RECORD OFFICE. Guide to the contents of the Public Record Office. London, H.M. Stationery Office, 1963. 2v. *100s.*

v. 1. *Legal records, etc.* 32s. 6d.
v. 2. *State Papers and Departmental records.* 67s. 6d.
Supersedes M. S. Giuseppi's *Guide to the manuscripts preserved in the Public Record Office* (1923-24. 2v.), of which it is largely a revision.
The Records transferred to the P.R.O. between 1923 and 1960 "have not only lengthened previously existing series but have added upwards of two thousand classes not known to Giuseppi's *Guide*" (*Preface*). Arrangement is by administrative provenance. General classes (*e.g.*, Records of the High Court of Admiralty) are allotted separate sections, with introductions. Each type of record (*e.g.*, Prize Appeal Records) is briefly annotated. Each volume has a key to regnal

numbers; chronological index to statutes cited in text; index of persons and places; index of subject. V. 1 also has a glossary.

Accessions since 1961 are recorded in the *Annual Report of the Keeper of the Public Records.*

941 (093):016

GREAT BRITAIN. PUBLIC RECORD OFFICE. Handbooks. London, H.M. Stationery Office, 1954-. 1-.

1. *Guide to seals in the Public Record Office.* 1954. 4s.
2. *Domesday re-bound. Notes on the physical features and history of the Record.* 1954. 4s.
3. *The records of the Colonial and Dominions Offices.* 1964. 10s.
4. *List of Cabinet papers, 1880-1914.* 1964. 10s.
5. *Shakespeare in the Public Records.* 1964. 3s. 6d.
6. *List of papers of the Committee of Imperial Defence, to 1914.* 1964. 3s. 6d.
7. *List of documents relating to the Household and Wardrobe, John to Edward I.* 1964. 13s. 6d.
8. *List of Colonial Office Confidential Print, to 1916.* 1965. 16s.
9. *List of Cabinet papers, 1915 and 1916.* 1966. 15s.
10. *Classes of Departmental papers for 1906-1938.* 1966. 5s.
11. *The Records of the Cabinet Office, to 1922.* 1966. 8s.
No. 11 (viii, 52p.) "aims to give some guidance in the use of a group of records which has been described as 'the most valuable single collection of modern material for historical purposes that can be obtained from official sources' " (*Introduction*). Pt. 2 gives 'Summary of Cabinet Office Records to 1922'. 4 plates.

941 (093):016

"Local archives of Great Britain". In *Archives,* v. 1, no. 1, 1948-.

A series of articles surveying the holdings of local record offices in Great Britain, *e.g.*:
1. "The County Record Office at Bedford."
2. "The Essex Record Office."
3. "The Glamorgan County Record Office."
4. "The County Record Office of Hertford."
5. "The Birmingham Reference Library."
6. "The Lincolnshire Archives Committee."
7. "The Lancashire Record Office."
The latest, no. 29: "The Dorset Record Office", by M. Holmes, in *Archives,* v. 7, no. 36, October 1966, p. 207-14.

941 (093):016

MACFARLANE, L. J. "The Vatican archives, with special reference to sources for British [and Irish] medieval history." In *Archives,* v. 4, no. 21, Lady Day 1959, p. 29-44; v. 4, no. 22, Michaelmas 1959, p. 84-101.

101 references. The second article has two appendices: 1. 'Transcripts and microfilms of British and Irish material extracted from the Vatican archives already available in Great Britain and Ireland'; 2. 'Sources in Rome other than the Vatican which contain British and Irish material'.
Supplemented by L. Macfarlane's "The Vatican archives, with special reference to sources for British medieval history" (*Archives,* v. 4, no. 21, 1959, p. 29-44; 92 references) and "The Vatican

archives, with special reference to British and Irish medieval history" (*Archives*, v. 4, no. 22, 1959, p. 84-101; 101 references). Dr. Macfarlane has a more general work in preparation on the Vatican archives.

941 (093) (02)
GALBRAITH, V. H. Introduction to the use of public records. 2nd ed. London, Oxford Univ. Press, 1952. 120p. 12s. 6d.

First published 1934; reprinted lithographically, with corrections.
Introduction (the subject of five lectures), for graduate students beginning their research, to the main classes of records in the Public Record Office, and to the administrations which produce them. A practical handbook containing invaluable hints to the beginner, a bibliography which no student of diplomatic or of the Public Records should miss, and appendices of regulations in force at the P.R.O.

941 (093) (02)
HEPWORTH, P. Archives and manuscripts in libraries. 2nd ed. London, Library Association, 1964. 69p. illus. (Library Association pamphlet, no. 18). 12s. (9s. to members).

First published 1958.
Contents: 1. Definition and history—2. Archives and manuscripts in libraries—3. Catalogues and guides to manuscripts in libraries (p. 20-61; arranged by countries—England, Scotland, Wales, N. Ireland, Eire—then by counties; with some descriptive notes)—4. The archivist in the library. 'Further reading', p. 69.

941 (093):026
GREAT BRITAIN. HISTORICAL MANUSCRIPTS COMMISSION, and BRITISH RECORDS ASSOCIATION. Record repositories in Great Britain: a list . . . 2nd ed. London, H.M. Stationery Office, 1966. xii, 49p. 5s.

First published 1956, by the British Records Association.
Aims to help the student "who wishes to know where the record material available in this country may be found and what organisations will help him to approach and use it" (*Introduction*). Directory of more than 150 repositories, excluding public libraries with collections of local record material. Arranged under country, etc. (England: London; counties—Wales—Scotland—Northern Ireland—Isle of Man—Channel Islands); name-index. Data: name and address; telephone number; name of archivist or librarian in charge; hours of opening; holiday closing; restrictions on consulting; microfilm; copying or micro-reading facilities.

Lists of accessions to archives were published in the *Bulletin* of the Institute of Historical Research from 1923 to 1953. From 1954 to 1956 this was covered by the *Bulletin* of the National Register of Archives (London, N.R.A. Limited circulation), and from 1957 they were published separately as *List of accessions to repositories*. The I.H.R. *Bulletin* still lists "migrations" of manuscripts, derived from booksellers' and auctioneers' catalogues.

941 (093) (08)
GALBRAITH, V. H., and MYNORS, R. A. B. Medieval texts. London & Edinburgh, Nelson, 1949-. v. 1-.

Originally entitled *Medieval classics*.
Parallel texts, Latin and English. Each edition and translation is by an authority. Often supersedes older editions in such series as the Rolls Series, Royal Historical Society Publications, and Bohn's Antiquarian Library.
Latest volume: *Chronica Buriensis. The Chronicle of Bury St. Edmunds, 1212-1301*; edited, with introduction, notes and translation, by A. Gransden (London, Nelson, 1964. 84s.).

941 (094.5)
POWELL, W. R. Local history from Blue Books: a select list of the Sessional Papers of the House of Commons. London, published for the Historical Association by Routledge & Kegan Paul, 1962. 43p. (Helps for students of history, no. 64). 6s.

A description of the Sessional Papers of the House of Commons (p. 3-12) is followed by a short bibliography (p. 13) and appendices: House of Lords Papers—Libraries in the British Isles holding Sessional Papers of the House of Commons—Select list of Sessional Papers, arranged under subjects A-Z (Agrarian history (with subdivisions); Charities; Church . . .). Index.

941:930
MACRAY, W. D. A manual of British historians to A.D. 1600: containing a chronological account of the early chroniclers . . ., their printed works and unpublished MSS. London, Pickering, 1845. xxiii, 110p. (Reprinted 1967. 100s.).

Recent research has corrected some of Macray's dates and ascriptions, but the *Manual* remains the only basic list of medieval British chroniclers and historians. Short biographical sketch, list of MS. texts and bibliography of printed editions are provided for each author. Arrangement, chronological. Two indexes and a bibliography.

The evolution of British historiography from Bacon to Namier, edited by J. R. Hale (London, Macmillan, 1967. 381p. 18s.; 35s.) was originally published in 1964 (Cleveland, Ohio, Meridian Books).

941:930.24
POWICKE, Sir F. M., and FRYDE, E. B., ed. Handbook of British chronology. 2nd ed. London, Royal Historical Society, 1961. xxxviii, 565p. (Royal Historical Society. Guides and handbooks, no. 2). 63s.

First published 1939.
Vade mecum for the serious student of British history. Lists of rulers with style and significant dates, of officers of state, bishops, dukes, marquesses and earls; tables of parliaments and councils; tables of regnal and legal years; lists of saints' days. These provide an essential chronological structure.
The 2nd ed. omits the section on the reckonings of time (now a separate pamphlet: Cheney, C. R.

Handbook of dates for students of English history. 1955. 12*s.* 6*d.*), but includes several new lists, *e.g.*, of Chief Justiciars to 1265, Lord Presidents of the Council. A list of the principal Scottish officers of state is included for the first time. 'Bibliographical guide to the list of English office-holders' (to *c.* 1800), p. xxi-xxxviii.

British Towns

941-201:016
GROSS, C. A bibliography of British municipal history. 2nd ed. Leicester, Univ. Press, 1966. vi, xvi, vii, xxxiv, 461p. 84*s.*

First published 1897, by Harvard Univ. Press.
A basic critical bibliography of 3092 numbered items (books, pamphlets and articles), with interpolations, on the constitutional history of the boroughs of Great Britain. *Introductory section*: Survey of principal public and local records for municipal history and town chronicles. *Part 1*: General works (including bibliographies, sources and secondary works) on municipal history, arranged by period and by subject (county histories included). *Part 2*: Works on individual towns, A-Z (including bibliographies, town records, general histories and individual aspects). Particularly important items (*e.g.*, Anderson) are asterisked.
The 2nd ed. is a reprint, with an introductory essay on Gross and his contributions to urban studies, by G. H. Martin, who is now preparing a continuation of Gross's work, to assimilate the literature published since 1897.

W. H. Chaloner's "Writings on British urban history, 1934-1956, covering the period 1700 to the present" (*Manchester review*, v. 7, Autumn 1956, p. 399-406) provides a running commentary on books, periodical articles, etc., under various headings, subject and geographical.

941-201 (084.4)
HARLEY, J. B.—"Maps for the local historian: a guide to British sources". In *The amateur historian,* v. 7, no. 6, 1967, p. 196-208; v. 7, no. 7, 1967, p. 223-31. facsims., maps.

The first two of a series of articles: 1. "Maps and plans of towns" (general and specialised town plans; facsimiles; bibliography)—2. "Estate maps" (their development and content; facsimiles; bibliography). Other articles will deal with enclosure and tithe maps, transport maps, and county and regional maps.

Noted: *Town plans of the British Isles: series appearing in atlases from 1580 to 1850,* by Angela Fordham (London, Map Collector's Circle, 1965. 17p. of text; 30p. of illus. Map Collector's series, 3rd year 1965/66, no. 22).

Scotland

941.1:016
British humanities index (previously *Subject index to periodicals*). Regional lists. **Scotland.** London, Library Association, 1954-. Annual. (1965, published [1966]. 68, [7]p. 25*s.*).

Arranged A-Z by subjects and localities, with adequate references. Entries indicate presence of

illustrations, plans and maps. Many cross-references. The list includes a 'Check list of books and pamphlets', compiled from the *British national bibliography.* To cease at the end of 1968.

941.1:016
HANCOCK, P. D., *comp.* **A bibliography of works relating to Scotland, 1916-1950.** Edinburgh, Univ. Press, [1960]. 2v. 84*s.*

A supplement, in itself entirely independent, to Mitchell and Cash's *Contribution to the bibliography of Scottish topography* (q.v.); *c.* 12,000 entries. V. 1 covers general works (maps, atlases, gazetteers, description and travel) and then records under shires, towns and parishes all books and major articles of topographical and general interest. V. 2 has A-Z subject arrangement. Details of author, title, format, publisher and date are given. No annotations, but entries are fuller than in Mitchell and Cash. Critically reviewed in *Times literary supplement,* no. 3,096, 30th June 1961, p. 408.

Two older bibliographies of importance are: *Early sources of Scottish history,* edited by A. O. Anderson (Edinburgh, Oliver & Boyd, 1923); and *List of works in the New York Public Library relating to Scotland,* compiled by George F. Black (New York Public Library, 1916), considered by J. D. Mackie (*Scottish history.* Cambridge, Univ. Press, for the National Book League, 1956) to be the best bibliography of Scottish history, with 25,000 entries.

H. W. Meikle's *A brief bibliography of Scottish history for the use of teachers* (London, Bell, 1937. 21p. (Historical Association pamphlet no. 109)) is the only thorough bibliographical introduction to the subject and is more comprehensive than the title suggests.

941.1:016
MATHESON, C. A catalogue of the publications of Scottish historical and kindred clubs and societies, and of the papers relative to Scottish history, issued by H.M. Stationery Office, including the Reports of the Royal Commission on Historical MSS., 1908-27. Aberdeen, Milne & Hutchison, 1928. viii, 232p.

Continues Terry's *Catalogue* and includes Terry's *Index to the printed papers relating to Scotland . . . in the H.M.C. reports* (1908). References to Terry are given as well as the volumes listed. Historical Manuscripts Commission reports are also indexed.

941.1:016
MITCHELL, Sir A., and CASH, C. G. A contribution to the bibliography of Scottish topography. Edinburgh, Univ. Press, 1917. 2v. (Scottish Historical Society. Second series, v. 14-15).

v. 1: General descriptions and guides, Aberdeenshire—Wigtownshire.
v. 2: Lists arranged under subject, Antiquities—Views.

Sir A. Mitchell's *List of travels and tours in Scotland, 1296 to 1900.* (Edinburgh, 1902) is reprinted from *Proceedings of the Society of*

Antiquaries of Scotland, v. 35. Arrangement is chronological; annotations; author index.

941.1:016

NATIONAL LIBRARY OF SCOTLAND. Shelf catalogue of the Blaikie Collection of Jacobite pamphlets, broadsides and proclamations. Boston, Mass., G. K. Hall, 1964. 42p. $15 (U.K. and British Isles).

Entries, photolithographically reproduced, for the 720 v. in the Jacobite Collection made by Dr. W. B. Blaikie (1847-1928). Includes prints and composite volumes of pamphlets.

941.1:016

TERRY, C. S. A catalogue of the publications of Scottish historical and kindred clubs and societies, and of the volumes relative to Scottish history issued by H.M. Stationery Office, 1780-1908. Glasgow, Maclehose, 1909. xiii, 253p.

Arranged under societies, giving contents of all volumes issued (*c*. 1,000 items), with author and subject index.

941.1 (02)

BROWN, P. H. History of Scotland. Cambridge, Univ. Press, 1899-1909 (reprinted 1911). 3v.

No subsequent large-scale histories of Scotland are as satisfactory. The period covered is from early times to 1843. There are critical bibliographies.

The same author's condensed and simplified *Short history of Scotland* has been edited by H. W. Meikle (Nelson, 1954). It is for general reading rather than for reference.

Sir Robert Rait and George S. Pryde's *Scotland* (2nd ed. Benn, 1954, 356p.) is more up-to-date and authoritative, within its compass, and particularly from 1707 onwards.

941.1 (02)

DICKINSON, W. C. A new history of Scotland. London, Nelson, 1961-2. 2v. map, tables.

v. 1. *Scotland from the earliest times to 1603,* by W. C. Dickinson. 1961.
v. 2. *Scotland from 1603 to the present day,* by W. C. Dickinson and G. S. Pryde. 1962.
Hume-Brown's *History of Scotland* virtually stopped at 1843. This new history corrects the political slant of that work by covering economic and social aspects. V. 2 of Dickinson has 26 chapters and an epilogue: 'Post-war Scotland'. Footnote references; select bibliography, p. 333-42. The author is the Fraser Professor of Scottish History and Palaeography in the University of Edinburgh.
V. 1 of a revised ed. appeared in 1965 (45s.).

941.1 (05)

The Scottish historical review. Edinburgh, Nelson, 1903-28, 1947-. 2 p.a. 30s.; 40s. p.a.

The v. 46, no. 1, April 1967 (no. 141) contains 3 well-documented articles on Scottish history; reviews of 17 books (p. 56-76); 'Notes and comments' (on 5 items, *e.g.,* 'Religion and the Massacre of Glencoe').
V. 45, no. 2, October 1966, includes "A list of artcles on Scottish history published during the year 1965" (p. 219-25).

941.1 (084.3)

ROYAL SCOTTISH GEOGRAPHICAL SOCIETY. The early maps of Scotland, with an account of the Ordnance Survey; by H. R. G. Inglis and others. Edinburgh, the Society, 1934. 120p. maps, diagrs. (2nd ed., rev. 1936).

Gives a description of some 1,400 maps and plans; many reproductions; bibliography (p. 91-92).
A 3rd ed. is due to be published in 1968.
A. B. Taylor's "Some additional early maps of Scotland" (*Scottish geographical magazine,* v. 77, no. 1, April 1961, p. 37-43) supplements the 2nd ed. of *The early maps of Scotland.*

Scotland: Public Records

941.1 (093)

DICKINSON, W. C., and others. A source book of Scottish history. London, Nelson, 1952-54. 3v.

v. 1: *From earliest times to 1424.*
v. 2: *1424 to 1567.*
v. 3: *1567 to 1707.*
Extracts and translations, with commentaries. The various sections are equipped with excellent introductions and references, especially to periodical articles. Index to v. 3 only; v. 1 and 2 are to be re-issued with index.

941.1 (093):016

GOULDESBROUGH, P., and others. Handlist of Scottish and Welsh record publications. The Scottish section, by P. Gouldesbrough and A. P. Kup; the Welsh section, by I. Lewis. London, British Records Association, 1954. 34p. (B.R.A. Publications pamphlet no. 4).

Complements the *Handlist of record publications* (1951) (at 942.0 (093):016) which was exclusively English. Analyses by subject the publications of the specialist societies (*e.g.,* lists parish registers); subject index. Wales occupies only one page.

941.1 (093):016

LIVINGSTONE, M. A guide to the public records of Scotland deposited in H.M. General Register House, Edinburgh. Edinburgh, General Register House, 1905. xxvii, 233p.

Descriptive lists in four classes: 1. Crown, Parliament, Revenue and Administration—2. Judicial records—3. Titles to land, dignities and offices — 4. Ecclesiastical and miscellaneous records. 4 appendices (*e.g.,* 3. Records of Chancery). Index.
On subsequent accessions down to 1946, see *The Scottish historical review,* v. 26, no. 101, April 1947. p. 26-46,—Angus, W. "Accessions to public records to the Register House since 1905".

J. M. Thomson's *The public records of Scotland* (Glasgow, Maclehose, 1922. ix, 175p.) comprises the Rhind Lectures for 1911 and explains the origin and scope of Scottish national records; full subject index. A briefer but more up-to-date introduction is H. M. Paton's *The*

Scottish records, their history and value (Historical Association of Scotland leaflet; new series, no. 7, 1933).

Scotland: Counties & Towns

941.11/.62

Shetland. Barratt, J. L. *The Shetland Islands: a bibliography of printed books on Shetland history written in English and published in Great Britain.* 1958. (University of London, School of Librarianship and Archives. *Cumulative list of bibliographies and theses accepted for Part II of the University of London Diplomas in Librarianship and Archives . . . 1946-1960,* entry no. 171).

Caithness. Mowat, J. *New bibliography of the county of Caithness, with notes.* Wick, Reid, 1940.

Inverness. Anderson, P. J. "Concise bibliography . . . of Inverness." In *Aberdeen University library bulletin,* v. 2-3, 1913-16.

Aberdeen. Johnstone, J. F. K., and Robertson, A. W. *Bibliographia Aberdonensis* [1472-1700]. Aberdeen Press, 1929-30. 2v.

Fifeshire. Fife County Library, and Kirkcaldy Public Libraries. *Check list on books for local subjects.* 1957; Fife County Library. *Books on local subjects.* 1962.

Lanarkshire. Wilson, J. A. *A contribution to the history of Lanarkshire.* Glasgow, Wylie, 1936 - 37. 2v. Glasgow University. *Catalogue of the Wylie Collection of books.* 1929.

Edinburgh. Cowan, W. *The maps of Edinburgh, 1544-1929.* 2nd ed., rev. Edinburgh Public Libraries, 1932. Edinburgh Public Libraries. *The Edinburgh scene: catalogue of prints and drawings . . .* 1951.

East Lothian. Jamieson, J. H., & Hawkins, E. *Bibliography of East Lothian.* Edinburgh, East Lothian Antiquarian & Field Naturalists' Society, 1936.

Peebles. Buchan, J. W., *ed. A history of Peeblesshire.* Glasgow, Jackson, Wylie, 1925-37. 3v.

Ireland

941.5:016

BELFAST PUBLIC LIBRARIES. Bibliographic Department. **Finding list of books added to the stock of the Irish and local history collection before 1956.** Belfast, 1965. 2v.

Section 1. *Main author and title entries arranged alphabetically.*
Section 2. *Main author and title entries arranged in classified order.*

941.5:016

CARTY, J. Bibliography of Irish history, 1870-1921. National Library of Ireland. Dublin, Stationery Office, 1936-40. 2v.

The first 2 v. in a proposed series of bibliographies on Irish history. Entries are confined to publications in the collections of the National Library of Ireland, but they include books, rare pamphlets, parliamentary papers and other official publications, and articles in periodicals.

V. 2, covering 1912-21, arranged by period, deals almost exclusively with political history; v. 1, covering 1870-1911 (2,727 items), arranged by subject, embraces political, economic, social, literary and ecclesiastical history, and as such serves as an excellent bibliography of Ireland for the period.

941.5:016

MAXWELL, C. A short bibliography of Irish history. London, Historical Association, 1921. 33p. (Leaflet no. 23 (1911), revised).

This brief annotated bibliography of 526 items is an introductory guide to the chief works on Irish history (general, political, ecclesiastical, literary, social and cultural) — bibliographies, periodicals, source collections, general histories, special periods and subjects. There is at present no larger work to replace it.

Bibliography of Irish history, by E. M. Johnston (London, Historical Association. Helps for students of history, no. 73) is in preparation.

A. E. Eager's *A guide to Irish bibliographical material* (London, Library Association, 1964) includes a sizeable section on Irish history, national and local, p. 282-337 (items no. 3163-3780).

941.5:016

Writings on Irish history; compiled by J. Carty and others, 1936-. (In *Irish historical studies,* v. 1-, 1938-).

An annual list of books and articles on Irish history published during the year under review. This useful guide to current research will in effect keep up to date existing bibliographies.

Irish historical studies carries an annual list of completed theses and those in progress under the heading "Research on Irish history in Irish universities".

941.5 (02)

CURTIS, E. A history of Ireland. 6th ed., rev. London, Methuen, 1950. xi, 434p. maps, tables.

The best general survey of Irish history, with more emphasis on the medieval period than on the modern. Bibliography, p. 413-6.

941.5 (03)

LEWIS, S. A topographical dictionary of Ireland, comprising the several counties, cities, boroughs, corporate market, and post towns, parishes, and villages, with historical and statistical descriptions . . . London, S. Lewis, 1837; 2nd ed., 1849. 2v. and atlas.

Despite its date, this gazetteer is indispensable for research of any nature involving topographical detail; an atlas volume was also issued but is now only of historical interest.

941.5 (05)

Irish historical studies: the joint journal of the Irish Historical Society and the Ulster Society for Irish Historical Studies. Dublin, Hodges, Figgis, 1938-. 2 p.a. 20s. p.a.

The v. 15, no. 59, March 1967 issue contains 4 articles (p. 213-302), an annual contribution, "Research on Irish history in Irish universities", 1966-7 (p. 303-7), and reviews and short notices (26 items; p. 308-56).

941.5 (084.3)
ANDREWS, J. Ireland in maps: an introduction; with a Catalogue of an exhibition mounted in the Library of Trinity College, Dublin, 1961, by the Geographical Society of Ireland, in conjunction with the Ordnance Survey of Ireland. Dublin, Dolmen Press, 1961. 36p. maps (facsims.). 5s.

The introduction, on the cartography of Ireland, makes references to the numbered entries in the Catalogue. 120 maps in 18 sections. Manuscripts are identified by giving their repository; printed books, by giving their place of publication. Where reproductions of manuscripts are exhibited, the location of the original is given in brackets. List of authorities, p. 34-35.
Supplemented by the same author's "Ireland in maps: a bibliographical postscript", in *Irish geography*, v. 4, no. 4, 1962, p. 234-43.

The Ordnance Survey map, *Monastic Ireland* (1:625,000) (Dublin, O.S., 1965), consists of 1 sheet, 29" × 23", with explanatory booklet.

941.5 (084.3)
IRISH MANUSCRIPTS COMMISSION. Ulster and other Irish maps, c. 1600. Edited by G. A. Hayes-McCoy. Dublin, Stationery Office, for the Irish Manuscript Commission, 1964. 36p. 120s.

Contains fine lithographic reproductions of 23 early manuscript maps (12 by Richard Bartlett (or Barthelet)), now preserved in the National Library of Ireland; also an authoritative text. "Makes a notable contribution to the history of Ireland and to that of Irish cartography" (*Times literary supplement*, no. 3,267, 8th October 1964, p. 926).

941.5:091
KENNEY, J. F. The sources for the early history of Ireland: an introduction and guide. v. 1. **Ecclesiastical.** New York, Columbia Univ. Press, 1929. xvi, 807p. fldg. maps. (Records of Civilization: sources and studies, v. 11).

No more published. It was intended to publish a guide to the printed sources of Irish history up to *c.* 1170 in 2v.

See entry at 282 (415):091.

941.5:091
NATIONAL LIBRARY OF IRELAND, Dublin. **Manuscript sources for the history of Irish civilisation.** Boston, Mass., G. K. Hall, 1965. 11v. $800 (U.S.A. and Ireland).

A union index (310,000 card entries photolithographically reproduced) to manuscripts relating to Ireland and the activities of Irishmen at home and abroad, 5th-20th century. As-

sembled from the collections of 678 libraries and archives in 395 places in 30 countries, and from more than 600 private collections. Four main divisions: persons and institutions; subjects; places; dates. The fifth division consists of lists of manuscripts by location. (G. K. Hall. *Annual catalog of reference works,* May 1968, p. 29.)

941.5 (093)
CURTIS, E., and **McDOWELL, R. B.,** *ed.* **Irish historical documents, 1172-1922.** London, Methuen, 1943. [iv], 331p.

A standard collection of constitutional and political documents, with spelling and punctuation modernised, and texts in Latin or French translated into English. Five sections; 135 documents. Detailed contents list.

941.6 (093)
NORTHERN IRELAND. PUBLIC RECORD OFFICE. Report of the Deputy Keeper of the Records for the year . . . Belfast, H.M. Stationery Office, 1924-.

Issued as a Command Paper annually 1924-37; consolidated reports 1938-45; thereafter irregularly. Each report contains a detailed index to the documents acquired during the year.

941.5 (093):016
GRIFFITH, M. "A short guide to the Public Record Office of Ireland". In *Irish historical studies* (Dublin), v. 8, 1952-3, p. 45-58.

Indispensable as a guide to the Public Record Office of Ireland collections.

The bulk of the records listed in H. Wood's *A guide to the records deposited in the Public Record Office of Ireland* (Dublin, Stationery Office, 1919. xvi, 334p.) were destroyed by fire in 1922.

The *Report of the Deputy Keeper of the Public Records and Keeper of the State Papers in Ireland* (Dublin, Stationery Office, 1928-. v. 55-. (In progress)) constitutes the key to the existing collection, read in conjunction with H. Wood's *Guide.* Only four reports have been issued since the destruction of records in 1922. (Although the Public Record Office of Ireland is the official record repository for Eire, it still acquires material relating to pre-1922 Ireland.)

Noted: "The Irish Record situation", by K. Darwin, in *Journal of the Society of Archivists,* v. 2, no. 8, October 1963, p. 361-6.

941.5 (093):016
O'NEILL, T. P. Sources of Irish local history. 1st series. Dublin, Library Association of Ireland, 1958. 38p. 4s.

A reprint of articles in *An Leabharlann,* "written to help librarians throughout Ireland in advising local historians" (*Introduction*). Chapters: 1. Early historical sources—2. Ecclesiastical records—3. Legal records—4. Maps and surveys—5. Newspapers—6. Pictures—7. Descriptive works. — British Parliamentary Papers. Chapter references.

It is hoped to provide notes on official collections of state papers, county and municipal records and family, estate and business collections, and on other topics in a further series of articles in *An Leabharlann,* beginning June 1958. "Archives of local authorities" appeared in v. 16, no. 1, June 1958, p. 31-36. "The bibliographical coverage of Irish local material", by H. J. Neaney, appeared in v. 20, no. 4, December 1962, p. 127-9.

Ireland: Counties & Towns

941.691:016
CULLEN, S. Books and authors of County Cavan. Cavan County Council, 1965. xvi, 132p. 30s.

More than 1,400 entries. Covers literary and topographical, as well as historical, aspects. Separate sections for newspapers, maps, portraits and topographical prints. Appendix 2: 'Bibliographically incomplete items'. Reviewed in *Irish historical studies,* v. 15, no. 59, March 1967, p. 309.

941.72:016
McTERNAN, J. C. A bibliography of Sligo. [1957].

Typewritten copy, for Fellowship of the Library Association of Ireland.
405 entries, with author and subject indexes, according to Eager, A. R. *A guide to Irish bibliographical material* (1964), entry no. 3555.

941.74:016
KAVANAGH, M. A bibliography of the County Galway. Galway, County Libraries, 1965. 187p. 30s.

1669 numbered items, grouped under 16 headings, A-Z: Antiquities — Biography — Botany — Commerce — Education — Fishery — Geology — History — Maps — Natural science—Printing — Topography — Transport — Travels — Valuation—Wills. 1476 of these items concern Antiquities, Biography, History and Topography. Brief notes follow some titles, by way of explanation. List of 53 journals consulted. Index nominum and index locorum, but no subject index, a distinct drawback to quick location. Sanserif type, with effective use of bold. Reviewed by A. R. Eager in *Library Association record,* v. 67, no. 12, December 1965, p. 455.

941.94:016
NAIS, R. de. A bibliography of Limerick history and antiquities. Limerick, County Library, [1962?]. [v], 61p.

581 numbered, unannotated items, with locations noted in the British Museum, National Library of Ireland, Limerick County Library and Limerick Municipal Library. 8 period sections (4th-20th century), preceded by 'General works', and followed by material on specific areas under areas A-Z. Includes many periodical articles (7 journals). Also lists of Limerick newspapers and magazines, maps and relevant Parliamentary Papers.

England & Wales

942:016
MULLINS, E. L. C. Texts and calendars: an analytical guide to serial publications. London, Royal Historical Society, 1958. xi, 674p. (Royal Historical Society. Guides and handbooks, no. 7). 50s.

Covers texts and calendars for English and Welsh history issued by the various Record Commissions, the Public Record Office and local authorities and record societies. Parts: 1. Official bodies—2. National bodies—3. English local societies—4. Welsh societies—5. Addenda. Index. Invaluable in supplying complete lists of the publications of such bodies as the Camden Society, Harleian Society, English Place-Name Society, Rolls series, etc., with a full subject index.

942 (058.7)
NORTON, J. E. Guide to the national and provincial directories of England and Wales, excluding London, published before 1856. London, Royal Historical Society, 1950. vii, 241p. (Royal Historical Society guides and handbooks, no. 5).

Complements *London directories, 1677-1855,* by C. W. F. Goss (1932) *(see at 942.1 (058.7)).*
878 numbered entries (English, national, chronologically arranged; English, local, by counties A-Z, then chronologically; Welsh, chronologically; addenda). Locations for each directory are given. Excludes directories of particular trades or professions, but includes "a number of histories and guide books to which directories have been added".
A valuable introduction deals with the origin and development of directories, and authorship, methods of compilation and tests of reliability. Index of authors, printers and publishers, and printers; general index.

942 (084.3)
HUDDY, E. J. Early printed topographical maps of the counties of England and Wales: a descriptive catalogue. 1960.

Listed in University of London, School of Librarianship and Archives. *Cumulative list of bibliographies and theses accepted for Part II of the University of London Diplomas in Librarianship and Archives . . 1946-1960,* entry no. 90.

942 (093)
EMMISON, F. G. Archives and local history. London, Methuen, 1966. xvi, 112p. illus. (pl.), diagrs. 18s. 6d.; 30s.

Gives a brief survey of the various repositories in England and Wales, plus a detailed account of all the main groups of local records. 7 sections: 1. Aids in using local archives—2. Local repositories—3. Visiting a local repository—4. Using local archives (p. 22-72)—5. Transcripts of selected illustrations—6. Extracts from archives (not illustrated)—7. Appendix: Selected pamphlets and articles (from *Amateur historian,* etc.). 32 pages of illustrations; index.

942 (093)
EMMISON, F. G., and GRAY, I. County records
(Quarter Sessions, Petty Sessions, Clerk of the
Peace and Lieutenancy). Rev. and re-set ed.
London, Historical Association, 1961. 32p.
(Helps for students of history, no. 62). 5s.

First published 1948.
Confined to England and Wales. Sections:
1. Introduction—2. Records of the Courts of
Quarter Sessions and of Petty Sessions—3. Other
county records—4. Topography and genealogy
in county records—5. Local and national history
in county records. Appendix 1: Printed catalogues
and transcripts of county records; 2: The County
Record Office and the student (tabulated: County
(address of repository) — Facilities — Selected records (types), p. 29-32.

England

942.0:016
**GROSS, C. Sources and literature of English
history,** from the earliest times to about 1485.
2nd ed. London, Longmans, Green, 1915. xxiv,
820p. (Reprinted Gloucester, Mass., Smith, 1952).

First published 1900. 2nd ed., published posthumously, included works up to 1910. 3rd ed. in
preparation.
Systematic critical bibliography of the sources
and secondary works for English history. The
fundamental guide for the historian of medieval
England, it contains sections on: (pt. 1), Auxiliary
studies, archives collections and libraries, printed
collections of sources, modern works on specific
topics; (pt. 2), Celtic, Roman and Germanic
origins; (pt. 3), Anglo-Saxon period; (pt. 4), 1066
to c. 1485. This last section has sub-divisions
on chronicles, law-writers, Exchequer, revenue,
Privy Council and Parliament, courts, foreign
relations, army and navy, feudalism, the Church,
local records and other miscellaneous material.

942.0:016
**HISTORICAL ASSOCIATION. English local
history handlist:** a short bibliography and list
of sources for the study of local history and
antiquities. Prepared by the Local History
Committee of the Historical Association. 2nd ed.
London, Philip, for the Historical Association,
1952. 74p.

First published 1947.
A valuable list of more than 1,500 items in
26 subject sections, covering many aspects of
local history, from topography and prehistoric
archaeology to dialect and local worthies. Some
annotations are given. Section 26: Societies and
institutions concerned with local history and
antiquities and their publications. Detailed subject
index.

942.0:016
HOSKINS, W. G. Local history in England.
London, Longmans, 1959. xi, 196p. illus., maps,
plans. 21s.

12 chapters. Chapter 3: "The old community"
(local directories; census schedules; census
reports, 1801-1951; old newspapers; reminis-
censes; local records: printed and manuscript;
parliamentary papers; maps; land tax assess-

ments; illustrations; diaries, letters and account
books; auctioneeers' catalogues and sales notices).
Additional references, p. 179-85; analytical index.
It "contrasts the older antiquarian approach
with the newer idea of studying the development
of the local community. It also illustrates how
neglected sources, *e.g.*, field remains and material
concerned with social and economic history,
should be utilized" (*Handbook for history
teachers,* p. 669). Attractively produced.

The National Council of Social Service's
Introducing local history (1960. 38p. 2s. 6d.),
published for the Standing Conference for Local
History, includes a directory of authorities and
organizations (p. 17-30).

*Readers' guide to books on the sources of local
history* (2nd ed., Library Association. County
Libraries Section, 1959. 27p. (Readers' guide, new
series, no. 54)) lists about 450 items under 30
headings, arranged A-Z. A few entries are
annotated.

942.0:016
KUHLICKE, F. W., and EMMISON, F. G., *ed.*
English local history handlist: a short biblio-
graphy and list of sources for the study of local
history and antiquities. Edited for the Local
History Committee of the Historical Assocation.
London, Historical Association, 1965. 73p. (Helps
for students of history, no. 69). 8s. 6d.

"A series of short lists intended to help the
student, who may not be an expert, to an understanding of such matters of historian and antiquarian interest as he may encounter in his local
studies" (*Introductory note*). 1609 numbered
items in 27 sections; section 28: 'Societies helpful
to students'; section 29: 'Year books and national
periodicals (selected)'. References to other material and numerous cross-references. Occasional
concise annotations. Covers a wide range of
subjects (the subject index lists c. 650 topics),
from 1. Topography—2. Names—3. Prehistory
. . . 22. Costume and dress—23. Genealogy and
heraldry—24. Local worthies and biography—25.
Folklore and dialect—26. Miscellaneous (*e.g.*,
Medicine and public health)—27. Other bibliographies and catalogues.

The National Council of Social Service has
published *A selection of books on local history*
(1949) and *A directory of authorities and organisations for the assistance of local historians.*
(1950. 11p.).

942.0 (02)
The Oxford history of England. General editor,
Sir G. N. Clark. Oxford, Clarendon Press, 1936-
65. 15v. tables, maps.

v. 1: *Roman Britain and the English settlements,*
by R. G. Collingwood and J. N. L. Myres. 2nd ed.
1937. 38s. (See at 930.26 (410) (02).)
v. 2: *Anglo-Saxon England,* by Sir F. M. Stenton.
2nd ed. 1947. 42s.
v. 3: *From Domesday Book to Magna Carta,
1087-1216,* by A. L. Poole. 2nd ed. 1955. 38s.
v. 4: *The thirteenth century, 1216-1307,* by Sir
F. M. Powicke. 2nd ed. 1962. 38s.
v. 5: *The fourteenth century, 1307-1399,* by M.
McKisack. 1959. 38s.
v. 6: *The fifteenth century, 1399-1485,* by E. F.
Jacobs. 1961. 38s.
v. 7: *The earlier Tudors, 1485-1558,* by J. D.
Mackie. 1952. 45s.

v. 8: *The reign of Queen Elizabeth*, by J. B. Black. 2nd ed. 1959. 38s.

v. 9: *The early Stuarts, 1603-1660*, by G. Davies. 2nd ed. 1959. 38s.

v. 10: *The later Stuarts, 1660-1714*, by Sir G. N. Clark. 2nd ed. 1956. 38s.

v. 11: *The Whig supremacy, 1714-1760*, by B. Williams. 1939. 30s.

v. 12: *The reign of George III*, by J. S. Watson. 1960. 38s.

v. 13: *The age of reform, 1815-1870*, by Sir E. L. Woodward. 2nd ed. 1960. 42s.

v. 14: *England, 1870-1914*, by R. C. K. Ensor. 1936. 38s.

v. 15: *English history, 1914-1945*, by A. J. P. Taylor. 1965. 45s.

Standard introductions to the periods concerned, with valuable critical bibliographies. V. 15, brilliantly and occasionally controversially written (see *Times literary supplement*, no. 3329, 16 December 1965, p. 1169-70, "History Taylor-made"), has a lengthy bibliography in the form of a running commentary (p. 602-39).

942.0 (02)

The Victoria history of the counties of England. Edited by H. A. Doubleday and W. Page. London, Constable (then St. Catherine Press and now Oxford Univ. Press for the Institute of Historical Research, Univ. of London), 1901-. illus. (pl.), maps.

An indispensable series. Only Cheshire, Northumberland and Westmorland have still to be covered. See entries under individual counties.

The general articles usually appear in the first 2v. or, for larger counties, in the first 3v., with topography or history of parishes and boroughs in later volumes. "The history of each county will be complete in itself, beginning with the natural features and the flora and fauna, followed by the antiquities, pre-Roman, Roman, and post-Roman; a translation and critical study of the Domesday Survey, and articles upon political, ecclesiastical, social and economic history; architecture, arts, industries, biography, folklore and sport" (*Introduction*).

In "The structure and aims of the Victoria history of the counties of England" (*Bulletin of the Institute of Historical Research*, v. 40, no. 101, 1967, p. 65-73), R. B. Pugh discusses the desirability of separate volumes for urban centres, comments on the practice of studying each county on the hundred and parish level, and considers the need for more cartographic illustration (*Geographical abstracts, D*, 1967, no. 67D/862).

W. G. Hoskins (*The listener*, v. 73, no. 1880, 8th April 1965, p. 531) criticises the 'Victorian' approach of the Victoria history. "It has made few concessions over the years to the growth of historical scholarship in social and economic history and in topography; and the arrangement of the sections splits up a parish in a confusing way. The old addiction to the minutiae of manorial history and church architecture is still there. . .".

Dictionaries

942.0 (032)

LEWIS, S. A topographical dictionary of England . . . 7th ed. London, Lewis, 1848-49. 4v. and atlas. illus., maps. 168s.

First published 1831-33.

The most valuable of the early gazetteers. The places are entered in A-Z order and substantial details, descriptive and historical, are given. The illustrations are restricted to coats-of-arms but there are maps for each county. The county maps in the atlas volume are particularly valuable as they indicate the smaller administrative areas.

G. E. Fussell's *The exploration of England: a select bibliography of travel and topography, 1570-1815* (London, Mitre Press, 1935. 56p.) lists 353 items chronologically, with occasional brief notes. Author index.

942.0 (032)

LOW, *Sir* S., and **PULLING, F. S. The dictionary of English history.** New ed., rev. and enl. by F. J. C. Hearnshaw, H. M. Chew and A. C. F. Beales. London, Cassell, 1928. x, 1154p.

First published 1884; new ed., rev. 1896.

33 principal contributors, articles being occasionally signed. Entries which deal with persons, events and topics in English history, vary in length according to the importance of the subject, and brief bibliographies are usually appended. For the layman, not the scholar.

942.0 (084.3)

LEE, J. English county maps: the identification, cataloguing and physical care of a collection. London, Library Association, 1953. 32p. (Library Association pamphlets, no. 13).

Includes a select classified list of forty items, confined to maps published in atlases or books. Reviewed by R. A. Skelton, in *Journal of documentation*, v. 12, no. 2, June 1956, p. 124-5.

J. Lee's "English carto-bibliography", in *Manchester review* (v. 8, Summer 1959, p. 304-16) has a bibliography of about 100 items appended: "Cartography: a selection of material available in the Manchester Reference Library". Sections: General — Early text books and techniques — *Mappae mundi* and other early maps (including facsimiles) — Catalogues and lists (excluding Great Britain)—Great Britain.

942.0 (093)

English historical documents; edited by D. C. Douglas. London, Eyre & Spottiswoode, 1953-. v. 1-. ea. 105s.

v. 1: *c. 500-1042*; edited by D. Whitelock. 1955.

v. 2: *1042-1189*; edited by D. C. Douglas and G. W. Greenaway. 1953 (reprinted 1961).

v. 5: *1485-1558;* edited by C. H. Williams. 1967. 147s.

v. 8: *1660-1714*; edited by A. Browning. 1953.

v. 9: *American colonial documents to 1776*; edited by M. Jensen. 1955.

v. 10: *1714-1783*; edited by D. B. Horn and M. Ransome. 1957.

v. 11: *1783-1832*; edited by A. Aspinall and E. A. Smith. 1959. 95s.

v. 12, pt. 1: *1833-1874;* edited by G. M. Young and W. D. Handcock. 1956.

The purpose of the series is "to make generally accessible a wide selection of the fundamental sources of English history" (*General preface. v. 12, pt. 1*).

Each volume has a lengthy general introduction and a select bibliography; each of its parts carries its own introduction and select bibliography. All documents (or selections from documents) are translated into English (as necessary), the text being well footnoted. V. 12, pt. 1 contains 12 parts and 269 items, including departmental and Royal Commission reports, leaders from *The times*, legislation and statistical data.

English historical documents, 1714-1815 (London, Methuen, 1967. 15 illus. 22s. 6d.) is a selection of v. 10-11 of the above.

942.0 (093)

TATE, W. E. The parish chest: a study of the records of parochial administration in England. 2nd ed., rev. and enl. Cambridge, Univ. Press, 1951. 346p. illus. (15 pl.).

First published 1946.
A well-illustrated guide. Includes a glossary, references, cumulated chapter bibliographies, and appendices (table of the principal statutes cited or referred to, the principal record and archaeology societies, field clubs, etc., of England and Wales). Invaluable and almost indispensable for the study of parish history. A new edition is in preparation.

J. C. Cox's *The parish registers of England* (London, Methuen, 1910) is narrower in scope. It deals with the history of parish registers and the light that they throw on customs and social life; ample citations.

R. B. Pugh's *How to write a parish history* (6th ed. London, Allen & Unwin, 1954. 148p.), first published in 1879 as J. C. Cox's work of that title, gives a good cross-section of resources on Essex, Surrey, Yorkshire and other counties. Well documented and indexed; sets a high standard.

W. G. Hoskins' *Local history in England* (London, Longmans, 1959. xi, 196p. pl., maps. 21s.) in contrast, is more accommodating for the beginner and insists on the need for field work.

942.0 (093):016

SOMERVILLE, R. Handlist of record publications. London, British Records Association, 1951. 36p. (B.R.A. Publications pamphlet no. 3).

Lists, arranged by administration and type of document, of records published by societies in England. Much abbreviated.

942.0 (093):016

UPTON, E. S. Guide to sources of English history from 1603 to 1660 in early reports of the Royal Commission on Historical Manuscripts. 2nd ed. New York & York, Scarecrow Press, 1964. 258p. $6.

First published 1952.
The main part is virtually a reprint: 'Subject index to materials on English history, 1603-1660 in the first nine reports' (p. 35-248). Appendix A: 'Parliamentary proceedings, 1621 to 10 February 1642, in print'; B: 'List of collections within the scope of this Guide' (*c.* 125 collections). Analytical index; asterisked entry indicates that the Report gives the contents of the manuscript item with a fair degree of detail.

942.0:930.24

CHENEY, C. R. Handbook of dates for students of English history. London, Royal Historical Society, 1945 (reprinted 1955, with revised bibliography). xvii, 164p. (Royal Historical Society. Guides and handbooks, no. 4).

Duplicates part of, and supplements, Powicke's *Handbook* (at 941:930.24). Reckonings of time, legal chronology, lists of rulers and of saints' days are revisions of chapters in Powicke. New matter included: bibliography; list of popes; Roman calendar; calendar for each year up to A.D. 2000; index.

See also 941:930.24.

England: Local History

942.1/.8:016

British humanities index (previously *Subject index to periodicals*). **Regional lists.** London, Library Association, 1954-. Annual.

Lists of periodical articles on English counties. Issues for 1964, published in November 1965, are as follows:

Bedfordshire. 4s. 6d.	Lincolnshire. 4s.
Berkshire. 3s. 6d.	London. 17s. 6d.
Buckinghamshire.	Middlesex. 6s. 6d.
4s. 6d.	Norfolk. 5s.
Cambridgeshire. 4s. 6d.	Northampton. 4s.
Cheshire. 4s.	Northumberland. 4s.
Cornwall. 4s.	Nottingham. 4s.
Cumberland. 3s.	Oxfordshire. 5s.
Derbyshire. 4s. 6d.	Shropshire. 3s.
Devon. 6s.	Somerset. 3s. 6d.
Dorset. 3s. 6d.	Staffordshire. 4s. 6d.
Durham. 4s.	Suffolk. 4s. 6d.
Essex. 7s. 6d.	Surrey. 5s. 6d.
Gloucestershire. 7s.	Sussex. 7s. 6d.
Hampshire. 8s.	Warwickshire. 8s
Herefordshire. 2s.	Westmorland. 3s. 6d.
Hertfordshire. 4s.	Wiltshire. 3s. 6d.
Kent. 11s.	Worcestershire. 4s.
Lancashire. 13s. 6d.	Yorkshire. 15s. 6d.
Leicestershire. 3s. 6d.	

Complete set (including *Scotland*, q.v.), 150s. The series is to cease at the end of 1968.

London

942.1:016

GUILDHALL LIBRARY, London. The County of London: a select book list. London, Library Association, Reference and Special Libraries Section, South Eastern Group, 1959. 32p. (Aids to reference service, no. 1). 4s. 6d. (3s. 6d. to members).

225 numbered items, with annotations. Sections: General—Physical aspects and geology, including water supply—Natural history—Religion—Government—Social services, including welfare, police, fire service, transport—Cultural aspects—Architecture—Town planning—Social life—Finance and commerce—General history and archaeology—Histories of special areas and localities—Pictorial record. Index of personal authors.

942.1:016

LONDON COUNTY COUNCIL. Library. **Members' library catalogue.** v. 1: **London history and topography.** London, L.C.C., 1939. [v], 142p.

The most extensive published London bibliography. Arrangement is by subjects alphabetically; author and subject indexes. A number of entries are annotated.

942.1:016

SMITH, F. R., *comp.* **The City of London:** a select book list . . . London, National Book League, [1951]. 38p. (N.B.L. Book lists. Second series). 1*s*.

Each title is followed by a helpful annotation.

942.1 (02)

BESANT, *Sir* **W. The survey of London.** London, Black, 1902-12. 10v.

Early London: prehistoric, Roman, Saxon and Norman. 1908. x, 370p.
Mediæval London. 1906. 2v. (v. 1: Historical and social; v. 2: Ecclesiastical).
London in the time of the Tudors. 1904. x, 430p.
London in the time of the Stuarts. 1903. xiii, 400p.
London in the 18th century. 1902. xv, 667p.
London in the 19th century. 1909. ix, 421p.
London: City. 1910. xi, 491p.
London: North of the Thames. 1911. xii, 682p.
London: South of the Thames. 1912. xiv, 372p.
Besant, who died in 1901, intended this survey to do for modern London what Stow did for the Elizabethan city. Still useful, especially for illustrations, although out of date in many particulars and lacks references to sources.

Only v. 1 of *The Victoria history of London* has appeared (London, Constable, 1909. 105*s*., 126*s*.).

942.1 (02)

CLUNN, H. P. The face of London . . . [4th ed.]. London, Phoenix House, [1951]. xiii, 630p. illus. (pl.). 30*s*.

A topographical survey showing development, demolition and change in London and its suburbs from about 1831. Arranged in a series of 25 "walks" covering the City, West End and old Metropolitan Boroughs, and 4 "drives" into the suburbs. Excellent index of *c.* 60p.

942.1 (02)

CUNNINGHAM, G. H. London; being a comprehensive survey of the history, tradition and historical associations of buildings and monuments arranged under streets in alphabetical order . . . London, Dent, 1931. xxviii, 887p.

The area covered is mainly metropolitan but some entries for suburban areas are also included. For the most part deals with the eminent people who have been associated with each street, and indicates the houses in which they lived.

942.1 (02)

GREAT BRITAIN. ROYAL COMMISSION ON THE ANCIENT AND HISTORICAL MONUMENTS . . . OF ENGLAND. An inventory of the historical monuments in London . . . [London, H.M. Stationery Office, 1924-28]. 5v. illus. (pl.). ea. 20*s*.

v. 1: *Westminster Abbey.* 1924.
v. 2: *West London, excluding Westminster Abbey.* 1925.
v. 3: *Roman London.* 1928.
v. 4: *The City.* 1928.
v. 5: *East London.* 1928.
V. 2, 4 and 5 consist of inventories of historic buildings erected before 1714 which are considered worthy of preservation. Architectural and descriptive notes on points of special interest are given, with copious illustrations; glossaries of technical terms.

The presentation of Roman London in v. 3 of the Royal Commission *Inventory* (above) has been transformed by subsequent extensive excavation. R. Merrifield's *The Roman City of London* (London, Benn, [1965]. xvii, 344p. illus. (pl.), maps. 63*s*.) is in 3 parts: (1) account of the history of archaeology in the City, outline of the history of Roman London, account of its topography with natural features, fortifications and principal buildings, and guide to its visible remains; (2) collection of 140 photographs and other illustrations, with full notes on each; (3) gazetteer of all Roman structures recorded in the Walled City and its immediate neighbourhood up to July 1964. These are plotted on a 25" : 1 mile map which revises that in the Royal Commission volume. The gazetteer (455 items) serves as a numbered key to the map and gives a summary of each find, with references to sources of fuller information.

942.1 (02)

LONDON COUNTY COUNCIL (now GREATER LONDON COUNCIL) and LONDON SURVEY COMMITTEE. Joint Publishing Committee. **The survey of London** . . . London, L.C.C. (then Univ. of London, Athlone Press), 1900-. v. 1-. illus., pl., maps.

v. 1: *Bromley-by-Bow.* 1900. o.p.
v. 2, 4, 7, 11: *Chelsea.* [1909]-27. 4 pts. v. 2. o.p.; v. 4 & 7. ea. 21*s*.; v. 11. 42*s*.
v. 3, 5: *St. Giles in the Fields.* 1912-14. 2 pts. ea. 21*s*.
v. 6: *Hammersmith.* 1915. 21*s*.
v. 8: *St. Leonard, Shoreditch.* 1922. 42*s*.
v. 9: *St. Helen, Bishopsgate.* 1924. 42*s*.
v. 10, 13, 14: *St. Margaret, Westminster.* 1926-30. 3 pts. v. 10. 42*s*.; v. 13-14. ea. 52*s*. 6*d*.
v. 12, 15: *All Hallows, Barking.* 1929-34. 2 pts. v. 12. 31*s*. 6*d*.; v. 15. 42*s*.
v. 16, 18, 20: *St. Martin-in-the-Fields.* 1935-40. 3 pts. v. 16. 52*s*. 6*d*.; v. 18. 20. ea. 21*s*.
v. 17, 19, 21, 24: *St. Pancras.* 1936-52. 4 pts. v. 17. o.p.; v. 19. 21*s*.; v. 21. 50*s*.; v. 24. 35*s*.
v. 22: *St. Saviour and Christchurch, Southwark.* 1950. 30*s*.
v.23, 26: *St. Mary, Lambeth.* 1951-56. 2 pts. v. 23. 30*s*.; v. 26. 40*s*.
v. 25: *St. George's Fields.* 1955. 40*s*.
v. 27: *Spitalfields and Mile End New Town.* 1957. 50*s*.
v. 28: *The parish of Hackney.* pt. 1: *Brooke House.* 1960. 30*s*.

v. 29, 30: *The parish of St. James, Westminster.* pt. 1: *South of Piccadilly.* 1960. 3v. 168s. (v. 3 consists of a plan pocket, with 4 plans).

v. 31-32: *The parish of St. James, Westminster.* pt. 2: *North of Piccadilly.* 1963. 2v. £10 10s.

v. 33-34: *The parish of St. Anne, Soho.* 1966. 2v. £12 12s.

The survey of London aims to provide, on completion, an historical survey of the administrative county of London. Each volume gives a detailed history of a parish or part of a parish, with descriptions and illustrations of historically important buildings.

The 34v. of the Survey published to date are supplemented by a series of 16 monographs on separate buildings of historic interest.

942.1 (02)

PEVSNER, N. B. L. The Cities of London and Westminster. 2nd ed., extensively rev. Harmondsworth, Middlesex, Penguin Books, 1962. 704p. illus. (pl.), maps. 25s.

—— **London except the Cities of London and Westminster.** Harmondsworth, Middlesex, Penguin Books, 1952. 496p. illus. (pl.). 8s. 6d.

These 2v. are in the *Buildings of England* series. The *Cities of London and Westminster* deals with religious buildings, public buildings and streets in separate alphabetical arrangement. In the other volume the old Metropolitan boroughs are arranged A-Z and under each borough heading a perambulation of the area follows sections on religious and public buildings. The main emphasis is on architecture with critical evaluations of new buildings, but brief historical notes are included. Both v. have indexes of artists and topographical names. The volume for *Middlesex* in the same series (1951, 204p. 7s. 6d.) comes under this heading now that the whole of Middlesex is within the Greater London Council area. Parts of Greater London are also included in the volumes on *Surrey* and *Essex*.

942.1 (02)

STOW, J. A survey of London . . . , reprinted from the text of 1603, with introduction and notes by C. L. Kingsford . . . Oxford, Clarendon Press, 1908. 2v. illus. (pl.) 55s.

The best modern edition of the 1603 ed. of Stow's *Survey.* The work was first published in 1598 and provides an invaluable pre-Fire survey of London and its early history.

942.1 (02)

WHEATLEY, H. B. London, past and present: its history associations and traditions . . . Based upon the "Handbook of London" by P. Cunningham . . . London, Murray, 1891. 3v.

Cunningham's *Handbook of London* was first published in 1849.

London past and present, which embraces the county of London, is arranged alphabetically by streets, localities and buildings. Authoritative historical accounts under each heading emphasize the historical personages connected with each. General index.

942.1 (03)

HARBEN, H. A. A dictionary of London: being notes topographical and historical relating to the streets and principal buildings in the city of London . . . London, Jenkins, 1918. xxiv, 641p. illus. (pl.), maps.

Indispensable reference book for the city of London, giving detailed topographical and historical information about buildings, streets, parishes, wards, etc. Origins and earlier forms of names are given with full documentation.

"The most important contribution to the topography and history of London" (E. Ekwall).

942.2 (03)

KENT, W. R. G. An encyclopaedia of London . . . [2nd ed.]. London, Dent, [1951]. xii, 674p. illus. (pl.).

First published 1937. This revised ed. includes the changes brought about by the War of 1939-45.

Arranged alphabetically by subjects and places; a useful modern historical survey of the county of London, its buildings and institutions.

942.1 (058.7)

GOSS, C. W. F. The London directories, 1677-1855: a bibliography, with notes on their origin and development. London, Archer, 1932. xi, 147p.

A list of the 285 directories then known to Goss, with locations of each. Arranged chronologically; scope of each directory is clearly indicated. The introduction (p. 1-35) surveys the history of early directories of London.

942.1 (084.4):016

DARLINGTON, I., and HOWGEGO, J. Printed maps of London, circa 1553-1850. London, Philip, 1964. ix, 257p. illus. (pl.), maps. 42s.

The only bibliography of London maps. Part 1 comprises a detailed historical introduction including chapters on the inclusion of canals and railways in London maps, and a select bibliography of sources in London map history. Part 2, the catalogue, lists chronologically, with brief annotations, 421 maps described as London (with their several editions) but excludes local plans. Their locations in the British Museum Map Room, Guildhall Library and the Greater London Council Members' Library are indicated, with locations elsewhere of items not found in any of these three. Well produced.

942.1 (093)

JONES, P. E., and SMITH, F. R., *comp.* **A guide to the records in the Corporation of London Records Office and the Guildhall Library muniment room.** Compiled by authority of the Corporation, under the direction of the Library Committee. London, English Universities Press, 1951. 203p. illus.

Pt. 1: The Corporation of London Records Office; pt. 2: The Guildhall Library muniment room. Pt. 1 systematically deals with the various types of records (administrative, judicial, etc.). Includes the records of the City Library Companies. Entries are given in some detail and brief annotations are provided, as necessary; adequate cross-references; detailed index. Pt. 2 now outdated through widespread accessions since 1951.

No new ed. contemplated but complete sectional lists of various classes of records available, viz. *Vestry minutes of City parishes* (1964. 2*s*. 6*d*.). *Churchwardens' accounts of City parishes* (1960. *Gratis*). *London rate assessments and inhabitants' lists* (1961. *Gratis*). Parish registers: (1) *Parishes within the City* (1966. 5*s*.) (2) *Other London parishes, nonconformist, etc.* (1964. 2*s*.). (3) *Foreign registers in the London Diocesan archives* (1967. 2*s*. 6*d*.).

Middlesex

942.19 (02)
ROBBINS, R. M. Middlesex. London, Collins, 1953, xxiii, 456p. 75 pl., maps.

The first volume of the *New survey of England* series. The first part covers the economic, political, and social history. The second part is devoted to topography (places, A-Z).

Though this plan is reminiscent of the *Victoria histories,* more attention is given to modern conditions and the text is more akin to the style of the *Highways and byways* series. Notes on the sources are relegated to a separate section.

942.19 (02)
The Victoria history of the county of Middlesex. London, Constable (subsequently Oxford Univ. Press for the Institute of Historical Research). 1911-, v. 2, 3. illus. (pl.), maps.

V. 2 (o.p.) covers the history, industries, and sport of the county. It concludes with a topographical account of seven parishes in the Spelthorne Hundred. V. 3 (1962. 147*s*., 189*s*.) comprises the history of the parishes in Spelthorne, Isleworth and Elthorne Hundreds.

Surrey

942.21:016
GUILDFORD. PUBLIC LIBRARY. Reference Department. **Catalogue of works in the library relating to the County of Surrey.** Guildford, Public Library, 1957. 80p.

942.21:016
MINET PUBLIC LIBRARY. Catalogue of the collection of works relating to the county of Surrey; compiled by W. Minet and C. J. Courtenay. Aberdeen, Univ. Press, 1901. 148p. **Supplements,** 1910, 1912, 1923.

942.21:016
WILLIAMS, M. Y. A short guide to the Surrey Collection. London Borough of Lambeth, 1965. 20p. illus.

A guide to the collection in the Minet Public Library, which covers the pre-1888 county of Surrey; this included the parishes of Battersea, Wandsworth, Lambeth, Camberwell, Southwark, Bermondsey and Rotherhithe.

942.21 (02)
The Victoria history of the county of Surrey. London, Constable, 1902-14. 4v. and index. illus. (pl.), maps. (Reprinted London, Dawsons, 1968. £84 11*s*.).

V. 1 comprises the archaeology, Domesday survey, and natural history of Surrey. The various aspects of economic and social history are contained in v. 2, and the topographical survey initiated. The last is completed in v. 4, which has additional chapters on antiquities and civil history. Supplemented by:

942.21 (02)
FORGE, J. W. L., ed. **List of antiquities in the administrative county of Surrey.** 5th ed. Kingston, Surrey County Council, 1965. 251p. illus., maps. 35*s*.

The standard older histories are: O. Manning's *The history and antiquities of the county of Surrey* . . . Continued to [1814] by W. Bray (London, Nichols, 1804-14. 3v.); and E. W. Brayley's *A topographical history of Surrey* (London, Willis, 1850. 5v.).

942.21 (058.7)
SURREY LIBRARIANS GROUP. Surrey people: a union list of directories and allied material held in the libraries of Surrey. Esher, Surrey County Library, 1965. 125p. 11*s*.

942.21:07
MYSON, W. Surrey newspapers: a handlist and tentative bibliography. Wimbledon, Surrey Libraries Group, 1961. v, 36p.

List arranged chronologically under places, giving titles, dates, place of publication and locations, with publisher for current titles. Index of titles; list of libraries and newspaper offices with files.

Preliminary ed. only; a definitive ed. is in preparation.

942.21 (084.4)
The story of Surrey in maps: catalogue of an exhibition arranged by the Surrey County Branch of the Royal Institution of Chartered Surveyors. Ipswich, Cowell, 1954. 64p.

Supplements H. A. Sharp's *An historical catalogue of Surrey maps* (Croydon, Public Libraries Committee, 1929. 56p.).

942.21 (093)
SURREY RECORD SOCIETY. Guide to archives and other collections of documents relating to Surrey. Guildford, etc., the Society, 1925-51. 9v. (Publications, no. 23, 24, 26, 28-29, 31-32). 147*s*.

no. 23. *General introduction and scheme,* by by Hilary Jenkinson. 1925.
no. 24. *The Public Record Office,* by M. S. Giuseppi. 1926.
no. 26. *Parish records, civil and ecclesiastical,* by D. L. Powell. 1927.
no. 28. *List of court rolls, with some notes on other manorial rolls.* 1928. 10*s*. 6*d*.
no. 29. *Borough records,* by D. L. Powell. 1929.
no. 31. *Records of schools and other endowed institutions.* 1930. 10*s*. 6*d*.
no. 32. *Quarter session records* . . ., by D. L. Powell. 1931-51. 5v.

Kent

942.23:016

GILLINGHAM. PUBLIC LIBRARIES. Local history catalogue. Gillingham, 1951. 20p.; 1st supplement, 1955. 22p.

Classified list of books on Kent, Medway towns, Chatham, Gillingham and Rochester; author and subject indexes.

942.23:016

JESSUP, F. W. The history of Kent: a bibliography. [Maidstone], Kent County Council, 1966. [ii], 12p.

Classified list, partly by period, of *c.* 300 items, including many periodical articles. Annotated, but does not state publishers of books.

942.23:016

KENT. COUNTY LIBRARY, Local history catalogue, 1939. Springfield, Maidstone, 1939. [1], 107p.

Sections: 1. General history and description— 2. A list of subjects—3. Towns and villages. Gives full sub-titles of books; includes periodical articles.

942.23:016

MARGATE. PUBLIC LIBRARY. Catalogue of books, pamphlets and excerpts dealing with Margate, the Isle of Thanet and the county of Kent in the local collection; compiled by A. J. Gritten. Margate, 1934. 166p.

942.23:016

SMITH, J. R. Bibliotheca Cantiana: a bibliographical account of what has been published on the history, topography, antiquities, customs and family history of the County of Kent. London, J. R. Smith, 1837. [xiv], 360p.

942.23 (02)

HASTED, E. The history and topographical survey of the county of Kent, containing the ancient and present state of it . . . Canterbury, Bristow, 1797-1801. 12v. and atlas. illus. (pl.), maps.

The best history of Kent. It is the 2nd ed., the first was published between 1778-99. The first volume comprises the general history of the county. The individual places are arranged under the Hundreds. Each volume has its own index.
A single additional volume—*The Hundred of Blackheath,* by H. H. Drake—was issued in 1886 (Mitchell).

942.23 (02)

The Victoria history of the county of Kent. London, Constable, and St. Catherine Press, 1908-32. v. 1-3 only. illus. (pl.), maps. ea. 105*s.*, 126*s.*

No topographical volumes for this county have been issued. The general introductory matter has been extended to more than the usual two volumes to allow for the detailed survey of the county's maritime history, and Roman remains.

942.23 (093)

KENT COUNTY COUNCIL. County Archives Committee. Guide to the Kent County Archives Office, by Felix Hull. Maidstone, the County Council, 1958. xvi, 290p. illus. 15*s.*

An excellent calendar of official and private (deposited) archives. 22 illus. Indexed.

Sussex

942.25:016

EAST SUSSEX. COUNTY COUNCIL. Record Office, and WEST SUSSEX, COUNTY COUNCIL. Record Office. A descriptive report on the Quarter Sessions, other official and ecclesiastical records in the custody of the County Councils of East and West Sussex, with a guide to the development and historical interest of the archives. Lewes, & Chichester, the County Councils, 1954. xii, 212p. (Record publications no. 2).

"A later volume, devoted to estate and family archives, is under compilation" (*Foreword*).

942.25:016

EASTBOURNE. PUBLIC LIBRARIES. Catalogue of the local collection, comprising books on Eastbourne and Sussex. Eastbourne, 1956. 36p.

Sections: Sussex: General; Sussex: Special topics (no sub-division); Sussex: Localities (A-Z). 901 items; occasional bibliographical notes. Index of authors; index of subjects and titles.

942.25 (02)

HORSFIELD, T. W. The history, antiquities, and topography of the county of Sussex. Lewes, Sussex Press, 1835. 2v. illus. (pl.), maps.

The best complete topography of Sussex. The introductory chapters cover the natural and civil history of the county. The places are described under their respective Hundreds, or Rapes. Each volume has its own index.

942.25 (02)

The Victoria history of the county of Sussex. London, Constable and Oxford Univ. Press, for the Institute of Historical Research, 1905-53. v. 1-4, 7, and 9 only. illus. (pl.), maps.

The various aspects of the county's history and antiquities are surveyed in v. 1-3. The topographical survey is commenced in v. 3, and continued in the subsequent volumes. V. 2 and 9, o.p.; others, ea. 84*s.*-105*s.*

Hampshire

942.27:016

GILBERT, H. M., and GODWIN, G. N. Bibliotheca Hantoniensis: a list of books relating to Hampshire, including magazine references, etc., with an additional list of Hampshire newspapers, by F. E. Edwards, Southampton, Ye Olde Boke Shoppe, 1891. [3], lxiii, [1]p.

The main sequence is by authors, catchword subjects and localities. Appended are lists of books and periodicals containing references to Hampshire (p. i-xxxv) and of Hampshire newspapers (p. xxxvii-lxiii).

Continued by: Wilson, S. *Supplementary Hampshire bibliography . . .; being a list of Hampshire topography not appearing in the 'Bibliotheca Hantomiensis'* [sic] (1897).

942.27 (02)
The Victoria history of Hampshire and the Isle of Wight. London, Constable, 1900-14. 5v. and index. illus. (pl.), maps.

V. 1 covers the county's archaeology, natural history, and Domesday survey. Religious history, education, and forestry are in v. 2, which also commences the topography. The last is concluded in v. 5 which also includes the economic and general history of the region.

Isle of Wight
942.28 (02)
The Victoria history of Hampshire and the Isle of Wight. London, Constable, 1900-14. 5v. and index.
See entry at 942.27 (02).

Berkshire
942.29:016
READING. PUBLIC LIBRARIES. Local collection catalogue of books and maps relating to Berkshire. Reading, Central Public Library, 1958. [v], 259p.

The catalogue is in two parts: classified (topographical classes with subject divisions) and author. The subject index is followed by an appendix, Berkshire maps, 1574-1900, with index of cartographers.

942.29 (02)
The Victoria history of Berkshire. London, Constable and St. Catherine Press, 1906-27. 4v. and index. illus. (pl.), maps.

V. 1-2 are devoted to the introductory chapters on natural history, and the various aspects of history, economic and social. The topographical survey, by Hundreds, is contained in v. 3-4. All volumes o.p. except v. 4, 105s., 126s.

The standard older history is E. Ashmole's *The history and antiquities of Berkshire . . .* (Reading, Carnan, 1736. xxvi, 342p.).

942.29 (093)
BERKSHIRE. COUNTY RECORD OFFICE. Guide to the Berkshire Record Office; prepared for the County Records Committee, by F. Hull. Reading, Berkshire County Council, 1952. 117p. 8 pl. (facsims.). 4s.

Official archives — Borough records — Parish records—Unofficial deposited archives—Facilities for students — Collections not in the British Record Office.

Wiltshire
942.31:016
GODDARD, E. H., *comp.* **Wiltshire bibliography:** a catalogue of printed books, pamphlets and articles bearing on the history, topography and natural history of the county. Trowbridge, Wilts. Education Committee, 1929. [3], 276p.

Pt. 1: Wiltshire as a whole (A-Z by subjects) (p. 1-29); pt. 2: Individual parishes, A-Z (p. 31-276). Many analytical references.

942.31 (02)
HOARE, Sir R.C., *and others.* **The ancient history of Wiltshire.** London, Miller; Lockington, Hughes, etc., 1812-21. 2v.

—— **The modern history of South Wiltshire.** London, Nichols, 1822-37. 5v.; v. 6-7, by R. Benson and H. Hatcher. 1843.

A monumental work, not yet replaced. All aspects of the county history are dealt with under the respective Hundreds.

942.31 (02)
The Victoria history of Wiltshire. London, Oxford Univ. Press, for the Institute of Historical Research, 1953-. illus. (pl.), maps. v. 1, pt. 1, v. 2-8. ea. 84s.-189s.

V. 1, pt. 1 is largely an archaeological gazetteer. V. 2 is devoted to the Anglo-Saxon period and the Wiltshire Domesday, the latter being treated in detail. V. 3 covers ecclesiastical history, and v. 5, political history (*i.e.,* city government from 1066 onwards, and parliamentary representation). V. 7 is topographical and deals with the Hundreds of Bradford, Melksham, Potterne and Cannings; v. 8 covers Salisbury.

492.31 (093)
WILTSHIRE COUNTY COUNCIL. County Records Committee. **Guide to the records in the custody of the Clerk of the Peace for Wiltshire;** compiled by Maurice G. Rathbone. Trowbridge, Wilts, the County Council, 1959. xiii, 41p. 6s.

Issued as pt. 1 of the Guide to the Record Office. Covers the judicial and civil records. Index.

—— County Record Office. **Guide to the Record Office. Part 2. Guide to the County Council, parish, poor law and other official records** in the Wiltshire County. Record Office; compiled by Pamela Stewart. Trowbridge, Wilts., the County Council, 1961. xi, 131p. 9s.

Part 3 of the *Guide* is to follow.

Dorset
942.33:016
MAYO, C. H. Bibliotheca Dorsetiensis: . . . account of printed books and pamphlets relating to the history and topography of the county of Dorset. London, Whittingham, 1885. x, 296p.

942.33 (02)
DOUCH, R. A handbook of local history: Dorset. Bristol, Univ. of Bristol, Department of Adult Education, 1952 [*i.e.,* 1953]. 143p.

Provides information on a much wider area than the county concerned.

942.33 (02)
HUTCHINS, J. The history and antiquities of the county of Dorset . . . 3rd ed., by W. Shipp

and J. W. Hodson. London, Nichols, 1861-73. 4v. illus. (pl.), maps.

First published in 1774.
The 3rd ed. is a fine example of detailed topography. The introductory chapters cover the history, natural history, and general topography of the county. The description of individual places follows, by Hundreds. The fourth volume has indexes of persons and places.

942.33 (02)
The Victoria history of the county of Dorset. London, Constable, 1908. v. 2 only. illus. (pl.), maps. 105s., 126s.

Covers the economic, political, religious, and social history of Dorset.

942.33 (093)
COX, A. C. Index to the county records in the Record Room at the County Offices and . . . at the Shire Hall, Dorchester. Dorchester, Dorset Natural History and Archaeological Society, 1938. 102p. 5s.

Channel Islands
942.34:016
LE PELLEY, J. C. A classified bibliography of books and pamphlets relating to the island of Guernsey. 1953.

Listed in University of London, School of Librarianship and Archives. *Cumulative list of bibliographies and theses accepted for Part II of the University of London Diplomas in Librarianship and Archives . . . 1946-1960,* entry no. 131.

942.34:016
SUMNER, J. Le C., *comp.* **A bibliography of Jersey, 1902-1938,** supplementing Eugene Duprey's 'Essai de bibliographie Jersiaise', 1898 and 1902. 1939.

Listed in University of London, School of Librarianship and Archives. *List of bibliographies and theses accepted for Part III of the University of London Diploma in Librarianship . . . 1936-1950,* p. 4

942.34 (02)
ANSTED, D. T., and **LATHAM, R. G. The Channel Islands.** Revised by E. T. Nicolle. 3rd ed. London, Allen, 1893. xiv, 476p. illus., maps.

First published 1862.
Provides a comprehensive account of the natural history, antiquities, and geography of these islands.

Devonshire
942.35:016
DAVIDSON, J. Bibliotheca Devoniensis: a catalogue of the printed books and pamphlets relating to the county of Devon. Exeter, Roberts, 1852. vi, 226p.; Supplement. 1862. 51p.

More than 1,000 items.

942.35:016
DREDGE, J. I. A few sheaves of Devon bibliography . . . Plymouth, Brendon, 1889-99. 276p.

Reprinted from the *Transactions,* Devonshire Association for the Advancement of Science.

942.35:016
EXMOOR SOCIETY, Bratton Fleming. **The Exmoor bibliography.** 3rd ed. [Bratton Fleming], 1966. 20l. Mimeographed.

About 300 items, systematically arranged.

942.35 (02)
HOSKINS, W. G. Devon. London, Collins, 1954. xxi, 600p. 59 pl., maps.

This is the second volume of the *New survey of England* series (no more published), and follows the plan adopted in the one on Middlesex. It offers a convenient condensation of the older works and includes up-to-date information. Details of manorial descents are kept to a minimum. The topographical section has only a brief survey of Exeter as it is planned to devote a separate volume to that city.

The standard older history is R. Polwhele's *The history of Devonshire* (Exeter, Cadell, 1797-1806. 3v.).

942.35 (02)
The Victoria history of the county of Devon. London, Constable, 1906. v. 1 only. illus. (pl.), map. 105s., 126s.

This single volume comprises the archaeology, natural history, and feudal survey of the county.

Cornwall
942.37:016
BOASE, G. C., and **COURTNEY, W. P. Bibliotheca Cornubiensis:** a catalogue of the writings, both manuscript and printed, of Cornishmen, and of works relating to the county of Cornwall. London, Longmans, Green, 1874-82. 3v.

And its supplement:

BOASE, G. C. Collectanea Cornubiensis: collection of bibliographical and topographical notes relating to the county of Cornwall. Truro, 1890. xi p., 1904 col.

942.37 (02)
BOASE, G. C., and **COURTNEY, W. P. Bibliothe county of Cornwall . . .** Truro, Lake, 1867-72. 4v. illus. (pl.).

The most recent, comprehensive survey of Cornwall. Each parish is surveyed in A-Z sequence. There is no overall index but each volume has an index of contents. The plates are not particularly good or numerous but the parochial topography is very detailed.

942.37 (02)
POLWHELE, R. History of Cornwall, civil, military, religious, architectural, agricultural, commercial, biographical and miscellaneous. Falmouth, Cadell & Davis, 1803-6. 5v. in 1.

942.37 (02)

The Victoria history of the county of Cornwall.
London, Constable and St. Catherine Press, 1906-
24. v. 1 and 2 (pts. 5 and 8) only. illus. (pl.), maps.
105s., 126s.; 17s. 6d.; 21s.

The archaeology, industries, and natural history of the county are contained in v. 1. Pts.
5 and 8 of the second volume cover Romano-
British antiquities and the Domesday survey,
respectively.

942.37 (084.4)

**RODGER, E. M. Printed maps of Cornwall,
1576-1800: a bibliography.** 1956.

Listed in the University of London School of
Librarianship and Archives. *Consolidated list of
bibliographies and theses accepted . . . 1946-1960*
(1960).

Somerset
942.38:016

**CHUBB, T. A descriptive list of the printed
maps of Somersetshire, 1575-1914,** with
biographical notes and illustrations. Taunton,
Somersetshire Archæological and Natural History
Society, 1914. xii, 232p.

942.38:016

GREEN, E. Bibliotheca Somersetiensis: a catalogue of books, pamphlets, single sheets, and
broadsides in some way connected with the
county of Somerset. Taunton, Barnicott & Pearce,
1902. 3v.

v. 1: Bath books and general introduction.
v. 2-3: County books; general index.

942.38 (02)

**COLLINSON, J., and RACK, E. The history and
antiquities of the county of Somerset . . .**
Bath, Cruttwell, 1791. 3v. illus. (pl.) map.

The standard survey of this county. V. 1 has
a general introduction which is followed by descriptions of the individual places, by Hundreds.
Each volume has a place index. A brief, general
index is included in v. 3. A complete index, by
F. W. Weaver and E. H. Bates, was published,
by Barnicott of Taunton, in 1898.

942.38 (02)

HUMPHREYS, A. L. Somersetshire parishes:
handbook of historical references to all places
in the county. London, Hatchard, 1906. 2v.

Arranged by parishes, A-Z.

942.38 (02)

The Victoria history of the county of Somerset.
London, Constable, 1906-11, v. 1-2 only. illus.
(pl.), maps. v. 1, 105s., 126s.; v. 2, o.p.

These volumes are restricted to the archaeology, economic, natural, and social history of
Somerset. The index to both volumes is in v. 2.

942.38:07

**BROOKE, L. E. J. Somerset newspapers, 1725-
1960.** Yeovil, Somerset, the Author, 1960. 103p.
15s.

Compiled principally from the British Museum

newspaper catalogue and Emanuel Green's
Bibliotheca Somersetensis. A valuable brief
survey of the development of the local newspaper in Somerset, with biographical notes (p.
3-30). 181 newspapers arranged A-Z, with details
on history and change of title. Index of publishers, editors, printers, etc.; chronological list;
indexes of places of publication. Appendices
include a list of institutes and newspaper offices
where files are located (12 libraries and museums:
16 newspaper offices) and a list of principal published works consulted (p. 103).

942.38 (093)

SOMERSET COUNTY COUNCIL. Records Committee. **Somerset in manuscript:** notes on the
main archive groups preserved in the Somerset
Record Office, with a description of documents
selected for exhibition. Taunton, [the County
Council], 1959. ix, 36, [iv]p. front. 2s.

A general description of the main classes of
records; not a calendar. Index to items exhibited.

942.38/B:016

MATHEWS, E. R. N., *ed.* **Bristol bibliography**
. . . a catalogue of the books, pamphlets, collectanea, etc., relating to Bristol, contained in the
Central Reference Library. Bristol, Libraries
Committee, 1916. x, 404p.

Gloucestershire
942.41:016

**GLOUCESTER. PUBLIC LIBRARY. Catalogue
of the Gloucestershire collection;** books,
pamphlets, and documents in the Gloucester
Public Library relating to the county, cities
towns and villages of Gloucestershire; compiled
by R. Austin. Gloucester, Public Library, 1928.
xii, 1236p. illus.

Arranged by locality, with further sub-
division.

942.41:016

HYETT, F. A., and **BAZELEY, W.** **Biblio-
grapher's manual of Gloucestershire literature;** being a classified catalogue of books,
pamphlets, broadsides and other printed matter
relating to the county of Gloucester or to the
city of Bristol. Gloucester, Bellows, 1895-97. 3v.

942.41 (02)

**FOSBROOKE, T. D. Abstracts of records and
manuscripts respecting the county of Gloucester;** formed into a history . . . Gloucester,
Harris, 1807. 2v. illus. (pl.).

The last, completed full-scale account of
Gloucestershire. It incorporates the earlier
labours of Sir R. Atkyns (*The ancient and present
state of Gloucestershire.* 2nd ed., 1768) and R.
Bigland (*Historical, monumental and genealogical
collections relating to the county of Gloucestershire.* London, Nichols, 1791-2. 2v.). The description and history of each parish is given, under
the appropriate Hundred. Each volume has a
name and a subject index.

942.41 (02)

The Victoria history of the county of Gloucester.
London, Constable, 1907-. v. 2, 6-. illus. (pl.),
maps.

V. 2 (105s., 126s.) covers the ecclesiastical, economic, industrial and sporting history of the county. V. 6 (1965. 147s.) deals with 30 parishes in the northern Cotswolds; v. 8 (1968. 168s.) covers 22 parishes in central Gloucestershire.

942.41 (093)
GLOUCESTERSHIRE COUNTY COUNCIL. County Records Committee. **Gloucestershire quarter sessions archives, 1660-1889,** and other official records: a descriptive catalogue, compiled for the County Records Committee by I. E. Gray and A. T. Gaydon. Gloucester, the County Council, 1958. xvi, 96p. illus. (pl.). 6s. 6d.

An excellent guide, with historical notes on various classes of documents; index.

942.41 (093)
GRAY, I., and **RALPH, E.,** *ed.* **Guide to the parish records of the city of Bristol and the county of Gloucester.** [Bristol], Bristol and Gloucestershire Archaeological Society, [1963]. 315p. 30s.

Arranged by parishes A-Z.

Monmouthshire
942.43 (02)
EVANS, C. J. O. Monmouthshire; its history and topography. Cardiff, Lewis, 1954. xii, 559p. illus. (pl.), maps.

One of a series conceived on a similar plan to the *New survey of England.* In the first part of the volume the economic, political, and social history of the county are surveyed. This is followed by a description of places, arranged A-Z.
No attempt is made to give the manorial history in detail. Such information is to be found in the *History of Monmouthshire* (1796), by David Williams.
J. A. Bradney's *The history of Monmouthshire* . . . (London, Hughes and Clarke, 1907-32. 4v.), arranged according to Hundreds, was not completed.

942.43 (093)
MONMOUTHSHIRE ARCHIVES COMMITTEE. Guide to the Monmouthshire Record Office; prepared for the Monmouthshire Archives Committee by W. H. Baker. Newport, Mon., Monmouthshire Archives Committee, 1959. 126p. 5s.

A first-rate calendar of archives and deposited records, with an index.

Herefordshire
942.44:016
ALLEN, J., *comp.* **Bibliotheca Herefordiensis;** or, A descriptive catalogue of books, pamphlets, maps, and prints relating to the county of Hereford. Hereford, Allen, 1821. xii, 118, [1]p.

942.44:016
HEREFORDSHIRE. COUNTY LIBRARY. Local history collection. **Herefordshire books:** a select list of books in the local collection of the Here-

fordshire County Library. Hereford, County Library, Local History Section, 1955. 23 l.

942.44 (02)
DUNCUMB, J. Collections towards the history and antiquities of the county of Hereford. [Continued by W. H. Cooke, M. G. Watkins, J. H. and T. H. Matthews.] Hereford, Wright; London, Murray; and Hereford, Jakeman & Carver, 1804-1915. 7v. illus. (pl.), map.

Duncumb's first volume gives a general description and history of the county. He then commenced a survey, by Hundreds. This series was added to by his successors.

942.44 (02)
The Victoria history of the county of Hereford. London, Constable, 1908. v. 1 only. illus. (pl.), maps. 105s., 126s.

This single volume covers natural history, archaeology, the Domesday survey, political history, and agriculture. The general topography of the county must be sought in the work of John Duncumb and his successors (*q.v.*).

Shropshire
942.45 (02)
LLOYD, E. Antiquities of Shropshire . . . ; edited by T. F. Dukes. Shrewsbury, Eddowes, 1844. xviii, 462p. illus.

There is no good, comprehensive work of topography for this county. This volume provides a complete, but indifferent survey. It cannot be compared with R. W. Eyton's *History and antiquities of Shropshire* (1854-60. 12v.), which is very scholarly but is restricted to the feudal period.

942.45 (02)
The Victoria history of Shropshire. London, Constable, 1908. v. 1 only. illus. (pl.), maps. 105s., 126s.

This volume embraces the archaeology, Domesday survey, industries, and natural history of the county.

942.45 (084.4)
COWLING, G. C. A descriptive list of printed maps of Shropshire, A.D. 1577-1900. Shrewsbury, Salop County Council, 1959. viii, 234, [2]p.

751 maps are listed chronologically, with lengthy descriptions; addenda of 2 pages. Tabular index (name, date, title, dimensions, work in which map was issued, entry number); supplementary index of authors, printers, publishers, publications, etc.

942.45 (093)
SHROPSHIRE. COUNTY COUNCIL. Record Office. **A guide to the Shropshire records.** Shrewsbury, Salop County Council, 1952. 172p. 32 facsims.

A brief list of all types of official records and a more detailed survey of transferred records and private papers.

Staffordshire

942.46:016

EMERY, N., *comp.* **North Staffordshire studies. Pt. 1. The geography, geology and natural history of North Staffordshire.** Stoke-on-Trent, Horace Barks Reference Library and Information Service, 1966. 10p.

Lists *c.* 60 items, plus maps. 6 parts: 1. General — 2. Geology — 3. Geomorphology — 4. Land utilisation, agriculture, historical geography, etc. —5. Meteorology—6. Natural history.

942.46:016

SIMMS, R. Bibliotheca Staffordiensis; or, A bibliographical account of books and other printed matter relating to, printed or published in, or written by a native, resident or person deriving a title from any portion of the county of Stafford . . . Litchfield, Lomax, 1894. xxv, 546p.

942.46:016

STAFFORD. PUBLIC LIBRARY. Staffordshire: a list of books in Stafford Public Library. [Stafford, Public Library], 1953. 14p.

942.46:016

STOKE - ON - TRENT PUBLIC LIBRARIES. Current bibliography of published material relating to North Staffordshire and South Cheshire. Stoke-on-Trent Public Libraries, May 1954-. v. 1, no. 1-. Quarterly.

942.46 (02)

ERDESWICKE, S., *and others.* **A survey of Staffordshire;** edited by T. Harwood. London, Nichols, 1844, cii, 588p. illus.

The best complete survey of this county. Harwood collated and enlarged the work of Erdeswicke and his successors. The text is continuous and in itinerary form. There are indexes of persons and places. Illustrations include portraits.

942.46 (02)

The Victoria history of the county of Stafford. London, Constable and Oxford Univ. Press, for the Institute of Historical Research, 1908-. v. 1-. illus. (pl.), maps. ea. 84*s.*-189*s.*

V. 1 covers the county's natural history, archaeology, and history, economic, social and political. V. 2 (1967) is mainly concerned with the industrial history of Staffordshire. V. 4 (1958) comprises the Staffordshire Domesday and the West Cuttlestone Hundred. V. 5 (1959) is devoted to the East Cuttlestone Hundred. V. 8 (1963) concerns the history of the city of Stoke-on-Trent and the borough of Newcastle-under-Lyme.

942.46 (058.7)

EMERY, N., and **BEARD, D. R.,** *ed.* **Staffordshire directories:** a union list of directories relating to the geographical county of Stafford. Stoke-on-Trent Public Libraries, 1966. 46p. 5*s.*

Warwickshire

942.48:016

WILSON, R. D. A hand-list of books relating to the county of Warwick. Birmingham, Wilson, 1955. 34p.

Material is divided into 16 sections; no annotations, but a useful introduction.

942.48 (02)

The Victoria history of the county of Warwick. London, Constable, and Oxford Univ. Press, for the Institute of Historical Research, 1904-64. 7v. & index. illus. (pl.), maps. v. 1, 2, 4, 6, o.p.; others, ea. 84*s.*-168*s.;* index, 52*s.* 6*d.,* 84*s.*

Archaeology, natural history, and the Domesday survey are in v. 1. V. 2 comprises the economic, political, religious, and social history of the county. The other volumes contain the topographical descriptions of places, by the Hundreds. V. 7 deals with the growth of Birmingham (1964); index, 1955.

The standard old history is Sir William Dugdale's *The antiquities of Warwickshire* (2nd ed. London, Osborn & Longman, 1730. 2v.).

942.48 (084.4)

HARVEY, P. D. A., and **THORPE, H. The printed maps of Warwickshire, 1576-1900.** Warwick, Records and Museums Committee of the Warwickshire County Council, in collaboration with the Univ. of Birmingham, 1959. x, [1], 279p. maps. 30*s.*

Pt. 1: Introduction. The personality of Warwickshire reflected in its printed maps (p. 1-59, with 12 half-tones—reproduction of portions of important maps, and appendix); pt. 2: Catalogue of the printed maps of Warwickshire, 1576-1900; Catalogue of county maps; Supplementary list of some other maps of Warwickshire. A short bibliography (p. 253-5), followed by detailed index. Well produced; "the result of co-operation between an archivist and a historical geographer" (*Geographical journal,* v. 125, pt. 3-4, September-December 1959, p. 417).

942.48/B:016

BIRMINGHAM. PUBLIC LIBRARIES. Reference Department. **Catalogue of the Birmingham collection;** including printed books and pamphlets, manuscripts, maps, views, portraits, etc. Birmingham, 1918. xvi, 1132p.

—— —— —— **Supplement, 1918-1931.** 1931, vii, 913p.

Author catalogue, with many cross-references. "The catalogue . . . cannot claim to be a Bibliography of Birmingham, but it is the nearest approach to such a work that has ever been issued" (*Preface*).

The main catalogue has two supplementary sections, listing books printed in, and published in Birmingham but not otherwise relating to Birmingham. Revised entries in the Supplement are marked with an obelisk. The 2v. together carry some 50,000 entries.

942.48/B(02)

BIRMINGHAM CORPORATION. History of Birmingham. London, Oxford Univ. Press for the Birmingham City Council, 1952. 2v. illus., maps.

v. 1: *Manor and borough to 1865,* by Conrad Gill.

v. 2: *Borough and city, 1865-1938,* by Asa Briggs.

V. 1 has 50 plates, with a list of sources at the end of each of the 18 chapters; v. 2 has 49 plates, footnote references and 7 appendices (including a select list of local acts of Parliament); index, p. 359-84. This definitive history invites comparison with the 3-volume *History of local government in Manchester,* by A. Redford and I. S. Russell (1939-40). It is much wider in scope and takes account of local industries and the city's role in national political life, but is also less detailed (see *Manchester Review,* v. 7, autumn 1956, p. 400-1).

Worcestershire

942.47:016
BURTON, J. R., and PEARSON, F. S. **Bibliography of Worcestershire . . .** Edited for the Worcestershire Historical Society. Oxford, Parker, 1898-1907. 3 pts. (252p.), facsims.

pt. 1: Acts of Parliament relating to the county.
pt. 2: Bibliography of Worcestershire, being a classified catalogue of books and other printed matter relating to the county, with descriptive and explanatory notes.
pt. 3: Works relating to the botany of Worcestershire.

942.47 (02)
The Victoria history of the county of Worcester. London, Constable and St. Catherine Press, 1901-26. 4v. and index. illus. (pl.), maps. v. 3, 4, o.p.; others, ea. 105s., 126s.; index, 35s., 52s. 6d.

The county's archaeology, Domesday survey, and natural history are covered in v. 1. V. 2 deals with ecclesiastical and political history, and begins the topography. V. 4 concludes the survey, by Hundreds, and has chapters on economic and social history.

The standard older history is T. Nash's *Collections for the history of Worcestershire* (London, White, 1799. 2v.).

Midlands

942.5:016
North Midland bibliography. Edited by R. A. H. O'Neal. Library Association, North Midland Branch, c/o The Library, Derby & District College of Technology, Derby, 1963-. v. 1, no. 1-. Quarterly. 42s. p.a.

Covers the counties of Derby, Nottingham, Lincoln, Leicester, Rutland, Northampton and the Soke of Peterborough. Compiled largely from reports sent in by the co-operating libraries in the area. Classified arrangement, with index of names and places. V.1, no. 1 contained *c.* 90 entries (v. 5, no. 1: 250-300); an unusual feature —analytical entries for books on more general topics. Gives 44 permanent locations (public libraries, university libraries and 1 Record Office). No index.

Derbyshire

942.51:016
DERBY. PUBLIC LIBRARIES. Derbyshire: a select catalogue of books about the county; [compiled by J. Ormerod]. Derby, Public Libraries, 1930. [vi], 128p.

Two parts: 1. The county (sub-divided alphabetically by subjects)—2. Towns, villages and other places (A-Z, with subject sub-division for larger towns, *e.g.,* Derby).

942.51 (02)
The Victoria history of the county of Derby. London, Constable, 1905-07. 2v. illus. (pl.), maps. o.p.

These 2v. contain the natural history, archaeology, the Domesday survey, economic and political history, and ecclesiastical foundations of Derbyshire. There are no topographical volumes giving details of individual localities.

There is little to supplement these volumes as the choice lies betwen the thin, but comprehensive topography of James Pilkington (*View of the present state of Derbyshire.* Derby, Drewry, 1789. 2v.), and the detailed but incomplete history by Stephen Glover (1829-33).

P. D. Hallsworth's *Histories of Derbyshire* (1956) is an unpublished bibliography, listed in Univ. of London School of Librarianship and Archives. *Consolidated list of bibliographies and theses accepted 1946-1960* (1960), entry no. 121.

Nottinghamshire

942.52:016
NOTTINGHAM. PUBLIC LIBRARIES. Nottinghamshire collection: list of books in the Nottingham Free Public Libraries; by J. P. Briscoe. Nottingham, 1890. 89p.

942.52:016
NOTTINGHAMSHIRE. COUNTY LIBRARY. Nottinghamshire: a catalogue of the County Library local history collection. 3rd ed. Nottingham, County Library, 1966. [6], 119p. illus.

First published 1953.

942.52:016
WARD, J. **Descriptive catalogue of books relating to Nottinghamshire** in the Library of J. Ward. Nottingham, privately printed, 1892. viii, 40p.; Supplement. 1898. 41p.

942.52 (02)
THOROTON, R. **History of Nottinghamshire.** 3rd ed, [enlarged] by J. Throsby. London, Throsby, 1797. 3v. illus. (pl.), maps.

The standard account of Nottinghamshire. Thoroton's work was originally published in 1677. V. 3 contains an index to the earlier volumes.

942.52 (02)
The Victoria history of the county of Nottingham. London, Constable, 1906-10. v. 1-2 only. illus. (pl.), maps. ea. 105s., 126s.

These two volumes contain the introductory chapters on the various aspects of the county's economy and history. There is no index.

942.52 (093)
KENNEDY, P. A. Guide to the Nottinghamshire County Records Office. Prepared for the Records Committee. [Nottingham], Nottinghamshire County Council, 1960. xii, 180p. illus., facsims., maps. 25s.

A detailed list of the public and private records in the custody of the Nottinghamshire County Council and Diocesan Record Office. Three sections: 1. Official records of the County Council (p. 1-39)—2. Ecclesiastical records (p. 40-92)—3. Private deposits (p. 93-152). Indexes of places, persons and subjects. By the County Archivist.

Lincolnshire

942.53:016
CORNS, A. R. Bibliotheca Lincolniensis: a catalogue of the books, pamphlets, etc., relating to the city and county of Lincoln, preserved in the Reference Department. Lincoln, Morton, 1904. 254p.

942.53:016
LINCOLNSHIRE LOCAL HISTORY SOCIETY. Local history: its interest and value. With a select list of books, both general and relating to Lincolnshire. 2nd ed. Lincoln, Lincolnshire Chronicle, for the Society, 1949. 52p.

List of books, p. 37-52 (including Lincolnshire, p. 43-52).

942.53 (02)
ALLEN, T. The history of the county of Lincoln, from the earliest period to the present time. London, Saunders, 1833-34. 2v. illus. (pl.), maps.

The best comprehensive survey of Lincolnshire. There is an account of the general character and history of the county. Individual places are described under their respective wapentakes, etc.

942.53 (02)
The Victoria history of the county of Lincoln. London, Constable, 1906-. v. 2 only. illus. (pl.), maps. 105s., 126s.

V. 2 is devoted to the ecclesiastical, economic, political and social history of the county.

Leicestershire

942.542:016
BELDOWSKI, L. M. Bibliography of books and pamphlets relating to the history of Leicestershire. 1959.

An unpublished bibliography, listed in the Univ. of London School of Librarianship and Archives. *Consolidated list of bibliographies and theses accepted 1946-1960* (1960), entry no. 143.

J. M. Lee's *Leicestershire history: a handlist to printed sources in the libraries of Leicester* (Vaughan College Papers, no. 4, 1958) "correlates and gives locations of the chief works dealing

with local history in eight of the city's libraries" (Hobbs, J. L. *Local history and the library* (1962), p. 145).

942.542:016
LEE, J. M. Leicestershire history: a handlist to printed sources in the libraries of Leicester. Leicester, Univ. of Leicester, 1958. viii, 64p. Mimeographed. 2s. 6d.

12 sections, each with an introductory note, ranging from published histories, collections of printed documents, special collections and parliamentary papers to reference works, maps of the city and county, commercial directories, journals and newspapers. Locations in 8 libraries in the area; special subject index.

942.542 (02)
NICHOLS, J. The history and antiquities of the county of Leicester. London, Nichols, 1795-1811. 4v. in 8. illus. (pl.), maps.

The standard, and most detailed work on Leicestershire. The county's general history and topography are contained in v. 1. In the other volumes the individual places are described under their respective Hundreds.

942.542 (02)
The Victoria history of the county of Leicester. London, Constable, and Oxford Univ. Press, for the Institute of Historical Research, 1907-. v. 1-. illus. (pl.), maps. v. 1, o.p.; others, 84s.-168s.

V. 1-5 have been published. V. 1 comprises natural history, archaeology, ecclesiastical history, and the Domesday survey. Religious, political, and agrarian history are covered in v. 2. V. 3 deals with industries, transport, population, education, and sport. V. 4 (1958. 126s.) is devoted to the City of Leicester; v. 5, to Gartree Hundred (1964. 147s.).

942.542 (084.4)
GIMSON, B. L., and RUSSELL, P. Leicestershire maps: a brief survey. Leicester, Backus, 1947. viii, 40p. illus.

Chronological arrangement; lengthy annotations; index.

942.542 (093)
LEICESTER CORPORATION. Museums and Art Gallery, Archives Department. **Handlist of Leicestershire parish register transcripts.** Leicester, 1953. 44p.

Rutland

942.545 (02)
The Victoria history of the county of Rutland. London, Constable, St. Catherine Press and Oxford Univ. Press, 1908-36. 2v. and index. illus. (pl.), maps. £12 8s., £13 7s.

V. 1 covers natural history, archaeology, the Domesday survey, and various aspects of economic and social history. V. 2 is purely topographical, the places being arranged under their respective Hundreds.

The standard older history is T. Blore's *History and antiquities of the county of*

Rutland, although only v. 1, pt. 2 (containing the East Hundred) was published (Stanford, Newcombe, 1811).

Northamptonshire

942.55:016
TAYLOR, J. Bibliotheca Northantonensis, 1800-83. Northampton, Taylor, 1884. 34p.

Lists *c.* 400 items.

942.55 (02)
BRIDGES, J. The history and antiquities of Northamptonshire; edited by P. Whalley. Oxford, Payne, 1791. 2v. illus. (pl.), map.

The only complete, full-scale history of this county. It contains a general history of Northamptonshire, followed by descriptions of individual places, by Hundreds. There are indexes of persons and places in v. 2.

942.55 (02)
The Victoria history of the county of Northampton. London, Constable, St. Catherine Press and Oxford Univ. Press, for the Institute of Historical Research, 1902-37. v. 1-4 only. illus. (pl.), maps. ea. 105*s.*, 126*s.*

The general chapters on antiquities, natural and social history are contained in the first two volumes. The topographical survey commences in v. 2. The only index is that to the Domesday survey, in the first volume. A genealogical volume was issued in 1906.

942.55 (084.4)
WHITAKER, H. A descriptive list of the printed maps of Northamptonshire, A.D. 1576-1900. Northampton, Northamptonshire Record Society, 1948. xvi, 216p. (Northampton Record Society Publications, v. 14).

942.55 (093)
KING, P. I. Summary guide to the Northamptonshire Record Office, [Northampton], Northamptonshire Archives Committee, 1954. 24p.

Ten sections, including: 5. Estate and family records—8. Ecclesiastical records—9. Official archives and records of statutory authorities. No index. By the County Archivist.

Huntingdonshire

942.562:016
HUNTINGDONSHIRE. COUNTY LIBRARY. Catalogue of the local history collection. 2nd ed. Huntingdon, the County Library, 1958. 59p. Unpriced.

First published 1950.
The main section, 'Subject groups' (p. 5-40) is followed by others on 'Bibliography', 'Aerial photographs', 'Prints' and 'Maps' (p. 43-51; 147 items). Very occasional annotations. Author index.

942.562 (02)
The Victoria history of the county of Huntingdon. London, St. Catherine Press, 1926-38. 3v.

and index. illus. (pl.), maps. v. 1, o.p., v. 2-3, ea. 105*s.*, 126*s.*; index, 35*s.*, 52*s.* 6*d.*

The natural history, antiquities, and religious history comprise the first volume. V. 2 surveys the general and economic history of the county and introduces the topographical chapters which are concluded in v. 3. Ecclesiastical and manorial antiquities are treated in detail.

942.562 (093)
HUNTINGDONSHIRE. COUNTY ARCHIVES COMMITTEE. Guide to the Huntingdonshire Record Office; prepared for the County Archives Committee by G. H. Findlay. Huntingdon, the County Council, 1958. viii, 33p. illus. (pl.). 3*s.*6*d.*

Includes the records of a number of private collections deposited at the Office. 8 plates.

Bedfordshire

942.565:016
CONISBEE, L. R. A Bedfordshire bibliography, with some comments and biographical notes. Luton, Bedfordshire Historical Record Society, 1962. 333p. 80*s.*

About 6,000 items, with locations in 17 libraries.
Three main sections: A. The county (subjects, A-Z)—B. Places (Bedford; Dunstable; Luton; other towns and villages)—C. Persons. Omits all manuscripts, since the *Guide to the Bedfordshire Record Office* (q.v.) contains a catalogue of its documents, official and unofficial archives, and a list of its local manuscript map collection. Well produced.

——— ———: 1967 supplement. Bedford, Historical Record Society, 1967. 85p.

313 items in 3 main sections, as in the parent work; 25 sub-sections Index of authors and editors.

942.565:016
NATIONAL UNION OF TEACHERS. Bedfordshire County Teachers Association. Local history in Bedfordshire: a handbook of guidance upon sources and materials available for teachers and historians. Kempton, Beds., [the Association], 1960. [iii], 32p. map.

"Compiled by members of the Bedfordshire County Teachers Association and the Bedfordshire branch of the Historical Association as a contribution towards the teaching of local history" (prefatory note). 7 chapters; 4: Book and pamphlet sources (including works on sources in Bedford Public Library); 5: Directory of Bedfordshire biography (p. 18-23); 7. Likely topics for study. Appendices: Churches.

942.265 (02)
BEDFORDSHIRE. COUNTY COUNCIL. Guide to the Bedfordshire Record Office. Bedford, Bedfordshire County Council, 1957. 163p. 18 facsims., map. 12*s.* 6*d.*

An annotated *Handlist of the Bedfordshire county muniments* had previously been published by the Bedfordshire County Records Committee in 1931 (24p.).

942.565 (02)
The Victoria history of the county of Bedford.
London, Constable, 1904-14. 3v. and index. illus.
(pl.), maps. o.p.

V. 1 comprises the county's natural history,
archaeology, the Domesday survey, and ecclesiastical history and foundations. In v. 2 is a
review of the political and economic history,
followed by accounts of the agriculture, schools,
and sport. The topographical chapters, arranged
by the Hundreds, commence in v. 2 and are
completed in v. 3. The topography is detailed but
the emphasis is on churches and manors.

Oxfordshire
942.572:016
CORDEAUX, E. H., and **MERRY, D. H.**
**A bibliography of printed works relating to
Oxfordshire** (excluding the University and City
of Oxford). Oxford, Univ. Press, 1955. xv. 411p.

Also issued by the Oxford Historical Society
(new series, v. 11).
Considered a model of its kind. Locations of
books not in the Bodleian Library are indicated.
Addenda and corrigenda (1st supplement) appeared in *The Bodleian Library record,* v. 6, no.
2, February 1958, p. 433-43.

The complementary work is: Madan, F. *Oxford
books: a bibliography of printed works relating
to the university and city of Oxford, or printed
or published there.* (Oxford, Clarendon Press,
1895-1912. 2v.).

*A bibliography of printed works relating to
the University of Oxford,* by E. H. Cordeaux
and D. H. Merry (Oxford, Clarendon Press, 1968.
xxvii, 809p. 168s.) comprises more than 10,000
entries, including periodical articles, under *c.*
500 headings.

942.572 (02)
The Victoria history of the county of Oxford.
London, Constable, and Oxford Univ. Press, for
the Institute of Historical Research, 1907-. v. 1-.
illus. (pl.), maps.

Natural history, archaeology, the Domesday
survey, political history, and education are
covered in v. 1 (105s., 126s.) V. 2 (105s., 126s.),
the first issued, is devoted to religious history,
industries, and sport. The University takes up
the whole of v. 3 (o.p.). V. 5 (1957. 100s.) covers
Bullingdon Hundred; v. 6 (1959. 126s.), the
Hundred of Ploughley; v. 7 (1962. 126s.), Dorchester and Thame Hundreds; v. 8 (1964. 147s.),
Lewknor and Pyrton Hundreds. V. 4 and 9 are in
course of preparation.
This series is particularly valuable as the
earlier works, like that of White Kennett (1818),
are incomplete.

942.572 (093)
**OXFORDSHIRE COUNTY COUNCIL. Summary
catalogue of the privately deposited records
in the Oxfordshire County Record Office.**
Oxford, Clerk of the County Council, 1966. x,
158p. 21s.

601 items; detailed, analytical index, p. 129-58.

Also noted: Oxford University. Bodleian
Library. *Summary catalogue of manuscripts in
the Bodleian Library relating to the City,
County and University of Oxford: accessions
from 1916-1962,* by P. S. Spokes (Oxford, Oxford
Historical Society, 1964. xiii, 207p. 42s.).

Buckinghamshire
942.575:016
GOUGH, H. Bibliotheca Buckinghamiensis: a
list of books relating to the county of Buckingham. Aylesbury, De Fraine, 1890. iv, 96.

Reprinted from *Records of Buckinghamshire,*
v. 5-6, 1885-90.

942.575 (02)
**The Victoria history of the county of Bucking-
ham.** London, Constable and St. Catherine Press,
1905-28. 4v. and index. illus. (pl.), maps. v. 3,
126s.; others, o.p.

V. 1 covers the natural history, archaeology,
ecclesiastical history, and Domesday survey of
the county. V. 2 deals with the economic and
social history and initiates the topographical
survey. The latter is concluded in v. 3-4.

The older standard history is G. Lipscomb's
*The history and antiquities of the county of
Buckingham* (London, Robins, 1847. 4v.), ar-
ranged by Hundreds.

942.575 (084.4)
**PRICE, U. E. "The maps of Buckinghamshire,
1574-1800: a bibliography."** In *Records of
Buckinghamshire,* v. 15, 1947-52, p. 107-33, 182-
207, 250-69.

This item also appears in the University of
London. School of Librarianship and Archives.
*Cumulated list of bibliographies and theses
accepted . . . 1946-1960* (item no. 91).

A hand-list of Buckinghamshire estate maps,
compiled by E. M. Elvey (Jordans, Bucks.,
Buckinghamshire Record Society, 1963. 60p. 15s.)
gives details of 353 old estate maps, with 17
facsimiles.

Hertfordshire
942.58:016
**HERTFORDSHIRE. COUNTY MUSEUM. Cata-
logue of the Lewis Evans Collection of books
and pamphlets relating to Hertfordshire.** St.
Albans, 1906-8. 2pts. ii, 97p.; ii, 99-154p.

Pt. 1: Subject catalogue; pt. 2: catalogue of
authors.

942.58:016
**JOHNSON, W. B. Local history in Hertford-
shire:** a brief retrospect and a Hertfordshire
local history directory. Hitchin, Herts., Hertfordshire Local History Council, 1964. 40p. 5s.

The 'brief retrospect' mentions significant
publications on and concerning Hertfordshire up
to 1964. The directory (p. 34-39) gives brief data
on 15 local history societies, the Hertfordshire
and Middlesex County Councils and other organisations, with a list of libraries and museums
having local collections.

942.58 (02)
The Victoria history of the county of Hertford.
London, Constable, and Oxford Univ. Press, for the Institute of Historical Research, 1902-37. 4v. and index. illus. (pl.), maps. o.p.

The topographical survey is contained in v. 2-4. The chapters on the antiquities, history, and natural history are comprised in v. 1, 2, and 4. A genealogical volume was published in 1907.

The standard older history is Sir Henry Chauncey's *The historical antiquities of Hertfordshire* (London, Griffin, 1700).

942.58:05
THWAITE, M. F., *comp.* **Periodicals and transactions relating to Hertfordshire:** a short guide and subject index. Bengeo, Hertfordshire Local History Council, 1959. [i], 109 l. Mimeographed. 12s. 6d.

Part 2 of the Council's county bibliography. Section 1 list 36 titles of Hertfordshire periodicals and transactions, with 12 locations. Section 3 is a subject index of *c.* 2,500 articles from these and more general periodicals; many cross-references.

942.58:07
—— **Hertfordshire newspapers, 1772-1955:** a list compiled for the County bibliography. Welwyn, Herts., Hon. Sec., Hertfordshire Local History Council, 1956. [i], 42 l. Mimeographed. 7s. 6d.

Part 1 of the Council's county bibliography. 99 newspapers, with locations in 13 museums and libraries, and 10 newspaper offices; A-Z list, with notes; chronological list.

942.58 (084.4)
FORDHAM, *Sir* **H. G. Hertfordshire maps:** a descriptive catalogue of the maps of the county, 1579-1900. Hertford, Austin, 1907. xii, 182p.

Re-issued with a supplement, 1914. Reprinted from *Transactions of the Hertfordshire Natural History Society and Field Club,* v. 11-13 (1901-07); also *Transactions,* v. 15, p. 73-104.

942.58 (093)
LE HARDY, W., *ed.* **Guide to the Hertfordshire Record Office.** Pt. 1, Quarter sessions and other records in the custody of the officials of the County. Hertford, County Hall, 1961. xvi, [1], [1], 283p. illus. 45s.

The first of an intended series of 5v. 957 items; analytical index, p. 235-83.

Cambridgeshire

942.59:016
BARTHOLOMEW, A. T. Catalogue of the books and papers for the most part relating to the university, town and county of Cambridge, bequeathed to the University by J. W. Clark. Cambridge, Univ. Press, 1912. xiv, [1], 282p. front.

942.59:016
BOWES, R. Catalogue of books printed at or relating to the university, town and county of Cambridge, from 1521 to 1893; with bibliographical and biographical notes. Cambridge, Macmillan & Bowes, 1894. xxxvi, 516p. and index of 67p. illus.

942.59:016
CAMBRIDGESHIRE. COUNTY LIBRARY. Cambridgeshire: an annotated list of the books, maps, prints, pamphlets and other material in the Cambridgeshire County Library local history collection. Cambridge, County Library, 1961. 57p. *Gratis.*

Subject list, with no author index. Includes articles in periodicals.

942.59 (02)
CARTER, E. The history of the county of Cambridge, from the earliest account to the present time; edited by W. Upcott. London, Bentley, 1819. iv, 376p.

This work, first published in 1753, gives a condensed, but complete, account of places in Cambridgeshire. An historical introduction is followed by the survey of Cambridge and then of other places alphabetically. There is an index.

942.59 (02)
The Victoria history of the county of Cambridgeshire and the Isle of Ely. London, Oxford Univ. Press, for the Institute of Historical Research, 1938-60. 4v., ea. 84s.-189s.; index, 42s., 70s. (Reprinted London, Dawsons, 1968. £89 5s.).

V. 1 comprises the county's natural history and the Domesday survey. Archaeology is completed in v. 2, which also covers ecclesiastical, economic, political, and social history. V. 3-4 are topographical, v. 3 being devoted to the City, University and colleges of Cambridge. Reviewed in *Times literary supplement,* no. 3,028, 11th March 1960, p. 163.

East Anglia

942.6:016
East Anglian bibliography: a check-list of publications not in the *British national bibliography.* Norwich, Library Association, Eastern Branch, July 1960-. Quarterly. 21s. p.a. (libraries, 42s.).

Covers the counties of Cambridge, Isle of Ely, Huntingdon, Norfolk and Suffolk; lists publications printed (or duplicated) locally, or of local interest. Topographical arrangement, with annual index. Library locations are given.

Norfolk

942.61:016
COLMAN, J. J. Bibliotheca Norfolciensis: a catalogue of writings of Norfolk men and of works relating to the county of Norfolk, in the library of Mr. J. J. Colman, at Carrow Abbey, Norwich. [Compiled by J. Quinton]. Norwich, privately printed, 1896. viii, 592p.

942.61 (02)

BLOMEFIELD, F., and **PARKIN, C. An essay towards a topographical history of the county of Norfolk.** London, Miller, 1805-10. 11v. illus. (pl.), maps.

The standard work on Norfolk. Blomefield's *Essay* was originally published, in 5v., in 1739-75. There is no general survey, the entire work being devoted to descriptions by Hundreds. V. 11 contains name and place indexes. A further index of names was compiled by J. N. Chadwick in 1862, and a supplementary volume by C. R. Ingleby, in 1929.

942.61 (02)

The Victoria history of the county of Norfolk. London, Constable, 1901-06. v. 1-2 only. illus. (pl.), maps. ea. 105s., 126s.

This series has never been completed. V. 1 covers the natural history and archaeology of the county. The Domesday survey, art, political and religious history comprise v. 2.

942.61 (084.4)

CHUBB, T. A descriptive list of the printed maps of Norfolk, 1574-1916, with biographical notes and tabular index; and, A descriptive list of Norwich plans, 1541-1914, by G. P. Stephens. Norwich, Jarrold, 1928. xvi, 289p.

Suffolk

942.64:016

BLOOM, J. H. A calendar of broadsides and single sheets relating to the county of Suffolk. London, Gandy, 1921. 14p.

—— **Early English tracts, pamphlets and printed sheets:** a bibliography. v. 1 (Early period): 1473-1650 (Suffolk). London, Gandy, 1922. xvi, 232p.

v. 2, 1473-1650 (1923) covered Leicestershire, Staffordshire, Warwickshire and Worcestershire.

942.64 (02)

PAGE, A. A supplement to the "Suffolk Traveller"; or, Topographical and genealogical collections concerning that county. Ipswich, Page, 1844. viii, 1054p.

A complete topographical survey of Suffolk. The places are arranged under their respective Hundreds. It includes indexes of families, and places. The standard of the work is not equal to that of A. Suckling's *History and antiquities of the county of Suffolk* (1846-48), which was not completed.

942.64 (02)

The Victoria history of the county of Suffolk. London, Constable, 1907-11. v. 1-2 only. illus. (pl.), maps. v. 1, o.p.; v. 2, 105s., 126s.

These volumes do not contain any topographical chapters, being devoted to a general review of the county's antiquities, economy, and general history. No index.

The standard older history is A. Suckling's *History and antiquites of the county of Suffolk* (London, Weale, 1846-8. 2v.).

Essex

942.67:016

CUNNINGTON, A. Catalogue of books, maps, and manuscripts, relating to or connected with the county of Essex . . . Braintree, privately printed, 1902. 90p.

942.67:016

O'LEARY, J. G. Supplement to the 'Essex bibliography'. Dagenham, the Author, 1962. 70p. 21s.

An unofficial supplement to the Bibliography volume of the *Victoria history of the county of Essex* (q.v.).

942.67:016

WARD, G. A., *comp.* **Essex local history:** a short guide to books and manuscripts, for the Essex Committee of the National Register of Archives. Brentwood (Essex), 1950. 36p. illus.

942.67 (02)

The Victoria history of the county of Essex. London, Constable, and Oxford Univ. Press, for the Institute of Historical Research, 1903-. v. 1-. illus. (pl.). maps. v. 1-2, 4. ea. 105s.-168s.; bibliography v. (1959), 105s., 147s.

V. 1-2 contain the natural history, archaeology, and general history of the county. The account of the local industries is particularly full but there is no place-by-place topography. V. 3, *Roman Essex,* is the only V.C.H. volume to be devoted exclusively to the Romano-British antiquities of a county. V. 4 deals with Ongar Hundred. V. 5 (1966) is the first of 2v. on the history of places in the Waltham Hundred, etc.

The Bibliography volume (*A history of the county of Essex: a bibliography*) has 3 pts.: (i) the county; (ii) biography and family history; (iii) individual places and regions. Author and subject indexes. This volume, edited by W. R. Powell, is the first volume in the Victoria history series to be devoted specially to bibliography. Supplemented by O'Leary (*see above*).

942.67 (02)

WRIGHT, T. The history and topography of the county of Essex . . . London, Virtue, 1836. 2v. illus. (pl.), map.

The latest general account of Essex. A survey of the economic and physical character of the county is prefixed to the detailed topography, arranged by Hundreds. Each volume has its own index to families and places.

An earlier history is P. Morant's *History and antiquities of the county of Essex* (London, Osborne, 1768. 2v.).

942.67 (084.4)

EMMISON, F. G., *ed.* **Catalogue of maps in the Essex Record office,** 1566-1855. [Chelmsford, Essex County Council], 1947. **First supplement.** 1952. **Second supplement.** 1964.

——**County maps of Essex, 1576-1852: a handlist.** Chelmsford, Essex County Council, 1955. 20p. (Essex Record Office publications, no. 25). 5s.

Chronologically arranged; annotated entries. Bibliography. Index to surveyors, engravers and publishers.

Cheshire

942.71:016

COOKE, J. H. Bibliotheca Cestriensis; or, A bibliographical account of books, maps, plates and other printed matter relating to, printed or published in, or written by authors resident in the county of Chester . . . Warrington, Mackie, 1904. A-W, iii, 218p.

942.71 (02)

ORMEROD, G. The history of the county palatine and city of Chester . . . 2nd ed., by T. Helsby. London, Routledge, 1882. 3v. illus. (pl.), maps. £20.

The standard work on this county. V. 1 deals with Chester and the Hundred of Buclow. The other volumes complete the survey, all places being arranged under the Hundreds. Most of the plates are engraved views. There are many pedigrees and tables of charities, clergy, and populations. V. 3 contains an index of families and places.

942.71 (084.4)

SYLVESTER, D., and NULTY, G., *ed.* **The historical atlas of Cheshire.** Rev. ed. Chester, Cheshire Community Council, 1966. viii, 64p. maps. 18s.

30 black-and-white maps on odd-numbered pages (p. 5-61, 62), with descriptive text facing. Coloured geological drift map as frontispiece. Bibliography, p. 63-64. Page size (oblong), $7\frac{2}{3}'' \times 9''$.

492.71 (084.4)

WHITAKER, H. A descriptive list of the printed maps of Cheshire, 1577-1900. Manchester, Chetham Society, 1942. xv, 220p. (Chetham Society, New series, 106).

668 items, chronologically arranged; index of authors, printers and publishers.

Lancashire

942.72:016

FISHWICK, H. The Lancashire library: a bibliographical account of books on topography, biography, history, science and miscellaneous literature relating to the County Palatine; including an account of Lancashire tracts, pamphlets and sermons printed before 1720 . . . Warrington, Pearse; London, Routledge, 1875. xi, 443p.

942.72:016

HAWKES, A. J., *ed.* **Lancashire printed books:** a bibliography of all the books printed in Lancashire down to the year 1800. Wigan, 1925. xxviii, 155p.

942.72:016

LIVERPOOL. PUBLIC LIBRARIES. Reference Library. **Liverpool prints and documents:** catalogue of maps, plans, views, portraits, memoirs, literature, etc., in the Reference Library relating to Liverpool. Liverpool, 1908. viii, 374p.

942.72:016

MANCHESTER LITERARY CLUB. List of Lancashire authors, with brief biographical and bibliographical notes; edited by C. W. Sutton. Manchester, Heywood, 1876. vii, 164p.

942.72 (02)

BAINES, E. The history of the county palatine and duchy of Lancaster. 3rd ed., by J. Croston. Manchester, Heywood, 1888-93. 5v. illus., maps. 80s.

The latest and best edition of a work first published in 1836. V. 1 embraces the general history of the county. Then follow the topographical surveys of each Hundred. There are many pedigrees of the local families. A general index is included in v. 5.

942.72 (02)

The Victoria history of the county of Lancaster. London, Constable, 1906-14. 8v. illus. (pl.), maps. o.p. (Reprinted London, Dawsons, 1967. £139 13s.).

V. 1 covers the archaeology, feudal survey, and natural history of the county. Economic, political, religious, and social history are in v. 2. The remainder are devoted to topography, the places being arranged under the Hundreds. V. 5 has an index to v. 3-5; v. 7 has one to v. 6-7, and v. 8 includes its own.

942.72 (058.7)

Lancashire directories, 1684-1957; edited by G. H. Tupling. Rev. ed., edited by S. Horrocks. Lancashire Bibliography Committee, Central Library, Manchester, 1968. 78p. (Lancashire bibliography, v. 1). 60s.

Progress on 'The Lancashire bibliography'—a union list of the holdings of Lancashire libraries, excluding Liverpool Public Libraries—was reported on by G. B. Cotton in *The Manchester review,* v. 10. Winter, 1964-65, p. 165-71.

942.72 (084.3)

WHITAKER, H. A descriptive list of the printed maps of Lancashire, 1577-1900. Chetham Society, 1938. xvi, 274p. illus.

942.72 (093)

FRANCE, R. S. Guide to the Lancaster Record office. 2nd ed. Preston, Preston, Lancashire County Council, 1962. [5], xii, 353p. facsims., maps.

First published 1948.

942.72/M (02)

THOMSON, W. H. History of Manchester, to 1852. Altrincham, Sherratt, 1968. xviii, 444p. ill. 42s.

942.72/M (084.4)

LEE, J. Maps and plans of Manchester and Salford, 1650 to 1843: a handlist. Altrincham, Sherratt, 1957. 43p.

"An attempt to list and classify, for the first time, all the published plans of Manchester and Salford from the first reasonably authenticated one, drawn about 1650, to the issue of the first large scale Ordnance Survey Plan in 1843." 65 items, in chronological order. Any identification features and size are stated.

Yorkshire

942.74:016

BOYNE, W. The Yorkshire library: a bibliographical account of books on topography, tracts of the seventeenth century, biography, spaws, geology, botany, maps, views, portraits, and miscellaneous literature relating to the county . . . London, Taylor, 1869. 304p.

942.74:016

DICKENS, A. G., and MacMAHON, K. A. A guide to regional studies on the East Riding of Yorkshire and the city of Hull. Hull, Univ. of Hull, Department of Adult Education and History, 1956. 66p.

942.74:016

YORKSHIRE ARCHAEOLOGICAL SOCIETY. Catalogue of the printed books and pamphlets in the library; compiled by G. E. Kirk. Wakefield, West Yorkshire Printing Co., 1933-36. 2v.

942.74 (02)

ALLEN, T. A new and complete history of the county of York. London, Hinton, 1828-31. 6v. illus. (pl.).

Though the standard of this work is not equal to that set by historians like Hunter and Thoresby, it is the best of the comprehensive surveys of this county. More detailed accounts of the particular regions of Yorkshire should be sought in the works of the other authors alluded to. V. 1 of Allen's *History* is devoted to the annals of the county. Subsequent volumes survey each Riding in turn. V. 6 contains an index to the whole work.

942.74 (02)

The Victoria history of the county of York. London, Constable and St. Catherine Press; subsequently published for the Institute of Historical Research by Oxford Univ. Press, London, 1907-. illus. (pl.), maps.

The 3v. and index, published 1907-25 (v. 1, 105s., 126s.; v. 2-3, o.p.; index, 35s.) comprise the general series and include the introductory surveys, for the whole county, which are usually contained in the first two volumes of the Victoria Histories. No topographical chapters are given. *North Riding* (1914-25. v. 1, 126s.; v. 1 & index, o.p.) is a complete survey, devoted to topographical description. *The city of York* (1961. 168s.) covers the history from Roman times to 1959 as well as particular institutions and aspects of the city.

942.74:07

LAUGHTON, G. E., and STEPHEN, L. R., *comp.* **Yorkshire newspapers:** a bibliography, with locations. Compiled for the Yorkshire Branch of the Library Association. [Harrogate], Yorkshire Branch of the L.A., 1960. x, 61p. Mimeographed. 7s. 6d. (interleaved, 10s. 6d.).

446 items, with locations in 37 public and university libraries, 41 newspaper offices, 6 museums (including the British Museum) and other institutions. Exact holdings are stated; microform is indicated. No correction has been made to the British Museum holdings to show losses from war damage.

The *Preface* refers to this publication as "this first instalment of a Yorkshire bibliography".

942.74 (084.4)

WHITAKER, H., *ed.* **A descriptive list of the printed maps of Yorkshire and its Ridings, 1577-1900.** Wakefield, Yorkshire Archæological Society, 1933. xiii, 261p. illus. (pl.).

This bibliography forms v. 86, for 1933, of the Yorkshire Archæological Society *Record series.* The introduction gives a concise survey of the development of English cartography. The 706 items are chronologically arranged; detailed descriptive notes.Tabular index (name; date; title; dimensions; work in which map was issued; number); supplementary index of authors, engravers, printers and publishers. Some of the 23 plates are facsimiles.

The Yorkshire Archæological Society's *Catalogues of the maps and plans in the library . . . ,* compiled by G. E. Kirk (Wakefield, the Society, 1937. [ii], 26p. has two parts—1, Maps: Yorkshire; Yorkshire Ordnance Survey maps; Yorkshire local maps. 2, Plans.

942.74/L:016

BONSER, K. J., and NICHOLS, H. Printed maps and plans of Leeds, 1711-1900. Leeds, Thoresby Society, 1960. xxiv, 148p. illus. (Publications of the Thoresby Society, v. 47). 21s.

374 items are listed chronologically; 12 plates of maps and plans.

942.74/S:016

FREEMANTLE, W. T. Bibliography of Sheffield and vicinity. Sheffield, Pawson & Brailsford, 1911. v. 1 (to the end of 1700).

942.74/L:016

LEEDS. PUBLIC LIBRARIES. Leeds and Yorkshire: a guide to the collections. Leeds, Libraries and Arts Committee, 1947. 30p.

942.74/S:016

SHEFFIELD. CITY LIBRARIES. Department of Local History and Archives. **Basic books on Sheffield history.** Rev. ed. Sheffield, City Libraries, 1958. 16p. *Gratis.*

First published 1950.
Sections: Bibliographies—General works, including geographical background — Selected record material available in print—Public and social services—Industrial history—Ecclesiastical history—Histories of particular districts—Biographies. 10-20 word annotations; no index.

942.74/S:091

SHEFFIELD. CITY LIBRARIES. Guide to the manuscript collections in the Sheffield City Libraries. Sheffield, Libraries, Art Galleries and Museums Committee, 1956. x, 115p. illus.

Sections: Family muniments—Solicitors' accumulations—Other professional and business records—Antiquaries' collections—Miscellaneous documents. The muniments described are almost all of a "private" (non-official) nature, and the guide is confined as strictly as possible to MS. material of a historical type. Analytical index.

Northern England

942.8:016

DONKIN, W. C. An outline bibliography of the Northern region. Newcastle-upon-Tyne, King's College; North East Industrial and Development Association; Cumberland Development Council, 1956. 40p.

Covers Cumberland, Durham, Northumberland, Westmorland and the North Riding of Yorkshire.

Durham County

942.81 (02)

SURTEES, R. The history and antiquities of the county palatine of Durham. London,Nichols, 1816-40. 4v. illus. (pl.).

The standard work on this county. A view of the general history of Durham precedes the excellent topographical survey to which the majority of the volumes are devoted. Pedigrees are given and the engraved plates are fine.

942.81 (02)

The Victoria history of the county of Durham. London, Constable and St. Catherine Press, 1905-28. v. 1-3 only. illus. (pl.), maps. ea. 105s., 126s.

The general chapters on the various aspects of the county's history are contained in the first two volumes. V. 3 is a topographical survey of the city of Durham and Stockton Ward.

942.81 (084.4)

TURNER, R. M., comp. **Maps of Durham, 1576-1872,** in the University Library, Durham; including some other maps of local interest: a catalogue. Durham, Bailes, for Univ. Library, 1954. 40p.

Chronological arrangement under three sections: maps of the county of Durham; maps of smaller areas within the county of Durham; and maps of the city of Durham.

Supplemented by A. I. Doyle's *Maps of Durham, 1607-1872, in the University Library, Durham: a supplementary catalogue* (1960. 16p. 1s. 3d.). This embodies corrections and addenda.

Northumberland

942.82:016

GREAT BRITAIN. MINISTRY OF TOWN AND COUNTRY PLANNING. Northumberland and Tyneside: a bibliography; by W. C. Donkin and E. F. Patterson. London, 1946. xvi, 101p.

475 entries, including periodical articles. 13 broad subject sections; some annotations; indexes of authors and subjects. Locations are given for books.

942.82:016

NEWCASTLE-UPON-TYNE PUBLIC LIBRARIES COMMITTEE. Local catalogue of material concerning Newcastle and Northumberland, as represented in the Central Public Library. Newcastle-upon-Tyne, Reid. 1932. vii, 626p.

Author list, followed by a classified list and subject index. Some annotations. Appendices:

Newcastle typography, 1639-1850; Index to Newcastle printers, 1639-1850.

942.82:016

TAYLOR, H. A., comp. **Northumberland history:** a brief guide to records and aids in Newcastle-upon-Tyne. Newcastle-upon-Tyne. Northumberland County Council, 1963. xi, 59p.

By the County Archivist. Printed sources (county histories, etc.); texts, calendars and lists; manuscript and other primary sources. Annotated, particularly for primary sources. Tithe maps, p. 19-40. Index.

942.82 (02)

NORTHUMBERLAND. COUNTY HISTORY COMMITTEE. A history of Northumberland. Newcastle, Reid, 1893-1940. 15v. illus. (pl), maps.

This monumental and excellent work was planned as a continuation of Hodgson's *History of Northumberland* (London, Longmans, 1841-57. 7v. £14 14s.), and follows it in its arrangement, which is by parishes. The topography as well as the history of each place is covered.

042.82 (084.4)

WHITAKER, H. A descriptive list of the maps of Northumberland, 1576-1900. Newcastle-upon-Tyne, Society of Antiquaries of Newcastle-upon-Tyne and the Public Libraries Committee of Newcastle-upon-Tyne, for the Chetham Society, 1949. xvi, 219p. illus.

Cumberland

942.85 (02)

The Victoria history of the county of Cumberland. London, Constable, 1901-05. v. 1-2 only. illus. (pl.), maps. ea. 105s., 126s.

V. 1 contains the archaeology, natural history, and the Domesday survey of the county. V. 2 covers ecclesiastical, economic, political, and sporting history. No topographical chapters are included.

942.85 (02)

WHELLAN, W. The history and topography of the counties of Cumberland and Westmorland . . . Pontefract, Whellan, 1860. viii, 896p.

The most modern, comprehensive history of these counties. The text is workmanlike but it is not illustrated. In this respect it is inferior to the publications of Nicolson and Burn (1777), and W. Hutchinson (*History of the county of Cumberland and some places adjacent.* Carlisle, Jollie, 1794. 2v.). Whellan gives chapters on geology and general history and arranges the topography by wards. There is an index of places.

Westmorland

942.88 (02)

WHELLAN, W. The history and topography of the counties of Cumberland and Westmorland . . . Pontefract, Whellan, 1860. viii, 896p.

See entry at 942.85 (02).

Isle of Man

942.89:016

CUBBON, W., *comp. and ed.* **A bibliographical account of works relating to the Isle of Man,** with biographical memoranda and copious literary references. London, Oxford Univ. Press, for the Manx Museum and Ancient Monuments Trustees, 1933-39. 2v. illus.

Systematically arranged. V. 2 includes annotated lists of Manx periodicals, newspapers, directories, etc. Detailed index in v. 2.

942.89 (02)

TRAIN, J. An historical and statistical account of the Isle of Man, from the earliest times to the present date . . . Douglas, Quiggin, 1845. 2v. illus. (pl.), maps.

Wider in scope than A. W. Moore's *History of the Isle of Man* (1900), which excludes topography. Train devotes several chapters to antiquities, commerce, customs, and history. The geographical descriptions are in v. 2.

942.89 (084.4):016

CUBBON, A. M. Early maps of the Isle of Man: a guide to the collection in the Manx Museum. Douglas, Manx Museum & National Trust, 1954. 44, [1]p. illus. (3rd rev. ed. 1967. 48p. 1s. 6d.).

Cites 6 items "for further reading".

Wales

942.9:016

WALES, UNIVERSITY OF. Board of Celtic Studies. **A bibliography of the history of Wales.** 2nd ed., edited by R. T. Jenkins and W. Rees. Cardiff, Univ. of Wales Press, 1962. xviii, 330p. 67s.

First published 1931.
The standard critical bibliography of Welsh history. The arrangement of material (printed bibliographies, sources and secondary works (English and Welsh languages)) is chronological, with appropriate subject sub-divisions. The treatment is selective rather than exhaustive and that three grades of reader have been provided, for the teacher, the research student and the general reader.
2nd ed. has 3,574 numbered entries (1st ed.: 1,587), 38 contributors. Sections A-K (A, General history; B. Topography and local history; C-K. Periods (ancient history, to 1914)). Very occasional brief annotations; valuable cross-references. List of historical, etc. journals, nos. 291-346. Some items are annotated. Index of subjects and others, p. 290-330.
Substantially supplemented in *The bulletin of the Board of Celtic Studies,* v. 20, pt. 2, May 1963, p. 126-64,—'Supplement 1 [1963]', mainly covering items published during the years 1959-1962 inclusive.

942.9 (02)

DAVIES, I. M. Welsh history: a handbook for teachers. Cardiff, National Union of the Teachers of Wales, 1947. xi, 149p.

An admirable teaching aid. The method adopted is to assign the early history to the younger age groups and modern history to the older age groups. Long and excellently arranged bibliography.

942.9 (02)

LLOYD, J. E. A history of Wales, from the earliest times to the Edwardian conquest. 3rd ed. London, Longmans, Green, 1939 (reprinted 1948). 2v. tables, map.

First published 1911.
A scholarly work, with profuse footnote references (chapter 20, Llywelyn ap Gruffydd, has 236 such references). Index of authors, works, MSS., etc., cited in the notes, v. 1, p. xv-xxviii. V. 2 includes genealogical tables, a folding map and analytical index.

Jane Williams's *A history of Wales, derived from authentic sources* [to 1603] (London, 1869) is one of the best of the older general histories of Wales.

942.9 (084.4)

NATIONAL MUSEUM OF WALES. The map of Wales [before 1600 A.D.]; by F. J. North. Cardiff, published for the National Museum of Wales, by the Press Board of the Univ. of Wales, 1935. iii, 69p. maps, facsims.

First published in *Archaeologia Cambrensis,* v. 90, 1935.
Sections: Wales on the early *Mappae Mundi* —Wales on the Ptolemy maps—Wales on the Portolan maps—Wales on some mediaeval maps of Britain—Wales on some early sixteenth century maps—Wales on the later sixteenth century maps. No index.

942.9 (084.4)

REES, W. An historical atlas of Wales, from early to modern times. 2nd ed. Cardiff, the Author, 1951. vii, 73p. 71 pl. of maps. (Reprinted London, Faber, 1966 [*i.e.,* 1967]. 25s.).

First published 1959.
71 line-maps illustrating various aspects of Welsh history (geological, political, ecclesiastical, social, economic, industrial and educational) from its origins to approximately the end of the 19th century, with adequate textual description.

942.9 (093):016

BRITISH RECORDS ASSOCIATION. Handlist of Scottish and Welsh record publications. The Scottish section, by P. Gouldesbrough and A. P. Kup; the Welsh section, by I. Lewis. London, the Association, 1954. 34p. (B.R.A. Publications pamphlet no. 4).

See entry at 941.1 (093):016.

942.9 (094.5)

JONES, T. I. J., *ed.* **Acts of Parliament concerning Wales, 1714-1901.** Cardiff, Univ. of Wales Press, 1959. xiv, 344p. 35s.

Contains a transcription of the long titles of private and public acts relating to Wales, arranged chronologically.

Caernarvonshire

942.92

CAERNARVONSHIRE. COUNTY RECORD OFFICE. Guide to the Caernarvonshire Record Office, by W. Ogwen Williams. Caernarvon, Caernarvonshire County Records Joint Committee, 1952. 45p.

Official records; deposited records; miscellanea.

Merioneth

942.925

BOWEN, E. G., and GRESHAM, C. A. History of Merioneth. Dolgelly, Merioneth Historical and Record Society, 1967-. v. 1-. illus. (incl. pl.) maps.

v. 1: *From the earliest times to the age of the native princes.* 1967. 63s.
v. 2: *The early Middle Ages to the making of the Shire.*
v. 3: *The modern period.*
Primary aim—"the study of the history of the county, including family history, literature, folklore, archaeology, and . . . antiquities" (*Foreword*); also a concise account of Merioneth up to the 20th century. (V. 3 will probably be in 2 parts.) V. 1 has abbreviated titles of reference, p. xiv-xv, 12 plates and appendices A-D (D: Maps of Roman roads in Wales).

Denbighshire

942.932

DENBIGHSHIRE. COUNTY LIBRARY. Bibliography of the county. Ruthin, Denbighshire County Library, 1935-37. 3v.

pt. 1: *Biographical sources.*
pt. 2: *Historical and topographical sources.*
pt. 3: *Denbighshire authors and their works.*

A rev. ed. of pt. 2 appeared in 1951 and a supplement, 1955-57 (56p.), in 1959 (Sections: list of periodicals; Denbighshire in general; towns, A-Z, with sub-dviisions).

The three parts are easily the most comprehensive printed bibliography for any Welsh county and together constitute a remarkable tool for the study of Denbighshire local history.

Flintshire

942.935

FLINT. COUNTY LIBRARY. Bibliography of the county of Flint. pt. 1, **Biographical sources,** compiled by E. R. Harries. Mold, Flint County Library, 1953. 70p.

A sound example of a county list of biographical sources.

Cardiganshire

942.95

JONES, G. L. Llyfryddiaeth Ceredigion, 1600-1964: a bibliography of Cardiganshire. Aberystwyth, Llyfryddiaeth Ceredigion, 1967. 3v. 40s.

1. *Ardaloedd Ceredigion—Cardiganshire localities.*

2. *Awduron Ceredigion—Cardiganshire authors, A—Jones, Joseph.*
3. *Awduron Ceredigion—Cardiganshire authors, Jones, Josiah—Y.*

Germany

943:016

DAHLMANN, F. C. Dahlmann-Waitz. Quellenkunde der deutschen Geschichte. Bibliographie der Quellen und der Literatur zur deutschen Geschichte. 10. Aufl. hrsg. in Max-Planck-Institut für Geschichte von H. Heimpel und H. Geuss. Stuttgart, Hiersemann, 1965-. Lfg. 1-. ea. DM.25.

First published 1830; 9th ed. 1931-32 (2v.). The 10th ed. is to be in 8v., with coverage up to 1945. The general plan of the 9th ed. is to be followed: a general section, including auxiliary subjects such as methodology, palaeography, diplomatic; sections on aspects of German history (*e.g.,* legal, military, economic, ecclesiastical, literary, art and music); and the major part, a chronologically arranged bibliography of German history. Sections (*Lieferungen*) are being published, as and when completed. Lfg. 6 (1967), items 45-176, deals with libraries, museums, palaeography, epigraphy, handwriting, diplomatic, etc. A list of *c.* 1,200 journals appears in Lfg. 1. A substantial revision of what is the basic bibliography for German history.

943:016

INSTITUT FÜR ZEITGESCHICHTE. Alphabetischer Katalog. Sachkatalog. Länderkatalog. Biographischer Katalog. Boston, Mass., G. K. Hall, 1966. 11v. $725 (U.S. and W. Germany); $797 (elsewhere).

A photolithographic reproduction of the author, subject, regional and biographical catalogues of the library of the Institute, which specialises in the history of National Socialism, the Third Reich and the Weimar Republic (*i.e.,* post-1918). The *Alphabetischer Katalog* (4v.) consist of *c.* 55,000 card entries; the *Sachkatalog* (5v.), of *c.* 78,000 card entries; and the other catalogues (each 1v.) of *c.* 19,000 and *c.* 13,500 entries respectively.

The Institute also produces a serial bibliography of current history, *Vierteljahreshefte für Zeitgeschichte,* 1953-.

943:016

JACOB, K. Quellenkunde der deutschen Geschichte des Mittelalters. Berlin, de Gruyter, 1949-52. 3v. (Sammlung Göschen, 279, 280, 284).

v. 1. 5th ed. 1949; v. 2. 4th ed. 1949; v. 3; edited by F. Weden. 1950.
The first two volumes, the work of K. Jacob, form a valuable bibliography for German history up to 1250; v. 3 is an unsatisfactory continuation, based partly on Jacob's notes, from 1250 to the end of the Middle Ages.

O. Lorenz's *Deutschlands Geschichtsquellen im Mittelalter seit der Mitte des dreizehnten Jahrhunderts* (3. Aufl. Berlin, Hertz, 1886-87. 2v.) gives comprehensive coverage of older material on the later Middle Ages from 1250, thus acting as a continuation of Wattenbach's bibliography.

943:016

Jahresberichte für deutsche Geschichte, Jahrg. 1-9/10, 11-14, 15/16. 1925-40. Leipzig, Koehler, 1927-42. 14v.; Neue Folge, Jahrg. 1-. 1949-. Berlin, Akademie Verlag, 1952-.

An annual bibliography which in effect brings the 9th ed. of Dahlmann-Waitz (*q.v.*) up to date, but is arranged on a different system. The first part of each volume is a bibliography (general works including auxiliary studies, sources and secondary works by period up to 1919, individual subjects); the second part is an evaluation of items listed in pt. 1, each section being written by a specialist in the field concerned. References to reviews.

So far the *Neue Folge* consists of bibliography; period covered is extended to 1945.

The annual *Bibliographie zur deutschen Geschichte* covered 1889-1927 (Leipzig, Teubner, 1889-1918; Dresden, Baensch, 1920-31). Issued as a supplement to the *Historische Vierteljahresschrift*, it dealt with books, pamphlets and periodical articles, plus references to reviews. Arrangement is by subject and period, with author index.

943:016

SCHOTTENLOHER, K. Bibliographie zur deutschen Geschichte im Zeitalter der Glaubensspaltung 1517-1585. Im Auftrag der Kommission zur Erforschung der Geschichte der Reformation und Gegenreformation. Leipzig, Hiersemann, 1933-40 (1956-58 reprint). 6v.; v. 7. (Supplement). 1962-.

v. 1-2: *Personnen*, A-L; M-Z; *Orte und Landschaften.* DM.170.

v. 3: *Reich und Kaiser; Territorien und Landesherren.* DM.70.

v. 4: *Gesamtdarstellung der Reformationszeit.* DM.90.

v. 5: *Nachträge und Ergänzungen.* DM.70.

v. 6: *Verfasser- und Titelverzeichnis.* DM.95.

v. 7: *Das Schrifttum von 1938-1960.* 1962-.

One of the most comprehensive bibliographies of its kind. V. 1 contains 14,652 numbered entries; v. 5, 52,199 entries (books and periodical articles). Sub-division is minute; many cross-references. V. 7 (1962-66) covers items 52,200-65,621 in 5 sections, plus supplement.

943:016

WATTENBACH, W. Deutschlands Geschichtsquellen im Mittelalter: Vorzeit und Karolinger; bearb. von Wilhelm Levison, Rudolf Buchner und Heinz Löwe. Weimar, Böhlaus, 1952-. Heft 1-.

Wattenbach's work, originally published in 1858, reached its 7th ed. in 2 v. in 1902/4. The present work is the 8th ed. of the first two sections of v. 1.

Fundamental guide to printed narrative sources for the history of the West, up to and including the Carolingians, with valuable additional material on legal sources in the *Beiheft.* Arrangement to a certain extent regional, or by schools of thought, but mainly on a personal basis, being a discussion of the works of the great philosophers and writers, *e.g.,* Alcuin.

943:016

——Deutschlands Geschichtsquellen im Mittelalter: Deutsche Kaiserzeit; hrsg. von R. Holtzmann. Tübingen, Matthiessen, 1948-. v. 1-.

8th ed. of v. 1 (section 3) and v. 2 of Wattenbach's complete work. Fundamental guide to printed sources for the history of the Holy Roman Empire from the time of the Ottos to 1250. Arrangement is mainly regional, but to some extent round certain writers, *e.g.,* Widukind von Korvei.

943:016

WIENER LIBRARY, London. **After Hitler: Germany, 1945-1963.** London, published for the Wiener Library by Vallentine, Mitchell, 1963. x, 261p. (Catalogue series, no. 4).

2,694 numbered entries (with interpolations) in 10 sections. 8: East Germany (p. 190-212). No annotations Jewish slant. Preceded by:

——From Weimar to Hitler: Germany 1918-1933. 2nd rev. and enl. ed. London, published for the Wiener Library by Vallentine, Mitchell, 1964. x, 269p. (Catalogue series no. 2).

2,990 numbered entries (with interpolations) in 6 sections. List of periodicals; index.

943 (02)

GEBHARDT, B. Handbuch der deutschen Geschichte. 8. völligneubearb. Aufl., hrsg. von H. Grundmann. Stuttgart, Union Deutsche Verlagsgesellschaft, 1954-68. 5v.

First published 1891-92.

v. 1. *Frühzeit und Mittelalter.* 1954.

v. 2. *Von der Reformation bis zum Ende des Absolutismus. 16. bis 18. Jahrhundert.* 1955.

v. 3. *Von der Französischen Revolution bis zum Ersten Weltkrieg.* 1960.

v. 4. *Die Zeit der Weltkriege*, von K. D. Erdmann. 1959.

v. 5. *Athenaion-Bilderatlas zur deutschen Geschichte.* 1968.

Arranged by period and subject, the articles in this massive compendium provide a bibliography and a framework of facts for German history from prehistoric times to 1945. V. 5 has 572 illus., 400 plates (with descriptive notes), 19 colour plates and 31 maps.

943 (03)

RÖSSLER, H., and **FRANZ, G. Sachwörterbuch zur deutschen Geschichte.** Unter Mitarbeit von Willy Hoppe [u.a.]. Munich, Oldenbourg, 1958. xl, iv, 1,472p. DM.100.

A companion volume to the authors' *Biographisches Wörterbuch zur deutschen Geschichte* (1952; see entry at 92 (43)), to which it makes references. Entries cover political and economic events (*e.g.,* Weltkrieg II), institutions (*e.g.,* Hanseatic League), countries (*e.g.,* Austria, Switzerland), places, battles (with plans) and cultural subjects (*e.g.,* Music, Literature). Compact, signed articles, with short bibliographies (*e.g.,* the article 'Hanse' runs to 6 columns, with a 6-line bibliography; 'Weltkrieg II'—15 columns, with a ½ column of bibliography). Many cross-references. An excellent work of its kind.

943 (093)
AMERICAN HISTORICAL ASSOCIATION.
Committee on War Documents. **Index of micro-
filmed records of the German Foreign
Ministry** and the Reich's Chancellery covering
the Weimar period, deposited at the National
Archives; prepared by Ernst Schwandt. Washing-
ton, the Association, 1958. vii, 95p.

Index to a series of guides to microfilms of
captured German records, containing a vast
amount of valuable information on all kinds of
economic, political and military questions from
1920 to 1945 (reviewed in *American archivist*,
v. 22, no. 4, October 1959, p. 445-9).

For the pre-Weimar periods, see the Com-
mittee's *A catalogue of files and microfilms of the
German Foreign Ministry Archives, 1867-1920*.
Washington, 1959. xliv, [643]p.

943 (093)
—— —— **Guides to German records microfilmed
at Alexandria, Va.** Washington, the Association,
1958-. v. 1-.

47 volumes of guides have so far (1958-65)
been published, ranging from v. 1, Records of
the Reich Ministry of Economics to v. 30,
Records of Headquarters of the German Army
High Command, pt. 3. A description of the
contents of the 15 most important groups of
records appears in *American Archivist*, v. 22, no.
4, October 1959, p. 433-43.

943 (093)
KENT, G. O., ed. **A catalog of files and microfilms of the German Foreign Ministry
archives, 1920-1945.** Stanford, Cal., Hoover
Institution on War, Revolution and Peace, 1962-.
v. 1-.

A joint project of the U.S. Department of
State and the Hoover Institution. "Continues and
completes the work of the *Catalogue of German
Foreign Ministry files and microfilms, 1867-1920*"
(*Preface*) (see above).

943 (-5) (03)
SCHNEE, H., ed. **Deutsches Kolonial-Lexikon.**
Leipzig, Quelle & Meyer, [c. 1920]. 3v. illus.,
maps.
See entry at 96 (03).

Austria
943.6:016
UHLIRZ, K., and **UHLIRZ, M. Handbuch der
Geschichte Österreich-Ungarns.** 2. Aufl. Graz,
Leuschner & Lubensky, 1963-. v. 1-.

First published 1927-44 (4v.) as *Handbuch der
Geschichte Österreichs und seiner Nachbarländer
Böhmen und Ungarn*.
A guide to the history of Austria-Hungary,
with ample bibliographies.

Österreichische historische Bibliographie, 1965,
by E. H. Boehm and F. Fellner, was announced
for publication in 1967 (Santa Barbara, Cal.).

943.6:930
LHOTSKY, A. Österreichische Historiographie.
Munich, Oldenbourg, 1962. 235p. (Österreich
Archiv).

A running commentary, in 20 chapters, on
Austrian historiography, from 1. 'Spätantike' to
20. 'Die Historiographie seit 1848'. 658 footnote
references. Index of names.

Czechoslovakia
943.7:016
**Bibliografie československé historie za rok
1955-.** Prague, Nákl. Československé Akademie
Ved, 1957-. Annual. (1961 v. 1965. Kcs.41.).

'Bibliography of writings in Czechoslovak history for the year 1955-'.
Continues the annual *Bibliografie české historie
za rok 1904 . . . 1941* (Prague, Nákl. Klubu His-
torického, 1905-51). Not confined to writings in
Czech.

943.7 (084.4)
Atlas československych dejin. Prague, 1965. 18,
45, 30p. maps. (London, Collet's. 195s.).

Historical atlas of Czechoslovakia. 45 pages of
coloured maps; 18 pages of text; index-gazetteer
of 30p. Page size, 20" × 16⅜".

Poland
943.8:016
Bibliografia historii polskiej. Pod red. H.
Madurowicz. Warsaw, Państwowe Wydawnictwo
Naukowe, 1965-. v. 1, pt. 1-.

Pts. 1-2, covering the bibliography of Polish
history from earliest times to 1795, form v. 1 of
a 3-volume bibliography that will extend to 1944.
V 1, pt. 1 covers general aids and history
auxiliary studies. (Reviewed in *College and
research libraries*, v. 27, no. 4, July 1966, p.
316-7).

Bibliographies covering the 19th-century:
Bibliografia historii Polski XIX wicku (Wroclaw,
1958-) and *Bibliografia historii Polski 1815-1914*
(Warsaw, P.W.N., 1954-); also the older *Biblio-
grafia historyi polskiej* by L. Finkel (Lwow (later
Cracow), 1891-1914. 3v. & 2 suppts.).

Current writings are listed in the annual
Bibliografia historii polskiej, 1944/47- (Wroclaw,
Ossolińskich, 1952-).

943.8 (02)
The Cambridge history of Poland; edited by
W. F. Reddaway [and others]. London, Cam-
bridge Univ. Press, 1941-50. 2v. maps.

v. 1: *From the origins to Sobieski* (*to 1696*).
1950. 70s.
v. 2: *From Augustus II to Pilsudski* (*1697-
1935*). 1941. o.p.
The standard work in English; a co-operative
effort still awaiting the volume of bibliography.

Noted: *Atlas historyczny Polski* (Warsaw,
P.P.W.K., 1967).

Hungary
943.91:016
Magyar történeti bibliográfía, 1825-1867. Budapest, Publishing House of the Hungarian
Academy of Sciences, 1950-. v. 1-.

Each volume of this bibliography of Hungarian history contains the following chapters: (1) General; (2) Economics; (3) Politics, law, education and schools, science, arts, the press, religion and churches; (4) Non-Hungarian peoples (national groups). Preceded by:

D. G. Kósáry's definitive *Bevezetés a magyar történelem forrásaiba és irodalmába* [Introduction to source materials and works on Hungarian history] (Budapest, Közokt. Kiadó [and other publishers], 1951-58. 3v.), which covers the period up to 1825.
A further series, covering the period 1867-1945, is planned.

France

944:016
Bibliographie annuelle de l'histoire de France du cinquième siècle à 1939. Année 1955-. Comité Français des Sciences Hstoriques. Paris, Éditions du Centre National de la Recherche Scientifique, 1956-. Annual. (Année 1964, published 1966).

Intended as a continuation of the *Répertoire bibliographique de l'histoire de France,* by P. Caron and H Stein (*q.v.*), with the terminal date advanced from 1914 to 1939, and, with the 1964 v. (published 1965), to 1945.
The 1962 v. has 8,200 entries, systematically arranged (Sciences auxiliaires de l'histoire—Histoire politique—Histoire des institutions—Histoire économique et sociale—Histoire religieuse—La France outre-mer—Histoire de la civilisation—Histoire locale). Periodical articles were drawn from *c.* 1,300 journals in a number of European languages. Detailed subject and author indexes.

944:016
CARON, P., and **STEIN, H. Répertoire bibliographique de l'histoire de France,** années 1920/21-1930/31. Paris, Picard, 1923-38. 6v. (Publicaton de la Société Française de Bibliographie).

A biennial bibliography of the history of France from the beginning to 1914, omitting the history of literature, art, science. Books and articles in periodicals published during the two years under review are listed, with explanations where necessary and notes of reviews, by subject. Indexes of persons and places.

Preceded by *Répertoire méthodique de l'histoire moderne et contemporaine . . .* (Paris, Rieder, 1899-1932. v. 1-7, 9-11), covering the years 1898-1912, with the exception of v. 8: 1907-9.

944:016
CARON, P., and others. **Répertoire méthodique de l'histoire moderne et contemporaine de la France,** pour l'année 1898-1912/13. Paris. Bellais, 1899-1914; Centre National de la Recherche Scientifique, 1965-. v. 1-.

Volumes for 1913/19 in preparation. 12v., to date V. 8: 1907-1909 (C.N.R.S., 1965. 20F.).
Planned as an annual bibliography of books and articles (arranged by subject with explanations and notes of reviews), on the lines of the *Répertoire méthodique du moyen âge français*

pour l'année, 1894-95, published by A. Vidier in *Le moyen âge* (1895-96), to cover French history from 1500. Vidier's bibliography of the Middle Ages was never continued.

944:016
COMITÉ FRANÇAIS DE SCIENCES HISTORIQUES. La recherche historique en France de 1940 à 1965. Paris, Centre National de la Recherche Scientifique, 1965. lxiv, 519p. 40F.

A classified list of French writings during the period on all areas and aspects. 6,460 entries, indicating presence of portraits, maps, etc. in classes A-U, with sub-divisions (p. 207-477). Preceded by sections. 1. 'L'enseignement et la recherche'—2. 'Les publications (Les inventaires et répertoires d'archives; Thèses; Revues)'. Author index.

944:016
MOLINIER, A., and others. **Les sources de l'histoire de France depuis les origines jusqu'en 1815.** Paris, Picard, 1901-35. 18v. (Manuels de bibliographie historique, 2-5).

Pt. 1. *Des origines aux guerres d'Italie (1494),* par A. Molinier. v. 1: Époque primitive, Mérovingiens et Carolingiens; v. 2: Époque féodale, les Capétiens jusqu'en 1180; v. 3: Les Capétiens, 1180-1328; v. 4: Les Valois, 1328-1461; v. 5: Introduction générale, Les Valois (suite), Louis XI et Charles VIII (1461-94); v. 6: Table générale. (Reprinted New York, B. Franklin, 1964. $97.50.).
Pt. 2. *Le XVIe siècle (1494-1610),* par H. Hauser. v. 1: Les premières guerres d'Italie, Charles VIII et Louis XII (1494-1515); v. 2: François I et Henri II (1515-59); v. 3: Les guerres de religion (1559-89); v. 4: Henry IV (1589-1610); provisional index of authors only.
Pt. 3. *Le XVIIe siecle (1610-1715),* par E. Bourgeois et L. André. v. 1: Géographie et histoire générales; v. 2: Mémoires et lettres; v. 3: Biographies; v. 4: Journaux et pamphlets; v. 5: Histoire politique et militaire; v. 6: Histoire maritime et coloniale, histoire religieuse; v. 7: Histoire économique, histoire administrative; v. 8: Histoire provinciale et locale. Essai sur les sources étrangères. Additions et corrections. Table générale.
The last part, covering the period 1715-1815, was never published.
A critical bibliography, arranged by subject, of the printed narrative sources for the history of France.

944:016
SAULNIER, E., and **MARTIN, A. Bibliographie des travaux publiés de 1866 à 1897 sur l'histoire de la France, de 1500 à 1789.** Paris. Presses Universitaires de France, 1932-38. 2v. (Publication de la Société d'Histoire Moderne).

A list of books and articles, with references to reviews, relating to the history of France during the period 1500 to 1789, published in the years 1866 to 1897. Arranged by subject.

Bibliographie de l'histoire de France: catalogue méthodique et chronologique des sources et des ouvrages relatifs à l'histoire de France depuis les origines jusqu'en 1789, by G. Monod (Paris,

Hachette, 1888. 420p.) is still valuable for earlier works, but it must be used in conjunction with Saulnier and Martin for more recent publications.

944 (02)
LAVISSE, E., *ed.* **Histoire de France depuis les origines jusqu'à la Révolution.** Paris, Hachette, 1900-11. 9v. in 18.

Continued by his *Histoire de France contemporaine* (Paris, Hachette, 1919. 10v.). No series for French history on a comparable scale has since been produced. The political attitude of the various contributors is moderately "left of centre".

Lavisse is still a standard work for its many sound chapters and its critical bibliographies. Relevant volumes of *Clio (see at 93 (02))* may be consulted to bring it up to date.

The less learned *Histoire de la nation française,* edited by G. Hanotaux (Paris, Plon-Nourrit, 1920-29. 15v.) is more conservative in approach.

J. Madaule, *Histoire de France* (Paris, Gallimard, 1943 2v.) is one of the best shorter histories.

944 (084.4)
BOUJU, P. M., *and others.* **Atlas historique de la France contemporaine, 1800-1965.** Paris, Colin, 1966. 234p.

461 maps and graphs, usually small (2-4 per page) in 8 chapters: 1. Le territoire national et l'administration—2. La population—3. Vie économique et financière—4. Forces politiques et opinions publiques—5. Forces et croyances religieuses—6. L'enseignement et l'instruction—7. Information, culture et loisirs—8. Les français hors de France. No index, but full contents-list. 'Orientation bibliographique', p. 218-21. "An extremely useful visual presentation of many aspects of French political, social, economic, religious and cultural life during the past 150 years" (*International affairs,* v. 43, no. 4, October 1967, p. 811.)

Sources

944 (093):016
COURTEAULT, H. État des inventaires des archives nationales, départementales, communales et hospitalières au 1er Janvier 1937. Paris, Didier, 1938. xvi, 703p. (Direction des Archives de France).

Complete list, corrected to 1 January 1937, of inventories (in print, in the press, in typescript, in manuscript, or on cards) of the collections in the national and local archive repositories of France.
Continuation: Direction des Archives de France. *État des inventaires des archives nationales, départementales, communales et hospitalières: supplément, 1937-1954* (Paris, Didier, 1955. xii, 344p.).

Les sources de l'histoire de France depuis 1789 aux Archives Nationales, by C. Schmidt (Paris, Champion, 1907. 288p.) is a guide to the resources of the Archives Nationales for the history of France since 1789, and to the use of the Archives Nationales, with notes on series worth consulting for certain specialised aspects, lists of départements, with dates of formation.

A. L. A. Franklin's *Les sources de l'histoire de France: notices bibliographiques et analytiques des inventaires et des recueils de documents relatifs à l'histoire de France* (Paris, Firmin-Didot, 1877. 681p.; reprinted New York, Kraus. $25.) is largely superseded, but it does bring together material in the great collections relating to France published up to the 1870s. Subject index.

944 (093):016
LANGLOIS, C. V., and **STEIN, H. Les archives de l'histoire de France.** Paris, Picard, 1891-93. [ii], xviii, 1000p (Manuels de bibliographie historique, 1)

Fundamental guide to the archive sources for French history in France and elsewhere, including a note on the repository concerned and a description of the classes of documents contained therein. Information on inventories is brought up to date in Courteault (*q.v.*).
Pt. 1: Archives Nationales, des ministères, départementales, municipales, et hospitalières; pt. 2: Archives relating to France in foreign archive repositories; pt. 3: Archives relating to France in French and other libraries.

944 "1789/ ":016
BIBLIOTHÈQUE NATIONALE, Paris. Département des Imprimés. **Catalogue de l'histoire de la Révolution française,** par A. Martin and G. Walter. Paris, Bibliothèque Nationale, 1936-55. 5v. in 6.

A catalogue of all the works published during the French Revolution, 1789-1799, held at the Bibliothèque Nationale. V. 1-4: authors; anonymous titles (52,144 items); v. 5: 'Journals et almanachs'.

Supplemented by *Répertoire de l'histoire de la Révolution française,* par G. Walter. *Travaux publiés de 1800 à 1940* (Paris, Bibliothèque Nationale, 1941-51. 2v.). V. 1 covers biographies; v. 2, places. V. 3 is to cover subjects.

944"1789/":016
CARON, P. Manuel pratique pour l'étude de la la Révolution française. 2. éd. [rev.] Paris, Picard, 1947. 324p.

First published 1912.
Guide for the student beginning research on the French Revolution. Chapter 1: Present state of studies, works published by commissions and societies, periodicals and collections of mémoires; chapter 2: Material in the central and departmental archives and other MS. sources; chapter 3: Contemporary printed sources; chapter 4: Bibliographies and secondary works; chapter 5: Works of reference. Valuable appendices contain hints on method, a Revolutionary calendar and list of départements.

P. Caron's *Bibliographie des travaux publiés de 1866 à 1897 sur l'histoire de la France depuis 1789* (Paris, Cornély, 1912. xlii, 831p.) is a comprehensive bibliography of 13,496 books and articles, continuing Saulnier and Martin (*q.v.*). It has references to book reviews.

944 "1789/":016
HARDY, J. D., *and others.* **The Maclure Collection of French Revolutionary materials.** Philadelphia, Pa., Univ. of Pennsylvania Press, 1964. xxix, [i], 456p.

About 12,000 entries, catalogued by volumes; v. 1-643 contain legislative proceedings, private journals and other serials; v. 644-1460, private works, topical series, miscellaneous works, etc. Meticulously arranged; no annotations. Indexes of deputies, authors (excluding deputies), committees and commissions. The Maclure Collection compares in variety with those at Cornell, Harvard, Chicago and Columbia Universities and New York Public Library. "An intelligent use of the collection, with the catalogue as a supervisor, might save the research student a year's work in French libraries" (*Times literary supplement,* no. 3411, 13th July 1967, p. 628).

944 "1789/":016
MONGLOND, A. **La France révolutionnaire et impériale:** annales de bibliographie méthodique et description des livres illustrés. Paris, Imprimerie Nationale, 1930-. v. 1-. illus.

V. 1-9: 1789-1812. To be completed in 10 v.; v. 10 to include index.
An exhaustive bibliography of books, pamphlets and articles on various aspects of life in France, 1789-1815. Arranged chronologically by years; under each year: La vie française—La tradition littéraire—Les relations littéraires avec l'étranger—La littérature nouvelle.

944 "1789/" (03)
ROBINET, J. F. E., *and others.* **Dictionnaire historique et biographique de la Révolution et de l'Empire, 1789-1815.** Paris, Librairie Historique de la Révolution et de l'Empire, 1899. 2v.

General historical, descriptive and biographical articles edited by A. Robert; constitutional and legal articles edited by J. Le Chaplain. Many biographical entries.

944-201
DOLLINGER, P., *and others.* **Bibliographie d'histoire des villes de France.** Paris, Klincksieck, 1967. xi, 755p. map. 60F.

A scholarly bibliography of 311 towns. Includes most of the towns with at least 5,000 population in 1801. Reviewed in *Bulletin critique du livre français,* v. 22, no. 5, May 1967, entry no. 70, 284.

944.1/.9:016
GANDILHON, R., and **SAMARAN, C.** **Bibliographie générale des travaux historiques et archéologiques,** publiés par les sociétés savantes de la France: **Période 1910-40.** Paris, Imprimerie Nationale, 1944-. v. 1-. (v. 1-5. 1944-61).

List of books and articles on historical and archaeological subjects published by French learned societies between 1910 and 1940; arranged A-Z by Département, then by place of publication, then by society; a note on each society and its publications is followed by an analysis of the contents of each volume of its

publications. V. 5: *Seine-et-Marne—Yonne. France d'Outre-mer et étranger* (1961. 583p.) records 19,138 publications, from 104 societies. No indication whether subject and author indexes are planned.

For earlier publications, see *Bibliographie générale des travaux historiques et archéologiques publiés par les sociétés savantes de la France* [-1885 and 1886-1900], compiled by Robert de Lasteyrie (*c.* 1888-1918), 6v. and its annual continuation: *Bibliographie annuelle des travaux historiques et archéologiques* under the same compiler, covering the years 1901-10 (1906-14 3v.; reprinted New York, 1965. £127).

944.3/.4
HILLAIRET, J. **Dictionnaire historique des rues de Paris.** Paris, Éditions de Minuit, [*c.* 1963]. 2v. illus. 180F.

Covers the streets, past and present, of Paris, A-Z. Entries give location, previous names, a house-by-house description of important buildings or other landmarks, names of celebrities who lived there and anecdotes associated with them. Index covers former street-names, hospitals, theatres, fountains, etc. mentioned in entries, but not names of celebrities. Based on the Préfecture de la Seine's *Nomenclature des voies publiques et privées* (7. éd. 1951). (Review in *College and research libraries,* v. 25, no. 4, July 1964, p. 324.)

Guide historique des rues de Paris, by C. Braibant and others (Paris, Hachette, 1965. xxxviii, 598p. illus. (Guides bleus). 38.41F.) has an entry on each street, with notes on origin. Appended list of prevôts des marchands, présidents du conseil municipal, lieutenants et préfets de police. Reviewed in *Bulletin critique du livre français,* v. 20, no. 12, December 1965, item no. 65,456.

Italy

945:016
Bibliografia storica nazionale, 1939-. Rome, Scalia Editore (subsequently Bari, Laterza), 1942-. (Giunta Centrale per gli Studi Storici). Annual. (Anno 23: 1961. 1963. L3,000).

Annual bibliography of books and articles published in Italy and outstanding foreign publications, relating mainly to Italian history and related historical subjects.

945 (02)
"Italia. Preistoria e storia". In *Enciclopedia italiana,* v. 19, p. 791-916. illus., maps.

A detailed history up to 1933 (p. 791-897) in 22 sections, followed by a list of sources (p. 897) and an extensive bibliography, arranged under periods (p. 898-916).

945 (093)
ITALY. MINISTERIO DELL' INTERNO. Archivi di Stato. **Gli archivi di stato italiani.** Bologna, 1944. x, 606p.

Separate bibliography and index are given for each archive depository.

—— — —— **Pubblicazioni.** Rome, 1951-. v. 1-.

V. 1: *Archivio di stato di Firenze* (1951) . . .
v. 54, 56: *Abbazia di Montecassino* (1964-65).

Vatican

945.61
FINK, K. A. Das Vatikanische Archiv: Einführung in die Bestände und ihre Erforschung. 2. verm. Aufl. Rome, Regenberg, 1951. xii, 185p. Published 1943.

Necessary tool for anyone proposing to work on the Vatican Archives. Introduction on the organization and history of the Archives; List of the archive groups, with brief description and notes on inventories and bibliography; List of published registers, accounts and reports of papal nuncios.

Noted: *Bibliografia dell Archivio Vaticano* (Vatican City, 1962-. v. 1-). On L. J. Macfarlane's account of the Vatican archives in *Archives,* v. 4, nos. 21 & 22, see entry at 941 (093):016.

Spain

946:016
FOULCHÉ-DELBOSC, R., and BARRAU-DIHIGO, L. Manuel de l'hispanisant. New York, Hispanic Society of America, 1920-25. 2v. (Reprinted New York, Kraus, 1959. £14.).

A basic bibliography of Spanish history and literature; almost 8,000 entries. V. 1, *Répertoires* (1. Généralités—2. Typo-bibliographies—3. Biographies et bio-bibliographies—4. Bibliographies monographiques—5. Archives, bibliothèques et musées—6. Collections dispersées. Additions). V. 2, *Collections* (check list, p. vii-x, followed by contents-listing of printed collections and series; author index).

946:016
Indice histórico español: bibliografía histórica de España e Hispano-América. Barcelona, Teide, 1953-. v. 1-, no. 1-. 3 p.a.

Produced by Centro de Estudios Históricos Internacionales, Universidad de Barcelona.
V. 9, 1963, comprises 4,143 indicative (and sometimes critical) abstracts on many aspects of Spain and, more selectively, Hispanic America. Preceded by a well-documented article (532 references), 'Historiografía de la guerra de la independencia y su epoca' desde 1952 a 1964, by J. M. Riba (p. xi-lxxiii). Annual. Indexes of authors and subjects (broad headings).

946:016
SÁNCHEZ ALONSO, B. Fuentes de la historia española e hispano-americana: ensayo de bibliografía sistemática de impresos y manuscritos que ilustran la historia política de España y sus antiguas provincias de ultramar. 3. ed. corr. y puesta al día. Madrid, Consejo Superior de Investigaciones Científicas, 1952. 3v.

First published 1919.
A comprehensive guide to printed sources and secondary works (books and periodical articles) covering Spain and Hispanic America. No evaluations. Systematically arranged within periods, with author and 3 subject indexes. About 24,000

items. Supplemented by *Indice histórico español* (q.v.).

B. Sánchez Alonso's *Historia de la historiografía española* . . . (Madrid, Sánchez de Ocaña, 1944-) is to be in 3v., of which only v. 1-2 have appeared.

The Dirección General de Archivos y Bibliotecas has as its *Publicaciones* (Madrid, 1952-. 1-.) a series of *Guías, Bibliografías* and *Catálogos de archivos y bibliotecas.* The fundamental collections in Madrid and Barcelona have already been described in the *Guías.*

946 (02)
MENÉNDEZ PIDAL, R., *ed.* **Historia de España.** Madrid, Espasa-Calpe, 1935-. v. 1-. illus., ports., facsim., maps.

v. 1,	i.	*España prehistórica.* 2. ed. 1954.
	ii.	*España protohistórica.* 1950.
	iii.	*España preromana.* 1954.
v. 2.		*España romana (B.C. 218-414 A.D.).* 2. ed. ampl. 1955.
v. 3.		*España visigoda (414-711).* 1940.
v. 4-5.		*España musulmana (711-1031).* 1950.
v. 6.		*España cristiana . . . 711-1038.* 1956.
v. 19.		*España en tiempo de Felipe II, 1556-1598.* 1958. 2v.

A monumental standard history by various authorities, with critical bibliographies appended to each chapter. V. 4-5 are simply translations of E. Lévi-Provençal's older history.

946 (02)
VICENS VIVES, J. Historia social y económica de España y América. Barcelona, Editorial Teide, 1957-59. 4v. in 5. illus., ports., facsims., maps.

1. *Colonizaciones, feudalismo, América primitiva.*
2. *Patriciado urbano, reyes católicos, descubrimiento de América.*
3. *Imperio, aristocracia, absolutismo.*
4. *Burguesia, industrialización, obrerismo.* 2 pts.
Excellent illustrations. V. 4, pt. 2 (to 1950) has about one illus. per page. a systematically arranged bibliography (p. 673-92) and a detailed, non-analytical index.

946 (03)
Diccionario de historia de España desde sus orígenes hasta al fin del reinado de Alfonso XIII. Madrid, Revista de Occidente, [1952]. 2v.

Signed articles, A-Z; the work of a team of specialists under the direction of Don Germán Bleiberg. Covers the period up to 1931. V. 2 has appended bibliography of sources (p. 1493-1519), chronology and 16 maps. "In every way scholarly and satisfactory" (*Times literary supplement,* no. 2832, 8th June 1956, p. 348).

Portugal
946.9:016
ACADEMIA PORTUGUESA DA HISTORIA. Guía da bibliografia histórica portuguesa. Lisbon, 1959-. v. 1, fasc. 1-.

Aims to cover Portugal from the 9th century to 1910 and meet the need for a comprehensive bibliography of Portuguese history.

A catalog of the William B. Greenlee Collection of Portuguese history and literature, and the Portuguese materials in the Newberry Library; compiled by D. V. Welsh (Chicago, Newberry Library, 1953. viii, 342p.) is a well-produced, systematically arranged, with author and anonymous title index.

W. B. Greenlee himself compiled "A descriptive bibliography of the history of Portugal" (*Hispanic American historical review,* v. 20, no. 3, August 1940, p. 491-516), which aims to give a survey of the chief sources, in both Europe and the Orient.

946.9 : 016
OLIVEIRA MARQUES, A. H. de. Guía do estudiante de história medieval portuguesa. Lisbon, Edições Cosmos, [1964]. 285, [39]p.

A running commentary in 7 chapters, covering bibliographies, atlases and dictionaries, handbooks, history auxiliaries, printed sources, archives and collections of manuscripts, and, finally, 'Apresentação dos resultados'. Author index.

946.9 (02)
ALMEIDA, F. de. História de Portugal. Coimbra, Almeida, 1922-29. 6v.

A standard history, with chapter bibliographies. Particularly valuable for its extensive treatment of medieval and modern constitutional and social institutions in v. 3 and 5.
The other standard history is *História monumental de Portugal,* edited by D. Peres and E. Cerdeira (Barcelona, 1928-), to be in 8v.

Russia

947 : 016
Istoriya SSSR. Ukazatel' sovetskoĭ literatury za 1917-1952 gg. Moscow, Izdatel'stvo Akademiya Nauk, 1956-58. 2v.

The basic retrospective bibliography of Soviet historical writings in Russian (books and articles) published between 1917 and 1952. V. 1 (18,825 items) covers the history of Russia from earliest times to 1861; v. 2 (10,508 items), the period 1861-1917. Arranged chronologically, with detailed sub-division. No annotations, but, explanatory extensions of title, where required, and references to reviews. Indexes of authors, place-names, etc.
V. 3 is to cover the Soviet period; pt .1 (Soviet writings on the history of the October Revolution of 1917) is scheduled for publication on the 50th anniversary, 1967.
Current writings are covered by *Novaya sovetskaya literatura po istorii, arkheologii i etnografii* (Moscow, 1934-. Monthly).

947 : 016
MAICHEL, K. Guide to Russian reference books. v. 2. **History, auxiliary historical sciences, ethnography and geography;** edited by J. S. G. Simmons. Stanford, Cal., Hoover Institution on War, Revolution and Peace, 1964. 297p. $12.

Section B, 'History of the U.S.S.R.' (p. 33-122): 633 excellently annotated entries, including atlases, biography and artists, encyclopaedias and dictionaries. Section D, 'Auxiliary historical sciences' (p. 147-170): 174 entries. Detailed author and subject index.

947 : 016
SHAPIRO, D. A select bibliography of works in English on Russian history, 1801-1917. Oxford, Blackwell, 1962. xii, [i], 106p. 10s. 6d.

Lists 1,070 books and periodical articles in 21 sections, with evaluative sectional annotations and references to reviews. Covers all aspects of Russian history. Material up to 1961, deliberately omitting more inclusive bibliographies and histories. Author index.

947 : 016 : 016
HAUPT, G. C. "Ouvrages bibliographiques concernant l'histoire de l'URSS". In *Cahiers du monde russe et soviètique,* v. 1, no. 3, April-June 1960, p. 502-12.

A survey of the material up to 1959; 51 footnote references.

L. H. Miller's "East European history" (*Library trends,* v. 15, no. 4, April 1967, p. 730-44) is mainly concerned with current bibliographies and reviewing journals on Russia and the U.S.S.R.

947 : 016 : 016
Istoriya SSSR. Annotirovannyi perechen' russkikh bibliografii izdannykh do 1965 g. Izd. 2., perer. i dop. Moscow, Kniga, 1966. 426p.

First published 1957 as *Bibliografiya russkoĭ bibliografii po historii SSSR . . . izdannykh do 1917g.* 'The history of the U.S.S.R.: an annotated list of Russian bibliographies [of the history of Russia and the Soviet Union] published up to 1965'. 1,000 annotated entries, arranged under broad subject and period headings; author and geographical indexes. Reviewed in *Library of Congress information bulletin,* v. 26, no. 5, 2nd February 1967, p. 88.

947 (084.4)
ADAMS, A. E., *and others.* **An atlas of Russian and East European history.** New York, Praeger, 1966; London, Heinemann, 1967. [xi], 204p. maps. 25s.

101 black-and-white maps, some of them with double-page spread, in five periods. The final two maps depict 'Industrial Eastern Europe, 1965' and 'The Communist world in 1961'. Text commentary on groups of maps. Sources, p. 197-8. Co-ordinates and compass-bearings not shown. Poor cartography. Reviewed in *Geographical journal,* v. 133, pt. 4, December 1967, p. 582-3. Page size, $8'' \times 5\frac{1}{4}''$.

A. F. Chew's *An atlas of Russian history: eleven centuries of changing borders* (New Haven, Conn. & London, Yale Univ. Press, 1967. x, 113p. spiral binding. 25s.) has 34 black-and-white maps (plus insets), with text facing on overleaf. Covers period from 9th century to post-1945. Clear, uncrowded maps. Spoilt, according to *Geographical journal,* v. 133, pt. 4, December

1967, p. 583, by exceptionally unimaginative and amateurish cartography. Page size, 8" × 5⅝".

947 (084.4)
KOVALEVSKII, P. E. Atlas historique et culturel de la Russie et du monde slav. Paris, Elsevier, [1961]. 216p. illus., maps. 59.50F.

16 plates of coloured maps, 630 black-and-white illustrations. Emphasis on cultural aspects. Bibliography of Western language publications (p. 202-4); author and place-name index. Well produced. Page size, 14⅜" × 10½".

947 (093)
Gosudarstvennye arkhivy Soyuza SSR: kratii spravochnik. Pod red. G. A. Belova [and others], Moscow, 1956. 508p.

'The state archives of the U.S.S.R.: a short guide'. 17 sections, the first devoted to the nine central archives and the rest to the archives of the various Soviet republics. Data on each archive: name; location; brief historical note; general description (type and extent of documents); chronological limits; and names of individuals whose papers are deposited. Bibliography on the archives covered for the period 1941-56 (p. 484-8); name index. (Based on entry B 38 in Maichel's *Guide to Russian reference books,* v. 2).

947:930
AKADEMIYA NAUK SSSR. Institut Istorii. **Istoriya istoricheskoĭ nauki v SSSR; do oktiabr'skii period. Bibliografiya.** Moscow, Nauka, 1965.

A bibliography (11,086 entries) of Russian historiography of the period up to 1917. Three main sections,—general historiography; activities of institutions and societies in the field of history; literature about regional historians.

A. G. Mazour's *Modern Russian historiography* (Princeton, N.J., Van Nostrand, 1958. 260p. illus.) is a much enlarged 2nd ed. of his *Outline of modern Russian historiography* (1939), with its short studies of individual Russian historians or groups of historians and their contributions from the 18th century onwards.

Scandinavia
948 (03)
Kulturhistorisk leksikon for nordisk middelalder fra vikingetid til reformationstid. Copenhagen, Rosenkilde & Bagger, 1956-. v. 1-. illus.

Associate publishers: Helsingfors, A-B Örnförlaget; Malmö, Allhems Förlag; Oslo, Gyldendal Norsk Förlag; Reykjavik, Bókaverzlun Ísafoldar.
v. 1-12 (1956-67): A—ORLOGSSKIB.
Encyclopædia of Scandinavian mediæval culture, published with the official support of all five countries and with five national editorial boards. Contributions are printed in Danish, both varieties of Norwegian and Swedish. Articles written originally in Finnish have been translated into Swedish, and those in Icelandic into one of the other three languages. Articles are of good length, are signed, and have excellent

bibliographies with detailed references to chapters and pages of books and periodicals. The article 'Metallhandel' (v. 11, p. 566-79) has sections on Sweden, Denmark and Norway, each with references. Two kinds of cross-reference in the text: between related topics, and between terms used in any two of the languages to a variant term used as the heading of an article in the third language. A general index is to follow; meanwhile the publishers are issuing a loose cumulative index with each volume. Some black and white illustrations in the text, usually of one column's width, and each volume has a colour plate and several half-tone plates at the end.

948-201
STOCKHOLM. UNIVERSITY. Sweden Institute for Urban History. **International bibliography of urban history. 1: Denmark, Finland, Norway, Sweden.** Stockholm, the Institute, 1960. 73p.

477 items, chiefly periodical articles. Under each country sections are: Introduction; General; Individual towns, A-Z (giving population figures in each case). Author and editor index.

Finland
948.0:016
VALLINKOSKI, J., and **SCHAUMAN, H. Suomen historiallinen bibliografia, 1544-1900.** Finsk historisk bibliografi. Bibliographie historique finlandaise. Helsinki, 1961. xix, 571p.

MALINIEMI, A. H., and **KIVIKOSKI, E. Suomen historiallinen bibliografia, 1901-1925 ...** Helsinki, 1940. xx, 527, 108p.

VALLINKOSKI, J., and **SCHAUMAN, H. Suomen historiallinen bibliografia, 1926-1950 ...** Helsinki, 1955-56. 2v.

A systematically arranged series of retrospective bibliographies of writings (books and periodical articles) on Finnish history. Includes items in other languages. Russian-language publications are included in the volumes for 1544-1900 and 1926-50, but omitted for 1901-25. Includes history of special subjects. Does not entirely displace the earlier annual bibliographies published in, or as appendices to, *Historiallinen aikakauskirja,* 1905-15, 1917, and covering 1905-16 (these also include research on Scandinavian and general history).

Norway
948.1:016
Bibliografi til Norges historie, 1916-1925; 1926-1935; 1936-1945; 1946-55. . . . Oslo, Grøndahl, 1927-.

Issued as annual supplements (*Norges historie. Bibliografi for . . .*) to *Historisk tidsskrift* (udg. av den Norske Historiske Forening), 1916- Covers books, pamphlets and periodical articles. Subject arrangement; 10-yearly author index.

Sweden
948.5:016
BRING, S. E. Bibliografisk handbok till Sveriges historia. Stockholm, Norstedt, 1934. xx, 780p.

Bibliographical guide to Swedish history. Chapters on historical method, bibliographical aids in general, archives and libraries, publishing societies, historiography, etc.; then chapters on periods of Swedish history. The index occupies the last 110 pages.

948.5:016

SETTERWALL, K. Svensk historisk bibliografi, 1771-1874. Systematisk förteckning över skrifter och uppsatser, som röra Sveriges historia. Uppsala, Appelberg, 1937.

————, **1875-1900** . . . Stockholm, Norstedt, 1907.

————, **1901-1920** . . . Uppsala, Appelberg, 1923.

948.5:016

SJÖGREN, P. Svensk historisk bibliografi, 1921-1935 . . . Stockholm, Norstedt, 1956.

948.5:016

BOHRN, H., and ELFSTRAND, P. Svensk historisk bibliografi, 1936-1950 . . . Stockholm, Norstedt, 1964.

Issued under the auspices of the Svenska Historiska Föreningen. Bibliographies of sources and secondary works (books and periodical articles), arranged by period and by subject; includes history of the arts.

Cumated from the annual *Svensk historisk bibliografi*, 1880- (1881-), supplement to *Historisk tidskrift* (Stockholm).

948.5 (093)

KUNGLIGA KRIGSARKIVET, Stockholm. A guide to the materials for Swedish historical research in Great Britain. Translated from the Swedish by Alan Tapsell. Stockholm, [Krigsarkivet], 1958, [4], 264p. illus. (Meddelanden från Kungl. Krigsarkivet, Stockholm, 5).

Arranged by repositories: Public Record Office (p. 19-59)—Parliament—Board of Customs and Excise—Commonwealth Relations Office—General Register Office—County record offices —British Museum (p. 72-152), etc. Concludes with 'Private archives in England' (p. 187-213); 'Scottish Record Office' (p. 214-26) and 'Private archives in Ireland' (p. 232-5). The main sources are briefly described. Index of persons, p. 236-64.

Denmark

948.9:016

Danske historisk bibliografi, 1943-1947. Udgivet af den Danske Historiske Forening, ved Henry Bruun. Copenhagen, Hagerup, 1956. 18, 594p.

The first of a series of 5-year bibliographies of Danish history. Systematically arranged, with subject and title indexes.

The volume covering 1932-42 (1966) has 11,830 systematically arranged entries.

Current coverage is given by the yearly bibliography in *Historisk tidsskrift* (udg. af den Danske Historiske Forening), 1896-.

948.9:016

ERICHSEN, B., and KRARUP, A. Dansk historisk bibliografi. Systematisk fortegnelse over

bidrag til Danmarks historie til udgangen af 1912. Copenhagen, Gad, 1917-27. 3v.

v. 1. *Danmarks historie. Danmarks stats- og kulturforhold.*
v. 2. *Danmarks topografi.*
v. 3. *Personalhistorie* [biography].

V. 1-2 list more than 20,000 references to sources and secondary works (books, articles, etc.); name and title indexes in v. 2. History of the arts included.

H. Bruun's *Dansk historisk bibliografi 1913 til 1942* (to be in 6v.) began publication in 1966 with v. 1. *Danmarks historie. Danmarks stats- og kulturforhold.*

Netherlands

949.2:016

PETIT, L. D., and RUYS, H. J. A. Repertorium der verhandelingen en bijdragen betreffende de geschiedenis des vaderlands in tijdschriften en mengelwerken tot op 1939 verschenen. Leiden, Brill, 1907-53. 5v.

V 1: up to 1900; v. 2: 1901-10; v. 3: 1911-20; v. 4: 1921-29; v. 5: 1930-39. Continued as *Repertorium van boeken en tijdschriftartikelen betreffende de geschiedenis van Nederland verschenen in het jaar.* 1940-. Leiden, Brill, 1943-. Triennial since the 1943 v. (*e.g., Repertorium . . . 1954-1956.* 1963. Gld. 32).

Failing a general bibliography of Netherlands history, this series provides valuable lists of material appearing in collections, serial and periodical publications up to 1939 and thereafter of similar material and separately published works. The first series may be supplemented by *Beknopte katalogus van de geschiedenis der Nederlanden (Nord en Zuid) in de Koninklijk Bibliotheek* (The Hague, K. Bibliotheek, 1922-1940?).

949.2 (084.4)

Geschiedkundige atlas van Nederland . . . Uit. door de Commissie voor den Geschiedkundigen Atlas van Nederland. The Hague, Nijhoff, 1913-[1938]. v. 1-19 (incomplete). maps.

'Historical atlas of the Netherlands'. 154 plates of maps, covering the Netherlands from prehistoric times to the present day. Page size, 20″ × 15″. 42v. of text.

949.2 (-5):016

COOLHAAS, W. Ph. A critical study of studies on Dutch colonial history. The Hague, Nijhoff, 1960. [viii], 154p.

A thoroughly revised and enlarged English ed. (commissioned and financed by the Netherlands Institute for International Cultural Relations) of Coolhaas' *Chronique de l'histoire coloniale outre-mer neérlandais* (*Revue d'histoire des colonies*, v. 44, 1957, p. 311-448).

Six main sections: 1. Archives—2. Journals, institutes, university chairs—3. Books of travel—4. The area covered by the charter of the V.O.C. (United East Indies Company)—5. The Netherlands East Indies after 1795—6. The area covered by the charter of the Westindische Compagnie . . . to the present day. Covers general works; sources; monographs; biographies; regional studies. List of abbreviated titles of the most important periodicals, A-Z. Index of personal names.

The basic bibliographies on Dutch colonial history are: Hooykaas, J. C. *Repertorium op de koloniale literatuur . . . 1595-1865* (Amsterdam, van Kampen, 1874-80. 2v. 8,410 entries) continued by *Repertorium op de literatuur betreffende de Nederlandsche kolonien* (The Hague, Nijhoff, 1895-1935. 1v. 21,373 entries; suppts. (covering 1940 onwards), 1943-).

Belgium

949.3:016

BELDER, J. de, and HANNES, J. Bibliographie de l'histoire de Belgique, 1865-1914. Louvain, Nauwelaerts, 1965. 301p. (Centre Interuniversitaire d'Histoire Contemporaine. Cahiers, 38).

The second in a series of bibliographies on the history of Belgium since 1789. The first, by P. Gérin, covered 1789-1831 (1960). A third, covering the intervening period, 1831-1865, by S. Vervaeck, is due for publication.

The Belder-Hannes volume has 2,442 numbered, unannotated entries covering all aspects of history,—general; law and institutions; internal politics and ideology; international relations of Belgium; military history; economic and social history; history of Belgian expansion (Congo, p. 159-211); intellectual and scientific life; education; religious history; press; local history. Author and subject indexes.

949.3:016

"Bibliographie de l'histoire de Belgique. Bibliografie van de geschiedenis van Belge." 1952-. In *Revue belge de philologie et d'histoire.* v. 31, 1953-. Annual.

The 1965 instalment, in *Revue belge de philologie et d'histoire,* v. 44, no. 4, 1966, p. 1217-1312, covers items 7575-9003. Three main sections: 1. Bibliographies et sciences auxiliaires—2. Travaux généraux—3. Histoire par époques (to 1965). Clear layout: authors in bold, titles in italics. Covers all aspects of Belgian history.

949.3:016

GÉRIN, P. Bibliographie de l'histoire de Belgique, 1789—21 juillet 1831. Louvain, Nauwelaerts, 1960. 430p. (Centre interuniversitaire d'histoire contemporaine. Cahiers 15).

3,385 numbered, unannotated entries, systematically arranged. Covers all aspects of history. Basic works are asterisked; locations in 7 libraries, including the Bibliothèque Nationale, Paris, Author index; subject index (non-analytical, *e.g.* more than 200 unspecified entries under 'Révolution de 1830').

949.3:016

PIRENNE, H. Bibliographie de l'histoire de Belgique: catalogue méthodique et chronologique des sources et des ouvrages principaux relatifs à l'histoire de tous les Pays-Bas jusqu'en 1598 et à l'histoire de Belgique jusqu'en 1914. 3. éd. rev. avec la collaboration de H. Nowé et H. Obreen. Brussels, Lamertin, 1931. viii, [7]-440p.

2nd ed. 1902.

The only work of its kind, being an essential guide to the sources and secondary works for the history of the Low Countries up to 1598 and of Belgium, thereafter, of individual provinces and periods.

Switzerland

949.4:016

BARTH, H. Bibliographie der Schweizergeschichte, enthaltend die selbständig erschienenen Druckwerke zur Geschichte der Schweiz bis Ende 1912. Basle, Basler Buch- und Antiquariatshandlung, 1914-15. 3v. (Allgemeine Geschichtforschenden Gesellschaft der Schweiz. Quellen zur Schweizer Geschichte, new series, section 4, v. 1-3). (Reprinted New York, Kraus. $85.50.)

A very full bibliography (35,000 items) of sources and secondary works (books and periodical articles, by period (v. 1) and by subject (v. 2-3). Includes history of the arts and a lengthy section, 'Personengeschichte'.

Supplemented annually by *Bibliographie der Schweizergeschichte,* appearing for the years 1913-19 as supplements to *Anzeiger für Schweizerische Geschichte,* and for 1920-34 as supplements to *Zeitschrift für schweizerische Geschichte.* Now published by Eidg. Drucksachen- und Materialzentrale.

949.4:016

SANTSCHY, J.-L. Manuel analytique et critique de bibliographie générale de l'histoire suisse. Berne, Lang, 1961. 250p. 60*s.*

506 numbered entries, with lengthy, critical annotations, and contents lists of issues of journals. Pt. 1, Introduction. Pt. 2, 'Les grands instruments de la bibliographie générale de l'histoire suisse' (4 chapters, covering general guides to Swiss history, and selective, exhaustive (*e.g.,* national bibliographies) and current bibliographies of Swiss history). Author and anonymous title index; subject index.

949.4 (03)

Dictionnaire historique et biographique de la Suisse, publié avec la recommandation de la Société Générale Suisse d'Histoire . . . Neuchâtel, Administration du Dictionnaire, 1921-34. 7v. & suppts. 1-2. illus.

German edition as *Historisch-biographisches Lexikon der Schweiz.*

A major Swiss reference tool, covering all aspects of history; particularly rich on biographies, with genealogical data. Signed articles, with bibliographies; well illustrated.

Byzantium

949.5:016

ASSOCIATION INTERNATIONALE DES ÉTUDES BYZANTINES. Dix années d'études byzantines: bibliographie internationale, 1939-48, publ. avec le concours de l'Unesco. Paris, École des Hautes Études, 1949. 180p.

Contributions from 10 countries, listing nearly 3,000 books and periodical articles published in those countries in the ten years under review on various aspects of Byzantine studies.

See also Cambridge medieval history, v. 4 (2nd ed. 1966-67. 2v.) *at 94 "04/14" (02).*

Yugoslavia

949.71:016

TADIC, J., *ed*. **Ten years of Yugoslav historio-graphy,** 1945-55, Belgrade, "Jugoslavija", 1955. 686p. (Yugoslav National Committee for Historical Studies).

Essays (with full bibliographical details) on ten years of historical studies in Yugoslavia written in French and English for the Tenth International Congress of the Historical Sciences in Rome, 1955.

Muslim East

95/96 (=927):016

SAUVAGET, J. **Introduction to the history of the Muslim East:** a bibliographical guide. [English ed.], based on the 2nd ed. as recast by Claude Cahen. Berkeley & Los Angeles, Univ. of California Press, 1965. xxi, 252p. $6.95.

Originally as *Introduction à l'histoire de l'Orient musulman* (1943; éd. refondue. 1961). Running commentary in 3 pts.: 1. The sources of Muslim history (chapters 1-9)—2. Tools of research and general works (chapter 10: General information; 11: Special disciplines; 12: Dynastic series and tribal genealogies; 13: The main outlines of Muslim history)—3. Historical bibliography (chapters 14-25). Index of names. Many references to periodical articles.

95/96 (=927) (02)

HITTI, P. K. **History of the Arabs,** from the earliest times to the present. 7th ed. London, Macmillan, 1960 (reprinted 1963). xxiii, 822p. (Papermacs series). 30s.

First published 1937.
The standard history in English, noted for command of sources and meticulous accuracy. The author, Professor Emeritus of Semitic Literature, Princeton University, has made repeated journeys to all the major countries treated in the book. Six parts: 1. The pre-Islamic age—2. The rise of Islam and the Caliphal state—3. The Umayyad and 'Abbāsid Empires—4. The Arabs in Europe: Spain and Sicily—5. The last of the medieval Moslem States—6. Under the Ottoman rule. Numerous footnote references. Detailed, analytical index, p. 759-822.

An English translation of pts. 1-2 of B. Spuler's *Geschichte der islamischen Länder* (Leiden, Brill, 1952-59, pts. 1-3. (Handbuch der Orientalistik, Bd. 6)) is entitled *The Muslim world: a historical survey* (pt. 1. The age of the Caliphs; pt. 2. The Mongol period). (Leiden, Brill, 1960. 2v. D.fl.41). Pt. 3 of the original German was entitled *Neuzeit* (1959).

95/96 (=927) (084.4)

HAZARD, H. W., *comp*. **Atlas of Islamic history.** 3rd ed., rev. and corr. Princeton, N.J., Princeton Univ. Press, 1954. 49p. maps. (Princeton Oriental studies, v. 12).

First published 1951; 2nd ed. 1952.
Maps cover the Islamic world up to 1953; also the Near East, the Crusades, the Ottoman Empire, the Middle East and the Far East. 20 maps on the right-hand page and historical data on the left-hand page facing. Appendices: conversion table of dates; index of place-names. Page size (oblong): $11'' \times 14\frac{1}{2}''$.

95/96 (=927) (084.4)

ROOLVINK, R., *and others*. **Historical atlas of the Muslim peoples.** Amsterdam, Djambatan, 1957; London, Allen & Unwin, 1958. x, [1], 40p. of maps.

52 coloured maps, covering the period 612 B.C. to the 20th century. The final map is 'Islam in the U.S.S.R.'. The maps themselves are not attractive: some are too small, colouring is not pleasing and hill shading is rather heavy. The Middle Ages receive a particularly generous quota of maps. No index-gazetteer. Page size, $10'' \times 12''$.

95/96 (=927):930.2

ROSENTHAL, F. **History of Muslim historio-graphy.** Leiden, Brill, 1952. xi, 558p.

Work of much erudition on a subject otherwise neglected. In the absence of a bibliography of Muslim history, this work, together with C. Brockelmann's *Geschichte der arabischen Literatur* (Weimar, 1898-1902), v. 1-2 (new ed., Leiden, 1943-49) and Supplement. v. 1-3 (Leiden, 1937-42), provides a necessary basis for work on Muslim history.
A 2nd revised ed. of Rosenthal is in preparation. It will include a new chapter on Al-Iji's methodology of historical writing.

Asia

95 (02)

PHILIPS, C. H. **Handbook of Oriental history.** London, Royal Historical Society, 1951 (reprinted 1963). viii, 265p. (Royal Historical Society. Guides and handbooks, no. 6). 60s.

A basic handbook for westerners embarking on studies relating to Oriental history. Five sections (on the Near and Middle East, India and Pakistan, South-East Asia and the Archipelago, China and Japan, each by a specialist on the area) contain guidance on the following subjects for each area: romanization of words; personal names; place-names; glossary of basic words; systems of dating; dynasties and rulers.

According to *Bibliography, documentation, terminology* (v. 8, no. 3, p. 126), the international Council on Archives' *Guide to the resources of the history of Asia* will be begun in 1969.

South-East Asia

95-012:016

HAY, S. N., and CASE, M. H. **South-East Asian history:** a bibliographic guide. New York, Praeger, 1962. [xi], 138p. map. Mimeographed.

632 entries for books, periodical articles and dissertations. Sections A-K: A. General biblio-

graphies and reference works—B. Burma—C. Cambodia—D. Ceylon—E. Indonesia—F. Laos—G. Malaya, N. Borneo, Sarawak and Singapore—H. The Philippines—I. Thailand—J. Vietnam—K. General books, articles and dissertations. Some entries are annotated. List of book dealers specialising in materials on South-East Asia. Author and subject indexes.

J. M. Pluvier's *A handbook and chart of South-East Asian history* (Kuala Lumpur & London, Oxford Univ. Press, 1967. [*i.e.,* 1968]. xii, 58p. illus., maps, tables. 21*s.*) consists largely of tables listing rulers, governors-general, major chiefs, etc. for Burma, Laos, Cambodia, Vietnam, Malaya, Borneo, Indonesia, the Philippines, etc.

(95-012):930.2
HALL, D. G. E., *ed.* **Historians of South-east Asia.** London, Oxford Univ. Press, 1961. viii, 342p. (Historical writing on the people of Asia, 2). 50*s.*

25 chapters, by various contributors—papers presented at conferences held at the School of Oriental and African Studies, London University, 1956-58. Pt. 1: Indigenous writings (9 chapters; p. 13-104); pt. 2: Western writings (chapters 10-25; p. 107-335) (*e.g.,* 'Some aspects of Spanish historical writing on the Philippines', by C. R. Boxer, p. 200-12). Covers Malaya, Burma, Indonesia, Vietnam. Numerous footnote references. Detailed index.

The same editor has written a brief general survey, "On the study of Southeast Asian history", in *Pacific affairs,* v. 33, no. 3, September 1960, p. 268-81.

Two articles in *Library trends,* v. 15, no. 4, April 1967, have a running commentary on current bibliographical activity,—"Far Eastern history", by E. Wolff (p. 745-59; 70 references), and "History and culture of Southern Asia", by C. Hobbs (p. 760-75).

Middle East

95-015:930.2
LEWIS, B., and **HOLT, P. M.,** *ed.* **Historians of the Middle East.** London, Oxford Univ. Press, 1962. xi, 519p. (Historical writing on the people of Asia, 4). 50*s.*

41 contributions—papers presented at conferences held at the School of Oriental and African Studies, London University, 1956-58. Parts: 1. Arabic, Persian and Turkish historiography to the 12th/19th century (1-22)—2. European (including Russian) historical writing on the Near and Middle East, from the Middle Ages to the present day (23-32)—3. Modern Middle Eastern historical writing (33-38)—4. General theories (39-41). Footnote references. Detailed index.

China

951:016
CHESNEAUX, J., and **LUST, J. Introduction aux études d'histoire contemporaine de Chine, 1898-1949.** Paris, Mouton, 1964. 148p. (Maison des Sciences de l'Homme. Matériaux pour l'Étude

de l'Extrême-Orient moderne et contemporain. Travaux 2). 40*s.*

About 600 briefly annotated entries. Author's name in romanised form precedes name in Chinese characters. 7 sections: 1. Introduction—2. Quelques points de repère—3. Bibliographie générale (including doctoral theses and research periodicals, ceased and current, p. 31-43)—4. Sources de caractère général (archives, etc.)—5. État des questions, par période—6. État des questions, par publications (*e.g.,* economic history; military history; biography)—7. Appendices (1. Transcriptions—2. Noms de personne). Index (romanised); index (Chinese characters). Attractively produced.

951 (084.4)
HERRMANN, A. An historical atlas of China. Redrawn under the supervision of N. S. Ginsburg. Chicago, Ill., Aldine Publishing Co.; Edinburgh, Univ. Press, 1966. xxxii, 88p. maps. $12.50; 80*s.*

First published 1935, as *Historical and commercial atlas of China.*

The new edition adds 10 new plates on contemporary China, bringing the total number of map plates to 64. The new maps cover China, 1936; Manchuria; and modern China (agriculture; ethnology; transportation; mining and industry). Appended: Selected bibliography and list of map sources (3p.)—Index of geographical and proper names—List of 2,922 Chinese characters—Corrigenda. Separate place-name index for historical as opposed to modern maps, possibly to avoid confusion between different spellings and to facilitate location. Reviewed in *Surveying and mapping,* v. 27, no. 2, June 1967, p. 335; and *Economic geography,* v. 43, no. 4, October 1967, p. 370-1.

951:930
BEASLEY, W. G., and **PULLEYBLANK, E. G.,** *ed.* **Historians of China and Japan.** London, Oxford Univ. Press, 1961 (reprinted 1962). viii, 351p. (Historical writing on the people of Asia, 3). 50*s.*

19 chapters, by various contributors—papers presented at conferences held at the School of Oriental and African Studies, London University. Typical contributions: 'Chinese biographical writing', by D. C. Twitchett; 'Modern Japanese economic historians', by Hugh Borton; 'British historical writing on Japan', by G. F. Hudson. Footnote references. Index, "chiefly of historians and histories".

951:930
HAN, Yu-shan. Elements of Chinese historiography. Hollywood, Hawley, 1955. x, 246p.

Valuable guide to the work of Chinese historians, indicating problems involved and the Chinese approach to history Important lists of historians and their works, and of terms used. Each work cited given in Chinese characters, in transliteration and in translation More emphasis is placed on works in Chinese than in the still valuable *Chinese traditional historiography,* by C. S. Gardner (1938).

Communist China

951.0:016

HSÜEH, Chün-tu. The Chinese Communist movement, 1921-1937: an annotated bibliography . . . Stanford, Cal., Hoover Institution on War. Revolution and Peace. 1960. viii, 131p. (Hoover Institution bibliographical series, 8). $2.50.

359 titles; preceded by a list of general reference works.

951.0:016

────── **The Chinese Communist movement, 1937-1949:** an annotated bibliography . . . Stanford, Cal., Hoover Institution on War, Revolution and Peace, 1962. x, 312p. (Hoover Institution bibliographical series, 11). $5.

The second volume comprises c. 863 titles "selected from the extensive holdings of books, pamphlets, periodicals, newspapers and transcripts in the East Asian Collection of the Hoover Institution". Excludes Chinese translations of works in other languages, literary publications by Communists and Communist-front organizations, and all articles except those preprinted in pamphlet form. 23 sections; authors and titles in Chinese characters, following romanised form. Appendix 1: A list of personal, corporate and geographical names appearing in annotation—2. List of publishers.
To be continued into the post-1949 period.

Japan

952:016

KOKUSAI BUNKA SHINKŌKAI. KBS bibliography of standard reference books for Japanese studies, with descriptive notes. V. 3. **History and biography,** pt. 1: History. Tokyo, K.B.S., 1963. [ii], 197p.

383 numbered and well annotated items. 6 sections, the first dealing with research, survey histories, special fields, dictionaries, chronologies, atlases and series) and the others with periods. Relevant biography is included. Title, author and publisher in romanised form with each followed by the Japanese characters. Glossary; author index.

952:016

HALL, J. W. Japanese history: a guide to Japanese reference and research materials. Ann Arbor, Univ. of Michigan Press, 1954. xi, 165p. (Univ. of Michigan, Center for Japanese Studies, Bibliographical series no. 4).

1,551 numbered and briefly annotated entries in 12 sections that are wide-ranging: 1. Bibliographies (nos. 1-202)—2. Reference works—3. Historical sources—4. Periodicals—5. Survey histories . . . 8. Education—9. History of religion, thought and philosophy—10. Literature—11. Arts and crafts—12. Applied science. Author and title in romanised form, then in Japanese characters. "It is assumed that Western materials pertaining to Japan are adequately covered in the bibliographies of Pagès, von Wenckstern, Nachod, Praesent-Haenisch, Pritchard, Gaskill, etc. . . . " *(Editor's Foreword)* Appended list of publishers.

Noted: *Index for 'Japanese history: a guide . . .',* prepared by the School of Oriental Studies, University College, Canberra (33p. Not for sale).

952:016

WENCKSTERN, F. von. A bibliography of the Japanese Empire; being a classified list of all books, essays and maps in European languages relating to Dai Nihon published in Europe, America and in the East. London, Kegan Paul, 1895-1907. 2v.

Continued by:

952:016

NACHOD, O. Bibliographie von Japan [1906-37] . . . Leipzig, Hiersemann, 1928-40. 6v.

Various publishers. V. 1-2 of Nachod were also published as *A bibliography of the Japanese Empire, 1906-26* (London, Goldston, 1928).
The two bibliographies cover books and periodical articles published 1859-1937, and range over all branches of knowledge. Wenckstern, v. 1, includes a facsimile reprint of: Pagès, L. *Bibliographie japonaise* (Paris, 1859. 68p.); v. 2 includes a supplement to Pagès, and 'A list of the Swedish literature on Japan', by V. Palmgren (21p.). Wenckstern has c. 16,000 entries; Nachod, 33,621.

952:930.2

BEASLEY, W. G., and **PULLEYBLANK, E. G.,** *ed.* **Historians of China and Japan.** London, Oxford Univ. Press, 1961. viii, 351p. (Historical writing on the people of Asia, 3). 50s.

See entry at 951:930.2.

India

954:016

CASE, M. H. South Asian history, 1750-1950: a guide to periodicals, dissertations and newspapers. Princeton, N.J., Princeton Univ. Press; London, Oxford Univ. Press, 1968. viii, 561p. 166s. 6d.

About 17,000 entries, some annotated, covering the Indian sub-continent. Periodical articles (p. 27-381) cover political, economic, social and cultural history. Author, univ. and subject indexes to dissertations.

Noted: Wilson, P. *Government and politics of India and Pakistan, 1885-1955: a bibliography of works in Western languages* (Univ. of California, Institute of East Asiatic Studies: Modern India project. Bibliographical study (no. 2). Berkeley, Cal., [1956]. [ii], viii, 357p.),—5,294 entries.

954:016

GREAT BRITAIN. INDIA OFFICE. Catalogue of European printed books. India Office Library, Commonweath Relations Office. Boston, Mass., G. K. Hall, 1964. 10v. $335.

110,000 card and sheaf-catalogue entries, plus sheaf entries, photolithographically reproduced on 7,225 pages. Covers c. 90,000 v. in European languages, but excludes translations from Oriental languages. V. 1-2, author catalogue in sheaf form for accessions up to 1936; since 1936, author and subject catalogues (v. 3-6); v. 7-9, subject catalogue (post-1936); v. 10, Periodicals catalogue. A companion volume reproduces the index of post-1936 European manuscript accessions. "Particularly strong in art and archaeology, history, philosophy and religion, linguistics, anthropology, and economics and politics, the collection includes many official British and Indian publications" (G. K. Hall. *Annual catalog of reference works, May 1968*, p. 29).

Noted: Marshall, D. N. *Mughals in India: a bibliographical survey* (London, Asia Publishing House, 1967-. v. 1-). V. 1: *Manuscripts*. xix, 634p. 100*s*.

954 (02)
The Cambridge history of India. Edited by E. J. Rapson and others. Cambridge, Univ. Press, 1922-53 (reprinted 1957-64). v. 1, 3-6 and supplementary v. illus. (pl.), maps. £15.

v. 1: *Ancient India*. 1922. xxii, 684p. 34 pl., 4 maps.
v. 2: Never published.
v. 3: *Turks and Afghans*. 1928. xxxii, 752p. 51 pl., 7 maps.
v. 4: *Mughal period*. 1937. xxvii, 693p. 25 pl., 6 maps.
v. 5: *British India, 1497-1858*. 1929. xxii, 683p.
v. 6: *The Indian Empire, 1859-1918*. New ed. (Delhi, S. Chand & Co.), 1964. xxix, 759p.

Supplementary volume: *The Indus civilization*, by Sir Mortimer Wheeler (3rd ed. 1968. xi, 144p. illus., pl., plans. 18*s*. 6*d*., 45*s*.), first published 1953.
V. 5-6 form v. 4-5 of the *Cambridge history of the British Empire* (entry at 941-44 (02)).
The new ed. of v. 6 comprises "The Indian Empire, with chapters on the development of administration, 1818-1858", edited by H. H. Dodwell, and "The last phase, 1919-1947", by R. R. Sethi (10 chapters added to the original volume). V. 5 contains 32 chapters by specialists; chapter bibliographies, p. 609-53; chronological table, p. 613-8. Footnote references; no maps or illustrations.

954 (02)
A Comprehensive history of India. Published under the auspices of the Indian History Congress and the Bharatiya Itihas Parishad. Bombay, Orient Longmans, 1957-. illus., maps.

To be completed in 12 v.
v. 2: *The Mauryas & Satavahanas, 325 B.C.-A.D. 300;* edited by K. A. Nilakanta Sastri.
V. 2 has 25 chapters by various contributors and covers religions, social life, language and literature. art and architecture, coinage, etc. Bibliography, p. 812-39; chronology, p. 840-4; analytical index, p. 855-918; 88 illustrations; 7 black-and-white folding maps.

954 (026):016
SUTTON, S. C. A guide to the India Office Library. London, H.M. Stationery Office, 1952. iv, 62p. illus. (pl.). (2nd ed. 1967. 196p. 27*s*. 6*d*.).

Coverage: Printed books (European and Oriental)—Manuscripts (European and Oriental) — Drawings — Photographs — Miscellaneous

properties. Appendix I: 'A handlist of the principal manuscript collections'.

954 (03)
BHATTACHARVA, S. A dictionary of Indian history. Calcutta, Univ. of Calcutta, 1967. 889p. Rs.40.

About 3,000 entries, arranged A-Z, covering all periods. The reviewer in *Times literary supplement* (no. 3,423, 5th October 1967, p. 945) finds in it an admixture of opinion and fact, with comments "not invariably impartial".

954 (084.4)
DAVIES, C. C. An historical atlas of the Indian peninsula. 2nd ed. Madras, Oxford Univ. Press, 1959 (reprinted 1963). 96p. maps. 6*s*. 6*d*.

First published 1949.
47 clearly lettered black-and-white maps. Maps 2-17 cover periods up to A.D. 1398; maps 18-36 cover the modern period up to 1908. The remainder deal with factors bearing on history: monsoons, rainfall, languages, economic products, population density, religions and railways, with a map of India in 1939, and a cover-map of the Indian Union and Pakistan, 1947. Maps are on the right-hand page, with relevant notes and bibliography on the page facing. Page size, $9\frac{3}{4}'' \times 7\frac{1}{4}''$.

954 (093):016
LANCASTER, J. C. A guide to lists and catalogues of the India Office records. London, Commonwealth Office, 1966. iii, 26p. *Gratis*.

The records of the India Office, indispensable source material for research in British-Indian historical studies, are "the product of successive administrations from the foundation of the East India Company in 1600 to the dissolution of the India Office and of the Burma Office in 1947" (*Preface*). Brief descriptions of 30 lists and catalogues of records.
Detailed guides to the records of particular departments of the E.I.C. and the India Office (*e.g.*, Accountant General's Department; Political and Secret Department; Military Department) are being prepared for publication. A revised ed. of Sir W. Foster's *Guide to the India Office records, 1600-1858* (1919) is also in preparation.

954:930.2
PHILIPS, C. H., *ed.* **Historians of India, Pakistan and Ceylon.** London, Oxford Univ. Press, 1961. x, 504p. (Historical writing on the people of Asia, 1). 50*s*.

Papers presented at conferences held at the School of Oriental and African Studies, London University, 1956-58. Pt. 1 deals with historiography current in the early empires; pt. 2 covers historical writings in the periods of European dominance and nationalist movements. Footnote references (for chapter 26, 115 such references). Index. Reviewed in *Pacific Affairs*, v. 36, no. 1, Spring 1963, p. 78-85.

Noted: Hardy, P. *Historians of medieval India: studies in Indo-Muslim historical writing* (London, Luzac, 1960. [vii]. 146p. 35*s*.).

Iran

955:016

WICKENS, G. M., and **SAVORY, R. M. Persia in Islamic times:** a practical bibliography of its history, culture and languages . . . ; edited by W. J. Watson. Montreal, Institute of Islamic Studies, McGill Univ., 1964. 57p.

The Cambridge history of Iran is to be published in 8 v. by the Cambridge Univ. Press. Board of editors: A. T. Arberry, H. W. Bailey, B. Gray, A. K. S. Lambton, R. Levy, L. Lockhart and R. C. Zachner. V. 1, *The land of Iran,* edited by W. B. Fisher and v. 5, *The Seljug and Mongol periods,* edited by J. A. Doyle, were both published in 1968, each at 75s.

Turkey

956.0:016

KORAY, E. Türkiye tarih yayinari bibliografyasi, 1729-1955. 2nd ed. Istanbul, Maarif Basimevi, 1959. xv, 680p.

First published 1954.
Bibliography of Turkish historical literature, in 2 parts: 1729-1928 and 1928-1955. Each part includes general works, collections, encyclopaedias, works on individual countries, and on special aspects. Index of titles and authors.

Türk traih kurumu yayinlarindan (12 seri. Ankara, Türk Tarih Kurumu Basimevi, 1948-. no. 1-.) is a series of bibliographies of various aspects of Turkish history, published by the Turkish Historical Association. V. 1: Archaeology, epigraphy and historical geography, by A. M. Mansel; v. 2: Coins of the classical period, by E. Bosch.

Malaysia

959.5 (093)

TREGONNING, K. G., *ed.* **Malaysian historical sources:** a series of essays on historical material, mainly in Malaysia on Malaysia. Singapore, History Department, Univ. of Singapore, 1962 (reprinted 1965). vi, 130p. 25s.

16 essays, by various hands (*e.g.,* 'Chinese sources for the history of the Malay Peninsula in ancient times'; 'Introduction to English language sources in Malaya'; 'Malay historical works'; 'The Jahore archives'; 'Indonesia's national archives'). Individual items are described; detailed inventory of archives.

Africa

96:016

MEYER-HEISELBERG, R. Bibliografi over Afrikansk historie: nyere litteratur om Afrika syd for Sahara. Udsendt af UNESCO-Skoleprojektet, 1963. [Copenhagen?], 1963. xi, 88p. Mimeographed.

'South of the South Sahara' here includes Sudan, Ethiopia, Somalia, Eritrea and Tchad. About 500 entries, with *c.* 20-word annotations. 31 chapters, 7-31 having sections of bibliography. (7. General handbooks on the African continent —8. Works on special subjects—9. Historical maps and atlases—10. African pre-history (including archaeology)—11. Art.—12. Folklore, customs—13. African history, south of the Sahara—14-27. Areas and countries—28. Exploration—29. Travel—30. Periodicals—31. Author index. Material listed is mostly in English.

German Africa: a select annotated bibliography, by J. Bridgman and D. E. Clarke (Stanford Cal., Stanford Univ., Hoover Institution on War, Revolution and Peace, 1965. ix, 120p. (Hoover Institution. Bibliographical series, 19). $3) records *c.* 800 books and pamphlets, microfilms, and periodical and newspaper files in four main groups: General—German East Africa—German Southwest Africa—Togo and Cameroon. Most items are in German; no index. Some important gaps (see review in *Library materials on Africa,* v. 3, no. 1, May 1965, p. 12).

96:016

MONIOT, H. Bibliographie pratique sur l'histoire de l'Afrique. Paris, Institut Pédagogique National, 1963. 55p. (Documentation pédagogique africaine, no. 6).

About 250 annotated entries, grouped under 8 headings: Les revues—Ouvrages généraux non historiques—Études historiques d'ensemble—Préhistoire et protohistoire—Afrique occidentale et centrale—Outre régions d'Afrique continentale —Colonisation, période coloniale, aspects du premier XXᵉ siècle—Madagascar. Important items are given one, two or three asterisks. No index.

Noted: Thomas, P. A. *Bibliographies on African history, anthropology and social studies* (2nd draft. Zaria, N. Nigeria, Ahmadu Bello Univ. (Kashim Ibrahim Library), 1967. 41p.).

96 (03)

SCHNEE, H., *ed.* **Deutsches Kolonial-Lexikon.** Leipzig, Quelle & Meyer, [*c.* 1920]. 3v. illus., maps.

An encyclopaedia covering all aspects of German colonial rule, particularly in Africa; entries (*e.g.,* flora and fauna; diseases; geography) A-Z. Includes map, town plans, illustrations (some coloured), tables. Many cross-references; bibliographies.

96 (084.4)

FAGE, J. D. An atlas of African history. London, Arnold, 1958. 64p. maps. 30s.

62 black-and-white maps, covering the continent and its parts from 410 A.D. to 1957. Considerable detail is included in the legends and the captions are usually descriptive. Good, clear lettering. Bibliography ('Acknowledgements'), p. 60; Index of proper names, p. 61-64. Page size, 8½″ × 11″.

966 (093)

Guide to materials for West African history in European archives. London, Univ. of London, Athlone Press, 1962-. v. 1-.

v. 1: *Materials for West African history in the archives of Belgium and Holland,* by P. Carson. 1962. 86p. 21s.
v. 2: *Materials for West African history in Portuguese archives,* by A. F. C. Ryder. 1965. vi, 92p. 25s.

v. 3: *Materials for West African history in Italian archives,* by J. R. Gray and D. S. Chambers. 1965. viii, 104p. 35s.

v. 4: *Materials for West African history in French archives,* by P. Carson. 1968. viii, 170p. 42s.

V. 2 deals with the main sources, in Lisbon, Coimbra, Evora and Porto. Individual volumes and documents are singled out for special mention. Detailed abstract of manuscript catalogues, indexes, etc., with an indication of inadequacies. Index. Most of the items in v. 3 are in Rome, notably the Vatican archives.

The International Council on Archives is to follow up its *Guide to sources of Latin American history* with a *Guide to the sources of the history of Africa.* (See *Bibliography, documentation, terminology,* v. 5, no. 4, July 1965, p. 111-2.)

967:016
INSTITUT PÉDAGOGIQUE NATIONAL. Service de Recherches Pédagogiques pour les Pays en Voie de Développement. **Notes de bibliographie sur l'histoire de l'Afrique noire.** Paris, the Institute, 1963.

967 (02)
History of East Africa. Oxford, Clarendon Press, 1963-. v. 1-. maps.

v. 1 [to 1898], edited by R. Oliver and G. Mathew. 1963. 63s.

v. 2 [from the 1890's to the close of World War II], edited by V. Harlow and E. M. Chilver. 1965. 84s.

To be completed in 3 volumes. The outcome of a parallel initiative on the part of the governments of Tanganyika and Uganda and of the Colonial Social Science Research Council. Studied from an African as well as a European standpoint.

V. 1 "directly surveys results of original research" (*Prefatory note*). 12 chapters; 10 contributors. Chapter bibliographies, p. 457-80; analytical index. The reviewer in *Commonwealth journal* (v. 6, no. 5, October 1963, p. 218), while conceding that it is an indispensable work of reference, complains of the lack of general maps locating the many place-names mentioned (the sketch-maps are no substitute), and of unevenness in treatment. "The strength of the book lies in its account of the political history of the indigenous societies of East Africa" (*Africa,* v. 34, no. 2, April 1964, p. 177-9).

968:016
MULLER, C. F. J., *and others, ed.* **A select bibliography of South African history:** a guide for historical research. Pretoria, Univ. of South Africa, 1966. xii, 215p. R.2.50; R.3.50.

2,521 numbered entries, sometimes annotated, for books only. 31 sections in 3 parts: 1. General (section 1: Aids to research—bibliographies; guides to archival and other sources; historiography; etc.)—2. Periods (sections 4-16)—3. Subjects (sections 17-31, including biographies and autobiographies). Authors' index; index to persons mentioned in titles, biographies and autobiographies.

968 (02)
The Cambridge history of the British Empire. v. 8. **South Africa, Rhodesia and the High Commission Territories.** 2nd ed. General editor, E. A. Walker. Cambridge, Univ. Press, 1963. 1087p. 105s.

First published 1936.

32 chapters, by specialists, covering the political, economy, cultural, ethnological, constitutional and legal history, from ancient times to date. Chapter bibliographies, p. 917-1017; analytical index, p. 1019-87.

A reprint of G. McCall Theal's classic and comprehensive *History of South Africa, 1505-1884* (London, Allen & Unwin, 1919-26. 11v.) appeared in 1964 (Cape Town, Struik. R.70). V. 1 deals with the ethnography and condition of South Africa before 1505; v. 2-11 cover the history in 3 periods: before 1795 (v. 2-4); since 1795 (v. 5-9); and 1873-84 (v. 10-11).

968 (093)
Archives year book for South African history. Pretoria, Government Printer, 1938-. Annual. ea. R.5.

"This important series consists of original contributions in Afrikaans, English and Nederlands, based on the South African archival sources. The series deals with numerous aspects of South African history and is regarded as a mirror of the activities of history students at South African universities" (R. Musiker. *Guide to South African reference books* (4th ed. 1965), p. 73).

Americas

97/98:016
INSTITUTO PANAMERICANO DE GEOGRAFÍA E HISTORIA. Comisión de Historia. **Program of the history of America.** Mexico, the Institute, 1953. 18v.

series 1: *Período indígena.* 10v.
2: *Período colonial.* 4v.
3: *Período nacional.* 4v.

Three series of introductory volumes, largely bibliographical in approach, each written in English, by either a North American or a Latin American specialist.

97/98:016
NEW YORK. PUBLIC LIBRARY. Reference Department. **Dictionary catalog of the history of the Americas.** Boston, Mass., G. K. Hall, 1960-61. 28v. $1280 (outside U.S., $1408).

A photolitho reproduction of the original dictionary catalogue on cards. 21 cards per page, reaching p. 13,774 with v. 14. About 600,000 cards will be reproduced eventually, in 28v. The cards include Library of Congress printed cards, handwritten entries, etc. Headings are only legible with difficulty. Entries cover many articles in learned periodicals. Entries under some headings are very extensive (*e.g.,* 'Folklore', p. 7255-7336). "Essentially a series of bibliographies", states the *Introduction,* which notes the material brought together under 'American languages', 'Indians, North America'; 'Indians, South America'; 'Pioneer life', 'U.S.-Foreign relations', 'Irish in the U.S.'; 'Germans in the U.S.', 'Cuba', 'Mexico', etc. There are 44 entries under 'Dwight Eisenhower'; entries under 'Brazil' occupy p. 2658-2821; entries under 'Cuba', p. 5516-5617. V. 28 ends on p. 26,397.

Canada

(See also 973:016.)

971:016
"Recent publications relating to Canada". In *The Canadian historical review.* Toronto, Univ. of Toronto Press, 1920-. v. 1-. Quarterly.

Preceded by *Review of historical publications relating to Canada;* edited by G. M. Wrong [and others] (v. 1-22: 1896-1918. Toronto, Briggs, for the Univ. of Toronto Press, 1897-1919. 22v.).
The *Review* lists *c.* 100 books and periodical articles p.a. in this section (1. Canada's Commonwealth and international relations—2. History of Canada—3. [Provinces]—4. Educational history —5. Religious history . . . 8. Arts and sciences). The June 1967 issue (v. 48, no. 2) also carries 23 book reviews (p. 159-89) and a list of books received (p. 190-5).

Canadian Public Archives. *Register of postgraduate dissertations on history and related subjects* (Ottawa, Canadian Historical Association, 1966-. v. 1-. Annual) continues the lists previously published in *The Canadian historical review.*

971.016
TORONTO. PUBLIC LIBRARY. A bibliography of Canadiana; being items in the Public Library of Toronto, Canada, relating to the early history and development of Canada. Toronto, Public Library, 1934. 828p. 1st supplement, 1959. 333p. $7.50.

Covers books, pamphlets and broadsides on Canada published 1534-1867. The two volumes contain 6,286 numbered and fully annotated entries in chronological order; author and selected subject index.

971 (02)
The Canadian centenary series: a history of Canada. W. L. Morton, executive chief. Toronto, McClelland & Stewart, 1963-. illus., maps.

To be completed in 17v. Each volume deals with a particular period and is assigned to a specialist, to be handled n his own way.
V. 12, *The critical years: the Union of British North America, 1857-1873,* by W. L. Morton (1964. xii, 322p. illus., maps) has 14 chapters; chapter notes (p. 279-304); bibliography (p. 305-14: manuscripts; printed sources; newspapers and contemporary periodicals; pamphlets; secondary authorities); analytical index. The outstanding multi-volume history of Canada.

The *Cambridge history of the British Empire.* v. 6. *Canada and Newfoundland* (Cambridge, Univ. Press, 1930) is still in print. (90s.).

971 (03)
BURPEE, L. J. S. Oxford encyclopaedia of Canadian history. Oxford, Univ. Press, 1926. 699p. illus. (Makers of Canada. Anniversary ed., v. 12).

Supersedes Burpee, L. J., and Doughty, A. C. *Index and dictionary of Canadian history* (1911). Well documented, including lists of source material.

971 (03)
STORY, N. The Oxford companion to Canadian history and literature. Toronto, London, New York, Oxford Univ. Press, 1967. [xx], 935p. maps. 120s.

Comprises *c.* 1,900 articles (1,500 on Canadian history). Valuable for entries on people, places, periodicals and societies of Canada; also extensive bibliographies (*e.g.,* 'Arcadia: bibliography', p. 5-6; 'Rebellion of 1837: bibliography', p. 699-700). 5 appendices (2: Governors General, etc.). List of titles referred to (title—date—author), p. 866-935,—*c.* 6,000 items.

971 (084.4)
KERR, D. G. G., *ed.* **A historical atlas of Canada.** 2nd ed. Toronto, Nelson, 1966. ix, [i], 120p. illus., maps.

First published 1960.
Sponsored by the Canadian Historical Association. 154 two-colour maps in 6 parts: 1. Environment and prehistory—2. Exploration and development, to 1763—3. British North America, 1763-1867—4. Founding a nation, 1867-1914—5. Wars and expansion since 1914—6. Main economic and political trends since 1867 (largely bar diagrams, with some explanatory text). 'Selected bibliography', p. 114-5; index of *c.* 1,250 entries. Clearly drawn, uncluttered maps. "This is altogether a most satisfactory atlas, both in appearance and for use" (*The geographical review,* v. 52, no. 3, July 1962, p. 426). Page size, 12¼″ × 9¼″.

Mexico

972:016
RAMOS, R. Bibliografía de la historia de México. Mexico, Cuadernos Americanos, 1956. viii, 772p. $10.

4,776 numbered items (books, pamphlets, manuscript sources) under authors, A-Z. Some anonymous items (*e.g.,* nos. 1, 2, 4, 11, 12, 14) are entered under the indefinite article). No subject index. Locations in 18 libraries.

The same author's *Bibliografía de la revolución mexicana* (2. ed. Mexico, 1959-60. 3v.) has 5,067 entries on the Mexican revolution of 1910.

972 (093.2)
MILLARES CARLO, A. Repertorio bibliográfico de los archivos mexicanos y de los europeos y norteamericanos de interés para la historia de México. Mexico, [Biblioteca Nacional de México, Instituto Bibliográfico Mexicano], 1959. 366p.

Entries, sometimes annotated, for books, pamphlets and periodical articles on archives and historical sources on Mexican history in Latin America, the U.S. and Europe.

Fuentes de la historia contemporánea de México. Libros y folletos. Estudio preliminar. Ordenamiento y compilación de Luís González (Mexico, El Colégio de Mexico, 1961-62. 3v.)

records 24,078 items, systematically arranged. V. 3 has author index.

Guatemala

972.81
MOORE, R. E. Historical dictionary of Guatemala. Metuchen, N.J., Scarecrow Press, 1967. 187p. $5.

Extends from pre-Columbus times to the early 1960s. "Many of the entries on historical figures constitute the only information to be found on them" (*Library journal*, v. 93, no. 8, 15th April 1968, p. 1618). Valuable bibliography, p. 179-87.

British West Indies

972.9:016
RAGATZ, L. J. A guide for the study of British Caribbean history, 1763-1834; including the abolition and emancipation movements. Washington, Government Printing Office, 1932. viii, 725p.

Comprehensive annotated bibliography, with full index. Notes MS. sources, printed official papers, books, pamphlets and articles. "Of outstanding value" (Murray, D. L. *The West Indies and the development of colonial government, 1801-1834* (1965)).

972.9:016
WILLIAMS, E. "A bibliography of Caribbean history: a preliminary essay. Part 1: 1492-1898". In *Caribbean historical review*, nos. 3/4, December 1954, p. 208-50.

A critical survey in 4 parts (general; 3 periods). Period 3 (p. 230-50): The British West Indies—The French West Indies—Haiti—The Spanish territories—The Danish territories—The Netherlands territories. Includes manuscript material, official sources (Commissions of Inquiry), memoirs and local histories.

972.9 (093)
BELL, H. C., and PARKER, D. W. Guide to British West Indian archive material in London and in the Islands. Washington, Carnegie Institution, 1926. 435p.

972.9:930.24
GOVEIA, E. V. A study on the historiography of the British West Indies to the end of the nineteenth century. Mexico, Instituto Panamericano de Geografia e Historia, Comisión de Historia, 1956. 183p.

A chronological survey, based on the printed histories available in the libraries of the University College of the West Indies and of the Institute of Jamaica. 867 footnote references to titles cited. Appended 'Chronological list of the chief works dealt with in this paper' (c. 80 titles).

972.97
BAKER, E. C. A guide to records in the Leeward Islands. Oxford, published for the University of the West Indies, by Blackwell, 1965. x, 102p. map. 63s.

Based on a survey made in 1962. An inventory

of records in Antiqua, Montserrat, Nevis, St. Christopher and the British Virgin Islands, with some descriptive notes. Includes newspapers; one of the appendices covers maps, plans and drawings. Very brief index (p. 102).

A similar guide to records in the Windward Islands, by E. C. Baker will be published in September 1968 at 63s.

972.986:016
BARBADOS PUBLIC LIBRARY, Bridgetown. **Barbadiana: a list of works** pertaining to the history of the island of Barbados; prepared . . . to mark the attainment of independence. Bridgetown, 1966. [i], 44p.

Lists c. 500 items in four sections: Historical, descriptive—Government and politics—Social and economic—Education. Includes numerous official publications. No index.

972.986 (093)
CHANDLER, M. J. A guide to records in Barbados. Oxford, published for the University of the West Indies, by Blackwell, 1965. xi, 204p. map. 63s.

Based on a survey made in 1960, and the first of a series of volumes that are to cover the records of all the territories in the West Indies. The full inventory (p. 1-164) is followed by appendices on special types of material (*e.g.*, acts and laws, newspapers, maps and plans). Detailed index.

U.S.A.

973:016
America: history and life—a guide to periodical literature. Santa Barbara, Cal., Clio Press, July 1964-. v. 1, no. 1-. Quarterly.

About 3,000 informative abstracts p.a., covering c. 500 U.S. and Canadian state and local historical society journals, plus upwards of a thousand foreign journals. Classified arrangement, with annual author and biographee index. Its fairly prompt appearance compensates for the time-lag in publication of *Writings on American history*.

973:016
Harvard Guide to American history, [edited by] O. Handlin [and others]. Cambridge, Mass., Belknap Press of Harvard Univ. Press, 1954. xxiv, 689p. 80s.

Does not supersede E. Channing, A. B. Hart and F. J. Turner. *Guide to the study and reading of American history* (Rev. ed. Boston, 1912), but lists uncritically a much greater range of material.
Pt. 1: "Status, methods and presentation": pt. 2: "Materials and tools"; pt. 3: "Colonial history and the Revolution"; pt. 4: "National growth, 1789-1863"; pt. 5: "The rise of modern America"; pt. 6: "America in the twentieth century". Detailed index.

973:016
NEVINS, A., and others, ed. Civil War books: a critical bibliography, Baton Rouge, for the U.S. Civil War Memorial Commission by Louisiana Univ. Press, 1967-. v. 1-. (v. 1. $11.50).

To be in 2v.

V. 1 has *c.* 2,500 entries, with *c.* 20-word evaluative annotations. 7 'categories': 1. Military aspects: Mobilization; organization; administration and supply)—2. Military aspects: Campaigns —3. Military aspects: Soldier life—4. Prisons and prisoners of war—5. The negro—6. The navies —7. Diplomacy. Arranged by authors, A-Z, under categories. No index.

V. 2 is to cover general works, biographies, and the government, politics, social and economic studies, state and local studies covering the Confederacy and the Union.

973:016

LARNED, J. N. The literature of American history: a bibliographical guide. Boston, American Library Association Publ. Board, 1902. 596p.; Supplements for 1900-04. 1902-05.

Classified annotated lists prepared by specialists and still of value. Author and subject indexes.

973:016

Writings on American history, 1906-. A bibliography of books and articles on United States history published during the year 1906-. New York, Macmillan, 1908-10; Washington, 1911-13; New Haven, Conn., 1914-19; Washington, 1921-40, 1948-. Price varies.

Publisher varies. Follows Larned's *Literature of American history* (q.v.) and an earlier volume, under same title, for 1902 and 1903, compiled by E. C. Richardson and others. No issues for 1904-05 and 1941-47, as yet. Now published as v. 2 of the American Historical Association's *Annual report.* From 1906-35 scope included Canada and West Indies. Latest volumes record only publications on U.S.A. and omit reviews of books. In the past 25 years only 10v. have appeared. The 1958 v. did not appear until 1966. An indispensable classified bibliography with author, subject and title index.

The cumulated *Index to the "Writings on American history", 1902-1940* (Washington, American Historical Association, 1956. 1115p.) contains additional references and subject entries not in the annual indexes, but subject entries are criticised as difficult to use and often misleading (White, C. M. *Sources of information in the social sciences,* p. 92).

973:016:016

BEERS, H. P. Bibliographies in American history; guide to materials for research. [Rev. ed.] New York, Wilson, 1942. 487p.

First published 1938.
Classifies over 11,000 titles of printed guides to materials on subjects arranged under broad headings, such as "Diplomatic history", "Economic history", "States", etc.

973 (02)

COMMAGER, H. S., and MORRIS, R. B., ed. New American nation series. New York, Harper, 1954-.

To be in 43 v.
Scholarly and readable; each volume has a bibliography and index. Examples:
English people on the eve of colonization.

1603-1660, by W. Nottestein. $5.
Coming of the Revolution, 1763-1775, by L. H. Gipson. $5.
American Revolution, 1775-1783, by J. R. Alden. $5.
America's rise to world power, 1898-1954, by F. R. Dulles. $5.
Woodrow Wilson and the progressive era, 1910-1917, by A. S. Link. $5.
Topical volumes are planned in addition to the chronological series.

So far volumes published do not supersede their predecessors, the scholarly *The American nation* series, edited by A. B. Hart (New York, Harper, 1904-18. 28v.). These were of high quality, often pioneering work, giving valuable guidance to sources and literature of each period covered.

973 (03)

ADAMS, J. T., *ed.* **Dictionary of American history.** 2nd ed., rev. New York, Scribner, 1942-63. 5v. and index; **Supplement 1, 1940-1960.** 1961; Index v. 1963. £34.

First published 1940.
Designed for general rather than scholarly use. More than 6,000 entries, with brief bibliographies after most articles. Biographies are not included, the *Dictionary* being published as a companion work to the *Dictionary of American biography.* Supplemented, in turn, by *Album of American history,* also edited by J. T. Adams (New York, Scribner, 1944-61. 5v. and index), for illustrations up to 1953, and *Atlas of American history* (q.v.). *Supplement 1, 1940-1960* updates and extends previous articles and adds new ones. The 1963 analytical index v. covers all articles in the 5v. and Supplement 1.

Concise dictionary of American history, edited by W. Andrews (New York, Scribner, 1962. 1156p. $19.50; London, Oxford Univ. Press, 1963. 105s.) is a one-volume version of the above. Some important articles are reprinted without change. Described as "admirably edited" (*Times literary supplement,* no. 3177, 18th January 1963, p. 44).

The encyclopedia of American history (New ed., edited by R. B. Morris. New York, Harper; London, Hamish Hamilton, 1961. 840p. illus., maps. 80s.) was first published in 1953. Unlike the *Concise dictionary of American history,* it does include biographical articles, but for the rest consists mainly of chronological outlines.

973 (03)

The Oxford companion to American history, by T. H. Johnson and H. Wish. New York, Oxford Univ. Press, 1966. vi, 906p. 84s.

4,710 entries (including 1,835 biographies and 699 cross-references), mostly "summaries of lives, events and places significant in the founding and growth of the nation. It gives attention to social, political and labor movements, the observations of travellers, both foreign and domestic, and includes the fields of art, science, commerce, literature, education, and law. There are also articles dealing with sports and entertainment" (*Preface*). Lengthier articles have references (*e.g.,* 'Supreme Court': 1½p.; 2 references). Tables give names and dates of persons who held high office (*e.g.,* Cabinet members). Appended text of Constitution and amendments. A reliable companion to the *Oxford companion to American literature* (3rd ed. 1956).

973 (05):016
BELLOT, H. H., *comp.* **Union list of American historical periodicals in United Kingdom libraries.** London, Univ. of London, Institute of Historical Research, 1959. viii, 41p. 10*s.*

Two main sequences—Journals; Reports of proceedings and transactions, each sub-divided into Federal, Regional, and State, territorial and local, with further divisions. About 400 entries, with locations in 97 libraries, including the British Museum, National Central Library, public, university and special libraries. Entry is under earliest form of name. Imperfections are noted. Corrects and supplements information on holdings in the *British union-catalogue of periodicals.*

973:06
AMERICAN ASSOCIATION FOR STATE AND LOCAL HISTORY. Historical societies in the United States and Canada: a handbook. [2nd ed.], compiled and edited by C. Crittenden and D. Godland. Washington, the Association, 1944. xi, 261p. $2.50.

First published 1936.
1,467 entries, giving descriptive and historical information on national, general and local societies, with notes on their publications. The main list of 904 items is supported by 564 supplementary items at the end of lists for each state.

The Association's *Directory of historical societies and agencies in United States and Canada* (Madison, Wis., the Association, 1956-. Biennial since 1959. 1963 ed. 124p. $2) updates the *Handbook* and gives address, name of secretary, date of founding, membership, number of staff, and days and hours of opening for *c.* 2,500 societies.

973 (084.4)
ADAMS, J. T., *ed.* **Atlas of American history.** New York, Scribner; London, Oxford Univ. Press, 1943 (reprinted 1967). xii, 360p. maps. 132*s.*

Designed to accompany the *Dictionary of American history* (q.v.). Carefully drawn black-and-white maps (*e.g.,* of battlefields), arranged chronologically, with index of places. "The Civil War maps do not stand up to the competition of *West Point atlas of American wars,* but, then, all history is not wars" (*Times literary supplement,* no. 3, 414, 3rd August 1967, p. 713); excellent lettering (*Cartographic journal,* v. 4, no. 2, December 1967, p. 139).

Atlas of American history, edited by E. W Fox (New York, Oxford Univ. Press, 1964. xvi, 48p. maps. 20*s.*) has 48 pages of colour maps drawn by the Cartographic Department of the Clarendon Press.

973 (084.4)
PAULLIN, C. O. Atlas of the historical geography of the United States, edited by J. K.

Wright. Washington and New York, Carnegie Institution of Washington and American Geographical Society, 1932. 162p. maps. (Carnegie Institution Publication, 401).

688 maps and descriptive text covering "Natural environment"; "Cartography, 1492-1867"; "Indians, 1567-1930"; "Explorations"; "Settlements, population and towns, 1650-1790"; "States, territories and cities, 1790-1930); and many special subjects. Excellent detail.

973 (084.4)
The West Point atlas of American Wars. Compiled by the Department of Military Art and Engineering, the United States Military Academy, West Point, New York. Chief editor, Vincent J. Esposito. New York, Praeger, 1959; London, Stevens, 1960. 2v. maps. $47.50; £15 15*s.*

V. 1 covers 1689-1900 and has 158 maps; v. 2 covers 1900-1953, with 256 maps. Maps in both volumes are printed on the right-hand page and the text on the left-hand page, giving a critical analysis of the campaign concerned. V. 2 contains 71 maps on World War I, 168 on World War II and 15 on the Korean War. Good use of outline base-maps in grey with colour overlays. Page size, $10\frac{1}{2}'' \times 14''$. According to *Military review* (v. 40, no. 2, May 1960, p. 107), "Many of the maps bear a striking resemblance to those in the two earlier volumes—*Atlas to accompany Steele's American Campaigns* and *A Military History of World War II, Atlas . . .* The new set, however, is much more complete in its coverage" and has the valuable narrative text. 'Recommended reading list' of 4 pages, a number of entries being annotated.

973 (093)
COMMAGER, H. S. Documents of American history. 7th ed. New York, Appleton-Century-Crofts, 1963. 2v.

6th ed. 1958.
Gives coverage up to 1962. Includes State charters, historic acts, proclamations and the like.

973 (093):016
CARMAN, H. J., and **THOMPSON, A. W. A guide to the principal sources for American civilization, 1800-1900, in the City of New York: Manuscripts.** New York, Columbia Univ. Press; London, Oxford Univ. Press, 1960. xlviii [1], 453p. $10; 80*s.*

Follows on *A guide to the principal sources for early American history (1600-1800) in the City of New York,* by E. B. Greene and R. B. Morris (2nd ed. New York, Columbia Univ. Press, 1953. 357p. $7.50).
30 classes, arranged alphabetically ('Architecture'; 'Boundary controversies', 'Cookery' to 'Societies'; 'Sports and recreation'; 'The theatre'). Sub-division is by states, with final chronological arrangement. A descriptive list of libraries and depositories in the City of New York precedes. Index of names, p. 405-53.

973 (093):016
CARNEGIE INSTITUTION, Washington. **Guides to manuscript materials for the history of the**

United States. Washington, Carnegie Institution, 1906-43. 23v. Prices vary. (Reprinted New York, Kraus, 1965. $275; $325).

Indispensable. Covers material in American and in European archives.

The following volumes are valuable for British as well as American history: *Guide to the manuscript materials for the history of the United States to 1783 in the British Museum, in minor London archives and in the libraries of Oxford and Cambridge,* by C. M. Andrews and F. G. Davenport (1908. 499p.); *Guide to the materials for American history, to 1783, in the Public Record Office of Great Britain,* by C. M. Andrews (1912-14 2v.); *Guide to materials in London archives since 1783,* by C. O. Paullin and F. L. Paxon (1914. 642p.); *Guide to British West Indian archive material in London and in the Islands,* by H. C. Bell and D. W. Parker (1926. 435p.).

Catalog of manuscripts of the Massachusetts Historical Society (Boston, Mass., G. K. Hall, 1969. 7v. $650; $715 (outside U.S.)) will reproduce *c.* 250,000 cards, with entries for authors, subjects and geographical areas.

973 (093)
CRICK, B., and **ALMAN, M.,** *ed.* **Guide to manuscripts relating to America in Great Britain and Ireland.** Under the general supervision of H. L. Beales. London, published for the British Association for American Studies by Oxford Univ. Press, 1961. xxxvi, 667p. 84*s.*

Locates and briefly describes "all manuscripts in Great Britain and Ireland relating to the history and literature of the American colonies and the United States" (*Introduction*) which do not fall within the scope of three previous, complementary works—Andrews, C. M. *Guide to the materials for American history, to 1783, in the Public Record Office of Great Britain;* Andrews, C. M., and Davenport, F. G. *Guide to the manuscript materials for the history of the United States to 1783, in the British Museum, in minor London archives, and in libraries of Oxford and Cambridge;* and Paullin, C. O., and Paxon, F. C. *Guide to materials in London archives for the history of the United States since 1783.* (For a full list of *Guides to manuscript materials for the history of the United States* (1906-43. 23v.), see Winchell, C. M. *Guide to reference books* (8th ed. 1967), p. 475.)

Includes political, economic, social and intellectual history as well as American domestic and international affairs, and direct U.S. influence in Great Britain and Ireland Arrangements is primarily by countries—England (p. 3-472), Wales and Monmouthshire (p. 475-88), Scotland (p 491-520), Northern Ireland (p. 523-30) and Eire (p. 533-53). 'England' is sub-divided alphabetically by counties (London, p. 119-346), and then into repositories—record offices, private collections, libraries, public churches, etc.

Supplements to Crick and Alman's *Guide to manuscripts relating to America . . .* are contained in the *Bulletin* of the British Association for American Studies (now superseded by *Journal of American studies* (April 1961-. v. 1-).

973 (093)
HAMER, P. M., *ed.* **A guide to archives and manuscripts in the United States.** Compiled for the National Historical Publications Commission. New Haven, Conn. & London, Yale Univ. Press, 1961. xxiii, 775p. $12.50; 100*s.*

"In the present guide there is information about the archival and manuscript holdings of some 1,300 depositories in the 50 states of the United States, the District of Columbia, Puerto Rico, and the Canal Zone" (*Introduction*). Holdings (brief title or descriptions) are listed in inventory form, with dates of coverage under the name of the depository (*e.g.,* Historical Society of Pennsylvania, p. 530-4). Reference is made to publications of the societies, etc., concerned. Notes on bibliographical guides, p. xix-xx. Index of proper names and subjects, p. 643-775. On the shortcoming of the index, see *Special libraries,* v. 52, no. 7, September 1961, p. 425; there is also a critical review in the *Times literary supplement,* no. 3,125, 19th January 1962, p. 48.

973 (093):016
UNITED STATES. NATIONAL ARCHIVES. List of National Archives microfilm publications. Washington, National Archives, 1953. vi, 98p. facsims.

Detailed lists of microfilms made since 1940 of the archives of the Supreme Court, Department of State, Department of the Interior and other national records, giving prices.

973:930.23
BELLOT, H. H. American history and historians. A review of recent contributions to the interpretation of the history of the United States. Univ. of London, Athlone Press; Norman, Univ. of Oklahoma Press, 1952. xi, 336p. maps. 25*s.*

Historiography of America in the United States, 1890-1940, with valuable bibliographical notes attached to each chapter.

The critical method in historical research and writing, by H. C. Hockett (New York, Macmillan, 1955. 330p.) is a rewritten and expanded ed. of his *Introduction to research in American history* (2nd ed. 1948) and is primarily concerned with American history; bibliography, p. 265-95.

973:930.24
CARRUTH, G., *ed.* **The encyclopedia of American facts and dates.** 3rd ed. New York, Crowell, 1962. vi, [i], 758p. $6.95.

First published 1956.
Chronologically arranged in four parallel columns, 986-1961, covering: politics, government, etc.; literature and art; science, industry, economics, etc.; sports, fashion, etc. Good use of bold type. 117-page analytical index (*c.* 15,000 entries).

J. N. Kane's *Famous first facts: a record of first happenings, discoveries and inventions in the United States* (3rd ed. New York, Wilson, 1964. 1165p. $18) has entries A-Z (p. 9-619), plus extensive indexes,—index by years; index by days of the month; index to personal names; geographical index.

973 "1763/1783"
BOATNER, M. M. Encyclopedia of the American Revolution. New York, McKay, [c. 1966]. xviii, [i], 1287p. illus., geneal. tables, diagrs., maps. $17.50.

About 1,616 entries and cross-references, including c. 600 biographies, for the period 1763-1783. Military emphasis; numerous maps of battlefields (e.g., Yorktown campaign, p. 1230-50; 2 maps; bibliography note of 1 page). Frequently quotes secondary authorities ('Permissions', p. v-vi) (e.g., the article on Henry Clinton (9 cols.) has many quotations. Bibliography and short-title index, p. 1253-73. The author was Assistant Professor of Military History at the U.S. Military Academy.

Manuscripts of the American Revolution in the Boston Public Library: a descriptive catalogue is to be published by G. K. Hall (Boston, Mass.) in 1969 ($15; $16.50 (outside U.S.)—c. 1,250 items, chronologically arranged, with a detailed index of topics.

973 "1861/1865" (03)
BOATNER, M. M. The Civil War dictionary. New York, McKay, 1959. xvi, 974p. illus., diagrs., maps. $15.

Similar in pattern to the author's *Encyclopedia of the American Revolution* (q.v.). Bibliography, p. 970-4.

973 "1861/1865" (093.2)
MUNDEN, K. W., and BEERS, H. P. Guide to Federal archives relating to the Civil War. Washington, U.S. General Services Administration, National Archives & Record Service, 1962. x, 721p.

Arranged by departments, with detailed notes; analytical index, p. 505-721. A companion volume, *Guide to the archives of the government of the Confederate States of America,* is being compiled.

Latin America

98:016
HUMPHREYS, R. A. Latin American history: a guide to literature in English. Issued under the auspices of the Royal Institute of International Affairs. London, Oxford Univ. Press, 1958. xiii, 197p. 25s.

First published 1941 as *Latin America: a selective guide to publications in English;* rev. ed. 1949.
2,089 numbered items, surveyed mostly in running commentary form. Covers books and periodical articles, but not Parliamentary and Congressional Papers; excludes the fields of archaeology and ethnology, and omits British, French and Dutch West Indies and U.S. possessions. 14 sections: 1. General reference works—2. Bibliographies and guides—3. Periodicals—4. General histories and comprehensive works—5. The land and the environment—6. Ancient peoples and cultures—7. The Spanish Empire in America . . . 12. The Republics of South America since 1830—13. The Central American and Island Republics since 1830—14. Mexico since 1830. Appended list of 69 periodicals cited. Biographical index; indexes of authors, editors and

translations. Author is Professor of Latin American History, University of London.

The 'History' section in the *Handbook of Latin American studies,* no. 26, *Humanities* (1964) covers items 344-1291, with a general introduction (p. 38-42) and appended list of abbreviations of periodicals cited (p. 131-4). Author index to v. 1-28 (1936-66) is to be published by Univ. of Florida Press in September 1968.

H. Keniston's *List of works for the study of Hispanic-American history* (New York, Hispanic Society of America, 1920. xviii, [1], 451p.) lists c. 20,000 items on the history up to 1830. 'Hispanic America in general', p. 1-141; individual countries (including the Antilles and the former Spanish provinces of the U.S. Starred items are those generally recognised as authoritative or fundamental. Index of territorial divisions.

Noted: Velásquez, M. del Carmen. *Guía bibliográfica para la enseñanza de la historia en Hispano-América* (Mexico, Instituto Panamericano de Geografía e Historia, Comissión de Historia, 1964. 507p.).

98:016
WILGUS, A. C. Histories and historians of Hispanic America. [Rev. ed.] New York, Wilson, 1942. xii, 144p. (Reprinted London, Cass, 1966. 55s.).

First published 1936.
Chapters on 16th, 17th, 18th, 19th and 20th century works, sub-divided geographically, with "A selected list of bibliographical and biographical collections and aids", and index of authors.

98 (03)
MARTIN, M. R., and LOVETT, G. H. An encyclopedia of Latin American history. New York, Abelard-Schumann, 1956. vi, [1], 392p. $6. (Rev. ed., revised by L. R. Hughes. Indianapolis, Bobbs-Merrill, 1968. vi, 368p. 105s.).

"The purpose is to provide in convenient form the essential information concerning the political, economic, and cultural development of all Latin-American nations from the earliest times to the present" (*Preface*). Includes biographies and defines some Spanish-American terms. About 3,000 brief entries, with data up to 1955. No illustrations, maps or bibliographies. A handy compendium for quick reference.

98 (093.2)
HILL, R. R., ed. The national archives of Latin America. Edited for the Joint Committee on Latin American Studies of the National Research Council, the American Council of Learned Societies and the Social Science Research Council. Cambridge, Mass., Harvard Univ. Press, 1945. xx, 169p. illus.

The archival resources of 20 republics are considered in as many chapters. That on *Brazil: Arquivo nacional* (Rio de Janeiro) (p. 17-35) has headings: History—Problems—Administrators—Regulations—Duties of the Director and Section chiefs—Indexes and inventories—Material in the Archive—Publications. Detailed, analytical index.

Noted: *Guide to materials on Latin America in the National Archives,* by J. P. Harrison (Washington, General Services Administration, National Archives and Records Service, National Archives, 1961-. v. 1-).

The first volume of the International Council on Archives' Sources of national history series, *Guide to sources of Latin American history,* was due to be published in 1966, but it has yet to appear.

98 (093.2)

SPAIN. MINISTERIO DE EDUCACIÓN NACIONAL. Dirección General de Archivos y Bibliotecas. **Guía de fuentes para la historia de Ibero-América** conservadas en España. Madrid, 1966-. v. 1-.

Archive repositories are systematically described in 5 groups. Data on each include address, hours of opening, services, general description, bibliography, and documents on America and The Philippines. Category and locality indexes.

Brazil

981:016

COMISSÃO DE ESTUDO DOS TEXTOS DA HISTÓRIA DO BRASIL. Bibliografia de história do Brasil. 1943-. [Rio de Janeiro], Ministério das Relações Exteriores, Seção de Publicações, 1944-.

The combined issue for 1953-54 (1962) has sections for books (with short signed reviews), p. 17-201; periodical and serial publications (Brazilian; foreign); periodical and journal articles (*c.* 1,800; p. 205-353). Author index.

An annotated bibliography which covers a wide range of subjects is *Manual bibliográfico de estudos brasileiros,* by R. Borba de Moraes and W. Berrien (Rio de Janeiro, Souza, 1949. xi, 895p.). The 5,845 items are arranged in sections—art, law, education, geography, history, literature, music, general reference books (p. 779-88) and sociology. Author index.

981 (02)

INSTITUTO HISTÓRICO E GEOGRÁFICO BRASILEIRO. Diccionario histórico, geográfico e etnographico do Brasil; commemorativo do primeiro centenário da independencia. Rio de Janeiro, Imprensa Nacional, 1922. 2v. illus., maps.

v. 1. *Brasil.* v. 2. *Estados.*

981:930.24

RODRIGUES, J. H. Historiografía del Brasil siglo XVI. Mexico, Instituto Panamericano de Geografía e Historia, Comisión de Historia, 1957. 102p.

V. 1 of a projected major work by Brazil's leading authority on historiography. "The volume is slightly marred by the hispanization of some titles" (*Handbook of Latin American studies,* no. 22 (1960), entry no. 3852).

—— **Historiografía del Brasil siglo XVII.** Mexico, Instituto Panamericano de Geografía e Historia, Comisión de Historia, 1965. 261p.

"Done with the meticulous care characteristic of the author's bibliographic works" (*Handbook of Latin American studies,* no. 28 (1966), entry no. 1320).

Argentina

982:016

Bibliografia argentina de historia. No. 1: 1960-. La Plata, Argentina, Ministerio de Educación de la Provincia de Buenos Aires, Instituto Bibliográfico, 1964-.

Annual listing of articles and books on Argentine history (in the broadest sense). Some entries are abstracts. No. 2: 1961 (published 1964): 1,570 references. Briefly reviewed in *Handbook of Latin American studies* (v. 28 (1966), entry no. 11).

982 (03)

Diccionario histórico argentino. Publicado bajo la dirección de Ricardo Piccinilli [and others]. Buenos Aires, Ediciones Históricas Argentinas, [*c.* 1955]. 6v.

A feature of this extensive dictionary is the large number of biographies (deceased persons only). Articles are unsigned and run to about ½ column to 1 column in length on the average. Important persons, places, etc., are given fuller treatment (*e.g.,* Manuel Belgrano: 9 columns; 5 lines of bibliography; Juan B. Alberdi: 6 columns; 12 lines of bibliography; Tucumán (city and province): 18 pages; ½ column of bibliography, including sources). About 2,500 double-columned pages in all; no illustrations.

982:930

CARBIA, R. D. Historia crítica de la historiografía argentina (desde sus orígenes en siglo XV). La Plata, [Universidad de la Plata], 1939. xi, 483p. Biblioteca humanidades, v. 22).

First published 1925.

A detailed survey, with 3 indexes—of persons mentioned, of works reviewed by the author, and of books and publications merely cited. "Unique in the bibliography of Latin American history. For no other country have we a survey so complete, so authoritative, so consonant with the methods and ideals of modern historical science" (*Hispanic American historical review,* v. 20, no. 4, November 1940, p. 581).

Supplemented by "Fuentes de la historiografía argentina en el siglo XX", by E. de Gandía (*Revista interamericana de bibliografía,* v. 17, no. 1, January/March 1967, p. 3-50), which includes subject histories, history auxiliaries and historical fiction.

Chile

983 (03)

FUENTES, J., and **CORTÉS, L. Diccionario histórico de Chile.** Santiago, Editorial del Pacifico, 1965. 329, [35]p. $12.50.

Articles A-Z on Chilean history, including precolonial and Spanish colonial periods. Weighted in favour of biographies, but includes articles on political events and organisations, historic sites and battles. No references appended to articles, but a bibliography at end of volume (p. 361-4). Reviewed in *College and research libraries*, v. 27, no. 1, January 1966, p. 50.

Indonesia

991:930
SOEDJATMOKO, M. A., *and others, ed.* **An introduction to Indonesian historiography.** Ithaca, New York, Cornell Univ. Press, 1965. xxviii, 427p. maps. 78s.

A symposium prepared under the auspices of the Modern Indonesia Project, Southeast Asia Program, Cornell University.
22 scholars survey available source materials in Asia, and Europe and discuss the current state and problems of Indonesian historical scholarship, suggesting approaches and methods that might be useful for future research (Ad Orientem. *Books on Africa and the Orient. Catalogue six, 1966,* item no. 1902). Includes bibliographical references.
See also entries at 949.2 (-5)=016.

Philippines

991.4:016
WELSH, D. V., *comp.* **A catalogue of printed materials relating to the Philippine Islands,** 1519-1900, in the Newberry Library, Chicago, Newberry Library, 1959. viii, 179p.

Catalogue of 1,938 items, systematically arranged: 1. General reference—2. Political history—3. Ecclesiastical history—4. Social and cultural history—5. Local history. Author index. Well produced.

New Zealand

993.1:016
HOCKEN, T. M. **A bibliography of the literature relating to New Zealand.** Wellington, J. Mackay, Government Printer, 1909. xii, 619p.

Arranged chronologically, 1643-1909 (p. 1-487), with a Maori bibliography appended (p. 499-547). About 4,000 annotated entries; index of authors and subjects.
Supplement to Hocken's 'Bibliography of New Zealand literature'; compiled by A. H. Johnstone (Auckland, Whitcombe & Tombs, 1927. ii, 73p.) adds items (unannotated) for the period 1694-1909, plus 'Principal additions to New Zealand literature since 1909' (p. 50-59). Index of authors and subjects.

Further supplemented, for the period up to 1909, by L. J. B. Chapple's *Bibliographical brochure containing addenda and corrigenda to extant bibliographies of New Zealand literature* (Dunedin, Read, 1938. 47p.).

993.1:016
"Writings on New Zealand history". In *Historical studies, Australia and New Zealand.* Melbourne, Department of History, Univ. of Melbourne, 1940-. 2 p.a. 35s. p.a.

An annual survey of books, with running commentary. Thus, the v. 11, no. 43, October 1964

issue contains "Writings on New Zealand history, 1/7/63—30/6/64" (p. 422-3), reviewing 17 items. *Historical* studies also annually records "Research work in Australian and New Zealand universities. Theses completed" and "Accessions of manuscripts" (arranged under libraries receiving), as well as reviewing *c.* 12 items at some length in each issue.

993.1 (02)
The Cambridge history of the British Empire. v. 7, pt. 2. **New Zealand.** Cambridge, Univ. Press. 1933. xiii, 309. o.p.

13 chapters by specialists. Bibliography, p. 259-90: pt. 1. Manuscript sources and official publications (Australia; Great Britain; New Zealand); pt. 2. Other works.

993.1 (093.2):016
NEW ZEALAND. DOMINION (now NATIONAL) ARCHIVES. **A guide to the Dominion Archives.** Wellington, Department of Internal Affairs, 1953. 27p.

Notes on arrangement of documents and access to them in the Dominion Archives precede a list of the principal archive groups. Appended: 'Government publications and bibliography'.
The New Zealand National Archives is publishing a *Preliminary inventory* of the archives of each of the provinces, etc. (1953-).

National Archives of New Zealand: a review and summary of work, 1966 ([Wellington], Department of Internal Affairs, 1967) includes a list of all groups and series of archives held by the National Archives, p. 25-63.

993.1 (094.5):016
WILSON, J. O. **A finding list of British Parliamentary Papers relating to New Zealand, 1827-1900.** Wellington, General Assembly Library, 1960. v, 28p. Mimeographed.

About 400 items, chronologically arranged under the following heads: Bills—Acts—Papers (House reports, accounts and papers; Command Papers) "wholly or principally concerned with New Zealand" (p. 6-17)—Minor papers. Excludes reports with some information about New Zealand where the matter is rather trivial or more readily or more lengthily available in official New Zealand reports.

Australia

994:016
FERGUSON, J. A. **Bibliography of Australia.** Sydney & London, Angus & Robertson, 1941-. v. 1-.

v. 1: *1784-1830.* 1941. 63s.
v. 2: *1831-1838.* 1945. 63s.
v. 3: *1839-1845.* 1951. 126s.
v. 4: *1846-1850.* 1955. 189s.
v. 5: *1851-1900:* A-G. 1963. £10 10s.
v. 6: *1851-1900:* H-P. 1965. £10 10s.
Covers all printed matter relating to Australia, wherever published, in the period concerned. Arranged chronologically under year of publication, with author and anonymous title index.

Covers books, pamphlets, broadsides, newspapers, periodicals and government publications. V. 4 includes addenda to v. 1-3. Locations of items in ten Australian libraries and also the British Museum. "Painstakingly compiled and spaciously and clearly set out" (*Times literary supplement*, no. 3333, 13th January 1966, p. 29). To be completed in 7 v., to 1900.

994:016

NATIONAL LIBRARY OF AUSTRALIA, Canberra. **Select list of works on Australian history.** Canberra, the Library, 1962 (revised 1965). [i], 13 l. Mimeographed.

About 200 unannotated items in this basic list. Three main sections: A. Documents and original source material—B. General works—C. Select list of biography, and works on particular questions.

The Cambridge history of the British Empire, v. 7, pt. 1: *Australia* lists all important material up to 1933 in the appended 'Bibliography: Australia and the Pacific Islands' (p. 645-718).

994:016

SPENCE, S. A. A bibliography of selected early books and pamphlets relating to Australia, 1610-1880. Mitcham, Surrey, the Author, 1952. xi, 88p. 30s.

About 1,000 items, arranged A-Z by author. "Most of the important works upon the subject are reported, including many small but desirable pamphlets whose scarcity is beyond doubt" (*Foreword*). Entries state full pagination, format, presence of maps, type of illustrations and cover reprints and various editions. Appendix: 'A list of Australian engraved portraits, etc.' (p. 85-88). Entries under Captain Cook occupy p. 18-22.

An enlarged ed., incorporates *Supplement, 1881-1900* (1955), (1956. vii, 102p. 45s.).

994:016

"Writings on Australian history". In *Historical studies, Australia and New Zealand.* Melbourne, Department of History, Univ. of Melbourne, 1940-. 2 p.a. 35s. p.a.

An annual survey, based mainly on the *Monthly book list of Australian publications,* compiled by the Commonwealth National Library. Thus v. 11, no. 41, November 1963 issue contains "Writings on Australian history, 1962" (p. 107-19), in 2 parts: 1. Separate publications (*c.* 200 items, with running commentary) —2. Periodicals (more than 150 items, arranged under authors A-Z; no annotations). Includes biography and local history. *Historical studies* also annually records "Research work in Australian and New Zealand universities. Theses

completed" and "Accessions of manuscripts" (arranged under libraries receiving), as well as reviewing *c.* 12 items at some length in each issue.

994 (02)

The Cambridge history of the British Empire. v. 7, pt. 1. **Australia.** Cambridge, Univ. Press, 1933. xix, [i], 759p. o.p.

24 chapters by specialists; includes economic, cultural and military aspects. Bibliography, p. 645-718: pt. 1, Manuscript sources and official papers and publications; pt. 2, Other sections (10 sections). Analytical index, p. 719-59.

994 (02)

CLARK, C. M. H. A history of Australia. Melbourne, Univ. Press; London, Cambridge Univ. Press, 1962-. v. 1-. pl., maps.

v. 1. *From the earliest times to the age of Macquarie.* xiv, 422p. 50s.
v. 2. *New South Wales and Van Diemen's Land, 1822-1838.* 1968. [xiii], 364p. 84s.
V. 1 covers the years up to *c.* 1824. A scholarly survey by the Professor of History, Australian National University. Many footnote references. 'A select bibliography', p. 389-410. Analytical index. Described in *Times* (2nd April 1964) as a "great bone of a book", upon which Australian historians immediately fell. V. 2 includes 'A note on sources' (p. 350-1), 17 plates (mostly portraits) and 3 maps. To be completed in 4v.

994 (091)

NATIONAL LIBRARY OF AUSTRALIA. Guide to collections of manuscripts relating to Australia. Canberra, National Library, 1965-. pt. 1-. Loose-leaf.

Pts. 1-3 describe 900 collections in 15 repositories. When completed, will contain 1,500 entries, with indexes. Noted in *Library of Congress Information bulletin,* v. 25, no. 29, 21st July 1966, p. 415-6.

994 (-013):016

CROWLEY, F. K. South Australian history: a survey for research students. Adelaide, Libraries Board of South Australia, 1966. xii, [1], 200p.

20 chapters, including 2. Australian bibliography—3. South Australian bibliography—4. General references—5. Foundation history—6. Exploration—7. Biography . . . 11. Government and politics—12. Economic history . . . 15. Social history—16. Religion—17. Education—18. War and defence—19. Aborigines. Index of names of persons. The author is Professor of History in the University of New South Wales.

INDEX

A page number followed by 'n' indicates a note.
Subject entries are in bold type.

Falley, M. D. Irish and Scotch-Irish ancestral research, 372
Familiengeschichtliche Bibliographie, 375
Family history, 373-5
Family names, 375-7
Family Welfare Association. Guide to the social services, 197
Fanning, D. Market research, 225
Far Eastern Economic Review. Yearbook, 131
Farquhar, J. N. Outline of the religious literature of India, 55
Fasti archeologia, 400
Fawcett, F. B. Court ceremonial and book of the court of King George the Sixth, 245
Feachem, R. Guide to prehistoric Scotland, 405
Feaveryear, A. E. Pound sterling, 143n
Federal Writers' Project. American guide series, 341
Federation of British Industries. E.F.T.A. sources of information, 226n
Federbush, S., *ed.* World Jewry today, 59
Fekete, M., *ed.* Prominent Hungarians, 353
Fellman, J. D., *jt. author. See* Harris, C. D., *and* Fellman, J. D.
Fellows, A. England and Wales, 333
Fêng, Yu-Lan. *See* Fung, Yu-Lan
Ferguson, J. A. Bibliography of Australia, 475
Ferguson, J. P. S., *comp.* Scottish family histories held in Scottish libraries, 374
Ferm, V. Encyclopedia of religion, 24n
Fernández de Villavicences, F., *and* Sola Canizares, F. de. Bibliografía jurídica española, 171
Ferrater Mora, J. Diccionario de filosofia, 5
Festival of Britain. Catalogue of an exhibition of 20th century Scottish books, 259
Festivals, 251
Festschriften: history, 386
Feuillet, A., *jt. author. See* Robert, A., *and* Feuillet, A.
Field, H. Bibliography of Soviet archaeology and physical anthropology, 407n
Fieldhouse's Income tax simplified, 149n
Fife County Library. Books on local subjects, 426n
Fife County Library *and* Kirkcaldy Public Libraries. Check list on books for local subjects, 426n
Fifeshire: history, 426
Fiji: area studies, 297n
Filby, P. W. Basic list of books on British genealogy and heraldry, 370n
Filip, J. Enzyklopädisches Handbuch zur Urand Frühgeschichte Europas, 397

Filosofskaya entsiklopediya, 4
Filson, F. V., *jt. author. See* Wright, G. E., *and* Filson, F. V.
Finance, 141-50
Financial Publishing Co. Consolidated tables of bond values, 146
Financial Times. Investor's guide, 146n
Finegan, J. Archeology of world religions, 53
— Handbook of Biblical chronology, 30
Fink, K. A. Vatikanische Archiv, 457
Finkel, L. Bibliografia historyi polskiej, 453n
Finland. Ministry of Finance. Economic survey, 130
— Tilastollinen Päätoimisto. Suomen tilastollinen vuosikirja, 81
— — Tilastokatsauksia-Statistiska Oversikter, 82n
Finland
area studies, 265
atlases, 323
biography, 355
economics, 130
history, 459
statistics, 81
First World War, 415-16
Firth, *Sir* C. H. Cromwell's army, 193n
Fischer, E., *and* Elliott, F. E. German & English glossary of geographical terms, 304
Fischer-Galati, S. A. Rumania, 267
Fisher, J., *jt. author. See* Baring-Gould, S., *and* Fisher, J.
Fisher, M. L. Cambodia, 279
Fishwick, H. Lancashire library, 447
Fitzgerald, B. Vesey-. *See* Vesey-Fitzgerald, B.
Fitzmyer, J. A., *jt. author. See* Glanzman, G. S., *and* Fitzmyer, J. A.
Fizicheskaya karta SSSR, 322n
Fiziko-geograficheskiĭ atlas mira, 311
Flag Research Center. Bibliography of flags of foreign nations, 384
Flags, 384-5
Fletcher, R. H. Arthurian material in the Chronicles, 250
Fliche, M. J. H. S. A., *and* Martin, V. Histoire de l'Église, 41n
Flint. County Library. Bibliography of the county of Flint, 451
Flint, J. E. Books on the British Empire and Commonwealth, 257n
Flintshire: history, 451
Florinsky, M. T., *ed.* McGraw-Hill Encyclopedia of Russia and the Soviet Union, 264
Flugel, J. C. Hundred years of psychology, 17
Flutre, L.-F. Tables des noms pro-

pres avec toutes leurs variantes figurants dans les romans du Moyen Age, 250
Focus, 302
Focus on world law, 174
Fodor, N., *comp. and ed.* Encyclopaedia of psychic science, 12
Fodor's Modern guides, 329
Folk literature, 249-50
Folk-Lore Society. Bibliography of folklore, 247
— British calendar customs, 251
Folklore, 246-54
Fondation Nationale des Sciences Politiques. Bulletin analytique de documentation, 62
— Index to post-1944 periodical articles, 62n
Food and Agriculture Organization. Bulletin of fishery statistics, 153n
— Cocoa statistics, 152
— FAO commodity review, 151
— Fertilizers, 151
— Monthly bulletin of agricultural economics and statistics, 151n, 230n
— Production yearbook, 151
— State of food and agriculture, 151
— Trade yearbook, 230
— World cocoa survey, 152n
— World crop statistics, 151
— World forest product statistics, 152
— World rice economy, 152
— Yearbook of fishery statistics, 152
— Yearbook of food and agricultural statistics, 151n
— Yearbook of forest product statistics, 152
Ford, G., *jt. author. See* Ford, P., *and* Ford, G.
Ford, P., *and* Ford, G. Breviate of Parliamentary Papers, 108
— Guide to Parliamentary Papers, 108
— Select list of Parliamentary Papers, 108
Fordham, A. Town plans of the British Isles, 424n
Fordham, *Sir* H. G. Hand-list of catalogues and works of reference relating to carto-bibliography, 420n
— Hertfordshire maps, 445
— Road-books and itineraries of Great Britain, 420
Foreign affairs, 101-6
Foreign affairs bibliography, 101
Foreign Office. *See* Great Britain. Foreign Office
Foreign Policy Association. Focus on world law, 174
Foreign trade, 226-31
Forge, J. W. L., *ed.* List of antiquities in the administrative county of Surrey, 434
Forke, A. Geschichte der alten chinesischen Philosophie, 11n
— Geschichte der neueren chinesischen Philosophie, 11n